conflict
and
consensus

conflict
and
consensus:
readings toward a sociological perspective

HAROLD M. HODGES, JR.
California State University at San Jose

Harper & Row, Publishers
New York, Evanston, San Francisco, London

CONFLICT AND CONSENSUS: Readings Toward a Sociological Perspective

Standard Book Number: 06-042844-9

LIBRARY OF CONGRESS CATALOG CARD NUMBER: 72-8263

In memory of my mother, Grace Inez Hodges,
whose brilliance, example, and encouragement
nurtured my fascination for sociology,
to my father for his understanding,
to my wife, Betty, and to Scott and Kenneth, in
gratitude for their patience.

contents

sociology : a preliminary overview

What is sociology? A shorthand answer—a terse and formal definition in the space of a paragraph or two—simply will not do. Nor, for that matter, will the half-dozen essays that comprise the first section of this book do anything more than merely suggest the full compass, the richness, the topicality, variety, and excitement of the sociological perspective. When the reader has sampled each of this book's 67 selections, however, he will have a reasonably firm and modern notion of what the discipline of sociology is all about.

He will have discovered, for one thing, that the student of sociology is concerned with virtually every facet of social life; that nothing—neither the most conspicuous element of everyday life nor the most obscure or exotic—escapes the scrutiny of the sociological imagination. He will have found, too, that the sociological quest for answers is rarely based upon merely playing hunches—that such quests depend instead upon sophisticated analytical procedures, and that the modes of analysis the sociologist has at his disposal are various and subtle.

The student will have realized, further, that because sociology is a relatively young and rapidly growing field, its practitioners are often at odds regarding the proper mission, means, and objectives of their endeavors. There are many time-tested parameters of interest in sociology, as well as other parameters that are constantly changing and continually expanding. Moreover, sociological interests, ranging from race, class, education, and religion to sex norms, riots, rebellions, and revolutions, are always topical.

The sociological dimensions of everyday life will have emerged in vivid and often compelling perspective in the articles that comprise this collection. A hint of the intellectual excitement, the sheer vitality, that pervades the sociological enterprise has been captured by two sociologists who have contributed to this volume. "By its use," C. Wright Mills observed of sociology, "men whose mentalities have swept only a series of limited orbits often come to feel as if suddenly awakened in a house with which they had only supposed themselves to be familiar. . . . Their capacity for astonishment is made lively again." And Peter Berger elaborates:

To ask sociological questions . . . presupposes that one is interested in looking some distance beyond the commonly accepted or officially defined goals of human actions. It presupposes a certain awareness that human events have different levels of meaning, some of which are hidden from the consciousness of everyday life. . . . We will not be far off if we see sociological thought as part of what Nietzsche called the "art of mistrust". . . . [the] sociological perspective involves a process of "seeing through" the facades of social structures. . . . The sociologist will be driven time and again, by the very logic of his discipline, to debunk the social systems he is studying.

Harold M. Hodges, Jr.

conflict
and
consensus

topic 1
the sociological enterprise: its scope and compass

What is the scope and compass of sociology? What is its range of concerns, its basic perspective, its distinctive frames of reference? What topics in the incredibly complex panorama of social life does the student of sociology focus upon? There are no elementary answers. For some understanding, the reader must wait—wait until he has sampled the range and diversity of subjects, analytical styles, and basic questions in the readings in this collection.

All the same there are a number of common themes that animate virtually all sociological inquiry. For one thing, the student of sociology is a student not of this or that distinctive event (the Afro-American awakening, for instance) or human being (Huey Newton or Malcolm X), but rather of social movements as a general and recurrent phenomenon and of man as a group animal. The sociologist is fundamentally concerned with man in the process of interaction with other men: with man's enduring relations, his recurrent and patterned social relationships. It follows, too, that he is concerned with both the abiding and persistent as well as the dynamic and changing qualities of such relationships. He attends at once to structure and fluidity, to the stable and the transient. He is at once a student of social order and of social change.

This explains the sociologist's concern with such things as man's institutions (his political, religious, economic, educational, and family arrangements), the communities and subcommunities in which he lives and works, his formal memberships and his informal affiliations, his social class and his racial or ethnic links. Nor do these exhaust the topics that excite the curiosity of the sociologist. But they do attest to the complex many-sidedness of his interests. They attest as well to the fact that nothing that he studies—however esoteric or humble—can be ripped from its larger social context, can be comprehended apart from the welter of variables (such as race, age, social class, or value configurations) with which it is enmeshed.

In the first essay, C. Wright Mills poses an elementary question: Why should we, why must we grasp the lessons of sociology? Because, he replies, all too few of us possess that sociological "imagination" that enables some to make sense out of the intricate interplay between man and the subtle social forces that enmesh him. Alan Bates, diagnosing the "sociological view of human behavior" in the second essay, calls attention to the fact that sociology is essentially a generalizing discipline which searches for the typical and the representative instead of the unique, the aberrant, and the happenstance or idiosyncratic aspects of social life. He pinpoints some of those essential qualities—the skeptical outlook, for instance, which helps un-cover the hidden meanings behind social facades—that animate the sociological quest to untangle the "mystery of human behavior." It is, moreover, a mystery that is forever elusive, never quite solva-ble. Thus its allure. For, as the ancient English adage put it, "the hunt's the thing."

chapter 1
the sociological imagination
c. wright mills

Nowadays men often feel that their private lives are a series of traps. They sense that within their everyday worlds they cannot overcome their troubles, and in this feeling they are often quite correct: What ordinary men are directly aware of and what they try to do are bounded by the private orbits in which they live; their visions and their powers are limited to the close-up scenes of job, family, neighborhood; in other milieux, they move vicariously and remain spectators. And the more aware they become, however vaguely, of ambitions and of threats which transcend their immediate locales, the more trapped they seem to feel.

Underlying this sense of being trapped are seemingly impersonal changes in the very structure of continent-wide societies. The facts of contemporary history are also facts about the success and the failure of individual men and women. When a society is industrialized, a peasant becomes a worker; a feudal lord is liquidated or becomes a businessman. When classes rise or fall, a man is employed or unemployed; when the rate of investment goes up or down, a man takes new heart or goes broke. When wars happen, an insurance salesman becomes a rocket launcher; a store clerk, a

radar man; a wife lives alone; a child grows up without a father. Neither the life of an individual nor the history of a society can be understood without understanding both.

Yet men do not usually define the troubles they endure in terms of historical change and institutional contradiction. The well-being they enjoy they do not usually impute to the big ups and downs of the societies in which they live. Seldom aware of the intricate connection between the patterns of their own lives and the course of world history, ordinary men do not usually know what this connection means for the kinds of men they are becoming and for the kinds of history-making in which they might take part. They do not possess the quality of mind essential to grasp the interplay of man and society, of biography and history, of self and world. They cannot cope with their personal troubles in such ways as to control the structural transformations that usually lie behind them.

Surely it is no wonder. In what period have so many men been so totally exposed at so fast a pace to such earthquakes of change? That Americans have not known such catastrophic changes as have the men and women of other societies is due to historical facts that are now quickly becoming "merely history." The history that now affects every man is world history. Within this scene and this period, in the course of a single generation,

From **The Sociological Imagination** by C. Wright Mills. Copyright © 1959 by Oxford University Press, Inc. Reprinted by permission.

one-sixth of mankind is transformed from all that is feudal and backward into all that is modern, advanced, and fearful. Political colonies are freed; new and less visible forms of imperialism installed. Revolutions occur; men feel the intimate grip of new kinds of authority. Totalitarian societies rise, and are smashed to bits—or succeed fabulously. After two centuries of ascendancy, capitalism is shown up as only one way to make society into an industrial apparatus. After two centuries of hope, even formal democracy is restricted to a quite small portion of mankind. Everywhere in the underdeveloped world, ancient ways of life are broken up and vague expectations become urgent demands. Everywhere in the overdeveloped world, the means of authority and of violence become total in scope and bureaucratic in form. Humanity itself now lies before us, the super-nation at either pole concentrating its most co-ordinated and massive efforts upon the preparation of World War III.

The very shaping of history now outpaces the ability of men to orient themselves in accordance with cherished values. And which values? Even when they do not panic, men often sense that older ways of feeling and thinking have collapsed and that newer beginnings are ambiguous to the point of moral stasis. Is it any wonder that ordinary men feel they cannot cope with the larger worlds with which they are so suddenly confronted? That they cannot understand the meaning of their epoch for their own lives? That—in defense of selfhood—they become morally insensible, trying to remain altogether private men? Is it any wonder that they come to be possessed by a sense of the trap?

It is not only information that they need—in this Age of Fact, information often dominates their attention and overwhelms their capacities to assimilate it. It is not only the skills of reason that they need—although their struggles to acquire these often exhaust their limited moral energy.

What they need, and what they feel they need, is a quality of mind that will help them to use information and to develop reason in order to achieve lucid summations of what is going on in the world and of what may be happening within themselves. It is this quality, I am going to contend, that journalists and scholars, artists and publics, scientists and editors are coming to expect of what may be called the sociological imagination.

The sociological imagination enables its possessor to understand the larger historical scene in terms of its meaning for the inner life and the external career of a variety of individuals. It enables him to take into account how individuals, in the welter of their daily experience, often become falsely conscious of their social positions. Within that welter, the framework of modern society is sought, and within that framework the psychologies of a variety of men and women are formulated. By such means the personal uneasiness of individuals is focused upon explicit troubles and the indifference of publics is transformed into involvement with public issues.

The first fruit of this imagination—and the first lesson of the social science that embodies it—is the idea that the individual can understand his own experience and gauge his own fate only by locating himself within his period, that he can know his own chances in life only by becoming aware of those of all individuals in his circumstances. In many ways it is a terrible lesson; in many ways a magnificent one. We do not know the limits of man's capacities for supreme effort or willing degradation, for agony or glee, for pleasurable brutality or the sweetness of reason. But in our time we have come to know that the limits of "human nature" are frighteningly broad. We have come to know that every individual lives, from one generation to the next, in some society; that he lives out a biography, and that he lives it out within some historical sequence. By the fact of his living he contributes, however minutely, to the shaping of this society and to the course of its history, even as he is made by society and by its historical push and shove.

The sociological imagination enables us to grasp history and biography and the relations between the two within society. That is its task and its promise. To recognize this task and this promise is the mark of the classic social analyst. It is characteristic of Herbert Spencer—turgid, polysyllabic, comprehensive; of E. A. Ross—graceful, muckraking, upright; of Auguste Comte and Emile Durkheim; of the intricate and subtle Karl Mannheim. It is the quality of all that is intellectually excellent in Karl Marx; it is the clue to Thorstein Veblen's brilliant and ironic insight, to Joseph Schumpeter's many-sided constructions of reality; it is the basis of the psychological sweep of W. E. H. Lecky no less than of the profundity and clarity of Max Weber. And it is the signal of what is best in contemporary studies of man and society.

No social study that does not come back to the problems of biography, of history, and of their intersections within a society has completed its intellectual journey. Whatever the specific problems of the classic social analysts, however limited or however broad the features of social reality they have examined, those who have been imaginatively aware of the promise of their work have consistently asked three sorts of questions:

1. What is the structure of this particular society as a whole? What are its essential components, and how are they related to one another? How does it differ from other varieties of social order? Within it, what is the meaning of any particular feature for its continuance and for its change?

2. Where does this society stand in human history? What are the mechanics by which it is changing? What is its place within and its meaning for the development of humanity as a whole? How does any particular feature we are examining affect, and how is it affected by, the historical period in which it moves? And this period—what are its essential features? How does it differ from other periods? What are its characteristic ways of history-making?

3. What varieties of men and women now prevail in this society and in this period? And what varieties are coming to prevail? In what ways are they selected and formed, liberated and repressed, made sensitive and blunted? What kinds of "human nature" are revealed in the conduct and character we observe in this society in this period? And what is the meaning for "human nature" of each and every feature of the society we are examining?

Whether the point of interest is a great power state or a minor literary mood, a family, a prison, a creed—these are the kinds of questions the best social analysts have asked. They are the intellectual pivots of classic studies of man in society—and they are the questions inevitably raised by any mind possessing the sociological imagination. For that imagination is the capacity to shift from one perspective to another—from the political to the psychological; from examination of a single family to comparative assessment of the national budgets of the world; from the theological school to the military establishment; from considerations of an oil industry to studies of contemporary poetry. It is the capacity to range from the most impersonal

and remote transformations to the most intimate features of the human self—and to see the relations between the two. Back of its use there is always the urge to know the social and historical meaning of the individual in the society and in the period in which he has his quality and his being.

That, in brief, is why it is by means of the sociological imagination that men now hope to grasp what is going on in the world, and to understand what is happening in themselves as minute points of the intersections of biography and history within society. In large part, contemporary man's self-conscious view of himself as at least an outsider, if not a permanent stranger, rests upon an absorbed realization of social relativity and of the transformative power of history. The sociological imagination is the most fruitful form of this self-consciousness. By its use men whose mentalities have swept only a series of limited orbits often come to feel as if suddenly awakened in a house with which they had only supposed themselves to be familiar. Correctly or incorrectly, they often come to feel that they can now provide themselves with adequate summations, cohesive assessments, comprehensive orientations. Older decisions that once appeared sound now seem to them products of a mind unaccountably dense. Their capacity for astonishment is made lively again. They acquire a new way of thinking, they experience a transvaluation of values: in a word, by their reflection and by their sensibility, they realize the cultural meaning of the social sciences.

■

Perhaps the most fruitful distinction with which the sociological imagination works is between "the personal troubles of milieu" and "the public issues of social structure." This distinction is an essential tool of the sociological imagination and a feature of all classic work in social science.

Troubles occur within the character of the individual and within the range of his immediate relations with others; they have to do with his self and with those limited areas of social life of which he is directly and personally aware. Accordingly, the statement and the resolution of troubles properly lie within the individual as a biographical entity and within the scope of his immediate milieu—the social setting that is directly open to his personal experience and to some extent his willful activity. A trouble is a private matter:

values cherished by an individual are felt by him to be threatened.

Issues have to do with matters that transcend these local environments of the individual and the range of his inner life. They have to do with the organization of many such milieux into the institutions of an historical society as a whole, with the ways in which various milieux overlap and interpenetrate to form the larger structure of social and historical life. An issue is a public matter: some value cherished by publics is felt to be threatened. Often there is a debate about what that value really is and about what it is that really threatens it. This debate is often without focus if only because it is the very nature of an issue, unlike even widespread trouble, that it cannot very well be defined in terms of the immediate and everyday environments of ordinary men. An issue, in fact, often involves a crisis in institutional arrangements, and often too it involves what Marxists call "contradictions" or "antagonisms."

In these terms, consider unemployment. When, in a city of 100,000, only one man is unemployed, that is his personal trouble, and for its relief we properly look to the character of the man, his skills, and his immediate opportunities. But when in a nation of 50 million employees, 15 million men are unemployed, that is an issue, and we may not hope to find its solution within the range of opportunities open to any one individual. The very structure of opportunities has collapsed. Both the correct statement of the problem and the range of possible solutions require us to consider the economic and political institutions of the society, and not merely the personal situation and character of a scatter of individuals.

Consider war. The personal problem of war, when it occurs, may be how to survive it or how to die in it with honor; how to make money out of it; how to climb into the higher safety of the military apparatus; or how to contribute to the war's termination. In short, according to one's values, to find a set of milieux and within it to survive the war or make one's death in it meaningful. But the structural issues of war have to do with its causes; with what types of men it throws up into command; with its effects upon economic and political, family, and religious institutions, with the unorganized irresponsibility of a world of nation-states.

Consider marriage. Inside a marriage a man and a woman may experience personal troubles, but when the divorce rate during the first four years of marriage is 250 out of every 1,000 attempts, this is an indication of a structural issue having to do with the institutions of marriage and the family and other institutions that bear upon them.

Or consider the metropolis—the horrible, beautiful, ugly, magnificent sprawl of the great city. For many upper-class people, the personal solution to "the problem of the city" is to have an apartment with private garage under it in the heart of the city, and forty miles out, a house by Henry Hill, garden by Garrett Eckbo, on a hundred acres of private land. In these two controlled environments—with a small staff at each end and a private helicopter connection—most people could solve many of the problems of personal milieux caused by the facts of the city. But all this, however splendid, does not solve the public issues that the structural fact of the city poses. What should be done with this wonderful monstrosity? Break it all up into scattered units, combining residence and work? Refurbish it as it stands? Or, after evacuation, dynamite it and build new cities according to new plans in new places? What should those plans be? And who is to decide and to accomplish whatever choice is made? These are structural issues; to confront them and to solve them requires us to consider political and economic issues that affect innumerable milieux.

Insofar as an economy is so arranged that slumps occur, the problem of unemployment becomes incapable of personal solution. Insofar as war is inherent in the nation-state system and in the uneven industrialization of the world, the ordinary individual in his restricted milieu will be powerless—with or without psychiatric aid—to solve the troubles this system or lack of system imposes upon him. Insofar as the family as an institution turns women into darling little slaves and men into their chief providers and unweaned dependents, the problem of a satisfactory marriage remains incapable of purely private solution. Insofar as the overdeveloped megalopolis and the overdeveloped automobile are built-in features of the overdeveloped society, the issues of urban living will not be solved by personal ingenuity and private wealth.

What we experience in various and specific milieux, I have noted, is often caused by structural changes. Accordingly, to understand the changes of many personal milieux we are required to look beyond them. And the number and variety of such structural changes increase as the institutions within which we live become more embracing and more intricately connected with one another. To be aware of the idea of social structure and to use it with sensibility is to be capable of tracing such linkages among a great variety of milieux. To be able to do that is to possess the sociological imagination.

■

What are the major issues for publics and the key troubles of private individuals in our time? To formulate issues and troubles, we must ask what values are cherished yet threatened, and what values are cherished and supported, by the characterizing trends of our period. In the case both of threat and of support we must ask what salient contradictions of structure may be involved.

When people cherish some set of values and do not feel any threat to them, they experience **well-being.** When they cherish values but **do** feel them to be threatened, they experience a crisis—either as a personal trouble or as a public issue. And if all their values seem involved, they feel the total threat of panic.

But suppose people are neither aware of any cherished values nor experience any threat? That is the experience of **indifference,** which, if it seems to involve all their values, becomes apathy. Suppose, finally, they are unaware of any cherished values, but still are very much aware of a threat? That is the experience of **uneasiness,** of anxiety, which, if it is total enough, becomes a deadly unspecified malaise.

Ours is a time of uneasiness and indifference—not yet formulated in such ways as to permit the work of reason and the play of sensibility. Instead of troubles—defined in terms of values and threats—there is often the misery of vague uneasiness; instead of explicit issues there is often merely the beat feeling that all is somehow not right. Neither the values threatened nor whatever threatens them has been stated; in short, they have not been carried to the point of decision. Much less have they been formulated as problems of social science.

In the thirties there was little doubt—except among certain deluded business circles—that there was an economic issue which was also a pack of personal troubles. In these arguments about "the crisis of capitalism," the formulations of Marx and the many unacknowledged reformulations of his work probably set the leading terms of the issue,

and some men came to understand their personal troubles in these terms. The values threatened were plain to see and cherished by all; the structural contradictions that threatened them also seemed plain. Both were widely and deeply experienced. It was a political age.

But the values threatened in the era after World War II are often neither widely acknowledged as values nor widely felt to be threatened. Much private uneasiness goes unformulated; much public malaise and many decisions of enormous structural relevance never become public issues. For those who accept such inherited values as reason and freedom, it is the uneasiness itself that is the trouble; it is the indifference itself that is the issue. And it is this condition, of uneasiness and indifference, that is the signal feature of our period.

All this is so striking that it is often interpreted by observers as a shift in the very kinds of problems that need now to be formulated. We are frequently told that the problems of our decade, or even the crises of our period, have shifted from the external realm of economics and now have to do with the quality of individual life—in fact with the question of whether there is soon going to be anything that can properly be called individual life. Not child labor but comic books, not poverty but mass leisure, are at the center of concern. Many great public issues as well as many private troubles are described in terms of "the psychiatric"—often, it seems, in a pathetic attempt to avoid the large issues and problems of modern society. Often this statement seems to rest upon a provincial narrowing of interest to the Western societies, or even to the United States—thus ignoring two-thirds of mankind; often, too, it arbitrarily divorces the individual life from the larger institutions within which that life is enacted, and which on occasion bear upon it more grievously than do the intimate environments of childhood.

Problems of leisure, for example, cannot even be stated without considering problems of work. Family troubles over comic books cannot be formulated as problems without considering the plight of the contemporary family in its new relations with the newer institutions of the social structure. Neither leisure nor its debilitating uses can be understood as problems without recognition of the extent to which malaise and indifference now form the social and personal climate of contemporary American society. In this climate, no problems of "the private life" can be stated and solved without recognition of the crisis of ambition that is part of the very career of men at work in the incorporated economy.

It is true, as psychoanalysts continually point out, that people do often have "the increasing sense of being moved by obscure forces within themselves which they are unable to define." But it is **not** true, as Ernest Jones asserted, that "man's chief enemy and danger is his own unruly nature and the dark forces pent up within him." On the contrary: "Man's chief danger" today lies in the unruly forces of contemporary society itself, with its alienating methods of production, its enveloping techniques of political domination, its inter-national anarchy—in a word, its pervasive transformations of the very "nature" of man and the conditions and aims of his life.

It is now the social scientist's foremost political and intellectual task—for here the two coincide—to make clear the elements of contemporary uneasiness and indifference. It is the central demand made upon him by other cultural workmen—by physical scientists and artists, by the intellectual community in general. It is because of this task and these demands, I believe, that the social sciences are becoming the common denominator of our cultural period, and the sociological imagination our most needed quality of mind.

chapter 2
the sociological perspective
allan p. bates

To the social aspects of human experience sociology brings a unique and valid perspective unlike any other. It is not a better perspective than those provided by alternative models; it is different.

Sociology overlaps its sister fields in many ways, but, like each of them, it has a distinctive orientation toward its subject matter. Most broadly and fundamentally, it is concerned with how human social behavior is organized and how this organization changes over time. Just now these words may convey little meaning, or may have a deceptive simplicity, but they state the case for what is unique in the point of view of sociology. The key words in this statement are "social behavior," "organization," and "change."

Social Behavior

As a specialist, the sociologist is not interested in all behavior which affects and is affected by other people, only in that which is interpersonally relevant. Social behavior, a very inclusive notion, refers to all behavior meeting this criterion. Quite a few specialists are interested in social behavior, so we must push further in order to grasp the sociologist's particular concern. We come close to the

From **The Sociological Enterprise** by Alan P. Bates. Boston: Houghton Mifflin Company, 1967. Reprinted by permission.

heart of the matter by stating that the sociologist is chiefly interested in being able to make **general** statements about social behavior—that under such-and-such circumstances a given kind of behavior is likely to occur. Inkeles puts it well in saying that the primary concern of the sociologist is "in the study of those aspects of social life which are present in all social forms."[1]

Such a statement means that the sociologist is interested in such things as the organization of American cities, the way in which power is distributed in groups, the relationship between masculine and feminine roles, the factors which produce conforming and deviating behavior, the ways in which change is induced or resisted (not to mention many other problems, of course). By the same token he is not, as a specialist, concerned with the Boston Tea Party, the Wagner Labor Relations Act, the family life of the American president, a quarrel between two young lovers of his acquaintance, or the personality of his mother-in-law.

We must be as clear as possible about this. In its purest form the sociological frame of reference does not take into account the idiosyncrasies of single persons or of separate historical occurrences. Or, looking at an individual case from this perspective, it will be seen as a single instance of a more general class of similar instances, deviating to a greater or lesser extent from the characteristics of the class. In other words, sociology is or aspires to be a generalizing science. In this it is like many other sciences. Human physiology is not the physiology of a single organism but of a class of organisms, and the characteristics of the class do not precisely describe all the attributes of a single case. As a science psychology is not concerned with the behavior of one particular human, but with that of classes of humans **seen as individuals.** The sociologist also is interested in the behavior of people, but only that behavior which links people together, at a level at which he can generalize about classes of such behavior.

Here is an example of a sociological generalization: "In American cities there is an inverse relation between the incidence of reported crime and distance from the center of the city." Note that there is no reference to any particular city, no mention of which persons actually commit crimes, or what kinds of personalities they have, only a statement of the relation between a condition and a class of social behavior. Here is another. "The higher the rank of a person within a group, the more nearly his activities conform to the norms of the group."[2] Again, no particular group is mentioned, the nature of the norms is not specified, and the many differences among group members are ignored.

When one first encounters the sociological perspective and begins to grasp its nature, an initial reaction may be that it omits one of the most important things about human behavior: that which is unique in each occurrence and in each person. Actually, the sociologist does not mean to belittle in any way such elements in human experience. In his personal life he is as sensitive to them as is anyone else. He does argue that there is a level of human behavioral organization, the social level, which is of enormous importance, and about which it is possible to develop a generalizing science which deliberately ignores the individual case in order to be able to discover how human behavior is socially organized.

Social Organization

The sociologist is interested in organized social behavior. But very generally, this means that behavior which links together individuals or groups of individuals is not random or haphazard. It has the properties of orderliness, pattern, repetitiveness, hence predictability. Here is a college classroom. During a particular semester at nine o'clock each morning, Monday through Friday, the room is filled with college students. Each goes without

hesitation to a certain chair. A minute or two later a professor enters, stands at the front of the classroom, facing the students, and begins to talk. Most of the students write in notebooks. A few whisper covertly to one another. At the end of fifty minutes a bell rings, the professor ends his comments, the students close their notebooks, and all leave the room. We have here an identification and short description of an instance of **social** organization even though it does not use the technical language of sociology. It is clear that the behavior of these persons with respect to each other is patterned. This is true even though there are minor variations in the specific sequence of actions from one class meeting to the next. Our example includes no information about the psychological characteristics of students or teacher; it does not even mention the nature of the course, or whether it is advanced or elementary. We recognize a single specimen of a large class of social situations having a familiar kind of social organization which, by the way, significantly channels a good deal of human activity.

It is the **pattern of interdependent behavior** which interests the sociologist. This is the kind of unit he studies, not the individuals who participate in the pattern. He knows perfectly well that there are important differences between the class members and that from the viewpoint of another model, say, the psychological, these differences would be of first importance. But not for the sociologist. What is crucial for him is that all these persons, **despite their differences,** behave with respect to each other in an orderly, predictable fashion. Furthermore, he is not at all surprised to find that the patterned behavior of the people in this class closely resembles that of innumerable other classes, each with its own set of "unique" personalities and other special characteristics. Without knowing anything of the attributes of individuals in a given class he can know a good deal about how people will behave in this category of situations precisely because such settings are socially organized. True, he can't say a great deal about the psychological organization of individual students from knowledge of this kind of social organization. But by the same token, we cannot learn much about the social structure of college classrooms from the summated personality characteristics of college students. These are simply different levels of behavioral organization, interdependent to be sure, but not the same.

The order the sociologist sees in the social life

of men is not perfect. Evidence of organization is sought in the pattern and predictability of actual behavior, but it is always true that some of the behavior in every situation does not fit the pattern and conform to the prediction. Similarly, if organization is described in cultural terms, it will be found that there is seldom, perhaps never, complete agreement among all the actors on what behavior is called for in a particular real-life drama. There may even be radical disagreement on the cultural prescriptions. On the other hand, the fact that a group exists at all testifies that it is to some degree socially organized. Social organization is a "more or less" matter, and the sociologist is interested in differences in the degree of organization and the consequences for understanding behavior.

Social Change

The general statement about the sociological outlook made a few pages back indicated that this orientation is concerned not only with stability in social life but also with change. Consider the college classroom illustration again. It is possible to describe this situation as though there were no time dimension, and the sociologist often does this when he is primarily concerned with revealing the "structural" characteristics of a social situation. So we say that the classroom is organized so that the students sit in orderly rows facing the front of the room, each student occupying a particular spot in the arrangement. The instructor faces them, standing at the front. Interaction flows between the students and the instructor for the most part, with little student-student communication; students show more deference to the teacher than vice versa; and so on.

Such a description has a static quality. The fact is that what we see as social organization only becomes manifest with the passage of time, as was better suggested in our first reference to the classroom. First this event takes place, then that. We say there is organization and structure because the **sequence** of events is repetitive and predictable. The next session of the class will correspond closely to this one. Paradoxically, one form of change is a kind of absence of change. Since the pattern of events repeats itself over and over, we can observe change only as we watch the unfolding of a single manifestation of a pattern which itself does not alter.

A more familiar notion of change as applied to social organization involves some alteration in the patterned character of social behavior. The

pattern is different, and presumably will not return to its former state. In a strict sense even very stable social organizations always undergo at least minor alterations through time. Our hypothetical college class will not have quite the same social organization ten weeks after its first session even though the main features of the structure appear to be the same. Similarly, on a larger scale, college classes in general are conducted somewhat differently today than their "sociological ancestors" were two or three generations ago.

Sociologists are interested in both cross-sectional, structural approaches to social phenomena and in time-dimensional, change approaches. Neither is inherently more important than the other. Both present fundamental problems to the discipline. The stability of social life and the inevitable accompanying change are taken for granted by laymen, but to sociologists they are a Janus-faced mystery that forever challenges.

THE SCOPE OF SOCIOLOGICAL INTEREST

The sociologist's interest in the general characteristics of all social behavior can take him into the study of any particular manifestation: economic, political, religious, educational, aesthetic, or any other. Also, for him the entire social world is subdivisible into innumerable progressively smaller units. For instance, the United States constitutes for him a single social structure, so incredibly complex that the social sciences cannot very adequately describe it at their present stage of development. Included within this single structure are a number of major social institutions, each a smaller social world within the larger. Below the institutional level are hundreds of thousands of organizations and associations of varying size and complexity. Still lower down the scale of size and complexity are millions upon millions of small, relatively informal, and transient face-to-face groups, each containing subgroups. Finally, there are, in astronomically large numbers, single social acts, which can, if desired, be abstracted from context for analysis.

As a discipline sociology is interested in this whole range of social organization, as manifested in every sector of society and at every level of size and complexity. Furthermore, it is concerned with the interdependence of organization among different sectors and levels. In physical science man is interested in the features of the planet earth, but recognizes that part of his understanding of earth depends upon recognition that it is part of the solar system. Hence, the solar system is a level of organization of matter and energy worth studying too. But the solar system is part of a still larger organization known as a galaxy, and the galaxy of which our solar system is a part is only one among incredibly large numbers of other galaxies, all of which respond to some larger order of organization. In the social life of man, too, there are worlds within worlds, and while there is a rough inverse relation between size and complexity, the sociologist has learned to have a most healthy respect for the complexity of even the smallest and seemingly most simple unit of social organization.

It is worth stressing that sociology is concerned with all forms of organized social behavior. One sociologist, to be sure, may be interested only in the study of large, formal organizations, another in the structure of communities, a third in family disorganization. Specialization is as inevitable here as in other fields of knowledge. But the general viewpoint of sociology excludes no arena in which organized social behavior is found, and by the same token, the general viewpoint of the discipline will inform the specialized research of any true sociologist. This means that the importance or visibility of a phenomenon as a layman would see it is no criterion of its sociological interest. The discipline is interested in events where decisions of huge importance are weighed, but just as interested in homely, seemingly trivial, and commonplace events of everyday life. It is committed to the study of behavior that society judges deviant, bizarre, "bad," such as crime, alcoholism, and far-out religious cults, but no more so than to the analysis of conforming, normal, "good" behavior.

SOME OTHER FEATURES OF SOCIOLOGY'S OUTLOOK

Like every scholarly field, sociology has some identifying features which are not, perhaps, essential to a minimum definition, yet are very much part of it. Some development of these additional characteristics will help to get a better "feel" of how it is to think sociologically about behavior.

Looking Beyond the Obvious

The professional posture of a sociologist requires him to stand apart from his subject matter, to detach himself and step outside the ongoing social scene in which he ordinarily participates like anyone else. He is a little like the drama critic who must write a review of a new play after its first performance. The critic sets aside the point of view of an ordinary audience member in order to analyze the structure of the play, its content, staging, and the performances of the actors.[3] Unlike the sociologist, however, the drama critic will usually also pass judgment on the quality of the play, while the sociologist tries to exclude value judgments from his analyses of social behavior.

The special nature of his interest causes the sociologist to look for and to see different things (or to see the same things in different ways) than the engaged participants. In a provocative discussion of this point Berger used the phrase "looking behind the façades" of social structures.[4] Here is a group whose members resent Bill's "bossy" behavior. A sociological observer notices almost at once that the admired leader of the group often acts in the same way as Bill (a low-ranking member), but the other members are not antagonized by the leader. The sociologist "sees" that the hostility of the members is produced not so much by the nature of Bill's behavior as by its incompatibility with his rank in the group.

The organization of behavior which is the sociologist's province is almost never immediately clear in the social scene as it appears to the people engaged in it. Therefore, the sociologist is always probing "below," "behind," "through" the immediate circumstances for the structure that is there. This is as true of the organization of a casual conversation among friends as it is of the most portentous social structures which exist.

The Sociologist as Skeptic

The sociologist is inevitably cast in the role of skeptic. He cannot help being skeptical of the easy answers people have learned to give for complex problems of social behavior. There cannot be a single sociologist who has not frequently listened while friends or acquaintances happily revealed their confusions and misunderstandings about a problem he recognizes as essentially sociological in character. The friend, of course, will not be discomfited in the least, since like most of the general public he has no idea of what sociology is, and it will not occur to him that the sociologist might have some special competence in the subject under discussion. Most specialists probably have this experience. Many an attorney has winced, no doubt, as a layman unknowingly revealed his misconceptions of the law.

But the sociologist's skepticism must not be thought of as wholly negative, an attitude which seeks the destruction of other men's cherished notions of reality. The point is that the sociologist has been trained to see a special class of problems in human behavior, and so he becomes highly sensitive to experiences in which the problem and the model applied to its understanding are mismatched. He finds that the answers given to sociological problems by others are sometimes not only inappropriate but terribly oversimplified as well.

Sociologists, particularly those who conduct original research, have a most healthy respect for the complexities of their subject matter. Nothing can be taken for granted, not even the most seductive generalizations of "common sense." The research sociologist is continually reminded of how little we know, scientifically speaking, about human behavior. He is aware that he and his colleagues are only pioneering in a small way on the edges of a trackless wilderness, whose size and complexity exceed the grasp of the imagination in almost the same sense that the human mind fails before the task of imaginatively laying hold of the physical universe revealed in modern physical science.

The practice of sociological research is not conducive to arrogance about knowledge of human affairs, but rather the converse. No wonder then that it is hard to capture the sociologist's

mind with the routine formulas that society uses in its attempts to cope with social problems large or small. At the same time, if he is a wise man as well as a sociologist, he will not be contemptuous of men's fumbling efforts to solve pressing problems since he will recognize that his own ability to do so is still strictly limited. The problems of the day cannot wait. They must be dealt with somehow. So he may cheerfully participate as a citizen in efforts to improve the human condition, even as he remains a skeptic, intellectually speaking. But back within his disciplinary perspective he will know vividly at times the mystery of human behavior, even the most ordinary behavior. His objective is to penetrate that mystery, and perhaps to reduce it a little.

NOTES

1. A. Inkeles, **What Is Sociology?** Foundations of Modern Sociology Series. Englewood Cliffs, N.J.: Prentice-Hall, 1964, p. 16.

2. G. C. Homans, **The Human Group.** New York: Harcourt, Brace, 1950, p. 141. This is Homans' famous "rank-conformity" hypothesis, which stimulated much research and discussion subsequent to its publication.

3. Homans, op. cit., p. 126.

4. P. L. Berger, **Invitation to Sociology,** Garden City: Doubleday, Anchor Books, 1963, p. 32.

topic 2
the sociological enterprise: modes of analysis

Is sociology an art? Or is it a science? Has it deeper affinities with the humanities, or with the physical sciences? These are not trivial matters. For the **raison d'être**—the complex of assumptions, convictions, and rationales that serve as guiding principles for an academic discipline—shapes and colors its modes of analysis. And the latter, the ways in which the sociologist goes about gathering and interpreting his data, are our concern in this chapter.

One need not delve far into the essays by Raymond Mack and by Jacqueline Wiseman and Marcia Aron to realize that the analytical procedures that dominate sociological inquiry are **scientific.** Yet we are not dodging the issue when we reply to the question "Is sociology more a science or an art?" by affirming that it is and must be both—that is, it is dependent upon the scientific canons of inquiry, yet it is at heart an art and a humanistic endeavor.

Sociology is essentially scientific because, in the words of Robert Redfield, "its propositions describe, in general terms, natural phenomena; in that it returns again and again to special experience to verify and to modify these propositions. It tells what is, not what ought to be. It investigates nature. It strives for objectivity, accuracy; . . . it employs hypotheses and formal evidence; it values negative cases; and, when it finds a hypothesis to be unsupported by the facts, it drops it for some other which is." All the same, adds Redfield, it is equally true that to **create** the hypothesis—to "get, often, the very first real datum as to what are A's motives or what is the meaning of this odd custom or that too-familiar institution, requires on the part of one who studies persons and societies, and not rocks or proteins, a truly humanistic and freely imaginative insight into people, their conventions and interests and motives. . . ."

Robert A. Nisbet would carry this logic a step further. "It is my contention," he writes, "that the science of sociology makes its most significant intellectual advances under the spur of stimuli and through processes that it largely shares with art; that whatever the differences between science and art, it is what they have in common that matters most in discovery and creativeness." Still others—Florian Znaniecki, for example—argue that the "humanistic coefficient" makes sociology more an art form than a technology, that it must rely as much upon intuition and **verstehen** (imaginative insight) as upon rational deduction and objectively verifiable facts. Sociology is humanistic, another sociologist argues, "because it attempts to understand whatever man does, in categories that acknowledge his humanity. . . . The great traditions of sociology are humanistic"

In sum, however much they might quibble regarding the worth of this or that technique or analytic procedure, most sociologists are committed to the ideal that the same basic logic of inquiry that characterizes the physical and natural sciences must characterize sociological analysis as well. They generally agree that science is "an organized enterprise, a style of inquiry, which begins with the realization that our present knowledge is inadequate for handling many problems. It deals with these problems by developing better knowledge through the conceptual and empirical investigation of current information, the collection of new data, and the continuous reassessment of our theories, beliefs, and practices."

In a contribution that is at once brief and comprehensive, Raymond Mack explains why the scientific method is so invaluable an instrument in sociological analysis. He explains, too, why the scientific practitioner—whether he is an historian, a botanist, sociologist, physicist, or anthropologist—accepts the canon that he must separate his own wishes and convictions from the process of observing and interpreting data. In equally unambiguous language (a rarity, sadly, among the many who feel that they are not truly "scientific" unless they indulge in esoteric gobbledygook), Jacqueline Wiseman and Marcia Aron point out the function and utility of such basic research procedures as sampling, observation, depth interviewing, descriptive surveys, and participant-observer studies.

chapter 3
science as a frame of reference
raymond w. mack

"A social scientist is a man who, if he has two little boys, sends one to Sunday School every Sunday and keeps the other one home as an experimental control group." So runs one of our bits of occupational in-group humor. Would that we more often knew such precision!

The scientific **method** in social science is the same scientific method which underlies the work done in the chemist's laboratory, the zoologist's dissecting room, and the astronomer's observatory. But the **techniques** of gathering information vary from discipline to discipline: the chemist has his Bunsen burner and his watch glass, the zoologist his scalpel and his microscope, the astronomer his radio telescope and his charts. The social scientist has his interview schedule and his questionnaire. For each, the controlled experiment is an ideal seldom achieved but often approximated. For all, the canons of the scientific method are identical.

The unity of the sciences lies in their method. The scientific method is a way of trying to make sense out of the booming, buzzing confusion of the universe. It is an intellectual stance toward information. The scientific method is a set of assumptions about when a fact is a fact. The method provides scientists with a set of guideposts for gathering information and for bringing order to congeries of data.

Persons using the scientific method as a frame of reference operate under three assumptions: (1) that the human senses are the most reliable medium for gathering data; (2) that human reason is the most valid tool for organizing data; and (3) that agreement among a number of competent observers is the best check on the efficiency of the data gathering and organizing process called for in the first two assumptions.

Knowledge is scientific, then, when (1) an observer gathers information through one or more of his senses—sight, hearing, touch, taste, or smell—and (2) uses logic to interpret his information, that is, to relate one fact to another, and (3) other scientists sufficiently well-trained in the observer's specialty to understand what he has done use their sense experience and human reason on the information and arrive at the same conclusion.

When one of these criteria is violated in the search for knowledge, the conclusions are not scientific. Science does not provide us with knowledge about God because, by definition, the supernatural cannot be experienced through human senses. A random collection of facts does not constitute a science because facts do not speak for themselves; human reason must be employed to explain the relationships among facts and among sets of facts.

Scientists often use instruments for collecting information: thermometers, stethoscopes, tape recorders, questionnaires. These are the techniques which vary from discipline to discipline. They are simply aids to implementing the scientific method, which is unvarying. These devices are auxiliaries to the human senses. Scientists use them to bring greater precision to their own sense experience.

But the most refined gauge does not measure anything. A human being does the measuring. The instrument extends the range and sharpens the precision of his observations. A yardstick does not measure, and a Geiger counter does not count: a man does. It is the eye and the ear of the scientist using them that translate their sensitive markings and murmurings into scientific facts.

It is hardly correct, then, to speak of facts as being more or less scientific. A set of observations may be more or less precise, but if they are the product of sense experience logically interpreted and independently verified, they are scientific.

While the method of science is unvarying, the bodies of knowledge accumulated via the scientific method are ever-changing. The scientific method does not change, but the content of a scientific discipline does. This does not necessarily mean that a set of facts is disproved, but often that the gaining of additional information leads to a reinterpretation of what is known. Einstein's theory of relativity does not disprove Newton's scientific facts; it explains more by adding to and reinterpreting Newton's observations.

When a man accepts science as a frame of reference, and uses it in his daily work life, it is bound to have some impact upon his frame of mind. The stereotype which nonscientists hold of the scientist offers a clue to that frame of mind. Laymen often see scientists as cold-blooded skeptics, uninvolved in the values of their culture or the issues of their society, and hard to convince of anything. Like most stereotypes, this one is organized around elements of truth. The scientist is neither as bad as some people think in his lack of capacity for emotional conviction, nor as good as others think in his ability to separate his personal preferences from his objective scholarly conclusions.

But his training and practice do lead a scientist to attempt to separate his own wishes and convictions from the process of observing and interpreting data. The scientific method, with its commitment to sense experience and independent verification, is an attempt to assure complete objectivity. A social scientist, even more than others, should be aware that his own experience and cultural conditioning will influence his choice of research problems. He has learned in his own society a set of rules and preferences and even a way of thinking. That is why he uses the scientific method: as a guard against confusing what he would like to find with what is actually there.

He may not be able to bring his scientific frame of mind to every problem he addresses as a Republican, as a Baptist, as a father, or as a friend, but when he is working, his commitment to the method helps him to get outside himself and his milieu and to see his physical and social environment objectively. In this sense, too, the stereotype is founded on fact: the scientist **at work** is a man alienated from his society. As a citizen, the bacteriologist may loathe the ravages of tuberculosis and want passionately to find a means of preventing the disease. As a citizen, a sociologist may love democratic concepts of justice and deplore the ways in which poverty and racial discrimination cause his society to fall short of its own ideals. But at work, the bacteriologist must measure, not curse, the virulence of the bacillus; the sociologist must invest his work time in analyzing the effectiveness of special interest groups, not in cheerleading.

Calling something science does not make it scientific, of course. Astrology remains more popular than astronomy. Alchemy preceded chemistry, and there were hosts of economic and political philosophers eager to turn the lead of their opinions into the gold of truth long before there were many economists and political scientists using the scientific method to further their understanding of human behavior. There are still people who call themselves social scientists, but who evidence little inclination to subject their pet theories to the hazards of empirical test.

Nonetheless, this century has seen a larger and larger proportion of scholars using the scientific method as a means to the end of learning more about human social behavior. Every year, more students are exposed to science as a frame of reference. The mass media report and comment upon information gathered by observation, interviews, and questionnaires. Political leaders, educators, businessmen, church administrators make policy decisions based upon data gathered by social scientists. The growing acceptance of science as a frame of reference can encourage belief that decision makers may come to feel more at home with science as a frame of mind.

chapter 4
basic research methods
jacqueline p. wiseman and marcia s. aron

Sociology—like anthropology, psychology, economics. political science, and history—is a commitment to learning how and why man behaves as he does in the many contexts in which he lives. To learn these things, researchers have found they must check their armchair speculations with hard facts from the real world. In so doing, they have developed various techniques of obtaining data about man and his social relationships.

Sampling

The goal of science is to find uniformities or "patterns" in nature, for it is a basic scientific assumption that such uniformities exist in the physical, biological, and social worlds. The scientist obviously cannot examine all instances of the data he is studying—the botanist does not look at all plants, or even all roses; the sociologist does not study all cases of juvenile delinquency, or even all cases of juvenile car theft; etc.

But even though he is unable to observe all cases in his area of study, the scientist wants to be able to **generalize to all similar cases** from the data he has collected. The problem is how to be certain that he has studied specimens that will be repre-

From **Field Projects for Sociology Students** by Jacqueline P. Wiseman and Marcia S. Aron. Copyright © 1970 Schenkman Publishing Co., Inc., Cambridge, Mass. Reprinted by permission.

sentative or typical of all similar cases of the phenomena he has chosen to investigate. To assure data representativeness, various sampling techniques have been developed. Students who decide to major in sociology will want to be familiar with them and their specific applications.

Validity

Validity refers to whether you are **really** measuring or classifying what you **say** you are measuring or classifying. For example, a yardstick measures inches or feet but **not** grams or pounds. You do not measure your height by standing on a scale! There is no ambiguity or doubt about this. But the social scientist faces the problem of creating measuring instruments and classification schemes to measure phenomena that do not have physical attributes. Therefore he must try to devise other kinds of tools, such as questionnaires, attitude tests, projective techniques, and so on, which presumably **do** measure or "get at" the social phenomena in which he is interested. How does he know he has succeeded? This is where various tests of validity are helpful and should be studied by the more advanced student.

Reliability

While validity refers to whether the measuring instrument **really** "gets at" the desired social phenomena, reliability refers to the consistency, dependability, or "repeatability" of the measuring instrument. Does the investigator get the same results with his instrument if he uses it more than once? If not, it is not a reliable measuring device. If you weigh the same book on the same scale day after day, you will get the same result each time. The reliability of the social scientist's instruments—for example, a questionnaire—also depends on whether he (or other investigators) could use it with the same sample or similar samples of respondents more than once and get the same results. It is clear that the reliability of the social scientist's tools of investigation is considerably more problematic than that of an instrument such as a thermometer or a scale. Methods of testing instruments for reliability are important for the more advanced sociology student.

No one claims that sampling, validity, and reliability are unimportant; in fact, they are so important that they apply to **every** method in this manual. We have omitted these concerns from your projects only because they take a great deal of time to explain and to execute, and they do not add measurably to your initial experience in handling a specific method in the field.

As your time is limited, you will have no way of testing the **validity** of the findings—though you **can** compare your findings with the results of other investigators who have used similar measuring and classifying instruments. Nor will you be able to check on **reliability**—whether you would find the same thing if you repeated the study.

OBSERVATION AS A RESEARCH TOOL

Observation as a means of increasing one's knowledge is basic to the investigation of almost any phenomenon. Some types of social action can only be truly understood and appreciated when they are actually witnessed—seen "in the flesh." The pomp and ceremony of rituals, the life conditions of men in prison, and the subtle nuances of flirting are but a few aspects of social life best grasped through firsthand observation. Many of the most memorable sociological studies have been conducted by investigators who used observation techniques. That such studies are often of interest far beyond the immediate application of their findings bears witness to the vitality of observation as a research tool.

Observation of social phenomena is obviously not restricted to the sociologist. All people observe social situations to which they are privy or about which they would like greater understanding.

Moreover, they offer amateur reports of such scenes by describing and interpreting them to friends or relatives who were not present, in order to increase these persons' understanding of what happened. There is an important difference between the observations of the sociologist and those of the lay observer, however. Because the sociologist must organize and analyze his data in terms of sociological theories and concepts, he is sensitized to attending to human group life in a far more systematic fashion than the average person is. The layman relies primarily on his memory, but the researcher attempts to keep written descriptions of what he sees, for he is interested in more detail than his memory can retain. For this reason the sociologist is forced to think of systematic ways to conduct his observations and record what happens **as** it happens, or soon after, without upsetting his subjects or missing significant actions. Such planning is a part of the observation technique for which laymen seldom have patience or need.

THE DEPTH INTERVIEW, A DEFINITION

One of the major tools of the social scientist—the depth interview—is also a favorite of the average citizen. Everyone at one time or another has used this technique to learn more about a subject of interest. A person will start by asking someone general questions. As he receives answers, he follows up on certain points with increasingly specific questions until he has acquired "an understanding" of the topic.

Depth interviewing, as generally conducted by sociologists, has the same pattern as that used by curious nonprofessionals. The major difference is that the answers social researchers receive are usually carefully recorded and reviewed in terms of concepts and theories of concern to the discipline. As an **exploratory** tool, depth interviewing is a way to locate important information for further study. It can also become an end in itself—that is, a way to get detailed descriptions or even explanations of certain types of social behavior.

The depth interview enables the investigator to probe the intensity of an individual's feelings about a given social phenomenon, the intricacies of his definition of it, and how he relates it to other areas of his social life. Respondents will often give their judgments of what the attitudes of others are and how these affect their own attitudes and behavior. Memories of past events (technically called retrospective longitudinal data) can be obtained through depth interviews, especially when respondents are allowed adequate time to recall past events and place them in proper order or perspective.

Depth interviewing can be viewed as a fishing expedition, because the sociologist does it to get information when he has so little knowledge on a subject that he cannot ask structured questions. He also uses it to obtain more detail than a formal questionnaire normally makes available. The depth interview is a major tool in the social sciences, one that every competent researcher should be able to handle.

THE DESCRIPTIVE SURVEY, A DEFINITION

Survey research is a method for collecting and analyzing social data via highly structured and often very detailed interviews or questionnaires in order to obtain information from large numbers of respondents presumed to be representative of a specific population. The best-known example of this type of research is the so-called Gallup Poll of the American Institute of Public Opinion, a full-time survey organization that probes public attitudes about matters of general interest. Several universities also have permanent survey research centers located on or near their campuses—e.g., the National Opinion Research Center at the University of Chicago; the Survey Research Center at the University of California, Berkeley; and the Survey Research Center at the University of Michigan, Ann Arbor.

Survey research is not a new method. It began to be important as a research tool in sociology shortly before World War II, but its use only became truly widespread with the development of electronic computers. These machines perform rapid, accurate compilation and analysis of enormous quantities of "social facts" that before their development would have taken months or even years to complete.

The major aim of a descriptive survey is to establish the range and distribution of such social characteristics as age, sex, occupation, and marital status, and to determine how these characteristics are related to a particular behavior pattern or attitude. For example, an investigator might want to learn how many high school graduates in Berkeley, California, attend movies weekly as compared to the number who watch television nightly or read at least one book a year. Another investigator might want to conduct a descriptive study to

discover the attitudes of students in a college toward the development of a new Ethnic Studies Department. In such a case, he undoubtedly would want to find out which particular campus groups (ethnic, religious, departmental) favor the plan and which do not.

In a **descriptive** survey the sociologist is interested in **describing** the population he is studying. Therefore he will usually include questions that ask for information about **ascribed** characteristics (age, sex, race, nationality, etc.) as well as for information about characteristics that arise from membership in social groups or categories (occupation, income, religious affiliation, etc.). Usually he will also want to know about past and present behaviors, beliefs, values, attitudes, or opinions.

Laymen constantly indulge in descriptive surveys. They collect such social statistics as: How many persons are home from the office with the flu? How many people got drunk at the party last night? Were there more friends of the bride or of the groom at the wedding? How many of that "old gang" are now married or engaged to be married? The professional survey researcher is often interested in the same types of information as the layman, but he wants to be able to generalize his findings to large populations.

In an **explanatory** survey the sociologist concerns himself with **explaining** the relationships that he has shown in the descriptive survey. Often he has a hunch about the cause or causes of a particular act or belief, and he will use the data gathered in the large descriptive survey to see if his hypothesis can be verified.

PARTICIPANT OBSERVATION, A DEFINITION

Now that you are acquainted with the field technique of observation, you should be ready to take a turn with its research cousin, participant observation. Both of these techniques are important sociological tools. It is only by observing what people **do** when they interact with one another, as well as by recording what they **say** they do, that we can begin to get an understanding of the dynamics of social processes.

The method of research known as participant observation differs from structured and unstructured observations in several important ways. As the name implies, the participant observer is a researcher who becomes a member of the group he is observing, while the nonparticipant observer tries to remain aloof from it. This distinction is not clear-cut since there is a wide range in the level of participation—from the sociologist who stays out of the group and just watches the action to the researcher who is actually a member. Usually a researcher participates to a degree somewhere between these two extremes by either **posing** as a member or announcing himself as a scientific investigator and hoping to be accepted by the group in that role. Inevitably, a time continuum parallels the degree of participation. The longer an observer stays on the scene, the more likely he is to be drawn into participating in the group's way of life. As a general rule, the **participant** observer commits himself to a group for a considerable period of time, ranging from several weeks or months to many years.

A second characteristic of the participant observer is that he tries to understand the frame of reference of the group he is investigating. He does this primarily by joining the members in their daily activities in order to experience things as they do. The autobiographies of those who have lived for many years in institutions such as prisons (Black, 1927) or convents (Baldwin, 1959) are particularly insightful studies of these "closed" societies. Though these individuals were not trained sociologists, they were participant observers **par excellence.**

There is a certain similarity between this approach and espionage. The observer must exist mentally on two levels. Instead of being socialized to the new way of life almost unknowingly, as are most individuals after they join a group, the scientific investigator must learn to be simultaneously "inside" and "outside" the group life he is studying. He must learn the meanings that behavior has for the members of the group, and he has to become sufficiently involved with the group to be able to understand what makes it tick. At the same time, he cannot be so involved that he is unable to report accurately what is happening and why. He cannot be so far "inside" that everything seems so "normal" as to be not worth reporting. And to top it all off, he must be able to report patterns of behavior and interrelationships objectively, without moral judgment or bias. The reason for this double frame of reference is that the participant observer wants to understand the group and its actions not only in its own terms—that is, how the members themselves live and feel the culture—but also in terms of a larger and more general set of sociological hypotheses or theories about the nature of human interaction.

Do these sound like impossible tasks? They are difficult, but with practice they can be handled fairly well. Anthropologists occasionally find some of the attitudes, beliefs, and behaviors of the societies they study repugnant or immoral. However, they are trained not to judge, but rather to try to faithfully record and to determine what meaning these behavior patterns have for the people who practice them.[1] Perhaps an even more common outcome of close contact with a new group over a prolonged period of time is the observer's identification with the group. He starts to accept their behavior patterns as his own and may find it hard to reenter his old way of life when he has finished his study. Many Peace Corps volunteers have had this problem after living for a year or two in a foreign culture with a way of life dissimilar from their own. These twin dangers—aversion and overidentification—can be partially neutralized if the researcher is aware that he is not **merely** a recording machine—and that he is going to have personal reactions to any new group he enters.

NOTES

1. The diary of Bronislaw Malinowski, the famous English anthropologist, was published recently, and a great many people, including social scientists, were shocked at the disclosures he made of his personal feelings about the Trobriand Islanders (Malinowski, 1967).

topic 3
the sociological enterprise: issues and controversies

One observes these grave young sciences hiding behind their precocious bears of "dispassionate research" and "scientific objectivity." They observe, record, and analyze, but they shun prediction. And, above all else, they avoid having any commerce with "values." Values, they say, may not be derived from science, and therefore science should have nothing to do with them.

Robert Lynd wrote these words a third of a century ago. Yet, as the articles by Anderson and Howard attest, they might just as well have been written yesterday, for they express a point of view that is as topical and controversial in the 1970s as it was on the eve of World War II. C. Wright Mills was referring to one facet of this issue when he charged that "those in the grip of the methodological inhibition often refuse to say anything about modern society unless it has been through the fine little mill of the Statistical Ritual." And when Alvin W. Gouldner alleges that "all the powers of sociology have entered into a tacit alliance to bind us to the dogma that 'Thou shalt not commit a value judgment,' " he is alluding to still another, yet closely related, theme.

In the selection "Toward a Sociology of Being," Henry Anderson advises us of the dangers inherent in a purely statistical view of man—a view that often seems to conceive of man as little more than a "collection of conditioned responses to situational stimuli." Another sociologist meant much the same thing when he attacked the "oversocialized conception of man" that would portray humans as robotlike bundles of culturally forged social roles. Anderson argues that the "sociology of the survey research method" is guilty of perpetuating a variety of other misconceptions; for instance, it belittles the crucial role of social change, and it confuses what may in reality be healthful social reorganization with what it deems to be pathological social disorganization.

Espousing a "radical perspective" in sociology, John Howard urges what growing numbers of younger scholars are demanding—that sociology must be a sociology of engagement, that the sociologist can no longer afford to be a mere passive observer "watching others do their thing." It is obvious, what is more, that the radical perspective touches other bases as well, among them the question of whose "side" a more applied and less theoretical sociology should be on and whose interests it should serve—for example, the political-industrial establishment or the impoverished ghetto dweller.

Elaborating on Howard's thesis, Thomas F. Hoult alludes to the counterargument that celebrates the importance of value-neutrality and the noninvolvement of sociologists in polemical or hotly debated issues. This interpretation, Hoult claims, "amounts to a permanent abrogation of responsibility because, of course, in the complex affairs of mankind we can be **absolutely** sure of nothing of importance." Nor does Hoult stop there: "Although greed and sloth may account for a significant number of those who choose to remain on what they **think** is dead center . . . I am personally convinced," he says, "that **cowardice** is the most important single explanation."

All the same, Hans Peter Dreitzel concludes, "in spite of this growing split between 'establishment sociology' and 'radical sociology,' the mainstream of the discipline is still the safe and shallow waters of academic empiricism." Perhaps. But two other sociologists speak for a growing number of younger academicians when they urge that "it is imperative for sociologists to analyze what is sick in American society and then to act to try to change and heal American society."

chapter 5
toward a sociology of being
henry anderson

The questions to be studied, the ways they are to be studied, and everything else that passes under the rubric of "sociology" depend on assumptions which are usually not articulated at all, and which most sociologists appear to avoid as "insusceptible of proof": assumptions about the nature of man. Sociologists usually do not openly utilize the terminology of behavioristic psychology. But without examining or acknowledging their debt, they commonly rest everything they do on these premises borrowed unwittingly and whole: that man is by his nature a collection of conditioned responses to situational stimuli. It is difficult otherwise to account for the orthodox sociological conception of man as a creature whose behavior is so patterned that one may sum up each person in terms of his roles and statuses; and, indeed, that one may abstract from the behavior of large numbers of persons such regularities that roles and statuses are often spoken of as though they were entities with an existence of their own.

Sociology has been able to survive as long as it has with this world view because people do indeed act in a fairly predictable way much of the time. This enables one, after interviewing a sample with a standardized questionnaire, to say, with an

From Manas, 21, January 27, 1968, pp. 1-2, 7-8. Manas Publishing Company. Reprinted by permission.

appropriate number of weasel words, that the people who live in Piedmont will more likely vote Republican than the people who live in East Oakland, and so forth. For some limited kinds of purposes such findings are doubtless meaningful. None of these is a particularly "sociological" application, however. Statistical methods are inherently unable to shed much light on most of the important questions about what is going on in society. The important questions are the ones that are hard to answer, and they are hard to answer precisely because man is not just a creature who acts out a series of social roles. Man is also a creative and cantankerous creature who sometimes kicks over the traces. Babbitts try their hand at abstract expressionism; crooks become honest men, and honest men sell out for the right price; ministers desert their wives and run off with organists, or leave the organists and return to their wives. And this kind of latent indeterminacy is not just individual. Sometimes substantial numbers of people kick over the traces in the same way at the same time. People get swept away by a demagogue; welfare recipients rise up in protest against being degraded, young people drop out to become hippies.

The entire range of social movements, fads, fashions, booms, panics, crazes, mobs, riots, revolutions, is incomprehensible in terms of man "programmed" to act and talk and think in a certain socially acceptable and predictable way. The sociology of the survey research method says almost nothing, and can say almost nothing, about this whole vast area of human behavior. Gagged by the consequences of its conception of the nature of man, it is virtually mute on the subject of social change—the area which should constitute the growing edge of sociology. Societies are obviously changing, and changing at an accelerating rate. They are changing primarily in the above mentioned ways—the "unacceptable" ways which lie outside the competence of polls and interviews.

The behavior of human beings—not only when they are running outside of established channels, but, for that matter, when they are acting more "stably"—is adequately accounted for only in terms of a radically different conception of the nature of man. Man is a creature, the only creature, with a sense of self. Given this sense of self, he is able to carry on internal dialogues with himself, and he does so during practically every waking moment. Some of the exchanges in this dialogue are more common than others, and in these cases the internal conversation may flow back and forth almost instantaneously and unreflectively. Shall I turn off the alarm clock? Yes. Shall I put on a clean pair of socks? Yes. Right foot first? Yes. Now left foot? Yes. White shirt next? No. Undershirt? Yes.

Repetition may cut down the transaction times of such dialogues to tenths or even perhaps hundredths of seconds, but the process never becomes purely "automatic." And the moment anything slightly out of the ordinary occurs—and there are hundreds of such moments in every human being's existence, every day—the internal communication slows down, blooms and proliferates in all manner of new directions. This razor blade is getting dull. Shall I change it or make do one more time? What's the matter with these blades, anyway? Should I pick up a box of that other brand today? Say, has my wife been shaving her legs with my razor again? How many times do I have to ask her not to? Is this a sign she is growing away from me? Am I being unreasonable? And so forth. These sequences cannot be accounted for by behavioristic theory.

A human life is built up of such rich, blooming, variegated give-and-take. It is "social" to the extent that the internal images which pass in review as one is thinking, speaking, or acting are derived from experiences one has had with others. This is a very great extent indeed. But "the

others"—i.e., society—can never completely control the content of the images, the sequences in which they will pass in review in the individual's private dialogue, or the selections which the individual will make on a particular occasion.

There is nothing esoteric about this conception of man's nature. Nor is it a sentimental view of the way one might like human beings to be. It is the way human beings are, and cannot help being. Whoever you are, you may verify this conception of the nature of your own nature by looking into yourself (your Self) during any waking minute. You cannot stop the flood of images and subvocal conversation even if you try—and the harder you try, the more will flood in through the back door. For example, as you have been reading this piece, hundreds of reactions, recollections, propositions, and possibilities have passed fleetingly in review within your perpetual dialogue.

Human behavior, then, is the outcome of dialogue, rather than any fixed stimulus-response arcs, instincts, or metaphysical imperatives such as "role" or "status." To account for human behavior, there is no substitute for "getting in on the dialogue." This is another way of saying that, for anything but the most superficial kinds of understandings, sociology requires a conception of the nature of man which is humanistic rather than mechanistic.

Let us consider a few examples of how orthodox, mechanistic sociology and a new humanistic sociology might differ in their approaches to the same problems. Let us say we are interested in the question of employee morale or job satisfaction. If we happen to be survey research sociologists, we prepare a battery of questions, and after a number of pretests, we select, say, a dozen questions which provide a "scalable" basis for ranking informants from very low job-satisfaction to very high job-satisfaction. We find, say, that 5 per cent rank in what we call a very low satisfaction category, 5 per cent in a very high satisfaction category, with other percentages distributed in a "normal curve" in whatever categories we have ordained between the two extremes.

Like the strictly objective scientists that we aspire to be, we let these statistics speak for themselves—but they speak neither very loudly nor very accurately about what is really going on in the job situations of our society. They cannot. For one thing, many informants are not in close enough touch with themselves and their internal dialogues to be aware of how they honestly feel toward their jobs. For another thing, many would not tell an interviewer the truth even if they were in touch with it. For example, it is commonplace for people to feel resentful toward bureaucracies for homogenizing them, and to "fight back" by subtle forms of sabotage, by boondoggling, by taking a whole day to do a task that might take no more than an hour if their morale were good. To observe these things is crucial to any serious understanding of what is happening in American working life and will happen increasingly as more jobs become bureaucratized.

People are unlikely to admit to an interviewer—even an interviewer highly skilled at manipulating their privacy—that they have been boondoggling. They usually do not openly admit it to themselves. It is probably not so much a matter of their fearing that they will be fired if the truth is known, as fear of a loss of esteem: self-esteem, and esteem by another. Most people crave the good opinion even of an interviewer they have never seen before and know they will never see again. The crucial understandings are a closed door as long as the researcher has a questionnaire in his hand. The door begins to open only as he grows sensitive to the **sub rosa** dialogues that lie behind overt dialogues—for example, what people are really saying as they engage in idle office gossip during coffee breaks. Or, perhaps even better, the researcher may work at a white-collar job himself and tune in on his own internal communication, moment by moment.

Another example, from among many which could be given, of the way a humanistic sociology, as distinguished from a mechanistic sociology, might operate in a given area: Traditional sociology collects data on divorces and classifies them by age of the principals, length of marriage, number of children, etc. These statistics usually appear in courses and sections of texts entitled "social pathology," "social disorganization," and the like. Such a perspective conceals more than it reveals. Behind the statistical curtain, a tremendous ferment is taking place, moving in the direction of redefining the relationships between men and women in our society—redefining love, sexuality, the family, maternity, paternity, masculinity, femininity. Some of this ferment, to be sure, is rebellion without a cause, and many people are being badly hurt to no constructive purpose. But much of what is going on might better be thought of as social reorganization than as social disorganization. The family is not going to be tomorrow

what it was yesterday or is today. If sociology is to make a useful contribution to the understanding of this deep tide, it must have almost totally new methods of observation.

The **reductio ad absurdum** of the survey research method was the census of orgasms conducted by Kinsey, who was, of course, a biologist, but was ever afterward called a "sociologist" because he used the orthodox sociological method of asking people some simple questions and adding up the simple answers. Any number of sociologists promptly went out to conduct similar censuses, and then quibbled over whose sampling technique was the best. All of it was so irrelevant to what is really happening in the relationships between the sexes that it was tantamount to outright falsification. If there is any one thing of which we may be sure about the present process of redefinition, it is that, amid all the fitful starts and blind alleys, it points in the direction of quality of relationship rather than quantity. Women are demanding that they be perceived not as sexual objects, or housekeepers, or nursemaids, but as full persons in their very own right. And so are men, a little more slowly perhaps, and in their own ways.

How does a researcher apprehend these things? He becomes attuned to the conversation of gestures. He learns what is meant by silences as well as by words. He learns what is meant by the sighs, frowns, giggles, tears. He has to get behind masks, to where the gropings, the agonies, the intimacies are. He cannot possibly do this in an interview. The instant he knocks at the door of a couple in the midst of a quarrel, or an act of love, or any other kind of authentic revelation, the authenticity ceases, and he gets answers from masks, not from the real people behind. His findings may be "true" in the sense that most people prefer to wear masks in the presence of interviewers and other strangers. But his findings will be false in the sense that there were critical dialogues taking place behind the masks, dialogues by definition inaccessible to strangers.

The survey research method is helpless in the face of most significant social questions because of a kind of Heisenberg effect which is far more serious than anything in the physical or biological sciences: the very act of observation distorts that which is being observed. But whereas the natural sciences accept the "uncertainty principle" with an appropriate humility, sociology tries to nullify it by investing more time and talent in sharpening the very methods that are trivializing human social life, cutting back its true boundaries, betraying it, falsifying it.

It is difficult to think of a precedent for this: a would-be science busily engaged in denying and eroding the character of its subject matter. Sociology, as the study of human relationships should, before anything else, have a clear conception of what genuine human relationships are, as distinguished from ersatz varieties.

If two people act like automatons toward one another—one consistently subordinate, one consistently superordinate, let us say, or one consistently aggressive, the other consistently passive—they are the beau ideal of orthodox sociological research. And if you multiply them by a million, you have the beau ideal of a stable, predictable, quantifiable society. But can they be said to have a human relationship? It would be more accurate to say that they have an inhuman relationship.

Sociology is going to fall farther and farther behind in its comprehension of what is actually happening in society, and what is going to happen, because people are growing more and more dissatisfied with inhuman relationships. What is taking place behind the masks is growing richer all the time. Social roles are not what they may have been. People are building their interior castles stronger, getting in touch with themselves better. That is the root reason why our society is growing increasingly dynamic: men are increasingly demanding that their essential human nature be recognized and fulfilled. All kinds of people are mounting this demand in one way or another, from the millionaire business executive who joins an "encounter group," to the man with the hoe who no longer dumbly accepts the blowing out of the light in his brain but is joining a union or asking for land of his own. It is dawning on vast numbers of people that they are real and they are individuals, unique in all the world, not just a bundle of projections of what their parents, teachers, employers, and others think they ought to be. It is dawning on people that they are entitled to demand that they be allowed to function and grow as authentic persons. This is the greatest revolution among all the revolutions of our time, and it is bound to spread. For after all the other revolutions are consummated—computerization, the guaranteed annual income, "black power," land reform, or whatever—the most basic of hungers will remain to be satisfied: the hunger to be a truly human being.

If sociologists devoted themselves to sensitivity rather than methodological rigor—if they spent more time looking behind social roles and less time at the facades (including a great deal more time looking behind their own roles and searching for their own selves)—would this be the abandonment of sociology as a "science"? It all depends on what one means by science. Yes, if science is the accumulation of numbers representing observations which can later be duplicated more or less exactly by some other observer. No, if science is the accretion of wisdom, insight, and understanding of the subject matter by means which are most appropriate to the nature of the subject itself.

The question of "subjectivity" and "objectivity" is a bugbear in any such discussion. The process envisaged here does not require that sociology take to the hustings and plump for the humanization of man, mount shot and shell against the dehumanization of man, or even use the naughty words that one is "good" and the other is "bad." Man's nature is his nature, no matter what sociology says, and man is going to struggle toward the fulfillment of his nature no matter what sociology does or does not do. What is envisaged here would not involve "taking sides," losing scholarly dignity, or whatever other red herrings the sociological establishment might try to draw across the trail. All that is suggested here is that, for the sake of its own survival if for no other reason, sociology begin asking the right kinds of questions—those which really get at the things which hold groups of human beings together, tear them apart, and enable them to reassemble themselves in some coherent way. These are the legitimate sociological questions. All questions which assume that human beings are mechanical are unrealistic, unsociological, and in the truest sense of the word "unscientific."

It is entirely proper that a work of literature—a novel by Dickens or Zola, for example—be considered also a work of sociology, quite possibly a greater work of sociology than a statistical study of nineteenth-century England or France could have been if there had been survey research sociologists at large in those days. It is entirely possible that more might be learned about family life in modern Mexico from five families telling their stories honestly than from any number of stilted interviews with any size sample.

The **sine qua non** of human science is not numbers; it is insights, and the power of prediction which insights confer. If plays by Ionesco announce to those who have ears to listen amidst the laughter, that communication between husbands and wives, teachers and pupils, has become absurd, and that people are growing restive with absurd communication, then these are major sociological statements, and may be said to have forecast such developments as the Free Speech Movement better than any academic sociological statements. If plays by LeRoi Jones anticipated, before Watts, that there was going to be violence between black and white in the North, they should be counted as better sociology than any of the surveys.

The best sociology is not usually by sociologists, but by those who are free from any obsession with statistical methods: anthropologists, existential psychologists, theologians, philosophers, novelists, playwrights. For example, Buber is most often thought of as a philosopher—the founder of the "philosophy of dialogue." But he was as much a sociologist as anything else, and he gave us the conceptual tools for a "sociology of dialogue," or what we have here called "humanistic sociology."

One of the most significant features of the survey method is that it precludes any dialogue between the interviewer and interviewee. The interviewer is carefully trained to stifle all his normal human impulses—to take from the informant, but to give nothing of himself in return. This cannot but perplex the informant, throw him off stride, render the entire situation counterfeit. In real life, people do not function without cues from others.

Without dialogue, there is no such thing as society. Without listening to this dialogue, tactfully, attentively, lovingly, there is no such thing as an adequate sociology.

If sociology continues to lag in its grasp of the nature of human nature, and what this nature implies for research problems and methods, it will increasingly be cast into the intellectual penumbras of our time. It will be overshadowed by the philosophers of being, psychologists of being, and others who are in touch and in sympathy with the great contemporary revolution in man's understanding of his own nature.

It does not strain the imagination excessively to visualize institutions of higher learning, twenty years or so from now, in which sociology departments occupy approximately the same kind of place that classics departments do today. Since the academy changes cautiously, a corner will be reserved for the present crop of bright, young,

mathematically oriented assistant professors of sociology, by then grown into full professors. They will still get grants from the National Institutes of Health and other federal agencies. They will be given a computer for their very own, and they may command a somewhat distant admiration from their less mathematically inclined colleagues who do not know how to write a computer program. But their version of sociology will be regarded as an anachronism by most students, and without students any academic field grows old, sere, crotchety, quaint, and irrelevant. Students will gravitate toward the promise of greater wisdom, which will lie in such areas as the psychology of Maslow, the philosophy of Kierkegaard, the theology of Tillich, and, even more, in areas we can presently only vaguely foresee: creative combinations of "talking about" the psychology, philosophy, theology, anthropology of Being, and actually Being through body movement, sensory awareness, self-revelation, painting, whatever.

It does not exhaust the imagination to visualize "courses" and perhaps even a whole "curriculum" in which "students" and "professors" begin by learning to shuck their masks by dance, improvisatory theater, and the like, and then go on simply to share their life stories. More might be learned about sociology, and a score of other "subjects," in these ways than from any number of formal lectures.

If this is the trend, why trouble to protest against the shortcomings of contemporary sociology? Why not let events take their course, and let sociology go into eclipse? What difference does it make where the insights come from, as long as they come;

It does make a difference whether the emphasis is on the dialogue of John and Mary Smith, or whether the question is, How are all the other Smiths doing with their dialogue, empathy, sharing, genuineness, joy, love, and other aspects of humanness? Are they going forward, by and large; are they going backward; or are they standing still? Why are some people moving more than others? What are the processes by which a fledgling human being, necessarily dependent on those around him for his images, identity, and very survival, grows beyond this dependency and becomes a unique person? How can people pass along the necessary continuities to the fledgling human beings who are born to them, and then, in due time, help those beings become less conforming and more fully human? What are the environmental influences which tend to assist this process? What influences hinder it? What can be done to encourage the influences which foster human development? What can be done to minimize the influences which retard it?

With exemplary modesty, most humanistic psychologists and others who are in the vanguard of the revolution in Being focus on the individual, and do not attempt to address the sweeping broad-gauge questions. But somebody must be so immodest as to do so, for these questions will determine whether society itself lives or dies. These questions constitute the province of what might be called a "sociology of dialogue" or "humanistic sociology." Since the word "humanistic" is subject to various misinterpretations, perhaps it would be preferable to say that what is advocated here is an ushering out of the old sociology of seeming, and an ushering in of a sociology of human becoming and of being.

chapter 6
notes on the radical perspective in sociology
john howard

Contemporary American sociology is probably viewed by many persons as being a radical discipline. In an article appearing in **The New York Times Sunday Magazine**, Irving Kristol suggested that much of the unrest on college campuses across the nation during the fall of 1968 had been inspired by sociologists—graduate students and faculty;[1] and even Vice-President Spiro Agnew was quoted during the 1968 election campaign as stating that policy with regard to urban problems should be guided by the hardheaded knowledge of the businessman and the engineer rather than the dubious nostrums of the sociologist.

In truth, sociology's reputation for daring is hardly deserved. Like the fake priest played by Humphrey Bogart in the movie **The Left Hand of God**, the discipline is not what most people think it is. It has neither posed a radical analysis of the society nor consistently concerned itself with alternatives and change.

In the last few years an increasing number of sociologists have begun to question the orientation of the discipline. In a piece appearing in **Transaction** magazine Herbert Gans criticized his colleagues for not choosing to do research having greater relevance for policy—particularly with regard to poverty.

Sociology has long limited itself to describing and explaining human behavior, using methods and concepts not easily adapted to the needs of policy. As a result, sociologists find it easier to catalogue behavior (and misbehavior) of the poor than to suggest experiments that would test ways of eliminating poverty.[2]

Many published studies, Gans commented, "are still small and narrow, often intended more for colleagues than for application to current social problems."

Alvin Gouldner,[3] Maurice Stein,[4] and Thomas Hoult[5] have also questioned some of the basic dicta of the discipline, particularly the principle of "ethical neutrality."

Discontent is to be found among graduate students as well as faculty. The November, 1968, issue of **The Human Factor,** the journal of the Graduate Students Union at Columbia University, was devoted to a self-proclaimed radical critique of the discipline. We quote from the conclusion of Albert Syzmanski's "Toward a Radical Sociology." Whatever the dismay felt by the elders of the sociological tribe, Syzmanski's article represents the thinking of at least some of the people who will play a role in shaping the future of the discipline.

We maintain that radical sociologists must have an integral conception of their role as radical sociologists, and avoid the schizophrenic dissociation of their academic and political activities. Radical sociology should not mean contributing money to radical causes, nor should it mean dropping out to organize slum dwellers, draft resisters, or guerrillas. The goal of radical sociologists should be above all the formulation and propagation of a sociology relevant to the practical problems facing man. We must conceive of our contribution to the building of a decent society in terms of (1) the development of an understanding of the organization and dynamics of our society; (2) the development of an understanding of how that society can be changed and a human social organization substituted; and (3) the dissemination of these understandings to our fellow social scientists, our students, and to men in general.[6]

The elders of the discipline probably view sentiments of this sort as the aberrations of youth, or as an expression of outrage at the multiple indignities of graduate student life—some academic equivalent of the Freudian drama of the slaying of the father. It is possible, however, that they bespeak more than momentary madness or infantile leftism.

This book forms a part of the dissent from the discipline as traditionally constituted. In this brief essay we shall explore the meaning of the term "radical sociology." Is it possible, in any scholarly sense, to speak of a radical sociology? Some might argue that it makes no sense to link words such as these: that on one level it is verbal magic, while on another level, it is like speaking of "Baptist sociology" or "Stalinist sociology"—that is, it connotes an ideological bias which precludes the objective analysis of behavior.

In the remainder of this essay we shall attend to these questions.

RADICAL SOCIOLOGY: NOTES FOR A DEFINITION

Radical sociology rests upon a certain conception of the social role of the sociologist. We are in accord with Thomas Hoult's observation that "it is both logical and necessary for sociologists to become involved in at least certain aspects of building the 'good society.' " That

It is appropriate for sociologists **acting as such**, to "take sides" relative to those controversial social issues which are functionally related to conditions that seem likely to enhance or undermine the development of the social sciences.[7]

Hoult argues that a sociology having any degree of integrity cannot exist except in a society with libertarian values. Therefore, involvement in the actions and passions of the times, in the continuing struggle to maintain and extend those values, should be part of the professional role of the sociologist.

In this sense, radical sociology tends to focus on what might loosely be termed "social problems." It is not the case, however, that all sociology dealing with social problems is **per se** radical. A number of attributes identify the radical perspective.

First, it is assumed that certain of the questions with which sociologists concern themselves are more important than others. Certain questions bear on deep and enduring cleavages in the society and on complexes of values which have great portent in terms of its character. Thus, issues and questions of class, race, and generation, of the distribution of power, and the management of dissent bear on what kind of society now exists and what kind of society it will become.

Second, even when important phenomena are studied, the manner in which questions are put may preclude radical analysis. Put somewhat differently, attendance to important issues is not **per se** radical; it is also, in part, a matter of how one asks one's questions. C. Wright Mills in "The Professional Ideology of Social Pathologists" indicated that many sociologists and social workers tended to view the difficulties of people as personal and psychological in nature rather than as consequences of social structure.[8] The radical raises questions with regard to social structure and whether it generates and sustains the problems of individuals.

There is an extensive literature in sociology which acknowledges the existence of certain kinds of social problems—poverty, racism, powerlessness—but often there is the accompanying assumption that these problems can be understood in terms of the characteristics of their bearers rather than in terms of system defects. For example:

—Regarding education, a vast literature attempts to account for the inferior performance of slum children in the public schools in terms of their "cultural deprivation," "impoverished home lives," "lower aspiration levels," and the like. The radical would at least raise questions as to whether the school system itself generates failure. Are there systematic differences in the quality of physical plant between slum and nonslum schools?[9] Do teachers expect lower-class children and nonwhite children to be stupid and therefore react to them as if they were in fact stupid?[10]

—Regarding the disproportionately high percentage of households among blacks headed by a female, does one seek an explanation in terms of the "self image of the Negro male" and the "historical legacy of slavery" or in the persistent exclusion of blacks from the job market by employers and trade unions?[11]

The radical perspective has important consequences for the formulation of policy. It is not simply a matter of preference or prejudice, but a question of how one accurately accounts for certain problems. Explanation governs the formulation of policy. Some of the work of E. White Bakke on unemployed whites during the depression revealed the same kind of family breakdown that the Moynihan report indicated for blacks.[12] The disintegration of the family among whites was directly and clearly a consequence of the breakdown of the economy and of course had nothing to do with "self-image" or "historical legacies." The radical perspective suggests that system analysis not only is likely to generate sounder explanations for the phenomena in question, but also holds more promising possibilities for the formulation of effective policy.

In short, then, radical sociology has recourse to the distinction which C. Wright Mills made between "the personal troubles of milieu and the public issues of social structure."[13] In other words, if a few people are poor, one may look to "case factors." If masses are poor, one has grounds for asking questions about social structure.

Radical sociology asks whether the problems generated by social structure are inherent within it (a consequence of "internal contradictions," if one will) or simply "mistakes" or unintended consequences? Poverty, for example, can be seen as simply a residual category, i.e., the poor are those people who have **not yet** been raised up in standard of living by the dynamic of an expanding economy. Alternatively, it may be viewed as an inevitable consequence of a certain kind of economy. The policy implications of these alternatives are quite profound. If problems are seen simply as accidents, then one poses policies which leave the fundamental structure of the system intact (in terms of education, for example, bonus pay for teachers willing to work in slum schools). On the other hand, if defects are discerned to be an integral part of the way the system normally operates, then policy calling for more fundamental kinds of restructuring becomes necessary (again, in terms of education, something such as "community control" of schools by ghetto people).

Further, the radical perspective generates its own definition of problems and system defects. It deals in an area where there is broad consensus— poverty and inequality, for example—but it does not assume that conventional definitions exhaustively identify what is. As John Seeley indicated in "The Making and Taking of Social Problems," one needs to ask who is doing the defining. Seeley commented on the inadequacy of conventional definitions.

> The table of contents of almost any "social problems" text shows a notable bias in the predictable direction. The text I have momentarily at hand lists among "Deviant Behavior" only Crime, Juvenile Delinquency, Mental Disorders, Drug Addiction, Suicide, and Prostitution; and among "Social Disorganization" Population Crisis, Race and Ethnic Relations, Family, Work, Military, Community and Traffic Disorganization, and Disaster. The presence of the military chapter is unusual and somewhat happenstantial, but otherwise this pretty well is the "mix as usual," representing our study of categories of persons sufficiently powerless to offer small resistance to violation by enquiry.
>
> . . . On the Social Disorganization side also we have a more or less customary collection of relatively unresistant units that could be disorganized and could be enquired into. Note no business disorganization, religious disorganization, intellectual anomie, political breakdown, or disorganization, debasement, and degradation of the most eminent candidate: post primary education.
>
> Safe. Safe. Safe.[14]

Radical sociology generates its own definition of social problems partly by asking questions about system defects and about the possible role of social structure in perpetuating problems and defeating the intentions of meliorative policy.

Lest it be said that the radical perspective involves the sociologist in making judgments which are properly foreign to any science, let us point out that there is no such thing as being "above the battle." A number of persons have indicated that the social scientist who refuses to take sides opts by default for the status quo. Beyond this, there is a respected body of theory in sociology which rationalizes and justifies the status quo. One need only mention Talcott Parsons's "Revised Analytic Theory of Social Stratification"[15] or the Davis-Moore theory of stratification.[16] The logical short-comings and analytic insufficiencies of the functionalist approach to stratification and inequality have already been commented upon at length in other places, and there is no need to discuss them here. As Howard Becker suggested, no matter how one approaches it, ultimately it is a question of "Whose Side Are We On?"[17]

Finally, radical sociology is a sociology of **engagement**. Traditionally the role of the sociologist in the field has been that of observer. He has confined himself to watching others do their thing. The radical perspective suggests that it is legitimate (in a scholarly sense) for the sociologist to play a vigorous role in the situations and organizations which he studies. Etzkowitz and Schaflander in their article "A Manifesto for Sociologists" gave several illustrations of engaged social science.

One social scientist who has gone beyond the non-involved, observer-participant category is Robert Coles, a psychiatrist. He went to study the Student Non-Violent Coordinating Committee in Mississippi during the Summer of 1964. Once down there he found that no one in SNCC was interested in talking to him. To them he seemed to be just another social scientist asking what they thought were irrelevant questions. But instead of just asking his questions and getting "put on" answers, he decided to stay for the summer and offered to become their doctor. Gradually he came to be trusted by them enough to begin group psychotherapy.

Coles came to occupy a key position in their organization. As part of the inner circle, he helped to make decisions and then partici-

pated in the action they took. He thus knew what was going on from the inside. The insight and knowledge he gained thereby was far greater than that of the sociologist who flies down on the "Civil Rights Special" to ask Stokely Carmichael "How's it going, baby?" over a one-night scotch-and-steak quiz session.

SNCC trusted Coles and he was able to tape record and take notes without having to ask any questions. He was interacting in a real life situation. His resources and materials were drawn from his daily life. He learned more about what was happening that summer than any sociologist could learn by any other socio-logical method. No outside observer, no one coming in with a questionnaire, or sending a questionnaire down, or coming down there to do depth interviewing, could learn as much as he did as part of the decision-making apparatus. Like any other social scientist, when he returned North he scientifically checked and evaluated his research.

It can be questioned, then, whether the purposes of scholarship are necessarily served by lack of involvement. Indeed, under some circumstances scholarly purposes may be properly attended to **only** if the sociologist becomes involved.

Etzkowtiz and Schaflander go beyond this; they suggest that the sociologist should play a positive role in the creation of institutions which embody humanist and libertarian values. They suggest that this is necessary both in terms of the professional obligation of the sociologist to use his skills in the alleviation of social ills, and in terms of the superior quality of the data which emerges when the sociologist has been deeply involved in a situation rather than riding the coattails of people who are involved.

NOTES

1. Irving Kristol, "A Different Way to Restructure the University," The New York Times Sunday Magazine, 4, No. 13:3, 50-53, 162-180, December 8, 1968.

2. Herbert Gans, "Where Sociologists Have Failed," Trans-action, October 1967, p. 2.

3. Alvin W. Gouldner, "Anti-Minotaur: The Myth of a Value-Free Sociology," Social Problems, 9, No. 3:199-213, winter 1962.

4. Maurice R. Stein, "Value Sterility, Value Neutrality, or Value Advocacy: The Choice Before Us," The Human Factor, 8, No. 1, November 1968.

5. Thomas Ford Hoult, "Who Shall Prepare Himself to the Battle," The American Sociologist, 1, No. 1:3-7, February 1968. [Steven E. Deutsch and John Howard (eds.), Where It's At. New York: Harper & Row, 1970.]

6. Albert Szymanski, "Toward a Radical Sociology," The Human Factor, 8, No. 1:21, November 1968.

7. Hoult, op. cit., p. 3.

8. C. Wright Mills, "The Professional Ideology of Social Pathologists," in Irving Louis Horowitz (ed.), Power, Politics, and People. New York: Oxford University Press, 1967.

9. Patricia Sexton, Education and Income. New York: Viking Press, 1961. See p. 241 in this text [Deutsch and Howard, op. cit.].

10. See for example, Robert Rosenthal and Lenore Jacobson, Pygmalion in the Classroom: Teacher Expectation and Pupils' Intellectual Development. New York: Holt, Rinehart & Winston, 1968.

11. See the section on "The Distribution of Work Opportunities," p. 283 in this text [Deutsch and Howard, op. cit.].

12. E. White Bakke, Citizens Without Work. London: Oxford University Press, 1940.

13. C. Wright Mills, The Sociological Imagination. New York: Oxford University Press, 1959, pp. 8-13. See p. 15 in this text [Deutsch and Howard, op. cit.].

14. John Seeley, "The Making and Taking of Social Problems: Toward an Ethical Stance," Social Problems, 14, No. 4:382-389, Spring 1967.

15. Talcott Parsons, "Revised Analytic Approach to the Theory of Social Stratification," in Reinhard Bendix and Seymour Lipset (eds.), Class, Status, and Power. Glencoe, Ill.: Free Fress, 1953.

16. Kingsley Davis and Wilbert Moore, "Some Principles of Stratification," American Sociological Review, 10:242-249, 1945.

17. Howard S. Becker, "Whose Side Are We On?" Social Problems, 14, No. 3:239-248, 1967.

topic 4

the cultural dimensions
of everyday life:
the cultural imperative

Culture. Few terms are so crucial to the sociological conception of human life. None is so pivotal, wide-ranging, and multidimensional. Moreover, perhaps no other concept is so slippery—so hard to grasp and employ—and meets with such stubborn if unconscious resistance on the part of the newcomer to sociology. Why? The reasons are various and significant, and the articles by Horace Miner and Clyde Kluckhohn tell us why.

Miner's essay affords vivid documentation of the fact that man is irreducibly culture bound. That the Nacirema people may seem so exotic—or on the contrary, perhaps, so normal—is confirmation of our inclination to judge "other tribes" as somehow unnatural, unpleasant, or not quite human. To observe the Nacirema through the trained vision of the anthropologist is to learn, too, how neatly meshed and patterned the culture of this or that society is: how interdependent and mutually supporting are people's webs of norms and values—their ways of behaving and their beliefs.

Kluckhohn's explanation of the meaning of culture is revealing and comprehensive, and yet succinct. Exploring the nature and functions of cultural behavior, he explains why so much of "human behavior can be understood, and indeed predicted, if we know a people's design for living."

Forearmed with the knowledge and the insights implicit in the cultural concept, the student of society is a critical step closer to that sociological imagination that will facilitate his understanding of the many-faceted lessons of sociology. All the same, a caveat—a warning—is in order.

When he has finished reading the Kluckhohn and Miner essays, the reader will be impressed—perhaps awed—by the way in which culture delicately yet decisively shapes us into the human beings that we are. The language and the symbols that enable us to communicate intelligibly, what we wear, what we deem ugly or beautiful, sublime or ridiculous, our tastes in food, our esthetic values, our religious persuasions, our political convictions, our notions of sexual attractiveness, of what is properly masculine and what feminine, are all products of our cultural inheritance.

Granting this, it is imperative that we not succumb to cultural determinism: to the belief that culture determines **everything**. We are indeed cultural animals; if we were not, there would be no such thing as **homo sapiens**. But we are also stubbornly unique creatures, at one and the same time culture bound and culture resistant. We are never cultural animals pure and simple. We are simultaneously cultural conformists and cultural misfits; we are identifiable products of our cultural heritage and milieu, yet forever at odds with it; we are convention abiding and still unique, idiosyncratic yet un-fathomably singular. Kluckhohn and Murray put the matter briefly but synoptically:

Everyman is in certain respects
    a.   like all other men,
    b.   like some other men,
    c.   like no other man.

chapter 7
body ritual
among the nacirema
horace miner

The anthropologist has become so familiar with the diversity of ways in which different peoples behave in similar situations that he is not apt to be surprised by even the most exotic customs. In fact, if all of the logically possible combinations of behavior have not been found somewhere in the world, he is apt to suspect that they must be present in some yet undescribed tribe. This point has, in fact, been expressed with respect to clan organization by Murdock.[1] In this light, the magical beliefs and practices of the Nacirema present such unusual aspects that it seems desirable to describe them as an example of the extremes to which human behavior can go.

Professor Linton first brought the ritual of the Nacirema to the attention of anthropologists twenty years ago,[2] but the culture of this people is still very poorly understood. They are a North American group living in the territory between the Canadian Cree, the Yaqui and Tarahumare of Mexico, and the Carib and Arawak of the Antilles. Little is known of their origin, although tradition states that they came from the east. According to Nacirema mythology, their nation was originated by a culture hero, Notgnihsaw, who is otherwise

known for two great feats of strength—the throwing of a piece of wampum across the river Pa-To-Mac and the chopping down of a cherry tree in which the Spirit of Truth resided.

Nacirema culture is characterized by a highly developed market economy which has evolved in a rich natural habitat. While much of the people's time is devoted to economic pursuits, a large part of the fruits of these labors and a considerable portion of the day are spent in ritual activity. The focus of this activity is the human body, the appearance and health of which loom as a dominant concern in the ethos of the people. While such a concern is certainly not unusual, its ceremonial aspects and associated philosophy are unique.

The fundamental belief underlying the whole system appears to be that the human body is ugly and that its natural tendency is to debility and disease. Incarcerated in such a body, man's only hope is to avert these characteristics through the use of the powerful influences of ritual and ceremony. Every household has one or more shrines devoted to this purpose. The more powerful individuals in the society have several shrines in their houses and, in fact, the opulence of a house is often referred to in terms of the number of such ritual centers it possesses. Most houses are of wattle and daub construction, but the shrine

Reproduced by permission of the American Anthropological Association from **American Anthropologist**, vol. 56, no. 3, 1958.

rooms of the more wealthy are walled with stone. Poorer families imitate the rich by applying pottery plaques to their shrine walls.

While each family has at least one such shrine, the rituals associated with it are not family ceremonies but are private and secret. The rites are normally only discussed with children, and then only during the period when they are being initiated into these mysteries. I was able, however, to establish sufficient rapport with the natives to examine these shrines and to have the rituals described to me.

The focal point of the shrine is a box or chest which is built into the wall. In this chest are kept the many charms and magical potions without which no native believes he could live. These preparations are secured from a variety of specialized practitioners. The most powerful of these are the medicine men, whose assistance must be rewarded with substantial gifts. However, the medicine men do not provide the curative potions for their clients, but decide what the ingredients should be and then write them down in an ancient and secret language. This writing is understood only by the medicine men and by the herbalists who, for another gift, provide the required charm.

The charm is not disposed of after it has served its purpose, but is placed in the charm-box of the household shrine. As these magical materials are specific for certain ills, and the real or imagined maladies of the people are many, the charm-box is usually full to overflowing. The magical packets are so numerous that people forget what their purposes were and fear to use them again. While the natives are very vague on this point, we can only assume that the idea in retaining all the old magical materials is that their presence in the charm-box, before which the body rituals are conducted, will in some way protect the worshipper.

Beneath the charm-box is a small font. Each day every member of the family, in succession, enters the shrine room, bows his head before the charm-box, mingles different sorts of holy water in the font, and proceeds with a brief rite of ablution. The holy waters are secured from the Water Temple of the community, where the priests conduct elaborate ceremonies to make the liquid ritually pure.

In the hierarchy of magical practitioners, and below the medicine men in prestige, are specialists whose designation is best translated "holy-mouthmen." The Nacirema have an almost pathological horror of and fascination with the mouth, the condition of which is believed to have a supernatural influence on all social relationships. Were it not for the rituals of the mouth, they believe that their teeth would fall out, their gums bleed, their jaws shrink, their friends desert them, and their lovers reject them. They also believe that a strong relationship exists between oral and moral characteristics. For example, there is a ritual ablution of the mouth for children which is supposed to improve their moral fiber.

The daily body ritual performed by everyone includes a mouth-rite. Despite the fact that these people are so punctillious about care of the mouth, this rite involves a practice which strikes the uninitiated stranger as revolting. It was reported to me that the ritual consists of inserting a small bundle of hog hairs into the mouth, along with certain magical powders, and then moving the bundle in a highly formalized series of gestures.

In addition to the private mouth-rite, the people seek out a holy-mouth-man once or twice a year. These practitioners have an impressive set of paraphernalia, consisting of a variety of augers, awls, probes, and prods. The use of these objects in the exorcism of the evils of the mouth involves almost unbelievable ritual torture of the client. The holy-mouth-man opens the client's mouth and, using the above mentioned tools, enlarges any holes which decay may have created in the teeth. Magical materials are put into these holes. If there are no naturally occurring holes in the teeth, large sections of one or more teeth are gouged out so that the supernatural substance can be applied. In the client's view, the purpose of these ministrations is to arrest decay and to draw friends. The extremely sacred and traditional character of the rite is evident in the fact that the natives return to the holy-mouth-men year after year, despite the fact that their teeth continue to decay.

It is hoped that, when a thorough study of the Nacirema is made, there will be careful inquiry into the personality structure of these people. One has but to watch the gleam in the eye of a holy-mouth-man, as he jabs an awl into an exposed nerve, to suspect that a certain amount of sadism is involved. If this can be established, a very interesting pattern emerges, for most of the population shows definite masochistic tendencies. It was to these that Professor Linton referred in discussing a distinctive part of the daily body ritual which is performed only by men. This part of the rite involves scraping and lacerating the surface of the face with a sharp instrument. Special women's rites are performed only four times during each lunar month, but what they lack in frequency is made up in barbarity. As part of this ceremony, women bake their heads in small ovens for about an hour. The theoretically interesting point is that what seems to be a preponderantly masochistic people have developed sadistic specialists.

The medicine men have an imposing temple, or *latipso*, in every community of any size. The more elaborate ceremonies required to treat very sick patients can only be performed at this temple. These ceremonies involve not only the thaumaturge but a permanent group of vestal maidens who move sedately about the temple chambers in distinctive costume and headdress.

The *latipso* ceremonies are so harsh that it is phenomenal that a fair proportion of the really sick natives who enter the temple ever recover. Small children whose indoctrination is still incomplete have been known to resist attempts to take them to the temple because "that is where you go to die." Despite this fact, sick adults are not only willing but eager to undergo the protracted ritual purification, if they can afford to do so. No matter how ill the supplicant or how grave the emergency, the guardians of many temples will not admit a client if he cannot give a rich gift to the custodian. Even after one has gained admission and survived the ceremonies, the guardians will not permit the neophyte to leave until he makes still another gift.

The supplicant entering the temple is first stripped of all his or her clothes. In everyday life the Nacirema avoids exposure of his body and its natural functions. Bathing and excretory acts are performed only in the secrecy of the household shrine, where they are ritualized as part of the body rites. Psychological shock results from the fact that body secrecy is suddenly lost upon entry into the *latipso*. A man, whose own wife has never seen him in an excretory act, suddenly finds himself naked and assisted by a vestal maiden while he performs his natural functions into a sacred vessel. This sort of ceremonial treatment is necessitated by the fact that the excreta are used by a diviner to ascertain the course and nature of the client's sickness. Female clients, on the other hand, find their naked bodies are subjected to the scrutiny, manipulation and prodding of the medicine men.

Few supplicants in the temple are well enough to do anything but lie on their hard beds. The daily ceremonies, like the rites of the holy-mouth-

men, involve discomfort and torture. With ritual precision, the vestals awaken their miserable charges each dawn and roll them about on their beds of pain while performing ablutions, in the formal movements of which the maidens are highly trained. At other times they insert magic wands in the supplicant's mouth or force him to eat substances which are supposed to be healing. From time to time the medicine men come to their clients and jab magically treated needles into their flesh. The fact that these temple ceremonies may not cure, and may even kill the neophyte, in no way decreases the people's faith in the medicine men.

There remains one other kind of practitioner, known as a "listener." This witch doctor has the power to exorcise the devils that lodge in the heads of people who have been bewitched. The Nacirema believe that parents bewitch their own children. Mothers are particularly suspected of putting a curse on children while teaching them the secret body rituals. The countermagic of the witch doctor is unusual in its lack of ritual. The patient simply tells the "listener" all his troubles and fears, beginning with the earliest difficulties he can remember. The memory displayed by the Nacirema in these exorcism sessions is truly remarkable. It is not uncommon for the patient to bemoan the rejection he felt upon being weaned as a babe, and a few individuals even see their troubles going back to the traumatic effects of their own birth.

In conclusion, mention must be made of certain practices which have their base in native esthetics but which depend upon the pervasive aversion to the natural body and its functions. There are ritual fasts to make fat people thin and ceremonial feasts to make thin people fat. Still other rites are used to make women's breasts larger if they are small, and smaller if they are large. General dissatisfaction with breast shape is symbolized in the fact that the ideal form is virtually outside the range of human variation. A few women afflicted with almost inhuman hypermammary development are so idolized that they make a handsome living by simply going from village to village and permitting the natives to stare at them for a fee.

Reference has already been made to the fact that excretory functions are ritualized, routinized, and relegated to secrecy. Natural reproductive functions are similarly distorted. Intercourse is taboo as a topic and scheduled as an act. Efforts are made to avoid pregnancy by the use of magical materials or by limiting intercourse to certain phases of the moon. Conception is actually very infrequent. When pregnant, women dress so as to hide their condition. Parturition takes place in secret, without friends or relatives to assist, and the majority of women do not nurse their infants.

Our review of the ritual life of the Nacirema has certainly shown them to be a magic-ridden people. It is hard to understand how they have managed to exist so long under the burdens which they have imposed upon themselves. But even such exotic customs as these take on real meaning when they are viewed with the insight provided by Malinowski when he wrote:

Looking from far and above, from our high places of safety in the developed civilization, it is easy to see all the crudity and irrelevance of magic. But without its power and guidance early man could not have mastered his practical difficulties as he has done, nor could man have advanced to the higher stages of civilization.[3]

NOTES

1. George P. Murdock, **Social Structure,** New York: The Macmillan Co., 1949, p. 71.
2. Ralph Linton, **The Study of Man,** New York: D. Appleton-Century Co., 1936, p. 326.
3. Bronislaw Malinowski, **Magic, Science, and Religion,** Glencoe: The Free Press, 1948, p. 70.

chapter 8
queer customs
clyde kluckhohn

Why do the Chinese dislike milk and milk products? Why would the Japanese die willingly in a Banzai charge that seemed senseless to Americans? Why do some nations trace descent through the father, others through the mother, still others through both parents? Not because they were destined by God or Fate to different habits, not because the weather is different in China and Japan and the United States. Sometimes shrewd common sense has an answer that is close to that of the anthropologist: "because they were brought up that way." By "culture" anthropology means the total life way of a people, the social legacy the individual acquires from his group. Or culture can be regarded as that part of the environment that is the creation of man.

This technical term has a wider meaning than the "culture" of history and literature. A humble cooking pot is as much a cultural product as is a Beethoven sonata. In ordinary speech a man of culture is a man who can speak languages other than his own, who is familiar with history, literature, philosophy, or the fine arts. In some cliques that definition is still narrower. The cultured person is one who can talk about James Joyce, Scarlatti, and Picasso. To the anthropologist, how-

ever, to be human is to be cultured. There is culture in general, and then there are the specific cultures such as Russian, American, British, Hotentot, Inca. The general abstract notion serves to remind us that we cannot explain acts solely in terms of the biological properties of the people concerned, their individual past experience, and the immediate situation. The past experience of other men in the form of culture enters into almost every event. Each specific culture constitutes a kind of blueprint for all of life's activities.

One of the interesting things about human beings is that they try to understand themselves and their own behavior. While this has been particularly true of Europeans in recent times, there is no group which has not developed a scheme or schemes to explain man's actions. To the insistent human query "Why?" the most exciting illumination anthropology has to offer is that of the concept of culture. Its explanatory importance is comparable to categories such as evolution in biology, gravity in physics, disease in medicine. A good deal of human behavior can be understood, and indeed predicted, if we know a people's design for living. Many acts are neither accidental nor due to personal peculiarities nor caused by supernatural forces nor simply mysterious. Even those of us who pride ourselves on our individualism follow most of the time a pattern not of our own making. We brush our teeth on arising. We put on pants—

not a loincloth or a grass skirt. We eat three meals a day—not four or five or two. We sleep in a bed—not in a hammock or on a sheep pelt. I do not have to know the individual and his life history to be able to predict these and countless other regularities, including many in the thinking process, of all Americans who are not incarcerated in jails or hospitals for the insane.

To the American woman a system of plural wives seems "instinctively" abhorrent. She cannot understand how any woman can fail to be jealous and uncomfortable if she must share her husband with other women. She feels it "unnatural" to accept such a situation. On the other hand, a Koryak woman of Siberia, for example, would find it hard to understand how a woman could be so selfish and so undesirous of feminine companionship in the home as to wish to restrict her husband to one mate.

Some years ago I met in New York City a young man who did not speak a word of English and was obviously bewildered by American ways. By "blood" he was as American as you or I, for his parents had gone from Indiana to China as missionaries. Orphaned in infancy, he was reared by a Chinese family in a remote village. All who met him found him more Chinese than American. The facts of his blue eyes and light hair were less impressive than a Chinese style of gait, Chinese arm and hand movements, Chinese facial expression, and Chinese modes of thought. The biological heritage was American, but the cultural training had been Chinese. He returned to China.

Another example of another kind: I once knew a trader's wife in Arizona who took a somewhat devilish interest in producing a cultural reaction. Guests who came her way were often served delicious sandwiches filled with a meat that seemed to be neither chicken nor tuna fish yet was reminiscent of both. To queries she gave no reply until each had eaten his fill. She then explained that what they had eaten was not chicken, not tuna fish, but the rich, white flesh of freshly killed rattlesnakes. The response was instantaneous—vomiting, often violent vomiting. A biological process is caught in a cultural web.

A highly intelligent teacher with long and successful experience in the public schools of Chicago was finishing her first year in an Indian school. When asked how her Navaho pupils compared in intelligence with Chicago youngsters, she replied, "Well, I just don't know. Sometimes the Indians seem just as bright. At other times they

just act like dumb animals. The other night we had a dance in the high school. I saw a boy who is one of the best students in my English class standing off by himself. So I took him over to a pretty girl and told them to dance. But they just stood there with their heads down. They wouldn't even say anything." I inquired if she knew whether or not they were members of the same clan. "What difference would that make?"

"How would you feel about getting into bed with your brother?" The teacher walked off in a huff, but, actually, the two cases were quite comparable in principle. To the Indian the type of bodily contact involved in our social dancing has a directly sexual connotation. The incest taboos between members of the same clan are as severe as between true brothers and sisters. The shame of the Indians at the suggestion that a clan brother and sister should dance and the indignation of the white teacher at the idea that she should share a bed with an adult brother represent equally nonrational responses, culturally standardized unreason.

All this does not mean that there is no such thing as raw human nature. The very fact that certain of the same institutions are found in all known societies indicates that at bottom all human beings are very much alike. The files of the Cross-Cultural Survey at Yale University are organized according to categories such as "marriage ceremonies," "life crisis rites," "incest taboos." At least seventy-five of these categories are represented in every single one of the hundreds of cultures analyzed. This is hardly surprising. The members of all human groups have about the same biological equipment. All men undergo the same poignant life experiences such as birth, helplessness, illness, old age, and death. The biological potentialities of the species are the blocks with which cultures are built. Some patterns of every culture crystallize around focuses provided by the inevitables of biology: the difference between the sexes, the presence of persons of different ages, the varying physical strength and skill of individuals. The facts of nature also limit culture forms. No culture provides patterns for jumping over trees or for eating iron ore.

There is thus no "either-or" between nature and that special form of nurture called culture. Culture determinism is as one-sided as biological determinism. The two factors are interdependent. Culture arises out of human nature, and its forms are restricted both by man's biology and by natural laws. It is equally true that culture channels biological processes—vomiting, weeping, fainting, sneezing, the daily habits of food intake and waste elimination. When a man eats, he is reacting to an internal "drive," namely, hunger contractions consequent upon the lowering of blood sugar, but his precise reaction to these internal stimuli cannot be predicted by physiological knowledge alone. Whether a healthy adult feels hungry twice, three times, or four times a day and the hours at which this feeling recurs is a question of culture. What he eats is of course limited by availability, but is also partly regulated by culture. It is a biological fact that some types of berries are poisonous; it is a cultural fact that, a few generations ago, most Americans considered tomatoes to be poisonous and refused to eat them. Such selective, discriminative use of the environment is characteristically cultural. In a still more general sense, too, the process of eating is channeled by culture. Whether a man eats to live, lives to eat, or merely eats and lives is only in part an individual matter, for there are also cultural trends. Emotions are physiological events. Certain situations will evoke fear in people from any culture. But sensations of pleasure, anger, and lust may be stimulated by cultural cues that would leave unmoved someone who has been reared in a different social tradition.

Except in the case of newborn babies and of individuals born with clear-cut structural or functional abnormalities we can observe innate endowments only as modified by cultural training. In a hospital in New Mexico where Zuñi Indian, Navaho Indian, and white American babies are born, it is possible to classify the newly arrived infants as unusually active, average, and quiet. Some babies from each "racial" group will fall into each category, though a higher proportion of the white babies will fall into the unusually active class. But if a Navaho baby, a Zuñi baby, and a white baby— all classified as unusually active at birth—are again observed at the age of two years, the Zuñi baby will no longer seem given to quick and restless activity—**as compared with the white child**— though he may seem so as compared with the other Zuñis of the same age. The Navaho child is likely to fall in between as contrasted with the Zuñi and the white, though he will probably still seem more active than the average Navaho youngster.

It was remarked by many observers in the Japanese relocation centers that Japanese who were born and brought up in this country, espe-

cially those who were reared apart from any large colony of Japanese, resemble in behavior their white neighbors much more closely than they do their own parents who were educated in Japan.

I have said "culture channels biological processes." It is more accurate to say "the biological functioning of individuals is modified if they have been trained in certain ways and not in others." Culture is not a disembodied force. It is created and transmitted by people. However, culture, like well-known concepts of the physical sciences, is a convenient abstraction. One never sees gravity. One sees bodies falling in regular ways. One never sees an electromagnetic field. Yet certain happenings that can be seen may be given a neat abstract formulation by assuming that the electromagnetic field exists. Similarly, one never sees culture as such. What is seen are regularities in the behavior or artifacts of a group that has adhered to a common tradition. The regularities in style and technique of ancient Inca tapestries or stone axes from Melanesian islands are due to the existence of mental blueprints for the group.

Culture is a **way** of thinking, feeling, believing. It is the group's knowledge stored up (in memories of men; in books and objects) for future use. We study the products of this "mental" activity: the overt behavior, the speech and gestures and activities of people, and the tangible results of these things such as tools, houses, cornfields, and what not. It has been customary in lists of "culture traits" to include such things as watches or lawbooks. This is a convenient way of thinking about them, but in the solution of any important problem we must remember that they, in themselves, are nothing but metals, paper, and ink. What is important is that some men know how to make them, others set a value on them, are unhappy without them, direct their activities in relation to them, or disregard them.

It is only a helpful shorthand when we say "The cultural patterns of the Zulu were resistant to Christianization." In the directly observable world of course, it was individual Zulus who resisted. Nevertheless, if we do not forget that we are speaking at a high level of abstraction, it is justifiable to speak of culture as a cause. One may compare the practice of saying "syphilis caused the extinction of the native population of the island." Was it "syphilis" or "syphilis germs" or "human beings who were carriers of syphilis"?

"Culture," then, is "a theory." But if a theory is not contradicted by any relevant fact and if it helps us to understand a mass of otherwise chaotic facts, it is useful. Darwin's contribution was much less the accumulation of new knowledge than the creation of a theory which put in order data already known. An accumulation of facts, however large, is no more a science than a pile of bricks is a house. Anthropology's demonstration that the most weird set of customs has a consistency and an order is comparable to modern psychiatry's showing that there is meaning and purpose in the apparently incoherent talk of the insane. In fact, the inability of the older psychologies and philosophies to account for the strange behavior of madmen and heathens was the principal factor that forced psychiatry and anthropology to develop theories of the unconscious and of culture.

Since culture is an abstraction, it is important not to confuse culture with society. A "society" refers to a group of people who interact more with each other than they do with other individuals— who cooperate with each other for the attainment of certain ends. You can see and indeed count the individuals who make up a society. A "culture" refers to the distinctive ways of life of such a group of people. Not all social events are culturally patterned. New types of circumstances arise frequently.

A culture constitutes a storehouse of the pooled learning of the group. A rabbit starts life with some innate responses. He can learn from his own experience and perhaps from observing other rabbits. A human infant is born with fewer instincts and greater plasticity. His main task is to learn the answers that persons he will never see, persons long dead, have worked out. Once he has learned the formulas supplied by the culture of his group, most of his behavior becomes almost as automatic and unthinking as if it were instinctive. There is a tremendous amount of intelligence behind the making of a radio, but not much is required to learn to turn it on.

The members of all human societies face some of the same unavoidable dilemmas, posed by biology and other facts of the human situation. This is why the basic categories of all cultures are so similar. Human culture without language is unthinkable. No culture fails to provide for aesthetic expression and aesthetic delight. Every culture supplies standardized orientations toward the deeper problems, such as death. Every culture is designed to perpetuate the group and its solidarity, to meet the demands of individuals for an orderly way of life and for satisfaction of biological needs.

However, the variations on these basic themes are numberless. Some languages are built up out of twenty basic sounds, others out of forty. Nose plugs were considered beautiful by the predynastic Egyptians but are not by the modern French. Puberty is a biological fact. But one culture ignores it, another prescribes informal instructions about sex but no ceremony, a third has impressive rites for girls only, a fourth for boys and girls. In this culture, the first menstruation is welcomed as a happy, natural event; in that culture the atmosphere is full of dread and supernatural threat. Each culture dissects nature according to its own system of categories. The Navaho Indians apply the same word to the color of a robin's egg and to that of grass. A psychologist once assumed that this meant a difference in the sense organs, that Navahos didn't have the physiological equipment to distinguish "green" from "blue." However, when he showed them objects of the two colors and asked them if they were exactly the same colors, they looked at him with astonishment. His dream of discovering a new type of color blindness was shattered.

Every culture must deal with the sexual instinct. Some, however, seek to deny all sexual expression before marriage, whereas a Polynesian adolescent who was not promiscuous would be distinctly abnormal. Some cultures enforce lifelong monogamy, others, like our own, tolerate serial monogamy; in still other cultures, two or more women may be joined to one man or several men to a single woman. Homosexuality has been a permitted pattern in the Greco-Roman world, in parts of Islam, and in various primitive tribes. Large portions of the population of Tibet, and of Christendom at some places and periods, have practiced complete celibacy. To us marriage is first and foremost an arrangement between two individuals. In many more societies marriage is merely one facet of a complicated set of reciprocities, economic and otherwise, between two families or two clans.

The essence of the cultural process is selectivity. The selection is only exceptionally conscious and rational. Cultures are like Topsy. They just grew. Once, however, a way of handling a situation becomes institutionalized, there is ordinarily great resistance to chance or deviation. When we speak of "our sacred beliefs," we mean of course that they are beyond criticism and that the person who suggests modification or abandonment must be punished. No person is emotionally indifferent to his culture. Certain cultural premises may become totally out of accord with a new factual situation. Leaders may recognize this and reject the old ways in theory. Yet their emotional loyalty continues in the face of reason because of the intimate conditionings of early childhood.

A culture is learned by individuals as the result of belonging to some particular group, and it constitutes that part of learned behavior which is shared with others. It is our social legacy, as contrasted with our organic heredity. It is one of the important factors which permits us to live together in an organized society, giving us ready-made solutions to our problems, helping us to predict the behavior of others, and permitting others to know what to expect of us.

Culture regulates our lives at every turn. From the moment we are born until we die there is, whether we are conscious of it or not, constant pressure upon us to follow certain types of behavior that other men have created for us. Some paths we follow willingly, others we follow because we know no other way, still others we deviate from or go back to most unwillingly. Mothers of small children know how unnaturally most of this comes to us—how little regard we have, until we are "culturalized," for the "proper" place, time, and manner for certain acts such as eating, excreting, sleeping, getting dirty, and making loud noises. But by more or less adhering to a system of related designs for carrying out all the acts of living, a group of men and women feel themselves linked together by a powerful chain of sentiments. Ruth Benedict gave an almost complete definition of the concept when she said, "Culture is that which binds men together."

It is true any culture is a set of techniques for adjusting both to the external environment and to other men. However, cultures create problems as well as solve them. If the lore of a people states that frogs are dangerous creatures, or that it is not safe to go about at night because of witches or ghosts, threats are posed which do not arise out of the inexorable facts of the external world. Cultures produce needs as well as provide a means of fulfilling them. There exists for every group culturally defined, acquired drives that may be more powerful in ordinary daily life than the biologically inborn drives. Many Americans, for example, will work harder for "success" than they will for sexual satisfaction.

Most groups elaborate certain aspects of their culture far beyond maximum utility or survival value. In other words, not all culture promotes physical survival. At times, indeed, it does exactly the opposite. Aspects of culture which once were adaptive may persist long after they have ceased to be useful. An analysis of any culture will disclose many features which cannot possibly be construed as adaptations to the total environment in which the group now finds itself. However, it is altogether likely that these apparently useless features represent survivals, with modifications through time, of cultural forms once useful.

Any cultural practice must be functional or it will disappear before long. That is, it must somehow contribute to the survival of the society or to the adjustment of the individual. However, many cultural functions are not manifest but latent. A cowboy will walk three miles to catch a horse which he then rides one mile to the store. From the point of view of manifest function this is positively irrational. But the act has the latent function of maintaining the cowboy's prestige in the terms of his own subculture. One can instance the buttons on the sleeve of a man's coat, our absurd English spelling, the use of capital letters, and a host of other apparently nonfunctional customs. They serve mainly the latent function of assisting individuals to maintain their security by preserving continuity with the past and by making certain sectors of life familiar and predictable.

Every culture is a precipitate of history. In more than one sense history is a sieve. Each culture embraces those aspects of the past which, usually in altered form and with altered meanings, live on in the present. Discoveries and inventions, both material and ideological, are constantly being made available to a group through its historical contacts with other peoples or being created by its own members. However, only those that fit the total immediate situation in meeting the group's needs for survival or in promoting the psychological adjustment of individuals will become part of the culture. The process of culture building may be regarded as an addition to man's innate biological capacities, an addition providing instruments which enlarge, or may even substitute for, biological functions, and to a degree compensating for biological limitations—as in ensuring that death does not always result in the loss to humanity of what the deceased has learned.

Culture is like a map. Just as a map isn't the territory but an abstract representation of a particular area, so also a culture is an abstract description of trends toward uniformity in the words, deeds, and artifacts of a human group. If a map is accurate and you can read it, you won't get lost; if you know a culture you will know your way around in the life of a society.

Many educated people have the notion that culture applies only to exotic ways of life or to societies where relative simplicity and relative homogeneity prevail. Some sophisticated missionaries, for example, will use the anthropological conception in discussing the special modes of living of South Sea Islanders, but seem amazed at the idea that it could be applied equally to inhabitants of New York City. And social workers in Boston will talk about the culture of a colorful and well-knit immigrant group but boggle at applying it to the behavior of staff members in the social-service agency itself.

In the primitive society the correspondence between the habits of individuals and the customs of the community is ordinarily greater. There is probably some truth in what an old Indian once said, "In the old days there was no law; everybody did what was right." The primitive tends to find happiness in the fulfillment of intricately involuted cultural patterns; the modern more often tends to feel the pattern as repressive to his individuality. It is also true that in a complex stratified society there are numerous exceptions to generalizations made about the culture as a whole. It is necessary to study regional, class, and occupational subcultures. Primitive cultures have greater stability than modern cultures; they change—but less rapidly.

However, modern men also are creators and carriers of culture. Only in some respects are they influenced differently from primitives by culture. Moreover, there are such wide variations in primitive cultures that any black-and-white contrast between the primitive and the civilized is altogether fictitious. The distinction which is most generally true lies in the field of conscious philosophy.

The publication of Paul Radin's **Primitive Man as a Philosopher** did much toward destroying the myth that an abstract analysis of experience was a peculiarity of literate societies. Speculation and reflection upon the nature of the universe and of man's place in the total scheme of things have been carried out in every known culture. Every people has its characteristic set of "primitive postulates." It remains true that critical examination of basic premises and fully explicit systematization of philosophical concepts are seldom found

at the nonliterate level. The written word is an almost essential condition for free and extended discussion of fundamental philosophic issues. Where dependence on memory exists, there seems to be an inevitable tendency to emphasize the correct perpetuation of the precious oral tradition. Similarly, while it is all too easy to underestimate the extent to which ideas spread without books, it is in general true that tribal or folk societies do not possess competing philosophical systems. The major exception to this statement is, of course, the case where part of the tribe becomes converted to one of the great proselytizing religions such as Christianity or Mohammedanism. Before contact with rich and powerful civilizations, primitive peoples seem to have absorbed new ideas piecemeal, slowly integrating them with the previously existing ideology. The abstract thought of nonliterate societies is ordinarily less self-critical, less systematic, not so intricately elaborated in purely logical dimensions. Primitive thinking is more concrete, more implicit—perhaps more completely coherent than the philosophy of most individuals in larger societies which have been influenced over long periods by disparate intellectual currents.

No participant in any culture knows all the details of the cultural map. The statement frequently heard that St. Thomas Aquinas was the last man to master all the knowledge of his society is intrinsically absurd. St. Thomas would have been hard put to make a pane of cathedral glass or to act as a midwife. In every culture there are what Ralph Linton has called "universals, alternatives, and specialties." Every Christian in the thirteenth century knew that it was necessary to attend mass, to go to confession, to ask the Mother of God to intercede with her Son. There were many other universals in the Christian culture of Western Europe. However, there were also alternative cultural patterns even in the realm of religion. Each individual had his own patron saint, and different towns developed the cults of different saints. The thirteenth-century anthropologist could have discovered the rudiments of Christian practice by questioning and observing whomever he happened to meet in Germany, France, Italy, or England. But to find out the details of the ceremonials honoring St. Hubert or St. Bridget he would have had to seek out certain individuals or special localities where these alternative patterns were practiced. Similarly, he could not learn about weaving from a professional soldier or about canon law from a farmer. Such cultural knowledge belongs in the realm of the specialities, voluntarily chosen by the individual or ascribed to him by birth. Thus, part of a culture must be learned by everyone, part may be selected from alternative patterns, part applies only to those who perform the roles in the society for which these patterns are designed.

Many aspects of a culture are explicit. The explicit culture consists in those regularities in word and deed that may be generalized straight from the evidence of the ear and the eye. The recognition of these is like the recognition of style in the art of a particular place and epoch. If we have examined twenty specimens of the wooden saints' images made in the Taos Valley of New Mexico in the late eighteenth century, we can predict that any new images from the same locality and period will in most respects exhibit the same techniques of carving, about the same use of colors and choice of woods, a similar quality of artistic conception. Similarly, if, in a society of 2,000 members, we record 100 marriages at random and find that in 30 cases a man has married the sister of his brother's wife, we can anticipate that an additional sample of 100 marriages will show roughly the same number of cases of this pattern.

The above is an instance of what anthropologists call a behavioral pattern, the practices as opposed to the rules of the culture. There are also, however, regularities in what people say they do or should do. They do tend in fact to prefer to marry into a family already connected with their own by marriage, but this is not necessarily part of the official code of conduct. No disapproval whatsoever is attached to those who make another sort of marriage. On the other hand, it is explicitly forbidden to marry a member of one's own clan even though no biological relationship is traceable. This is a regulatory pattern—a Thou Shalt or a Thou Shalt Not. Such patterns may be violated often, but their existence is nevertheless important. A people's standards for conduct and belief define the socially approved aims and the acceptable means of attaining them. When the discrepancy between the theory and the practice of a culture is exceptionally great, this indicates that the culture is undergoing rapid change. It does not prove that ideals are unimportant, for ideals are but one of a number of factors determining action.

Cultures do not manifest themselves solely in observable customs and artifacts. No amount of questioning of any save the most articulate in the most self-conscious cultures will bring out some of the basic attitudes common to the members of the group. This is because these basic assumptions are taken so for granted that they normally do not enter into consciousness. This part of the cultural map must be inferred by the observer on the basis of consistencies in thought and action. Missionaries in various societies are often disturbed or puzzled because the natives do not regard "morals" and "sex code" as almost synonymous. The natives seem to feel that morals are concerned with sex just about as much as with eating—no less and no more. No society fails to have some restrictions on sexual behavior, but sex activity outside of marriage need not necessarily be furtive or attended with guilt. The Christian tradition has tended to assume that sex is inherently nasty as well as dangerous. Other cultures assume that sex in itself is not only natural but one of the good things of life, even though sex acts with certain persons under certain circumstances are forbidden. This is implicit culture, for the natives do not announce their premises. The missionaries would get further if they said, in effect, "Look, our morality starts from different assumptions. Let's talk about those assumptions," rather than ranting about "immorality."

A factor implicit in a variety of diverse phenomena may be generalized as an underlying cultural principle. For example, the Navaho Indians always leave part of the design in a pot, a basket, or a blanket unfinished. When a medicine man instructs an apprentice he always leaves a little bit of the story untold. This "fear of closure" is a recurrent theme in Navaho culture. Its influence may be detected in many contexts that have no explicit connection.

If the observed cultural behavior is to be correctly understood, the categories and presuppositions constituting the implicit culture must be worked out. The "strain toward consistency" which Sumner noted in the folkways and mores of all groups cannot be accounted for unless one grants a set of systematically interrelated implicit themes. For example, in American culture the themes of "effort and optimism," "the common man," "technology," and "virtuous materialism" have a functional interdependence, the origin of which is historically known. The relationship between themes may be that of conflict. One may instance the competition between Jefferson's theory of democracy and Hamilton's "government by the rich, the wellborn, and the able." In other cases most themes may be integrated under a single dominant theme. In Negro cultures of West Africa the mainspring of social life is religion; in East Africa almost all cultural behavior seems to be oriented toward certain premises and categories centered on the cattle economy. If there be one master principle in the implicit culture, this is often called the "ethos" or **Zeitgeist**.

Every culture has organization as well as content. There is nothing mystical about this statement. One may compare ordinary experience. If I know that Smith, working alone, can shovel 10 cubic yards of dirt a day, Jones 12, and Brown 14, I would be foolish to predict that the three working together would move 36. The total might well be considerably more; it might be less. A whole is different from the sum of its parts. The same principle is familiar in athletic teams. A brilliant pitcher added to a nine may mean a pennant or may mean the cellar; it depends on how he fits in.

And so it is with cultures. A mere list of the behavioral and regulatory patterns and of the implicit themes and categories would be like a map on which all mountains, lakes, and rivers were included—but not in their actual relationship to one another. Two cultures could have almost identical inventories and still be extremely different. The full significance of any single element in a culture design will be seen only when that element is viewed in the total matrix of its relationship to other elements. Naturally, this includes accent or emphasis, as well as position. Accent is manifested sometimes through frequency, sometimes through intensity. The indispensable importance of these questions of arrangement and emphasis may be driven home by an analogy. Consider a musical sequence made up of three notes. If we are told that the three notes in question are **A**, **B**, and **G**, we receive information which is fundamental. But it will not enable us to predict the type of sensation which the playing of this sequence is likely to evoke. We need many different sorts of relationship data. Are the notes to be played in that or some other order? What duration will each receive? How will the emphasis, if any, be distributed? We also need, of course, to know whether the instrument used is to be a piano or an accordion.

Cultures vary greatly in their degree of integration. Synthesis is achieved partly through the overt statement of the dominant conceptions, assumptions, and aspirations of the group in its religious lore, secular thought, and ethical code;

partly through habitual but unconscious ways of looking at the stream of events, ways of begging certain questions. To the naïve participant in the culture these modes of categorizing, of dissecting experience along these planes and not others, are as much "given" as the regular sequence of daylight and darkness or the necessity of air, water, and food for life. Had Americans not thought in terms of money and the market system during the depression they would have distributed unsalable goods rather than destroyed them.

Every group's way of life, then, is a structure—not a haphazard collection of all the different physically possible and functionally effective patterns of belief and action. A culture is an interdependent system based upon linked premises and categories whose influence is greater, rather than less, because they are seldom put in words. Some degree of internal coherence which is felt rather than rationally constructed seems to be demanded by most of the participants in any culture. As Whitehead has remarked, "Human life is driven forward by its dim apprehension of notions too general for its existing language."

In sum, the distinctive way of life that is handed down as the social heritage of a people does more than supply a set of skills for making a living and a set of blueprints for human relations. Each different way of life makes its own assumptions about the ends and purposes of human existence, about what human beings have a right to expect from each other and the gods, about what constitutes fulfillment or frustration. Some of these assumptions are made explicit in the lore of the folk; others are tacit premises which the observer must infer by finding consistent trends in word and deed.

In our highly self-conscious Western civilization that has recently made a business of studying itself, the number of assumptions that are literally implicit, in the sense of never having been stated or discussed by anyone, may be negligible. Yet only a trifling number of Americans could state even those implicit premises of our culture that have been brought to light by anthropologists. If one could bring to the American scene a Bushman who had been socialized in his own culture and then trained in anthropology, he would perceive all sorts of patterned regularities of which our anthropologists are completely unaware. In the case of the less sophisticated and less self-conscious societies, the unconscious assumptions characteristically made by individuals brought up under approximately the same social controls bulk even larger. But in any society, as Edward Sapir said, "Forms and significances which seem obvious to an outsider will be denied outright by those who carry out the patterns; outlines and implications that are perfectly clear to these may be absent to the eye of the onlooker."

All individuals in a culture tend to share common interpretations of the external world and man's place in it. To some degree every individual is affected by this conventional view of life. One group unconsciously assumes that every chain of actions has a goal and that when this goal is reached tension will be reduced or will disappear. To another group, thinking based upon this assumption is meaningless—they see life not as a series of purposive sequences, but as a complex of experiences which are satisfying in themselves, rather than as means to ends.

The concept of implicit culture is made necessary by certain eminently practical considerations. Programs of the British Colonial services or of our own Indian service, which have been carefully thought through for their continuity with the overt cultural patterns, nevertheless fail to work out. Nor does intensive investigation reveal any flaws in the setup at the technological level. The program is sabotaged by resistance which must be imputed to the manner in which the members of the group have been conditioned by their implicit designs for living to think and feel in ways which were unexpected to the administrator.

What good is the concept of culture so far as the contemporary world is concerned? What can you do with it? Much of the rest of this book will answer these questions, but some preliminary indications are in order.

Its use lies first in the aid the concept gives to man's endless quest to understand himself and his own behavior. For example, this new idea turns into pseudoproblems some of the questions asked by one of the most learned and acute thinkers of our age, Reinhold Niebuhr. In his recent book **The Nature and Destiny of Man** Niebuhr argues that the universally human sense of guilt or shame and man's capacity for self-judgment necessitate the assumption of supernatural forces. These facts are susceptible of self-consistent and relatively simple explanation in purely naturalistic terms through the concept of culture. Social life among human beings never occurs without a system of conventional understandings which are transmitted more or less intact from generation to generation. Every individual is familiar with some of these and they constitute a set of standards against which he judges himself. To the extent that he fails to conform he experiences discomfort because his childhood training put great pressure on him to follow the accepted pattern, and his now unconscious tendency is to associate deviation with punishment or withdrawal of love and protection. This and other issues which have puzzled philosophers and scientists for so long become understandable through this fresh concept.

The principal claim which can be made for the culture concept as an aid to useful action is that it helps us enormously toward predicting human behavior. One of the factors limiting the success of such prediction thus far has been the naïve assumption of a minutely homogeneous "human nature." In the framework of this assumption all human thinking proceeds from the same premises; all human beings are motivated by the same needs and goals. In the cultural framework we see that, while the ultimate logic of all peoples may be the same (and thus communication and understanding are possible), the thought processes depart from radically different premises—especially unconscious or unstated premises. Those who have the cultural outlook are more likely to look beneath the surface and bring the culturally determined premises to the light of day. This may not bring about immediate agreement and harmony, but it will at least facilitate a **more** rational approach to the problem of international understanding and to diminishing friction between groups within a nation.

Knowledge of a culture makes it possible to predict a good many of the actions of any person who shares that culture. If one knows how a given culture defines a certain situation, one can say that the betting odds are excellent that in a future comparable situation people will behave along certain lines and not along others. If we know a culture, we know what various classes of individuals within it expect from each other—and from outsiders of various categories. We know what types of activity are held to be inherently gratifying.

Many people in our society feel that the best way to get people to work harder is to increase their profits or their wages. They feel that it is just "human nature" to want to increase one's material possessions. This sort of dogma might well go unchallenged if we had no knowledge of other cultures. In certain societies, however, it has been found that the profit motive is not an effective incentive. After contact with whites the Trobriand Islanders in Melanesia could have become fabulously rich from pearl diving. They would, however, work only long enough to satisfy their immediate wants.

Administrators need to become conscious of the symbolic nature of many activities. American women will choose a job as hostess in a restaurant rather than one as waitress at a higher salary. In some societies the blacksmith is the most honored of individuals while in others only the lowest class of people are blacksmiths. White children in schools are motivated by grades; but children from some Indian tribe will work less hard under a system that singles the individual out from among his fellows.

Understanding of culture provides some detachment from the conscious and unconscious emotional values of one's own culture. The phrase, "some detachment," must be emphasized, however. An individual who viewed the designs for living of his group with complete detachment would be disoriented and unhappy. But I can prefer (i.e., feel affectively attached to) American manners while at the same time perceiving certain graces in English manners which are lacking or more grossly expressed in ours. Thus, while unwilling to forget that I am an American with no desire to ape English drawing-room behavior, I can still derive a lively pleasure from association with English people on social occasions. Whereas if I have no detachment, if I am utterly provincial, I am likely to regard English manners as utterly ridiculous, uncouth, perhaps even immoral. With that attitude I shall certainly not get on well with the English, and I am likely to resent bitterly any modification of our manners in the English or any other direction. Such attitudes clearly do not make for international understanding, friendship, and cooperation. They do, to the same extent, make for a too rigid social structure. Anthropological documents and anthropological teachings are valuable, therefore, in that they tend to emancipate individuals from a too strong allegiance to every item in the cultural inventory. The person who has been exposed to the anthropological perspective is more likely to live and let live both within his own society and in his dealings with members of other societies; and he will probably be more flexible in regard to needful changes in social organization to meet changed technology and changed economy.

Perhaps the most important implication of

culture for action is the profound truth that you can never start with a clean slate so far as human beings are concerned. Every person is born into a world defined by already existing culture patterns. Just as an individual who has lost his memory is no longer normal, so the idea of a society's becoming completely emancipated from its past culture is inconceivable. This is one source of the tragic failure of the Weimar constitution in Germany. In the abstract it was an admirable document. But it failed miserably in actual life partly because it provided for no continuity with existent designs for acting, feeling, and thinking.

Since every culture has organization as well as content, administrators and lawmakers should know that one cannot isolate a custom to abolish or modify it. The most obvious example of failure caused by neglect of this principle was the Eighteenth Amendment. The legal sale of liquor was forbidden, but the repercussions in law enforcement, in family life, in politics, in the economy were staggering.

The concept of culture, like any other piece of knowledge, can be abused and misinterpreted. Some fear that the principle of cultural relativity will weaken morality. "If the Bugabuga do it why can't we? It's all relative anyway." But this is exactly what cultural relativity does **not** mean.

The principle of cultural relativity does not mean that because the members of some savage tribe are allowed to behave in a certain way that this fact gives intellectual warrant for such behavior in all groups. Cultural relativity means, on the contrary, that the appropriateness of any positive or negative custom must be evaluated with regard to how this habit fits with other group habits. Having several wives makes economic sense among herders, not among hunters. While breeding a healthy skepticism as to the eternity of any value prized by a particular people, anthropology does not as a matter of theory deny the existence of moral absolutes. Rather, the use of the comparative method provides a scientific means of discovering such absolutes. If all surviving societies have found it necessary to impose some of the same restrictions upon the behavior of their members, this makes a strong argument that these aspects of the moral code are indispensable.

Similarly, the fact that a Kwakiutl chief talks as if he had delusions of grandeur and of persecution does not mean that paranoia is not a real ailment in our cultural context. Anthropology has given a new perspective to the relativity of the normal that should bring greater tolerance and understanding of socially harmless deviations. But it has by no means destroyed standards or the useful tyranny of the normal. All cultures recognize some of the same forms of behavior as pathological. Where they differ in their distinctions, there is a relationship to the total framework of cultural life.

There is a legitimate objection to making culture explain too much. Lurking, however, in such criticism of the cultural point of view is often the ridiculous assumption that one must be loyal to a single master explanatory principle. On the contrary, there is no incompatibility between biological, environmental, cultural, historical, and economical approaches. All are necessary. The anthropologist feels that so much of history as is still a living force is embodied in the culture. He regards the economy as a specialized part of the culture. But he sees the value in having economists and historians, as specialists, abstract out their special aspects—so long as the complete context is not entirely lost to view. Take the problems of the American South, for example. The anthropologist would entirely agree that biological (social visibility of black skin, etc.), environmental (water power and other natural resources), historical (South settled by certain types of people, somewhat different governmental practices from the start, etc.), and narrowly cultural (original discrimination against Negroes as "heathen savages," etc.) issues are all inextricably involved. However, the cultural factor is involved in the actual working out of each influence—though culture is definitely not the whole of it. And to say that certain acts are culturally defined does not always and necessarily mean that they could be eliminated by changing the culture.

The needs and drives of biological man, and the physical environment to which he must adjust, provide the stuff of human life, but a given culture determines the way this stuff is handled—the tailoring. In the eighteenth century a Neapolitan philosopher, Vico, uttered a profundity which was new, violent—and unnoticed. This was simply the discovery that "the social world is surely the work of man." Two generations of anthropologists have compelled thinkers to face this fact. Nor are anthropologists willing to allow the Marxists or other cultural determinists to make of culture another absolute as autocratic as the God or Fate portrayed by some philosophies. Anthropological knowledge does not permit so easy an evasion of

man's responsibility for his own destiny. To be sure, culture is a compulsive force to most of us most of the time. To some extent, as Leslie White says, "Culture has a life and laws of its own." Some cultural changes are also compelled by economic or physical circumstances. But most of an economy is itself a cultural artifact. And it is men who change their cultures, even if—during most of past history—they have been acting as instruments of cultural processes of which they were largely unaware. The record shows that, while situation limits the range of possibility, there is always more than one workable alternative. The essence of the cultural process is selectivity; men may often make a choice. Lawrence Frank probably overstates the case:

In the years to come it is possible that this discovery of the human origin and development of culture will be recognized as the greatest of all discoveries, since heretofore man has been helpless before these cultural and social formulations which generation after generation have perpetuated the same frustration and defeat of human values and aspirations. So long as he believed this was necessary and inevitable, he could not but accept this lot with resignation. Now man is beginning to realize that his culture and social organization are not unchanged cosmic processes, but are human creations which may be altered. For those who cherish the democratic faith this discovery means that they can, and must, undertake a continuing assay of our culture and our society in terms of its consequences for human life and human values. This is the historic origin and purpose of human culture, to create a human way of life. To our age falls the responsibility of utilizing the amazing new resources of science to meet these cultural tasks, to continue the great human tradition of man taking charge of his own destiny.

Nevertheless, to the extent that human beings discover the nature of the cultural process, they can anticipate, prepare, and—to at least a limited degree—control.

Americans are now at a period in history when they are faced with the facts of cultural differences more clearly than they can take with comfort. Recognition and tolerance of the deeper cultural assumptions of China, Russia, and Britain will require a difficult type of education. But the great lesson of culture is that the goals toward which men strive and fight and grope are not "given" in final form by biology nor yet entirely by the situation. If we understand our own culture and that of others, the political climate can be changed in a surprisingly short time in this narrow contemporary world providing men are wise enough and articulate enough and energetic enough. The concept of culture carries a legitimate note of hope to troubled men. If the German and Japanese peoples behaved as they did because of their biological heredity, the outlook for restoring them as peaceful and cooperative nations would be hopeless. But if their propensities for cruelty and aggrandizement were primarily the result of situational factors and their cultures, then something can be done about it, though false hopes must not be encouraged as to the speed with which a culture can be planfully changed.

topic 5

the cultural dimensions of everyday life: subcultures and contracultures

There is no belittling the usefulness of the culture concept. All the same, we are compelled to ask whether the notion of "the" American culture—or "the" Japanese or French
or Israeli—is altogether serviceable. Granted, the characteristic American shares much of
his cultural heritage with his fellow Americans, just as the Scot does with his Scottish
peers. But what about the American who is a hobo, pimp, heroin addict, member of a
"Jesus Freak" commune, inhabitant of a Chicago **barrio**, or lower-middle-class college
student? What, in other words, about the American who is as much a member of a **subculture** (or even a **contraculture**) as he is of the wider American society?

Subcultural distinctions are critical to an understanding of any but the simplest and
most homogeneous tribal societies, for the web of subcultural affiliations (religion, sex,
age, social class, race, residential, or ethnic) are as decisive in determining one's personality
and character as is nationality. This is even truer of those with hyper-loyal ties to such
contracultural groups as the Black Muslims, the Ku Klux Klan, the Weatherman, or a delinquent gang.

A subculture shares much in common with the dominant culture, yet it contains
elements—norms, values, attitudes, and life styles—that differ from those of the larger
society and are peculiar to that subculture. A particular subculture, moreover, differs in
degree from the dominant culture; members of a Hutterite religious community, for instance, will differ far more markedly from their fellow Americans than will, say, suburbanites, middle-agers, Italo-Americans, or Christian Scientists. So, too, will prostitutes or
career officers in the Navy or members of a Mafia "family" be much more sharply differentiated from the average citizen than will, say, schoolteachers, dentists, or secretaries.
Yet each is a member of what the sociologist chooses to designate an occupational subculture.

If most subcultures exist in a more or less harmonious relationship with the larger
social system, echoing and reinforcing most of its values and styles of life, there are other
subcultures—**contracultures**—that are keenly and consciously at odds with many or most
of the values and life styles of the dominant society. Take Albert K. Cohen's description

of characteristic slum-dwelling lower-class juvenile delinquents:

> They are caught up in a game in which others are typically the winners and they are the losers and also-rans. One way they can deal with this problem is to repudiate and withdraw from the game, to refuse to recognize the rules as having any application to them, and to set up new games with their own rules or criteria of status—rules by which they **can** perform satisfactorily. . . . They not only reject the dominant value system, but do so with a vengeance. They "stand it on its head"; they exalt its opposition; they engage in malicious, spiteful, "ornery" behavior of all sorts to demonstrate not only to others, but to themselves as well, their contempt for the game they have rejected.

The boundaries that distinguish a subculture from a contraculture are occasionally ill defined. This is especially apparent in the first of the two selections that comprise this section. The "counter culture" that Jesse Pitts describes is many-stranded and in a constant state of flux and redefinition, now amorphous, now distinct. If it is mainly contracultural, it is also at least partially subcultural. And the "outlaw" motorcycle gangs that Hunter Thompson analyzes illustrate how self-definitions and the definitions of others mesh and react in a subtle give-and-take manner to define what is "deviant" or "pathological" and what is "normal" or "appropriate."

chapter 9
the counter culture: tranquilizer or revolutionary ideology?
jesse pitts

In an essay I wrote a while back, "The Hippies as Contrameritocracy," (**Dissent**, July-August 1969), I argued that the movement was essentially a response to meritocratic pressures bearing down not only upon youth but upon the society as a whole, and that it represented a first-line structural response that probably would not endure in its initial form. This argument seems to me still decidedly to the point, but I would now like to go a little further. As of the early 1970s the hippie movement has divided itself into four major cultural streams and organizational patterns: the commune, the drug culture, the music culture, and the political youth movement. While all of these could be found in some form prior to the rise of the hippies, it is the hippies who provided them with momentum, style, and legitimation, so that the hippie look came to serve as their badge of allegiance. Various writers have described this phenomenon under the generic term of "counter culture"; I have described it, with an eye toward its structural origins, as a contrameritocracy.

In some form or other, communes have always existed in the United States. There are some in Europe as well, and a number have lasted for several generations, like the Communauté Boismondeau which, with an 1848 ideology, makes watch cases as a producers' cooperative.

From **Dissent**, 18, June 1971. Reprinted by permission.

Such groups have flourished in the U.S., in part because of our abundance of land and space, so that people have been able to "do their thing" without too much popular opposition. Popular historiography presents the Pilgrims as a band of men and women whose religious principles led them to come to the New World and found a commune of their own. **Newsweek** guesses that there now may be 500 communes functioning at any one time, with a total membership of 10,000.

But the significance of this movement goes beyond these small figures. On any campus there are a number of students who experiment with "communal living," which means sharing the money and housework. During the summer and after graduation there are many who try with more or less conviction to live in a communal way in the country and share in the farm labor. The rural commune is where the hippies have retreated in order to escape being swamped by the young "premoral" types and exploited by individuals ready to use any kind of violence that will insure them bed, board, drugs, and sex. Communes can select their members and impose some sort of vows upon them. And if the mortality rate of communes and the turnover of members seem rather high, only in the communes do the nonviolent themes of hippie culture retain some vigor.

The hippie communes feature a persistent attempt to organize group life without overt leadership and with a minimum of sex-role differentiation. Yet rural life, because of the premium it places upon physical strength, tends to sharpen the division of labor by sex, especially if there are children around who require close watching. The girls find themselves working in the kitchen, doing the sewing, and caring for the babies—while the men work in the fields, fix the fences, repair the barn, and make expeditions to the square world for canned goods, pot, and spare parts for cars. The urban communes, by contrast, find it easier to reduce, if not abolish, the sexual division of labor.

Leadership is repressed as sex was repressed by the Victorians, and just about as successfully. Commune dwellers avoid words like "directed," "requested," "ordered," as Victorians avoided "thigh" and "belly." Efforts are made to resist the crystallization of leadership, and when they are successful during the season when much hard and monotonous work is necessary, the result is often disastrous for the capacity of the commune to survive on its own. Tools are lost or broken through careless use. Weeding is not done. People disappear at harvest time. Luckily enough, there are checks from home or dividend checks, and people can go away to work for wages and return when they have accumulated enough to buy brown rice and beans for several months.

"Group marriage" also creates problems. Some girls are better looking than others, and prejudices against homeliness die hard among liberated men and even liberated women. There seems to be an irresistible tendency for the leading "nonleaders" to exercise a powerful attraction upon the more beautiful girls, a tendency that has also been observed in "encounter" and "sensitivity" training groups. Most communes have more men than women and hence some men are always left out. Luckily, commune life does not seem to raise the level of sexual desire among men. Communes frown on "playboy" types, and we know that the threshold of "sexual frustration" is determined more by the norms of the group than by any sort of "biological urge." What seems to work best is some form of monogamy plus some 10-20 percent adultery. In the commune one would speak less of "adultery" than of "experiences" or "switching." Some switching takes place without too much overt pain. In other cases the best way to describe what happens is to say that a top male is replaced in the affections of one of the best-looking females by another male, with the displaced male leaving for another commune or

deciding it is time to go to work outside in the flatland for the wages that will replenish the cash pool. Another common way that resolves the shortage of women is for one or two girls to be on a "promiscuous kick." As long as they don't try to seduce the top males away from their women, their constant state of availability will receive gratitude and amused condescension.[1]

Successful farming or even gardening requires a good deal of repetitive and careful work. Urban types tend, after a while, to miss the excitement and variety, or even more the **privacy** of city life. Indeed, the commune is different from the urban hippie community in tha people in the commune are forced to interact and reach some form of harmony. In standard rural life a sharp division of labor, clear-cut lines of authority, and a stress on getting the work done reduces the areas of "problematic intimacy." But in the commune problematic intimacy is the rule rather than the exception. Some are helped by this atmosphere, some put off.

Communes may allow for greater role shifts in their members than do most other forms of small group organization. A personality in search of its identity and strong enough to face the demands of others may find in the commune greater support for the changes he is going through than he can find in his own parents. Communes that are successful in limiting the contacts of their members with the outside world can develop private cultures that are very demanding and also sometimes rather deviant. These, however, are rare. Lack of discipline is so much more frequent that it reduces the capacity of the commune to test systematically new forms of social relations. The mystery, the rich fantasies that surround communes, from the Satanic with Manson, to the humorous as with the Hog Farm, will insure a steady supply of mass-media interest. **Time-Life** waxes sentimental over communes.

The urban-based Hare Krishna, which has an involved set of rules and real discipline, is limited in its impact by its conservatism in regard to sex roles and its Hinduist spiritual and vestimentary transvestism. Since communes have the same appeal for people with sexual hang-ups as nudist camps used to have—and with the same sedative effects—the Hare Krishna also suffer the public relations consequence of their apparent sexual frugality.

Many communes, even those made up of dropouts from Ivy League and New York universities, attempt a pathetic imitation of Indian life: a search of roots for the rootless; an identification with those too powerless to be guilty; a put-down of the WASP majority for having chased the Red Man from his God-given territory.

Still the communes represent the **hubris** of the Puritan tradition, the attempt of men and women who feel moved by the spirit to create a perfect community, where the person can meet God face-to-face and be as unique, as true, as giving as God must be: Promethean arrogance that is the dignity and the curse of our Judeo-Puritan civilization, and will always deserve our respect and our hope that one day we can make it work. The communes remind us that no man is free not to search for God and that in this search resides his honor even if in the end he meets but his fallible self.

■

The second major cultural stream picked up and amplified by the hippie movement is the drug culture. Before the late fifties, marijuana smoking was limited to blacks, Puerto Ricans, and Mexicans, and among whites to jazz musicians who had picked it up from black colleagues. In the Eastern colleges, only the few students who were real jazz aficionados might have some casual contact with marijuana. The radical movement, in its Communist, Trotskyite, or other varieties, was dead set against all drugs.

In the mid-fifties a new phenomenon began: the widespread use of drugs in the treatment of mental disorders. For those not so sick, Miltown became a fashionable remedy against anxiety and tension. In many professional families, where anxiety, hypochondria, and nonconformity describe the social climate, taking tranquilizers became a fashionable exhibit of how many of the world's troubles one had to carry.

The children of these families went to college and there met with at least two currents that would help their conversion to drugs. The first was the poetry-reading fad, often against a background of jazz music, with its heroes the beat poets, Allen Ginsberg, Gregory Corso, Lawrence Ferlinghetti, Gary Snyder, Kenneth Rexroth, and Brother Antoninus, who gave recitals in colleges followed by late-hour gatherings where the "in" crowd would "turn on."

The second current was the civil rights movement, whose undeniable greatness was marred by the transformation of the Negroes into angels with black faces: a form of **ouvrièrisme**, probably inevitable, which led some to imitate the objects of compassion in their speech, their ghetto separation, their music, and even their "vices." Since blacks smoked marijuana it had to be a good thing. Heroin addiction, instead of being horrible, became a sort of secret cult—dangerous, of course, but also a curse of greatness that revealed to the initiates how many jazz musicians were addicted to it.

At the same time, one of the barriers to the diffusion of drugs, the frat culture of football games and beer busts, began to disintegrate. A new elite appeared on Eastern and California campuses; instead of claiming upper-class and old-settler connection, it claimed legitimacy on the basis of political awareness and intellectual activism. Its name-dropping related more to the **New York Review of Books** than to the Social Register. The smoking of marijuana became one of its rituals of solidarity, just as the heavy drinking of alcoholic beverages had been the ritual of the frats. Many professors who looked with disdain on the frats looked with approval, if not fondness, on the new student leaders. Whatever their antics, political or recreational, these students supported values in tune with high culture even if the search for the "golden screw" did not allow them to turn in papers on time. Although they might come from prestigious private schools and have rich parents, they did not snub their professors. Many even wanted to join the profession. The period 1957-66 saw the height of the post-Sputnik meritocratic campus, where professors attempted to impose upon adolescents from all social classes the ideals of the intellectual jock.

By 1963-64, however, the ideals of the contrameritocracy—affirming the right, nay the superiority, of dropping out, and the claim that drugs gave access to a knowledge superior to rational knowledge—all became part of the hippie "backlash," which gave the diffusion of marijuana, soon followed by other drugs, a new impulse and legitimacy. By 1964 the whole college scene (i.e., the 200 most selective establishments) was permeated with marijuana, and by 1965 LSD became widely available. In 1967 drugs had begun to infiltrate the high schools. In 1970 a questionnaire, distributed in two middle-class high schools located in the suburbs of a large midwestern metropolis, showed that only one-third of the students had never taken any drugs, one-third had had only an occasional experience with them, and one-third took drugs (overwhelmingly marijuana or hashish) once a week or more. A tenth of the student body could be called "serious" users. Heroin users (not necessarily addicts) were rare, but 1 percent in a student body of 1,500 still makes 15 users.

The drug culture gets its organization from "dealers" who in turn secure their supplies from wholesalers. The dealer is a semibenevolent merchant who barely makes expenses **over the long run**, wholesalers being the real money-makers. The small-time dealers "turn on" frequently with their customers. Although sales promotion is not unknown, the dealer prefers to think of himself as servicing a need rather than creating it. Gifts to customers are not uncommon. The small-time dealer becomes a "taste leader" to his clients and this leadership is not necessarily limited to drugs. Clients and dealers meet in an "underground" atmosphere that seems exciting. For many personalities at loose ends the drugs provide a motivational center, a substitute identity, and an occasion to relate meaningfully to others, even if in the process they may kill a certain percentage of those who use them.

Drugs are used, of course, by members of other hippie cultures such as the communes, the music culture, and the political culture. And with time, drugs have lost much of the mystical aura with which the hippie movement had surrounded them. But, especially among some teenagers, drugs have become an end in themselves, a subject of interminable conversations, part tranquilizer, part escape, part dare, a form of Russian roulette with which the middle-class adolescent can demonstrate to himself he has "heart" without engaging in the fights and gang bangs dear to the "grease." It is a juvenile delinquency with low risks, where prosecution does not alienate you from your peers; a means of self-assertion and rebellion, yet a way of imitating older adolescents in the search for maturity. As such, it is already spreading to the junior high schools. The drug culture has its own scale of prestige where the bottom rung belongs to the marijuana experimenter and the top rung to the users of the needle, who inject methedrine, seconal, or heroin.

Drugs were publicized heavily by the underground press until 1968. Such youth movies as **Easy Rider** and **Getting Straight** (there is a lame attempt in **Getting Straight** to oppose the heavy use of drugs by showing the "head" to be unreliable), and the rock songs have glamorized marijuana and LSD.[2] At the present time the irony of

drug education programs (it is one way of employing excess language teachers) is that they finish the publicity job the rock songs and the movies have begun.

Drugs serve an antiestablishment function through the promise of unconditional pleasure (pleasure without having to "earn" the right to it), and through their relation to an antirationality where astrology and good or bad "vibes" replace the belief that hard work, learning, and persistence will get you where you want to go. They promote "dropping out" of structures that require postponement of gratification (college). Through instant nirvana they lure some of the young away from the Puritan establishment culture. Drugs also have an antiestablishment function through the dissonance of illegality. During Prohibition alcohol rarely had this effect, if only because it was part of a traditional male culture resonant with the aggressive toughness of the Puritan ethos and therefore lacking, even in illegality, the tone of subversion.

■

To evaluate the future of drug consumption in the U.S. one might look at the problems of the legalization of marijuana. The proponents of legalization find themselves caught in several cross pressures. It is difficult to press for restrictions on tobacco and pollution while advocating the legalization of a hallucinogen about which little is known as to long-range effects. One cannot press for limits to fertilizers, pesticides, and cyclamates, and wish to generalize the unsupervised use of a drug that has a powerful and little understood impact upon the brain.

Another cross pressure is that the steady use of marijuana **does** lead frequently to further experimentation with other drugs. (A colleague of mine doing research on marijuana effects and using medical students as his subject population, noted that it was hard to find cases where marijuana smoking had not been followed by more or less broad experimentation of other drugs, so that it became difficult to distinguish between the effects of marijuana smoking and those of other drugs.) Although the great bulk of drug experimenters settles down eventually to a "Martini-type" consumption of marijuana or hashish, a certain percentage is sucked into a process of hard-drug addiction, which may last for years before death or remission occurs. Thirty years ago, 17-year-old alcoholics were practically unknown. Today middle-class drug addicts on pills or heroin or plain "pot-heads" are not uncommon, and the group most affected is that of children who participate in the antiestablishment culture centering around the school's swingy teachers. Many a potential candidate for an Ivy League college turned on as a high school junior and found in his senior year his grades slipping to the point where even graduation was in danger.

In liberal circles which dabble in depth psychology one frequently hears that "if it had not been marijuana or barbiturates it would have been something else." This sort of fatalism, based on no data whatsoever, is not very convincing. It comes from the same ideological outlook that sees in the concept of "bad company" an authoritarian or segregationist prejudice, and ignores the insight it contains. The fact is, there are times when in the necessary process of emotional disengagement from parents adolescents do become very vulnerable to outside influences, even if their upbringing has given them "good" principles. In most cases there will be a return to these principles, but the experiences that the adolescent may in the process go through can sear his mind and body for life.[3]

Those whose interest in the legalization of marijuana comes mainly from an antagonism to the Puritan ethos must accept the fact that the illegality of drugs reinforces their antiestablishment significance. The legalization of marijuana would destroy the social influence of the benevolent dealer, as well as the dissonance of illegality which tends to promote allegiance to the counter culture. Legalization might also accentuate the pacifier aspect of drug intake and facilitate the co-opting of the drug users into the system. This seems to have been one of the major functions of drugs in relation to the lower strata of India, China, the Arab countries, and the South American Indians.

Yet the legalization of marijuana, like the legalization of pornography (already accomplished sub rosa by the courts), could have a strong impact as a symbol of the weakening of the Puritan ethos. But if the Puritan ethos were not mortally wounded in the process, the violent attacks upon it could lead to a fundamentalist reassertion which might crush liberalizing movements and lead to drastic changes in the personnel that mans the gates of the mass media.

Under these conditions the pros and cons of the legalization of marijuana are complex and there is not likely to be a major push in that direc-

tion, certainly not while Mr. Nixon is in the White House. Heavy drug use will probably lose its fad appeal as it reaches the junior high schools where it can be controlled more effectively by parents. One frequently meets college freshmen who have already been "heavy" into the drug scene and are ready to leave it, now that drug use is becoming identified with the "freak" part of high school culture, rather than with college sophistication.

Marijuana and hashish will probably remain illegal as prostitution is illegal. Drug use of a heavy and prolonged nature will be the tranquilizer of the stagnant and the defeated, the novocaine of downward mobility. For some middle-class adults who follow the **New York Times Magazine** in asserting the chicness of marijuana smoking,[4] it will become the equivalent of bathtub gin in the 1920s. For others it may become a middle-class equivalent of what the gin shop in Zola's **L'Assommoir** was to the working class.

■

Now to the third and most creative cultural form in the hippie movement—the music culture. Reaching an apex in the Woodstock festival, it derives its organization from the musicians, the promoters, the disc jockeys, and the record industry.

This movement has its roots in several strands of American popular music. There is the folk singing strand, which had remained an antiquarian interest until it began its slow climb to popularity under the aegis of the Popular Front. Folk singing expressed the wisdom of the American folk and as such deserved the support of the progressive. This was the period when the movement took to square dancing and Pete Seeger was a major troubadour. It continued during the war in "Café Society Downtown" and "Uptown" and eventually developed its own momentum in the 1950s to culminate in the TV Hootenanny (with a little assist from Tennessee Ernie Ford's "Sixteen Tons"). Joan Baez with her voice and Bob Dylan with his poetical talent were to give a new dimension to folk singing in the first half of the 1960s.

Other strands of the music culture were the rock and roll of black popular music and the blues, the latter being one of the great contributions made by the blacks to American and world culture. A synthesis between the two at the end of the 1950s and the beginning of the sixties gave us the particular Detroit sound known as "Motown."

Meanwhile Elvis Presley had made a national fad out of his particular fusion of "mountain" music and rock, getting white audiences to accept a much more orgiastic and openly sexual message within the medium.

The Beatles created the new music by synthesizing the rock of Elvis Presley with Motown sound. They brought to the states their "rocker" or young British working-class style, and it caught fire immediately. One might have expected the hippies to look down their nose at the Beatles and return to the records of Ornette Coleman and Leadbelly; but they did not. On the contrary, the Beatles and the Rolling Stones became new culture heroes. Hippie musicians, combining rock, blues, and English sound (the Yard Birds, the Cream) and using Dylan-type lyrics, gave young America a music all its own, relegating jazz to the paternal generation. It was partially on the wings of the music created and played by John Mayall, Paul Butterfield, Mike Bloomfield, the Fugs, the Jefferson Airplane, the Grateful Dead, Jimi Hendrix, the Canned Heat, and many others that the hippie movement became a mass movement, only to explode under the strains of its success, leaving the music culture to develop on its own. The musicians are also close to the drug culture, which they have popularized by their songs and example. Rock musicians (AM rock in working-class districts, FM rock in middle-class districts) have become in the high schools an alternative to the athlete as nonacademic and even antiacademic models.

There is little doubt that the youths who become either players, band followers, or aficionados of the rock culture have a strong antimeritocratic bias. Yet even for them the requirements of professionalization conflict with the cult of spontaneity. Long practice is necessary if one is to obtain proficiency. There is much competition in the music field and the rewards for excellence are enormous, both in prestige and money. The discipline of playing, and the organization of the show that accompanies the playing, stimulate self-control and self-distance. Drugs, however, are a constant temptation for an ego that is put on the block at each performance. But the instability of rock musicians, whether due to their personality types, drugs, life on the road, or the temporary allegiance to music as a career, makes such groups transitory and the quality of their music hard to sustain. Because of their talent, their unusual stability as a group, and the widespread belief that

financial success had not spoiled them, the Beatles were the role models. Now that they have disbanded, there seems to be a certain exhaustion of inspiration throughout the rock movement.

Rock music has become a transmission belt for antiestablishment views, through both the lyrics and the orgiastic color of the music. It has contributed to the isolation of youth culture from adult culture by creating a much sharper break between big band music and rock than there was between ragtime and big band songs—a process symbolized by the end of the "Hit Parade" program in the late 1950s.

The music culture does not lead per se to political commitment. Musicians tend to be "situationists," prompt to underline and act out the absurd. They find political rhetoric boring, and at the rock festivals the mood seems hardly conducive to radicalization. How much lasting alienation from the Puritan ethos the music creates is a moot point. It may promote a commitment to the "counter culture" through the prestige it gives to deviant life styles and also has impact in promoting the counter culture among a segment of working-class white youth who enjoy the contact and occasional sexual opportunities that rock will give them with college youth.

Drugs and music have made a much bigger impact on youth society than has the "dropout" message of the hippie movement. Yet dropping out can take place, even while serving time in high school or college, simply by the withdrawal of motivation from occupational and family roles. For most, the moratorium is temporary; for some, even beneficial.

■

Perhaps both the drug and music cultures would have developed without the hippie phenomenon. The connection with the latter's love and freedom ethos gave the "practitioners" a feeling of group membership and self-righteousness, which greatly increased their proselytizing capacity. The same can be said about the political culture, which was born separately from the hippie movement and eventually merged into it without losing its identity—just as the communal movement, the drug and music cultures have done.

It was probably the collapse of the Communist party as a vital political force after the 1956 Hungarian uprising that provided an opportunity for the development of a tenderhearted and expressive oppositional movement, free of the bureaucratic discipline and "rule or ruin" tactics characteristic of Bolshevik politics. This was the New Left. It received considerable momentum from the FSM movement at Berkeley (1964), where it first discovered the vulnerability of the university to political protest.

Three social forces were to give unexpected impetus to the New Left. The first was the development of the "technico-professional complex" as a political tendency led by left-wing academics. The civil rights battles were their first experience with mass politics, after which came the peace movement as it found its real start on the campus in the 1965 "teach-in" organized at the University of Michigan.

The second force was the cooperation of the mass media, especially the TV networks and the national news magazines (**Time, Life, Look, Newsweek**), which saw in these movements not only a source of dramatic news happenings but also of an ideology commonly shared by cameramen, reporters, news commentators, and even the vice-presidents in charge of editing the six-thirty news show. The mass media and especially TV will give favorable exposure to the New Left, but with this proviso: it must fit the interests of the technico-professional complex of which they are a part. Their coverage of the Vietnam war in 1967-68 was an extraordinary boost to the peace movement and yet remained "invisible" in its political intent.[5] "The Breaking of the President 1968" was also a major success, although of course they had a major assist from their victim.

The third force was the hippyization of antiwar students and the New Left. From the hippies the New Left took its life style, clothing, hair, language, sex life; and from 1967 onward many hippies renounced nonviolence and political indifference.

The hippyization of the New Left enabled it to attract the drug and the music fans, giving them a political identity of sorts as well as feelings of solidarity. For nonpolitical but disaffected youth, the musicians legitimated the hippie garb. Though it would create difficulties with the world of square adults, the fact that the mass media customarily saw the hippyfied youth as the exemplars of the new style and the new rebellion also helped to push antiwar students toward the New Left. For when the mass media speak of "youth" or "the students," they certainly don't mean the average youth with a vocational orientation

toward college, good relations with his parents, coolness toward drugs and promiscuous sex, and a political outlook slightly to the left of Hubert Humphrey. No Stalinist front has ever been so successful in endowing the young with its distinctive aura as has the coalition of antiwar students, New Left, hippies, and the mass media, operating without any formal committees, secret accomplices, or central apparatus.

■

From this coalition two major currents have emerged as the standard-bearers of the counter culture. The first is the literary-sociological assault on the Puritan ethos and the WASP establishment; the second, the Ché Guevara type of political activism where the effectiveness of the action is subordinated to the exaltation of the participants.

The literary-sociological assault has been carried out by a group essentially marginal to the academy, but which desires to keep the aura of the academic commitment to scientific truth. Yet it cannot accept the uncertainty of scientific truth, its perpetual renewal, its rejection of the temptation of power. This group, which might be called the "intellectuoids," searches for a theology in science, a fighting faith which will help to destroy the country club set, the yacht club set, the deanery, the professorial establishment, Palm Beach, the military-industrial complex, and install in their place a brotherhood of freedom.

Inevitably many of these "intellectuoids" are young instructors and assistant professors who in their professional fields are ready to accept the burdens of uncertainty but revert to self-serving ideologies when it comes to social issues. It is probably too much to ask that they should approach social science in an intellectual fashion when many of their own peers in sociology, psychology, and political science seem to have transformed their disciplines into a sort of muckraking journalism where the basic "theoretical" orientation is a new version of **delenda est Carthago** or Voltaire's **Écrasons l'infâme**. Too often when opening **Trans-action** and even **Psychology Today** one can predict the argument of the article from a mere knowledge of the title, at least if one follows the principle that the WASP establishment and the Silent Majority are oppressive, dehumanizing, pig-dominated, exploitative, polluting, inefficient, sexist, afraid of sex, racist, authoritarian, rigid, frigid, fearful, paranoid, white-collar crimi-

nals, desperate, sick, sadistic, infantile, and ignorant.

Besides **Trans-action**, **Ramparts**, the **New
York Review of Books**, the intellectual ammunition of the counter culture on campus is provided
by the radical paperbacks dealing with street
violence, racism, and the Third World. Marcuse,
Fanon, Kenneth Keniston [6] (who sees in the student radicals a breed of moral supermen as, more
realistically, Richard Flacks sees in them the new
Social Register), and Jerry Rubin's and Abbie
Hoffman's nonbooks, Roszak's **Counter Culture**
and Charles Reich's **Greening of America** are typical resources of the radical faculty. They have
organized courses entitled **Where It's At** and **The
Revolution of the Sixties**, the prototype of which
was Harvard's full-year course **Social Relations
148-149**, taught to some 600 students rewarded
by easy A's. Part of this counter culture is seeping
down to the high schools and private schools
where, in conjunction with the drug and music
culture, it contributes to the development of the
"freak" grouping, somewhere between the "frats"
and the "grease."

The literary-sociological assault has "radicalized" the culture of "Proper bohemia," to
which belong the young college instructors, the
civil liberties lawyers, the Unitarian militants, the
Quaker work camps, the mass media specialists
(especially those below the $40,000 level), the
publishing-house readers and editors, movie direc-
tors, actors and actresses between jobs, and other
professionals and paraprofessionals who gravitate
around the university. A few rich businessmen
contribute heavily to the financing of the local
underground press and often own the FM stations
which provide them with tax write-offs and their
younger friends with job opportunities.

The counter culture takes from the upper
class its casualness about rules, and also its willingness to use four-letter words that show it to be
above middle-class constraints. Most exponents of
the counter culture are of petty-bourgeois origin,
and most petty bourgeois, not having been raised
in bourgeois manners, try to bypass them. They
imitate the aristocracy's disregard for proper form,
believing that they thereby partake of its elegance.
They assume the permissiveness of the upper class
but not its **noblesse oblige.**

The hippies have provided a pattern of dress
which, interpreted by the jet-set boutiques,
becomes a badge of being "with it" and a challenge to the status of the traditional Puritan elites.

The doctrine of "crystallized establishment violence" has facilitated the transition from the
pacifism of the civil rights movement to the legitimation of the violence perpetrated (way downtown) against the establishment and its Irish cops.
The worship of the Black Panthers whereby Proper
bohemia atones its guilt—sometimes intellectual
guilt, sometimes a disguise for ethical vanity,
sometimes guilt as to the sources of the parental
fortunes—has become another badge of membership and a gambit for claiming moral superiority
over the conservative old rich.

In the 1930s Proper bohemia, besides being
much smaller, was influenced by the Stalinist version of Marxism and held real power in some
publishing houses.[7] At the present time the ideological tenets are more of the hippie variety. Not
that hippies invented them (the sophisticates will
refer to young Marx and Wilhelm Reich), but they
provided the symbolic rejuvenation for some of
the old utopian standbys: arts-and-crafts communism, elegant pastoralism, the poor as noble
savages (more specifically the black and Indian
poor, certainly not the Polack poor). The hippie
cultivation of mood has become the emotionalism
of sensitivity training; hippie work avoidance,
hippie stress on equality of the sexes, the promotion of career aggressiveness in women and of
sensualism in men. While the Puritan ethos implied
a commitment to abstract values and a suspicion
of ascriptive group ties and unearned pleasure, the
counter culture promotes a sort of organic group-
ism in battle against the enemy camp and an
existential concern with body pleasures from
which active sports are usually excluded.

■

The meaning of the counter culture is not
exhausted by referring to its obvious protection
against the pains of possible failure and its utilization as a weapon of class struggle. There are other
aspects which might turn out to be effective solutions to major problems of the postindustrial
world: the development of an international community of the young; a blurring of the lines
between work and play; a considerable decline in
status formalism; a greater equality for women.

Everywhere, perhaps even in Soviet Russia,
there seems to be an erosion of classical patriotism. By contributing to this erosion the counter
culture orients the search for the sacred toward an
international community of students. On the other

hand, the critique of nationalism too often takes on a shrill quality that denies any obligation of the citizen to the nation. Instead of replacing nationalism by a thoughtful dedication to an entity beyond the nation that requires even more self-sacrifice, there is a tendency toward a premoral affirmation of the primacy of self-interest. The counter-culture hatred for the nation is parochial, often too bitter to be the result of a greater love.

Similarly, the counter culture seems to be trying to create the elements whereby the traditional division between work and play can be overcome by a new synthesis. What seems to be wanted is an end to the guilt that attends some of the processes necessary to creative work: the careless as well as the careful experimentation, the trials and errors, the sloth of discovery and the failure to discover anything, the painful fact that most innovations are useless. If we are to solve the problem of work meaninglessness (and I am aware that there is a lot of romantic drivel being peddled under that expression), it is likely that a definition of work less associated with the routine deprivations of discipline must become more generally accepted. Professors know this problem well who feel guilty when they have an enjoyable conversation with their colleagues, a conversation that often leaves a sediment of new ideas, while their superego associates work with the careful reading of Talcott Parsons or the thorough preparation of a lecture which leaves little room for response to the audience.

In the process of this search for a new definition of work the counter culture seems to have been instrumental in the destruction of the post-Sputnik university, whose excesses contributed to the development of the hippie movement and to the spread of drugs. In the present permissive atmosphere of academe most students can accommodate a commitment to the music, drug, and political cultures without any need to drop out from either the university and/or their families. It is possible that the revival of Rousseau's ideas on education, which the counter culture is promoting, may have a positive impact on teaching. So far the older faculty, puzzled and frequently demoralized, laments the passing of the post-Sputnik university, while young faculty want to transform academe into a sanctuary from which to lead students into forays against the establishment. Meanwhile, little is done about teaching, and the decreased power of the deanery makes it less likely that anything constructive (hence somewhat painful) will be

done. It is unlikely that the impulse will come from the students now that they have gained soft grading, Mickey Mouse courses, and mixed dormitories.

A greater rate of discovery and change, even if limited to the expressive spheres of life, will demand a greater solidarity, a willingness to put up with the higher rate of obsolescence and disorder that creativity implies. Thus the counter culture's stress upon the legitimacy of ephemeral art, the poetry of mood, the immediate sensitivity and positive response to others, may just possibly create conditions for a solution to the problem of work, play, and rank in the postindustrial world.

Meanwhile, its search for intimacy often seems like a Hollywood version of the shoe salesman's pseudo-**Gemeinschaft**, a ploy for Portnoy on the make. It mocks work discipline and suspects the poor of "Uncle Tomism" if they take "blind-alley jobs." Since most of its adherents work in bureaucratic organizations where they do not own the means of teaching or administration, contempt for private property may seem to have a revolutionary meaning: the property is that of the pig landlord, the pig stockholders, the pig establishmentarian government. It seeps down to the youth society as indulgence for "ripping off." Solid bases for comparison are lacking, hence we cannot be sure that there is really more stealing in the stores than 40 or 50 years ago, or much more cheating in school. On a short-run basis, we all know that cheating and thievery on campuses have reached epidemic proportions. Some of it may be the result of the changing composition of the student body, or of a redefinition of stealing by middle-class students as a matter of taste.

The decline in status formalism may facilitate social mobility and reduce the costs of marginality. Yet the intolerance that the straight upper-middle class reserves for bad manners is more than matched by the intolerance the counter culture shows to those who disagree with its views. In many localities it has created a level of political contentiousness and law-suit proneness that did not exist before it gained a substantial following.

One might hope that the positive advantages of destruction and reconstruction created by the counter culture will be gained without disorder and reaction. But this hope seems unrealistic. New solutions for tomorrow may come from a few of the communes, but so far the intellectual caliber of the blueprints for tomorrow proposed by the literary-sociological assault has been disappointingly low. Again the medium has been the message.

The weakness of the counter-culture analysis, once it tries to go beyond the exaltation of mood and personal freedom, is partly reflected by the weakness of the political movement it sustains, and which I here describe as the Ché Guevara movement. This movement contains the political spectrum that made up the non-Bolshevik section of SDS of 1968-69, and independent groups like the White Panthers, whose leader John Sinclair was one of the original Midwest hippies and a good jazz critic. The core of the Guevarist movement is made up of the more romantic and antibureaucratic revolutionaries who remind one of the Russian Narodniks (Populists) of the 1860-70s, except that our Narodniks have little desire to convert the white working class and peasantry, and are not often welcomed by the blacks. They meet their best response in the "swinging" and "Proper bohemians" of the middle class, and of course among the college students and/or middle-class dropouts from either high school or college. The Weathermen might well take for their hero Nechaev, who wrote with Bakunin the famous **Revolutionary Catechism** (1869). They have seized the imagination of the revolutionary students by their undeniable courage and flamboyant actions, as well as their luck in avoiding arrest. It will be a while before the police effectively penetrate the organization and corrupt it—which seems to be the fate of all underground movements unable to come quickly above ground and relate directly to the political public.

While the original hippie movement had many aspects of radical Puritanism, this tendency is now found mostly in the rural commune; the Che Guevara tendency is much more overtly anti-Puritan. In contrast with the ascetic patterns of the Bolsheviks, the strength of the American Narodniks resides in their capacity to combine the delights of moral righteousness with the underwriting of sensual release through drugs, sex, music, vandalism, "ripping off," and violence. They have developed a style of leadership that permits their roving bands or campus-based groups to have the benefit of direction without the penalty of felt subordination. To middle-class youth this seems to have more appeal than the authoritarian "delegate from the Central Committee" typical of the Bolshevik tradition.

The Guevara movement has had some success (though more apparent than real) because it was carried along for a time by the peace movement created by professors of the elite colleges and universities. Within that movement—which, for instance, in the mainstream (Michigan) campuses of the University of Michigan, and of Oakland, Michigan State, and Wayne State universities receives the support of 70 percent of the liberal arts students[8]—the Ché Guevarists were like fish in water. As a result, until 1969-70 the revolutionary activists benefited not only from the support of Proper bohemia, but from the indulgence of some antiwar professors, and the favorable publicity of the mass media which played down their provocations but gave maximum publicity to police excesses in repression. The Guevarists (and the Bolsheviks) thus used the peace movement as a cover and a resonance box, and in return provided an energy and drama that academics could not supply. They also benefited from the inexperience of college administrators and police in coping with the type of disorder created by a group that amounts at most to 1.5 percent of the student body in the Michigan universities, and probably to no more than 3-4 percent of the Ivy League undergraduates.[9]

The present fading of the peace movement has left the Ché Guevara groups stranded. Its activists try to take the leadership of a new mass of American **bezprizorniki**, the "street people." The latter are quite different from the hippies and their teeny boppers, even if their hair and dress are similar. While the hippies were attached to nonviolence even when it delivered them to the exactions of hoodlums, the "street people" use knives and guns without much reluctance. Their panhandling is aggressive while the hippies' was humorous, hiding behind a joke the guilt they experienced. While heroin was considered uncool by the hippies, its usage is not rare among street people. While hippies would delight in "blowing the mind" of an ogling tourist, the street people are more ready to roll him. No doubt hippie centers were not without some of these pathologies, but they were recognized as deviant. The norm of universal love and keeping one's cool worked toward self-control and personal responsibility. "Keeping one's cool" is not an expression one hears very frequently among street people, and this means more than a mere passing of argot.

The street people, roaming, turning on, panhandling, ripping off, raping (i.e., a "gang bang" with a bit of force at the beginning), once in a while getting killed (and killing), hanging around the universities (preferably the prestige ones) from which they secure some crumbs and protection, resemble the sometime students, sometime bums, sometime hoodlums that lived around the medieval universities. The connection to high culture, more and more fictitious, saves the street people from being defined as common juvenile delinquents. The Ché Guevarists are trying to dignify the amoral violence that prevails in this group by politicizing it. They hope for rehabilitation through revolutionary uplift and opportunity. Meanwhile the result is more often the spreading of a new set of hip rationalizations for aggressive acting out, which includes bombing and arson, and a rip-off on the new brand of self-appointed social workers.

■

On the basis of this diagnosis, two scenarios can be constructed. The first is based on the hypothesis that the academic community will not be further influenced by the counter culture and will not attempt to increase its own political power—and that the liberal-left faculty will let the peace movement die on the vine and not allow the Guevarists to use the university as a sanctuary. Thus, the faculty would take toward the student movement the same stance it took toward the jock and fraternity cultures which provided much of the contrameritocratic ideology before 1960. Through an interval in the student movement, an irresistible momentum of social assimilation would be imparted to the ethnic and racial minorities that provide its more determined militants. The 1970s would then see a period of university and social adjustments to the strains of the meritocracy, which would motivate a new creative surge at the end of the decade. The counter culture would be preempted of its useful elements and the rest encapsulated, so as to provide a permanent justification for those whose rewards in the capitalist-bureaucratic society do not seem commensurate with their ambitions. This, paradoxically, would contribute to the long-range stability and productivity of the meritocracy.

Another scenario requires at least two postulates. First, that the faculty—partly because of the threat of downward mobility implicit in the "high-schoolization" of college, partly because of the charisma of science which it generates, and partly

because it is the most articulate segment of the technico-professional class—will try to develop the peace movement into a political battering ram, using masses of students and new voters as its army. Second, that the counter culture will reach the white working-class youth.

The politicization of the colleges and universities would lead to the growth of influence of "Proper bohemia" over the "straight" faculty. The disaffection of the intelligentsia and the near-monopoly of the mass media held by groups hostile to the WASP establishment would result in widespread alienation of the youth for whom meritocracy would cease to be meaningful. The result is that economic and military institutions could not be staffed with adequate talent. At the other end of the scale, there would be an accumulation of college diplomates or partial diplomates having to settle for jobs which in the generation of their parents did not even require a high school degree. The experience of downward mobility from the college student status, if not tranquilized sufficiently by the counter culture, would create much resentment and smoldering aggression, especially in a climate where the dignity of labor, the last fortress of pride, had been debunked out of existence.

Meanwhile the WASP establishment, bereft of the symbols of legitimacy, as well as of intellectual advice and support, would lose its nerve and its capacity for social control. The United States would then enter a phase of disorganization, with lesser growth in industrial productivity leading to relative deprivation among the working class. From there one can choose his climax: Berlin 1930 with a fundamentalist reaction, or St. Petersburg October 1917 with the assumption of power by a theocracy of politicized intellectuoids, which would bring back order and the comforts of a sacred orthodoxy. Of course, such a disequilibrium of the capitalist order in America might lead to atomic war.

Somehow, the pessimistic scenario does not seem convincing. The mass media have a way of banalizing and sterilizing new cultural forms by giving them instant success. A movement in the United States soon becomes a fad, overwhelmed by the problems of success before it has had time to deepen its insights. Were this Czarist Russia, the disaffection of the mass media gatekeepers (if not of the intellectuals) might herald revolution. But this is multicentered America.

Most of history is dull rather than dramatic, and the 1970s seem more likely to result in the stabilization of a contrameritocratic movement, which would blunt the cutting edges of meritocratic competition. Furthermore, the professional intellectuals have begun a criticism of the counter culture, which should soon result in a decline of its prestige with the mass media.

The professional intellectual has a crucial role to play in the solution of the problems created by the meritocracy if he can find a way to show the society that the true goal of man is the understanding of nature and that the face of God "can be found in the anatomy of the louse." In this contemplation the search for the sacred finds a solution in which achieved rank differences, so emphasized by the meritocracy, are shriveled to insignificance by the cosmic perspective of learning. Within a generation, more than half our population may well be involved in the learning process, as teacher, as student, and more often as both. What an opportunity for the professional intellectual to expand his influence if he will only resist the temptation of power! Meanwhile he must put his house in order, dampen his snobbery, strengthen the community of equals and the international community of scholars, take more seriously his teaching responsibilities. He must incorporate the adult community into the universities, and recuperate his legitimacy as the leader in the search for elusive truth. In the disenchanted world of the meritocracy people long for a sense of purpose and meaning. It is the intellectual's urgent task, at this juncture of history, to teach through the word and his example that the passion to know must replace the passion to conquer.

NOTES

1. Commune dwellers would fiercely deny that they show amused condescension. New value conflicts lead to new areas of repression. Freudianism is not "in" within the commune.

2. The retort by record companies that most listeners cannot tell the meaning of the words and care only about the music neglects the fact that those who understand the words operate as translators. This is certainly one case where the medium is the message.

3. In many suburbs, therapeutic youth centers have sprung up with batteries of phones available to give help to anxious youths whose problems range from boredom to "bad trips" to a need for an abortion. Such centers, heavily steeped in the counter culture, are often directed by a swingy psychologist or psychiatrist aided by mother types out of Alice's Restaurant. The bulk of the aid they give is precisely the chance to find a congenial group with a new form of self-righteousness which abates the adolescent's guilt. Here it is not a question of learning to dream in a Freudian manner so as to please the "shrink," but becoming innocent through a put-down of the establishment. It probably does help the youth in getting himself "together."

4. Cf. Sam Blum, "Marijuana Clouds the Generation Gap," New York Times Magazine, August 23, 1970.

5. Richard W. Jencks, head of the CBS broadcast group, declared in a recent conference on the problems of broadcasting, where he was being attacked from the Left ("T.V. Neglects Social Needs"): "History will assign television a major role in the black revolution and in the anti-Vietnam war revolution. . . ."

6. Kenneth Keniston seems to be having some second thoughts as he discovers the self-serving aspects of moral righteousness in the student radical. Some of the writers used by the counter culture can become quite distressed by their fans.

7. For a good description of this milieu, see Mary McCarthy's The Company She Keeps (1942).

8. This is the result of a poll of 1,200 students in these universities in May-June 1970.

9. Figures derived from the Michigan survey mentioned above. There is a higher percentage of revolutionaries among the students at the University of Michigan than at the three other universities.

chapter 10
the motorcycle gangs: losers and outsiders
hunter s. thompson

Last Labor Day weekend newspapers all over
California gave front-page reports of a heinous
gang rape in the moonlit sand dunes near the
town of Seaside on the Monterey Peninsula. Two
girls, aged 14 and 15, were allegedly taken from
their dates by a gang of filthy, frenzied, boozed-up
motorcycle hoodlums called "Hell's Angels," and
dragged off to be "repeatedly assaulted."

A deputy sheriff, summoned by one of the
erstwhile dates, said he "arrived at the beach and
saw a huge bonfire surrounded by cyclists of both
sexes. Then the two sobbing, near-hysterical girls
staggered out of the darkness, begging for help.
One was completely nude and the other had on
only a torn sweater."

Some 300 Hell's Angels were gathered in the
Seaside-Monterey area at the time, having
convened, they said, for the purpose of raising
funds among themselves to send the body of a
former member, killed in an accident, back to his
mother in North Carolina. One of the Angels, hip
enough to falsely identify himself as "Frenchy of
San Bernardino," told a local reporter who came
out to meet the cyclists: "We chose Monterey
because we get treated good here; most other
places we get thrown out of town."

But Frenchy spoke too soon. The Angels

weren't on the peninsula twenty-four hours before
four of them were in jail for rape, and the rest of
the troop was being escorted to the county line by
a large police contingent. Several were quoted,
somewhat derisively, as saying: "That rape charge
against our guys is phony and it won't stick."

It turned out to be true, but that was another
story and certainly no headliner. The difference
between the Hell's Angels in the papers and the
Hell's Angels for real is enough to make a man
wonder what newsprint is for. It also raises a question as to who are the real hell's angels.

Ever since World War II, California has been
strangely plagued by wild men on motorcycles.
They usually travel in groups of ten to thirty,
booming along the highways and stopping here
and there to get drunk and raise hell. In 1947,
hundreds of them ran amok in the town of Hollis-
ter, an hour's fast drive south of San Francisco,
and got enough press notices to inspire a film
called **The Wild One**, starring Marlon Brando. The
film had a massive effect on thousands of young
California motorcycle buffs; in many ways, it was
their version of **The Sun Also Rises**.

The California climate is perfect for motorcycles, as well as surfboards, swimming pools and
convertibles. Most of the cyclists are harmless
weekend types, members of the American Motorcycle Association, and no more dangerous than
skiers or skin divers. But a few belong to what the

From **The Nation**, May 17, 1965. Reprinted by
permission.

others call "outlaw clubs," and these are the ones who—especially on weekends and holidays—are likely to turn up almost anywhere in the state, looking for action. Despite everything the psychiatrists and Freudian casuists have to say about them, they are tough, mean, and potentially as dangerous as packs of wild boar. When push comes to shove, any leather fetishes or inadequacy feelings that may be involved are entirely beside the point, as anyone who has ever tangled with these boys will **sadly** testify. When you get in an argument with a group of outlaw motorcyclists, you can generally count your chances of emerging unmaimed by the number of heavy-handed allies you can muster in the time it takes to smash a beer bottle. In this league, sportsmanship is for old liberals and young fools. "I smashed his face," one of them said to me of a man he'd never seen until the swinging started. "He got wise, He called me a punk. He must have been stupid."

The most notorious of these outlaw groups is the Hell's Angels, supposedly headquartered in San Bernardino, just east of Los Angeles, and with branches all over the state. As a result of the infamous "Labor Day gang rape," the Attorney General of California has recently issued an official report on the Hell's Angels. According to the report, they are easily identified:

The emblem of the Hell's Angels, termed "colors," consists of an embroidered patch of a winged skull wearing a motorcycle helmet. Just below the wing of the emblem are the letters "MC." Over this is a band bearing the words "Hell's Angels." Below the emblem is another patch bearing the local chapter name, which is usually an abbreviation for the city or locality. These patches are sewn on the back of a usually sleeveless denim jacket. In addition, members have been observed wearing various types of Luftwaffe insignia and reproductions of German iron crosses.[1] Many affect beards and their hair is usually long and unkempt. Some wear a single earring in a pierced ear lobe. Frequently they have been observed to wear metal belts made of a length of polished motorcycle drive chain which can be unhooked and used as a flexible bludgeon. . . . Probably the most universal common denominator in identification of Hell's Angels is their generally filthy condition. Investigating officers consistently report these people,

both club members and their female associates, seem badly in need of a bath. Fingerprints are a very effective means of identification because a high percentage of Hell's Angels have criminal records.

In addition to the patches on the back of Hell's Angels jackets, the "One Percenters" wear a patch reading "1%-er." Another badge worn by some members bears the number "13." It is reported to represent the 13th letter of the alphabet, "M," which in turn stands for marijuana and indicates the wearer thereof is a user of the drug.

The attorney general's report was colorful, interesting, heavily biased and consistently alarming—just the sort of thing, in fact, to make a clanging good article for a national news magazine. Which it did; both barrels. **Newsweek** led with a left hook titled "The Wild Ones," **Time** crossed with a right, inevitably titled "The Wilder Ones." The Hell's Angels, cursing the implications of this new attack, retreated to the bar of the De Pau Hotel near the San Francisco waterfront and planned a weekend beach party. I showed them the articles. Hell's Angels do not normally read the news magazines. "I'd go nuts if I read that stuff all the time," said one. "It's all bullshit."

Newsweek was relatively circumspect. It offered local color, flashy quotes, and "evidence" carefully attributed to the official report but unaccountably said the report accused the Hell's Angels of homosexuality, whereas the report said just the opposite. **Time** leaped into the fray with a flurry of blood, booze, and semen-flecked wordage that amounted, in the end, to a classic of supercharged hokum: "Drug-induced stupors . . . no act is too degrading . . . swap girls, drugs and motorcycles with equal abandon . . . stealing forays . . . then ride off again to seek some new nadir in sordid behavior. . . ."

■

Where does all this leave the Hell's Angels and the thousands of shuddering Californians (according to **Time**) who are worried sick about them? Are these outlaws really going to be busted, routed, and cooled, as the news magazines implied? Are California highways any safer as a result of this published uproar? Can honest merchants once again walk the streets in peace? The answer is that nothing has changed except that a few people calling themselves Hell's Angels have a new sense of identity and importance.

After two weeks of intensive dealing with the Hell's Angels phenomenon, both in print and in person, I'm convinced the net result of the general howl and publicity has been to obscure and avoid the real issues by invoking a savage conspiracy of bogymen and conning the public into thinking all will be "business as usual" once this fearsome snake is scotched, as it surely will be by hard and ready minions of the establishment.

Meanwhile, according to Attorney General Thomas C. Lynch's own figures, California's true crime pictures makes the Hell's Angels look like a gang of petty jack rollers. The police count 463 Hell's Angels: 205 around Los Angeles and 233 in the San Francisco-Oakland area. I don't know about L.A. but the real figures for the Bay Area are thirty or so in Oakland and exactly eleven— with one facing expulsion—in San Francisco. This disparity makes it hard to accept other police statistics. The dubious package also shows convictions on 1,023 misdemeanor counts and 151 felonies—primarily vehicle theft, burglary, and assault. This is for all years and all alleged members.

California's overall figures for 1963 list 1,116 homicides, 12,448 aggravated assaults, 6,257 sex offenses, and 24,532 burglaries. In 1962, the state listed 4,121 traffic deaths, up from 3,839 in 1961. Drug arrest figures for 1964 showed a 101 per cent increase in juvenile marijuana arrests over 1963, and a recent back-page story in the **San Francisco Examiner** said, "The veneral disease rate among [the city's] teen-agers from 15-19 has more than doubled in the past four years." Even allowing for the annual population jump, juvenile arrests in all categories are rising by 10 per cent or more each year.

Against this background, would it make any difference to the safety and peace of mind of the average Californian if every motorcycle outlaw in the state (all 901, according to the police) were garroted within twenty-four hours? This is not to say that a group like the Hell's Angels has no meaning. The generally bizarre flavor of their offenses and their insistence on identifying themselves make good copy, but usually overwhelm—in print, at least—the unnerving truth that they represent, in colorful microcosm, what is quietly and anonymously growing all around us every day of the week.

"We're bastards to the world and they're bastards to us," one of the Oakland Angels told a **Newsweek** reporter. "When you walk into a place where people can see you, you want to look as repulsive and repugnant as possible. We are complete social outcasts—outsiders against society."

A lot of this is a pose, but anyone who believes that all of it is has been on thin ice since the death of Jay Gatsby. The vast majority of motorcycle outlaws are uneducated, unskilled men between 20 and 30, and most have no credentials except a police record. So at the root of their sad stance is a lot more than a wistful yearning for acceptance in a world they never made; their real motivation is an instinctive certainty as to what the score really is. They are out of the ball game and they know it—and that is their meaning; for unlike most losers in today's society, the Hell's Angels not only know but spitefully proclaim exactly where they stand.

I went to one of their meetings recently, and halfway through the night I thought of Joe Hill on his way to face a Utah firing squad and saying his final words: "Don't mourn, organize." It is safe to say that no Hell's Angel has ever heard of Joe Hill or would know a Wobbly from a Bushmaster, but nevertheless they are somehow related. The IWW had serious plans for running the world, while the Hell's Angels mean only to defy the world's machinery. But instead of losing quietly, one by one, they have banded together with a mindless kind of loyalty and moved outside the framework, for good or ill. There is nothing particularly romantic or admirable about it; that's just the way it is, strength in unity. They don't mind telling you that running fast and loud on their customized Harley 74s gives them a power and a purpose that nothing else seems to offer.

Beyond that, their position as self-proclaimed outlaws elicits a certain popular appeal, however reluctant. That is especially true in the West and even in California where the outlaw tradition is still honored. The unarticulated link between the Hell's Angels and the millions of losers and outsiders who don't wear any colors is the key to their notoriety and the ambivalent reactions they inspire. There are several other keys, having to do with politicians, policemen, and journalists, but for this we have to go back to Monterey and the Labor Day "gang rape."

∎

Politicians, like editors and cops, are very keen on outrage stories, and state Senator Fred S. Farr of Monterey County is no exception. He is a leading light of the Carmel-Pebble Beach set and no friend of hoodlums anywhere, especially gang rapists who invade his constituency. Senator Farr demanded an immediate investigation of the Hell's Angels and others of their ilk—Commancheros, Stray Satans, Iron Horsemen, Rattlers (a Negro club), and Booze Fighters—whose lack of status caused them all to be lumped together as "other disreputables." In the cutoff world of big bikes, long runs, and classy rumbles, this new, state-sanctioned stratification made the Hell's Angels very big. They were, after all, Number One. Like John Dillinger.

Attorney General Lynch, then new in his job, moved quickly to mount an investigation of sorts. He sent questionnaires to more than 100 sheriffs, district attorneys, and police chiefs, asking for information on the Hell's Angels and those "other disreputables." He also asked for suggestions as to how the law might deal with them.

Six months went by before all the replies were condensed into the fifteen-page report that made new outrage headlines when it was released to the press. (The Hell's Angels also got a copy; one of them stole mine.) As a historical document, it read like a plot synopsis of Mickey Spillane's worst dreams. But in the matter of solutions it was vague, reminiscent in some ways of Madame Nhu's proposals for dealing with the Vietcong. The state was going to centralize information on these thugs, urge more vigorous prosecution, put them all under surveillance whenever possible, etc.

A careful reader got the impression that even if the Hell's Angels had acted out this script—eighteen crimes were specified and dozens of others implied—very little would or could be done about it, and that indeed Mr. Lynch was well aware he'd been put, for political reasons, on a pretty weak scent. There was plenty of mad action, senseless destruction, orgies, brawls, perversions, and a strange parade of "innocent victims" that, even on paper and in careful police language, was enough to tax the credulity of the dullest police reporter. Any bundle of information off police blotters is bound to reflect a special viewpoint, and parts of the attorney general's report are actually humorous, if only for the language. Here is an excerpt:

On November 4, 1961, a San Francisco resident driving through Rodeo, possibly under the influence of alcohol, struck a motorcycle belonging to a Hell's Angel parked outside a bar. A group of Angels pursued the vehicle, pulled the driver from the car and attempted to demolish the rather expensive vehicle. The bartender claimed he had seen nothing, but a cocktail waitress in the bar furnished identification to the officers concerning some of those responsible for the assault. The next day it was reported to officers that a member of the Hell's Angels gang had threatened the life of this waitress as well as another woman waitress. A male witness who definitely identified five participants in the assault including the president of the Vallejo Hell's Angels and the Vallejo "Road Rats" advised officers that because of his fear of retaliation by club members he would refuse to testify to the facts he had previously furnished.

That is a representative item in the section of the report titled "Hoodlum Activities." First, it occurred in a small town—Rodeo is on San Pablo Bay just north of Oakland—where the Angels had stopped at a bar without causing any trouble until some offense was committed against them. In this case, a driver whom even the police admit was "possibly" drunk hit one of their motorcycles. The same kind of accident happens every day all over the nation, but when it involves outlaw motorcyclists it is something else again. Instead of settling the thing with an exchange of insurance information or, at the very worst, an argument with a few blows, the Hell's Angels beat the driver and "attempted to demolish the vehicle." I asked one of them if the police exaggerated this aspect, and he said no, they had done the natural thing: smashed headlights, kicked in doors, broken windows, and torn various components off the engine.

Of all their habits and predilections that society finds alarming, this departure from the time-honored concept of "an eye for an eye" is the one that most frightens people. The Hell's Angels try not to do anything halfway, and anyone who deals in extremes is bound to cause trouble, whether he means to or not. This, along with a belief in total retaliation for any offense or insult, is what makes the Hell's Angels unmanageable for the police and morbidly fascinating to the general public. Their claim that they "don't start trouble" is probably true more often than not, but their idea of "provocation" is dangerously broad, and their biggest problem is that nobody else seems to understand it. Even dealing with them personally, on the friendliest terms, you can sense their hair-trigger readiness to retaliate.

■

This is a public thing, and not all true among themselves. In a meeting, their conversation is totally frank and open. They speak to and about one another with an honesty that more civilized people couldn't bear. At the meeting I attended (and before they realized I was a journalist) one Angel was being publicly evaluated; some members wanted him out of the club and others wanted to keep him in. It sounded like a group-therapy clinic in progress—not exactly what I expected to find when just before midnight I walked into the bar of the De Pau in one of the bleakest neighborhoods in San Francisco, near Hunters Point. By the time I parted company with them—at 6:30 the next morning after an all-night drinking bout in my apartment—I had been impressed by a lot of things, but no one thing about them was as consistently obvious as their group loyalty. This is an admirable quality, but it is also one of the things that gets them in trouble: a fellow Angel is **always right** when dealing with outsiders. And this sort of reasoning makes a group of "offended" Hell's Angels nearly impossible to deal with.

Here is another incident from the attorney general's report:

On September 19, 1964, a large group of Hell's Angels and "Satan's Slaves" converged on a bar in South Gate (Los Angeles County), parking their motorcycles and cars in the street in such a fashion as to block one-half of the roadway. They told officers that three members of the club had recently been asked to stay out of the bar and that they had come to tear it down. Upon their approach the bar owner locked the doors and turned off the lights and no entrance was made, but the group did demolish a cement block fence. On arrival of the police, members of the club were lying on the sidewalk and in the street. They were asked to leave the city, which they did reluctantly. As they left, several were

heard to say that they would be back and tear down the bar.

Here again is the ethic of total retaliation. If you're "asked to stay out" of a bar, you don't just punch the owner—you come back with your army and destroy the whole edifice. Similar incidents—along with a number of vague rape complaints—make up the bulk of the report. Eighteen incidents in four years, and none except the rape charges are more serious than cases of assault on citizens who, for their own reasons, had become involved with the Hell's Angels prior to the violence. I could find no cases of unwarranted attacks on wholly innocent victims. There are a few borderline cases, wherein victims of physical attacks seemed innocent, according to police and press reports, but later refused to testify for fear of "retaliation." The report asserts very strongly that Hell's Angels are difficult to prosecute and convict because they make a habit of threatening and intimidating witnesses. That is probably true to a certain extent, but in many cases victims have refused to testify because they were engaged in some legally dubious activity at the time of the attack.

In two of the most widely publicized incidents the prosecution would have fared better if their witnesses and victims **had** been intimidated into silence. One of these was the Monterey "gang rape," and the other a "rape" in Clovis, near Fresno in the Central Valley. In this latter, a 36-year-old widow and mother of five children claimed she'd been yanked out of a bar where she was having a quiet beer with another woman, then carried to an abandoned shack behind the bar and raped repeatedly for two and a half hours by fifteen or twenty Hell's Angels and finally robbed of $150. That's how the story appeared in the San Francisco newspapers the next day, and it was kept alive for a few more days by the woman's claims that she was getting phone calls threatening her life if she testified against her assailants.

Then, four days after the crime, the victim was arrested on charges of "sexual perversion." The true story emerged, said the Clovis chief of police, when the woman was "confronted by witnesses. Our investigation shows she was not raped," said the chief. "She participated in lewd acts in the tavern with at least three Hell's Angels before the owners ordered them out. She encouraged their advances in the tavern, then led them to an abandoned house in the rear. . . . She was not robbed but, according to a woman who accompanied her, had left her house early in the evening with $5 to go bar-hopping." That incident did not appear in the Attorney General's report.

But it was impossible not to mention the Monterey "gang rape," because it was the reason for the whole subject to become official. Page one of the report—which **Time**'s editors apparently skipped—says that the Monterey case was dropped because ". . . further investigation raised questions as to whether forcible rape had been committed or if the identifications made by victims were valid." Charges were dismissed on September 25, with the concurrence of a grand jury. The deputy district attorney said "a doctor examined the girls and found no evidence" to support the charges. "Besides that, one girl refused to testify," he explained, "and the other was given a lie-detector test and found to be wholly unreliable."

This, in effect, was what the Hell's Angels had been saying all along. Here is their version of what happened, as told by several who were there:

One girl was white and pregnant, the other was colored, and they were with five colored studs. They hung around our bar—Nick's Place on Del Monte Avenue—for about three hours Saturday night, drinking and talking with our riders, then they came out to the beach with us—them and their five boy friends. Everybody was standing around the fire, drinking wine, and some of the guys were talking to them—hustling 'em, naturally—and soon somebody asked the two chicks if they wanted to be turned on—you know, did they want to smoke some pot? They said yeah, and then they walked off with some of the guys to the dunes. The spade went with a few guys and then she wanted to quit, but the pregnant one was really hot to trot; the first four or five guys she was really dragging into her arms, but after that she cooled off, too. By this time, though, one of their boy friends had got scared and gone for the cops—and that's all it was.

But not quite all. After that there were Senator Farr and Tom Lynch and a hundred cops and dozens of newspaper stories and articles in the national news magazines—and even this article, which is a direct result of the Monterey "gang rape."

When the much-quoted report was released, the local press—primarily the **San Francisco Chronicle,** which had earlier done a long and fairly objective series on the Hell's Angels—made a point of saying the Monterey charges against the Hell's Angels had been dropped for lack of evidence. **Newsweek** was careful not to mention Monterey at all, but the **New York Times** referred to it as "the alleged gang rape" which, however, left no doubt in a reader's mind that something savage had occurred.

It remained for **Time,** though, to flatly ignore the fact that the Monterey rape charges had been dismissed. Its article leaned heavily on the hairiest and least factual sections of the report, and ignored the rest. It said, for instance, that the Hell's Angels' initiation rite "demands that any new member bring a woman or girl [called a 'sheep'] who is willing to submit to sexual intercourse with each member of the club." This is untrue, although, as one Angel explained, "now and then you get a woman who likes to cover the crowd, and hell, I'm no prude. People don't like to think women go for that stuff, but a lot of them do."

We were talking across a pool table about the rash of publicity and how it had affected the Angels' activities. I was trying to explain to him that the bulk of the press in this country has such a vested interest in the **status quo** that it can't afford to do much honest probing at the roots, for fear of what they might find.

"Oh, I don't know," he said. "Of course I don't like to read all this bullshit because it brings the heat down on us, but since we got famous we've had more rich fags and sex-hungry women come looking for us than we ever had before. Hell, these days we have more action than we can handle."

NOTES

1. Purely for decorative and shock effect. The Hell's Angels are apolitical and no more racist than other ignorant young thugs.

topic 6

the acquisition of personality: interpersonal interaction, social roles, and the social self

That man is a role-playing animal, that he is so because he must be, is one of the fundamental wisdoms with which the student of sociology must come to immediate grips. For unless we recognize that "humanness" is intrinsically a social product—that every individual in many crucial respects mirrors the culture in which he has grown up—we lose sight of the fact that social life implies coercion. It implies coercion because all societies, whether small, isolated, and tribal, or vast, cosmopolitan, and industrial, require that individuals fit into a web of social relationships that depend upon a high degree of routinization, congruity, and uniformity.

Thus the universality of **social roles**: every human being who has progressed from infancy toward adulthood has acquired an ever more complex repertoire of roles—age roles, sex roles, occupational roles, family roles, and an infinitude of other roles (i.e., boy-girl, husband-wife, parent-child, boss-employee) that stipulate appropriate behavior in a vast variety of interpersonal situations.

To emphasize the centrality of social roles is not to contend that role is the only element in the socialization process—the process through which cultural norms and behavior patterns are transmitted to successive generations. Nor is it to allege that the human being is a compliant creature who meekly internalizes all that he is taught without fighting back or asserting his individuality. Not at all. To subscribe to such an "oversocialized" conception of man is to bypass the crucial truth that man is simultaneously conformist and nonconformist, a tribal or cultural animal, and an autonomous, self-actuating creature who never entirely succumbs to society's demands for conformance and conventionality. Endleman, a student of this give-and-take between culture and personality, sums it up succinctly:

> There is not only a duality, but a perpetual interplay, a dialectic, between man and culture. Man is ever living culture and in tension with it. He can never fully live without it, yet he can never fully be at ease with it.

The three articles in this section vividly illustrate the complexity and richness of the role concept. In the opening essay, Peter Berger compares everyday role-playing to the parts enacted by the **dramatis personae** in a theatrical production. Erving Goffman, too, relies on what he calls a "dramaturgic" approach to role analysis, wherein "social interaction is likened (not as a true analogy, but as a scaffold for insight) to a theatrical production or play-in-progress consisting of individual and team performances in a complex patterning of intersecting roles and setting." And Stanford Lyman and Marvin Scott use a variety of theatrical analogies in their analysis of "coolness"—an unruffled performance of one's role during a time of crisis (in comparison with "blowing" one's cool).

chapter 11
society
in man
peter berger

Society can exist by virtue of the fact that most of the time most people's definitions of the most important situations at least coincide approximately. The motives of the publisher and the writer of these lines may be rather different, but the ways the two define the situation in which this book is being produced are sufficiently similar for the joint venture to be possible. In similar fashion there may be quite divergent interests present in a classroom of students, some of them having little connection with the educational activity that is supposedly going on, but in most cases these interests (say, that one student came to study the subject being taught, while another simply registers for every course taken by a certain redhead he is pursuing) can coexist in the situation without destroying it. In other words, there is a certain amount of leeway in the extent to which response must meet expectation for a situation to remain sociologically viable. Of course, if the definitions of the situation are too widely discrepant, some form of social conflict or disorganization will inevitably result—say, if some students interpret the classroom meeting as a party, or if an author has no intention of producing a book but is using his

contract with one publisher to put pressure on another.

While an average individual meets up with very different expectations in different areas of his life in society, the situations that produce these expectations fall into certain clusters. A student may take two courses from two different professors in two different departments, with considerable variations in the expectations met with in the two situations (say, as between formality or informality in the relations between professor and students). Nevertheless, the situations will be sufficiently similar to each other and to other classroom situations previously experienced to enable the student to carry into both situations essentially the same overall response. In other words, in both cases, with but a few modifications, he will be able to **play the role** of student. A role, then, may be defined as a typified response to a typified expectation. Society has predefined the fundamental typology. To use the language of the theater, from which the concept of role is derived, we can say that society provides the script for all the **dramatis personae**. The individual actors, therefore, need but slip into the roles already assigned to them before the curtain goes up. As long as they play their roles as provided for in this script, the social play can proceed as planned.

The role provides the pattern according to

which the individual is to act in the particular situation. Roles, in society as in the theater, will vary in the exactness with which they lay down instructions for the actor. Taking occupational roles for an instance, a fairly minimal pattern goes into the role of garbage collector, while physicians or clergymen or officers have to acquire all kinds of distinctive mannerisms, speech and motor habits, such as military bearing, sanctimonious diction, or bedside cheer. It would, however, be missing an essential aspect of the role if one regarded it merely as a regulatory pattern for externally visible actions. One feels more ardent by kissing, more humble by kneeling, and more angry by shaking one's fist. That is, the kiss not only expresses ardor but manufactures it. Roles carry with them both certain actions and the emotions and attitudes that belong to these actions. The professor putting on an act that pretends to wisdom comes to feel wise. The preacher finds himself believing what he preaches. The soldier discovers martial stirrings in his breast as he puts on his uniform. In each case, while the emotion or attitude may have been present before the role was taken on, the latter inevitably strengthens what was there before. In many instances there is every reason to suppose that nothing at all anteceded the playing of the role in the actor's consciousness. In other words, one becomes wise by being appointed a professor, believing by engaging in activities that presuppose belief, and ready for battle by marching in formation.

Let us take an example. A man recently commissioned as an officer, especially if he came up through the ranks, will at first be at least slightly embarrassed by the salutes he now receives from the enlisted men he meets on his way. Probably he will respond to them in a friendly, almost apologetic manner. The new insignia on his uniform are at that point still something that he has merely put on, almost like a disguise. Indeed, the new officer may even tell himself and others that underneath he is still the same person, that he simply has new responsibilities (among which, en passant, is the duty to accept the salutes of enlisted men). This attitude is not likely to last very long. In order to carry out his new role of officer, our man must maintain a certain bearing. This bearing has quite definite implications. Despite all the double-talk in this area that is customary in so-called democratic armies, such as the American one, one of the fundamental implications is that an officer is a superior somebody, entitled to obedience and respect on the basis of this superiority. Every military salute given by an inferior in rank is an act of obeisance, received as a matter of course by the one who returns it. Thus, with every salute given and accepted (along, of course, with a hundred other ceremonial acts that enhance his new status) our man is fortified in his new bearing—and in its, as it were, ontological presuppositions. He not only acts like an officer, he feels like one. Gone are the embarrassment, the apologetic attitude, the I'm-just-another-guy-really grin. If on some occasion an enlisted man should fail to salute with the appropriate amount of enthusiasm or even commit the unthinkable act of failing to salute at all, our officer is not merely going to punish a violation of military regulations. He will be driven with every fiber of his being to redress an offence against the appointed order of his cosmos.

It is important to stress in this illustration that only very rarely is such a process deliberate or based on reflection. Our man has not sat down and figured out all the things that ought to go into his new role, including the things that he ought to feel and believe. The strength of the process comes precisely from its unconscious, unreflecting character. He has become an officer almost as effortlessly as he grew into a person with blue eyes, brown hair, and a height of six feet. Nor would it be correct to say that our man must be rather stupid and quite an exception among his comrades. On the contrary, the exception is the man who reflects on his roles and his role changes (a type, by the way, who would probably make a poor officer). Even very intelligent people, when faced with doubt about their roles in society, will involve themselves even more in the doubted activity rather than withdraw into reflection. The theologian who doubts his faith will pray more and increase his church attendance, the businessman beset by qualms about his rat-race activities starts going to the office on Sundays too, and the terrorist who suffers from nightmares volunteers for nocturnal executions. And, of course, they are perfectly correct in this course of action. Each role has its inner discipline, what Catholic monastics would call its "formation." The role forms, shapes, patterns both action and actor. It is very difficult to pretend in this world. Normally, one becomes what one plays at.

Every role in society has attached to it a certain identity. As we have seen, some of these identities are trivial and temporary ones, as in some occupations that demand little modification in the being of their practitioners. It is not difficult to change from garbage collector to night watchman. It is considerably more difficult to change from clergyman to officer. It is very, very difficult to change from Negro to white. And it is almost impossible to change from man to woman. These differences in the ease of role changing ought not to blind us to the fact that even identities that we consider to be our essential selves have been socially assigned. Just as there are racial roles to be acquired and identified with, so there are sexual roles. To say "I am a man" is just as much a proclamation of role as to say "I am a colonel in the U.S. Army." We are well aware of the fact that one is born a male, while not even the most humorless martinet imagines himself to have been born with a golden eagle sitting on his umbilical cord. But to be biologically male is a far cry from the specific, socially defined (and, of course, socially relative) role that goes with the statement "I am a man." A male child does not have to learn to have an erection. But he must learn to be aggressive, to have ambitions, to compete with others, and to be suspicious of too much gentleness in himself. The male role in our society, however, requires all these things that one must learn, as does a male identity. To have an erection is not enough—if it were, regiments of psychotherapists would be out of work.

This significance of role theory could be summarized by saying that, in a sociological perspective, identity is socially bestowed, socially sustained and socially transformed. The example of the man in process of becoming an officer may suffice to illustrate the way in which identities are bestowed in adult life. However, even roles that are much more fundamentally part of what psychologists would call our personality than those associated with a particular adult activity are bestowed in very similar manner through a social process. This has been demonstrated over and over again in studies of so-called socialization—the process by which a child learns to be a participant member of society.

Probably the most penetrating theoretical account of this process is the one given by Mead, in which the genesis of the self is interpreted as being one and the same event as the discovery of society. The child finds out who he is as he learns what society is. He learns to play roles properly belonging to him by learning, as Mead puts it, "to take the role of the other"—which, incidentally, is the crucial sociopsychological function of play, in

which children masquerade with a variety of social roles and in doing so discover the significance of those being assigned to them. All this learning occurs, and can only occur, in interaction with other human beings, be it the parents or whoever else raises the child. The child first takes on roles vis-à-vis what Mead calls his "significant others," that is, those persons who deal with him intimately and whose attitudes are decisive for the formation of his conception of himself. Later, the child learns that the roles he plays are not only relevant to this intimate circle, but relate to the expectations directed toward him by society at large. This higher level of abstraction in the social response Mead calls the discovering of the "generalized other." That is, not only the child's mother expects him to be good, clean, and truthful, society in general does so as well. Only when this general conception of society emerges is the child capable of forming a clear conception of himself. "Self" and "society," in the child's experience, are the two sides of the same coin.

In other words, identity is not something "given," but is bestowed in acts of social recognition. We become that as which we are addressed. The same idea is expressed in Cooley's well-known description of the self as a reflection in a looking glass. This does not mean, of course, that there are not certain characteristics an individual is born with, that are carried by his genetic heritage regardless of the social environment in which the latter will have to unfold itself. Our knowledge of man's biology does not as yet allow us a very clear picture of the extent to which this may be true. We do know, however, that the room for social formation within those genetic limits is very large indeed. Even with the biological questions left largely unsettled, we can say that to be human is to be recognized as human, just as to be a certain kind of man is to be recognized as such. The child deprived of human affection and attention becomes dehumanized. The child who is given respect comes to respect himself. A little boy considered to be a **schlemiel** becomes one, just as a grown-up treated as an awe-inspiring young god of war begins to think of himself as, and act as is appropriate to, such a figure—and, indeed, merges his identity with the one he is presented with in these expectations.

Identities are socially bestowed. They must also be socially sustained, and fairly steadily so. One cannot be human all by oneself and, apparently, one cannot hold on to any particular identity all by oneself. The self-image of the officer as an officer can be maintained only in a social context in which others are willing to recognize him in this identity. If this recognition is suddenly withdrawn, it usually does not take very long before the self-image collapses.

Cases of radical withdrawal of recognition by society can tell us much about the social character of identity. For example, a man turned overnight from a free citizen into a convict finds himself subjected at once to a massive assault on his previous conception of himself. He may try desperately to hold on to the latter, but in the absence of others in his immediate environment confirming his old identity he will find it almost impossible to maintain it within his own consciousness. With frightening speed he will discover that he is acting as a convict is supposed to, and feeling all the things that a convict is expected to feel. It would be a misleading perspective on this process to look upon it simply as one of the disintegration of personality. A more accurate way of seeing the phenomenon is as a reintegration of personality, no different in its sociopsychological dynamics from the process in which the old identity was integrated. It used to be that our man was treated by all the important people around him as responsible, dignified, considerate, and aesthetically fastidious. Consequently he was able to be all these things. Now the walls of the prison separate him from those whose recognition sustained him in the exhibition of these traits. Instead he is now surrounded by people who treat him as irresponsible, swinish in behavior, only out for his own interests, and careless of his appearance unless forced to take care by constant supervision. The new expectations are typified in the convict role that responds to them just as the old ones were integrated into a different pattern of conduct. In both cases, identity comes with conduct and conduct occurs in response to a specific social situation.

Extreme cases in which an individual is radically stripped of his old identity simply illustrate more sharply processes that occur in ordinary life. We live our everyday lives within a complex web of recognitions and nonrecognitions. We work better when we are given encouragement by our superiors. We find it hard to be anything but clumsy in a gathering where we know people have an image of us as awkward. We become wits when people expect us to be funny, and interesting characters when we know that such a reputation has

preceded us. Intelligence, humor, manual skills, religious devotion, and even sexual potency respond with equal alacrity to the expectations of others. This makes understandable the previously mentioned process by which individuals choose their associates in such a way that the latter sustain their self-interpretations. To put this succinctly, every act of social affiliation entails a choice of identity. Conversely every identity requires specific social affiliations for its survival. Birds of the same feather flock together not as a luxury but out of necessity. The intellectual becomes a slob after he is kidnapped by the army. The theological student progressively loses his sense of humor as he approaches ordination. The worker who breaks all norms finds that he breaks even more after he has been given a medal by management. The young man with anxieties about his virility becomes hell-on-wheels in bed when he finds a girl who sees him as an avatar of Don Giovanni.

To relate these observations to what was said in the last chapter, the individual locates himself in society within systems of social control, and every one of these contains an identity-generating apparatus. Insofar as he is able the individual will try to manipulate his affiliations (and especially his intimate ones) in such a way as to fortify the identities that have given him satisfaction in the past—marrying a girl who thinks he has something to say, choosing friends who regard him as entertaining, selecting an occupation that gives him recognition as up-and-coming. In many cases, of course, such manipulation is not possible. One must then do the best one can with the identities one is thrown.

Such sociological perspective on the character of identity gives us a deeper understanding of the human meaning of prejudice. As a result, we obtain the chilling perception that the prejudging not only concerns the victim's external fate at the hands of his oppressors, but also his consciousness as it is shaped by their expectations. The most terrible thing that prejudice can do to a human being is to make him tend to become what the prejudiced image of him says that he is. The Jew in an anti-Semitic milieu must struggle hard not to become more and more like the anti-Semitic stereotype, as must the Negro in a racist situation. Significantly, this struggle will only have a chance of success when the individual is protected from succumbing to the prejudiced program for his personality by what we could call the counterrecognition of those within his immediate community. The Gentile world might recognize him as but another despicable Jew of no consequence, and treat him accordingly, but this nonrecognition of his worth may be balanced by the counterrecognition of him within the Jewish community itself as, say, the greatest Talmudic scholar in Latvia.

In view of the sociopsychological dynamics of this deadly game of recognitions, it should not surprise us that the problem of "Jewish identity" arose only among modern Western Jews when assimilation into the surrounding Gentile society had begun to weaken the power of the Jewish community itself to bestow alternate identities on its members as against the identities assigned to them by anti-Semitism. As an individual is forced to gaze at himself in a mirror so constructed as to let him see a leering monster, he must frantically search for other men with other mirrors, unless he is to forget that he ever had another face. To put this a little differently, human dignity is a matter of social permission.

The same relationship between society and identity can be seen in cases where, for one reason or another, an individual's identity is drastically changed. The transformation of identity, just like its genesis and its maintenance, is a social process. We have already indicated the way in which any reinterpretation of the past, any "alternation" from one self-image to another, requires the presence of a group that conspires to bring about the metamorphosis. What anthropologists call a rite of passage involves the repudiation of an old identity (say, that of being a child) and the initiation into a new one (such as that of adult). Modern societies have milder rites of passage, as in the institution of the engagement, by which the individual is gently led by a general conspiracy of all concerned over the threshold between bachelor freedom and the captivity of marriage. If it were not for this institution, many more would panic at the last moment before the enormity of what they are about to undertake.

We have also seen how "alternation" operates to change identities in such highly structured situations as religious training or psychoanalysis. Again taking the latter as a timely illustration, it involves an intensive social situation in which the individual is led to repudiate his past conception of himself and to take on a new identity, the one that has been programmed for him in the psychoanalytic ideology. What psychoanalysts call "transference," the intense social relationship between analyst and

analysand, is essentially the creation of an artificial social milieu within which the alchemy of transformation can occur, that is, within which this alchemy can become plausible to the individual. The longer the relationship lasts and the more intensive it becomes, the more committed does the individual become to his new identity. Finally, when he is "cured," this new identity has indeed become what he is. It will not do, therefore, to dismiss with a Marxist guffaw the psychoanalyst's claim that his treatment is more effective if the patient sees him frequently, does so over a long time and pays a considerable fee. While it is obviously in the analyst's economic interest to hold to this position, it is quite plausible sociologically that the position is factually correct. What is actually "done" in psychoanalysis is that a new identity is constructed. The individual's commitment to this new identity will obviously increase, the more intensively, the longer, and the more painfully he invests in its manufacture. Certainly his capacity to reject the whole business as a fake has become rather minimal after an investment of several years of his life and thousands of dollars of hard-earned cash.

The same kind of "alchemistic" environment is established in situations of "group therapy." The recent popularity of the latter in American psychiatry can again not be interpreted simply as an economic rationalization. It has its sociological basis in the perfectly correct understanding that group pressures work effectively to make the individual accept the new mirror-image that is being presented to him. Erving Goffman, a contemporary sociologist, has given us a vivid description of how these pressures work in the context of a mental hospital, with the patients finally "selling out" to the psychiatric interpretation of their existence that is the common frame of reference of the "therapeutic" group.

The same process occurs whenever an entire group of individuals is to be "broken" and made to accept a new definition of themselves. It happens in basic training for draftees in the army; much more intensively in the training of personnel for a permanent career in the army, as at military academies. It happens in the indoctrination and "formation" programs of cadres for totalitarian organizations, such as the Nazi SS or the Communist Party elite. It has happened for many centuries in monastic novitiates. It has recently been applied to the point of scientific precision in the "brainwashing" techniques employed against prisoners of totalitarian secret-police organizations. The violence of such procedures, as compared with the more routine initiations of society, is to be explained sociologically in terms of the radical degree of transformation of identity that is sought and the functional necessity in these cases that commitment to the transformed identity be fool-proof against new "alternations."

Role theory, when pursued to its logical conclusions, does far more than provide us with a convenient shorthand for the description of various social activities. It gives us a sociological anthropology, that is, a view of man based on his existence in society. This view tells us that man plays dramatic parts in the grand play of society, and that, speaking sociologically, he is the masks that he must wear to do so. The human person also appears now in a dramatic context, true to its theatrical etymology (persona, the technical term given to the actors' masks in classical theater). The person is perceived as a repertoire of roles, each one properly equipped with a certain identity. The range of an individual person can be measured by the number of roles he is capable of playing. The person's biography now appears to us as an uninterrupted sequence of stage performances, played to different audiences, sometimes involving drastic changes of costume, always demanding that the actor be what he is playing.

Such a sociological view of personality is far more radical in its challenge to the way that we commonly think of ourselves than most psychological theories. It challenges radically one of the fondest presuppositions about the self—its continuity. Looked at sociologically, the self is no longer a solid, given entity that moves from one situation to another. It is rather a process, continuously created and re-created in each social situation that one enters, held together by the slender thread of memory. How slender this thread is, we have seen in our discussion of the reinterpretation of the past. Nor is it possible within this framework of understanding to take refuge in the unconscious as containing the "real" contents of the self, because the presumed unconscious self is just as subject to social production as is the so-called conscious one, as we have seen. In other words, man is not also a social being, but he is social in every aspect of his being that is open to empirical investigation. Still speaking sociologically, then, if one wants to ask who an individual "really" is in this kaleidoscope of roles and identities, one can answer only by enumerating the situations in which he is one thing and those in which he is another.

chapter 12

encounters
erving goffman

In sociology there are few concepts more commonly used than "role," few that are accorded more importance, and few that waver so much when looked at closely.

ROLE CONCEPTS

The classic formulation of role concepts comes from the social-anthropological tradition[1] and has led to the development of a conceptual framework sometimes called "role theory." A **status** is a position in some system or pattern of positions and is related to the other positions in the unit through reciprocal ties, through rights and duties binding on the incumbents. **Role** consists of the activity the incumbent would engage in were he to act solely in terms of the normative demands upon someone in his position. Role in this normative sense is to be distinguished from **role performance** or role enactment, which is the actual conduct of a particular individual while on duty in his position. (Accordingly, it is a position that can be entered, filled, and left, not a role, for a role can only be performed; but no student seems to hold to these consistencies, nor will I.) In describing a role there is, of course, a problem of how much detail to give, the amount sometimes being tacitly determined unsystematically by the degree of familiarity the reader is assumed to have with the role in question.

The individual's role enactment occurs largely through a cycle of face-to-face social situations with **role others,** that is, relevant audiences. These various kinds of role others for an individual in role, when taken together, have recently been termed a **role-set.**[2] The role-set for a doctor, for example, contains colleagues, nurses, patients, and hospital administrators. The norms relating the individual to performers of one of the roles in his role-set will have a special and nonconflictful relation to one another—more so than the norms relating the individual to different kinds of role others. The overall role associated with a position falls into **role sectors**[3] or subroles, each having to do with a particular kind of role other. Doctor-nurse is a role sector of the doctor role; doctor-patient, another. Social changes in a role can be traced by the loss or gain to the role-set of types of role other. However, even within the special sector of a role relating the performer to one type of role other, the activities involved may themselves fall into different, somewhat independent parcels or bundles, and through time these may also be reduced or added to, a bundle at a time. In any case, we ought not to be embarrassed by the fact that what is handled from one kind of position in one organization may be apportioned to two or three kinds of positions in another organization. We need only claim to know how a role is likely to be broken up should it come to be divided—the points of cleavage—and what roles are likely to be combined at times of organizational retrenchment.

The elementary unit of role analysis, as Linton was at pains to point out,[4] is not the individual but the individual enacting his bundle of obligatory activity. The system or pattern borrows only a part of the individual, and what he does or is at other times and places is not the first concern. The role others for whom he performs similarly represent only slices of these others. Presumably his contribution and their contribution, differentiated and interdependent, fit together into a single assemblage of activity, this **system** or pattern being the real concern of role analysis.

The role perspective has definite implications of a social-psychological kind. In entering the position, the incumbent finds that he must take on the whole array of action encompassed by the corresponding role, so role implies a social determinism and a doctrine about socialization. We do not take on items of conduct one at a time but rather a whole harness load of them and may anticipatorily learn to be a horse even while being pulled like a wagon.[5] Role, then, is the basic unit of socialization. It is through roles that tasks in society are allocated and arrangements made to enforce their performance.

Recruitment for positions is restrictively regulated in some way, assuring that the incumbents will possess certain minimal qualifications, official and unofficial, technically relevant and irrelevant.[6] Incumbency tends to be symbolized through status cues of dress and manner, permitting those who engage in a situation to know with whom they are dealing. In some cases there will also be a role term of reference and address. Each position tends to be accorded some invidious social value, bringing a corresponding amount of prestige or contamination to the individual who fills it.

For this paper, it is important to note that in performing a role the individual must see to it that the impressions of him that are conveyed in the situation are compatible with role-appropriate personal qualities effectively imputed to him: a judge is supposed to be deliberate and sober; a pilot, in a cockpit, to be cool; a bookkeeper, to be accurate and neat in doing his work. These personal qualities, effectively imputed and effectively claimed, combine with a position's title, when

there is one, to provide a basis of **self-image** for the incumbent and a basis for the image that his role others will have of him. A self, then, virtually awaits the individual entering a position; he need only conform to the pressures on him and he will find a **me** ready-made for him. In the language of Kenneth Burke, doing is being.

Sociologists have added several concepts to round out the Lintonian perspective; these can be introduced here, along with some effort at clarification.

It can be useful to distinguish between the **regular performance** of a role and a **regular performer** of a role. If, for example, a funeral parlor is to stay in business, then the role of the director, of the immediately bereaved, and of the deceased must be performed regularly; but, of these regularly performed roles, only the director will be a regular performer. The immediately bereaved may play the same role on a few other occasions, but certainly the role of the deceased is played but once by any one individual. We can now see that to speak in commonsense terms of an "irregular" performer is to refer to someone performing only a few times what is usually performed by a regular performer.

The **function** of a role is the part it plays in the maintenance or destruction of the system or pattern as a whole, the terms **eufunction** and **dysfunction** sometimes being employed to distinguish the supportive from the destructive effects.[7] Where the functional effect of a role is openly known and avowed, the term **manifest** function is sometimes employed; where these effects are not regularly foreseen and, especially, where this foresignt might alter effects, the term **latent** is sometimes used.[8]

A concept that is often employed in the discussion of roles is that of **commitment**. I propose to restrict this term to questions of impersonally enforced structural arrangements. An individual becomes committed to something when, because of the fixed and interdependent character of many institutional arrangements, his doing or being this something irrevocably conditions other important possibilities in his life, forcing him to take courses of action, causing other persons to build up their activity on the basis of his continuing in his current undertakings, and rendering him vulnerable to unanticipated consequences of these undertakings.[9] He thus becomes locked into a position and coerced into living up to the promises and sacrifices built into it. Typically, a person will become deeply committed only to a role he regularly performs, and it is left to gallants, one-shot gamblers, and the foolhardy to become committed to a role they do not perform regularly.

The self-image available for anyone entering a particular position is one of which he may become affectively and cognitively enamored, desiring and expecting to see himself in terms of the enactment of the role and the self-identification emerging from this enactment. I will speak here of the individual becoming **attached** to his position and its role, adding only that in the case of larger social units—groups, not positions—attachment is more likely to have a selfless component.[10] An appreciation can grow up concerning how attached an individual ought properly to be to a particular role, giving rise to the possibility that, compared to this moral norm, a performer may be overattached to his role or alienated from it. For example, it is said that a new capitalist of the seventeenth century in Europe who entered and left an area of trade according to the temporary profit in it was felt by members of crafts and guilds to be sinfully unattached to what he dealt in.[11]

ROLE DISTANCE

The occurrence of explanations and apologies as limitations on the expressiveness of role leads us to look again at what goes on in concrete face-to-face activity. I return to our example, the merry-go-round.

A merry-go-round horse is a thing of some size, some height, and some movement; and while the track is never wet, it can be very noisy. American middle-class two-year-olds often find the prospect too much for them. They fight their parents at the last moment to avoid being strapped into a context in which it had been hoped they would prove to be little men. Sometimes they become frantic halfway through the ride, and the machine must be stopped so that they can be removed.

Here we have one of the classic possibilities of life. Participation in any circuit of face-to-face activity requires the participant to keep command of himself, both as a person capable of executing physical movements and as one capable of receiving and transmitting communications. A flustered failure to maintain either kind of role poise makes the system as a whole suffer. Every participant, therefore, has the function of maintaining his own poise, and one or more participants are likely to have the specialized function of modulating activity so as to safeguard the poise of the others. In many situated systems, of course, all

contingencies are managed without such threats arising. However, there is no such system in which these troubles might not occur, and some systems, such as those in a surgery ward, presumably provide an especially good opportunity to study these contingencies.

Just as a rider may be disqualified during the ride because he proves to be unable to handle riding, so a rider will be removed from his saddle at the very beginning of the ride because he does not have a ticket or because, in the absence of his parents, he makes management fear for his safety. There is an obvious distinction, then, between qualifications required for permission to attempt a role and attributes required for performing suitably once the role has been acquired.

At three and four, the task of riding a wooden horse is still a challenge, but apparently a manageable one, inflating the rider to his full extent with demonstrations of capacity. Parents need no longer ride alongside to protect their youngsters. The rider throws himself into the role in a serious way, playing it with verve and an admitted engagement of all his faculties. Passing his parents at each turn, the rider carefully lets go one of his hands and grimly waves a smile or a kiss—this, incidentally, being an example of an act that is a typical part of the role but hardly an obligatory feature of it. Here, then, doing is being, and what was designated as a "playing at" is stamped with serious realization.

NOTES

1. Principally Ralph Linton, **The Study of Man** (New York: Appleton-Century, 1936), especially chap. 8, "Status and Role."

2. R. K. Merton, "The Role-Set: Problems in Sociological Theory," **British Journal of Sociology**, 8 (1957), pp. 106-120. Presumably, a term will be needed to refer to the complement of individuals within one element in the role set, so that we can discuss the fact that some role others, such as wife, contain only one performer, while other role others, such as patient, contain many.

3. Neal Gross, Ward Mason, and Alexander McEachern, **Explorations in Role Analysis** (New York: Wiley, 1958), especially p. 62. This book provides a very useful treatment of role. See also the helpful article by F. L. Bates, "Position, Role, and Status: A Reformulation of Concepts," **Social Forces**, 34 (1956), pp. 313-321.

4. Linton, op. cit., p. 113.

5. See Orville Brim, unpublished paper, "Socialization as Role Learning."

6. E. C. Hughes, "Dilemmas and Contradictions of Status," **American Journal of Sociology**, 50 (1945), pp. 353-359.

7. M. J. Levy, Jr., The Structure of Society (Princeton: Princeton University Press, 1952), pp. 76-79. It sometimes seems to be the hope of so-called functional analysis to transform all role analysis into role-function analysis.

8. R. K. Merton, Social Theory and Social Structure (revised ed.; Glencoe: The Free Press, 1957), chap. 1, "Manifest and Latent Functions," pp. 19-84, especially definitions, p. 51.

9. This last point is based on the thorough statement by Philip Selznick, TVA and the Grass Roots (Berkeley: University of California Press, 1953), pp. 255-259. A general consideration of the term commitment may be found in Howard S. Becker, "Notes on the Concept of Commitment," American Journal of Sociology, 66 (1960), pp. 32-40.

10. Strictly speaking, while it is possible for an individual to become attached to a position (as when a Queen becomes convinced of the public value of monarchical government), to be attached to a position usually means to be attached to one's own incumbency of it.

11. See, for example, Werner Sombart, The Jews and Modern Capitalism (Glencoe: The Free Press, 1951), chap. 7, "The Growth of a Capitalistic Point of View in Economic Life."

chapter 13
coolness in everyday life
stanford lyman and marvin scott

"Don't lose your cool!"

A common enough phrase and one easily recognized in contemporary urban America. But, sociologically speaking, what does this new moral imperative mean? What does one lose when he loses his cool? Our task is to answer these questions by analyzing the social arrangements whereby coolness gained and coolness lost are readily observable features in everyday life.[1]

Coolness is exhibited (and defined) as poise under pressure. By pressure we mean simply situations of considerable emotion or risk, or both. Coolness, then, refers to the capacity to execute physical acts, including conversation, in a concerted, smooth, self-controlled fashion in risky situations, or to maintain affective detachment during the course of encounters involving considerable emotion.[2]

We may distinguish three types of risk under which an individual might display coolness. First there is **physical risk** to the person in the form of danger to life and limb. The moral worth of many of the heroes of the Western world is displayed in their willingness and ability to undergo trials of pain and potential death with stylized equanimity and expert control of relevant motor skills. Modern fictional heroes, such as James Bond and Matt Dillon, for example, face death constantly in the form of armed and desperate killers; yet they seem never to lose their nerve or skill. It is not merely their altruistic service in the cause of law and country that makes them attractive, but also, and perhaps more importantly, their smooth skill—verbal and physical—that never deserts them in times of risk.

Secondly, there is **financial** risk. Financial risk entails not only the possible loss of income and status, but also the loss of character associated with the venture. Captains of industry, professional gamblers, and those who play the stock market are supposed to withstand the losses sometimes occasioned in the process with calmness, detachment, even cavalier abandon.

Finally, the most crucial for our concerns, there is **social** risk. Social risks may arise whenever there is an encounter. In every social encounter a person brings a "face" or "mask"—which constitutes the value he claims for himself.[3] Given that an individual stakes this value in every encounter, it follows that encounters are morally serious occasions fraught with great risks where one puts on the line a public face. This is the most serious of risks, for in risking it—he risks his very selfhood. When the interactants are **aware** that each is putting on a public face, they will look for cues to

Stanford M. Lyman and Marvin B. Scott, "Coolness in Everyday Life," in Marcello Truzzi, ed., **Sociology and Everyday Life**, © 1968. Reprinted by permission of Prentice-Hall, Inc., Englewood Cliffs, New Jersey.

glean some "real self" presumably lurking beneath the mask.[4] The capacity to maintain face in such situations constitutes a display of coolness.

As suggested, encounters are hazardous because of the ever present possibility that identity and status will be disconfirmed or damaged by behavior. Whenever an individual or a group has to stage an encounter before a particular audience in order to establish a distinctive identity and meaning, the management of the staging becomes crucial to the endeavor. The effort can fail not simply because of the inadequacies or the conflict of the presented material, but also, and perhaps more importantly, because of the failure to maintain expressive identity and control. Thus individuals and teams—for a successful performance—must not only manage what they have planned, but also carry off the presentation smoothly in the face of interruptions, intrusions, and prop failures.

Smoothness of performance can be seriously interrupted by "prop" failure. Some engagements involve the maintenance in good order of a particular setting. Included here at the minimum is the apparel of the actor. A professor lecturing before his class might be completely discomfited if he discovers his fly is unzipped; and he is indeed hard pressed to reestablish his seriousness of purpose if he is unable to repair the situation with discretion. Professional stage actors must immediately and smoothly construct dialogue to suit a situation in which the stage sets unexpectedly collapse.

Smooth performance can also be challenged by interruption or intrusion. In certain societies—England, for example—public political speeches are traditionally interrupted by hecklers, and on some occasions, objects are flung at the speaker. English politicians try to develop a style that prepares them for responding to such interrutpions by having in readiness a repertoire of clever remarks. Interruption can also be occasioned by a sudden and unexpected event that would normally upset the average man. During the Second World War many actors and concert performers earned reputations for coolness under extreme situations when they continued to play out their performances after an air raid had begun.

Interruptions, intrusions, and prop failures are of two sorts with respect to coolness. The first type requires deft and casual repair of self or self-possessions in order for coolness to be displayed. The professor who, aware that the class perceives his unzipped fly, casually zips it up without inter-rupting the flow or tone of his lecture is likely to be recognized as cool. Similarly, the Walter Mitty-like flyer who sets the broken bone of his arm while maneuvering his plane to a safe landing under hazardous conditions will be known for his coolness.

The second type of intrusion, interruption, or prop failure involves those situations that require immediate action because the entire situation has been altered by their presence. Fires in theaters, air raids, tornados, assassinations of presidents, and other major calamities are illustrations. Those who maintain presence of mind in the face of the disastrous event, and especially those who by their own example prevent others from riotous or panicky behavior, place a stamp of moral worth upon themselves.

The exhibition of coolness under situations of potential panic can be a source of leadership. Formal leaders may be thrust from their posts because they panic, and unknown persons raised to political heights because of their publicly displayed ability to remain calm. Much popular folklore perceives calamitous situations as those providing just the right opportunity for a person otherwise unqualified to assume a dominant position. Indeed, if his acts are sufficiently skillful and smooth, the displayer of coolness may be rewarded with future rights of charismatic authority. A doctor who performs delicate surgery in the midst of an earthquake may by that act establish rights to administer the hospital in which he works. And a teacher who manfully but nonviolently prevents a gang of hoodlums from taking over a school may by his performance take over the school himself.

Embarrassment is one of the chief nemeses of coolness. Any encounter is likely to be suddenly punctured by a potentially embarassing event—a gaffe, a boner, or uncontrollable motor response—that casts new and unfavorable light upon the actor's performance. In some instances, the audience will save the actor from needless embarrassment by studiously overlooking the event; however, this tactful inattention may itself cause embarrassment as each person in the engagement manfully seeks to overlook the obvious. In other instances, the actor himself will be on his mettle to attend or disattend to the disturbance in such a manner that it does not detract from his performance. A skillful self-rescue from a potentially embarrassing situation can win the actor more than he intended, since he may gain not only his directly intended objective but also a boost in his moral worth as well.

Thus, coolness is both a quality to be lost and a prize to be gained in any engagement. That is, coolness may be lost or gained by qualities exhibited in the behavior. A failure to maintain expressive control, a giving way to emotionalism, flooding out, paleness, sweatiness, weeping, or violent expressions of anger or fear are definite signs of loss of cool.[5] On the other hand, displays of **savoir-faire**, aplomb, **sangfroid**, and especially displays of stylized affective neutrality in hazardous situations are likely to gain one the plaudits associated with coolness.

Coolness does not, therefore, refer to routine performance in a role. However, an affectively manifest departure from a role can disconfirm the presence of an actor's coolness just as a remarkable exhibition of **sangfroid** can gain for one the reputation of having it. To be cool, then, is to exhibit a definite form of expressive control during the performance of a role. Thus, we can distinguish three kinds of role performance: cool role behavior, routinized role behavior, and role behavior that indicates loss of cool.

Card playing is one type of social gathering in which all three kinds of role behavior might be exhibited. The "cool player" may push the deed to his family home into the pile of money in the center of the table with the stylized casualness of a Mississippi gambler, neither his smooth, softly smiling face nor his calm, unshaking hands indicating that he is holding only a pair of deuces. The "routine player" may take his bet with a grimace indicating seriousness of purpose and awareness of risk, but not entirely losing composure or calling undue attention to himself. The "uncool player" may become ashen, burst into tears, shriek obscenities, or suddenly accuse his opponents of cheating when his prized and final bet is raised beyond his ability to respond. The card game, like the battlefield, is a moral testing ground.

While the display of coolness is a potential in all encounters, there are certain typical situations where such a display is a social expectation. These involve situations in which the risks are patently obvious –e.g., bullfighting, automobile racing, and war. Literature dealing with these subjects typically portrays characterological coolness and invests it with honor and virtue. Indeed, if one wishes to find examples and evidence of coolness one need but look in the literature about activities considered risky.

Two other types of situations calling for the display of coolness are the **innovative** and the **anomic**. Innovative situations include activities associated with the rites of passage—all those "first times" in the life cycle in which one has to be poised in the face of the as yet unexperienced event. Examples include the wedding night for virgins, first days in school, and the first witnessing of death. Anomic situations are those in which at least one of the actors does not know the rules of conduct and must carry off an engagement in the face of those who do. Typically immigrants, newcomers, and parvenus find themselves in such situations—situations in which poise is at a premium.[6]

A display of coolness is often a prerequisite to entrance into or maintenance of membership in certain social circles. Since in nearly all societies coolness is taken to be part of the character syndrome of elites, we may expect to find a universal condition and a variety of forms of character testing of the elite. European nobility were expected to acquire adeptness at coquetry and repartee; the stylized insult and the witty return were highly prized and regularly tested.[7] Among would-be samurai in Japan, the martial skills were highly prized but even more highly prized was presence of mind. A samurai in training was constantly subjected to contrived sudden dangers, but if he exercised little cathectic control over his skill and strength he would be severely reproved by his zen master.[8] Another coolness test for membership—one involving sexual self-control—is a commonplace of college fraternity initiations. A "stag" film will be shown, and immediately upon its completion, the lights will be flashed on and the initiates ordered to stand up. Those who have "lost their cool" are then observable.

Tests of coolness among peers usually take the form of some contest relation. Teen-age Italian-American slum dwellers engage in "a series of competitive encounters intended to assert the superiority and skillfulness of one individual over the other, which take the form of card games, short physical suffles, and endless verbal duels."[9] And American ghetto-dwelling Negroes have developed a highly stylized dialogue of insult which reaches its quintessential manifestation in "sounding" or the game known as "the dozens."[10]

To successfully pass coolness tests one must mobilize and control a sizable and complex repertoire of material and moral forces. First one must master all those elements of self and situation whose unmastered presence constitutes the condition of embarrassment. These include spaces, props, equipment, clothing, and body.[11] Maladroit usage of these often constitutes a definite sign of loss of coolness, while deft and skillful management of any intrusive action by these can signify the presence of coolness.

Coolness tests also require one to control all those elements of self which, if evidenced, constitute the sign of emotional incapacity. In addition to the body—and here we refer to its carriage, litheness, deftness and grace—there is the special case of the face, perhaps the most vulnerable agent of, as well as the most valuable instrument for, poise under pressure.[12] The eyes, nostrils, and lips are all communicators of one's mental ease and personal control. Failures here—such as a look of fear in the eyes, a flare of the nostrils, or quivering lips—communicate characterological faults that deny coolness. Finally, the color of the face must be kept neutral if coolness is to be confirmed. Those who blush or pale quickly are hard put to overcome the outward physical sign that they are not poised.

Among the most significant instruments for coolness is the voice. Both form and content are relevant here, and each must be coordinated in the service of **savoir-faire** if that character trait is to be confirmed. In institutionalized verbal contests— such as the Negro game of the "dozens"—vocal controls are the principal element of style. For these games as for other verbal artistic endeavours "style is nothing if it is not an overtly conscious striving for design on the part of the artist."[13] To engage expertly in "the dozens," and other Negro word games, one has to employ "noncasual utterances"—i.e., use of language for restricted purposes—in subculturally prescribed but seemingly effortless syntactic constructions and specified elements of diction. Of course voice control as an element of the establishment and maintenance of poise under pressure has its place in circles beyond that of the ghetto Negro. In parlor repartee, covert exchanges of hostility among colleagues, joking relations, and teasing, not only the content but also the tone and timbre count for much.

Courtship and mating are perhaps the most widespread institutions in which poise is expected and thus they require mobilization of those material, anatomical, physiological, and moral forces which together, under coordinated control, constitute the armamentarium by which the coolness game may be won.[14] Activities which require for their execution a mobilization of passions—e.g.,

sexual intercourse—are sometimes regarded as peculiarly valuable for testing poise through affective detachment. Italian-American men admire a person "who is able to attract a good-looking woman and to conquer her without becoming involved."[15] Chinese clan rules warn husbands about the dangers created by emotional expression in sexual relations with their wives.[16] And youthful male prostitutes count it as a proof of their strong character that they do not become emotionally excited during professional acts of sexual intercourse.[17]

Where coolness is considered a positive trait, attempts will be made to demonstrate it. However, there are those statuses and situations that typically are thought to be devoid of risk and whose incumbents must therefore search out or create situations in which coolness can be demonstrated if that trait is desired. For some, then, coolness must be staged. Since, as we have said, coolness is imputed to individuals only insofar as the person's actions are seen to occur in risk-taking situations, those who strive after a reputation for coolness will seek out risky situations wherein it can be manifested. Thus, children often attempt to show emotional poise by "risky" riding on merry-go-round horses.[18] Adolescents escalate both the nature of the risk and the poise required in games of "chicken." Not surprisingly we find that slum-dwelling adolescents—who highly prize the character attribute of coolness—distinguish time in terms of its potential for action (and by inference, for displays of character). "Dead" time is time devoid of such potential.[19]

CONCLUSIONS

Although the term "coolness" is of recent vintage, the phenomenon or trait to which it refers is universal, appearing under a variety of rubrics: nonchalance, sophistication, **savoir-faire**, "blasé character," and so on. For Simmel, coolness—or blasé character, as he called it—was a trait of urbanized man.[20] Although Simmel attributes this blasé character to the preponderance of a money economy, the rapidity of change, and the interdependence of roles in cities, it would seem that these are but major sources of risk that generate the conditions for displaying the character trait of coolness. These sources of risk may be matched by other types of risk, and thus other forms of coolness and character development appropriate to them may be found in nonurban settings.[21]

Coolness is often associated with nobility and

wealth; indeed, it is from among the ranks of the risk-taking rich that savoir-faire and finesse are usually noted and often expected, but it is not exclusively so. Bandits and burglars exhibit many of the traits associated with coolness and sometimes explicitly link these up to aspirations toward or identification with the nobility. Thus Robin Hood is protrayed as a wronged lord who, although forced to flee into the forest and adopt the outlaw life, remains noble, courageous, temperate, and capable of considerable finesse.[22]

Note, too, that coolness is not only associated with those of high rank but also with those who are so low in the social order that the most prized possession they have is personal character—a personal status that can be acknowledged or disconfirmed in everyday encounters and demonstrated particularly in the skill and finesse with which word games are played. Such people, Negroes in America are an outstanding example, develop considerable verbal ability, a pervasive pride in their own individuality, and—because of the permanent danger of character as well as physical assassination—skill in social and personal defense. And it is among quite ordinary American Negroes and persons similarly situated that we find the creative imagination developed toward posturing and prevarication and characterological coolness.[23]

On the contemporary American scene, however, the trait of coolness is not limited to any one segment of the social order. David Riesman and others have suggested that the era of moral absolutism, accompanied by the trait of inner-directedness, has declined, and among the concomitant changes is a shift in the concept of strong character.[24] In the era of inner-directedness moral character was summed up in the admonition to do one's duty. Today, such a seemingly simplistic moral model has been exchanged for the chameleonlike, radar-attuned actor who keeps pace with the rapid changes in form, content, and style. Although poise under pressure was an issue in the era of rugged individualism and unfettered capitalism, the nature of the risks involved was both different in content and differentially distributed. Modern society has changed the issue in risk and democratized it.[25] Keeping cool is now a problem for everyone.

In the place of the earlier isolated individuality accompanied by morally clear doctrines of guilt and shame, there has arisen the coordinated group accompanied by loneliness and affected by a ubiquitous sense of anxiety. The fictional heroes

of the eras reflect these changes. The Lone Ranger—perhaps the last fully developed prototype of morally correct inner direction—was a silent, skillful devotee of law and order. He traveled the uncharted trails of the frontier West accompanied only by an Indian, both in but not of their society. He spoke seldom and then in short, clipped, direct statements. He seemed to have no needs; neither women, wealth, nor power attracted or wounded him. The problems he solved were simple in form; they were only dangerous to life and limb: a gang of evil-doers threatened the town. Only their removal from the scene would restore the unquestionably desirable status quo ante.

By contrast Maverick is the prototype hero of the modern age. He is a gambler and, like Riesman's other-directed man, a cosmopolitan. For Maverick, the problems are not simple. His interest is to get through life with the maximum of pleasure, the minimum of pain. He recognizes no moral absolutes except physical and characterological survival. For him the only weapon is his wits; the only skill, verbal repartee. Only if he loses his cool will he lose to his more powerful and often ill-defined and impersonal opponents. The moral lesson implied in Maverick is quite clear. The modern age is one of permanent complex problems. They neither lend themselves to direct solution nor do they gradually disappear.[26] It is rather that the hazardous nature of life becomes ordinary, the impermanence of things and relationships becomes fixed, and to survive man must adopt the character associated with the routinization of anxiety. Its most salient feature is what we call coolness. Its manifestations are the recognition of danger in the presentation of self in everyday life, the risk in attachment to things or people, and the positive value of what Goffman calls "role distance."[27]

Despite the ubiquity of coolness in the modern world, its study may be enhanced if we look at the form and content of life for those who are relatively permanent outsiders in society. Career deviants must manifest a considerable display of savoir-faire if they are to survive and especially—if like abortionists[28]—they deal with a clientele who are only situationally deviant. Minorities whose status is both anomalous and precarious have evidenced a remarkable ability to build a subculture resting in large part on the artful development of coolness forms. Here, then, are the strategic research sites.

The study of coolness—its meaning, manifestations, and metamorphosis—is surely a topic deserving further investigation, for all men in society are subject to the problems of personal risk and the preservation of poise under pressure.

NOTES

1. This paper explores a theoretical avenue opened up by Erving Goffman. Our orientation and some of the conceptual categories used here are derived from the various writings of this seminal thinker.

2. This definition closely follows the one suggested by Goffman in "Where the Action Is," unpublished manuscript, University of California, Berkeley, p. 29.

3. Goffman, "On Face Work," Psychiatry, 18 (August, 1955), pp. 213-231.

4. The hazards of social encounters are not universally recognized with the same degree of seriousness. Thus, in Japanese culture the face engagements of individuals are always regarded as character tests. Individuals are expected to be aware at all times of the proprieties. Loss of face can occur at any time. On the other hand, in American culture it would appear that social risks are not recognized as an ingredient of every encounter, but only of those that have a retro- or pro-active effect on the participants. For an analysis of the Japanese as veritable models of poise under pressure, see Nyozekan Hasegawa, The Japanese Character, Tokyo: Kodansha International, 1966, esp. pp. 29-34 and 90-94. See also George De Vos, "A Comparison of the Personality Differences in Two Generations of Japanese Americans by Means of the Rorschach Test," Nagoya Journal of Medical Science, (August, 1954), pp. 164-165, 252-261; and William Caudill, "Japanese American Personality and Acculturation," Genetic Psychology Monographs, 45 (1952), pp. 3-102.

5. The loss of cool is not everywhere a stigma. Among Shtetl Jews, for example, displays of overt emotionalism are culturally approved. See Mark Zborowski and Elizabeth Herzog, Life is With People: The Culture of the Shtetl, New York: Schocken Books, 1962, p. 335.

6. In some instances the fears and apprehensions among newcomers are so great that not even ordinary calmness can prevail until special restorative measures are employed. For a most dramatic illustration of the point see Equiano's Travels: The Interesting Narrative of the Life of Olaudah Equiano or Gustavus Vassa the African, edited by Paul Edwards, New York: Praeger, 1967 (originally published in 1789), pp. 30-31.

7. Repartee and other word games apparently came into full bloom in courtly circles after women and intellectuals were admitted to participate. See Florian Znaniecki, Social Relations and Social Roles, San Francisco: Chandler, 1965, pp. 175-76.

8. Hasegawa, op. cit., p. 88.

9. Herbert J. Gans, The Urban Villagers, New York: The Free Press of Glencoe, 1962, p. 81.

10. See John Dollard, "The Dozens: Dialectic of Insult," The American Imago, vol. 1 (November, 1939), pp. 3-25; Rolph E. Berdie, "Playing the Dozens," Journal of Abnormal and Social Psychology, vol. 42 (January,

1947), pp. 120-121; Corneleus L. Golightly and Israel Scheffler, "Playing the Dozens: A Research Note," Journal of Abnormal and Social Psychology, vol. 43 (January, 1948), pp. 104-105; Roger D. Abrahams, Deep Down in the Jungle, Hatboro, Penn.: Folklore Associates,, 1964, pp. 41-65, 89-98, 259-262. Abrahams (p. 50) describes sounding as follows: "Sounding occurs only in crowds of boys. One insults a member of another's family; others in the group make disapproving sounds to spur on the coming exchange. The one who has been insulted feels at this point that he must reply with a slur on the protagonist's family which is clever enough to defend his honor (and therefore that of his family). This, of course, leads the other (once again, due more to pressure from the crowd than actual insult) to make further jabs. This can proceed until everyone is bored with the whole affair, until one hits the other (fairly rare), or until some other subject comes up that interrupts the proceedings (the usual state of affairs)."

11. Edward Gross and Gregory P. Stone, "Embarrassment and the Analysis of Role Requirements," American Journal of Sociology, 70 (July, 1964), pp. 6-10. See also Erving Goffman, "Embarrassment and Social Organization," American Journal of Sociology, 62 (November, 1956), pp. 264-71.

12. See Georg Simmel, "The Aesthetic Significance of the Face," in Kurt Wolff, editor, Georg Simmel, 1858-1918, Columbus: Ohio State University Press, 1959, pp. 276-281. Also Goffman, "On Face Work," op. cit.

13. Charles T. Scott, A Linguistic Study of Persian and Arabic Riddles: A Language-Centered Approach to Genre Definition, unpublished Ph.D. dissertation, University of Texas, 1963, p. 12.

14. For a piquant instance in which these forces were unexpectedly tested by a Kikuyu youth studying in America see R. Mugo Gatheru, Child of Two Worlds: A Kikuyu's Story, Garden City: Doubleday-Anchor, 1965, pp. 153-154.

15. Gans, op. cit., p. 190.

16. Hui-chen Wang Liu, The Traditional Chinese Clan Rules, Locust Valley, N.Y.: J. J. Augustin, 1959, pp. 60-93.

17. Albert J. Reiss, "The Social Integration of Queers and Peers," in Howard S. Becker, ed., The Other Side, N.Y.: The Free Press of Glencoe, 1964, pp. 181-210.

18. For a discussion of the behavioristic elements in riding a merry-go-round and other games of equipoise see Erving Goffman, "Role Distance," in Encounters, Indianapolis: Bobbs-Merrill, 1961, pp. 105-110. [See excerpt from that work published as Chapter 12 in the present volume.]

19. Gans, op. cit., pp. 27-32; Jules Henry, "White People's Time, Colored People's Time," Trans-Action (March-April, 1965), pp. 31-34; John Horton, "Time and Cool People," Trans-Action (April, 1967), pp. 5-12.

20. Georg Simmel, "The Metropolis and Mental Life," in Sociology of Georg Simmel, New York: The Free Press, 1950, pp. 413-414.

21. One such setting is the chivalric ideal of the fifteenth century. See Diaz de Gamez, "The Chivalric Ideal," in James B. Ross and Mary M. McLaughlin, eds., The Portable Medieval Reader, New York: Viking Press, 1949, esp. pp. 91-92.

22. See Maurice Keen, **The Outlaws of Medieval Legend**, London: Routledge and Kegan Paul, 1961. For further evidence of the generalized character of bandits and outlaws see Eric J. Hobsbawm, **Social Bandits and Primitive Rebels**, Glencoe: Free Press, 1959, pp. 1-29. For a characterological analysis of the modern day fictional Robin Hood, namely, Raffles, see George Orwell, "Raffles and Miss Blandish," in **Dickens, Dali and Others**, New York: Reynal and Co., 1946, pp. 202-221. These legendary bandits—Robin Hood, Raffles, etc.—are characterized by taking extra risks in the name of sportsmanship, or aesthetic reasons, and in so doing amply display strong character.

23. See Richard Wright, "The Psychological Reactions of Oppressed People," in **White Man, Listen!**, Garden City: Doubleday Anchor, 1957, pp. 17-18.

24. David Riesman, Nathan Glazer, Reuel Denny, **The Lonely Crowd**, Garden City: Doubleday-Anchor, 1950, 1953.

25. See Talcott Parsons and Winston White, "The Link Between Character and Society," in S. M. Lipset and L. Lowenthal, eds., **Culture and Social Character**, New York: The Free Press of Glencoe, 1961, pp. 89-135.

26. For an analysis of the modern world in these terms see Robert Nisbet, **Community and Power**, New York: Oxford Galaxy, 1962.

27. Goffman, "Role Distance," **Encounters**, op. cit.

28. See Donald Ball, "An Abortion Clinic Ethnography," **Social Problems**, vol. 14 (Winter, 1967), pp. 203-301.

topic 7

the enduring self and the changing self: the total institution and resocialization

Recall Peter Berger's account of a man who is turned overnight from a free citizen into a convict: "With frightening speed he will discover that he is acting as a convict is supposed to, and feeling all the things that a convict is expected to feel." Berger's depiction sharply disputes the long-cherished notion that the socialization process is all but completed during the formative years—that our repertoire of roles and our sense of self are firmly and ineffaceably implanted during the first years of life.

Our self-conceptions, the roles we play, and the norms, values, and life styles that we adopt as our own are in fact in a continual state of flux and redefinition. We are literally never quite the same person from one day to the next. This truth is apparent in the essays by Erving Goffman and Robert Lifton.

Goffman's description of the "moral career" of the mental patient vividly recalls similar accounts of life in monasteries, convents, ships at sea, prisons, boarding schools, Marine Corps boot camps, and military academies. And well it should. For he is portraying the way of life in a **total institution**—"a place of residence and work," Goffman writes elsewhere (1961), "where a large number of like-situated individuals, cut off from the wider society for an appreciable period of time," lead isolated, tightly controlled lives.

Thus just as the intractable cadet or prisoner is bullied, humiliated, punished, and intimidated until he finally accepts the rigid norms of behavior laid out for him, so does the patient in the mental hospital go through "degradation ceremonies" which at last succeed in divesting him of his old self-identities. Literally "broken," he is ultimately "reborn" with what amounts to a new sense of self.

Lifton's characterization of the "protean" mentality, which, he contends, is increasingly characteristic of today's postindustrial youth, is a conjectural attempt to identify a "new style of self-process that is emerging everywhere." Forever young in spirit no matter what his chronological age, continually questing for new forms of rebirth, the protean man is constantly "starved for ideas and feelings that can give coherence" to a world that never stands still. In consequence, the protean style of self-process "is characterized by an interminable series of experiments and explorations—some shallow, some profound—each of which may be readily abandoned in favor of still new psychological quests."

If the reader finds man's plasticity disturbing, he should recall the two-sided nature of man. Man is, in the main, a conforming "tribal" creature; he is dependent for behavioral cues upon those "significant others" who people his world, dependent upon them for indications that this act is praiseworthy and that one blameworthy. Yet man is also both an obstinate, nonconforming animal and an individual with deeply buried and often quite unconscious traits that make him unlike any other human being who has ever lived. He is, in sum, simultaneously hidebound, orthodox, and conventional, and yet eccentric and a maverick. That is precisely why he is human.

chapter 14
the moral career of the mental patient: the inpatient phase
erving goffman

The last step in the prepatient's career can involve his realization—justified or not—that he has been deserted by society and turned out of relationships by those closest to him. Interestingly enough, the patient, especially on a first admission, may manage to keep himself from coming to the end of this trail, even though in fact he is now in a locked mental-hospital ward. On entering the hospital, he may very strongly feel the desire not to be known to anyone as a person who could possibly be reduced to these present circumstances, or as a person who conducted himself in the way he did prior to commitment. Consequently, he may avoid talking to anyone, may stay by himself when possible, and may even be "out of contact" or "manic" so as to avoid ratifying any interaction that presses a politely reciprocal role upon him and opens him up to what he has become in the eyes of others. When the next-of-relation makes an effort to visit, he may be rejected by mutism, or by the patient's refusal to enter the visiting room, these strategies sometimes suggesting that the patient still clings to a remnant of relatedness to those who made up his past, and is protecting this remnant from the final destruc-

From Psychiatry, 22, 1959, pp. 123-142. Copyright © 1959 by The William Alanson White Psychiatric Foundation, Inc. Reprinted by special permission of The William Alanson White Psychiatric Foundation, Inc.

tiveness of dealing with the new people that they have become.[1]

Usually the patient comes to give up this taxing effort at anonymity, at not-hereness, and begins to present himself for conventional social interaction to the hospital community. Thereafter he withdraws only in special ways—by always using his nickname, by signing his contribution to the patient weekly with his initial only, or by using the innocuous "cover" address tactfully provided by some hospitals; or he withdraws only at special times, when, say, a flock of nursing students makes a passing tour of the ward, or when, paroled to the hospital grounds, he suddenly sees he is about to cross the path of a civilian he happens to know from home. Sometimes this making of oneself available is called "settling down" by the attendants. It marks a new stand openly taken and supported by the patient, and resembles the "coming-out" process that occurs in other groupings.[2]

Once the prepatient begins to settle down, the main outlines of his fate tend to follow those of a whole class of segregated establishments—jails, concentration camps, monasteries, work camps, and so on—in which the inmate spends the whole round of life on the grounds, and marches through his regimented day in the immediate company of a group of persons of his own institutional status.

Like the neophyte in many of these total institutions, the new inpatient finds himself cleanly stripped of many of his accustomed affirmations, satisfactions, and defenses, and is subjected to a rather full set of mortifying experiences: restriction of free movement, communal living, diffuse authority of a whole echelon of people, and so on. Here one begins to learn about the extent to which a conception of oneself can be sustained when the usual setting of supports for it are suddenly removed.

While undergoing these humbling moral experiences, the inpatient learns to orient himself in terms of the "ward system."[3] In public mental hospitals this usually consists of a series of graded living arrangements built around wards, administrative units called services, and parole statuses. The "worst" level often involves nothing but wooden benches to sit on, some quite indifferent food, and a small piece of room to sleep in. The "best" level may involve a room of one's own, ground and town privileges, contacts with staff that are relatively undamaging, and what is seen as good food and ample recreational facilities. For disobeying the pervasive house rules, the inmate will receive stringent punishments expressed in terms of loss of privileges; for obedience he will eventually be allowed to acquire some of the minor satisfactions he took for granted on the outside.

The institutionalization of these radically different levels of living throws light on the implications for self of social settings. And this in turn affirms that the self arises not merely out of its possessor's interactions with signficant others, but also out of the arrangements that are evolved in an organization for its members.

There are some settings that the person easily discounts as an expression or extension of him. When a tourist goes slumming, he may take pleasure in the situation not because it is a reflection of him but because it so assuredly is not. There are other settings, such as living rooms, which the person manages on his own and employs to influences in a favorable direction other persons' views of him. And there are still other settings, such as a work place, which express the employee's occupational status, but over which he has no final control, this being exerted, however tactfully, by his employer. Mental hospitals provide an extreme instance of this latter possibility. And this is due not merely to their uniquely degraded living levels, but also to the unique way in which significance

for self is made explicit to the patient, piercingly, persistently, and thoroughly. Once lodged on a given ward, the patient is firmly instructed that the restrictions and deprivations he encounters are not due to such blind forces as tradition or economy—and hence dissociable from self—but are intentional parts of his treatment, part of his need at the time, and therefore an expression of the state that his self has fallen to. Having every reason to initiate requests for better conditions, he is told that when the staff feel he is "able to manage" or will be "comfortable with" a higher ward level, then appropriate action will be taken. In short, assignment to a given ward is presented not as a reward or punishment, but as an expression of his general level of social functioning, his status as a person. Given the fact that the worst ward levels provide a round of life that inpatients with organic brain damage can easily manage, and that these quite limited human beings are present to prove it, one can appreciate some of the mirroring effects of the hospital.[4]

The ward system, then, is an extreme instance of how the physical facts of an establishment can be explicitly employed to frame the conception a person takes of himself. In addition, the official psychiatric mandate of mental hospitals gives rise to even more direct, even more blatant, attacks upon the inmate's view of himself. The more "medical" and the more progressive a mental hospital is—the more it attempts to be therapeutic and not merely custodial—the more he may be confronted by high-ranking staff arguing that his past has been a failure, that the cause of this has been within himself, that his attitude to life is wrong, and that if he wants to be a person he will have to change his way of dealing with people and his conceptions of himself. Often the moral value of these verbal assaults will be brought home to him by requiring him to practice taking this psychiatric view of himself in arranged confessional periods, whether in private sessions or group psychotherapy.

Now a general point may be made about the moral career of inpatients which has bearing on many moral careers. Given the stage that any person has reached in a career, one typically finds that he constructs an image of his life course—past, present, and future—which selects, abstracts, and distorts in such a way as to provide him with a view of himself that he can usefully expound in current situations. Quite generally, the person's line concerning self defensively brings him into appropriate alignment with the basic values of his society, and so may be called an apologia. If the person can manage to present a view of his current situation which shows the operation of favorable personal qualities in the past and a favorable destiny awaiting him, it may be called a success story. If the facts of a person's past and present are extremely dismal, then about the best he can do is to show that he is not responsible for what has become of him, and the term sad tale is appropriate. Interestingly enough, the more the person's past forces him out of apparent alignment with central moral values, the more often he seems compelled to tell his sad tale in any company in which he finds himself. Perhaps he partly responds to the need he feels in others of not having their sense of proper life courses affronted. In any case, it is among convicts, "winos," and prostitutes that one seems to obtain sad tales the most readily.[5] It is the vicissitudes of the mental patient's sad tale that I want to consider now.

In the mental hospital, the setting and the house rules press home to the patient that he is, after all, a mental case who has suffered some kind of social collapse on the outside, having failed in some overall way, and that here he is of little social weight, being hardly capable of acting like a full-fledged person at all. These humiliations are likely to be most keenly felt by middle-class patients, since their previous condition of life little immunizes them against such affronts, but all patients feel some downgrading. Just as any normal member of his outside subculture would do, the patient often responds to this situation by attempting to assert a sad tale proving that he is not "sick," that the "little trouble" he did get into was really somebody else's fault, that his past life course had some honor and rectitude, and that the hospital is therefore unjust in forcing the status of mental patient upon him. This self-respecting tendency is heavily institutionalized within the patient society where opening social contacts typically involve the participants' volunteering information about their current ward location and length of stay so far, but not for reasons for their stay—such interaction being conducted in the manner of small talk on the outside.[6] With greater familiarity, each patient usually volunteers relatively acceptable reasons for his hospitalization, at the same time accepting without open immediate question the lines offered by other patients. Such

stories as the following are given and overtly accepted.

> I was going to night school to get a M.A. degree, and holding down a job in addition, and the load got too much for me.
>
> The others here are sick mentally but I'm suffering from a bad nervous system and that is what is giving me these phobias.
>
> I got here by mistake because of a diabetes diagnosis, and I'll leave in a couple of days. [The patient had been in seven weeks.]
>
> I failed as a child, and later with my wife I reached out for dependency.
>
> My trouble is that I can't work. That's what I'm in for. I had two jobs with a good home and all the money I wanted.[7]

The patient sometimes reinforces these stories by an optimistic definition of his occupational status. A man who managed to obtain an audition as a radio announcer styles himself a radio announcer; another who worked for some months as a copy boy and was then given a job as a reporter on a large trade journal, but fired after three weeks, defines himself as a reporter.

A whole social role in the patient community may be constructed on the basis of these reciprocally sustained fictions. For these face-to-face niceties tend to be qualified by behind-the-back gossip that comes only a degree closer to the "objective" facts. Here, of course, one can see a classic social function of informal networks of equals: they serve as one another's audience for self-supporting tales—tales that are somewhat more solid than pure fantasy and somewhat thinner than the facts.

But the patient's apologia is called forth in a unique setting, for few settings could be so destructive of self-stories except, of course those stories already constructed along psychiatric lines. And this destructiveness rests on more than the official sheet of paper which attests that the patient is of unsound mind, a danger to himself and others—an attestation, incidentally, which seems to cut deeply into the patient's pride, and into the possibility of his having any.

Certainly the degrading conditions of the hospital setting belie many of the self-stories that are presented by patients, and the very fact of being in the mental hospital is evidence against these tales. And of course there is not always sufficient patient solidarity to prevent patient discrediting patient, just as there is not always a sufficient number of "professionalized" attendants to prevent attendant discrediting patient. As one patient informant repeatedly suggested to a fellow patient: "If you're so smart, how come you got your ass in here?"

The mental-hospital setting, however, is more treacherous still. Staff have much to gain through discreditings of the patient's story—whatever the felt reason for such discreditings. If the custodial faction in the hospital is to succeed in managing his daily round without complaint or trouble from him, then it will prove useful to be able to point out to him that the claims about himself upon which he rationalizes his demands are false, that he is not what he is claiming to be, and that in fact he is a failure as a person. If the psychiatric faction is to impress upon him its views about his personal makeup, then they must be able to show in detail how their version of his past and their version of his character hold up much better than his own.[8] If both the custodial and psychiatric factions are to get him to cooperate in the various psychiatric treatments, then it will prove useful to disabuse him of his view of their purposes, and cause him to appreciate that they know what they are doing, and are doing what is best for him. In brief, the difficulties caused by a patient are closely tied to his version of what has been happening to him, and if cooperation is to be secured, it helps if this version is discredited. The patient must "insightfully" come to take, or affect to take, the hospital's view of himself.

The staff also have ideal means—in addition to the mirroring effect of the setting—for denying the inmate's rationalizations. Current psychiatric doctrine defines mental disorder as something that can have its roots in the patient's earliest years, show its signs throughout the course of his life, and invade almost every sector of his current activity. No segment of his past or present need be defined, then, as beyond the jurisdiction and mandate of psychiatric assessment. Mental hospitals bureaucratically institutionalize this extremely wide mandate by formally basing their treatment of the patient upon his diagnosis and hence upon the psychiatric view of his past.

The case record is an important expression of this mandate. This dossier is apparently not regularly used, however, to record occasions when the patient showed capacity to cope honorably and effectively with difficult life situations. Nor is the case record typically used to provide a rough average or sampling of his past conduct. One of its purposes is to show the ways in which the patient is "sick" and the reasons why it was right to commit him and is right currently to keep him committed; and this is done by extracting from his whole life course a list of those incidents that have or might have had "symptomatic" significance.[9] The misadventures of his parents or siblings that might suggest a "taint" may be cited. Early acts in which the patient appeared to have shown bad judgment or emotional disturbance will be recorded. Occasions when he acted in a way which the layman would consider immoral, sexually perverted, weak-willed, childish, ill-considered, impulsive, and crazy may be described. Misbehaviors which someone saw as the last straw, as cause for immediate action, are likely to be reported in detail. In addition, the record will describe his state on arrival at the hospital—and this is not likely to be a time of tranquillity and ease for him. The record may also report the false line taken by the patient in answering embarrassing questions, showing him as someone who makes claims that are obviously contrary to the facts:

> Claims she lives with oldest daughter or with sisters only when sick and in need of care; otherwise with husband, he himself says not for twelve years.
>
> Contrary to the reports from the personnel, he says he no longer bangs on the floor or cries in the morning.
>
> Conceals fact that she had her organs removed, claims she is still menstruating.
>
> At first she denied having had premarital sexual experience, but when asked about Jim she said she had forgotten about it 'cause it had been unpleasant.[10]

Where contrary facts are not known by the recorder, their presence is often left scrupulously an open question:

> The patient denied any heterosexual experiences nor could one trick her into admitting that she had ever been pregnant or into any kind of sexual indulgence, denying masturbation as well.
>
> Even with considerable pressure she was unwilling to engage in any projection of paranoid mechanisms.

No psychotic content could be elicited at this time.[11]

And if in no more factual way, discrediting statements often appear in descriptions given of the patient's general social manner in the hospital:

When interviewed, he was bland, apparently self-assured, and sprinkles high-sounding gneralizations freely throughout his verbal productions.

Armed with a rather neat appearance and natty little Hitlerian mustache this 45-year-old man who has spent the last five or more years of his life in the hospital, is making a very successful hospital adjustment living within the role of a rather gay liver and jim-dandy type of fellow who is not only quite superior to his fellow patients in intellectual respects but who is also quite a man with women. His speech is sprayed with many multi-syllabled words which he generally uses in good context, but if he talks long enough on any subject it soon becomes apparent that he is so completely lost in this verbal diarrhea as to make what he says almost completely worthless.[12]

The events recorded in the case history are, then, just the sort that a layman would consider scandalous, defamatory, and discrediting. I think it is fair to say that all levels of mental-hospital staff fail, in general, to deal with this material with the moral neutrality claimed for medical statements and psychiatric diagnosis, but instead participate, by intonation and gesture if by no other means, in the lay reaction to these acts. This will occur in staff-patient encounters as well as in staff encounters at which no patient is present.

In some mental hospitals, access to the case record is technically restricted to medical and higher nursing levels, but even here informal access or relayed information is often available to lower staff levels.[13] In addition, ward personnel are felt to have a right to know those aspects of the patient's past conduct which, embedded in the reputation he develops, purportedly make it possible to manage him with greater benefit to himself and less risk to others. Further, all staff levels typically have access to the nursing notes kept on the ward, which chart the daily course of each patient's disease, and hence his conduct, providing for the near present the sort of information the case record supplies for his past.

I think that most of the information gathered in case records is quite true, although it might seem also to be true that almost anyone's life course could yield up enough denigrating facts to provide grounds for the record's justification of commitment. In any case, I am not concerned here with questioning the desirability of maintaining case records, or the motives of staff in keeping them. The point is that, these facts about him being true, the patient is certainly not relieved from normal cultural pressure to conceal them, and is perhaps all the more threatened by knowing that they are neatly available, and that he has no control over who gets to learn them.[14] A manly looking youth who responds to military induction by running away from the barracks and hiding himself in a hotel-room clothes closet, to be found there, crying, by his mother; a woman who travels from Utah to Washington to warn the President of impending doom; a man who disrobes before three young girls; a boy who locks his sister out of the house, striking out two of her teeth when she tries to come back in through the window—each of these persons has done something he will have very obvious reasons to conceal from others, and very good reason to tell lies about.

The formal and informal patterns patterns of communication linking staff members tend to amplify the disclosive work done by the case record. A discreditable act that the patient performs during one part of the day's routine in one part of the hospital community is likely to be reported back to those who supervise other areas of his life where he implicitly takes the stand that he is not the sort of person who could act that way.

Of significance here, as in some other social establishments, is the increasingly common practice of all-level staff conferences, where staff air their views of patients and develop collective agreement concerning the line that the patient is trying to take and the line that should be taken to him. A patient who develops a "personal" relation with an attendant, or manages to make an attendant anxious by eloquent and persistent accusations of malpractice, can be put back into his place by means of the staff meeting, where the attendant is given warning or assurance that the patient is "sick." Since the differential image of himself that a person usually meets from those of various levels around him comes here to be unified behind the scenes into a common approach, the patient may find himself faced with a kind of collusion against him—albeit one sincerely thought to be for his own ultimate welfare.

In addition, the formal transfer of the patient from one ward or service to another is likely to be accompanied by an informal description of his characteristics, this being felt to facilitate the work of the employee who is newly responsible for him.

Finally, at the most informal of levels, the lunchtime and coffee-break small talk of staff often turns upon the latest doings of the patient, the gossip level of any social establishment being here intensified by the assumption that everything about him is in some way the proper business of the hospital employee. Theoretically there seems to be no reason why such gossip should not build up the subject instead of tear him down, unless one claims that talk about those not present will always tend to be critical in order to maintain the integrity and prestige of the circle in which the talking occurs. And so, even when the impulse of the speakers seems kindly and generous, the implication of their talk is typically that the patient is not a complete person. For example, a conscientious group therapist, sympathetic with patients, once admitted to his coffee companions:

I've had about three group disrupters, one man in particular—a lawyer [sotto voce] James Wilson—very bright—who just made things miserable for me, but I would always tell him to get on the stage and do something. Well, I was getting desperate and then I bumped into his therapist, who said that right now behind the man's bluff and front he needed the group very much and that it probably meant more to him than anything else he was getting out of the hospital—he just needed the support. Well, that made me feel altogether different about him. He's out now.

In general, then, mental hospitals systematically provide for circulation about each patient the kind of information that the patient is likely to try to hide. And in various degrees of detail this information is used daily to puncture his claims. At the admission and diagnostic conferences, he will be asked questions to which he must give wrong answers in order to maintain his self-respect, and then the true answer may be shot back at him. An attendant whom he tells a version of his past and his reason for being in the hospital may smile dis-

believingly, or say, "That's not the way I heard it," in line with the practical psychiatry of bringing the patient down to reality. When he accosts a physician or nurse on the ward and presents his claims for more privileges or for discharge, this may be countered by a question which he cannot answer truthfully without calling up a time in his past when he acted disgracefully. When he gives his view of his situation during group psychotherapy, the therapist, taking the role of interrogator, may attempt to disabuse him of his face-saving interpretations and encourage an interpretation suggesting that it is he himself who is to blame and who must change. When he claims to staff or fellow patients that he is well and has never been really sick, someone may give him graphic details of how, only one month ago, he was prancing around like a girl, or claiming that he was God, or declining to talk or eat, or putting gum in his hair.

Each time the staff deflates the patient's claims, his sense of what a person ought to be and the rules of peer-group social intercourse press him to reconstruct his stories; and each time he does this, the custodial and psychiatric interests of the staff may lead them to discredit these tales again.

Behind these verbally instigated ups and downs of the self is an institutional base that rocks just as precariously. Contrary to popular opinion, the "ward system" insures a great amount of internal social mobility in mental hospitals, especially during the inmate's first year. During that time he is likely to have altered his service once, his ward three or four times, and his parole status several times; and he is likely to have experienced moves in bad as well as good directions. Each of these moves involves a very drastic alteration in level of living and in available materials out of which to build a self-confirming round of activities, an alteration equivalent in scope, say, to a move up or down a class in the wider class system. Moreover, fellow inmates with whom he has partially identified himself will similarly be moving, but in different directions and at different rates, thus reflecting feelings of social change to the person even when he does not experience them directly.

As previously implied, the doctrines of psychiatry can reinforce the social fluctuations of the ward system. Thus there is a current psychiatric view that the ward system is a kind of social hothouse in which patients start as social infants and end up, within the year, on convalescent wards as resocialized adults. This view adds considerably to the weight and pride that staff can attach to their work, and necessitates a certain amount of blindness, especially at higher staff levels, to other ways of viewing the ward system, such as a method for disciplining unruly persons through punishment and reward. In any case, this resocialization perspective tends to overstress the extent to which those on the worst wards are incapable of socialized conduct and the extent to which those on the best wards are ready and willing to play the social game. Because the ward system is something more than a resocialization chamber, inmates find many reasons for "messing up" or getting into trouble, and many occasions, then, for demotion to less privileged ward positions. These demotions may be officially interpreted as psychiatric relapses or moral backsliding, thus protecting the resocialization view of the hospital; these interpretations, by implication, translate a mere infraction of rules and consequent demotion into a fundamental expression of the status of the culprit's self. Correspondingly, promotions, which may come about because of ward population pressure, the need for a "working patient," or for other psychiatrically irrelevant reasons, may be built up into something claimed to be profoundly expressive of the patient's whole self. The patient himself may be expected by staff to make a personal effort to "get well," in something less than a year, and hence may be constantly reminded to think in terms of the self's success and failure.[15]

In such contexts inmates can discover that deflations in moral status are not so bad as they had imagined. After all, infractions which lead to these demotions cannot be accompanied by legal sanctions or by reduction to the status of mental patient, since these conditions already prevail. Further, no past or current delict seems to be horrendous enough in itself to excommunicate a patient from the patient community, and hence failures at right living lose some of their stigmatizing meaning. And finally, in accepting the hospital's version of his fall from grace, the patient can set himself up in the business of "straightening up," and make claims of sympathy, privileges, and indulgence from the staff in order to foster this.

Learning to live under conditions of imminent exposure and wide fluctuation in regard, with little control over the granting or withholding of this regard, is an important step in the socialization of the patient, a step that tells something important about what it is like to be an inmate in a mental hospital. Having one's past mistakes and present progress under constant moral review seems to

make for a special adaptation consisting of a less than moral attitude to ego ideals. One's shortcomings and successes become too central and fluctuating an issue in life to allow the usual commitment of concern for other persons' views of them. It is not very practicable to try to sustain solid claims about oneself. The inmate tends to learn that degradations and reconstructions of the self need not be given too much weight, at the same time learning that staff and inmates are ready to view an inflation or deflation of a self with some indifference. He learns that a defensible picture of self can be seen as something outside oneself that can be constructed, lost, and rebuilt, all with great speed and some equanimity. He learns about the viability of taking up a standpoint—and hence a self—that is outside the one which the hospital can give and take away from him.

The setting, then, seems to engender a kind of cosmopolitan sophistication, a kind of civic apathy. In this unserious yet oddly exaggerated moral context building up a self or having it destroyed becomes something of a shameless game, and learning to view this process as a game seems to make for some demoralization, the game being such a fundamental one. In the hospital, then, the inmate can learn that the self is not a fortress, but rather a small open city; he can become weary of having to show pleasure when held by troops of his own, and weary of having to show displeasure when held by the enemy. Once he learns what it is like to be defined by society as not having a viable self, this threatening definition—the threat that helps attach people to the self society accords them—is weakened. The patient seems to gain a new plateau when he learns that he can survive while acting in a way that society sees as destructive of him.

A few illustrations of this moral loosening and moral fatigue might be given. In state mental hospitals currently a kind of "marriage moratorium" appears to be accepted by patients and more or less condoned by staff. Some informal peer-group pressure may be brought against a patient who "plays around" with more than one hospital partner at a time, but little negative sanction seems to be attached to taking up, in a temporarily steady way, with a member of the opposite sex, even though both partners are known to be married, to have children, and even to be regularly visited by these outsiders. In short, there is licence in mental hospitals to begin courting all over again, with the understanding, however, that nothing very per-

manent or serious can come of this. Like ship-
board or vacation romances, these entanglements
attest to the way in which the hospital is cut off
from the outside community, becoming a world of
its own, operated for the benefit of its own citizens. And certainly this moratorium is an expression of the alienation and hostility that patients
feel for those on the outside to whom they were
closely related. But, in addition, one has evidence
of the loosening effects of living in a world within
a world, under conditions which make it difficult
to give full seriousness to either of them.

The second illustration concerns the ward
system. On the worst ward level, discreditings
seem to occur the most frequently, in part because
of lack of facilities, in part through the mockery
and sarcasm that seem to be the occupational
norm of social control for the attendants and
nurses who administer these places. At the same
time, the paucity of equipment and rights means
that not much self can be built up. The patient
finds himself constantly toppled, therefore, but
with very little distance to fall. A kind of jaunty
gallows humor seems to develop in some of these
wards, with considerable freedom to stand up to
the staff and return insult for insult. While these
patients can be punished, they cannot, for example, be easily slighted, for they are accorded as a
matter of course few of the niceties that people
must enjoy before they can suffer subtle abuse.
Like prostitutes in connection with sex, inmates
on these wards have very little reputation or rights
to lose and can therefore take certain liberties. As
the person moves up the ward system, he can manage more and more to avoid incidents which discredit his claim to be a human being, and acquire
more and more of the varied ingredients of self-
respect; yet when eventually he does get toppled—
and he does—there is a much farther distance to
fall. For instance, the privileged patient lives in a
world wider than the ward, containing recreation
workers who, on request, can dole out cake, cards,
table-tennis balls, tickets to the movies, and writing materials. But in the absence of the social control of payment which is typically exerted by a
recipient on the outside, the patient runs the risk
that even a warmhearted functionary may, on
occasion, tell him to wait until she has finished an
informal chat, or teasingly ask why he wants what
he has asked for, or respond with a dead pause and
cold look of appraisal.

Moving up and down the ward system means,
then, not only a shift in self-constructive equip-

ment, a shift in reflected status, but also a change
in the calculus of risks. Appreciation of risks to his
self-conception is part of everyone's moral experience, but an appreciation that a given risk level is
itself merely a social arrangement is a rarer kind of
experience, and one that seems to help to disen-
chant the person who undergoes it.

A third instance of moral loosening has to do
with the conditions that are often associated with
the release of the inpatient. Often he leaves under
the supervision and jurisdiction of his next-of-relation or of a specially selected and specially watch-
ful employer. If he misbehaves while under their
auspices, they can quickly obtain his readmission.
He therefore finds himself under the special power
of persons who ordinarily would not have this
kind of power over him, and about whom, moreover, he may have had prior cause to feel quite
bitter. In order to get out of the hospital, however,
he may conceal his displeasure in this arrangement,
and, at least until safely off the hospital rolls, act
out a willingness to accept this kind of custody.
These discharge procedures, then, provide a built-
in lesson in overtly taking a role without the usual
covert commitments, and seem further to separate
the person from the worlds that others take seriously.

The moral career of a person of a given social
category involves a standard sequence of changes
in his way of conceiving of selves, including, importantly, his own. These half-buried lines of
development can be followed by studying his
moral experiences—that is, happenings which mark
a turning point in the way in which the person
views the world—although the particularities of
this view may be difficult to establish. And note
can be taken of overt tacks or strategies—that is,
stands that he effectively takes before specifiable
others, whatever the hidden and variable nature of
his inward attachment to these presentations. By
taking note of moral experiences and overt personal stands, one can obtain a relatively objective
tracing of relatively subjective matters.

Each moral career, and behind this, each self,
occurs within the confines of an institutional system, whether a social establishment such as a mental hospital or a complex of personal and
professional relationships. The self, then, can be
seen as something that resides in the arrangements
prevailing in a social system for its members. The
self in this sense is not a property of the person to
whom it is attributed, but dwells rather in the
pattern of social control that is exerted in connec-

tion with the person by himself and those around him. This special kind of institutional arrangement does not so much support the self as constitute it.

In this paper, two of these institutional arrangements have been considered, by pointing to what happens to the person when these rulings are weakened. The first concerns the felt loyalty of his next-of-relation. The prepatient's self is described as a function of the way in which three roles are related, arising and declining in the kinds of affiliation that occur between the next-of-relation and the mediators. The second concerns the protection required by the person for the version of himself which he presents to others, and the way in which the withdrawal of this protection can form a systematic, if unintended, aspect of the working of an establishment. I want to stress that these are only two kinds of institutional rulings from which a self emerges for the participant; others, not considered in this paper, are equally important.

In the usual cycle of adult socialization one expects to find alienation and mortification followed by a new set of beliefs about the world and a new way of conceiving of selves. In the case of the mental-hospital patient, this rebirth does sometimes occur, taking the form of a strong belief in the psychiatric perspective, or, briefly at least, a devotion to the social cause of better treatment for mental patients. The moral career of the mental patient has unique interest, however; it can illustrate the possibility that in casting off the raiments of the old self—or in having this cover torn away—the person need not seek a new robe and a new audience before which to cower. Instead he can learn, at least for a time, to practise before all groups the amoral arts of shamelessness.

NOTES

1. The inmate's initial strategy of holding himself aloof from ratifying contact may partly account for the relative lack of group formation among inmates in public mental hospitals, a connection that has been suggested to me by William R. Smith. The desire to avoid personal bonds that would give licence to the asking of biographical questions could also be a factor. In mental hospitals, of course, as in prisoner camps, the staff may consciously break up incipient group formation in order to avoid collective rebellious action and other ward disturbances.

2. A comparable coming out occurs in the homosexual world, when a person finally comes frankly to present himself to a "gay" gathering not as a tourist but as someone who is "available." See Evelyn Hooker, "A Preliminary Analysis of Group Behavior of Homosexuals," **Journal of Psychology,** XLII (1956), pp. 217-225; see

especially p. 221. A good fictionalized treatment may be found in James Baldwin's **Giovanni's Room** (New York: Dial, 1956), pp. 41-57. A familiar instance of the coming-out process is no doubt to be found among prepubertal children at the moment one of these actors sidles back into a room that had been left in an angered huff and injured amour propre. The phrase itself presumably derives from a rite-de-passage ceremony once arranged by upper-class mothers for their daughters. Interestingly enough, in large mental hospitals the patient sometimes symbolizes a complete coming out by his first active participation in the hospital-wide patient dance.

3. A good description of the ward system may be found in Ivan Belknap, **Human Problems of a State Mental Hospital** (New York: McGraw-Hill, 1956), ch. ix, especially p. 164.

4. Here is one way in which mental hospitals can be worse than concentration camps and prisons as places in which to "do" time; in the latter, self-insulation from the symbolic implications of the settings may be easier. In fact, self-insulation from hospital settings may be so difficult that patients have to employ devices for this which staff interpret as psychotic symptoms.

5. In regard to convicts, see Anthony Heckstall-Smith, **Eighteen Months** (London: Allan Wingate, 1954), pp. 52-53. For "winos" see the discussion in Howard G. Bain, "A Sociological Analysis of the Chicago Skid-Row Lifeway" (unpublished M.A. thesis, Department of Sociology, University of Chicago, September 1950), especially "The Rationale of the Skid-Row Drinking Group," pp. 141-146. Bain's neglected thesis is a useful source of material on moral careers.

Apparently one of the occupational hazards of prostitution is that clients and other professional contacts sometimes persist in expressing sympathy by asking for a defensible dramatic explanation for the fall from grace. In having to bother to have a sad tale ready, perhaps the prostitute is more to be pitied than damned. Good examples of prostitute sad tales may be found in Henry Mayhew, **London Labour and the London Poor,** vol. IV, **Those That Will Not Work** (London: Charles Griffin and Co., 1862), pp. 210-272. For a contemporary souce, see **Women of the Streets,** edited by C. H. Rolph (London: Secker and Warburg, 1955), especially p. 6: "Almost always, however, after a few comments on the police, the girl would begin to explain how it was that she was in the life, usually in terms of self-justification. . . ." Lately, of course, the psychological expert has helped out the profession in the construction of wholly remarkable sad tales. See, for example, Harold Greenwald, **The Call Girl** (New York: Ballantine Books, 1958).

6. A similar self-protecting rule has been observed in prisons. Thus, Alfred Hassler, **Diary of a Self-Made Convict** (Chicago: Regnery, 1954), p. 76, in describing a conversation with a fellow prisoner: "He didn't say much about why he was sentenced, and I didn't ask him, that being the accepted behavior in prison." A novelistic version for the mental hospital may be found in J. Kerkhoff, **How Thin the Veil: A Newspaperman's Story of His Own Mental Crack-up and Recovery** (New York: Greenberg, 1952), p. 27.

7. From the writer's field notes of informal interaction with patients, transcribed as nearly verbatim as he was able.

8. The process of examining a person psychiatrically and then altering or reducing his status in consequence is known in hospital and prison parlance as bugging, the assumption being that once you come to the attention of the testers you either will automatically be labeled crazy or the process of testing itself will make you crazy. Thus psychiatric staff are sometimes seen not as discovering whether you are sick, but as making you sick; and "Don't bug me, man" can mean, "Don't pester me to the point where I'll get upset." Sheldon Messinger has suggested to me that this meaning of bugging is related to the other colloquial meaning, of wiring a room with a secret microphone to collect information usable for discrediting the speaker.

9. While many kinds of organizations maintain records of their members, in almost all of these some socially significant attributes can only be included indirectly, being officially irrelevant. But since mental hospitals have a legitimate claim to deal with the "whole" person, they need officially recognize no limits to what they consider relevant, a sociologically interesting licence. It is an odd historical fact that persons concerned with promoting civil liberties in other areas of life tend to favor giving the psychiatrist complete discretionary power over the patient. Apparently it is felt that the more power possessed by medically qualified administrators and therapists, the better the interests of the patients will be served. Patients, to my knowledge, have not been polled on this matter.

10. Verbatim transcriptions of hospital case-record material.

11. Verbatim transcriptions of hospital case-record material.

12. Verbatim transcriptions of hospital case-record material.

13. However, some mental hospitals do have a "hot file" of selected records which can be taken out only by special permission. These may be records of patients who work as administration-office messengers and might otherwise snatch glances at their own files; of inmates who had elite status in the environing community; and of inmates who may take legal action against the hospital and hence have a special reason to maneuver access to their records. Some hospitals even have a "hot-hot file," kept in the superintendent's office. In addition, the patient's professional title, especially if it is a medical one, is sometimes purposely omitted from his file card. All of these exceptions to the general rule for handling information show, of course, the institution's realization of some of the implications of keeping mental-hospital records. For a further example, see Harold Taxel, "Authority Structure in a Mental Hospital Ward" (unpublished M.A. thesis, Department of Sociology, University of Chicago, 1953),pp. 11-12.

14. This is the problem of "information control" that many groups suffer from in varying degree. See Goffman, "Discrepant Roles," in The Presentation of Self in Everyday Life (New York: Anchor Books, 1959), ch. iv. pp. 141-166. A suggestion of this problem in relation to case records in prisons is given by James Peck in his story, "The Ship that Never Hit Port," in Prison Etiquette, edited by Holley Cantine and Dachine Rainer (Bearsville, N.Y.: Retort Press, 1950), p. 66:

"The hacks of course hold all the aces in dealing with any prisoner because they can always write him up for inevitable punishment. Every infraction of the rules is noted in the prisoner's jacket, a folder which records all the details of the man's life before and during imprisonment. There are general reports written by the work detail screw, the cell block screw, or some other screw who may have overheard a conversation. Tales pumped from stoolpigeons are are also included.

"Any letter which interests the authorities goes into the jacket. The mail censor may make a photostatic copy of a prisoner's entire letter, or merely copy a passage. Or he may pass the letter on to the warden. Often an inmate called out by the warden or parole officer is confronted with something he wrote so long ago he had forgot all about it. It might be about his personal life or his political views—a fragment of thought that the prison authorities felt was dangerous and filed for later use."

15. For this and other suggestions, I am indebted to Charlotte Green Schwartz.

chapter 15

protean
man
robert jay lifton

I should like to examine a set of psychological patterns characteristic of contemporary life, which are creating a new kind of man—a "protean man." As my stress is upon change and flux, I shall not speak much of "character" and "personality," both of which suggest fixity and permanence. Erikson's concept of identity has been, among other things, an effort to get away from this principle of fixity; and I have been using the term self-process to convey still more specifically the idea of flow. For it is quite possible that even the image of personal identity, insofar as it suggests inner stability and sameness, is derived from a vision of a traditional culture in which man's relationship to his institutions and symbols are still relatively intact—which is hardly the case today. If we understand the self to be the person's symbol of his own organism, then self-process refers to the continuous psychic re-creation of that symbol.

I came to this emphasis through work in cultures far removed from my own, studies of young (and not so young) Chinese and Japanese. Observations I was able to make in America also led me to the conviction that a very general process was taking place. I do not mean to suggest that everybody is becoming the same, or that a totally new

"world-self" is taking shape. But I am convinced that a new style of self-process is emerging everywhere. It derives from the interplay of three factors responsible for human behavior: the psychobiological potential common to all mankind at any moment in time; those traits given special emphasis in a particular cultural tradition; and those related to modern (and particularly contemporary) historical forces. My thesis is that this third factor plays an increasingly important part in shaping self-process.

My work with Chinese was done in Hong Kong, in connection with a study of the process of "thought reform" (or "brainwashing") as conducted on the mainland. I found that Chinese intellectuals of varying ages, whatever their experience with thought reform itself, had gone through an extraordinary set of what I at that time called identity fragments—of combinations of belief and emotional involvement—each of which they could readily abandon in favor of another. I remember particularly the profound impression made upon me by the extraordinary history of one young man in particular: beginning as a "filial son" or "young master," that elite status of an only son in an upper-class Chinese family; then feeling himself an abandoned and betrayed victim, as traditional forms collapsed during civil war and general chaos, and his father, for whom he was to long all his life, was separated from him by political and military duties; then a "student activist" in rebellion against the traditional culture in which he had been so recently immersed (as well as against a Nationalist Regime whose abuses he had personally experienced); leading him to Marxism and to strong emotional involvement in the Communist movement; then, because of remaining "imperfections," becoming a participant in a thought reform program for a more complete ideological conversion; but which, in his case, had the opposite effect, alienating him, so he came into conflict with the reformers and fled the country; then, in Hong Kong, struggling to establish himself as an "anti-Communist writer"; after a variety of difficulties, finding solace and meaning in becoming a Protestant convert; and following that, still just thirty, apparently poised for some new internal (and perhaps external) move.

Even more dramatic were the shifts in self-process of a young Japanese whom I interviewed in Tokyo and Kyoto from 1960 to 1962. I shall mention one in particular as an extreme example of this protean pattern, though there were many others who in various ways resembled him. Before the age of twenty-five he had been all of the following: a proper middle-class Japanese boy, brought up in a professional family within a well-established framework of dependency and obligation; then, due to extensive contact with farmers' and fishermen's sons brought about by wartime evacuation, a "country boy" who was to retain what he described as a life-long attraction to the tastes of the common man; then, a fiery young patriot who "hated the Americans" and whose older brother, a kamikaze pilot, was saved from death only by the war's end; then a youngster confused in his beliefs after Japan's surrender, but curious about rather than hostile toward American soldiers; soon an eager young exponent of democracy, caught up in the "democracy boom" which swept Japan; at the same time a youthful devotee of traditional Japanese arts—old novels, Chinese poems, kabuki, and flower arrangement; during junior high and high school, an all-round leader, outstanding in studies, student self-government, and general social and athletic activities; almost simultaneously, an outspoken critic of society at large and of fellow students in particular for their narrow careerism, on the basis of Marxist ideas current in Japanese intellectual circles; yet also an English-speaking student, which meant, in effect, being in still another vanguard and having strong interest in things American; then, midway through

high school, experiencing what he called a "kind of neurosis" in which he lost interest in everything he was doing and, in quest of a "change in mood," took advantage of an opportunity to become an exchange student for one year at an American high school; became a convert to many aspects of American life, including actually being baptized as a Christian under the influence of a minister he admired who was also his American "father," and returned to Japan only reluctantly; as a "returnee," found himself in many ways at odds with his friends and was accused by one of "smelling like butter" (a traditional Japanese phrase for Westerners); therefore reimmersed himself in "Japanese" experience—sitting on **tatami**, indulging in quiet, melancholy moods, drinking tea and so on; then became a **ronin**—in feudal days, a samurai without a master, now a student without a university—because of failing his examinations for Tokyo University (a sort of Harvard, Yale, Columbia, and Berkeley rolled into one), and as is the custom, spending the following year preparing for the next round rather than attend a lesser institution; once admitted, found little to interest him until becoming an enthusiastic **Zengakuren** activist, with full embrace of its ideal of "pure Communism" and a profound sense of fulfillment in taking part in the planning and carrying out of student demonstrations; but when offered a high position in the organization during his junior year, abruptly became an **ex-Zengakuren** activist by resigning, because he felt he was not suited for "the life of a revolutionary"; then an aimless dissipator, as he drifted into a pattern of heavy drinking, marathon mah-jongg games and affairs with bargirls; but when the time came, had no difficulty gaining employment with one of Japan's mammoth industrial organizations (and one of the **bêtes noires** of his Marxist days) and embarking upon the life of a young executive or **sarariman** (salaried man)—in fact doing so with eagerness, careful preparation and relief, but at the same time having fantasies and dreams of kicking over the traces, sometimes violently, and embarking upon a world tour (largely Hollywood-inspired) of exotic and sophisticated pleasure-seeking.

■

There are, of course, important differences between the protean life styles of the two young men, and between them and their American counterparts—differences which have to do with cultural emphases and which contribute to what is generally called national character. But such is the intensity of the shared aspects of historical experience that contemporary Chinese, Japanese, and American self-process turn out to have striking points of convergence.

I would stress two historical developments as having special importance for creating protean man. The first is the worldwide sense of what I have called **historical** (or **psychohistorical**) **dislocation**, the break in the sense of connection which men have long felt with the vital and nourishing symbols of their cultural tradition—symbols revolving around family, idea systems, religions, and the life cycle in general. In our contemporary world one perceives these traditional symbols (as I have suggested elsewhere, using the Japanese as a paradigm) as irrelevant, burdensome, or inactivating, and yet one cannot avoid carrying them within or having one's self-process profoundly affected by them. The second large historical tendency is the **flooding of imagery** produced by the extraordinary flow of postmodern cultural influences over mass communication networks. These cross readily over local and national boundaries, and permit each individual to be touched by everything, but at the same time cause him to be overwhelmed by superficial messages and undigested cultural elements, by headlines, and by endless partial alternatives in every sphere of life. These alternatives, moreover, are universally and simultaneously shared—if not as courses of action, at least in the form of significant inner imagery.

We know from Greek mythology that Proteus was able to change his shape with relative ease—from wild boar to lion to dragon to fire to flood. But what he did find difficult, and would not do unless seized and chained, was to commit himself to a single form, the form most his own, and carry out his function of prophecy. We can say the same of protean man, but we must keep in mind his possibilities as well as his difficulties.

■

The protean style of self-process, then, is characterized by an interminable series of experiments and explorations—some shallow, some profound—each of which may be readily abandoned in favor of still new psychological quests. The pattern in many ways resembles what Erik Erikson has called "identity diffusion" or "identity confusion," and the impaired psychological functioning which

those terms suggest can be very much present. But I would stress that the protean style is by no means pathological as such, and, in fact, may well be one of the functional patterns of our day. It extends to all areas of human experience—to political as well as sexual behavior, to the holding and promulgating of ideas, and to the general organization of lives.

I would like to suggest a few illustrations of the protean style, as expressed in America and Europe, drawn both from psychotherapeutic work with patients and from observations on various forms of literature and art.

One patient of mine, a gifted young teacher, spoke of himself in this way:

> I have an extraordinary number of masks I can put on or take off. The question is: is there, or should there be, one face which should be authentic? I'm not sure that there is one for me. I can think of other parallels to this, especially in literature. There are representations of every kind of crime, every kind of sin. For me, there is not a single act I cannot imagine myself committing.

He went on to compare himself to an actor on the stage who "performs with a certain kind of polymorphous versatility"—and here he was referring, slightly mockingly, to Freud's term, "polymorphous perversity," for diffusely inclusive (also protean) infantile sexuality. And he asked:

> Which is the real person, so far as an actor is concerned? Is he more real when performing on the stage—or when he is at home? I tend to think that for people who have these many, many masks, there is no home. Is it a futile gesture for the actor to try to find his real face?

My patient was by no means a happy man, but neither was he incapacitated. And although we can see the strain with which he carries his "polymorphous versatility," it could also be said that, as a teacher and a thinker, and in some ways as a man, it served him well.

In contemporary American literature, Saul Bellow is notable for the protean men he has created. In **The Adventures of Augie March**, one of his earlier novels, we meet a picaresque hero with a notable talent for adapting himself to divergent social worlds. Augie himself says: "I touched all sides, and nobody knew where I belonged. I had no good idea of that myself." And a perceptive young English critic, Tony Tanner, tells us: "Augie indeed celebrates the self, but he can find nothing to do with it." Tanner goes on to describe Bellow's more recent protean hero, Herzog, as "a representative modern intelligence, swamped with ideas, metaphysics, and values, and surrounded by messy facts. It labours to cope with them all."

A distinguished French literary spokesman for the protean style—in his life and in his work—is, of course, Jean-Paul Sartre. Indeed, I believe that it is precisely because of these protean traits that Sartre strikes us as such an embodiment of twentieth-century man. An American critic, Theodore Solotaroff, speaks of Sartre's fundamental assumption that "there is no such thing as even a relatively fixed sense of self, ego, or identity—rather there is only the subjective mind in motion in relationship to that which it confronts." And Sartre himself refers to human consciousness as "a sheer activity transcending toward objects," and "a great emptiness, a wind blowing toward objects." These might be overstatements, but I doubt that they could have been written thirty years ago. Solotaroff further characterizes Sartre as

> constantly on the go, hurrying from point to point, subject to subject; fiercely intentional, his thought occupies, fills, and distends its material as he endeavors to lose and find himself in his encounters with other lives, disciplines, books, and situations.

This image of repeated, autonomously willed death and rebirth of the self, so central to the protean style, becomes associated with the themes of fatherlessness—as Sartre goes on to tell us in his autobiography with his characteristic tone of serious self-mockery:

> There is no good father, that's the rule. Don't lay the blame on men but on the bond of paternity, which is rotten. To beget children, nothing better; **to have** them, what iniquity! Had my father lived, he would have lain on me at full length and would have crushed me. . . . Amidst Aeneas and his fellows who carry their Anchises on their backs, I move from shore to shore, alone and hating those invisible begetters who bestraddle their sons all their life long. I left behind me a young man who did not have time to be my father

and who could now be my son. Was it a good thing or bad? I don't know. But I readily subscribed to the verdict of an eminent psychoanalyst: I have no Superego.

We note Sartre's image of interchangeability of father and son, of "a young man who did not have time to be my father and who could now be my son"—which, in a literal sense refers to the age at which his father died, but symbolically suggests and extension of the protean style to intimate family relationships. And such reversals indeed become necessary in a rapidly changing world in which the sons must constantly "carry their fathers on their backs," teach them new things which they, as older people, cannot possibly know. The judgment of the absent superego, however, may be misleading, especially if we equate superego with susceptibility to guilt. What has actually disappeared—in Sartre and in protean man in general—is the **classic** superego, the internalization of clearly defined criteria of right and wrong transmitted within a particular culture by parents to their children. Protean man requires freedom from precisely that kind of superego—he requires a symbolic fatherlessness—in order to carry out his explorations. But rather than being free of guilt, we shall see that his guilt takes on a different form from that of his predecessors.

There are many other representations of protean man among contemporary novelists: in the constant internal and external motion of "beat generation" writings, such as Jack Kerouac's **On the Road**; in the novels of a gifted successor to that generation, J. P. Donleavy, particularly **The Ginger Man**; and of course in the work of European novelists such as Günter Grass, whose **The Tin Drum** is a breathtaking evocation of prewar Polish-German, wartime German and postwar German environments, in which the protagonist combines protean adaptability with a kind of perpetual physical-mental "strike" against any change at all.

In the visual arts, one of the most important postwar movements has been aptly named "action painting" to convey its stress upon process rather than fixed completion. And a more recent and related movement in sculpture, called Kinetic Art, goes further. According to Jean Tinguely, one of its leading practitioners, "artists are putting themselves in rhythm with their time, in contact with their epic, especially with permanent and perpetual movement." As revolutionary as any style or approach is the stress upon innovation per se which now dominates painting. I have frequently heard artists, themselves considered radical innovators, complain bitterly of the current standards dictating that "innovation is all," and of a turnover in art movements so rapid as to discourage the idea of holding still long enough to develop a particular style.

We also learn much from film stars. Marcello Mastroianni, when asked whether he agreed with **Time** magazine's characterization of him as "the neo-capitalist hero," gave the following answer:

> In many ways, yes. But I don't think I'm any kind of hero, neo-capitalist or otherwise. If anything I am an **anti**-hero or at most a **non**-hero. **Time** said I had the frightened, characteristically 20th-century look, with a spine made of plastic napkin rings. I accepted this—because modern man is that way; and being a product of my time and an artist, I can represent him. If humanity were all one piece, I would be considered a weakling.

Mastroianni accepts his destiny as protean man; he seems to realize that there are certain advantages to having a spine made of plastic napkin rings, or at least that it is an appropriate kind of spine to have these days.

John Cage, the composer, is an extreme exponent of the protean style, both in his music and in his sense of all of us as listeners. He concluded a recent letter to the **Village Voice** with the sentence: "Nowadays, everything happens at once and our souls are conveniently electronic, omniattentive." The comment is McLuhan-like, but what I wish to stress particularly is the idea of omniattention—the sense of contemporary man as having the possibility of "receiving" and "taking in" everything. In attending, as in being, nothing is "off limits."

■

To be sure, one can observe in contemporary man a tendency which seems to be precisely the opposite of the protean style. I refer to the closing off of identity or constriction of self-process, to a straight-and-narrow specialization in psychological as well as in intellectual life, and to reluctance to let in any "extraneous" influences. But I would emphasize that where this kind of constricted or "one-dimensional" self-process exists, it has an essentially reactive and compensatory quality. In

this it differs from earlier characterological styles it may seem to resemble (such as the "inner-directed" man described by Riesman, and still earlier patterns in traditional society). For these were direct outgrowths of societies which then existed, and in harmony with those societies, while at the present time a constricted self-process requires continuous "psychological work" to fend off protean influences which are always abroad.

Protean man has a particular relationship to the holding of ideas which has, I believe, great significance for the politics, religion, and general intellectual life of the future. For just as elements of the self can be experimented with and readily altered, so can idea systems and ideologies be embraced, modified, let go of, and reembraced, all with a new ease that stands in sharp contrast to the inner struggle we have in the past associated with these shifts. Until relatively recently, no more than one major ideological shift was likely to occur in a lifetime, and that one would be long remembered as a significant individual turning-point accompanied by profound soul-searching and conflict. But today it is not unusual to encounter several such shifts, accomplished relatively painlessly, within a year or even a month; and among many groups, the rarity is a man who has gone through life holding firmly to a single ideological vision.

In one sense, this tendency is related to "the end of ideology" spoken of by Daniel Bell, since protean man is incapable of enduring an unquestioning allegiance to the large ideologies and utopian thought of the nineteenth and early twentieth centuries. One must be cautious about speaking of the end of anything, however, especially ideology, and one also encounters in protean man what I would call strong ideological hunger. He is starved for ideas and feelings that can give coherence to his world, but here too his taste is toward new combinations. While he is by no means without yearning for the absolute, what he finds most acceptable are images of a more fragmentary nature than those of the ideologies of the past; and these images, although limited and often fleeting, can have great influence upon his psychological life. Thus political and religious movements, as they confront protean man, are likely to experience less difficulty convincing him to alter previous convictions than they do providing him a set of beliefs which can command his allegiance for more than a brief experimental interlude.

Intimately bound up with his flux in emotions

and beliefs is a profound inner sense of absurdity, which finds expression in a tone of mockery. The sense and the tone are related to a perception of surrounding activities and belief as profoundly strange and inappropriate. They stem from a breakdown in the relationship between inner and outer worlds—that is, in the sense of symbolic integrity—and are part of the pattern of psychohistorical dislocation I mentioned earlier. For if we view man as primarily a symbol-forming organism, we must recognize that he has constant need of a meaningful inner formulation of self and world in which his own actions,and even his impulses, have some kind of "fit" with the "outside" as he perceives it.

The sense of absurdity, of course, has a considerable modern tradition, and has been discussed by such writers as Camus as a function of man's spiritual homelessness and inability to find any meaning in traditional belief systems. But absurdity and mockery have taken much more extreme form in the post-World War II world, and have in fact become a prominent part of a universal life style.

In American life, absurdity and mockery are everywhere. Perhaps their most vivid expression can be found in such areas as Pop Art and the more general burgeoning of "pop culture." Important here is the complex stance of the pop artist toward the objects he depicts. On the one hand he embraces the materials of the everyday world, celebrates and even exalts them—boldly asserting his creative return to representational art (in active rebellion against the previously reigning nonobjective school), and his psychological return to the "real world" of things. On the other hand, everything he touches he mocks. "Thingness" is pressed to the point of caricature. He is indeed artistically reborn as he moves freely among the physical and symbolic materials of his environment, but mockery is his birth certificate and his passport. This kind of duality of approach is formalized in the stated "duplicity" of Camp, a poorly-defined aesthetic in which (among other things) all varieties of mockery converge under the guiding influence of the homosexual's subversion of a heterosexual world.

Also relevant are a group of expressions in current slang, some of them derived originally from jazz. The "dry mock" has replaced the dry wit; one refers to a segment of life experience as a "bit," "bag," "caper," "game" (or "con game"), "scene," "show" or "scenario"; and one seeks to "make the scene" (or "make it"), "beat the system" or "pull it off"—or else one "cools it" ("plays it cool") or "cops out." The thing to be experienced, in other words, is too absurd to be taken at its face value; one must either keep most of the self aloof from it, or if not one must lubricate the encounter with mockery.

A similar spirit seems to pervade literature and social action alike. What is best termed a "literature of mockery" has come to dominate fiction and other forms of writing on an international scale. Again Günter Grass's **The Tin Drum** comes to mind, and is probably the greatest single example of this literature—a work, I believe, which will eventually be appreciated as much as a general evocation of contemporary man as of the particular German experience with Nazism. In this country the divergent group of novelists known as "black humorists" also fit into the general category—related as they are to a trend in the American literary consciousness which R. W. B. Lewis has called a "savagely comical apocalypse" or a "new kind of ironic literary form and disturbing vision, the joining of the dark thread of apocalypse with the nervous detonations of satiric laughter." For it is precisely death itself, and particularly threats of the contemporary apocalypse, that protean man ultimately mocks.

The relationship of mockery to political and social action has been less apparent, but is, I would claim, equally significant. There is more than coincidence in the fact that the largest American student uprising of recent decades, the Berkeley Free Speech Movement of 1965, was followed immediately by a "Dirty Speech Movement." While the object of the Dirty Speech Movement—achieving free expression of forbidden language, particularly of four-letter words—can be viewed as a serious one, the predominant effect, even in the matter of names, was that of a mocking caricature of the movement which preceded it. But if mockery can undermine protest, it can also enliven it. There have been signs of craving for it in major American expressions of protest such as the Negro movement and the opposition to the war in Vietnam. In the former a certain chord can be struck by the comedian Dick Gregory, and in the latter by the use of satirical skits and parodies, that revives the flagging attention of protestors becoming gradually bored with the repetition of their "straight" slogans and goals. And on an international scale, would say that, during the past decade, Russian intellectual life has been enriched by a leavening spirit of mockery—against which the Chinese leaders are now, in the extremes of their "Cultural Revolution," fighting a vigorous but ultimately losing battle.

Closely related to the sense of absurdity and the spirit of mockery is another characteristic of protean man which can be called "suspicion of counterfeit nurturance." Involved here is a severe conflict of dependency, a core problem of protean man. I first began to think of the concept several years ago while working with survivors of the atomic bomb in Hiroshima. I found that these survivors both felt themselves in need of special help, and resented whatever help was offered them because they equated it with weakness and inferiority. In considering the matter more generally, I found this equation of nurturance with a threat to autonomy a major theme of contemporary life. The increased dependency needs resulting from the breakdown of traditional institutions lead protean man to seek out replacements wherever he can find them. The large organizations (government, business, academic, etc.) to which he turns, and which contemporary society more and more holds out as a substitute for traditional institutions, present an ambivalent threat to his autonomy in one way; and the intense individual relationships in which he seeks to anchor himself, in another. Both are therefore likely to be perceived as counterfeit. But the obverse side of this tendency is an expanding sensitivity to the unauthentic, which may be just beginning to exert its general creative force on man's behalf.

Technology (and technique in general), together with science, have special significance for protean man. Technical achievement of any kind can be strongly embraced to combat inner tendencies toward diffusion, and to transcend feelings of absurdity and conflicts over counterfeit nurturance. The image of science itself, however, as the ultimate power behind technology and, to a considerable extent, behind contemporary thought in general, becomes much more difficult to cope with. Only in certain underdeveloped countries can one find, in relatively pure form, those expectations of scientific-utopian deliverance from all human want and conflict which were characteristic of eighteenth- and nineteenth-century Western thought. Protean man retains much of this utopian imagery, but he finds it increasingly undermined by massive disillusionment. More and more he calls forth the other side of the God-devil polarity generally applied to science, and sees it as a pur-

veyor of total destructiveness. This kind of profound ambivalence creates for him the most extreme psychic paradox: the very force he still feels to be his liberator from the heavy burdens of past irrationality also threatens him with absolute annihilation, even extinction. But this paradox may well be—in fact, I believe, already has been— the source of imaginative efforts to achieve new relationships between science and man, and indeed, new visions of science itself.

I suggested before that protean man was not free of guilt. He indeed suffers from it considerably, but often without awareness of what is causing his suffering. For his is a form of hidden guilt: a vague but persistent kind of self-condemnation related to the symbolic disharmonies I have described, a sense of having no outlet for his loyalties and no symbolic structure for his achievements. This is the guilt of social breakdown, and it includes various forms of historical and racial guilt experienced by whole nations and peoples, both by the privileged and the abused. Rather than a clear feeling of evil or sinfulness, it takes the form of a nagging sense of unworthiness all the more troublesome for its lack of clear origin.

Protean man experiences similarly vague constellations of anxiety and resentment. These too have origin in symbolic impairments and are particularly tied in with suspicion of counterfeit nurturance. Often feeling himself uncared for, even abandoned, protean man responds with diffuse fear and anger. But he can neither find a good cause for the former, nor a consistent target for the latter. He nonetheless cultivates his anger because he finds it more serviceable than anxiety, because there are plenty of targets of one kind or another beckoning, and because even moving targets are better than none. His difficulty is that focused indignation is as hard for him to sustain as is any single identification or conviction.

Involved in all of these patterns is a profound psychic struggle with the idea of change itself. For here too protean man finds himself ambivalent in the extreme. He is profoundly attracted to the idea of making all things, including himself, totally new—to the "mode of transformation." But he is equally drawn to an image of a mythical past of perfect harmony and prescientific wholeness, to the "mode of restoration." Moreover, beneath his transformationism is nostalgia, and beneath his restorationism is his fascinated attraction to contemporary forms and symbols. Constantly balancing these elements midst the extraordinarily rapid change surrounding his own life, the nostalgia is pervasive, and can be one of his most explosive and dangerous emotions. This longing for a "Golden Age" of absolute oneness, prior to individual and cultural separation or delineation, not only sets the tone for the restorationism of the politically Rightist antagonists of history: the still-extant Emperor-worshipping assassins in Japan, the Colons in France, and the John Birchites and Ku Klux Klanners in this country. It also, in more disguised form, energizes that transformationist totalism of the Left which courts violence, and is even willing to risk nuclear violence, in a similarly elusive quest.

Following upon all that I have said are radical impairments to the symbolism of transition within the life cycle—the **rites de passage** surrounding birth, entry into adulthood, marriage and death. Whatever rites remain seem shallow, inappropriate, fragmentary. Protean man cannot take them seriously, and often seeks to improvise new ones with whatever contemporary materials he has available, including cars and drugs. Perhaps the central impairment here is that of symbolic immortality—of the universal need for imagery of connection predating and extending beyond the individual life span, whether the idiom of this immortality is biological (living on through children and grandchildren), theological (through a life after death), natural (**in** nature itself which outlasts all) or creative (through what man makes and does). I have suggested elsewhere that this sense of immortality is a fundamental component of ordinary psychic life, and that it is now being profoundly threatened: by simple historical velocity, which subverts the idioms (notably the theological) in which it has traditionally been maintained; and, of particular importance to protean man, by the existence of nuclear weapons, which, even without being used, call into question all modes of immortality. (Who can be certain of living on through children and grandchildren, through teachings or kindnesses?)

Protean man is left with two paths to symbolic immortality which he tries to cultivate, sometimes pleasurably and sometimes desperately. One is the natural mode we have mentioned. His

attraction to nature and concern at its desecration has to do with an unconscious sense that, in whatever holocaust, at least nature will endure—though such are the dimensions of our present weapons that he cannot be absolutely certain even of this. His second path may be termed that of "experiential transcendence"—of seeking a sense of immortality in the way that mystics always have, through psychic experience of such great intensity that time and death are, in effect, eliminated. This, I believe, is the larger meaning of the "drug revolution," of protean man's hunger for chemical aids to "expanded consciousness." And indeed all revolutions may be thought of, at bottom, as innovations in the struggle for immortality, as new combinations of old modes.

■

We have seen that young adults individually, and youth movements collectively, express most vividly the psychological themes of protean man. And although it is true that these themes make contact with what we sometimes call the "psychology of adolescence," we err badly if we overlook their expression in all age groups and dismiss them as "mere adolescent phenomena." Rather, protean man's affinity for the young—his being metaphorically and psychologically so young in spirit—has to do with his never-ceasing quest for imagery of rebirth. He seeks such imagery from all sources: from ideas, techniques, religious and political systems, mass movements and drugs; or from special individuals of his own kind whom he sees as possessing that problematic gift of his namesake, the gift of prophecy. The dangers inherent in the quest seem hardly to require emphasis. What perhaps needs most to be kept in mind is the general principle that renewal on a large scale is impossible to achieve without forays into danger, destruction, and negativity. The principle of "death and rebirth" is as valid psychohistorically as it is mythologically. However misguided many of his forays may be, protean man also carries with him an extraordinary range of possibility for man's betterment, or more important, for his survival.

topic 8
social systems:
the human group

If man is a social animal, a cultural animal, he is even more preeminently a **group** animal. In point of fact, our cultural habitat—the whole complex of norms that encase us, the values that define our goals and preferences, and the roles that shape our patterns of interaction—amounts, in effect, to a series of organized **social systems**. Some, such as the poker group and the military academy, which are analyzed in this section, are relatively small. Others, like "underdogs," "outsiders," a small town, and a suburban community, which we will encounter in the following two sections, have different characteristics.

To explore the structure and the dynamics of social organization is to search for the common properties of these systems. It is to become aware that the human group and the human community are microcosms—smaller-scale versions—of the macrocosm we know as society. It is to learn, too, that the designation **system** denotes an always-shifting, adaptive process: something that is never static or rigid. It is to discover, finally, that social systems, large or small, consist of a number of strikingly analogous, virtually identical, structured social relationships—of group norms, values, role prescriptions, "pecking orders," and communications systems that are invisible to the sociologically untutored eye.

The poker group analyzed by Louis Zurcher is as small, intimate, relaxed, and informally structured as cadet life in the Coast Guard Academy, described by Sanford Dornbush, is impersonal, hierarchical, and tightly structured. The poker gang is a **primary** group—small, informal, personal, and spontaneous—while the military academy, with its system of clear-cut ranks, its protocol, its specialization, and its complexity, is a characteristic **secondary** group. Yet it will be immediately apparent that these two social systems share many qualities in common. Both are human groups: an aggregate of individuals who interact with one another on a regularized, routinized face-to-face basis.

But if the Coast Guard Academy is characterized by rigid rules, regulations, and codes of conduct that stipulate how occupants of subordinate and superordinate statuses are to treat one another, it is also in all likelihood rife with a welter of unofficial, perhaps "underground" social groups and interpersonal relationships that are both informal and primary in nature. Some such groups are small and intimate cliques, others larger but still unceremonious and "old shoe." Occasional primary-type relations even allow a degree of informality and casualness between officers and cadets and between upperclassmen and plebes, who are normally constrained, by the dictates of officially prescribed behavior, from intermingling informally.

In sum, then, in the smallest human group as much as in the macrocosm we call society freedom and conformity, spontaneity and constraint, inevitably thread their reciprocal ways. However uninhibited and free flowing the nature of interpersonal give-and-take in the small and informal group, **contrary** forces are at work, patterning and structuring social relationships. For, lacking boundaries and constraints, the human group would be a nongroup—without configuration, consciousness of identity, and social texture.

chapter 16
the "friendly" poker game: a study of an ephemeral role
louis a. zurcher

The participants of the friendly game are not gamblers in the social-problem sense of the word. Their game is not part of a commercial enterprise, yet they are drawn together regularly, take their participation seriously, and usually thoroughly enjoy themselves. What social-psychological functions does the friendly game serve for the participants? What is its attraction? What aspects of society-at-large are reflected in its dynamics?

The structure and some of the social-psychological functions of a friendly game were observed by a participant, yielding an analytical ethnography of the poker group and highlighting the theoretical concept "ephemeral role." An ephemeral role is a temporary or ancillary position-related behavior pattern **chosen** by the enactor to satisfy social-psychological needs incompletely satisfied by the more dominant and lasting roles he regularly must enact in everyday life positions.[1]

PROCEDURE

For twelve months the author attended the twice-monthly friendly game of a long-established poker group. He was a "complete participator" in Gold's (1958) classification. That is, he played

"The 'Friendly' Poker Game: A study of an Ephemeral Role," by Louis A. Zurcher, in **Social Forces**, December 1970, published by University of North Carolina Press. Reprinted by permission.

and the other players did not know they were being observed. No notes were taken during the game, nor were any recording devices used. Though such techniques would have enhanced reliability, they may have disrupted the game. The author did, however, outline his observations immediately following adjournment of the session, and dictated a narrative based on the outline within eight hours.

Recreation, and not detached research was the primary reason for the author's joining the friendly game. However, after the first session he felt that the social dynamics of the game and the manifest benefits of participation for the players were important to record and analyze.

The day after his last game (the day before his departure to a job in another state), the author conducted semistructured individual interviews with all of the regular players concerning their reasons for playing, criteria for selecting new players, socialization processes, group rituals, and group argot.

THE PLAYERS

The seven "core" players who attended almost every game during the period of observation were all college educated, married, professional men: a lawyer, a college coach, a high school coach, an engineer, a sociologist, a social psychologist (the author), and an insurance broker. Four had been playing poker together for over ten years, and two others for over five years. They ranged in ages from early thirties to late forties, and all were in the middle, salaried, socioeconomic bracket. Four had been reared and educated in the midwestern city (population 125,000) where the game took place, and where all of the players then resided. When the friendly game first formed, the players had been associated with a small local college. Three of the current players still were employed by the college, each in a separate department. A second common characteristic of the founding members and four of the current members was experience in coaching scholastic athletic teams.

Since three core players, because of job transfers or time conflicts, were going to leave the group, members were actively recruiting "new men." Those new men invited during the course of the observation included, after the author: an accountant, a rancher, a sports writer, a high school teacher, and a purchasing agent. The author had been brought into the group by the sociologist, who was a co-worker at a local psychiatric research facility.

The games were held twice monthly, between 7:30 p.m. and 12:00 p.m. on Monday nights, in rotation at each of the core player's homes. One of the players hosted the game in a den; the others in dining rooms, kitchens, or spare rooms. Three had purchased commercially produced, green felt covered, poker tables; the others used whatever large table was available. The playing table was surrounded by smaller tables containing ashtrays, and bowls of chips and pretzels. Hot coffee and soft drinks were available throughout the game, but no alcoholic beverages were allowed during the game. Then, after the completion of the "last deal around the table," which started at 12:00 p.m., the hosting player was responsible for a meal of hors d'oeuvres, sandwiches, and desserts.

The evening's leisure was divided into three major components: (1) the informal discussion while waiting for all the players to arrive and the poker chips to be distributed; (2) the game itself; (3) the meal following the game. During the game it was understood that there were to be no "outside" interruptions. There were no radios or television sets playing, no wives serving beverages, no children looking over shoulders. The atmosphere was quite relaxed and the dress casual (although on occasion a member arrived in suit and tie following a business meeting). There was no apparent seating preference around the table ex-

cept that if there was an empty chair, it generally would be next to a new man.

At the beginning of the game each player purchased $3 worth of chips (blue, 25 cents; red, 10 cents; white, 5 cents). One had the option to buy additional chips at any time, although frequently cash was introduced in place of chips. The host player was responsible for being the banker, and also for dragging a dime or so out of each pot to defray the cost of the post-game meal. The betting limit was established at 25 cents, with a three-raise limit. Drawing "light" (borrowing money) from the pot or purchasing chips by check was tolerated.

The general rules of poker were closely followed, but the games played under "dealer's choice" were more varied than in a commercial poker setting. Use of the joker or naming of wild cards was forbidden. Often the "draw" and "stud" games were dealt with the stipulation that the high hand split with the low hand, or the high hand split with the low spade. Rarely, low ball (where low hand wins) was played. Each player seemed to have one or two favorite games which he dealt regularly and which were called "his" games.

BECOMING A MEMBER:
SELECTION AND ROLE SOCIALIZATION

The criteria by which a new man was judged for membership revealed much about the group dynamics and functions. The core players, when being interviewed by the author, reflected about these criteria:

A fellow coming into the game almost must feel like he's walking into a closed group, because we've been playing together for quite a while. I guess some newcomers leave the game sometimes feeling "will they ever ask me back again" or "I don't want to play with that bunch of thieves again." Sometimes we have fellows join us who we decide we don't want to come back. In particular, we don't like people who slow up the game, or bad players who get wiped out. They have to be capable of playing with the other players, or we don't want them.

In our game the group is the thing. We invite people in who we think are nice persons, and who we can be friends with. That's the important thing. But he has to be more than a nice person. He has to be able to play poker with the rest of us. It's no fun to sandbag a sucker! So to get invited to sit in regularly, we've got to like the person, and he's got to know what he's doing so that he adds to the game and doesn't subtract from it. The group has to be kept in balance. One dud can throw the whole thing out of focus. Another thing too. In our group, he has to be able to take a lot of teasing, and maybe give out some too. We have a good time teasing each other.

The new man therefore had to be friendly and experienced enough to learn, compete, and to maintain the pace and stability of the game.

Lukacs (1963:58) has observed that "there are a thousand unwritten rules in poker, and continuous social standards and codes of behavior." The new man, as a prerequisite to invitation was expected to know the basic rules and etiquette of poker. He was to be socialized, however, in accordance with the group's idiosyncratic expectations. He was to learn the local rules of the game, the style and tempo of play, and the patterned interactions. In other words, he was not going to be taught how to play poker, but how to be a member of this poker group.

Many of the socialization messages were verbal instructions from the core members, particularly with regard to betting rules, games allowed, quitting time, and borrowing money. Other socialization messages were more subtle, though no less forceful. The player who slowed the pace of the game might hear the drum of fingers on the green felt or an annoyed clearing of the throat. The player who talked too lengthily about a topic unessential to the game might be reminded that it was his deal, or his turn to bet.

The new man would be strongly reinforced for behavior that conformed to the group's expectations by verbal compliment, camaraderie, or a simple but effective "now you've got it!" One new man, for example, unwittingly disrupted the group's unwritten strategy, that of killing large raises from a strong hand by exhausting the three-raise limit with nickel bets. Three of the core players immediately made pleasant comments about the "lack of insurance" in that particular hand. They did not directly admonish the new man for not having enacted his part of the "insurance." When on a later occasion he did carry out the strategy, he was immediately reinforced by a hearty, "good play!" from two core players.

At no point during the entire period of ob-

servation did any of the core players show overt anger at a new man's violation of group expectations. They did on a few occasions invoke what appeared to be their most severe sanction, an absence of response cutting the errant player momentarily from group interaction. When, for example, a new man challenged a dealing core player's choice of game, the dealer dealt and the rest continued to play their cards as if the new man had not said a word. On another occasion, when a new man angrily threw down his cards in disgust, two of the core players quietly gathered them up, handed them to the dealer, and there was otherwise a total absence of response.[2] If someone suggested a game be played which was not in the group's repertoire, he would be met with a lack of enthusiasm that was more crushing than any verbal negation could have been.

One of the core players commented about the "silent communication that takes place" within the group:

> We've been playing together for so long that we can read each other's expressions for the opinions that we have about something. If one of the fellows who's new or who is just sitting in for the night does something out of line, there's a quick and silent communication that takes place, and almost simultaneously we know what to do about it. We tease him or we give him instruction or something.

Sometimes the core players united in humorously expressed sanctions of a player's behavior. One new player had committed the cardinal sin of criticizing the play of core members. He had also lectured on the "right way to play poker." As if on cue, a core player deliberately checked his bet and, when the bet came around to him again, laughingly announced he was going to raise (an act which actually was forbidden by the group, as the bettor knew). The new man exploded: You can't do that! You can't check and then raise! What kind of a game is this! Where did you learn to play poker!

A second core member with straight face replied, We always do that! We do some strange things in our group!

A third added, Yes, sometimes we allow ourselves to take back our discards if we think they can improve our hand.

A fourth added, Well, but we have to match the pot first!

Shortly thereafter, when the man won his first pot, a core member again with straight face asked for 25 percent of the pot to put into the kitty, since "it is a custom that you always donate one-fourth of your first pot in this game." The new man, who was not asked to return, was effectively excluded from the group interaction, even though he was present for the remainder of the evening.

One core player told how novices were covertly appraised:

It's hard to put your finger on it, but there's a secret evaluation of a new player during the game. You know, we look at each other, and seem to be able to come to a conclusion about whether or not we want him to come back and play with us again, even before the game is over. Sometimes we talk about the player after the game, or during the week if we see each other before the next game. But most of the time we know even before that.

Of six new men, including the author, invited to "sit in for a night" three were asked to return. Each of these had manifested during their first night, behavior which corresponded to group expectations and which was openly reinforced. In two cases, the new men at the end of the session were welcomed to "our group" and told where the game would be held two weeks hence. The third man was informed by telephone after some of the core members had "talked it over," and agreed to invite him back. When core members felt unsure about inviting a new man back, or when they were certain that they did not want to invite him back, there was no post-game discussion of the next meeting.

A new man who was being accepted could be observed increasingly identifying himself as a member. During the early hours of the game he would ask questions about specific rules that "you fellows have." In the later hours he might phrase his questions differently, asking what "we" do in certain situations.

The core players clearly seemed to enjoy instructing a new man, overtly and covertly, about their expectations. In fact, his receptivity to those socialization messages was a key criterion for acceptance. A core player expressed how he felt about the socialization process:

I think there is a certain enjoyment in teaching the rules of our game to people that can learn them. It's a kind of pride. Maybe it's a simple pride, but it's still a matter of pride to be able to show other people how to play in our game, when you know all the rules, but they don't.

Once accepted as a core member the individual retained that status even if circumstances precluded his regular participation. This was clearly illustrated when three core members terminated regular attendance. The author was present when the first member announced he was being transferred to a job in another state. The players were eating their post-game meal, when he said:

I may as well tell you fellows this before you find out from somewhere else. I won't be able to play anymore because I got orders to go to Wisconsin. I hate to tell you this, because I hate to leave my contacts here with all my friends, and especially I hate to leave the poker club.

The group was silent for several seconds, and a few players stopped eating. Finally, one said, sadly, "That's too bad." Several inquiries were made about the specifics of his transfer, and players commented that he would be missed. One added that "the gang won't be the same without you." They talked briefly about the "breaking up of the group," and discussed the importance of starting to recruit new men for permanent positions. As they left, they warmly said goodbye to the departing member, and several of them earnestly asked him to "get in touch" whenever he visited the city. "Remember," encouraged one, "there will always be a chair open for you in the game." The offer of "an open chair" was similarly made to two core members who subsequently had to terminate regular attendance; one of them has played while in town at the time of a scheduled session.

A returning core member was not immune from socialization, however. During the author's participation one returned to "sit in for a night" after an absence of two years. Throughout the evening he inadvertently violated some of the group norms. He started to bet beyond the limit, and he began to deal a game not in the repertoire. One of the core members smilingly reminded him of the norms, and said, "You've been away so long you've forgotten our standing rules." The visitor was gently being resocialized.

BENEFITS OF MEMBERSHIP: SATISFACTIONS FROM THE EPHEMERAL ROLE

Participation in the friendly game seemed to provide the individual with several rewarding social-psychological experiences, including opportunities for: scripted competition; self- and situation-control; event brokerage; normative deception and aggression; micro-institutionalizing; and retrospective conquest.

Scripted Competition: "Knocking Heads"

The criteria for acceptance as a core member included one's ability to "hold his own" in the game. He was not to be "easy" or a "pigeon," but rather should be able to "put up a fight" and maintain the "balance" of the play. The new man was expected to be a competitor, to have "guts" and not be a "feather merchant."

Zola (1964) has pointed out that the importance and relevance of competition to gambling varies with the social context in which it occurs. Competition among the players seemed to be a carefully scripted and central dynamic in the friendly game. Competition involved money, but more importantly accomplishments of skill, daring, and bluffing, as two core players indicated:

> We cut each other's throats while the game is going on. We forget about it after the game, but it's that very competitive part of the game that I enjoy so much. Maybe it's a carry-over from my sports days, but I just like to compete. There aren't many places anymore where I can really get eye to eye with someone and "knock heads." A hand starts and you try to get other players to drop out. Then there's just two or three of you left, and you really start putting the pressure on. You can really slug it out, but it's only a game, and you forget about it when you leave the table.
>
> It's sort of like when you were a kid, and you were testing yourself all the time. Poker is like the good old days; you get a chance to test yourself.

Several other observers have reported that competition in gambling, whether against others or "the system," provides individuals with opportunities to demonstrate self-reliance, independence, and decision-making abilities which for some reason or other are unavailable to them in their major life roles (cf. Herman, 1967b; Bloch, 1951; Crespi,

1956; Goffman, 1967). All of the core players were employed in bureaucracies. It may have been that their jobs made impossible the kind of competition, the kind of "testing" that they desired—particularly in the case of those members who had histories of athletic competition. Within the friendly game they could carefully and normatively script for themselves satisfactory and safe competitive experiences.

Self- and Situation-Control: "Showing Skill"

Each of the players was expected to possess considerable skill in dealing, betting, playing his hand, and bluffing. A player who noticeably showed skill was pleased with his accomplishment, whether or not he won the hand. Core members rewarded his demonstration of skill with compliments and verbal recounting ("instant replay") of the action.

Skill was closely related to competition, as illustrated by the following:

> I like to keep a mental file about the way people play. I like to think about how a person acts when he has something, and how I might act myself when I have something, and try and change that periodically. I think about how someone played a hand last time, and then try to figure out what he has by the way he's playing this time. You decide how to play your hand by the way you see others playing. That's the real skill in the game.
>
> It's a beautiful thing to see a guy play a hand of poker well. It's better, of course, if you are the one who's doing it, but it's still nice to watch somebody else make a good bet, play his cards right, and then win. I don't like to lose, but if I've got to lose, I'd much rather lose to someone who's showing some skill in the game than to somebody who just steps into it.

Crespi (1956) pointed out that "skill players of necessity play frequently and by preference with others who are also highly skilled," and that they "seek to demonstrate their mastery of the necessary skills and, if possible, their skill superiority." Zola (1964:255) concurred when he observed in the horse parlor that "the handicapper gains and retains prestige not because of monetary profits or preponderance of winners, but because he demonstrates some techniques of skill enabling him to select winners or at least come close."

Skill, as it appeared in the friendly game, seemed also to be related closely to control over other players, over self (e.g., "poker face;" resisting temptations to bet or draw cards impulsively), and to a large extent over luck. Lukacs (1963:57) considered "the uniqueness of poker to consist of its being a game of chance where the element of chance itself is subordinated to psychological factors, and where it is not so much fate as human beings who decide." Zola (1964:260) extrapolated this interpretation to gambling in general, and felt that it "occasionally allows bettors to beat the system through rational means, and thus permits them to demonstrate to themselves and their associates that they can exercise control, and for a brief moment that they can control their fate. . . . [It] denies the vagaries of life and gives men a chance to regulate it." Skill in this sense indeed has a rational character, but also seems to have a kind of magical quality.

Event Brokerage: "Feeling the Action"

The poker group did not tolerate disruption of the "pace" of the game. Some players commented about the rapid series of "thrills" that were strung together in a night's playing—the thrill of the "chance" and the "risk." Gambling, according to Bloch (1951:217-218), allows the player to "escape from the routine and boredom of modern industrial life in which the sense of creation and instinctive workmanship has been lost. Taking a chance destroys routine and hence is pleasurable." Bergler (1957:117) wrote of the "mysterious tension" that is "one of the pivotal factors in deciphering the psychology of gambling. . . . This tension is a mixture, part pleasurable, part painful. It is comparable to no other known sensation."

Goffman (1967:155, 185) saw gambling as being most thrilling when it requires "intense and sustained exercising of relevant capacity," and when, as "action," "squaring off, determination, disclosure and settlement occur over a period of long enough time to be contained within a continuous stretch of attention and experience." Each hand of poker met the criteria for "action" and the requirement for "intensive and sustained exercising of relevant capacities" (skill and competitiveness). Central to this process was the opportunity for the player to make decisions concerning his participation in the play, decisions which were perceived to influence the outcome of his "action." Herman

(1967b:101) wrote that the function of money, in the context of the gambling institution, is primarily to reify the decision-making process, establishing "the fact of a decisive act" and "verifying the involvement of the bettor in the action."

Both Goffman and Herman, in their discussions of "action" and "decision-making," referred to commercial gambling establishments. However, these factors, particularly as they relate to the stimulation of players and their experiencing of "thrill," were clearly manifested in the friendly game. A core member explained, when the author first joined, "We don't eat sandwiches and things like that during the game, and we don't shoot the bull, because it causes a break in the action." Another remarked, "It's like a new game every hand. There's a new dealer, you get a new set of cards, and it's a whole new ball game. You get your new cards dealt to you and you've got to think all over again what you are going to do with this hand." Each player was a broker of events potentially thrilling to himself and his colleagues.

Normative Deception and Aggression: "You're a Liar!"

To "bluff" in poker is to attempt by a pattern of betting, physical cues, and playing the cards to deceive other players about the quality of your hand. In poker the bluff is

> not only occasional but constant, not secondary but primary. Like certain other games of chance, poker is played not primarily with cards but with money; unlike other games the money stakes in poker represent not only our idea of the value of cards, but our idea of what the other player's idea of the value of cards might be (Lukacs, 1963:57).

Goffman (1961:38-39) observed that, "assessing a possible bluff is a formal part of the game of poker, the player being advised to examine his opponents' minor and presumably uncalculated expressive behavior."

Bluffing is related to the dynamics of competition, skill, decision-making, and action. Each player attempts to "fake out" the others. By giving the appearance that the cards randomly dealt to him are really something other than what they appear to be, he tries symbolically to control fate. With each succeeding hand the player must decide whether to try to "run one by" or to "play them straight."

Shortly after the author joined the group, he was shown a cartoon sketch of the players that one had drawn. The drawing caricatured the core members at play. They were addressing one another, and strikingly every comment referred to self, others, or the whole group "lying." In the friendly game, to "lie" or "speed" meant to bluff, and the performance of this act, successful or not, brought great pleasure to all, as indicated by the following interview responses:

> I really enjoy slipping one by the other guys. . . . Putting one over on them—that's really a great feeling. I get a kick out of that.
>
> I like the teasing that goes on in the game. You can say things there to people that you couldn't say elsewhere. I tell one of the other players he's a damned liar, for example, and he might take offense at that under other circumstances. But here it's almost a form of endearment. You'll say something to the rest like "nobody here is telling the truth. Everybody is a phony." Well, some of the guys may hit you on the head with something if you said that anywhere else.

To be called a "liar" or to be accused of speeding was a compliment, a sign that one could engage in the intense personal interaction that bluffing stimulated. The game, and particularly the bluff established the kind of "focused gathering" that Goffman (1961:17-18) described as providing "a heightened and mutual relevance of acts; an eye to eye ecological huddle" quite generative of a gratifying "we rationale."

Core members often discussed their ability to catch one another "speeding," and the cues that would give fellow players away:

> When he puts a big stack of chips on his cards like that, I know he's bluffing. . . . When he puffs his pipe like that, he's trying to speed. . . . He's got that funny look in his eye. . . . When he says, 'I don't know why I'm doing this' or 'I must be stupid to stay in this,' you better look out!

Lukacs (1963:57) commented, "Since the important thing to poker is not the cards but the betting, not the value of the player's hands but the player's psychology, as one gets to know the habits, the quirks, the tendencies, the strengths, the weaknesses of the other players, the play becomes increasingly interesting."

To be caught speeding and then teased as a liar seemed to be a *rite de passage* for a new man. On his first night, a new player was caught attempting to bluff and lost to a better hand. The men burst into laughter, and a core player loudly commented, "Now you're a member of this thieving group! You've been caught lying! Trying to speed, huh? Now you're one of us!" The new man was asked to return for subsequent sessions.[3]

On the other hand, not to have the capacity or inclination to bluff, or to be considered "honest," was flatly an insult. A new man in exasperation asked during his first and only night why it was that everyone dropped out whenever he initiated a bet or a raise. A core player shook his head and responded, "because you are too honest." This was said unsmilingly, and was based upon the new man's tendency to bet only when he had cards to validate the size of his bet. He was not inclined to bluff or lie. He was too predictable. One didn't have to read subtle cues or study the pattern of his play in order to approximate whether or not he was speeding or "for real." Potentially, he was a "pigeon" who would destroy the group "action."

Ironically, a player had to be caught bluffing if others were to know that he was a "speeder." Once caught and appropriately teased, he established his potential for speeding and further stimulated the intense personal interaction, competition, and opportunity for cue-reading skill that generated from the bluff. In essence, the speeder contributed to the uncertainty in the game and to cognitive imbalance for the players. The resolution of this uncertainty and cognitive imbalance seemed to be pleasurable and thus rewarding.

When a core player was caught in a particularly gross bluff, there were comments from others about historically memorable "lies," and the former culprit, if present, was again teased for his attempt. Usually someone would add, "Well, that's a time we caught him. Nobody knows how many times his lying is successful!" The uncalled winner does not have to show his hand in poker, so players are never really certain when he was bluffing. A common poker strategy used occasionally in the group is deliberately to be caught bluffing so that on subsequent occasions the relation between betting and hand strength is less clear.

The lie can also be interpreted as an opportunity to engage safely in behavior which might be considered "deviant" according to norms outside the friendly game.[4] "Honesty" became a negative attribute and "dishonesty" became a positive attribute. A fellow player could be called a liar and he would laugh. To have called him such in public would probably have invited anger. Within the game, delimited aggression and deception were normative and functional.

Micro-Institutionalizing: "Almost a Law"

Ritual, magic, and tradition, complexly interrelated, have often been described as central components in human play. That component complex is present in poker, and was dramatically apparent in the friendly game. In addition to the more explicit rules governing play discussed above, there were instances of at least implicit "rules of irrelevance." According to Goffman (1961:19-21), rules of irrelevance are an important aspect of focused interactions. They strengthen idiosyncratic norms and the cohesion and "separateness" by declaring irrelevant certain characteristics of the participants or setting which may have considerable saliency in the world "outside."

In the friendly game, even though a player's occupational status may have had some influence in his being invited that status became irrelevant. The author was, for example, asked by a new man what his occupation was. Before he could answer, a core player laughingly but nonetheless forcefully exclaimed, "Right now he's a poker player, and it's his deal!"

Although all the core players were married, family roles were also deemed irrelevant. One might talk about family problems or items of mutual interest in the "socializing" before the game began or during the meal after the game but certainly not in the game. The mere presence of wives or children was prohibited, and even the thought of allowing wives to play was, as one core player summarized it, "horrible!" Another commented, "My son would like to come and watch us, but I won't let him. It's kind of an invasion of privacy, and you don't want **people** to be butting in at times like that."

During the game virtually all topics of conversation not appropriate to the action were deemed irrelevant. "My wife asked me what we talk about when we play cards," observed a core player. "I tell her we don't talk about anything, we play cards. She can't understand that, because they gossip when they play bridge. But they aren't really playing a game then." On one occasion a core player

worriedly interjected, "My God, how about this war in Viet Nam!" The others were silent for a few seconds, then one answered, "Whose deal is it?" The player who had commented about the war continued his statements, and quickly was interrupted by another who somewhat sternly though not angrily advised, "I didn't come here to hear you give a speech. I came here to play poker. I could give a speech myself you know." "Who will sell me some chips," inquired another, and the game continued.

Along with the accepted and expected verbal interactions of teasing and "game talk," the players enjoyed, indeed institutionalized, a core member's occasional references to the sagacity of his grandfather as a poker player. Whenever he was facing a particularly difficult decision, he would lean back in his chair, puff on a cigar (all but one of the players smoked either pipes or cigars during the game), and reflectively comment, "Well, my grandfather used to say," (for example) "never throw good money after bad." Often other players would make similar statements when they were faced with problem situations. The "grandfather" quotes had reference to betting, bluffing, soundness of decision, or competition. The content of the messages might accurately be described, as suggested by an interviewee, as "a poker player's Poor Richard's Almanac." The quotes seemed to be an important mechanism for bringing into the friendly game, as a lesson of a wise, "pioneer" man, considerations of the Protestant Ethic. The advice of grandfather was often cited to new men, thus serving a socialization function.

The verbal rituals, rules of irrelevance, and various behavioral taboos seemed to support valued group dynamics. The no-alcohol rule, for example, was adopted early in the group's history when an inebriated player had disrupted the pace. Similarly, the no-eating rule was inaugurated when players were observed to drop cards, or get them sticky. A number of specific games or methods of playing split-pot games were outlawed because they had in the past caused anger among players.

Although the players stressed the use of skill, particularly as a manifestation of control over fate, they also invoked what Malinowski (1948:38, 88) called "practical magic," primarily in an attempt to control the flow of cards or to change their luck. They would, for example, talk to the deck, urging it to give them good cards; rap the table with their knuckles just before receiving a card; slowly "squeeze out" a hand dealt to them, particularly after having drawn another card or cards, in order to "change the spots"; make a "fancy cut" as a luck changer; bet a hand "on the come" or "like you had them," as a means of guaranteeing getting the card or cards desired; deal a different game in order to "cool off" or "heat up" the deck; get up and stretch, or get a cup of coffee, in order to "change the way the money is flowing on the table"; stack their chips in a "lucky" way. On one occasion a player reached over and disordered another's chips, laughingly saying, "That should change your luck! You're winning too much!"[5]

The most striking example of magical behavior within the friendly game was the clearly understood and always followed rule that a player must bet fifteen cents, no more and no less, on the first face-up ace he received in a hand. It was agreed that if one did not follow this rule he would "insult the ace" and would inevitably lose. No one seemed to know where the "rule" originated, but all followed it and made a point of instructing new men to do likewise. Three members specifically referred to the fifteen-cent rule when interviewed about "specific rules." "I don't know why we do that," commented one, 'but that's our precious ritual. I do remember one time I forgot to bet in that way, and by God I lost!" The second member thought betting fifteen cents on the ace was "a funny rule, but still a rule." The third man referred to the fifteen-cent bet as "almost a law. It's stupid, I guess, but it makes the game more fun." In this case, the magic served not only the function of insuring against possible loss but also as another contributor to group cohesion. It may have been a "stupid" law, but it was "our" law.

The meal following the game might be considered a ritual feast. The strict poker rules and interactions were loosened, and the players discussed various topics deemed inappropriate during the game itself.

Retrospective conquest: "If I had only ..."

In the friendly game, winners necessitate losers. Unlike forms of betting games in which the participants play against the "house," not every player in poker can win.

The most a member could win or lose was approximately $30. Generally, there was one "big winner," one "big loser," and the rest were distributed in between. One core player was a "big winner" more often than the others, but not

enough to disrupt the balance of the group. There was no consistent "big loser." All of the members were in approximately the same income bracket, and thus winning or losing $30 had a similar impact upon them. Goffman (1961:69) pointed out that if betting is low relative to the financial capacities of the players, interest may be lacking in the game and they may not take it seriously. If, conversely, players feel that betting is too high then interest may be "strangled" by concern for the money they could lose. The core members understood the impact of someone who "couldn't afford to lose" or "didn't care about losing." In their view the former "makes you feel guilty if you win," and the latter "is no challenge, because if he's not really losing anything, you're not really winning anything." It was important that the financial conditions of the players be such that they maintained the dynamic equilibrium of the group.

The players knew that someone had to lose and inevitably at times it would be themselves. All agreed it was better to win than lose, but losing was not a disgrace so long as one did so through no lack of skill. For the member who had "played well" but nonetheless ended up a loser at the end of the evening the group offered and accepted several rationalizations, most commonly sympathizing about a plague of "second-best hands." This meant that the loser had played his cards well, "knocked heads" to the very end, and then come up with a slightly inferior hand. In essence, the cards were being blamed for his loss. It was no fault of his, because he "played well." When a player of this quality lost, luck was the culprit. But, when he won, it was by virtue of his skill; luck had nothing to do with it.

The core members looked with disfavor upon anyone who won by luck alone. A skillful player might invest some money early in a hand, but should not consistently "ride the hand out" hoping subsequently to be dealt some good cards. He should assess the odds, appraise through observation of cues and actions the quality of others hands, and if evidence warranted he should decide to drop out and take his temporary loss.

Those who had lost a hand were often seen to "relive" the play. They would utter such statements as: "I figured that you ..."; "If I hadn't thrown away those ..."; "All I needed was another spade and ..."; "I thought you had three of a kind because you were betting ..." Zola (1964:256) observed this phenomenon, which he called "the hedge," in the horse parlor, and described it as a means of maintaining some status even when losing. The loser would give a series of reasons why he lost, and how he wouldn't have if he had done some minor thing differently.

Goffman (1967:247) pointed out instances where in competitive interactions "both parties can emerge with honor and good character affirmed." This opportunity was clearly provided in the friendly game for those players who would "knock heads." There was potential in that situation for a "good winner" and one or more "good losers."

If a core player clearly had made a blunder, he would be teased by the others. Often the blunderer, in defense, would narrate a blunder historical for the group, whether made by himself or some other player. "Remember the time when Joe bet like crazy on his low hand because he thought the game was high-low split, and it was a high hand take all!" Considerable detail would be shared about the nature of the epic mistake. The current blunderer effectively would have anchored his own current error on a point somewhere less gross than a historical one. The core players appreciated and were comforted by the fact that all of them made mistakes. As one interviewee pointed out, "Nobody likes to play poker against a machine."

The player who had lost despite his skill might choose some other form of rationalization. He might consider the evening to have been "cheap entertainment," or "the cost of some lessons in poker." He might indicate that it was "his turn to lose tonight," or he had "let the host win." Nobody ever really complained about losing (although frustration was expressed concerning "second-best hands.") "I have more fun losing in this group," commented a core member, "than I do winning at roulette, or something like that."

The amount of money won or lost was discussed only in the most offhand manner. Specific figures were seldom mentioned, only estimates given, and then only sporadically and without pattern by different players. A core member reflected,

> At the end of the evening the game is over. Who cares how much you win or lose on one evening because each of us wins or loses, and it balances it out. It's each hand during the game that counts, and whether you win or lose that hand. The overall thing doesn't mean as much.

The money, out of the context of group interaction, seemed unimportant.

CONCLUSION: THE EPHEMERAL ROLE

The core members perceived themselves to be in a "different world" when they were playing. The friendy game, with its idiosyncratic roles, norms, rituals and rules of irrelevance, maintained clearly established boundaries. New men were selected carefully, and anyone or anything that disrupted the group dynamics or reduced the satisfactions experienced was eliminated or avoided. The players testified to their awareness that the poker group was "separate" from their other, broader, day-to-day social relationships:

> I look forward every other Monday to getting away from it all. I can do that when I'm playing poker with the guys. I forget about my job, and other problems that I have, and I can just sort of get lost in the game.
>
> It's a chance to get away from our wives and families. Every man needs a chance to get away from that once in awhile.
>
> When that first card hits the table, it's like we're on an island, you know, all to ourselves. Nobody bothers us. You're your own man! I miss it whenever we have to cancel a game for some reason or another.

In this sense, the friendly game seemed, as did Zola's (1964:248-249) horse parlor, to allow the players to effect "disassociation from ordinary utilitarian activities."

Goffman (1961:36, 67-68) described a "gaming encounter" as having social participants deeply involved in a focused interaction, and as such has "a metaphorical membrane around it." When the core players had all arrived, they formed the metaphorical membrane, and the friendly game became "a little cosmos of its own" (Riezler, 1941:505). Within the group boundaries, each member enacted the "ephemeral role" of core member, providing him the opportunity for scripted competition, self- and other-control, event brokerage, normative deception and aggression, micro-institutionalizing, and retrospective conquest. More specifically it provided him with the following opportunities for satisfaction: to share in the establishing and/or maintaining of a personally relevant group structure and interaction pattern; to compete vigorously but safely with equals; to bluff, tease, or otherwise "one-up" equals; to demonstrate and be admired for skill in betting and playing; to become deeply involved in intense but controlled personal inter-action; to read, analyze, and utilize cues emitted from other players; to control and become immersed in action, including a series of thrills and the exhilaration of "pace;" to enjoy the fellow-ship of a chosen and mutually developed primary group; to exert control over self, others, and luck or fate; to capture or relive some of the com-petencies and freedoms of youth; to reaffirm one's masculinity; to enjoy legitimized deviancy; to implement, in rapid succession, a great number of significant decisions; to declare as irrelevant, norms and roles which society-at-large deems mandatory in favor of idiosyncratic group norms and roles; and to escape the routine and "ordinary" social dynamics of everyday life.

The core member appeared to enter and leave the metaphorical membrane and ephemeral role through two buffer zones structured into the friendly game. The first buffer zone was the pre-game socializing period during which players waited and discussed various topics until all had arrived. The transition from everyday social inter-action to the contrived interaction in the game, the "easing" into the ephemeral role, was facilitated by this short delay. Players who had arrived late and thus missed the socializing period were heard to comment, for example, "give me a second to shift gears," or "let me put on my poker hat."

The other buffer zone, the meal after the game, served a similar function. The players then were behaving as members of any other group sit-ting down to have a snack together. The topics of conversation were unrestricted, and only rarely and briefly were any comments made concerning the game itself. During that period of the evening, the players were being "eased back" into their day-to-day complex of social roles.

Those who could not make the transition into the ephemeral role were disruptive to the group. This happened on only two occasions observed by the author. The first occasion involved a new man whose home had some months before been destroyed by a severe tornado. Shortly before the game had begun a tornado watch had been an-nounced for the area; the sky was heavy with clouds and the wind was noticeably increasing. The new man kept looking over his shoulder and out of the window, rose several times to walk to the front porch and look up at the sky, and twice dropped

out of the game to phone his wife. A core player commented, in an uncriticizing manner, "Your mind is wandering, isn't it." The distracted man commented that since he was "so nervous" it might be a "good idea" for him to go home. The group quickly agreed with him, and he left. A minute or so later a core player announced, "Okay, let's settle down and play some poker," and the game went on.

In the second incident, a core player seemed to be distracted throughout the game. He told short jokes, talked about "irrelevant" topics, and generally slowed down the pace. "What the hell's the matter with you!" inquired another, "Why are you so talkative tonight?" The reasons for his be-havior were not clear until later, during the meal, when he announced that he was being moved to another area and would no longer be able to partici-pate. He apparently had found it difficult to enact fully the ephemeral role, since he realized he would no longer be part of the friendly game. His dis-traction by the world "out there" had distracted the other players. As Goffman (1957) observed, in a gaming encounter "the perception that one participant is not spontaneously involved in the mutual activity can weaken for others their own involvement in the encounter and their own belief in the reality of the world it describes."

Core member of the friendly game is only one example of an ephemeral role. Other examples might include such diverse behavioral patterns as LSD "tripper," encounter "grouper," adulterer, volunteer work crew member (Zurcher, 1968), vacationer, weekend fisherman, or whatever is in-tense and intermittent and defined in contrast to one's day-to-day social world. Hopefully, we may see more systematic and comparative studies show-ing why people choose to develop or enact specific ephemeral roles, the satisfactions they gain, and the relation between ephemeral roles and major "life" roles.

NOTES

1. For an earlier definition and example of the concept, see Zurcher (1968).
2. See Goffman (1956) for a description of emo-tionally "flooding out" from group interaction.
3. The "liar" in the poker group seems honorifically similar to the "handicapper" in horse playing (cf. Zola, 1964:255).

4. For a relevant treatment of group norms for deviance, see Erikson (1962).

5. For a fascinating discussion of such behavior among craps shooters, see Henslin (1967).

REFERENCES

American Institute of Public Opinion. 1948. "The Quarter's Polls." *Public Opinion Quarterly* 12 (Spring): 146-176.

BERGLER, E. 1957. *The Psychology of Gambling.* New York: Hill & Wang.

BLOCH, H. A. 1951. "The Sociology of Gambling." *American Journal of Sociology* 57(November):215-221.

CAILLOIS, R. 1961. *Man, Play and Games.* New York: Free Press of Glencoe.

CRESPI, I. 1956. "The Social Significance of Card Playing as a Leisure Time Activity." *American Sociological Review* 21(December):717-721.

EDWARDS, W. 1955. "The Prediction of Decisions Among Bets." *Journal of Experimental Psychology* 50(September):201-214.

ERIKSON, E. 1950. *Childhood and Society.* New York: Norton.

ERIKSON, K. 1962. "Notes on the Sociology of Deviance." *Social Problems* 9(Spring):307-314.

GOFFMAN, E. 1956. "Embarrassment and Social Organization." *American Journal of Sociology* 62(November):264-271.

_____1957. "Alienation from Interaction." *Human Relations* 10(February):47-60.

_____1961. *Encounters: Two Studies in the Sociology of Interaction.* Indianapolis: Bobbs-Merrill.

_____1967. *Interaction Ritual.* Chicago: Aldine.

GOLD, R. 1958. "Roles in Sociological Field Observation." *Social Forces* 36(March):217-223.

HENSLIN, J. M. 1967. "Craps and Magic." *American Journal of Sociology* 73(November):316-330.

HERMAN, R. D. (ed.) 1967a. *Gambling.* New York: Harper & Row.

_____1967b. "Gambling as Work: A Sociological Study of the Race Track." Pp. 87-104 in R. D. Herman (ed.), *Gambling.* New York: Harper & Row.

HUIZINGA, J. 1955. *Homo Ludens, The Play Element in Culture.* Boston: Beacon Press.

LUKACS, J. 1963. "Poker and American Character." *Horizon* 5(November):56-62.

MALINOWSKI, B. 1948. *Magic, Science and Religion.* New York: Doubleday.

MARTINEZ, T. M., and R. LAFRANCI. 1969. "Why People Play Poker." *Transaction* 6(July-August):30-35, 52.

PIAGET, J. 1951. *Play, Dreams and Imitations in Childhood.* New York: Norton.

RIEZLER, K. 1941. "Play and Seriousness." *The Journal of Philosophy* 38(September):505-517.

ROBBINS, F. G. 1955. *The Sociology of Play, Recreation and Leisure Time.* Dubuque, Iowa: Brown.

STRAUSS, A. 1956. *The Social Psychology of George Herbert Mead.* Chicago: University of Chicago Press.

SUTTON-SMITH, B., and J. M. ROBERTS. 1963. "Game Involvement in Adults." *Journal of Social Psychology* 60(First Half):15-30.

ZOLA, I. K. 1964. "Observations on Gambling in a Lower Class Setting." Pp. 247-260 in H. Becker (ed.). *The Other Side.* New York: Free Press.

ZURCHER, L. A. 1968. "Social Psychological Functions of Ephermeral Roles." *Human Organization* 27 (Winter):281-297.

chapter 17
the military academy as an assimilating institution
sanford m. dornbusch [*]

The function of a military academy is to make officers out of civilians or enlisted men. The objective is accomplished by a twofold process of transmitting technical knowledge and of instilling in the candidates an outlook considered appropriate for members of the profession. This paper is concerned with the latter of these processes, the assimilating function of the military academy. Assimilation is viewed as "a process of interpenetration and fusion in which persons and groups acquire the memories, sentiments, and attitudes of other persons and groups, and, by sharing their experience and history, are incorporated with them in a common cultural life. . . . The unity thus achieved is not necessarily or even normally like-mindedness; it is rather a unity of experience and of orientation, out of which may develop a community of purpose and action."[1]

Data for this study consist almost entirely of retrospective material, based on ten months spent as a cadet at the United States Coast Guard Academy. The selective nature of memory obviously may introduce serious deficiencies in the present formulation. Unfortunately, it is unlikely

that more objective evidence on life within the Academy will be forthcoming. Cadets cannot keep diaries, are formally forbidden to utter a word of criticism of the Academy to an outsider, and are informally limited in the matters which are to be discussed in letters or conversations. The lack of objective data is regrettable, but the process of assimilation is present here in an extreme form. Insight into this process can better be developed by the study of such an explicit, overt case of assimilation.

The Coast Guard Academy, like West Point and Annapolis, provides four years of training for a career as a regular officer. Unlike the other service academies, however, its cadet corps is small, seldom exceeding 350 cadets. This disparity in size probably produces comparable differences in the methods of informal social control. Therefore, all the findings reported here may not be applicable to the other academies. It is believed, however, that many of the mechanisms through which this military academy fulfills its assimilating function will be found in a wide variety of social institutions.

THE SUPPRESSION OF PREEXISTING STATUSES

The new cadet, or "swab," is the lowest of the low. The assignment of low status is useful in producing a correspondingly high evaluation of successfully completing the steps in an Academy

From Social Forces, 1955, published by University of North Carolina Press. Reprinted by permission.

*The writer is indebted to Harold McDowell, Frank Miyamoto, Charles Bowerman, and Howard S. Becker for their constructive criticism of this paper.

career and requires that there be a loss of identity in terms of preexisting statuses. This clean break with the past must be achieved in a relatively short period. For two months, therefore, the swab is not allowed to leave the base or to engage in social intercourse with noncadets. This complete isolation helps to produce a unified group of swabs, rather than a heterogeneous collection of persons of high and low status. Uniforms are issued on the first day, and discussions of wealth and family background are taboo. Although the pay of the cadet is very low, he is not permitted to receive money from home. The role of the cadet must supersede other roles the individual has been accustomed to play. There are few clues left which will reveal social status in the outside world.[2]

It is clear that the existence of minority-group status on the part of some cadets would tend to break down this desired equality. The sole minority group present was the Jews, who, with a few exceptions, had been informally excluded before 1944. At that time 18 Jews were admitted in a class of 162. Their status as Jews made them objects of scrutiny by the upper classmen, so that their violations of rules were more often noted. Except for this "spotlight," however, the Jews reported no discrimination against them—they, too, were treated as swabs.

LEARNING NEW RULES AND ADJUSTMENT TO CONFLICTS BETWEEN RULES

There are two organized structures of rules which regulate the cadet's behavior. The first of these is the body of regulations of the Academy, considered by the public to be the primary source of control. These regulations are similar to the code of ethics of any profession. They serve in part as propaganda to influence outsiders. An additional function is to provide negative sanctions which are applied to violations of the second set of expectations, the informal rules. Offenses against the informal rules are merely labeled as breaches of the formal code, and the appropriate punishment according to the regulations is then imposed. This punitive system conceals the existence of the informal set of controls.

The informal traditions of the Academy are more functionally related to the existing set of circumstances than are the regulations, for although these traditions are fairly rigid, they are more easily forgotten or changed than are the formal regulations. Unlike other informal codes, the

Academy code of traditions is in part written, appearing in a manual for entering cadets.

In case of conflict between the regulations and tradition, the regulations are superseded. For example, it is against the regulations to have candy in one's room. A first classman orders a swab to bring him candy. Caught en route by an officer, the swab offers no excuse and is given 15 demerits. First classmen are then informally told by the classmate involved that they are to withhold demerits for this swab until he has been excused for offenses totaling 15 demerits. Experience at an Academy teaches future officers that regulations are not considered of paramount importance when they conflict with informal codes—a principle noted by other observers[3]

Sometimes situations arise in which the application of either form of control is circumvented by the commanding officer. The following case is an example. Cadets cannot drink, cannot smoke in public, can never go above the first floor in a hotel. It would seem quite clear, therefore, that the possessor of a venereal disease would be summarily dismissed. Cadets at the Academy believed that two upper-class cadets had contracted a venereal disease, were cured, and given no punishment. One of the cadets was an outstanding athlete, brilliant student, and popular classmate. Cadets were told that a direct appeal by the commanding officer to the Commandant of the Coast Guard resulted in the decision to hush up the entire affair, with the second cadet getting the same treatment as his more popular colleague. The event indicated the possibility of individualization of treatment when rules are violated by officers.

THE DEVELOPMENT OF SOLIDARITY

The control system operated through the class hierarchy. The first class, consisting of cadets in their third or fourth year at the Academy, are only nominally under the control of the officers of the Academy. Only one or two officers attempt to check on the activities of the first classmen, who are able to break most of the minor regulations with impunity. The first class is given almost complete control over the rest of the cadet corps. Informally, certain leading cadets are even called in to advise the officers on important disciplinary matters. There are one or two classes between the first classmen and the swabs, depending on the existence of a three- or four-year course. These middle classes haze the swabs. Hazing is forbidden by the regulations, but the practice is a hallowed tradition of the Academy. The first class demands that this hazing take place, and, since they have the power to give demerits, all members of the middle classes are compelled to haze the new cadets.

As a consequence of undergoing this very unpleasant experience together, the swab class develops remarkable unity. For example, if a cadet cannot answer an oral question addressed to him by his teacher, no other member of his class will answer. All reply, "I can't say, sir," leaving the teacher without a clue to the state of knowledge of this student compared to the rest of the class. This group cohesion persists throughout the Academy period, with first classmen refusing to give demerits to their classmates unless an officer directly orders them to do so.

The honor system, demanding that offenses by classmates be reported, is not part of the Coast Guard Academy tradition. It seems probable that the honor system, if enforced, would tend to break down the social solidarity which the hazing develops within each class.

The basis for interclass solidarity, the development of group feeling on the part of the entire cadet corps, is not so obvious. It occurs through informal contacts between the upper classmen and swabs, a type of fraternization which occurs despite the fact it traditionally is discouraged. The men who haze the swab and order him hazed live in the same wing of the dormitory that he does. Coming from an outside world which disapproves of authoritarian punishment and aggressiveness, they are ashamed of their behavior. They are eager to convince the swab that they are good fellows. They visit his room to explain why they are being so harsh this week or to tell of a mistake he is making. Close friendships sometimes arise through such behavior. These friendships must be concealed. One first classman often ordered his room cleaned by the writer as a "punishment," then settled down for an uninterrupted chat. Such informal contacts serve to unite the classes and spread a "we-feeling" through the Academy.

In additon, the knowledge of common interests and a common destiny serves as a unifying force that binds together all Academy graduates. This is expressed in the identification of the interest of the individual with the interest of the Coast Guard. A large appropriation or an increase in the size of the Coast Guard will speed the rate of promotion for all, whether ensign or captain. A winning football team at the Academy may familiarize more civilians with the name of their common alma mater. Good publicity for the Coast Guard raises the status of the Coast Guard officer.

The Coast Guard regulars are united in their disdain for the reserves. There are few reserve officers during peacetime, but in wartime the reserve officers soon outnumber the regulars. The reserves do not achieve the higher ranks, but they are a threat to the cadets and recent graduates of the Academy. The reserves receive in a few months the rank that the regulars reach only after four grueling years. The Academy men therefore protectively stigmatize the reserves as incompetents. If a cadet falters on the parade ground, he is told, "You're marching like a reserve." Swabs are told to square their shoulders while on liberty, "or else how will people know you are not a reserve?" Myths spring up—stories of reserve commanders who must call on regular ensigns for advice. The net effect is reassurance that although the interlopers may have the same rank, they do not have equal status.

Another outgroup is constituted by the enlisted men, who are considered to be of inferior ability and eager for leadership. Segregation of cadets and enlisted men enables this view to be propagated. Moreover, such segregation helps to keep associations within higher-status social groups. There is only one leak in this insulating dike. The pharmacist mates at sick bay have direct contact with the cadets, and are the only enlisted personnel whom cadets meet on an equal basis. The pharmacist mates take pleasure in reviling the Academy, labeling it "the p——k factory." Some of the cadets without military experience are puzzled by such an attitude, which is inconsistent with their acquired respect for the Academy.

THE DEVELOPMENT OF A BUREAUCRATIC SPIRIT

The military services provide an excellent example of a bureaucratic structure. The emphasis is upon the office with its sets of rights and duties, rather than on the man. It is a system of rules with little regard for the individual case. The method of promotion within the Coast Guard perfectly illustrates this bureaucratic character. Unlike the Army or Navy, promotions in the Coast Guard up to the rank of lieutenant-commander do not even depend on the evaluation of superior officers. Promotion comes solely according to seniority, which is based on class standing at the Academy. The 50th man in the 1947 class will be lieutenant-commander before the 51st man, and the latter will be promoted before the 1st man in the 1948 class.

The hazing system contributes directly to acceptance of the bureaucratic structure of the Coast Guard, for the system is always viewed by its participants as not involving the personal character of the swab or upper classman. One is not being hazed because the upper classman is a sadist, but because one is at the time in a junior status. Those who haze do not pretend to be superior to those who are being hazed. Since some of those who haze you will also try to teach you how to stay out of trouble, it becomes impossible to attribute evil characteristics to those who injure you. The swab knows he will have his turn at hazing others. At most, individual idiosyncrasies will just affect the type of hazing done.[4]

This emphasis on the relativity of status is explicitly made on the traditional Gizmo Day, on which the swabs and their hazers reverse roles. The swabs-for-a-day take their licking without flinching and do not seek revenge later, for they are aware that they are under the surveillance of the first classmen. After the saturnalia, the swabs are increasingly conscious of their inability to blame particular persons for their troubles.

Upper classmen show the same resentment against the stringent restrictions upon their lives, and the manner in which they express themselves indicates a feeling of being ruled by impersonal forces. They say, "You can't buck the System." As one writer puts it, "The best attitude the new cadet can have is one of unquestioning acceptance of tradition and custom."

There is a complete absence of charismatic veneration of the Coast Guard heroes of the past and present. Stirring events are recalled, not as examples of the genius of a particular leader, but as part of the history of the great organization which they will serve. A captain is a cadet thirty years older and wiser. Such views prepare these men for their roles in the bureaucracy.

NEW SATISFACTIONS IN INTERACTION

A bureaucratic structure requires a stable set of mutual expectations among the occupants of offices. The Academy develops this ability to view the behavior of others in terms of a preordained set of standards. In addition to preparing the cadet for later service as an officer, the predictability of the behavior of his fellows enables the cadet to achieve a high degree of internal stability. Although he engages in a continual bustle of activity, he al-

ways knows his place in the system and the degree to which he is fulfilling the expectations of his role.

Sharing common symbols and objects, the cadets interact with an ease of communication seldom found in everyday life. The cadet is told what is right and wrong, and, if he disagrees, there are few opportunities to translate mental reservations into action. The "generalized other" speaks with a unitary voice which is uncommon in modern societies. To illustrate, an upper classman ordered a swab to pick up some pieces of paper on the floor of a washroom. The latter refused and walked away. There was no repercussions. The swab knew that, if he refused, the upper classman would be startled by the choice of such an unconventional way of getting expelled from the Academy. Wondering what was happening, the upper classman would redefine his own behavior, seeing it as an attack on the high status of the cadet. Picking up litter in a washroom is "dirty work," fit only for enlisted men. The swab was sure that the upper classman shared this common universe of discourse and never considered the possibility that he would not agree on the definition of the situation.

Interaction with classmates can proceed on a level of confidence that only intimate friends achieve in the outside world. These men are in a union of sympathy, sharing the same troubles, never confiding secrets to upper classmen, never criticizing one another to outsiders. Each is close to only a few but is friendly with most of the men in his class.

When interacting with an upper classman in private, a different orientation is useful. The swab does not guess the reason why he is being addressed, but instead assumes a formal air of deference. If the upper classman says, "Aw cut it out," the swab relaxes. In this manner the role of the upper classman is explicitly denoted in each situation.

In addition to providing predictability of the behavior of others, the Academy provides a second set of satisfactions in the self-process. An increase in the cadet's self-esteem develops in conjunction with identification in his new role. Told that they are members of an elite group respected by the community, most cadets begin to feel at ease in a superordinate role. One may be a low-ranking cadet, but cadets as a group have high status. When cadets visit home for the first time, there is a conflict between the lofty role that they wish to play and the role to which their parents are accustomed. Upon return to the Academy, much conversation is concerned with the way things at home have changed.

This feeling of superiority helps to develop self-confidence in those cadets who previously had a low evaluation of themselves. It directly enters into relationships with girls, with whom many boys lack self-confidence. It soon becomes apparent that any cadet can get a date whenever he wishes, and he even begins to feel that he is a good "catch." The cadet's conception of himself is directly influenced by this new way of viewing the behavior of himself and others. As one cadet put it, "I used to be shy. Now I'm reserved."

SOCIAL MOBILITY

A desire for vertical social mobility on the part of many cadets serves as one means of legitimizing the traditional practices of the Academy. The cadets are told that they will be members of the social elite during the later stages of their career. The obstacles that they meet at the Academy are then viewed as the usual barriers to social mobility in the United States, a challenge to be surmounted.

Various practices at the Academy reinforce the cadets' feeling that they are learning how to enter the upper classes. There is a strong emphasis on etiquette, from calling cards to table manners. The Tactics Officer has been known to give long lectures on such topics as the manner of drinking soup from an almost empty bowl. The cadet must submit for approval the name of the girl he intends to take to the monthly formal dance. Girls attending the upper-class college in the vicinity are automatically acceptable, but some cadets claim that their dates have been rejected because they are in a low status occupation such as waitress.

Another Academy tradition actively, though informally, encourages contact with higher status girls. After the swabs have been completely isolated for two months, they are invited to a dance at which all the girls are relatives or friends of Coast Guard officers. A week later the girls at the nearby college have a dance for the swabs. The next weekend finds the swab compelled to invite and acceptable girl to a formal reception. He must necessarily choose from the only girls in the area whom he knows, those that he met during the recent hours of social intercourse.

JUSTIFICATION OF INSTITUTIONAL PRACTICES

In addition to the social mobility theme which views the rigors of Academy life as obstacles to up-ward mobility, there is a more open method of justifying traditionally legitimated ways of doing things. The phrase, "separating the men from the boys" is used to meet objections to practices which seem inefficient or foolish. Traditional standards are thus redefined as further tests of ability to take punishment. Harsh practices are defended as methods by which the insincere, incompetent, or undisciplined cadets are weeded out. Cadets who rebel and resign are merely showing lack of character.[5]

Almost all cadets accept to some extent this traditional view of resignations as admissions of defeat. Of the 162 entering cadets in 1944, only 52 graduated in 1948. Most of the 110 resignations were entirely voluntary without pressure from the Academy authorities. Most of these resignations came at a time when the hazing was comparatively moderate. Cadets who wish to resign do not leave at a time when the hazing might be considered the cause of their departure. One cadet's history illustrates this desire to have the resignation appear completely voluntary. Asked to resign because of his lack of physical coordination, he spent an entire year building up his physique, returned to the Academy, finished his swab year, and then joyously quit. "It took me three years, but I showed them."

Every cadet who voluntarily resigns is a threat to the morale of the cadet corps, since he has rejected the values of the Academy. Although cadets have enlisted for seven years and could theoretically be forced to remain at the Academy, the usual procedure is to isolate them from the swabs and rush acceptance of their resignation. During the period before the acceptance is final, the cadets who have resigned are freed from the usual duties of their classmates, which action effectively isolates them from cadets who might be affected by their contagious disenchantment.

REALITY SHOCK

Everett C. Hughes has developed the concept of "reality shock," the sudden realization of the disparity between the way a job is envisaged before beginning work and the actual work situation.[6] In the course of its 75-year history the Coast Guard Academy has wittingly or unwittingly developed certain measures to lessen reality shock in the new ensign. The first classmen, soon to be officers, are aided in lessening the conflict between the internalized rules of the Academy world and the standards for officer conduct.

On a formal level the first classmen are often

reminded that they are about to experience a relative decline in status. On their first ship they will be given the most disagreeable duties. The first classmen accept this and joke about how their attitudes will change under a harsh captain. On a more concrete level, first classmen are given weekend leaves during the last six months of their stay at the Academy. These leaves allow them to escape from the restrictive atmosphere of the nearby area. It is believed wise to let them engage in orgiastic behavior while still cadets, rather than suddenly release all controls upon graduation.

Rumors at the Academy also help to prepare the cadets for their jobs as officers. Several of the instructors at the Academy were supposed to have been transferred from sea duty because of their incompetence. Such tales protect the cadets from developing a romantic conception of the qualities of Coast Guard officers, as well as providing a graphic illustration of how securely the bureaucratic structure protects officers from their own derelictions. In addition, many stories were told about a junior officer whose career at the Academy had been singularly brilliant. He had completely failed in his handling of enlisted men because he had carried over the high standards of the Academy. The cadets were thus oriented to a different conception of discipline when dealing with enlisted personnel.

CONCLUSION

The United States Coast Guard Academy performs an assimilating function. It isolates cadets from the outside world, helps them to identify themselves with a new role, and thus changes their self-conception. The manner in which the institution inculcates a bureaucratic spirit and prevents reality shock is also considered in this analysis.

The present investigation is admittedly fragmentary. Much of the most relevant material is simply not available. It is also clear that one cannot assume that this analysis applies completely to any other military academy. However, as an extreme example of an assimilating institution, there is considerable material which can be related to other institutions in a comparative framework.

NOTES

1. Robert E. Park and Ernest W. Burgess, **Introduction to the Science of Sociology** (Chicago: University of Chicago Press, 1921), pp. 735, 737.

2. Cf. Arnold Van Gennep, **Les Rites de Passage** (Paris: Emile Nourry, 1909). Translated by Everett C. Hughes in **Anthropology-Sociology 240, Special Readings** (Chicago: University of Chicago Bookstore, 1948), pt. II, p. 9.

3. Ralph H. Turner, "The Navy Disbursing Officer As a Bureaucrat," **American Sociological Review**, XII (June 1946), 344 and 348; Arnold Rose, "The Social Structure of the Army," **American Journal of Sociology**, LI (March 1946), 361.

4. Compare this viewpoint with that expressed in Hugh Mullan, "The Regular Service Myth," **American Journal of Sociology**, LIII (January 1948), 280, where hazing is viewed as the expression of "pent-up sadism." Such individualistic interpretations do not take into account the existence of an institutional structure, or else they give psychological interpretations to social processes.

5. "At each step of the ceremonies he feels that he is brought a little closer, until at last he can feel himself a man among men." A. R. Radcliffe-Brown, **The Andaman Islanders** (Glencoe, Illinois: The Free Press, 1948), p. 279.

6. Miriam Wagenschein, "Reality Shock." Unpublished M. A. thesis, Department of Sociology, University of Chicago, 1950.

topic 9

the human community: views from below and outside

Skid row, home for alcoholics and vagrants, and the contracultural commune in a remote mountain valley are both inhabited by "outsiders," perhaps unwilling outcasts, or perhaps self-conscious rebels who have rejected conventional morality, goals, and life styles. Yet both, skid row and the commune, are human communities. Both, however impermanent their residents, are human groups. And both are substantially identical to sister communites elsewhere.

Jacqueline Wiseman's "Stations of the Lost" has look-alike counterparts in the skid rows of Chicago, Denver, and Atlanta, and Vivian Gornick's hippies in and around Taos, New Mexico, would be equally at home in communal settlements in Hawaii or in the Cascade Mountains of Oregon.

Thus what one denizen of Pacific City confided to Professor Wiseman might have been said by a counter part in any other metropolitan skid row:

After you've bummed around for a while you develop sort of
an instinct so you know where you'll be safe overnight. . . . So
you sleep under a bridge, under an awning, on a loading platform, or in a patch of weeds, having your bottle with you

Nor is the alcoholic's quest for shelter often a lone-wolf operation: he is quickly joined by fellow boozers and a new inchoate and transient community evolves:

We found a place under the freeway entrance. . . . The next
thing you know, we had half the city livin' with us. There was
John, Bob, and Pots coming up there, and one night Poloock
came up there, him and Rickey. We had a houseful

A portrayal of the itinerant inhabitants of the New Buffalo commune outside of Taos has a kindred ring, for it is a description as well of other rural communes, at far-flung points of the compass:

Some have migrated to this site from the high-rise anonymity of New York: some come from defunct communes; some are California hips who've fled inland. Some are ex-motorcycle outlaws or artists or black militants or one-time burglars or present fugitives from the law or dropped-out drifters who have . . . erased all traces of their past life. . . .

And what is more, these agrarian communes are, as one reporter put it, "an effort to forge a oneness, a semi-mythical new rapport with air and soil and other souls. The result, in most intentional communities, is a feeling of 'us-ness' in everything undertaken." Whether they are the homes of tramps, homosexuals, drug addicts, juvenile gangs, prostitutes, or lesbians, the homes of outsiders everywhere are human communities with much in common.

chapter 18
skid row:
the professional overview
and the participant close-up
jacqueline p. wiseman

To the average person, the term Skid Row immediately brings to mind a grey, slumlike section of town peopled with society's misfits and castoffs, poverty-striken men who have failed to make it in the competitive world and are now eking out an existence in an alcoholic haze amid environmental squalor and human misery. The literature concerning the subject concurs. One description of Skid Row summed up the prevailing symbolism of the area with the following picturesque statement:

> Skid Row, U.S.A., belches despair. Skid Rowers consider it "the last step before the grave." They wash their hands of themselves and say they're beyond caring what happens to them any more. Nobody else cares either.[1]

All metropolitan cities tend to develop slum areas, that is, older, deteriorated clusters of buildings where the down-and-out tend to live. Skid Row, however, is a unique asylum for the homeless man. It is thought to have first developed in the United States at the close of the Civil War when countless unemployed men, newly discharged

from the army, roamed the cities.[2] Today a Skid Row is found in every fairly large American city[3]

Skid Row, and more especially its inhabitants, has been highly resistant to the pressures of assimilation. No city has been successful in eradicating either the area or the inhabitants through social engineering alone. Some of them have resorted to the bulldozer—and the homeless male moves on geographically,[4] but does not move up socially. During good times, the Skid Row population shrinks, and during bad times it grows, but never does it wither away from lack of inhabitants, despite the fact that its predominantly male society is replenished almost entirely by adult recruits.

Not only has Skid Row proved tenacious as a continuing urban pattern but the area and its culture are strikingly similar from city to city and from time period to time period. In fact, the descriptions of Skid Row have been remarkably stable over the past 50 years: the filth and stench of the hotels, the greasy cheapness of the restaurants, the litter in the streets, the concentration of "low-type" bars, or "dives." All of these aspects are mentioned again and again in both the research and the romantic literature from the 1920s until today.[5]

This consistency overrides the changes in Skid Row demographic composition from itinerant workers to more stable local spot jobbers and retired men living on social security.[6] The social silhouette of these men has not changed to any degree—idle, ill-kempt, living hand to mouth. Even the special jargon used by the habitués of Skid Row is amazingly consistent from city to city and through time. This would seem to suggest both a persistence of common meanings as well as a good deal of traveling from one Skid Row to another Skid Row by itinerants.

Equally persistent—and most pertinent in terms of this study—is the fact that the majority of Skid Row residents are men alone, without families, whose heavy drinking orientation outweighs efforts toward maintaining steady employment or improving living standards. In this way, Skid Row is different from other urban low-income areas where some struggle to sustain family life and regular employment is attempted. As Wallace puts it:

> To be completely acculturated in skid row subculture is to be a drunk—since skid rowers place strong emphasis on group drinking and the acculturated person is by definition a conformist. The drunk has rejected every single one of society's established values and wholly conformed to the basic values of skid row subculture. Food, shelter, employment, appearance, health and all other considerations are subordinated by the drunk to the group's need for alcohol. This group constitutes the drunk's total social world and it in turn bestows upon him any status, acceptance, or security he may possess.[7]

When the existence of a phenomenon is apprehended by concerned groups as inherently bad for society at large, a great deal of professional energy usually is expended on eradication and/or prevention of the presumed problem. Skid Row has attracted its share of all types of social reformers and they (and their hired agents) have, over the years, become an integral part of the scene there. Thus, as Skid Row alcoholics view their world, they must take into account these agents of social control who, in turn, see the area within a rehabilitation framework.

The purpose of this chapter is to present descriptions of Skid Row in Pacific City as seen by two types of persons who must cope with it: agents of social control, and those male residents who are also alcoholics. The problems of each group are different as are some of their goals. The several frameworks each group develops for under-

standing what is going on in Skid Row are sharply divergent and yet strikingly self-reinforcing. As a result, the phenomena each group encounters are selected and sorted in radically different ways. The meaning of the situations each group apprehends and the actions planned as a result have possibly only one overlapping feature—both groups see the Row as "the bottom of the barrel."

THE PROFESSIONALS' VIEW OF SKID ROW

The general attitudes of agents of social control toward Skid Row and the Skid Row alcoholic can best be apprehended by looking at two determinants of their frame of reference: (1) **their professional training**, influenced as it is by psychological and sociological literature on the subject, including the language these studies employ; and (2) **their social background** of middle-class decency, responsibility, cleanliness, and enterprise, which most of them have absorbed. (This is not to say that there are no differences in attitude among various agents of social control. Rather, this chapter dwells on the general agreement of outlook, while the next chapter highlights specific divergences based on theoretical approaches to treatment of alcoholism.)

From a review of the literature on the subject of Skid Row, it seems reasonable to say that to social workers, psychiatrists, psychologists, and many sociologists, Skid Row is seen as a prime manifestation of social pathology.[8] Like a cancer embedded in healthy tissue, Skid Row is viewed as a potential danger to an entire city. The physical deterioration of the buildings and resultant lowering of property values of adjacent areas is but one aspect of this threat.[9] The social and psychological deterioration of its residents, inevitably resulting in added cost to the city for police surveillance and humane care, is the other.

The Physical Area and Social Environment Seen as Blighted

The language selected to describe the area, an important part of the judgmental frame of reference, includes such professional terms as "below code," "deteriorated property," "dilapidated structures," "blighted zone," "detrimental land use," and then goes beyond these to such pejorative labels as "firetraps," "depressing rooms," "dismal," and "grimy."

When an official of the Pacific City Urban Renewal Agency spoke of Skid Row, he said:

There are about 50 dilapidated hotels in the area that ought to be torn down. It is a place of dismal, grimy buildings, disreputable bars, and degrading social conditions. The alleys are dirty. The buildings are crumbling. Sanitary conditions are unspeakable. Any sort of fire would end in a disaster. On top of that, there is a bad conflict of land use here that cannot go on if Pacific City is not to suffer. There are fine stores and shopping areas side by side with Skid Row.

The Residents Seen as Pathological

If the physical conditions of the Skid Row neighborhood are accepted as not only inherently unattractive and undesirable but also as conveying a pathological gestalt, certain implications inevitably arise about the moral character, the psychological make-up, and the physiological state of the man who would live in such an environment. Thus the cited studies that speak of stench, degrading social conditions, and urban blight also describe the essential character of the residents as depressed, down-and-out, apathetic, mentally and physically ill, the dregs of society, having a dependency problem, lacking in religious belief, needing counseling and psychic support, needing rehabilitation, requiring institutional care, discouraged, and frustrated.[10]

The manner in which the appearance of the area is linked with the character of the men by agents of social control can be apprehended in the following excerpts taken from professional conference papers concerning Skid Row.

Residents of Skid Row are the most poorly housed group in the urban population. The "normal" population would refuse to live in the housing occupied by these men.[11]

The Skid Row men considered that Skid Row was foul and dirty and grudgingly uncomfortable and they hated it.[12]

It [Skid Row] still stinks just as bad, and the inhabitants wander aimlessly about, just as they used to.[13]

The physical appearance of the men is also taken as at least surface evidence that the character diagnoses are correct. The following passages, excerpted from a journalist's diary on his Skid Row adventures in Pacific City, illustrate the transmu-

tation by the press of environmental variables into social and personality characteristics.

I have just come home from Skid Row. I have scrubbed myself with laundry soap and water as hot as I could stand. But I could not wash the stench out of my mind.

Skid Row is another world—a world of crutches, of boarded-up stores, of broken clocks, peeling plaster, cracked windows, and worn-out stairs. It is a world of flophouses, greasy hash joints, and the battered inside of the patrol wagon.

But above all, Skid Row is a world of sickness. The men I lived with there were sick with the all-pervading sickness of alcoholism. They could sink no lower on the social scale. Their goal each day was to drink enough wine to get them through the next. The next day was the same and the next day and the next day.

The men I lived with had given up and in giving up they had lost the thing which once made them men.

I have scrubbed my body until it is tingling clean. My wife says the smell has gone. But it hasn't.

In my mind I still smell with the smell of the human wreckage who accepted me as a friend.[14]

The literature of the Pacific City Urban Redevelopment program also is particularly apt to illustrate the mental connection between blighted buildings and blighted individuals in the minds of professional agents of social control. The excerpt quoted below is part of an urban renewal publicity campaign to move men out of condemned hotels that are to be replaced by a sports arena. Note how disease, disaster, and arrest statistics are used as evidence the buildings should be demolished:

Some people think it's all right for you to live in the midst of all this. Compared to the rest of Pacific City, in 1964 Skid Row had:
4 times more fires per acre
9 times more deaths from fires*
8 times more tuberculosis*
3 times more venereal disease*

5 times more major crimes*
30 times more drunk arrests*
(*per 1,000 population)
WE SAY YOU DESERVE BETTER. MUCH BETTER[15]

Another approach used to extract the moral and psychological character of a given group of people is to outline their life style as perceived by observing their daily round. Again it should be kept in mind that where a person's frame of reference utilizes depressing physical conditions as an indication of social and physical pathology, it also will tend to influence the **selection** of daily round incidents and the **meanings** attributed to them.

For instance, in his demographic and attitudinal study of Skid Row, Donald Bogue asked his respondents to describe a typical day and night. He then coded the answers into gross activity categories, of which the most frequently cited are:

Working	Getting extra sleep
Looking for work	Drinking in a
Walking along Skid	tavern
Row	Going to the reading
Talking with other	room
Skid Row men	Play pool, cards,
Sitting in the hotel	other games
lobby	Go to mission ser-
Watching TV	vices[16]
Reading newspapers	
or books	

From this rather neutral empirical data, plus some verbatim descriptions, Bogue reconstructs life on Skid Row as brutish and mean at the very least, with some pathological overtones, both social and personal:

The major finding of this study is that Skid Row life is very different from what may be the popular impression. Instead of being a carefree, anarchistic seventh heaven, life for the typical Skid Row resident is boring, insecure, and often lonely. Fear of robbery, worry about where the next meal is coming from, alcoholic shakes from need of a drink, physical discomfort, despondency, and self-hate are daily feelings of these men. . . . Moreover, each day is almost like every other day, punctuated only by changing seasons or a run of unusually good or bad luck.[17]

The police of Pacific City see Skid Row and its inhabitants in a framework derived from their major experiences there. They liken it to a jungle. Although a good deal of time goes into preventing the Skid Row alcoholic from being exploited and beaten up, police feel this barely scratches the surface of such activities on their beat.

Tough guys from the Tenderloin area come down here and take advantage of these bums . . . take them to their room and beat them and rob them.

Taxi drivers often roll a drunk from this area. They know he can't prove anything. Restaurant owners overcharge whenever they know a guy is too drunk to know better or make a fuss.

The men rob and beat up on each other here. One day you'll see two men being buddies, the next day they are beating hell out of each other in some bar.

There is very little permanent buddying up here. They are too afraid and suspicious of each other.

This latter remark is also a key to a major impression of Skid Row social relationships—they are attenuated when existing at all.[18] One officer of the Christian Missionaries, a major charitable organization that works with Skid Row men, stated:

Loneliness is their major problem. Sometimes they will come in here for help with their drinking problem, but it always comes out in the end—how lonely they are. Sometimes they cry right here in the office. These men have no families, no one who cares about them. They don't even have any real friends.

Many studies of the daily activities of Skid Row regulars reflect a similar theme: the alcoholic ambles through the day, alone a great deal of the time, sleeping in a cheap hotel, drinking in a tavern if he can afford it, or with a bottle gang if he is short on funds. He eats in a "greasy spoon" restaurant, watches television in the lobby of his hotel (if he is lucky enough to have one), and goes to bed. If he is without a bed for the night, he goes to a reading room to keep warm or drops in on a mission for soup and salvation. Then he "carries the banner" (walks around all night).[19]

In addition to being without close friends, the Skid Row alcoholic is almost completely without the social anchorages—the personal ties—that most middle-calss men take for granted. If the Skid Row man ever had a wife and children, he has long ago lost them for one reason or another and he often does not even know where they are. Most in-laws avoid him. With the possible exception of his mother, he has usually lost all track of his parents, brothers, and sisters. Friends from his previous days of semirespectability have long ago given up on him. So have employers. Hence he lacks the usual social life that accompanies most jobs. By most standards he is seen to have a very constricted social life.

It is from these characteristics, of course, that the so-called undersocialization hypothesis arises concerning the Skid Row man. His apparent lack of long-term friendships, family commitments, or steady job is considered to be indicative of some flaw in his personality and upbringing, making it impossible for him to make commitments to others.[20]

Perhaps the most important indicator of the pathological character of the Skid Row alcoholic is his physical and mental state as it is affected by ingestion of copious quantities of alcohol over extended periods of time.[21] Skid Row drunks, with their lack of permanent housing, their bottle sharing, their fights, their passing out in doorways and sleeping out in all weather, the lack of ordinary cleanliness standards in restaurants and hotels, the impermanency of sex arrangements, and the dangerous jobs they often have to accept in order to make a little money, are easy prey to all types of disease and debility.[22]

Because of these conditions, Skid Row men have high rates of tuberculois, venereal disease, pneumonia, influenze, injuries to limbs, and eye and teeth defects, as indicated by surveys sponsored by Pacific City Urban Redevelopment Association.

Table 1, that follows, shows mortality rates, by cause, found in the general Pacific City population as compared to that of the Skid Row area.

Thus a constant alcoholic haze, punctuated by blackouts, vomiting spells, and agonizing withdrawal pangs, all compounded by other physical ailments and disabilities, leaves the Skid Row man so weakened physically and mentally as to be

TABLE 1.
Male Mortality Rates by Cause in Pacific City and the Skid Row Area (Death by Cause per 100,000 Population)

CAUSE	ALL CITY (Male)	SKID ROW AREA (Mostly male)
All causes	1461.6	3159.6
Cardiovascular	526.8	2681.3
Cancer (malignant neoplasms)	256.9	349.1
Cirrhosis	107.7	650.9
Accidents	85.0	210.3
Suicide	34.7	23.6
Tuberculosis	8.1	47.2

Source: Pacific City Health Department. The citywide rates are not age-adjusted because the necessary information was not available for this computation. Rates are restricted to males to match more closely the Skid Row area (which is represented here by three Census Tracts and does not quite match Bogue's boundaries). Inasmuch as cancer is primarily a disease of the aged, the cancer death differential of the two areas can be taken as a rough indicator of the relatively slight weight added to the Skid Row rates due to its older population. Age alone then would not account for the dramatically higher mortality from other causes on Skid Row as compared to the rest of the city.

nearly unfit to cope with the ordinary daily problems. As one public health official commented:

> You think they look bad when you see them on the streets? You ought to see them in their rooms—lying in their own vomit, no bath or clean clothes for weeks, their bodies covered with open sores from drinking. Sometimes they don't even know where they are.

NOTES

1. Sarah Harris, **Skid Row USA** (Garden City, N. Y.: Doubleday and Company, Inc., 1956), p. 16. The pictures of Skid Row used to illustrate the various books and studies about the area show what can only be described as squalor and filth. The faces of the men look resigned and expressionless.

2. Samuel E. Wallace, **Skid Row as a Way of Life** (Totowa, N. J.: The Bedminister Press, 1965), pp. 13-15.

3. Donald J. Bogue, **Skid Row in American Cities** (Chicago: University of Chicago Press, 1963), chap. 1, reported the existence of 45 cities with identifiable Skid Rows.

4. As indicated by studies and the experience of cities, the Skid Row man will move to another Skid Row area in another city if his present area is destroyed. He may also move to other areas in the same city where food and rent is inexpensive or where social welfare agencies are available nearby, and gradually attract enough cohorts

to establish a second Skid Row. Seventeen of the 41 cities mapped by Bogue had more than one separate and distinct Skid Row area. Bogue, ibid.

5. See, for example, Nels Anderson, **The Hobo, The Sociology of the Homeless Man** (Chicago: University of Chicago Press, 1923); Howard G. Bain, **A Sociological Analysis of the Chicago Skid Row Lifeway** (unpublished M.A. dissertation, University of Chicago, 1950); Sarah Harris, **Skid Row USA**; Elmer Bendiner, **The Bowery Man** (New York: Thomas Nelson and Sons, 1961); Bogue, **Skid Row in American Cities**; Philip O'Connor, **Britain in the Sixties, Vagrancy** (Baltimore: Penguin Books, 1963); Edward Rose et al., **The Unattached Society** (University of Colorado, Institute of Behavioral Science, Bureau of Sociological Research, no. 24, September 1965).

6. Wallace, **Skid Row as a Way of Life**, pp. 23-25.

7. Estimates as to what proportion of Skid Row residents are heavy drinkers vary with the investigator and the area under discussion. Wallace, **Skid Row as a Way of Life**, p. 182, suggests that almost all in the Skid Row of his study are heavy drinkers. Donald J. Bogue, **Skid Row in American Cities**, pp. 92-93, estimates that 65 percent of Chicago Skid Row residents have been arrested as drunk, but that only about 30-35 percent are alcoholics.

8. The social pathology point of view is best explained in C. Wright Mills, "The Professional Ideology of the Social Pathologists," **American Journal of Sociology**, 49, no. 2, September 1943, 165-80. An alternative view, that a social problem is what men decide and define it to be, is found in Richard C. Fuller and Richard R. Myers, "The Natural History of a Social Problem," **American Sociological Review**, 6, June 1941, 320-29.

9. So cognizant are Pacific City's Urban Redevelopment leaders of the effect of deteriorated buildings on the property value of adjacent structures that they plan to have a sort of neutral or buffer zone (i.e., an area of improved buildings) between the remainder of Skid Row and that portion destined to be torn down and replaced with an expensive sports arena and shopping mall.

10. Not all social theorists agree that men will automatically and uniformly improve if their surroundings do. W. I. Thomas and Florian Znaniecki were among pioneer sociologists to point out a possible fallacy in the idea that men's behavior automatically and uniformly reflected their physical conditions. See "Methodological Note" in **The Polish Peasant in Europe and America** (New York: Dover Publications, Inc., 1918-20), p. 12. See Albert K. Cohen and James F. Short, Jr., "Juvenile Delinquency," in Merton and Nisbet (eds.), **Contemporary Social Problems** (New York: Harcourt, Brace and World, Inc., 1961), pp. 104-5 for a discussion of the lack of correspondence of delinquency rates with improvement of economic conditions in an area.

11. "Report on First Annual International Institute on Homeless Alcoholics" (Detroit, 1955).

12. Capt. Andrews, Christian Missionaries, "Report on Conference with Eastern City Center Team" (n. d.), p. 1.

13. Discussion of a return to Skid Row by Arthur Stine, Executive Director of the New Mexico Alcoholic Rehabilitation Commission, "Report on First Annual International Institute on Homeless Alcoholics," December 27, 1955.

14. Newspaper reporter for paper in Pacific City,

1956. Editor's introduction mentions that Skid Row is an ugly world and the story he [the reporter] tells is not a pretty one."

15. Partial text of Pacific City Redevelopment Agency pamphlet (1966) designed to attract Skid Row residents to the agency for relocation assistance before their hotel was demolished.

16. Bogue, **Skid Row in American Cities**, p. 117.

17. Ibid., pp. 116, 117.

18. By middle-class standards, the men on Skid Row do not appear to make lasting social commitments. They have no family, no permanent employer, change hotel addresses often, and seldom have a roommate. (This latter appears partly to be a result of hotel rules.) The type of social relationships they do have appear to be extremely temporary (usually based on a bottle) and not dependent on what sociologists would term a primary group relationship. Yablonsky's description of the informal structure of the "near group" in connection with teen-age gangs seems also to fit the structure of the bottle gang. See "The Delinquent Gang as a Near Group," **Social Problems**, 7 (1959). (See also footnote 20, this chapter.)

19. See especially Bogue, **Skid Row in American Cities**, chap. 4, pp. 116-33.

20. For a detailed discussion of the undersocialization hypothesis, see James F. Rooney, "Group Processes Among Skid Row Winos, A Reevaluation of the Undersocialization Hypothesis," **Quarterly Journal of Studies on Alcohol**, 22, no. 3 (September 1961), 444-60. Pittman's discussion of undersocialization epitomizes this theory: "By undersocialization we mean that the person is characterized by limited participation in the primary groups which are necessary for personality formation, by minimum participation in social activities, and by inadequate opportunities for sharing experiences with others. His [the police case inebriate] life history is one that has been and continues to be deficient in membership in those associations of sharing that are found in the family of orientation and procreation, in the peer groups that stretch from preadolescence to old age, and in community activities." See David J. Pittman and C. Wayne Gordon, **Revolving Door: A Study of Chronic Police Case Inebriate** (New Haven: Yale Center of Alcohol Studies, 1958), p. 10. See also Robert Straus, "Alcohol and the Homeless Man," **Quarterly Journal of Studies on Alcohol**, 7, no. 3 (1946), 360-404.

21. For instance, a recent Health, Education and Welfare study of 1,343 patients in California alcoholic treatment centers found that: ". . . accidents kill seven times as many alcoholics as non-alcoholics, cirrhosis ten times as many, influenza and pneumonia 6.2 times, and suicide . . . 3.5 Times. A sampling of 922 drinkers (532 known to be and 390 thought to be alcoholics) and 922 nondrinkers at E. I. du Pont de Nemours indicates that various other degenerative diseases, including some not popularly associated with alcohol, strike drinkers with measurably greater frequency than nondrinkers: e.g. hypertension 2.3 times as frequently, cerebrovascular disease 2 times, stomach ulcer 1.9 times, asthma 1.7 times. . . . More alcoholics . . . die of cardiovascular catastrophe than from all other causes combined." See Herrymon Mauer, "The Beginning of Wisdom about Alcoholism," **Fortune**, 67, no. 5 (May 1968), 176. Courtesy of **Fortune Magazine**.

22. Anderson, **The Hobo.**, pp. 133-36; Bogue, **Skid Row in American Cities,** pp. 199-223; and Wallace, **Skid Row as a Way of Life,** pp. 119-21, all suggest that the Skid Row man's health problems are usually much more serious than those of the average population of the same age.

chapter 19
the hippie as survivor: a mecca on the mesa
vivian gornick

Taos, New Mexico—Taos is a village and a county (a "country" say its passionate partisans) spread out across the top of a 7000-foot mesa 70 miles north of Santa Fe, in the heart of the Sangre de Cristo Mountains. It is, as Mabel Dodge Luhan said, "a region of magic," a country of deep beauty and immense variety. The mesa stretches for miles and miles, some of it fertile lovely farmland, much of it magnificent sagebrush desert, all of it gathering itself at last, at a distant horizon, into the misted purple ridges and peaks which throw a ring around the world out here. On the other hand, one may turn from the mesa and descend into the Rio Grande Gorge (10 miles from Taos), where the river, being awesomely geological, has created one of the great canyons of the world, in its stubborn push toward Mexico. And yet another world lies, away from the canyon and from the mesa, up in the mountains. There one climbs up, up, up to heights of 10,000 and 12,000 feet through dense, green, primeval forests overflowing with the wildlife created by the endless gush of rivers and streams moving irresistibly across these slopes to mate with the Rio Grande. It is something to see, all of this.

Taos, for a variety of reasons, has for the past

From **The Village Voice**, May 29, 1969. Reprinted by permission of **The Village Voice.** Copyrighted by The Village Voice, Inc., 1969.

60 years attracted the serious artist, the casual bohemian, the beauty lover, the adventurer, the man who wants to get away from it all. Most notably, of course, it attracted D. H. Lawrence, who came and settled here in the '20s on a ranch about 20 miles north of the village and around whom there collected a colony of artists, a number of them still alive and kicking in Taos.

If, however, you should come to Taos (as I did) expecting to see the village dominated by Indians, Spanish-Americans, and ladies with gray bangs and wooden beads who knew DHL when, forget it. What you will see is Indians, Spanish-Americans, tourists from Texas, and—hippies. Hippies everywhere. On the streets, in the plaza, on the roads around town. Everywhere, one sees floppy hats, long skirts, Indian beads, bare feet, and thin wan faces framed by masses and masses of hair. And slowly, as one spends more and more time here— that is, hours and days—one realizes that the hippies are indeed living everywhere, not only all over Taos, but in every village, valley, and canyon for miles around, as far south as Albuquerque, as far north as Colorado. In fact, the hippies are entrenched in New Mexico. The word has come down from Hashbury and from the Lower East Side: New Mexico is the new mecca. And the faithful have not been recalcitrant in their response.

When I say the hippies are "everywhere" I

mean that theirs is the presence that exerts the most unexpected impact upon the newly arrived eye.

For instance: We drive into Taos to shop. Hippies line the road, some reading paperbacks, while an indolent hand is raised in a semblance of the traditional hitchhiker's gesture.

For instance: We go into the village two miles from our house on a Saturday night for a beer. In this village nine miles from Taos, 50 Spanish families have lived in absolute rural quiet for generations. Suddenly, from a house behind the church, strobe lights terrify the sky and acid rock splits the air.

For instance: In a driving rain on the rim road descending into our valley an emaciated couple hails our Saab. We stop. His incredibly blond hair and beard is matted and dripping. She looks heartbreakingly hopeless in her long red velvet skirt and her silver jewelry. Suddenly three kids and two dogs appear from nowhere and throw themselves about their drenched master and mistress. It turns out they are going in another direction altogether. We leave them there, all of us feeling helpless and dismal.

For instance: We visit a friend of ours, a schoolteacher from Texas who has settled here with her three kids, her potter's wheel, and her easygoing ways. She lives in cheerful bohemian disorder and the house is always full of spaced-out hippies. The place is like a stop on the underground railway: they arrive, get processed, and depart. One never sees the same face twice but there's always a wordless beard sitting in one corner or another of the room you're in.

For instance: We go hiking one day across the sagebrush mesa out near the Rio Grande Gorge. We are looking for the Mamby Hot Springs (fabled mineral springs, used by the Indians many years ago, as well as by DHL). We get lost in the desert, but find our way, circuitously, up through a canyon of volcanic rock to the rim of the gorge, coming out at the right place, just above the trail leading down to the hot springs. We look around in the utter stillness of the silent afternoon filled by the massive beauty of the gigantic canyon, the mesa stretching away from it, and the distant purple mountains. I turn to my partner in crime: "Oh, sweetheart!" I murmur. "Imagine! Just you and me and all of this!" At that moment Jesus Christ rounds the corner. He is tall and concentration-camp thin. Long hair, Indian headband, naked except for a loin cloth. About 21, his eyes are filled

with weary tolerance. He raises his hand in benediction. "Peace," he says to us, and passes on. "what . . . does he mean by that?" my unenlightened, over-30 husband wonders.

For instance: When we were looking for a house, nine out of ten Spanish landlords closed the door to us, saying "We no rent to heepies." This because we are "Anglos" (anyone who is not Spanish or Indian out here is, by default, "Anglo"), look younger than we are, and one of us sports a big black mustache. And they "no rent to heepies" because the hippies have often vandalized and abandoned their houses.

For instance: In the village of Truchas, many miles from Taos, where everyone is Spanish and so poor the place could double for a Mexican slum, suddenly a psychedelic bus comes careening down the central street, with 15 strong, straight out of Los Angeles, honking and waving.

For instance: One day on an errand we stop to speak to a neighbor about making a wood run (our houses are all heated by wood and coal). Out of the trailer parked on our neighbor's land there suddenly emerges a disheveled feverish-looking girl. She is blonde, barefoot, and wears only a thin tiny chemise. She comes straight up to us: "Ya goin' to Hondo?" (She means Arroyo Hondo, a village out on the mesa, where a huge crash pad is currently in operation.) We are. Okay, get in. She sits in the back seat, eyes closed, lips moving, swaying frantically to some rock record of the mind. Her name, she finally volunteers, is Linda.

Where are you from? we ask.

Now? she responds.

Come off it, the driver says. Where're ya from?

The Bronx, she says sullenly.

She's 22 years old and she's been making the scene for four years: L. A., Big Sur, Mendocino. She's been **everywhere**. She came to New Mexico because the scene in California was getting up-tight and she heard it was the new mecca out here. What does she do here, and where has she been living? "I don't know," she says vaguely. "We've had so many encampments, from Santa Fe to Taos . . . right now we're in Hondo. It's been groovy . . . some places have had some beautiful souls. What do I do? Why, whatever please me when I wake up. I consult my heart and my wishes and I do whatever they instruct me to do. I tune into nature. I eat, listen to music, I turn on. I mean, whaddaya do? If I make a few meals for the family, or give some yoga lessons, I'm happy. There's no script. I threw it away and I forgot my lines a long time ago."

■

The hippies exist here in every size, shape, and philosophical persuasion. And, inevitably, there are many people here who are called hippies who would not willingly so call themselves. But in the largest sense they all are, if one accepts as a broad definition of the word **hippie**: one who aggressively refuses, in any sense, to participate in middle-class life. And certainly if what you are is determined by the way you are treated, then many who would not subscribe to the title must, nevertheless, for, in the eye of the average Taoseno, hippies include: the acid-rock crash pad dwellers, the schoolteacher from Texas, the many ex-Berkeley swingers now living here in order to get away from it all (!), the Yippies, generally from the East and fresh from the Chicago front, who are now making New Mexico a stop on their way to the West Coast, and the commune dwellers.

The communes out here are the most interesting, the most exciting, and the most disturbing manifestation of hippie life and hippie point. It is there that one begins to grasp the meaning of what is happening in this place at this time.

Out on a plain in the mesa about 10 miles from Taos, a group of young men and women, mainly from the cities of the East, are living in tepees, building an adobe house, planting bean and corn fields. They draw water from a well, cook on a wood stove, have lived through a hellish winter. They intend to be self-sufficient, to live off the land, to rediscover functionalism. Above all, they intend to survive. Although they wear the long skirts and Indian things common to this part of the world, they look not so much like hippies as like those blurred photos of the pioneers of 100 years ago.

Up in the mountains, on 125 acres of magnificent land overlooking the Taos mesa and the purple sea of ridges and peaks beyond, another commune. Here, another group (not farming pioneers but rather "students of life," intensely influenced by eastern spiritualism), this one with the avowed purpose of attempting to "awaken consciousness," has left the cities to make a stab at cooperative living, far from the urban industrial life which removes men more and more from the sources of decision, the flow of consequences, the connection between a man's labor and the good it renders him.

Down in Placitas, near Albuquerque, another commune. Up in Trinidad, Colorado, another commune. Someplace else, just above the Colorado border, another commune.

■

If what is happening here in New Mexico were an isolated phenomenon, it would be only interesting. But what is happening here is happening all over the country, and that makes it significant.

Two years ago I crossed the country by automobile and was struck, as usual, by the presence of the continent. This past summer I crossed the country by automobile and was struck by the presence of the hippies. Everywhere, literally everywhere, across the entire nation: dustbowl faces and gypsy clothes. In college towns, on highways, in city parks, near mountain streams. In villages, on farms, in encampments on the coast, and out on the prairies. Hippies.

"There's been nothing like it since the hobo movement of the '30s," said a veteran observer of the scene. And, indeed, the analogy is irresistible. In the 1930s thousands of perfectly respectable men, feeling demoralized and betrayed by the nation, cut loose, set themselves adrift, joined the ranks of the wandering hobo. Soon, everywhere, the sight of these men: dead-eyed, silent, drifting. Often, when one looks at the hippies one is assailed by this image as by a peculiar whiff of memory, a memory all the stranger as it is a part not of one's actual experience but of one's sense of history.

But the Depression hobo's face is not the only one that haunts the hippie. Like the multiple edges that surround a figure on an unfocused camera lens, so the faces of a number of spiritual ancestors can be detected in the figure of this contemporary wanderer. Behind the hobo stands the "Grapes of Wrath" migrant. Behind him the frontier pioneer. Behind him the homeless immigrant and the war refugee. All those images whose restless wanderings signify unwilling uprootedness, emotional despair, spiritual bitterness, turmoil, and cynical bewilderment are there, not quite filling the hippie's shadow, overflowing the edges. For there is about the hippie's presence the unmistakable feeling that something in the nation is terribly wrong, that a gut-wrenching turbulence in the belly of the country is taking place, and that the hippie has stepped aside to utter prophecies of doom until the seizure runs its course, kills its victim, and allows the hippie to preside over the burial. For the hippie is, despite the Yippie's call to arms, not at all a traditional revolutionary, but rather a harbinger of social decay, a significant victim standing at the edge of a dying civilization, announcing by his separateness his intent to survive a lost cause.

■

The hippies are almost universally disliked. Here in New Mexico the Indians dislike their playing Indian and the Spanish look with puzzled distaste on their deliberate poverty, their irresponsibility, their dirtiness. (A diner in Taos sports the sign: "Keep America Beautiful. Take a Hippie to a Carwash." Across the country pretty much the same response. Out in Monterey, on the California coast, close to the Big Sur (which is crawling with hippies), old, once-beat friends say: "Can't stand these kids. They shit in the creek, out in the woods, won't use lime, don't give a damn about the disease they're spreading. They burn up the picnic tables for firewood. The business communities everywhere get worse, more reactionary after the hippies hit town. Everybody knows they're playing poor and papa's gonna pick up the tab eventually."

On one of the communes, a lovely, grave-eyed girl in a trailing cerise gown said: "Yes, I know they hate them in the Big Sur. We were there two years ago and they laid that stuff on us. We've never been back since. I know what you mean about the kids being offensive to people. But I think they're beautiful. I mean there's some beautiful souls among them and they're real searchers. Sure they do a lot of bad things and are irresponsible but that's because they're confused and their minds are hurting. They've lost their way and are true searchers after the good way. What I mean is: if a man was a poet and he lived as an alcoholic and a thief and he beat his wife, still he was a poet, right?"

■

What are they searching for? I don't really know. I think most of them don't really know. It would be easy to look at the worst of them, the acid-rock crash-pad kids out having a joyride of a nervous breakdown, the kids for whom papa is indeed going to pick up the tab, and say nothing. But it is impossible to so dismiss the best of them. For the best of them put one in mind of the man

in Plato's parable. Like him, they know the shadows they are watching in the cave are not the genuine forms and, having come up out of the cave, they are now blinded and groping in the light.

To go among the people of the communes (which, incidentally, number in the hundreds now, and extend from New Jersey to Oregon), to live and work with them as they live and work, was, I thought, to make a seriously coherent attempt at understanding what the hippies are groping toward. So, for a brief time I stayed at a number of the communes here in New Mexico. The longer I stayed the less I knew and the more impressed I became. Here, then, are no answers to the question originally posed, but rather a composite portrait only, based on very brief visits, of what I found on the communes out here.

The people, first of all, are an extraordinarily heterogeneous bunch. They come from everywhere and they have been everything. They are from New York, Boston, Denver, Dallas, Los Alamos, Santa Barbara, Seattle. They are painters, nurses, engineers, teachers. They are students of philosophy, Russian, sociology. They are farm boys from the Ozarks, waitresses from Fort Worth, construction workers from Oklahoma. They are the children of regular Army men, dentists, physicists. Some have intensely alert, responsive minds, some are dogmatic and plodding. Some are very worldly and theoretical, some are concrete, down-home types. What all share, however, is a profound conviction that in the places from which they come, out of the cities and families and lives they have known, there is a deadened and diluted life which is sapping their energies, a life that is intellectually sterile and spiritually empty, a life in which a vital sense of the self constantly eludes one. And, into the bargain, a life which threatens from all sides: Vietnam, IBM Is Watching You, Dr. Strangelove in Washington, Mayor Daley in Chicago.

Coming as they do from places where they have performed years of meaningless labor, they are determined that now their labor shall be with meaning. They plant fields to feed themselves, they build houses to protect themselves, they cook meals to sustain themselves. They take as much pleasure in the doing as in the accomplishing: bread is baked lovingly because the baking is as significant as the bread that is to be eaten. Earth is dug thoughtfully as it is as good to feel your body in use while wielding a shovel as it is to turn that earth into the adobe that will become your house. A lady painter from the Lower East Side had come to one of these communes with her husband and three kids. Hardly a suburban housewife, she never-the less said to me (standing, thin in a long skirt and with a smudged face, over a huge black pot filled with rice, in a kitchen that looked exactly like an army field kitchen on maneuvers): "All those years I was cooking and cleaning and doing the laundry—because that's where you're at when you've got kids no matter what else—and I hated it. Oh God, how I hated it! But here, it's somehow different. Here"—and she waved her arm to include the fields, the men on the distant building site, the women moving about at their various tasks, the mountains beyond, the kitchen itself—"it's . . . it's all, somehow, **obvious!**"

Children are everywhere, definitely a part of the hippie scene. (And, I might add, a very good answer to James Baldwin's old charge that Negro girls have children while white girls have abortions. It just ain't so anymore. Hippie girls have children. And if there is no husband to bear the conventional burden of fatherhood, then the kid gets absorbed into the communal life, just as the illegitimate off-spring of Negro girls got absorbed into the fabric of family life. Once on a psychedelic bus I saw four children of varying colors and sizes being handed around among the 15 or so people who live on the bus as though each one was the child of each person there.) On the communes the mothers of young children plan their work around their kids, but their kids do not prevent them from working. Chil-dren are handed around to all men and women like common property, so that there is an intimacy there between all children and all men and women, even though every kid is ultimately accountable to his own mother. How do the kids respond? They thrive! Almost all the children I saw were beautiful and healthy and a good deal sweeter and less hys-terically selfish than they are where I come from. (Oh yes, it is true that last year a group out here all came down with hepatitis because their methods of hygiene were simply idiotic and their children were endangered. But whose children are not en-dangered by the occasional grave mistakes of the group in which they are growing?) Another thing about the kids: they are all present and watching while their mothers and fathers work. To those kids daddy is not someone who disappears at 8 A.M. and reappears at 6 P.M. and God knows what he does in between. These kids know where their fathers are and, more important, what they are doing. They are growing up along with their parents, sharing intimately in this virgin effort,

understanding in their bones, before they can speak, what their parents are all about.

But the most important thing about the chil-dren is that they are the key to the most vital phenomenon of the commune, the re-creation, the redefinition, so to speak, of the family. Here, on the communes, I am deeply convinced, a new, a **real** family is being formed. What I mean is this: there isn't a person in the Western world who doesn't bear the psychic scars of family life. You're supposed to love your father and your mother, and you don't. You're supposed to be close to your brothers and your sisters, and you're not. And this terrible discrepancy rips you apart as long as you live. Here, I think, the gap begins to be closed, the wound begins to heal. People find they are close to those they're **supposed** to be close to—i. e., those they are living with—because they feel spiritually akin. One feels, and in some places this spirit is alive with power, that here on the communes af-fection, and therefore concern, grows out of a bond deeper by far than automatic attachment. That bond is the acceptance that comes of intimate knowledge born in an atmosphere of stress and spiritual confusions shared. These people **know** each other, in a true sense. They live together, work together, share an idea, a feeling; they watch each other under stress, and, above all, they share ad-versity and deprivation. These are the binding fac-tors in a life. These are the things that lead to a true sense of family.

"As far as I'm concerned," said one tall, lean, wildly bearded young man, leaning on a rake in the sun, "there's the brothers and the sisters, and there's everyone else." Needless to say, I was "everyone else." Needless to say, he would do whatever was necessary for the brothers and sisters.

This sense of the family is prevalent, all over, among the hippies. Even among the crash-pad acid trippers, even on the psychedelic buses, there is constant allusion to "the family." One girl on a bus said to me: "This is my home. I am more at home here than I ever was in the homes of my parents or my brother."

In each place I visited, it was the custom for the entire community to gather in a circle just be-fore the evening meal. All bowed their heads in a kind of prayer. In some places all were silent. In some, one among them made a brief prayer of thanks to a "heavenly father." In some, as at Quaker meetings, whoever felt like it addressed his prayers aloud. The first night I experienced the circle, I bowed my head in silent cynicism, smiling uneasily to myself. The second night, I listened to what people were praying for. The third night, I was moved.

Everywhere, there is an aggressive pursuit of one form or another of spiritualism: Hinduism, drugs, Tarot cards, astrology, meditations, the Native American Church (the peyote-using Indian cult). Everything but the conventional forms of Christian worship common to the Western World. At first it all looks absolutely nuts. But after a while one grasps the genuine sincerity of the pursuit and one is stirred to new realizations of the powerful need in men to which it testifies.

They live, many of the commune dwellers, in dreadfully primitive circumstances. They do so without affectation or complaint. And once you've experienced a cold, dirty wind blowing across that open mesa or a tepee in a rainstorm or an open A-frame in the freezing cold mountains or an attack of hepatitis or day after day after day of rice or corn for breakfast, lunch, and dinner or an outhouse half a mile from your sleeping bag, you begin to realize that a year of this kind of life is no mean feat. And you also begin to realize these people are serious. They are serious about themselves and about their life here. Their present is their future. They are living today but building for tomorrow. They intend to survive, grow, and prosper, they intend for their children to grow in the living, concrete light of their felt ideas. What is most amazing to me is that this instinct is alive in them to discover themselves within a community, despite the oppressive bureaucracy from which they have fled. But the fact is there is a penetrating realization here that men find out who they are and what they are not off by themselves in the woods, but watching themselves respond to other men's actions; that one restricts one's freedoms in order to taste the sweetness of freedom earned, freedom defined, freedom marked off; that one gains the whole of oneself by giving up a part of oneself; that men, in order to call themselves anything, must call themselves members of a nation.

And then, suddenly it hits you like a ton of bricks. These hippies, these rebels, these dropouts, left to their own devices, what have they done? What new and dangerous things have they done? Why, they have fashioned a life composed of community, hard work, the family, religion. They have re-created (in their own image, to be sure) an old knowledge fired by a new passion, born of original discovery. They have given new life to old, old needs. Because what they want, in a word, is only

a real life. Not a novel life. Not an aboriginal, orgiastic fantasy of a life. Only a real life.

The urgency of this need, and only the urgency of this need, accounts for the continued existence of the communes. After all, it is difficult enough to live with just one other person, much less 25. On the communes one sees evidence of strained nerves, clashing temperaments, subtle (and sometimes not so subtle) bids for authority or attention, the screaming need for privacy, the sometimes insane and exhausting unwieldiness of a consistently participating democracy. But these facts of life do not dominate the atmosphere. Just as one can tell when the irritations and bickerings between a man and his wife indicate the normal strains of togetherness felt by two people who are nevertheless vitally bound to each other, so one feels on those communes that are working that all these strains of living are subordinated to a larger need, a really convincing belief among the commune dwellers that for them now there is no alternative to this life.

■

At one commune, a tall young man, sweating in the sun after six hours on a tractor, said to me, his blue eyes intent and serious:

"After the bomb who's going to know how to be? We here are trying to learn how to be." I took his words metaphorically, although I knew that he meant them literally.

Our civilization has produced a race of men painfully out of touch with themselves, a strain of humanity which has some interesting features but God knows is diluted and without appetite. This generation, this group of hippies, is the first to successfully challenge the irreversible direction in which this life is going, the first to insist on attempting the full strength of manhood. Mine was the so-called Silent Generation. It was a generation caught in the struggle between the desire, on the one hand, to succeed and the desire, on the other hand, to change the world. What made it silent was the very real fears caused by an inquisitorial government and fed by our own passionless liberalism. We paid for our fears: we got pasted to the wall.

This cool generation has resolved the conflict by simply refusing to succeed. It looks middle-class America in the eye with an unwavering, unblinking expression. "Not interested," it says. "No, man. Simply not interested. No. Don't sweat it. Just not interested. We won't go to your schools. We won't be drafted into your army. We won't hold your jobs. We won't administrate your bureaucracy. We will not, in a word, become the heirs apparent. We won't go into the business. We won't perpetuate the life."

What is most astonishing about all this is that it has worked. The kids are doing their thing and, in so doing, have called their parents' bluff.

On the East Coast a mother I know recently listened respectfully while her 19-year-old daughter calmly informed her that she smoked pot and kept the stuff in the house. If her mother objected she would move out. The mother did not object. But then later, while the daughter was at school, she panicked and threw the stuff out. Afterward she apologized profusely to her daughter (who was really her pal). The daughter solemnly and generously accepted her mother's apology.

On the West Coast, another mother I know, herself a former San Francisco swinger, lost the LSD battle with her dropout son. She threw him out, then tearfully begged him to come back. He did. With his acid.

"What can I do?" the mother said sadly. "I need him more than he needs me."

And that's it in a nutshell. The loss of power in the middle-class parent is due to the fact that his extension or withdrawal of love, his promises, his threats, his rewards, his punishments, no longer carry any weight. They are simply not needed. And in an odd circular way, they are not needed because the middle class, having been challenged, has lost faith in itself, has lost the conviction of right-

ness which originally gave it its power, and now quavers like a humbled bully before its indifferent children.

My friend the Texas schoolteacher laughed to hear her house described as a stop on the underground railroad. Then, intensely serious, she said:

"Anyone who's out here is welcome at my house. Because if you're out here I feel you're searching for something. Why, dammit, you're not just a searcher, you're a refugee!"

Pioneer? Searcher? Refugee? Slightly different descriptions of the same condition: displaced by the fortunes of warring life, men become pioneer-searcher-refugees. The figure is not a new one, but always in the past he has been created by the hard objective fact of economic or political upheaval. What makes the hippie ominously significant is that he now makes this figure live in a time when economic affluence nourishes all and America is a leading political power.

So where does that leave us? Well, I for one, being very much drawn to the theory that history is made by the alternate stage-front-center position of progressive and decadent forces, and that the life of a nation or a civilization is determined by the force of its rising passion, its conviction of rightness (progressive force) which, once lost, can never be regained (decadent force), am rather taken with the idea that middle-class America is apparently on the declining end of its history and the hippies are its poster-figure symbol of the brave "life-affirming" victim, determined to rise from its own civilization's ashes.

topic 10

the human community: suburb and village in the posturban world

"Small Town, U.S.A." and "surburbia." Few designations evoke more stereotypical and more surprisingly uniform reactions than these. And few call for more cautious scrutiny.

The reader can readily elaborate on a host of suburban clichés: neat, look-alike rows of ready-made houses, each with its picture window, its well-trimmed lawn, its station wagon, its well-scrubbed children, its kaffeeklatsching wife, and its gray-flannel-suited, organization-man husband hurrying home from the commuter train, attaché case in hand. So too with the small-town American: we all know him, narrow-minded, given to busy-body gossip, provincial, unprogressive, or—paradoxically, for we have a split image here—homespun, warm, kindly, sentimental, hospitable.

Good and well. But what of the truth? Even a casual analysis of the growing body of empirical evidence is revealing. It is apparent for one thing that if all small towns and all suburbs share certain common properties, it is even more fundamentally true that they differ from one another. There are upper-middle-class suburbs, blue-collar suburbs, and "honky-tonk" suburbs—in part residential and in part a conglomeration of night clubs, pizza parlors, used-car lots, and bowling alleys. There are industrial suburbs where more people work than live, and there are slum suburbs abandoned to racial minorities by their former white working-class inhabitants. So also with small towns and villages: their dis-similarities and their heterogeneity are as impressive as their similarities and their homo-geneity.

The essay by Arthur Vidich and Joseph Bensman is extracted from their **Small Town in Mass Society**, one of the latest and most perceptive in a long line of community studies (among the earliest of which were the analyses of "Middletown" by Robert and Helen Lynd, the first of them conducted shortly after World War I). A poignant theme threads its way through the Vidich-Bensman description of Springdale, for this isolated town of about 1000 in upstate New York is gradually losing its distinctive flavor. Its uniqueness and autonomy are slowly but surely being erased by what one observer labels the "cul-tural and corporate tentacles . . . of mass society".

In Springdale, as in so many such communities elsewhere in the industrial world, urban controls and urban norms and values are supplanting the traditional patterns that have prevailed until now. Everywhere in Springdale there is an abiding conflict between the illusions of the past and the realities of the present and future, a conflict, Vidich and Bensman note, "which is avoided, it appears, by the unconscious altering and falsification of memories"—thus the almost strident insistence on such big-city evils as corruption and impersonality and such Springdale virtues as equality, neighborliness, and "just plain folks" wholesomeness.

In like vein, Dennis Wrong's essay examines suburban myths and suburban realities. In this case, however, the myths have been perpetrated and nurtured more by social scientists and journalists than by suburbanites. Wrong's analysis of the origins of the "suburban myth" are revealing. His conclusions warn that "conventional wisdom" in the social sciences can often be as stubbornly misinformed as the stereotypes that becloud the thinking of the man on the street.

chapter 20
suburbs and myths of suburbia
dennis h. wrong

Suburbia is no longer a very fashionable topic. In the 1950s, social critics and sociologists subjected the growing numbers of suburban dwellers to endless scrutiny, seeing them as especially representative of an affluent postwar America whose complacency and flaccidity were mirrored in Eisenhower's presidency. The suburb was the new habitat of the American middle class, whose taste, intellect, spiritual vigor, and mental health were savagely attacked in best-selling assaults, both journalistic and fictional, on "split-level traps," "cracks in the picture window," and "gray-flannel-suited" commuters. Social scientists, meanwhile, discovered new "styles of life" developing in the suburbs and linked suburban expansion to the revival of the Republican party, higher birth rates, and the upward mobility of the erstwhile urban masses.

An image of the suburbanite as a new kind of American possessing a distinctive outlook shaped by his residential environment emerged from these accounts. He was pictured as a former plebeian city-dweller who, benefiting from postwar prosperity, fled to the suburbs to escape his origins. He changed his political affiliation from Democratic to Republican to express his sense of social elevation and refurbished his religious and ethnic loyalties by rejoining the church and choosing to live among those of like background, seeking in particular communities that excluded Negroes and other minorities. His insecurity about his newly won higher status revealed itself, however, in the frantic pursuit of material status symbols purchased to impress his neighbors, who were similarly striving to impress him. The inevitable result was a pervasive standardization of life externally manifested in the monotonous similarity of houses, furnishings, clothing, gardens, and cars. The cultural and leisure pursuits of suburbanites were also uniform: watching TV, reading mass magazines and the latest bestsellers, gardening, and outdoor barbecuing.

But common interests and possessions failed to create true "togetherness" in suburbia, for they existed in the context of the wary status-seeking that had motivated the move to the suburbs in the first place. And in spite of the proclaimed virtues of roots and local community spirit, each suburb remained a temporary resting place for many of its residents, who on climbing still higher up the social ladder were apt to move to a more prestigious, higher-income suburb and start the whole process all over again. This transience gave the busy suburban social life, both informal and in such organized groups as the church, the PTA, the women's clubs, a synthetic and compulsive quality, belying

Reprinted with permission of the Macmillan Company, from **Readings in Introductory Sociology** by Dennis H. Wrong and Harry L. Gracey. Reprinted with permission of the MacMillan Company. © Copyright by the Macmillan Company, 1967.

the vaunted neighborliness so often extolled in contrast to the cold impersonality of city life.

This portrait of the suburban lifestyle possessed an initial plausibility, because it managed to link all the new developments in American life during the late 1940s and the 1950s to suburbanization. The postwar economic boom was bringing relative affluence to many who had not previously known it, the moderation of class conflicts in our politcs enabled the Republicans to win office under Eisenhower, obsession with the Cold War created a spirit of political timidity, marriage rates and birth rates were soaring to the highest levels in two generations,there was evidence of a religious revival in the land, and the mass media, particularly the new medium of television, were reaching more and more Americans. All of these trends seemed to attain their maximum intensity in suburbia, and the mass migration to the suburbs after 1945 represented one of the largest and most visible population movements in American history. Whether described in the neutral language of the sociologists or in the satirical and rejecting epithets of social critics deprived temporarily of their usual targets of political attack, the suburbs seemed to exhibit all that was most contemporary and most typical in American life. Thus was born a composite portrait of suburbanism as a way of life that has been dubbed by those who have recently challenged its accuracy the "myth of suburbia."

All this seems very passé nowadays. With the return to power of the Democratic party in 1960, the growth of the civil rights movement, and the rediscovery of poverty, our attention today is directed to social problems arising out of inequality and economic deprivation rather than to the psychological burdens of newly won affluence. The Negroes and the poor are overwhelmingly concentrated in the center of the city or in such rural slums as those in Appalachia rather than in the outlying metropolitan districts. Moreover, the cities, responding to the flight of so many of their former inhabitants to the suburbs, have launched programs of urban renewal that have created a host of new and hotly debated political issues. Sociologists have turned to the investigation of blue-collar rather than white-collar ways of life. And social critics now assail middle-class America less for its allegedly trivial leisure pursuits and compulsive conformism than on moral grounds, charging it with racial bigotry and insensitivity to the sufferings of the urban poor and the Negroes trapped in black ghettos.

Yet a social reality does not simply disappear when the spotlight of publicity is no longer focused upon it. The suburbs are still very much with us. Nor has the process of suburbanization slowed up: there is every indication that the movement of population to the suburbs has continued and will continue during the sixties at a rate equal to or surpassing that of the forties and fifties. By 1960, just over one-fifth of the American people (roughly forty million of them) lived in the suburbs; by 1970 the proportion is likely to be closer to one-third. Politically, the suburbs stand to gain the most from the reapportionment of congressional and state legislative districts required by recent Supreme Court and lower court decisions, even though few of the cases heard by the courts were suits brought by suburban voters. It is therefore worth taking another look at received views of the suburban way of life, examining not only their validity when first put forward but also how continuing suburban growth and change affects their accuracy as descriptions of social reality.

A suburb is an area adjacent to the political boundaries of a city that is more densely settled than the open countryside, but less so than the central city. It depends on the city economically and culturally; politically, however, it is a self-governing municipality. A suburb, then, is a **place** defined by its location in relation to a city, both geographically and along transportation lines. This elementary fact needs to be stressed in view of the prevalent tendency to treat suburbia as if it were a state of mind or a moral and spiritual condition. Thus defined, virtually all cities and towns in the United States—large, middle-sized, and small—have in the present century produced suburbs forming a population belt encircling their original political boundaries. But the distinctive social and political outlook that commentators have attributed to suburbia is clearly intended to characterize chiefly the suburban populations surrounding the metropolitan giants among Amercian cities. At the 1960 census, twenty-one million people (about 12 percent of the total American population) lived in the suburban belt surrounding the central cities of our ten largest metropolitan areas. This figure, however, includes residents of industrial suburbs with working-class populations engaged in varied economic activities, whereas the popular generalizations about suburbia apply only to middle-class residential or "dormitory" suburbs whose inhabitants commute some distance to work, usually to the central city.

Most of the earlier accounts of the suburbs failed to distinguish between the traits of the residents that were acquired as a result of living in suburban communities with their special relation to cities, and traits that suburban migrants possessed before moving to the suburbs and continued to share after moving with fellow citizens who remained in the city. Just as "urban" attitudes may exist in rural areas—say, among Great Plains farmers, a fair number of whom are today sufficiently prosperous and literate to own private planes, vacation in Hawaii, and subscribe to the Book-of-the-Month Club—so may the so-called suburban way of life flourish outside of the suburbs. Urban tastes and attitudes, nevertheless, could scarcely have **originated** outside of those dense concentrations of people of different occupations that we call cities. It is far less certain, on the other hand, that the outlook imputed to suburbia could have developed only in the special physical and demographic setting of the suburbs.

Sociologists who have continued to study the suburbs have recently concentrated their efforts on debunking the so-called "myth of suburbia" created by the popular writers of the 1950s and earlier sociological studies. Bennett Berger, for example, investigated a new working-class "mass-produced" suburb in California and found little evidence among its residents of the changes in attitudes and behavior alleged to result from the move to the suburbs. Their class identification remained working-class, their occupational and income aspirations were no higher than formerly, they did not participate more actively in the church or in other local community affairs, they regarded the suburb as their permanent home, and they continued to vote regularly for the Democratic party. William Dobriner, studying Levittown, Long Island, found that since 1950 Levittown has been "steadily drifting from monolithic homogeneity into heterogeneity" as far as the income, occupational, and even ethnic and religious composition of its population is concerned. S. D. Clark, a Canadian sociologist, has, in effect, insisted that the move to the suburbs is largely a search for cheap family housing and that status-seeking and mobility striving do not have to be invoked to account for it. Finally, Herbert Gans has criticized the general proposition that location, population density, and housing have the influence on attitudes and ways of life assumed by many writers on urban communities, whether slums, residential neighborhoods in the city, or suburbs. Gans argues that the styles of life associated with the upper-middle, lower-middle, and working classes are determined by social and economic conditions having little to do with place of residence within the metropolitan community.

The enormous pluralities won by Eisenhower in the two presidential elections of the 1950s gave rise to the claim that migrants to the suburbs were prone to change their party preferences from Democratic to Republican. But detailed analyses of the vote in 1952 and 1956 suggest that most of the suburban Republicans would have voted for Eisenhower even if they had remained in the city. Indeed, voters resembling the migrants in their social and economic characteristics who did remain voted just as overwhelmingly for Eisenhower, cutting deeply into the "normal" Democratic big-city majorities. Moreover, it is now plain that 1952 and 1956 were what Angus Campbell and his associates at the University of Michigan Survey Research Center call "deviating elections," elections in which the result was determined largely by the personal popularity of one candidate rather than by regular party preferences. In the more normal 1960 presidential election, Nixon was unable to hold the huge suburban margins run up by Eisenhower, and in 1964, central cities and suburbs alike, outside of the South, were carried by the Democrats in the Johnson landslide.

Both Angus Campbell and political scientist Robert C. Wood have shown that migrants to the suburbs in the 1950s were indeed more likely to vote Republican, but not because of the impact of suburbia on their political preferences. Rather, Republicans were more likely to move to the suburbs than Democrats with the same social and economic characteristics, perhaps because big-city Republicans more often came from families who had grown up in traditionally Republican small towns and rural areas a generation or more ago. Such family histories would explain both their Republicanism and their greater disposition to move to the suburbs in an attempt to recapture something of the uncongested, small-town atmosphere of their forebears. Angus Campbell has also shown that movers to the suburbs, though preponderantly Republican, had not achieved greater upward social mobility than those they left behind them in the city. So much for the view that suburban Republicanism is the result of party-switching reflecting the new conservatism of the upward mobile.

The high birthrates of the 1950s, linked by many commentators to the family and child-centered way of life of suburbanites, have declined in the 1960s and many demographers expect them to decline still further. TV sets are now as ubiquitous in city neighborhoods and even in the slums as in the suburbs. Studies of local government have shown suburbanites to be just as apathetic as residents of city wards and small towns when it comes to voting in local elections and participating in civic affairs. The trend toward increased church attendance by Americans has leveled off in recent years. Sociological studies have shown that all Americans, whether they live in the suburbs, the city, or the country, attach greater significance to their religious affiliations than was the case before World War II. More new churches and synagogues have certainly been built in the suburbs, but this is to be expected, because the suburbs have been growing more rapidly than other areas and does not result from any stimulus to greater religious activity peculiar to the suburban environment.

Social scientists, of course, greatly enjoy debunking popular myths. Some of them, indeed, appear to believe that the refutation of common beliefs about contemporary society provides the main justification for the existence of social science. (Sometimes it almost seems as if social scientists initially help create new stereotypes in order to make work for other social scientists in testing and correcting them.) Debunking is clearly not enough, for one also wants to know why a particular myth won such wide currency. The myth of suburbia may be no more than a mid-twentieth-century version of the old intellectual's game of deriding the middle class (épater le bourgeois), but even so it possessed and still possesses in many circles a surface plausibility that needs to be accounted for.

The myth partly owes its origin to emphasis on extreme and vivid cases in the earlier accounts of the suburbs. The various Levittowns, Park Forest, Illinois, as described by William H. Whyte in **The Organization Man**, the mass-produced housing developments quickly thrown up by private realtors described by John Keats in **The Crack in the Picture Window**—these are the initial sources of the myth. It is relatively easy to show that mass-produced or "packaged" suburbs, springing up overnight like earlier boomtowns, are not the only, or even the most typical, kind of suburb. Their standardized house types all similarly priced and the absence of the contrasts between old and new residents found in most communities obviously promote the social homogeneity and the busy

creation of new formal and informal groups that have been seen as characteristic of suburbia in general. Yet there are many other kinds of suburbs: traditional, upper-class suburbs, often dating back to the turn of the century; old rural towns that have gradually been engulfed by migrants from the city; stable, middle-income residential suburbs with individually styled houses, in addition to industrial satellites with noncommuting working-class populations. All have been increasing in population in the past two decades, though not necessarily at the same rate.

If the suburbs have long been more heterogeneous than the myths of suburbia suggest, it is also the case that they have been becoming even more heterogeneous. Suburbanization is, after all, a **process**, and one that is by no means completed. William Dobriner's study of Levittown, Long Island, built in the late 1940s, finds that commuting to the central city—that presumably universal characteristic of suburbanites—is less common than formerly as a growing number of Levittown residents take shorter journeys to work, often to new industrial cities within the suburban ring. Dobriner concludes that the suburbs are losing their sociological distinctiveness and becoming merely the most recent extensions of the city. "In our efforts to capture the sociological soul of the suburbs," he writes, "perhaps we turned away from the basic and most fascinating question . . . the way in which cities create suburbs only to turn them into cities in their own image."

Yet suburban life possesses one unique feature that helps explain the resonance of the myth: what Dobriner calls the "visibility principle." Middle-class ways of life that are concealed from public view in city apartments or residential backstreets become highly visible in the suburbs, with their open lawns and gardens, on-the-street parking, backyard barbecue pits and swimming pools, and, more important, the more informal visiting and friendship patterns that are possible in a smaller, less densely settled and more like-minded community than a city neighborhood. The suburb is middle-class America fully exposed to public observation. Take the status-seeking, for example, that is alleged to be a peculiar trait of the suburban style of life. In the city there is not only less opportunity publicly to display one's possessions as "status symbols," but there is far less incentive to do so when they will be observed by the vulgar throng in all its variety, as well as by one's own circle of class and ethnic equals, one's own "reference group," to use the sociological term. In the suburb, surrounded by neighbors of similar class and ethnic background, this inhibition disappears. It is not that suburban life breeds a frenetic concern with status lacking in city-dwellers; it is merely that the status-seeking propensities of the latter must necessarily be expressed in more limited, less public ways.

Although there is little difference between suburban communities and many home-owning middle-class residential neighborhoods inside the city line (except for the local government independence of the former), the suburbs are more visible to strangers. They are located in proximity to major highways and transportation lines into the city and, in the case of new subdivisions, have been suddenly and dramatically created by bulldozing out of exisence areas of the nearby countryside long visited by city-dwellers for picnics and walks through the woods on Sunday outings. On the other hand, middle-class residential neighborhoods in the city are often isolated from the rest of the city and protected from close contact with it by ecological barriers: hills in San Francisco or Montreal, ravines in Washington or Toronto, lakeshore enclaves in Chicago or Detroit.

From a broader perspective, it is clear that the myth of suburbia very well suited the prevailing style of cultural criticism during the politically quiescent 1950s. In the 1920s, also a decade of political complacency, intellectuals assailed the philistinism, sexual puritanism, and moral hypocrisy of the American middle class, seeing the small town or city as the place of residence of most Americans and the breeding ground of these attitudes. Suburbia played a similar role in the 1950s with

Whyte's organization man replacing Sinclair Lewis' Babbitt, and the oppressive togetherness of the suburb supplanting the zenophobic provinciality of Main Street, as targets of satire. Conversely, celebrators of the American way of life saw the small town in the 1920s and the suburb in the 1950s as the locus of its virtues: in the earlier period **Saturday Evening Post** covers of frame houses and tree-lined streets played the same symbolic role as glossy advertising layouts depicting ranchhouse living thirty years later. With civil rights, poverty, and international peace becoming major political issues in the 1960s, delineations of the suburban life cycle have lost the immediacy and sense of relevance they possessed a decade ago, just as the Depression and the New Deal ended the **Zeitgeist** of the 1920s and the cultural revolt against the small town that played so large a part in it.

Yet the small town was indeed becoming a backwater of American life by the 1930s as more and more Americans moved to metropolitan areas, whereas the suburbs are still expanding and even now contain more Americans than central cities, small urban communities, or rural areas. We cannot therefore dismiss them as objects of interest, regarding the obsession with them in the 1950s as no more than a fad of yesterday. The image of a homogenized suburban sameness was always a caricature and is becoming an even more distorted one with the passage of time. The increasing heterogeneity of suburbia, however, means merely that the distinction between **suburbanization** and **urbanization** as social processes is becoming a less meaningful one. The continuing growth and differentiation of cities remains one of the most significant social trends of our time.

chapter 21
small town in mass society: springdale's image of itself
arthur j. vidich
and joseph bensman

"Just Plain Folks"

When one becomes more intimately acquainted with the people of Springdale, and especially with the more verbal and more prominent inhabitants, one finds that they like to think of themselves as "just plain folks." The editor of the paper, in urging people to attend public meetings or in reporting a social event, says, "all folks with an interest" should attend or "the folks who came certainly had a good time." Almost any chairman of a public gathering addresses his audience as folks—"all right folks, the meeting will get under way"—and the interviewer in his work frequently encounters the same expression—"the folks in this community," "the townfolk," "the country folk," "good folks," and "bad folks." Depending on context, the term carries with it a number of quite different connotations.

First and foremost, the term serves to distinguish Springdalers from urban dwellers, who are called "city people," an expression which by the tone in which it is used implies the less fortunate, those who are denied the wholesome virtues of rural life. City people are separated from nature and soil, from field and stream, and are caught up in the inexorable web of impersonality and loneliness, of which the public statement in Springdale is: "How can people stand to live in cities?" In an understandable and ultimate extension of this valuation one may occasionally hear references to the rural or country folk, in contrast to the villagers, the former being regarded by Springdalers as the "true folk."

The self-designation as "folk" includes everyone in the community; by its generality of reference it excludes neither the rich nor the poor, for everyone can share equally in the genuine qualities ascribed by the term. This is not to say that the community does not recognize scoundrels and wastrels in its own environment; quite the contrary, the scoundrel and allied types become all the more noticeable in the light of the dominant genuineness of rural life. It is rather to say that the standard of judgment by which character is assessed in Springdale includes no false or artificial values. To be one of the folks requires neither money, status, family background, learning, nor refined manners. It is, in short, a way of referring to the equalitarianism of rural life.

The term also includes a whole set of moral values: honesty, fair play, trustworthiness, good-neighborliness, helpfulness, sobriety, and clean-

From "Springdale's Image of Itself" in Arthur J. Vidich and Joseph Bensman, Small Town in Mass Society: Class, Power and Religion in a Rural Community (rev. ed., copyright © 1968 by Princeton University, Princeton Paperback, 1968), pp. 29-39. Reprinted by permission of Princeton University Press.

living. To the Springdaler it suggests a wholesome family life, a man whose spoken word is as good as a written contract, a community of religious-minded people, and a place where "everybody knows everybody" and "where you can say hello to anybody." The background image of urban society and city people gives force and meaning to the preferred rural way of life.

Rural Virtues and City Life

The sense of community-mindedness and identification has its roots in a belief in the inherent difference between Springdale and all other places, particularly the nearby towns and big cities. For the Springdaler, surrounding towns all carry stigmata which are not found in Springdale: the county seat is the locus of vice and corruption, the Finnish settlement is "red," University Town is snobbish and aloof, and Industrial Town is inhuman, slummy, and foreign. In the big city the individual is anonymously lost in a hostile and dog-eat-dog environment. Being in the community gives one a distinct feeling of living in a protected and better place, so that in spite of occasional internal quarrels and the presence of some unwholesome characters, one frequently hears it said that "there's no place I'd rather live . . . there isn't a better place to raise a family . . . this is the best little town in the whole country." In the face of the outer world, Springdalers "stick up for their town."

The best example of community identification occurs when newspapers of neighboring towns choose to publicize negative aspects of Springdale life: making banner headlines over the dismissal of a school principal, publishing the names of youthful criminal offenders who come from good families. In such instances, irrespective of issue or factional position, anyone with an interest in the community comes to its defense: "We may have our troubles, but it's nothing we can't handle by ourselves—and quicker and better if they'd leave us alone." A challenge to the image of Springdale as a preferred place cuts deep and helps to re-create the sense of community when it is temporarily lost.

It is interesting that the belief in the superiority of local ways of living actually conditions the way of life. Springdalers "make an effort to be friendly" and "go out of their way to help newcomers." The newspaper always emphasizes the positive side of life; it never reports local arrests, shotgun weddings, mortgage foreclosures, lawsuits,

bitter exchanges in public meetings, suicides or any other unpleasant happening. By this constant focus on warm and human qualities in all public situations, the public character of the community takes on those qualities and, hence, it has a tone which is distinctly different from city life.

Relationships with nearby towns, in spite of the occasional voicing of hostility, also have a sympathetic and friendly competitive aspect. No one in Springdale would gloat over another town's misfortunes, such as a serious fire or the loss of an industry. Athletic rivalries have long histories and although there is a vocabulary of names and yells for "enemies," these simply stimulate competitiveness and arouse emotions for the night of the contest. No one takes victory or defeat seriously for more than a day or two and only in a very rare instance is there a public incident when outsiders visit the town. "Nobody really wants trouble with other towns."

When one goes beyond neighboring communities, the Springdaler leaps from concrete images of people and places to a more generalized image of metropolitan life. His everyday experiences give him a feeling of remoteness from the major centers of industry, commerce and politics. His images are apt to be as stereotyped as those that city people hold concerning the country. Any composite of these images would certainly include the following:

1. Cities breed corruption and have grown so big and impersonal that they are not able to solve the problems they create.
2. Cities are an unwholesome environment for children and families, and have had an unhealthy effect on family morals.
3. Urban politicians and labor leaders are corrupt and represent antidemocratic forces in American life.
4. Washington is a place overridden with bureaucrats and the sharp deal, fast-buck operator, both of whom live like parasites off hard-working country folk.
5. Industrial workers are highly paid for doing little work. Their leaders foment trouble and work against the good of the country.
6. Cities are hotbeds of un-American sentiment, harbor the reds, and are incapable of educating their youth to Christian values.
7. Big universities and city churches are centers of atheism and secularism and in spite of occasional exceptions have lost

touch with the spiritual lesson taught by
rural life.

8. Most of the problems of country life have
their origin in the effects which urban life
has on rural ways.

What is central, however, is the feeling of the
Springdaler that these things do not basically affect him. While he realizes that machinery and
factory products are essential to his standard of
life and that taxation and argricultural policy are
important, he feels that he is independent of other
features of industrial and urban life, or, better,
that he can choose and select only the best parts.
The simple physical separation from the city and
the open rural atmosphere make it possible to
avoid the problems inherent in city life. Personal
relations are face to face and social gatherings are
intimate, churchgoing retains the quality of a
family affair, the merchant is known as a person,
and you can experience the "thrill of watching
nature and the growth of your garden." Springdalers firmly believe in the virtues of rural living,
strive to maintain them and defend them against
anyone who would criticize them.

"Neighbors are Friends"

Almost all of rural life receives its justification
on the basis of the direct and personal and human
feelings that guide people's relations with each
other. No one, not even a stranger, is a stranger to
the circumambience of the community. It is as if
the people in a deeply felt communion bring themselves together for the purposes of mutual self-help
and protection. To this end the community is
organized for friendliness and neighborliness, so
much so that the terms "friends" and "neighbors"
almost stand as synonyms for "folk."

In its most typical form neighborliness occurs
in time of personal and family crisis—birth, death,
illness, fire, catastrophe. On such occasions friends
and neighbors mobilize to support those in distress:
collections of money are taken, meals are prepared
by others, cards of condolence are sent. A man
whose house or barn has burned may unexpectedly find an organized "bee" aiding in reconstruction. Practically all organizations have "sunshine"
committees whose sole purpose is to send greeting
cards. These practices are so widespread and ultimately may include so many people that an individual, unable to acknowledge all this friendliness
personally, will utilize the newspaper's "card of

thanks" column to express his public appreciation.

Borrowing and "lending back and forth" is
perhaps the most widespread act of neighborliness.
Farmers say they like to feel that "in a pinch"
there is always someone whom they can count upon for help—to borrow tools, get advice, ask for
labor. In spite of the advent of mechanized and
self-sufficient farming and consequently the reduction of the need for mutual aid, the high public
value placed on mutual help is not diminished.
Though a farmer may want to be independent and
wish to avoid getting involved in other people's
problems and, in fact, may privately resent lending his machinery, it is quite difficult for him to
refuse to assist his neighbor if asked. Even where
technological advance has made inroads on the
need for the practice, to support the public creed
remains a necessity.

For housewives in a community where "stores
don't carry everything" domestic trading and
borrowing is still a reality; they exchange children's clothing and **do** borrow salt and sugar. In
Springdale they say "you never have to be without . . . if you need something bad enough you can
always get it: of course, sometimes people overdo
it and that makes it bad for everybody, but after a
while you find out who they are." The process of
selectively eliminating the bad practitioners makes
it possible to keep the operation of the practice on
a high plane.

Neighborliness has its institutional supports
and so is given a firm foundation. Ministers and
church groups make it a practice to visit the sick in
hospitals and homes and to remember them with
cards and letters, and all other organizations—the
Legion, Masons, Community Club, book clubs—
designate special committees to insure that remem-
brance is extended to the bereaved and ill. The
Legion and Community Club "help our own" with
baskets of food and clothing at Christmas time and
organize fund drives to assist those who are
"burned out." The ideology of neighborliness is
reflected in and reinforced by the organized life of
the community.

To a great extent these arrangements between
friends and neighbors have a reciprocal character: a
man who helps others may himself expect to be
helped later on. In a way the whole system takes
on the character of insurance. Of course some
people are more conscious of their premium payments than others and keep a kind of mental bookkeeping on "what they owe and who owes them

what," which is a perfectly permissible practice so long as one does not openly confront others with unbalanced accounts. In fact, the man who knows "exactly where he stands" with his friends and neighbors is better advised than the one who "forgets and can't keep track." The person who is unconsciously oblivious of what others do for him and distributes his own kindness and favor without thinking is apt to alienate both those whom he owes and those he doesn't owe. The etiquette for getting and giving in Springdale is an art that requires sensitive adjustments to the moods, needs, and expectations of others. This ability to respond appropriately in given situations is the sign of the good neighbor. That this sensitivity is possessed by large numbers of people is attested to by the fact that friendliness and neighborliness contribute substantially to the community's dominant tone of personalness and warmth.

Of course, everyone does not participate equally or at the same level in being a good friend and neighbor. Deviations and exceptions are numerous. Neighborliness is often confined to geographical areas and to socially compatible groups. The wife of the lawyer is on neighborly terms with others like herself rather than with the wife of a carpenter. Farmers necessarily have less to do with people in the village and teachers are more apt to carry on friendly relations with each other. Those who are not willing to both give and take find themselves courteously eliminated from this aspect of local life. "People who are better off" simply by possessing sufficient resources do not find it necessary to call on friends and neighbors for help, though "everyone knows that if you went and asked them for something, they'd give it to you right away." Others have a more "independent turn of mind" and "will get by with that they have, no matter what, just to be free of mind"; the ideology of neighborliness is broad enough to include them "so long as they don't do anyone harm." The foreign elements, particularly the Poles, limit their everyday neighboring to their own group, but by community definitions they are good neighbors because "you can always trust a Pole to deal square . . . if they owe you anything, they will always pay you back on time." Some folks are known as "just good people" who by choice "keep to themselves." By isolating themselves within the community they neither add nor detract from the neighborly quality of community life and so do not have an effect on the public character of the town.

The only group which does not fall within the purview of the conception of friend and neighbor is the 10 percent of the population that live "in shacks in the hills." The people who live in shacks "can't be trusted"; "they steal you blind"; "if you're friendly to them, they'll take advantage of you"; "if you lend them something you'll never see it again"; "they're bad . . . no good people . . . live like animals." Hence by appropriately extending the social definition to give it a broader base than mutual aid, all groups in the community, except the shack people, fulfill the image of good friend and neighbor. The self-conception then reinforces itself, serves as a model for achievement and adds to the essential appearance of community warmth.

Good Folks and Bad Folks

"Of course, there are some people who just naturally have a dirty mouth. You'll find them anywhere you go and I'd be lying if I said we didn't have a few here." The "dirty mouth" is a person who not only fabricates malicious gossip about his enemies but also wantonly and carelessly spreads his fabrications. He commits the double **faux pas** of being deliberately malicious and of not observing the etiquette of interpersonal relations, and he is perhaps the most despised person in the community.

There are a whole range of personal qualities which are almost unanimously disapproved in Springdale. These are identified in the person

"who holds a grudge . . . who won't ever forget a wrong done to him"

"who can't get along with other people . . . who won't ever try to be friendly and sociable"

"who gives the town a bad name . . . always raising up a ruckus . . . always trying to stir up trouble"

"who trys to be something he isn't . . . the show-off . . . the braggart"

"who thinks he's better than everybody else . . . who thinks he's too good for the town . . . who thinks he's a cut above ordinary folks"

"who is bossy . . . thinks his ideas are always the best . . . tries to run everything . . . wants to be the center of attention all the time without working for it"

"who makes money by cheating people . . . who hasn't made his money honestly . . . you can't figure out where he got all that money"

"whom you can't trust . . . whose word is no good

. . . who doesn't do what he says he was going to do . . . who doesn't carry through on anything"

In almost the exact reverse, the qualities of a good member of the community are found in the person who

"forgives and forgets . . . lets bygones be bygones . . . never dredges up the past . . . lets you know that he isn't going to hold it against you"
"is always doing something for the good of the town . . . gives willingly of his time and money . . . supports community projects . . . never shirks when there's work to be done"
"gets along with everybody . . . always has a good word . . . goes out of his way to do a good turn . . . never tries to hurt anybody . . . always has a smile for everybody"
"is just a natural person . . . even if you know he's better than you, he never lets you know it . . . never tries to impress anybody just because he has a little more money . . . acts like an ordinary person"
"always waits his turn . . . is modest . . . will work along with everybody else . . . isn't out for his own glory . . . takes a job and does it well without making a lot of noise"
"worked hard for what he's got . . . deserves every penny he has . . . doesn't come around to collect the first day of the month . . . you know he could be a lot richer"
"stands on his word . . . never has to have it in writing . . . does what he says . . . if he can't do it he says so and if he can he does it . . . always does it on time"

Springdalers affirm that on the whole most people have these qualities. They are the qualities of "average folk" and "we like to think of ourselves as just a little above the average." "Average people can get things done because nobody has any high-blown ideas and they can all work together to make the community a better place to live."

What is interesting about the usual definitions of good and bad people are the types that are excluded entirely. At this level those who go unrecognized, even in the negative statements, are the intellectuals, the bookish, and the introverts. In a community that places a high premium on being demonstrably average, friendly, and open, the person who appears in public and "doesn't say much" is a difficult character to understand: "he's a good fellow, but you never know what he's thinking." "Book reading and studying all the time," while they have a place, "shouldn't be carried too far . . . you have to keep your feet on the ground, be practical." The intellectual is respected for his education, is admired for his verbal facility and sometimes can provide the right idea, but nevertheless he is suspect and "shouldn't be allowed to get into positions of responsibility." It is apparent that where stereotyped public definitions do not easily fit, nonconformity is still tolerated so long as it does not seriously interfere with the workings of the town.

In the community setting the test case of the toleration and sympathy for nonconformity lies in attitudes toward cranks, psychotics, and "odd" personalities: the ex-minister who writes poetry, the hermit who lives in the woods, the woman obsessed with the legal correctness of her husband's will, the spinster who screams at callers, the town moron, and the clinical catatonic. Needless to say these represent only a small percentage of the population. The point is that Springdale is able to absorb, protect, and care for them; when in the infrequent instance they intrude on the public scene, they are treated with the same sympathy and kindness accorded a child. So long as nonconformity does not interfere with the normal functioning of the town, no price is exacted from the nonconformist. At the worst, the nonconforming types are surrounded by humor. They become local "characters" who add color and interest to the everyday life of the community; because they are odd and different, they are always available as a standard conversational piece. In this way the community demonstrates its kindness and "lives and lets live."

"We're All Equal"

With the exception of a few "old cranks" and "no-goods," it is unthinkable for anyone to pass a person on the street without exchanging greetings. Customarily one stops for a moment of conversation to discuss the weather and make inquiries about health; even the newcomer finds others stopping to greet him. The pattern of everyone talking to everyone is especially characteristic when people congregate in groups. Meetings and social gatherings do not begin until greetings have been exchanged all around. The person who feels he is above associating with everyone, as is the case with

some newcomers from the city, runs the risk of
being regarded a snob, for the taint of snobbishness
is most easily acquired by failing to be friendly to
everyone.

It is the policy of the Community Club to be
open to "everyone, whether dues are paid or not"
and hardly a meeting passes without a repetition of
this statement. Those who are the leaders of the
community take pride in this organization specifically because it excludes no one, and this fact is
emphasized time and again in public situations.
Wherever they can, community leaders encourage
broad participation in all spheres of public life:
everyone is urged and invited to attend public
meetings and everyone is urged to "vote not as a
duty, but as a privilege." The equality at the ballot
box of all men, each according to his own conscience, in a community where you know all the
candidates personally, where votes can't be
bought, and where you know the poll-keepers, is
the hallmark of equality that underpins all other
equality. "Here no man counts more than any
other"; this is stated in every affirmation of rural
political equality—"if you don't like the rascals,
use your vote to kick them out."

In the private sphere—at what is commonly
regarded as the level of gossip, either malicious or
harmless—Springdalers tend to emphasize the negative and competitive qualities of life. One learns
about domestic discords, sexual aberrations, family
skeletons, ill-gained wealth, feuds, spite fences,
black sheep, criminal records, and alcoholism. The
major preoccupation, however, is reserved for
"what he's worth" in the strictly monetary and
material meaning of the expression. The image of
the sharp-trading farmer, the penny-wise homemaker and the thrifty country folk is reflected in
reverse in this concern with the state of other
people's finances and possessions. All men, from
the bartender to the clergyman, are capable of such
concern typically expressed as follows:

"I'd say he's worth at least $30,000. Why the cows
    and buildings are worth that alone."
"You'd think a man with his money would give
    more than $50 to the church."
"The reason he's got so much is because he never
    spends any, hasn't taken a vacation for thirty
    years, never contributes a cent to anything."
"There's a man who's got a fortune and you'd
    never guess it."
"What I couldn't do with his dough."
"The way they spend money, you'd think it was

like picking leaves off a tree."
"There's a guy making $2,800 and he's got a new
    Pontiac."
"Up to his neck in debt and he walks around like
    he had a million."
"Lend him a cent and you'll never see it again."
"He cleaned up during the war."
"There isn't anything he can't turn into a dollar."
"Figure it out. He's working, his wife's working,
    they haven't got any kids, and they're collect-
    ing rent on two houses besides."
"He could be doing well if he stopped drinking."
"He may be taking in more than me, but then he's
    killing himself doing it."
"If he'd loosen up and be human, this town would
    be a better place for everybody."
"But, then, I haven't done so bad myself. There's
    the car, only four years left on the house, and
    two kids through school."

These and similar statements, however, serve
the function of enabling a person to calculate his
relative financial standing. They are encountered
almost everywhere in private gossip, but remain
unspoken and hidden in ordinary public situations.

The social force of the idea finds its most positive expression in a negative way. The ladies of the
book clubs, the most exclusive and limited membership groups in Springdale, find themselves in
the ambiguous position of having to be apologetic
for their exclusiveness. Because they are select in a
community which devalues standoffishness, they
are the only groups that are defensive in meeting
the rest of the public. To the observer, they explain, "It's not that we want to be exclusive. It's
just that sixteen is all you can manage in a book
club. If anybody wants to be in a book club, she
can start her own, like the Wednesday Group." By
the same token they receive a large share of resentment; any number of vulgar expressions refer to
this feminine section of the community.

The public ideology of equality has its economic correlates. One must not suppose that inequalities in income and wealth go unnoticed;
rather, they are quite closely watched and known
in Springdale. However, such differences, as in the
image of the frontier community, are not publicly
weighed and evaluated as the measure of the man.

In everyday social intercourse it is a social
faux pas to act as if economic inequalities make a
difference. The wealthiest people in town, though
they have big homes, live quite simply without
servants. The serviceman, the delivery boy, and the

door-to-door canvasser knock at the front door and, though they may feel somewhat awkward on carpeted floors, are asked to enter even before stating their business. A man who flaunts his wealth, or demands deference because of it, is out of tune with a community whose "upper class" devalues conspicuous consumption and works at honest pursuits. "What makes the difference is not the wealth but the character behind it."

It is not a distortion to say that the good man is the working man and in the public estimation the fact of working transcends, indeed explains, economic differentials; work has its own social day of judgment and the judgment conferred is self-respect and respectability. Work, in the first instance, is the great social equalizer, and the purest form of work, which serves as a yardstick for all other work, is farm work. By this mechanism the "hard-working poor man" is superior to the "lazy rich man." The quotation marks are advised and indicate the hypotheticalness of the case because in common usage the two, work and wealth, go together. Where they don't it is because of misfortune, catastrophe, bad luck, or simply because the man is young and work has not yet had a chance to pay its dividends. But even wealth is the wrong word. Work is rather juxtaposed beside such terms as rich, solvent, well-off; wealth implies more economic differentiation than Springdalers like to think exists in their community. Thus, the measure of a man, for all public purposes, is the diligence and perseverance with which he pursues his economic ends; the "steady worker," the "good worker," the "hard worker" in contrast to the "fly-by-night schemer," the "band-wagon jumper," and the "johnny-come-lately." For the Springdaler the test case is the vulgar social climber, the person who tries to "get in with the better people" by aping them in dress and possessions which only money can buy. In spite of the social and economic differences visible to the outside observer, the pervading appearance of the community is that of a social equality based on the humanness of rural life.

The Etiquette of Gossip

Like other small rural communities Springdale must face the classic problem of preserving individual privacy in the face of a public ideology which places a high valuation on positive expressions of equalitarianism and neighborliness. The impression of community warmheartedness which is given by the free exchange of public

greetings and the easy way "everybody gets along with everybody else" has its counterpart in the absence of privacy implied by the factor of gossip. The observer who has been in the community for a length of time realizes that "everybody isn't really neighborly . . . that some people haven't talked to each other for years . . . that people whom you might think are friends hate each other . . . that there are some people who are just naturally troublemakers . . . that he'd skin his own grandmother for a buck." However, such statements are never made in public situations. The intimate, the negative, and the private are spoken in interpersonal situations involving only two or three people. Gossip exists as a separate and hidden layer of community life.

That is why it is at first difficult for the observer to believe the often-repeated statement that "everybody knows everything about everybody else in Springdale," or, as stated otherwise, "in a small town you live in a glass house." It develops that the statements are true only to a degree: while one learns intimate and verifiable details of people's private lives, these never become the subject of open, public discussion.

What is interesting about gossip is that in Springdale it seldom hurts anyone. Because it occurs in small temporarily closed circles and concerns those who are not present, the subject of the gossip need never be aware of it. Moreover, the **mores** demand, or better still one should say that it is an iron law of community life, that one not confront the subject of gossip with what is said about him. For this reason, though everyone engages in the practice, no one **has** to learn what things are being said about him. In the rare instance where one hears about gossip about oneself, it comes as a distinct shock "to think that so-and-so could have said that about me."

In a way, then, it is true that everyone knows everything about everyone else but, because of the way the information is learned, it does not ordinarily affect the everyday interpersonal relations of people; in public view even enemies speak to each other. When the victim meets the gossiper, he does not see him as a gossip and the gossiper does not let the privately gained information affect his public gestures; both greet each other in a friendly and neighborly manner and, perhaps, talk about someone else. Because the people of the community have this consideration for other people's feelings ("we like to think of ourselves as considerate and kind, not out to hurt anybody . . . that's one of the main reasons you live in a small town") relationships between people always give the impression of personalness and warmth.

The etiquette of gossip which makes possible the public suppression of the negative and competitive aspects of life has its counterpart in the etiquette of public conversation which always emphasizes the positive. There are thus tow channels of communication that serve quite different purposes. In public conversation one hears comments only on the good things about people—"a man who has always done good things for the town"; "a swell guy"; "she's always doing good things for people"; "a person who never asks anything in return." More than this, the level of public conversation always focuses on the collective success of the community and the individual successes of its members. People comment on the success of a charitable drive, on the way a money-raising project "went over the top," on "what a good program it was," on the excellence of the actors' performance. These same themes become the subject of self-congratulatory newspaper articles. When failures occur, when the play "was a flop," as of course must happen from time to time, one senses what is almost a communal conspiracy against any further public mention of it. So too with the successes of individuals—the man who after many years of diligence finally gets a good job, the person who completes a correspondence course, the local girl who gets a college degree, the local boy who makes good in the city, the man who finally succeeds in establishing himself in business, the winner of a contest, the high scorer, the person who has his name in a city newspaper— all such successes are given recognition in conventional conversation and in the press. At the public level all types of success are given public recognition while failure is treated with silence. It is because of the double and separate set of communication channels that negative gossip seldom colors the friendly ethos and the successful mood of the public life of the community.

topic 11

structured social inequality: the underclass in america

We would be hard put to find diagnoses of the ills of the impoverished as apt as the two quoted below, because—when it comes down to it—poverty amounts to **powerlessness.**

Poverty is the lack of power to command events.
[John Seeley, 1966]

The people of the other America do not . . . belong to
unions . . . or to political parties. They are without lobbies of
their own; they put forward no legislative program. As a
group, they are atomized. They have no face; they have no
voice. [Michael Harrington, 1962]

Powerlessness is a fundamental incapacity to determine one's life-chances in the face of others' ascendency in the same sphere. It is the primary determinant of social-class position in this and all systems of social inequality (which is to say everywhere in all times).

The powerless were the underclass in the classical civilizations of China, India, and the Fertile Crescent, in medieval Europe and Japan, and in the slave states of our own Deep South, and they are today in Third-World haciendas and in the ghettos, barrios, and hinterlands of industrial societies everywhere. To be powerless, moreover, is to have too little food, meager education, dilapidated and overcrowded dwellings, a host of unattended physical and psychological disabilities, and—perhaps most significant of all—no avenue to the jobs and incomes that allow one to escape from the vicious circle.

Thus there is the paradox, which is only seemingly paradoxical—the stubborn reality that poverty can and does endure even in the midst of material plenty, rising standards of living, and growing spending power. The United States, like such other thriving, industrial, mass-consumption giants as Japan and West Germany, is a vivid case in point. To hunger in such nations as these, where so many are overfed, is a degrading insult—and surely even more demoralizing than to live in poverty in a country where there is no televized promise of plenitude and luxury with which to compare one's own deprivation.

The selections in this section deal with the plight of the underdog: with the itinerant farm laborers who are herded from one of America's shabby migrant camps to another (Truman Moore, "Slaves for Rent: The Shame of American Farming"); with the helplessness of the elderly poor (Ben Seligman, "The Poverty of Aging"); and with the underfed, unemployable inhabitants of Appalachia (Harriette Arnow, "The Gray Woman of Appalachia").

This section does not allude to the millions of other Americans who suffer sporadic or total poverty: those, for instance, who live in big-city ghettos, in the barrios and Indian reservations of the Southwest, and in a myriad of impoverished hamlets, sharecroppers' shacks, and tenements. Nor does it mention the majority of Americans who are in the middle and upper reaches of the stratification system. Nonetheless, we shall repeatedly come to grips with all these facets of structured social inequality in other portions of this book as we explore the many-sidedness of social life in our posturban world.

chapter 22
slaves for rent: the shame of american farming
truman moore

Each year when the harvest begins, thousands of buses haul thousands of crews to fields across America as millions of migrant workers hit the road. They ride in flatbed trucks or old condemned school buses patched together for just one more season. They go by car: Hudson bombers with engines knocking, laying a smoke screen of oil; prewar Fords packed with bags, bundles, pots and pans, children crying. They go in pickups made into mobile tents—a home for the season. They ride the rods of the "friendly" Southern Pacific.

They come from farms in the Black Belt, from closed mines in the mountains of Kentucky and West Virginia, from wherever men are desperate for work. They come by whatever means they can find. These are the migrants—the gasoline gypsies, the rubber tramps—crossing and recrossing America, scouring the countryside in a land where the season never ends. There's always a harvest somewhere.

From Florida to Oregon the fruit tramp pursues the orchards. From Texas to Michigan the berry migrants work from field to field. Two million men, women, and children invade every state of the Union to pick fruit, to chop cotton, to scrap beans, to top onions, to bunch carrots, to pull corn, to fill their hampers with the richest harvest earth every yielded to man.

The circus and the college house parties leave Florida after Easter. The first week of April, the major league clubs wind up their spring training and go home to play ball. The snowbirds start back to the cities of the North with their tans. And the migrants form crews and follow the sun. Sometimes a single bus will carry a crew; sometimes they pass in ragged convoys as the migrant battalions rumble out of Florida and up the Eastern seaboard.

The invasion hits South Carolina in May, North Carolina and Virginia by June. By late summer they have passed through Pennsylvania into New Jersey and New York State. Some go into Delaware and Maryland, others to Long Island, and a few on to Maine. By October the upstate crops are in, and the migrant tide flows back to the southern tip of Florida.

The workers find little to do in November. It is after a lean Thanksgiving and a bleak Christmas that hands are needed again in the fields and groves of the winter gardens.

From Texas the pattern is much the same. This is the home base of the largest migrant group. The exodus begins in early spring. Storekeepers close down for the season as the little towns depopulate. Everyone who can bend and stoop starts for the great corporate farms of the North and the West. From the steaming valleys of Arizona and California to the great Pacific Northwest comes a string of harvests. There is no crop in the world that can't be grown on the Pacific coast, and relatively few that aren't. Where once was a vast desert wasteland, there are now the rich irrigated valleys, principally the Imperial and the San Joaquin. In steady sun and several inches of water, crop after crop is produced with factorylike precision.

Into all these fields, through state after state, the migrants cut a footpath across America. But in spite of their mobility, the migrants are shut off in their own world. Migrant America is a network of side roads, of farm towns and labor camps and riverbanks, of fields and packing sheds. The famous cities are not New York, Boston, and San Francisco, but the capitals of the agricultural empire of the big growers: Homestead and Belle Glade in Florida; Stockton in California; Riverhead on Long Island; and Benton Harbor in Michigan. For the migrants, no roadside motel or tavern offers a neon welcome. The host community sees them not as a potential payroll but as a blight to the community's health and a threat to the relief rolls. Businessmen, dance bands, and tourists making their way across the country find many services and comforts at their disposal. The migrant can hope at most for good weather, a grassy bank, and a filling station that will permit him to use the rest room.

There is always blood on the harvest moon. No one knows how many luckless migrants have died on their way to gather the harvest. Only a few of the more spectacular crashes make their way to America's breakfast table by way of the local newspaper. A few years ago, a half-ton truck left Texas for the sugar-beet fields of Wyoming. In it were fifty-four migrant workers. As the truck neared the outskirts of Agate, Colorado, the driver suddenly hit the brakes. The truck spun around and turned over twice, scattering workers across the highway. There was one death, a baby who died in a Denver hospital shortly after the accident. In October, 1963, not three miles from the spot in Fayetteville, North Carolina, where a truckload of migrants died in 1957, a truck carrying twenty-four bean-pickers turned over when a tire blew out, strewing its human cargo like a handful of oats. Fortunately no one was killed.

When the ICC was considering regulation of migrant transportation in 1957, a representative of the "jolly" Green Giant Company complained that restriction of travel between 8 p.m. and 6 a.m. was a hardship on the workers and employers. "It has been been our experience," said the company's man, "that these trucks can complete the trip from Texas to Wisconsin in from fifty to sixty hours with stops only for meals, gasoline, and general stretching."

A vegetable packer said that it was practically impossible to attach seats securely and still use the trucks to haul produce. He did not advance this as an argument against carrying workers in produce trucks, but against using seats. Many crew leaders use trucks because of the extra money they can make hauling the crops from the fields to the processors. Jon Misner, the director of migrant labor at Stokely-Van Camp in Indianapolis, said he knew crew leaders who made $15,000 hauling vegetables—in an eight-week season.

THE CREW LEADER

Little Jim was a good crew leader. His bus, the Bean-picker Special, was a bit run-down, and the tires were slick. But the driver was sober and careful. The camps that Little Jim found for his crew while they were on the road were not always what he had promised them, but he could hardly help that. He couldn't demand that the grower put the crew up in the Holiday Inn.

The crew went hungry before the crop came in, but Little Jim never told them he was going to feed them. If he lent them money to buy food before they got work, he charged them no more than the going rates, just as a bank would. And he had not been greedy about the money he took from their pay. A dime out of every dollar was his take. He stuck to it. And he charged a couple of dollars for each job he got them, and there were no more than three or four a season. While they were on the road, he got them to "help on the gas." When he deducted for social security, he always turned it in, as he was supposed to. If there was a big shopping center near the camp, he'd stop on the way back from the field so that the crew could do their shopping there instead of in the little stores near the camps, which always overcharged.

His wife thought he was stupid to pass up any chance to make money. So he sold moonshine. There was a good profit in that. "I keep a little around because some of them—they won't work without it. If you don't have it for them, they'll go out and get it." He bought from a bootlegger for

$1.00 a quart and sold it in the fields at $.50 a shot. A heavy drinker gets thirsty in the field. But Little Jim had to be careful not to give a bad drinker too much. He had one worker named Leroy Small, who was a mean drunk. He pulled out a homemade machete one afternoon and almost took a man's head off. After that Little Jim was more careful.

He was usually on the road with the crew four to five months a year. During that time, he was the crew's official representative. It is the crew leader, not the grower or the corporate farm, who is recognized as the employer. Whether or not a migrant ends the season money ahead or money behind often depends on his crew leader.

There are more than 8000 crew leaders in the migrant streams. They come in all shades of reliability and honesty. Good or bad, the crew leaders perform a service that is invaluable to the grower. A grower in Maryland can make a simple agreement with a crew leader to supply a given number of migrants at a specified date and for a stipulated price. The farmer, theoretically, can rest assured that his labor problems will be taken care of. In practice, however, he can never rest easy until he sees the crew pull into camp. An unscrupulous crew leader can shift his crew to a higher-paying farm at the last minute. The first farmer can easily lose his crop for lack of a harvest crew. Because both the migrants and the farmers depend on the crew leader, he is in a good position to take advantage of both. Hamilton Daniels was like that.

You had to admire Hamp. He was a thorough professional, with imagination and style. He usually honored his obligations to deliver the promised number of workers at the agreed price and time. Sometimes he came a little late though, because he would stop for a few small unscheduled jobs on the way. Born in New Orleans, a diplomat and a shrewd judge of character, Hamp had a quick intelligence far beyond what five years in school had given him. He knew how to get along with the white growers. He just played Uncle Tom.

Sometimes when the grower was around, Hamp would ride herd on the crew just to let the man know he was in charge. But the growers knew that. They depended on Hamp to bring the migrants in on time and get them out when the work was done. Neither Hamp nor the grower would profit by argument. His dealings with the growers were usually cordial; a balance of power existed that neither cared to test.

Hamp could make a flat price for harvesting and then cut the crew's pay as low as they'd stand for. On a flat-fee basis, Hamp's profit was the difference between what the grower paid him and what he paid the crew. Hamp didn't care for this because if the weather was too hot or it rained too much, he might even lose money.

If there was a good crop and a high market, the grower might agree to an hourly rate so the crew would take their time and not damage the crop. But the usual agreement was a piece rate. This fixed the cost for Hamp and the grower. The rates were usually set up on a sliding scale. When the crop was good, the rates were lower, and as the fields thinned out, the rates went up. When the fields thinned out, the crew didn't want to work them because it was hard to make any money. So the grower would pay a bonus at the end of the harvest to all the workers who stayed on the job. But it really wasn't a bonus. He just withheld some of their money until the job was finished.

Whatever arrangement was made, the crew seldom knew the details. If the grower gave his camp rent free as part of the payment, Hamp might still charge the crew rent. He was careful never to cut into a man's pay directly, except to take out social security, which he never turned in to the government.

His dealings with the migrant crew were complex. For one thing, he lived closely with them. His impression on them was important. If a crew leader looked too prosperous, the crew might think he was crooked. If he looked too poor, they might doubt he was a good crew leader. Hamp managed to look just right. He has a pair of brown pants and a red shirt that were ragged to the point of fascination. He was the raggedest man they'd ever seen. Close examination of this costume would have revealed patches sewn over whole cloth, but the effect was one of arresting poverty. To contrast with this, Hamp drove a Cadillac. His garments attested to his humility and his car to his success.

In picking a crew, Hamp seemed to work with little thought or design. Actually, he was very careful about whom he took on. He wouldn't take boys who looked as if they were trying to save money for college in the fall. They held too tight to their money, and most of them would leave the crew to go back to school before the season was over.

Hamp looked for the quirk, the twist: the reason this man or that woman wanted to work the crops. He preferred workers, either male or female, in the first stages of alcoholism. Some crew leaders wouldn't hire the drinkers, but Hamp knew better. You had to wait until a man was hooked. Then he didn't seem to know or care what you took out of his pay as long as he had enough to eat and drink. He might get mad, but he didn't leave. Of course, a hardened wino was worthless. He couldn't stand the pace. It isn't easy to bend over in the broiling sun all day.

Hamp kept a good supply of white mule and had places along the way where he could get it. There was good money in it. He also kept little white packets of dope. There was the real money. But sometimes it was hard to get. You really had to push it all the time to make it pay, and it was too bad if the government men caught you with junk.

He kept his hand in the ordinary rackets, too. He got a 15 percent cut from the grocery store near the camp. If the storekeeper refused to pay a kickback, Hamp would take the crew to another store. The crew seldom had cash, so Hamp worked out a credit system with the storekeeper. The crew members were never shown an itemized bill; they just paid what Hamp said they owed. Hamp also had beer and cigarettes in his trailer at double the store prices. For a $.50 bottle of wine, he charged $1.45. None of the crew stocked up on these things because they never had cash. With one thing and another, Hamp cleared about $20,000 in a fair year.

On the West Coast, the crew leader is called a labor contractor. (The term "crew leader" refers to the foreman.) Nick Peronni is a labor contractor in California. He has a fleet of buses and trucks that haul workers in and out of the San Joaquin Valley. He operates out of the "slave market," a big fenced-in lot that serves as a hiring hall, just up the street from the Farm Placement Service in the skid-row section. Before a man can work, he has to get a white card from the placement office. If he changes crews, he can't get another card. Even if the grower cheats him, he can't quit without losing his white card.

Most of the growers that Nick works for prefer to contract workers from elsewhere. Part of Nick's job is to keep too many of the local workers from getting on the crews. Nick does not travel with the crews. He loads the buses out of the slave market each day for short hauls into the valley. He also handles the paper work. No one is sure how much Nick makes, but estimates run high. As he

himself puts it, "If this thing blows up tomorrow, I'll go fishing. It'll be a long time before I get cold and hungry."

These men are representative of crew leaders. For the most part their lives are hard to trace. Some use colorful pseudonyms like Sugar Daddy, Cool Breeze, or Meatball. A few years ago, the **New York Times** reported that only half of the crew leaders coming into New York State gave addresses that could be located. Tax investigators in Oregon found that relatively few crew leaders had ever filed personal income taxes, and almost none had filed social security returns for the crew, even though all presumably deducted from their migrants' paychecks.

In 1964, Congress passed a crew-leader registration law designed to put dishonest crew leaders out of business. The crews have just started to move now. It remains to be seen what effect the new law will have.

THE TAR-PAPER CURTAIN

Across America there are tens of thousands of migrant camps. They are in the valleys and in the fields, on the edges of cities and towns. Some are half deserted. Some are behind barbed wire and even patrolled by armed guards. Migrant camps are within commuting distance of Times Square, under the vapor trails of Cape Kennedy, and surrounded by missile sites in the Southwest. They have names like Tin Top, Tin Town, Black Cat Row, Cardboard City, Mexico City, The Bottoms, Osceola (for whites), Okeechobee (for blacks), and Griffings Path.

Negroes from the Black Belt are dismayed by camps they find up North. Okies and Arkies who migrate today find camps much like those the Joads found in **The Grapes of Wrath**. You can drive from New York to California and never see a migrant camp. You have to know where to look. To borrow a popular analogy, a tar-paper curtain separates the migrants from the rest of America.

Let us look at a typical migrant camp which we will call Shacktown. Shacktown is owned by a corporate farm, one of whose foremen is in charge of the camp. "But mostly," he says, "we just turn it over to the people to run for themselves." In other words, no one collects garbage or maintains the camp in any way. The camp is built on the grower's sprawling farm. It cannot be reached without trespassing, and several signs along the road remind the visitor of this fact. Even finding it is difficult. Local residents are suspicious of out-siders who are interested in migrant camps. Re-quests for directions are met with icy stares.

Shacktown was built about fifteen years ago. No repairs to speak of have been made since then. Most of the screen doors are gone. The floors sag. The roofs leak. The Johnsons, a Shacktown fam-ily, have a six-month-old baby and five older chil-dren. "When it rains," says Mr. Johnson, "it leaks on our bed and all over the room. At night when it rains, we have to stand up with the baby so he don't get wet and catch pneumonia."

All the rooms in Shacktown are the same size, eight feet by sixteen. When the Johnsons moved in, they found they needed much more space. They sawed through the wall, a single thickness of one-by-six-inch pine, and made a door to the next cabin, which was not occupied. The exterior walls are unpainted and uninsulated. They keep out neither wind nor rain, sight nor sound. Cracks between the boards are big enough to put your hand through. There is no privacy, and the John-sons, like most Shacktown families, have learned to live without it. The windows are simple cutouts with a hatch propped open from the bottom. Some have a piece of clothlike screening tacked on.

The only touch of the twentieth century in the Johnsons' cabin is a drop cord that hangs down from the ceiling. It burns a single light bulb, plays a small worn radio, and when it works, an ancient television set that Mr. Johnson bought for ten dollars, through which they get their only glimpse of urban, affluent America.

Although there are trees nearby, the camp is built on a barren red-clay hill, baked by a blazing summer sun. There are four barrack-type frame buildings, dividided into single rooms. Behind the barracks are two privies, both four-seaters. The door to the women's privy is missing, but the rank growth of weeds serves as a screen. There are no lights, and no one uses the toilets after dark. The Johnsons use a slop jar at night. It is kept in the kitchen and used for garbage, too.

There is virtually no hope of keeping out the flies that swarm around the privies. But one coun-ty health inspector found an unusual way of get-ting the growers interested in the problem. The inspector would drop by the grower's house just before lunch and ask to see the migrant camp. When they came to the privy, the inspector would throw a handful of flour over the seats, which

invariably swarmed with flies. On the way back to the house, the inspector would manage to get in-vited to stay for lunch. At the table he would re-mark, "Well, I'm sure glad you asked us all to lunch." And there crawling around on the fried chicken would be a floured, white-backed privy fly.

During most of the season in Shacktown there will be several full- or part-time whores. The going price is $3. Prostitution thrives behind open doors. Venereal diseases are sometimes epidemic. In a crew near Morehead City, North Carolina, one woman infected ten men in the course of three days. Six out of eight crews working in the area had at least one syphilitic.

There are two hasps on the Johnson's door in Shacktown. One is for the family to use. The other is for the grower. If the rent is not paid, the family will find when they return from the field that they have been locked out. Some growers provide cab-ins free. Some charge according to the number of able-bodied workers. Rents run from as low as $10 a month to as high as $50.

The Johnsons, like most Shacktown families, do their own cooking. But grocery shopping is not easy. There is a small cracker-barrel store near the camp, run by the grower, but the prices are a third higher than in town. "We got a ten-cent raise," says Mr. Johnson, "and everything in the store went up a quarter. He wants us to buy from him or move out. It don't seem right."

Cooking is done on a small, open-flame, un-vented kerosene stove which serves as a heater in the cold weather. Fires and explosions are not uncommon. The cabins are not wired for electric heaters; natural gas is not available. Bottled gas requires a deposit and an installation fee. Asked if the tenants didn't suffer from the cold nights, the camp manager replied, "Oh, heat's no problem. You'd be surprised how hot it gets in one of them little cabins with so many people."

For most of the year the cabins are miserably hot. Refrigeration is nonexistent, and perishable foods seldom find their way to the migrant's table. The baby's milk sours quickly, and he is given warm Coke. Good water is always scarce in Shacktown. Between the long buildings there is a single cold-water tap. The faucet leaks, and there is no drainage. A small pond has developed, and the faucet is reached by a footbridge made of boards propped on rocks. This is the only water in camp.

Just keeping clean is a struggle. Water must be

carried in from the spigot, heated over the kerosene stove, and poured into the washtub. In the evening, the oldest children are sent out with buckets to stand in line for water. Sometimes when the line is too long, the Johnsons buy their water from a water dealer, who sells it by the bucket. "We get some of our water down the road about five miles," says Mrs. Johnson. "Sometimes I get so tired I'd just like to go in and die. We have to boil the water and then take it to the tub to wash the clothes. We have to boil water for washing dishes. The last camp we was in had a shower, but you had to stand in line for it half a day, especially in the summer."

The problem of getting water is widespread in migrant camps. A Mexican national in California said his camp was without water for a week. "The contractor said the pump broke. There was a small rusty pipe that brought enough water for washing the hands and the face, but we could not wash our clothes, and we could not take a bath for a week. The inspector ordered the pump be fixed right away. Now the water from the baths is pumped out of a big hole, and it flows through a ditch between the bunkhouse and the tents. When it makes warm weather it smells very bad. To me it looks like the contractor is not afraid of the inspector."

When several children in a Swansboro, North Carolina, camp became ill, a young minister named Jack Mansfield had the water in the camp tested. It was found to be contaminated. He reported this to the county health office, but they said nothing could be done since the camp had been condemned long ago.

Shacktown is a typical migrant camp, but not all migrants live like the Johnsons. Some find better camps. Many will find no room at all, and unfortunate workers will live, as they say in Arkansas, "under the stars." Three hundred migrants were stranded in Nevada when the harvest was late. "For days they had barely enough food to keep alive," the Associated Press reported. "They camped—men, women, and children—in the open, along ditch banks, without protection from winter rains and freezing night temperatures. They took their drinking water from irrigation ditches used by cattle. Many children were sick. And they had no work."

Migrant workers are often housed with the livestock. A Mexican worker in California described his camp this way: "We are installed in a barn which was used for the cows when we moved in. You have to slide the big door and go in and

out the same as the cows. The cracks between the wall planks are about eight or ten centimeters wide. This makes very good ventilation for the cattle, but it allows the wind to pass over our bunks at night. It is strong and fresh cow smell. It is necessary to use much Flit, and the smell of this chemical also affronts us. The Americans are very inventive. Perhaps someday they will invent a Flit with perfume. . . . The only person who comes to see us is the Father, who hears confessions and says the Rosary. We are ashamed to have him come on account of the smell of the cows and the stink of the Flit."

As bad as conditions are in the camps where the migrants live, they are worse in the fields where they work. A Florida Health Department report noted that at times crews refused to harvest fields because of the human waste deposited there by an earlier crew.

Americans are probably the most dirt-conscious people in the world. We are a bathroom-oriented society. Chains of restaurants, motels, and hotels across the country appeal to customers almost solely on the contention that their establishments are spotlessly clean. In such a society, it is not pleasant to imagine that beneath the cellophane wrapper lies a head of lettuce that has been urinated on. A storm of controversy erupted when a labor union showed a movie of field workers urinating on a row of lettuce. Growers charged that the picture was posed by union men in old clothes. Perhaps it was, but it need not have been faked.

The fields of the modern factory farm are immense. And there are no bathrooms. A Catholic priest observed that "most consumers would gag on their salad if they saw these conditions, the lack of sanitary conditions, under which these products are grown and processed."

After a tour of leading farm states, Senator Harrison Williams of New Jersey said: "In the fields . . . sanitation facilities are a rarity. Unlike other sectors of our commerce, agriculture generally does not provide migrant farm workers with field-sanitation facilities such as toilets, hand-washing facilities, and potable drinking water.

"We as consumers have good reason to be uneasy about this situation. Much of our soft food and other products are picked, and often field packed, by migratory farm workers. If we object to filth anywhere, we certainly should object to it in any part of the process that brings the food from the fields to our tables."

One grower, a woman, docked the workers an

hour's pay if they left the field to go to the bathroom. The woman stayed with the crew most of the day. The men had to relieve themselves in front of her. They found this humiliating but were unwilling to lose the wage.

Antonio Velez, a field worker in the San Joaquin Valley, said he was told by the grower to drive a pickup truck, which carried two chemical toilets, into the fields. The grower told him to drive fast so that the toilets would slosh around and be dirty, and no one would want to use them. He was afraid the workers "would lose too much time going to the bathroom." The idea of providing field workers with toilets and clean water strikes most growers as an unnecessary refinement. Consumers who realize that diseases such as amebic dysentery, polio, and infectious hepatitis (to name only a few) can be transmitted through human excreta may not be so convinced of the frivolity of field sanitation.

Dysentery is often considered a joke. It is called by a host of humorous euphemisms. The facts about dysentery are not funny. It kills 6000 Americans a year, finding its heaviest toll among children less than two years old, many of whom are the children of migrant workers.

It will be argued that to supply field workers with rest rooms would be prohibitively expensive. In 1955, as a result of newspaper articles and state investigations about the lack of bathrooms and a hand-washing facilities, a group of Western lettuce growers started a voluntary program. A novel type of mobile toilet and hand-washing facility was developed and tried out in the lettuce fields and found to be successful. Forty of the units were built and put into the fields in the spring of 1956. None of the other growers picked up the idea; so when the pressure abated, the project was abandoned.

THE CHILDREN OF HARVEST

The man put down his hamper. "It sure looks like rain," he said. The skies were a bright crystal blue, with only a trace of clouds to the east. The crew kept working, but a few looked up and saw the three men coming down the row. One was the grower, who seldom came around. The other was the crew leader. The third man was a stranger. He carried a brown leather case and a clipboard. The men just nodded as they passed.

They went up and down the rows, the first two walking easily. The third man, the stranger, stumbled now and then—a city man used to flat

sidewalks. They crossed the red-clay road and went into the south field. A woman looked up as they came past the stacks of empty crates. Before they were close enough to hear, she turned to the busy crew. "Sure looks like rain." Two small pickers dropped their boxes and darted through the vines and ran into the woods. Someone on the next row passed the word. "Sure looks like rain." Two more children ducked into the vines and ran.

The children hid beyond the road in a small clearing in a clump of scrub oaks. From here they could see the man leave. It was their favorite game. Hiding from the inspector was about the only thing that broke up the long hours in the field. In the camp they played hide-and-seek this way. When you were "it" you were the inspector. But it was more fun when there was a real inspector.

Luis at twelve was the oldest of the children. He had been to school off and on since he was six, but he was only in the fourth grade. If he ever went back he would be in the fifth grade, because he was older and bigger now. But Luis didn't want to go back. He wanted to run away. He had been around the country a lot. Last year his family went to California and Oregon. One year they went to Arkansas. Once, long ago—he was too young to remember when—his father took them to Florida for the winter citrus harvest. Luis was an ageless child. He had a way of taking a deep weary drag on a cigarette, and after a long while letting the smoke curve slowly out of his nostrils. His face was wrinkled, marked with a tiny network of fragile lines at the corners of his eyes and deeper lines across his forehead.

Still a child, he liked to play games. He enjoyed the gaiety at the Christmas feast. But at the end of the working day, he would stand stooped over slightly with his hands stuck flat into his back pockets. From behind he looked like a dwarf, a tiny old man whose bones had dried up and warped with age.

Billy was the youngest of the children. He was not quite five but old enough to do a little work. He didn't earn much, but it was better, his father said, than having him sit around the day-care center costing them $.75 every single day. His mother kept the money he earned in a mason jar. When fall came, he'd get a pair of shoes if there was enough money. He could start school, if there was one nearby, in new shoes.

His brother lay beside him in the clearing. John was ten. In the years that separated Billy and John, a brother and sister had died, unnamed, a day after birth. John kept them alive in his imag-ination. There were few playmates in the camps and fields that he ever got to know.

"I got two brothers and a sister," he would say. "And they's all in heaven but Billy there."

He called his invisible brother Fred, which is what he wanted to be called instead of John. Faith was the name he gave his sister. He saw her as soft and gentle, wearing a dress with white frills, like a china doll. He played over in his mind a single drama with endless variations. Faith was hurt or being picked up by some bully. He would come to her side to help or defend her. Then he and Faith and Fred would sit beneath a tree, and they would praise him for his bravery, and he would say it was nothing. They would have something cold to drink and maybe some candy to eat. He retreated more and more into this pleasant world. His mother had noticed his blank gaze many times and had heard him say, "Faith." She thought he was going to be called to the ministry to be a gospel preacher or a faith healer.

Robert was almost as old as Luis. He had been on the season for two years. His father came from the sawmill one day and said, "They don't need me any more. They hired a machine." His father had tried to make a joke of it, but late at night Robert could hear his mother crying. He knew it wasn't a joke about the machine being hired. They sold their house and packed everything into the car. Robert left school, and now they lived in one camp after another. Sometimes they slept in the car.

The man with the clipboard left. The children came out of the bushes, picked up their boxes. They bent over in silence and began to pluck at the vines. These are the children of harvest. "The kids that don't count" they are sometimes called. "The here-today-gone-tomorrow kids."

Inspectors from the Department of Labor find children working illegally on 60 percent of the farms they inspect. And no one knows how many hide in the woods when it "looks like rain." No one really knows how many migrant children there are. Estimates run from 10,000 to 600,000. The most frequently used figure is 150,000. One sur-vey in the olive groves of California showed that nearly three-fourths of the workers were children. An Oregon survey showed the importance of the child's labor to the family. There the average mi-grant worker earned $32 a week during the weeks he worked. But his wife and children together

earned $48. In some crops women and children do more than half the harvest work.

The birth of the migrant child will most likely be in a migrant shack or, at best, in the emergency room of a county hospital. His nursery is the field and his toys the things that grow there. A few camps have day-care centers. There are twenty-four such registered centers in the United States, with a total capacity of less than a thousand chil-dren.

The migrant child may never develop any idea of home. His family is never in any place long enough, and home to him is wherever he happens to be. He seldom sees a doctor. It is almost certain that he will have pinworms and diarrhea. Other common ailments untreated are contagious skin infections, acute febrile tonsillitis, asthma, iron deficiency anemia, and disabling physical handi-caps. A poor diet condemns the child from the start. A report on a camp in Mathis, Texas, showed that 96 percent of the children had not drunk milk in six months. Their diet consisted mainly of corn-meal and rice. A doctor commenting in the report said there was evidence of ordinary starvation. The migrant child is prone to scurvy, rickets, and kwashiorkor—a severe protein deficiency. Some reports have put the incidence of dental abnormal-ities at 95 percent, and others said that bad teeth were universal.

Epidemics, like the one in the San Joaquin Valley a few years ago, take a heavy toll. Shigel-losis, a form of dysentery, had been rampant in the valley for years. The infant mortality rate was extremely high. Within a short time, twenty-eight babies died of dehydration and malnutrition. The migrant child is also prey to a host of diseases now rare in the nonmigrant world: smallpox, diphthe-ria, and whooping cough. A medical survey in California showed that two-thirds of the children under three years of age were never immunized against diphtheria, whooping cough, lockjaw, or smallpox. Two-thirds of the children under eigh-teen had not received polio shots.

There have been many brave attempts to pro-vide migrant workers with medical service, usually on a shoestring budget and through the energy of a few determined people in a community. In the little farming towns around Morehead City, North Carolina, the Reverend Jack Mansfield got to-gether the first mobile medical clinic, a white trail-er called the Rocking Horse, equipped with the rudiments of a doctor's office. The Rocking

Horse—so named because it tilted back and forth when you walked around in it—was staffed by a group of local doctors who took turns going out to the migrant camps. The welfare department was persuaded to provide a social worker. The National Council of Churches provided a migrant minister.

By the light of a flickering kerosene lantern, the lines of workers waited to see the doctor. Some had unnamed miseries of the head and the chest, aches and pains that move up the back and sieze the neck in a vise. Colds, bad teeth, rheumatism, and chronic headaches could only be treated by the same white pills.

It would take a full staff of psychologists to evaluate the psychic condition of the migrant children. But even in the absence of any thorough-going study, the symptoms of frustration, bitterness, and disorganization are easy to see. A day-care center was started in the basement of an Arkansas church for migrant children. One of the most successful parts of the center was a workshop run by a young man named Alec Johnson. The shop was set up in a corner room with small windows for ventilation at the top. It was cool and pleasant on the hottest days.

Alec had assembled the usual carpentry tools and some leatherworking tools. By the end of the season, when the migrants pulled out, he had learned several things about migrant children by watching them at play. Joey Smith was a blond blue-eyed boy from Kentucky. The family had been on the road for almost ten years, which was most of Joey's life. He was two when the coal mine was closed and his father lost his job. When Joey first came to the shop, he was quiet; by the end of the second week, he was racing around the room banging the chairs with a hammer. Alec had to take the hammer away from him, and Joey sulked and refused to do anything.

Alec got Joey interested in making a leather billfold. "I got all the material together," said Alec, "and Joey started with a flurry of energy. But within an hour, he had put it aside and was toying with some pieces of lumber. I started him back on the billfold. Joey hit it a few whacks with the mallet and then looked around for something else to do. Joey wanted the billfold and had been excited about making it. But he didn't seem to be able to stay with it and finish. There were many of the kids who were like this. It seemed to be a characteristic. They start out with great enthusiasm, but as soon as they hit a snag, they toss whatever

it is aside and go to something else. They haven't had any experience in building anything or in solving problems. They have no confidence in themselves." Teachers, doctors, and ministers have the most contact with the migrant children. They are, understandably, not optimistic about the future.

Children have worked on farms since the first farmer had a son, and it has always been considered part of the rural way of life. But there is a difference between the farmer's boy doing his chores and the migrant child topping onions and digging potatoes. The two are blurred together in the minds of people outside agriculture. The blurring gets help from such spokesmen as North Carolina's Congressman Cooley, who enunciated the Blue Sky Doctrine: "There are no sweat shops on the farms of America," he said. "On the farms of our nation, children labor with their parents out under the blue skies."

Under the blue skies of Idaho, a twelve-year-old girl got her ponytail caught in a potato-digging machine. It ripped off her scalp, ears, eyelids, and cheeks. She died shortly afterward in a hospital. On a farm in California, a ten-year-old girl came back from the fields exhausted from a day's work. She fell asleep on a pile of burlap bags as she waited for her parents. As other workers returned from the fields, they tossed the empty bags on the stack, and the little girl was soon covered up. A two-ton truck backed across the pile and drove off. They did not find her body until the next day.

If children were mangled in steel mills, there would be a storm of public protest. But death and injury on the mechanized farms seem to pass unnoticed. Under the blue sky of the farm factory is no place for little children. Agriculture is one of the three most hazardous industries. In California alone, more than five hundred agricultural workers under the age of eighteen are seriously injured every year.

The migrants who follow the harvest are the only people in America who are desperate enough for this work to take it. Their children will be another generation of wanderers, lost to themselves and to the nation.

FACTORIES IN THE FIELD

The family farm used to be the citadel of virtue in the American rural tradition. Life was made hard by the vagaries of the weather and complicated only by the bureaucrats in Washington, who always meddled with farming. In 1900, when the population of the United States was under seventy-six million, 40 percent of the people lived on the farm. Today, only 8 percent live on farms, and more leave every year.

Today, the important farms, as units of production, are more like factories. Great cultivators and harvesting machines lumber through endless fields. Gangs of workers bring in the harvest. One cannot ride past these giant farms after the harvest is over and the crew has left without an eerie feeling of being in a land without people. A verse from Isaiah rides the wind: "Woe to those who join house to house, who add field to field, until there is no more room, and you are made to dwell alone in the midst of the land."

The importance of making the distinction between the big farm and the little farm—between the homestead and the factory in the field—is essential to the story of migrant labor. To begin with, the family farmer and the migrant worker are in the same sinking boat. The family farm, while providing an income and a place to live, no longer contributes significantly to America's food production.

If the earth suddenly swallowed up a million and a half small family farms in America—nearly half the total number—food production would drop by only 5 percent. Half of our food is produced by only 9 percent of the farms. These highly mechanized, capitalized, and integrated companies use most of the seasonal labor. Only a relatively few big growers (5 percent of the total number) use more than $2000 worth of labor a year. The real giants—the top 3 percent—hire more than a third of all farm labor.

It is through the fields of the farm factories that the migrant stream flows. And these are the growers that have brought foreign farm workers to America each year. The growth of corporation farming and its effect on the traditional family farm have been watched with concern for many years. In 1923 a North Carolina land commission issued a still-urgent report: "It is quite conceivable that under capitalistic or corporation farming, greater gains might be secured than under a system of small individual holdings.

"It is quite inconceivable, however, that the . . . farmer would be as good or as efficient a citizen, that he would get as much contentment and happiness for himself and his family out of his home, or that he could develop as satisfactory a community for himself and neighbors as he could and would if he owned the house in which he lives

and the farm he cultivates. The problem, then, is that of life on the farm, the development of rural communities and the building of rural civilization with which, after all, we are most concerned. . . . The late Governor Bicket said: 'the small farm owned by the man who tills it is the best plant-bed in the world in which to grow a patriot. . . .' Every consideration of progress and safety urges us to employ all wise and just measures to get our lands into the hands of many and forestall that most destructive of all monopolies—the monopoly of the soil."

The policy of the federal government has always more or less agreed with this. Nearly every administration has declared itself in favor of preserving the family farm. It is ironic that each, in turn, has brought it closer to extinction.

In 1963 the government spent $4.7 billion on surplus commodities. Most of the money went to prosperous commercial farms, with only pennies trickling down to the hard-pressed family farms. The government-support price is often more than the production costs of the big commercial farms. This means they can produce without worrying about the market since "Uncle Sucker"—as some of the farmers say—will buy what they can't sell elsewhere.

In 1961 two corporate cotton farms received government subsidies of $2 million each; thirteen great farms each received $649,753 on the average; and 332 farms received $113,657 each. By contrast, 70 percent of the cotton farms were given an average of $60.

The government has subsidized the big operators in a more important way. Until this year the commercial farms have been allowed to draw on the pools of cheap labor from other countries, principally Mexico. The presence of hundreds of thousands of foreign workers has naturally disrupted the domestic labor market, resulting in low wages and poor working conditions. The family farmer, who hires little outside help, has to value his and his family's labor at no more than the commercial farmer pays for gang labor.

The exodus from the farm is proceeding at the rate of about 800,000 people a year, although cities and towns have as little immediate need for surplus rural populations as the nation has for surplus farm production. It has been seriously proposed many times that overproduction is caused by a surplus of farmers and that we should let the natural laws of competition weed out the less successful. This way, the problem of surplus production and surplus farmers would solve itself at no expense to the taxpayers. But, as we have already seen, most of the food is produced by a relatively few big farms. And, of course, when the small farmer finally gives up and goes to the city, his land is taken over eventually by another farmer and remains in production.

As a unit, the larger family farm is not without merit. According to a 1962 government report, "Family farms [in this case those using 1.5 man-years of hired labor] are more efficient than large corporate-type farms. . . . When the management of a farm is taken away from those who supply the labor, there is a loss of incentive, diligence, skill and prudent judgment which are necessary to maintain efficiency." The report said that the advantages of the corporate farm lay primarily in superior financing and control of the market.

No farmer, of course, whether big or small, can dominate the market. But the vertically integrated farm is its own market. The perishable harvest from the field goes to the farm's own processing and canning plants and is sold canned or frozen under less urgent conditions. (In 1962, however, the government bought up $1.3 million worth of California canned apricots.) The small farmer selling perishable produce is completely at the mercy of the market, or specifically, the buyer.

Today the position of the buyer is stronger than it has ever been. In 1958, supermarket buying agencies handled 60 percent of the food dollar. At the present time, it is said that chain buyers account for 90 percent of the food dollar.

There are about 3.7 million farms in the United States. What seems to be happening is this: the 312,000 first-class farms are big and getting bigger; the 1,755,000 middle-class farms are struggling, and to survive they need a more equitable marketing structure, some government aid, and an orderly farm labor force; the third-class farms, of which there are 1,641,000, are marked for certain death if agriculture continues for much longer on its present path.

The farm of the classic rural tradition, the family farm, required little outside labor. A hired man or two were enough on the bigger farm for most of the year. And at planting or harvest, neighboring farm families joined together and did the work, going from farm to farm.

THE EXPLOITATION OF LABOR.

The history of migrant labor is sketchy, but its dominant themes are quite clear. The rise of the corporate farm and the growth of the migrant labor force were twin developments. It is arguable which came first. Some say the industrialized farm developed because growers saw a chance to utilize a growing pool of unemployed labor. Others say that the development of the giant farm created a demand for gangs of itinerant labor, and the migrants came to fill the need. Whichever way it happened, the result has been that the corporate farm is, and always has been, dependent on cheap, migrant labor.

The migrant force of today still bears the marks of our history. Since early America was largely rural, farm interests dominated the government. While manufacturers adjusted to the industrial revolution early, agriculture was able to win exemption from most of the social legislation passed since the turn of the century. Agriculture has grown from a society, or way of life, into a complex food industry without coming to terms with its labor force. Had the automobile industry been able to import cheap labor from underdeveloped countries, it is unlikely that the automobile union would have made much headway.

The commercial farm has never adjusted to the realities of modern labor conditions or wages. Furthermore, the modern commercial farmer holds on to the idea that he somehow has a God-given right to unlimited cheap labor. Never has he had to enter the labor market and make serious efforts to attract farm labor. If anything characterizes the history of the seasonal farm worker, it is this—fate, through famine or depression, war or revolution, has time and again delivered to the commercial grower an ample supply of cheap and docile labor.

The migrant drama caught the nation's attention in the thirties. Great dust storms swept the plains and dimmed the sun as far away as the east coast. Long lines of tenant families, the gasoline gypsies, crossed the desert into California looking for work. The dust bowl refugees were only one set of characters in the migrant epic that began long before the Joads of **The Grapes of Wrath**.

By 1934 the Anglo population in the labor camps reached 50 percent. As the bitter years of dust storms and depression set in, Okies and Arkies continued to stream into California in caravans of jalopies. It was ironic that after so many years of coolies and peons, American workers took over in a time of widespread unemployment. Hence wages and working conditions, bad as they were, got worse. For every job that was open, there was a hungry carload of migrants. Men fought in the field over a row of beans. For the first time Western growers admitted there was a labor surplus. The Farm Security Administration reported that by 1938, 221,000 dust bowlers had entered California.

THE BRACEROS

With the coming of World War II, shipyards and aircraft industries drained off the surplus labor left by the draft board. Food demands climbed to wartime levels. Another source of cheap labor had to be found. The government was induced to sanction the wetbacks. And in 1944 the United States spent nearly $24 million to supply the growers with 62,170 braceros—Mexican farm laborers.

As the war progressed, prisoners of war were turned over to growers, along with convicts. Japanese-Americans, impounded in concentration camps, were released to the custody of the big growers. Armed guards patrolled the fields. When the war ended, the P.O.W.'s went back to Italy and Germany, and the convicts went back to their cells.

The wetbacks remained, and their questionable legal position became more and more evident. Border patrols, on orders from Washington, looked the other way during the harvest season, and the wetbacks streamed in. The federal government not only condoned wetback traffic during the harvest season but actually encouraged it. The President's commission studying the problems of migratory labor discovered this incredible situation:

Wetbacks (who were apprehended) were given identification slips in the United States by the Immigration and Naturalization Service which entitled them, within a few minutes, to step back across the border and become contract workers. There was no other way to obtain the indispensable slip of paper except to be found illegally in the United States. Thus violators of law were rewarded by receiving legal contracts while the same opportunities were denied law-abiding citizens of Mexico. The United States, having engaged in a program giving preference in contracting to those who had broken the law, had encouraged violation of the immigration laws. **Our government thus has become a contributor to the growth of an illegal traffic which it has the responsibility to prevent** [Italics mine].

In 1950 when the "police action" began in Korea, President Truman appointed a commission to study the problems of migrant labor. The pressure was building up for more cheap labor to meet the anticipated new demands for food. The McCarran-Walter Act (Public Law 414) had just been passed over the President's veto. This was a new Immigration and Naturalization Act, which permitted the temporary importation of foreign labor under contract for periods up to three years.

Following completion of the report of the President's commission, the 82nd Congress, on July 12, 1951, passed Public Law 78. The commission had recommended a few months earlier that "no special measures be adopted to increase the number of alien contract workers beyond the number admitted in 1950." In that year 192,000 legal braceros (literally arm-men) came in under contract to work in the fields of the Southwest. Illegal wetback traffic began to decline, but by the end of the decade the number of braceros had risen far above the wartime emergency levels of either World War II or the Korean War. In 1959 there were 437,000 Mexican nationals scattered across the United States from Texas to Michigan.

Over the years growers have shown a decided preference for the foreign farm workers. The reasons are many. The foreigner many times does not speak English. He is uninformed about his rights and in a poor position to defend them if they are violated. He is willing to work for less and under poorer conditions. Imported farm workers are always single males. Housing and transportation are simpler. And when the farmer has done with them, they can be shipped back where they came from. And if any of them make trouble, they can be shipped home a little early.

Shortage of workers amid mass unemployment; foreign workers in record numbers while American workers can't find jobs—these are long-standing contradictions in farm labor. Growers say they can't find workers. Workers say they can't find jobs. Part of the answer lies in the definition of the terms. A shortage of labor exists for many growers when they don't have more than twice the number of workers they can get by with. Extra hands keep the wages down and the union out. The workers' idea of the proper labor supply is when he can choose between jobs and take the one that pays the most.

The theory of the laws that enable growers to import labor was that both worker and grower could be served. In practice these laws crushed the worker and gave the grower an almost limitless supply of cheap labor. Obviously, when a worker refuses a job at $.35 an hour (the prevailing wage for field workers in Arkansas, for example), he only makes it possible for the grower to get Mexicans. Until very recently, Arkansas was the third-largest user of braceros, employing about 40,000 annually.

An interesting example of the law in action was the shifting wages in the Imperial Valley. For many years domestic workers in the winter lettuce harvest were paid a piece rate of a penny a head for harvesting lettuce. This amounted to an hourly wage of from $1.25 to $2.00, good money for harvesting.

As growers began to use more braceros, the piece rate was finally dropped and the wage level in the valley fell. For several years prior to 1961, it was frozen at about $.70 an hour. When President Kennedy signed the extension of Public Law 78 in 1961 (for two years), he instructed the Secretary of Labor to see to it that the program had no adverse effect on domestic labor. As a result, Imperial Valley growers who sought to use braceros were instructed to reinstate the old piece rate of a penny a head. (It can be noted in passing that if harvest wages were doubled, the labor cost would be only $.02 a head.)

In anticipation of this change, growers had increased the hourly wage from $.70 to $1.00. But as soon as the Labor Department called for the old piece rate, 200 growers flew to Washington to protest. The department backed down and agreed that the growers could pay either $1.00 an hour **or** the piece rate of $.24 a carton. **The choice was to be left to the worker.** That the growers were satisfied with the new arrangement indicated that they didn't intend the workers, most of whom were braceros, to have much say in the matter after all. And the nature of the choice—between $1.00 an hour or $2.00 an hour—indicated that the Department of Labor was either naive or cynical.

The mystery was cleared up when an accountant employed by an El Centro lettuce company announced that she had falsified the payroll records. What she had done, on the orders of the company owners, was to pad the hours reported by the labor crews. This lowered, on paper, the hourly wage. Thus the Labor Department was unaware of what the piece-rate earnings actually were. Apparently the wage surveyors had asked the growers what they were paying. But no one bothered to ask the workers what they were earning. If it had been discovered that the piece rate was equal to $2.00 an hour, then the bracero wage of $1.00 would have had to be doubled. It would have been clear that the use of the Mexicans had definitely had an adverse effect on other wages in the valley.

The low wages in agriculture may seem to be of little importance to the rest of society. But "agriculture as a whole," according to the California Democratic Council, "still remains our largest single industry. Depressed farm purchasing power contributes directly and significantly to fewer sales, fewer jobs, lower business profits, and a lower general level of national output and income than what the U.S. economy should be producing."

MEASURED IN PENNIES

The marketing of agriculture products needs a thorough investigation. In many cases neither the grower nor the worker is getting a fair shake. Tomatoes grown in McAllen, Texas, and sold in Denver, for instance, produced a net income to the grower of $68.85 per acre. But the consumers paid $9,660 for this acre of tomatoes. Only a small fraction of retail food prices reflects farm crop prices. And a much smaller fraction represents harvesting wages.

There is room here for fair profits to growers and honest wages to workers. What the harvesters need is the dignity of work done under conditions meant for farm workers, not farm animals. The issues that are fought over are cabin space, hot water, and piece rates, but the real issues are basic human rights and fair play. The migrant doesn't want charity or handouts. He wants a chance, a start, to build his strength and manage his own life.

The wages paid harvest labor constitute a tiny fraction of the retail cost of food. In many cases, an increase in wages as much as 100 percent would barely affect the retail price. The price to consumers of eliminating migrant poverty is measured in pennies.

Legislation designed to help migrant labor is urgently needed. In 1964 a number of bills were enacted which will help states improve migrant education, expand the restrictions on child labor, provide some new day-care centers for children, and help farmers provide field sanitation. Congress could, if it would, establish a minimum wage for migratory workers, improve the methods of recruiting, training, transporting, and distributing farm workers, and extend the National Labor Relations Act to cover agriculture.

The ingrained poverty and underemployment that exist among the seasonal farm workers will be difficult to eliminate. Our agricultural system has made harvest work shameful. It has made the welfare check often more honorable than harvest work. It has made pride and satisfaction impossible. No man goes into a field to harvest crops if there is any other choice open to him. The new laws passed in 1964 do not constitute a complete solution. But they would make a start.

■

NOTHING BUT DESPAIR

The Brent family is typical of many thousands of migrant families. They were forced off their land in Georgia. They blundered into the migrant stream when the owner combined it with five other "mule and nigger" farms. One afternoon a placard appeared in the window of the filling station-grocery store near their home. It offered "employment opportunities" in the harvest in Homestead, Florida. The family was desperate for work. They loaded their household goods into their 1940 Dodge and started for Homestead.

After a long, hot, and dusty trip, they stopped in Belle Glade, north of Homestead, where the harvest was under way. Once there, they found plenty of work, and the whole family went to the fields. In a month it was all over. They never got to Homestead. Work was finished there, too. They realized, too late, that they would have to go where the crops were. They sold their car and joined a crew headed for Pennsylvania. They had become migrants.

Crew leaders and roving bus drivers make recruiting drives into the South, and many workers enter the migrant stream this way. The promise of "a hundred dollars a week and live in a ho-tel" sounds good. A favorite target of the recruiters is the debt-ridden tenant family. Cash earnings and a place to live are heady inducements.

Some families enter the stream to search for a better place to live. One member will go on the season to look around up north or out west. Still, many of them wind up in the rural slums that lie at the fringes of the suburbs across the land. There are, for example, many Negroes from North Carolina living in Riverhead, Long Island. They came with migrant crews first and later brought their families.

Settling is a slow and difficult process. A Long Island woman explained it this way: "A man comes alone with a crew and picks a place to settle down. Next season, he may come back with another of the men in the family. If they decide it's OK, he'll come next year with his wife. At the end of the season, they stay in Riverhead. No one wants to hire a migrant because they're supposed to be wild and unstable; no one will rent him a house for fear he'll tear it up. So the first place the family lives is a real chicken house. If he finds a job, he can move his family out of the ex-migrant slum into a regular slum. After that, he's got it made. A lot of them don't, and they get stranded. Sometimes the husband has to leave so the wife can get welfare."

The valleys of California and Arizona and the suburbs of the Middle West are filled with the cabin slums of Mexican-Americans, Negroes, and poor whites trying to settle down. After a few years a migrant who cannot escape the stream is broken by it. The poverty, anxiety, homelessness, and isolation wear away his spirit. It is this apathy that is often called acceptance and makes people say, "They like things that way."

"We're always goin' someplace," said a sandy-haired Oklahoma migrant, "but we never git noplace." In a tired, flat voice, an old woman in a Michigan field put it only a little differently: "I been ever' place, and I got no place."

A migrant minister in a Belle Glade camp asked a woman in his camp church if she was going on the season again. "I don't know. Ever' year I go up broke, and I come back broke. I don't know why I go even."

A migrant in Arkansas sat on the steps of his one-room cabin. For an hour he had talked about where he had been, and the things he had done to keep his family alive. Suddenly it seemed as if the memory of the years crushed him. "I get sick of the world sometimes and ever'body in it. I don't know what's goin' to happen. Used to make a livin' pickin' cotton. Then they started bringin' in them Mexicans by the truckload. Now they're gettin' them machines every day."

Few urban Americans have any awareness of this vast impoverished army that tramps through their country to bring the crops in from the fields. It cannot be seen except as a broken-down car or bus here, a truck there, a ragged crew working somewhere off in a field.

But the harvest cycle yields its own fruits: ignorance, poverty, death, and despair. Until we see the connection between migrancy—the corpses piled up on the roadway, the children left to the darkness of ignorance and illiteracy, the despairing, destitute families groping for a way to live —and the bountiful supply of fruits and vegetables on every corner fruit stand or in every supermarket, no changes will come. Without this understanding, no war on poverty can hope to win more than a few skirmishes.

chapter 23
the poverty
of aging
ben b. seligman

Americans are proud of the fact that the nation is becoming young. Nearly half the population is now under 25 years of age and about a third under 15. While this may mean crowded colleges or teen-age unemployment, the problems of **senior** citizens, who are increasing in numbers, do not diminish because older people become a smaller portion of the population. In fact, in an industrial society the position of the aged tends to worsen. The long-run decline in death rates, signifying greater longevity, coupled with the inability of older persons to compete for jobs, makes the problem of the aged more visible, despite a desire on the part of the rest of us to push them out of sight and out of mind.

The final stages of human existence can be a protracted period of human obsolescence. As in so many other societies, we would prefer simply to discard our aged. While we do not burn the villages of the aged dead, or fill the air with cries of joy over the departed,[1] we do stuff our aged into institutions to let them await death slowly. There they are given care of a sort. Unfortunately, as Jules Henry has revealed, such care is of the order that might be accorded to an inanimate object.[2] Often, the names of the inmates are not known to the staff that takes care of them. Institutions for the aged are likely to be tombs for those still alive, and as in a tomb, silence prevails.

A resident of an old-age home must foster the illusion that he is among the living, although awareness that he has been discarded by relatives, friends, and society is not uncommon. In some private profit-making homes, the inmates ". . . suffer most from [a] sense of being dumped and lost; [from] the . . . vacant routine, the awareness of being considered a nuisance and of being inferior to the most insensitive employee."[3] Soon ordinary human functions are distorted, so that the resident of an old-age institution undergoes a "pathogenic metamorphosis" akin to that experienced by characters in the tales of Franz Kafka. If he reaches pathetically for reality, the inmate is apt to be rebuffed by a staff member: the latter do not want reality, for the transformation of their charges is the only reality available to **them**. Ordinary human dignity would represent too serious a challenge to the apparatus of the institution, the main purpose of which is to create hopelessness. When this has been achieved, persons of sound mind and body can then withdraw from the aged without qualms of conscience. The sense of doom that the aged suffer hastens their passage through the vestibule to death.[4]

From **Dissent**, March/April, 1968. Reprinted by permission.

■

The aged may be among us, but they are not part of us. The aged are simply an embarrassment. They are poor, unable to provide medical care for themselves: they violate the canon of self-help, and so we dishonor them. Irving Rosow has demonstrated that a secure position for the aged can exist only under conditions that cannot be found in a modern industrial society. If the aged owned or controlled property on which younger persons depended, if they were transmitters of culture, in possession of key blocks of knowledge, if they provided significant links to the past, if the extended family were still central to our mode of life, if our society were tradition-oriented, and if the output of the aged were in any way economically useful, then they would still be honored.[5]

An older person has a chance for a fruitful existence if he is married and living with his spouse, but many of those over 65 years of age have no spouse, and widowhood increases with age at the rate of 20 percent with each decade after 65. An old person has a chance if he is still at work, but most of the aged do not work. Today only a third of persons 65 years of age or older are in the work force, as contrasted with two-thirds at the turn of the century. Escape from poverty and hopelessness is possible if there is no loss of income, but the data show a drop of as much as 50 percent in income after retirement. Life might be meaningful if one's health were good, but most of the aged suffer from a large assortment of illnesses. Says Rosow, the chances of a man over 65 having a favorable rating on all four counts is seven in a hundred, for a woman 65, one in a hundred.[6]

To be sure, there has been some improvement in institutional homes in recent years. The recognition that the aged need to have a choice in living arrangements has been growing, and some better homes have been provided by religious denominations and fraternal organizations. The private proprietary institutions, though they are proliferating, rarely set up responsible lay boards to review both policy and day-to-day operations. With social security payments as a base, the aged poor can turn to private services when no others are available; yet few of these institutions tie their services to a medical care system or rehabilitation effort that would minimize the "disuse syndrome" among their clients. In the final analysis, proprietary homes are commercial enterprises and generally isolated from community health services.[7]

Living with relatives has not been a viable solution either. In one study two-thirds of the persons interviewed were opposed to having aged parents live with their children.[8] It was evident that little contact or understanding between the generations existed. Only 13 percent of the respondents in this study saw virtue in some semblance of an extended family. The higher the educational level, the more undesirable did joint living appear to be: educated persons were less likely to provide a home for their older relatives. A similar attitude prevailed among the aged: older persons with incomes of at least $5000 a year expressed preferences for separate domiciles. And older persons in states that provide higher Old Age Assistance appear to live alone more frequently than in states where OAA is minimal.

■

How difficult living alone must be is underscored by the income data for the aged. The largest proportion of aged married couples—79 percent—derive their income from social security payments. Other government retirement programs, such as railroad retirement systems, provide income for 12 percent, while private retirement schemes lend support to 16 percent.[9] Earnings were a source of income for somewhat more than half the aged couples. For the nonmarried aged this ratio dropped to 24 percent. More important is the size of the income: the median for married couples was $2875; for nonmarried persons, $1130. Almost all of the latter had incomes under $3000 a year: this was also true for 54 percent of the married couples. Set against the standards of "modest but adequate" budgets, these data suggest that at least 2 million couples and 6 million unmarried aged are in dire straits.

It is often argued that older persons do not need as much as younger ones, because the aged spend less for clothing, housing, food, and medicine. But as Harold Sheppard has said, this reflects a curious reversal of logic, since the aged spend less only because they have less.[10] The patent fact is that those aged who do not sustain a loss in income do consume as much as anyone else in their income level. No doubt, the aged would be worse off were there no social security payments. Yet a large percentage of social security beneficiaries still require public assistance, mainly because the benefits are too small to maintain them at even low levels of existence.

Families headed by older persons represent one-third of all poor families, a ratio substantially higher than the one in seven for the total number of aged in the general population. As we have suggested, the nonmarried are worse off than couples: they tend to be older and poorer, so that one in six requires old-age assistance, as contrasted with one in twelve for the married aged. A large number of social security beneficiaries receive the minimum benefit: women who select "early" retirement get even less.

There may have been some improvement in the income position of the aged in recent years; yet as late as 1962, 5 percent of aged married couples and 44 percent of aged nonmarried persons had incomes of less than $1000 a year.[11] While the proportion of all families and individuals in dire poverty has decreased since 1900, the proportion of the aged in such circumstances has not decreased markedly.[12] Nor do they have accumulations of savings on which they can fall back. The aged may have homes with mortgages fully paid, some insurance, and some liquid assets; but in 1960, 30 percent of spending units with heads over 65 years of age had no liquid assets, and 20 percent had such assets amounting to less than $1000. And more than half the home equities were worth less than $10,000. Liquid assets are not available for the usual emergencies that afflict the aged.

■

There have been improvements, of course, in the last few years. Amendments to the Social Security Act have helped, and the beneficiaries now coming onto the rolls with better earnings records than those in past years have added to average benefits. Yet in December, 1964, the average social security payment was $79 a month. At the end of 1964, there were 13.7 million aged persons receiving such benefits; on the average this represented three out of every four aged persons in the nation. In 1965 it was estimated that 35 percent of all social security recipients were poor and that another 38 percent would fall below the Social Security Administration's poverty standard in the absence of social security payments.

Of course, social security encourages withdrawal from the work force.[13] The proportion of the aged who work appears to have fallen sharply in recent years, although it is conceivable that illness or changes in attitudes toward retirement may have accounted for the decline.[14] Curiously enough, social security is structured in such a manner that the income transfers flow from lower-middle-income groups to lower-income groups, with upper-income groups contributing very little. In effect, support of the poor comes from those quite close to them in the income scale. Further, because of the retirement tests, the law limits beneficiaries in supplementing benefits in any effective fashion. Furthermore, widows must surrender part of their benefits if they marry another beneficiary, leading to "the St. Petersburg sin," couples living together to overcome loneliness, but in an unmarried state.[15]

After some years of agitation, improvements were made in 1965. Monthly cash benefits were increased by 7 percent, so that the range is now from $44 a month to $136 a month, with the maximum scheduled to rise to $168 a month in future years. The tax base was raised to $6600 a year and the tax rate stepped up to reach 4.85 percent by 1973. For a family the maximum benefit may reach $368 a month. The retirement test was altered, allowing earnings up to $1500 a year. Benefits were continued for children still in school up to the age of 22. Disability allowances were liberalized and the standards made less restrictive. Widows could receive benefits at the age of 60 on an actuarially reduced basis. These changes do indeed offer some improvements, but whether they will take the aged poor out of poverty remains to be seen. (The foregoing data do not take into account more recent changes in Social Security.)

■

All too often an aged person receiving benefits must ask local authorities for additional help. And for the aged poor who do not have recourse to the federal program there is no alternative to Old Age Assistance (OAA). Yet more than half the states fail to make OAA payments sufficient to meet their own income tests. The Senate Committee on Aging noted numerous cases of local agencies reducing their aid when other sources were made available.[16]

As with all forms of public assistance at local levels, OAA is conditioned by the perennial clash between proponents of low taxes and those who express a concern for the poor. Yet assistance to the aged, as well as other categorical forms of aid, has become much too severe a problem to be handled by private charity, as is frequently suggested by low-tax advocates; moreover, the private agencies have developed their own specialized clientele and they are now reluctant to become involved in aid programs rooted in economic distress. They prefer to deal with such matters as family counseling, leaving economic need to public authorities.[17]

So large is the bill for public assistance that on occasion a local authority gives up in frustration and simply closes down its program. When Clermont County in Ohio cut off aid in 1961 because the voters rejected a tax levy for public assistance, the burden was simply shifted to landlords, grocers, doctors, and other agencies. Debt in the county rose 54 percent in a 15-month period, and evictions increased alarmingly. Clearly, cutting the aged and other needy off the rolls was no solution. But neither does increased aid make the problem disappear. Although survivor's insurance may lighten the widow's burden and help the orphans, no one anticipated that illegitimacy and desertion would in turn crowd the public assistance rolls.

While two-fifths of the total public-assistance burden goes for OAA, its distribution is quite unequal. A higher proportion of the rural aged are reached through OAA than of the urban aged. Yet there is no consistent pattern among the states: Louisiana reaches 49 percent of its aged poor; Delaware only 3 percent. But this doesn't mean that Delaware's level of aid is munificent—its average monthly payment is $63. In practice, there is no rational economic explanation for the sort of benefits the individual states bestow on their aged poor. Worse yet, the state-run programs are frequently conducted in an irregular manner. Confidentiality requirements may be flouted or recipients classified on some arbitrary basis other than need.[18] The eligibility standards usually mean emotional agony for the recipient who is willing to run a bureaucratic gauntlet to obtain aid. All too often the public agency tends to blame his situation on the client himself.

Recipients, especially those on OAA, cannot influence the level or administration of the programs that serve them. As Gilbert Steiner says, farmers have their lobbyists, publishers express their views on mail subsidy to Congress, and trade associations speak for industry, but the aged—or for that matter, any recipient of public assistance—are not asked what they need. (Some change in this regard is being sought by some civil rights groups.)[19]

■

One might think private pension benefits would relieve the situation of the aged. In 1960 total payments to retirees from private pensions were about $1.3 billion, four times larger than a decade before. The various plans cover over 20 million workers, or about 43 percent of the employed private work force, almost double the ratio in 1950. Much progress had been made in ten years. Nevertheless, the income derived from private pensions represented less than 6 percent of the income of the aged. And most of the recipients could be classified as "higher-income aged." Less than 3 percent of social security beneficiaries who receive under $1200 a year obtain any income from private pension plans.

To rely on private pension income to relieve the condition of the aged poor would be disastrous. Small firms are less apt to have pension arrangements than large ones. Low-wage industries, in which many of the aged poor have spent their working lives, have not instituted pension programs in any widespread fashion. Federal tax regulations are so cumbersome that entrepreneurs in these industries are discouraged from even trying. The most serious problem is the lack of airtight legal protection for pensioners. Despite some improvement, stemming from the Welfare and Pension Disclosure Act, it is still possible for an employee to discover that he really has no pension. For in the last analysis, the contract is between the employer or trustees and the carrier, and all too often trustees can escape penalties for negligence or misconduct. Many private plans have poor vesting—an absolute right to a pension—or none at all; and in the absence of portability—the transfer of pensions from one company to another—a feature conspicuous by its rarity, workers lose years of accumulated rights when they change jobs.

■

Meeting health costs is a major problem for the aged. Private insurers could not solve the problem of offering adequate benefits for a high-risk, low-income population, nor were they especially interested in doing so. Despite the American Medical Association's crude effort in 1960 to demonstrate that the aged weren't suffering from sickness and could easily meet their health bills, the fact was that four out of five aged persons had chronic ailments as contrasted with two out of five for younger persons. Mental, as well as physical illness, was a problem for the aged: first admissions in mental hospitals were two-and-a-half times greater than those for patients under 65. The aged stay in hospitals longer; they need more home care and more drugs; they visit the doctor more often. Set against this record the mounting hospital costs—an increase of 27 percent between 1960 and 1962—and it is patent that the health problem of the aged has been indeed serious.[20]

The demand for health insurance as part of the social security system grew without abatement. At the eleventh hour, private insurance companies sought to offer plans for aged health coverage within their underwriting perspective, but these were inadequate. They were almost all hospital-oriented and did not deal with other needs, i.e., they were not comprehensive. The industry failed to convince anyone—not even itself—that it could do the job. In 1959 hospital insurance coverage for the aged covered 46 percent of that group as compared with 67 percent in the total population; surgical coverage was 37 percent, a little over half of what everyone else had; and only 10 percent of the aged had insurance for doctors' visits, as contrasted with 19 percent for the general population. The lower the income, the less coverage: only a third of the aged with incomes under $2000 a year had hospital insurance.

All too frequently the insurance the aged did have provided lower benefits at higher premiums.[21] Furthermore, the shift from a community rating basis in setting costs to an experience basis tended to force up rates. In any case, the usual commercial coverage offered fixed dollar benefits according to some predetermined schedule rather than in terms of need. And the deductible corridors—that part borne directly by the insured—placed a substantial part of the cost on the policy holder. Ordinary health insurance did not meet more than 7 percent of the total cost of the aged's health requirements.

Nor did the Kerr-Mills Act in 1960 solve the problem. Admittedly passed as a substitute for health care through the social security system, it asked the states to develop their own medical aid programs for the aged as a condition for obtaining federal grants. Numerous restrictions were instituted—means tests and family responsibility—which severely limited coverage. The administrative costs were inordinately high. Moreover, since most of the states had failed to provide even adequate general assistance to the aged, it was un-

likely that they would assume the added burden of Kerr-Mills. By 1962 only one in every 200 eligibles was receiving aid through Kerr-Mills. Many refused to utilize the "service" when they discovered that they would have to pauperize themselves. Quite simply, Kerr-Mills was a failure.

■

It remained for Medicare—medical aid through social security—to make the first sensible step toward an adequate health scheme for the aged. While Medicare, as passed in 1965, fell short of the original proposals, it was a significant advance, one that took 20 years to achieve. Its impact will probably go far beyond the 10 percent of the population for whom it has been devised. It is more than likely that private health insurance plans for younger persons will be altered and Medicare will no doubt affect proposals developed through collective bargaining.

In brief, the 1965 amendments to the Social Security Act provide hospital and medical insurance for beneficiaries. The hospital plan is financed by a separate earnings tax and separate fund. Enrollment in the medical plan is voluntary, paid for by a monthly premium of $3 to be matched by the federal government. Benefits include a maximum of 90 days hospitalization for each illness, post-hospital extended care for 100 days, and outpatient diagnostic services. The law also stresses the need for community health planning.

Opponents apparently have accepted Medicare as a **fait accompli**, and indeed are getting on the bandwagon. Medical practitioners are helping the government to set up the necessary standards, and the AMA, after spending almost $1 million in the first three months of 1965 to forestall the passage of Medicare, is now urging its members to cooperate. Nevertheless, it was reported that some 20,000 physicians have decided not to participate. Private insurance companies, on the other hand, are cooperating. No doubt, it was their influence that resulted in all of Medicare's deductible corridors, for these allow dovetailing private plans with government plans. There is still some business they hope to get. A query remains: Will not those aged who do not buy private "dovetailed" policies continue to suffer a financial burden by virtue of the deductible corridors?

It was predicted that Medicare would enforce

vast changes in hospital administration. Fees for some services provided by hospitals would be raised; the prices of other services would be reduced. Thus, charges for rooms, x-rays, and medicines were expected to fall, whereas service costs for obstetrics and pediatrics might increase. New arrangements might be worked out for staff doctors, and it was hoped that Medicare would speed up integration in Southern hospitals. In any case, it was expected that the aged of the nation would flock into the 7200 hospitals across the country and overtax already limited facilities. No one thought that the deductible corridors would provide some restraint.[22]

■

Most observers overlooked Medicaid—Title 19 of the 1965 amendments to the Social Security Act—while plans for Medicare were being formulated. Unnoticed for months, attention was called to Title 19 when New York State took advantage of its provisions by adopting enabling legislation in April, 1966. This amendment is a liberalized and expanded version of the 1960 Kerr-Mills law. Financed by general revenues, not through social security, it provides for certain kinds of health care for the aged poor, but on a broader scale than Kerr-Mills. In fact, Title 19, sponsored by Rep. Wilbur Mills, offers benefits through matching grants to the disabled, ADC families, and to those who may have enough for other needs, but not for medical care. In effect, funds would be made available to all medically needy persons under 21 and over 60 and to the blind or disabled and ADC cases between those ages. By mid-1966 seven states had obtained approval for their programs and a number of others have applied for approval. It was expected that Medicaid would eventually reach some 35 million people. The initial cost to the federal government was expected to be more than $350 million. Quite significant too was the marked easing of eligibility rules, residence requirements, and family responsibility regulations. Further, there was a prospect that some of the deductible corridors under Medicare would be covered.

When it was suddenly realized that New York's plan alone would cost over a billion dollars a year in combined federal, state, and local payments, the legislators in Washington were stunned. They hurriedly tried to amend the law, but it

seemed too late—the welfare state had barged through the cautious legislative barriers with a resounding crash. For the members of Congress had left the definition of "medically indigent" up to the states, and some of the latter were prepared to be as liberal as New York has been. Under the latter's program up to 40 percent of its inhabitants could qualify for Medicaid. Moreover, the states were not permitted to substitute Medicaid for existing welfare programs in order to prevent new federal monies from paying for old state welfare programs, thus encouraging liberality.

Senators and congressmen were chagrined at their extraordinary **faux pas** and tried to scale down the generous program. Yet by October, 1966, some 41 states and Puerto Rico had taken advantage of Title 19. Although most of the state plans were modest, California and Massachusetts had devised fairly ambitious ones, and their representatives in Washington made it known that they would not tolerate any changes in the law. Congress proposed to bar able-bodied adults whose children were receiving assistance under other welfare programs, but the income standards were still open for aid to such adults. Only $80 million would be cut from the estimated half-billion-dollar federal cost in the year beginning July, 1967: the original estimate for federal contributions had been $238 million a year. It was feared that Washington's Medicaid bill would reach $2 billion annually.[23]

For all these improvements, social security remained inadequate. It was clear that much still had to be done if the country was to catch up with standards elsewhere in the West. One problem was the erosion that resulted as prices continued their upward drift. Somehow social security benefits would have to be tied to a "cost of living" formula if the retired were not to lose ground. It was obvious too that the structure of social security taxes, which provided the "trust fund," could not be expected to do the whole job. Sentiment increased for recourse to the general revenues, although a sharp increase in the tax base—perhaps up to $15,000 a year—was not unthinkable. It has been argued that the steep increase in payroll taxes that this entailed would generate resistance, and discourage firms from increasing their work force because of rising costs. Further, no matter what the base limit, a payroll tax remains regressive: with the present $6,600 limit, those receiving income under this figure pay proportionately more than those whose income exceeds $6,600 a year. The prospect seems to be that social security benefits will come less and less from direct contributions to a special fund.

■

The aged need decent housing as well as adequate income, yet the limitations from which they suffer in income impose severe restrictions on what they can purchase in shelter. This was underscored by the Senate Committee on Aging in 1962, and despite existing legislation little genuine progress has been made. Local housing authorities have available certain instrumentalities under the Housing Act to allow the construction of special facilities for the aged: by the end of 1962 about 8,000 such units had been built. New rental housing for the aged can be supplied through government-insured mortgages: by 1962, about 26,000 units had been built. Direct loans are also available to nonprofit organizations sponsoring housing for the aged: by 1962, about 8,800 such units had been constructed. It seems obvious that these programs have provided a tiny fraction of the need.

Even in the one agency primarily concerned with proverty—the Office of Economic Opportunity—the aged have been relegated to secondary status. For months during 1965-1966 a bureaucratic battle raged in OEO on whether the aged poor should become a prime target group or remain a minor concern of the agency. Budgeting outlays in OEO through 1966 for the aged were about 2 percent of the total. Said some bureaucrats in justification of the policy: "We're a youth-oriented nation." Yet Congress made it clear in 1965 that OEO was to consider the special problems of the aged "wherever possible." The only program for the aged to which OEO gave any priority was "Medicare Alert," under which older persons were given temporary jobs at $1.25 an hour to brief other aged on the benefits available under Medicare. Their job was done by March 31, 1966, the deadline for registering for Medicare. While President Johnson specified in August, 1965, a many-sided crash program for the aged poor, only one of these, "Foster Grandparents," a program to train older persons to serve as "substitute parents" for neglected children, was in operation six months later. The program was small in scale, employing about 1200 elderly persons in March, 1966; in the meantime, OEO's original allotment for this venture was cut back from $10

million to $5.5 million; and total OEO funds for aged programs were cut in half.

■

Yet there are numerous services the aged could be trained to perform—library assistants, recreation aides, school crossing guards, toll collectors, helpers to shut-in persons, and subprofessional social workers are just a few. The cost-benefit philosophy that had begun to infect many federal agencies, however, impelled some OEO officials to question the payoff of investment in the aged. The brutalizing habits of the larger society seemed to have undermined what would appear to be the moral obligations of an agency concerned with poverty.

The outstanding feature of such an effort as "Foster Grandparents" was the remarkable reliability and sense of responsibility of the participants. After eight months one could detect no demonstration, no dropouts, no absenteeism in the project. While the lives of hundreds of rejected children were brightened for a brief time, a sizable group of aged men and women, all poor, were given a new interest in life. Even congressmen who had expressed some doubts were pleasantly surprised at the results. Some children's institutions were horrified at the prospect of "caring" for older persons in addition to what they had to do: within weeks of the inception of the program they were asking for more "foster grandparents."

If one suggests an utter failure of imagination on the part of OEO in dealing with the aged, he would not be far from the truth. All Sargent Shriver could do was to tell a Senate Committee that little could be done for the aged: older persons, said Shriver, have low educational levels, are in poor health, and cannot compete for jobs. Besides, it was more difficult to get local communities excited about the aged poor. Other agencies, insisted Shriver, had a greater responsibility for the aged; OEO could at best play a minor role. The only way to help the aged seemed to be direct cash benefits. Perhaps, in **our** society this may be the only way—give the aged poor money and let them stand aside, silent and unseen.[24]

NOTES

1. Cf. J. Campbell, **The Masks of God: Primitive Mythology**, New York, 1959, p. 118 ff.

2. J. Henry, Culture Against Man, New York, 1963, p. 391 ff.

3. Ibid., p. 407.

4. Ibid., p. 437.

5. I. Rosow, "And Then We Were Old," Transaction, Jan.-Feb. 1965. p. 21.

6. Rosow, ibid., p. 25.

7. Senate Committee on Aging, Developments in Aging: 1959 to 1963, Washington, 1963; New York Times, July 19, 1966.

8. J. N. Morgan et al., Income and Welfare in the United States, New York, 1962, p. 158, ff.

9. L. S. Epstein, "Income of the Aged in 1962: First Findings of the 1963 Survey of the Aged," Social-Security Bulletin, March 1964.

10. H. L. Sheppard, "The Poverty of Aging," in B.B. Seligman, ed., Poverty As a Public Issue, New York, 1965, p. 98.

11. H. S. Gordon, "Aging and Income Security," in C. Tibbitts, ed., Aging and Society, Chicago, 1960, p. 212

12. Ibid., p. 211.

13. C. D. Long, The Labor Force Under Changing Income and Employment, Princeton, 1958, p. 163.

14. M. Gordon, The Economics of Welfare Policies, New York, 1963, p. 35.

15. Ibid., p. 44.

16. Senate Committee on Aging, op. cit., pp. 69-70.

17. G. Y. Steiner, Social Insecurity: The Politics of Welfare, Chicago, 1966, p. 11.

18. Ibid., p. 84.

19. Ibid., p. 153 ff.

20. Senate Committee on Aging, op. cit., passim.

21. Ibid., p. 15.

22. New York Times, May 29, 1966, June 13, 1966, and June 19, 1966; Wall Street Journal, June 15, 1966; Baltimore Sun, Dec. 21, 1965.

23. New York Times, May 29, 1966; National Observer, June 20, 1966; Boston Globe, June 5, 1966; Wall Street Journal, July 11, 1966, and October 20, 1966; Business Week, June 25, 1966.

24. New York Times, Dec. 22, 1965, and Jan. 20, 1966; Washington Post, May 13, 1965, and Jan. 20, 1966; Chicago Tribune, May 1, 1966; National Observer, March 7, 1966.

chapter 24
the gray woman of appalachia
harriette simpson arnow

The region known as Southern Appalachia was once rich in natural resources. Most of the land was covered with dark, fertile soil, much of it thin, but still able to support an enormous stand of timber, chiefly hardwoods. Still greater wealth lay in minerals, especially oil and coal.

Yet by mid-20th century, when most of the United States was enjoying a boom, parts of Appalachia were wastelands: oil gone, timber gone, soil washed away, farmers gone or near starvation. Much of Appalachia was prospering—and still is—but in spite of constant and heavy migration, the percentage of those on the dole at home was much higher than in the rest of the nation. For the region as a whole, median income, years spent in school, and employment were all below national averages.

Unemployment in the coal fields degenerated to disaster proportions when, in the early 1960s, strip and auger mining became the chief methods. Highly mechanized, these are the cheapest means yet found to mine coal. But they use few men, and these mostly truckers and manipulators of heavy machinery, and have no use for the many pit and drift miners who live in the coal country. The general wretchedness of once thriving mining communities, especially in eastern Kentucky and West

Virginia, brought passage, after long debates, of the Appalachian Redevelopment Act of 1965. A territory of around 160,000 square miles, containing about 15 million people living in 320 counties that comprise the mountains and lowlands of nine different states and one whole state, West Virginia, was designated as an underdeveloped area to receive extra federal aid.

Passage of the bill after years of discussion was something of a tragedy. The Act gave false hope to many who needed help most; at the same time, the general public got the idea that Appalachia's most pressing problems would soon be solved. Five years later, most of these problems remain.

The reasoning of the lawmakers who eventually passed the bill was that Appalachia ought not to get too much preferential treatment. Other sections of the country, as their congressmen were quick to point out, also had special needs. Furthermore, by no means all of Appalachia was suffering. Thus it was decided that most of the extra federal funds earmarked for the region should go to programs that would help the nation as a whole. Throughways, it was felt, would encourage tourists and industry to come to Appalachia, and at the same time be of great help to overland travelers and truckers. The percentage of state money required for these roads is smaller than for states outside the region. Still, it comes to a good deal

From **The Nation**, December 28, 1970. Reprinted by permission.

and could have benefited more people in Appalachia had it been spent on state and county roads.

The great throughways, only extensions of those already built, do not come near most rural and small-town Appalachians. The roads of eastern Kentucky, for example, have long been infamous, yet the two new throughways that cross at Lexington only skirt the northern and western edges of the coal fields.

■

Traveling the only east-west road into the heart of the coal country, one soon realizes that, whatever improvements have been made by the Redevelopment Act, Kentucky 80 is not one of them. Leaving Pulaski County, the road soon collapses into a narrow-shouldered, cracked and worn thread twisting into and out of narrow, smoke-filled valleys. The coal country has been reached, and business is good. Such is the demand for electricity that coal-fed, steam-powered generators are at full burn.

The signs of prosperity along the highway are the roaring, oversize coal trucks, now and then a shiny car and, newest of all, the clawed-out earth, rock and trees from active strip mines. Everything else is old, worn out, cast off, a smoke- and coal-dust-wreathed landscape of weed-grown railroad tracks, derelict tipples, mud and weed-choked streams strewn with debris, including abandoned cars. Often looming above the road are sliding mountains of slack and other mine refuse, on which no plant will risk its life. Here and there in rows along the hillsides, the miners' little houses, many of them knocked up during World War I, stand windowless, doors missing, some roofless.

Yet a good many have tenants. And it is here that one sees the gray woman—gray like everything about her. She sits on a sagging porch step, knees lax, puffy with fat, motionless, as she appears to stare straight ahead, seeing nothing. Around her, children are sitting, standing among the rusty tin cans, bottles and weeds in the narrow strip of hillside between house and road.

Driving on, you see the woman again and again. Often near her is a man; he, too, stares, and both seem waiting. For what? The next welfare check? A job? The men are out-of-work miners, sick or crippled miners. The women are their wives or the widows of miners.

What can a jobless pit miner expect in this time of mining prosperity? Some few have

been able to return to mining; others have taken low-paying, part-time jobs in truck mines or whatever they can get. Some have enrolled in the job-retraining courses sponsored by the federal government; in one project a man with children was paid while he trained. But these training programs have not been much help to the older miners. Some have never heard of them; others, living 15 or 20 miles from a training center and with no means of transportation, could not participate.

As one goes deeper into the smoke-filled, gritty world, the unkempt women, children and men multiply. It is futile to berate these idle, seemingly lazy people in one's mind, or to think how the women could neaten up themselves and children, the men mend broken steps and sagging porches, the children clean up the bits of yard. They have lived in this junk heap of a world too long; dirt all around, crawling down the hillsides, scumming the streams. Their houses are part of the debris, in a place where laws, if any, about dumping rubbish and garbage are not enforced, and where there's no getting ahead of the coal dust and smoke that fall like rain, but a rain that never stops.

■

A rejuvenation of the mess surrounding these people would undoubtedly help to restore hope and pride. Such a program would also mean employment for the idle men. If the owners of the slack piles and other debris of abandoned drift mines cannot or will not clean up their mess, the government could take the land by eminent domain, as it has taken many thousands of acres above the water level of many artificial lakes. If local and state governments in Kentucky and elsewhere cannot do the regrading and reforestation that West Virginia managed to do, the federal government should take over. Heavy machinery would be needed for much of the regrading, but the remainder of the work could be accomplished through a program much like the WPA of the 1930s.

Once the work was done, every effort would be needed to check and remedy the ravages of day-to-day mining. Strip and auger mining are the worst offenders. The mobility of the equipment cuts mining costs, but adds immeasurably to the amount of damage one outfit can do to the land in a short time. When one mountain is scalped, the machinery can move to another. Bad roads or none at all are no great handicap; bulldozers and giant pushers can soon knock over the trees and claw out a way. Kentucky fines the operator who fails to regrade, but it is cheaper to pay the fine and leave the loosened rock and earth to go where they will; often onto the dwellings below.

The ravaging of the earth is the most obvious effect of strip and core mining, but it is only the beginning of the bigger pollution problems in most of Appalachia's coal counties. Both the Appalachian Planning Commission and the framers of the Act hoped to find more uses for coal within the region. Their specific suggestion was that more coal-fired, steam generators be located in or near the coal fields. The plants were to be built by private utility firms that would find it cheaper to transmit electricity than to build generators near big cities and ship coal to them.

Part of that hope has been realized. One cannot drive very far in any direction in Appalachia without seeing, and usually smelling, a generator. At mid-afternoon in the valley of the Big Sandy, twilight thickens until the road is scarcely visible, and from the car one catches only smudged glimpses of big chimneys shooting out black smoke. The generators on the Big Sandy are small compared to those on the Monongahela. The REA generator on Lake Cumberland, near Burnside, Kentucky uses 100 tons of coal a day; much larger are some of the eleven—a twelfth is being built—in the TVA system. All emit coal fumes, and all are built by a body of water. Large generators may use thousands of gallons per minute, and this water is returned to the lake or stream several degrees warmer than when pumped out.

In addition to smoke, noise and the warming of the nearby water, other deadlier pollutants are less easily detected. Mixed with the smoke are poisonous gases, among them a sulfur compound that sooner or later gets into the soil and water to the detriment of life in both. The need for pollution control concerns not only Appalachia but also areas far down the Mississippi Valley, since most Appalachian rivers are parts of the Ohio-Mississippi complex.

A good deal of effort is put forth in Appalachia to check pollution, but the biggest single complaint among the well-to-do and the townspeople of the coal country is lack of flood control. Some had hoped for a replication of TVA that would build dams on the upper tributaries of their rivers

to power hydroelectric plants and at the same time control floods. These hydroelectric plants would not have precluded the building of steam plants using local coal. TVA's coal-powered generators furnish 80 percent of the electricity produced by the program. However, the framers of the Appalachian Act wanted everything to be built by free enterprise, and it is much less expensive to produce electricity with coal-fired generators than to build dams for hydroelectric plants. Thus yearly floods continue to destroy life and property in West Virginia, eastern Kentucky and the mountainous sections of Pennsylvania and Virginia.

Many in the coal counties also complain of strip mining, but few condemn it, for the money is rolling in. The biggest town in a coal county may seem at first nothing more than a row of squat, brick buildings, begrimed with years of coal smoke and dust, and jammed together in a narrow valley. However, traffic is heavy, parking places are filled with cars, often new and expensive, and business in the stores, better restaurants and chain motels is brisk. A few miles outside such a town the visitor will discover handsome houses, half hidden in trees and shrubbery and served by private roads.

Splendid homes and other marks of wealth are fairly common in Appalachia. Huntsville, Alabama, and the surrounding region have prospered greatly since the Marshall Space Flight Center was established there in 1960. Western North Carolina, east Tennessee and counties in northern Georgia serviced by TVA have high levels of income and little unemployment. West Virginia, though still suffering, has cut the number of its unemployed miners in half. It has also, and with scant federal aid, regraded, grassed or reforested most of the land ruined by mining.

Thanks to state aid and good planning at the local level, school consolidation is more common than not in Appalachia. County health units have done much, especially to lower the rate of most contagious diseases. More and better medical centers have been built. Agricultural methods and forestry have also improved.

However, many sections are untouched by any of these improvements. In contrast to the remainder of the nation, about 50 percent of Appalachia's people are rural. Yet less than 10 percent own enough land to qualify as farmers under the census. There are prosperous farming communities in the region, mostly in Georgia, Pennsylvania and Maryland, with a few others on the eastern and western fringes; but one-third of all Appalachian farmers were earning less than $2500 a year when the Appalachian Act was passed. In eastern Kentucky, where there are more farmers than miners, their average yearly income was $1844 in 1965, or less than some miners on the dole receive in cash and food.

■

The subsistence farmer often lives in a poor county in which bad roads, an inadequate educational system, and no medical facilities make life difficult. Nevertheless, if he can keep off the dole, hanging onto his farm until death or decrepitude overtakes him, he is well off compared to many of Appalachia's rural poor.

Such a farmer may live in an old house with a sagging porch, but almost always there are flowers by the front gate and vines on the porch. Apples and peaches dry in the sun while the glint of fruit jars upside down on the picket fence tell that the housewife's canning is not yet done. The hillside may be in corn because there's no place else to put it, and the milk cow grazes in the surrounding woods—against the law in most counties—with only the calf in the barnyard to bring her home. There are fruit trees, chickens and, surrounded by a picket fence to keep out chickens and hogs, a large vegetable garden that supplies much of the family's food.

The family usually has an abundant, healthful diet during summer, fall and most of winter; but by early spring the one milk cow is dry, meat and most of the canned and stored food are gone. However, food is scarce only part of the time, which is more than can be said for money. Cash for anything—school shoes or taxes—is almost impossible to come by.

A great many small farmers in Appalachia and elsewhere in the United States take part-time jobs, usually in the nearest town or city. But the farmer with no car, a road unfit for a car if he had one, and no place of employment within walking distance, cannot even look for a job.

The few sharecroppers and farm laborers left in the area are even worse off; there is less farm work to be done and the abandoned farms are not worth renting. Most are on the dole: not an easy

way of life. They usually have to walk many miles to get their surplus food or to spend welfare checks and food stamps.

■

The back-hill communities grow smaller and smaller. The very poor, the young and ambitious, and often even the middle-aged go to the cities. During wars and boom times the exodus quickens. Some find steady employment and in time move into good communities. But more of them, badly educated, with no marketable skills, strange to all the ways of the city, their children behind in school, find nothing but misery and disappointment. Hope is lost and pride crushed when, as often happens, they end up on welfare.

Such families would often rather be back home in the hills, but for most there is no longer a home in the hills. Everybody they once knew is gone; the community has disappeared, the abandoned farms gone into a national forest or sold to an absentee owner for unpaid taxes. Those who do hang on find life increasingly difficult in the dwindling community. As the population decreases there are no longer enough children for the one-room school. The few left are either forced to walk much farther to another one-room school, or even more miles to the nearest school bus route; a long ride over dangerous roads often follows the walk; some young children spend twelve hours a day away from home. One wishes all consolidated school systems could serve breakfasts as well as lunches to those who need them.

In the dying community, roads and paths grow up in brush; help in time of trouble is hard to get in a place with no telephones. The few people left seldom see one another. The community gathering place, the post office to which everybody went on mail days, has been replaced by rural routes. The government did away with the rural postmasters, since one mail carrier can serve more people. The mail box may be miles from the owner's home, but he can walk.

It is true that within the last three or four decades there has been great improvement in Appalachia's agriculture as a whole. There are many farm programs, usually instituted by the county agricultural agent whose salary is paid in part by the federal government. The Appalachian Redevelopment Act contained measures for helping farmers with loans, forest management and pasture improvement. However, the backwoods farmer on small acreage has not enough land or money to take advantage of any of these. He is still less able to get any of the billions spent on farm subsidies or crop control.

■

Industry is increasing in Appalachia; more than 30 percent of the labor force is employed in manufacturing and the figure is rising. Tourism has increased until it is now big business in many sections. Most business and industry are in the developed regions, though a good many rural counties have benefited from tourism or the coming of some industry, such as a small wood-working plant.

However, neither business nor tourism can benefit the back-hill farming community in a poor county. And there seem to be no plans for doing so. Most agronomists, rural economists, and many government officials welcome the disappearance of the subsistence farmer and his community. The sooner all the people get out the better. They reason that a farmer with a small acreage of worn-out land, most of it submarginal to begin with, adds nothing to the national economy. He's probably never had earnings high enough to pay income tax; he doesn't even have Social Security.

And the small farmers are leaving, and have left, for the cities. In most of Appalachia the decline in the farm population is much greater than for the nation as a whole. Considering the many

problems of our cities, too often caused by Appalachian migrants, semiliterate and unsuited for city living, it might be sounder economics to improve living conditions in the poorer counties. Build, with federal funds if need be, at least all-weather, gravel roads into the vanishing communities. Bring in electricity; in spite of REA, many rural homes do not have it. And at the same time try to fill the most important need—better educational facilities for all.

Lack of even the rudiments of an education is one of the greatest problems of Appalachian migrants to the city. In Clay County, Kentucky, a few years ago, median years spent in school for all over 25 was only 6.5. What is still more disheartening is that only 52 percent of the county's 16- and 17-year-olds are in school. In parts of Appalachia a dropout is not a student who quits high school but one who never reaches the 8th grade. Many of these dropouts were handicapped from the beginning: school or the bus route too far away for the very young; no background of education at home; poverty that meant insufficient clothing. There are school attendance laws, but what county judge will jail a penniless father for not sending his shoeless children to school in January?

The backward parts of Appalachia need to be improved, at least until the young are educated enough to take care of themselves. This may mean a good deal of direct aid from the federal government in road building, education and medical services, but considering the present cost in wasted life, it would be worth it.

topic 12

the economic sector: the realm of power

Who rules America? Old-fashioned political rhetoric—conventional wisdom—would have it that the **people** do. But do they? Who in truth makes the ultimate decisions that shape and control the destinies of the mass of Americans? The responses to so sweeping a question are varied, and many of them are worth heeding, for whether we are controlled by a monolithic power elite, by a plurality of lesser yet still potent power blocs, or by ourselves is surely one of the most crucial issues of our times.

Few students of the matter, whether they be sociologists, economists, political scientists, or historians, would take serious issue with C. Wright Mills' contention that the "history of modern society may readily be understood as the story of the enlargement and the centralization of the means of power." The ultimate problem is less a matter of whether the growth of power and modernization, industrialization, and urbanization go hand in hand, than it is of the **degree** to which—and the **manner** in which—power has become progressively concentrated in the hands of the few.

As varied as the interpretations of this issue are, most fit into one of two fundamental diagnostic categories. Mills voiced one of these views when he wrote that "the top of modern American society is increasingly unified, and often seems willfully coordinated: at the top there has emerged an elite of power. The middle levels are a drifting set of stalemated, balancing forces; the middle does not link the bottom with the top. The bottom of this society is politically fragmented, and even as a passive fact, increasingly powerless." Thus goes the most celebrated elaboration of the "power elite" thesis, a thesis that has been sharply challenged by the "pluralists." David Riesman has contended, for instance, that there is no single unified power bloc at the pinnacle of our society—that, instead, there is an "amorphous power structure," which consists of a "series of groups, each of which has struggled and finally attained a power to stop things . . . inimical to its interests and, within far narrower limits, to start things." Still other pluralists such as Parsons assert that the key political decisions are reached by alliances among an ever-shifting constellation of many pressure groups.

Pilisuk and Hayden spell out a middle-ground explanation. They admit that elite groups do endanger the democratic process, because our economic and political institutions are continually biased by the requisites of military preparedness, and yet they maintain that there is no ruling group in the United States. "Nor is there," they add, "any easily discernible ruling institutional order, so meshed have the separate sources of power become." All the same, Pilisuk and Hayden conclude, ours is a social structure that tends to encourage and protect power centers, with only partial accountability to the masses of citizens.

We are concerned here with the economic dimensions of power, yet we can no more pinpoint pure "economic" power than we can a purely "economic" man. In this and in the next two sections, as we attend to **homo economicus**, we must recognize that "economic" man, like "political" or "religious" man, is nothing more than a conceptual fiction—an analytical convenience, which, while helping us focus on a given dimension of life, must not be studied outside of the larger social context in which it functions.

This reciprocal and sensitively interdependent nature of the components in institutional life is attested to in the articles by Vernon K. Dibble and Seymour Melman, both of whom are concerned with what they take to be the centrality of the military establishment in the major institutional spheres—political, economic, educational—of the United States. "Handmaidens of the military, out of uniform," Dibble advises, "abound in politics, in scholarship, in the mass media, and in business." And Melman claims that "a basic alteration has been effected in the governing institutions of the United States." He deplores the emergence of a "state military machine" characterized by "an institutionalized power-lust" and a 1970 budget ($83 billion) that exceeds the gross national product of Italy and Sweden combined.

chapter 25
the garrison society
vernon k. dibble

The brazen disregard of law in the Korean enterprise and in the setting up of an international army in Europe is further evidence that our State Department has long since repudiated any serious respect for law and justice . . . My own feeling is that this policy in the field of foreign affairs, unless restrained, can only lead to arbitrary and totalitarian government at home, as foreign affairs come more and more to dominate our domestic activities, and to war in the world [Senator Robert A. Taft, 1951].

The United States today is a garrison society. A garrison society is one in which it makes no sense to ask whether or not civilians control the military. It is a society in which the institutions and the men who hold military, economic, and political power have become so dependent upon one another; in which their goals and interests are so complementary; and in which the traditional boundaries between military and civilian spheres have broken down to such an extent that the very conception of civilian versus military control has no meaning.[1]

In militia societies, too, it makes no sense to talk of civilian control of the military. For in

From New University Thought, 5, Spring 1967. Reprinted by permission.

militia societies—England before the English Civil War, for example—there are few or no full-time soldiers, and no independent military establishment, for civilians to control.[2]

In a civilian society—the United States before World War II—there are full-time soldiers and an independent military establishment. Professional soldiers live, in large measure, within their own, somewhat isolated world. Many of their values—obedience to hierarchical superiors, discipline, physical courage, military honor—are at odds with, or are at least different from, the values of the rest of the society.[3] But they remain subordinate to civil authority.

In an old-fashioned militarist society—Bismarck's Germany, in some respects—the military establishment was not subordinate to civil authority. For example, military budgets in Imperial Germany did not require the approval of the Reichstag. Distinctly military values and styles, of which the duels in German fraternities are the best known example, spill over into civilian society.

But these old-fashioned distinctions between civilian or militarist societies, or between civilian versus military control, have no meaning in the United States today. For example, when hundreds of civilian institutions are closely involved with the military, civilian censorship of the public utterances of officers does not prevent them from having their say in public debate, or in public indoctrination. In August, 1914, President Wilson wrote to the Secretary of War as follows:[4]

> My dear Secretary, I write to suggest that you request and advise all officers of the service, whether active or retired, to refrain from public comment of any kind upon the military and political situation on the other side of the water. . . . It seems to me highly unwise and improper that officers of the Army and Navy of the United States should make any public utterances to which any color of political or military criticism can be given where other nations are involved.

That policy still holds. The White House or civilian secretaries censor the speeches of officers, or forbid their presentation altogether. But in a garrison society the silencing of men in uniform is irrelevant. For handmaidens of the military, out of uniform, abound in politics, in scholarship, in the mass media, and in business.

It makes little difference whether the men who make speeches are generals; or retired generals working for armaments firms; or professors whose research is paid for by the Pentagon, or by the CIA; or journalists whose bread and butter depend upon good relations with Pentagon sources; or congressmen whose reelection may be jeopardized if the bases in their districts are shut down; or researchers in institutes and think shops that survive on military contracts; or corporate executives whose firms manufacture missiles or napalm.

Whoever makes the speeches, and whatever their disagreements with one another—missiles or manned bombers, bomb Hanoi or hold up in enclaves, get tough with Russia or try peaceful coexistence—we will hear no challenge to the basic assumptions of American foreign and domestic policy. We will hear no challenge to the false view that freedom versus communism is what our cold wars and our hot wars are all about.

The point, then, is not simply the size and power of the American military establishment. To be sure, its size and power are basic features of the garrison society. The Pentagon is the headquarters of the largest corporation in the world. As Bert Cochran describes it:[5]

> The sprawling bureaucracy housed in this enormous fortress . . . controls an empire that elicits the respectful attention of any of the heads of our leading corporations. The Cordiner Report of several years ago set a valuation of $160 billion on the property owned by the Defense Department, "by any yardstick of measurement, the world's largest organization." This wealth includes weapons arsenals, air bases, naval stations, army reservations, in all, more than thirty-two million acres of land in the United States, and another two and a half million acres abroad. The total is larger than the combined area of Rhode Island, Connecticut, Massachusetts, Maryland, Vermont, and New Hampshire.
> . . . The assets of the military are three times the combined assets of United States Steel, American Telephone and Telegraph, Metropolitan Life Insurance, General Motors, and Standard Oil Company of New Jersey. Its paid personnel is three times as large as that of these corporations. Of a grand total of five million federal employees, more than three and one-half million are working for the Defense Department: two and a half million in the armed forces, one million civilian workers. The civilian payroll alone is $11 billion a year, equal to one and half times the combined payrolls of the iron and steel industry and of all other basic metal producers, and equal to twice the payroll of the automobile industry. The annual military budget is larger than the annual net income of all the corporations in the country.

But these figures alone do not define the garrison society. The garrison society consists, rather, of (1) a large and powerful military that penetrates deeply into civilian life; of (2) the great importance of civilians in military affairs, the increasing resemblance between military officers and civilian executives in politics and business, and the greater contact and cooperation between officers and civilians in politics, in science, and in business; such that (3) the traditional boundaries between civilian and military society break down; and (4) the military are blended into an alliance with government and with large corporations, whose goals include (a) counterrevolution and American hegemony abroad and (b) a large dose of centralized, executive control of the economy and of politics at home.

PENETRATION INTO CIVILIAN LIFE

You cannot administer a military outfit as big as the Pentagon's without penetrating deeply into civilian society. And even if you could, the largest corporation in the world, like all large corporations, seeks to expand, and to reach out for monopoly control over its environment. It sets up or takes over subsidiary corporations like the non-profit think shops. It diversifies its products. These products now include not only weapons, strategic theories, and military skills. They also include ideological indoctrination, social research, and, in Secretary McNamara's proposal to "salvage" the rejects of the draft, social work, pedagogical theory, an implicit denunciation of the failures of the welfare state, an attack upon the teaching profession, a veiled attack upon the humanities,[6] and "advanced educational and medical techniques." If our schools have failed, the Department of Defense will rescue us.[7]

> The imperatives of national security in our technological age make the Defense Department the world's largest educator of highly skilled men. Those same imperatives require that it also be the world's most efficient educator.

The military penetrates into education, into research and scholarship, into labor unions, into the political decisions of senators and congressmen, and, most crucially, into business and the economy. In education, the use of class standing as a basis for student deferments requires every college instructor in the country to confront his students as an agent of the state. He helps to decide which of his students shall live and which shall die. The selective service system has intruded into the internal government of colleges and universities, has appropriated the ordinary relations between students and teachers for its own administrative convenience, and has transformed these relations into instruments of the garrison society.[8]

The military's penetration into research and scholarship is even more direct. "There was a period after the war," writes Louis J. Halle, "when various departments of the Government tried to marry themselves to the universities." That marriage did not work well in the case of the State Department. But it "worked in the case of the Pentagon and the faculties of science and technology, a wartime precedent having already been established at Oak Ridge and Los Alamos."[9]

Since that time, the military has continued to purchase some of the best minds in the country. Professor Melman has described some of the consequences of that fact for civilian research and development, for the internal structure of American universities, and for the financially neglected fields outside the natural sciences.[10] The military provides large percentages of the annual budget of many major universities.[11] And it, along with the CIA, have transformed scholars and researchers into intelligence analysts, military technicians, and apologists. Michigan State University's fronting for the CIA in Vietnam, and the University of Pennsylvania's secret research for the Pentagon are extreme, but not unique, instances. For example, at last count thirty-eight universities and institutes affiliated with universities were conducting research on chemical and biological warfare for the Department of Defense.[12]

Government money for research has consequences, in turn, for education. A professor who has research money from outside his university acquires an economic base that tends to free him from collegial and departmental control. Whether he operates alone with his assistants or in a research institute with colleagues, he is under less pressure to be concerned with all the varied tasks of a university, including the task of teaching students. He is more free, if so inclined, to regard his university as a home base for his operations elsewhere. One result, even among some teachers in undergraduate colleges, is professorial disdain for teaching and for education, as opposed to the specialized training of selected students. From the students' point of view, some of the best of them are suspicious of all scholars and of all scholarship, because they see the confusion of scholarship with military intelligence or apologetics.

In many labor unions, members and dues depend upon war plants. I doubt (as Isaac Deutscher recently expressed it) that most American workers are happy about working for death instead of for life. But a man needs a job. And a union needs members. Hence, unions help munitions firms to secure or retain military contracts, or lobby to prevent the closing down of shipyards and airplane plants. And some labor leaders are among the most chauvinistic heralds of the American counterrevolution abroad.

The no-strike pledge during World War II is to the unions' relations with the government as Oak Ridge and Los Alamos are to the postwar marriage between the Pentagon and departments or institutes of science and technology. That is, the organizational mobilization of American society that World War II brought about has continued ever since. For the managers of unions, business firms, research institutes, and governmental agencies find advantages—less militant unions, access to power, money for research, or whatever—in continuing cooperation with one another. These advantages are quite independent of their original military significance. Hence, the organizational coordination of World War II goes on, but, of course, with a new definition of the enemy.

Thus, during the Korean War the Research Director of the Textile Workers Union wrote:[13]

The present emergency found American trade-unions prepared to unite with other groups on a common program of national mobilization. They were keyed to an all-out extended battle against Communist totalitarianism, for they knew its dangers and the threat it represented to the people's well-being.

One decade later the Executive Council of the AFL-CIO declared, "The nation's defense requirements obviously have top priority."[14] And in 1963, Secretary McNamara awarded the AFL-CIO a well-deserved citation for, among other things, military propaganda. The Secretary praised the union for "utilizing extensive communications media to promote greater understanding among its millions of members and the public of the vital objectives of defense programs."[15]

In Congress, we read, many silent senators are "concerned" about Vietnam. But only three voted against the latest Vietnam appropriation. Dozens of congressmen signed a statement of "concern" about escalation, and proceeded to vote in favor of the appropriation. In contrast, the draft was reinstated in 1948 by a vote of 70 to 10 in the Senate and 259 to 136 in the House.[16] For (except when they want to appropriate more money than the Pentagon requests) a mere senator or congressman does not tangle with the largest corporation in the world, whether his state or district wants to keep the bases and war plants it already has, or feels neglected and wants to acquire some. Its economic importance stifles debate. And with most labor unions, or their leaders, committed to the garrison system, one potential source of pressure on congressmen to behave differently is eliminated.

The acquiescence of Congress and of the labor movement has repercussions, in turn, on education. Many of the most intelligent and most serious college students today spend more time on political activity than on their studies. For as they see it, and they see it correctly, America faces desperate problems that almost no one in public life is willing to face. If a dozen silent senators

who are "concerned" about Vietnam would only speak up, political activists on college campuses would feel free to spend more time on chemistry formulae and the Greek dative.

In the economy, some ten to twenty percent—depending on what you include and how you measure it—of the national product depends on the military. And some ten to twenty percent of the labor force work at jobs that also depend upon the military. About 25,000 private industrial plants operate under systems of military security, over four million employees were required to obtain security clearance during a period of ten years, and, to be on the safe side, some firms have extended military security to all of their operations, including those which have nothing to do with military work.[17]

To be sure, many, perhaps most, American firms do not benefit directly from the garrison society. If twenty percent depend upon it, eighty percent pay taxes to make it possible. Nor would all munitions firms, even, be hurt seriously by sudden disarmament. And some firms, in banking and in men's clothing for example, have been hurt by the war in Vietnam. But we cannot look to businessmen who are left out of the profits of the garrison society, or to firms that are hurt by the war, to lead the way toward "dismantling the cold war institutional machine."[18] For to do so would be a basic challenge to their aerospace colleagues; to the existing system of political power; in some cases to the unions that operate in their plants; and to the entire ideology of anticommunism from which they, too, derive strength and comfort in these trying times. Terminating the war in Vietnam tomorrow would be in the economic interest of many American firms. But adherence to the reigning ideology, and class solidarity with other businessmen more directly involved in the garrison society, seem thus far to be stronger than immediate economic interests. In short, as concerns the military and the American economy, a little penetration goes a long, long way.

THE BOUNDARIES BREAK DOWN

But, as noted in the second element in our definition of the garrison society, the penetration of the military into civilian society is only part of the story. While civilian life has become increasingly militarized, civilians have become more important in military affairs, military men have more contact with civilians, and military men come to resemble civilians more than ever before.

The office of the Secretary of Defense is no longer that of a coordinator. The Secretary and his civilian aides are makers of military policy. The number and the influence of civilian military theorists, in and out of the Department of Defense, moved General Thomas D. White, former Air Force Chief of Staff, to remark, "in common with other military men I am profoundly apprehensive of the pipe-smoking, trees-full-of-owls type of so-called defense intellectuals who have been brought into this nation's capitol."[19] And no longer do armaments firms simply manufacture what the military orders. They have their own staffs to devise their own weapons systems, which they try to sell to Congress and to the Pentagon.

But the military, too, is developing its own generation of military intellectuals and technological specialists. Advanced technology and a complex, sprawling organization (no longer limited to a simple command structure plus some staff positions) make brains and managerial talent more important than old-fashioned heroism in the upper reaches of military hierarchies. And, of course, constant dealings with corporate executives, plus the prospect of a career in business after retirement from the service, reinforce tendencies within the services themselves toward making the work of military leaders increasingly similar to the work of corporate executives.[20] More generally, as Allen Guttman suggests, the end of laissez faire liberalism in this country—the transformation, in Guttman's words, "from an imperfect liberal democracy to an imperfect social democracy"—means that "the American soldier can for the first time in our history square the dictates of his professional ethic with the accepted values and institutions of our society."[21]

In short, the traditional social and cultural boundaries between civilian and military society have broken down. The military, civilian government, and large corporations do not form a single, monolithic ruling group. There are conflicts within, and between, each party to the alliance. But on all essentials—American world power, the Cold War and anticommunism, and the shape of our domestic economy and social structure—they are as one.

The historical origins of the garrison society are reflected in this coalescence of military and civilian executives, and in this fading away of traditional boundaries. The garrison society did not come about because a military clique imposed itself on the rest of America. It was built—base by

base, contract by contract, and professor by professor—through the cooperation of military leaders, politicians, and corporate executives that began during World War II. Universities, labor leaders, intellectuals, and the mass media followed along.

One of the earliest prophets of the garrison society was Charles E. Wilson, former president of General Electric. In January, 1944, in an address before the Army Ordnance Association, Wilson proposed an alliance of the military, the executive branch of the federal government, and large corporations in "a permanent war economy." He proposed that every large corporation have on its roster a colonel in the reserves for liaison with the military, and he spelled out the role of the federal executive, of Congress, and of business as follows:[22]

> First of all such a [preparedness] program must be the responsibility of the Federal government. It must be initiated and administered by the executive branch—by the President as Commander-in-Chief and by the War and Navy Departments. Of equal importance is the fact that this must be, once and for all, a continuing program and not the creature of an emergency. In fact one of its objects will be to eliminate emergencies so far as possible. The role of Congress will be limited to voting the needed funds. . . .
>
> Industry's role in this program is to respond and cooperate . . . in the execution of the part allotted to it; industry must not be hampered by political witch hunts, or thrown to the fanatical isolationist figure tagged with a 'merchants of death' label.

The cooperation that Wilson proposed, and that in fact came about, does not create a monolithic ruling group. But it does create a system in which each party has a great stake in the other party's interests and success. That is one of the system's strong points. If one party to the alliance were imposing itself on the other two, the whole system would be weaker than it is. The economy is dependent in an important degree on the military. But it is equally true that the military are dependent on big business. If armaments firms acted like old-fashioned entrepreneurs, keeping their capital mobile and seeking out the most profitable markets, they might go in for pea canning plants in Sicily instead of missiles. The military and the

government depend upon their continued preference for government-sponsored, low-risk capitalism.

Another source of the alliance's strength is the
fact that most participants—politicians, generals,
corporate executives, and professors—really believe
in what they are doing. They are, by their lights,
patriotic servants of the public weal. And the combination of power, profits, and sincerity is more
powerful than power and profits alone.

INTERNATIONAL POWER
AND DOMESTIC CONTROLS

This powerful combination, of motives and of
institutions, has profound consequences for American society. The world-wide goals of the garrison
society—preventing social revolution and preserving both capitalism and American world power
abroad—have repercussions on domestic politics
and on the domestic political economy. The preservation of the American imperial system requires
economic stability and steady, manageable, predictable economic growth at home. Management
and predictability are crucial.

Suppose the United States had a free market
economy, subject to uncontrolled fluctuations.
Think of the international consequences. A big
depression, a great and sudden decline in profits
and in employment, would mean a great decline in
federal revenues. There would also be increased
political pressure to use these declining revenues
for more domestic relief of one kind or another.
Foreign aid programs might be threatened. American purchases abroad, public and private, would be
curtailed. American multinational corporations
might import more of their undistributed profits
from abroad and engage in less foreign investment,
especially if low prices in capital goods made the
depression a good time to invest here. And imports
of the products of other nations, including unstable and potentially revolutionary nations, would
go down. Previously friendly governments and
businessmen in foreign countries would have to
look elsewhere for friends. And, what is more crucial, what would happen to our counterrevolution
in Colombia if we could not buy Colombian coffee?

On the other hand, a boom that is too big or
too sudden is no good either. For one thing,
booms tend to produce their opposite. But apart
from that fact, too great an increase in dividends
and in corporate investment creates inflationary

pressure and invites social conflict in the form of
wage demands and perhaps crippling strikes. Inflation means that foreign nations have less purchasing power in the United States and would take
their business elsewhere, while production at high
capacity forces American business to purchase
more from abroad than they otherwise would.
Both developments place further strain on the
balance of payments, which might require, at some
later point, either great cuts in foreign purchases,
or a great cut in the foreign military bases of the
United States.

In short, some of the international repercussions of a big boom are identical to those of a big
depression. Both must be avoided if the American
imperial system is to remain intact.

Avoiding both the big boom and the big
depression requires an increasingly guided economy—guidelines, dumping surplus commodities on
the market to prevent an increase in price, the
confrontation between President Kennedy and the
steel industry, using the White House instead of
old-fashioned bargaining sessions to settle strikes,
and using tax policy to make investment and consumption go up or down as the moment requires.
These policies, in turn, have further consequences
for the society.

For example, labor leaders come under pressure to suppress any signs of an active internal life,
and of mass rank-and-file involvement in labor
unions. Such things are unmanageable. They have
unpredictable consequences. To cite a second example, we cannot permanently abolish unemployment—the classic test of the success of the welfare
state—because we must worry about attendant
inflationary pressure. That fact, in turn, makes any
genuine integration of the mass of Negroes into
American society most unlikely, so long as the
garrison system lasts.

There are, to be sure, strains in the system.
The airline machinists did not go along. The guidelines are breaking down. And there is probably an
inherent contradiction between the requirements
of the system and the interests of each single firm
or industry. Guidelines are most advantageous to
you if your firm or your union is the only one that
does not go along with them.

But suppose, for the moment, that the economic management that is inherent in the garrison
society works well enough for the foreseeable
future. What, then, are the lessons of Vietnam?
The obvious lesson is that future garrison govern-

ments, in time of peace, must always manage to keep unemployment relatively high and production well below capacity. For reasons that Professor Terence McCarthy has expounded, that extra slack is needed in order to fight our next colonial war without overheating the economy. That is how you incorporate Keynesian economics and the historic achievements of the New Deal and of American liberalism into the garrison society.

NOTES

1. The term "garrison society" is, of course, a variation of Harold Lasswell's term, "garrison state." But the two terms do not refer to the same phenomena. In Lasswell's words, "The simplest version of the garrison-state hypothesis is that the arena of world politics is moving toward the domination of specialists in violence." See Lasswell, "The Garrison State Hypothesis Today," in Samuel P. Huntington, ed., Changing Patterns of Military Politics, The Free Press of Glencoe: New York, 1952, pp. 51-70.

2. For more details about this example, see the section entitled "Lords Lieutenant And Their Deputies" in Vernon K. Dibble, "The Organization of Traditional Authority: English County Government, 1558-1640," in James G. March, ed., Handbook of Organizations, Rand McNally: Chicago, 1965, pp. 879-909. See also the relevant chapters in Thomas G. Barnes, Somerset, 1625-1640: A County's Government During the Personal Rule, Harvard University Press: Cambridge, 1961.

3. Samuel P. Huntington, in The Soldier and the State, notes a number of ways in which "the military ethic" is in conflict with the liberal ideology that has been dominant in American political history. For example, "The heart of liberalism is individualism. It emphasizes the reason and moral dignity of the individual, and opposes political, economic, and social restraints upon individual liberty. In contrast, the military ethic holds that man is evil, weak, and irrational and that he must be subordinated to the group. The military man claims that the natural relation among men is conflict." Quoted in Allen Guttman, "Political Ideals And The Military Ethic," The American Scholar, 34:2, Spring, 1965, p. 22.

4. Quoted in Jack Raymond, Power At The Pentagon, Harper and Row: New York, 1964, p. 178.

5. Bert Cochran, The War System, Macmillan: New York, 1965, pp. 138-139.

6. I take it that the Secretary's statement that "One of the department's key concepts is that traditional classroom training is often largely irrelevant to actual on-the-job performance requirements" and his reference to "pruning from existing courses all nonessential informa tion" are veiled attacks on the humanities.

7. The quotation which follows, the quotation in the previous sentence and the quotation in note 3 are from the excerpts from Secretary McNamara's address to the Veterans of Foreign Wars, New York Times, August 24, 1966, p. 18.

8. The administration of a number of colleges (including Wayne State, Haverford, Cornell, and a few others) have indicated that their colleges will either submit no class standings to draft boards or will otherwise refuse to go along (for example, by refusing to compute class standings separately for male and female students). The faculties of a few other colleges, including Columbia College, have voted in favor of this position.

9. Louis J. Halle, "On Teaching International Relations," Virginia Quarterly Review, 40:1, Winter, 1964, p. 13.

10. Semour Melman, Our Depleted Society, Dell Publishing Co.: New York, 1965, Chapter 4, entitled "Cold War Science and Technology."

11. Ibid., Appendix C, "Index of 500 Largest Military Prime Contractors for Experimental Development, Test and Research Work." See also Raymond, op. cit., Chapter VIII, "Research and the Federal Government" and Cochran, op. cit., pp. 155-161.

12. This figure is from Carol Brightman, "The 'Weed Killers'—A Final Word," Viet Report, 2:7, 1966, pp. 3-5. Miss Brightman relies on "a Pentagon spokesman" as reported in the Washington Post.

13. Solomon Barkin, "American Trade-Unions in the Present Emergency," Monthly Labor Review, the Bureau of Labor Statistics 73:4, October, 1951, p. 409.

14. Proceedings of the AFL-CIO Fourth Constitutional Convention, 1961, vol. II, p. 70.

15. Proceedings of the AFL-CIO Fifth Constitutional Convention, 1963, vol. I, p. 355.

16. New York Times, June 11, 1948 and June 23, 1948.

17. The information on military security in business is from Raymond, op. cit., pp. 154-156. On the extent to which the economy depends upon military spending, Harry Magdoff, using the estimates of the U.S. Arms Control And Disarmament Agency in its volume, Economic Impacts of Disarmament (Washington, D.C., 1962), writes as follows: "The more than $55 billion spent annually on what the government agencies classify as 'national defense' has a chain-reaction effect on the rest of the economy, just as other forms of investment and spending have a 'multiplier' effect. It is estimated that for every $1 spent on 'national defense' another $1 to $1.40 of economic product is stimulated. A crude, but conservative, calculation shows that in addition to the approximately 7.4 million people engaged in some phase of 'national defense,' another 6 to 9 million are employed due to the economic stimulus of defense spending." Harry Magdoff, "Problems of United States Capitalism," in R. Miliband and J. Savile, eds., The Socialist Register: 1965, Monthly Review Press: New York, 1965, p. 63. See also Cochran, op. cit., pp. 140-141.

18. This phrase is the title of Chapter 12 of Melman, op. cit.

19. Quoted in Raymond, op. cit., p. 289. More generally, see Raymond's Chapter 16, "The 'McNamara Monarchy'."

20. See Morris Janowitz, The Professional Soldier: A Social and Political Portrait, The Free Press: Glencoe, Illinois, 1960. Especially Section II, "Organizational Realities: Heroic And Managerial" and Chapter 20, "The Future of the Military Profession."

21. Guttmann, op. cit., p. 237. See note 3, above, for further explanation of this point.

22. Quoted in Fred J. Cook, **The Warfare State,** Macmillan: New York, 1962, pp. 76-77. Mr. Cook, in turn, quotes from an article by John M. Swomley in **The** **Progressive,** January 1959. I was unfortunately not able to locate the full text of Mr. Wilson's speech in any of the usual sources such as **Vital Speeches** or **The New York Times.** Note that this man is Wilson of G.E., not Wilson of General Motors.

chapter 26

pentagon capitalism: the political economy of war

seymour melman

In the name of defense, and without announcement or debate, a basic alteration has been effected in the governing institutions of the United States. An industrial management has been installed in the federal government, under the Secretary of Defense, to control the nation's largest network of industrial enterprises. With the characteristic managerial propensity for extending its power, limited only by its allocated share of the national product, the new state-management combines peak economic, political, and military decision-making. Hitherto, this combination of powers in the same hands has been a feature of statist societies—communist, fascist, and others—where individual rights cannot constrain central rule.

This new institution of state-managerial control has been the result of actions undertaken for the declared purposes of adding to military power and economic efficiency and of reinforcing civilian, rather than professional, military rule. Its main characteristics are institutionally specific and therefore substantially independent of its chief of the moment. The effects of its operations are independent of the intention of its architects, and may ever have been unforeseen by them.

The creation of the state-management marked

the transformation of President Dwight Eisenhower's "military-industrial complex," a loose collaboration, mainly through market relations of senior military officers, industrial managers, and legislators. Robert McNamara, under the direction of President John Kennedy, organized a formal central-management office to administer the military-industrial empire. The market was replaced by a management. In place of the complex, there is now a defined administrative control center that regulates tens of thousands of subordinate managers. In 1968, they directed the production of $44 billion of goods and services for military use. By the measure of the scope and scale of its decision-power, the new state-management is by far the largest and most important single management in the United States. There are about 15,000 men who arrange work assignments to subordinate managers (contract negotiation), and 40,000 who oversee compliance of submanagers of subdivisions with the top management's rules. This is the largest industrial central administrative office in the United States—perhaps in the world.

The state-management has also become the most powerful decision-making unit in the United States government. Thereby, the federal government does not "serve" business or "regulate" business. For the new management is the largest of them all. Government is business. That is state capitalism.

The normal operation, including expansion, of the new state-management has been based upon preemption of a lion's share of federal tax revenue and of the nation's finite supply of technical manpower. This use of capital and skill has produced parasitic economic growth—military products which are not part of the level of living and which cannot be used for further production. All this, while the ability to defend the United States, to shield it from external attack, has diminished.

From 1946 to 1969, the United States government spent over $1,000 billion on the military, more than half of this under the Kennedy and Johnson administrations—the period during which the state-management was established as a formal institution. This sum of staggering size (try to visualize a billion of something) does not express the cost of the military establishment to the nation as a whole. The true cost is measured by what has been foregone, by the accumulated deterioration in many facets of life, by the inability to alleviate human wretchedness of long duration.

Here is part of the human inventory of depletion:

1. By 1968, there were 6 million grossly substandard dwellings, mainly in the cities.
2. 10 million Americans suffered from hunger in 1968-1969.
3. The United States ranked 18th at last report (1966 among nations in infant mortality rate (23.7 infant deaths in first year per 1,000 live births). In Sweden (1966) the rate was 12.6.
4. In 1967, 40.7 percent of the young men examined were disqualified for military service (28.5 percent for medical reasons).
5. In 1950, there were 109 physicians in the United States per 100,000 population By 1966 there were 98.
6. About 30 million Americans are an economically underdeveloped sector of the society.

The human cost of military priority is paralleled by the industrial-technological depletion caused by the concentration of technical manpower and capital on military technology and in military industry. For example:

1. By 1968, United States industry operated the world's oldest stock of metal-working machinery; 64 percent was 10 years old and over.

2. No United States railroad has anything in motion that compares with the Japanese and French fast trains.
3. The United States merchant fleet ranks 23rd in age of vessels. In 1966, world average age of vessels was 17 years, United States 21, Japan 9.
4. While the United States uses the largest number of research scientists and engineers in the world, key United States industries, such as steel and machine tools, are in trouble in domestic markets: in 1967, for the first time, the United States imported more machine tools than it exported.

As civilian industrial technology deteriorates or fails to advance productive employment opportunity for Americans diminishes.

All of this only begins to reckon the true cost to America of operating the state military machine. (The cost of the Vietnam war to the Vietnamese people has no reckoning.) Clearly, no mere ideology or desire for individual power can account for the colossal costs of the military machine. A lust for power has been at work here, but it is not explicable in terms of an individual's power drive. Rather, the state-management represents an institutionalized power-lust. A normal thirst for more managerial power within the largest management in the United States gives the new state-management an unprecedented ability and opportunity for building an empire abroad. This is the new imperialism.

The magnitude of the decision-power of the Pentagon managment has reached that of a state. After all, the fiscal 1970 budget plan of the Department of Defense—**$83 billion**—exceeds the gross national product (GNP) of entire nations: in billions of dollars for 1966—Belgium, $18.1; Italy $61.4; Sweden $21.3. The state-management has become a para-state, a state within a state.

In its beginning, the government of the United States was a political entity. The managing of economic and industrial activity was to be the province of private persons. This division of function was the grand design for American government and society, within which personal and political freedom could flourish alongside of rapid economic growth and technological progress. After 1960, this design was transformed. In the name of ensuring civilian efficiencies of modern management, Secretary of Defense Robert McNamara redesigned the organization of his Department to include, within the office of the Secretary, a central administrative office. This was designed to control operations in thousands of subsidiary industrial enterprises undertaken on behalf of the Department of Defense. Modeled after the central administrative offices of multidivision industrial firms—such as the Ford Motor Company, the General Motors Corporation, and the General Electric Company—the new top management in the Department of Defense was designed to control the activities of subsidiary managements of firms producing, in 1968, $44 billion of goods and services for the Department of Defense.

By the measure of industrial activity governed from one central office, this new management in the Department of Defense is beyond compare the largest industrial management in the United States, perhaps in the world. Never before in American experience has there been such a combination of economic and political decision-power in the same hands. The senior officers of the new state-management are also senior political officers of the government of the United States. Thus, one consequence of the establishment of the new state-management has been the installation, within American society of an institutional feature of a totalitarian system.

The original design of the American government was oriented toward safeguarding individual political freedom and economic liberties. These safeguards were abridged by the establishment of the new state-management in the Department of Defense. In order to perceive the abridgement of traditional liberties by the operation of the new managerial institution, one must focus on its functional performance. For the official titles of its units sound like just another government bureaucracy: Office of the Secretary of Defense, Defense Supply Agency, etc.

The new industrial management has been created in the name of defending America from its external enemies and preserving a way of life of a free society. It has long been understood, however, that one of the safeguards of individual liberty is the separation of roles of a citizen and of an employee. When an individual relates to the same person both as a citizen and as an employee, then the effect is such—regardless of intention—that the employer-government official has an unprecedented combination of decision-making power over the individual citizen-employee.

In the Soviet Union, the combination of top economic and political decision-power is a formal part of the organization and ideology of that soci-

ety. In the United States, in contrast, the joining of the economic-managerial and top political power has been done in an unannounced and, in effect, covert fashion. In addition to the significance of the new state-management with respect to individual liberty in American society, the new organization is significant for its effects in preempting resources and committing the nation to the military operations that the new organization is designed to serve. Finally, the new power center is important because of the self-powered drive toward expansion that is built into the normal operation of an industrial management.

The preemption of resources takes place because of the sheer size of the funds that are wielded by the Department of Defense. Its budget, amounting to over $80 billion in 1969, gives this organization and its industrial-management arm unequalled decision-power over manpower, materials, and industrial production capacity in the United States and abroad. It is, therefore, predictable that this organization will be able to get the people and other resources that it needs whenever it needs them, even if this requires outbidding other industries and other organizations—including other agencies of the federal and other governments.

Regardless of the individual avowals and commitments of the principal officers of the new industrial machine, it is necessarily the case that the increased competence of this organization contributes to the competence of the parent body—the Department of Defense. This competence is a war-making capability. Hence, the very efficiency and success of the new industrial-management, unavoidably and regardless of intention, enhances the war-making capability of the government of the United States. As the war-making department accumulates diverse resources and planning capability, it is able to offer the President blueprint-stage options for responding to all manner of problem situations—while other government agencies look (and are) unready, understaffed, and underequipped. This increases the likelihood of recourse to "solutions" based upon military power.

Finally, the new government management, insofar as it shares the usual characteristics of industrial management, has a built-in propensity for expanding the scope and intensity of its operations—for this expansion is the hallmark of success in management. The chiefs of the new state-management, in order to be successful in their own eyes, strive to maintain and extend their decision-power—by enlarging their activities, the number of their employees, the size of the capital investments which they control, and by gaining control over more and more subsidiary managements. By 1967-68, the scope of the state-management's control over production had established it as the dominant decision-maker in the U.S. industry. The industrial output of $44 billion of goods and services under state-management control in 1968 exceeded by far the reported net sales of American industry's leading firms (in billions of dollars for 1968): A.T.&T., $14.1; Du Pont, $3.4; General Electric, $8.4; General Motors, $22.8; U.S. Steel, $4.6. The giants of United States industry have become small-, and medium-sized firms, compared with the new state-management—with its conglomerate industrial base.

The appearance of the new state-managerial machine marks a transformation in the character of the American government and requires us to reexamine our understanding of its behavior. Various classic theories of industrial capitalist society have described government as an essentially political entity, ideally impartial. Other theories depict government as justifiably favoring, or even identifying with, business management, while the theories in the Marxist tradition have depicted government as an arm of business. These theories require revision.

THEORIES OF
GOVERNMENT—BUSINESS POWER

The classic theory of imperialism explained the behavior of government, in part, as the result of the influence of private industrial managers and chiefs of financial organizations. In this view, a ruling class, located in private enterprise, used the political instruments of government in the service of private gain. Thereby, the central government's political, legal, and military powers were utilized at home and abroad to maintain and extend the decision-power of this ruling class, through sponsoring and protecting private property rights, foreign trade, and foreign investment.

These classic theories of imperialism do not help us understand one of the most important of recent United States government policies—participation in the war in Vietnam and preparation for a series of such wars. At the time of this writing, the United States government had expended not less than $100 billion in military and related activities in connection with the Vietnam war. This excludes the economic impacts of an indirect sort within the United States caused by this war.

No one has demonstrated any past, present, or foreseeable volume of trade or investment in Vietnam and/or adjacent areas that would justify an outlay of $100 billion. The accompanying data on location and size of United States foreign investments speak for themselves (see table). Indeed, there is substantial evidence to indicate that an important segment of the industrial corporations of the United States are not beneficiaries of participation by the American industrial system in military and allied production. (Thus, a Marxist political economist, Victor Perlo, has judged that about one-half of the major American industrial firms would gain materially from a cessation of military production.) Moreover criticism of the Vietnam war by important institutions of the American establishment, such as **The Wall Street Journal** and **The New York Times**, is not consistent with the idea that the war has been conducted to suit the requirements of private finance and industry.

U.S. Private Direct Long-Term Investments Abroad 1966 (In Billions of Dollars)

Total	$54.2
Canada	$16.8
Western Europe	16.2
Latin American republics	9.8
Other Western hemisphere	1.6
Africa	2.0
Middle East	1.6
Far East	2.2
Oceania	2.0
Miscellaneous international	2.0

Source: Statistical Abstract of the United States, 1968, U.S. Department of Commerce, 1968, p. 792.

However, the operation of Vietnam war policies by the federal government is quite consistent with the maintenance and extension of decision-power by the new industrial management centered in the Department of Defense—for the management of the Vietnam war has been the occasion of major enlargement of budgets, facilities, manpower, capital investment and control over an additional million Americans in the labor force and more than one-half million additional Americans in the armed forces.

In his notable volume **The Power Elite**, C. Wright Mills, writing in 1956, perceived a three-part system of elites in the United States: economic, military, and political. At different times in American history, Mills wrote, this elite has been variously composed. That is, one or another of these three principals exercised primary decision-power. Mills concluded:

The shape and the meaning of the power elite today can be understood only when these three sets of structural trends are seen at their point of coincidence: the military capitalism of private corporations exists in a weakened and formal democratic system containing a military order already quite political in outlook and demeanor.

Mills stated further:

Today all three are involved in virtually all ramifying decisions. Which of the three types seems to lead depends upon the tasks of the period as they, the elite, define them. Just now, these tasks center upon defense and international affairs. Accordingly, as we have seen, the military are ascendent in two senses: as personnel and as justifying ideology. That is why, just now, we can most easily specify the unity and the shape of the power elite in terms of the military ascendancy.

In a similar vein, Robert L. Heilbroner, writing of **The Limits of American Capitalism**, supports the Mills analysis that a system of elites wields primary decision-power in American society: the military, professionals—including technical experts—and government administrators. "There is little doubt," Heilbroner wrote,

that a military-industrial-political interpenetration of interests exists to the benefit of all three. Yet in this alliance I have seen no suggestion that the industrial element is the dominant one. It is the military or the political branch that commands, and business that obeys: . . . the role of business in the entire defense effort is essentially one of jockeying for favor rather than initiating policy.

The analysis by C. Wright Mills was a reasonable one for his time. It was appropriate to a period of transition, whose closing was marked by the famous farewell address of President Dwight Eisenhower.

In his final address as President, Eisenhower gave his countrymen a grave message. "In the councils of government we must guard against the acquisition of unwarranted influence, whether sought or unsought, by the military-industrial complex. The potential for the disastrous rise of misplaced power exists and will persist." [For the full text, see Ap-

pendix B of Seymour Melman, **Pentagon Capitalism: The Political Economy of War**, New York: McGraw-Hill, 1970—Ed.] Here and in subsequent addresses, Eisenhower did not offer a precise definition of what he meant by military-industrial complex. It is reasonable, however, to see the meaning of this category in the context in which it was stated. Military-industrial complex means a loose, informally defined collection of firms producing military products, senior military officers, and members of the executive and legislative branches of the federal government—all of them limited by the market relations of the military products network and having a common ideology as to the importance of maintaining or enlarging the armed forces of the United States and their role in American politics.

The military-industrial complex has as its central point an informality of relationships, as befits the market form which underpins its alliances. The understanding, therefore, is that the main interest groups concerned tend to move together, each of them motivated by its own special concerns, but with enough common ground to produce a mutually reinforcing effect. It is noteworthy that neither Eisenhower nor anyone else has suggested that there was a formal organization, or directorate, or executive committee of the military-industrial complex. The new industrial management in the federal government is, by contrast, clearly structured and formally organized, with all the paraphernalia of a formal, centrally managed organization, whose budget draws upon 10 percent of the gross national product of the richest nation in the world.

The formal organization and powers of the new state-management also bear on the meaning of the various elite theories. It is true that various groups in society obviously have greater power over the course of events than ordinary citizens. But the elites are not equal. Some are "more equal than others." Primacy in decision-power among major elites is determined by the extent of control over production and by the ability to implement policies whose consequences are favorable to some elites, even while being hurtful to the others. By these tests the new state-management dominates the field. It manages more production than any other elite. Its policies of military priority, military buildups, and the Vietnam wars program have been damaging to the decision-power of other elites. [For further discussion, see later chapters in Melman, **Pentagon Capitalism: The Political Econ-**

omy of War—Ed.] In sum, an understanding of the normal operation of the new state-management and its consequences is essential for a meaningful theory of contemporary American economy, government, and society.

During recent years, many writers have been intrigued by the panoply of technological power displayed by the immense and complicated stockpile of weapons fashioned for the Department of Defense. There has been a tendency in some quarters to focus on control over weaponry rather than on decision-power over people. In December, 1967, Arthur I. Waskow told the American Historical Association, "The first major trend event of the last generation in America has been the emergence of what could almost be seen as a new class, defined more by its relation to the means of total destruction than by a relation to means of production."

In a somewhat similar vein, Ralph E. Lapp, in his recent volume **The Weapons Culture,** concluded: "It is no exaggeration to say that the United States has spawned a weapons culture which has fastened an insidious grip on the entire nation." While I admire the excellence of Lapp's analyses of military organization and weaponry and the consequences of their use, it seems to me that to emphasize the idea of a weapons culture, implying a kind of weapons-technological Frankenstein, is less than helpful for appreciating the sources of recent changes in the American government and its policy.

Lapp declared: "The United States has institutionalized its arms-making to the point that there is grave doubt that it can control this far-flung apparatus." He may be correct in his judgment that the whole affair has gone beyond the point of being halted or reversed. But in order to make this judgment, it seems altogether critical to define exactly what it is that has been institutionalized. Where is the location of critical decision-power over "the weapons culture," with several million Americans involved directly or indirectly in military organization and in its support? Should we understand that one person, or one part, of this network is as important as any other?

In my estimate, it is important to identify the crucial decision-makers of the largest military organization (including its industrial base) in the world. Apart from these considerations, I am uneasy about theories viewing man as the captive of his weapons. This is a self-defeating mode of understanding, rather different from identifying the top decision-makers and their mode of control. Men may be captives, but only of other men. The concept of man in the grip of a Frankenstein weapons system has a severely limiting effect on our ability to do anything about it, if that is desired.

Recently, two writers have developed theories of convergence between military industry and government. Better-known are the ideas of John Kenneth Galbraith, as formulated in his volume **The New Industrial State.** Galbraith states: "Increasingly, it will be recognized that the mature corporation, as it develops becomes part of the larger administrative complex associated with the state. In time the line between the two will disappear." In this perspective, the major military-industrial firms, as part of the larger family of major enterprises, merges with governmental organization. But this theory does not specify which of the managerial groups involved becomes more important than the other. Indeed, one of the theoretical contributions of **The New Industrial State** is the idea of a "technostructure," a community of technically trained managers operating on behalf of enterprises, public and private, with their movements among these enterprises serving as a bond between public and private institutions. But the technostructure idea homogenizes the men of the managerial-industrial occupations on the basis of their skills and work tasks. This bypasses the fact that an accountant, for example, in the state-management participates in a power-wielding institution of incomparably greater scope than the management of any private firm. Being in the state-management amplifies the significance of his work tasks, which may be qualitatively undifferentiable from those in a private firm.

In a similar vein, a former economist for Boeing, Murray L. Weidenbaum (now Professor of Economics at Washington University), presented another convergence hypothesis before the American Economic Association in December, 1967. In Weidenbaum's view,

> The close, continuing relationship between the military establishment and the major companies serving the military establishment is changing the nature of both the public sector of the American economy and a large branch of American industry. To a substantial degree, the government is taking on the traditional role of the private entrepreneur while the companies are becoming less like other corporations and acquiring much of the characteristics

of a government agency or arsenal. In a sense, the close, continuing relationship between the Department of Defense and its major suppliers is resulting in a convergence between the two, which is blurring and reducing much of the distinction between public and private activities in an important branch of the American economy.

The Weidenbaum thesis is close to the analyses which I am presenting in this book. My purpose here, however, is to underscore not convergence but the managerial primacy of the new managerial control institution in the Department of Defense, and the consequences for the character of American economy and society that flow from this.

When the Kennedy-Johnson administration took office in 1961, the President's aides were impressed with the problem of ensuring civilian White House control over the armed forces. From this vantage point, one of the main accomplishments of Robert S. McNamara was to reorganize the Department of Defense so as to give top decision-power to the newly enlarged and elaborated office of the Secretary of Defense—clearly a civilian control office superior to and separate from the Joint Chiefs of Staff. McNamara obviously drew upon his experience as a top manager of the Ford Company central office to design a similar organization under the Office of the Secretary of Defense. There is a similarity between these two central offices, but the difference in decision-power is very great. The Pentagon's management is by far the more powerful in the industrial sphere, and is tied to top decision-power in the military and political spheres as well.

It is true that the top echelons of the Department of Defense were reorganized in a manner consistent with the goal of establishing firmer civilian control. This result, however, was achieved by methods that also established an industrial management of unprecedented size and decision-power within the federal government. One result is that it is no longer meaningful to speak of the elites of industrial management, the elites of finance, and the elites of government and how they relate to each other. The elites have been merged in the new state-management.

This development requires a review of many of our understandings of the role of the federal government in relation to individual freedom in our society. For example, antitrust laws, and their enforcement by the executive branch of the government, have been designed to preserve individual freedom by limiting combinations and preventing conspiracies in the economic realm. The laws have been enforced with varying intensity, but have pressed in particular on the largest firms by restraining them in their growth relative to smaller firms in the same industry.

These laws exempted government because government, in particular its executive branch, was seen as acting for the nation as a whole. With the new development of the state-management, the government-management is now acting for the extension of its own managerial power.

It is worth recalling that Eisenhower warned against the acquisition of unwarranted influence by the military-industrial complex, "**whether sought or unsought.**" One of the controlling features of the new industrial management is that, like other managements, it may be expected to act for the acquistion of additional influence; such behavior is normal for all managements.

topic 13

the economic sector: the bureaucratic ethos

Bureaucracy: the word is at once an epithet—a stereotype that evokes a variety of images, in the main invidious—and a designation that depicts our age. For this is indisputably the era of bureaucratic organization. A standard mode of formal organization endemic to industrial societies in all quadrants of the globe, bureaucracy characterizes every facet of institutional life, educational, religious, and political, as well as economic.

Bureaucracy suffuses so many aspects of our everyday lives for a reason: It is for better or worse, a **necessity.** Max Weber, the pioneering sociologist who was the first to analyze the phenomenon systematically, explains why:

> The decisive reason for the advance of bureaucratic organization
> has always been its purely technological superiority over any
> other form of organization. . . . Precision, speed, unambiguity,
> knowledge of the files, . . . strict subordination, reduction of
> friction and of material and personal costs—these are raised to
> the optimum point in the strictly bureaucratic administration.

The pervasiveness of bureaucratic organization has bred a variety of reactions, and many have been negative: Some critics claim that bureaucratic societies tend to ignore human needs and feelings, that they encourage inflexibility, that they require a kind of specialization that prevents the creative side of man from developing, and that in the long run they are dehumanizing.

But **do** such features of beaucracy as a clearly hierarchial sequence of subordinate-superordinate relationships, specialized roles, an emphasis upon "doing it by the book" and formality and social distance dehumanize those who are enmeshed in bureaucratic routines? Are such features invariable corollaries of this form of organization? A number of critics think not. Michael Crozier contends that bureaucratic organization has made it possible for the institutions involved to be **more** tolerant of the personal needs and idiosyncracies of their members, and many point out that most bureaucratic organizations, in both the private and public sectors of the economy are characterized by a number of **informal** primary groups that help to satisfy the individual's need for contact and spontaneity.

Other critics, such as Bennis, argue that bureaucracy as we know it is changing, and that
"new shapes, patterns, and models are emerging
which promise drastic changes in the conduct of
the corporation and of managerial practices in
general." In consequence, fantasy, imagination,
and creativity will be legitimate in ways that today
seem strange. Social structures, Bennis concludes,
"will no longer be instruments of psychic repression but will increasingly promote play and freedom on behalf of curiosity and thought."

At first blush, the two selections that follow
may seem somewhat circumscribed: The action of
both takes place in a university community, and,
what is more, the same institution: the University
of California at Berkeley. Yet these illustrations of
bureaucratic technicalism and insensitivity to currents of change will surely be familiar, perhaps
painfully familiar, to many readers. The readings
by Michael Otten and by Sheldon Wolin and John
Schaar raise crucial questions regarding the legitimacy, nature, and functions of bureaucratic organization and the bureaucratic mentality in a world
that is changing with dazzling rapidity.

chapter 27
rebellion
and
bureaucracy
michael otten

Only a few short years ago the Free Speech Movement at Berkeley electrified the academic world. It was a revolution! Students were all at once demanding—not respectfully petitioning, as before—the right to solicit money and members for political causes and the right to invite any speaker they wished, whether approved by the administration or not. And not only did they demand these rights, but instead of discussion to gain their ends, they sat in and struck against the university. While the American flag waved over the campus demonstrations, Joan Baez came by to sing the "Lord's Prayer." From the perspective of the early seventies, the free speech revolution is bound to seem rather quaint. In 1969, the National Guard was patrolling the Berkeley campus. Black militants were threatening to burn the administrative records at Duke University. San Francisco State College was virtually closed for four months. And students and faculty of Columbia University were still binding up their wounds from their fierce encounter with policemen's Mace, clubs, fists, and words. Each month and each week the list of disturbances grew, as the smell of tear

From **University Authority and the Student: The Berkeley Experience** by Michael Otten, 1970. Originally published by the University of California Press; reprinted by permission of The Regents of the University of California.

gas drove out the nostalgic odor of autumn leaves burning in front of the fraternity house.

Clearly, something is happening to American colleges. Students have always been rebels, but they have never before been so openly defiant and morally righteous in their mass rebellions. For instance, in contrast to the contemporary militancy, in 1881 nearly every member of the sophomore class at Berkeley was expelled, and they did not so much as write a complaint against the authorities. In fact, "they expressed themselves perfectly willing to abide by the consequences [of their actions]." To show what good sports they were about it, they "shouted the 'jolly sophomore'," after which they formed a long procession and, "class pins inverted" and "crepe on their arms," solemnly marched off the campus.[1]

University authority is under attack. Students do not typically "abide by the consequences," but question, confront, defy, and then demand amnesty. What is happening? Where is university control headed?

The dynamics of college crises bring several issues to the surface. First, as to the role of the university in modern society, American colleges have been famous (or infamous depending on one's values) for their ability to serve the more privileged classes and established economic institutions of the country. But such services are called into question as more and more students become sensitive to the problems of racism, militarism, imperialism, and bureaucracy. The new vision, hoping to broaden educational opportunity so as to service large numbers of the poor and non-white—the students of the "Third World"—is in effect pressuring the colleges and universities into becoming agencies of social change. It is thought by some, however, that such a radical alteration of function—from teaching and research to social change through political action—would undermine the precarious equilibrium that the universities have worked out with the larger society, and it is this conflict that lies at the heart of the problems at Berkeley and elsewhere.

Second, there is the issue of the ultimate control of university governance. Most if not all American colleges and universities have absentee managers called trustees or regents. These officials, who are usually appointed, are predominantly wealthy and conservative, besides being quite far removed from the immediate campus situation. Of this group, it has been reliably reported that "64 percent . . . would exclude professors from decisions regarding academic tenure and only 1 percent would include students in these decisions. 96 percent still cling to the notion that college attendance is a privilege, not a right."[2] Professors, not to mention students, are seldom represented on these boards of control. Indeed, judging from this report, trustees by and large do not think either group should be represented. Only in the late 1960s were some moves made to appoint young recent graduates to these boards. Not only do trustees usually adhere to a managerial authoritarianism, they back up their perspectives with genuine power.

The third problem has to do with disciplinary procedures and due process. Student involvement with serious political issues and rights has raised important questions about student liberties versus institutional functions. To handle student protest against war and racism by the methods that were once applied to the drunken, brawling sophomore is clearly inappropriate. Deprivation of a college degree amounts to a denial of citizenship in an advanced technological society, and such deprivation cannot justly be allowed for exercise of lawful civil liberties—no matter how obnoxious that exercise may seem to the political moderate. Nor can the colleges justly punish the student for crimes which are properly a matter for the civil courts and not the college administration. Yet order must be maintained if the traditional university func-

tions of teaching and research are to be protected. Most campus crises indeed involve very complicated questions of due process.

One further important issue concerns campus rule-making procedures. To put it in political terms, this problem has to do with "legislative," as opposed to the "judicial" concerns—rule enforcement and due process—touched on above. At Berkeley and most other academic institutions, the boards of trustees and the chief campus officers make the major policy decisions. Seldom are students seriously represented at administrative meetings. Furthermore, student government, which operates best in the context of the traditional collegiate activities, is increasingly ignored by the new generation of student activists. Students frequently view their existing government as an impotent pastime devoid of any real power.

To disagree on such fundamental issues as university function, control, rule making, and discipline is to deny the very legitimacy of academic authority. Such disagreement underlies the presence of armed control on the campuses. The case of Columbia University provides a good example of this. The **Cox Commission Report**, an independent study of the Columbia campus crisis in early 1968, concluded that the major difficulty was that the authoritarian structures did not allow the "natural student leaders" to participate in university governance.[3] The **Report** urged that ways be found immediately to allow students to "meaningfully influence the education afforded them and other aspects of the University's activities."[4] The Columbia student government provided no meaningful lever of change, influence, or representation. Similarly, the university's "outmoded disciplinary procedures" were better suited to a past era of personalized paternalism than to a period when a student's current draft status "may even attain life and death importance."[5] And yet, although the students had undergone a remarkable transformation over only a couple of generations, the old rigid and authoritarian control by the Columbia administration continued. This new generation of students is, according to the **Cox Report**, the "best informed, most intelligent, and most idealistic the country has ever known, . . . the most sensitive to public issues, . . . the most sophisticated in political tactics."[6]

Thus, the clash between the new kind of student and the old style of governance underlies most campus conflict today. Again, the **Cox Report** stated the basic issue: "At a time when the spirit of self-determination is running strongly, the administration of Columbia affairs too often conveyed an attitude of authoritarianism and invited distrust."[7] This "spirit of self-determination" that manifests itself so strongly must be taken seriously into account. To ignore it is to invite disorder. While it is possible to maintain order with the help of local and state police forces, it is a fact that "the government of a University depends, even more than that of a political community, upon the consent of the governed to accept the decisions reached by constitutional processes."[8] There are, unfortunately, few "constitutional processes" by which the voice, not to say the power, of students can be heard within the university. The gulf between students and administrators only widens and the crisis spreads.

The situation can also be stated in more general terms. University authority, as it stands, is not a legitimate form of government in the eyes of a large number of students. And because it is not legitimate, it finds itself unable to govern by moral persuasion and must increasingly fall back on physical force to control dissent. Only the radical restructuring of the present system would appear to offer a possible alternative to the ever increasing use of force.

AUTHORITY IN AN ORGANIZATIONAL SOCIETY

The outcome of the struggle within the universities is important in itself, but perhaps even more important, the universities' struggle brings to trial the very nature of modern society. The modern world is an organizational society increasingly controlled by large bureaucratic structures. Whether it is called "corporate capitalism," the "technological society," the "techno-structure," or the "organizational society," the fact is that the focus of power, the shape and tone of our society, indeed the very way we think is dependent upon the products and information processed by large organizations.[9] Such being the case, either the power of organizations must be constrained to render justice to the individual and service to the larger society or modern man will live under tyranny. It may be air-conditioned, tastefully decorated, artificially scented, and oppressively friendly, but it will be tyranny nonetheless. Max Weber saw the problem—though in somewhat different terms—and he consistently emphasized the notion that bureaucratic organization, not class conflict, is the

dominant feature of the times. Who will control? How will organizational power be constrained? These are the central questions, and the universities are just one setting—albeit the most dramatic— where the questions are being asked.

The revolt in the colleges, then, is not simply a revolt against college administrators; it is the clash of a new mentality against the older forms of organization. The universities and colleges just happen to be the most immediate and at present most vulnerable target for the new generation of antiorganizational militants. But what will happen when these battle-hardened, risk-taking militants begin to direct their individualistic, antiorganizational attitudes toward General Motors, the major political parties, the Army, the local zoning board, and the PTA?

To comprehend the challenges to organizational authority, the present must be seen in a historical context. Given their total impact on society, large-scale organizations are an extraordinarily recent phenomenon. Indeed, the rapidity of organizational emergence, coupled with its far-reaching implications, may account in large part for the spontaneous, ad hoc nature of the challenges. There is a sense of groping for a comprehension of organizational reality as well as for control of its centralized, bureaucratically structured authority. The antiorganizational movements are open to experimentation, and their participants often "flow with it," making sense out of the situation as it develops. Lacking a clear understanding of organizations, the movements for change are frequently criticized for not having any clear goals other than destruction of the "system." But it would seem that the myriad of protests are all responses to essentially the same complaint, since all reflect the same effort to cope with the reality of organizational dominance in every area of life, ranging from medical care to food production, from birth to burial.

It is little wonder that the antiorganizational New Left groups seem confused. Their "enemy" is too new to be fully comprehended. Until very recently technology was simple, and a man could prosper with little more than hard work. Now 85 percent of the population works for someone else. It is estimated that just five hundred huge corporations control two-thirds of the economy, and the centralizing trend increases with every corporate merger. The very complexity of modern technology requires immense organizations capable of rationally coordinating a great number of intricate and specialized tasks. Whether we are concerned with the possibility of a nationwide, computer-controlled, centralized credit bureau or with the inability of a student to obtain the courses needed to graduate, the problem of individual freedom in the large organization becomes the central issue in modern society.

Since organization means power, what will be the ideological guidelines for authority? What will be the structural constraints—which are usually quite inefficient in terms of time, temper, and money—against organizational dominance? In the political sphere, elaborate controls such as elections, a bill of rights, a constitution, courts, petitions, etc., already exist. These were developed during a period when the government was the only real power over the individual citizen. But we are in a new era where power is not the monopoly of government but dispersed throughout the organizational fiefdoms. The college president usually affects the student's livelihood and liberties far more than the town mayor; the employer more than the local congressman; the credit bureau more than the state assemblyman. Yet where the individual has channels of redress against the elected official, he has few, if any, formal channels against the all-important nonpolitical powers. Evidence abounds that a restless few are groping toward a containment of expanding organizational power. Bishops are challenged, teachers go on strike, the poor demand a voice in government. Welfare recipients fight the agencies, professors are forced to make their classes relevant, college trustees are picketed, old union leaders are thrown out, Catholics even ignore the Pope. Some observers look out from behind the once secure ramparts of the status quo and see anarchy. They feel that society is coming apart. This study offers another interpretation. These manifestations of unrest, no matter what their immediate cause, reflect the same issues—who will be in control and how will organizational power be constrained.

In the past, the compliance of the governed could often be gained by little more than an ap-peal to a generalized deference toward established authority. Now the once revered voices are sometimes drowned out by the shouts of protest. University authority, along with other kinds of authority, is being stripped of the traditional justifications for its existence. Demands are being made to justify it on the basis of public purposes and membership needs, and not simply on the basis of private property, sacred founding, God's will, or a charter from the government. This trend can be called the "secularization" of authority. Persons assuming authority roles are being relieved of the magic aura of those roles and of the privileges accruing from their prestigious positions—which is, parenthetically, one of the reasons irreverent style is so important to contemporary protest. Such ideological rationales as private ownership are no longer sufficient to justify certain types of managerial decisions, nor are the chancellor's appeals to old-time institutional loyalty enough to placate the advocates of student power. To repeat the telling phrase of the **Cox Report**, "The spirit of self-determination is running strongly."

NOTES

1. Berkeleyan, October 31, 1881.
2. The San Francisco Chronicle, February 24, 1969, reporting on the results of a survey conducted by Rodney T. Hartnett for the Educational Testing Service, Princeton, New Jersey.
3. Crisis at Columbia, The Cox Commission Report, Report of the Fact Finding Commission Appointed to Investigate the Disturbances at Columbia University in April and May 1968 (New York: Vintage Books, 1968).
4. The Cox Report, p. 198.
5. The Cox Report, p. 96.
6. The Cox Report, p. 4.
7. The Cox Report, p. 193.
8. The Cox Report, p. 197.
9. A great many authors have commented on the growing dominance of large-scale organizations. Among the more recent books are Michael Harrington, **Toward a Democratic Left** (New York: The Macmillan Co., 1968), and David T. Bazelon, **Power in America** (New York: The New American Library, 1964).

chapter 28
berkeley: the battle of people's park
sheldon wolin and john schaar

Shortly before 5:00 A.M., on Thursday, May 16, a motley group of about fifty hippies and "street-people" were huddled together on a lot, 270 by 450 feet, in Berkeley. The lot was owned by the Regents of the University of California and located a few blocks south of the Berkeley campus. Since mid-April this lot had been taken over and transformed into a "People's Park" by scores of people, most of whom had no connection with the university. Now the university was determined to reassert its legal rights of ownership. A police officer approached the group and announced that it must leave or face charges of trespassing. Except for three persons, the group left and the area was immediately occupied and surrounded by about 200 police from Berkeley, Alameda County, and the campus. The police were equipped with flak jackets, tear gas launchers, shotguns, and telescopic rifles. At 6:00 A.M. a construction crew arrived and by mid-afternoon an eight-foot steel fence encircled the lot.

At noon a rally was convened on campus and about 3000 people gathered. The president-elect of the student body spoke. He started to suggest various courses of action that might be considered. The crowd responded to the first of these by spon-

taneously marching toward the lot guarded by the police. (For this speech, the speaker was charged a few days later with violating numerous campus rules, and, on the initiative of university officials, indicted for incitement to riot.) The crowd was blocked by a drawn police line. Rocks and bottles were thrown at the police, and the police loosed a tear gas barrage, scattering the crowd. Elsewhere, a car belonging to the city was burned. Meanwhile, police reinforcements poured in, soon reaching around 600. A rock was thrown from a rooftop and, without warning, police fired into a group on the roof of an adjacent building. Two persons were struck in the face by the police fire, another was blinded, probably permanently, and a fourth, twenty-five-year-old James Rector, later died. Before the day was over, at least thirty others were wounded by police gunfire, and many more by clubs. One policeman received a minor stab wound and six more were reported as having been treated for minor cuts and bruises.

Meanwhile, action shifted to the campus itself, where police had herded a large crowd into Sproul Plaza by shooting tear gas along the bordering streets. The police then formed small detachments which continuously swept across the campus, breaking up groups of all sizes. Tear gas enfolded the main part of the campus and drifted into many of its buildings, as well as into the surrounding city. Nearby streets were littered with

Reprinted with permission from **The New York Review of Books**, October 9, 1969. Copyright © 1969 NYREV, Inc.

broken glass and rubble. At least six buckshot slugs entered the main library and three .38 calibre bullets lodged in the wall of a reference room in the same building. Before the day ended, more than ninety people had been injured by police guns and clubs.

Under a "State of Extreme Emergency" proclamation issued by Governor Reagan on February 5 in connection with the "Third World Strike" at Berkeley late last winter and never rescinded, a curfew was imposed on the city. Strict security measures were enforced on campus and in the nearby business districts, and all assemblies and rallies were prohibited. The proclamation also centralized control of the police under the command of Sheriff Frank Madigan of Alameda County.

Roger Heyns, the chancellor of the university, saw none of this, for he had left the previous day for a meeting in Washington. His principal vice-chancellor had gone to the Regents' meeting in Los Angeles. The Regents took notice of the events by declaring, "It is of paramount importance that law and order be upheld." The governor said that the lot had been seized by the street-people "as an excuse for a riot." A Berkeley councilman called the previous use of the lot a "Hippie Disneyland freak show."

The next day, May 17, 2000 National Guardsmen appeared in full battle dress, armed with rifles, bayonets, and tear gas. They were called into action by the governor, but apparently the initiative came from local authorities acting in consultation with university administrators. Helicopters weaved back and forth over the campus and city. Berkeley was occupied. (The next day one helicopter landed on campus and an officer came out to ask that students stop flying their kites because the strings might foul his rotors. A collection was promptly taken and the sky was soon full of brightly colored kites.)

During the next few days a pattern emerged. Each day began quietly, almost like any other day, except that people awoke to the roar of helicopters and the rumble of transports. As university classes began (they have never been officially canceled), the Guardsmen formed a line along the south boundary of the campus. The Guard and the police would cordon off the main plaza and station smaller detachments at various points around the campus. Gradually the students crowded together, staring curiously at the Guardsmen and occasionally taunting them. The Guard stood

ready with bayonets pointed directly at the crowd. This standoff would continue for an hour or two, and then the police would charge the crowd with clubs and tear gas. The crowd would scatter, the police would give chase, the students and street-people would curse and sometimes hurl rocks or return the tear gas canisters, and the police would beat or arrest some of them.

On Tuesday, May 20, the pattern and tempo changed. Previously the police had sought to break up gatherings on the campus, so now the protesters left the campus and began a peaceful march through the city. This was promptly stopped by the police. The marchers then filtered back to campus and a crowd of about 3000 assembled. The group was pressed toward the Plaza by the police and Guardsmen and, when solidly hemmed in, was attacked by tear gas. A little later a helicopter flew low over the center of the campus and spewed gas over a wide area, even though the crowd had been thoroughly scattered. Panic broke out and people fled, weeping, choking, vomiting. Gas penetrated the university hospital, imperiling patients and interrupting hospital routines. It caused another panic at the university recreation area, nearly a mile from the center of campus, where many people, including mothers and children, were swimming. The police also threw gas into a student snack bar and into an office and classroom building.

The next day, May 21, was a turning point. More than 200 faculty members announced their refusal to teach; a local labor council condemned the police action; some church groups protested; and the newspapers and television stations began to express some criticism. Controversy arose over the ammunition which the police had used the previous Thursday. Sheriff Madigan was evasive about the size of birdshot issued, but the evidence was clear that buckshot had killed James Rector. The tear gas was first identified as the normal variety (CN) for crowd disturbances, but later it was officially acknowledged that a more dangerous gas (CS) was also used. The American army uses CS gas to flush out guerrillas in Vietnam. It can cause projectile vomiting, instant diarrhea, and skin blisters, and even death, as it has to the VC, when the victim is tubercular. The Geneva Conventions outlaw the use of CS in warfare.

On the same day the chancellor issued his first statement. He deplored the death which had occurred, as well as "the senseless violence." He warned that attempts were being made "to polarize the community and prevent rational solutions," and he stated that a university has a responsibility to follow "civilized procedures." Heyns made no criticism of the police or National Guard tactics: that same day a Guardsman had thrown down his helmet, dropped his rifle, and reportedly shouted, "I can't stand this any more." He was handcuffed, taken away for a physical examination, and then rushed off to a psychiatric examination. He was diagnosed as suffering from "suppressed aggressions."

In Sacramento, where a deputation of Berkeley faculty members was meeting with the governor, aggression was more open. The governor conceded that the helicopter attack might have been a "tactical mistake," but he also insisted that "once the dogs of war are unleashed, you must expect things will happen. . . . " Meantime, the statewide commander of the Guards defended the gas attack on the grounds that his troops were threatened. He noted that the general who ordered the attack had said, "It was a Godsend that it was done at that time." The commander regretted the "discomfort and inconvenience to innocent bystanders," but added: "It is an inescapable by-product of combating terrorists, anarchists, and hard-core militants on the streets and on the campus."

The next day, May 22, a peaceful march and flower planting procession began in downtown Berkeley. With little warning, police and Guardsmen converged on the unsuspecting participants and swept them, along with a number of shoppers, newsmen, people at lunch, and a mailman, into a parking lot, where 482 were arrested, bringing the week's total near 800. As those arrested were released on bail, disturbing stories began to circulate concerning the special treatment accorded "Berkeley types" in Santa Rita prison.

These stories, supported by numerous affidavits and news accounts submitted by journalists who had been bagged in the mass arrest, told of beatings, verbal abuse, and humiliation, physical deprivations, and refusal of permission to contact counsel. Male prisoners told of being marched into the prison yard and forced to lie face down, absolutely motionless, on gravel and concrete for several hours. The slightest shift in posture, except for a head movement permitted once every half hour, was met with a blow to the kidneys or testicles. On May 24 a District Court judge issued an order restraining Sheriff Madigan's subordinates from beating and otherwise mistreating the arrestees taken to Santa Rita prison.

Despite all the arrests, the shotguns, gas, and clubs, the protesters have thus far shown remarkable restraint. Although both police and Guards have been targets of much foul language and some hard objects, nothing remotely resembling sustained violence has been employed against the police; and the Guard has been spared from all except verbal abuse. At this writing, the only damage to campus property, other than that caused by the police, has been two broken windows and one flooded floor.

After the mass arrests, the governor lifted the curfew and the ban on assemblies, saying "a more controlled situation" existed. But he warned that no solution was likely until the troublemaking faculty and students were separated from the university. "A professional revolutionary group," he said, was behind it all. Charles Hitch, the president of the University of California, issued his first statement. (Much earlier, his own staff issued a statement protesting campus conditions of "intolerable stress" and physical danger.) The president ventured to criticize "certain tactics" of the police, but noted that these "were not the responsibility of university authorities."

In a television interview, the chancellor agreed with the president, but added that negotiations were still possible because "we haven't stopped the rational process." A published interview (May 22) with the principal vice-chancellor found him saying, "Our strategy was to act with humor and sensitivity. For instance, we offered to roll up the sod in the park and return it to the people. . . . We had no reason to believe there would be trouble." Meanwhile the governor was saying, "The police didn't kill the young man. He was killed by the first college administrator who said some time ago it was all right to break laws in the name of dissent."

The governor also accused the president of the university, a former assistant secretary of defense and RANDsman, of "trying to weasel" to the side of the street-people. Two days later the governor refused the request of the Berkeley City Council to end the state of emergency and recall the Guard—requests, it might be added, that the university itself has not yet made. At this time the mayor of Berkeley suggested that police tactics had been "clumsy and not efficient," to which Sheriff Madigan retorted: "If the mayor was capable of running the city so well without problems we wouldn't be here. I advise the mayor to take his umbrella and go to Berkeley's Munich."

On Friday, May 23, the Faculty Senate met. It listened first to a speech by the chancellor in which he defined the occupation of the lot as an act of "unjustified aggression" against the university, and declared that the "avoidance of confrontations cannot be the absolute value." He said that the fence would remain as long as the issue was one of possession and control, and, pleading for more "elbow room," he asserted that the faculty should support or at least not oppose an administrative decision once it had been made. The faculty then defeated a motion calling for the chancellor's removal (94 voted for, 737 against, and 99 abstained). It approved, by a vote of 737 to 94, a series of resolutions which condemned what was called "as irresponsible a police and military reaction to a civic disturbance as this country has seen in recent times."

The resolutions demanded withdrawal of "the massive police and military presence on campus"; the "cessation of all acts of belligerency and provocation by demonstrators"; an investigation by the attorney general of California and the Department of Justice; and the prompt implementation of a plan whereby part of the lot would become "an experimental community-generated park" and the fence would be simultaneously removed. The faculty also resolved to reconvene in a few days to reassess the situation.

There is where events now stand (May 26). But pressures from all sides are increasing. A student referendum, which saw the heaviest turnout in the history of student voting, found 85 percent of the nearly 15,000 who voted favoring the use of the lot as it had been before the occupation. The students also voted to assess themselves $1.50 each quarter to help finance an ethnic studies department previously accepted by the university but now foundering. As of this writing, college students from all over the state are planning direct protests to Governor Reagan. Leaders of the protesters are preparing for a huge march against the fence on Memorial Day. The governor remains committed to a hard line. All the issues remain unsettled.

■

What brought on this crisis? Like many of its sister institutions, the Berkeley campus has been steadily advancing its boundaries into the city. Back in 1956 it had announced its intention to purchase property in the area which includes the present disputed lot. Owing to lack of funds, very little land was actually purchased. Finally, in June, 1967, the monies were allocated and the university announced that ultimately dormitories would be built on the land, but that in the interim it would be used for recreation.

The lot itself was purchased in 1968, but no funds were then available for development. Undoubtedly the university was aware of the disastrous experience of other academic institutions which had attempted to "redevelop" surrounding areas. In fact, a short time ago the university announced, with much fanfare, its intention to mount a major attack on the problems of the cities. Despite these professions, the university's treatment of its own urban neighbors has consisted of a mixture of middle-class prejudice, aesthetic blindness, and bureaucratic callousness.

The victims in this case, however, have not been so much the blacks as another pariah group, one whose identity is profoundly influenced by the university itself. For many years, Telegraph Avenue and "the south campus area" have constituted a major irritant to the university, the city fathers, and the business interests. It is the Berkeley demimonde, the place where students, hippies, drop-outs, radicals, and run-aways congregate. To the respectables, it is a haven for drug addicts, sex fiends, criminals, and revolutionaries. Until the university began its expansion, it was also an architectural preserve for fine old brown shingle houses and interesting shops. It is no secret that the university has long considered the acquisition of land as a means of ridding the area not of substandard housing, but of its human "blight." The disputed lot was the perfect symbol of the university's way of carrying out urban regeneration: first, raze the buildings; next let the land lay idle and uncared for; then permit it to be used as an unimproved parking lot, muddy and pitted; and finally, when the local people threaten to use and enjoy the land, throw a fence around it.

Around mid-April, a movement was begun by street-people, hippies, students, radicals, and a fair sprinkling of elderly free spirits to take over the parking lot and transform it. Many possibilities were discussed: a child care clinic; a crafts fair; a baseball diamond. Soon grass and shrubs were planted, playground equipment installed, benches built, and places made for eating, lounging, and occasional speechmaking. About 200 people were involved in the beginning, but soon the park was intensively and lovingly used by children, the

young, students and street-people, and the elderly.
A week after the park began, the university announced its intention to develop a playing field by
July 1, and the park people responded by saying
that the university would have to fight for it. Discussions followed, but not much else. The university said, however, that no construction would be
started without proper warning and that it was
willing to discuss the future design of the field.

On May 8 the chancellor agreed to form a
committee representing those who were using the
lot as well as the university. But he insisted as "an
essential condition" of discussions about the future of the land that all work on the People's Park
cease. In addition he announced certain guidelines
for his committee: university control and eventual
use must be assured; the field must not produce
"police and other control problems"; and no political or public meetings were to be held on the
land. Suddenly, on May 13, he announced his decision to fence in the area as the first step toward
developing the land for intramural recreation.
"That's a hard way to make a point," he said, "but
that's the way it has to be. . . . The fence will also
give us time to plan and consult. Regretfully, this
is the only way the entire site can be surveyed, soil
tested, and planned for development . . . hence the
fence."

Why did it have to be this way? Because, as
the chancellor explained, it was necessary to assert
the university's title to ownership. Concerning the
apparent lack of consultation with his own committee, he said that a plan could not be worked
out because the park people had not only refused
to stop cultivating and improving the land, but
they had "refused to organize a responsible committee" for consultative purposes. In addition, he
cited problems of health, safety, and legal liability,
as well as complaints from local residents.

The first response came from the faculty
chairman of the chancellor's committee. He declared that the chancellor had allowed only two
days (the weekend) for the committee to produce a
plan and that the "university didn't seem interested in negotiations." On May 14 a protest rally
was held and the anarchs of the park, surprisingly,
pulled themselves together and formed a negotiating committee. Although rumors of an impending fence were circulating, spokesmen for the
park people insisted that they wanted discussion,
not confrontation.

On May 15, the day immediately preceding
the early morning police action, the chancellor

placed an advertisement in the campus newspaper
inviting students to draw up "ideas or designs" for
the lot and to submit them by May 21. The ad was
continued even after the military occupation. On
May 18, three days after the occupation had begun, the chancellor announced that there would be
"no negotiations in regard to the land known as
People's Park," although discussions might go on
"while the fence is up anyway." His principal vice-
chancellor, in an interview reported on May 22,
stated that the university had not turned down a
negotiating committee.

He also noted—and this was after the helicopter attack—that "the fence was necessary to
permit the kind of rational discussion and planning
that wasn't possible before." Once more the faculty chairman had to protest that he had not been
informed of meetings between the administration
and representatives of the People's Park and that
the chancellor had consistently ignored the committee's recommendations. However, the principal
vice-chancellor had an explanation for this lack of
consultation: "I guess that's because the chancellor didn't want him to get chewed up by this
thing."

■

Why did the making of a park provoke such a
desolating response? The bureaucratic nature of
the multiversity and its disastrous consequences
for education are by now familiar and beyond
dispute. So, too, is the web of interdependence
between it and the dominant military, industrial,
and political institutions of our society. These
explain much about the response of the university
to the absurd, yet hopeful, experiment of People's
Park.

What needs further comment is the increasingly ineffectual quality of the university's responses, particularly when its organizational apparatus attempts to cope with what is spontaneous, ambiguous, and disturbingly human. It is
significant that the Berkeley administration repeatedly expressed irritation with the failure of the
park people to "organize" a "responsible committee" or to select "representatives" who might "negotiate." The life-styles and values of the park
people were forever escaping the categories and
procedures of those who administer the academic
plant.

Likewise the issue itself: The occupants of the
park wanted to use the land for a variety of proj-

ects, strange but deeply natural, which defied customary forms and expectations, whereas, at worst, the university saw the land as something to be fenced, soil-tested, processed through a score of experts and a maze of committees, and finally encased in the tight and tidy form of a rational design. At best, the most imaginative use of the land which the university could contemplate was as a "field-experiment station" where faculty and graduate students could observe their fellow beings coping with their "environment." In brief, the educational bureaucracy, like bureaucracies elsewhere, is experiencing increasing difficulty, because human life is manifesting itself in forms which are unrecognizable to the mentality of the technological age.

This suggests that part of the problem lies in the very way bureaucracies perceive the world and process information from it. It was this "bureaucratic epistemology" which largely determined how the university responded to the People's Park. Bureaucracy is both an expression of the drive for rationality and predictability, and one of the chief agencies in making the world ever more rational and predictable, for the bureaucratic mode of knowing and behaving comes to constitute the things known and done themselves.

Now this rational form of organizing human efforts employs a conception of knowledge which is also rational in specific ways. The only legitimate instrument of knowledge is systematic cognition, and the only acceptable mode of discourse is the cognitive mode. Other paths to knowledge are suspect. Everything tainted with the personal, the subjective, and the passionate is suppressed, or dismissed as prejudice or pathology. A bureaucrat who based his decisions upon, say, intuition, dialectical reason, empathic awareness, or even common sense, would be guilty of misconduct.

The bureaucratic search for "understanding" does not begin in wonder, but in the reduction of the world to the ordinary and the manageable. In order to deal with the world in the cognitive mode, the world must first be approached as an exercise in "problem-solving." To say there is a problem is to imply there is a solution; and finding the solution largely means devising the right technique. Since most problems are "complex," they must be broken down by bureaucrats into their component parts before the right solution can be found. Reality is parsed into an ensemble of discrete though related parts, and each part is assigned to the expert specially qualified to deal

with that part. Wholes can appear as nothing more than assemblages of parts, just as a whole automobile is an assemblage of parts. But in order for wholes to be broken into parts, things that are dissimilar in appearance and quality must be made similar.

This is done by abstracting from the objects dealt with those aspects as though they were the whole. Abstraction and grouping by common attributes require measuring tools that yield comparable units for analysis: favorite ones are units of money, time, space, and power; income, occupation, and party affiliation. All such measurements and comparisons subordinate qualitative dimensions, natural context, and unique and variable properties to the common, stable, external, and reproducible. This way of thinking becomes real when campus administrators define "recreation" in fixed and restrictive terms so that it may accord with the abstract demands of "lead-time." In a way Hegel might barely recognize, the Rational becomes the Real and the Real the Rational.

When men treat themselves this way, they increasingly become this way, or they desperately try to escape the "mind-forged manacles," as Blake called them, of the bureaucratic mentality and mode of conduct. In the broadest view, these two trends increasingly dominate the advanced states of our day. On the one side, we see the march toward uniformity, predictability, and the attempt to define all variety as dissent and then to force dissent into the "regular channels"—toward that state whose model citizen is Tocqueville's "industrious sheep," that state whose only greatness is its collective power.

On the other side we see an assertion of spontaneity, self-realization, and do-your-own-thing as the sum and substance of life and liberty. And this assertion, in its extreme form, does approach either madness or infantilism, for the only social institutions in which each member is really free to do his own thing are Bedlam and the nursery, where the condition may be tolerated because there is a keeper with ultimate control over the inmates. The opposing forces were not quite that pure in the confrontation over the People's Park, but the university and public officials nearly managed to make them so. That they could not do so is a comforting measure of the basic vitality of those who built the park and who have sacrificed to preserve it.

■

But this still does not account for the frenzy of violence which fell on Berkeley. To understand that, we must shift focus.

Clark Kerr was perceptive when he defined the multiversity as "a mechanism held together by administrative rules and powered by money." But it is important to understand that the last few years in the university have seen more and more rules and less and less money. The money is drying up because the rules are being broken. The rules are being broken because university authorities, administrators and faculty alike, have lost the respect of very many of the students. When authority leaves, power enters—first in the form of more and tougher rules, then as sheer physical force, and finally as violence, which is force unrestrained by any thought of healing and saving, force whose aim is to cleanse by devastation.

Pressed from above by politicians and from below by students, the university administration simultaneously imposes more rules and makes continual appeals to the faculty for more support in its efforts to cope with permanent emergency. It pleads with the faculty for more "elbow room," more discretionary space in which to make the hard decisions needed when money runs short and students run amuck. That same administration is right now conducting time-and-motion studies of faculty work and "productivity." Simultaneously, both faculty and administration make spasmodic efforts to give the students some voice in the governance of the institution. But those efforts are always too little, too late, too grudging.

Besides, as soon as the students get some power, unseemly things happen. Admit the blacks on campus and they demand their own autonomous departments. Give the students limited power to initiate courses and they bring in Eldridge Cleaver and Tom Hayden. The faculty sees student initiative as a revolting mixture of Agitprop and denial of professional prerogatives. The administration sees it as a deadly threat to its own precarious standing within the university and before the public. The politicians see it as concession to anarchy and revolution. The result is more rules and less trust all around—more centralization, bureaucratization, and force on one side, more despair and anger on the other.

Under these conditions, the organized system must strive to extend its control and reduce the space in which spontaneous and unpredictable actions are possible. The subjects, on the other hand, come to identify spontaneity and unpredic-

tability with all that is human and alive, and rule and control with all that is inhuman and dead. Order and liberty stand in fatal opposition. No positive synthesis can emerge from this dialectic unless those who now feel themselves pushed out and put down are admitted as full participants. But that is not happening. More and more, we are seeing in this country a reappearance of that stage in the breakdown of political societies where one segment of the whole—in this case still the larger segment—determines to dominate by force and terror other segments which reject and challenge its legitimacy.

This dynamic largely accounts for the crushing violence and terror that hit Berkeley. When spontaneity appeared in People's Park, it was first met by a restatement of the rules governing possession and control of land. When that restatement did not have the desired effect, the university failed to take the next step dictated by rule-governed behavior—seeking an injunction. Nor did it take the step which would have acknowledged itself as being in a political situation—talking on a plane of equality, and acting in a spirit of generosity, with the other parties. Instead, it regressed immediately to the use of physical measures. In the eyes of the administration, the building of People's Park was an "unjustified aggression," and the right of self-defense was promptly invoked.

Once force was called into play, it quickly intensified, and the university cannot evade its share of responsibility for what followed. He who wills the end wills the means; and no university official could have been unaware of the means necessary to keep that fence standing. But the administrators did not quite understand that their chosen agents of force, the police, would not limit their attention only to the students and streetpeople, who were expendable, but would turn against the university and the city as well.

Ronald Reagan reached Sacramento through Berkeley because, in the eyes of his frightened and furious supporters, Berkeley is daily the scene of events that would have shocked Sodom and revolutionary Moscow. All this came into intense focus in the behavior of the cops who were on the scene.

The police were numerous and armed with all the weapons a fertile technology can provide and an increasingly frightened citizenry will permit. Their superiority of force is overwhelming, and they are convinced they could "solve the problem" overnight if they were permitted to do it their own way: one instant crushing blow, and

then license for dealing with the remaining recal-
citrants. All the trouble-makers are known to the
police, either by dossier and record or by appearance and attitude. But the police are kept under
some restraints, and those restraints produce
greater and greater rage.

The rage comes from another source as well.
Demands for a different future have been welling
up in this society for some years now, and while
those demands have not been unheard they have
gone unheeded. Vietnam, racism, poverty, the
degradation of the natural and manmade environment, the bureaucratization of the academy and
its active collaboration with the military and industrial state, unrepresentative and unreachable
structures of domination—all these grow apace. It
seems increasingly clear to those who reject this
American future that the forces of "law and
order" intend to defend it by any means necessary. It becomes increasingly clear to the forces of
law and order that extreme means will be necessary, and that the longer they are delayed the
more extreme they will have to be.

Those two futures met at People's Park. It
should be clear that what is happening this time is
qualitatively different from 1964 and the Free
Speech Movement. The difference in the amount
of violence is the most striking, but this is largely a
symptom of underlying differences. In 1964, the
issues centered around questions of civil liberties
and due process within the university. The issues
now are political in the largest sense.

■

The appearance of People's Park raised questions of property and the nature of meaningful
work. It raised questions about how people can
begin to make a livable environment for themselves; about why both the defenders and critics of
established authority today agree that authority
can be considered only in terms of repression,
never in terms of genuine respect and affection.
These questions cannot be evaded. Those who
honestly and courageously ask them are not imperiling the general happiness but are working for
the common redemption.

It is increasingly clear that legitimate authority is declining in the modern state. In a real sense,
"law and order" is the basic question of our day.
This crisis of legitimacy has been visible for some

time in just about all of the nonpolitical sectors of
life—family, economy, religion, education—and is
now spreading rapidly into the political realm. The
gigantic and seemingly impregnable organizations
that surround and dominate men in the modern
states are seen by more and more people to have at
their center not a vital principle of authority, but a
hollow space, a moral vacuum. Increasingly,
among the young and the rejected, obedience is
mainly a matter of lingering habit, or expediency,
or necessity, but not a matter of conviction and
deepest sentiment.

The groups who are most persistently raising
these questions are, of course, white middle-class
youth and the racial and ethnic minorities. The
origins of protest are different in the two cases:
The former have largely seen through the American Dream of meaning in power and wealth and
have found it a nightmare; the latter have been
pushed aside and denied even the minimal goods
of the Dream. But the ends of the protest are remarkably similar: Both are fighting against distor-
tions and denials of their humanity. Both reject
the programmed future of an America whose only
imperative now seems to be: more.

The people who built the park (there will be
more People's Parks, more and more occasions for
seemingly bizarre, perverse, and wild behavior)
have pretty much seen through the collective
ideals and disciplines that have bound this nation
together in its conquest of nature and power. Having been victimized by the restraints and authorities of the past, these people are suspicious of all
authorities and most collective ideals. Some of
them seem ready to attempt a life built upon no
other ideal than self-gratification. They sometimes
talk as though they had found the secret which has
lain hidden through all the past ages of man: that
the individual can live fully and freely with no
authority other than his desires, absorbed completely in the development of all his capacities
except two—the capacity for memory and the
capacity for faith.

No one can say where this will lead. Perhaps
new prophets will appear. Perhaps the old faith
will be reborn. Perhaps we really shall see the new
technological Garden tended by children—kind,
sincere innocents, barbarians with good hearts.
The great danger at present is that the established
and the respectable are more and more disposed to
see all this as chaos and outrage. They seem prepared to follow the most profoundly nihilistic

denial possible, which is the denial of the future through denial of their own children, the bearers of the future.

In such times as these, hope is not a luxury but a necessity. The hope which we see is in the revival of a sense of shared destiny, of some common fate which can bind us into a people we have never been. Even to sketch out that fate one must first decide that it does not lie with the power of technology or the stability of organizational society. It lies, instead, in something more elemental, in our common fears that scientific weapons may destroy all life; that technology will increasingly disfigure men who live in the city, just as it has already debased the earth and obscured the sky; that the "progress" of industry will destroy the possibility of interesting work; and that "communications" will obliterate the last traces of the varied cultures which have been the inheritance of all but the most benighted societies.

If hope is to be born of these despairs it must be given political direction, a new politics devoted to nurturing life and work. There can be no political direction without political education, yet America from its beginnings has never confronted the question of how to care for men's souls while helping them to see the world politically. Seeing the world politically is preparatory to acting in it politically; and to act politically is not to be tempted by the puerile attraction of power or to be content with the formalism of a politics of compromise. It is, instead, a politics which seeks always to discover what men can share—and how what they share can be enlarged and yet rise beyond the banal.

People's Park is not banal. If only the same could be said of those who build and guard the fences around all of us.

the economic sector: the age of cybernation and technetronic man

There is no disputing the fundamental wisdom of the distinguished microbiologist René Dubos when he remarks that "the largest part of life is now spent in an environment conditioned and often entirely created by technology." However indecipherable the ultimate ramifications of the technological revolution, it is crucial that we explore its shorter-term implications. This is one of the basic questions to which sociology addresses itself, and, in fact, virtually everything we encounter in this book substantiates how all-embracing technology is.

All the same, it is best that we confine ourselves to one of the more central aspects of what has been called the "technetronic revolution." The matter of automation will do nicely. And we no sooner confront the question of automation and all that it encompasses than it becomes apparent that here—just as in the debate about power—there are two fundamentally **opposing** points of view. One is essentially optimistic, the other far less so. At one level this debate reflects disagreement about the quality of life in the future:

> Some observers of the cybernetic revolution . . . envision a
> future where it will become increasingly difficult for the aver-
> age citizen to make his voice heard on matters related to his
> interests. A less pessimistic view recognizes the growing com-
> plexity of society which makes direct individual participation
> in government increasingly difficult, but sees the needs and
> interests of the average citizen being represented through the
> federal government [Perrucci and Pilisuk, 1968].

Other observers are concerned about the dangers implicit in the computer-assisted collection, storage, retrieval, and assessment of personal information, about the ascendancy of scientist-engineers whose esoteric "expertise" is beyond the comprehension or control of ordinary citizens, or about social engineering that makes use of computer-linked techniques of persuasion in such areas as advertising, television programming, the communications media, and electioneering.

"Technological man," Victor Ferkiss retorts, "will be man in control of his own development." Instantaneous language translation, computerized education, computer-operated households, shorter workweeks, computerized medical diagnoses, and greater material abundance at a lesser cost: These and a plenitude of other automated technological breakthroughs will, it is argued, make our lives in the 1980s far easier than they are today.

But of all the points of disagreement among students of automation, none has elicited more controversy than the purported links between automation and employment. And it is here that the more pessimistic sentiments prevail. Robert Theobald's position is representative:

Whatever we do, we can only succeed in delaying the inevitable: the attempt to keep demand growing as fast as supply and thus create enough conventional jobs will inevitably fail. The effects of the computer in developing abundance and eliminating jobs will inevitably exceed our capacity to create jobs [Dechert, 1967].

The essays that comprise this section come to direct grips with these and related matters. Both authors, Robert Theobald and Bernard J. Muller-Thym, however, go far beyond the question of automation and unemployment. Both raise larger questions: How will our leisure time as well as our workaday lives be affected by automation? What new values, life styles, and institutions will emerge? What new human rights will become ascendant? How will wealth be equally distributed?

chapter 29
cybernation and human rights
robert theobald

My use of the word cybernation instead of automation does not stem from a desire to **seem** to be saying something new. On the contrary, I use the word cybernation because it represents something quite different from automation. Automation was the process by which you could take a block of metal, put it in at one end of a series of machines and it would come out at the other as a finished engine block, without the need for human intervention. Automated machinery could do some things fast and well; nevertheless, its potential to organize people out of work was limited because it was inflexible.

Cybernation, however, is highly flexible and will become more so as time passes. Cybernation is the process of linking a computer, which is effectively a machine which will make decisions, with, and using it to control, automated machinery. These interlocking machine-systems can often be controlled by a few people sitting at computers, while the requirements for other workers are very small, for not only will the machines do all the work but the latest ones are being built practically to repair themselves. The potential to organize human beings out of work in order to increase the efficiency of machine-systems is already large and rapidly growing. In other words, the present type

of change in technology cannot be considered merely a continuation of the organizational process of the last one hundred and fifty years—it means something completely new which is quietly taking place all around us. Cybernation involves a production revolution which has two major consequences. First, in the field of production it is challenging and will increasingly challenge the supremacy of man's mind, and it will do this just as surely as the industrial revolution challenged and overcame the supremacy of man's muscle. In the relatively near future the machine-systems will take over all repetitive physical and mental production tasks and huge numbers of people will be thrown out of work. It has been estimated by some authorities that as little as 10% or even 2% of the labor force will be required for conventional work in the future.

The idea that we can continue to aim at finding a job for everybody is obsolete. A large proportion of those born in the fifties and sixties have no prospect of ever holding an ordinary job. There is no role in today's economy for those teenagers who are high-school dropouts and there is increasingly little place for those over fifty-five.

Such a picture seems bleak to many: they seem afraid that there will not be enough toil to go round. To me, on the other hand, it appears like the lifting of the curse of Adam, for it will no longer be necessary for man to earn his bread in

From **Liberation**, August 1964, Reprinted by permission.

the sweat of his brow. Machines could perform the productive toil and men could receive the resulting abundance, for machines would not only take over all the toil, they would also make it possible to turn out effectively unlimited quantities of both goods and services. U Thant, Secretary-General of the United Nations, has expressed it in the following terms:

> The truth, the central stupendous truth, about developed countries today is that they can have—in anything but the shortest run—the kind and scale of resources they decide to have. . . . It is no longer resources that limit decisions. It is the decision that makes the resources. This is the fundamental revolutionary change—perhaps the most revolutionary mankind has ever known.

There is no need—and no excuse—for poverty in the America of the second half of the twentieth century. Why, then, does it exist, and what can be done? Before I discuss this I want to present a few figures which will show that there is already too much unemployment, that there is the ability to produce more goods and services, and that we will have more unemployment and more ability to produce additional goods and services in coming years.

First, unemployment rates have remained around or above the excessive rate of 5.5% during the sixties. (The last few months have seen a decline to 5.1%.) The unemployment rate for teenagers has been rising steadily, reaching 17% in 1963; the unemployment rate for Negro teenagers was 27% in 1963, while the unemployment rate for teenagers in minority ghettos often exceeds 50%. Unemployment rates for Negroes are regularly above twice those for whites, whatever their occupation, educational level, age or sex. The unemployment position for other racial minorities is also unfavorable.

These official figures seriously underestimate the true extent of the unemployment problem. In 1962, in addition to the percentage of the labor force who were officially unemployed, nearly 4% of the labor force wanted full-time work but could find only part-time jobs. Methods of calculating unemployment rates—a person is only unemployed if he has actively sought a job recently—ignore the existence of a large group who would like to find jobs but who have not looked for them because they know there are no employment opportuni-

ties. Underestimation for this reason is particularly severe for people in groups whose unemployment rates are high—the young, the old and racial minorities. Willard Wirtz, Secretary of Labor, has stated that at least 350,000 young men between 14 and 24 have stopped looking for work. Many people in the depressed agricultural, mining, and industrial areas, who officially hold jobs but who are actually grossly underemployed, would move if there were real prospects of finding work elsewhere. It is therefore reasonable to estimate that around eight million people are looking for jobs today as compared to the 3.6 million shown in the official statistics.

Even more serious is the fact that the number of people who have voluntarily removed themselves from the labor force is not static but increases continually. For these people the decision to stop looking for employment and to accept the fact that they will never hold a job or will not hold a job again is largely irreversible, not only in economic but also in social and psychological terms. The older worker calls himself "retired"; he cannot accept work without affecting his social security status. The worker in prime years is forced onto relief: in most states the requirements for becoming a relief recipient bring about such fundamental alterations in an individual's total material situation that a reversal of the process is always difficult and often totally infeasible. The teenager knows that there is no place for him in the labor force but at the same time is unaware of any realistic alternative avenue for self-fulfillment.

Statistical evidence of these trends appears in the decline in the proportion of people claiming to be in the labor force. The recent apparent stabilization, and indeed decline, of the unemployment rate is therefore misleading: it is primarily a reflection of the discouragement and defeat of people who cannot find employment rather than a measure of the economy's success in creating enough jobs for all those who want to find a place in the labor force.

Second, we could produce far more goods and services if we would only find more ways to allow people to buy them—for the past eight years there has been the potential to produce some sixty billion dollars of additional goods and services. We are able every year to produce at least another thirty billion dollars of additional goods and services; this will rise to forty billion dollars per year before the end of the sixties, fifty billion dollars during the first half of the seventies, and at least sixty billion dollars well before the end of the seventies. We will be able to produce an additional one hundred and fifty billion dollars of extra goods and services every year by the end of the century. The children born in 1964 will be only about half way through their lives at this time. I should add that these estimates are certainly conservative.

Third, the forward movement of cybernation is raising the skill level of the machine. If a human being is to compete with such machines, he must **at least** possess a high school diploma. The Department of Labor has estimated, however, that on the basis of present trends as many as thirty percent of **all** students will be high-school dropouts in this decade.

Fourth, a permanently depressed class is developing in the United States. Scattered throughout the land, some thirty-eight million Americans, or almost one-fifth of the population, are living in a condition of chronic poverty which is daily becoming more evident to the rest of the nation. The percentage of total income received by the poorest 20% of the population has fallen from 4.9% to 4.7% since 1944. Movement out of the ranks of the poor is increasingly difficult, for it depends on an adequate education, while conscription of new and apparently permanent recruits continues.

The best summary of the effects of these trends was perhaps made by the Secretary of Labor at the beginning of 1964:

> The confluence of surging population and driving technology is splitting the American labor force into tens of millions of "haves" and millions of "have-nots." In our economy of sixty-nine million jobs, those with wanted skills enjoy opportunity and earning power. But the others face a new and stark problem—exclusion on a permanent basis, both as producers and consumers, from economic life. This division of people threatens to create a human slag-heap. We cannot tolerate the development of a separate nation of the poor, the unskilled, the jobless, living within another nation of the well-off, the trained and the employed.

Is it surprising that the news media are full of reports of violence? There is no need to remind you of these reports nor of the climate which has created them—we all live too close to these problems. But I want to discuss with you the response, or rather the reaction, which is growing among many people. I will quote from the police chief, William H. Parker, in Los Angeles. This report appeared in the magazine **U.S. News and World Report** in the form of a question and answer interview.

Question: Has the crime picture changed much in [the last 37 years]?

Answer: Not only has the crime picture changed, but the entire attitude of the American people toward crime, I think, has undergone quite a definite change. I think there is a tendency to accept crime as part of the American scene, and to tolerate it.

Question: Do you mean that people now feel that wrong-doing is normal?

Answer: More than that—they seem to think that we must have a certain amount of crime not only because of man's inherent weakness, but because we are enlarging upon the scope of individual liberty.

Question: America might have a choice, eventually, between a criminal state and a police state?

Answer: I believe that will become the option before us if crime becomes so troublesome that we are no longer able to control it.

But Chief Parker did not mention what is to me the most serious aspect of the present situation. He did not deal with the passive apathy of individuals recently demonstrated in several notorious cases in the New York area. In one of these, at least 38 people failed to call the police although they became progressively more aware that a woman was being murdered in the street below their windows. He did not deal with the fact that there is now a desire to witness violence, to participate vicariously, as when a crowd of 40 interested spectators remained indifferent to the appeals of an 18-year-old bruised and bloodied office worker as she tried to escape from a rapist. (Only the accidental arrival of two policemen eventually resulted in her rescue.)

It is understandable, if regrettable, when those accidentally present at the scene of a crime or disaster flee through fear. It is incomprehensible as rational behavior when they remain as interested spectators or even active participants. During an attempted suicide which took place in Albany recently, numerous spectators participated in this novel type of sports event, urging the mentally-disturbed youth to jump to his death and betting on the outcome. Two comments reported in **The New York Times** are hardly believable: "I wish he'd do it and get it over with. If he doesn't hurry up we're going to miss our last bus." And another: "I hope he jumps on this side. We couldn't see him if he jumped over there."

I believe this indifference to violence, and indeed increasing encouragement of it, are products of a society which is rapidly coming to regard interrace conflict as inevitable; a society which fails to challenge the individual to anything more than economic goals and responsibilities and which has now deprived many people of even an opportunity to achieve the self-respect which would result from reaching these economic goals. Although we are confronted with the symptoms of incipient total breakdown in our society, we are unwilling to face reality. We refuse to recognize that the survival of American values depends on fundamental changes which will reverse the process toward alienation. We refuse to recognize that the economically poor and the culturally alienated, who are the young and the minorities, have and should have little interest in the goals our society presently espouses. Instead of looking for the new and better society that cybernation makes possible we continue the drift into a worse society: we then propose that the way to arrest this drift is through measures which must necessarily be categorized as movements toward a centralized authoritarian state: teen-age curfews and all-day seven-day-a-week retention of children within the confines of the school plant.

SOME PROPOSALS

Now I want to set out a program which might suffice to reverse the drift toward a centralized authoritarian state.

The first necessity is to guarantee every individual within the United States a decent standard of living whether he can find work or not. We should provide every individual with an absolute constitutional right to an income adequate to allow him to live with dignity. No governmental agency, judicial body, or other organization whatsoever should have the power to suspend or limit any payments by this guarantee. Such an absolute constitutional right to an income will recognize that in an economy where many jobs already represent make-work in any social, and indeed economic, sense and where the requirements for workers will decrease in coming years, it is nonsensical to base the right to an income on an ability to find a job.

Many people have attacked this proposal, but their arguments have failed to convince me. I remain quite sure that the guaranteed income is the first necessary step if we are to achieve the new and better society made possible by cybernation, that it is the only practical means of preserving our fundamental goal of individual freedom, the only method of allowing the individual to make his own decisions and pursue his own interests. The guaranteed income is not one of many solutions to the problems of cybernation: On the contrary it is the economic prerequisite for the solution of the real problems of the second half of the twentieth century, many of which have not yet even begun to be discussed in realistic terms.

The first of these problems is education. One of the key principles of the cybernated era is that society must make an unlimited commitment to produce the conditions in which every individual can develop his full intellectual potential. The acceptance of this principle would make me highly optimistic for the long run. I believe that we have so far developed only a tiny proportion of the potential of most human beings. I believe that acceptance of an absolute right to an income and complete education would allow a flowering of the spirit and mind whose dimensions cannot even be guessed today.

If we are to achieve the complete education of every individual, we must recognize that the student is "working" at least as relevantly as the man in the factory. The time has come when we must introduce the concept of a student salary, starting possibly at 14 and increasing with age, payable to all students attending school or university. This salary would be tangible proof of the recognition by society of the value of this young individual and its acceptance by the child would be a recognition by him of his obligation to the society which has accorded him this right.

Society must not only be concerned with the individual's mental abilities but also with his physical health. We must develop a system which will ensure that everybody can obtain the best medical care—both preventive and curative. Income levels should be seen as totally irrelevant to rights to health and life.

Rights to an income sufficient to live with dignity, to the opportunity to develop oneself fully and to obtain meaningful activity are only extensions of present values, although many people will be shocked by the direction of the proposed extension. However, the coming of the cybernated society not only forces us to live up to past ideals but it also requires the development of new human rights. I want to talk about the need for three rights which seem highly important to me. (There are others which should be mentioned if space permitted.)

The first of these new human rights is for the individual to be provided with guarantees about the quality of all the goods he purchases. It has always been a fundamental principle of marketing in the Western world that the purchaser should discover the quality, condition, and quantity of the goods he is purchasing. The seller simply offers a product and it is held to be the responsibility of the purchaser to inform himself as to whether it is satisfactory. This is the famous legal doctrine of **caveat emptor** (let the buyer beware).

Today, the consumer cannot reasonably be expected to examine a television set or any other complex product to discover if it is well made: The makers of many types of goods have recognized this fact and have steadily lengthened their periods of guarantee. We now need to take the next step and acknowledge that the total responsibility for determining whether a product is satisfactory lies with the seller and not with the buyer. Each seller should become responsible for the claims made on behalf of his product and should be forced to refund some multiple of the purchase price if the product does not meet his claims. In some cases, when injury to the purchaser results, the seller should be liable for damages. The manufacturer will therefore have a direct financial interest in living up to the claims made for his product.

In upper Manhattan, we are all used to the shoddy-goods salesman with the foot in the door on a Sunday afternoon or late on a weekday evening. We fail to translate our momentary irritation into terms of national waste. The proposed human right would not only minimize the time wasted by the individual in purchasing, repair, or replacement; it would also meet desirable social criteria. The time and money the manufacturer saves by selling unsatisfactory products is wasted many times over by the troubles of the user. We need a productive system which will turn out goods which will render the services for which they were designed with the minimum possible number of breakdowns.

In addition, the long-run necessity, if mankind is to survive on this planet, is maximum economy in the use of raw materials. Every pressure should therefore be placed on the manufacturer to maximize the life of the product. This measure would be a first step in this direction.

The second new human right is the right to buy from any seller. Originally the buyer and seller were in close human contact and they naturally wished to choose to whom they would sell and from whom they would buy. Today, business desires to move goods and services at a profit without entangling social problems. As a result it is not only desirable but also necessary for society to state that in return for the right granted the businessman to sell goods and services, he has the obligation to serve all comers. Those who do not want to accept the obligation to sell to all comers should not be granted the right to sell at all.

It is, of course, **only** the establishment of such a principle in law which will provide a completely satisfactory answer to present discrimination practices. It is an answer which must be eventually passed as a constitutional amendment: It must be clearly recognized that private property ceases to be private **just as soon as** the individual or company makes the decision to sell to the public.

It would be naïve, of course, to expect that these new rights, and many others, could be effectively established without a major reform in our legal system. Today, the government has all the resources in a criminal case; the private individual, unless he is wealthy, has no opportunity to hire legal talent of comparable skill. In a civil case, the large corporation controls enough funds to hire a battery of lawyers; the private individual rarely has enough resources to match this ability to spend. We require a new institution: the public defender. Public defenders would be paid by the government and would have the power of government officials but their responsibility would be to take the cases of private individual whose interests they felt had been unjustly damaged by the use of private and governmental power. They would possess enough resources to challenge the large institution effectively. A system similar to this has already been established in Scandinavia, and Arthur Goldberg has proposed it be introduced into the United States.

The third new human right is that every individual should have the right to receive information undistorted by desires to mislead for the purposes of private gain. This is, in today's world, a very novel proposal for it means that society must develop effective sanctions against individuals and groups who distort information deliberately. That such a proposal seems novel is perhaps a good measure of the degree of malfunction in our society. The framers of the American Constitution intended that the right of free speech and a free press should be a method of achieving free debate, not a justification of deliberate distortion with consequent fragmentation of the society.

What types of distortion am I condemning? I condemn the advertisers who play on the weakness of the individual in order to increase their sales. I condemn the propagandists of any country who unhesitatingly distort the unfavorable and bury the undesirable news. I condemn the academics who distort the truth as they see it in order to gain reputations or power. On the other hand, I do not condemn but resolutely uphold the right of the individual to put forward all the truth as he sees it, however unpalatable it may be. I believe, indeed, that we must smooth the path of individuals who are willing to dissent, for the costs of disagreement with existing social norms are always high. The granting of an absolute constitutional right to an income will be helpful here.

Indeed, I go further. The existence of lively controversy which allows the discovery of the truth in constantly changing circumstances is one of the prime necessities of today. Only a lively democracy can lead to the adoption of appropriate policies to deal with changing situations. Concentration of power in the hands of a few not only is against our past ideals but also fails to meet present necessities.

I would like to suggest that this is, in fact, the major role which has been played by the civil rights movement in recent years, and particularly in recent months. The attention of the civil rights groups themselves, and of outside observers, has been concentrated on the degree of success or failure achieved in striving for stated goals. There is a considerable feeling that they have consistently fallen short of their goals and this has been called failure. This is an excessively naive view of social change. Very few commentators discuss the real success of the civil rights movement—the fact that it has, almost single-handed, wrested America out of the apathy in which it was mired and forced it to face the problems of unemployment and inadequate education, the problems of poverty, and the long-run dangers of cybernation. The drive of the civil rights movement is forcing America to reexamine itself and to recognize that the rights of the Negro cannot be achieved without fundamental social and economic change. The civil rights movement has provided America with another

chance, and possibly its last one, to recognize that in conditions of abundance every citizen both can and should be provided with the means to obtain enough food, clothing, shelter, education, and health care: in effect to be a first class citizen.

Martin Luther King has taken this theme and proposed in his new book "that the United States launch a broad-based and gigantic Bill of Rights for the Disadvantaged." He adds: "It is a matter of simple justice that the United States, in dealing creatively with the task of raising the Negro from backwardness, should also be rescuing a large stratum of the forgotten white poor. A Bill of Rights for the Disadvantaged could mark the rise of a new era, in which the full resources of the society could be used to attack the tenacious poverty which so paradoxically exists in the midst of plenty."

How can this goal be achieved? Clearly the civil rights movement must be joined by other supporting groups. Only if all those who are concerned with the improvement of our society unite to bring about major change will it be possible to achieve the pace of development in social values which will allow us to benefit from technology and consequent abundance rather than be destroyed by it.

The civil rights and labor movements stand, indeed, at a crossroads. They can become the rallying point for true social change, for demands which in any other period of history would clearly have been Utopian but which are today completely practical and indeed essential. The decision to take the route proposed would deprive the civil rights movement of the support of some sections. It would alienate those who are only concerned with obtaining justice for the Negro, who refuse to recognize that justice for the Negro cannot be secured in a society which does not secure justice for all its citizens; in the same way that present injustice to the Negro is progressively involving injustice to others. In addition, this decision would deprive the unions of the support of those who are concerned solely with people who still are, or might become, union members.

If we plan and carry out the necessary actions our common future has a brighter aspect but we must face up to the unkind fact that much of the potential benefit from cybernation and abundance will be reaped not by us but by our children. We are in many ways the truly lost generation: We are torn adrift from the certainties by which our parents still lived and we will never fully understand the new set of apparent certainties which will seem totally natural to the children growing up today. These children, in their turn, will never understand how we could have allowed our defunct concepts of economics to prevent us from providing everybody with food, clothing, shelter, education, and health care.

In one sense, we will remain chained to our past, unable to enter the promised land. But our generation, and **only** our generation, can bring humanity to this promised land. The challenge is uniquely ours: if we fail to rise to it we will destroy our values, the values of our children and very possibly the whole world. If we succeed we have laid the groundwork for the Great Society.

chapter 30
the meaning
of
automation
bernard j. muller-thym

Automation today is bringing us face to face
with problems and potentialities beyond our previous experience, and its impact is forcing us to
question some of the basic assumptions we have
made about the design of machinery, our concepts
of organization, and even our basic concepts of
work and wealth.

The assumption we made about the design of
work done by machines has dominated industrial
practice for half a century. Our assumption has
been that work will be performed more efficiently
if the entire piece of work or the total sequence of
operations is broken down into relatively fine
pieces, and if our work forms are simpler and more
specialized. Although we have achieved a great
amount of progress working within this framework, it was actually a curious set of assumptions,
since it goes counter to all the rest of our experience with nature. Man, for example, is far more
complex than the dinosaur—yet man survives, and
the dinosaurs perished. Hands are among the most
complex and general-purpose things in nature;
with very few elements of specialization, they can
perform a tremendous variety of tasks. Yet we
made exactly the opposite assumption—that simplification and specialization are more efficient

than complexity—when we designed the machines
that run our factories all over the world.

As a result, we have had to make our machine
tools increasingly larger and more specialized in
order to get greater production from them. And as
machines get larger, they require proportionately
greater investments of capital. So in order to get
the incremental cost advantage out of a new machine, a company has to use it to produce ever
greater quantities; instead of a run of one hundred,
it becomes necessary to have runs of a thousand,
ten thousand, or a million of the same item. In
consequence, our factories have become larger and
more cumbersome, and it has become very difficult to optimize the productive facility. A businessman who bought a machine tool three years
ago is at the mercy of a competitor who buys one
this year, because the new machine is not only
more efficient but incorporates additional technological advances. And even if the three-year-old
machine is paid for, the businessman simply does
not have the courage to start all over—to tear up
his factory and redesign it from scratch.

The new generation of machine tools is not
like this at all. It represents a completely different
set of assumptions—a complete reversal of past
practice. To take a simple example, consider the
methods of making automobile tailpipes. The
older types of machines with which we are familiar
consist of jigs, dies, and fixtures, and once the

Reprinted by permission of the publisher from **Management Review**, June 1963, by the American Management Association, Inc.

settings are made, they make a hundred, a thousand, or ten thousand of the same kind of tailpipe. The new type of machine for making tailpipes is small—perhaps the size of a desk—and it has no dies, no fixtures, no settings of any kind. It consists of certain general-purpose things like grippers, benders, and advancers, and it is programmed by tape. On this machine, which costs less than its predecessors, it is possible to make eighty different kinds of tailpipes in succession, just as rapidly and as cheaply as eighty of the same type. This is simple and primitive, but it is an indication that the prototypes of the new generation of machines are already in existence. Their characteristics are general purpose, flexibility, and ability to be programmed with constant changes of program, and hence to be part of a network or society of such machines that form a completely flexible productive array.

By reason of the development of such machines and the development of the concepts and technology of information management, it has become possible to manage the productive matrix directly. In previous years, we have done this in a rather clumsy way by the use of such devices as production control, material control, and the like. What is now within our grasp is a kind of productive capability that is alive with intelligence, alive with information, so that at its maximum it is completely flexible; one could completely reorganize the plant from hour to hour if one wished to do so, and inventories would begin to approach the zero point. It may never be possible to achieve this maximum potential, but it will be possible to come close enough to change radically the allocation of capital as well as the allocation of the productive capabilities themselves.

Automation will also have an impact on our forms of organization, on work structure, and on the institutions of authority and control within the organization itself. Here, again, we have been operating for perhaps half a century on the basis of certain assumptions about the organization of work done by human beings. We have always assumed, for example, that there must be someone who is superior over workers, that everyone must have a boss, that no one should have more than one boss, that a limited number of people should report to the same boss, and so on. As a result of these assumptions, we have inevitably created a management work structure illustrated by the classical organization chart—a structure that is pyramidal and many-layered. As a business orga-

nized in this way grows larger and larger, not only does the base of the pyramid broaden, but the number of intermediate layers (consisting of supervisors and managers) is multiplied.

We are already, and we have been for some time, beyond the tolerable limits of inefficiency that result from running a business with this kind of organizational structure. There is no need to go into detail about the communications problems and the decay of action that result—not as a consequence of individual incompetence, but as a consequence of the structure itself. Once an organization has grown to any size at all, such a work structure diffuses and dissipates competence and creates organization distances and separations between the parties responsible for action. It results in a decay in action and communication that is directly proportional to the number of intermediaries through whom the action or the message must be transmitted.

It was possible to run our businesses with this kind of work structure one, two, or three generations ago, because businesses were smaller, rates of change in the society and in the economy were slower, and the kinds of competence required to run a business were fewer. This is no longer true. Not only are our businesses larger and more complicated, but the kinds of competence required to run an enterprise have multiplied, and the required competence levels are constantly rising. It has already become impossible to run a large business efficiently with the old kind of structure.

We already have working models of the new kind of organizational structure that increasing complexity will require. If you were to diagram them, they would look somewhat like diagrams of a nervous system, or the kind of diagrams nuclear scientists make. We might consider the present-day organization chart as a two-dimensional Euclidean structure in which any increase in size automatically creates greater distances between the various points. The new type of organization, in contrast, exists in a kind of curved space, where points of competence mobilization, points of decision-making, and points of information management are so arrayed that one can go directly, or almost directly, from any action-taking, decision-making, information-handling point to any other point.

We are fortunate that computer technology has arrived on the scene when its potentials—the capability of handling information nonselectively, totally, and in configurations that can be changed at will—will enable us to be much more daring in designing organization structures. Up to now, business information (e.g., accounting, controls) has been handled piecemeal and selectively. Instead of total information, our information systems have reported samples of business behavior or managerial action, both qualitatively (selected costs, selected money allocations, selected items of sales performance) and in time. These systems were supplemented by having some middle-level manager try to find out what was wrong at a lower level in order to pass the information to this superior, or by managers in a chain trying to force information from the top down through many layers to the point where, hopefully, work would be done. This "bucket brigade" approach is extremely inefficient: There is about a 50 percent slop, a 50 percent loss at each transmission.

Analyses of managerial action indicate that people in middle management spend 80 percent of their time simply handling information—and handling it in a very primitive and inadequate manner. We are fortunate, therefore, that at the very moment when we need to optimize the managerial work structure, we have available to us a computer technology through which we can handle the total information in a system nonselectively, instantaneously, and with random access. This makes it possible for us to create a flexible managerial organizational structure that will enable us to manage the integer of work, the points or concentrations of competence, and the entire business network. And because profit and the creation of wealth is a function of the business network, and is not (as classical economists thought) simply a matter of adding value through production, we now have the capability of managing wealth itself.

This brings us to the third point: the social consequences of automation. We are living in a period in human history that might be considered the end of the Neolithic age. At the very beginning of the Neolithic Age (8,000-10,000 B.C.) we abandoned our nomadic ways and settled down, and after we became static and attached to the land, we invented the wheel. We also invented property, as defined by an object, primarily land; and we invented ownership as a moral act that focused on and had as its terms such an object.

We are living at the end of the age of the wheel; we are living at the end of the electromechanical age. We have abandoned Neolithic weaponry like spears, arrows, and bullets—selective, single-purpose weaponry that is used to kill the enemy seriatim, one after another—and have adopted nuclear weapons that are total, instantaneous, and with random access. And now we are abandoning property as well.

One of the characteristics of the world in which we live is that property and work are disappearing. This process is going on inexorably; it is further advanced in some parts of the world than in others, but all parts of the world will be involved in it. Automation is accelerating the process, although automation did not bring it about. Property as a thing-type object is disappearing; it is doubtful whether any group of people in the history of the world could measure themselves against their ancestors of comparable wealth and find that they owned so little in comparison.

A house, for example, used to be a thing to be born in, to live in throughout one's life, and to leave to one's son or heir. In recent years, the average length of time a person in the United States lives in a particular house has dropped from eight years to five years, and it is still going down. A house today is a kind of space valve in which a married couple and their children live for increasingly shorter periods of time before moving on to another house or to an apartment; it is a place where a family spends the semiprivate part of their lives between trips to the more public centers of worship, work, education, and play.

To take another example: Americans, at a startlingly increasing rate, are leasing personal automobiles rather than owning them. (One of the largest auto manufacturers believes that the majority of our people will have cars through lease within not too many years.) When the leasing company owns the car but does not use it, and the driver uses it but does not own it, the result is something quite different from classic ownership.

One could cite other instances to indicate that property and the thing-element of property are disappearing. (The description of the disappearance of both property and work has already been made eloquently by Gerard Piel in **Consumers of Abundance**, published in 1962 by the Fund for the Republic.) The fact is that we are relatively more wealthy than our Neolithic ancestors; there is an increasingly richer abundance of goods and services for us to enjoy; but there are also increasingly less property and less ownership.

We have brought business into being as the prime wealth-generating organ of our society. The only sources of **new** wealth up to now have been the household of the ancient world, increase from nature, and independent, sporadically occurring invention. Now we have added to the technology of generating wealth by designing a modern business, for a business is a system in which output is greater than input. That output—newly created wealth—is a function of organized innovation and of the total business as a system. But to an increasing extent, the wealth that is created is not so much resident in the hardware as in the competence—the software—of the objects that enter into economic exchanges; and the wealth itself is created at and exists only as a point of intersection in a matrix of economic exchanges.

At the same time, work, in the sense of servile work, is disappearing. It is futile to talk of relieving "chronic unemployment"; the rate is going up, and it is going up much more rapidly than in the past decade. A substantial amount of retraining is going to be necessary, for there is going to be a radical change in the skill mix of people found in a business. But no amount of retraining is going to provide the amount of work that human beings now perform as sources of power, servomechanisms, levers, and things of this sort. No amount of work for human beings is going to replace the work that is being destroyed by automation.

In a world in which the prime mechanism for distributing the wealth we have learned to create has been pay for work, the disappearance of work has serious implications. It means that we are able to generate wealth, to invent almost anything we decide to invent, and to achieve command over nature for the first time—yet no one will have money; no one will be able to buy anything.

It would be foolish to try to reverse the direction of this trend; it is basically not bad. It is, in fact, an extension of the noble work of freeing man from slavery, from the curse of Adam, from having to earn his bread by the sweat of his brow. It is a direction that is generally good, and should be regarded by any normal human being as good.

The task before us, therefore, is to invent a new kind of money, new institutions for the distribution of wealth. None of us is ready to describe what these new institutions will be—after all, we have only now identified the phenomenon. But one can describe something of what that society will be like and some of the design criteria for that money or those monies that will replace or supplement pay.

It will be a world in which two of the largest industries will be education and the management

of information. Add to these communications—both electronic communication and physical communications in an intricate and sensitive space-time network whose management will require both people and computers. Some factories will produce long rows of standard commodities, but most of them will produce a marvelous variety of different end-products to the requirements of individual customers as well as of markets. (Even buildings—houses, laboratories, and the like—can be produced this way now, and more cheaply than the inflexible structures we now build.) There will be many more wants and many more goods and services to satisfy them. But while there will be an opportunity for people to be very active and engaged, there will be increasingly less opportunity for them to to do the kind of work that has represented the great bulk—perhaps 90 percent— of the world's work up to now.

The displacement we expect, therefore, will not be like the kind that occurred after the Industrial Revolution—the cycle of temporary employment, followed by greater productivity and then by a greater requirement for workers to satisfy the new orders of demand in a mechanized world. It will rather be a displacement or shift towards kinds of activity, nonservile and sometimes even wealth-producing, that have not been considered work and for which people generally have not been paid in the past.

We know that wealth exists only at a moment of exchange in an economic network. We know that we are also in a society where people are getting married younger, expect to have some children, and look forward to a life of opportunity with a reasonable right to education, health, pleasure, and a life of useful activity in the economy, the society, the polity—and at whatever age may be appropriate. We need, therefore, a kind of "money" that will enable them to have enough such opportunities on a random and timely basis. This would be a money with no thing component: It would be only a language. But the thing part of money—gold, cattle, women—has practically disappeared anyway.

We have barely enough time in which in an evolutionary but planned way to invent such a network and the money-language to make it operational. As a practical strategy, we might use that time to sell our present competences abroad and bring the rest of the world as rapidly as possible to equality with us. A world so dominated by science and electronic communications has to be one world, and economic exchanges can take place in greater volume and with greater enrichment to both parties in such measure as the parties are equal and strong.

This strategy of working simultaneously to design the new networks and to bring the world to our higher level of well-being is the only one we see at the moment to buy our way out of the dislocations that will otherwise occur as we head into an age wherein automation can be either tyrant and malignant, or servant and benign.

topic 15

institutional change: the family in transformation

Yesterday . . . today . . . tomorrow: This is the context, the only **revealing** context, in which our institutional complex can be fully comprehended. For if any word is descriptive of institutional structure in industrial and postindustrial societies, that word, surely, must in some way connote transient, kaleidoscopic, or changing.

Granted, the institutional spheres of life—economic, political, educational, religious, familial—are commonly defined as organized, patterned, and traditional ways of doing something (designations that imply durability and stability). All the same, we must attach an essential proviso. If institutions prevail in every known human society because they enable those societies to meet their more enduring or persistent needs, institutions in our protean modern societies are and must be more **dynamic** than they are static, more **flexible** than inflexible, and continually **innovative** instead of stubbornly unchanging.

That is our rationale as we shift our attention to the family. What is more, we need not delve far into the essays by Frank Furstenberg, Mervyn Cadwallader, and Morton Hunt before realizing that the family in the United States is at one and the same time resistent to change and changeable, stable and plastic. It simultaneously mirrors the past and anticipates the future.

The contribution by Furstenberg attests to the more durable, more constant aspects of the American family structure—to its essential continuity in the face of the social dislocations wrought by rapid industrialization. Granting that yesterday's American families differed from today's in many substantial respects, Furstenberg takes strong issue with the common assumption that parent-child relations, the system of mate selection, and the pattern of husband-wife relations have undergone radical transformations since the early nineteenth century.

Cadwallader, on the other hand, attacks the very validity of the middle-class American family. Charging that contemporary marriage is a wretched institution that spells "the end of voluntary affection, of love freely given and joyously received," he calls for a flexible marriage contract with periodic options to renew or cancel the arrangement. Cadwallader's argument is similar to Barrington Moore's. Moore challenges the conventional notion "that the family is a universally necessary social institution and will remain such through any foreseeable future." Moore contends that today's American family has been progressively shorn of all the functions—affectional, economic, and even procreational—that it has traditionally performed. In this section's final article, Hunt, analyzing contemporary trends, suggests that the family system that we take for granted today is due for major changes. His conclusions will seem as startling to many readers as Cadwallader's.

chapter 31
industrialization and the american family: a look backward
frank f. furstenberg, jr.

The proposition that industrialization destroys traditional family structures has long been accepted by sociologists and laymen alike. In industrial societies a new kind of family, the "isolated nuclear family," has been recognized; in societies presently industrializing, the older family systems are thought to be under great strain.[1] Analysts of the American family have both assumed and asserted that the transition from an agricultural to an industrial economy is accompanied by the weakening of a family system characterized by such traits as low social and geographical mobility, high parental authority over children, marital harmony and stability, dominance of husband over wife, and close ties within the extended family. It is similarly assumed that the modern family possesses few of the characteristics of the preindustrial family. Just as the older family pattern served the needs of a farming economy, it is frequently said that the modern family serves the needs of an industrial economy.[2]

Widespread acceptance of an ideal image of the preindustrial family has limited empirical investigation of family change. Waller wrote some years ago: "According to the Victorian ideology, all husbands and wives lived together in perfect

amity; all children loved the parents to whom they were indebted for the gift of life; and if these things were not true, they should be, and even if one knew that these things were not true he ought not mention it."[3] Few sociologists today would want to conceal unflattering truths about the family of three or four generations ago. However, certain widely shared beliefs about the family of today have helped to preserve what Goode has labeled "the classical family of Western nostalgia."[4]

Goode's recent analysis of change in some of the world's major family systems suggests some general propositions that cast doubt on the traditional view of the relationship between industrialization and the family. Goode concludes: (1) there are indigenous sources of change in family systems, before industrialization takes place; (2) the relations between industrialization and family patterns are complex and still not sufficiently understood; (3) the family system itself may be an independent source of change facilitating the transition to industrialization; and (4) some apparently recent characteristics of the family may actually be very old social patterns.[5]

Each of these general propositions may be partially tested by using historical data from the United States. While this paper will touch on all four, it will concentrate on data pertaining to the fourth proposition—that certain "recent" family

From American Sociological Review, 31, June 1966, pp. 326-337. Reprinted by permission of the author and the American Sociological Association.

patterns are in fact evident in the family of a century ago. This is a particularly important theoretical point, for relatively stable family patterns would weaken the hypothesis that industrialization necessarily undermines the traditional family form. Further, it would force us to examine more carefully just which elements in the family are most responsive to changes in the economic system. A refutation of the assumption that trends in family change are well known may stimulate historians and historical sociologists to develop more precise descriptions of family systems at different periods in the past and of the family's relations with other social institutions during these periods.

It is important to recognize that the sharp contrast between the preindustrial family and the modern family has already been diminished to some extent. Recent research has brought into question the validity of the conception of the "isolated nuclear family."[6] Increasing evidence suggests that we must modify our picture of the modern family. It seems not to be nearly so isolated and nuclear as it has been portrayed by some sociologists.[7]

Thus, we may attack from two ends the view that considerable family change has occurred in the past century. On the near end, we are beginning to get a more balanced picture of what the family of today looks like. On the far end, we have less information. This paper attempts to assemble some limited but highly useful information on the family of a hundred or more years ago. This information may be used to explore certain theoretical issues concerning family change. Although industrialization may have placed added strains on the family, the extent to which the industrial system affected the family has been greatly exaggerated. Further, I contend that not only did strains exist prior to industrialization, but some of these very tensions in the family may have facilitated the process of industrialization. The long-recognized effect of the economy on the family has too often obscured the converse—that the family may have important consequences for the economic system. To understand the complicated relationship between the economy and the family, we cannot simply view the family as the dependent variable in the relationship.

METHOD

The data supporting these views are drawn from the accounts of foreign travelers visiting this country during the period 1800-1850.[8] Although prior to and during this period American technical achievements were many—a canal system, the cotton gin, the steamship, a spreading rail network, etc.—the nation was almost entirely agricultural until the decade before the Civil War. In 1850 only 16 per cent of the labor force was engaged in manufacturing and construction industries, and this percentage had not greatly changed since 1820.[9] Although the country was beginning to industrialize and urbanize, over four-fifths of the population still resided in rural areas.[10] About two out of every three workers were farmers. This ration had decreased only slightly over the previous four decades.[11] Thus, it seems safe to assert that the impact of industrialization on the American family cannot have been great prior to 1850.[12]

Travelers' accounts are a rich source of data on the American family in the first half of the nineteenth century.[13] Many of these accounts have both literary and historical merit, and some of the writings have become famous because of their perceptive observations on American society. While the writings of Alexis de Tocqueville, Harriet Martineau, and Frances Trollope are well known thousands of little-known accounts were written during this period.[14] Europeans, anxious to observe what was still referred to as "the New World" became the precursors of the more systematic participant observers of today.

To what extent can we place confidence in these travelers' accounts? Do they accurately portray American society as it actually was in the nineteenth century? Naturally the same cautions apply in using this source of historical data as apply to any other source of data. There are several methodological qualifications about the use of travelers' accounts that should be made. While these travelers may be viewed in certain respects as sociological observers of the nineteenth century, it must be remembered that they did not possess the basic qualifications of trained sociological observers. Many of the accounts of American society lack a neutral and value-free perspective. The biases of the observers are especially evident in the area of the family. For many travelers, the family was the source of great moral concern.

Without dismissing the possibility of distortion, such moral sentiments may to a degree enhance the value of these accounts as sociological data when we can ascertain and control for such biases. Generally, liberal and conservative Europeans evaluated the American family differently, reflecting their own biases. Liberals, as one might expect, viewed the American family in a more favorable light; conservatives, in an unflattering glare.[15] The possibility of bias from political persuasion is not great, however, because most of the observations reported in this paper are common to observers of all political points of view. That travelers of very different prejudices made **similar** observations enhances the reliability and validity of these observations. Where, on the other hand, the observer's bias may have affected the accuracy of his accounts, I shall try to note such bias. When they do occur, these biases are more likely to be the result of the traveler's sexual status than his political status.[16]

The accounts used here do not represent a systematically selected sample of European travelers during the period. There are literally thousands of published and unpublished accounts, and a good sample of the observations of European travelers would be difficult to obtain. The sample used here is composed of forty-two accounts and selections from accounts, most of them containing extensive commentary on the family. To arrive at this sample, I examined over one hundred accounts, the majority of which made either no reference, or only an oblique reference, to family life in America.[17]

One final caution: Most of the travelers base their comments on a view of the middle-class American family.[18] These travelers usually observed the family during their stay in residential hotels or during brief visits to American homes in rural areas of the country. More likely than not, these homes were middle-class. Since most of the comments and generalizations about the modern family of today also apply largely to the middle class, this limitation in the data will probably not affect the comparison adversely.

FAMILY OBSERVATIONS

Courtship and Mate Selection

To begin this discussion with the first stage in the life cycle of the family, we shall discuss some of the foreign travelers' observations on the courtship patterns of American youth. The American system of courtship and mate selection is sometimes said to be one of the consequences of the urbanized and industrialized economy in the United States.[19] Free mate selection and the "romantic-love complex" are often linked to the demands of the economic system or to the weakened control by family elders in an industrialized society.[20] In fact, however, the same system of mate selection and emphasis on romantic love appear to have existed here prior to industrialization.

Although few of the travelers described the actual process of courtship in America, it is evident from their accounts that free choice of mates was the prevailing pattern as well as the social norm. Foreign visitors expressed diverse opinions on the desirability of this norm, but there was complete agreement that such a norm existed. Chevalier wrote in the 1830s that the dowry system, common in France, was almost nonexistent in the United States. He observed that American parents played only a nominal role in selecting the person their child married.[21] Parental consent was formally required, but this requirement was seldom taken very seriously. In 1842, Lowenstern wrote:

> A very remarkable custom in the United States gives girls the freedom to choose a husband according to their fancy; practice does not permit either the mother or the father to interfere in this important matter.[22]

The general expectation in America was that the choice of a mate should be based on love. Some travelers were skeptical about whether love actually dictated the marriage selection. Buckingham writes, "Love, among the American people, appears to be regarded rather as an affair of the judgement, than of the heart; its expression seems to spring from a sense of duty, rather than from a sentiment of feeling."[23] A few travelers already noted that, in spite of the previously mentioned tendency of young people to spurn financial considerations in choosing a mate, there were matches that seemed to be based on material considerations. This touch of cynicism, however, occurs in only a minority of the travelers' writings. Most of the observers praised the American marriage system because it permitted young people to select mates whom they loved and with whom they could enjoy a happy marriage. Some persons, however, noted that free mate selection resulted in certain family strains. Lowenstern states that marriage between people of different social classes, a pattern sometimes asserted to be typical of an industrial society, was not uncommon.[24] Several other travelers support this view. By no means were all the comments on interclass marriages favorable. Women, it was sometimes noted with bitterness, not infrequently married beneath themselves.[25]

Another source of strain of the marriage system, in the view of some travelers, was the American habit of marrying at an extremely early age. Many observers noted that there seemed to be a great pressure for young people to marry. "In view of the unlimited freedom of the unmarried woman," Moreau writes, "it is astonishing to discover the eagerness of all to be married, for marriage brings about an absolute change in the life of the girl."[26] The tendency for an early marriage and the feelings of pressure to marry may be related to the "unlimited freedom" of which Moreau speaks.

Almost half of the travelers in the sample comment on freedom given to youth before marriage. Particularly striking to the travelers was the amount of freedom given to young women. But this freedom was tempered by considerable self-restraint. Adolescents were permitted to be alone together, but they were expected to behave according to strict moral standards. In the view of at least one observer, apparently his restraint led to a pronounced lack of responsiveness. Moreau stated that a young couple could be left alone in the house together without any fear of improper behavior. In fact, "sometimes on returning, the servants find them fallen asleep and the candle gone out—so cold is love in this country!"[27]

While these extraordinary feats of self-restraint may be reminiscent of the privileges of courtly love, lauded by poets but not reported by objective observers,[28] there is general consensus among the travelers that the behavior of American women, particularly of young women, was exemplary. More often, young women in America came under criticism for being cold. No doubt, the combination of the freedom granted and the strong sanctions against misbehaving have something to do with the common observation that American women lacked warmth and spontaneity. On this matter, though, there is a dissenting view. Abdy commented: "Many women, who seem cold as flint in general, give out fire enough when they find a 'blade' that suits them."[29]

The pressure to marry at an early age may have been generated by strains on the young woman. She was permitted to travel alone, to so-cialize with the opposite sex, and even to leave home alone for extended periods; but with this freedom went an enormous responsibility. She was expected to remain chaste, to conform to strict standards of propriety, and to respect the privileges of her freedom. The strain created by such a combination of freedom and moral restraint could well explain the tendency toward early marriage.[30]

Several observers note the problems that arise from early marriage. In her characteristically incisive way, Frances Trollope commented:

> They marry very young; in fact, in no rank of life do you meet with young women in that delightful period of existence between childhood and marriage, wherein, if only tolerably well spent, so much useful information is gained, and the character takes a sufficient degree of firmness to support with dignity the more important parts of wife and mother.[31]

The Pulszkys concurred with Trollope that American girls got too little opportunity to see life before they settled down to marriage.[32] It was also suggested that the rapid push toward marriage led young people to marry without knowing each other sufficiently; courtships were considered excessively casual. As one observer wrote, "Meet your girl in the morning, marry in the afternoon, and by six in the evening you are settled in your home, man and wife."[33] To sum up, travelers perceived several strains in the American system of courtship and mate selection. Freedom of choice did not always lead to the selection of a mate on the basis of love; and it sometimes resulted in crossing of class lines and unwise marriages. The pressures toward early marriage seemed to result in inadequate preparation for marriage. These strains were observed by both critics and supporters of America alike. Their frequency and consistency suggest that they were very real problems. It is perhaps obvious to point out similarities in the criticisms of American marriages that were observed in the nineteenth century and the criticisms of American marriages today. At the time these criticisms were made, they were not thought to be related to incipient industrialization. The problems in the courtship process were regarded as the consequence of other political and economic factors, such as American ideological commitment to democracy, the opportunity for achievement in the society, and the emphasis on equality and individualism.[34]

The Conjugal Relation

The aspect of married life which drew the most attention was the great loss of freedom the woman suffered when she married. As already noted, single girls were granted considerable freedom before marriage. Almost a fourth of all the travelers commented on the loss of this freedom for the woman in married life. On this situation, there are no views to the contrary. Although Tocqueville[35] and Murat[36] see the loss of this freedom as voluntary on the part of the female, other observers view it as imposed upon her. A number of writers state their belief that the American wife is neglected in favor of the single woman. She is, as one traveler put it, "laid on the shelf."[37]

Why this was so, few travelers ventured to speculate. Several travelers imply that the retirement of married women from social life gives them greater moral protection.[38] Most of the writers feel that married women suffer unnecessary discrimination. Some of our contemporary sociological notions might suggest that the women, after consenting to marry, had little left to bargain with.[39] Furthermore, there were really no alternatives open to the women which would permit them to get out of the home more often and at the same time fulfill their domestic obligations. It is also possible that the intense pressures for early marriage prohibited married women from competing with single girls for men's attentions.

The primary cause for the withdrawal of married women from social life seems to have been their demanding domestic obligations. It is commonly assumed that women were more satisfied in their domestic role a century ago, before industrialization tempted them into the job market.[40] Yet the frequent complaint that married women were "laid on the shelf" belies this picture of domestic felicity. Lacking the alternative of employment, women did not face the possibility of role conflict that the modern woman may encounter. Yet boredom and dissatisfaction with this domestic withdrawal may have encouraged women into the labor market when the possibility arose some decades later.

There was general consensus that American women made dutiful and affectionate wives. Lieber wrote:

I must mention the fact, that American women make most exemplary wives and mothers, and strange, be a girl ever so

coquettish—yea, even a positive flirt, who, in Europe would unavoidably make her future husband unhappy as soon as she were married, here she becomes the domestic and retired wife.[41]

The coldness that was attributed to single girls was not mentioned in the descriptions of married women. Even the most critical observers acknowledged the braveness and devotion that pioneer wives demonstrated in following their husbands into the Western wilderness.

There were a few travelers who dissented from the prevailing view that American women made good wives and mothers. A single traveler, Israel Benjamin, wrote, "The women have a characteristic, innate, and ineradicable aversion to any work and to household affairs."[42] This opinion, however, is so disparate from the vast majority of observers that it may indicate nothing more than Benjamin's generally negative attitude toward family life in America.

Although observers seemed to agree that the young women gave up an advantageous position when they married, several travelers noted that women wielded considerable power inside the home. Along with Tocqueville, these observers felt that the division of labor between husband and wife permitted the wife to have a great deal of authority over household matters.[43] One observer commented bitterly: "The reign of the women is here complete."[44] But, generally, observers remarked that women deferred to their husbands' decisions in cases of disagreement. Clearly, the picture of the patriarchal household is only partially accurate. The authority of the husband was uncontested, but it seemed to be a limited authority which did not interfere with the woman's domestic power.[45] Bremer sums up the situation: "Of the American home I have seen and heard enough for me to say that women have, in general, all the rule there they wish to have. Woman is the centre and lawgiver in the home of the New World, and the American man loves that it should be so."[46]

There is a lack of consensus among the travelers on the closeness of the American family. Some observers commented that family members are united. Tocqueville interprets the close ties between husband and wife, father and sons, and between siblings as resulting from the greater equality of family members and the absence of arbitrary authority.[47]

Although Tocqueville's theory of family relations is probably sound, there was considerable opinion that family ties were not as close as in Europe. Here, the particular experiences of travelers to the United States may have created certain observational biases which cannot easily be checked. Specifically, many travelers did not observe families in their homes, but saw them in hotels and boardinghouses. Families that lived in such residences were frequently engaged in business and represented the urban middle class. The observations of the urban middle-class family tend to increase the appearance of similarity between the nineteenth-century family and the family of today.

Most of the travelers who commented on family life in boardinghouses were appalled at what they saw. Young married couples neither desired nor got privacy.[48] Young women were denied the opportunity to develop domestic skills which they would need when they moved into their own homes. Above all, boardinghouse life for women was exceedingly dull. Men went off to work leaving women with nothing to do. Trollope remarked that she saw the most elaborate embroidered apparel there because women had little else with which to occupy their time.[49] Several descriptions of life in the boardinghouse paint a dismal picture of women's pathetic attempts to occupy themselves until their husbands came home from work. A few travelers also felt the inactivity and lack of privacy endangered the wife's morals.

The claim that husbands neglected their wives for business was not restricted to accounts of boardinghouse life. It was one of the most frequent criticisms of American marriages. Vivid detail is supplied to give testimony to this situation. The husband left for his business early in the morning, perhaps came home for lunch, but usually did not return until late at night. This situation was frequently used to explain the dull marriages and the lack of intimacy between family members. Bishop gives a curious picture of the husband's role in the family:

> The short period which they can spend in the bosom of their families must be an enjoyment and relaxation to them; therefore, in the absence of any statements to the contrary, it is but right to suppose that they are affectionate husbands and fathers.[50]

Marryat, among others, felt that the family

was disintegrating in America though he was not specific about why this was so.

> Beyond the period of infancy there is no endearment between the parents and children; none of that sweet spirit of affection between brother and sisters; none of those links which unite one family; of the mutual confidence; that rejoicing in each other's success; that refuge, when they are depressed or afflicted, in the bosoms of those who love us.[51]

Thus we find there is some disagreement about the closeness of the family in America at this time, despite the widespread assumption in our generation that family life then was cohesive and intimate. Perhaps the most interesting insight on this problem is offered by Chevalier, who wrote:

> It may be objected that in the United States family sentiment is much weaker than it is in Europe. But we must not confound what is merely accidental and temporary with the permanent acquisitions of civilization. The temporary weakness of family sentiment was one of the necessary results of the general dispersion of individuals by which the colonization of America has been accomplished. . . . As soon as they have their growth, the Yankees whose spirit now predominates in the Union quit their parents, never to return, as naturally and with as little emotion as young birds desert forever their native nests as soon as they are fledged.[52]

This statement suggests a reformulation of the common latter-day hypothesis that industrialization and urbanization weaken family cohesion. There are a number of general centrifugal forces which may weaken the family. These forces are not always accompanied by industrialization and urbanization. When, for example, the family cannot offer opportunities locally to its younger men and women that are equal to those opportunities elsewhere, we would expect that family ties will be weakened.

American morality drew praise from many of the European visitors. The American woman's self-imposed restraint was often attributed to the childhood freedom granted to her. Though a few of the travelers scoffed at the reputed moral purity of American women, the great majority of travelers who commented on morality found American women to be almost beyond reproach. Tocqueville[53] and Wyse[54] even indicate that there is less of a double standard for men than in Europe; moral restraints are binding on the males as well as the female. But Marryat counters, "To suppose that there is no conjugal infidelity in the United States is to suppose that human nature is not the same everywhere."[55] Several travelers heard stories of infidelity but few actual encounters are reported. Martineau claims that disgrace is less permanent in the United States.[56]

Divorce

Although divorce is touched upon in the travelers' accounts, it obviously is not a matter of intense concern for most of the observers.[57] Grattan[58] and Griesinger[59] point out that a divorce is more difficult to obtain in America than in Europe. Marryat[60] and Marjoribanks[61] report just the opposite. Several observers found that divorce was increasing in this country. Wyse notes that the problem had grown to the point where divorces were said to exceed two thousand a year.[62] The fact that all the mention of divorce occurs in accounts written after 1845 suggests an increasing concern in the latter part of the century. Still, this subject was relatively neglected, and did not take on great significance until after the Civil War.

Aging

One family problem is conspicuous by its absence. This is the problem of aging. Not a single account discusses the place of old people in the society or even the position of the grandparent in the family. Indeed, the subject of the extended family is rarely, if ever, discussed. There are several possible explanations for this absence. The proportion of older persons in the population was quite small: less than 4 percent of the population was over 60 years old.[63] Not only were there proportionally fewer old people, but they were less likely to be living in urban areas where they might be viewed as a problem to the family. In rural areas, the older person might easily live with his children. The accounts make no mention of parents living with their grown children. However, it is likely that foreign travelers, accustomed to seeing the same pattern in their own country, did not think it was worthy of notice. A careful historical study of how old people were cared for in this country would be most interesting.

Parent-Child Relations

Many travelers point out the loving care that was given to children in America. Because of early marriages and the domestic emphasis placed on the married woman's role, large families were common.[64] There was almost complete agreement that children were well taken care of in America.

The most significant observation about American children was the permissive child-rearing patterns that apparently were widespread at this time. A fifth of the sample states that youth in America were indulged and undisciplined. Marryat put it bluntly, "Now, anyone who has been in the United States must have perceived that there is little or no parental control."[65] Many of the Europeans were shocked by the power children had over their parents, their defiance of their parents' authority, and the way the children were spoiled and pampered.

The lack of restraints on children was justified by some travelers who felt this rejection of authority was a necessary preparation for a democratic citizen. Martineau argues:

> Freedom of manners in children of which so much complaint has been made by observers . . . is a necessary fact. Till the United States ceases to be republican—the children there will continue as free and easy and as important as they are.[66]

Some observers even took delight in the spontaneity and independence shown by American children.

The above suggests that the controversy between permissive and authoritarian child-rearing has not been confined to the twentieth century.[67] Also the great respect and reverence for parental authority that is generally assumed to have existed at this time is not as pervasive as the defenders of the traditional nineteenth-century family would suggest. Furthermore, the picture of the close Victorian family is not entirely supported by these accounts. Some travelers observed disharmony as well as harmony in the family, though not enough observers commented on this subject to make any conclusive statements.

Grattan, among others, comments on the enormous push for children to grow up and become independent of their families.[68] This may be part of the "business" stereotype that is present in some of these writings, but the move toward early maturity is consistent with the prevalence of early marriages. Girls over the age of 21 were considered by some as old maids, and boys, according to Marryat,[69] left home in their middle teens. This picture may be somewhat exaggerated. Yet the impression is that children were not inclined to stay in the bosom of the family for any longer than they had to. Children are frequently characterized as self-confident, independent, poised, and mature.

This contention is supported by description of the American adolescent. Freedom is the most frequent word used to describe adolescent behavior in America. However, as already noted, the freedom which existed between the sexes was tempered by considerable restraint.

There is surprisingly little criticism of the behavior of adolescents. It is said by a few observers that there was much frivolous dancing and partying. Adolescents were not given nearly as much attention in these accounts as would be devoted to the subject today. The stress on growing up and assuming adult responsibilities seems to take precedence over what is today called "youth culture."[70]

From the little information that is reported, there appeared to be less discontinuity between the role of an adolescent and the role of an adult. This is one point where the industralized society may have placed added strains on the family. At least there is some reason to believe that adolescence as a period of great stress had not yet been generally identified in America.

The Position of Women in Society

The final topic that emerges from the travelers' accounts is the position of women in American society. This subject has been touched upon throughout the paper. There are, however, some additional observations to be reported. Over a fourth of the travelers comment favorably on female beauty in America. Cobden describes the ladies as "petite but elegant."[71] At the same time, he notes that Boston ladies were "still deficient in preface and postscript."[72] Several writers consider the women unhealthy in appearance. It is quite interesting that so many observers find that American looks fade at an early age. Moreau expresses a common view when he writes about American women: "They are charming, adorable at fifteen, dried-up at twenty-three, old at thirty-five, decrepit at forty or fifty."[73] This observation is consistent with the comments discussed earlier about the withdrawal of the older women from social life. There was probably little motivation or need for the women to keep up their appearance. In view of the strong emphasis on morality, the attractive older woman may have been viewed with a certain suspicion.

Almost all of the sample remarked that American women were treated with extraordinary deference and respect. As a matter of course, men were expected to give women any seat they desired in a public place even though someone might be sitting there and other seats be available. One traveler commented that he saw a man grab a chicken wing off another man's plate to give to a woman who had asked for it.[74] Some Europeans found this almost compulsive chivalry quite proper. To them it indicated the high esteem in which the female was held in America. Thornton wrote, "Attention and deference to women, if carried to a faulty extreme, is an error on the right side; but I deem it rather praiseworthy than faulty."[75] Tocqueville suggested that the respect for women was a sign of a growing equality between the sexes.[76]

Many observers do not agree with these views. They saw the respect as superficial and deceptive. The Pulszkys had an extremely sophisticated analysis of this cult of politeness:

> It appears as if the gentlemen would atone for their all-absorbing passion for business by the privilege they give to the ladies of idling time away. . . . And as business is a passion with the Americans, not the means, but the very life of existence, they are most anxious to keep this department exclusively to themselves; and, well aware that there is no more infallible way to secure noninterference, than by giving the general impression that they never act for themselves, **the lady's rule** has become a current phrase, but by no means a fact in the United States.[77]

Though others do not see the degree of rationalization in the cult of politeness, there is support for the Pulszkys' view. Hall[78] and Martineau[79] state that women occupy an inferior position in American society. The elaborate courtesy and deference are only substitutes for real respect.

Although several of the observers see the American woman as satisfied with her place in society and two visitors see her fulfilling a valuable function of maintaining morality in the society, others feel strongly that the woman occupies an ambiguous position. Her lower status in the society is at odds with the democratic ideology. She cannot be considered an equal to men as long as she is confined completely to the home. The single woman must give up a good deal of her freedom when she marries. This loss of freedom is not fully compensated for by the respect she gains by mothering her husband's children and supervising his household. The discontinuity in the role of a woman is, in certain respects, similar to the conflict between career and family that exists today. It would be valuable to look at the diaries and letters of women from this period to see whether there is any indication of such a strain.

The great deference paid to women may have compensated them, in part, for this loss of standing. But many of the observers seemed to feel that the reward was not adequate compensation. It should be said, however, that some of the observers were crusaders for women's rights in Europe, and their dissatisfaction with the cult of politeness is to be expected.

Finally, it should be noted that this kind of strain, like many of the other strains in the family which we have pointed out, did not directly derive from emerging industrialization. No doubt, post-Civil War industrialization aggravated the ambiguous position of women in American society, but women by this time may have been ripe for emancipation from the home. Thus, we might find a convergence of social patterns rather than the often-assumed cause-and-effect relationship between industrialization and the emancipation of women.

CONCLUSION

The accounts of foreign travelers visiting the United States in the first half of the nineteenth century contain valuable observations on the American family. These observations suggest the following conclusions:

1. Changes in the American family since the period of industrialization have been exaggerated by some writers. The system of mate selection, the marital relationship, and parent-child relations in the preindustrial family all show striking similarities to those in the family of today. Family strains commonly attributed to industrialization are evident to observers of the family prior to industrialization.

2. Although the American family is for the most part viewed favorably by the foreign travelers, it is in no way viewed as a tension-free, har-

monious institution. Strains resulting from the voluntary choice of mates, the abrupt loss of freedom for women at marriage, women's discontent arising from total domesticity, lack of discipline of American children, the inferior position of women in American society—these were some of the common points of stress in the American family at that time.

3. It is not unlikely that some of these tensions may have eased the adaptation to an industrial society. The lack of parental restrictions on American children and the desire for women to improve their position in society and escape the demands of domestic duties may have facilitated the growth of the industrial system.

4. It should also be pointed out that certain strains in the American family which are sources of widespread concern today were not noted by foreign travelers. Few comments were directed at adolescence, old age, or divorce, perhaps indicating that at that time these areas were not sources of strain.

NOTES

1. Talcott Parsons discusses how the family and the economy affect each other in **Family, Socialization and Interaction Process**, Glencoe, Ill.: The Free Press, 1955, especially Chapter 1. The most forceful expression of this view was made by William F. Ogburn in his **Technology and the Changing Family**, New York: Houghton Mifflin, 1955. This view is also expressed in George C. Homans, **The Human Group**, New York: Harcourt, Brace and Company, 1950, pp. 276-280. See also David and Vera Mace, **Marriage East and West**, Garden City, N.Y.: Dolphin Books, 1959, chap. 1.

2. Two excellent books on the social consequences of industrialization summarize the supposed changes in the family produced by industrialization: Harold L. Wilensky and Charles N. Lebeaux, **Industrial Society and Social Welfare**, New York: Russell Sage Foundation, 1958, pp. 67-83; and Eugene V. Schneider, **Industrial Society**, New York: McGraw-Hill Book Company, Inc., 1957, chap. 18.

3. **The Family: A Dynamic Interpretation**, New York: Cordon Company, 1938, p. 13.

4. William J. Goode, **World Revolution and Family Patterns**, New York: The Free Press of Glencoe, 1963, p. 6

5. Ibid., chap. 1.

6. See Marvin B. Sussman's "The Isolated Nuclear Family: Fact or Fiction" in his book of readings **Sourcebook in Marriage and the Family**, Boston: Houghton Mifflin Company, 1963, pp. 48-53.

7. Marvin Sussman has done several studies on the relationship between middle-class couples and their families. See especially, "The Help Pattern in the Middle-Class Family," in Sussman, **Sourcebook in Marriage and the Family**, ibid., pp. 380-385. Note the article by Gordon F.

Streib in the same reader entitled "Family Patterns in Retirement." Also see Eugene Litwak, "Occupational Mobility and Extended Family Cohesion," Bobbs-Merrill Reprint Series in the Social Sciences, Sociology-177.

8. Accounts of foreign travelers have been used in a few studies of the family. Arthur W. Calhoun made extensive use of such accounts in his three-volume study of the American family, **A Social History of the American Family**, 3 vols., New York: Barnes & Noble, Inc., 1960 (first published 1917-1919). See also Willystine Goodsell, **A History of Marriage and the Family**, New York: The Macmillan Company, 1939, chap. 11. More recently, Lipset has used foreign travelers' accounts in making some observations about the early American family (Seymour Martin Lipset, **The First New Nation: The United States in Historical and Comparative Perspective**, New York: Basic Books Inc., 1963, especially chap. 3.)

9. U.S. Bureau of the Census, **Historical Statistics of the United States: Colonial Times to 1957**, Washington, D.C.: U.S. Government Printing Office, 1960, Series D, 57-71. It should be noted that more change appeared in the decade between 1840-1850 than in previous decades.

10. Ibid., Series A, 34-50.

11. Ibid., Series D, 36-45.

12. A limited amount of industrialization could be found in the Northeastern states prior to 1850. However, Wilensky and Lebeaux, and Schneider report that industrialization was quite confined until after the Civil War. Wilensky and Lebeaux, op. cit., p. 49; Schneider, op. cit., chap. 4. The beginnings of an industrial economy, however, were apparent in such places as Lowell, Massachusetts. A number of travelers visited Lowell during this period and commented with great interest on the Lowell factories.

13. There are many bibliographies of accounts of foreign travelers written during this period. Two extensive bibliographies are: Max Berger, **The British Traveler in America**, New York: Columbia University Press, 1943, and Frank Monagham, **French Travelers in the United States 1765-1932**, New York: The New York Public Library, 1953.

14. Berger and Monagham each list many thousands of accounts and they are only partial listings for two countries.

15. Portions of the travelers' accounts used in this study were rated by the author and an associate and placed into three categories: positive, neutral, or negative. It was found that accounts could be reliably coded. There was complete agreement in 78 percent of the cases. Where disagreement occurred, it never involved cases where one person coded a positive evaluation and the other a negative evaluation. The traveler's general evaluation was related to his political ideology. Although this information could be obtained for only about half of the sample, it showed a distinct relationship to evaluation. All three travelers who were conservatives had a negative view of America, while only one of twelve liberals had an overall negative impression of the country.

16. The females in the sample were inclined to view the position of married American women less favorably. They were more skeptical about the desirability of the position of women in the United States.

17. The sample of accounts examined does not represent a systematic selection of travelers' accounts. A large proportion of the sample was located from the

bibliography of Oscar Handlin et al. (eds.), **Harvard Guide to American History**, Cambridge, Mass.: The Belknap Press, 1954, pp. 151-159, which includes a diverse selection of accounts. Handlin also edited a book of selections from travelers' accounts. This book contains some writings not listed in the **Harvard Guide**. See **This Was America**, New York: Harper & Row, 1949.

18. Middle-class, in this context, refers to persons engaged in small business, professionals, and prosperous landowners. Travelers in the sample were more likely to comment on the habits and customs of the farmer than the farmhand.

19. This is suggested in Harry Johnson's chapter on the family in **Sociology: A Systematic Introduction**, New York: Harcourt, Brace and Company, 1960, chap. 6. Parsons advocates this view in his article "Age and Sex in the Social Structure" in his **Essays in Sociological Theory**, Glencoe, Ill.: The Free Press, 1954.

20. David and Vera Mace, op. cit., chap. 5; also Robert F. Winch, **The Modern Family**, rev. ed., New York: Hold, Rinehart and Winston, 1963, pp. 318-320.

21. Michael Chevalier, **Society, Manners, and Politics in the United States**, New York: Doubleday Anchor Books, 1961, p. 294. Six other travelers substantiate Chevalier's observations on the freedom of mate selection.

22. Isidore Lowenstern, "Les Etats-Unis et La Havane: souvenirs d'un Voyage, 1842," in Handlin, **This Was America**, op. cit., p. 183.

23. James Silk Buckingham, **The Eastern and Western States of America**, 2 vols., London: Fisher, Son & Co., 1867, p. 479.

24. Lowenstern, op. cit. James Fenimore Cooper, the American novelist, in a book on his observations of American life, notes the same pattern of interclass marriage. See his **Notions of the Americans**, vol. I, London: Henry Colburn, 1828.

25. Among others, Sir Charles Lyell made this observation in his **A Second Visit to the United States of North America**, New York: Harper & Brothers, 1849.

26. Mederic Louis Elie Moreau de Saint-Mery, "Voyage aux Stat-Unis de L'Amerique, 1793-1798," in Handlin, **This Was America**, op. cit., p. 100. Similar observations on the early marriage age were made by nine other travelers.

27. Ibid., p. 99.

28. Sidney Painter in his book, **French Chivalry**, Ithaca, N.Y.: Great Seal Books, 1957, presents a superb account of courtly love in mediaeval France. See especially chap. 4.

29. E. S. Abdy, **Journal of a Residence and Tour in the United States of North America**, vol. I, London: John Murray, 1935, p. 74.

30. It is possible to develop a fourfold table based on the two variables of amount of moral restraint (permissiveness toward sexual expression before marriage) and degree of freedom permitted young people to associate together. I predict that marriage age will be early when freedom to associate is high and moral restraint is also high. Where freedom to associate is high and moral restraint is low, marriage age will be somewhat later. It may be even later when freedom to associate is low and moral restraint is high. It is difficult to predict how the fourth case would turn out. A study on this problem is being undertaken.

31. Frances Trollope, **Domestic Manners of the**

Americans, New York: Alfred A. Knopf, 1949, p. 118.

32. Theresa and Kossuth Pulszky, "White Red Black" in Handlin, This Was America, op. cit.

33. Karl T. Freisinger, "Lebende Bilder Aus America," Handlin, This Was America, op. cit., p. 254.

34. This view is advocated by Tocqueville throughout his writings on the American family. Alexis de Tocqueville, Democracy in America, 2 vols., New York: Vintage Books, 1954. See especially vol. 2, chap. 8.

35. Ibid., chap. 10.

36. Achille Murat, The United States of America, London: Effingham Wilson, 1833.

37. Alex Macay uses this expression in The Western World, vol. I, London: Richard Bentley, 1850.

38. Grattan suggests that married women are particularly visible and thus, to a great extent, safeguarded from moral dangers. He also notes that American women do not stop flirting after they are married. Thomas Colley Grattan, Civilized America, 2 vols., second edition, London: Bradbury and Evans, 1859.

39. This notion of a role bargain is implicit in Willar Waller's article "The Rating and Dating Complex," American Sociological Review, 2 (October, 1937), pp. 727-734, and in his book on the family, op. cit., pp. 239-254. Goode uses the conception of a "role bargain" in "A Theory of Role Strain," American Sociological Review, 25 (August, 1960), pp. 483-496.

40. Ralph Linton, in an otherwise quite illuminating discussion of the dilemma of the modern woman, states, "Even fifty years ago the comfortably married woman looked with smug pity on the poor working girl in her drab, mannish clothes." "Women in the Family" in Marvin B. Sussman, op. cit., p. 170.

41. Francis Lieber, The Stranger in America, London: Richard Bentley, 1835, p. 132.

42. Israel Joseph Benjamin, "Drei Jahre in Amerika 1859-1862," in Handlin, This Was America, op. cit., p. 274.

43. Tocqueville, op. cit.

44. Benjamin, op. cit., p. 273.

45. Rose Coser identifies the same pattern in the Eastern European Jewish family in her article, "Authority and Structural Ambivalence in the Middle-Class Family" in the book of readings she edited, The Family: Its Structure and Functions, New York: St. Martin's Press, 1964, pp. 370-383.

46. Fredrika Bremer, The Homes of the New World, 2 vols., New York: Harper & Brothers, 1853, p. 190.

47. Tocqueville, op. cit.

48. Boardinghouse life is discussed by W. E. Baxter in America and the Americans, London: Geo. Routledge & Co., 1855. Auguste Carlier associated the spread of boardinghouses with the decline of domestic life in America. See his Marriage in the United States, Boston: De Bries, Ibarra & Co., 1867.

49. Trollope, op. cit.

50. Anne Bishop, The Englishwomen in America, London: John Murray, 1856, p. 365.

51. Frederick Marryat in Sydney Jackman (ed.), A Diary in America, New York: Alfred A. Knopf, 1962, p. 355.

52. Chevalier, op. cit., p. 398.

53. Tocqueville, op. cit.

54. Francis Wyse, America, Its Realities and Resources, vol. I, London: T. C. Newby, 1846.

55. Marryat, op. cit., p. 431.

56. Harriet Martineau in Seymour M. Lipset (ed.), Society in America, New York: Anchor Books, 1962.

57. The intense concern with divorce does not begin until the rise of industrialization in the post-Civil War period. Then the divorce rate slowly rises, and public discussion of divorce rapidly increases. The Census did not begin to report divorce rates until after the Civil War.

58. Grattan, op. cit.

59. Griesinger, op. cit.

60. Marryat, op. cit.

61. Alexander Marjoribanks, Travels in South and North America, New York: Simpkin, Marshall, and Company, 1853.

62. Wyse, op. cit.

63. Historical Statistics, op. cit., Series A, 71-85.

64. Calhoun reports the frequency of large families in his study of the American family, op. cit., vol. II, chap. 1.

65. Marryat, op. cit., p. 351.

66. Martineau, op. cit., p. 28. Four other travelers concur with Martineau.

67. Miller and Swanson make a similar observation in their review of childrearing practices. Daniel R. Miller and Guy E. Swanson, The Changing American Parent, New York: John Wiley & Sons, Inc., 1958, pp. 8-9.

68. Grattan, op. cit.

69. Marryat, op. cit.

70. Parsons, "Age and Sex in the Social Structure," op. cit.

71. Richard Cobden in Elizabeth Hoon Cawley (ed.), The American Diaries of Richard Cobden, Princeton: Princeton University Press, 1952, p. 89.

72. Ibid., p. 14.

73. Moreau, op. cit., p. 98. Eight other travelers make the same observation.

74. Marryat, op. cit.

75. Major John Thornton, Diary of a Tour Through the Northern States of the Union and Canada, London: F. Barker . . . and Co., 1850, p. 110.

76. Tocqueville, op. cit.

77. Pulszky and Pulszky, op. cit., p. 239.

78. Captain Basil Hall, Travels in North America in the Years 1827 and 1828, Edinburgh: Robert Cadell, 1830.

79. Martineau, op. cit.

chapter 32
marriage as a wretched institution
mervyn cadwallader

Our society expects us all to get married. With only rare exceptions we all do just that. Getting married is a rather complicated business. It involves mastering certain complex hustling and courtship games, the rituals and the ceremonies that celebrate the act of marriage, and finally the difficult requirements of domestic life with a husband or wife. It is an enormously elaborate round of activity, much more so than finding a job, and yet while many resolutely remain unemployed, few remain unmarried.

Now all this would not be particularly remarkable if there were no question about the advantages, the joys, and the rewards of married life, but most Americans, even young Americans, know or have heard that marriage is a hazardous affair. Of course, for all the increase in divorce, there are still young marriages that work, unions made by young men and women intelligent or fortunate enough to find the kind of mates they want, who know that they want children and how to love them when they come, or who find the artful blend between giving and receiving. It is not these marriages that concern us here, and that is not the trend in America today. We are concerned with the increasing number of others who, with mixed intentions and varied illusions, grope or fling themselves into

marital disaster. They talk solemnly and sincerely about working to make their marriage succeed, but they are very aware of the countless marriages they have seen fail. But young people in particular do not seem to be able to relate the awesome divorce statistics to the probability of failure of their own marriage. And they rush into it, in increasing numbers, without any clear idea of the reality that underlies the myth.

Parents, teachers, and concerned adults all counsel against premature marriage. But they rarely speak the truth about marriage as it really is in modern middle-class America. The truth as I see it is that contemporary marriage is a wretched institution. It spells the end of voluntary affection, of love freely given and joyously received. Beautiful romances are transmuted into dull marriages, and eventually the relationship becomes constricting, corrosive, grinding, and destructive. The beautiful love affair becomes a bitter contract.

The basic reason for this sad state of affairs is that marriage was not designed to bear the burdens now being asked of it by the urban American middle class. It is an institution that evolved over centuries to meet some very specific functional needs of a nonindustrial society. Romantic love was viewed as tragic, or merely irrelevant. Today it is the titillating prelude to domestic tragedy, or, perhaps more frequently, to domestic grotesqueries that are only pathetic.

Reprinted by permission from **The Atlantic Monthly**, November 1966.

Marriage was not designed as a mechanism for providing friendship, erotic experience, romantic love, personal fulfillment, continuous lay psychotherapy, or recreation. The Western European family was not designed to carry a lifelong load of highly emotional romantic freight. Given its present structure, it simply has to fail when asked to do so. The very idea of an irrevocable contract obligating the parties concerned to a lifetime of romantic effort is utterly absurd.

Other pressures of the present era have tended to overburden marriage with expectations it cannot fulfill. Industrialized, urbanized America is a society which has lost the sense of community. Our ties to our society, to the bustling multitudes that make up this dazzling kaleidoscope of contemporary America, are as formal and superficial as they are numerous. We all search for community, and yet we know that the search is futile. Cut off from the support and satisfactions that flow from community, the confused and searching young American can do little but place all of his bets on creating a community in microcosm, his own marriage.

And so the ideal we struggle to reach in our love relationship is that of complete candor, total honesty. Out there all is phony, but within the romantic family there are to be no dishonest games, no hypocrisy, no misunderstanding. Here we have a painful paradox, for I submit that total exposure is probably always mutually destructive in the long run. What starts out as a tender coming together to share one's whole person with the beloved is transmuted by too much togetherness into attack and counter attack, doubt, disillusionment, and ambivalence. The moment the once-upon-a-time lover catches a glimpse of his own hatred, something precious and fragile is shattered. And soon another brave marriage will end.

The purposes of marriage have changed radically, yet we cling desperately to the outmoded structures of the past. Adult Americans behave as though the more obvious the contradiction between the old and the new, the more sentimental and irrational should be their advice to young people who are going steady or are engaged. Our schools, both high schools and colleges, teach sentimental rubbish in their marriage and family courses. The texts make much of a posture of hard-nosed objectivity that is neither objective nor hard-nosed. The basic structure of Western marriage is never questioned, alternatives are not proposed or discussed. Instead, the prospective young

bride and bridegroom are offered housekeeping advice and told to work hard at making their marriage succeed. The chapter on sex, complete with ugly diagrams of the male and female genitals, is probably wedged in between a chapter on budgets and life insurance. The message is that if your marriage fails, you have been weighed in the domestic balance and found wanting. Perhaps you did not master the fifth position for sexual intercourse; or maybe you bought cheap term life rather than a preferred policy with income protection and retirement benefits. If taught honestly, these courses would alert the teenager and young adult to the realities of matrimonial life in the United States and try to advise them on how to survive marriage if they insist on that hazardous venture.

But teenagers and young adults do insist upon it in greater and greater numbers with each passing year. And one of the reasons they do get married with such astonishing certainty is because they find themselves immersed in a culture that is preoccupied with and schizophrenic about sex. Advertising, entertainment, and fashion are all designed to produce and then to exploit sexual tension. Sexually aroused at an early age and asked to postpone marriage until they become adults, they have no recourse but to fill the intervening years with courtship rituals and games that are supposed to be sexy but sexless. Dating is expected to culminate in going steady, and that is the beginning of the end. The dating game hinges on an important exchange. The male wants sexual intimacy, and the female wants social commitment. The game involves bartering sex for security amid the sweet and heady agitations of a romantic entanglement. Once the game reaches the going-steady stage, marriage is virtually inevitable. The teenager finds himself driven into a corner, and the one way to legitimize his sex play and assuage the guilt is to plan marriage.

Another reason for the upsurge in young marriages is the real cultural break between teenagers and adults in our society. This is a recent phenomenon. In my generation there was no teen culture. Adolescents wanted to become adults as soon as possible. The teenage years were a time of impatient waiting, as teenage boys tried to dress and act like little men. Adolescents sang the adults' songs ("South of the Border," "The Music Goes Round and Round," "Mairzy Doats"—notice I didn't say anything about the quality of the music), saw their movies, listened to their radios, and waited confidently to be allowed in. We had no money, and so there was no teenage market. There was nothing to do then but get it over with. The boundary line was sharp, and you crossed it when you took your first serious job, when you passed the employment test.

Now there is a very definite adolescent culture, which is in many ways hostile to the dreary culture of the adult world. In its most extreme form it borrows from the beats and turns the middle-class value system inside out. The hip teenager of Macdougal Street or Telegraph Avenue can buy a costume and go to a freak show. It's fun to be an Indian, a prankster, a beat, or a swinging troubadour. He can get stoned. That particular trip leads to instant mysticism.

Even in less extreme forms, teen culture is weighted against the adult world of responsibility. I recently asked a roomful of eighteen-year-olds to tell me what an adult is. Their deliberate answer, after hours of discussion, was that an adult is someone who no longer plays, who is no longer playful. Is Bob Dylan an adult? No, never! Of course they did not want to remain children, or teens, or adolescents; but they did want to remain youthful, playful, free of squares, and free of responsibility. The teenager wants to be old enough to drive, drink, screw, and travel. He does not want to get pushed into square maturity. He wants to drag the main, be a surf bum, a ski bum, or dream of being a bum. He doesn't want to go to Vietnam, or to IBM, or to buy a split-level house in Knotty Pines Estates.

This swing away from responsibility quite predictably produces frictions between the adolescent and his parents. The clash of cultures is likely to drive the adolescent from the home, to persuade him to leave the dead world of his parents and strike out on his own. And here we find the central paradox of young marriages. For the only way the young person can escape from his parents is to assume many of the responsibilities that he so reviles in the life-style of his parents. He needs a job and an apartment. And he needs some kind of emotional substitute, some means of filling the emotional vacuum that leaving home has caused. And so he goes steady, and sooner rather than later, gets married to a girl with similar inclinations.

When he does this, he crosses the dividing line between the cultures. Though he seldom realizes it at the time, he has taken the first step to adulthood. Our society does not have a conventional "rite of passage." In Africa the Masai adolescent

takes a lion test. He becomes an adult the first time he kills a lion with a spear. Our adolescents take the domesticity test. When they get married they have to come to terms with the system in one way or another. Some brave individuals continue to fight it. But most simply capitulate.

The cool adolescent finishing high school or starting college has a skeptical view of virtually every institutional sector of his society. He knows that government is corrupt, the military dehumanizing, the corporations rapacious, the churches organized hypocrisy, and the schools dishonest. But the one area that seems to be exempt from his cynicism is romantic love and marriage. When I talk to teenagers about marriage, that cool skepticism turns to sentimental dreams right out of **Ladies' Home Journal** or the hard-hitting pages of **Reader's Digest**. They all mouth the same vapid platitudes about finding happiness through sharing and personal fulfillment through giving (each is to give 51 percent). They have all heard about divorce, and most of them have been touched by it in some way or another. Yet they insist that their marriage will be different.

So clutching their illusions, young girls with ecstatic screams of joy lead their awkward brooding boys through the portals of the church into the land of the Mustang, Apartment 24, Macy's, Sears, and the ubiquitous drive-in. They have become members in good standing of the adult world.

The end of most of these sentimental marriages is quite predictable. They progress, in most cases, to varying stages of marital ennui, depending on the ability of the couple to adjust to reality; most common are (1) a lackluster standoff, (2) a bitter business carried on for the children, church, or neighbors, or (3) separation and divorce, followed by another search to find the right person.

Divorce rates have been rising in all Western countries. In many countries the rates are rising even faster than in the United States. In 1910 the divorce rate for the United States was 87 per 1000 marriages. In 1965 the rate had risen to an estimated figure of well over 300 per 1000 in many parts of the country. At the present time some 40 percent of all brides are between the ages of fifteen and eighteen; half of these marriages break up within five years. As our population becomes younger and the age of marriage continues to drop, the divorce rate will rise to significantly higher levels.

What do we do, what can we do, about this wretched and disappointing institution? In terms of the immediate generation, the answer probably is, not much. Even when subjected to the enormous strains I have described, the habits, customs, traditions, and taboos that make up our courtship and marriage cycle are uncommonly resistant to change. Here and there creative and courageous individuals can and do work out their own unique solutions to the problem of marriage. Most of us simply suffer without understanding and thrash around blindly in an attempt to reduce the acute pain of a romance gone sour. In time, all of these individual actions will show up as a trend away from the old and toward the new, and the bulk of sluggish moderates in the population will slowly come to accept this trend as part of social evolution. Clearly, in middle-class America, the trend is ever toward more romantic courtship and marriage, earlier premarital sexual intercourse; earlier first marriages, more extramarital affairs, earlier first divorces, more frequent divorces and remarriages. The trend is away from stable lifelong monogamous relationships toward some form of polygamous male-female relationship. Perhaps we should identify it as serial or consecutive polygamy, simply because Americans in significant numbers are going to have more than one husband or more than one wife. Attitudes and laws that make multiple marriages (in sequence, of course) difficult for the romantic and sentimental among us are archaic obstacles that one learns to circumvent with the aid of weary judges and clever attorneys.

Now the absurdity of much of this lies in the fact that we pretend that marriages of short duration must be contracted for life. Why not permit a flexible contract perhaps for one to two or more years, with periodic options to renew? If a couple grew disenchanted with their life together, they would not feel trapped for life. They would not have to anticipate and then go through the destructive agonies of divorce. They would not have to carry about the stigma of marital failure, like the mark of Cain on their foreheads. Instead of a declaration of war, they could simply let their contract lapse, and while still friendly, be free to continue their romantic quest. Sexualized romanticism is now so fundamental to American life—and is bound to become even more so—that marriage will simply have to accommodate itself to it in one way or another. For a great proportion of us it already has.

What of the children in a society that is moving inexorably toward consecutive plural marriages? Under present arrangements in which marriages are ostensibly lifetime contracts and then are dissolved through hypocritical collusions or messy battles in court, the children do suffer. Marriage and divorce turn lovers into enemies, and the child is left to thread his way through the emotional wreckage of his parents' lives. Financial support of the children, mere subsistence, is not really a problem in a society as affluent as ours. Enduring emotional support of children by loving, healthy, and friendly adults is a serious problem in America, and it is a desperately urgent problem in many families where divorce is unthinkable. If the bitter and poisonous denouncement of divorce could be avoided by a frank acceptance of short-term marriages, both adults and children would benefit. Any time husbands and wives and ex-husbands and ex-wives treat each other decently, generously, and respectfully, their children will benefit.

The braver and more critical among our teen-agers and youthful adults will still ask, But if the institution is so bad, why get married at all? This is a tough one to deal with. The social pressures pushing any couple who live together into marriage are difficult to ignore even by the most resolute rebel. It can be done, and many should be encouraged to carry out their own creative experiments in living together in a relationship that is wholly voluntary. If the demands of society to conform seem overwhelming, the couple should know that simply to be defined by others as married will elicit married-like behavior in themselves, and that is precisely what they want to avoid.

How do you marry and yet live like gentle lovers, or at least like friendly roommates? Quite frankly, I do not know the answer to that question.

chapter 33
the future
of
marriage
morton hunt

Over a century ago, the Swiss historian and ethnologist J. J. Bachofen postulated that early man lived in small packs, ignorant of marriage and indulging in beastlike sexual promiscuity. He could hardly have suggested anything more revolting, or more fascinating, to the puritanical and prurient sensibility of his time, and whole theories of the family and of society were based on his notion by various antrhopologists, as well as by German socialist Friedrich Engels and Russian revolutionist Pëtr Kropotkin. As the Victorian fog dissipated, however, it turned out that among the hundreds of primitive peoples still on earth—many of whom lived much like early man—not a single one was without some form of marriage and some limitations on the sexual freedom of the married. Marriage, it appeared, was a genuine human universal, like speech and social organization.

Nonetheless, Bachofen's myth died hard, because it appealed to a longing, deep in all of us, for total freedom to do whatever we want. And recently, it has sprung up from its own ashes in the form of a startling new notion: Even if there never was a time when marriage didn't exist, there soon will be. Lately, the air has been filled with such prophecies of the decline and impending fall of marriage. Some of the prophets are grieved at this

prospect—among them, men of the cloth, such as the Pope and Dr. Peale, who keep warning us that hedonism and easy divorce are eroding the very foundations of family life. Others, who rejoice at the thought, include an assortment of feminists, hippies, and anarchists, plus much-married theater people such as Joan Fontaine, who, having been married more times than the Pope and Dr. Peale put together, has authoritatively told the world that marriage is obsolete and that any sensible person can live and love better without it.

Some of the fire-breathing dragon ladies who have given women's lib an undeservedly bad name urge single women not to marry and married ones to desert their husbands forthwith. Kate Millet, the movement's leading theoretician, expects marriage to wither away after women achieve full equality. Dr. Roger Egeberg, an Assistant Secretary of HEW, urged Americans in 1969 to reconsider their inherited belief that everyone ought to marry. And last August, Mrs. Rita Hauser, the U.S. representative to the UN Human Rights Commission, said that the idea that marriage was primarily for procreation had become outmoded and that laws banning marriage between homosexuals should be erased from the books.

So much for the voices of prophecy. Are there, in fact, any real indications of a mass revolt against traditional marriage? There certainly seem to be. For one thing, in 1969 there were 660,000 divorces in America—an all-time record—and the divorce rate seems certain to achieve historic new highs in the next few years. For another thing, marital infidelity seems to have increased markedly since Kinsey's first surveys of a generation ago and now is tried, sooner or later, by some 60 percent of married men and 30 to 35 percent of married women in this country. But in what is much more of a departure from the past, infidelity is now tacitly accepted by a fair number of the spouses of the unfaithful. For some couples it has become a shared hobby; mate-swapping and group-sex parties now involve thousands of middle-class marriages. Yet another indication of change is a sharp increase not only in the number of young men and women who, dispensing with legalities, live together unwed but also in the kind of people who are doing so; although common-law marriage has long been popular among the poor, in the past few years it has become widespread—and often esteemed—within the middle class.

An even more radical attack on our marriage system is the effort of people in hundreds of communes around the country to construct "families," or group marriages, in which the adults own everything in common, and often consider that they all belong to one another and play mix and match sexually with total freedom. A more complete break with tradition is being made by a rapidly growing percentage of America's male and female homosexuals, who nowadays feel freer than ever to avoid "cover" marriages and to live openly as homosexuals. Their lead is almost certain to be followed by countless others within the next decade or so as our society grows ever more tolerant of personal choice in sexual matters.

Nevertheless, reports of the death of marriage are, to paraphrase Mark Twain, greatly exaggerated. Most human beings regard whatever they grew up with as right and good and see nearly every change in human behavior as a decline in standards and a fall from grace. But change often means adaptation and evolution. The many signs of contemporary revolt against marriage have been viewed as symptoms of a fatal disease, but they may, instead, be signs of a change from an obsolescent form of marriage—patriarchal monogamy—into new forms better suited to present-day human needs.

Marriage as a social structure is exceedingly plastic, being shaped by the interplay of culture and of human needs into hundreds of different forms. In societies where women could do valuable productive work, it often made sense for a man to acquire more than one wife; where women were idle or relatively unproductive—and, hence, a burden—monogamy was more likely to be the pattern. When women had means of their own or could fall back upon relatives, divorce was apt to be easy; where they were wholly dependent on their husbands, it was generally difficult. Under marginal and primitive living conditions, men kept their women in useful subjugation; in wealthier and more leisured societies, women often managed to acquire a degree of independence and power.

For a long while, the only acceptable form of marriage in America was a lifelong one-to-one union, sexually faithful, all but indissoluble, productive of goods and children and strongly husband-dominated. It was a thoroughly functional mechanism during the 18th and much of the 19th centuries, when men were struggling to secure the land and needed women who would clothe and feed them, produce and rear children to help them, and obey their orders without question for an entire lifetime. It was functional, too, for the women of that time, who, uneducated, unfit for other kinds of work and endowed by law with almost no legal or property rights, needed men who would support them, give them social status and be their guides and protectors for life.

But time passed, the Indians were conquered, the sod was busted, towns and cities grew up, railroads laced the land, factories and offices took the place of the frontier. Less and less did men need women to produce goods and children; more and more, women were educated, had time to spare, made their way into the job market—and realized that they no longer had to cling to their men for life. As patriarchalism lost its usefulness, women began to want and demand orgasms, contraceptives, the vote, and respect; men, finding the world growing ever more impersonal and cold, began to want wives who were warm, understanding, companionable, and sexy.

Yet, strangely enough, as all these things were happening, marriage not only did not lose ground but grew more popular, and today, when it is under full-scale attack on most fronts, it is more widespread than ever before. A considerably larger percentage of our adult population was married in 1970 than was the case in 1890; the marriage rate, though still below the level of the 1940s, has been climbing steadily since 1963.

The explanation of this paradox is that as marriage was losing its former uses, it was gaining new ones. The changes that were robbing marriage of practical and life-affirming values were turning America into a mechanized urban society in which we felt like numbers, not individuals, in which we had many neighbors but few lifelong friends and in which our lives were controlled by remote governments, huge companies and insensate computers. Alone and impotent, how can we find intimacy and warmth, understanding and loyalty, enduring friendship and a feeling of personal importance? Why, obviously, through loving and marrying. Marriage is a microcosm, a world within which we seek to correct the shortcomings of the macrocosm around us. Saint Paul said it is better to marry than to burn; today, feeling the glacial chill of the world we live in, we find it better to marry than to freeze.

The model of marriage that served the old purposes excellently serves the new ones poorly. But most of the contemporary assaults upon it are not efforts to destroy it; they are efforts to modify and remold it. Only traditional patriarchal marriage is dying, while all around us marriage is being reborn in new forms. The marriage of the future already exists; we have merely mistaken the signs of evolutionary change for the stigmata of necrosis.

Divorce is a case in point. Far from being a wasting illness, it is a healthful adaptation, enabling monogamy to survive in a time when patriarchal powers, privileges, and marital systems have become unworkable; far from being a radical change in the institution of marriage, divorce is a relatively minor modification of it and thoroughly supportive of most of its conventions.

Not that it seemed so at first. When divorce was introduced to Christian Europe, it appeared an extreme and rather sinful measure to most people; even among the wealthy—the only people who could afford it—it remained for centuries quite rare and thoroughly scandalous. In 1816, when president Timothy Dwight of Yale thundered against the "alarming and terrible" divorce rate in Connecticut, about one of every 100 marriages was being legally dissolved. But as women began achieving a certain degree of emancipation during the 19th Century, and as the purposes of marriage changed, divorce laws were liberalized and the rate began climbing. Between 1870 and 1905, both the U.S. population and the divorce rate more than doubled; and between then and today, the divorce rate increased over four times.

And not only for the reasons we have already noted but for yet another: the increase in longevity. When people married in their late 20s and marriage was likely to end in death by the time the last child was leaving home, divorce seemed not only wrong but hardly worth the trouble; this was especially true where the only defect in a marriage was boredom. Today, however, when people marry earlier and have finished raising their children with half their adult lives still ahead of them, boredom seems a very good reason for getting divorced.

Half of all divorces occur after eight years of marriage and a quarter of them after 15—most of these being not the results of bad initial choices but of disparity or dullness that has grown with time.

Divorcing people, however, are seeking not to escape from marriage for the rest of their lives but to exchange unhappy or boring marriages for satisfying ones. Whatever bitter things they say at the time of divorce, the vast majority do remarry, most of their second marriages lasting the rest of their lives; even those whose second marriages fail are very likely to divorce and remarry again and, that failing, yet again. Divorcing people are actually marrying people, and divorce is not a negation of marriage but a workable cross between traditional monogamy and multiple marriage; sociologists have even referred to it as "serial polygamy."

Despite its costs and its hardships, divorce is thus a compromise between the monogamous ideal and the realities of present-day life. To judge from the statistics, it is becoming more useful and more socially acceptable every year. Although the divorce rate leveled off for a dozen years or so after the postwar surge of 1946, it has been climbing steadily since 1962, continuing the long-range trend of 100 years, and the rate for the entire nation now stands at nearly one for every three marriages. In some areas, it is even higher. In California, where a new ultraliberal law went into effect in 1970, nearly two of every three marriages end in divorce—a fact that astonishes people in other areas of the country but that Californians themselves accept with equanimity. They still approve of, and very much enjoy, being married; they have simply gone further than the rest of us in using divorce to keep monogamy workable in today's world.

Seen in the same light, marital infidelity is also a frequently useful modification of the marriage contract rather than a repudiation of it. It violates the conventional moral code to a greater degree than does divorce but, as practiced in America, is only a limited departure from the monogamous pattern. Unfaithful Americans, by and large, neither have extramarital love affairs that last for many years nor do they engage in a continuous series of minor liaisons; rather, their infidelity consists of relatively brief and widely scattered episodes, so that in the course of a married lifetime, they spend many more years being faithful than being unfaithful. Furthermore, American infidelity, unlike its European counterparts, has no recognized status as part of the marital system; except in a few circles, it remains impermissible, hidden and isolated from the rest of one's life.

This is not true at all levels of our society, however: Upper-class men—and, to some extent, women—have long regarded the discreet love affair as an essential complement to marriage, and lower-class husbands have always considered an extracurricular roll in the hay important to a married man's peace of mind. Indeed, very few societies have ever tried to make both husband and wife sexually faithful over a lifetime; the totally monogamous ideal is statistically an abnormality. Professors Clellan Ford and Frank Beach state in **Patterns of Sexual Behavior** that less than 16 percent of 185 societies studied by anthropologists had formal restrictions to a single mate—and, of these, less than a third wholly disapproved of both premarital and extramarital relationships.

Our middle-class, puritanical society, however, has long held that infidelity of any sort is impossible if one truly loves one's mate and is happily married, that any deviation from fidelity stems from an evil or neurotic character and that it inevitably damages both the sinner and the sinned against. This credo drew support from earlier generations of psychotherapists, for almost all the adulterers they treated were neurotic, unhappily married or out of sorts with life in general. But it is just such people who seek psychotherapy; they are hardly a fair sample. Recently, sex researchers have examined the unfaithful more representatively and have come up with quite different findings. Alfred Kinsey, sociologist Robert Whitehurst of Indiana University, sociologist John Cuber of Ohio State University, sexologist/therapist Dr. Albert Ellis and various others (including myself), all of whom have made surveys of unfaithful husbands and wives, agree in general that:

Many of the unfaithful—perhaps even a majority—

are not seriously dissatisfied with their marriages nor their mates and a fair number are more or less happily married.
Only about a third—perhaps even fewer— appear to seek extramarital sex for neurotic motives; the rest do so for nonpathological reasons.
Many of the unfaithful—perhaps even a majority— do not feel that they, their mates nor their marriages have been harmed; in my own sample, a tenth said that their marriages had been helped or made more tolerable by their infidelity.

It is still true that many a "deceived" husband or wife, learning about his or her mate's infidelity, feels humiliated, betrayed and unloved, and is filled with rage and the desire for revenge; it is still true, too, that infidelity is a cause in perhaps a third of all divorces. But more often than not, deceived spouses never know of their mates' infidelity nor are their marriages perceptibly harmed by it.

The bulk of present-day infidelity remains hidden beneath the disguise of conventional marital behavior. But an unfettered minority of husbands and wives openly grant each other the right to outside relationships, limiting that right to certain occasions and certain kinds of involvement, in order to keep the marital relationship all-important and unimpaired. A few couples, for instance, take separate vacations or allow each other one night out alone per week, it being understood that their extramarital involvements are to be confined to those times. Similar freedoms have been urged by radical marriage reformers for decades but have never really caught on, and probably never will, for one simple reason: What's out of sight is not necessarily out of mind. What husband can feel sure, despite his wife's promises, that she might not find some other man who will make her dream come true? What wife can feel sure that her husband won't fall in love with some woman he is supposed to be having only a friendly tumble with?

But it's another matter when husband and wife go together in search of extramarital frolic and do their thing with other people, in full view of each other, where it is free of romantic feeling. This is the very essence of marital swinging, or, as it is sometimes called, comarital sex. Whether it consists of a quiet mate exchange between two couples, a small sociable group-sex party or a large orgiastic rumpus, the premise is the same: As long as the extramarital sex is open, shared, and purely recreational, it is not considered divisive of marriage.

So the husband and wife welcome the baby sitter, kiss the children good night and drive off together to someone's home, where they drink a little and make social talk with their hosts and any others guests present, and then pair off with a couple of the others and disappear into bedrooms for an hour or so or undress in the living room and have sex in front of their interested and approving mates.

No secrecy about that, certainly, and no hidden romance to fear; indeed, the very exhibitionism of marital swinging enforces its most important ground rule—the tacit understanding that participants will not indulge in emotional involvements with fellow swingers, no matter what physical acts they perform together. Though a man and a woman make it with each other at a group-sex party, they are not supposed to meet each other later on; two swinging couples who get together outside of parties are disapprovingly said to be going steady. According to several researchers, this proves that married swingers value their marriages: They want sexual fun and stimulation but nothing that would jeopardize their marital relationships. As sociologists Duane Denfeld and Michael Gordon of the University of Connecticut straight-facedly write, marital swingers "favor monogamy and want to maintain it" and do their swinging "in order to support and improve their marriages."

To the outsider, this must sound very odd, not to say outlandish. How could anyone hope to preserve the warmth and intimacy of marriage by performing the most private and personal sexual acts with other people in front of his own mate or watching his mate do so with others?

Such a question implies that sex is integrally interwoven with the rest of one's feelings about the mate—which it is—but swingers maintain that it can be detached and enjoyed apart from those feelings, without changing them in any way. Marital swinging is supposed to involve only this one segment of the marital relationship and during only a few hours of any week or month; all else is meant to remain intact, monogamous and conventional.

Experts maintain that some people swing out of neurotic needs; some have sexual problems in their marriages that do not arise in casual sexual relationships; some are merely bored and in need of new stimuli; some need the ego lift of continual conquests. But the average swinger, whatever his (or her) motive, normal or pathological, is apt to believe that he loves his spouse, that he has a pretty good marriage and that detaching sex—and sex alone—from marital restrictions not only will do the marriage no harm but will rid it of any aura of confinement.

■

In contrast to this highly specialized and sharply limited attitude, there seems to be a far broader and more thorough rejection of marriage on the part of those men and women who choose to live together unwed. Informal, nonlegal unions have long been widespread among poor blacks, largely for economic reasons, but the present wave of such unions among middle-class whites has an ideological basis, for most of those who choose this arrangement consider themselves revolutionaries who have the guts to pioneer in a more honest and vital relationship than conventional marriage. A 44-year-old conference leader, Theodora Wells, and a 51-year-old psychologist, Lee Christie, who live together in Beverly Hills, expounded their philosophy in the April 1970 issue of **The Futurist**: " 'Personhood' is central to the living-together relationship; sex roles are central to the marriage relationship. Our experience strongly suggests that personhood excites growth, stimulates openness, increases joyful satisfactions in achieving, encompasses rich, full sexuality peaking in romance. Marriage may have the appearance of this in its romantic phase, but it settles down to prosaic routine. . . . The wife role is diametrically opposed to the personhood I want. I [Theodora] therefore choose to live with the man who joins me in the priority of personhood."

What this means is that she hates homemaking, is career oriented and fears that if she became a legal wife, she would automatically be committed to traditional female roles, to dependency. Hence, she and Christie have rejected marriage and chosen an arrangement without legal obligations, without a head of the household and without a primary money earner or primary homemaker—though Christie, as it happens, does 90 percent of the cooking. Both believe that their freedom from legal ties and their constant need to rechoose each other make for a more exciting, real, and growing relationship.

A fair number of the avant-garde and many of the young have begun to find this not only a fashionably rebellious but a thoroughly congenial attitude toward marriage; couples are living together, often openly, on many a college campus, risking punishment by college authorities (but finding the risk smaller every day) and bucking their parents' strenuous disapproval (but getting their glum acceptance more and more often).

When one examines the situation closely, however, it becomes clear that most of these marital Maoists live together in close, warm, committed, and monogamous fashion, very much like married people; they keep house together (although often dividing their roles in untraditional ways) and neither is free to have sex with anyone else, date anyone else, nor even find anyone else intriguing. Anthropologists Margaret Mead and Ashley Montagu, sociologist John Gagnon and other close observers of the youth scene feel that living together, whatever its defects, is actually an apprentice marriage and not a true rebellion against marriage at all.

Dr. Mead, incidentally, made a major public pitch in 1966 for a revision of our laws that would create two kinds of marital status: individual marriage, a legal but easily dissolved form for young people who were unready for parenthood or full commitment to each other but who wanted to live together with social acceptance; and parental marriage, a union involving all the legal commitments and responsibilities—and difficulties of dissolution—of marriage as we presently know it. Her suggestion aroused a great deal of public debate. The middle-aged, for the most part, condemned her proposal as being an attack upon and a debasement of marriage, while the young replied that the whole idea was unnecessary. The young were right: They were already creating their own new marital folkway in the form of the close, serious but informal union that achieved all the goals of individual marriage except its legality and acceptance by the middle-aged. Thinking themselves rebels against marriage, they had only created a new form of marriage closely resembling the very thing Dr. Mead had suggested.

■

If these modifications of monogamy aren't quite as alarming or as revolutionary as they seem to be, one contemporary experiment in marriage **is** a genuine and total break with Western tradition. This is group marriage—a catchall term applied to a wide variety of polygamous experiments in which small groups of adult males and females, and their children, live together under one roof or in a close-knit settlement, calling themselves a family, tribe, commune or, more grandly, intentional community and considering themselves all married to one another.

As the term intentional community indicates, these are experiments not merely in marriage but in the building of a new type of society. They are utopian minisocieties existing within, but almost wholly opposed to, the mores and values of present-day American society.

Not that they are all of a piece. A few are located in cities and have members who look and act square and hold regular jobs; some, both urban and rural, consist largely of dropouts, acidheads, panhandlers and petty thieves; but most are rural communities, have hippie-looking members and aim at a self-sufficient farming-and-handicraft way of life. A very few communes are politically conservative, some are in the middle, and most are pacifist, anarchistic and/or New Leftist. Nearly all, whatever their national political bent, are islands of primitive communism in which everything is collectively owned and all members work for the common good.

Their communism extends to—or perhaps really begins with—sexual collectivism. Though some communes consist of married couples who are conventionally faithful, many are built around some kind of group sexual sharing. In some of these, couples are paired off but occasionally sleep with other members of the group; in others, pairing off is actively discouraged and the members drift around sexually from one partner to another—a night here, a night there, as they wish.

Group marriage has captured the imagination of many thousands of college students in the past few years through its idealistic and romantic portrayal in three novels widely read by the young— Robert Heinlein's **Stranger in a Strange Land** and Robert Rimmer's **The Harrad Experiment** and **Proposition 31**. The underground press, too, has paid a good deal of sympathetic attention— and the establishment press a good deal of hostile attention—to communes. There has even been, for several years, a West Coast publication titled **The Modern Utopian** that is devoted, in large part, to news and discussions of group marriage. The magazine, which publishes a directory of intentional communities, recently listed 125 communes and the editor said, "For every listing you find here, you can be certain there are 100 others." And an article in **The New York Times** last December stated that "nearly 2000 communes in 34 states have turned up" but gave this as a conservative figure, as "no accurate count exists."

All this sometimes gives one the feeling that group marriage is sweeping the country; but, based on the undoubtedly exaggerated figures of **The Modern Utopian** and counting a generous average of 20 people per commune, it would still mean that no more than 250,000 adults—approximately one-tenth of one percent of the U.S. population—are presently involved in group marriages. These figures seem improbable.

Nevertheless, group marriage offers solutions to a number of the nagging problems and discontents of modern monogamy. Collective parenthood—every parent being partly responsible for every child in the group—not only provides a warm and enveloping atmosphere for children but removes some of the pressure from individual parents; moreover, it minimizes the disruptive effects of divorce on the child's world. Sexual sharing is an answer to boredom and solves the problem of infidelity, or seeks to, by declaring extramarital experiences acceptable and admirable. It avoids the success-status-possession syndrome of middle-class family life by turning toward simplicity, communal ownership and communal goals.

Finally, it avoids the loneliness and confinement of monogamy by creating something comparable to what anthropologists call the extended family, a larger grouping of related people living together. (There is a difference, of course: In group marriage, the extended family isn't composed of blood relatives.) Even when sexual switching isn't the focus, there is a warm feeling of being affectionally connected to everyone else. As one young woman in a Taos commune said ecstatically, "It's really groovy waking up and knowing that 48 people love you."

There is, however, a negative side: This drastic reformulation of marriage makes for new problems, some of them more severe than the ones it has solved. Albert Ellis, quoted in Herbert Otto's new book, **The Family in Search of a Future,** lists several categories of serious difficulties with group marriage, including the near impossibility of finding four or more adults who can live harmoniously and lovingly together, the stubborn intrusion of jealousy and love conflicts, and the innumerable difficulties of coordinating and scheduling many lives.

Other writers, including those who have sampled communal life, also talk about the problems of leadership (most communes have few to start with; those that survive for any time do so by becoming almost conventional and traditional) and the difficulties in communal work sharing (there are always some members who are slovenly and lazy and others who are neat and hardworking, the latter either having to expel the former or give up and let the commune slowly die).

A more serious defect is that most group marriages, being based upon a simple, semiprimitive agrarian life, reintroduce old-style patriarchalism, because such a life puts a premium on masculine muscle power and endurance and leaves the classic domestic and subservient roles to women. Even a most sympathetic observer, psychiatrist Joseph Downing, writes, "In the tribal families, while both sexes work, women are generally in a service role. . . . Male dominance is held desirable by both sexes."

Most serious of all are the emotional limitations of group marriage. Its ideal is sexual freedom and universal love, but the group marriages that most nearly achieve this have the least cohesiveness and the shallowest interpersonal involvements; people come and go, and there is really no marriage at all but only a continuously changing and highly unstable encounter group. The longer-lasting and more cohesive group marriages are, in fact, those in which, as Dr. Downing reports, the initial sexual spree "generally gives way to the quiet, semipermanent, monogamous relationship characteristic of many in our general society."

Not surprisingly, therefore, Dr. Ellis finds that most group marriages are unstable and last only several months to a few years; and sociologist Lewis Yablonsky of California State College at Hayward, who has visited and lived in a number of communes, says that they are often idealistic but rarely successful or enduring. Over and above their specific difficulties, they are utopian—they seek to construct a new society from whole cloth. But all utopias thus far have failed; human behavior is so incredibly complex that every totally new order, no matter how well planned, generates innumerable unforeseen problems. It really is a pity; group living and group marriage look wonderful on paper.

■

All in all, then, the evidence is overwhelming that old-fashioned marriage is not dying and that nearly all of what passes for rebellion against it is a series of patchwork modifications enabling marriage to serve the needs of modern man without being unduly costly or painful.

While this is the present situation, can we extrapolate it into the future? Will marriage continue to exist in some form we can recognize?

It is clear that, in the future, we are going to have an even greater need than we now do for love relationships that offer intimacy, warmth, companionship, and a reasonable degree of reliability. Such relationships need not, of course, be heterosexual. With our increasing tolerance of sexual diversity, it seems likely that many homosexual men and women will find it publicly acceptable to live together in quasi-marital alliances.

The great majority of men and women, however, will continue to find heterosexual love the preferred form, for biological and psychological reasons that hardly have to be spelled out here. But need heterosexual love be embodied within marriage? If the world is already badly overpopulated and daily getting worse, why add to its burden—and if one does not intend to have children, why seek to enclose love within a legal cage? Formal promises to love are promises no one can keep, for love is not an act of will; and legal bonds have no power to keep love alive when it is dying.

Such reasoning—more cogent today than ever, due to the climate of sexual permissiveness and to the twin technical advances of the pill and the loop—lies behind the growth of unwed unions. From all indications, however, such unions will not replace marriage as an institution but only precede it in the life of the individual.

It seems probable that more and more young people will live together unwed for a time and then marry each other or break up and make another similar alliance, and another, until one of them turns into a formal, legal marriage. In 50 years, perhaps less, we may come close to the Scandinavian pattern, in which a great many couples live together prior to marriage. It may be, moreover, that the spread of this practice will decrease the divorce rate among the young, for many of the mistakes that are recognized too late and are undone in divorce court will be recognized and undone outside the legal system, with less social and emotional damage than divorce involves.

If, therefore, marriage continues to be important, what form will it take? The one truly revolu-

tionary innovation is group marriage—and, as we have seen, it poses innumerable and possibly insuperable practical and emotional difficulties. A marriage of one man and one woman involves only one interrelationship, yet we all know how difficult it is to find that one right fit and to keep it in working order. But add one more person, making the smallest possible group marriage, and you have three relationships (A-B, B-C and A-C); add a fourth to make two couples and you have six relationships; add enough to make a typical group marriage of 15 persons and you have 105 relationships.

This is an abstract way of saying that human beings are all very different and that finding a satisfying and workable love relationship is not easy, even for a twosome, and is impossibly difficult for aggregations of a dozen or so. It might prove less difficult, a generation hence, for children brought up in group-marriage communes. Such children would not have known the close, intense, parent-child relationships of monogamous marriage and could more easily spread their affections thinly and undemandingly among many. But this is mere conjecture, for no communal-marriage experiment in America has lasted long enough for us to see the results, except the famous Oneida Community in Upstate New York; it endured from 1848 to 1879, and then its offspring vanished back into the surrounding ocean of monogamy.

Those group marriages that do endure in the future will probably be dedicated to a rural and semiprimitive agrarian life style. Urban communes may last for some years but with an ever-changing membership and a lack of inner familial identity; in the city, one's work life lies outside the group, and with only emotional ties to hold the group together, any dissension or conflict will result in a turnover of membership. But while agrarian communes may have a sounder foundation, they can never become a mass movement; there is simply no way for the land to support well over 200,000,000 people with the low-efficiency productive methods of a century or two ago.

Agrarian communes not only cannot become a mass movement in the future but they will not even have much chance of surviving as islands in a sea of modern industrialism. For semiprimitive agrarianism is so marginal, so backbreaking and so tedious a way of life that it is unlikely to hold most of its converts against the competing attractions of conventional civilization. Even Dr. Downing, for all his enthusiasm about the "Society of

Awakening," as he calls tribal family living, predicts that for the foreseeable future, only a small minority will be attracted to it and that most of these will return to more normal surroundings and relationships after a matter of weeks or months.

Thus, monogamy will prevail; on this, nearly all experts agree. But it will almost certainly continue to change in the same general direction in which it has been changing for the past few generations; namely, toward a redefinition of the special roles played by husband and wife, so as to achieve a more equal distribution of the rights, privileges, and life expectations of man and woman.

This, however, will represent no sharp break with contemporary marriage, for the marriage of 1971 has come a long way from patriarchy toward the goal of equality. Our prevalent marital style has been termed companionship marriage by a generation of sociologists; in contrast to 19th century marriage, it is relatively egalitarian and intimate, husband and wife being intellectually and emotionally close, sexually compatible, and nearly equal in personal power and in the quantity and quality of labor each contributes to the marriage.

From an absolute point of view, however, it still is contaminated by patriarchalism. Although each partner votes, most husbands (and wives) still think that men understand politics better; although each may have had similar schooling and believes both sexes to be intellectually equal, most husbands and wives still act as if men were innately better equipped to handle money, drive the car, fill out tax returns, and replace fuses. There may be something close to equality in their homemaking, but nearly always it is his career that counts, not hers. If his company wants to move him to another city, she quits her job and looks for another in their new location; and when they want to have children, it is seldom questioned that he will continue to work while she will stay home.

With this, there is a considerable shift back toward traditional role assignments: He stops waxing the floors and washing dishes, begins to speak with greater authority about how their money is to be spent, tells her (rather than consults her) when he would like to work late or take a business trip, gives (or withholds) his approval of her suggestions for parties, vacations, and child discipline. The more he takes on the airs of his father, the more she learns to connive and manipulate like her mother. Feeling trapped and discriminated against, resenting the men of the world, she thinks she makes an exception of her husband, but in the hidden recesses of her mind he is one with the

others. Bearing the burden of being a man in the world, and resenting the easy life of women, he thinks he makes an exception of his wife but deep down classifies her with the rest.

This is why a great many women yearn for change and what the majority of women's liberation members are actively hammering away at. A handful of radicals in the movement think that the answer is the total elimination of marriage, that real freedom for women will come about only through the abolition of legal bonds to men and the establishment of governmentally operated nurseries to rid women once and for all of domestic entrapment. But most women in the movement, and nearly all those outside it, have no sympathy with the antimarriage extremists; they very much want to keep marriage alive but aim to push toward completion the evolutionary trends that have been under way so long.

Concretely, women want their husbands to treat them as equals; they want help and participation in domestic duties; they want help with child rearing; they want day-care centers and other agencies to free them to work at least part time, while their children are small, so that they won't have to give up their careers and slide into the imprisonment of domesticity. They want an equal voice in all the decisions made in the home— including job decisions that affect married life: they want their husbands to respect them, not indulge them; they want, in short, to be treated as if they were their husbands' best friends—which, in fact, they are, or should be.

All this is only a continuation of the developments in marriage over the past century and a quarter. The key question is: How far can marriage evolve in this direction without making excessive demands upon both partners? Can most husbands and wives have full-time uninterrupted careers, share all the chores and obligations of homemaking and parenthood, and still find time for the essential business of love and companionship?

From the time of the early suffragettes, there have been women with the drive and talent to be full-time doctors, lawyers, retailers, and the like, and at the same time to run a home and raise children with the help of housekeepers, nannies, and selfless husbands. From these examples, we can judge how likely this is to become the dominant pattern of the future. Simply put, it isn't, for it would take more energy, money, and good luck than the great majority of women possess and more skilled helpers than the country could possibly provide. But what if child care were more efficiently handled in state-run centers, which would make the totally egalitarian marriage much more feasible? The question then becomes: How many middle-class American women would really prefer full-time work to something less demanding that would give them more time with their children? The truth is that most of the world's work is dull and wearisome rather than exhilarating and inspiring. Women's lib leaders are largely middle-to-upper-echelon professionals, and no wonder they think every wife would be better off working full time—but we have yet to hear the same thing from saleswomen, secretaries, and bookkeepers.

Married women **are** working more all the time—in 1970, over half of all mothers whose children were in school held jobs—but the middle-class women among them pick and choose things they like to do rather than **have** to do for a living; moreover, many work part time until their children have grown old enough to make mothering a minor assignment. Accordingly, they make much less money than their husbands, rarely ever rise to any high positions in their fields and, to some extent, play certain traditionally female roles within marriage. It is a compromise and, like all compromises, it delights no one—but serves nearly everyone better than more clear-cut and idealistic solutions.

Though the growth of egalitarianism will not solve all the problems of marriage, it may help solve the problems of a **bad** marriage. With their increasing independence, fewer and fewer wives will feel compelled to remain confined within unhappy or unrewarding marriages. Divorce, therefore, can be expected to continue to increase, despite the offsetting effect of extramarital liaisons. Extrapolating the rising divorce rate, we can conservatively expect that within another generation, half or more of all persons who marry will be divorced at least once. But even if divorce were to become an almost universal experience, it would not be the **antithesis** of marriage but only a part of the marital experience; most people will, as always, spend their adult lives married—not continuously, in a single marriage, but segmentally, in two or more marriages. For all the dislocations and pain these divorces cause, the sum total of emotional satisfaction in the lives of the divorced and remarried may well be greater than their great-grandparents were able to achieve.

Marital infidelity, since it also relieves some of the pressures and discontents of unsuccessful or boring marriages—and does so in most cases without breaking up the existing home—will remain an alternative to divorce and will probably continue to increase, all the more so as women come to share more fully the traditional male privileges. Within another generation, based on present trends, four of five husbands and two of three wives whose marriages last more than several years will have at least a few extramarital involvements.

Overt permissiveness, particularly in the form of marital swinging, may be tried more often than it now is, but most of those who test it out will do so only briefly rather than adopt it as a way of life. Swinging has a number of built-in difficulties, the first and most important of which is that the avoidance of all emotional involvement—the very keystone of swinging—is exceedingly hard to achieve. Nearly all professional observers report that jealousy is a frequent and severely disruptive problem. And not only jealousy but sexual competitiveness: Men often have potency problems while being watched by other men or after seeing other men outperform them. Even a regular stud, moreover, may feel threatened when he observes his wife being more active at a swinging party than he himself could possibly be. Finally, the whole thing is truly workable only for the young and the attractive.

There will be wider and freer variations in marital styles—we are a pluralistic nation, growing more tolerant of diversity all the time—but throughout all the styles of marriage in the future will run a predominant motif that has been implicit in the evolution of marriage for a century and a quarter and that will finally come to full flowering in a generation or so. In short, the marriage of the future will be a heterosexual friendship, a free and unconstrained union of a man and a woman who are companions, partners, comrades, and sexual lovers. There will still be a certain degree of specialization within marriage, but by and large, the daily business of living together—the talk, the meals, the going out to work and coming home again, the spending of money, the lovemaking, the caring for the children, even the indulgence or nonindulgence in outside affairs—will be governed by this fundamental relationship rather than by the lord-and-servant relationship of patriarchal marriage. Like all friendships, it will exist only as long as it is valid; it will rarely last a lifetime, yet each marriage, while it does last, will meet the needs of the men and women of the future as no earlier form of marriage could have. Yet we who know the marriage of today will find it relatively familiar, comprehensible—and very much alive.

topic 16

the religious factor: zen and sects, black muslims and jesus freaks

As with the economic and familial spheres of American society, so with the religious. If change is the only constant, change itself rarely goes unchallenged. It evokes unceasing and stubborn resistance. Thus we again see the "eternal dialectic of life"—the incessant give-and-take between the impulses promoting change and the impulses that would resist change. The religious dimension affords a legion of striking examples. Nor need we turn the calendar back to the struggles of the Reformation and the Counterreformation or the Puritan Revolution in England to find examples. Religious life today as then is rife with colorful instances of movement and inertia, adventurousness and orthodoxy.

The dissimilarities as well as the parallels in the two selections in this section illustrate the range of phenomena we can legitimately call religious; they illustrate, too, the truth of Robin Williams' assertion (1970) that "all societies have some system of beliefs and practices that may be termed religious." For if we accept the classical definition of religion proposed by the pioneer sociologist Emile Durkheim—that religion is "a unified system of beliefs and practices relative to sacred things, uniting into a single . . . community all those who adhere to those beliefs and practices"—then we must agree that the allegiances of Muhammad Ali, Kareem Jabbar, and Malcolm X to the Nation of Islam are legitimate illustrations of religious behavior. So too are Scientology, Sufism, Naturalism, astral projection, and black magic as religious as Episcopalianism, Zen Buddhism, and Christian Science.

In any collection of essays designed to illustrate the scope and portray the topical concerns of sociology, much more is left unsaid than is said. Thus there is no mention here, as there might have been, of the relationships between religion and such variables as structured social inequality, race, power or powerlessness, political radicalism or political conservatism, and bigotry or tolerance. Nor do we analyze the links between sect and denomination or the differences between sectarian religion and denominational religion.

The contributions by Sara Davidson and I. F. Stone make it clear that religion in America today is not "dead." Far from it. Many students of the matter contend that today's religion is becoming more exotic and that the novel and evanescent qualities of the Jesus Freaks, Hare Krishna, and the underground church are affecting, indeed enlivening, the older, more established churches. In the words of Martin E. Marty (1969):

In the new age of technology and urban living, churches are experimenting to find a new role for themselves. In some ways it is a great deal like the religious turmoil of the 1840s, when the Mormons and the Transcendentalists emerged in what was then a new era of industrialism. . . . There is restlessness with intellectualism, a desire for "feeling," a dissatisfaction with authority—the same things you find on the campus.

chapter 34
the rush for instant salvation
sara davidson

It is the third day of our quest for enlightenment. We are wandering through leaves, in a birch grove, solitary figures, not speaking, asking silently, intoning repeatedly until we are dizzy and numb: "Who am I?" We have suffered through intense desire and despair, weakness and exhilaration, doubt and calm disinterest. And now we are waiting.

What has kept us here is the wish, the hope for and the need to seek inner peace. We are sweating, and the men have three-day growths of stubble. We have eaten millet and swallowed great handfuls of vitamins, and slept on the floor, head to toe. We have screamed and cried and hugged and stared into space. What has carried us is the power of what we are promised: a sudden crack in the consciousness, a splitting open of the soul, when we are flooded with joyous certainty. A direct experience of who, exactly, we are. Salvation!

There is a movement easing across the land, a movement in which individuals are trying to work out personal salvation—a way to proceed through life with harmony and peace, a minimum of tension, and a maximum of fulfillment. What we are

From Harper's, July 1971. Reprinted by permission of Curtis Brown, Ltd. Copyright © 1971 by The Minneapolis Star and Tribune Company, Inc.

witnessing is the flowering of a generation of seekers, a generation whose world boundaries were shattered by drugs, politics, street-fighting, encounters, communes, or rapid social change, and who came to believe in the possibility of an answer, a key that would make life better immediately.

The keys now being taught, traded, and sold do not require withdrawal from the world or total rejection of straight society. One will not have to spend thousands of dollars, or five years in psychoanalysis, or twenty years of meditation in a cave. The methods are practical: exercise, chants, ritual, diet, relating systems, learning to control brain waves. They promise to bring a natural high, ecstasy while living the life of your choice. Each person cultivating his garden, seeking inner peace, will lead, it is felt, to world peace. Swami Kriyananda, an American who was initiated as a swami in the Self-Realization Fellowship, tells his disciples: "People must be saved and peaceful, before they can save the world and make it peaceful." Scott Wren, a thoughtful, twenty-year-old student in California, who has been practicing yoga for two years, says, "It's not a cop-out. I don't want to withdraw from the world, I want to change it. But how can we have a peaceful society if there's no peace within us?"

Because of doomsday warnings, which seekers take literally, there is an urgency to reach satori now. Crash programs are appealing. Many groups have accelerated enlightenment devices, and the Silva Mind Control Institute guarantees that after a four-day course, each person will be able to exercise psychic powers, to tap into the universal consciousness—or get his money back ($150). Charles Berner, who founded a religion called Abilitism and developed an "enlightenment intensive" which produces dramatic results in three to five days, says, "The emphasis everywhere is on technique. Kids are coming by the droves out of the drug experience into the spiritual movement, and they won't tolerate nonsense. They say, your ideas are wonderful but show me what to do. The sharper and more exact the technique, the more the kids respond. If the kids try your technique and it doesn't do what you say, they drop you. Those teachings which are doing well now are the ones that deliver the goods."

Success has not been limited, though, to groups which teach effective techniques. Virtually any spiritual organization that has outlined a path outside the establishment churches and synagogues has been flooded with seekers over the past several years. The 3H (Happy, Healthy, Holy) Organization, founded by Yogi Bhajan, who teaches kundalini yoga, opened more than fifty ashrams in three years. All schools of yoga have had wild bursts of growth, as have groups dedicated to Zen, transcendental meditation, Krishna consciousness, Jewish mysticism, Scientology, Abilitism, Gurdjieff, eductivism, light radiation, channeling, macrobiotics, Jesus Freaks, Fundamentalist Christianity, Sufism, mountain Buddhism, Taoism, Naturalism, psycho-cybernetics, and astral projection. The trend has also been reflected in rock music. **Jesus Christ Superstar** stayed at the top of the album charts for nine months, and record companies are investing heavily in "soft rock" that carries a spiritual message.

In none of the spiritual practices, except Zen, are there any formal qualifications or public certification for leaders. Anyone may call himself a swami, a guru, or a reverend, place an ad in the local underground paper, and wait for the phone to ring. An Indian student in New York did so as a practical joke. "Guru recently arrived from India now accepting students," read the ad in the **East Village Other**. For three days, wearing a ratty silk bathrobe and a turban made of towels, he received applicants in his apartment. He giggled and told riddles while a friend snapped Polaroid pictures, but to his shock, only one out of thirty who visited him gave any indication of suspecting fraud.

While the Eastern and occult religions flourish, Christian churches last year showed the lowest gain in membership in this century. It is no coincidence that, in a period when young people are increasingly suspicious of and hostile to all authority, those religions which see God as the supreme authority to whom man must bow have failed to inspire interest. The notion of God being experienced and sought now is that of a force within us all, not outside sitting in judgment. The experience is found by taking Christ's word literally: "the kingdom of God is within you." Each person comes to his own experience of the truth, and all experiences are valid. It is an anarchic, egalitarian, self-determinist strain. Each man is seen as a continuous spirit, with the power to understand everything if he can just bring that power into consciousness!

■

It is 10:00 A.M., the first Sunday of spring. On the luxuriant grass mall of the Davis campus of the University of California, 1,000 people sit cross-legged, palms turned upward and resting on their knees, with the thumb and first finger meeting in little o's. Two women in saris, their hair pulled into topknots, bring flowers and burning incense to a makeshift stage. A bell tolls, and Yogi Bhajan strides out. He is a towering, heavyset man with the air of a potentate—jet-black eyes and beard, a turban, coral rings, and a costume all of white, with cloth wrapped like adhesive tape around his legs. "Children," he says, in a surprisingly shrill voice, "you are searching all the time for a teacher. Well, you are to become teacher for your own self. Who is teacher and who is student? Same one." He laughs. "Don't start on spiritual path unless you want to end up as a teacher."

The audience sits perfectly still, while dogs race pell-mell around the bodies. Bhajan says, "Let us meditate. Close your worldly eyes and see the sky within you. Breathe deep, and vibrate loud: 'Sat Nam.' " The crowd drones the syllables. Bhajan: "Inhale in you the kundalini, mother of creation—more, more! Pull the kundalini higher, towards the neck. Breathe deeper! That is vibration!" Sweat is pouring down his face. "Now chant: OM. Meditate on the sound current. Keep going—time is now! Three minutes only will give you an experience. Vibrate more powerfully!" He mops his brow, reaches out his arms and shouts:

"Continuous! Infinity! Keep on, pull it up. Get over your hangup, man! Strike when iron is hot! Add more power!" They om furiously, spines rigid, faces straining in the sun. "Inhale—meditate on the third eye. Now exhale, powerfully!" There is a loud, collective whoosh. Bhajan smiles. "Relax. This experience is your own. You got it, you did it. It is you alone who can raise the consciousness within you. Feel free, learn from everybody. Whatever can help you to reach the truth is the most beautiful thing. God bless you."

He walks away with slow steps, trailed by his retinue, and sits down on a blanket under a fir tree. Behind him, members of the 3HO ashram in San Rafael are selling candles, natural perfumes, organic fruit-nut balls, and T-shirts that have Bhajan's picture—a giant grinning head—silk-screened across the chest. A plump girl with auburn braids approaches one of Bhajan's aides. The girl says she is a teacher in Oakland. "I'm into kundalini, but I have a lot of hesitations, and I'd like to find out what those hesitations are." She rattles on for fifteen minutes, while the yogi listens, no hint of reaction on his face. At length, he asks what she is looking for. The girl puts a finger to her lips. "Well, I was seeking integration, psychologically. Realization of myself. I'd never thought about enlightenment. That's just recently come into the picture."

The yogi smiles.

■

Ten years ago, according to George Peters, who, as the founder of Naturalism, has been playing "salvation games" for almost that long, "no one in this country had ever heard of enlightenment. Now it's being offered in mail-order courses." As the notion of enlightenment is popularized, its meaning, predictably, becomes diluted. Many seekers anticipate it as a "blinding flash of white light" which will set them apart from their fellow men. Others see it as a continual, steady growth toward realization of the truth; when the ego falls away, one transcends the mind and body, and merges with absolute being. The definition on which most spiritual teachers would agree is that enlightenment is a direct, personal experience of the truth. It is a truth which comes to one intuitively, which cannot be proved rationally but is felt so strongly as to be beyond doubt. Enlightenment has led to many different perceptions of truth, but consistent in all enlightenment experiences has been a sense of unity and continuity, of oneness with infinity.

When most people first come into the spiritual movement, though, they are not looking for much more than relaxation, or help in solving problems. Yoga institutes are constantly being referred people with back trouble, who have been advised by doctors that the exercise will be beneficial. These people may be confirmed atheists, but after a period of exposure to spiritual seekers, some begin to question the certainty of their atheism. In addition, they see teachers who, unlike psychiatrists, put themselves forward as models of tranquillity. A forty-nine-year-old dress manufacturer in Los Angeles, who has been in yoga classes a year, says, "You see people like Swami Satchidananda and Indra Devi, who have eyes that shine, who radiate so much love that you feel great just being around them, and you start to think, well, maybe they know something, maybe they're right. I've even started to consider enlightenment. The more I think about it, the more irresistible it becomes."

■

"We are here for you," reads a brochure taped outside the Los Angeles ashram of the Institute of Ability. Dozens of shoes lie in rows on the porch. Inside the stucco bungalow, fifteen people sit hushed on the floor, in front of Charles Berner, founder of the Institute. He is a soft-voiced man of forty-one, with blue eyes, a blondish-brown beard, and a round, open face that, if clean-shaven, would recall that all-American freshness projected in the fifties by members of the Kingston Trio.

Before meeting Charles, I had read his booklet, "Abilitism, a New Religion." The theory he outlined seemed preposterous: Each human being is a God, which is defined as "infinite ability." Before time, all of the Gods floated freely, unconscious of one another. Then, billions of Gods agreed to create time, space, energy, and mass, in order to be able to understand and experience each other. The purpose of life, Berner says, is for the Gods to open up and relate completely with each other. "Life is the courtship of the Gods."

Now, sitting in a corner of the bungalow, he talks about his background. "I had a happy childhood in Colton, near Los Angeles," he says. "When I was eight, I had the experience of waking up to life." He began asking himself who he was, and what life was about. He "searched fervently" through 134 religions from the orthodox to the esoteric cults, read philosophy, and studied physics and engineering. "I was very disappointed to find that science didn't have all the answers." For nine years, he worked as a counselor in the Church of Scientology, then threw out everything he had learned to start over from scratch. Enlightenment came in the year 1964, on a day like any other. Charles was standing at the orange and white pickup counter of an A and W Root Beer stand, "when this direct, conscious experience occurred. I realized that I am a God of infinite ability, and that the purpose of life is for us all to become conscious of each other as the individual Gods we are. I experienced this as the truth—beyond the realm of doubt. It's pure experience."

Soon afterward, Berner founded the Institute of Ability, and he and his wife Ava worked out a technique for enlightenment in which people would sit opposite each other, trying to experience who they are, and then present that experience to a partner. The stress is on communicating, unlike most other disciplines, where meditation is a solitary affair and enlightenment lies beyond words. Charles and Ava found that after a three-day "enlightenment intensive," about half the participants would become enlightened "wham—like that. The others make good gains, become more open and increase their awareness," Charles says. "If they just follow the technique, they can't help but have experiences. Their enlightenment may not match the Buddha's, but if they work, it will grow deeper and deeper." I ask if the intensive would benefit someone who couldn't conceive of himself as a God. Berner says, "We don't ask you to accept our ideas. Most people who go on intensives don't know a thing about Abilitism. Our masters never say one word about what you are or are not. But it's funny. Everyone always comes up with the same thing, in different words. No one has ever come up with, 'I'm a sack of mud,' or the Communist Manifesto. They could, but they never have."

∎

And so I find myself on a Thursday midnight lugging a sleeping bag around the cavernous waiting room of the Philadelphia railroad station. A ragtag group gathers by the main door. We have come from all over the East Coast to pay $75 for a three-day intensive with Ava and Charles Berner. Charles, we learn, is sick with hepatitis, so Ava will preside with Leila Zimmermann, another Abilitist

master. On the ride to Drexel Lodge, the driver, Arnie (I am changing the names of all participants), passes out incense sticks. Although he has the face of an undergraduate—sandy hair and freckles—he is thirty-seven, an engineer. "After my last meditation, it took me an hour to get up off the ground. Meditation is a better high than pot, you know? It's cheaper, no bum trips, and no hassles with the law." A girl asks why he is taking the intensive. "I want to become more aware. I'm sort of at loose ends."

"Watch out!" Arnie slams on the brakes; the car swerves around a bus. He mentions, later, that he took up yoga after wrenching his back in a car accident. Two more near-collisions and we pull up to the lodge: a quaint, pink saltbox with a green roof and rows of white windows. Inside is a single sparsely furnished room, logs sputtering in the fireplace, dark forms in sleeping bags sprawled on the floor, and a funny little stage with a dusty piano. Two of the men calmly remove their clothes and lie down on their backs. Two others are sitting in front of the fire, staring into each other's eyes. Judy, a travel agent from Washington, lingers nervously in the upstairs bathroom. "I've never been to anything like this. Some of these people have been on two or three intensives, I heard." Shrugging, she adds, "They seem to keep coming back."

"Start waking up. Start waking up." It is 5:45 A.M. A girl circles the room, speaking in a detached monotone. All the forms move at once—shuffling, sneezing, surveying each other in the gray, gloomy light. There are twenty-two of us, thirteen men and nine women, ranging from nineteen to forty-five, although most are in their twenties. In addition, there are the masters, Ava and Leila, four monitors, and a cook. While waiting to register, people assume twisted postures, some bowing to the trees, others doing violent kundalini breathing while jumping in place. No behavior is regarded with any surprise. Ava gives us our instructions. For the next three days, we are to do only what we are told, "don't eat or sleep unless we say so," no smoking, no sex, no drugs or medication, "except the natural vitamins we'll be giving you to keep your body in a balanced state," and no talking or thinking about anything but enlightenment. Ava says, "If you do the exercise perfectly for the next three days, you can't help but get enlightened. But the exercise is so simple, a lot of people don't do it."

We are to hold the question, "Who am I?" for

the entire time. Those who have been on previous intensives work on other questions: what am I, what is life, or what is another? We will choose a different partner every hour, and alternate talking and listening for five-minute periods. The partner will say, "Tell me who you are" and we are to sit, open to whatever arises. "Anything that occurs to you as to who you are, tell your partner. Then go back to the question. Who? Who? You should have no expectations, you shouldn't want to experience this or that, you shouldn't even want to become enlightened. As a consequence, something will happen," Ava says.

When our partner is talking, we are to listen without judging. "To be open to your partner, don't analyze what he's saying or try to respond. Keep your mouth shut and just experience him. This is your chance to change your life-style, to be an open, flowing person. The complete end result of this is happiness."

We pair up and sit on the floor in two rows. My partner, Ruth, a social worker in her forties, says, "I'm here because I need inner peace, and I have to be less hard on my kids." Next to me, a girl is talking about her parents. Farther down, Fred, a young man with a frizzy beard and hawk nose, is shouting: "I am infinite ability! I am you. I am us." A timer goes off, and the monitor says, "Change over." The first five-minute session is insufferably long; the hour seems unendurable. When the final bell rings, it is only 7:00 A.M.

We break to have tea and vitamin pills, which are arranged in bowls with signs, "Take one," or, "Take three." Ava says, "Keep holding your question. Who am I, drinking tea?" My next partner, Tim, a thirty-year-old computer programmer, laughs self-consciously. "It's hard to hold a one-way conversation. Who cares anyway? This is absurd. I know the answer to who I am—me. I'll probably go away with the same thing I started with. I guess the question is just a way of focusing your attention for three days so other things can happen. Like hallucinations, mind trips. I once drove to Mexico nonstop, and at the end, I had road hypnosis. I saw myself from the back seat."

Breakfast is a bowl of hot millet with honey, and more vitamins. Ava says, "If you get a red heat in your body, that's the vitamin. If you get nauseous, let me know about it." In midmorning we bundle up for walking meditation. Spreading out from the lodge, we cross streams and weave over a hillside of silver birches. Some stand frozen, staring nowhere, bug-eyed. Others crunch rapidly

through the leaves, sweating it: Who is walking? What is walking?

The next period, Miles, a slender, wry biologist from Australia, says, "I'm just a mind and a body." We hear Fred shout: "I am the sun!" Miles says, "Seems like a lot of nonsense going on around me. I think some are faking it." He shakes his head. "I wonder if in three days I'll get through this blankness. I've got no thoughts."

The sessions change drastically with each partner. Some speak in highly personal, human terms and are always influenced by what their partner has just said. Others talk only in abstractions, straight past their partner on a separate beam. Some who insist, "I am you," or, "I am us," do not really communicate or feel their partner at all. And one man, Simon, is totally beyond reach. He sits in a rigid, catatonic lotus pose, and when not sitting, moves dreamily in a perpetual yoga exercise, eyes half-closed. He cannot look at anyone's face and is skittish about sitting close to others. In the exercises, he speaks with a lisp, feathery and babylike. "I find it very distracting to be near people. I feel as if I am in the presence of a snake." His mouth twitches to one side. "I need someone to make me feel the presence of the God. There is no one here to do that."

After lunch—cottage cheese with bananas and sunflower seeds, plus eight pills—Ava gives a lecture about enlightenment. "Don't worry about whether you're going to get enlightenment or not. Somehow it will just come to you. Then you should spend a few more hours working until you can articulate it extremely well. That's the only kind of experience we're looking for, because that's the kind that will stay with you in life."

Ava is twenty-nine, with a childlike laugh and the radiance of a young girl. Her parents were both atheists, she says, "but when I was eight, I got enlightened and joined the Catholic Church. I saw a movie about Joan of Arc, which reminded me of an enlightenment from a previous lifetime, when I had spent all my time meditating from the age of thirteen until I died." In the present incarnation, she says, she became disenchanted with the Church at sixteen, and turned to occult religious ceremonies and flying-saucer meetings. She married Charles when she was nineteen, and worked with him in Scientology. "I've been like this since my last lifetime—just a religious nut!"

Ava stresses that we should have no preconceived ideas about how we'll experience ourselves, but there is subtle pressure as to what would be acceptable. At one point, she makes a derisive reference to the "mud theory—we are mud, we come from mud," and everyone laughs. I tell my next partner, a young nurse, that the mud theory makes more sense to me than any theology I've been exposed to. She screws up her face and says, laboriously, "I try very hard not to feel like a speck of dust. Sometimes when viewed in the infinite river of time, I seem very insignificant. But today, in this room, I feel much closer to that flow—it's as if it's coursing right through me, through you as well, through everything." She looks transfixed as the timer goes off.

The hours wear on, and exhaustion sets in. Legs are stiff from sitting, and muscles ache. We massage each other between each exercise. Any break in the schedule is a relief, even the period of "karma yoga"—work. We chop vegetables, mop floors, wash windows. One of the monitors says, "Try to be one with the task you're doing. Who am I, cleaning toilets?"

During dinner (brown rice, beets, and carrots) the monitors patrol to check that no one is "gossiping." There is a walking meditation in the dark, and many more exercises, more pairs of eyes, more of what sounds like sophomoric prattling. "I am what is! It just came to me," from a boy who, an hour later, keels over and is diagnosed as having the flu. Fred's shouts punctuate each session: "I am shock. Boo! I am God. Dammit!" Lee, a Japanese boy who glows with joy, says he has the urge to leave. "I don't care about enlightenment. I don't believe there should be a separation between the enlightened and those who aren't. Just love everybody." Lee is always the first partner to be chosen. People rush for him and make dibs for the next session. Simon is the last; he asks no one, and waits on the side, eyes averted.

Finally, midnight: time for "sleep meditation," after we swallow thirteen bioplasma pills. "Let your body go now," the monitor says, "but **you** hold the question."

■

I sit up during the night. A girl is walking by the windows, giving instructions: "Let your body rise and fall. The mind never sleeps. . . . " Angrily, I pull a blanket over my head. Won't they even let us sleep in peace? Twice more, I wake up and the girl is still talking. In the morning, I ask the monitors who was patrolling all night. Leila stares at me. "It wasn't any of us." The others concur. "It

was probably someone walking around in her astral body. These phenomena happen all the time."

Before the first exercise, Ava says, "I want to give you a standard for being open. If, when it's your turn to speak, you feel the need to respond in all sorts of ways to your partner, and don't get right back to your question, you're not being open."

Judy, the travel agent, says, "In life, don't people like you to respond to them? If you just sat there with a blank look . . . " Ava: "If everybody could do that for just one month—be open and listen, without trying to rescue each other—we'd have the most beautiful world you'd ever want to live in."

I have the sensation of floating, peacefully, not caring and not resisting. Around me, others are booming their questions like the caterpillar in **Alice in Wonderland**. "Whhhhhooo . . . are . . . YOU!" Ruth pounds her fists on the floor. Fred, who has been quiet for a time, yells: "I don't give a shit about this intensive! I don't give a shit about yoga. I don't give a shit about anything in my life!" Almost everyone giggles uncontrollably. Miles, the frail-looking biologist, laughs convulsively until he cries, flushing red. "It's the first time I've felt anything in these two days."

During our walk, the grounds take on the air of a loony farm. It is snowing, and Fred and two others run in circles, oinking and cackling. A man lies down in the river with all his clothes on. From afar comes a feminine shriek: "Fuuuck!" During the meals, hardly anyone talks. The monitors are content. Melvin, a young man with a haunted look, approaches a girl who is a monitor. "I feel rejected by you. I feel lonely," he says. The monitor, with a lack of emotion that is chilling, says, "Is that all?" Melvin: "I guess I want to make love to you. Do you love me?" The monitor takes regular bites of her cottage cheese. "Umm hmmm." Melvin: "I feel weak now. I feel like everything I do is just a release of steam, to avoid an explosion." She waits several minutes. "Well, I appreciate your telling me all that stuff. I understand it. You shouldn't let it keep you off the track from holding your question."

Late in the day, Leila, the co-master, says, "Okay, you should all be standing on the edge of the cliff, ready to jump off into enlightenment. We're going to narrow the field now. Don't say anything you're not experiencing directly as you. If you're not sure, if it can be argued, if you wouldn't stake your life on it, it's not an experience. Don't intellectualize or speculate. You're not looking for an answer, you're looking for yourself." She suggests we try asking, "Who's asking who am I?" and then, "Who's asking who's asking who am I?" and so on, "until you back yourself into a corner."

I try it, and my body starts to tingle. I review, palpably, everything that contributes to who I am: eyes, nerves, voice, skin, senses, mind, feelings, needs, opinions, humor, particular way of looking at the world, a way I have always had. On the night walk, seeing the stars, smelling the trees, and moving through space make me feel acutely, dizzyingly alive until I am drunk with it. When we return to the lodge, Ava announces, "Someone had an enlightenment this afternoon, and it was Ruth." The veterans of previous intensives clap their hands; the rest of us, slightly stunned, join in. One man gives a low whistle. "Today is really different from yesterday." Arnie says, "I'm beginning to feel something, a feeling of happiness and contentment all through me. But I can't verbalize it yet." Tim is getting his road hallucination. "When I stare at one spot," he tells his partner, "your whole face disappears." After each session, the pairs linger together, whispering and hugging.

A twenty-year-old premed student, Jimmy, delivers each word with his whole body shaking. "I am ev-ery-thing. The fire, the tree, the dog, the wind. I am any-thing. I feel to-tally enlightened." How can one doubt that his eyes, dilated and red, are perceiving a blinding white flash? He requests an interview, and later, Ava announces the enlightenment of Jimmy, and of Melvin, who has been repeating for thirty-six hours, "I am infinite ability!" Roger, who is a Zen student, shakes his head with disgust. "All I've heard from them is bullshit. If that's what it takes to get certification of enlightenment here, I don't know about the whole thing."

■

In the night, I have more hallucinations—no body this time, just a voice coming from all sides. I wake up feeling colossally down, with paralyzing aches in the back and neck. I'm fed up with people's bad breath and tired of being ordered around. It doesn't help to work with Fred, who belches at me and then proclaims, "I am burp!" Everyone except Fred is subdued today. We are all talking straight past each other, hearing what the other says but not responding, not taking his trip. We are into our own heads, on a depersonalized, metaphysical plane.

I ask Ava how she judges an enlightenment. "I acknowledge it if I see it coming directly from the person. But it's not important if I'm right or wrong. What's important is that the person lives a better life, and the way to a better life is to open up to others."

By midday, I feel so drained and dejected that I'm overcome with terror that I won't live through this. Leila tells us: "You're coming up against the last barrier now—the fear that you'll die, that what you've identified yourself with is gonna die and you'll die." In the next exercise, I work with Dan, one of the monitors, who has an Indianlike face with soft green eyes. I look at him through tears, trembling, and everything in the room—sounds, images—dissolves. It is as if we are spinning in a circle together, our eyes in the center, still. The room alternately lights up and grays over. We can barely talk, moving our lips but producing little sound. Somehow, his gentleness and intense warmth flow into me. At the end of the hour, I feel purged and calm.

Later, giddiness takes over. People say anything that pops into their head. Tim says, "Remember I started this thing saying I was me? Well, now I'm at this: Who am I? Not me. I'm the illusion of me." Fred is into announcing himself as objects: Coca-Cola, a shoe, a razor blade. When a potato is dropped on his dinner plate, he says, "I am a baked potato!"

We wait our turn for interviews with Ava, like subjects filing up to see the Queen. She sits by herself "so her aura can be clear," wearing a black gown of cut velvet, her dark hair curling down her shoulders. After dinner, she announces two more enlightenments: Tim and Lee. Lee shakes his head. With his clipped Japanese accent, he says, "No, there is no enlightenment. It's her trip to say I'm enlightened." I ask Lee what he said in his interview. "I just told her I feel I have more courage to be who I am. And when I open up to another, it makes my life richer."

Lee is my partner during the next session, and I feel great power and love shooting between us like electricity. Everyone, it seems, is flashing on the energy within them. You can't spend three days looking at your soul and come up with mud. Instead, you get high on your power and strength, your love, warmth, and elemental goodness. Lee, his eyes glistening, says, "I never knew contacts between people could be so joyful. It blows my mind that you open yourself so totally to me. You don't tell me anything about your job, your family, your home—you just show me your power. I can hold it in my hands. If I never see you again, you will always be close to me."

And then Fred shouts: "I am the great pumpkin!" The whole room cracks up. Five minutes later, Ava announces Fred's enlightenment. As we applaud in disbelief, Fred claps his hands and punches them jubilantly over his head, like a boxing champ. "I just had a deepening enlightenment— I'm Chicken Little!"

The intensive ends promptly at 9:00 P.M. Ava says, "Okay. That's it. Everyone has showed a great increase in his ability to become conscious of who he is. Those of you catching the train must leave now." There is a euphoric flurry of hugging and dancing in circles. For the first time in three days, we learn each other's last names, what we do in life, where we live. Only six of the twenty-two have been acknowledged as enlightened, and all but one of these had been on previous intensives.

Roger drives seven of us in his Volkswagen to the station. "I'm disappointed," he says. "I thought everyone there would already know there is a God, and we're all part of God. The place was full of atheists!" He laughs. "If I'd known that, I wouldn't have come. I'm going back to Buddha."

I did not enjoy most of the enlightenment intensive and would not want to go through it again. Once home, though, I notice surprising effects. I am far more interested in listening to people; when I do so, they seem to unfold, with great pleasure and trust. Most of us, apparently, are not used to being truly listened to, or to listening in a totally open state. I find, also, that I can be freed from unconscious dependency on the moods and emotions of the other person. I can absorb and understand someone's anger, or pain, or depression, without getting embroiled—feeling anger or depression in return. I keep in touch with some of the people who took the intensive; they are all trying to stay open and serene. One young man writes: "For the first time in my life, peace is mine to give."

■

In every major city, there are ashrams and institutes where those who wish to make a life in the spiritual movement live and work communally. The groups form a supportive national network.

Members receive no salary, but their needs are taken care of while they study and teach. They can go anywhere in the country and be assured of a place to stay and a welcoming, loving "family." They have a culture all their own: food (vegetarian), language (they refer to the world, for example, as "this planet"), dress (Oriental fabrics, designs inspired from India, many choosing all white), and music (flutes, drums, and, for chants, the harmonium). In many of the disciplines, people tend to withdraw from sensual pleasures. The most serious are expected to be celibate. They give up smoking, liquor, and drugs. Convinced of the possibility of healing their own bodies, they avoid straight doctors, and would rather see a chiropractor, whose methods are felt to be more natural.

The intolerance of drugs is ironic, because the spiritual movement has reaped tremendous benefit from the drug culture. Acid and mescaline gave many people their first intimations of infinity and oneness with the universe. Since the acid experience could not be controlled, though, many began turning to techniques such as meditation by which people through the centuries have, by their own will, altered their states of consciousness. the success of spiritual groups in leading people away from drugs is one of their main sources of income. Almost every group has an antidrug rehabilitation program, funded by charitable agencies and, in some cases, the government.

One of the dangers of immersion in the spiritual movement, especially for young dropouts, is that it is possible to lose perspective, to suspend critical judgment, as one loses touch with the larger society. Quite rapidly, anything seems plausible. Nothing is too bizarre or outrageous. A nineteen-year-old boy in Berkeley, whose current trip is kundalini, says "I don't know what common sense is anymore. I can't tell what's valid and what isn't." He fails to discern hype, or techniques that smack of quackery. He does not consider the evidence when a spiritual teacher is charged in court with fraud or financial mismanagement. When a yogi who has a large following in this country was sued in New Delhi for allegedly taking money to procure American wives for Indian men, his disciples dismissed it as a frameup by jealous rivals.

Despite claims throughout the movement that each person is to be his own guru, many teachers, in fact, expect unquestioning devotion. Ronwen Proust, when she was eighteen, joined the staff of the Integral Yoga Institute. She was given the Sanskrit name Vathsala by the Institute's founder, Swami Satchidananda, the most charismatic and beloved spiritual figure in the counterculture. Vathsala says, "I got into this spacy kind of peace, but it was a false peace that was easily disrupted if I went somewhere else. Nobody at the Institute was asking any questions, like: Why do you meditate? Who are you? What is this peace? What's happening to you? The peace didn't come from my own consciousness. It was like I was stepping into someone else's aura and absorbing his peace."

There is a tendency, also, to lose sight of how closely related many spiritual techniques are to self-hypnosis, how they depend on the power of suggestion. Katherine Da Silva, a twenty-seven-year-old yoga teacher, met with hostility when she pointed this out to a crowd at a spiritual festival. Katherine lived for six years as a renunciate in the ashrams of Paramahansa Yogananda. Toward the end, because she was having what she calls "healthy, honest doubts," she felt it would be better to continue her spiritual work outside the cloister. "I'm so convinced of the power of suggestion," she says. "Things like breathing through your skin, and channeling light through your body—if you hear and believe these things, you actually start to feel yourself doing them."

Katherine is a dark beauty, with almond-shaped eyes, a graceful manner, and a voice whose cadences are highly pleasing. Despite her persistent questioning, men in the spiritual movement are magnetized by her; many declare love at first sight, and tell her they recall being her lover in previous incarnations. She suspects that being an ex-nun contributes to her attraction. Katherine has a school in New Jersey, and also teaches yoga to psychiatric patients at St. Joseph's Hospital in Paterson. One schizophrenic, she says, described experiences similar to those yogis talk of—traveling outside the body, and being flooded with light. She asked the doctors how they would distinguish between the experience of a yogi and a psychotic. "They told me they would look at the person's total behavior."

Katherine is aware that in yoga she uses techniques similar to hypnosis: the soft voice, the methodical way of speaking, and the concentration on parts of the body. Staring at a candle or chanting with eyes closed are used in meditation to induce a trance. "One of my problems now is that most mystics say their experiences come from an outside force—the hand of God. But when I see

that, with self-hypnosis, people can induce similar states in themselves, I'm not convinced it's an outside force."

■

I know a person who's used an Alpha Wave headset for nine months, and he's almost enlightened.
—Peter Max

The ads show Buddha with electrodes pasted to his skull. "Now you can be taught to control your brain waves. Enhanced states of consciousness easily attained!!" For $250, you can buy a headset made by one of the companies that have rushed into business to capitalize on biological-feedback training (BFT). In the past few years, bio-feedback training has excited the scientific community, become an underground cult and the darling of the popular media. With BFT, people learn, through conditioning, to control functions of the mind and body that have long been considered involuntary: heart rate, blood pressure, muscle control, body temperature, brain waves, and thereby, states of mind. Example: A subject sits in a darkened cubicle; an electroencephalograph traces the electrical impulses of his brain, and each time he produces alpha waves—one of four identified brain waves—a color flashes on a screen. After a number of sessions, the subject can learn to keep the color onscreen indefinitely, or prevent it from appearing. At this point he has learned to create, at will, a state of consciousness in which there is almost no anxiety, a state generally described as "calm, relaxed wakefulness."

In early experiments, it was found that the alpha state is similar to a state achieved during meditation by yogis and Zen masters. But conditioning is easier to learn than meditation, and you know immediately if you are "doing it right." As the alpha cult grew, droves rushed to volunteer as subjects in BFT experiments. Dr. Barbara Brown, a brilliant, salty, utterly captivating philosopher-scientist, has to fend off applicants from her office at the Veterans Hospital in Sepulveda, California, where she has assembled one of the country's most sophisticated BFT laboratories. Dr. Brown says alpha conditioning is not a miracle-agent. "I'd put it in the category of aspirin, which is a useful drug for general annoyances but doesn't do anything specific that we know of." She says alpha conditioning could raise the threshold of our overall mental and physical state. "It's fairly well known that in a state of emotional well-being, people are highly resistant to infections and colds. Through mind control, there's great hope that people could chug along for long periods without having extreme anxiety attacks or developing any illness."

Dr. Brown has worked for thirty years in pharmacology, biology, psychiatry, and electronics. She has invented a number of mind-altering drugs, and administered one of the first does of LSD to Aldous Huxley. Although she has read mystic and religious philosophy all her life, she says, "I never believed a bit of it. When you ask enough questions, you've shot it—there's nothing left to believe in. I don't believe in scientific facts. I suppose if I believe anything, it's that man's mind can do whatever it wants to do if it tries." She says our culture has never attempted to nourish the mind, "to see if it has any abilities beyond those we know of. We've stuffed it with facts, but we've been bloody repressive about all kinds of mental phenomena like ESP, and astral projection, which I prefer to call depersonalization. We're such a materialistic, exterior-oriented culture that we've squashed the mind and the brain under.

Sitting in her office, with walls of green blackboard, she utters a dreamy-eyed "whew," as she describes her future projects, in which people will paint canvases with their brain waves and create symphonies of "mind music." In five years, she predicts, there will be bio-feedback centers across the country, where people can learn, under supervision, to control all types of mind and body functions. "But that's just the beginning. We don't know where it will all lead. Individuals will be reproducing states of consciousness that are not well known to us at the moment. We're just approaching the foothills of the next evolutionary step—the evolution of the mind."

Dr. Brown has a sense of ironic resignation about "fringe groups" feeding on the interest in BFT. "Those headsets are utterly stupid and misleading, because it would be impossible, for $250, to construct an instrument that could accurately isolate brain waves. The components alone would cost $600." As to courses run by laymen, which advertise alpha conditioning as "the key to the promised land," Dr. Brown says: "It's true. Conditioning could be the key. Any of these techniques around now could help some people. LSD would have been a beautiful key to a better life, if it hadn't been misused. But people shouldn't accept anything as **the** final answer, or they will be disap-

pointed. It might be a key for you, but make sure, by comparing and asking: What does it do for me? Does it last? Is it real? Is it valid?"

∎

How, indeed, is one to judge the legitimacy of or find a sane path through the exotic array of salvation techniques? We all have urges and at some point have given in to the impulse to try a device that promised miracles: Lose ten pounds in three days; free yourself from worry with this mental routine; experience bliss and Godhead by repeating a mantra. When it failed, some of us found it difficult to trust or try any similar techniques. The spiritual movement, however, is filled with people who search endlessly from one teacher or system to the next. When I began looking into it, I thought this insatiable seeking was a sign of desperation and delusion. Now I'm not sure. There are, of course, people who flit about in confusion, but I have met others who manage to glean the best and ignore the nonsense in whatever technique they try, and who say that with each experience, they learn more and gain more love, quietude, and detachment from fear and conflict. Vathsala, who has been a seeker all her life, says, "There's no end, that's the beautiful thing. There's no end to life, no end to seeking consciousness, no end to the peace and joy you can realize." The search becomes, in itself, the salvation.

∎

The time has come for America to help the whole world with spirituality.
—Swami Satchidananda

Around the backyard swimming pool of the Integral Yoga Institute in Los Angeles, on a Sunday in March, sixteen spiritual teachers and their followers are gathered for a meeting of the World Congress for Enlightenment. The teachers take chairs in a circle, the followers sit on the grass, straining to hear, as Charles Berner explains what has happened to date: "Last fall, Swami Satchidananda, Yogi Bhajan, and I met by chance in Santa Cruz, and we talked about the need for better understanding between the spiritual teachers of this planet. We came up with the idea of holding a World Enlightenment Festival this August, where a large number of people could be with the teachers for a week, camping on the land, eating vegetarian food, with no drugs or alcohol, living in love and peace and thus demonstrating to the world the Aquarian way of life." Berner says he and his staff sent out hundreds of invitations to religious leaders in all countries. "We have over 200 acceptances. No one has turned us down. The idea is irresistible, because of the rising tide of spiritual awareness, because of the Aquarian Age."[1]

Swami Vishnu-Devananda, head of the Sivananda Yoga Centers and Camps, who flies about in a private airplane, asks where they'll get the money for the festival. Berner suggests selling tickets for $5. Another teacher protests. "This site will be a temple, holy ground. I won't go near it if there's any money changing hands." Muriel Tepper-Dorner, who teaches light radiation, says, "Money is not good or bad, it's just energy. It can work to spread the light."

There is discussion later of how all the gurus at the festival can interact and "experience each other." Berner proposes meeting in groups of five. Laura Huxley, widow of Aldous Huxley, says, "Why don't we all fast for twenty-four hours?" Swami Vishnu shakes his head and giggles. "You can't tell all the teachers to fast, because if they don't agree they won't do it. Silence is the best thing—fifteen minutes' silence, everyone praying his own way." "No no," says another swami. "The emphasis should be on communicating, not silence." A Hawaiian "kahuna" (high priest) says the answer is to chant—a Polynesian chant. Berner disagrees. "Everyone here can come up with something like that, and I can show you 600 more. Everybody chants, everybody prays, everybody's into something. If we make any one technique mandatory, we're finished."

One month later, many of the same teachers assemble in Davis, 500 miles to the north, for a three-day Earth Rebirth Festival at the University of California. It is a test run, in many ways, of the great festival to come. About a thousand young people are camping in a field, wearing Indian print clothes and farm coveralls. They wander about carrying incense, wood flutes, and finger cymbals. Almost every hour, there is a speech, class, or spiritual entertainment being given in the quad. Only a small portion of the crowd are Davis students. Most have come from surrounding areas for the "holy man jam." Remarkably, there are no drugs being hawked, no beer cans or wine bottles to be seen. On the mall, girls are selling organic apple cider, pumpkin bread, vegetables, and caracoa cookies.

Katherine Da Silva gives a yoga class to several hundred people on the grass. Many hold infants in their laps during the exercises. A two-year-old tow-head, who is named Siddhartha Greenblatt, wiggles between his parents, aping their movements. When the group does the dead man's posture, lying on their backs, it is an eerie sight: yards and yards of bodies, motionless in the sun, with only the dogs and babies crawling about. Later, people dance and gyrate to bongo drums, the men barechested, their stomachs sunken from fasting.

As the weekend progresses, the vibrations grow increasingly bizarre and increasingly ecstatic. There is a speaker who claims to be a messenger from Venus. The Rev. Kirby Hensley, an ex-Baptist who lives in Modesto, and who has a pink complexion and fly-away ears, offers to ordain everyone as ministers in his Universal Life Church. With one hand on his hip, the other sawing the air, he describes how the ministers will be able to perform marriages and divorces, get draft exemptions, fly at reduced rates on Ozark Airlines, and attend a new school Hensley is starting "where boys and girls can come to **practice** sex. You don't know how many homes get busted up because boys and girls didn't have no experience." "Far out, Reverend!" a boy yells. "Hallelujah." There is a scramble to get minister's credentials, and 116 are ordained, including one collie dog.

At sundown, Muriel Tepper-Dorner, who says she is a channel for the White Brotherhood, gives a demonstration of light radiation. "Breathe in the golden light, and see yourself as a sun. Radiate the light out to each other until we see this whole room filled with light. Now radiate more light, and see it flowing all over this campus, and now all over the planet." A freshman in a neat shirtdress whispers to her date, "I swear I can feel it coming out of my skin." The boy nods. "I have to be careful, or I'll get drained."

Next comes George Peters, the Abbie Hoffman of the spiritual movement, founder of Naturalism. George is thirty-two, a fast-talking New Yorker who sometimes says he is a psychiatrist. Wearing lavender suede pants, with black hair to his waist, he tells the crowd he gets people enlightened by locking them in black sensory-deprivation boxes for forty days, or by giving them knockout drops, stripping them, and letting them wake up in a deserted field.

Indra Devi, a seventy-two-year-old woman yogi who lives in Tecate, Mexico, shows films of Satya Sai Baba, who is believed by millions in India to be an avatar (an incarnation of God), and is said to have the power to materialize anything from thin air. Afterward, she plays tapes of Baba chanting, and everyone sings along. They walk off reeling, euphoric, having given up long ago any attempt to fit things into some rational framework.

The next day, Yogi Bhajan gives a mass meditation, followed by Swami Satchidananda, who is mobbed like a rock star. His disciples float about him in clumps, singing softly in adoration: "Sri Ram, Jai Ram." Wherever the Swami walks, he is surrounded by this celestial singing, while crowds push and scramble to get near him, touch his orange gown, kiss his hand, or snap his picture.

After lunch, the teachers meet in the student union to discuss the World Enlightenment Festival. As at previous meetings, only teachers can sit in the inner circle and speak. A few staff members are disgruntled. "It's cronyism, like the smoke-filled room. Only this is the incense-filled room." Charles Berner suggests they break up into groups of five, as they hope to do for three days during the August festival. Yogi Bhajan says, "Good. I want five negative people, because I'm in a very fine mood." Berner, Bhajan, and Swami Satchidananda each start a separate circle. Ava Berner says, "The one rule is that you talk only about yourself, not about theology or your ashrams or disciples. Talk about what makes you unique, so the others can become conscious of you."

George Peters turns to Swami Satchidananda: "I once tried wearing an orange robe and getting people to hum, and I felt ridiculous. How do you manage?" The Swami says, "The robe is only an outward symbol of a person who dedicates his life to serving others. Because I feel this dedication, I have no hesitation to wear it." Jack Horner, a tall, gaunt man who created a technique called eductivism, tells the swami, "You're one of the most beautiful human beings I've ever seen. How did you get there?" Swami laughs. "It just happened, as a natural growth. I never even decided to renounce the world. I didn't plan to come to this country and start yoga centers. Things just happen. I believe in that. I feel that I'm always at ease, no worry, no disturbance."

After an hour, Ava says, "All right, we're through. At the festival, hopefully we could continue longer and have a chance to go deeper." Charles says, "We had a good time here." Yogi Bhajan announces: "We had very fine time." Swami Satchidananda fairly rises into the air with glee. "We had a **wonderful** time." Charles says, "After three days, I think you're gonna get onto each other and will have the greatest high on this planet!"

The schedule calls for the teachers to conduct closing ceremonies on the Davis quad at nightfall. They learn, though, that in their absence all afternoon, the field has been taken over by rowdy students and teenagers from nearby high schools. While the holy men are experiencing each other, the scene outside looks like the last days of Rome. Much marijuana, liquor, people shedding clothes, dancing, and making love on blankets. A high-decibel rock band blares across the campus.

Secluded in the pea-green conference room, the gurus are standing in concentric circles, eyes closed, arms entwined as they chant: "OM Shanti, OM Shanti, OM Shanti, OOOOOMMMMM."

NOTES

1. Astrologers are in disagreement **as** to what and when the Aquarian Age is. One school says it started in the nineteenth century and is dominated by science. Other authorities say it won't begin until 2150, and will bring renewed spirituality. This seems certain: The Age lasts 2000 years, and at the rate pop culture is exploiting it, we'll be sick of it before it even gets rolling.

chapter 35
the pilgrimage of malcolm x
i. f. stone

Malcolm X was born into Black Nationalism. His father was a follower of Marcus Garvey, the West Indian who launched a "Back to Africa" movement in the twenties. Malcolm's first clash with white men took place when his mother was pregnant with him; a mob of Klansmen in Omaha, Nebraska, waving shotguns and rifles, warned her one night to move out of town because her husband was spreading trouble among the "good" Negroes with Garvey's teachings. One of his earliest memories was of seeing their home burned down in Lansing, Michigan, in 1929, because the Black Legion, a white Fascist organization, considered his father an "uppity" Negro. The body of his father, a tall, powerful black man from Georgia, soon afterwards was found literally cut to pieces in one of those mysterious accidents that often veil a racial killing.

His mother was a West Indian who looked like a white woman. Her unknown father was white. She slowly went to pieces mentally under the burden of raising eight children. When the family was broken up, Malcolm was sent to a detention home, from which he attended a white school. He must have been a bright and attractive lad, for he was at the top of his class and was elected class president in the seventh grade. Many years later, in a speech

on the Black Revolution which is included in the collection, **Malcolm X Speaks,** he was able to boast bitterly, "I grew up with white people. I was integrated before they even invented the word." The reason for the bitterness was an incident that changed his life. His English teacher told him he ought to begin thinking about his career. Malcolm said he would like to be a lawyer. His teacher suggested carpentry instead. "We all here like you, you know that," the teacher said, "but you've got to be realistic about being a nigger."

Malcolm X left Lansing deeply alienated and in the slums of Boston and New York he became a "hustler," selling numbers, women, and dope. "All of us," he says in his **Autobiography** of his friends in the human jungle, "who might have probed space or cured cancer or built industries, were instead black victims of the white man's American social system." Insofar as he was concerned, this was no exaggeration. He was an extraordinary man. Had he been wholly white, instead of irretrievably "Negro" by American standards, he might easily have become a leader of the bar. In the underworld he went from marijuana to cocaine. To meet the cost he took up burglary. He was arrested with a white mistress who had become his lookout woman. In February, 1946, not quite twenty-one, he was sentenced to ten years in prison in Massachusetts. The heavy sentence reflected the revulsion created in the judge by the discovery that Malcolm had made a white woman his "love slave." In prison, he went on nutmeg, reefers, Nembutal, and benzedrine in a desperate effort to replace the drugs. He was a vicious prisoner, often in solitary. The other prisoners nicknamed him "Satan." But the prison had an unusually well stocked library to which he was introduced by a fellow prisoner, an old-time burglar named Bimbi. Through him, Malcolm first encountered Thoreau. Prison became his university; also he was converted to the Nation of Islam, the sect the press calls Black Muslims.

The important word here is conversion. To understand Malcolm's experience, one must go to the literature of conversion. "Were we writing the history of the mind from the purely natural history point of view," William James concluded in his **Varieties of Religious Experience**, "we would still have to write down man's liability to sudden and complete conversion as one of his most curious peculiarities." The convert's sense of being born anew, the sudden change from despair to elation, bears an obvious resemblance to the manic-depressive cycle, except that the change in the personality is often permanent. But those who experience it must first—to borrow Gospel language—be brought low. James quotes the theological maxim, "Man's extremity is God's opportunity." It is only out of the depths that men on occasion experience this phenomenon of renewal. The success of the Black Muslims in converting and rehabilitating criminals and dope addicts like Malcolm X recalls the mighty phrases James quotes from Luther. "God," he preached, "is the God . . . of those that are brought even to nothing . . . and his nature is . . . to save the very desperate and damned." Malcolm had been brought to nothing, he was one of those very desperate and damned when he was "saved" by Elijah Muhammad, the self-proclaimed Messenger of Allah to the lost Black Nation of that imaginary Islam he preaches.

The tendency is to dismiss Elijah Muhammad's weird doctrine as another example of the superstitions, old and new, that thrive in the Negro ghetto. It is not really any more absurd than the Virgin Birth or the Sacrifice of Isaac. The rational absurdity does not detract from the psychic therapy. Indeed the therapy may lie in the absurdity. Converts to any creed talk of the joy in complete surrender; a rape of the mind occurs. "**Credo quia absurdum**," Tertullian, the first really cultivated apologist for Christianity, is said to have

exulted, "I believe because it **is** absurd." Tertullian was himself a convert. Black Nationalists may even claim him as an African, for his home was Carthage.

There is a special reason for the efficacy of the Black Muslims in reaching the Negro damned. The sickness of the Negro in America is that he has been made to feel a nigger; the genocide is psychic. The Negro must rid himself of this feeling if he is to stand erect again. He can do so in two ways. He can change the outer world of white supremacy, or he can change his inner world by "conversion." The teachings of the Black Muslims may be fantastic but they are superbly suited to the task of shaking off the feeling of niggerness. Elijah Muhammad teaches that the original man was black, that Caucasians are "white devils" created almost 6000 years ago by a black genius named Yakub. He bleached a number of blacks by a process of mutation into pale-faced blue-eyed devils in order to test the mettle of the Black Nation. This inferior breed has ruled by deviltry but their time will soon be up, at the end of the sixth millennium, which may be by 1970 or thereabouts. To explain the white man as a devil is, as Malcolm X says in the **Autobiography**, to strike "a nerve center in the American black man" for "when he thinks about his own life, he is going to see where, to him personally, the white man sure has acted like a devil." To see the white man this way is, in Gospel imagery, to cast out the devil. With him go his values, as he has impressed them on the Black Man, above all the inner feeling of being a nigger. To lose that feeling is to be fully emancipated. For the poor Negro no drug could be a stronger opiate than this black religion.

With rejection of the white man's values goes rejection of the white man's God. "We're worshipping a Jesus," Malcolm protested in one of his sermons after he became a Black Muslim Minister, "who doesn't even **look** like us." The white man, he declared, "has brainwashed us black people to fasten our gaze upon a blond-haired, blue-eyed Jesus." This Black Muslim doctrine may seem a blasphemous joke until one makes the effort to imagine how whites would feel if taught to worship a black God with thick African lips. Men prefer to create a God in their own image. "The Ethiopians," one of the pre-Socratic Greek philosophers observed a half millennium before Christ, "assert that their gods are snub-nosed and black" while the "Nordic" Thracians said theirs were "blue-eyed and red-haired." When Marcus Garvey, the first apostle of Pan-Africanism, toured Africa, urging expulsion of the white man, he called for a Negro religion with a Negro Christ. Just as Malcolm Little, in accordance with Black Muslim practice, rejected his "slave name" and became Malcolm X, so Malcolm X, son of a Baptist preacher, rejected Christianity as a slave religion. His teacher, Elijah Muhammad, did not have to read Nietzsche to discover that Christianity was admirably suited to make Rome's slaves submissive. In our antebellum South the value of Christian teaching in making slaves tractable was widely recognized even by slaveholders, themselves agnostic. The Negro converted to Christianity was cut off from the disturbing memory of his own gods and of his lost freedom, and reconciled to his lot in the white man's chains. Here again the primitivistic fantasies of the Black Muslims inerringly focus on a crucial point. It is in the Christian mission that what Malcolm X called the "brainwashing" of the blacks began.

Racism and nationalism are poisons. Sometimes a poison may be prescribed as a medicine, and Negroes have found in racism a way to restore their self-respect. But black racism is still racism, with all its primitive irrationality and danger. There are passages in the **Autobiography** in which Malcolm, recounting some of his Black Muslim sermons, sounds like a Southern white supremacist in reverse, vibrating with anger and sexual obsession over the horrors of race pollution. There is the same preoccupation with rape, the same revulsion about mixed breeds. "Why," he cried out, "the white man's raping of the black race's woman began right on those slave ships!" A psychoanalyst might see in his fury the feeling of rejection by the race of his white grandfather. A biologist might see in the achievements of this tall sandy-complexioned Negro—his friends called him "Red"—an example of the possibilities of successful racial mixture. But Malcolm's feelings on the subject were as outraged as those of a Daughter of the Confederacy. He returned revulsion for revulsion and hate for hate. He named his first child, a daughter, Attilah, and explained that he named her for the Hun who sacked Rome.

But hidden under the surface of the Black Nationalist creed to which he was won there lay a peculiar anti-Negroism. The true nationalist loves his people and their peculiarities; he wants to preserve them; he is filled with filial piety. But there is in Elijah Muhammad's Black Muslim creed none of the love for the Negro one finds in W. E. B. du

Bois; or of that yearning for the ancestral Africa which obsessed Garvey. Elijah Muhammad—who himself looks more Chinese than Negro—teaches his people that they are Asians, not Africans; that their original tongue is Arabic. He turns his people into middle-class Americans. Their clothes are conservative, almost Ivy League. Their religious services eschew that rich antiphony between preacher and congregation which one finds in Negro churches. The Nigerian, E. U. Essien-Udom, whose **Black Nationalism** is the best book on the Black Muslims, was struck by their middle-class attitudes and coldness to Africa and African ways. In Black Muslim homes, when jazz was played, he writes that he was "often tempted to tap his feet to the tune of jazz" but was inhibited because his Black Muslim hosts "listened to it without ostensible response to the rhythm." In their own way the Black Muslims are as much in flight from Negritude as was Booker T. Washington. Indeed Elijah Muhammad's stress on Negro private business and his hostility to trade unionism in his own dealings with Negroes are very much in the Booker T. Washington pattern. The virtues of bourgeois America are what Elijah Muhammad seeks to recreate in his separate Black Nation. This is the banal reality which lies behind all his hocus-pocus about the Koran, and here lie the roots of his split with Malcolm X.

For Elijah Muhammad practices separation not only from American life but from the American Negro community, and from its concrete struggles for racial justice. Malcolm X was drawn more and more to engagement in that struggle. In the midst of describing in the **Autobiography** his happy and successful years as a Black Muslim organizer, Malcolm X says:

> If I harbored any personal disappointment, whatsoever, it was that privately I was convinced that our Nation of Islam could be an even greater force in the American black man's overall struggle—if we engaged in more **action**. By that I mean I thought privately that we should have amended or relaxed, our general non-engagement policy. I felt that, wherever black people committed themselves, in the Little Rocks and Birminghams and other places, militantly disciplined Muslims should also be there—for all the world to see, and respect and discuss. It could be heard increasingly in the Negro communities: "Those Muslims **talk** tough, but they never **do**

anything, unless somebody bothers Muslims."
[Italics in original.]

This alone was bound to divide the prophet
and disciple. But there were also personal factors.
Elijah Muhammad won Malcolm's devotion by his
kindness in corresponding with the young convict
when Malcolm was still in prison. But Malcolm's
intellectual horizons were already far wider than
those of the rather narrow, ill-educated, and suspicious Messenger of Allah. In the prison library
Malcolm X was finding substantiation for the
Black Muslim creed in **Paradise Lost** and in Herodotus; this passionate curiosity and voracious reading were bound to make him outgrow Elijah's
dream-book theology. On the one side envy and
on the other disillusion were to drive the two men
apart. The crowds drawn by Malcolm and his very
organizing success made Elijah Muhammad and his
family jealous. On the other hand, Malcolm, who
had kept the sect's vows of chastity, was shocked
when former secretaries of Elijah Muhammad filed
paternity suits against the prophet. Malcolm had
nothing but a small salary and the house the sect
had provided for him. Elijah Muhammad's cars
(two Cadillacs and a Lincoln Continental), his
$200 pin-striped banker-style suits, his elegantly
furnished 18-room house in one of the better sections of Chicago's Hyde Park, began to make a
sour impression on Malcolm. The hierarchy lives
well in practically all religions, and their worldly
affluence fosters schism. Malcolm was too big, too
smart, too able, to fit into the confines of this
little sect and remain submissive to its family oli-
garchy. He began to open up a larger world, and
this endangered Elijah Muhammad's hold on the
little band of unsophisticated faithful he had recruited.

Muhammad Speaks, the weekly organ of the
Black Muslims, had begun to play down Malcolm's
activities. The break came over Malcolm's comment on Kennedy's assassination. Within hours
after the President's killing, Elijah Muhammad sent
out a directive ordering the cult's ministers to
make no comment on the murder. Malcolm, speaking at Manhattan Center a few days afterward, was
asked in the question period what he thought of
the assassination. He answered that it was a case of
"the chickens coming home to roost" Malcolm
explains in the **Autobiography**, "I said that the
hate in white men had not stopped with the killing
of defenseless black people but . . . finally had
struck down the President." He complains that

"some of the world's most important personages
were saying in various ways, and in far stronger
ways than I did, that America's climate of hate
had been responsible for the President's death. But
when Malcolm X said the same thing it was ominous." Elijah Muhammad called him in. "That was
a very bad statement," he said. "The country
loved this man." He ordered Malcolm silenced for
ninety days so that the Black Muslims could be
"disassociated from the blunder." Malcolm agreed
and submitted. But three days later he heard that a
Mosque official was suggesting his own assassination. Soon after, another Black Muslim told him of
a plan to wire his car so that it would explode
when he turned the ignition key. Malcolm decided
to build a Muslim Mosque of his own, and open its
doors to black men of all faiths for common action. To prepare himself he decided to make the
pilgrimage to Mecca.

This visit to Mecca was a turning-point for
Malcolm. His warm reception in the Arabic world,
the sight of white men in equal fraternity with
black and brown, marked a second conversion in
his life. "For the past week," Malcolm wrote
home, "I have been utterly speechless and spell-
bound by the graciousness I see displayed all
around me by people **of all colors**." The italics
were his. The man who made the seven circuits
around the Ka'ba and drank the waters of Zem-
Zem emerged from his pilgrimage no longer a
racist or a Black Muslim. He took the title of El
Hajj earned by his visit to Mecca and called himself
henceforth El-Hajj Malik El-Shabazz. He turned
Muslim in the true sense of the word. How indeli-
bly he also remained an American go-getter is deli-
ciously reflected in a passage of the **Autobiography** where he says that while in Mecca:

> I saw that Islam's conversions around the
> world could double and triple if the colorful-
> ness and the true spiritualness of the Hajj pil-
> grimage were properly advertised and com-
> municated to the outside world. I saw that
> the Arabs are poor at understanding the
> psychology of non-Arabs and the importance
> of public relations. The Arabs said "Inshah
> Allah" (God willing)—then they waited for
> converts, but I knew that with improved pub-
> lic relations methods the new converts turning
> to Allah could be turned into millions.

He had become a Hajj, but remained in some
ways a Babbitt, the salesman, archetype of our

American society. A creed was something to **sell**. Allah, the Merciful, needed better merchandising.

Malcolm returned from abroad May 21, 1964. Several attempts were made on his life. On February 21, 1965, he was killed by gunmen when he got up to speak at a meeting in New York's Audubon Ballroom. He was not quite forty when he died. The most revealing tribute paid him was the complaint by Elijah Muhammad after Malcolm was killed. "He came back preaching that we should not hate the enemy. . . . He was a star who went astray." What nobler way to go astray? In Africa and in America there was almost unanimous recognition that the Negro race had lost a gifted son; only the then head of the U.S. Information Agency, Carl Rowan, immortalized himself with a monumental Uncle Tomism. "All this about an ex-convict, ex-dope peddler who became a racial fanatic," was Rowan's obtuse and ugly comment; it ranks with his discovery, as USIA Director, of what he called the public's "right **not** to know."

From tape-recorded conversations, a Negro writer, Alex Haley, put together the **Autobiography**; he did his job with sensitivity and with devotion. Here one may read, in the agony of this brilliant Negro's self-creation, the agony of an entire people in their search for identity. But more fully to understand this remarkable man, one must turn to **Malcolm X Speaks**, which supplements the **Autobiography**. All but one of the speeches were made in those last eight tumultuous months of his life after his break with the Black Muslims when he was seeking a new path. In their pages one can begin to understand his power as a speaker and to see, more clearly than in the **Autobiography**, the political legacy he left his people in its struggle for full emancipation.

Over and over again in simple imagery, savagely uncompromising, he drove home the real truth about the Negro's position in America. It may not be pleasant but it must be faced. "Those Hunkies that just got off the boat," he said in one of his favorite comparisons, "they're already Americans. Polacks are already Americans; the Italian refugees are already Americans. Everything that comes out of Europe, every blue-eyed thing, is already an American. And as long as you and I have been over here, we aren't Americans yet. They don't have to pass civil rights legislation to make a Polack an American." In a favorite metaphor, he said, "I'm not going to sit at your table and watch you eat, with nothing on my plate, and call myself a diner. Sitting at the table doesn't

make you a diner, unless you eat some of what's on the plate. Being here in America doesn't make you an American. Being born here in America doesn't make you an American." He often said, "Don't be shocked when I say that I was in prison. You're still in prison. That's what America means—prison." Who can deny that this is true for the black man? No matter how high he rises, he never loses consciousness of the invisible bars which hem him in. "We didn't land on Plymouth Rock," Malcolm was fond of saying. "It landed on us."

He counselled violence but he defended this as an answer to white violence. "If they make the Klan nonviolent," he said over and over again, "I'll be nonviolent." In another speech he said, "If violence is wrong in America, violence is wrong abroad. If it is wrong to be violent defending black women and black children and babies and black men, then it is wrong for America to draft us and make us violent abroad in defense of her." He taunted his people in the same speech that "As long as the white man sent you to Korea, you bled. . . . You bleed for white people, but when it comes to seeing your own churches being bombed and little black girls murdered, you haven't any blood." In a speech he made about the brutal beating of Fannie Lou Hamer of Mississippi, he said of the white man, "If he only understands the language of a rifle, get a rifle. If he only understands the language of a rope, get a rope. But don't waste time talking the wrong language to a man if you really want to communicate with him." In preaching Pan-Africanism, he reached down into the aching roots of Negro self-hatred as few men have ever done. "You can't hate Africa and not hate yourself," he said in one speech. "This is what the white man knows. So they make you and me hate our African identity. . . . We hated our heads, we hated the shape of our nose, we wanted one of those long dovelike noses, you know; we hated the color of our skin, hated the blood of Africa that was in our veins. And in hating our features and our skin and our blood, we had to end up hating ourselves." No man has better expressed his people's trapped anguish.

Malcolm's most important message to his people is muted in the **Autobiography**, perhaps because Alex Haley, its writer, is politically conventional, but it comes out sharply in **Malcolm X Speaks** which was edited and published by a group of Trotskyists. This was the idea that while the Negro is a minority in this country, he is part of a majority if he thinks of common action with the rest of the world's colored peoples. "The first thing the American power structure doesn't want any Negroes to start," he says in the **Autobiography**, "is thinking internationally." In a speech at Ibadan University in Nigeria, he relates in the **Autobiography**, he urged the Africans to bring the American Negro's plight before the United Nations: "I said that just as the American Jew is in political, cultural, and economic harmony with world Jewry, I was convinced that it was time for all Afro-Americans to join the world's Pan Africanists." Malcolm persuaded the Organization of African Unity at its Cairo conference to pass a resolution saying that discrimination against Negroes in the United States was "a matter of deep concern" to the Africans, and **The New York Times** in August 1964 reported that the State and Justice Departments had begun "to take an interest in Malcolm's campaign because it might create 'a touchy problem' for the U.S. if raised at the UN." In the UN debate over U.S. intervention to save white lives in the Congo, African delegates at the UN for the first time accused the United States of being indifferent to similar atrocities against blacks in Mississippi. This is what Malcolm wanted when he spoke of putting the Negro struggle in a world context.

An Italian writer, Vittorio Lanternari, published a remarkable book five years ago, which appeared here in 1963 as **The Religions of the Oppressed: A Study of Modern Messianic Cults**. It suggests that wherever white men have driven out or subdued colored men, whether in the case of the American Indians, or in Africa, or with the Maoris in New Zealand, as with the Tai-Pings in China and the Cao Dai in Vietnam, or among the uprooted blacks and harried Indians in the Caribbean and Latin America, Messianic cults have arisen, rejecting white men's values and seeking the restoration of shattered cultural identities as the first step toward political freedom. He did not include in his survey the cults which thrive in our Negro ghettos though they are of the same character. One striking common bond among all these sects of the oppressed has been their effort to free their people from drinking the white man's "firewater" or (in China) smoking his opium. To see the Black Muslims and Malcolm's life in this perspective is to begin to understand the psychic havoc wrought around the world by white imperialism in the centuries since America was discovered and Afro-Asia opened up to white penetration. There are few places on earth where whites have not grown rich robbing the colored races. It was Malcolm's great contribution to help make us all aware of this.

His assassination was a loss to the country as well as to his race. These two books will have a permanent place in the literature of the Afro-American struggle. It is tantalizing to speculate on what he might have become had he lived. What makes his life so moving a story was his capacity to learn and grow. New disillusions, and a richer view of the human condition, lay ahead for the man who could say, as he did in one of his last speeches, when discussing the first Bandung conference, "once they excluded the white man, they found they could get together." Since then India and Pakistan, Singapore and Malaysia, the rebellion against the Arabs in Zanzibar and the splits in Black Africa itself have demonstrated that fratricide does not end with the eviction of the white devil. Various Left sects, Maoist and Trotskyist and Communist, sought to recruit him, but he was trying to build a movement of his own. He was shopping around for new political ideas. He was also becoming active in the South instead of merely talking about a Dixie Mau-Mau from the relative safety of Harlem. I believe there was in him a readiness painfully to find and face new truths which might have made him one of the great Negroes, and Americans, of our time.

topic 17

the institutional matrix:
the political realm

Scarcely ten years ago it was argued that ideological fervor and political passion were dead. The "silent fifties," the era of anti-Communist witch-hunts and Senator Joseph McCarthy, had just ended, and the general feeling prevailed that the fundamental political problems of the day had been solved. Clark Kerr, then president of the University of California, said with confidence, "The employers will love this generation. They are going to be easy to handle. There aren't going to be any riots."

There is little need to recount what happened within the next few years: In Europe as in Japan, Latin America, the United States, and even in the Iron Curtain countries, political dissent and political activism ignited with dramatic explosiveness. SDS, the Weatherman, Young Americans for Freedom, and the Ku Klux Klan: The far Left and the far Right were at it in a lively display of ideological frenzy.

The New Left, disdainful of what it took to be the sluggish consensus and coalition politics of the traditional Left and convinced that liberalism had been corrupted by its successes during the New Deal era, became enmeshed in the "politics of confrontation." Launched with the birth of the Students for a Democratic Society in 1962 and the Free Speech Movement at Berkeley two years later, and sustained by growing opposition on college campuses to the war in Vietnam, the New Left and its allies in "the movement" engaged in often bitter and sometimes violent confrontations with federal, civic, police, military, and university authorities. The radical Right, more or less quiescent since the McCarthy era, also experienced a renascence: The Christian Anti-Communist Crusade, the Liberty Lobby, White Citizens' Councils, and the John Birch Society found uncounted thousands of sympathetic ears. The culmination of demonstration versus counterdemonstration may have occurred in 1970, with the invasion of Cambodia.

And today? Conventional wisdom would have it that the radical Left and the radical Right have spent their energies, that the winding down of the Vietnam War, together with the alleged progress of minority and impoverished Americans on the one hand and the ascendancy of a moderate Republican administration on the other hand have effectively defused radical indignation—perhaps. Yet it is also possible that the resentments that gave rise to organized action in the 1960s may still be smoldering.

Granted, the counterculture has apparently "split" from activist engagement, to seek more peacful asylums in far-flung communes. And the far Right has muted its outspokenness and sought more benign allies (George Wallace, Spiro Agnew, and Ronald Reagan, for instance) to replace the Birch Society's Robert Welch or the Christian Crusade's Billy James Hargis. Nonetheless, as the authors of the following three selections note, the student of political sociology has learned to be skeptical of the irreversibility of "trends." Ours, after all, is a peculiarly volatile world—a truth that has been increasingly obvious during the capricious 1960s and the early 1970s.

In discussing the new sociopolitical coalition that is rising to take the place of the old amalgam of interests that has helped usher in the welfare state, Irving Howe—an Old Left socialist—states that there must be a "radicalization of American liberalism: a politics unqualifiedly devoted to democratic norms but much more militant, independent and combative than the Left-liberal world of today." He urges, in effect, that the New Left and the Old Left join forces. Benjamin Epstein and Arnold Foster, authors of our second selection, maintain that radical Right politics is anything but moribund—that its $20,000,000 propaganda offensive marks it as a political force to be reckoned with. In the final selection, Frank Donner warns that the many different forms of restraint on political expression (criminal anarchy statutes, sedition laws, deportations, loyalty oaths) that have marked this century are hardly about to disappear in a new era of benevolence. In fact, he advises, a new system of "political intelligence" is coalescing into what amounts to a potent national network. His is a chilling documentation that will remind some readers of the fictional world of Orwell's **1984**.

chapter 36
notes on
here and
now
irving howe

Ferment, conflict, innovation, violence, a measure of madness—all these and more characterize the American scene in 1967. The image of social stability, a sort of low-keyed containment of grasp and goal, which dominated both liberal and conservative thought only a few years ago, has proved to be an illusion. The welfare state in which we live is strained by tension and clash. But before examining these, let's look at the welfare state as an idea or model—a fixed abstraction, an "ideal type"—in order to gain some historical perspective.

THE ABSTRACT MODEL

A model is not a picture, either still or moving; it lacks, and in order to serve its purpose it must lack, the dynamics of reality. It may articulate skeletal structures but it cannot describe either the processes of change or idiosyncratic traits.

Among current models the most useful, I think, is that of the welfare state. By the welfare state one signifies a capitalist economy in which the interplay of private and/or corporate owners in a largely regulated market remains dominant but in which the workings of the economy are so modified that the powers of free disposal by property owners are controlled politically.

From Partisan Review, vol. 34, no. 4, 1967, p. 564.

The welfare state is constantly being reconstructed. The model we advance for it may suggest an equilibrium, but in the actuality from which the model is drawn there persist serious difficulties, conflicts and breakdowns. If the welfare state could reach, so to say, a point of internal perfection, the point at which it would all but approach its "ideal type," it would comprise a system of regulated conflicts making for pluralist balance and stability. (Indeed, it is a characteristic error of its apologists that they write about the reality as if it were in fact a good deal closer than it is to the model.) But this point of perfection cannot be reached, if only because the welfare state appears within a given historical context, so that it must always be complicated by the accumulation of problems provided by a capitalist economy and a specific national past; complicated, further, by concurrent international conflicts which, as we now see, can crucially affect and distort its formation; and complicated, as well, by a series of pressures, ranging from status ambition to moral idealism, which it is not, as a society, well equipped to handle.

Within certain limits having to do with basic relations of power and production, the welfare state remains open to varying sociopolitical contents, since it is itself the visible evidence of a long and continuing struggle among classes and groups for greater shares in the social product. That the welfare state exists at all is due not merely to autonomous processes within the economy, or enlightened self-interest on the part of dominant classes, or moral idealism which over decades has stirred segments of the population into conscience; no, the welfare state is primarily the result of social struggle on the part of the labor movement. If the working class has not fulfilled the "historic tasks" assigned to it by Marxism and if it shows, at least in the advanced industrial countries, no sign of revolutionary initiative, it has nevertheless significantly modified the nature and softened the cruelties of capitalist society. The surrender of the Marxist revolutionary perspective should by no means be equated with the view that there will not or need not be major social change.

In a curious way—the analogy need not be stressed—the welfare state has served a function similar to that of Communism in the East. I do not suggest an equivalence in value, since for myself, as a socialist, there can be no question that it is immensely more desirable to live in a society that allows political freedom and thereby organized struggle and independent class action. Yet, from a certain long-range perspective, one could say that both the welfare state and the Communist societies have had the effect of raising the historical expectations of millions of people, even while offering radically different kinds of satisfaction and sharing in common failures. Both have enabled previously mute segments of society to feel that the state ought to act in their behalf and that perhaps they have a role in history as active subjects demanding that the state serve their needs. The contrast with earlier societies is striking, for in them the dominant conviction was, as Michael Walzer writes, that

> the state always **is** more than it **does.** Pre-welfare theorists described it as a closely knit body, dense and opaque, whose members were involved emotionally as well as materially, mysteriously as well as rationally, in the fate of the whole. The members ought to be involved, it was said, not for the sake of concrete benefits of any sort, but simply, for the sake of communion. Since loyalty was a gift for which there was to be no necessary return, it could not be predicated on anything so clear-cut as interest. It depended instead on all sorts of ideological and ceremonial mystification. . . . The state still does depend on ideology and mystery, but to a far less degree than

ever before. It has been the great triumph of liberal theorists and politicians to undermine every sort of political divinity, to shatter all the forms of ritual obfuscation, and to turn the mysterious oath into a rational contract. The state itself they have made over . . . into a machine, the instrument of its citizens (rather than their mythical common life) devoted to what Bentham called "welfare production." It is judged, as it ought to be, by the amounts of welfare it produces and by the justice and efficiency of its distributive system.

What occurs characteristically during the growth of the welfare state is a series of "invasions," by previously neglected or newly cohered social groups demanding for themselves a more equitable portion of the social product and appealing to the common ideology of welfarism as the rationale for their demands. (Again an analogy with Communism: The dominant ideology is exploited and violated by the ruling elite, yet can be turned against its interests.)

In its early stages, the welfare state is "invaded" mostly by interest groups—economic, racial, ethnic—which seek both improvements in their condition and recognition of their status. An interest claim that is made through norms the entire society says it accepts is harder to reject than one which sets up new norms not yet enshrined in the society's formal value system—and that, in passing, is one reason it is today easier to press for desirable domestic legislation that to affect foreign policy. In its later stages—which I believe we are just beginning to approach in the United States—the welfare state is subjected to a series of pressures that morally are both more grandiose and more trivial than those of the usual interest groups; since now it becomes possible for claims to be entered with, and against, the welfare state by those who yearn forward to what they hope will be a splendid future and those who yearn backward to what they imagine was a golden past.

This course of "invasions" is by no means completed in the United States, and indeed is scandalously frustrated by racial and social meanness. As long, however, as there are groups trying to break in and powers trying to keep them out, we can be certain that the welfare state will be marked by severe conflict, even though the "invading" groups may differ from decade to decade. Nor is there any certainty whatever that the welfare state will prove receptive to all the claims likely to be made by groups largely outside its system of dispensation. It is possible that the legitimate demands of the Negroes will not be met and that this would, in turn, lead to the virtual destruction of the welfare state as we know it; but if that were to occur it would not, I believe, be the result of an inherent dynamic or ineluctable necessity within the welfare state as a socioeconomic system; rather it would be the result of a tradition of racism so deeply ingrained in American life that it threatens to overwhelm any form of society.

This process of "invasion" is one that a good many of the younger American radicals find troublesome and concerning which I find a good many of them confused. Except for a few who have developed a snobbish contempt for the working class, they acknowledge the justice of the claims made by deprived groups trying to gain a larger share of power, goods, and recognition; but they fear that once this happens there must follow among the once-insurgent groups an adaptation to detested values and a complacent lapse into material comfort. In part, the young radicals are right. At a particular moment, a once-insurgent group may settle for what seems too little—though we ought to be suspicious of contemptuous judgments made by people who have not shared in past struggles or have merely grown up to enjoy their rewards. At a particular moment, a once-insurgent group may move from the drama of popular struggle to the politics of limited pressure. Right now, for example, the trade unions seem relatively quiescent; having won major victories, they may for a time content themselves with minor adjustments; but with time they are likely to raise their horizons of possibility and again come into conflict with the existing order; and in any case, it takes a peculiarly sectarian mentality not to see the tremendous potentialities of the recent UAW demand for something approaching a guaranteed annual wage for blue-collar workers.

Simply to stop at the point where formerly rebellious groups are "absorbed" into society is—to miss the point. For what the young radicals fail sufficiently to see is that when a major social group breaks into the welfare society, then—even though full justice is by no means done—the society nevertheless undergoes an important betterment. The United States after the "absorption" of the labor movement is a different and, on the whole, better society than it was before. By a certain judgment the unions have succumbed to the system, though we should remember that only

rarely had they claimed to be its intransigent opponents. Yet even in their relative quiescence of the last few decades, the unions have performed an extremely valuable function: They have maintained a steady pressure, more than any other institution, in behalf of domestic social legislation which benefits not only their own members but a much wider segment of the population.

If—it is a large if—the Negroes succeed in establishing themselves within the society to the extent that the labor unions have, there will occur changes which can only be described as major and perhaps revolutionary—though there will not have occurred that "revolution" which various kinds of ideologues hope the Negroes will enact for them. Were such victories to be won by the Negroes, there would probably occur a settling-down to enjoy the fruits of struggle. But if past experience is any guide, there would follow after a certain interval a new rise in social appetites among the once-insurgent group, so that it would continue to affect the shape of society even if no longer through exclusively insurgent methods.

Is there, however, a built-in limit to this process of "invasion"? Almost certainly, yes; and by habit one would say, the point where fundamental relations or power seem threatened. But we are nowhere near that point, a large array of struggles awaits us before reaching it, and we cannot even be sure, certainly not as sure as we were a few decades ago, that this point can be located precisely. The history of the Left in the twentieth century is marked by a series of dogmatic assertions as to what could not be done short of revolutionary upheaval; the actuality of history has consisted of changes won through struggle and human will which have in fact achieved some of the goals that were supposed to be unattainable short of apocalypse.

SOME OTHER MODELS

The model of the welfare state I have been using here is of course an extrapolation from the complexities of history, and even if we are to content ourselves with it we must acknowledge the presence in our society of elements it cannot account for and which, indeed, conflict with it. Even the traditional laissez-faire model of capitalism, which by common consent is now obsolete, retains some importance. There are aspects of the society—certain segments of the economy, certain sectors of the country, certain strands of our ideological folklore—in regard to which the traditional model of capitalism retains much relevance, so that in discussing the welfare state, or welfare capitalism, one must bear in mind the earlier historical form out of which it emerged. More immediately, however, there are several models which should be looked at, not merely or even so much as competitors but rather as supplements, necessary complications, to the welfare state model.

The Garrison State

The war economy is like a parallel structure, a double aorta, of the welfare state, at some points reinforcing it through an economic largesse which a reactionary Congress might not otherwise be willing to allow, and at other points crippling it through sociopolitical aggrandizement such as we can observe at this very moment. In consequence, we can never be free of the haunting possibility that if our military expenditure were radically cut there would follow a collapse or a very severe crisis in the welfare state. Nor can we be sure that gradually the military arrangement will not overwhelm and consume welfare. But these, I would stress, are matters of political decision and thereby of social struggle; they will be settled not through some mysterious economic automatism but through the encounter of opposing classes and groups.

The Mass Society

This theory proposes a model of society in which traditional class distinctions have become blurred and in which there occurs a steady drift toward a bureaucratic and prosperous authoritarianism, with a population grown atomized, "primary" social groups disintegrated and traditional loyalties and associations become lax. Herbert Marcuse writes: "Those social groups which dialectical theory identified as forces of negation are either defeated or reconciled within the established system." This means that the working class which Marxism assigned to revolutionary leadership seems either unwilling or incapable of fulfilling the assignment. That there is a tendency in modern society toward a slack contentment it would be foolish to deny. But I think it sentimental to slide from an abandonment of traditional Marxist expectations to a vision of historical stasis in which men are fated to be the zombies of bureaucratic organization, zombies stuffed with calories, comfort and contentment; or to slide from the conclusion that revolutionary expectations no longer hold in the West to a Spenglerian gloom in

which we must yield the idea of major social change.

The trouble with the "mass society" theory is that, if pushed hard enough, it posits a virtual blockage of history. Yet the one thing that history, including the history of the last several decades, teaches us is that, for good or bad, such an eventuality seems most unlikely. Even in what seems to some disenchanted intellectuals the murk of stability, change is ceaseless. Twenty years ago who would have supposed that Russia and China would be at each other's throats, or that the seeming monolith of Communism would disintegrate? That a conservative French general would succeed in ending a colonial war in Algeria after both the liberal and radical parties failed? That in the United States Catholic students would be picketing Cardinal Spellmen's residence? That a silent generation would appear, to be followed by a remarkably articulate one, which in turn . . . well, who knows? What looks at a given moment like the end of days turns out to be a mere vestibule to novelty.

One interesting offshoot of the mass society theory, popular in some academic and student circles, declares that in a society where revolution is impossible and reform ineffectual, the only remaining strategy of protest is a series of dramatic raids from the social margin, akin to the guerrilla movements of Latin America. Insofar as this strategy draws upon the American tradition of individual moral protest, it has a decided respectability if only, I think, a limited usefulness. Insofar as it is meant to satisfy an unearned nostalgia, it is utterly feckless. Raising hell is a fine American habit, and if hell is even approximately identified, a useful one. But in contemporary society there is always the danger that the desperado exhausts himself much sooner than he discomfits society, and then retires at the ripe age of thirty and a half muttering about the sloth of the masses. Or he may be crushed in the embrace of a society always on the lookout for interesting spectacles.

A far more serious and honorable version of this strategy is that of absolute moral conscience, for example, that of the young people who, while not religious, refuse the Vietnam war on moral grounds. Their protest is to be respected. If they are simply bearing witness, then nothing more need be said. If, however, it is claimed that they stir other, more conventional and sluggish segments of the mass society into response, we have abandoned the ground of moral absolutes and moved to the slippery terrain of effectiveness and expediency—and then what they do must be scrutinized as a political tactic, open to the problem of consequences both expected and unexpected.

Liberal Pluralism

This theory, associated with the name of Daniel Bell, sees the society as a pluralist system in which competing pressure groups—some reflecting socioeconomic interests and others refracting the aspirations of status groups—tacitly agree to abide by the "rules of the game" and to submit their rival claims to the jurisdiction of technical experts. Superficially, this approach is congruent with the one I have here outlined, insofar as it traces the effects of political clash within a given society; fundamentally, it is divergent from the approach I have taken, insofar as it accepts the society as a given and fails to penetrate beneath political maneuver to the deeper contradictions of social interest. Still, whether we like it or not, this theory helps describe a good part of what has been happening in the United States these last few decades, especially when one confines oneself to the local texture of political life. I think, however, it is a theory inadequate on several counts:

1. It fails to consider sufficiently that within the society there remain long-range economic and technological trends threatening the stability, perhaps the survival, of the pluralist system: That is, it asserts a state of equilibrium too readily.

2. It fails to recognize, as a rule, that even when the society is operating at a high degree of efficiency and what passes for a notable benevolence, it does not sufficiently satisfy human needs and instead gives rise to new kinds of trouble with which it is poorly equipped to deal.

3. It fails to acknowledge sufficiently that the very "rules of the game" are prearranged so as to favor inequities of power and wealth.

SOME COMPLICATIONS OF REALITY

The welfare state does not appear in a vacuum; it arises at a certain point in the development of capitalist society and must therefore confront the accumulated traditions and peculiarities of that society. In Britain it comes to a society where serious problems remain of a premodern and predemocratic kind, difficulties having to do with aristocracy and caste. In France it comes to a society where the necessary industrialization has just been completed. In Sweden it comes to a society

with a minimum of historical impediments or world political entanglements and therefore functions best of all—though here, as Gunnar Myrdal describes it, the welfare state tends to break down organs of rural and village self-government. In the United States it comes at a time of severe historical and moral tensions: the former concerning our role as a world power and the latter a long-term shift in the country's pattern of values. Let us glance at the second.

For some decades now there has been noticeable in this country a slow disintegration of those binding assumptions which, operating almost invisibly, hold a society together and provide its moral discipline. These values can hardly be evoked in a phrase but we can at least point to a few: a creed of individualist self-reliance linked with a belief that the resultant of unrestrained struggle among private persons (atomized economic units) will be to the common good; a conviction that the claims of conscience, seriously entertained, and the promptings of will, persistently accepted, are in fact equivalent; a belief in work as salvation and therapy; a steady devotion to privacy, rigor, control, and moral sobriety. In short, the whole American mythos which we have inherited from the nineteenth century and which in retrospect has been remarkably successful in unifying the country.

During the last few decades, however, this creed has proven inadequate to the American reality, with the evidence ranging from the crisis of urbanization to the gradual decay of religious belief. Perhaps the most striking evidence has been the way in which the WASP elite has slowly been losing its hegemony in American society. So far as I can tell, this loss of hegemony, accompanied by a decline in self-confidence, has occurred more on the social surface than at the economic base, but with time it is bound also to affect the latter.

The American creed served to unify a nation that in its earlier years had largely consisted of a loose compact of regions. Once these regions were gradually melted into a nation, the unifying ideology began to lose some of its power and the sociocultural elite articulating the ideology began to decline. Precisely the unification of the country through the cement of this ideology gave an opportunity for new interest groups and competing moral styles to press their claims.

This process could not, of course, act itself out autonomously. It was always intertwined with social struggles. And as it slowly unfolds itself at the center of society there occur crisis reactions at the extremes: on the Right, a heartfelt cry that morality is being destroyed, religion mocked, our way of life abandoned; on the Left, an impatience to be done with old ways and to plunge joyously, sometimes merely programmatically, into experiment. The earnest suburban middle class which only a few years ago was shaking with indignation at the collapse of standards and the hippies of Haight-Ashbury and the East Village—these form symmetrical polarities along the spectrum of American moral life, each reacting to the gradual decay of American convictions and neither absorbed by the kind of pluralistic moderation and maneuvering encouraged by the welfare state. Both the little old lady in tennis shoes and the young hippie in sandals are demonstrating their hostility to the "role playing" of the current scene. Both provide complications of response which our increasingly rationalized and rationalistic society finds it hard to handle. For in a sense, the kind of issues raised by Barry Goldwater and the SDS are symmetrical in concern, if sharply different in moral value. Both of these metapolitical tendencies are reacting to long-range historical and cultural developments at least as much as to immediate political issues.

What then are the political consequences of this gradual deterioration of the American value system?

1. The traditional elite can no longer assert itself with its former powers and self-assurance. One reason Adlai Stevenson roused such positive reactions among intellectuals was that it seemed to them that he was a figure in the old style, for which, in their conservative disenchantment, they had developed a sudden fondness.

2. The image of America inherited from folklore, textbooks, and civic rhetoric proves unusable, and the result is an enormous barrier of intellectual and emotional fog which prevents people from apprehending their true needs.

3. At the margins of the welfare state there spring up apocalyptic movements and moods, seemingly political but often in their deepest impulses antipolitical (they want not a change in power relations but an end of days). Reflecting the pressures of the fading past and the undiscovered future, these movements confound, yet sometimes also refresh, the politics of the welfare state.

INNER PROBLEMS OF THE WELFARE STATE

It is not only the distinctive American setting which affects our version of the welfare state; there are also certain characteristics which seem to be intrinsically dysfunctional or at least unattractive. A few of them:

1. Especially in America, the welfare state fails to live up to its formal claims. At best it is a semi-welfare state; at worst an anti-welfare state. It allows a significant minority, the chronic poor, to be dumped beneath the social structure, as a **lumpen** deposit of degradation and pathology.

2. The welfare state may gratify the interests of previously deprived minorities and thereby benefit the society as a whole; but while doing this, and perhaps because of it, the welfare state tends to dampen concern with such larger values as justice, fraternity, equality and community. At least for a time, one consequence is that fundamental issues of power are muted; for better or worse—I think for worse—the system as such is hardly an issue in public debate.

Yet here again we ought to beware of a sin prevalent among intellectuals: the sin of impatience with history. For even in its brief existence, and with its own "historical tasks" far from fulfilled, the welfare state has witnessed the growth of an enormous body of social criticism, as well as the appearance of the militantly idealistic young, both of which insist that we pay attention to precisely the larger issues. If the welfare state lulls some groups into acquiescence, it also grants a succeeding generation the relative affluence to experiment with its life styles and cry out against the slumbers of their elders. The crucial question, to which no answer can yet be given, is whether this concern will remain limited to a tiny segment of the population, driven wild with frustrated reachings towards transcendence.

3. In its own right, the welfare state does not arouse strong loyalties. It seems easier, if no more intelligent, to die for King and Country, or the Stars and Stripes, or the Proletarian Fatherland than for Unemployment Insurance and Social Security. The welfare state makes for a fragmentation of publics and, at a certain point, a decline in political participation. By one of those accursed paradoxes history keeps throwing up, the welfare state seems to undercut the vitality of the democratic process even while strengthening both its formal arrangements and its socioeconomic base.

But again a word of caution. It should not be assumed that in a country like the United States, despite the rise of group interest politics and the atomization of social life, the traditional claims of the nation no longer operate. For they do, even in a muted and more quizzical way. Millions of people still respond to the call of patriotism and the rhetoric of democracy, even in their corniest versions. The centrifugal tendencies set into motion by the welfare state must always, therefore, be seen against a background of historical traditions and national sentiments which lie deeply imbedded in collective life.

4. The welfare state cannot, within the limits of the nation-state, cope with the growing number of socioeconomic problems that are soluble only on an international level or do not really fit into the received categories of class or group conflict. As Richard Titmuss says:

> It is much harder today to identify the causal agents of change—the microbes of social disorganization and the viruses of impoverishment—and to make them responsible for the costs of "disservices." Who should bear the social costs of the thalidomide babies, of urban blight, of smoke pollution, of the obsolescence of skills, of automation, of the impact on the peasants of Brazil of synthetic coffee which will dispense with the need for coffee beans?

5. The welfare state provides no clear or necessary outlook concerning the role of the nation in the modern world. It is almost compatible with any foreign policy, despite our too-easy assumption that domestic liberalism is likely to go together with restraint abroad. The welfare state can be yoked to a foreign policy which saves Titoist Yugoslavia and destroys Vietnam, which provides food to India and shores up dictators in Asia, which proclaims and begins a little to enable the Alliance for Progress and sanctions the Dominican intervention. The consequences are severe dislocations within the welfare state, splits between groups oriented primarily toward the improvement of their own conditons and groups oriented primarily toward improving the place our society occupies within the world. Of this, more later.

6. Within its terms and limits the welfare state finds it very difficult to provide avenues of fulfillment for many of the people whose conditions it has helped to improve—the workers displaced by automation, the Negroes given the vote but little else, the young seeking work that makes sense. That is why there now appear new formations, such as the subculture of the alienated young, responding primarily to their felt sense of the falseness of things. If the revolt of the Radical Right was, in Richard Hofstadter's phrase, an outburst of status politics—the anxious need of an insecure segment to assert itself in the prestige hierarchy—then the revolt of the alienated young is, among other things, an antistatus outburst—a wish to break loose from the terms of categorization fixed by the society. That, in the course of this effort, the young sometimes settle into categories, styles, and mannerisms quite as rigid as those against which they rebel, is still another testimony to the power of repressive social arrangements.

POLITICS OF THE WELFARE STATE

The politics of the welfare state extends back into the early twentieth century, through a variety of parallel and competing traditions—the labor movement, the Socialist movement, the various liberal groups, the moral pressures exerted through Christian action, the increasing role of the Jews as a liberal force. But for our present purposes we can date the beginning of welfare-state politics as a style of coalition to the early thirties and perhaps even more precisely to the election of 1932, one of the few in American history which marked a major realignment of political forces. In that election the unions began to play the powerful role they would command during the next few decades; large numbers of Negroes began their historic switch to the Democratic Party; the city machines found it expedient to go along with Roosevelt's policies. And soon significant numbers of intellectuals would begin their entry into practical politics. This coalition would remain a major force in American life during the next three or so decades. When all or most of its component parts could be held together, formally or informally, and it could command the practical issues and/or moral appeals to win a good cut of the middle-class vote, this coalition could often win elections on a national scale and in many industrialized states. When there were group defections, victory went to the Right. In general one can say that this coalition was most successful whenever it managed to link strong economic interests with moral urgencies, the politics of pressure with the traditions of American liberalism and populism. I believe that this lesson still holds, despite sharply changed circumstances.

What specific forms did this coalition take? It could be one or more of the following:

a bloc of organizations and movements cooperating for a legislative or electoral end;
a long-range concurrence in electoral behavior, so that certain expectations could reasonably be

inferred—e.g., that even if we do not have
self-conscious classes or disciplined publics
there are at least certain fundamental recognitions of common interest;
intermittent activization of class and interest
groups when aroused by specific issues—e.g.,
"right to work" laws, Negro rights, etc.;
various electoral and political arrangements within
and across the political parties.

Now one way of looking upon recent American politics is to conclude that in recent years the
liberal-left coalition has gradually disintegrated
and with the Vietnam war, seems virtually to have
come to an end.

There are plenty of signs. The electoral blocs
seem to function with less assurance and predictability than ten or twenty years ago. Workers
reaching a measure of affluence are less likely to
follow the signals of their union leadership; they
may veer off into middle-class styles or lapse into
racialism. Still, when certain issues are clearly
drawn along class lines, as for example during the
last presidential election or the earlier struggles
around "right to work" laws, the labor vote can
still cohere into a major force.

Similar signs of change seem to be occurring
among the Negroes, where the massive commitment to the Democratic Party may—though it
certainly has not yet—come to an end. And among
younger people there is a growing inclination to
respond to politics as if group interest were somehow vulgar or even reprehensible and what mat-
tered most were political "styles" and moral, or
pseudomoral, appeals rising above socioeconomic
concerns.

Why then has this coalition devoted to defending and extending the welfare state come to
a condition of crisis? A few answers suggest themselves:

1. As the interest groups become increasingly
absorbed into the welfare state, their combative-
ness decreases, at least for a time. They develop a
stake in the status quo and become economically
and psychologically resistant to new kinds of insurgency. Thus, while a general case can and
should be made out for a community of interests
among the unions, the Negroes, and the unorganized poor, these groups will often clash both
in their immediate demands and their political
styles.

2. What I would call the "rate of involvement" among the interest groups and moral issue

groups is likely to be sharply different at various
moments, and the result is unavoidable friction.
When the unions were surging ahead in the thirties,
they received little help from the churches; it did
not even occur to anyone at that time to expect
much help. The Catholic Church in particular was
regarded as a major center of political reaction.
Today we witness the astonishing and exhilarating
rise of ferment within the Catholic community,
while the unions, though still fierce guardians of
yesterday's gains, are not notable as centers of
innovation.

3. Ideally there ought to be cooperation between those committed to a politics of pressure
and those committed to a politics of insurgency;
but in practice the latter often tend to define
themselves through dissociation from the former
(perhaps on the "principle" that you strike out
most violently against your closest relatives) while
the former feel their survival and even their honor
to be threatened by the latter. As long as the
wretched Vietnam war continues and social stagna-
tion consequently characterizes our domestic life,
this conflict is likely to be exacerbated.

4. The programmatic demands advanced by
the liberal-left groups for domestic reforms during
the thirties have by now either been mostly
realized or require merely—but that's **some**
merely!—quantitative implementation. By itself
this does not yield a dramatic or inspiring perspective; it does not excite the young, it barely arouses
those in whose behalf it is advanced, and it proves
more and more inadequate for coping with the
new problems we all experience more sharply than
we can define.

5. There has occurred over the Vietnam war a
split between groups focusing primarily on domestic issues, mostly the unions, and the groups focusing primarily on foreign policy, mostly the middle-
class peace organizations and radical youth. During the twentieth century, with the possible
exception of the 1916 election, foreign policy has
never played a decisive role in American elections;
or, to modify that a bit, disputes over foreign
policy, such as the interventionist/isolationist
quarrel in the thirties, did not threaten the survival
of the liberal coalition. Today this is no longer
true, and cannot be true—even though I am unhappily convinced that in an electoral showdown
the moral protestants, among whom I wish to include myself, would prove to be a very small minority. Never in the past has it been possible to
rally a successful liberal-left movement on issues of

foreign policy alone or predominantly. Whether it can be done today remains very much an open question.

6. We are living through an exhaustion, perhaps temporary, of American liberalism. It is not, at the moment, rich in programmatic suggestions. It has lost much of its earlier élan. It has become all too easily absorbed into establishment maneuvers, so that it shares a measure of responsibility for the Vietnam disasters and ghetto outbreaks. It has not developed new leaders. In short, as its most intelligent spokesmen know, it is in a state of moral and intellectual disarray.

Yet in fairness one should add that pretty much the same difficulties beset most or all other political tendencies in the United States. One of the remarkable facts about our political life is the paucity of specific proposals to come from the far Left or far Right. A comparison with the thirties is instructive, for whatever else was wrong with American radicalism (almost everything) at that time, it did advance specific proposals for legislation and thereby agitation. Today that is hardly the case. "Participatory democracy" may be a sentiment as noble as it is vague, but even its most ardent defenders cannot suppose it to be a focused proposal for our national life. And by a similar token, it is interesting that Governor Reagan did not really try to dismantle the welfare state against which he had mock-raged during his campaign.

I think that for the next period we shall have to live and work within the limits of the welfare state. There is only one possibility that this perspective will be invalidated, and that is a racial civil war pitting white against black—a tragedy which even the most puerile advocates of "nose-to-nose confrontation" must recognize as utterly disastrous. Unless we are to delude ourselves with the infantile leftism of the talk about "Negro revolution" (sometimes invoked most fiercely by guerrillas with tenure), the first point on the political agenda must be a renewed struggle for the fulfillment of the claims advanced by the welfare state. And that, in turn, means a simultaneous struggle to end the Vietnam war and to bring large-scale economic help to the Negro ghettos.

A WORD ABOUT THE FUTURE

If one could view the present moment with detachment, one might say that we are witnessing the breakdown of the old political coalition which helped usher in the welfare state and perhaps the

slow beginnings of a new coalition to improve and transcend the welfare state. In this new coalition the labor movement would still have—it would have to have—a central role, but no longer with the decisive weight of the past. The churches would matter a great deal more, and so would the American "new class," that scattered array of intellectuals, academicians, and technicians. Issues of foreign policy would occupy a central place in the program of such a coalition, as would those concerning "quality of life"—though the immediate major domestic concern remains the realization of the welfare-state expectations for the American Negroes. In such a coalition there might come together the tradition of moral protest and the bearing of witness with the tradition of disinterested service. All of this could occur only through a radicalization of American liberalism: a politics unqualifiedly devoted to democratic norms but much more militant, independent, and combative than the left-liberal world of today.

Whenever in the past American radicalism has flourished somewhat, it has largely been in consort with an upsurge of liberalism. There have been two major periods: first during the years immediately preceding World War I and then during the thirties. The notion that radicalism can grow fat on the entrails of liberalism is a crude error, an absurdity.

But all of this remains hope and speculation. Before such a new coalition emerges, if ever it does, there is likely to be severe tension and conflict among its hoped-for component parts. The Vietnam war stands as a harsh barrier, political and psychological, which must be broken down in order to take care of our business at home—which is by no means to accept the quietistic and reactionary argument that until the war is ended nothing can or should be done at home.

■

Even the full realization of the "idea" of the welfare state would not bring us to utopia or the good society. The traditional socialist criticisms in respect to the maldistribution of power, property, and income would still hold. But to continue the struggle for such a realization is both a political and human responsibility. And through the very struggle to realize the "idea" of the welfare state— if I may offer a "dialectic" observation—it is possible to gain the confidence, strength, and ideas through which to move beyond the welfare state. Unfortunately, American intellectuals do not seem

well equipped for keeping to this dual perspective: They either lapse into a genteel and complacent conservatism or they veer off into an ul-
timatistic and pseudo-utopian leftism. Yet, when
one comes to think of it, why should it be so
difficult to preserve a balance between the struggle to force the present society to enact the reforms it claims to favor and the struggle to move
beyond the limits of the given society? Tactically,
to be sure, this creates frequent difficulties; but
conceptually, as a guiding principle, I think it
our only way.

chapter 37
radicals
of
the right
arnold foster
and benjamin r. epstein

It happened in Amarillo, Texas—population 140,000.

A shadow of fear and suspicion moved in across the city, in 1961, pitting people against people, and setting off a wave of antics so bizarre it appeared that some outlandish circus had encamped in town.

Brigadier General William L. (Jerry) Lee, a retired Air Force officer who was the area coordinator of the John Birch Society, the growing phenomenon of America's Right Wing, charged that a local clergyman was a Communist sympathizer. Shortly thereafter, he proclaimed that the National Council of Churches, representing an overwhelming proportion of the nation's Protestants, was infiltrated by Communists—for almost a decade a favorite and never-documented allegation of certain fundamentalist preachers and Extreme Rightists.

The community was immediately up in arms, disbelief fighting credence, townsman debating townsman. Leading Amarillo clergymen demanded that General Lee present to the Federal Bureau of Investigation his professed evidence that Communists had infiltrated the National Council of

From **Danger on the Right** by Arnold Forster and Benjamin R. Epstein. Copyright © 1964 by Anti-Defamation League of B'Nai Brith. Reprinted by permission of Random House, Inc.

Churches, or keep quiet. But Lee only repeated the scandalous charges and ignored the cries for proof.

Amarillo's mayor, Jack Seale, was an avowed member of the John Birch Society. With his help, and that of a strong Birch membership in the city, General Lee's charges were spread everywhere and reached everyone. Before long, members of congregations delivered angry ultimatums to their pastors demanding that they break with the National Council of Churches or suffer the stoppage of contributions in the collection baskets. The ministers, fortunately, stood firm, insisting that first they be shown evidence of the charges. Proof, uncharitably, was never forthcoming.

While the split grew worse, Birchers instigated a second drive, this one to get rid of "Communist" reading matter in local schools and libraries. As a result, nine books were removed from the city's four high schools and from the library at Amarillo College—among them four Pulitzer Prize novels: John Steinbeck's **The Grapes of Wrath**, Oliver LaFarge's **Laughing Boy**, MacKinlay Kantor's **Andersonville**, and A. B. Guthrie's **The Way West**. Ironically, another of the purged novels was George Orwell's **1984**, a book generally regarded as a devastating critique of life under communism. Amarillo College eventually cleared all the books for general circulation except **Andersonville** which, peculiarly, was placed on the reserve shelf.

The book-purging campaign and the search for Reds fell with an upsetting impact on many Amarillo high school students. Suddenly they "discovered" they had teachers who were Communists, and they leveled accusations of disloyalty and dark hints of treason. In a town torn by hatred, recriminations, and wild, unsupported Birch charges, many old friendships were soon broken.

As an almost palpable hostility crept across the small city, even the local Girl Scouts were drawn into the fight when Birchers questioned the patriotism of scout leaders. At that juncture, Amarillo's Birchite mayor, Jack Seale, decided to run for Congress against the incumbent Democrat and, in the ensuing campaign, received the enthusiastic help of the Birchers and their fellow travelers. Before election day finally arrived, the Birch Society and charges of "communism" had become the major issues in the bitter campaign, and politics in Amarillo might never be quite the same again.

This was not an isolated instance. Similar frenzy has not been wholly unknown to other communities in the United States. The circus encamps for a while here, for a while there, arousing the citizenry and then leaving bitterness and unresolved suspicions in its wake. It has been part of the pattern of the current resurgence of the Radical Right in this county.

And this is where it has been happening—not on Capitol Hill but in Amarillo, in Midlothian, in Levittown and Los Angeles. Not so often in the far-off halls of political theory, it's usually found just down the block, particularly if there is a school, a church, or a charitable institution there. And when the circus comes to town, everybody gets caught up in it.

∎

The climate is right.

In the long history of the United States, extremist groups—born of the problems of their times—have played a recurrent role. Most of these have been transients on the national scene. Some have lasted for a short time, others have stayed on longer. Eventually, as the real or the fancied need for such organizations has dwindled, most of them have disintegrated and have disappeared—to become short chapters or footnotes in the history books.

Today's Radical Right is the direct lineal descendant of ultra-Rightist organizations that flashed across the national scene in the 1930s and the 1940s—from the Liberty League to the isolationist America First Committee and the Constitutional Educational League, and thence to the whole amorphous carload of patrioteers and Communist-hunters that came to be called the McCarthy movement, or McCarthyites, after the late senator from Wisconsin.

Many of those whose names stud the rolls of today's Radical Right are veterans and leaders of those earlier political wars, and of those propaganda campaigns to save the nation from the "evils" of the New Deal, or the Fair Deal, or from "Communist infiltration" in Washington—particularly in the State Department. These old-time leaders have been joined by countless thousands who marched in their ranks in bygone years. They march today along with younger recruits who share the view of a United States heavily infiltrated by Communists and pro-Communists, and ripe for an imminent Red "take-over."

Still the question remains: Why did the Radical Right, which in various forms had been kicking and screaming about for many years, emerge around 1960 as a force to be reckoned with in American life?

In 1963, a group of social scientists from Stanford University, Washington University in St. Louis, and the California Department of Public Health published a depth study of the kind of American who is drawn to a Radical Right organization, and provided some clues on the question of why the Extreme Right Wing soars higher and higher at certain times. The study was made at one of the "schools of anti-Communism" conducted by Dr. Frederick C. Schwarz, head of the Christian Anti-Communism Crusade.

One conclusion drawn by the study was that those who paid to attend a Schwarz school in Oakland were in the majority Republican. It was possible, then, that the presence in the White House of a Republican President from 1952 to 1960 had acted as a restraining factor on the Radical Right.

"The allegations of Communist influence that play so large a part in right-wing propaganda," the study said, "are less convincing to the public when a Republican is President. Hope, party loyalty and organizational alliances all restrain right-wing leaders at this time." And it added: "All these conditions are reversed when the White House changes hands. There is no incumbent President to restrain right-wing dissidents. . . . During a Democratic administration, alarmism about Communism is more plausible to many people, particularly those with very conservative ideas.

"Recent fluctuations in radical right activity conform to this pattern. The current resurgence occurred after the 1960 Presidential election. While the John Birch Society was founded in 1958, it was not until 1961 that it grew enough to attract public attention. The Christian Anti-Communism Crusade was an obscure organization for the first seven years of its existence, but in the first year of the Kennedy Administration its income increased 350%."

There are, of course, reasons other than Democratic Party dominance for the upsurge of the Radical Right in the last four or five years. A complex of factors seems to have converged with unusual impact since 1960:

The cold war frustrations of the American people and the recurrent international crises and confrontations with the Communists in Korea, Berlin, Laos, Vietnam, and Cuba, together with the lack of clear-cut American "victory" in a number of these crises—a new kind of experience for Americans, accustomed to climactic triumphs on the battlefield and unprepared for "a long, twilight struggle" lasting years. Then there have been crises and tensions at home: the need for high taxes to support the nation's defense, rising costs of living, the conflicts of the racial struggle over integration—not to mention the return to Washington of a Democratic administration generally regarded as "liberal." For political or propaganda activity which flourishes in a climate of frustration and confusion, the climate was indeed right.

Some five hundred Right Wing organizations, national and local, have been identified on the American political scene in recent years. By 1964 many were inactive or moribund, but some were louder and lustier than ever. These groups have ranged from somewhat right of center to the Extremists of the Radical Right, and beyond—into the lunatic fringe, where racism and religious bigotry of the gutter variety supplement the Radical Rightist gospel.

Of these hundreds of organizations only twenty-six or twenty-seven can be considered major groups, and of these, perhaps fourteen can be viewed as Radical Right. The others, often less extreme, are the conservative allies of the Radical Right who, through a lavish lack of discrimination or through an excess of zeal, are sadly "soft" on radicals of the Right and prone to make common cause with them.

These two dozen or so organizations manifestly make an impact on the nation, and on the Republican Party in particular. Their activities reflect dissatisfaction with the course of national policy in the past three decades, and their propaganda thunders that GOP leaders are only "me-too" with respect to Democratic Party policies at home and abroad. The greater number of Republicans are undoubtedly embarrassed by their self-appointed supporters from the extreme edge of the political spectrum, having grown up in a complex, twentieth-century world that has ceased looking for final answers in the waving of a flag or in hair-raising escapes from responsibility.

Many of these outfits of the Radical Right and its conservative fellow travelers enjoy tax-exempt status. A number of them have been incorporated as "educational," "charitable," or religious" organizations, which qualifies them for tax exemption by the United States Treasury, although in fact much of their activity, and most of their publications and materials, appear to be at all times essentially political and partisan.

Virtually the only thing the Internal Revenue Service requires of a tax-exempt body is an annual report on its income and expenditures. Such reports show increased receipts and expenditures by Right Wing organizations in 1958 and 1959. As the 1960 Presidential campaign went into its final lap, the contributions reached a peak, and after the votes were in, contributions dwindled. In 1961 they began to rise again, and reached another high point in 1962, a congressional election year. Reports for 1963 indicated another sharp rise and, as this is written, point to a high level in the 1964 Presidential election year. It is not unfair to conclude that one immediate aim of those who contribute the money, and of those who spend it, is to influence the outcome of political elections.

As to political philosophy, the Right Wing ranges extremely wide as well as extremely far out. On one hand, the minions of the Radical Right, armed with those peculiar powers of intelligence denied most of us, see the country as ripe for a take-over by an internal conspiracy of secret Communist agents and socialist planners who have craftily burrowed into every facet of American life, saddling us with a domestic tyranny and a foreign policy made in Moscow. The Extreme Conservatives, on the other hand, are quite convinced that since the Roosevelt New Deal, America has been going socialist and that its foreign policy has been at least soft on communism. But, whereas the

Radical Right blames an internal conspiracy for the alleged sorry situation, its conservative allies attribute it to blindness, stupidity, and bungling on the part of Liberals who they say have controlled the nation's affairs these three decades.

From either viewpoint, however, the look of things is obviously frightening, and in the ideological war the Extremists are now waging, fear itself is a basic weapon. To convert Americans to their alarmist views, the crusaders of the Extreme American Right—the Radicals and their conservative allies—are currently spending at least $14,000,000 a year. In addition, about $1,300,000 goes to an ignoble potpourri of anti-Semitic, racist, and other fanatical bodies which also would like to make a hard Rightist impact on American political life.

A substantial portion of the $14,000,000 that goes to the Radical Rightists and their conservative allies comes from the wellsprings of 70 foundations (almost all of them tax-exempt), 113 business firms and corporations (most of which can deduct contributions to "religious" or "educational" organizations), 25 public utility companies, and some 250 individuals who have been identified as contributing at least $500 each to Rightist causes in the last few years.

Another sizeable portion of the total is scared up from ordinary citizens—through dues, appeals at rallies, mailing-list pleas, etc.—literally scared up, so potent is the pull of fear, and so fearful is the Rightist view of things.

In addition to these officially reported millions, other money is poured into the American Right Wing for specific projects such as TV and radio programs, special broadcasts, publications, and reprints—all of which are charged off as business expenses. Such costs, met by business firms, are not always reported by Right Wing organizations because the money does not pass through their hands. It is difficult to estimate such "side" expenditures precisely, but the total is known to be substantial.

Some of the nationally known organizations—for example, Dr. Schwarz's Christian Anti-Communism Crusade and Billy James Hargis' Christian Crusade—encountered difficulties in maintaining membership and financial support after a nationwide avalanche of critical publicity directed at the Radical Right during 1961 and 1962.

Hargis' crusade grossed almost $1,000,000 in 1961. The evangelist reasonably anticipated a million and a quarter in the following year, but instead he had to cut his operations for a time.

Schwarz suffered even more serious difficulties. But even with the widespread criticism of the Radical Right, Schwarz and Hargis might not have encountered such reversals were there not a basic difference between their operations and those of the Birch Society. Neither Schwarz nor Hargis sought to build a permanent membership organization from the grass roots up, but instead merchandised anticommunism by hitting the sawdust trail. Their unending appeals were for money for the cause, not permanent members. They sought to mobilize dollars to support their crusades. The John Birch Society, on the other hand, sought to mobilize the people whom it wanted to participate in an action program—a program in which money is only one necessary ingredient. As a result, the Birch Society grew, despite hostile publicity, while the Schwarz and Hargis crusades dwindled.

Politically, it was the 1962 congressional election which provided the first real test of Radical Right strength. Although most of its candidates were defeated, the Radical Right made its presence obvious in the political picture in a number of states, and in some of them exerted a political impact far out of proportion to its numerical strength.

In California, where the Radical Right in general and the John Birch Society in particular were strongest, the two known Birch members in the Eighty-seventh Congress—Representatives John Rousselot and Edgar Hiestand—were defeated in their bids for reelection. Superficial observers concluded that the Birchers and their allies had suffered a resounding defeat. The conclusion was not justified; the Rousselot and Hiestand districts had been redrawn by the California state legislature and neither of the men was given much chance of winning. Despite this handicap, the two ran surprisingly strong races, Rousselot polling 46 percent and Hiestand 45.5 percent of the vote cast. A third Bircher—H. L. Richardson, later to become one of the Society's paid coordinators—polled 44.2 percent in still another district.

In other primary and general election campaigns that year—including those in such politically important states as New York, Texas, Michigan, Wisconsin, and Washington—the John Birch Society and its Rightist allies wrought an impact on the course and the character of the campaigns far greater than the numerical strength and voting power of their adherents. The Birchers themselves became fired up with hopes for future victories.

In the June, 1964, California primaries at least

five members of the Society were successful in
bids for Republican nominations as candidates to
the House of Representatives and to the state legislature; three others publicly reported to have ties
to the Birch Society were also victorious. Assessing
the results of the 1964 primaries in California,
Rousselot, as western states governor for the Birch
Society, rejoiced—declaring that "it was a good
day" for the cause.

Despite their political impact on the 1962
elections, and even in the face of the successes of
Birchite candidates in the June, 1964, West Coast
primaries, Radical Right groups do not essentially
seek to create new political parties. Rather, they
seek by concerted propaganda drives to change the
political climate in the United States, to turn the
winds slowly their way. They do so by penetrating
and influencing both major political parties. And
in this effort, the John Birch Society has emerged
as the strongest of such organizations, geared as it
is for the long pull, and growing as it is, slowly but

steadily, in membership and in the influence of its
propaganda activities.

Thousands of words have been published in
the last few years exposing and criticizing the John
Birch Society and its founder, Robert Welch. . . .
John F. Kennedy, . . . Richard M. Nixon, and
United States senators in both political parties
have assailed the society and its leader, as have the
National Council of Churches, the United Presbyterian Church, the General Assembly of the Southern Presbyterian Church, leading Episcopalian
clerics and prominent Catholic churchmen and
laymen, and leaders in business, labor, and education. Even such Right Wing publicists as William F.
Buckley, Jr., and Russell Kirk have added their
own sharp criticism. Yet, despite this national
wave of rebukes, the Birch Society is still in business. It is still expanding its operations year by
year, and growing ever more arrogant against the
dupes, cowards, atheists, and traitors that it sees
directing the main stream of American life.

chapter 38
the theory and practice of american political intelligence
frank donner

The twentieth century has been marked by a succession of different forms of restraint on political expression: criminal anarchy statutes, sedition laws, deportations, Congressional antisubversive probes, loyalty oaths, enforced registration. These and related measures still survive. But in recent years new, more formidable ways of responding to political and social movements on the left have emerged. The most important of these is the system of political intelligence, which is rapidly coalescing into a national network.[1]

Despite the efforts of intelligence officials to keep intelligence operations secret, reliable information about our intelligence system is steadily accumulating. We now have a clearer picture of the methods and targets of political surveillance. As a result, we can no longer seriously doubt that the main purpose of such activity is political control of dissent or that the frequently advanced justifications of law enforcement or national security are often no more than a "cover."

■

On March 21, 1971, a group calling itself the Citizens' Commission to Investigate the FBI mailed

or delivered to a congressman and senator as well as to the Washington **Post, The New York Times,** and the Los Angeles **Times** a packet containing fourteen documents, selected from over 1000 stolen from a small FBI office in Media, Pennsylvania, a suburb of Philadelphia. The fourteen documents, all of them of recent date and undisputed authenticity, show that the FBI concentrates much of its investigative effort on college dissenters and black student groups. According to a memorandum from J. Edgar Hoover such groups "pose a definite threat to the Nation's stability and security," a conclusion that he has not been able to support and that both the Washington **Post** and **The New York Times** have challenged.

When conducting surveillance of a Swarthmore College philosophy professor regarded as a "radical," the FBI enlisted the assistance of the local police and postmaster, as well as a campus security officer and switchboard operator. In one of the documents, the FBI agent in charge of the Philadelphia bureau instructs his agents at Media that more interviews are

. . . in order for plenty of reasons, chief of which are it will enhance the paranoia endemic in these circles and will further serve to get the point across that there is an FBI agent behind every mailbox. In addition, some will be overcome by the overwhelming personalities of the contacting agent and will volunteer to tell all—perhaps on a continuing basis.

Dramatic disclosures of this sort as well as the recent Senate hearings on Army intelligence will undoubtedly help to cure the surviving skepticism about these practices. Until fairly recently even the targets of surveillance were reluctant to credit the existence of police activities which violate the most deeply held premises of their society. But political surveillance has become so obtrusive and its targets so numerous that it can no longer be easily ignored or justified. A sharper awareness of intelligence has, in turn, opened up new sources of data about a field which I have been researching since the McCarthy era.[2]

Of course dossiers, informers, and infiltrators are hardly new. But since the early Sixties, when attorneys general in the South formed a rudimentary intelligence network in order to curb the integrationist activities of students, political surveillance and associated practices have spread throughout the nation.

Surveillance has expanded largely because of the scale and militance of the protest movements that erupted in the Sixties. Policy makers and officers of intelligence agencies were then faced with the need to identify and control new actors on a new political stage—no easy matter in view of the anarchic radical milieu, characterized by highly mobile and anonymous young people, who tend to be hostile to formal organization and leadership. The social remoteness of new radicals concentrated in "tribal," self-contained groups made it all the more difficult to identify them.

Most of the existing intelligence agencies at that time were no more effective than other institutions in our society. Their techniques were as outmoded as their notions of subversion dominated by an old Left composed of "Communists," "fellow travelers," and "fronts." Intelligence files were choked with millions of dossiers of aging or dead radicals. At the same time, new gadgetry—miniaturization, audio-electronics, infrared lens cameras, computers, and data banks—gave intelligence possibilities undreamed of by the most zealous practitioners of the repressive arts of the nineteenth century.

According to the herald of the "technetronic" society, Zbigniew Brzezinski, new developments in technology will make it "possible to assert almost continuous surveillance over every citizen and maintain up-to-date files, containing even personal information about the . . . behavior of the citizen, in addition to the more customary data." Full access to critical data, he adds, will give the undercover agent and the roving political spy greater flexibility in planning and executing countermeasures.[3]

◾

Twenty federal agencies are engaged in intelligence activities. The most important are:

the FBI, with an estimated 2,000 agents on political investigative assignments in charge of thousands of undercover informers

the ARMY, which concededly had at one time 1,200 agents in the field, together with a huge staff operating a dossier bank of 25 million "personalities"

the CIA

the INTERNAL REVENUE SERVICE (for several weeks in 1970 its agents requested access to the circulation records of public libraries in a number of cities in order to learn the names of borrowers of books on explosives and other "militant and subversive" subjects, a practice which it defended as "just a continual building of information")

the INTELLIGENCE DIVISION OF THE POST OFFICE

the SECRET SERVICE (where names of 50,000 "persons of interest" are on file)

the CUSTOMS BUREAU OF THE TREASURY DEPARTMENT

the CIVIL SERVICE COMMISSION (15 million names of "subversive activity" suspects)

the IMMIGRATION AND NATURALIZATION SERVICE

the NAVY, AIR FORCE, COAST GUARD

the PASSPORT DIVISION OF THE STATE DEPARTMENT

the DEPARTMENT OF JUSTICE COMMUNITY RELATIONS SERVICE which feeds information into its computerized Inter-Divisional Intelligence and Information Unit[4]

civil rights and poverty projects sponsored by the DEPARTMENT OF HEALTH, EDUCATION AND WELFARE and the OFFICE OF ECONOMIC OPPORTUNITY. The Executive Department agencies cooperate with and are supplemented by the Congressional antisubversive committees.

Intelligence operations are also flourishing in states and counties. A typical state intelligence agency is the Massachusetts Division of Subversive Activities which conducts investigations in response to complaints by private citizens and acts as a central repository for information about subversion. The Division's Annual Report for 1969 is revealing:

A file is kept of peace groups, civil rightists and other such groups where, due to their enthusiasm, they might have a tendency to adopt or show a policy of advocating the commission of acts of force or violence to deny other persons their rights under the Constitution. These files are kept up-dated by communications with the Federal Bureau of Investigation, the House Internal Security Committee, Subversive Activities units in other states and decisions of the United States Supreme Court.

The files in this Division have grown to such an extent that the Federal Bureau of Investigation, Immigration and Naturalization Service, Department of Defense, U.S. Army Intelligence, Federal Civil Service Commission, Treasury Department, several departments of the Commonwealth, Industrial Plants and Educational Institutions now clear with this Division on security checks.

Requests for investigations, or assistance in investigations, received from various police departments, Federal Bureau of Investigation, House Committee on Un-American Activities and the Subversive Activities Control Board, complied with such requests [sic].

Members of the Division attended demonstrations conducted in the area by various groups. Note was made of the leaders and organizations participating, occasionally photographs are taken, the persons identified, and a file was made.

The Division is continuing to compile and tabulate a check on new organizations in the Civil Rights area so as to be sure of any inclinations toward communist-front activities or the infiltration into these organizations of known communists or communist sympathizers.

During the past year, as a result of the increased activity of the Communist and Subversive Groups in racial demonstrations throughout the country, this Division has kept a watch on these developments so as to note any trend toward that end in Massachusetts.

During the past year, this Division continued to submit information relative to subversive organizations and individuals to several local police departments who are in the process, or have started, Intelligence Units within their respective departments.

Sometimes state intelligence agencies operate under concealed or obscure auspices. For example, the Ohio Highway Patrol runs an intelligence unit which claims to have recruited student informers on every campus in the state. According to the head of the unit, "We have actually had informers who are members of the board of trustees [sic] of various dissident groups." State intelligence units are also at work in several universities in Maryland and Illinois.

Urban intelligence units ("red squads") have multiplied greatly and are becoming a standard tool in local police practice. Increasingly powerful, they operate under a variety of names (Anti-Subversive Squad, Intelligence Unit, Civil Disobedience Unit); in some cases they use a "Human Relations" or "Community Relations" cover, which is considered an efficient means of penetrating the ghetto.[5]

Black communities swarm with urban intelligence agents and informers, as do university and peace groups; invitations to young people to defect or to sell information at high prices are becoming routine. Young college graduates—black and white —are offered "career opportunities" in urban intelligence; courses in intelligence and surveillance are being taught to municipal police units and campus security police.[6]

In fact, the campus constabulary is spreading throughout the country's higher education community. Its functions are expanding to include clandestine intelligence activities such as undercover work and wiretapping and are meshed with the work of other intelligence agencies. We get a glimpse of this new collaboration in one of the recent Media documents, dated November 13, 1970.

On 11/12/70 MR. HENRY PEIRSOL, Security Officer, Swarthmore College, Swarthmore, Pa. advised that DANIEL BENNETT is a Professor of Philosophy at that School and in charge of the Philosophy Department. He has been there about three years having previously taught at University of Mass. MRS. BENNETT is not employed and there are two small children in the family ages about 8 to 12 years.

The BENNETTs reside in a semi-detached

house located near PEIRSOL's residence although he does not have any social contact with them. PEIRSOL has noted that there does not appear to be anyone other than the BENNETTs residing at their home but that numerous college students visit there frequently. BENNETT drives a two tone blue, VW station wagon, bearing Penna. license 5V0245. There are no other cars in the family and no other cars normally parked in their driveway.

PEIRSOL was funished [sic] with the wanted flyers on the subjects and he stated he would remain alert in his neighborhood for their possible appearance. Also he will alert his sources at the college for any information about the subjects particularly any information that subjects might be in contact with the BENNETTS.

(Those who are familiar with the quality of FBI reporting will not be surprised to learn that some of this report is not true. As Professor Bennett has pointed out, he is unacquainted with the subject of the "wanted flyers," has one child not two, and owns two cars not one.)

Many of the red squads run by city police are growing so fast that they are hard put to find enough agents. The permanent intelligence staffs are frequently augmented by detectives and plainclothesmen—as Chicago's regular intelligence unit was doubled for the SDS convention in 1969. There are also many informer recruits and trainees who report to intelligence units but are not counted as employees or officers. The official membership of Detroit's intelligence unit, which was formed in 1961, grew by 1968 to seventy members. In 1968, Boston had forty agents, New York had at least sixty-eight on its intelligence staff (ninety as of 1970) and fifty-five more line agents planted undercover; Chicago had more than 500, Houston fourteen. The Los Angeles Police Department doubled its Intelligence Division personnel from eighty-four in 1969 to 167 in 1970.

Intelligence is not a wholly public function. Political surveillance has been routinely practiced by private detectives since the nineteenth century, when objections to a political police force left the Pinkerton and Burns agencies free to engage in these activities without official competition. Today the private agencies are an important channel for political intelligence. Often they recruit employees with access to official files from government intel-

ligence agencies and sell such information to private industry.[7]

Local and national intelligence agencies are beginning to coalesce into an "intelligence community." For example, the young demonstrators who came to Chicago in 1968 encountered red squad operatives from their home towns. The overheated reports of these visiting local agents led Mayor Daley's office to conclude that a plot to assassinate Johnson had been hatched. The urban agents cooperated with their federal counterparts, as well as with the Army and Navy secret operatives at the Chicago demonstrations. During the subsequent conspiracy trial no fewer than thirty of about forty substantive prosecution witnesses were police agents or infiltrators associated with governmental surveillance at various levels.

The FBI plays a central role in coordinating the intelligence system; it exchanges information with other agencies, performs investigative work for intelligence groups with limited jurisdiction, and trains intelligence agents for service in other agencies. Its intelligence techniques and political standards serve as a model for local operations. It compiles albums of photographs and files of activists which are transmitted to agencies throughout the United States.[8]

Congressional antisubversive committees have also expanded their intelligence activities beyond the passive compilation of dossiers available only to government investigative personnel. They now provide a forum for local intelligence agencies, publish dossiers, mug shots, and other photographs of subjects obtained by surveillance and supplied by police witnesses.[9] They also independently engage in intelligence activities.

■

The changing role of the police in carrying out surveillance was described a few years ago by Inspector Harry Fox of the Philadelphia police. In his Senate testimony, he said:

Police now have become "watchdogs" and "observers" of vocal, subversive and revolutionary minded people. This function has been institutionalized in Philadelphia in a "civil-disobedience unit" composed of selected and highly trained plainclothesmen. They cover all meetings, rallies, lectures, marches, sit-ins, laydowns, fasts, vigils, or any other type of demonstration that has ominous overtones. . . .

These officers know by sight the hard core men and women who lead and inspire demonstrations. They know their associates, family ties, techniques, and affiliations with organizations leaning toward Communism both on and off the Attorney General's list. They see them day in and day out recruiting, planning, carrying signs, and verbally assaulting the principles of democracy.

Yes, the police role has become one of . . . surveillance, taking photographs, identifying participants, and making records of the events. On this basis, local police are able to piece together this jigsaw puzzle and see the widespread activity of the hard core demonstrators and instigators.

This account naturally omits the harassing and "guerrilla warfare" aspects of police tactics. To the policeman, public protest is an unwelcome disruption of the tranquillity which he regards as natural and proper. His response to antiwar activities is particularly hostile because he sees himself as a beleaguered defender of "patriotic" values, which he tends to protect by abusing his power, harassing demonstrators, and intimidating suspects. His resentment and anger are provoked in the same way by the nonconformity and personal style of many young people, who are now the principal targets of heavy surveillance and who are constantly subjected to detention and arrest on flimsy charges.

Protest activities have inevitably served to draw the police into politics and to expand their intelligence functions. Especially ominous is the widening use of photographic surveillance by intelligence units. Police in communities throughout the country systematically photograph demonstrations, parades, confrontations, vigils, rallies, presentations of petitions to congressmen and senators, and related activities. The photographers attached to the Philadelphia intelligence unit, for example, cover more than a thousand demonstrations a year. Any "incident" considered "controversial" is a predictable subject for the police photographer. Protest demonstrations against the Vietnam war are automatically considered "controversial," but not those in favor. In the South, photographing integrationist protesters is given top priority.

Subjects are often photographed from as close as three to five feet. Sometimes police photographers openly ridicule the demonstrators. Children who accompany their parents are photographed as are casual bystanders and nonparticipants. To con-

vey and conceal photographic equipment, panel trucks are sometimes used, occasionally camouflaged to look like the equipment of a television station (referred to by veteran surveillance subjects as "WFBI"). Surveillance photographers acquire spurious press credentials; bona fide cameramen often moonlight as police or FBI informers.[10] Supplementary photographic data are occasionally obtained from cooperating newspaper and television stations.

Photographs are sometimes covertly taken by unobtrusive plainclothesmen when a "respectable" group is involved—for example, parents picketing a school. Usually, however, policemen, sometimes in uniform, do not bother to conceal their activities: they either man the cameras themselves or direct their aides by pointing out individuals or groups to be photographed. The deterrent effect of open photography is not lost on the police but is justified on the ground, among others, that it "cools" the "subversive agitator" and prevents potential lawlessness.[11]

Photographs of individuals not already known to the police are submitted to informers and undercover agents for identification. Sometimes tentative identifications are verified by automobile license numbers which the police systematically collect at meetings and rallies and in front of the houses of "known militants." Then they ask other agencies, urban, state, and federal, to help to identify the subjects.

Once the individual is identified, his name is entered in an index. The local intelligence unit then sets out to obtain information about the subject—solely on the basis of his or her attendance at a single "controversial" event—from other intelligence sources, state and federal. In addition, the contents of the file are passed on, as Captain Drake, Commander of the Intelligence Division of the New Orleans Police Department, has explained, to "every conceivable authority that might have an interest in causing any prosecution or further investigation of these persons."

■

Photography describes the subject. But other techniques must also be used to obtain political data. These include interrogation of associates, employers, landlords, etc., collection of data about financial resources, bank deposits and withdrawals, and about the subject's background. Where meetings are held publicly, whether indoors or out, the speeches are monitored by portable tape recorders, a practice which is common in large cities but which also is growing in smaller communities, especially in college towns.

Wiretapping and electronic bugging are also common, in spite of judicial restraints on their use.[12] Local police specialists use these devices not only for their own purposes but also on behalf of the FBI. The 1968 Crime Control Law has authorized electronic eavesdropping in certain criminal cases; twelve states have passed similar legislation, while six others are now considering it. A variety of electronic devices is now being offered by commercial supply houses to state and local police departments to implement this legislation. Once they become available for even limited purposes, it is extremely unlikely that they will not be used for political surveillance as well.

Still, personal surveillance is necessary in those areas where technology cannot—at present anyway —replace human beings. Thus infiltration of dissident groups by informers remains a common procedure. Ironically, the Warren Court's limitations on wiretapping and bugging have themselves led to a heavier reliance on informers as a substitute. Moreover, these limitations encourage the use of informers because they can supply "probable cause" of a crime and so justify a wiretap order.[13]

Informers are indispensable to political intelligence systems. Electronic eavesdropping and wiretapping are ill-suited to the slow pace, confusion, ambiguity, and factionalism of the dissenting political activities that are the targets of intelligence. Besides, wiretaps can be circumvented once the subject becomes aware of them. Indeed, nothing can quite take the place of the classic tool of intelligence, the informer. But in addition to the moral stigma attached to informing in Western culture,[14] informers have always been regarded anyway as unreliable and treacherous observers, reporters, and witnesses. Most of them become informers for money. Their income, tenure, and future usefulness depend on their capacity to produce material useful to the police.[15] Others are "hooked" because of previous involvements with the law, or are recruited for ideological reasons—either as police plants or as defectors.

Both the pressures and the inducements, along with the sense of guilt that requires the betrayer to find some justification for his betrayal, tend to produce tainted information. All too frequently it is inaccurate, highly selective, and based on sinister and unwarranted inferences. Where a literal version

of a target's utterances would seem innocent, the informer will insist on stressing the connotations; conversely, where the language is figurative or metaphysical the informer reports it as literally intended. Most important of all, he seizes on the transient fantasies of the powerless—rhetoric and images not intended to be acted upon—and transforms them into conspiracies whose purpose and commitment are wholly alien to their volatile and ambiguous context.

It need only be added that the hazards inherent in the testimony of political informers are especially great in conspiracy cases. The vague, inchoate character of the conspiracy charge and the atmosphere of plotting and hidden guilt which accompanies it make it a perfect foil for the undercover agent who surfaces on the witness stand, a hero returned from the dark wood.[16]

The informer is not only a reporter or an observer, but also an actor or participant, and he frequently transforms what might otherwise be idle talk or prophecy into action. Professor Zachariah Chaffee, Jr., once remarked, "The spy often passes over an almost imperceptible boundary into the **agent provocateur.**" The purpose of such provocations, as Allen Dulles wrote in **The Craft of Intelligence**, is to "provide the pretext for arresting any or all of [the group's] members. Since the agent report[s] to the police exactly when and where the action is going to take place, the police [have] no problems."

There are powerful reasons for viewing provocation as the handmaiden of infiltration, even when it is not part of a planned intelligence strategy. A merely passive, "cool" infiltrator-observer cannot hope to play more than a lowly "Jimmy Higgins" role in the target group, if he gains entry at all. In order to enhance his usefulness he must penetrate planning circles by becoming highly active. Moreover, the pressure to produce results in the form of concrete evidence of illegal activity often drives the infiltrator into provocative acts, regardless of the official cautionary advice which he may be given when he receives his assignment. Such advice is routinely conveyed by the agent's "handler" for the record, as a defense against a possible charge of entrapment.

Convincing evidence of provocation has emerged in a number of recent cases.[17] But the motives of the **agent provocateur** are frequently complex and difficult to reconstruct from the materials available. The most common **provocateur** is simply a professional police agent who coldly engineers a single provocative act designed to "set up" leaders for roundup and arrest.

Another type (of which Tommy the Traveler is an example) is the ultrarightist who becomes a spy in order to destroy the target group. He is often driven to act out his paranoid fantasies with bombs and guns when his delusions about the group's sinister goals fail to conform to reality.

On the other hand, as the FBI student informer William T. Divale has disclosed in his recently published confessions, **I Lived Inside the Campus Revolution**, a planted informer may come to share the values of his victims, with the result that his newly acquired convictions carry him far beyond the call of duty—a form of conversion characteristic of infiltrators of black and youth groups. The infiltrator's secret knowledge that he alone in the group is immune from accountability for his acts dissolves all restraints on his zeal. He does, of course, take the risk of exposure and punitive reprisal, but this possibility itself encourages him to disarm suspicion by acting as a supermilitant. This almost schizoid quality of the behavior of informers seems inherent in political surveillance and has recurred throughout its history.

Many student informers who have surfaced or recanted have been revealed as operating for two intelligence agencies at the same time—usually a local and a federal one. Several informers commonly penetrate a single organization; indeed this is prescribed as sound intelligence practice, because each surveillance report can cross-check the others.[18] Attempts to recruit young leftists as police spies have also recently become common: For example, in the fall of 1969, young volunteers for the New Mobilization Committee to End the War in Vietnam were solicited to become informers by FBI agents. "Will you work for us?" they were asked as they entered the elevator on their way to the Committee's office. The FBI has recently acquired official jurisdiction on college campuses, which will result in even more extensive subsidy of student informers.

As the FBI Media documents make clear, Bureau agents now have formal authority from Washington to recruit informers as young as eighteen, including those attending two-year junior and community colleges. One of these documents quoted earlier appears below in full:

NEW LEFT NOTES—PHILADELPHIA

9/16/70
Edition #1

This newsletter will be produced at irregular intervals as needed to keep those persons dealing with New Left problems up to date in an informal way. It is not a serial and is considered an informal routing slip. It should be given the security afforded a Bureau serial, classified confidential, but may be destroyed when original purpose is served.

The New Left conference at SOG 9/10-11/70 produced some comments:

In disseminating reports recommending for the SI it is preferable to designate and disseminate to Secret Service immediately and put the FD-376 (the buck slip to Secret Service) on the second Bureau copy.

There was a pretty general consensus that more interviews with these subjects and hangers-on are in order for plenty of reasons, chief of which are it will enhance the paranoia endemic in these circles and will further serve to get the point across there is an FBI Agent behind every mailbox. In addition, some will be overcome by the overwhelming personalities of the contacting agent and volunteer to tell all—perhaps on a continuing basis. The Director has okayed PSI's and SI's age 18 to 21. We have been blocked off from this critical age group in the past. Let us take advantage of this opportunity.

In payments to informants, if the **total** of services and expenses to an informant is less than $300 in a lump sum payment or per month, our request for such payment is handled within division 5. If the lump sum payment or monthly authorization is $300 or more, it must be approached on a much higher level. **Note:** If an informant is to travel outside our division and we initially go in and request expense payment of less than $300, it can be handled simply while the services payment can be requested later based on what he has produced.

J. Oconnor [sic]

[From the FBI Media documents]

This authorization of September, 1970, made official a practice which long preceded the issuance of the directive but was consistently denied for public relations reasons. In fact, J. Edgar Hoover repeated this denial as recently as February of this year.

Moreover, local police—especially in university communities—have lately been given special funds to hire secret informers. For this purpose at least one state, Wisconsin, has made available the sum of $10,000.[19]

■

In the past the police agencies (whether federal or local) preferred to act as the informer's "handler," "controller," or "contact." Police officers themselves only rarely resorted to impersonation, dissembling loyalties, the fabrication of false cover identities—techniques made familiar by foreign intelligence practice and regarded as abhorrent to our traditions. It was one thing to hire an agent as an independent contractor to do the dirty work of political snooping, but quite another for a public servant to do it himself.

Today, however, the police themselves often go underground. In New Orleans an intelligence division officer gained access to the Black Panther headquarters by impersonating a priest. At least six agents of New York's Special Service Division infiltrated the Black Panthers, and appeared as witnesses in their current trial.

Three members of Chicago's intelligence unit infiltrated the Chicago Peace Council. One of them, in order to enhance his credibility, exposed another to Council leaders as a policeman. According to Karl Meyer, the Council's chairman, "At our meetings they invariably took the most militant positions, trying to provoke the movement from its nonviolent force to the wildest kind of ventures." "They were," he concluded, "about our most active members." The Peace Council became suspicious of possible spies when it and other Chicago groups—the Latin American Defense Organization, Women Strike for Peace, the Fellowship of Reconciliation—suffered a number of burglaries of files and records. (Office machines and small amounts of money were also stolen but subsequently returned.)

Agents of the Chicago intelligence unit are scattered throughout Illinois, and sometimes do not report to their superiors for days or even months. Their real identities are concealed even from their colleagues. Their methods include disguises, wiretapping, and the creation of elaborate "covers," such as dummy businesses. In numerous cities, including San Diego, Houston, Oakland, Los Angeles, New Orleans, and Columbus, the agent-informer is becoming a familiar phenomenon. We are moving toward the classic European model of political infiltration, in which the planted police agent lives a double life for years if necessary, clandestinely reporting to his superiors. This kind of intelligence requires skill and training; so one should not be surprised to see the emergence of schools of instruction in the deceptive arts, similar to those run by the CIA for indoctrination in foreign intelligence and guerrilla activity.

■

At an ever increasing rate the activities of antiwar, antiestablishment, civil rights, black militant, student, and youth groups are being recorded and compiled. Lists and dossiers are coded, computerized, stored, and made accessible to all branches of the intelligence network. Here is how Lt. George Fencl, head of Philadelphia's civil disobedience unit, describes its filing system:

> We've been acquainted with quite a number of people throughout the years we've been handling demonstrations. We have made a record of every demonstration that we've handled in the city of Philadelphia and reduced this to writing, first by report and then taking out the names of persons connected with the different movements.
>
> We have some 18,000 names and we've made what we call an alphabetical file. We make a 5 x 8 card on each demonstrator that we know the name and so forth that we handle. This card shows such information as the name, address, picture if possible, and a little rundown on the person . . . which group he pickets with and so forth.
>
> Also on the back of the card, we show the different demonstrations, the date, time and location and the groups that the person picketed with. We have some 600 different organizations that we've encountered in the Philadelphia area.

This new intelligence system concentrates more on compiling names than on the content of speeches or other activities. For example, a report submitted to the Detroit Criminal Investigation Bureau by two undercover agents reads as follows:

> At 8:00 P.M. on Thursday, November 11, 1965, the WEST CENTRAL ORGANIZA- TION held a special meeting which was com- prised primarily of executives, delegates and clergy. The meeting was called for a briefing by MR. SAUL ALINSKY of the INDUS- TRIAL AREAS FOUNDATION, Chicago, Illi- nois, who was in the Detroit area on November 10 and 11, 1965. Thirty-seven persons at- tended this meeting.
>
> The following persons were identified as be- ing in attendance at the above meeting, identi- fications being made by surveilling officers as well as by Confidential Informant 059. [A list of twenty-one names follows.]
>
> The following vehicles were observed parked in the immediate vicinity of 3535 Grand River, occupants entering same. [There follows a list of eleven automobiles together with the names and addresses of eleven indi- viduals who are presumably the title regis- trants.]

There is nothing in the report which suggests the reason for the surveillance or what took place at the meeting.

Experience with other official record systems suggests that it is only a matter of time before the intelligence now being collected by thousands of federal and local agencies will be codified and made accessible on a broad scale. Indeed, we are not far away from a computerized nationwide system of transmittal and storage.

■

While the recent bombings and the hunt for fugitives have supplied justification for some sur- veillance practices, the emerging system as a whole is oriented toward the future and is justified as pre- ventive: the security of the nation against future overthrow is said to require the present frenzy of surveillance. In cases where such an argument makes no sense, surveillance is justified on grounds that it is necessary to prevent local violence and disorder in the future.

Political intelligence indiscriminately sweeps into its net the mild dissenters along with those drawn to violence; when the national security is at

stake, so the argument runs, it is folly to take risks. The quarry is pursued long before expressions or associations of radicals are likely to incubate into violent or revolutionary acts. The fear of waiting "until it is too late" conditions the intelligence mind to suspect all forms of dissent as signs of po- tential "subversion."[20]

Thus peaceful, moderate, lawful organizations —from the NAACP to the Fellowship for Recon- ciliation—become intelligence targets on the theory that they are linked to communism or subver- sion.[21] This lack of selectivity, a familiar phenom- enon to students of intelligence, has now been abundantly documented by the Senate testimony of former Army Intelligence agents and the recent Media documents.

To equate dissent with subversion, as intelli- gence officials do, is to deny that the demand for change is based on real social, economic, or politi- cal conditions. A familiar example of this assump- tion is the almost paranoid obsession with the "agi- tator." Intelligence proceeds on the assumption that most people are reasonably contented but are incited or misled by an "agitator," a figure who typically comes from "outside" to stir up trouble. The task is to track down this sinister individual and bring him to account; all will then be well again.

Since the agitator is elusive and clever, one never knows who he will turn out to be or where he will show his hand. Indeed, the striking charac- teristic of the agitator, according to the rhetoric and testimony of the intelligence people, is not his views nor his actions but his persistence. A subject who keeps coming to meetings or rallies or is re- peatedly involved in "incidents" is soon marked as an agitator[22] (more sophisticated terms: "mili- tant," "activist," sometimes preceded by "hard core").

The outside agitator is a descendent of the "foreign agitator" or the "agent of a foreign power," as he came to be called. The thesis that domestic radicals are either tools or dupes of for- eign manipulation provides intelligence agencies with their most effective way of exploiting popu- lar fears, one which is also cherished by legislators. All movements on the left—and especially groups such as the Panthers—have come under attack as agents for foreign powers.[23]

Such ideological stereotypes give intelligence a powerful bias against movements of protest from the center leftward. To be sure, a handful of ultra- rightist groups such as the Klan and the Minutemen are also under surveillance, but for political intelligence, the presumption of innocence is largely confined to the defenders of the status quo. For individuals and groups committed to social or political protest, the presumption is reversed:[24] Peaceful nonviolent activity must be constantly scrutinized because it may turn out to be a vital clue to a vast subversive conspiracy.

■

While intelligence is developing new clandestine activities, it is also becoming highly visible. American political activity is plagued by an intelligence "presence" which demoralizes, intimidates, and frightens many of its targets—and is intended to do so. And it is not merely a "presence." A variety of sanctions are improvised to punish politically objectionable subjects. These include "information management" (such as inclusion on the "ten most wanted" list), press leaks, harassment, prosecution on drug charges, legislative inquisition, physical violence, the vandalizing of cars, blacklisting, the refusal to give police protection when needed, illegal searches and raids on pretexts.

One prevailing assumption of intelligence officers is that "subversion" is financed and supported by respectable "front" institutions (churches, foundations, and universities, for example) and individuals (such as lawyers). Special pressures are brought by intelligence agencies to cut off such suspected subsidies—for example, J. Edgar Hoover's attacks on white contributors to Black Panther defense funds and the listing by the House Internal Security Committee of honoraria paid to liberal and radical campus speakers.

Intelligence is thus becoming an end in itself, rather than an investigative means—a transformation all too clearly reflected in the encouragement of FBI agents to confront subjects in order to "enhance" their "paranoia," as one of the Media documents states. But its claim to be conducting a never-ending investigation into some future unspecified threat to the national security is consistently used to legitimize its expansion. Few want to shackle the police in their hunt for wrongdoers, especially those who threaten the safety of the Republic. Why should one question a "mere" investigation, even if tons of constitutional ore may have to be excavated in order to find a single subversive nugget?

What are the standards that intelligence agencies must follow for selecting subjects of surveillance, for the techniques they use or the data they develop? In fact, there are no effective standards, and there are no effective authorities in this country to insist on such standards. Every surveillance unit claimes its own authority to deal with "subversion" or "subversive activities," terms which mean whatever the agency wants them to mean. The head of the Chicago intelligence unit, Lt. Joseph Healy, summed up the matter when he testified at the conspiracy trial that his squad maintained surveillance over "any organization that could create problems for the city or the country." That Army Intelligence took the same view is shown by recent disclosures that it was snooping into a virtually unlimited range of civilian activity.

In most cases, the jurisdiction to engage in political intelligence activities is wholly improvised. This is true not merely of many local agencies but of the FBI itself. The authority the FBI claims it has to stalk nonconformists can be justified neither by its law enforcement powers nor by its domestic spy-catching jurisdiction. The latter, in fact, is based on an obscure 1939 directive which J. Edgar Hoover has interpreted as conferring upon the FBI the power, in his words, "to identify individuals working against the United States, determine their objectives and nullify their effectiveness." Who are these "individuals"? Those whose activities involve "subversion and related internal security problems."

The unlimited scope of their jurisdiction and their virtual autonomy encourage intelligence institutions to consolidate and expand. Intelligence thus constantly enlarges its operations by exaggerating the numbers, power, and intentions of the subversive enemy.[25]

Ironically, this exaggeration is further stimulated by the need to develop some plausible political and constitutional justification for violating democratic rights. Intelligence not only continually expands the boundaries of subversion in its operations, but inevitably generates a stream of fearmongering propaganda in its evaluation of intelligence data. A troubled period such as the present intensifies this process: the number of surveillance subjects increases greatly as the intelligence agencies circulate propaganda dramatizing their life-and-death struggle with subversion.

■   ■

The link between drug use and political radicalism has also served to expand the scope of political surveillance. In the past, narcotics law enforcement and the policing of political crimes have drawn on similar surveillance techniques. This was so because both involve conduct to which the parties consent and both frequently leave little proof that any crime was committed. Today the "nark" and undercover intelligence operatives are frequently in pursuit of the same prey. The same agents sometimes function in both areas and political militancy is a common cover for the "nark," especially on college campuses.

Similarly, students under surveillance for drug use are frequently selected for their political nonconformity, a link manifest in the background of both the Kent State and Hobart College cases, as well as in the conviction of Dr. Leslie Fiedler of the State University of New York at Buffalo for maintaining premises where marijuana was used. The pot bust has become a punitive sanction against political dissent and the threat of prosecution is a favorite method of "hooking" student informers. Lee Otis Johnson, former head of Houston's Student Non-Violent Coordinating Committee, is now serving a thirty-year jail term for the sale of a single marijuana cigarette to a Houston undercover policeman.

■

Many young radicals are finding ways of evading undercover surveillance of their political activities. Intelligence inevitably generates countermeasures ("security"), driving its targets into protective secrecy and sometimes underground even though they are usually engaged in legal protest. Such furtiveness is then cited as further proof of subversion and conspiracy ("What have they got to hide?") and reinforces the justification for surveillance.

Radicals in the past few years have tried to protect themselves by rigorously checking the backgrounds of possible infiltrators, isolating a suspected agent or feeding him bogus information, giving him test assignments, banning the use of drugs, cars, and private phones, and forming affinity groups. The radicals themselves sometimes use disguises and false names. The ultimate response to intelligence is counterintelligence, including the penetration of intelligence institutions to thwart their effectiveness. Some groups are beginning to boast about their double agents, counter-spies, and

pipelines to police sources. One Berkeley police officer has already complained (and not very convincingly): "I'm afraid they do a better job spying on us than we do on them."

The pilferage and circulation of the Media FBI documents seem to suggest an escalation in counterintelligence tactics. The group responsible for the action has already announced, as a follow-up measure, a planned exposure of a "first group" of FBI informers whose names appear in as yet unreleased stolen documents. This listing of a "first group" is presumably to be followed by publication of lists of others.

Such a tactic will not only create a painful dilemma for present Philadelphia area informers but may vastly complicate the FBI's problems in future recruitment. Because political spies are the keystone of the entire federal political intelligence system, the FBI goes to extraordinary lengths to shield their identities and stresses these protective practices as an inducement for recruits. A breach in the FBI security system may well scare off potential informers not only in the Philadelphia area, but everywhere—who knows where the Citizens' Commission will strike next? The increased risk is bound to boost the price of the informers' services. At the very least, it will "enhance" among the hunters the same "paranoia" now "endemic" among the hunted.

■

Our political intelligence apparatus has begun to exert a dangerous influence on the exercise of political power. The attempt by the Los Angeles Chamber of Commerce to use intelligence data to discredit and destroy a group of Los Angeles poverty agencies is a dramatic example of a spreading phenomenon. A candidate for public office learns that he has been made an intelligence target by orders of his opponent, the incumbent. A lawyer for a victim of police brutality is threatened with being disbarred as a "subversive" because of leaks in the police department's intelligence files.

Mayor Alioto of San Francisco discovers that unevaluated intelligence files compiled by federal and urban agencies, full of smears and unverified rumors, are opened up to the press for an article which threatens his political ruin.[26] A check of the California Un-American Activities Committee files discloses dossiers on many legislators, including the Senate president, with notations reflecting intensive surveillance. A courageous Chicago newsman, Ron Dorfman, who has vigorously attacked intelligence practices in that city, is confronted with a detailed dossier on himself in a session with the Illinois Crime Commission.

It is chilling enough to learn that in this country literally millions of people are systematically suffering invasions of privacy, and what is worse, are forced to exercise their rights of free expression and assembly under the fear of surveillance. But when a secret political police begins to play an important role in political decisions and campaigns, the democratic process is in grave danger.

Nor is there much comfort in the notion that our current intelligence mania is only a transient response to a particular emergency. History—and for that matter the annals of J. Edgar Hoover's FBI —painfully teaches that once a political intelligence system takes root, it is almost impossible to eradicate it. Fear and blackmail ensure its autonomy and self-perpetuation. How many of us can be expected to challenge a system which has such power to do injury to its critics?[27]

Americans will now have to answer the question whether the risks that we face—and some of them are real enough—outweigh the danger of a national secret police. One can hardly question the right of the government to inform itself of potential crimes and acts of violence. The resort to bombing as a political tactic obviously creates a justification for intelligence to forestall such practices. But the evolving intelligence system I have been describing clearly exceeds these limited ends. Before it is too late we must take a cold look at our entire political intelligence system: not to determine whether one aspect or another is repressive—whether, for example, it is possible to keep a dossier confidential—but to decide whether internal political intelligence as an institution, divorced from law enforcement, is consistent with the way we have agreed to govern ourselves and to live politically.

Eighteen cases have now been filed throughout the country, with American Civil Liberties Union support, to challenge various surveillance and filing practices by police agencies as violating constitutional rights of free expression, assembly, privacy, and the protection against unreasonable search and seizure. The constitutional issues imbedded in these cases will undoubtedly be presented ultimately to the Supreme Court. These challenges are important if for no other reason than that they will drag undercover surveillance out of the shadows.

But the political intelligence system cannot be controlled by piecemeal attacks in the courts. If our past experience is a guide, even successful litigation may leave unchecked the particular abuses involved by limiting surveillance in ways that are readily ignored or circumvented by a bureaucracy which is a law unto itself.

Political intelligence is both a symbol of a dying politics and the means of keeping it alive through powerful myths and constraints. A truly effective attack on the evils of intelligence cannot be mounted apart from the political process. A legislative investigation, more sharply focused and more searching than Senator Ervin's investigation, is vital in order to scour this area as thoroughly as Senator LaFollette's investigation scoured labor espionage in the thirties. Such a probe could develop a fuller understanding of political intelligence and might lay the basis for dismantling a system which, if it is allowed to grow, may choke all possibility of real change in this country. But it is illusory to talk of an effective investigative and statutory attack on the powerful intelligence system at present. The elimination of the evils of political surveillance and dossiers is yet another reason why we need a new politics.

NOTES

1. The term "intelligence" as used in this article is adapted from foreign intelligence usage and practice. It describes a body of techniques for collecting political information about a "subject" (physical surveillance, photography, electronic eavesdropping, informers—planted or recruited "in place"—and other deceptive or clandestine practices), the product of these activities (files and dossiers), and a set of political assumptions (the intelligence mind).

2. This article is a distillation of verified materials, many of them documentary, drawn from the files of the ACLU political surveillance project and based on the following sources: court proceedings; legislative and administrative hearings; reports by informers and police agents to intelligence units; intelligence evaluations and summaries by intelligence staff and command personnel; interviews and correspondence with subjects, informers, and intelligence officers; the files of lawyers and civil liberties groups; TV scripts, police journals and manuals, graduate theses, newspaper and magazine articles; and the responses to a detailed questionnaire.

3. To hasten the arrival of this brave new world, federal funds allocated by the Law Enforcement Assistance Administration are being channeled to state and local police units to subsidize such surveillance gear as twenty-four hour infrared lens closed circuit TV cameras which are being attached to telephone poles on the streets of American cities. Sensors and other electronic gadgetry developed for the military in Indochina are being adapted for internal intelligence use and tested on an experimental basis in a number of cities.

4. It was on the basis of information supplied by this unit that Attorney General Mitchell was informed in a confidential memorandum that the likelihood of violence during the November, 1969, moratorium was "extremely high . . . beyond the violence which was witnessed during the Pentagon demonstration in October, 1967, the Democratic National Convention in Chicago, in August, 1968, and the demonstration in Chicago on October 11th conducted by the Students for a Democratic Society." This prophecy turned out to be unfounded.

5. Police departments have in recent years been loaded with recommendations from commissions and professional groups to develop intelligence techniques as a means of curbing crime—especially organized crime. But the intelligence units which have come into being as a result have been converted into instruments for political surveillance—especially of the ghetto.

The day and night surveillance of blacks, as a group, by these newly constituted units is considered self-justifying, very much like the surveillance of aliens in the twenties. This is true even of small and medium-sized cities, which are rife with mounting crime and corruption, but proud of their "mod squads" and the increasing number of intelligence "inputs" to the ghetto, the "long-hair" community, and the campus.

As for the large cities, there are, according to Illinois Police Superintendent James T. McGuire, more police in the Chicago area on political intelligence assignments than are engaged in fighting organized crime. The same is true in Philadelphia.

6. The campus has become the theater of intensive intelligence activities by undercover urban police agents and paid informers. A recent investigation by the Committee on Academic Freedom of the University of California, Los Angeles Division, Academic Senate, concludes that "there are undercover activities by governmental agencies on campus, that some of these activities are conducted by operatives of the Los Angeles Police Department and that it is unclear what other agencies, if any, are involved."

7. A Dayton, Ohio, firm which calls itself Agitator Detection, Inc., advertises a "sure-fire method for keeping radical America out of work": "We have," the company boasts, "complete computerized files on every known American dissident. . . . And all 160 million of their friends, relatives and fellow travelers."

A scattering of right-wing organizations and publications across the country also has access to intelligence data. For example, the Church League of America, headed by Edgar Bundy, boasts of its over 7 million cross-indexed files of political suspects, its "working relationships" with "leading law enforcement agencies," and its cooperation with undercover agents.

These organizations are prized by intelligence agencies because they share the basic intelligence assumption that the country is in the grip of a widespread subversive conspiracy. Intelligence agents and informers use the platform and publications of the far right to document this thesis with "inside" information.

8. The FBI circulates through its own internal intelligence channels a document known as the "agitator index," which is made available to local agencies. In the spring and summer of 1968 the Washington field office of the FBI compiled an elaborate collection of dossiers and photographs for use in connection with the Resurrection City demonstration.

That material was thereafter augmented and organized into an album; multiple copies were made and transmitted to the Chicago police for use in dealing with protest activity around the Democratic convention. The FBI agent who was responsible for the idea received a special commendation. Such albums of "known leftists" are now widely circulated.

9. In a hearing last year, Chief Counsel Sourwine of the Senate Internal Security Subcommittee described the subcommittee's mission in these words:

"We seek information with respect to the persons who head these subversive organizations and are active in them and who participate in them, the persons who support them: about the interconnections, the channels of authority, and the sources of funds.

"We are asking police departments from all across the country to sift their records and bring these facts here for the committee. . . . By gathering all of the available information from leading police departments throughout the country, the committee hopes to be able eventually to present a picture. We are charting the organizations in each area, the persons in each area who are connected . . . and we hope when we finish we will have a picture which will show just what this country is up against."

The appendix to the volume from which this is quoted contains a series of documents from the intelligence files of the Flint, Michigan, Police Department including a "steno pad" which "was owned by one of the top members of the SDS," taken from a car in a raid which had no justifiable basis.

10. In view of the overwhelming need for identification it is hardly surprising that informers with photographic skills are paid a bonus. Louis Salzberg, a New York photographer, received about $10,000 in the two years he served as an FBI informer. He used this money to finance a studio which sold pictures to Left publications, the negatives of which were turned over to the FBI. He surfaced at the Chicago conspiracy trial and subsequently testified before the House Internal Security Committee which was also supplied with the negatives as well as with documents and correspondence taken by Salzberg from the files of the Veterans for Peace and the Fifth Avenue Peace Parade Committee.

11. The importance of photography in the new intelligence scene was amusingly demonstrated during the Chicago conspiracy trial. By court order, to safeguard the integrity of the judicial process, photographers were excluded from the federal courthouse during the trial. But this prohibition unwittingly closed a valuable surveillance channel and the order was amended to permit intelligence photographers to continue to ply their trade.

12. Attorney General Mitchell has asserted an inherent power flowing from executive responsibility for the national security (a term of enormous looseness) to disregard constitutional restraints in this area whenever, in his unreviewable discretion, an individual may be seeking "to attack and subvert the government by unlawful means." And even before the Mitchell regime, wiretapping and bugging were systematically used by the FBI in cases (such as those of Martin Luther King, Jr., and Elijah Muhammad) not even remotely linked to national security.

13. For example, the primary basis for successful application for, and repeated renewals of, wiretap authorization orders against a group of New York City Panthers consisted of an account by an informer of a conspiracy by

the Panthers to engage in the ambush and murder of policemen—a story admittedly invented by the informer, one
Shaun Dubonnet, to secure leniency in a criminal case,
earn a little money, and further his career as a double
agent. Neither Dubonnet's substantial prior criminal record—including two convictions for impersonation—nor
his repeated hospitalization for mental illness served to
impair his credibility with the police.

The tips and reports of informers, frequently fabri-
cated, provide pretexts for raids. One example of many
that could be cited is the alleged tip by the undercover
agent to the FBI that the Chicago Black Panthers had
assembled an arsenal of guns. This led to a predawn raid
in which Fred Hampton and Mark Clark were killed. Only
a few guns were found.

14. Judge Anderson tersely summed up the matter
when he wrote in 1920 in the case of Colyer v. Skeffing-
ton, "A right-minded man refuses such a job."

15. According to information from an FBI source,
"informants" (as the FBI prefers to call them; "informers" is a subversive usage) submit vast quantities of data of
a highly inflammatory character. The "contact" does not
challenge it because he is afraid to lose the informant.
Frequently he ignores this suspect material in his own reports either because he is convinced that it is incredible
or that the informant would have to surface, to testify, if
it became the basis for a criminal charge. This would again
result in losing the informant and require the "contact"
to recruit a replacement. It is infinitely preferable, I was
told, to cover up for an informant even if his reports are
wholly false than to be forced to go to the trouble of finding a replacement.

16. Conspiracy is a classic vehicle for the political informer for another reason. Under conspiracy law, evidence of acts and statements of co-conspirators to bring
about the purposes of the conspiracy agreement are ad-
missible against all the co-conspirators even though, without the agreement (frequently proved by flimsy and
remote evidence), it would be incompetent and inadmis-
sible as hearsay.

The informer's tale in this way becomes binding on
all of the alleged co-conspirators including individuals he
has never seen or met. The conspiracy charge thus econo-
mizes on the number of informer witnesses needed to
make a case. This is a highly important consideration to
intelligence agencies, which are traditionally reluctant to
surface informers.

The general question of the reliability of informer
witnesses as well as their role in conspiracy cases is dramatized by the current conspiracy indictment of the Berri-
gans, which is based on evidence supplied by a prison
informer, Boyd Douglas, Jr., who also inspired and arranged for a number of the "overt acts," allegedly in
furtherance of the "conspiracy."

17. Thomas Tongyai (Tommy the Traveler), an undercover agent on the campus of Hobart College (an
Episcopalian school with a tradition of nonviolence),
was charged by students with preaching revolution, using
violent rhetoric to gain converts, and demonstrating the
M1 carbine and the construction of various types of
bombs. He did not deny these allegations but explained,
"The best cover for an undercover agent who wanted to
get into the campus was portraying the part of a radical
extremist which I did."

According to Alabama Civil Liberties Union lawyers,

in May of 1970 a student infiltrator for the FBI and the
Tuscaloosa police on the University of Alabama campus,
Charles Grimm, Jr., committed arson and incited acts of
violence, which were then used as a reason for declaring a
campus protest meeting an unlawful assembly, a ruling
which resulted in criminal charges against 150 students.
One of the attorneys contended that the agent had admitted the violent acts to him and that the FBI and local
police had spirited the agent away to make him unavailable in the court cases.

William Frapolly, a Chicago police spy at Northeastern Illinois State College, was the leader of an SDS sit-in
and participated in a Weatherman action which culmi-
nated in throwing the institution's president off a stage,
conduct which led to his expulsion for two semesters. As
the only Weatherman SDS representative on Northeastern's campus, Frapolly actively recruited young students
to join the SDS Weatherman faction and to participate in
the Weatherman-sponsored "Days of Rage" in Chicago in
the fall of 1969. He surfaced as a prosecution witness in
the Chicago conspiracy trial, where he conceded on the
witness stand that during convention week he proposed a
number of schemes for sabotaging public facilities and
military vehicles, although his assigned duties as a mar-
shal were to maintain order.

There are half a dozen comparable cases. The UCLA
Academic Freedom Committee report which I have already cited states that its probe revealed suggestive evidence of "the presence of undercover agents as agents pro-
vocateurs, engaging in or precipitating the behavior they
are charged with suppressing."

18. There is no optimal number of infiltrators. An
FBI agent whom I recently interviewed said that at a
Washington Peace Mobilization meeting in 1969, of the
thirty-two individuals present, nine were undercover
agents. The number of informers an FBI agent can recruit
is limited only by his budget for this purpose. An informer
is first used ad hoc and is paid a small stipend. He is
known in the Bureau's records as a potential security informant (PSI) or a potential racial informant (PRI). When
he proves his worth he becomes a "reliable informant,"
acquires a file, cover name, and is paid a fixed salary
(sometimes disguised or augmented as "expenses"), which
is increased from time to time as his usefulness grows.

19. Some students are paid a fixed stipend but the
practice is growing, especially in urban intelligence units,
of paying them for each item of information. Houston
pays them from $5 to $400, depending on the value of
the information.

20. Or, in the talismanic intelligence usage, "threats
to the national security."

21. The informer's supermilitance in such groups,
his proclaimed impatience with the slow pace of his associates, clothe him with the requisite credibility when he
seeks ultimate entry into the more inaccessible organizations, in spite of his possible differences in social class and
personal style.

22. The special loathing with which grass-roots intelligence functionaries perceive the "agitator" is expressively
conveyed in Congressional testimony presented in October, 1970, by Michael A. Amico, sheriff of Erie County,
New York, who has organized an elaborate informer and
surveillance system in the Buffalo area. Referring to the
target groups under surveillance, he testified:

"Many of these organizations start their meetings

clandestinely by burning the American flag before they go into their rituals. It is difficult to get young undercover agents to remain disciplined to withstand, if you know the reaction, what does happen upon the burning of the flag. These are the rituals and different practices and, as said by the undercover man, orgasms are obtained by the different activities that follow because of the burning of the flag."

23. Recently declassified Army Intelligence documents (Annex B—Intelligence—to the Department of the Army Civil Disturbance Plan and Department of the Army Civil Disturbance Information Collection Plan), the most revealing intelligence material in the literature, suggest that peace and antidraft movements are foreign-directed because "they are supporting the stated objectives of foreign elements which are detrimental to the USA."

24. It is hardly surprising that intelligence is most at home with noncrimes such as "subversion" or inchoate crimes such as conspiracy in which innocent conduct is treated as criminal because it is claimed to be enmeshed in an illegal agreement and performed with evil intent. The affinity of the intelligence mind for the conspiracy offense can be illustrated by the testimony of Detective Sergeant John Ungvary, head of the Cleveland intelligence squad, before a Senate committee. He urged that "if we had a law whereby we can charge all of them [black nationalists] as participants or conspirators . . . it would be far better than waiting for an overt act."

25. The technique of broadening the boundaries of subversion has been developed and refined by the Congressional antisubversive committees; first, by the application of notions of vicarious, imputed, and derived guilt; second, by a process of cross-fertilization which proscribes an organization through the individuals associated with it and the individuals through their relationship to the organization; third, by increasing the number of condemned organizations through their links to one another; fourth, by treating subversion as permanent, irreversible, and even hereditary, with the result that a dossier, no matter how old, never loses its importance nor a subject his "interest."

This technique has been ingeniously applied in a remarkable document, A Report on the SDS Riots, October 8-11, 1969, issued by the Illinois Crime Investigating Commission, April, 1970, and reprinted in June, 1970, by the Senate Internal Security Subcommittee. Ostensibly concerned with the Weatherman demonstration ("Days of Rage"), this 400-page report is a virtual encyclopedia of militant radicalism among youth, replete with dossiers, photographs, personal letters, diaries, and documents relating not merely to the SDS figures with whom it purports to be primarily concerned, but to a host of other individuals and organizations about whom the Commission had collected intelligence information and whom it linked in the most tortured fashion to the subject matter of the Commission's report. This information, much of it highly inaccurate, was published purely for the purpose of punitive exposure of intelligence targets.

26. The mayor's charges against federal agencies have not been denied. The Los Angeles Police Department has admitted supplying confidential files to the writer of the article. The coordinator of intelligence, Sergeant George Bell, stated: "I would pull the index cards and let him go over the resumés, and some of them he asked to see the copy [of the file itself]."

27. Political files and dossiers give bureaucratic continuity to intelligence agencies and are a powerful reason for their survival in the face of the most hostile attack. When intelligence spokesmen cry, "What will happen to these valuable files which alone stand between us and a Commie takeover?" critics are usually silenced. After a motion was carried in January, 1945, to terminate the House Committee on Un-American Activities, the House reversed itself on the pleas of Congressman Rankin that "these valuable records that probably involve the fate of the Nation, the safety of the American people, would be dissipated—I want to see that these papers are kept; that is the one thing I am striving for."

the educational establishment: the precollege scenario

Fear, boredom, resistance—they all go to make what we call
stupid children. To a very great degree, school is a place
where children learn to be stupid.

John Holt, 1964

John Holt's indictment of today's American schools is echoed by many thoughtful
authorities who have examined America's public schools and found them wanting. Their
conclusions are not to be dismissed lightly; if their criticism is valid, it is crucial that we
reevaluate the missions and the methods of our educational establishment. As perhaps
never before, the quality of a nation's schools—particularly a nation that relies on mass
education—is intimately linked with that nation's material welfare and the quality of its
life.

There is no denying the fundamental role played by schools in a mass, postindustrial
society. Edgar Friedenberg, in the selection reprinted here, puts the matter bluntly: "The
central function of education in a complex society is the allocation of the various credentials that define the status of the bearer and the range of social roles that he may be permitted to fill." If, moreover, that society is essentially technological, bureaucratic, centralized, and hierarchical—if it demands workers who will fit into its occupational
structure like so many pegs into so many holes—then the odds are overwhelming that its
schools will fashion students to fulfill such needs. Conformity—not autonomy or self-fulfillment or creativity or discovery—becomes the overriding goal of the school system.

Small wonder, then, that Peter Marin's proposal that we start again from scratch to
rethink our notions of education and childhood strikes a respondent chord among many
students of the American educational system. In a related argument Paul Goodman urges
that American education somehow free itself from those bureaucratic restraints that
effectively cripple it; we must, he says, dismantle our whole school system and rebuild it
anew on the basis of free choice. Freedom of choice is central, Ronald and Beatrice Gross
contend, "because it is the necessary condition of finding the way to visible teaching and
learning. Breaking out of the constraints and compulsions of the surrounding culture and
society, of the hierarchical and authoritarian structure of educational institutions, of
obsolete attitudes toward children—these are necessary preconditions to basic change."

Many students of America's schools are demanding that we reexamine a number of
basic postulates that we have come to take for granted. Gross and Gross are more explicit.
They insist that we must ask such fundamental questions as these: "Is formal education
necessary or desirable? Should there be schools? Should education be compulsory? Should

teachers and school administrators run the schools? Should there **be** a curriculum? Nor can we stop here, for as the selection by Arthur Pearl makes clear, if we have fallen woefully short in educating middle-class Americans, we have failed altogether in the schooling we provide for the children of the impoverished. The articles by Friedenberg and Harold Taylor raise questions about the quality of America's elementary schools and high schools that will surely give serious pause to those who have held the uncritical assumption that "all's well" in the world's most costly public school system.

chapter 39
educational change: why –how –for whom
arthur pearl

WHY THE POOR AND DISADVANTAGED DON'T LEARN: TWO THEORIES

Current theory underlying most compensatory programs set up to help disadvantaged children assumes that their learning difficulties result from lack of basic preparation—that is, they are inadequately socialized, haven't sufficient male figures in their lives, have no books in their homes, can't delay gratification, suffer from accumulated environmental and cultural deficits, etc., etc. Therefore, teachers believe their primary role in working with these children is to "repair" them and deal with their handicaps. Programs are based on the premise that poor children are out of step and need reshaping. On the basis of such orientation, programs are generated that reinforce the inequality of education and the humiliation of the children.

As a working premise, start assuming that all children want to learn until somehow or other, they become "unmotivated." There is substantial evidence to support this position. Martin Deutsch and others note eagerness for schooling when children first enter and a declining enthusiasm the longer the exposure to the school. Schools have

From "Slim and None—The Poor's Two Chances" in C. W. Hunnicutt, ed., Urban Education and Cultural Deprivation, 1964. Reprinted by permission of Syracuse University School of Education.

been part of the problem, not part of the solution. Rather than helping, we, as society, have placed barriers in the way of the education of the poor.

I would argue that alleged disfunctionality of disadvantaged youth is the result of being locked out of society. Lack of motivation and apathy are the consequences of denial of opportunity. We are not properly sifting out cause and effect.

Some years ago in New York I was involved in programs for disadvantaged youth that were similar to the school compensatory programs, the Job Corps and Neighborhood Youth Corps programs. The programs, by all established criteria, were excellent—well designed, competent staff, and workable pupil-staff ratios. The programs included rigorous research and evaluation. At the end of a year it was pretty clear that there was no payoff despite the belief of everyone that such programs were sure to work. The youth in the program were no better off at the end of the year than were a comparable (control) group who had not been offered the programs.

It was out of these kinds of failure experiences over some years that it occurred to me that perhaps we are dashing off headlong in the wrong direction—that instead of trying to save people, salvage people, and help people, we should be offering disadvantaged youths the opportunities to belong, to help, and to salvage themselves and others. Rather than developing programs which emphasize failure, inadequacy, and thus continue to stigmatize and spoil the image of youth, focus on the structural barriers standing in the way of their success.[1]

Social scientists for some time have noted the difference between the socialization patterns of the poor and the nonpoor. The poor operate on the pleasure principal—they don't know how to delay need gratification. They have to get their kicks right now. We good middle-class people, who have been adequately socialized, operate on the reality principal—we delay our gratifications for future reward. We never buy a house until we save $20,000, and we never buy a car until we save $3,000. But the poor just aren't like that. What is not understood in this formulation is that the poor don't suffer from a lack of future orientation—they they suffer from a lack of future.

There must be a restructuring of employment opportunities so that the poor can find a place. Our schools must provide a learning experience which gives children a sense of contribution, of personal worth, a feeling of anticipation about the future, and a certainty that they have a place in it. This is not happening now for the poor youth. The school is an alien land from which he "cuts out." This exclusion leads to another exclusion—from a society which cannot employ him because he didn't learn. Without change, we face a frightening prospect of millions of people who are literally expendable—totally unnecessary to the functioning of the society and living with the terrible self-destructive knowledge that they are leaving no imprint on the sands of time, that they are "nobody" and functioning "no place."

Our education system can build in a future for our children only if educators look for what's wrong with current practice and start to truly test their theories. Is a child's noncommitment to education, is his dropping out of school, the result of prior handicap—or are these things due to lack of choice, to lack of future, to being locked out? There is a very important difference. If the handicap thesis is fraudulent, everything we're going makes little sense—whether it's the Job Corps program, the Neighborhood Youth Corps, or the compensatory programs in the schools. More and more the evidence supports the contention that opening up opportunities has a greater impact on poor children than do programs to "repair" them.

WHY IS EDUCATION SO IMPORTANT TODAY?

Around the turn of the century, about 94 percent of our people didn't graduate from high school. It caused little concern because there were a whole variety of absorption systems—albeit imperfect—available to the poor. But today, at least four years of education beyond high school are necessary for upward movement in our economic system—and this becomes increasingly more true as traditional ways of making a living become obsolete. At one time there were many possibilities for entrance and upward mobility for most of our citizens.

1. First, they could market their unskilled labor, learn on the job, and move up. Many of the people who command high positions in industry today started out as unskilled laborers. But today machines are replacing men. Despite the fact that we've had well over a 30 percent increase in productivity over the past five years, there are no more people turning out products than five years ago. And the better jobs demand credentials.

2. Another entrance was farming. But today agriculture is our most automated industry—over a million jobs have been eaten up by machines in the last six or seven years, despite the fact that agricultural surpluses continue to grow, and another million jobs will be destroyed in the next decade.

3. Still another possibility was entrepreneurial enterprise. But today the street peddler cannot compete seriously with a department store; the small machinist, with the major auto companies.

4. Finally, the fields of education, welfare, and recreation were available to the poor because there were not the prerequisites for education which are currently demanded. Ralphe Bunche says that the teacher that had the most profound effect on him had an 8th-grade education when she began to teach.

These absorption systems are today closed off. Two fundamental things have affected dramatically the way we can become absorbed into society: (1) automation—eating up the jobs or dead-ending them; and (2) the need for a credential to get into the largest and fastest-growing industries.

The biggest, fastest-growing industry in the country is education. It has to be the biggest 10 years from now because by 1975 there will be 40,000,000 more people in the country, and the median age will be less than 25. With preschool education, fewer dropouts, more people going to college, the lowering of the teacher-pupil ratio, the 2.3 million teachers we now have could easily be expanded to 5 or even 10 million. The equivalent is true in medicine, recreation, welfare—for all the human services and for all the skilled jobs for which we demand a college education for any significant involvement.[2]

Without credentials for the professions and for the new skilled and managerial jobs in private industry—the poor are locked out of participation in the economic life of the country. And yet the poor need education more than anyone else. It wasn't a great tragedy that Barry Goldwater couldn't get through the first year of college because his family could find things for him to do around the store. But the poor have no such resources—they must have an education. **Education is the only equalizer they have.**

Nevertheless, because of the way education is now structured, it's unlikely that very many of the poor will get the credential. Why?

WHAT HAPPENS TO DISADVANTAGED YOUTH IN SCHOOL

We "sort."

The teachers' responsibility is to teach, but instead we engage in self-fulfilling prophecy. We decide that certain people cannot be educated; we refuse to educate them; they grow up uneducated; and we pride ourselves on our exceedingly accurate predictive index. This sorting principle puts a stamp on pupils very early in the game, which follows them all the way through the production line until they come out labeled "dumb" or "smart" because there has been very little done to change the initial judgment. This distorts the educational function—teachers are supposed to **change** persons; they are not there only to sort and stamp.

To show you how important role expectation is in determining what you do in school—in Scotland, a few years ago, the IBM machine made a mistake and the school sent a bunch of stupid kids into the smart track and a bunch of smart kids into the dumb track. About a year later they discovered their mistake, and they checked to see what had happened. They found that those so-called stupid kids were acting just as if they were smart, just as if they had the innate ability to do the job, and the so-called smart kids were behaving just as though they were stupid[3]—**because** the role expectation to a large extent determines what you're going to do in a classroom. If the school believes you're incapable of doing anything, you're never going to get an opportunity to show what you're capable of doing.

We Refuse to Educate the Poor

Very few of the poor will get a chance to get the all-important credential because very few will be placed into tracks that lead to a college degree. As an example, consider the schools in Washington, D.C. In a school where middle-class white students go, where the median income for the parents is over $10,000 a year—92 percent of all students are in college-bound tracks. In another school in Washington, D.C., where 100 percent of the students are Negro and parents make less than $4,000 a year, 86 percent are in noncollege-bound tracks.[4] In other words, almost 9 out of 10 of the Negro children are being told they are not college material (and thus they cannot get a credential).

If you accept the proposition that without college in the coming years, you cannot get into meaningful work, these kids are being told that they have no future except possibly in menial service occupations. Thus, selective education imposes a rigid class structure upon the poor—especially the Negro poor. At the present time, the **best** predictor of a future college education is the occupation of the student's father. If the student has a parent with less than a college education, who works at a blue-collar job if he works at all, and is from a racially discriminated minority group, the probability of being a dropout is more than three times greater than if a student is reared by professional, well-educated, white parents.

Unless one holds to the belief that the poor are constitutionally inferior (and nice people don't believe that anymore), then you have to assume that the poor are not being educated; otherwise, the "bright" and the "stupid" would be more evenly distributed through all economic levels of the population.

Homogeneous or Heterogeneous Grouping

How do we appraise peoples' intelligence or lack of it. If they talk like we do, or act like we do, obviously they have to be intelligent. If they don't, equally obviously, they must be nonintelligent. Nothing could be more logical. So we establish a series of tests—that we devise for us, standardize on us, operate in situations in which we feel comfortable, and on this basis we determine who is educable or noneducable. And then we spend millions of dollars—because some people think this process isn't really fair—to look for that culture-free or culture-fair test. It's a totally unrealizable goal. We don't even try to discover whether it's essential to try to find this kind of test at all. Why is it really important to start labeling kids as being dumb or smart early in the game?

This is not to say that all people are equal, but

rather that no valid measures of intellectual capacity have been developed, nor does it really matter since none of us functions anywhere near capacity.

The argument for homogeneous grouping is that it makes it easier to teach; that is, we're setting up a system for the convenience of the teacher. The teacher takes the position—quite logically—how can I teach a whole bunch of different people if they all have different abilities? But even in homogeneous groups the children are not all identical. No matter how you group them, they're different people. They just happen to be somewhat similar on a particular score, but they're different in background, sex, learning styles, tempo, and timing. Only one variable has been isolated as a result of this grouping, but the teacher believes her job will be easier because she can operate at the same pace.

By the same token, we begin to water down the curriculum successively as we begin to label people as slower learners or less able. Those who learn slower are going to get less. Those in the second track are going to get a second-class education, and a third-class education will be offered those in the third track. This is what happens when one assumes that it is easier and more logical to teach people who learn roughly at the same pace.

Evidence, however, doesn't support the thesis. No evidence shows that homogeneous groupings work better **for the students.** Both here and in England it appears that a bright child learns no better when placed with a bunch of bright kids than when grouped heterogeneously. And the poor kid—the so-called dumb kids—**are** hurt by the grouping. They end up doing worse than the so-called dumb kid left in a heterogeneous group. It is fairly obvious why. Grouping doesn't help the educational process. Most of these kids aren't stupid, despite our judgment. They know who's being grouped with whom even if the labeling is couched innocuously as "bluebirds." If **they** don't know, the other kids will tell them. They soon learn to fulfill the role expected of them and—most destructive of all—learn to believe in the "truth" of the school's judgment of them.

If you're put in basic tracks, if you're given a watered-down curriculum, if you're treated as if you're dumb, there is not much you can get from school.

Although evidence does not support homogeneous grouping as educationally valid, it **is** definitely discriminatory. There's no question that the

child that goes into the smart track tends to be the youth whose parents are well educated. Those who go into the dumb class are those who didn't choose their parents very well. The track system is a discriminatory process—and it reinstitutes a segregated school system right within the school. There are interracial schools in this country where almost all the kids on the honor track are white and almost all the kids in nonhonor tracks are Negro or Spanish-speaking. This is not a "racially balanced" school. It's a totally segregated school, but the segregation takes place within a building. The segregation is just as intense, just as invidious, just as pernicious, as if it **were** a racially exclusive school.

WHY ARE THE SCHOOLS ALIEN TO THE POOR?

The Rules

There is no logic or rationale for most school rules. There is a minimum tolerance for differences—and much more tolerance if you're nonpoor than if you're poor. For example, if students don't dress or wear their hair in middle-class determined style, they can be asked to leave school. This can happen despite the fact that there's no data rationale to support the contention that learning is disturbed when students wear boots or long hair.

It is not surprising that youth try to establish an identity, often through bizarre dress and hairdos. What is surprising is that adults have the effrontery to meddle in what is essentially someone's own private business. **The real issue is:** Why do young people decide to express themselves in these ways? Why are there so few gratifications for poor youth in our society that they reject becoming part of the establishment? Whenever I see bizarre behavior in students, my initial reaction is to look to what the school is doing to **cause** the behavior.

School rules are differentially enforced. What is tolerably deviant and what is not depends on the child's background. In the case of middle-class boys, deviant behavior is often interpreted as a childish prank, a phase which the student will outgrow; in cases involving poor youth, it is interpreted as a signal of emerging criminality, which must be nipped in the bud.

It's important to insist on logical reasons for the rules of behavior in the schools. If education is to be rational—if it is to be a system which enables youth to learn to think clearly, to learn to work through problems—then a rule shouldn't be ad hoc; a rule shouldn't be made off the top of one's head; it shouldn't conform to the personal prejudices of a school board or the personal whim of principals. School rules should be backed by empirical evidence that they are supportive or negative to the learning process; that they endanger health or safety of another person or school property.

Powerlessness

The more deprived the background of the child, the less power he has in our educational system. To be totally powerless is to be placed in a terribly disquieting and uncomfortable position. Humans do not like to feel that they're nothing, that they have no control over their destiny. No one likes that feeling. It's quite clear that there's a great difference between the poor and nonpoor in their ability to defend themselves in the school system. A child of white middle-class parents has things going for him when he gets into trouble. He can talk the language of the system, and teachers and principals are much more likely to listen to him. But he can also turn to his parents. His parents also talk the language; they can negotiate for their child. The middle-class parent can do things for his child—he can hire a tutor, a psychologist, a lawyer; if worse comes to worse, he can take his child out of the system and put him in a private school. The poor have no escape, no voice. The whole system is a colonial imposition on them— made up by others, for others.

Meaningless Material

For the poor, education is totally removed from their life experience. It cannot be related to their backgrounds or immediate circumstances. In middle-class families, parents can talk "algebra" with their child; the material he gets has some meaning in the context of his life. The material is presented in a familiar language, in an understandable style, and at an acceptable pace. None of this is true for most disadvantaged youngsters.

Some social scientists have advocated replacing teachers with machines, insisting that machines can do everything teachers can do. There may be sense in this postulate because machines are more flexible (more human) than teachers. Machines, at least, can be made to change their pace. The child operates a learning machine and he operates it at the pace at which he is learning. Teachers cannot be manipulated that way. They operate at one

pace; at one track; and with one language style.

At the University of Oregon a counselor was simulated on a 1620 computer by collating the responses of a live counselor and developing a program based on queries to him from clients. The capacity of the computer was not taxed—very few unique responses were required, regardless of the questions asked. The students were asked to describe and evaluate the machine and compare it with a human counselor. They found the machine more warm, more understanding, more sympathetic. Schools must stop dehumanizing teachers. The teacher has a unique quality which no machine can replace, and that is the ability to challenge students constructively, to reach out and help, to exercise flexibility and judgment. Those qualities must be liberated if education is to have meaning to the poor.

Linkage with a Future

Where do youth go with schooling? A middle-class child may find rules stupid; may bridle because of his powerlessness; may find most of the courses meaningless—but these are obstacles he is willing to suffer because he knows at the end there's a place for him.

What about the noncollege-bound youth? What is that track leading to? What is he getting out of the educational experience? He's being told to stay in school to become an unemployed high school graduate. Dropouts I've worked with told me they felt worried about not having a high school diploma until they discovered you could lie about it. For the most part, a high school diploma leads to menial dead-ended jobs. There is no meaningful linkage with the future for anyone who is not in a college-bound program in school. Vocational education is, to a large extent, antiquated. It's antiquated because the job may be disappearing. Or if the job is still viable, the youth does not have the informal credentials; for example, many of the building trades offer preference to union members' children in apprentice programs. (We can't really reshuffle fathers as part of the vocational education program). Much of the vocational educational is delusional—a complex fabrication which disguises the reality of the world out there and the inappropriate nature of current procedures which ostensibly prepare youth for the world of work.

Gratification

Jobs aren't everything. Man does not live for bread alone. Dignity and a sense of self-worth are also extremely important. And here the school's effect is the most devastating of all. We rarely allow a student the opportunity to become a person in the school. We rarely allow students to have a sense of competence. Schools permit some to obtain competence and these are the "brains" and the "athletes." But the largest number are subjected to a humiliating and degrading experience. The middle-class child gets the rewards bestowed by teachers who understand him because he dresses and behaves appropriately. The deprived youngster, for the most part, goes to school every day to be punished. He gets no reward out of the system. Psychologists and social workers all treat his "deficiencies." But these are only some more overlords reinforcing humiliation.

Not only do the poor fail to develop a sense of mastery, they are not permitted a sense of contribution. They are not allowed to be important to anyone else.

These gratifications must come out of the school system if it's going to have real value to our children. If they have no sense that they're learning something, that they're contributing to others, that they're members of something, then it's hard to expect them to give very much to the school program. If they feel that the school is run by outsiders, with rules made by outsiders, in which they have little power to make any decisions and no understanding of those that are made; if it leads nowhere and they're getting no kicks out of it— how do we expect them to put out very much for that kind of school?

HOW DO WE CONSTRUCT A DIFFERENT KIND OF SCHOOL?

Before We Can Build Anew, We Have to Test Whether Our Cherished Beliefs Are True

We "know" that if we reduce class size, education will be better. We "know" it's true that if we give teachers time to prepare for classes, they will do better. We "know" that if we improve pupil personnel services and pour in psychologists and social workers, we can overcome children's handicaps. And yet there is no evidence to support this "knowledge." And if we researched it, I would predict that very little of the above would pay off one iota over an extended period of time.

Looking at what data there is, it is clear that none of these things by themselves produce better education. In fact, we have increasing evidence that nothing positive takes place in the classroom.

Omar Milton, a psychology professor at the University of Tennessee, is considered to be an effective teacher. He is dynamic, interesting, well liked by his students. One semester, he took a random half of his students and ordered them not to show up in class. These students took the midterms and the final, and at the end of the semester he found that the half that didn't show up at class did better than those that did. Two years later, they were still doing better. They were more interested in psychology; they had a higher grade-point average, fewer had dropped from school. On every possible objective and subjective index, they were doing better for **not** having been in class. This experiment has been repeated in many places with the same findings. I am sure that we would find it true in secondary schools if it were tested. If we ordered kids to stay home, they'd be better off. In the Omar Milton experiment, despite the fact that teacher-pupil ratio was down because half the students were home, there was absolutely no gain for those attending class.

We had better begin to look at some of our most treasured, heartfelt assumptions and test them out. If education is to pay off, we have to recognize that it wasn't set up for the convenience of the teacher. We didn't really set up public education to keep middle-class people off the streets. Schools were established to help the students, and we'd better test if it is working as intended.

Teachers have to accept the responsibility for teaching human beings to learn. One of the things I have tried to get across in my classes is that when I give a test it is not a test of my students. It is a test of me. I am testing whether or not I am a good teacher. If the students get poor grades, I interpret that as an indication that I failed to get the course material across. After one of my tests, one of my students came up and patted me on the back and said: "Hate to break it to you, buddy, but you flunked." And he was right. But this attitude is hard for teachers to accept. There is no other system in the world in which we flunk a product. We do a rotten job, and we flunk the kids. We fail to teach, and the kids are held accountable.

The Student As Teacher

We have to build in the gratification which comes from having a sense of contribution—a sense that you are of value to someone else. The student role as a passive sitter and absorber of knowledge is not particularly gratifying. The teacher role is.

So one of the things to recognize is that it would be better if teachers did some learning and the learners did some teaching right from the very beginning.

In a residential school for delinquents and abandoned kids in Oregon, a 7-11 club has been started. The 11th graders are teaching the 7th graders. One of the things that has happened is that most of the 11th graders didn't want to go home for Christmas because they had to work on lesson plans over the holiday; the 7th graders felt the same way. The school no longer just belongs to the teacher, but now the students have a stake in the system and suddenly school swings. The school is an entirely different school because the kids themselves are involved in the teaching process. And the teacher becomes somebody who is pretty important to the kids because he is needed to help them prepare lectures and work with each other. They find they need the teacher to help work through problems, to suggest ways of teaching, and to refer children who need special help.

In another school there was a youth who appeared to be absolutely unmanageable. He threw darts at the teacher, broke windows, was the one arrested if anything was stolen. He was not the kind of kid you would have suspected would be an optimal teacher, but almost in desperation it was suggested that he be allowed to teach. He was in the 8th grade, so he went to work helping 6th graders in spelling and 2nd graders in tumbling. Three or four weeks later, he's doing much better in all his classes because he has to keep up his work and stay out of trouble if he's going to be allowed to work with the other kids. His whole idea about education has changed. In fact, where once his life's aspiration was to be a Marine, he now wants to be a teacher.

Another way in which you inject the idea of making a contribution is to have the kids teach each other in the classroom. Instead of a classroom where the teacher does it all, some courses in some experimental programs in which I am involved are set up in teacherless led groups. The youth decide upon projects that interest them. This is being done with an 8th grade science course. The teacher initially thought it was absolutely insane. She saw her job as lecturing for a whole hour whether anybody listened or not. She saw her primary obligation as reaching the kids who cared, and those who didn't—too bad. We prevailed upon her to break the room into groups and let them have some alternatives as to what they might like to do. They

began to do things that the teacher thought only 11th and 12th graders could do. When she gave a test out of the text—in spite of the fact that they were doing almost nothing out of the text—the whole class had gone up in performance. Why?

Because now these kids had an investment. They were working on things themselves. They had some control over their own destiny—they had some concern for their own educational process; it was no longer something forced upon them. And the teacher found that teaching had become fun. She used to hate to come to school and look at the hostile faces, and the kids felt much the same about her. Now the whole educational experience has become exciting. She's playing essentially a consultative role—she answers questions, she helps individuals—and the kids are learning as they never learned before.

The principal keeps worrying because he doesn't know what he'll say when the parents come storming in complaining because their kids say school is fun. Many people feel that agony is a necessary part of the learning process. But he can demonstrate performance. There are kids in that school getting A's who never got anything better than an F. Kids are participating and asking questions who before were able only to incur wrath and be sent to the principal's office where, of course, all education takes place in our system.

A change has taken place because the kids are getting opportunities for gratification, an opportunity to develop a competence. They're working in heterogeneous groups where they all have a chance. Moreover, the so-called dumb kids are better in some things than the bright ones; for example, when the 8th grade kids were constructing tests for the 7th graders, the bright ones made up "catch" questions that no one could get; the slower kids asked fruitful questions that made real sense—and got a big kick out of being the best test-makers. The whole school is a different school—for both teachers and students.

What we are creating is cooperative team learning. Holding people up in individual competition is inherently unfair, especially when mixing middle-class and poor children. We've had team learning in this country for a long time—only we call it cheating. I suggest that we buy into cheating and help our kids work together. The pioneers could never have gotten across the country if they hadn't pulled together, with those who had helping those who hadn't. School also should be a cooperative effort.

Quality-Control Research

We must begin to incorporate quality-control research into the teaching process. We must begin to test some of the basic hypotheses that we "know" are correct. We can't just do outcome research—which is the type of research that checks, for instance, whether reducing pupil-teacher ratio leads to better school performance without ever determining what factor in the classroom situation has actually occasioned change. There must be another type of research—a process research, which checks on what is happening in the classroom. It doesn't help to reduce class size if the person with 15 in the class is doing precisely what he was doing with 35. His paper work may be up-to-date, but his relationship with individuals is no different.

We must begin to monitor school activities systematically. Discover what is being done and feed that back to the teachers. When I first go into a school, I try to give to the teachers a theoretical orientation pertaining to student disaffection with school. Graduate students then monitor what's going on in the school by observing classes at random moments. Students, especially those who are troublemakers, are interviewed and asked to discuss their school experiences. Every week we convene with the teachers and present the observations or play back tape recordings of the interviews. We attempt to determine whether some behavior might be ignored. We consider means by which we could make material more meaningful or interesting. We consider how the student could be more actively involved in school—could he teach or tutor? Is there any way he could be involved in class activity so that he may gain a better picture of self or derive the satisfaction of helping others? After analyzing a number of alternatives, a strategy is devised to help the student in question. The class is again monitored to determine if the agreed-upon approach is followed as planned, and whether it's having the desired effect. This kind of quality control is essential, or we could start adulterating a program and not know that it is happening.

In our initial seminars, many teachers listen to the tapes and start every response with "I'd like to start by saying something in my own defense." But since teachers get profound gratification from seeing their students "come alive," they soon begin to commit themselves to participation in the learning process, and we find that this continuous evaluation results very soon in basic changes in classroom relationships.

EXPERIMENT AT HOWARD UNIVERSITY: NEW METHODS—NEW PEOPLE

The school, transformed as I've described it, will create the alive, thinking, absorbed children that result when teachers have respect for each child's intelligence, competence, and need to participate actively in the teaching-learning process. Meanwhile, however, millions of young people have already given up the school system, and unless they are to remain permanently and dangerously nonfunctional appendages to our society, we have to move towards programs where you get your job first and your education afterwards.

At Howard University, in 1963, we took a look at some failures of the school system—a group of hard-core delinquent school dropouts—to determine what would happen if we stopped trying to compensate for handicaps and instead tried to open up opportunities for useful work, combined with a relevant education.

We created jobs in research, child care, and recreation for a group of youths, who would appear to have no potential to make it. The minimum requirements for the program were that youths had to (1) be high school dropouts; (2) live in the most economically disadvantaged neighborhoods in Washington, D.C.; (3) have no **pending** legal action; (4) have no **active** venereal disease.

The ten youths chosen for this original program were between the ages of 16 and 20, had a measured 77 IQ on a group test, and had between 8th and 11th grade education. None had worked more than a month in his life. Four of the seven boys had extensive delinquency histories, including time in institutions; two of the three girls had borne children out of wedlock. One of the girls was diagnosed by our psychiatrist as a catatonic schizophrenic. Our psychiatrist said it was ridiculous to include her in the program. We insisted she be included—we would test the proposition that her condition was not a psychological disorder, but the result of a locked-out condition with no future.

A number of tasks were structured which we thought it would be possible for persons with these backgrounds to learn. In six weeks of research training we expected them to learn to conduct and tape-record interviews; to code and prepare these interviews for key punch; to run a counter-sorter; to wire an IBM 407; to prepare instructions for a programmer in a 1620 computer; to operate desk calculators sufficiently well to compute percentages, means, medians, standard deviations, chi squares, rank-order correlations, product moment correlations, and other statistical manipulations. They were doing all these things and more, including helping design research experiments, in six to ten weeks. Similar performance was expected in the day-care and recreation programs, and **we grossly underestimated their ability.**

We discussed with the youths our orientation and told them we were going to see if our point of view made any sense.

On the question of tolerable deviance: Our position was that no rule would be imposed unless we could provide strong justification of its need. We didn't care how they dressed, how they wore their hair—unless we could prove to them that these things would affect their performance on the job. The fact that their appearance might outrage a professional was **his** problem.

On power: We established that they were the policy-making group for the program. They would determine in which of the three job areas they wished to work; they would decide the discipline to be applied if people were late or continuously absent, etc. They established the rules. Our role would be that of a review court. If the rules they made could not be supported, we would refer them back to them for review and consideration. Often we found the kids too tough, and our policy was to tell them their discipline seemed inconsistent with their complaints about how they had always been treated by others. We would ask them what **their** problems were—Why did they find it difficult to adjust to each other's differences when these caused them no personal harm? In time, they became very supportive to each other.

On meaningfulness of curricula: Everything we taught related to the work they were doing. We gave them a course in growth and development that you would find on a university level, but we keyed it into the behavior of the children they were dealing with in the preschool program. We gave them a course in group work, not too dissimilar to what you'd find in a school of social work, but again we keyed it into their activities in recreation. We oriented them to statistics by pointing out to them that they already knew a lot about probability theory. They knew it was a 2 to 1 bet not to make a 10 in a crap game. But as much as they knew, I knew more, and we went through a simulated crap game and I showed them how much money I'd have won if we'd really been playing "for real," because it isn't an even money bet against a 6 or an 8; it's 6 to 5 against the

shooter. They got quite interested and excited about probability theory and really wanted to know more.

On linkage: We pointed out that their jobs could lead possibly to a career in the fields in which they were now engaged.

On gratification: They got tremendous joy from discovering competencies they never knew they had and in knowing that they were making a contribution to each other and to those with whom they worked.

Our success was beyond wildest expectation. Despite late paydays (depriving them of the supposedly essential "instant" gratification), a staff that made hundreds of mistakes, we not only had no dropouts from the program, but we couldn't have beat those kids out with sticks. This created some difficulty because, considering the kind of intake criteria we set up and our previous experience with more traditional ways of helping kids, we didn't expect to have anyone left after 12 weeks and we had raised only 12 weeks worth of funds. At the end of that time we were scrambling around for additional money, since all 10 kids were still there. Two years later all 10 were still involved in a whole series of activities, and all had displayed spectacular competency—including our catatonic schizophrenic who was "chattering like a mynah bird," according to a friend. In addition, we had no dropouts; most had returned to school. None of them walked the same, talked the same, or acted the same. Their whole lives had changed as a result of getting to show what they could do.

Initially, these kids were drawn at random from a group of 20—the other 10 constituted a control group which had been matched for sex, age, employment, education, and delinquency records. Checking these 10 after a year, we found one person had been arrested for a felony (homicide), two others for burglary; none had gone back to school. This was not just a question of statistical differences—there was no overlap. The two groups were just not operating in the same universe.

It's important to note that these changes could not be attributed to the Hawthorne effect; that is, the initial effect which results from almost any novel program which incorporates special teachers, special attention, special equipment, etc. The effects usually wear off very soon. But in our experiment, there was no wearing out even after two years, or any lessening of success when staff was changed or when dozens of others were added to the program.[5]

HOW DO WE OPEN UP A
PARALLEL ROUTE TO THE CREDENTIAL?

If the war in Vietnam ended, unemployment would soar. Even in the midst of war, the more-skilled jobs remain unfilled, and unemployment and low-wage employment are prevalent. Since employment at the expense of lives will hopefully not be a permanent way of life, peace and the inevitable increase in automation will leave the human services as the area with the greatest potential for massive job creation.

The skilled jobs in industry and in the human services require credentials. Millions now unskilled and untrained cannot get credentials because they cannot go to college. We must begin to test the value of the proposition that education can come first and then the job. As the Howard experiment showed, it is not motivation, but opportunity that is lacking for the poor. A parallel route to the credential should be available. In essence, the educational facility should be moved to where the people are, instead of making people go to the educational facility. In terms of the teaching credential, this is important—not only to get the poor working—but it is educationally valid to do teacher training right in the schools, dealing with problems as they come up with monitoring and discussion and combining the research and training functions.

One of our problems in education is that we have taken a whole series of different functions and labelled them "teacher." If we analyze what a teacher does, we find many things that require little skill, training, or experience; many things that require some skill; and some things that require all the professional experience at his command. We have lumped all these functions together and call them teaching.

I would suggest that we establish an alternative route to the teaching credential. We can begin with a teacher aide position. Teacher aides could operate audio-visual equipment, monitor hallways and lunch yards, perform clerical functions, read to children, and tutor students in need of special attention.

As they demonstrate ability, they should be given college credit for their on-the-job experience and be encouraged to enroll in essential college courses offered at a city college, university, or extension division. These aides, with experience and some backup courses, in two years can advance to the position of **teacher assistant**. The assistant can take on additional responsibility, can teach under the supervision of a professional and

lead small group discussions. In another two or three years, having gained additional college credit for the increased work experience, and having taken some additional needed courses, the teaching assistant could become a **teaching associate**, performing much as a teacher does now. In another couple of years, the associate could become a **fully certified teacher**. The role of the fully certified teacher would necessarily be considerably different from his role today. The certified teacher would be a specialist, a consultant, a trainer, and a supervisor for those in training.

These various subprofessionals can liberate the teacher to truly reach every child in the classroom. Her assistants can lead small groups, while the teacher can give individual attention to those who need special aid. Aides can help children with homework in the evenings; or they can communicate with the parents and pull them more closely into the educational experience.

Getting a teaching credential via the route of job first, education later, could take 8 to 10 years. But throughout those years, a person is doing useful work. If motivation or ability are limited, he can remain at a landing and still make a contribution. If he wishes to go all the way, the system is open all the way to the credential. This is not merely a proposal for aides in the schools. We have had aides in the schools for years. But aides to date have been limited to menial, dead-ended tasks, and a menial dead-ended job in the school is not much different from the menial, dead-ended job in any other field. It's the opportunity to move up that is the essence of a "new careers" program.

If we don't create this parallel road—this apprentice approach of on-the-job training, backup college courses, and increasing responsibility, which can ultimately lead to a professional status—we create two problems: (1) We'll continue to have alien schools—schools which belong to outsiders and never can attract and hold the students; and (2) we'll lock out the poor from the largest and fastest-growing industry in our country.

The teachers' aides should be recruited from the neighborhoods around the school. If this is done, a different atmosphere can be created in the school. That school is then no longer a place where some people drop in from the peninsula at 8:00 A.M. and are sure they're on the way home by 3:30. Today, slum schools cannot be accurately described as neighborhood schools because the teachers never live in the neighborhood. One of the problems of the slum school is that it is difficult for a working parent to talk to a teacher because the teacher is miles away by the time the parent comes home from work. One way to create a neighborhood school is to have teaching resources in the neighborhood.

There are some who feel that this concept tends to further enclose the ghetto. However, if career development is institutionalized in the school system, and the indigenous poor are able to move in the system, they become eleigible to move anywhere such jobs are available, thus facilitating a move out of the ghetto. At the present time, there's no way in the world to truly eliminate segregation because true integration requires economic liberation. Housing and school segregation will be reduced much faster when many more people have the credentials to work in higher-paying jobs, giving them the financial resources to buy houses anywhere.

HOW CAN UNIVERSITIES RESPOND TO SOCIETY'S NEED FOR "NEW CAREERS"?

There are many who oppose any tinkering with higher education procedures, even though the great need to replenish the "vanishing professional" in all the expanding human services will not be met by the universities as they function today. It is somehow assumed that the model of higher education has stood the test of time and any effort to provide an alternative path in which "learning by doing" is heavily emphasized would be retrogressive.

I think that higher education needs to be critically evaluated. Universities have not achieved the ultimate. In fact, it may not be straining truth to suggest that higher education is the most atavistic of all systems—that it was made obsolete with the invention of the printing press. It made sense to go to the place where the book was when there was only one book. However, since books are both plentiful and relatively inexpensive, some of the palpable weaknesses of the system should be explored.

Higher education as currently constituted in the helping services provides very little truly simulated experience before a person is exposed to the pressure of the job. Practice teaching and field experience are trivial and only minimally relevant to job experience. A person may go to school for· four years before he is exposed to a classroom situation and can then decide whether teaching is for him. Similar agonizing reappraisals are forced

upon prospective candidates for careers in social work, medicine, law, etc. The problem of this "all-or-nothing" nature of training is further complicated because there are no intermediate landings in human service professions. A person can train for nearly a decade and become an almost-doctor (and probably then sell pharmaceutical supplies), go to school for seven years to become an almost-lawyer, psychologist, social worker, teacher, etc. The lack of intermediate positions in the professions puts considerable pressure on credentialing agencies to pass unqualified candidates to professionnal status because the alternative of giving no reward for such investment of time, money, and energy is unconscionable.

The new careers proposal, providing an alternative path to a credential, allows for much greater flexibility in the education process. A person unable to attain the terminal position can be offered an intermediate office commensurate with his ability and competences. A person can utilize a number of combinations of training experiences to obtain a degree. Some might start off in the on-the-job training and in a few years cross over to a university experience (at the equivalent grade); or a person may be at loose ends at the end of two years at a university and cross over to the learning-on-the-job alternative at an intermediate position (e.g., teacher assistant). The existence of a number of career landings and the possibility of cross over allows for much greater opportunity for persons to make meaningful contributions to society. While this increased flexibility would be of particular significance to the poor who are denied the conventional path to professional status, such a program would be valuable to affluent students as well who have difficulty negotiating the current route to a credential.

WHY WE MUST BEGIN TO MAKE CHANGE IN PUBLIC SCHOOLS

Pressure for educational change will continue to increase because of the "functional illiterates" that the schools are graduating or pushing out by the millions; because of the expanding need for more professionals; because of the millions who are locked out of the economic system for lack of a credential. There will be an increasing need to link up the population that needs jobs with the jobs that need doing.

Total change in the schools is not possible quickly. But demonstration projects can be set up which can be beachheads from which more extensive efforts can be launched. Demonstration projects can be started with "soft" money—funds from the Elementary and Secondary Education Act, the Anti-Poverty Act, the National Institute of Mental Health, or the Ford Foundation. Start with small demonstrations and continue to expand as effectiveness is demonstrated.

There's a need to work out a coherent educational package. Presently, we are all going full speed in all directions. One group says the solution to everything is busing; another, that paying teachers twice as much will make the difference; another, that homogeneous groups are the answer. Some believe in providing an instant reward for good grades; some want even more credentials for teachers; some want more social workers or psychologists. Some say we are too permissive; others say we are too repressive. We need to discuss a total school—what is it to look like? What kind of staffing do we need? How do we get the funds for it? How do we demonstrate that it works? And then how do we institutionalize it on a larger scale? Each year, more and more funds for education are authorized by Washington and Sacramento, but these funds are not drawn together into one package. Most of the programs offer compensatory education for those who didn't get the education the first time around, but such programs, without drastic changes in teacher-student relationship, won't be any more successful the second time around.

There is much concern about the expense involved in creating vast changes in the institutions of the country. It is expensive to be sure, but the cost of maintaining a large spectator population is great, too. It costs money to "welfare" people and to "warehouse" people. It costs about $10,000 to build one cell in a maximum security prison; it costs over $4,000 to keep one youth in the California Youth Authority for a year. Watts was also an expensive proposition.

If the human service systems are not opened to the poor, there will be the "costs" due to a lack of teachers, doctors, social workers, etc., and yet the majority of the people who need work will be unemployed or dead-ended in poverty-income jobs. Poverty is pretty simple. Even Calvin Coolidge figured it out. He pointed out that when a lot of people are out of work, unemployment results.

There can be no reality to human rights or

civil rights if, instead of being discriminated against because of color, people can be discriminated against because they lack credentials. The two are so highly correlated that it amounts to the same thing. **The basis of a poverty program must begin with job creation.** And the huge education system must share the social responsibility of creating a portion of the jobs in ways that have proved to be educationally valid.

Much of the money needed for changes in the school system already exists in the flood of educational and antipoverty legislation. But most of it is used for programs that have long since proved unproductive. We need programs that do not "bandage" the poor, but rather give a fair break to every child.

THE IMPORTANCE OF EDUCATIONAL CHANGE FOR ALL CHILDREN

Most school problems militate particularly against the poor and disadvantaged children. But schools tend to degrade all children. The irrational rules, the sense of powerlessness, the dependency, the insistence upon conformity, is destructive to the development of all children—and is antagonistic to preparing citizens for democratic responsibility.

What has been suggested here to remedy the ailments in education is a strategy which offers a better education for all youth. It allows for democratic decision-making, creates a link with the future, provides gratifications, and puts meaning into the educational experience for all youth regardless of background, neighborhood, or learning style.

NOTES

1. See, for example, Erving Goffman, **Stigma**, for further elaboration of the spoiled image concept.
2. For a full discussion on how to create millions of jobs in the human services, read: Arthur Pearl and Frank Riessman, **New Careers for the Poor.**
3. As reported by Martin Deutsch.
4. Elias Blake, "Teaching in Washington, D.C. Schools," **Integrated Education,** June 1965.
5. Send for "Community Apprentice Program" from the Center for Youth and Community Studies, Howard University, Washington, D.C. ($2.00) for the full story of this experiment.

chapter 40
status and role in education
edgar z. friedenberg

The central function of education in a complex society is the allocation of the various credentials that define the status of the bearer and the range of social roles that he may be permitted to fill. The role that an individual comes to occupy in society on the basis of his credentials from school virtually determines his social identity in both his own eyes and those of society. By "credential," of course, I mean far more than a transcript or a diploma; these certainly, but, properly speaking, the credential includes the entire dossier collected, preserved, and transmitted by the school or used by it as a basis for recommendations to those authorities on whom the student's life-chances depend.

Much of the emphasis placed on the credential in modern society is an expression of its commitment to universalistic values. Formal education is expected to further universalism by promoting achievement—doing rather than being—and appraising it impersonally regardless of the needs of or other claims to consideration by the candidate.

And to the degree that the society is egalitarian as well as universalistic in its values, the school will also be expected to admit candidates for credentials to its programs solely on the basis of potential or actual competence in the skills the

This article first appeared in **The Humanist**, September/October, 1968, and is reprinted by permission.

program demands. Such a society conceives itself as engaged in a continuous talent search, which it is obligated to conduct competitively and impartially for the purpose of maintaining a graded talent pool adequate to its enterprises and, generally speaking, without much concern for what the process does to those who are placed in the pool's shark-infested waters. And it regards the schools as its instrument for this purpose and hardly any other.

The schools' devotion to the task of keeping the talent pool stocked with properly labeled and fairly priced items wins it the public support it depends on, but also involves it in fundamental conflicts both internally and with its community. It affronts those students who dislike being processed and labeled as a product. It creates cynicism and despair among students and educators who perceive that, in any case, the credential is awarded in recognition of qualities quite different from the competences it is supposed to certify. And, because of its universalism, the school's talent searching involves it in continuous, covert conflict with its local community, of which, maneuvering over school integration provides the best examples.

School systems in the United States are locally controlled, and local control of education is rooted in local political and status systems. It must therefore often conflict with commitments to universalism in an increasingly cosmopolitan society. The intensity, and hence the capacity for damage, in such conflicts tends, however, to be limited by the steady attrition of real local power in an increasingly centralized society. As the scope of local control is reduced by the application of state-aid formulas, the control of textbook production and instructional services by the mass media, and the push toward uniformity exerted by a geographically mobile population that demands interchangeable schools, the local response tends to become more ritualized as it becomes impotent. This does not make it less acrimonious, but merely more passive, so that conflict serves neither to clear the air nor to exert a clear influence on policy.[1]

But local control remains an important influence on the process of status allocation in the schools because it retains considerable veto power and manages thereby to impose local norms on enterprises of great pith and moment. The character of these norms and their relationship to more cosmopolitan norms profoundly affect the outcome of this process. Local assessment of students, on the basis of values that may be unrelated or even negatively related to the abilities that will actually be required of them in the roles for which they are becoming qualified, may largely determine their life-chances. As an extreme example of this process, one may conceive of a beard or long hair ultimately costing a youth his life by occasioning his suspension from school, barring him from college admission, and leading to his induction into the armed services. At the level of higher education, it seems to me fair to observe that the Regents and administration of the University of California, by invoking narrowly authoritarian norms of personal conduct when confronted by the hippy cosmopolitanism of student activists and causing their leaders to be jailed, have managed to make a criminal record an essential part of the credential by which those students of the university who were most deeply concerned about education may be recognized; the Ph.D., surely, is a less reliable index.

Ultimately, what any credential comes to certify will be determined by the play of political forces among the groups who participate in the certification, whether they represent local customs, scholarly interests, or the burden of investment. The school, functioning as a certifying agency, serves partly as the vessel within which these contending forces are contained and reach equilibrium, and partly as one of the forces that contribute to the outcome. School personnel themselves judge students according to norms derived from their position in life that express their values and anxieties as well as—and doubtless far more than—academic standards. A school or university credential is in many ways a political document that expresses the vector sum of a set of social forces that determine what kinds of people will be accredited and on what terms; and hence what kinds of people may legitimately influence policy in a given situation. This aspect of the credential's function may or may not involve the way the competences it is supposed to certify are defined, but this does not usually matter crucially. Our society does not value competence very highly. It depends more on the rationalization of production and maintenance than on craftsmanship for quality control, and learns to content itself with lowered standards in those areas—of which teaching is a prime example—where rationalization does not work.

At the level of general education, I need look no further than the last graduation exercise I attended for an example of unconcern with the relevance of the credential to competence even during the very ceremony at which it is being awarded. At this institution, it is customary for the president of the senior class to make a short speech presenting the senior class gift to the university. The young man who did so stated that, instead of giving the school some costly object, the senior class had decided to spend its money on repairs for a dilapidated old fountain, which, he justly observed, "hadn't ran for several years." He further noted that this was "the most expensive gift any senior class had ever given the university." Nobody even winced.

It is possible, perhaps, to define liberal education in such a way that proficiency in its arts need not exclude either graceless and ungrammatical use of language or an unimaginatively materialistic sense of values, but I do not believe that many of my colleagues at that graduation would accept such a definition. Their conceptions of a college education were pretty conventional. They had simply ceased to expect the degree to mean anything at all in terms of the conventions they still accepted. In less striking ways we have all been living with our disillusionment for years, gradually adjusting to it by ceasing to expect high school graduates to show any real mastery of the "fundamentals" required for college entrance, expecting employers in turn to retrain our graduates on the job instead of relying on the competences for which we had certified them. Except for the advanced physical scientists, who don't really graduate anyway since they are hired by their own major professor or his colleagues to work in another part of the military-academic complex, employers usually have to retrain graduates, since, if they are hired to work with machines, the equipment they learned on at school is usually obsolete by industrial standards; and if they are hired to work with people—as for example, teachers or lawyers—the ideology they were taught in school is usually so naïve as to impede their function and must be unlearned on the job.

School credentials, though they determine access to status and role, then, I would maintain, are not thought of as certificates of competence. But they certainly mean something, and something society regards as important. And society is right; the process of allocating this access is indeed vital, at least in the sense that the chorus in **The Mikado** use the word:

Behold the Lord High Executioner:
A personage of noble rank and title.
A dignified and potent officer
Whose function is particularly vital.

Ko-ko himself, it will be recalled, proved incompetent to perform the duties of his post, but satisfied his sovereign with an affidavit that he had done so and an explanation that the affidavit should not be interpreted literally. His very professional deficiencies proved essential to the preservation of the Royal House, while his symbolic discharge of his function tended to preserve freedom and order in the community. In his case, the personnel-selection system of Titipu worked; it put the right man in the job, thereby ensuring that the job never really got done. And this was exactly what was required.

In the more complex society of the United States, the function of the credential is often analogous, though not strictly so. What we require of a credential is that it reliably designate its holder as a person who will get part of his job done, will provide a symbolic substitute for those aspects of it that cannot be publicly denied without creating intolerable social strain but cannot really be performed without creating even more intolerable social strain, and who will unfailingly and discreetly discharge those of his functions that can-

not be included in the job-definition or even admitted to be part of it, but which the actual power distribution of his community requires. This is really more than was demanded of Ko-ko; for a public executioner's role provides little opportunity for partial fulfillment and hence little complexity. But it is no more than is demanded of a school superintendent as he struggles to reconcile what his community really wants to do about its Negro youth with what is officially required; or of a lawyer, or a business executive—indeed, of the practitioner of any profession old enough to have defined its obligations and its ethics under conditions very different from those under which it must now be practiced.

Therefore, when we award a social role and the status that goes with it to a candidate, we want to be sure that he has some skills that cannot tactfully be attributed to practitioners of the role he is seeking; and these will strongly affect his appraisal, though in disguised or covert terms. Communities want to be sure that teachers will control children whether or not this impedes learning; that policemen will enforce their mores regardless of what may have been formally taught about civil rights, before they hire them for the job. Few communities, however, would rest content merely with the reassurance that new recruits to positions of social responsibility understood the requirements of their position well enough to be willing and able to betray its traditions when these became socially dysfunctional. We demand that the credential also tell us something positive about the incompetence that we require as a part of a candidate's qualifications—about what Veblen calls his trained incapacity, or a horse-trader calls being well broken. We expect it to assure us that the bearer will respect the conventional limits of the roles it makes available to him. To permit the members of a profession to make the fullest use of their technical powers would spoil the existing fit among society's various roles, impede the operation of its status system, and generate such hostility and mistrust as to jeopardize the place of the profession in the society. What tact and diplomacy do for individuals, trained incapacity does for role definitions and role expectations; and the credential must certify to that incapacity. A social worker must not only understand the dynamics of social stratification and of group work; he must be incapable of turning the poor on and using his skills to organize them into an effective political action group if he is to earn a good credential.

This is ironical, but not unusual, and is probably as true of most societies as of our own. What is new is that, in the United States, the accrediting function of the school has expanded so far that it issues not just licenses to enter particular trades or professions, or to continue more specialized education, but what amount to licenses to live. The schools have simply accepted the responsibility of recording and transmitting the kind of judgment of the candidate's personal qualities that a society less guilty about social stratification and less concerned to provide equality of opportunity would have left to private judgment, either of individuals or of cliques. Such judgments still affect recruitment and advancement crucially, even in our society; but they are acceptable as much more legitimate if supported by the credential of an official agency. The school grades students on citizenship and emotional adjustment, but this is less important than the fact that value judgments about the student's acceptability within the social structure permeate course grades as well, and at this level they cannot effectively be challenged as reflecting cultural bias. Similar judgments, as Aaron Cicourel and John Kitzuse have observed in **The Educational Decision-Makers** (Bobbs-Merrill, 1963), also strongly affect high school counselors' judgments as to whether students should be admitted to a college-preparatory program and hence whether they will ever obtain a college degree at all.

I am not certain whether it would be fairer to say that in this way the school introduces into the student's credential a personal judgment masked as a bureaucratic assessment, or that it depersonalizes its students by in fact reducing what is most human about them to a rationalistic appraisal. Both, perhaps; and either would be bad enough in my judgment. Yet, even granting that these processes occur, it would still be logically possible for the school to alter its assessment according to the role the student was preparing to fill, to leave him with a dossier indicating that he might make a very good scientist but a poor office worker, an excellent revolutionary but a rather unpromising naval officer, and so on. And of course the school does this insofar as it takes account of different aptitudes and levels of performance in various subject-matter fields and records variations in personality among students as it perceives them. I am very skeptical, however, that these ways of accounting for variability and suiting the student to the available opportunities are effective over a very wide range of behavior or personality. Despite their

terrifying array of testing and psychological services against which even the Constitution provides little defense, schools usually seem bent on turning out and labeling an all-purpose grind that will keep nobody awake.

This uniformity of viewpoint expresses a school mystique that pervades to a considerable degree every school I have observed, despite differences in location, curriculum, or social class served, even nationality. The mystique seems to be international. Of course there are tremendous differences as well; there are no up and down staircases, or any other kind, in glassy new suburban schools. But sooner or later, if one stays around, the characteristic flavor breaks through. I recall, for example, a five-day visit I made within the past year as a consultant to a high school widely—and justly—esteemed as one of the best in the United States for its academic standards and level of instruction. It had also just opened a magnificent new plant and was run with unusual urbanity. My hosts, or clients, had generously arranged for me to meet with student groups as well as staff under as little supervision as the routines of the place permitted. They could not, however, transcend the routines. There just was no way to permit a group of students to meet with me longer than a period unless we planned it that way—and then they had to. There was no place the students and I could sit together and smoke, even tobacco, while we talked. Nevertheless, after several days I had about concluded that this school was enough like a college in its atmosphere and its intellectual level to make the experience of attending it qualitatively different. Then, on the last day there was a fire drill during the morning, and the façade collapsed. Classes were interrupted, of course. Those like myself who happened to be in the library at the time were turned out hurriedly. The teachers and vice principals who had seemed bright and reasonably flexible during the discussions we had been having during the past four days turned into a horde of up-tight little men, blowing whistles and screaming at the youngsters, who were forbidden to talk as they marched out of the new glass and ferroconcrete structure into the snow. Several of the teachers looked a good deal more turned on, too, than they had during our seminars, now that they were really doing their thing.

Even in this nearly completely college-preparatory high school, its college-bound youngsters were still being assessed and recorded by a staff committed to a pattern of values that disparages qualities our colleges and our society could use a great deal more of. What kind of credential does the student get who refuses to interrupt intellectually exacting work in order to act out an imposed collective civic fantasy? Can he still get into a good college? Or are we going to make do with the talents of those who don't take themselves quite that seriously, or possess quite that much autonomy? What kind of credential does the student get who responds as I did to the principal's insistence that fire drills are required by law with the observation that extreme zeal in obeying the law is itself a **ressentient** way of behaving, and that a school that turns compliance with regulations into a devotional pageant is indoctrinating its students in servility as surely as it would be if it decked its halls with "Support your local police!" banners? This is, after all, a useful insight for a student of the social sciences to have, and one that comes rather easily at least to hippier high school students; and there is a good chance that those who develop it earlier will make more honest artists and even more effective executives.

And if the school is justified in insisting, for the sake of its own internal order and commitment to the official values of the community, that fire drills take precedence over and must be used to disrupt its regular instructional activities, then where does a youngster turn to get away from this constraint and learn more freely, doing his own thing, unconcerned with fires, neither setting nor fleeing them? What kind of credential does he get? The answer is clear enough; he gets a term in juvenile hall as a truant and a credential that says he is either a delinquent or mentally ill. And, of course, he has even less chance to learn on his own than he has of sneaking through the meshes of school routines.

We must still explain, however, why society has become so rigidly insistent on subjecting all its youth to protracted formal socialization, and why, in any case, it has made the public school system the single instrument of that process—except for the use of the Selective Service System, which, in effect, extends the compulsory school-attendance age to 21 or so for for middle-class male youth and provides an alternative form of compulsory socialization for school dropouts who are usually of lower status. As Paul Goodman has so often pointed out, our society permitted many alternative ways of growing up until a decade or so ago. Moreover, standardized testing has developed so massively in the United States, both in quality and

in the scale of its enterprise, that it would be both simple and economical to furlough young people from school as long as they reported to the testing center for a day or two each year and demonstrated that they were making normal progress toward the prescribed goals of the curriculum. That no such social arrangement is provided suggests very strongly that the achievement of these goals, which must be defined in terms of openly demonstrable competence, constitutes little more than a pretext for compelling the student to submit to schooling and submerge himself in its routines. The content of the curriculum is of little significance except insofar as what is done with it conveys to the student the values, threats, and anxieties whose impact he is required to sustain. In schooling more than any other kind of communication the medium is surely the message.

And the school mystique provides the medium. Those who accept it well enough to emerge after 16 years with a favorable credential can usually be trusted to have sufficiently conventional goals, motives, and anxieties to find the larger social system into which they are released rewarding. To those who have learned to endure and even have fun in a small trap, the big trap built to a similar plan but on a much more lavish scale and with much richer bait looks like freedom. It offers, in any case, all they are likely to have learned to desire or even imagine. "TV dinner by the pool! Aren't you glad you finished school?" the Mothers of Invention chant, succinctly and sardonically, in "The M.O.I. American Pageant." Most youngsters probably are.

But saturation of the young with the school mystique has, I believe, more fundamental functions than creating a respect for our common cultural heritage as exemplified by a desire for gracious suburban living. To survive the school and earn its commendation and support in gaining access to desirable roles and status, the student must come to accept as virtually inevitable certain value positions that determine his most intimate responses to other people and to his own experience. These responses get built into his very nervous system in the form of an anxiety gradient, and they set the limits of his life space by limiting how far he can swing and how confidently he can resist the inroads of social sanctions on his self-esteem. This, after all, is what socialization means.

Wide acceptance of the value positions conveyed by the school mystique keeps our social institutions going and reduces conflict; it stabilizes our society. But this is just another way of saying that the schools support the status quo, and, particularly, that the restriction of opportunity to those who come to terms with it virtually ensures that our society, in all its echelons, will be led by people who either cannot conceive of better social arrangements or despair of ever getting them adopted, and with good reason. This seems to me the final irony—the school, by controlling access to status on terms that perpetuate the characteristics of mass society, while serving simultaneously as the registrar and guarantor of competence, holds competence in escrow. And it does not release it until competence has demonstrated, over a period of years and under a variety of provocations, that its bearer has other qualities that make him unlikely or even unable to direct his competence toward major social change. By placing the school in control of the only legitimate channel to status and power, we virtually ensure that those who gain status and power will use them to perpetuate our difficulties rather than to create new and radical solutions.

The problem is not that the schools are conservative—offical social institutions are inevitably conservative. The problem is in the nature of what is to be conserved, of the specific social values of which the school is custodian, and to which it demands adherence as the price of accreditation. What are these values? They constitute a complex and seamless pattern, but the following emphases are revealing: There is first an anxious and sometimes brutal intolerance of deep feeling between persons, of emotional commitment to others. This permeates school routines; love and loyalty are violations of its code and are severely punished. In some ways this is evident—the school forbids any kind of physical expression of affection at the same time that it maintains and supports a teasing attitude toward sexual attraction; its erotic ethos is basically that of a key club with unpaid bunnies. Love between members of the same sex, though a real and valid aspect of adolescent growth, is of course even more brutally punished, and hippiness, which refuses to limit itself by considerations of gender at all, is perhaps most condemned. Calm, gentle, long-haired boys arouse genuinely pathological hatred in physical education teachers.

But it is not only physical love and honest, personally expressive sexuality that get the school up tight. Affectionate regard and care among peers is contrary to standard operating procedure, which prescribes instead jolly, antagonistic cooperation

and competition. The school breaks up what it calls peer groups bound together by strong personal ties as cliques, which it sees as antidemocratic and potential sources of resistance and subversion. In class, cooperation between friends is cheating. It is evident that this pattern of values is, or has been, functional in breaking youth to the demands of middle-class life in a mobile society dominated by impersonal bureaucratic structure. But the middle class itself has begun a strong revolt against the emptiness and lack of feeling this way of life imposes; not only is hippy youth primarily middle class, but industrial executives as well as isolated professionals have begun seeking a restoration of feeling and authenticity in group therapy sessions, T-groups, and other prostheses intended to replace the functions that friendship and respect for one's neighbor perform in cultures that do not stifle them.

For lower-status, or otherwise "culturally deprived" youth, the schools' insistence on impersonality is anathema. Murray and Rosalie Wax, in a continuing series of published studies of the effect of imposing formal education on the Oglala Sioux, have made it clear that this issue is the focus of a complete educational stalemate. Sioux children will not adopt American competitive folkways and refuse to respond to the teacher at all; adolescents sit in third grade year after year in derisive silence rather than meet the teacher's terms. Similar difficulties, as the Waxes point out, arise in encounters between lower-status urban youth and the schools; and one wonders why so common and serious a source of educational frustration has not resulted in a more flexible response to the children. But in the allocation of status and role the frustration is functional; it ensures that youngsters, whether Indian, Negro, or just unusually autonomous, who refuse to be depersonalized will get bad credentials that will stigmatize them as lazy or slow learners, keeping them down without involving the school in a disagreeable overt conflict about values.

A related, and perhaps even more fundamental, aspect of the school mystique is its support of vulgarity, especially shabby-genteel vulgarity. If there is one single social function of the school on which, more than any other, a mass society depends for stability, it is this: the hazing of potential poets and critics into submission, depriving them of the self-confidence that might have turned them into prophets rather than technologists.

This is accomplished by investing authority in personnel who themselves obviously either do not understand the material they are dealing with or are either intolerant of contradiction or defend themselves by treating the whole issue as a "fun thing"; and by grouping together in class students of such different backgrounds that no meaningful discussion is possible. It is all in **Up the Down Staircase**; but though life in Calvin Coolidge High and its counterparts is sometimes farcical, its social function is deadly serious, and it works. By defining the role of the teacher and school officials as fairly low in status, society ensures that, though there will be many competent teachers, all students will nevertheless be exposed for significant periods of time to the cognitive style and emotional attitudes that pervade life at the "common man" level. The fact that higher-status students are unlikely to accept this view as their own, and that students of whatever social status who feel a need for freedom and personal expression will loathe it as constrictive is all to the good. The school does not perform its integrative function by convincing its students that the way of life of the common man is beautiful and his view of reality profound. Rather, it demonstrates to them, over and over, that the common man is going to win and they are going to lose, no matter who is right, so that if they are wise they will learn to avoid challenging him. The lesson is not that the system is admirable but that you can't beat it.

Most of us learn this lesson; later, if we become professors at a state university we simply assume that we mustn't buck the legislature. Our administrators depend on our having this insight to assist them in their funding. Most of the good credentials go to those who learn them early and well. And in this way a shifting sea of unhappy and resentful people who live by wheeling and dealing keep their society going and avoid breaking one another up in direct confrontation. But the poets become frightened and sound the alarm; they, at least, are faithful to their function:

> Face the day
> And walk around
> Watch the Nazis
> Run your town
> Then go home
> And check yourself—
> You think we're singing
> 'Bout someone else!
> But you're plastic people!
> I know that love
> Will never be
> A product of
> Plasticity![2]

The Mothers sing. And the schools bear some of the responsibility for the truth of their vision of the Great Society.

NOTES

1. For a vivid descriptive analysis of this process at work, see Arthur D. Vidich and Joseph Bensman, **Small Town in Mass Society**, Princeton University Press, 1958.

2. "Plastic People" is from "Absolutely Free," words and music by Frank Zappa. © 1968 by Frank Zappa Music Inc. All rights reserved.

chapter 41
students
as teachers
harold taylor

When a university sets out to reform its educational program in direct collaboration with students, the quality of teaching and learning is immediately affected. In the first place, the academic departments have to be much more careful in making appointments to the faculty exclusively on the basis of publication records and academic reputation. Inability to teach, or even disinterest in teaching, then becomes a potential source of embarrassment to the administration and to the departmental chairmen and their advisory committees. Too much concern with academic prestige and research ability, for even a limited period of time, means that soon there are not enough good teachers to go around, not enough scholars who enjoy working with students, or, what is worse for the departmental interest, not enough students to fill the classes and therefore not enough appointments available to sustain the size and position of the department in the university structure.

On the positive side, the academic faculty, when it collaborates with students in the development of courses and educational policy, has the very great advantage of working within its own disciplines with students whose talents and motivation in these fields begin to flourish at a higher

level, both in teaching and in learning. Among the cooperating students, a far greater proportion than before becomes interested in working at an even higher level, with intellectual capacities of a broader range because of the experience they have had in their beginning courses and projects. The faculty thus finds itself with a breeding ground for future teaching and research talent and for the development of intellectual interests directly related to their own.

As for policy-making and government in student affairs, a great deal of this can be better arranged by students than by faculty members and administrative officers. The experimental colleges, particularly Antioch, Goddard, and Sarah Lawrence, have given students responsibilities in student affairs which in other colleges are handled entirely by college staff, and have found that not only the policy-making but the administration works in ways which call upon resources in students which would otherwise remain undeveloped. By bringing the students actively into the administration itself, the administrative problems of college life confront the students directly, and refute the idea that anyone who is an administrator belongs to the enemy camp.

The Sarah Lawrence pattern is one in which the Student Council not only has the power of deciding on the rules for the student community, from dormitory hours to chartering organizations, but the responsibility for administering their own rules through a council of vice presidents of the student houses. In the case of student legislation which in the view of the administration or faculty is unwise or misguided, the opportunity exists for a reconsideration in a joint committee of elected faculty members, elected students, and administration. The joint committee holds the power of ultimate decision in matters of college policy in general. An appeal could of course be made beyond that body to the board of trustees, but to make such an appeal would mean to admit the failure of the very system which brings the students into a position of responsibility for their own college.

In view of the time and energy absorbed by the administration of student affairs by students, it is also necessary to consider that factor in planning a student schedule of education in the college, and in some cases to relieve a student of course work during a given semester or college year, and to pay a stipend for the services rendered to the community. When the educational program is arranged in such a way that the experience of organizing education on behalf of others is a genuine opportunity for the student, he may learn more from that kind of responsibility over a limited period of time than he would in the formal studies which would otherwise occupy him.

This is especially true of those who intend to become teachers or to enter one of the professions where the ability to organize oneself and to develop programs of use to others is a necessary corollary to whatever scholarship and learning one may possess in the field. The experience in personal relationships, in sustaining the delicate lines of connection which flow between persons and groups who are working in voluntary ways to achieve a common end, is a very important one for students in the entire field of the human services and the arts. The student of theater who has not learned to collaborate with others in the work of the theater, and who has not learned what is involved on the practical side in putting a production on the stage, is in the same position as a student who has not learned to do what has to be done when any useful human enterprise involving cooperative effort is set in motion.

■

This brings me to another matter basic to the reconstruction of the learning-teaching system, the matter of graduate students and their role in teaching. Their present status as teaching assistants to professors is a function of the lecture system and all its parts, not the result of an examination of how education may best be conducted through the talents which students of all kinds can bring to the teaching system. It is now a truism to say that in most cases in the big universities the graduate students provide one of the few opportunities for personal contact by the undergraduates with the teaching faculty. The rest is a matter of sitting in lectures. The graduate students know this, and are fully aware of the dependence of the present economic and cultural structure of the university on their work in teaching. At many universities they have organized Graduate Student Unions both to advance their economic interests and to influence educational policy. Their ranks contain some of the most intelligent, imaginative, and energetic educators the country has ever seen. The fact that they do not yet possess teaching credentials and higher degrees cannot disguise the fact that they are already functioning as teachers, regardless of faculty status—teachers who are working under wraps by the status they now occupy.

What is true of the graduate schools is true of the whole educational system and the society at large. Everywhere the idea of specified and certified professional and vocational skills, only available for public use after certified institutional training programs, has taken hold of the country's institutional life. It has substituted itself for the idea that anyone who can demonstrate in action the quality of what he knows and what he can do has no need of diplomas and credentials in order to do it. Except in the case of brain surgeons and a limited range of professional talents, the certification is unjustified.

A move away from the pattern of the credential society is essential as the first step toward breaking down the barriers to the full use of all human talent, certified or uncertified. Psychiatric aides, for example, who spend more time with patients than anyone in the mental hospital staff and who have a serious degree of influence on the progress of the patient's recovery, should be given the recognition and responsibility that comes with their function. So should teachers' aides, student assistants in child-care centers, community volunteers, community workers without formal education. Once the obvious fact is recognized that education is an amalgam of influences and not simply a transaction between academic professionals and pupils who appear before them, the way is open for the full use of human resources of all kinds within the schools, the colleges, and the universities.

The students who have organized store-front colleges and street academies have already recognized the ability of ordinary people, without certificates and formal training, both to teach and to learn. Among those recruited by the students as tutors for their projects are high school dropouts, mothers of children, automobile mechanics, former convicts, college professors. Others at the University of North Carolina and elsewhere have organized "poor people's universities" and in one instance have developed a category of university professor whom they call "poor professors," which, although open to wide misinterpretation, refers to poor people in the community who come to college classes in the humanities and social sciences to talk about social issues and realities from their position in the middle of poverty.

In the case of teachers like David Riesman, in whose undergraduate courses graduate assistants are given an opportunity to collaborate directly both in the teaching and in the educational planning, there is no particular status problem, since Riesman and others like him deal with the assistants as intellectual and teaching colleagues, not as hired hands to carry out tasks for which professors have no time or inclination. But in the system as a whole the graduate assistant, whose maturity of outlook and practical teaching experience qualify him as a full-fledged teacher, finds himself in the absurd situation of acting as a handy man when he should be recognized as a major element in the conduct of university instruction.

There is no need to repeat again the account of how this situation is related to failures of graduate education in general, and the lack of connection between the requirements for the doctoral degree and the preparation of students for teaching assignments in the colleges and universities. What is needed is a conception of teaching and learning which reaches back into the undergraduate student body and considers undergraduates and graduate students as members of one community, capable of teaching each other. There are many juniors and seniors in the colleges and universities whose gifts as teachers and educational leaders are presently ignored, and, were a different attitude to the curriculum and its operation taken by the university, could become a major element in the improvement of undergraduate learning.

I have already referred to the organic unity of undergraduates and graduate students within the civil rights and activist groups, and their intellectual and practical collaboration in educational and political projects without regard to age level or academic status. There is no reason why that kind of collaboration cannot be made a regular part of the teaching system. It requires only the initiative of the faculty to set it in motion, with or without an educational plan for the whole university. A faculty member is free to call upon individual members of his undergraduate classes, both those in the present classes and those whose work in previous classes recommended itself to their teachers, to act as seminar and discussion leaders, tutors, organizers, and aides in educational planning and teaching.

A budget should be provided to allow a teacher or group of teachers to appoint undergraduates with teaching talent who had previously worked within particular courses, with the students invited to reduce their course schedule in a given semester in order to give teaching assistance as aides in a course, with a stipend to match. Freshmen entering the university could be given the advantage of choosing a student adviser from among those appointed to such a student staff; the staff could organize a seminar and tutorial plan by which the freshmen could become involved in the discussion and clarification of the problems of becoming educated at the university. This simply pushes to a larger dimension the informal advising system which already exists among students, but which at present bears the handicap of not being part of a serious effort to give the entering student a chance to find his bearings and to establish a sense of colleagueship with students more advanced than himself in the educational system.

There are many in the ranks of the graduate students who have earned the right to teach students of their own, and who could supply the basic resources for the teaching staff of the freshman and sophomore years, as well as in the upper division. If they were invited to collaborate with the faculty in planning seminars and programs, this could replace the lecture system with one more in keeping with the needs of the undergraduates. Whenever lectures were needed, these could be supplied by calling together a number of the individual seminars into one class for a joint session to be addressed by a lecturer chosen for the particular contribution he could make to the problems under consideration in the seminars. Collaboration among the seminar teachers would be possible, not only in this way, but in many others. Individual students could combine their talents in symposia to be presented to a group of the seminars; outside visitors from the community, the faculty, and the graduate-student roster could also be included.

This would entail a different kind of organization within the graduate divisions themselves. In a given semester, as part of the master of arts or doctoral degree program, a student would spend the whole of his time, with an appropriate stipend, in the work of an undergraduate seminar, with the seminar materials and supervision of undergraduate projects considered as an integral part of the work of the graduate student in developing his own body of knowledge within his chosen field. There is no more effective way of organizing such a body of knowledge of one's own than by teaching it. The rationale for the semester or year of work of a graduate student as teacher is not simply that it would give the future college professor experience in teaching as a necessary component of his preparation, but that it would deepen his scholarship and his intellectual resources by the process of discovering what it was he had learned which was useful to others in the culture.

The rationale could also be extended to the undergraduate curriculum, where, in connection with work in psychology, anthropology, literature, sociology, physics, biology, or mathematics, the students would be asked, as part of their regular work to volunteer for tutoring assignments with children or with high school students in areas and subjects where help was needed and in which the undergraduate had competence.

When the entire educational system is seen in terms of its interconnections through teaching and learning, not as a series of interlocking social and cultural agencies separated from each other by bureaucratic rules and testing devices, the stream of consciousness which runs from the child to the adolescent to the young adult and beyond then becomes the most vital and important thing about it. Links between one consciousness and another become the crucial matter, not the discontinuities and separations which the institutions make within temselves and among each other. The continuity of experience between the internal life of the school and college and the life of the society becomes a natural educational concept, with broad implications for the union of talents found within the educational institution and the need for these

talents for education in the community. The curriculum of the college is then joined to the reality of the society, and through their union the student can learn to locate himself in the wider world and to act upon it. It is this continuity in consciousness which gives the basis for planning the internal life of the university so that at every point the students are linked to others, and education for students becomes the series of influences and experiences through which they teach and are taught.

■

How then do we proceed, finally, to accomplish the reforms? Where do we take hold? Who makes the next moves?

It will be clear from what I have been saying up to now that my view is that the moves must be collaborative; they must be made by the faculty, the administration, and the students together. I would add that it does not matter who moves first, as long as the students are centrally involved in what is done. The students can become involved by invitation of the faculty or the administration, by their own initiative, by a new curriculum, by the student's natural attachment to a student organization which is itself involved in educational reform. But in the last analysis, it is the responsibility of the university of which they are a part to find ways of creating the involvement by the structure of the internal life of the college.

The movement in reform can therefore start at any point, without the necessity of another faculty report, by simply taking seriously the proposition already stated that the best place to start a reform movement to improve a student's education is directly in the area of his intellectual life as this is lived at the university—that is, in the courses, on the campus, with his teachers.

The simplest way to set in motion a reform movement which starts in the working areas of the student's intellectual life is to take the educational questions one year at a time, that is, to set a group of interested faculty members and students to work on rethinking the freshman year, with some relation between their work and that of another group considering how the freshman year develops into the sophomore year. This would be linked to plans for the junior and senior years, with students drawn into the planning from each of the years in view of the recency of their experience and the degree of their talent and interest. In the case of the freshman year, many of the universities have their only connection with the high schools through the admissions office, in the review of transcripts and sometimes interviews with candidates. In some cases, the universities invite high school students to come to the campus for a day's visit, or they show films in the high schools and before community groups of football games or documentaries about the university. In other cases, in connection with some of the new programs for the relatively unprepared entrants, summer sessions are arranged to get the new students ready for entry in the fall.

An extension of the idea of linking each year of education with its preceding one, and the idea of involving students in the university curriculum, would entail the appointment of students, with an appropriate stipend, not merely to the faculty admissions committee, but to a student admissions staff drawn from a list of students recommended by the faculty. These students could visit local high schools, possibly taking a sabbatical leave during the first semester of the sophomore or junior year; they could visit high school classes, talk to the students and teachers there, and lead discussions of the courses and programs presently available to freshman students, and of other ones which the high school students would like to see organized in view of what they have already learned in high school and what they would most like to do when they first enter the university.

From the body of material collected by the student-traveler and reports made to the student-faculty committee on the freshman year, ideas for patterns of study and programs could be developed for the entering freshmen, each of whom could be asked to prepare for himself a study plan, or general outline of courses and their content, to be included among other materials presented as qualification for admission. Or the applicants could be asked to join with other students in the high school who were applying for admission, and to organize groups among themselves, on the basis of common interests, to develop ideas for projects and areas of study in which they would like to work during their freshman year at the university.

A program of this kind would have a direct effect in stimulating some new educational thinking among students and teachers in the high school about what to do with the junior and senior years aside from carrying out the obligatory academic exercises necessary to meet the present admissions requirements. There could emerge from this an internal curriculum in the high school through

which the students, in order to improve their qualifications for admission to the university, could work with elementary and junior high school students as tutors and assistant teachers. Again, the rationale, as in the case of the graduate students, is that the best way to learn how to organize one's own education is to learn how to help others with theirs.

This could then serve a double purpose for the university. It would give to the faculty members who were planning the freshman year some fresh and interesting material for use in developing the freshman curriculum. It would help the admissions office to select the most promising students for admission, not exclusively in terms of their grades, rank in class, and academic credits, but by reference to the level of their intellectual interests and capacities, their talent for self-education, their potential contribution to the student community, their potential ability as teachers, community workers, artists, educational aides, and reformers once they arrived at the university.

The student appointee to the staff of the admissions office and the admissions committee, working with the committee on the freshman year, could review the study plans of high school students, along with the other admissions material from the applicants, some of which would be coming from students in the schools he had visited and whom he would know. From that material the student staff member could present ideas to the committee on the freshman year for various kinds of grouping within fields of study, distributing the freshmen throughout the university in terms of their interests, and organizing the teaching program around them.

One of the assignments for the entering freshmen could be to a seminar of the kind I have already suggested, similar to the exploratory courses taught at Sarah Lawrence by the faculty, to which freshmen are assigned on the basis of the account they have given of their past education and study plans in the admissions materials submitted to the college. The purpose of the exploratory course at Sarah Lawrence is to give a central place in the freshman year to each student, a place where, with whatever help and advice is needed from the teacher of the course, the student can explore the methods and materials for learning in an area of his interest and can raise a variety of questions on topics of concern, ranging from problems in handling the college life to issues of college policy or public affairs.

This kind of seminar provides the common

intellectual experience for which the curriculum makers have been in search, along with a sense of identification with the university, by the directly personal way in which the freshman seminar conducts its business, and the possibility of coming to know intimately and in the setting of a university class other students with similar interests and similar problems. In our experience at Sarah Lawrence, the exploratory course gave to each student a place to begin, a set of intellectual companions, and a central person in the faculty to whom one could go for advice and help on any matter connected with the experience of being in college.

When graduate students and upperclassmen are involved in advising and teaching this kind of freshman seminar, and sophomores and others are involved in the work of the admissions committee and the development of the freshman year, they create a completely new style of educational thinking. They bring to their colleagues in the faculty a wealth of empirical knowledge about students, and educational thinking can proceed on the basis of that knowledge rather than on generalizations about the student as an abstraction. They break down the barriers which separate the academic faculty from the student body, and introduce the idea of the learning-teaching community to replace the concept of the manufactured curriculum taught by hired hands.

They also produce a way of bridging the gap between the administration and the students, by carrying out some of the administrative tasks in cooperation with the administrators. In the case of the student members of the admissions staff, for example, there is no reason why such students should not correspond with high school applicants about their study plans, and prepare mimeographed material which would be useful to the high school student in understanding what would be expected of him when he comes to the university, and what he could expect to find available to him once he arrives there. Entering students can then learn to identify the university with its student body and not simply with its officials and their offical pronouncements.

The same kind of approach through student-faculty planning can be taken to the sophomore year, with the returning sophomores asked to prepare preliminary study plans for themselves during the spring of the freshman year. Student members of the student-faculty committee staff could work during the summertime on the collation of the student plans into general outlines of possible **courses, projects, and study groups, for use by the**

faculty in preparing the sophomore course offerings. In the case of the junior and senior years, when most students want to work in a major field, something approximating the student Council of Majors recommended by the Berkeley Commission on University Governance could be organized to work with the departments in making plans for courses in special fields of study.

Liberal allowances of choice could be made for students not yet ready for a full commitment to a specialized field; their programs could include a wider spread of courses, independent study under the supervision of graduate students, or work on a student research team with similar supervision. Not only would this keep the departments in touch with the changing needs of their clientele, but it would give them the benefit of many new ideas for undergraduate course offerings and different forms of organization, while linking their graduate students to the problems of the scholar-teacher.

In this way, from the freshman to the senior year and beyond, a new and sizeable internal network of student teachers and policy makers would be created on a university-wide scale. There would then be a basis for a far greater cohesion of interest in the student body as a whole and a wealth of opportunity for the undergraduates to combine forces among themselves in creating their own education and in finding close associates and colleagues who shared their interests. Out of that network can come the formal structure of student involvement in basic university policy questions, by elections from the student body, by nominations from both the students and faculty for appointments of students to the faculty bodies, administrative committees, and staff of the university. Through the existence of this internal structure, the primary elements of a true community of learning would have been assembled to carry out the tasks in which it is the business of that community to engage itself.

■

The task of reform in education and society has no end, but only new beginnings. Reform goes on, planned or unplanned, in one way or another way, usually at a pace many years behind the need, by the efforts of those few who cannot be satisfied with what they find, and look for better ways, and by the necessities of historical change which keep pressing upon all institutions and testing their capacity for alteration and survival.

This is the first age in which so many untamed and unmanageable necessitites have been pressing all at once, and the first age in which the historical circumstances have combined to produce a younger generation so fully aware of those circumstances. In other times it was possible to say that that is the way things go in the universities. The students enter and leave, the society changes and moves on, the universities stay at the quiet center, giving the mind its due, keeping the ideals of civilization alive.

It is clear that this is no longer a possible attitude, although the necessity for the quiet center continues to exist, and the protection of the ideals of civilization was never more urgent or necessary. The difference now is that the university is already engaged with the necessities and must act to engage itself with them now, on its own terms, without the time to speculate, but only time to confront. The society will not stand still, even to be studied and observed. It insists on acting.

In this situation of the university, once more the students are its greatest allies, and if some of them have declared themselves to be its enemies, let them be met by those in the universities who know and can teach that the real enemy of the university is ignorance, force, and violence, and that the way to overcome these is by knowledge, a passion for justice, and a commitment to truth.

For it is in the ideal of a community of concerned persons who share a common interest in the life of the mind and the quality of human experience that the genius of the university lies. The rest is a matter of how that community can best be constructed by the best efforts of all concerned. There is nobility and strength in the lovely old words "fraternity," "equality," "liberty and justice for all"—and the university is the place where these words can become names for the living experience of those within its environs. Unless the reality of that experience is to be found there, it is unlikely to be found in the larger world. Unless students learn through what they do there that equality is a two-edged sword, that fraternity means giving part of oneself away, that liberty is an affectionate state of mind, and that justice in a democracy is willingness to be faithful in action to agreed-upon principles, all the protest, controversy, radical action, and appeal to the big abstractions of moral enthusiasm will come to nothing

but a continual attrition of the very ideals of which the young are in search.

That is why education and the university must both be redefined so that they may become instruments through which the influence of persons on each other may act to secure the elevation of spirit and quality of life which it is the purpose of all education to induce. The university should be a place where students help their teachers to teach them, where teachers help their students to learn, where administrators help both to accomplish what they have come together to do. That is why the role of the students must also be redefined, in order to make clear to them and to all others that students are the foundation of the university, that when everything else is taken away, as in fact it can be—the government contracts, the isolated research institutes, the alumni bodies, the services to industry, the traveling faculty, the organization men—what is left are persons working together to learn and to teach.

Learning and teaching in this sense have to do with the totality of human conduct, in which the conduct of the affairs of the mind is by turns political, social, public, private, intellectual, emotional, external, internal, and, in the last analysis, personal. Otherwise conduct has no meaning, the human act is stripped of motivation, empty of content, lacking in truth.

The education of students, therefore, means nothing less than their personal involvement in the conduct of the affairs of the mind. An equality of position in the polity of the community is a necessary condition of their involvement; otherwise they are playing a game the necessity for whose rules they never learn to understand—the commitment to play is never completely made. What the world needs above all is a large and increasing supply of incorruptibles, men and women who have learned to act in the interest of mankind, who are capable of noble action as an outcome of unpremeditated thought, and are capable of clarity of thought as a natural and intuitive result of their experience in thinking and in acting. It is the responsibility of the university so to arrange its affairs that the experience of its students in thinking and acting can teach them what it means to serve mankind and what it means to honor the intellect.

topic 19

the educational establishment: the realm of higher education

There is no denying the sensitive ties between our public schools and the technobu-
reaucratic employment structure. But what are the links between higher education and
the larger society? What, in a word, is the basic mission of the American college? Is it
designed to help its students grow, to better comprehend themselves, their world, and our
accumulated store of wisdom? Or are colleges and universities simply servants of power—
training depots where their charges' marketable talents are shaped and honed so that they
can better fulfill the occupational demands imposed by the corporate and bureaucratic
world?

Most students of the sociology of education have few doubts. David Riesman and
Christopher Jencks put the matter bluntly: "Looked at in terms of a theory of the labor
force, one might describe colleges primarily as personnel offices, feeding properly certified employees into business and the professions." And James Ridgeway speaks for many
when he spells out a related but more detailed charge:

> Few people are aware of the extent to which the worlds of
> higher education, big business, and banking are linked through
> interlocking relationships among professors, college presidents,
> and trustees, industry, and government—relationships whose
> chief victims are the more than six million students the univer-
> sities are supposed to teach. In fact the American university
> today resembles a giant conglomerate corporation.

Some analysts have uncovered evidence that the trustees who govern American colleges favor authoritarian norms that are at fundamental odds with the tenets of academic
freedom. One investigator, Hartnett, concludes that "trustees generally favor a hierarchical system in which decisions are made at the top and passed 'down.' "

We have read Schaar and Wolin's condemnation of the rigid bureaucratic controls
that characterize so many of our giant "multiversities." Still other critics have attacked
the narrow professionalism, the petty jealousies, and the parochial outlooks that typify so
many segments of the professorial world. Some, finally (and this hardly exhausts the cata-

log of accusations), have questioned the very **raison d'être** of higher education. Thus the members of a commission appointed by the University of California to reassess the political structure of the university conclude that:

> Some of the most thoughtful and serious students have come to repudiate many of the social goals and values they are asked to serve in the university and upon graduation. That repudiation is directed, in part, at the conditions of technological society that seem to threaten human dignity. The new world emerging seems to exact greater conformity, more routinized lives, more formalized relationships among individuals, and a deeper sense of helplessness amid an increasingly abstract world devoid of humane values.

[Study Commission on University Governance, in Skolnick and Currie, 1970]

The arraignments advanced by the authors of our first two selections are unique in their candor. The one by John Weiss traces the evolution of the American university and examines the origins of many of the phenomena that have alienated so many of today's students: the mass lecture system, objective testing, the growth of administrative bureaucracy, and the shunning of undergraduates in favor of graduate students. Kingsley Widmer's "Rebellion as Education" raises similar questions, but his ire is aroused in particular by the stifling nature of educational bureaucracy. The anonymous author of the final selection, "The New Students," asks "Who is the young man or woman who comes to college today?" His answers will strike many readers as uncommonly perceptive, but his conclusion can hardly be comforting.

chapter 42
the university
as corporation
john weiss

The basic historical fact about higher education in the United States is this: in the late nineteenth century, a transformation began which ended by changing the theology-ridden, narrow, and classical college of the eighteenth century into a vast and truly social institution, broad in scope, secular and pragmatic in nature, and above all prepared to be of great use to a rising industrial society. The college became, and deliberately became, a necessary and major social institution for outstripping in aim and reality anything comparable in the American or European past. From this transformation have come both the major achievements and the tenacious defects of the beast.

The most basic change in the nineteenth century was the very conception of what and who should be taught. Led largely by administrative heads, often presidents, (and resisted often by faculty), the vast areas of knowledge which had been developing since the early eighteenth century, in both the natural and social sciences, were admitted into the college, where they assumed equal rank with the traditional Latin, Greek, and allied classical studies. The college, and later the university, became for the first time the place where new knowledge in academic disciplines was not only admitted and passed on, but, with time,

actively cultivated. Moreover, the disciplines themselves were being professionalized along with the college. National associations of scholars and disciplines were organized, with their meetings, journals, standards, and pedantic guildism. Slowly the college came to be regarded as the natural place for those who hoped to follow a life of scholarship. The advantages for the advance of knowledge and its teaching in all this are evident. What was not so evident then, however, was the way in which a unique and often destructive dialectic was set up between the claims of specialized research and the demand for mass education.

Hand in hand with scholarly or professional specialization went what one might call the democratization—or perhaps socialization—of the college curriculum and student body. Higher education was not really particularly useful or necessary in America before the last quarter of the nineteenth century. Previously the college had simply passed on, rather mechanically, the classical tradition plus a little advanced moral philosophy or deism. Its students were mainly future clergy and a thin slice of the upper crust. Normally, one would not find future lawyers, physicians, engineers, journalists, teachers, and business managers in attendance. They acquired their training outside the college, as apprentices. Had things remained this way, higher education in America would hardly play such a prominent social role today, nor

From New University Thought, Summer 1965. Reprinted by permission.

could it possibly have the vast influence it has attained as the teacher of each new segment of the rising meritocracy.

In the late nineteenth century, dynamic administrators, usually presidents, transformed the college by professionalizing its educational offerings and bureaucracy, and by opening it to the managerial and professional elites. Increasingly, the professions required theoretical, hence teachable, knowledge. In a swiftly changing mass industrial society, theory becomes crucial in all occupations—even farming, as any faculty member at one of our agricultural colleges can testify. At first, independent schools, uncontrolled by the college, met the new need as scientific, technical, and business institutes. A steady decline in college enrollments, however, made obvious the irrelevance of a solely classical or liberal education in an industrial society. Furthermore, the new presidents of the most advanced institutions of higher education were the first to sense that the traditional college would play an increasingly minor role in a market-oriented society, dedicated to democracy and utility. Under men like White of Cornell, Eliot of Harvard, Tappen of Michigan, and Wayland of Brown, the college began to preempt professional training and to assure itself of a really massive role in modern America. Francis Wayland, the President of Brown, put it all in compelling and businesslike fashion in 1850, when reporting to the Trustees of Brown University:

> Our colleges are not filled, because we do not furnish the education desired by the people. . . . We have produced an article for which the demand is diminishing. We sell it at less than cost, and the deficiency is made up by charity. We give it away, and the demand still diminishes.

I take it that oversensitivity to market terms is out of place here. The college and the university could not have become major social institutions without the insistence that higher education become a market commodity. And the American college president has, since the great transformation, known how to emphasize the commodity value of education as an article of trade. The rewards have been obvious: Higher education in America has found ample room at the public trough. Typically, the important Morrill Land-Grant Act of 1862 set the market conditions which were the price for the unique ability of the American college to gain wealth from the public domain. The Act insisted that for this wealth each favored state or territory must set up at least one college:

> where the leading object shall be . . . to teach such branches of learning as are related to agriculture and the mechanic arts . . . in order to promote the liberal and practical education of the industrial classes in the several pursuits and professions of life.

From the eighties on, then, the great transformation began. The college, to paraphrase Ezra Cornell, was to become a place where any man could study anything. Courses in the useful arts—agriculture and engineering—applied science courses, even military studies and that favorite abomination of liberal arts professors, domestic economy, shouldered their way in alongside the classics and the natural and social sciences. Some of the first public relations activities of the colleges were expanded, and at first in vain, to convince local farmers that education and science could improve farming. Wives were to be better for having formal training in cooking (enobled as domestic economy) and engineers and future business managers were to find college courses and degrees in the theoretical aspects of their vocations offered. One regent of Illinois University—limitless in his ambitions and also normal in other respects —held that his institution ought to teach "every form of human learning which it has fallen to the fortune of mankind to devise or acquire."

Thus, higher education in the United States began its modern career as a social institution, capable of shaping the intellectual habits of a nation. Vast changes, still going on, were required to adjust the college to its role as a social utility subject to market conditions in a democratic business and mass culture. Entrance requirements, grading and credit systems, financial structure, administrative bureaucracies, course offerings, student life, and a general departmentalization and bureaucratization of all aspects of the college had to be undertaken. Essentially, the failure of many of the critics of higher education has been a failure to comprehend the necessities and limitations of such changes, as well as the opportunities they afford to those who develop a strategy for working within a given system for serious and radical reforms.

The social role of the American college helps

to explain the brutal fact that ultimate authority is vested in men who are quite ignorant of education. The boards and trustees who hold final power have been, since the end of clerical influence in the nineteenth century, overwhelmingly composed of wealthy and prestigious businessmen and (secondarily) the professional elite of the community. Such men may have met a payroll but they have rarely taught a class. They are there because they are able to attract wealth and prestige as leaders of the business community, and to emphasize the social value of higher education. Critics have not been lacking to demonstrate that their control means that American higher education is a conservative bulwark of American society. It is not so much that university administrations do not believe in free speech, nor is it really a major defect that Communists are only reluctantly, if at all, allowed to speak on campus. What is really crucial is that as a social institution supported by those most satisfied with American society and unwilling to take seriously major criticisms of it, the university has simply refused to use its virtual monopoly of brains to stand apart from society and view it critically. The universities' knowledge and expertise are used only to train people for the given tasks of society—among them the task of scholarship. It is not so much that the university is not leftish or radical. The basic trouble is that in its marketplace-wisdom of maximizing demand, the university has ignored its duty to press for change and reform in all directions.

Perhaps even more crucial, however, has been the increasing power of the administrative officers over their boards and trustees. Lack of time and lack of interest coupled with the increasing complexity of running a major social institution (in education as elsewhere) has given increased power to managers rather than owners. The administration, of course, acts within the limits set by the business and professional groups. At the same time they act as neutralizers and buffers as well as administrative specialists. The result seems to be that though the university and the college are part of the ruling establishment and work entirely in its uncritical spirit, few see the extent of such indirect control. And this is so because the subtle management techniques of bureaucratic administrators are designed to avoid the crude thrust of manly dictatorship, even while forcing all to yield to market pressures and dominant values. The stuffy, patronizing, and even parental air of the average dean confronting his employees (called faculty) is one

of the results. Furthermore, bureaucratic administrators in any vast social corporation consider it their primary duty to work according to policy as they find it. They simply refuse to lead the university in radical new paths unless outside pressures or a united and singleminded internal constituency group force them to it. How amusing and disheartening to discover that the editor of **Oxford Magazine**, a semiofficial organ of Oxford University (England), senses the same compulsion at work as England moves to the socialization of her narrow-based education system. I quote:

> The University cannot in a democracy give the lead to public opinion . . . because it is more and more a public institution under public pressures. . . . Enlightened patronage of advanced principles is a privilege more easily exercised by a private rather than a public corporation.

Beyond these implications of the socialization of American higher education come the long-term consequences of having to justify the entire curriculum as useful to society but at the same time not critical and reformist. Within the college, natural selection works to give increase and funds to those programs which seem of obvious social utility, defined often enough as training upcoming members of the business and professional classes in their trade. This pragmatic community pressure was felt most strongly in the large state and land-grant institutions of the West, and still is. Their lack of a liberal arts tradition and more or less primitive cultural surroundings, their extreme need of public funds, and the financial power of the competing established private institutions have combined to make these institutions the most vulnerable and responsive to establishment attitudes.

As befits a corporate institution in a democratic economy, the college has had to introduce a vast array of new courses (commodities) and create a more or less free market for the exercise of consumer choice (the free elective system). Fortunately, a central concern with the liberal arts has managed to survive. Students of other things are still required to take courses in liberal arts. But is it too much to say that the contemporary trade school atmosphere of most liberal arts colleges has stifled that original sense of communicating an independent and critical lay culture to professional and business people?

Along with professional specialization there has been as well a fragmentation of the intellectual life of undergraduates. Whatever its defects, the eighteenth century college provided a unified and related intellectual life. We have multiplied our course offerings again and again with the excuse that knowledge has been similarly fragmented. But why has the college taken its task to be the representation of all disciplines fairly, rather than the purposeful communication of a unified intellectual culture? Basically, this is because the college has assumed the task of research as well as teaching and has insisted that its people do both—but especially research. The consequences for student life are apparent. Departmentalization shatters the student body and replaces it with student bodies. After the freshmen year, students have no intellectual life in common. As for political activism, it cannot function where there is no true community. Students soon see that in spite of all the pseudodemocratic rhetoric indulged in by deans of students, no shreds of power will come to them. As elsewhere, we train our young in college to refuse responsibility for the society as a whole and retreat to their private concerns. As for the few student lefties, shrewd administrative techniques can frustrate them and make them look foolish. If all else fails, one can always distribute a few tame faculty here and there in student government.

The student is pushed toward a mindless apathy to all but his career by virtue of the structure of the college itself. After some feeble exposure to highly simplified snippets of "surveyed" professional knowledge in several disciplines, the student gets on to his real business of preparing for a trade or profession. The parts are all there, but, except where general studies have been worked out, no one helps the student perceive the relationship between the various fields and, more importantly, between the knowledge he acquires and the culture he inhabits. Consequently, the student is aware above all of the vast irrelevance of most of the stuff he reads and hears—and on top of all that he must patiently listen to our accusations of apathy and conformity! Little wonder that he retreats to the at least real attractions of **Mad** magazine and the various gatefold girls! Those students who still cannot deny their intellectual curiosity most sensibly pick up bits and pieces of existentialist and revolutionary attitudes, and decide that their superiors are fools, that all most be redone, and that the only true education is self-education.

Correspondingly, the faculty and lower ad-

ministration have been divided into all sorts of distinct interest and professional groups which have little or no intellectual or social unity. This is, of course, a result of the great diversity in curriculum of the modern college. We don't really have colleges, we have many departments in search of a college. Colleges, divisions, departments; each require administrative heads, and the whole follows the same political pattern prevalent in America at large—that is, the clash of small power units for power and affluence under the managerial supervision of higher establishment or upper administration. Only the upper administration is regarded, even by the faculty, as speaking for the college, and this because only they have a sense of the total and are concerned with the whole. But unfortunately the upper administration can only be concerned with the bureaucratic and financial management of the whole, and not with its intellectual life. Educational reforms, for example, in our vast state institutions, are almost always confined to departments. General, college-wide, and serious educational reforms usually take place only in our small and private liberal arts colleges. Meanwhile the vast bulk of American students remain undirected and unreformed. Typically, the college teacher is ignorant of the total educational experience he and his colleagues are imparting to the students. The best of them can hardly find out what other courses their students take. Hence, even the faculty reformer is primarily concerned with improving his own course—not the complete intellectual life of his student.

The average faculty member, however, is, like the average student, concerned with his private career and his department's private fate in the college power struggle. The departmental interest in the struggle to improve its competitive position vis-à-vis other departments is the reality underlying most of the important changes in college offerings and requirements. No department or division has responsibility for the total intellectual life of the student. And no department will surrender its claim to student time and budget allotment by bowing before an educational reform that lessens their credit hour requirement. The free election and major system, meanwhile, gives power (in liberal arts at least) to those departments and teachers who can command or attract the largest number of students. Such departments become the great powers on campus, and gain larger budgets, more faculty, and more influence over college decisions. The temptation is usually too strong for any to resist. Success is not defined as successful guidance of the general intellectual life of the student—it comes to mean recruiting the largest possible number of apprentices for one's guild.

Perhaps the most serious defects in undergraduate teaching stem ultimately from the refusal of the national guilds of scholars to consider teaching their major professional responsibility. Historians, sociologists, economists, anthropologists, and others, united in their professional association, distribute their awards of prestige and, indirectly, faculty rank and pay, according to their single-minded devotion to research and scholarship. Such groups rarely take any responsibility for teaching methods, holding that such concern is nonsense emanating from the (unjustly) despised professors of education, and that, in any event, any research scholar can teach adequately. It is not too much to say that your average scholar confuses good teaching with smooth-flowing lecture rhetoric, mildly tough grading, and being liked by his students. Within such organizations, those who are devoted to the improvement of undergraduate education must form associations designed to remind the scholars of their neglect of duty. Someone must represent the teaching interest.

Any vital and sizeable institution designed to process large numbers of clients requires a businesslike administrative bureaucracy. The rise of the college to such status has meant the increase and prospering of the bureaucratic type and his dominance over higher education. The skill of such men has nothing to do with teaching or scholarship—though that is often their background. An administrator is one who knows how not to offend the powerful, and how to tread carefully the tightrope drawn tight by contending forces. He is a "moderate" in the sense in which we use that much abused word, that is, one who attempts no changes which will force him to move against the social pressures which surround him in any clearly defined way. The best administrator, as normally defined, is one who knows how to take advantage of prevailing conditions and gain students, status, and wealth for his administration. He will know how to stress the immediate utility of his medical and engineering schools; he will know how to represent, at one remove, the market demand for his various products. For the administrator must naturally look upon the college as producing a product (education) more or less efficiently (cost per credit hour per student) and competing for customers (students) and private and public

funds with other and similar corporations.

The teaching staff often assumes an air of superiority to their administrative superiors, though it is hard to see any justification for this. For most of them treat students more or less as apprentice specialists—whether they are to be future literary scholars, electrical engineers, social scientists, dentists, undertakers, or chemists. Captured by the ideal of feeding his profession with ever more skilled apprentices, the college teacher pays little heed to the general intellectual life of the undergraduate. He can hardly be persuaded to give serious attention to those undergraduates—the vast majority—who attend his courses but do not intend to become majors in his discipline. Before the student stands not a trained intellectual and generalist to help him reach an understanding of the world he inhabits, but a scholarly specialist, prepared only to communicate the lore and skills of his special field. The general student often becomes apathetic simply because he senses that his teachers have no real interest in improving his awareness as an educated layman. His instructor's work and prestige relates only to his fellow specialists and any in class who might become such.

The matter of prestige and status within one's specialty has been crucial for this trade-school orientation of modern liberal arts institutions. A college in America generally becomes famous and prestigious to the extent that it is able to purchase scholars of note who have achieved fame (among their few colleagues) through publication and paper-reading. This is the academic version of the "star" system. We hear it said again and again that there is no conflict between research and teaching. This would be true were it not for the simple fact that undergraduate teaching requires wide-ranging but not superficial generalists; whereas the only way to scholarly fame and higher wages is through steady and constant focus on a narrow area. One makes oneself a marketable commodity by developing intellectual skills that have little to do with general knowledge. Hence that extraordinary combination one so often finds among academic intellectuals: highly refined specialist knowledge but superficial irrelevance in all that pertains to general education. Increasingly, the academic intellectual does not regard himself as an intellectual and comes to scorn the very term, even as he condemns, perhaps, so-called American antiintellectualism! In short, American higher education, by becoming socially useful and professionally competent, has drawn talent and energy away from a serious concern with stimulating an informed, general, and critical awareness of our society and culture among those who need it most.

■

The evidence for all this is increasingly available. The administration, bent on decreasing costs, works for the introduction of the large lecture system, objective examinations, and flexible standards. Departmental chairmen, confronted with fixed budgets, are anxious to cram more students in the lecture halls so that the money thus saved may be used for hiring prestigious scholars, giving scholarships to their graduate students, and thereby obtaining budget increases, more staff, and campus power. The better and more ambitious faculty member, aware that promotion, scholarly fame, and the best posts go to the publisher rather than the teacher, will head for the nearest research grants, the most graduate seminars, and the fewest undergraduate courses.

The mass lecture system solves everybody's problem, even if at the expense of the undergraduate. Two hundred are taught, or shall we say "processed," where only twenty were before, and the professor can content himself with delivering two or three lectures a week. Exam grading and discussion sections can be left to graduate fellows who thus pay for their own fellowships. Teaching quality suffers because all real contact between teacher and student is lost, and ideas and facts cannot be related to the individual student's capacities and interests. All is tailored to fit the minimal needs of what one might call the mythical lecture room's most common denominator. The lecturer does not personally check the examinations, and he has little notion of what is happening to his students. The student is bereft of all opportunity to communicate his own grasp of the subject through extensive essay examination. This is not simply a matter of ignoring the rare creativity of a genius, it is a quite practical concern having to do with the daily work of all students. Examinations are merely graded in a mass system because there is no time to go over them carefully and demonstrate to the student **in writing** his own strengths and weaknesses of knowledge and understanding. If the individual student's mind and understanding are not revealed, discussed, and guided or enhanced at the junior college level, then teaching has not occurred. The whole system is simply and endlessly pumping out useless energy. The student level

of performance is checked but not raised. Improvement, when it occurs, will be a chance by-product of irrelevance. In any sensible educational system, such utter failure would be recognized as a teaching failure. It is not so recognized because the administrator is concerned with efficiency and the teacher with scholarship. In the midst of a mass educational system we all become cynics and anti-democrats, because we have only the students left to blame.

Correspondingly, the all-pervading objective examination, though often shown up for the absurdity it almost always is, increasingly dominates the college. And the reasons are clear. Few are really interested in giving the student a fair or so-called "objective" grade, and that is not in any event an important goal of college education. But efficiency and free time for research welcome an exam which can be graded swiftly and surely by anyone who can read and write. Objective exams have not been introduced because they measure the student's performance more accurately than the essay, they have been introduced because they save time and money. Only those who misunderstand the meaning of the word "objective" could continue to apply it to our proliferating multiple-choice examinations. **Just as with an essay exam, a multiple-choice exam requires some person (i.e., subject, not object) to select the questions and approve the answers.** Barring the simple parroting of brute names, dates, and semi-narratives (never anybody's educational ideal) all testing, **including** true-false and multiple-choice is subjective **and must be.** The nature of mind and knowledge is such that all testing of one mind by another must be subjective, tentative, and open to doubt—and one does not change matters by hiding one's inevitable subjectivity behind a graph, curve, percentage point, or numerical value. As for the usual textbook, it oversimplifies and describes where it should debate and analyze, and contrary to the way of the real world, avoids all strong opinions and thematic treatment. It remains one of the most depressing obstacles to the communication of the ability to judge, generalize, and weigh evidence. But the textbook, like the mass lecture and objective exam, is there because it saves the teacher the trouble of building the course anew each time it is taught, and fitting his perceptions to the individual abilities of the students. Most importantly, the avoidance of strong opinion and complex interpretation makes the average liberal arts textbook a perfect product for a mass market of captive readers. Such texts are intended for the professors' convenience, not the students' needs. The end result is the overvaluing of passive memory over intelligent comprehension. One is asked to react, not think, and one aims at the selection of correct responses, rather than the careful composition of thematic statement by the perception of relevant facts and ideas, skillfully presented in a written essay. Meanwhile, we grade students as we grade beef, with no concern for improving the quality as we stamp the product.

As one contemplates the general run of undergraduate courses in our vast state institutions one wonders if much of what goes under the name of a liberal education doesn't simply dull the intellect. It doesn't really help matters to mitigate the lecture system by introducing graduate section men to conduct weekly discussion sections, as is often done. Only the lecturer can guide a worthwhile discussion in a course which is otherwise his; and in any event, the graduate student soon learns that he is primarily expected to keep his own research and course work up. Short of annoying female students, he will not be judged by what goes on in his classroom. Why are graduate assistants used? Simply because, once again, they lower costs and increase their department's power and quantity of teaching on the graduate level. By teaching, the graduate student pays for his fellowship and is available for the graduate seminars. All this increases the graduate program of the department. A further step, already taken in many institutions, is simply to hand over the hapless undergraduates to the graduate assistants—untrained, inexperienced, and overburdened. And these graduate students soon become faculty somewhere themselves, and have learned before they even start, that only fools, incompetents, or hopeless idealists take undergraduate teaching for anything more than the farce it so often is. As for the progressive administrator and department chairman, they are privy to the most saddening fact: The old system wasn't any better except here and there and just potentially. Over the loss of a here and there and a mere potential, no administrator can be expected to linger, but it is this loss of potential which is the most serious loss.

As Paul Goodman has rightly pointed out, this vast corporate educational system monopolizes the available brains, talent, and wealth. The potential reformers disappear into the machinery, quietly muttering witty remarks at their own expense and coming even to despise those students who, with

crude naïveté, take their own education and their teachers seriously—for a while. Aside from perhaps attempting to attract many students to his courses, the teacher wastes little time on his undergraduates. He will concentrate on research, majors, and graduate students. Most teachers in academia, unlike many of their high school counterparts. don't even know the difference between good and bad teaching. The wise chairman, meanwhile, will manipulate his teaching system so as to increase that portion of the budget he may spend to attract academic stars and graduate students. A man becomes an academic star or world class competitor in the marketplace by his ability to publish in accepted academic journals, read papers before his national association, and publish books that are well received by his well-known colleagues. (Here there is, in the inexact studies, an amount of chicanery involved. For example, your publisher will ask you to name those who will be likely to give your book a favorable review and will act accordingly.) But however adequately set up, the standards of professional associations are not directly relevant to teaching; and increasingly these guilds set the standards for college and university appointment and promotion. For beyond this the terrible fact is that the system has no standards of its own.

The result is plain to see. In most large junior college classes, the majority of the students are not interested in the subject, and the instructors are not really interested in teaching them. At the same time, the department wants as many students in its classes as possible, and so, for that matter, does the teacher, unless he is concerned with teaching standards. To gain power with legislators, the corporation needs a vast number of customers. The situation is only made more absurd by the fact that the department genuinely feels its subject should be taught and for the best of reasons. As always, college politics are made all the more intense because ideals are at stake, and felt to be so. The students, for the most part, rarely know why, say, a future dentist or electrical engineer should be required to study sociology or history. And because courses are mainly taught by scholars on the lookout for potential scholars in the same discipline, the average student is right to assume that no rationale relevant to his needs lies behind his required presence. To suggest that the real purpose of liberal arts education for nonspecialists is to teach them to help make their society and culture express the best that is in man would be to risk being labeled Victorian, naive, radical, or simply absurd. He will certainly find that a serious attempt to suggest that knowledge exists to be used will cause doubt to be cast on his credentials as an "objective" scholar. Meanwhile, in the classroom the tension and alertness which should follow the sensible teaching of a subject that undergraduates are brought to sense they want and need is rarely to be found. Instead one finds boredom, apathy, or, worse, ignorant submissiveness and the drone of endless lectures—the whole permeated by a strong sense of sham and fundamental questions never asked. There are exceptions, even glorious exceptions, but they are exceptions. They arise, perhaps, because of the extraordinary difficulty of destroying the natural curiosity of the young and true intellectual commitment even by the most well-contrived system.

The instructor who begins his career anxious to teach, too often ends as the professor bored at the very thought. Presented with a self-defeating task, he finds that the truth is complex, rarely spectacular, and cannot be imparted without the direct meeting of mind and mind: All this the system avoids. Some few become campus characters—known as great teachers—who win student favor by purging their material of all but its dramatic and spectacular elements, and shouting these out with much effect. Most, however, unwilling or unable to "stimulate" (why not simply hook the chairs up to the nearest electric outlet?) yet plagued by the notion that they are boring their students, end by developing the appropriate cynical attitudes and concentrating on research and graduate students. The student may be entertained, he may be bored, or he may be trained. He is hardly ever taught anything of general significance beyond his trade that makes a difference to him, his society, or his culture.

The administration will and can do little to correct unaided what is more or less the responsibility of the faculty. Usually, administrations cooperate with curriculum reforms that do not increase costs, but few such proposals are forthcoming from the faculty. As with all bureaucracies, the administration is primarily interested in extending the power, prestige, and wealth of their institution. Left unopposed, they will always press for graduate school status, and they will encourage all means available for decreasing expenditures on undergraduates to that end. Hence the prevailing mood in the most progressive state universities is to dilute undergraduate education by doubling up the students. Given the system, individual departments dare not resist and must themselves press for Ph.D.-granting programs whether they feel they have the resources or not—because that is how one gets resources. The more graduate students and academic "stars" one can boast, the more one can gain greater resources from the administration. As a result, there is a vast waste of resources in many states as major public universities set up competing graduate programs.

■

Ever since the great change of the late nineteenth century, the university has used public relations techniques to impress the businessmen of the community with its utility. Often, reading the press releases of the fraudulent professionals involved, one gets the impression that the faculty, with rocklike unity and earthy practicality, is working down to the last instructor for "better things for better living." There is, of course, nothing wrong with campus research for business and industry, especially when it is well paid. Why we must continue to train business executives without pay in our colleges of business administration is not clear until one understands how convenient it is to have the business classes pass through the college and develop appropriate loyalties. Who ever bothered to establish a college of labor union administration? Funds for research prospects increasingly hinge on the good will of business foundations and the approval of Pentagon defense research dispensers. If you don't think this determines where the bulk of research talent will direct itself, try applying to the Ford Foundation for a grant to study taxdodging in the modern corporation, or to the Pentagon for a grant to study ways of drastically reducing our arms budget. But I am unfair. A considerable sum of money is available for conferences in the fine arts, and festivals for the celebration of pure culture abound, peopled with somewhat surprised poets and novelists. More money for research and culture is not to be despised, and one does not expect, say, the Rockefeller Foundation to finance a symposium on the defects of modern capitalism. Still, this is another powerful temptation for the university and college to neglect their primary role as neutral critic and intellectual leader for progress and reform. To those who complain that this would mean a loss of scholarly objectivity, one can only say that scholarly objectivity is not to be equated with neutralism or letting others direct one's research. The university now deducts administrative expenses from all grants. Could it not find means of establishing a fund from its grants for the kind of research which society needs but which no wealthy group in the community can be expected to support? We should not allow the university to become merely an affluent research branch of government and business, with a few deviant groups of scholars pushing forward the frontiers of knowledge for their respective national guilds.

chapter 43
rebellion as education: what we should learn from campus confrontations
kingsley widmer

We need not be at one with campus rebels to give them our sympathy and support. Granted, often their rhetoric comes out raspy, their tactics pyrrhic, and their programs simplex. All decent citizens decry the rebels' arrogant dogmatism, even when it but matches official obtuseness; all deplore calling policemen and other administrators animals, even if they do behave bestially; and all disapprove of erratic violence, even if provoked by arbitrary domination. But, at its worst, we may be getting the style of revolt that we as a society deserve. History may judge the quality of a civilization by its rebels as well as by its official heroes, and that may sometimes shame us. All good and representative Americans, our rebels might, and perhaps will, learn to do better if they continue their education in rebellion.

Among their present limitations we must include the recent curriculum of insurrection. The rebellious are as much chosen by as choosers in such issues as academic subordination to the military state and the corporate business order, the universities' structural bias against the underclasses, and the academic domination by the fatuous ideologies of autocratic elites. Only those who swim against the currents of our exploitative and

arbitrary institutional ocean sense the forces. The glitter looks warmly bright on a cold distant sea. One must, as do our militants, wade into attempts at change, or get splashed with typical American righteousness, to realize how rough and bitter can be our social and political waters.

But, goes the stock "moderate" retort, why should the campuses of higher education be the scenes for these rough confrontations? Why don't the mistreated minorities go after the business and other leaders instead of the academic administrators? the draftable young men fight government officials instead of local police? the leftist students attack the corporate offices instead of the university halls? Probably they would if they could. But because academic institutions half-fraudulently claim to be sanctuaries from the worst aspects of our society, they become especially and justifiably vulnerable. Historic insurrections, we might recall, occurred more often among the half-free than among the fully oppressed. The minorities in our universities, including the militants from the underclasses, the dissident middle-class students, and the intellectual-radical teachers, are advantaged enough to rebel though not to carry out revolutionary actions in the society at large. If this insurgency could move from the academic purlieus and other ghettos to the headquarters of power, this would already be a quite transformed society. Thus those of us with a critical view of our

Author's revision of an essay originally published in *The Nation*, 208, April 27, 1969. Reprinted by permission of the copyright holder, Kingsley Widmer.

social order must support dissent and protest and rebellion where they are at.

In recent history they often rightly arise in and against academic institutions. Our ambitious extensions of higher education long ago claimed to go beyond antiquarianism and specialism to engaged social pertinence. And in insurgency and disruption, they achieve it. Relevance is trouble. Student revolt as education may be epitomized in the remark of a charming young woman, a social science major, on an urban university campus: "I learned and felt more about just what American society is in the few days of the student strike than in four years of taking courses about it." In our schools, it is quite an achievement to, even briefly, fuse social role and individual intelligence and feeling. Such responsive experience, rather than the sometimes outré styles and radical mannerisms, should be the abrasive in bringing out the grain of our attitudes to the troubles. Apparently it takes rebellion, and perhaps some official roughing up, to truly learn many of the realities of our culture and society.

In and of itself, our higher education demands its troubles and deserves its disruptions, most of which can only improve it. And they have been doing so, as those of us around for several decades can see in the considerable, though inadequate, decline in authoritarian and repressive academic styles, whether of dress, admissions, requirements, teaching, "disciplines," or thinking. Poignantly, even many of our rebellious ones only reluctantly learn that contention unto revolt is required to make perfectly reasonable changes. They, too, often remain trapped in the American religiosity about institutional education. I've heard more than one avowed revolutionary echo administrators in "not wishing to destroy the educational process." But the very notions of processing people are much of what is wrong.

When I taught in and attended meetings with the student administrators of a "free university," or listened to an SDS chapter I was advising on "university reform" (before that went Maoistically out of fashion), or joined debates in and on "the New Student Left," or discussed polemical targets with the editors of an "underground" newspaper, or sat through interminable quasi-therapeutic sessions of a "Student-Faculty Committee for Change," or chaired protest rallies, I sometimes cringed at what many of the rebellious thought was pertinent and tough criticism of the Hired Learning. Classroom habit tempted me to rush to

a blackboard and list satiric novels about academic life for them to read, or to quote the lovely aphorisms, from Diogenes through Veblen to Goodman and others, of biting contempt for official education, or to start telling personal anecdotes of the pathology of half a dozen universities. Only as the rebellious literally dramatize their discontents against inauthentic education do they more fully discover that the institutional authorities are usually liars and intransigent, that the faculties are often selfish, narrow-minded and cowardly, and that much of academic work is arbitrary, incompetent, and false.

Once rebelling, many of the discontented suffer from "institutional shock" due to the unexpected lack of sympathy for their earnest efforts and the righteous refusal of any real attempts at change. Hence they sometimes respond erratically and with accelerating belligerence. The "liberal professors," the rebels discover, all too often provide melancholy confirmation of the usual truths about sophists, mandarins, clerics, technologues, and other orthodox rationalizers. Baroque professorial ways hardly obscure the primary drive of the hirelings to self-perpetuation and self-justification.

In countering student complaints about the usual mediocre teaching and mendacious disciplines, my colleagues often fall back on one or another appeal to "our scientific and humanistic traditions." Disingenuous and comic, for such traditions in America are rather like instant beverages: the bland result of a little synthetic dust and a lot of hot water. The majority of academic courses and fields, and other devices, including professors, result from made-up and inflated conventions. The muddle and fakery is not without virtue, if not taken literally, since it allows some variety and freedom.

We academicians sound more sincere, I suppose, when we speak of defending universities as sanctuaries for the pursuit of truth and art and dissent in a hostile and corrupting society. But what do we really do? Logically enough, rebellious students begin to wonder why our protestations of the separate and dissenting role of the universities don't even allow them amnesty, much less sanctuary and other support, when suppression comes. But how could our faculties, with their majority of careerists and technicians and time-serving bureaucrats, sanctify a dissenting intellectual community? Much of the deepest appeal of the insurgent movements comes from an intense desire for a sense of just such a community, an élan for communal responsiveness and responsibility as against the frequently fake "community of scholars." Rather more than the mainline faculties, the dissidents want to create autonomous places of order and joy within America's repressive fragmentation.

Academic rebelliousness can also be viewed as a symptom of the end of the naïve hopes implicit in the almost limitless expansion of higher education which, somehow, was to answer not only most technological and economic needs but produce a more egalitarian society of liberated individuals. The discontents, become visible, may mark a radical turn in the liberal faith in more schools and schooling—curiously parallel to the authoritarian faith in more police and policing—as the answer to all problems. Our rebellions show us that massive educational bureaucracies provide poor surrogates for a good society.

The campus insurrections may also educate us into the grimmer learned traditions, such as that academic institutions not only behave like our other state and corporate organizations, with similar built-in prejudices and crass manipulations (whether of real estate, public relations, science, or psychiatry) and fatuous hierarchies, but are equally anti-intellectual. Poets and saints and acute critics and original thinkers have always had a hard time in universities. Significant intellectual and moral work remains peripheral to most of formalized education or in subversion of its orderings. Tough academics claim large roles for their disciplines, they tend to operate as mere technicians of them, and especially these days in a society that glorifies techniques. Not incidentally, any current list of the exceptional professors must include a classicist doing the most provocative metapsychology, an historian serving as the major mentor of protest politics, a linguist carrying on the tradition of learned liberal polemics, an overage temporary professor of philosophy propounding next generation's revolution, and obscurely scattered critics of things-as-they-are and poets-of-change contributing to a radical sensibility breaking through in unexpected places. To be concerned about authentic intellectual and moral experience still, as always, includes assaulting traditional learned disciplines, accepted and honored views, and official higher education.

The odds run against most of the academic caste doing this barnyard labor. While academics currently confuse their trades with civilization itself, most vocally in the humanities and social sciences, their narrow and fearful tones belie such pretensions. As peasants, in their isolation and rigidity, suffer from congential idiocy, in Marx's aphorism, so professors, in their bureaucratization and rigidity, suffer from constitutional pettiness and become the peasants of culture. Nothing mysterious about it. Modern academicians do not come from the best practitioners of a profession or an intellectual activity but from one of the most elaborate of our processings. It takes about thirty years of formalized indenture, from nursery school to associate professorship—a generation of subservient schooling routines—to become a full member. No wonder most of them have so little left of passionate intelligence. These days, more, not less, are selected and advanced by institutional conformity rather than by autonomous achievement.

And no wonder universities suffer from ornate law-and-order arbitrariness and so many of their members feel threatened by any criticism or disruption. Next thing you know someone will question academic hierarchy. Are most full professors (I am one) one hundred to five hundred percent more competent and harder working than assistant professors? A joke! The percentages, except for salaries and related perogatives, usually run the other way. However, the differential (spread) in salaries has for some years been growing even faster than the excessive general increases in academic compensation. There can be no justice in any claims for critical intellectuals to receive corporate middle-management rewards and bribes. Professors deserve no more than anyone else, and probably less than those in more controlled and unpleasant occupations. Administrators, of course, merit less than garbagemen. With good reason, much of the public suspects all of us of crass self-interest. The step-by-crawling fraudulence of licking and booting one's way up the crypto-military ranks—and up the chain-of-being from the provincial animal farms to the "big twenty" prestige zoos—takes a considerable human toll. Internal as well as external exploitation creates the proper atmosphere for rebellion.

From their captive clientele (students) through their indentured servants (teaching assistants, etc.) into their arbitrary hierarchy (professorial as well as administrative) to their dubious packaging ("liberal education" and various psuedo-sciences), the universities illustrate, just as much as American advertising and foreign policy, grievous mislabeling and an ideology of competitive aggrandizement. Academic hiring and rewards exhibit all the ethical delicacy of, say, real estate brokerage. Sycophantic salesmanship controls prestige jobs and awards and publications. In the frenetic expansion of hired learning the traditional elitist and paternal (master-protégé) placement became manipulated "connections" and professional career "images." "Publication" and "research grants" serve as advertising but also become a self-generating "productivity" of which, even in the more rigorous fields, as a noted scientist advises me, "about 80 percent is pretty much nonsense."

The appropriate morals and manners for all this racketeering determine what happens in the classroom. The effects also show up, in quiet times, in the wary apathy of students or, in rebellious times, on the embattled steps of the administration building. Behind the rhetoric of student rebels grows the sense that when one speaks of a "power elite" or an "authoritarian bureaucracy" or more generally of exploitation and abused power, they do not just exist out yonder but right on campus. Even when the militant focus seems political, nonacademic, as on the issues of war and racism, the protest also goes against academic subservience to such order. But the essence of New Leftism has been, and is, **depowering**, on as well as beyond campuses. The rhetoric of "Power to the people!" as well as of "participatory" and "initiatory" democracy aims at replacing power structures with community order. Because of our institutional indoctrination and our corrupt recruitment and hierarchy and production, we hardly notice the lack of a community of scholars until the radicals rebel in its name. They teach us what we should be teaching them.

Most of us serve large, mediocre undergraduate state institutions. (Perhaps the problems in the "very best" colleges and universities would require some difference of emphasis but, having taught in several which claim such pretensions, I doubt it.) In social function, the majority of our educational bureaucracies serve to indoctrinate what used to be called the lower-middle classes, now relatively affluent, in the techniques and attitudes necessary for submissive service in the middle ranges of corporate and public bureaucracies. How well they do that job usually doesn't interest me. As with a large minority of teachers, I like to believe that my allegiances belong elsewhere, to critical intelligence and humanistic studies and libertarian values. But in fact most of us get caught in schizophrenic loyalties. Split between the orderings of the educational bureau-

cracies and our claims to separate moral and intellectual values, we end unpleasantly ambivalent. Only thus can one explain some of the weird and even hysterical faculty responses to rebellious demands for change. It is hard to blame schooling personnel, after years of institutional processing, for themselves becoming bureaucratic devices. At our best, I suppose, many of us secretly hope that we can provide some countereducation, some involvement in literature and thought which will work against the restricted indoctrination the schools officially pursue. One positive result, the rebellious, makes the secret public, and therefore outrages us. We want to carry on in what has become comfortable ambivalence, and is our very self-definition, with its wheezing rationalizations such as our "objectivity" and "value neutrality." We honorifically dress this up as "Socratic" (that is, playing question games as a substitute for a sustained view and for class preparation). But our methodological excuses turn out to have midwifed a rebelliousness which threatens to justly put us down and out.

Many professors long to escape such problems by narcissistically teaching only for those who will supposedly become graduate students in their subject. After all, this provides the orthodox ideal of the profession, systematically inculcated in graduate schools. Education, then, consists of an infinite regress with, say, professors of English passing on the word to an endless series of future professors of English. Mathematically as well as morally silly—even literary men should be able to calculate the geometric end of that, once expansion slows—this makes professionalism into one of our major educational pathologies. The ruthless climbers manage to make a career out of their illness. For the many others, recuperation is uncertain as they mouth symptoms about "research" and "finishing the book" (rewriting a dreary dissertation) and get spastically rigid about "maintaining professional standards." Students rightly find such teachers a bit puzzling in many of their demands, not understanding that academic bureaucrats want, above all, to breed more academic bureaucrats as their self-justification.

From the perspective of most students these days, interesting intellectual experience comes in inverse proportion to what passes for a "professional" or "scholarly" (usually meaning a technical) emphasis. But, some of my colleagues will reply, that is because the students came to college for the wrong reasons. True enough, but they don't have adequate other places to go in this society. A case might also be made that their professors, employed in one of our more lavish industries, stay in colleges for the wrong reasons. Students, of course, come to campuses for all sorts of non-scholarly motives: to remain adolescent a while longer, to look for sex, to acquire a trade the slow way, to avoid the draft, to gain social status, to play games, to join a counterculture community, or just because they have been mind-rinsed to believe they ought to stay in school no matter what. Probably many of our students should not be involved in higher education, at least in traditional scholarly and intellectual senses, and should be encouraged to more direct ways of learning skills and social activities. Surely a later age for study would be both personally and intellectually more appropriate. The effects of many of the young enduring years of inappropriate academicization warp the universities into doing all sorts of anti-scholarly things and the students into rebellious-ness which sometimes reveals a crude anti-intellectual side.

Those colleagues who piously assume that years of student submission to bureaucratic edu-cation only produces psychologically liberating and socially liberal benefits reveal themselves as schooling quacks. College may well be a net loss for many, including some who don't disgustedly drop out or get pushed out, as many do. Students who don't learn some resistance and confidence in their dissatisfactions, who don't become autonomously hip or radical, must find the pro-cessing an anxiously competitive and morally de-grading effort to make them less truly responsive and integral human beings.

Professorial self-interest has been used to deny many inappropriate students, with their guilt about "not finishing" or "not doing well," both candor and compassion. The proper end of this exploitation of students would not only be the recostuming called "university reform" but the relocation of tens of thousands of "researchers" and other dubious "teachers" and the dispersal of millions of "students" to more suitable ways of initiation into the larger society. That would leave much of our arbitrary programs and degrees and certifications but quaint mementos of what was once the fungoid spread of the academic for its own sake. In a society truly structured for merit, mechanics would become engineers, medical aides doctors, line-employees executives, and so on, with the academic only a critical accessory and reflec-

tive retreat. (And professors certainly would not be mere specialists in conning their way through schooling systems.) Our present system of hired learning deserves but little democratic as well as intellectual allegiance.

Our colleges and universities partly serve as custodial institutions for many who lack adequate place and role in our amorphously restrictive society, students and faculty. Periodically, those treated as inmates do naturally rebel. Professors get well paid for their institutionalization; students often do not, though they should, and therefore feel freer to express their discontents than we custodians. As one finds in reading most of the apologies for higher education, the basic ideologies glorify the separation of knowing and doing—one is preparing for rather than being now—and there-fore of culture and living. Rebelliousness, no matter what the immediate, and usually generous, "cause," must be partly understood as defiance of that moral schizophrenia. Activists vehemently attempt to bridge those gaps of knowing-doing and culture-living by breaking away from custodial controls.

Whatever many of my colleagues, and myself, might claim in scholarly allegiances, our devotion to busywork, to arbitrary requirements, to competi-tive procedures, to specialist propaganda, and to professional-class decorum reveals us as primarily keepers. The horrendous processing—selective ad-missions, requirements, rigid courses, tests, majors, minors, patterns, units, grades, averages, honors, recommendations, etc.—is both stupifying and nasty. Even at its best it rests on the obvious fallacies that competitive accumulation is learning and that institutionalization can be equated with education. Students who do not identify with the processing, as their professors did, can Schweikishly soldier or systematically cheat (as a majority ap-parently now do) or collectively disrupt. The real issue, then, is not whether one is for or against rebellion but merely which kind of rebellion is preferable. I think openly critical revolt is, in its negations, the more positive kind.

That rebellious students display little respect for our "scholarly" justifications means that they see them as just more of the processing. Rightly enough. In my own field of "literary scholar-criticism," in which I'm sufficiently published to confess rather than complain, most of the produc-tion is hobbyism: the overelaborate doctoring of texts, the compulsive collection of historical and biographical trivia, and the rather willful interpretation of interpretations. Such antiquarianism and gamesmanship should certainly not be confused with the need for responsive passion and critical intelligence. I don't mean to reject this learned hobbism as such, for it is a pleasant pastime which merits gracious support. But turned into professionalist ideology and institutional aggrandizement, and used to control jobs and social access for the young, "scholarship" provides trivial and inhumane molds which deserve to be broken. I am not arguing for the reduction of faculties to cosy commune leaders and intellectual scoutmasters—educational bureaucracies are inappropriate places for adolescent collectives—though this often seems to be the position of the "antipublication" factions among faculty and students. (Currently in some institutions we find that the intellectual incompetent plays the popular role of student-centered reformer.) True higher learning has very limited functions, and can only corrupt itself by not staying with them. My argument would be that cultivated and contentious people, those with something to profess, should be recognized as a good in themselves. Given the lack of other harboring institutions, or even room, for them in this society, they should be the major part of higher education, far more so than the sinecured technicians and bureaucratic manipulators. Sartre comments in his biography that to be a teacher is to be an intellectual monk. I don't care for the desexed metaphor but the quality of intellectual commitment may be hard to describe in a postreligious way. Certainly it suggests the proper contrast with our hired learning in which business and bureaucratic production, if not sheer racketeering, replace any deep sense of vocation. Critical intellectuals, as both teacher-students and student-teachers, constitute the main community of scholars worth preserving. The rest of the university, which would be the larger part of it, can well be done away with.

Given the illegitimacy of our educational institutions, we should recognize that rebellions are against the faculties as well as the officials. In past years, campus revolt aimed mostly at the administrators, especially when they asserted paternalistic and police powers. That partly justified the contemptuous interpretation that students were symbolically "father killing." But for some time it has been evident that this, like fatherhood itself, has become increasingly **pro forma**. Granted that the superjanitors who now ambitiously administer most academic institutions often deserve and incite rebellions. On good Jeffersonian principles,

one can agree that there should be student disruptions of power every generation (academically, every four or five years). And surely the hired help, such as presidents and deans, must be closely watched and warned between revolutions so that they don't arrogantly try to tidy up people and ideas as well as buildings and bookkeeping. However, the stock antiadministration rebellions simply wanted to dethrone the rulers but carry on much as before, like the liberal theologians admitting that God was dead but wanting to keep His show going. These rebellions, as in the middle sixties, brought some worthy changes which now look extreme only in their moderation. The later and broader revolts brought a further loosening, or its appearance. But deeper failures have become evident. The changes didn't develop adequate community and autonomy in education because it wasn't really allowed. It was also discovered that American abilities at fuller participation have been deeply eroded, not least by years of phony playyard democracy in our schools and other institutions. But most importantly, as I have been arguing, the whole process of mass hired learning started coming into question. Fighting administrations is not sufficent answer to that. Even lesser changes, it became evident, were difficult to achieve because of the basic subordination of universities to the state, because of the self-interest of faculties dominated by mediocre academic bureaucrats, and because the main functions of the universities were custodial indoctrination. If direct revolt continues, it exacerbates until it fractions the faculty and incites government and public suppression. Yet to end revolt requires not only major internal changes in universities but the reduction of their whole custodial role in the society. The controlled alternative is even sadder—a return to the dominant tone of careerist and other cynical apathy.

The whole of higher education, not merely its obvious contradictions, becomes the issue. As student **enragés** keep trying to tell us, intellectual commitment cannot be separated from moral passion. Institutional humanism long ago settled for the liberal ideology of certain limited academic freedoms separated from the aim for a more just and liberated society. But even at best such protected pools stagnate, then evaporate, unless the rebellious bring new streams, connecting with the larger society, to them. We academicians may be justly accused of denaturing the professor, who no longer professes much but supposedly neutral methodologies. The ideologies of technicians may no longer get by. Students, of course, should rebel against us as well as against the manipulative administrators and the power forces in the larger society. Almost any critical éclat amidst the hired learning becomes self-justifying to break the narcissitic routines and the institutional denaturing. However messy, it may well be true that nothing less than disruption of the academic will bring most of us to the perplexity and passion of a larger reality.

But, it is fearfully asked, can the universities bear the disruption? More grandiloquently, can our liberal humanism endure such uncouth assaults? If the institutions be so brittle, and our culture so anemic, that they can only maintain themselves by hiding in fearful unchange behind massed troopers, then there is little to be saved. If the universities must be arbitrary and deceitful bureaucracies and all learning must be reduced to academic institutionalization, then there is little to be lost, and the militants are right when they chant "Shut it down!"

No historical evidence suggests that a culture dominated by massive bureaucracies retains much vitality in the long run. Intellectual whores, contrary to classic American sentimentality, do not create great passions. And, of course, we should never confuse education and understanding with the Hired Learning. Even we dissident professors have probably been warped by decades of institutionalization and excessive engagement to official culture and therefore must make conscious efforts to support rebellious discontents. That does not mean forgoing criticism of the rebellious: Minority group demands sometimes contain a second-rate

nationalism and chauvinism; New Leftism, especially in its later developments, desperately moved to a doctrinaire abstraction of reality; and the "counterculture" rebellions, though delightfully bringing to the dreary academic scene what Fourier called "the butterfly passion," contain a good bit of mindless mystagoguery and cultism. Discrimination is our intellectual obligation but it should be part of a continuing radical critique to achieve the disequilibrium that allows rebellion to surface and change to come about. Radicalism may, and must at times, take other forms than overt insurrection. But either way, professors cannot claim privileged refusal of the essential struggles of the society for which they often are an exploitative part and dishonest parcel.

Only when we resist our institutionalization do we truly teach, turning topsy-turvy accepted orderings and helping transform ways of life. If we mostly play professional hacks and academic custodians, we will end up not teaching at all. Nor do we really profess any humanism or science by mainly channeling students into more bureaucratic schooling and the corporate elites and the non-dimensional sensibility for a counterfeit society. But the nastiest hypocrisy of professors these days comes out in those who demand intellectual and social and political change—but not where they are at.

Academic rebellions should educate us, not just the students, into seeing education as rebellion. Somewhere Nietzsche writes: "One repays a teacher badly if one remains a student." By educating ourselves in rebellion, we may allow them to create something different. Dissidence remains our saving grace, rebellion our educational possibility.

chapter 44
the new students
editors of
the hazen foundation

In discussions of the university, the education of students is too often relegated to the end of the list of unsolved problems. And most American universities devote far more attention to every conceivable research question than they do to trying to understand their own students. To be sure, everyone acknowledges that without students there can be no university; and so too, "education" is widely admitted to be one of the functions of a university. Yet the characteristics of students—the fact that they have commitments, aspirations, dreams, needs, psyches, and perhaps souls even **before** being admitted to college—are largely ignored in the concentration on more easily describable features of the university.

Who is the young man or woman who comes to college today? He has been tested, analyzed, studied, and speculated about more than any young person in human history, but we still do not understand him very well. All our research does not lead us away from generalizations about the student, his needs, his problems, and his aspirations; it only adds a note of considerable hesitancy to the same generalizations. We know the new student is not the aristocrat or even the fun-loving "big man on campus" of the not so distant

From "The Student in Higher Education" in **How Many Roads: The 70's,** by Herman A. Estrin and Esther Lloyd-Jones, 1968. Reprinted by permission of The Hazen Foundation.

past. We know that he is earnest and works hard, that he is frequently worried and anxious, and that his amusements are often frantic or even frenzied. We also know that on occasion he may expend his energies on something as serious as a sit-in or as frivolous as a panty raid. But we are not sure who he is or what he wants, and sometimes it seems that we don't much care.

From the literature we have read and the observations we have made and the experiences we have endured, the members of this committee feel that at least some assertions can be made about who the student is. To begin with, our student is not one person but many. He is the senior at Harvard who is planning graduate work in nuclear physics and the freshman girl at Michigan State crying softly to herself at night because she is homesick. He is a model of diversity, and he needs many different types of higher educational institutions to serve his diversity. It is not good that every American school, no matter how small or how specialized, aspires to imitate Harvard, for not every student wants or needs a Harvard education.

Some students represent a third or fourth generation of college graduates in their family; others are the first from their ethnic group to venture beyond secondary schools. Some are very young men with clearly defined career goals, and others are young women who expect college to provide them with a mate. A few are seeking knowledge for its own sake, and others, equally few in number, are interested purely in vocational training. In between lies the majority who are realistic enough to know that a college degree is required for occupational success, but idealistic enough to want to learn something in the process of getting a degree. A few are so brilliant that top-level schools fall over each other competing for them; others are so undistinguished that their schools accept them only because of state laws. The rest, who are the greatest number, are capable of being stimulated to creative thought by challenging ideas and willing, even eager, to learn to think for themselves.

There are some, perhaps as many as ten per cent, who are constricted by serious emotional problems, and there are others, probably even fewer, who are singularly free of such problems. But the majority are at neither extreme, for though they are haunted by self-doubts and insecurity, they can learn their way out of them, if only they meet the right set of circumstances. Some are leftists dedicated to tearing down the established power structure and come to college with sophisticated political skills that cause nightmares for student personnel officials; others are radical rightists dedicated to reestablishing the simplicities of the good old days which never existed. But the greatest number are politically and socially apathetic, ready to make peace with society's demands, yet vaguely resentful because they feel that society is cheating them. Some are extraordinarily sensitive to the artistic and cultural dimensions of life, while the literary taste of others is exhausted by the comic book. However, somewhere in between are the vast majority whose tastes are relatively undeveloped but still relatively unspoiled.

A minority will graduate at the age of 21 after four uninterrupted years at the same college; a majority will be dropouts in some sense, taking many years to finish, transferring from college to college, or never graduating at all. Some few are veterans of the Vietnamese war, and others are doing everything in their power not to be involved in that war. Some are profoundly religious, others convinced agnostics, and still others agonizing through a search for religious meaning. Some commute across the length of the continent, and others merely walk a few blocks to a community college. Some have never been out of the county in which they were born, and others have traveled to the farthest points of the earth. Some aspire to greatness; others are content with a life prospect

of moderate mediocrity. Some have had almost as much sexual experience as they claim, and others scarcely know the facts of life.

All of them, wherever they come from, are reflections of the extraordinarily rich, complicated, and nerve-wracking culture that has been built in these United States. If they often feel lost in the contemporary university, it is because they often feel lost in contemporary society. This fact, and all it portends about both university and society, is probably the central fact about American students today. They are enmeshed from kindergarten to the grave in the complex, specialized, bureaucratic, and impersonal institutions of American life. Whether we like it or not, we all—students and teachers alike—live in the most advanced technological nation of the world; and in such a society, as in its educational institutions, individuals tend to feel lost and to look for new ways to assert their individuality and justify their lives.

Perhaps for this very reason these diverse students all have at least one characteristic in common: **They want to learn.** The degree of willingness varies; the ability to learn varies; even the definition of what learning is and the motivation for it varies, but the desire for learning is very much alive when they first arrive on our college campuses.

Beyond this almost universal willingness to learn, several more assertions can be made about many college students. The assertions made in the pages that follow might very well be called characteristics of an elite minority, and the relationship between elites and masses is a question which social science has yet to answer satisfactorily. To state, for example, that the present college scene is characterized by "hippies" is as much an exaggeration as to say that the same scene several years ago was characterized by the "volunteers." The hippies are no more typical of 1967 than the volunteers were of 1962. Changes in the whole student scene proceed very slowly, and differences between the typical students of 15 or 20 years ago and those of today are probably not very great. Nevertheless, the untypical are worth discussing, both because they give color and tone to the university environment and because they are likely to have an influence far greater than their actual number. During the volunteer era, the young people who flocked off to the Peace Corps unquestionably attracted a considerable number of fellow volunteers for work in this country. Similarly, it seems very likely that far more students are inclined to tune out at the present time than those who actually go on LSD trips.

But the most important reason for trying to characterize at some length the new college students is that they present some of the critical problems which educators must respond to. There may be far more of the new students in the multiversities than there are in the state colleges, community colleges, and junior colleges to which more than half of the college population goes. There is unquestionably far more concern about "meaning" at the multiversity than at the junior college. Yet it seems reasonable to assume that the needs for meaning, purpose, community, and love which the multiversity's new student articulates so passionately also exist, if less charged and vocal, in the smaller colleges.

SOME CHARACTERISTICS OF THE NEW STUDENT

We can say at least the following about American students:

1. Students are seeking enduring commitments but are skeptical about the ideologies and orthodoxies that clamor for their loyalty.

Anyone who has dealt with college students for any length of time is aware that the quest for meaning, significance, and commitment is stronger than ever before in our students. Young men and women view the chaos, confusion, and disorder in the world around them with profound skepticism. Having experienced neither real peace nor total war, they are disturbed by the chronic disorder of international society. Lacking faith in the inevitability of human progress, they are doubtful about the possibility of a peaceful solution to the nation's racial crisis. Learned in the complexities of the American economy, they cannot side with either participant in a labor-management dispute or in the perennial conflict between liberals and conservatives—of another generation—about the relationship between government and industry. Although they know they need professional competence to earn the material rewards of the good life, they are not convinced that professional careers will yield personal meaning. The more sophisticated find themselves increasingly entertaining the same reservations about romance, marriage, and family. They feel that much is wrong with the world, but they are hard put to articulate clearly what the social ills of mankind are, much less what ought to be done about them

or what vision of the good life is possible in contemporary society.

They have no heroes, at least since the death of John Kennedy, and only on occasion can they be moved to turn someone into a villain. Faintly suspicious of the wisdom of their elders—and anyone over 30 is presumed to be irrevocably old—they are sophisticated enough to know that there is little point in blaming elders for the mess they made of the world and less hope of convincing them that it is indeed a mess.

The chaotic disorder of the world today, with the threat of thermonuclear destruction always hovering above it, is enough to dissuade young people from taking the ideologies of the past very seriously or from listening to the advice of a generation responsible for a state close to anarchy. Traditional left-wing ideologies are, for most students, as irrelevant and archaic as the ideologies of the right. Traditional religions hold their own as far as church attendance goes, but are less able to persuade their members to take their cosmogonies seriously as a map of life. Dogmatic ideology is no longer seen as a useful tool with which to face life; articulate social criticism based on a clear vision of what the world ought to be seems largely impossible. Personal witness, direct protest, insistence on the importance of the interpersonal, the authentic, and the genuine are replacing systematic ideologies as a basis of action among substantial numbers of students.

The new college student therefore would like to be able to believe in something or someone, but as a matter of principle virtually rejects the possibility. He is not incapable of commitment or conviction, but his sales resistance is very strong.

2. Because of their suspicion about formal ideology, the new students turn to human relationships as the source of most of the purpose and meaning they seek in their lives.

The student leftist who when queried about the nature of his ideology replied, "Our ideology is Love," spoke for his whole generation; and the hippies with their demand for "flower power" represent in caricature the kind of honest, open, trusting, and undemanding relationships the student thinks will be the key to personal happiness. Man has always wanted to love and be loved, but the explicit, self-conscious, and agonized pursuit of love as a rationale for existence has not been so much a part of Western culture since the age of the medieval troubadors. Unfortunately, love is easy to talk about and more difficult to practice. For all their ability to quote from the **Art of Loving**, most students are only remotely conscious of the need for self-sacrifice and self-discipline in the love relationship. To speak of love which is "spontaneous" and "makes no demands" is to describe a relationship which is necessarily transitory and unreal, since once love goes beyond the initial stage of infatuation, it must be reflective and must make demands. An ideology based on love may produce brilliantly mystical rhetoric, but it is a poor basis on which to attempt to organize either a total society or a small group within society. Since most young adults are only beginning to learn the "art of loving," their adoption of an ideology of love is bound to lead to disappointment and frustration.

3. **The contemporary college student feels strongly the need to belong but is profoundly skeptical about most of the organizations he encounters, particularly an organization that claims to offer him an education.**

Ever since Western man left behind the warmth, intimacy, and social support of the rural village, he has striven to create within the industrial metropolis a community structure with some of the merits of the old folk society. On the whole, Western man shows little more than poetic regret over the loss of bucolic joys of the past; for him, the affluence and comfort of modern life have been worth the price. Nonetheless, it has been his dream through the years of migration to the metropolis that he could have his cake and eat it too, that he could by some kind of free contract reestablish the tribe in the metropolis. Until very recently, this quest for community had been a conscious quest for only a few. But among the younger generation the search for meaningful group relationships has become quite explicit. "Belonging," "participating," "sharing," and the skills they demand are, for the generation currently going through colleges and universities, among the most important goals of human existence. The desire to belong, to be part of an intimate fellowship, and to serve others in a face-to-face community seems to be more articulate and more dominant than ever before. Nor should we be surprised that a generation reared on Freud, Kafka, Kierkegaard, and Camus in the apartments and Levittowns of modern America is deeply anxious over its search for belonging, its needs for roots.

Despite all his enthusiasm about belonging, the new college student is anything but impressed by the organizations which he might join. He looks at the big university, the big government, big business, big labor, the big research enterprise, and the big church with considerable dismay, and asks with a mixture of Martin Buber and Sören Kierkegaard, "Where in all this bigness and impersonality is there room for my lonely suffering soul; where can I find a meaningful I-Thou dialogue?"

The new college student wants solidarity, participation and fellowship unequivocally and passionately. But he views most organizations of our computerized, bureaucratized, rationalized, formalized, urban industrial society as almost by their nature inimical to the freedom and spontaneity of the human spirit. The organized society can be cold, heartless, and impersonal. It can turn you into a cog in the machine, an IBM card processed through a computer. One must, of course, make one's peace with organizations, and students are usually prepared to concede in theory that organizations are necessary for pooling human resources and that without a division of labor, modern society would be impossible. But in practice many of the organizations with which they come in contact seem subtly depersonalizing; few provide any real community.

4. **The new student is generous and idealistic in his own fashion but is frequently fearful that any long-term commitment to social service may destroy his idealism and thwart his freedom.**

While much of the student population remains apathetic and it is difficult to compare the idealism of one generation with that of another, the spectacular growth of volunteer movements is stiking evidence of the extraordinary generosity and enthusiasm in today's students, if touched by the right kind of appeal uttered by the right kind of person. Whether the volunteer era will continue and whether it will have a substantial impact on American society is not yet clear, but it is clear that the college has generally ignored the marvelous opportunities for integrating education and life that the volunteer movements provided. From the point of view of the youthful volunteers who have served in their country and abroad, however, the critical question is not whether the volunteer movement will continue, but whether in fact it has any meaning.

The volunteer very quickly discovers that the love and service he wishes to bring to his fellow men is not always warmly received and may be quite inadequate. Worse still, he may learn that two years of hard work and enthusiastic commitment have only a marginal effect on the social evils he has dedicated himself to eliminate. He apparently has the alternative of withdrawing from active social reform into some relatively secure domain where his generosity and idealism will not be contaminated by the mess and exhaustion of social action (like a career in higher education), or of acquiring the skills that are required for social action and committing himself to a long period, perhaps a lifetime, of grueling and frequently dissatisfying efforts to correct the causes of social distress. The volunteer realizes all too well that such a commitment will plunge him into a world of uncertainty and ambiguity, where frequent compromise is necessary and where he runs the risk of sacrificing his ideals for the sake of getting something done. It sometimes seems preferable to be an alienated radical critic than to run the risk of being an involved but compromising activist.

5. The new students, for all their apparent poise and sophistication, are frequently hesitant and uncertain.

Their self-distrust and self-suspicion make them vulnerable to self-hatred and on occasion despair. Middle-class and particularly upper middle-class society in the United States continues to stress achievement as much as ever, although currently achievement is measured by more subtle indicators than annual income. The young person who has arrived at college has already passed through a series of rankings, evaluations, and comparisons with his fellow students and knows full well that such rankings will continue until the day he dies. Since successful and skillful performance is expected relatively early in life, and since reward is contingent on performance, it is rare for a middle-class youth to experience unconditional acceptance in the course of his growing up. Under such circumstances self-doubt, self-rejection, self-hatred, and self-punishment become almost endemic to the collegiate culture. Feelings of rejection and worthlessness, although they may be obscured by a veneer of poise and sophistication, occasionally incapacitate the student and frequently impair his real abilities. With greater or lesser vigor, the new college student hates and fears the rankings, evaluations, the comparisons, the gradings, of the higher educational system. But he is inclined to concede ruefully that there is not much he can do about it and that it is a good preparation for what he has to face the rest of his life.

6. Because of his doubts about himself, about organizations, and the possibility of faith and commitments, the new college student has a tendency to be suspicious and distrustful of the administration, and to a lesser extent, the faculty of his college.

The college is the most obvious manifestation of the organized society. The school and its officers become inkblots into which the students can project their frustrations, not only with the college experience, but also with the larger society. Most students will not attack the president in the school paper; they will not picket the administration building; they will not call the school officers obscene names or caricature them on placards. But they will be deeply suspicious in their relationships with the representatives of the college administration, whether they are personnel officers, clerks, secretaries, or campus police. The student's relationships with faculty are apt to be somewhat less resentful, if only because through sheer frequency of exposure he gets to know a little more about his teachers and at least on occasion has a meaningful, if fleeting, relationship with a few. The large number of college students who aspire to careers in professional academia is an indication of the relatively good image that the college professor has been able to maintain among his students. That the image remains so untarnished is an interesting commentary on the naïveté of the students, most of whom apparently do not realize that the organization and goals of the academic guilds are among the principal reasons for their own disadvantaged position in the college.

7. Students come to college with a great deal of excitement and willingness to do the work demanded of them, but their expectations and performance usually decline very rapidly during the first months of the freshman year.

Incoming students expect the college years to be exciting and challenging, both intellectually and socially; they are eager for this new adventure in their life. Almost as quickly as their expectations about work fade, so do their expectations about the excitement and challenge of higher education. Students learn that college is rather like high school, that most of what one does is still "Mickey Mouse," and that boredom and dullness are just as prevalent in college. Most teachers are uninteresting and many are uninterested. Course requirements frequently seem to be make-work, and programs of study appear to have little connection with career goals, personal concerns, or intellectual curiosity. As a practical expert in the game of making peace with the system, the student soon adjusts his needs and expectations to fit its requirements. At the end of four years, he even has a certain loyalty to his college. To be sure, it has not provided what he hoped it would as a freshman, but at least it has furnished him with the degree that is a prerequisite for employment or for further education, has offered social diversions to vary the routine, perhaps has found him a spouse, and has enabled him to prolong his youth—and his entry into the System—a bit longer than would otherwise have been possible.

8. Most students apparently expect that the college years will mark the definitive end of their dependence on their parents.

Even those who do not live away from home anticipate that college will provide the environment necessary for them to acquire the independence, initiative, and sense of responsibilty that are expected of adults. The final breaking of family ties, expecially when postponed as in American society, is bound to be a painful and ambivalent experience, filled with a yearning for adulthood and at the same time a regret for the loss of childhood. Since the break only becomes possible when a sufficient sense of selfhood has evolved, many students enter college ill prepared to depart from the confines of their family, however eager to do so they may be.

PROFILE OF THE NEW STUDENT

The background, the needs, the abilities, and the aspirations of the student entering college today are as diverse as the complex country which gave him birth. The great variety in American higher education reflects the equal variety in American culture. But there are some constants. Most students are curious, eager to learn, and willing to work, though they may not understand fully what learning is or what higher education is supposed to be for. They are seeking a meaningful explanation of the complex phenomena of life. They are also looking for a system of intimate relationships that will provide the dimension of belonging, which seems to them such a crucial part of life. Their generosity may lack depth and sophistication, but it has also produced volunteer movements the like of which the nation has never seen. They are afraid that they are not tough enough or ruthless enough to succeed in the competitive game that is required for success in American society. They are puzzled about who they are and whether they can be strong enough to stand on their own two feet, independent of parental support. Suspicious of the irrationality and corruption of adult society, they are, nevertheless, willing to make a deal with it since they see no feasible alternatives. Like all young people, they are immensely interested in and concerned about sex and expect that the college years will provide an opportunity for considerable sexual experimentation. The new students may also vaguely expect to have a good time in college, but they quickly adjust to a style of life which permits good times only as a periodic escape from the deadly serious business of classroom competition and achievement.

From the point of view therefore of someone seriously interested in education, the students of the midsixties are a mixed bag. They are too rebellious to expect to learn from the wisdom of those who have gone before them, and yet most of them are too docile to contemplate serious revolt. They are curious, open, and willing to work, but all too ready to make their peace with the system when they realize that it places little dividend on intellectual adventuresomeness. For all their weaknesses and ambivalences, however, their intelligence, curiosity, and capacity for work certainly ought to provide the educator with an extraordinary challenge. Unfortunately, most educators have little time to recognize or consider these qualities, much less to speculate on how educational programs might be developed to serve and strengthen them.

topic 20
collective behavior: fads and fashions in life styles

To many sociologists, collective behavior is—or ought to be—what their discipline is all about. The wide-range of topical concerns embraced by the rubric collective behavior —such things as riots, crazes, mobs, panics, and fads, as well as social movements—suggest the drama, the animation, and the immediacy that are such visible qualities of everyday life. But not all sociologists are interested in such phenomena; many find social statics, social structure, and social organization more fascinating than the more illusive and hard-to-pinpoint qualities that characterize social dynamics and social change.

It can nevertheless be argued that to comprehend the sources and qualities of collective behavior is to gain a new and critical measure of insight into the structural properties of social order. Lewis Coser puts the matter succinctly:

> Sociologists, in their preoccupation with social structure and institutionalized types of behavior, often tend to neglect those forms of social behavior which are relatively unorganized and lack the stability and predictability of cohesive social groups. Yet collective behavior arising spontaneously, and not based on pre-established norms and traditions, should be studied closely if only because such behavior may enlighten us as to how an old order dies and a new social order emerges.

Every component in the institutional complex—from economic to religious—is characterized by an inherent strain toward consistency, harmony, stability, and symmetry; yet at the same time each is impelled by forces that make for tension, instability, innovation, and discord. It is as though a dialectical push-and-pull, action-and-reaction, is at work in every institutional sphere. It follows, then, that the student of collective behavior is more alert to change and diversity than he is to permanance, uniformity, and the traditions.

We must be wary, however, that the volatile and often unanticipated nature of such phenomena as riots or fads does not blind us to the fact that much of collective behavior is obvious, and often trivial and ephemeral. Hula-hoops, turtleneck sweaters, new slang, frisbees: these are facets of collective behavior too.

All collective behavior has certain common features. If it did not, if in fact it were altogether random and helter-skelter—devoid of recurrent or patterned qualities—it would not be proper grist for sociological analysis. For example, collective behavior is especially likely to flourish in relatively unstructured situations; the more unfamiliar a situation, the more prone people are to turn to others, perhaps even to strangers, for behavioral cues. This in turn tends to heighten their suggestibility and make them less rational and more "other-directed" than they would otherwise be. In a word, people are more suggestible, less tradition-bound, and more open to novel ideas in the contexts in which collective behavior prospers.

The articles in this section attest to the variety and appeal of one facet of collective behavior: fads and fashions. The contributions by Ralph Gleason and Warren Brown, in particular, lend substance to Orrin Klapp's assertion:

> Fashion. . . is basically a matter of self-typing, and effort to mold oneself according to certain social types which currently have prestige. . . . While it may seem that fashion is simply blind imitation by thousands, it is for each person a highly selective process of picking one's type and avoiding other types which are now square, vulgar, or passé.

The selection by Carl Couch calls sociologists to task for the many stereotypes—most of them overgeneralizations, or simply untrue—that they have traditionally entertained regarding collective behavior.

chapter 45
like a rolling stone
ralph j. gleason

Forms and rhythms in music are never changed without producing changes in the most important political forms and ways.

Plato said that.

There's something happenin' here. What it is ain't exactly clear. There's a man with a gun over there tellin' me I've got to beware. I think it's time we STOP, children, what's that sound? Everybody look what's goin' down.

The Buffalo Springfield said that.

For the reality of politics, we must go to the poets, not the politicians.

Norman O. Brown said that.

For the reality of what's happening today in America, we must go to rock 'n roll, to popular music.

I said that.

■

From **American Scholar**, 36, Autumn 1967. Reprinted by permission of the author.

For almost forty years in this country, which has prided itself on individualism, freedom, and nonconformity, all popular songs were written alike. They had an eight-bar opening statement, an eight-bar repeat, an eight-bar middle section or bridge, and an eight-bar reprise. Anything that did not fit into that framework was, appropriately enough, called a novelty.

Clothes were basically the same whether a suit was double-breasted or single-breasted, and the only people who wore beards were absentminded professors and Bolshevik bomb throwers. Long hair, which was equated with lack of masculinity—in some sort of subconscious reference to Samson, I suspect—was restricted to painters and poets and classical musicians, hence the term "longhair music" to mean classical.

Four years ago a specter was haunting Europe, one whose fundamental influence, my intuition tells me, may be just as important, if in another way, as the original of that line. The Beatles, four long-haired Liverpool teenagers, were busy changing the image of popular music. In less than a year, they invaded the United States and almost totally wiped out the standard Broadway show—Ed Sullivan TV program popular song. No more were we "flying to the moon on gossamer wings"; we were now articulating such interesting and, in this mechanistic society, unusual concepts as "Money can't buy me love" and "I want to hold your hand."

"Societies, like individuals, have their moral crises and their spiritual revolutions," R. H. Tawney says in **Religion and the Rise of Capitalism.** And the Beatles appeared ("a great figure rose up from the sea and pointed at me and said 'you're a Beatle with an "a"'"—Genesis, according to John Lennon). They came at the proper moment of a spiritual cusp—as the Martian in Robert Heinlein's **Stranger in a Strange Land** calls a crisis.

Instantly, on those small and sometimes doll-like figures was focused all the rebellion against hypocrisy, all the impudence and irreverence, that the youth of that moment was feeling vis-à-vis his elders.

Automation, affluence, the totality of instant communication, the technology of the phonograph record, the transistor radio, had revolutionized life for youth in this society. The population age was lowering. Popular music, the jukebox, and the radio were becoming the means of communication. Huntley and Brinkley were for mom and dad. People now sang songs they wrote themselves, not songs written **for** them by hacks in grimy Tin Pan Alley offices.

The folk music boom paved the way. Bob Dylan's poetic polemics, "Blowin' in the Wind" and "The Times They Are A-Changin'," had helped the breakthrough. "Top-40" radio made Negro music available everywhere to a greater degree than ever before in our history.

This was, truly, a new generation—the first in America raised with music constantly in its ear, weaned on a transistor radio, involved with songs from its earliest moment of memory.

Music means more to this generation than it did even to its dancing parents in the big-band swing era of Benny Goodman. It's natural, then, that self-expression should find popular music so attractive.

The dance of the swing era, of the big bands, was the fox-trot. It was really a formal dance extended in variation only by experts. The swing era's parents had danced the waltz. The fox-trot was a ritual with only a little more room for self-expression. Rock 'n roll brought with it not only the voices of youth singing their protests, their hopes, and their expectations (along with their pathos and their sentimentality and their personal affairs from drag racing to romance), it brought their dances.

"Every period which abounded in folk songs has, by the same token, been deeply stirred by Dionysiac currents," Nietzsche points out in **The Birth of Tragedy.** And Dionysiac is the word to describe the dances of the past ten years, call them by whatever name from bop to the Twist to the Frug, from the Hully Gully to the Philly Dog.

In general, adult society left the youth alone, prey to the corruption the adults suspected was forthcoming from the song lyrics ("All of me, why not take all of me," from that hit of the thirties, of course, didn't mean **all** of me, it meant, well . . . er . . .) or from the payola-influenced disc jockeys. (Who ever remembers about the General Electric scandals of the fifties, in which over a dozen officials went to jail for industrial illegalities?) The TV shows were in the afternoon anyway and nobody could stand to watch those rock 'n roll singers; they were worse than Elvis Presley.

But all of a sudden the **New Yorker** joke about the married couple dreamily remarking, when a disc jockey played "Houn' Dog" by Elvis, "they're playing our song," wasn't a joke any longer. It was real. That generation had suddenly grown up and married and Elvis was real memories of real romance and not just kid stuff.

All of a sudden, the world of music, which is big business in a very real way, took another look at the music of the ponytail and chewing gum set, as Mitch Miller once called the teenage market, and realized that there was one helluva lot of bread to be made there.

In a short few years, Columbia and R.C.A. Victor and the other companies that dominated the recording market, the huge publishing houses that copyrighted the music and collected the royalties, discovered that they no longer were "kings of the hill." Instead, a lot of small companies, like Atlantic and Chess and Imperial and others, had hits by people the major record companies didn't even know, singing songs written in Nashville and Detroit and Los Angeles and Chicago and sometimes, but no longer almost always, New York.

It's taken the big ones a few years to recoup from that. First they called the music trash and the lyrics dirty. When that didn't work, as the attempt more recently to inhibit songs with supposed psychedelic or marijuana references has failed, they capitulated. They joined up. R.C.A. Victor bought Elvis from the original company he recorded for—Sun Records ("Yaller Sun records from Nashville" as John Sebastian sings it in "Nashville Cats")—and then bought Sam Cooke, and A.B.C. Paramount bought Ray Charles and then Fats Domino. And Columbia, thinking it had a baby folk singer capable of some more sales of

"San Francisco Bay," turned out to have a tiny demon of a poet named Bob Dylan.

So the stage was set for the Beatles to take over—"with this ring I can—dare I say it?—rule the world!" And they did take over so thoroughly that they have become the biggest success in the history of show business, the first attraction ever to have a coast-to-coast tour in this country sold out before the first show even opened.

With the Beatles and Dylan running tandem, two things seem to me to have been happening. The early Beatles were at one and the same time a declaration in favor of love and of life, an exuberant paean to the sheer joy of living, and a validation of the importance of American Negro music.

Dylan, by his political, issue-oriented broadsides first and then by his Rimbaudish nightmare visions of the real state of the nation, his bittersweet love songs and his pure imagery, did what the jazz and poetry people of the fifties had wanted to do—he took poetry out of the classroom and out of the hands of the professors and put it right out there in the streets for everyone.

I dare say that with the inspiration of the Beatles and Dylan we have more poetry being produced and more poets being made than ever before in the history of the world. Dr. Malvina Reynolds—the composer of "Little Boxes"—thinks nothing like this has happened since Elizabethan times. I suspect even that is too timid an assessment.

Let's go back to Plato, again. Speaking of the importance of new styles of music, he said, "The new style quietly insinuates itself into manners and customs and from there it issues a greater force . . . goes on to attack laws and constitutions, displaying the utmost impudence, until it ends by overthrowing everything, both in public and in private."

That seems to me to be a pretty good summation of the answer to the British rock singer Donovan's question, "What goes on? I really want to know."

The most immediate apparent change instituted by the new music is a new way of looking at things. We see it evidenced all around us. The old ways are going and a new set of assumptions is beginning to be worked out. I cannot even begin to codify them. Perhaps it's much too soon to do so. But I think there are some clues—the sacred importance of love and truth and beauty and interpersonal relationships.

When Bob Dylan sang recently at the Masonic

Memorial Auditorium in San Francisco, at intermission there were a few very young people in the corridor backstage. One of them was a long-haired, poncho-wearing girl of about thirteen. Dylan's road manager, a slender, long-haired, "Bonnie Prince Charlie" youth, wearing black jeans and Beatle boots, came out of the dressing room and said, "You kids have to leave! You can't be backstage here!"

"Who are you?" the long-haired girl asked.

"I'm a cop," Dylan's road manager said aggressively.

The girl looked at him for a long moment and then drawled, "Whaaaat? With those boots?"

Clothes really do **not** make the man. But sometimes . . .

I submit that was an important incident, something that could never have happened a year before, something that implies a very great deal about the effect of the new style, which has quietly (or not so quietly, depending on your view of electric guitars) insinuated itself into manners and customs.

Among the effects of "what's goin' on" is the relinquishing of belief in the sacredness of logic. "I was a prisoner of logic and I still am," Malvina Reynolds admits, but then goes on to praise the new music. And the prisoners of logic are the ones who are really suffering most—unless they have Mrs. Reynolds' glorious gift of youthful vision.

The first manifestation of the importance of this outside the music—I think—came in the works of Ken Kesey and Joseph Heller. **One Flew Over the Cuckoo's Nest**, with its dramatic view of the interchangeability of reality and illusion, and **Catch-22**, with its delightful utilization of crackpot realism (to use C. Wright Mills's phrase) as an explanation of how things are, were works of seminal importance.

No one any longer really believes that the processes of international relations and world economics are rationally explicable. Absolutely the very best and clearest discussion of the entire thing is wrapped up in Milo Minderbinder's explanation, in **Catch-22**, of how you can buy eggs for seven cents apiece in Malta and sell them for five cents in Pianosa and make a profit. Youth understands the truth of this immediately, and no economics textbook is going to change it.

Just as—implying the importance of interpersonal relations and the beauty of being true to oneself—the under-thirty youth immediately understands the creed patiently explained by Yossarian in **Catch-22** that everybody's your enemy who's trying to get you killed, even if he's your own commanding officer.

This is an irrational world, despite the brilliant efforts of Walter Lippmann to make it rational, and we are living in a continuation of the formalized lunacy (Nelson Algren's phrase) of war, any war.

At this point in history, most of the organs of opinion, from the **New York Review of Books** through the **New Republic** to **Encounter** (whether or not they are subsidized by the CIA), are in the control of the prisoners of logic. They take a flick like **Morgan** and grapple with it. They take **Help** and **A Hard Day's Night** and grapple with those two beautiful creations, and they fail utterly to understand what is going on because they try to deal with them logically. They complain because art doesn't make sense! Life on this planet in this time of history doesn't make sense either—as an end result of immutable laws of economics and logic and philosophy.

Dylan sang, "You raise up your head and you ask 'is this where it is?' And somebody points to you and says 'it's his' and you say 'what's mine' and somebody else says 'well, what is' and you say 'oh my god am i here all alone?' "

Dylan wasn't the first. Orwell saw some of it, Heller saw more, and in a different way so did I. F. Stone, that remarkable journalist, who is really a poet, when he described a **Herald Tribune** reporter extracting from the Pentagon the admission that, once the first steps for the Santo Domingo episode were mounted, it was impossible to stop the machine.

Catch-22 said that in order to be sent home from flying missions you had to be crazy, and obviously anybody who wanted to be sent home was sane. Kesey and Heller and Terry Southern, to a lesser degree in his novels but certainly in **Dr. Strangelove**, have hold of it. I suspect that they are not really a **New Wave** of writers but only a last wave of the past, just as is Norman Mailer, who said in his Berkeley Vietnam Day speech that "rational discussion of the United States' involvement in Viet Nam is illogical in the way surrealism is illogical and rational political discussion of Adolf Hitler's motives was illogical and then obscene." This is the end of the formal literature we have known and the beginning, possibly, of something else.

In almost every aspect of what is happening today, this turning away from the old patterns is making itself manifest. As the formal structure of the show business world of popular music and television has brought out into the open the Negro performer—whose incredibly beautiful folk poetry and music for decades has been the prime mover in American song—we find a curious thing happening.

The Negro performers, from James Brown to Aaron Neville to the Supremes and the Four Tops, are on an Ed Sullivan trip, striving as hard as they can to get on that stage and become part of the American success story, while the white rock performers are motivated to escape from that stereotype. Whereas in years past the Negro performer offered style in performance and content in song—the messages from Leadbelly to Percy Mayfield to Ray Charles were important messages—today he is almost totally style with very little content. And when James Brown sings, "It's a Man's World," or Aaron Neville sings, "Tell It Like It Is," he takes a phrase and only a phrase with which to work, and the Supremes and the Tops are choreographed more and more like the Four Lads and the Ames Brothers and the McGuire Sisters.

I suggest that this bears a strong relationship to the condition of the civil rights movement today in which the only truly black position is that of Stokely Carmichael, and in which the NAACP and most of the other formal groups are, like the Four Tops and the Supremes, on an Ed Sullivan-TV-trip to middle-class America. And the only true American Negro music is that which abandons the concepts of European musical thought, abandons the systems of scales and keys and notes, for a music whose roots are in the culture of the colored peoples of the world.

The drive behind all American popular music performers, to a greater or lesser extent, from Sophie Tucker and Al Jolson, on down through Pat Boone and as recently as Roy Head and Charlie Rich, has been to sound like a Negro. The white jazz musician was the epitome of this.

Yet an outstanding characteristic of the new music of rock, certainly in its best artists, is something else altogether. This new generation of musicians is not interested in being Negro, since that is an absurdity.

The clarinetist Milton Mezzrow, who grew up with the Negro Chicago jazzmen in the twenties and thirties, even put "Negro" on his prison record and claimed to be more at home with his Negro friends than with his Jewish family and neighbors.

Today's new youth, beginning with the rock band musician but spreading out into the entire movement, into the Haight-Ashbury hippies, is not ashamed of being white.

He is remarkably free from prejudice, but he is not attempting to join the Negro culture or to become part of it, like his musical predecessor, the jazzman, or like his social predecessor, the beatnik. I find this of considerable significance. For the very first time in decades, as far as I know, something important and new is happening artistically and musically in this society that is distinct from the Negro and to which the Negro will have to come, if he is interested in it at all, as in the past the white youth went uptown to Harlem or downtown or crosstown or to wherever the Negro community was centered because there was the locus of artistic creativity.

Today the new electronic music by the Beatles and others (and the Beatles' "Strawberry Fields" is, I suggest, a three-minute masterpiece, an electronic miniature symphony) exists somewhere else from and independent of the Negro. This is only one of the more easily observed manifestations of this movement.

The professional craft union, the American Federation of Musicians, is now faced with something absolutely unforeseen—the cooperative band. Briefly—in the thirties—there were co-op bands. The original Casa Loma band was one and the original Woody Herman band was another. But the whole attitude of the union and the attitude of the musicians themselves worked against the idea, and co-op bands were discouraged. They were almost unknown until recently.

Today almost all the rock groups are cooperative. Many live together, in tribal style, in houses or camps or sometimes in traveling tepees, but always **together** as a **group**; and the young girls who follow them are called "groupies," just as the girls who in the thirties and forties followed the bands (music does more than soothe the savage breast!) were called "band chicks."

The basic creed of the American Federation of Musicians is that musicians must not play unless paid. The new generation wants money, of course, but its basic motivation is to play anytime, anywhere, anyhow. Art is first, then finance, most of the time. And at least one rock band, the Loading Zone in Berkeley, has stepped outside the American Federation of Musicians entirely and does not play for money. You may give them money, but they won't set a price or solicit it.

This seems to me to extend the attitude that gave Pete Seeger, Joan Baez, and Bob Dylan such status. They are not and never have been for sale in the sense that you can hire Sammy Davis to appear, as you can hire Dean Martin to appear, any time he's free, as long as you pay his price. You have not been able to do this with Seeger, Baez, and Dylan any more than Allen Ginsberg has been for sale either to **Ramparts** or the CIA.

Naturally, this revolt against the assumptions of the adult world runs smack dab into the sanctimonious puritan morality of America, the schizophrenia that insists that money is serious business and the acquisition of wealth is a blessing in the eyes of the Lord, that what we do in private we must preach against in public. Don't do what I do, do what I say.

Implicit in the very names of the business organizations that these youths form is an attack on the traditional, serious attitude toward money. It is not only that the groups themselves are named with beautiful imagery: the Grateful Dead, the Loading Zone, Blue Cheer, or the Jefferson Airplane—all dating back to the Beatles with an A—it is the names of the nonmusical organizations: Frontage Road Productions (the music company of the Grateful Dead), Faithful Virtue Music (the Lovin' Spoonful's publishing company), Ashes and Sand (Bob Dylan's production firm—his music publishing company is Dwarf Music). A group who give light shows is known as the Love Conspiracy Commune, and there was a dance recently in Marin County, California, sponsored by the Northern California Psychedelic Cattlemen's Association, Ltd. And, of course, there is the Family Dog, which, despite **Ramparts**, was never a rock group, only a name under which four people who wanted to present rock'n roll dances worked.

Attacking the conventional attitude toward money is considered immoral in the society of our fathers, because money is sacred. The reality of what Bob Dylan says—"money doesn't talk, it swears"—has yet to seep through.

A corollary of the money attack is the whole thing about long hair, bare feet, and beards. "Nothing makes me sadder," a woman wrote me objecting to the Haight-Ashbury scene, "than to see beautiful young girls walking along the street in bare feet." My own daughter pointed out that your feet couldn't get any dirtier than your shoes.

Recently I spent an evening with a lawyer, a brilliant man who is engaged in a lifelong crusade to educate and reform lawyers. He is interested in the civil liberties issue of police harassment of hippies. But, he said, they wear those uniforms of buckskin and fringe and beads. Why don't they dress naturally? So I asked him if he was born in his three-button dacron suit. It's like the newspaper descriptions of Joan Baez's "long stringy hair." It may be long, but **stringy**? Come on!

To the eyes of many of the elder generation, all visible aspects of the new generation, its music, its lights, its clothes, are immoral. The City of San Francisco Commission on Juvenile Delinquency reported adversely on the sound level and the lights at the Fillmore Auditorium, as if those things of and by themselves were threats (they may be, but not in the way the Commission saw them). A young girl might have trouble maintaining her judgment in that environment, the Commission chairman said.

Now this all implies that dancing is the road to moral ruin, that young girls on the dance floor are mesmerized by talent scouts for South American brothels and enticed away from their happy (not hippie) homes to live a life of slavery and moral degradation. It ought to be noted, parenthetically, that a British writer, discussing the Beatles, claims that "the Cycladic fertility goddess from Amorgos dates the guitar as a sex symbol to 4800 years B.C."

During the twenties and the thirties and the forties—in other words, during the prime years of the Old Ones of today—dancing, in the immortal words of Bob Scobey, the Dixieland trumpet player, "was an excuse to get next to a broad." The very least effect of the pill on American youth is that this is no longer true.

The assault on hypocrisy works on many levels. The adult society attempted to chastise Bob Dylan by economic sanction, calling the line in "Rainy Day Woman," "everybody must get stoned" (although there is a purely religious, even biblical, meaning to it, if you wish), an enticement to teenagers to smoke marijuana. But no one has objected to Ray Charles's "Let's Go Get Stoned," which is about gin, or to any number of other songs, from the Kingston Trio's "Scotch and Soda" on through "One for My Baby and One More [ONE MORE!] for the Road." Those are about alcohol and alcohol is socially acceptable, as well as big business, even though I believe that everyone under thirty now knows that alcohol is worse for you than marijuana, that, in fact, the only thing wrong about marijuana is that it is illegal.

Cut to the California State Narcotics Bureau's chief enforcement officer, Matt O'Connor, in a TV interview recently insisting, à la Parkinson's Law,

that he must have more agents to control the drug abuse problem. He appeared with a representative of the state attorney general's office, who predicted that the problem would continue "as long as these people believe they are not doing anything wrong."

And that's exactly it. They do not think they are doing anything wrong, any more than their grandparents were when they broke the prohibition laws. They do not want to go to jail, but a jail sentence or a bust no longer carries the social stigma it once did. The civil rights movement has made a jailing a badge of honor, if you go there for principle, and to a great many people today, the right to smoke marijuana is a principle worth risking jail for.

"Make Love, Not War" is one of the most important slogans of modern times, a statement of life against death, as the Beatles have said over and over—"say the word and be like me, say the word and you'll be free."

I don't think that wearing that slogan on a bumper or on the back of a windbreaker is going to end the bombing tomorrow at noon, but it implies something. It is not conceivable that it could have existed in such proliferation thirty years ago, and in 1937 **we** were pacifists, too. It simply could not have happened.

There's another side to it, of course, or at least another aspect of it. The Rolling Stones, who came into existence really to fight jazz in the clubs of London, were against the jazz of the integrated world, the integrated world arrived at by rational processes. Their songs, from "Satisfaction" and "19th Nervous Breakdown" to "Get Off of My Cloud" and "Mother's Little Helper," were antiestablishment songs in a nonpolitical sort of way, just as Dylan's first period was antiestablishment in a political way. The Stones are now moving, with "Ruby Tuesday" and "Let's Spend the Night Together," into a social radicalism of sorts; but in the beginning, and for their basic first-thrust appeal, they hit out in rage, almost in blind anger and certainly with overtones of destructiveness, against the adult world. It's no wonder the novel they were attracted to was David Wallis' **Only Lovers Left Alive**, that Hell's Angels story of a teenage, future jungle. And it is further interesting that their manager, Andrew Loog Oldham, writes the essays on their albums in the style of Anthony Burgess' violent **A Clockwork Orange**.

Nor is it any wonder that this attitude appealed to that section of the youth whose basic position was still in politics and economics (re-

member that the Rolling Stone Mick Jagger was
a London School of Economics student, whereas
Lennon and McCartney were artists and writers).
When the Stones first came to the West Coast, a
group of young radicals issued the following proclamation of welcome:

> Greetings and welcome Rolling Stones, our
> comrades in the desperate battle against the
> maniacs who hold power. The revolutionary
> youth of the world hears your music and is
> inspired to even more deadly acts. We fight in
> guerrilla bands against the invading imperial-
> ists in Asia and South America, we riot at
> rock 'n roll concerts everywhere. We burned
> and pillaged in Los Angeles and the cops
> know our snipers will return.
>
> They call us dropouts and delinquents and
> draftdodgers and punks and hopheads and
> heap tons of shit on our heads. In Viet Nam
> they drop bombs on us and in America they
> try to make us make war on our own com-
> rades but the bastards hear us playing you on
> our little transistor radios and know that they
> will not escape the blood and fire of the anar-
> chist revolution.
>
> We will play your music in rock 'n roll
> marching bands as we tear down the jails and
> free the prisoners, as we tear down the State
> schools and free the students, as we tear down
> the military bases and arm the poor, as we
> tatoo BURN BABY BURN! on the bellies of
> the wardens and generals and create a new
> society from the ashes of our fires.
>
> Comrades, you will return to this country
> when it is free from the tyranny of the State
> and you will play your splendid music in fac-
> tories run by the workers, in the domes of
> emptied city halls, on the rubble of police
> stations, under the hanging corpses of priests,
> under a million red flags waving over a million
> anarchist communities. In the words of
> Breton, THE ROLLING STONES ARE THAT
> WHICH SHALL BE! LYNDON JOHNSON
> —THE YOUTH OF CALIFORNIA DEDI-
> CATES ITSELF TO YOUR DESTRUCTION!
> ROLLING STONES—THE YOUTH OF CALI-
> FORNIA HEARS YOUR MESSAGE! LONG
> LIVE THE REVOLUTION!!!

But rhetoric like that did not bring out last
January to a Human Be-In on the polo grounds of
San Francisco's Golden Gate Park twenty
thousand people who were there, fundamentally,
just to see the other members of the tribe, not to

hear speeches—the speeches were all a drag from
Leary to Rubin to Buddah[1]—but just to BE.

In the Haight-Ashbury district the Love Generation organizes itself into Job Co-ops and committees to clean the streets, and the monks of the
neighborhood, the Diggers, talk about free dances
in the park to put the Avalon Ballroom and the
Fillmore out of business and about communizing
the incomes of Bob Dylan and the Beatles.

The Diggers trace back spiritually to those
British millenarians who who took over land in
1649, just before Cromwell, and after the Civil
War freed it, under the assumption that the land
was for the people. They tilled it and gave the
food away.

The Diggers give food away. Everything is
Free. So is it with the Berkeley Provos and the
new group in Cleveland—the Prunes—and the Provos in Los Angeles. More, if an extreme, assault
against the money culture. Are they driving the
money changers out of the temple? Perhaps. The
Diggers say they believe it is just as futile to fight
the system as to join it and they are dropping out
in a way that differs from Leary's.

The Square Left wrestles with the problem.
They want a Yellow Submarine community be-
cause that is where the strength so obviously is.
But even **Ramparts**, which is the white hope of the
Square Left, if you follow me, misunderstands.
They think that the Family Dog is a rock group
and that political activity is the only hope, and
Bob Dylan says, "There's no left wing and no right
wing, only up wing and down wing," and also, "I
tell you there are no politics."

But the banding together to form Job Co-ops,
to publish newspapers, to talk to the police (even
to bring them flowers), aren't these political acts?
I suppose so, but I think they are political acts of a
different kind, a kind that results in the Hell's
Angels being the guardians of the lost children at
the Be-In and the guarantors of peace at dances.

The New Youth is finding its prophets in
strange places—in dance halls and on the jukebox.
It is on, perhaps, a frontier buckskin trip after a
decade of Matt Dillon and "Bonanza" and the other
TV folk myths, in which the values are clear (as
opposed to those in the world around us) and right
is right and wrong is wrong. The Negro singers
have brought the style and the manner of the Negro gospel preacher to popular music, just as they
brought the rhythms and the feeling of the gospel
music, and now the radio is the church and Everyman carries his own walkie-talkie to God in his
transistor.

Examine the outcry against the Beatles for John Lennon's remark about being more popular than Jesus. No radio station that depended on rock 'n roll music for its audience banned Beatles records, and in the only instance where we had a precise measuring rod for the contest—the Beatles concert in Memphis where a revival meeting ran day and date with them—the Beatles won overwhelmingly. Something like eight to five over Jesus in attendance, even though the Beatles charged a stiff price and the Gospel according to the revival preacher was free. Was my friend so wrong who said that if Hitler were alive today, the German girls wouldn't allow him to bomb London if the Beatles were there?

"Nobody ever taught you how to live out in the streets," Bob Dylan sings in "Like a Rolling Stone." You may consider that directed at a specific person, or you may, as I do, consider it poetically aimed at plastic uptight America, to use a phrase from one of the Family Dog founders.

"Nowhere to run, nowhere to hide," Martha and the Vandellas sing, and Simon and Garfunkel say, "The words of the prophets are written on the subway walls, in tenement halls." And the Byrds sing, "A time for peace, I swear it's not too late," just as the Beatles sing, "Say the word." What has formal religion done in this century to get the youth of the world so well acquainted with a verse from the Bible?

Even in those artists of the second echelon who are not, like Dylan and the Beatles and the Stones, worldwide in their influence, we find it. "Don't You Want Somebody to Love," the Jefferson Airplane sings, and Bob Lind speaks of "the bright elusive butterfly of love."

These songs speak to us in our condition, just as Dylan did with "lookout kid, it's somethin' you did, god knows what, but you're doin' it again." And Dylan sings again a concept that finds immediate response in the tolerance and the antijudgment stance of the new generation, when he says, "There are no trials inside the Gates of Eden."

Youth is wise today. Lenny Bruce claimed that TV made even eight-year-old girls sophisticated. When Bob Dylan in "Desolation Row" sings, "At midnight all the agents and the superhuman crew come out and round up everyone that knows more than they do," he speaks true, as he did with "don't follow leaders." But sometimes it is, as John Sebastian of the Lovin' Spoonful says, "like trying to tell a stranger 'bout a rock 'n roll."

Let's go back again to Nietzsche.

Orgiastic movements of a society leave their traces in music [he wrote] . Dionysiac stirrings arise either through the influence of those narcotic potions of which all primitive races speak in their hymns [—dig that!—] or through the powerful approach of spring, which penetrates with joy the whole frame of nature. So stirred, the individual forgets himself completely. It is the same Dionysiac power which in medieval Germany drove ever increasing crowds of people singing and dancing from place to place; we recognize in these St. John's and St. Vitus' dancers the bacchic choruses of the Greeks, who had their precursors in Asia Minor and as far back as Babylon and the orgiastic Sacea. There are people who, either from lack of experience or out of sheer stupidity, turn away from such phenomena, and strong, in the sense of their own sanity, label them either mockingly or pityingly "endemic diseases." These benighted souls have no idea how cadaverous and ghostly their "sanity" appears as the intense throng of Dionysiac revelers sweeps past them.

And Nietzsche never heard of the San Francisco Commission on Juvenile Delinquency or the Fillmore and the Avalon ballrooms.

"Believe in the magic, it will set you free," the Lovin' Spoonful sing. "This is an invitation across the nation," sing Martha and the Vandellas, and the Mamas and the Papas, "a chance for folks to meet, there'll be laughin', singin' and music swingin', and dancin' in the street!"

Do I project too much? Again, to Nietzsche. "Man now expresses himself through song and dance as the member of a higher community; he has forgotten how to walk, how to speak and is on the brink of taking wing as he dances . . . no longer the artist, he has himself become a work of art."

"Hail hail rock 'n roll," as Chuck Berry sings. "Deliver me from the days of old!"

I think he's about to be granted his wish.

NOTES

1. The Be-In heard speeches by Timothy Leary, the psychedelic guru, Jerry Rubin, the leader of the Berkeley Vietnam Day movement, and Buddah, a bartender and minor figure in the San Francisco hippie movement who acted as master of ceremonies.

chapter 46
why "hair" has become a four-letter word
warren brown

Back in 1964, a band of rock 'n' roll singers suddenly became the idols of America's youth, and this—of course—disgusted and disgruntled a great many American adults. Robert P. Odenwald, a disgusted, disgruntled psychiatrist, even made a stab at explaining the appeal of these raucous upstarts (in **The Disappearing Sexes**, 1965): "Surely they were not being mobbed by thousands of screaming youngsters because of their musical talent; any small town could produce a quartet with equal ability." No, the secret of their success, like Samson's, lay in their long hair—their long hair made them sexually neutral and permitted boys as well as girls to identify with them. "And the songs they sing are essentially sexless," the mad doctor went on. To clinch his point, he quoted the sour comment of an anonymous critic: "Who are these Beatles? You look at their faces and hairdos and you think they are women."

Yes, it was those sexless, talentless Beatles who launched the hypertrichosis revolution, who made the amount of one's hair the official determinant of which side of the generation gap you stood on. And ever since the Beatles' brief visit, this country has been busy fighting those bitter 17th-century English wars—the wars between the gay Cavaliers, with their long-flowing locks, and

the Roundheads, those dour Puritans who cut their hair short. Only, in modern times the Roundheads are called Skinheads.

Alas, the Skinheads—being more numerous, in higher positions of authority, and more given to brutish violence—have won almost all of the battles. In Norwalk, Connecticut, the Skinhead principal of the Brian McMahon High School suspended 51 boys whose hair, the principal had unanimously decided, was too long. A student at Seton Hall University in New Jersey was informed that he could keep either his beard or his scholarship—and cravenly chose the scholarship. A more courageous student, a bearded junior at the Colorado School of Mines, bristled when the seniors ordered all underclassmen to shave, and in defense of his beard fired off four shots, one of them wounding an upperclassman. In San Diego, a teacher forcibly cut off a student's hair (the student later filed suit, and won); in High Bridge, New Jersey, another teacher did the same thing, "on a dare." Indeed, high schools and institutions of higher learning all over the country have expelled, supended, or segregated long-haired young men, from DeWitt Clinton High School in New York to Marlboro High School in Boston to schools in New Augusta, Mississippi, and New Milford, New Jersey. Judges often order youthful defendants to get shaves and haircuts, and the youngsters comply—because the judges have them by the short hairs (an abominable ex-

From **Avant Garde**, May 1970. Reprinted by permission.

pression used as long ago as 1880, by Mark Twain in **A Tramp Abroad**). Once they are convicted—as in the case of the Chicago defendants—the youngsters have no choice at all. And it isn't only American youngsters who suffer—in Indonesia, 150 long-haired boys from wealthy families were forcibly given Army haircuts; cops in Buenos Aires, Argentina, made 200 young men get haircuts; police in Punta Arenas, Chile, shaved the heads of 10 long-haired boys. And it isn't only long-haired **youths** who get the shaft—a man was dismissed from Con Edison in New York because of his beard; New York University refused to hire a long-haired mail carrier; a New York City subway dispatcher got a misconduct charge because of his beard; Northwest Orient Airlines suspended 12 hairy airflight employees; a 24-year-old man in Southhampton, England, lost his unemployment benefits because he refused to cut his hair. One teacher at the John Muir High School in Pasadena, California, went to court rather than remove his whiskers, and in his defense pointed to a statue of the bearded naturalist John Muir—to no avail. A bearded prisoner in the Nassau County Jail, in Mineola, Long Island, was placed in solitary confinement when the refused to take up a razor. A black man in the Air Force wouldn't modify his Afro haircut, and was sentenced to three months hard labor. And in Carbon County, Wyoming, two men were being held by the police on a hitchhiking charge—and somehow had their heads and beards shaved.

Three recent films tell the same story. In **Alice's Restaurant**, the Skinheads abuse that noble Cavalier Arlo Guthrie, then toss him through a plate-glass window, where other Skinheads, the cops, arrest him (the incident actually happened). In **Easy Rider**, the Skinheads harass, then murder, two long-haired motorcyclists. In **Prologue**, a long-haired boy is roughed up by Skinheads who call him "a dirty Commie."

All over the land, in short, the anal-sadistic Skinheads are ganging up on the fun-loving Cavaliers, and though further evidence is not needed, read this recent letter to the **New York Times** from Tom Andrews of Kent, Connecticut:

> After viewing **Alice's Restaurant**, I sat in a cab that had stopped for a red light at 59th Street and Lexington Avenue. The driver and I watched a long-haired teen-age boy cross 59th Street. . . . His long, blond hair fell below his shoulders. Except for his hair he was all masculine in appearance.

> The driver turned to me just before the light changed, and, with deliberate hatred in his voice, said, "You see that? Boy, if I could get outa this cab right now, I'd go up and whip that kid and shave his hair naked." Judging from the cabbie's tone and physique, I didn't doubt for a moment his ability to carry out his threat. . . .

On the way home to Kent, Conn., I picked up two young hitchhikers near Bedford, N.Y. They wore long hair, unkempt beards. . . . When we reached Brewster, we had coffee together before parting. . . . While our treatment in the café didn't resemble that of the three travelers in the café in **Easy Rider**, . . . the waitress was hardly civil to us. And my two companions told me their experience:

> While traveling with a young salesman, just outside New Orleans, a few days before I met them, the three had stopped at a roadside café for coffee. Inside, they were completely ignored by the waitress. Two parties of teen-age boys began a barrage of caustic remarks. Two local policemen entered the café, approached the travelers, yanked them out of their chairs, threw them against the counter and searched them. Finding a pocketknife on one of them, the police put the two hitchhikers in jail overnight for illegal possession of a dangerous weapon.

But while the Skinheads have been scoring all of the runs, the Cavaliers have managed to get a few scratch singles. Joan Cook writes in the **New York Times** that nowadays "Rich man, poor man, beggarman, thief, doctor, lawyer, merchant, chief, not to mention teacher, stockbroker, and corporation executive," have begun to sprout long hair, sideburns, beards, and moustaches. The very word "hair" was chosen as the title of a zesty, frolicsome new musical. In New York, labor mediator Theodore W. Kheel recently ruled that bus drivers are entitled to grow beards—although he based his decision upon a passel of misinformation.[1] What's more, like all good revolutionaries, the Cavaliers have even added a few new words to our vocabulary, such as **grotty**—"used in connection with masculine long hair worn Beatle style," according to linguist Mario Pei in his highly unrecommended **Words in Sheep's Clothing** (1969), and possibly derived from "grotesque"—and **hairy**—defined by Wentworth and Flexner in their **Dictionary of American Slang** (1960) as "old," "lousy," or "virile," but in point of fact having now assumed the meaning of "formidable," as in this quotation from Gary Jennings' excellent **Personalities of Language** (1969): "When [Mark] Twain and Rudyard Kipling became friends, they engaged in a sort of competition to see who could write the hairiest obscenity. It is said that one of Kipling's sketches (which began, '"Shit!" said the Queen . . . ') was somehow brought to Victoria's attention. She was not amused." The Cavaliers have also popularized the term "fuzz," meaning "cops," in recognition of the fact that their enemies-to-the-death are short-haired.

■

THE 1000-YEAR WAR

What neither the Skinheads nor the Cavaliers seem to be aware of is that their war has been raging not just for a few years or merely for a few centuries, but for a few millenia. Herodotus tells us that the ancient Egyptians, who were clean-shaven, loathed the sight of the bearded Greeks, for which reason no Egyptian lassie or laddie could bear to kiss a Greek laddie or lassie. The estrangement between King David and his son Absolom no doubt stemmed in part from Absolom's grotty hairdo (it weighed "two hundred shekels after the king's weight"). Indeed, the Skinhead-Cavalier controversy was one of the causes of the schism between the Roman Catholic Church and the Eastern Church, Roman Catholic clerics insisting on being clean-shaven, Eastern clerics insisting on remaining bearded. In the 15th century, according to a contemporary, Père Fangé, the learned Cardinal Bessariom missed out becoming pope because the other cardinals objected to his long beard. Throughout the Middle Ages, in fact, hairy men led a perilous existence, being subject on occasion not only to excommunication but to involuntary barbering—the latter so common that lawyers for the Cavaliers (to quote Reginald Reynolds' **Beards**, 1949) "maintained that such compulsorary pogotomy was equal to the severance of a limb, meriting the same punishment."

Even in the so-called land of the free, the alleged home of the brave, persecution of the hirsute is old hat. In the 1700s, his fellow Quakers discriminated against Joshua Evans of New Jersey, a vegetarian, opponent of slavery, friend of the Indians, and—worst of all—wearer of a beard. In 1830, Joseph Palmer of Fitchburg, Massachusetts—the Arlo Guthrie of his day—was refused communion because of his beard. Later, according to Reginald

Reynolds, Palmer was "assaulted by four men who attempted to shave him forcibly. He routed them with the aid of a jackknife, wounding two of them, and soon found himself in court, charged with **unprovoked assault.** . . . Having been fined on this outrageous charge, Palmer refused to pay, and was put in the county jail." He was eventually released, over his own objections, and lived happily ever after. He is buried in Leominster, Massachusetts, and his tombstone to this day carries a carving of his likeness, complete with magnificent moustache and Brobdingnagian beard, along with the inscription, **Persecuted for wearing the beard.** (A photograph can be seen in Gerald Carson's **The Polite Americans,** 1965). A few score years later, George Armstrong Custer, while attending West Point, was given demerits for wearing his hair too long. In retaliation, Custer—who always was a little batty—shaved all of his head-hair off, for which he also received demerits.

Just what is the Skinhead-Cavalier brouhaha all about? Why does long-haired Tiny Tim arouse smirks, but baldheaded Yul Brynner arouse admiration? Why are priests clean-shaven, but Fidel and his followers hairy? Why did Joey Bishop get a costly hair transplant, why does Carl Reiner wear a wig, and why does Richard M. Nixon (as John Osborne charges in **The New Republic**) touch up his graying hair?

Stay tuned to this station.

To understand why hair has become a four-letter word, we must first brush up on our knowledge of symbolism. A symbol is something that is associated with something else. A primary symbol is something that has a direct, unambiguous association with something else—another word for it is "sign." For instance, this drawing ⟑ is a primary symbol of a horseshoe, while this drawing ⟍ is a primary symbol of a lipstick cartridge.

A **secondary** symbol has a vague, imprecise association with something else—whereas a primary symbol is apparent to the conscious mind, a secondary symbol is apparent only to the subconscious mind. The drawing of a horseshoe may have, as its secondary symbols, horses, sports, or masculinity. The drawing of a lipstick cartridge may have as its secondary symbols the world of cosmetics, or femininity.

A **tertiary** symbol is only very dimly associated with something else—and the referent is usually something basic, like sex or death. The tertiary symbol can reinforce the primary or secondary symbols, or even flatly contradict them. The examples we have chosen show contradictions. A horseshoe may be a secondary symbol of masculinity, but it is a tertiary symbol of **femininity**—because of its resemblance to the female sex organ. A lipstick cartridge may be a secondary symbol of femininity, but it is a tertiary symbol of **masculinity**—because of its phallic shape, and because it is extensible and retractable. We are usually unconscious of tertiary symbols, and can become aware of their existence only by studying dreams, slips of speech, free associations, folklore and myth, manifestations of the irrational, and so forth. And because, as we've seen, human hair is so often linked with irrational behavior, it is obvious that hair must have some interesting tertiary symbolism.

THE PRIMARY SYMBOLISM OF HAIR

But let us begin at the beginning. A primary symbol is readily apparent to all, and it is readily apparent that **long hair** symbolizes femaleness and **short hair** symbolizes maleness. As St. Paul put it, "Does not nature itself teach you that if a man have long hair it is a shame unto him? But if a woman have long hair it is a glory to her." Or as Mrs. Jane G. Austin writes in Frank Leslie's **Popular Monthly** (January, 1881), "Among the minor mysteries of human nature may be ranked the feeling, deeper than custom or fashion, in favor of long hair upon a woman's head, short upon that of a man. True, caprice occasionally dictates the reverse, but these caprices generally indicate an unnatural and unhealthy state of mind in people or individuals who exhibit them."

The tradition that men have short hair and women long hair is an important one, because modern men and women have obliterated a few other clues to their gender—they bathe often, removing their distinctive scents, and they wear clothing that conceals their distinctive genitals and bosoms. Children have it even worse than adults, because a little girl doesn't wear lipstick or rouge and she doesn't have a bosom—a little boy can identify her as a she, short of actually undressing her, only by observing whether she is wearing a dress and whether she has long hair. So the long hair = female, short hair = male equations are something we have learned, and used as a guide, ever since childhood.

We can now understand why cops, taxicab drivers, and other lower-class authoritarians become enraged when they encounter a man with long hair. The long hair acts as a female sexual **stimulus**; but because the person giving the stimu-

lus is male, the cops and taxicab drivers have caught themselves in a compromisingly homosexual situation. And their guilt is all the greater if the long-haired person turns out to be someone who is "otherwise all masculine in appearance." If the long-haired person, however, also sang in a falsetto, wore strange clothes, allowed himself to be verbally abused (as Arlo Guthrie did not), and went by the self-castrating appellation "Tiny Tim," the anxiety of the cops and taxicab drivers would express itself not in anger but in sadistic laughter.

If follows that long hair upon a man and short hair upon a woman are also primary symbols of dissent, of a yearning for freedom from convention—and so is a man's beard if the men around him go clean-shaven. Women cut their hair short during the French revolution and during the 20th-century suffragette movement. Men have let their hair grow during the artistic and political revolutions of the 19th and 20th centuries—"The connection between beards and freedom," writes Reginald Reynolds, "is . . . a long one." No wonder that nowadays, when we think of hairy men, we think of Karl Marx, Bernard Shaw, Garibaldi, Fidel and his followers, anarchists, wobblies, and Sinn Feiners—not to overlook hippies, yippies, and the New Left, Allen Ginsberg, the former Jerry Rubin, and the former Abbie Hoffman.

Tyrants have therefore always trembled at the thought of the hirsute. In the 1830s, Turkey, by imperial decree, banned beards; the King of Bavaria outlawed moustaches. In Naples, according to one 19th-century observer, men were being "dragged daily into the barbershops by the police, and their beards trimmed according to the political creeds of the authorities." In 1967, the military dictators of Greece announced that long-haired tourists would no longer be allowed into the country, and barbershops would be set up at all entry points to turn Cavaliers into Skinheads. (The ban was soon lifted because of travel-industry protests.) Modern-day Cuba, having had its revolution, wants no more truck with revolutionaries, and in 1968 the Cuban military banned beards, long hair, and moustaches from Havana University. As for the United States, our official position was taken in 1968 also, when the Supreme Court refused to overturn the expulsion of three long-haired students from a Dallas high school. The lone dissenter was that honorary Cavalier William O. Douglas, who stated that he believed that a country founded upon the Declaration of Independence could permit "idiosyncracies to flourish, especially when they concern the image of one's personality and his philosophy toward Government and his fellow men."

Conservatives, by the same token, are almost always shorthaired—it is unthinkable that William F. Buckley, Jr., Barry Goldwater, or Strom Thurmond would grow beards. And servants, waiters, judges, doctors, congressmen, policemen, and soldiers all show their obeisance to convention by their relative hairlessness.

THE SECONDARY SYMBOLISM OF HAIR

Though long hair is a primary symbol of femaleness, hairiness in general is a secondary symbol of masculinity. For while women have longer hair on their heads, men have more hair on their faces, chests, and everywhere else on their bodies, including the genital region (despite certain exceptions listed by Havelock Ellis: "Jahn delivered a woman whose pubic hair was longer than that of her head, reaching below her knees; Paulini also knew of a woman whose pubic hair nearly reached her knees and was sold to make wigs; Bartholin mentions a soldier's wife who plaited her pubic hair behind her back"). A hairy chest is almost universally considered a sign of virility, while a bald head is almost universally considered just the opposite. Men boast of how tough their whiskers are, or of how often they have to shave. Strong men, from Goliath to Steve Reeves playing Hercules, have been depicted as hairy.

Because hairiness is so masculine a symbol, women shave the hair on their legs and axilla, pluck their eyebrows, and electrocute their moustaches. Girls just reaching puberty suddenly develop a loathing for spiders—"The only clue here," writes Desmond Morris in **The Naked Ape** (1967), "is the repeated female reference to spiders being nasty, hairy things." A study by A. Frazier and L. K. Lisonbee (**School Review**, 1950) found that many tenth-grade girls are seriously concerned about their heavy eyebrows; Karl Garrison reports (**Psychology of Adolescence**, 1965 edition) that "The appearance of axillary hair is in some cases a source of disturbance for girls; the lack of hair on the arms and legs is regarded by many boys as a weakness."

Because hairiness = virility, men with beards or long hair have always been a bit smug about it, while the less hairy have always been a bit envious. In the Bible, King David wreaks a terrible vengeance upon the Ammonites when they desecrate

the beards of his ambassadors. When Rome was sacked, the senators did nothing to protect themselves—until the invaders began tweaking their beards. "In the Middle Ages," John Brophy writes in **The Human Face** (1946), "to pluck a man by the beard was a gross insult." Among the medieval Moslems, Père Fangé informs us, "A man who spits on the beard of another person, or who, while spitting on the ground, says to him, 'That's for your beard,' or a man who, while breaking wind, says, 'I fart on your beard,' will be rigorously punished." Returning to Mr. Brophy, we find that "until a few centuries ago men swore, without facetiousness, by their beards, and even today in Moslem countries . . . it is still conventional to take a sacred oath by the Prophet's beard."

The short-haired have traditionally included court jesters, slaves, prisoners, and priests—in fact, Pope Gregory the Great ordered priests to be clean-shaven at about the same time he insisted that they remain celibate ("perhaps by association? "Reginald Reynolds asks naively). Royalty, on the other hand, has been partial to hairiness (the Caesars took their name from a word meaning "long-haired"), while God and Jesus are traditionally depicted with beards (although the earliest portraits of Jesus, in the fourth century, show him clean-shaven).

Perhaps we can now understand why a student at the Colorado School of Mines reacted so irrationally when his beard was threatened. And we can understand the magical power of Yul Brynner's bald head (without, as some have done, considering it phallic). Mr. Brynner is asserting that he is so very virile he can dispense with a common symbol of virility. If he were simply incapable of growing hair on his head, and the public knew of this defect, Mr. Brynner would be considered not a sex symbol but a freak.

THE TERTIARY SYMBOLISM OF HAIR

But if hairiness is so virile, why don't more men wear beards and grow long hair? One answer is that hair, as a **tertiary** symbol, represents excrement—like excrement, hair is produced by the body and must be removed periodically. This is why hirsute men are often called "dirty" (William Pynne, an English pamphleteer, in 1628 criticized wigs as "the hairie excrements of some other person"; the Skinheads in **Prologue** call Jesse a "dirty Commie," linking hair = dirt with long hair as the sign of rebellion); why it is so disgusting to find a hair in your food, even if it came from the woman you love, or from your own head; why many barbers refuse to cut the hair of black men; why Good Guys have white beards (Merlin, Santa Claus, Father Time, God) and Bad Guys have dark beards (Svengali, Bluebeard, Satan); and why blonds have more fun (one brunette even told her psychiatrist that she was turning blonde in order to become cleaner—see "Reasons Why Blondes Have More Fun," **Pageant**, the author, November 1963). Charles Berg, an English psychiatrist, notes in **The Unconscious Significance of Hair** (1951) "how uncomfortable and guilty we feel in public if we forgo our morning shave. . . . Must we be clean—free from anal guilt?" And he proceeds to speculate that women who are always straightening or tidying their hair have a hangup about their "dirtiness."

Hair has other tertiary symbols. Just what long hair upon a woman can symbolize is indicated by a dream that one of Charles Berg's patients had:

> I was sitting in a bus close beside a young woman with brilliant red hair. I put my hand on her head and pressed her hair and experienced feelings of great pleasure. . . . I don't know anyone with red hair like this girl had. My girl has fair, golden hair. . . . The other day I succeeded in exposing her pubic region and was delighted to find that her pubic hair had a distinct reddish tinge. I laughed . . . and put my hand on it—just as I put my hand on the girl's head in my dream. I have only just thought of this.

Clearly, long hair upon a woman is pubic hair—because of what Freud would have called a displacement from below to above, and what the ethologists would call sexual self-mimicry. This explains why, among orthodox Jews, women are not supposed to show their hair in public; why, in the Middle Ages, Christian women were not supposed to reveal their head-hair until they were married; why the barbaric custom once prevailed, as Reginald Reynolds reports, "of offering to women the choice of losing their hair or their chastity"; and why, after World War II, women who collaborated with the enemy had their hair cut off in punishment. And then there is the story of Rapunzel, a folk tale collected by the brothers Grimm. Rapunzel is imprisoned in a

tall tower by a witch (representing the girl's puritanical mother), but lets down her long hair for a prince to climb up on (her blooming sexuality makes up for his impotence).

It is partly because long hair is symbolic of public hair that men are so attracted by a woman's crowning glory. Mrs. Austin shrewdly writes, "Another of the minor mysteries of human sentiment is the tenderness, the romance, the pathos attaching to the hair of one we love. Looking at the matter in the calm light of reason, there seems to be no better cause for treasuring the shorn hair of our darling than her shorn finger and toe nails." (Mrs. Austin, by the way, struck a blow for racial understanding in her 1881 article: "It is often stated that negro hair is not hair at all, but wool, like that of sheep. The microscope, however, contradicts this error." Someone should rush out and tell Strom Thurmond.) But while all men are hair fetishists to a degree, there are some in whom this passion is overly developed—men who, to this day, go around snipping off women's hair (Havelock Ellis: "Sexual excitement and ejaculation may be produced in the act of touching or cutting off the hair, which is subsequently, in many cases, used for masturbation").

HAIR AND THE VANITY OF FEMALES

The equation female head-hair = pubic hair explains why women are so vainglorious about their hair ("pride in its appearance, in its prettiness or social acceptability," Charles Berg notes, "is a displacement of exhibitionistic satisfaction"). It explains why nuns have their hair cut short, and why women who lose their head-hair feel so wretched (Berg had as a patient a woman who was bald, and she gave up her job and any opportunities for romance lest she be discovered—"She thought the absence of an arm or a leg would not be so bad"). And it explains the extraordinary though brief popularity of the movie actress Veronica Lake, who, with her peek-a-boo bang that covered half her face, made the symbolism almost explicit.

Curly female hair is an even more emphatic symbol of pubic hair. "The essential association to curly hair," Berg states, "is . . . a direct one to the curly hair of the pubic region. Men with naturally curly hair are often at pains to keep it brushed flat, as though it were a public disgrace."

Or perhaps curls have a direct relation to the female sex organ.

Very long female head-hair is no longer pubic but phallic, and consequently strikes terror in the hearts of many men. To quote Mrs. Austin again, "In the waters . . . float the mermaidens, whose beautiful sea-green tresses are at once the admiration and destruction of their victims. Upon the rocks of the Rhine sits the Lorelei, softly singing and 'combing her golden hair,' as the surest lure to the unwary fisherman. Below the waters again, in the lurid realms of Pluto, the horror of Medusa's head is augmented by the transformation of its crowning glory to writhing snakes." Snakes are, of course, phallic symbols. Recently an attractive member of the Women's Liberation Movement was talking on the **David Susskind Show,** and bitterly complained about the obscene remarks that men are always making to her, the lewd propositions she is forever getting. She couldn't understand why, even though the hair on her head was so long it hung down to her poop.

Tiny Tim may be willing to dispense with other conventional symbols of virility, but not with his virile head-hair. For while hairiness, as we've seen, is a secondary symbol of masculinity, it is a tertiary symbol of the phallus itself. Hair is springy and flexible; it begins to flourish just when sexuality is blossoming, and decays—falls out or turns grey—when sexuality is on the wane; and, in certain unusual circumstances, it even "stands on end." Samson's strength lay in his hair, and when Delilah cut it off, all of Samson's great strength disappeared. Greek youths dedicated their head-hair to local rivers. Roman youths sacrificed their hair to the gods, and many ancient warriors swore not to cut their beards until they had killed an enemy soldier. In Arabia and Syria the hair of adolescents was cut off as a puberty rite. In many other places, to this day, hair cutting is considered a terrible ordeal: Sir James Frazier informs us that "The chief of Nanomea in Fiji always ate a man by way of precaution when he had his hair cut"; in parts of New Zealand, the hair is cut only on the most sacred day of the year. The Persians, as war trophies cut off their enemies' beards, just as the American Indians cut off the scalps of theirs (a custom they borrowed from white men). In **The Death of Arthur** Thomas Mallory tells of King Ryons, who boasted of capturing 11 kings and cutting off their beards—and now

demanded King Arthur's beard. Arthur considered the request "the most villanous and lewdest message that ever a man sent unto a king," and refused, for "this is the most shamefullest message that ever I heard spoke of." Charles Berg reports, "according to the evidence revealed by dreams, the unconscious has no doubt whatsoever about the identity . . . of penis and beards for it constantly presents the latter when it means the former."

If we accept the male hair = phallus equation, we can understand why certain 19th-century women collected "hair albums"—locks from their lovers—and why Mrs. Austin loathed "these hideous trophies one sometimes sees in country houses or city attics"; why, as Charles Berg wrote in 1936 (**International Journal of Psycho-Analysis**), the typical father "cannot bear to see his sons allowing their hair to grow long"; and we can understand, all too clearly, why the United Daughters of the Confederacy, to this very day, stand watch over the sacred locks from the head of Jefferson Davis. "These historic filaments," Carson reports, "repose today under tight security at 'Beauvoir,' the Davis shrine on U.S. 90, midway between Biloxi and Gulfport, Mississippi." We can also understand why certain women prefer hairy men and why others prefer hairless men: "Women who like the male's hairiness (e.g., men with beards)," Charles Berg writes, "are commonly highly heterosexual and not averse to the male sexual organ, while scruples in this respect commonly imply sexual scruples also." And finally, we can understand the following dispatch from Reuters:

> Lancing, England, Feb. 11 [1966]—A 15-year old fan of the Rolling Stones, long-haired entertainers, committed suicide because he had been forced to get a haircut, a coroner here said today.
>
> The boy, Christopher Holligan, was found dead on a railroad line near his home. He had been killed by a train.
>
> Less than two hours earlier his guardian had made him get a "short back and sides" haircut.

As for Joey Bishop's hair transplant and Richard Nixon's touching up his greying hair, Berg explains that "The normal concern or anxiety about the hair becoming thin or falling out, alopecia, or becoming grey, are displacements of castration anxiety." It is significant that when a man does get a hair transplant, the transplanted hair is often taken from his pubic region.

The male head-hair = phallus equation further explains why women, and especially men, who comb their hair in public are frowned upon—"The act of combing or brushing our hair," says Charles Berg, ". . .is associated to as a masturbation equivalent." The equation even explains why customarily women, but not men, have long head-hair—women, Berg suggests, are being given "a compensatory indulgence, compensatory for the fantasied genital castration." Finally, the equation explains why modern man shaves—to indicate that he has renounced aggressive, invidious, overt sexuality. The all-knowing Charles Berg states: "It is as though the hair which we display in our clothed social state were the only phallus permitted us by society—the only phallus we are permitted to **reveal**. There is the tendency to show how fine it is, to be proud of it and sue for its approval, alternating with a fear lest it should not be approved. The fear is expressed by brushing it flat, by being sure it is tidy, or even by hastening to cut it off ourselves, as in shaving, lest we should suffer still more serious castration at the hands of society." Later on he writes, "There is a tendency for civilized man to brush his hair down flat, and even to guard against the contingency of erection by using various pastes or creams."

American men, curiously, were probably the most clean-shaven, short-haired men in the world until the Beatle revolution. In 1935, a bearded Englishman, Ernest Boyd, visited our shores and was aghast at the sight of "ubiquitously clean-shaven" men and "the astounding spectacle of the national cult of cold razor steel." Why, a hairy man was so uncommon that "a bearded man in America enjoys all the privileges of a bearded woman in the circus." In 1950, Frazier and Lisonbee found that tenth-grade boys were more liable to be ashamed of their facial growth than proud of it. John F. Kennedy, before he ran for the Presidency, drastically trimmed his long head-hair; his brother Robert was frequently criticized for letting his hair grow long. Indeed, no President of the United States has been moustached since Teddy Roosevelt (elected 1912), no President has been bewhiskered since Benjamin Harrison (elected 1889 with a minority of the popular vote). The last candidate to be bearded was Harrison, the last candidate to be moustached was Thomas E. Dewey.

Why are the great majority of American men still averse to hairiness? One answer is that the great majority of American women, as Charles Berg put it, still have scruples about the phallus, so they still have scruples about a hairy man—no hairy man has even run for the Presidency since women got the vote, and you will recall that many women admitted that they wouldn't vote for Thomas Dewey because of his moustache.

■

THE SKINHEADS
VERSUS THE CAVALIERS

Having concluded our investigation into the complex symbolism of hair, we are now in a position to understand just what the war between the Skinheads and the Cavaliers is all about. A Skinhead, as mentioned, sees a long-haired man, becomes sexually confused (because long hair is a symbol of femininity), and feels that he has been guilty of homosexual yearnings. After identifying the object of his sexual interest as male, the Skinhead proceeds to regard the Cavalier as a Communist, anarchist, Bonapartist, or whatever the latest radicals are (because long hair upon a man = rebellion); to regard the Cavalier as "dirty" (because hair = excrement); and to regard the Cavalier as a sexual rival, someone who is boasting. "Mine is longer than yours" (because hair = the phallus). The Skinhead's response is a gnawing desire to cut off the offending long hair or beard—to castrate the Cavalier (throwing him through a plate-glass window is a perfectly acceptable symbolic gesture).

The Cavalier, in his turn, grows his hair long because he is rebellious, because he is not so worried and anxious about whether he is male or not, because he is not hung up on anality and because he is proud of his genitality. Charles Berg put it succinctly: "When we attend, preserve, or love our hair, we are expressing in displaced form our appreciation of, and pleasure in, our genital sexuality. When we remove, cut, or control our hair we are giving expression to reaction formations against the genital (and anal) libido."

The Skinhead-Cavalier controversy, then, is no temporary altercation, like the Thirty Years' War, but symbolic of the age-old antagonism between the healthy and the neurotic, between self-actualizing people and self-strangling people. And even though the Skinheads vastly outnumber the Cavaliers, and even though John Lennon has cut his head-hair short and even though Ringo Starr is

quoted in **Look** as saying, "Long hair is going out
for me," as long as the spirit of rebellion breathes
in the human breast, as long as there are men and
women who have satisfactorily passed from the
anal phase of sexuality to the genital phase of
sexuality, there will be men eager to grow hair on
their faces and long hair upon their heads—and there
will be women who appreciate and value such men.

NOTES

1. Such as that Uncle Sam has "always" worn a beard
(he didn't grow one until about 1858); that Aristotle was
bearded (following the preference of his famous pupil,
Alexander the Great, Aristotle shaved); and that all over
the world beards have stood for wisdom and strength
(most Chinese are beardless, and thoroughly despise
beards).

chapter 47
collective behavior: an examination of some stereotypes
carl j. couch

After years of relative neglect there has been a recent resurgence of interest in collective behavior. However, with the exception of Smelser's work[1] there has been almost no effort to apply a general theory to collective behavior, nor have there been many empirical studies testing propositions about human conduct in collective behavior situations.[2] One common theme presented in many of the discussions of collective behavior holds that collective behavior is a form of deviant behavior.

This state of affairs is partly the consequence of the continuing influence of LeBon's characterization of collective behavior (crowd behavior).[3] LeBon viewed collective behavior as a different order of behavior than that manifested in other human associations[4] and as a pathological form of behavior.

Several have taken issue with LeBon's characterization of the crowd[5] but nearly all who have attempted to present a "theory" of crowd behavior have incorporated many of the ideas of LeBon. Almost without exception, contemporary statements explicitly state or imply that crowd behavior is pathological or, at best, a more primitive form of conduct than noncrowd behavior.

From **Social Problems**, Winter 1968, published by The Society for the Study of Social Problems. Reprinted by permission.

LeBon's central thesis was this: "The conclusion to be drawn from what precedes is, that the crowd is always intellectually inferior to the isolated individual, but that, from the point of view of feelings and of the acts these feelings provoke, the crowd may, according to circumstances, be better or worse than the individual."[6]

Fifty years after LeBon's classical statement, Blumer (who has been widely used as an authoritative source) suggested:

Instead of acting, then, on the basis of established rule, it (the acting crowd) acts on the basis of aroused impulse. Just as it is, in this sense, a noncultural group, so likewise it is a non-moral group. In the light of this fact it is not difficult to understand that crowd actions may be strange, forbidding, and at times atrocious. Not having a body of definitions or rules to guide its behavior and, instead, acting on the basis of impulse, the crowd is fickle, suggestible, and irresponsible.[7]

Nor did Smelser differ greatly from LeBon when he observed:

We can suggest already, however, why collective behavior displays some of the crudeness, excess, and eccentricity that it does. By short-circuiting from high-level to low-level components of social action, collective episodes by-pass many of the specifications, contingencies, and controls that are required to make the generalized components operative. This gives collective behavior its clumsy or primitive character.[8]

None of the theorists of collective behavior have accepted LeBon's formulation of crowd behavior without qualification. Some have given attention to "mechanisms" of crowd behavior in attempts to explain its behavior. Brown presented a rather comprehensive review of mechanisms to account for crowd behavior;[9] others, particularly Turner and Killian,[10] have centered on the interaction within the crowd; many have focused on the social conditions giving rise to crowds.[11]

Relatively little attention has been given to the structure (relationships between self and others) or interaction patterns within crowds. Many discussions of crowd behavior have followed LeBon's lead and directed attention to delineating the "nature" of the behavior of members of crowds. Often the delineation focuses attention on the primitive and/or pathological nature of the behavior. As a consequence, the significance of social relationships has been slighted.

This essay does not try to delineate the social relationships and processes distinctive of the acting crowd.[12] Rather it examines some widespread beliefs about the nature of crowd behavior. In short, it examines some stereotypes held by sociologists and others about the acting crowd. Hopefully, this examination will stimulate the reanalysis of the crowd as a social system.

SUGGESTIBILITY

It is generally agreed that crowds are highly suggestible.[13] But if crowds are as suggestible as some critics claim, they would pose no problem for authorities; all that would be necessary to disperse a crowd would be to suggest they break up and go for a cold swim. In fact, one of the distinctive features of a crowd is its lack of receptivity to suggestions offered by outside authorities. Members of institutionalized social systems regularly follow the directive of others. Workmen commonly follow the instructions of foremen. Very few label workmen as suggestible because they follow instructions of accepted authorities.

In his laboratory study of the acting crowd, Swanson states, "They [members of acting crowds] are faced with an urgent problem for which they have no solution. This being true, they grasp at such ideas as are available as a guide for their behavior."[14] He found that laboratory groups composed of members who had not previously worked together and with no previous experience with the task gave more attention to outside suggestions than those who had worked together previously and had experience with the task. This finding is not of special relevance to the acting crowd; rather it demonstrates that in problematic situations persons are receptive to suggestions.

Acting crowds probably confront problematic situations more frequently than other social systems. In these situations suggestions are commonly offered, one or more of which may be accepted. The behavior within a crowd is no different from the behavior in other social systems when they confront unanticipated situations—except in institutionalized systems, those who formulate the plans of action are vested with the authority to do so by the institutional structure.

Most members of an acting crowd have strong feelings about some object; any suggestions (directions) calling for behavior that is defined as incompatible with their desires is likely to be rejected. Directions that come from within the crowd which are perceived as facilitating their aims may be adopted.

DESTRUCTIVENESS

The destructiveness of crowds is legendary.[15] Conflict engenders destruction; crowds do destroy property and human lives; participants in race riots do kill each other. But destructiveness is not restricted to crowds.

Crowds acting against the established authority system as part of a general movement to modify the authority structure have generally been as gentle as a loving mother when compared with the established authority. The outstanding current example is the civil rights movement in the United States. Nor is this case unique.

In the Gordon Riots of 1780, the demonstration took a heavy toll in property and freed inmates of prisons (a destructive act?) but there is no evidence that the demonstrators killed anyone. However, 285 rioters were killed during the riots and another 25 were hanged afterwards.[16] Another extreme case was the rebellion riots during the French Revolution when the rioters killed no one, but several hundred of them were killed by representatives (police and military) of the established authorities.[17] In most, if not all, cases of crowds attempting to overthrow the authorities and to establish a less authoritarian political system the number of people killed or maimed by crowds is smaller than the number killed or maimed by those suppressing the crowd.[18]

Lang and Lang in a description of riots provide an illustration that violence is not a one-way affair. In the Shanghai riot, "The police responded [to bricks and stones being thrown at them] by arresting several 'agitators' in the crowd, whom they pulled, one by one, into the station, beating them as they were being dragged."[19] In the same account they state, "The crowd was finally dispersed by machine-gun fire followed by a police charge, with bayonets and clubs, against the crowd."[20] It was only after this that "the crowd began its rampage of Shanghai."[21]

Riots between ethnic groups are often marked by extensive destruction of life. Negro-white riots in the United States, religious riots in India, and other similar outbursts often have resulted in the death of many participants. Almost invariably a larger number of the minority are killed than are representatives of the dominant group;[22] this is, in part, because the dominant group is most likely to have greater access to instruments of destruction. Some of the differential probably is a function of fear of reprisals by the minority group.

Lynch crowds of the United States have often been used to illustrate the lack of respect for human life by a crowd. However, a substantial number of Negroes have been killed by law enforcement agencies—from deputy sheriffs to the court system. Probably far more Negroes have been killed in the southern part of the United States by the constituted authorities than by lynch mobs.

LeBon and others dealt extensively with the reign of terror of the French revolutions.[23] After the revolutionaries were in power a large number of the opposition were killed. An extreme case was the killing of over 1000 people in September of 1792. The bulk of the victims were first given a "trial" and then executed. In more recent times, after the Cuba revolution, several of the opposition were killed. While these situations are often used to illustrate the results of a so-called crowd, the overlooked fact is that the action was taken by the authority of the day.[24] Whether the new authorities destroy more lives than the old is difficult to answer. But the significant factor is that most of the killing is accomplished by the established authority, not by the crowd. This suggests that it is something about the social relationships inherent in authority that is responsible for the widespread destruction of life—not the social system of crowds nor the personalities of members of the crowd.

The destruction of leaders of the opposition after a successful revolution is usually well publicized. The killing of revolutionaries by the entrenched authority receives much less publicity, often because the revolutionaries killed are less well known, other times because it is conducted secretly.

In the entire history of mankind, crowds have been responsible for only a very small percentage of the lives taken by fellow humans. In fact, it appears that systems with a highly authoritarian structure are more given to killing humans and are far more effective at it. Armies are the ultimate instance of an authoritarian social system and they are the social system par excellence for the destruction of human life.

IRRATIONALITY

Most students of the crowd have commented, in one form or another, on the irrationality of crowds.[25] The concepts of rationality and irrationality have limited applicability for a sociological analysis.[26] The concepts are an attempt to characterize the nature of ideas or beliefs: they direct attention away from social processes. However, if we tentatively accept the definition of rational action as that action which represents the most effective means for achieving some goal, then acting crowds are frequently highly rational endeavors.

The potential lyncher, the striker in a plant without a union, and the student wishing to change rules governing students know that their chances of success as individuals are almost nil. They would be highly irrational if they attempted to achieve the the desired results as individuals. At the same time, those enforcing the rules want to deal with dissatisfied personnel through established channels. Those wishing to strike out against the system know that numbers are a critical element to any chance of success.

Another basis of the charge of irrationality of crowds is the demands of crowds. As Katz noted, the member of parliament who defends the prevailing economic system is behaving on the basis of delusions as much as the members of the crowd crying for liberty and equality.[27]

Coordinated human endeavor demands at least tacit acceptance of shared beliefs. The crowd is attempting to produce a situation where people organize their behavior on the basis of a different set of norms than those currently extant. Many economists well versed in traditional economics of the time knew that the programs proposed by the labor unions during the 1930s could not work. Similarly, most of the noted scholars of political systems knew that the programs voiced by the crowds of the French Revolution were unrealistic and irrational.

Rational thought is that which is supported by the established institutions of the day; irrational thought is that which is not supported by the current institutions. Irrational thought of today often forms the social institutions of tomorrow.

EMOTIONALITY

Compatible with the charge of irrationality is the one of emotionality. Crowd behavior usually does occur within a context of strong emotions. This does not distinguish crowd behavior from many other instances of human behavior. A sequence of interaction between a husband and wife or employer and employee can also be highly charged with emotion.

A crowd situation elicits a high level of emotion from both the participants and those they are acting against. The wrath of the factory owner confronted for the first time by a crowd of defiant workers is something to behold. School administrators confronted by demonstrating students and Southern white officialdom confronted by civil rights demonstrators are seldom placid.

There is strong feeling among members of crowds because many are behaving to acquire rights they feel are justifiably theirs.[28] Those they are acting against usually feel that the crowd is making demands or taking liberties that they have no right to.

Another set of factors assures a high level of emotion—most members of an acting crowd know they are running high risks. The shooting of demonstrators is not unknown; unsuccessful demonstrations often result in some of the participants losing statuses that are important to them; organizers of unsuccessful strikes often lose their jobs; demonstrating strdents are often expelled.

Emotion among those in opposition to the crowd is also assured for their status is threatened. If the crowd is successful, this will result in

restricting the rights of the opposition. When demonstrating strikers are successful, the owner loses his rights to hire and fire at his own discretion and to set work and wage levels. People seldom easily relinquish rights they have exercised for some time, especially when they are supported by established institutions. Many have commented on the "righteous" nature of beliefs of crowds. In most instances, there is probably a greater degree of righteousness on the part of those opposing the crowd.

MENTAL DISTURBANCES

Several have noted a similarity between the beliefs of crowd members and some forms of mental illness. One of the more extreme statements is Martin's. "Probably the most telling point of likeness between the crowd-mind and the psychoneurosis—paranoia especially—is the 'delusion' of persecution."[29] The farmer who was receiving fifteen cents a bushel for his corn in the early 1930s and joined the Farmer's Holiday Association knew that he had more than that invested in it and he thought something was wrong. He may have felt persecuted but to call it a delusion hardly illuminates the situation. The miner working 56 hours a week and unable to provide a doctor for his family often felt that things were against him and that someone somewhere was responsible for it. When he got into a crowd he often gave voice to these ideas.

In a way there is some similarity between the thought processes of crowd members and some forms of mental illness. The error in views such as Martin's is that mental illness is usually conceptualized as being a function of shortcomings of the individual, and it has been these so-called individual shortcomings of the same nature that have been designated as the causal factors of crowd participation.

Lemert offered an analysis of paranoia based on relationships between the person classified as suffering from paranoia and others. "The paranoid relationship includes reciprocating behaviors with with attached emotions and meanings which, to be fully understood, must be described cubistically from at least two of its perspectives."[30] Once the actor, who becomes classified as paranoid, develops a feeling that others are opposed to him he tends to behave in a manner that causes others to systematically exclude him from their interaction patterns. The exclusion furthers the actor's definition of the situaion that others are "ganging up" on him.

In a highly parallel manner, some of the participants of a crowd or protest movement have attempted to correct undesirable situations prior to the formation of crowds. Such action usually elicits negative evaluations and sometimes repressive acts. The person then feels the authority figure is persecuting him and this will strengthen his conviction that the opposition is against him. Reciprocally, his actions will elicit a still more negative evaluation and more repressive action.

The result is a decrease in the sharing of points of view and a decrease in meaningful communication. Open conflict becomes the only mode left for a resolution of the situation, each side having only negative evaluations of the other.

LOWER-CLASS PARTICIPATION

Of all of the ideas current about crowds the one that is probably most strongly entrenched holds that crowds tend to be composed of the lower echelons of society. Examination of the evidence lends little support for this idea. Members of the crowd are not composed of those in positions of power, authority, or policy formation. Usually a crowd is acting against current social relationships formulated by policymakers and enforced by authorities, so policymakers and authorities seldom participate in acting crowds. However, those protesting are seldom if ever representatives of social categories with the lowest prestige and fewest rights. The farmers who formed picket lines to prevent sale of produce during the withholding action of the National Farmers' Organization in 1964 were not the poorest farmers, nor were they farm laborers.[31] Rudé, in an analysis of several crowds in England and France, supplies evidence that members of the crowds were not those with the lowest prestige and fewest privileges. He asks the question, "If, then, slum dwellers and criminal elements were not the main shock troops of the pre-industrial crowd or the mainstay of riot and revolution, who were?"[32] The answer he supplies is that they were of "the lower orders" as compared to the aristocracy, but those with an occupation and often from skilled occupations.

College administrators and other authorities often write off demonstrators as being ne'er-do-wells. The participants in student demonstrations are very likely to be some of the outstanding students.[33] It is not the uneducated, uninformed Negro who organizes or participates in demonstrations. Nor are those who organize a crowd for throwing bricks at the home of Negroes who have just moved into a previously all-white suburb, the riffraff. Nor are the organizers of a lynching mob the down-and-outers. Those of the very lowest prestige do not command sufficient respect to organize others; nor do they usually have the skill and know-how to organize others.

An accepted axiom of human behavior is that dissatisfaction is an essential ingredient of any collective endeavor to strike out against established social institutions. There is a large body of evidence that the level of satisfaction is directly associated with position in the prestige hierarchy·and with privileges and rights.[34] From this it would follow that those with the fewest rights and least prestige would be most likely to participate in crowd behavior.

The paradox can be explained by taking cognizance of the fact that crowd behavior is an instance of coordinated social behavior. Those of the lowest status are the ones least likely to have stable role relationships with a number of others similar to themselves. Middle- and upper-class people are much more likely to have stable relationships with others similar to themselves than the unemployed are with others who are unemployed. The lack of consistent and widespread stable associations with others similar to themselves prevents the lowest categories from developing consensus on the cause of dissatisfaction, on the solution to the situation, and on plans for coordinated action. A low status does not carry with it any features that make its occupants more satisfied with the established order. The crucial factor in explaining their lack of action is the absence of an opportunity to coordinate their behavior. Kerr and Siegel found those workers in industries where there is ample opportunity to interact with fellow workers have a higher rate of striking than do those who are isolated from each other.[35] Miners have one of the highest rates whereas farm laborers have the lowest rate. The failure of those of the very lowest status to participate in crowds cannot be accounted for by by a lower level of dissatisfaction among those of very low status but by the lack of an opportunity to coordinate their behavior.

The formation of crowds composed largely of middle-class members—e.g., suburban home owners demonstrating against the purchase of a home by a Negro—is similar to that of other crowds. Such crowds also are opposing the policies formulated by authorities. They are a reaction to members of subordinate categories gaining access to the authority structure.

SPONTANEITY

Many commentators have assumed that crowds develop when a number of unconnected individuals suddenly and simultaneously strike out against some grievous condition or imagined wrong.[36] The formation of crowds and other protesting collectivities depends upon a plurality having common dissatisfying experiences. To share these common dissatisfactions and formulate a line of action, those with common dissatisfactions must engage in some planning.

In most cases, the crowd will act against those in authority and hide as much of the planning from authorities as possible. The first knowledge authorities and other outsiders have of the event is when the crowd is formed. They assume that as they were not aware of any prior activity, none had occurred.

Some observers have noted the presence of interaction among participants prior to the formation of a crowd, usually under the rubric of rumor. Allport and Postman state, "No riot ever occurs without rumors to incite, accompany and intensify the violence."[37] Certainly not all prior interaction (rumors) incite or intensify violence. Some of it is planning for the purpose of preventing or minimizing violence. The organizer who goes from person to person prior to the formation of the crowd pleading for no violence and instructing members on how to behave when the crowd is formed is not unknown. The advocating of violence by crowd participants is not unknown, but this does not distinguish them from generals of the army, governors, or other authorities.

Nor does the planning of the crowd activity distinguish most crowds from institutionalized social systems. Prior to any act on the part of a large social system some members of the system plan the activities of others; for example, school administrators planning a new building program, or a police department organizing a new push on delinquency, plan before the system acts. The crowd is distinctive in this dimension only by the fact that those planning the affair are not expected by tradition to plan the activities of collectivities.

In one account provided by Raper, an effort was made on three continuous nights to round up enough people to conduct a lynching, certainly evidence the crowd did not spring up without prior planning.[38] Rudé offers considerable indirect evidence that most crowds are preceded by extensive planning ahead of the actual formation of the crowd.[39] Quite in contrast to the idea of spontaneous formation, there is probably more time spent in the planning of crowd action than in the planning for action by more established social units of comparable size.

CREATIVENESS

In contrast to the idea that crowds operate on a primitive intellectual level, others have developed the proposition that crowds are creative. The crowd is not a particularly inventive social system. A crowd does involve people relating themselves to each other in a fashion different from that of routine relationships. However, the ideas used to organize their behavior are seldom developed (invented) during the interaction within the crowd. The plans of action used to organize their behavior nearly always have a history that predates the formation of the crowd. The peasants' hatred and their plans to burn the manor were current long before the formation of the crowd. The desire for the opportunity to vote and the idea of confrontation of the white authority were current among many Negroes, and a topic of discussion, long before the crowds were formed.

The crowd is not more emergent than other forms of interaction. It involves a number of people organizing themselves to participate in nontraditional behavior. But many of the ideas used to organize their behavior are developed outside the crowd situation. The ideas of equality and liberty were current long before any crowd was formed to force their implementation.

Most innovations are developed in social situations that are vastly different from a crowd. The formation of new ideas results from people being reflective. Members of a crowd are not highly reflective. They have a narrow focus of attention. They do not stand back and wonder about how something can be done in a different fashion than ever done before. This activity most commonly occurs in small groups or by persons in relative isolation. Neither the ideas germane to democracy nor knowledge of how to produce more food nor any similar set of ideas were formulated within the context of a crowd.

Joint action by members of a crowd often forces the adoption of new norms but is seldom the original formulator of new norms.

LACK OF SELF-CONTROL

Because people in a crowd behave differently within an acting crowd than in other situations is no reason to assume a loss of self-control.[40] The crowd participant often behaves without the concern for others that he normally takes into account in organizing his behavior. When the disenchanted worker hurls obscene words at management in a crowd, this is hardly evidence of lack of self-control. It is evidence that he is organizing his behavior by incorporating management into his acts in a different fashion than usual. Within the prior social system the worker incorporated the wishes and directions of management into his action. In the acting crowd, he is not organizing his behavior by incorporating the desires of management into his action.

Instead of a lack of self-control, it would be more accurate to characterize crowds as exhibiting a lack of control by others, particularly others who are in control within the institutional situations. "Normal social control is effective largely because the individual is known and identified and held responsible for his actions."[41] A crowd is formed to modify this condition.

ANTISOCIAL BEHAVIOR

Nearly all discussions of the crowd assume that the members of a crowd become dehumanized —more specifically that they are antisocial. Quite the contrary is the case. The acting crowd is an instance of social conduct. The human organism becomes and remains a human being by engaging in a joint coordinated endeavor with other humans, by taking the role of others, or by a fusion of self and others. The social act requires that a plural of humans integrate or incorporate within their activity the acts of others; that is, social behavior is behavior that incorporates the activity of others. Clearly, some members of a crowd identify with each other and they incorporate the acts of other members into their own activity.

In only a very limited sense is the behavior of the acting crowd anti- or non-social. As members of an institutionalized social system, humans incorporate into their acts the acts of the authorities of the system; a driver of an automobile incorporates the anticipated acts of the highway patrolman and other drivers into his own behavior; the student incorporates the anticipated acts of the school principal, teachers, and other students; and the "good" Southern Negro incorporates the ongoing and anticipated acts of the white men. What members of the crowd do not do that has resulted in crowd activity being regarded as antisocial or dehumanized is this: they do not incorporate the norms carried and sanctioned by the authorities

into their behavior. The demonstrating Negro takes policemen into account and guides his behavior accordingly, but not in terms of the norms the policeman is attempting to enforce. Such behavior may stamp him as antiauthority, but hardly as antisocial.

CONCLUSION

Sociologists have emphasized "cultural" factors in their analysis of behavior, and deemphasized the interaction among people. The tendency has been to examine how cultural factors influence or direct human behavior at the expense of questions of how cultural elements are created, modified, and adopted in interaction. Consequently, they find it hard to account for behavior that does not follow the "cultural patterns."

Discussions of crowd behavior often observe that cultural factors no longer provide the basis for the observed conduct. In the search for factors to account for crowd behavior many sociologists have employed concepts that suggest an explanation can be formulated by noting the traits and characteristics of the behavior. However, many of the ascriptions of these traits to crowd behavior are not empirically valid. Furthermore, the concepts commonly employed have restricted utility for a sociological analysis of crowds. Instead of directing attention to social processes and social relationships, concepts such as suggestibility, emotionality, and rationality suggest the explanation of crowds is to be made in terms of characteristics of the individual members.

The patterning of behavior by culture is much less marked than current sociological thought implies. Study of societies, particularly complex ones, leads one to conclude that numerous groups and collectivities are continually attempting to change their social structure. This should lead to the conclusion that many members of a society are dissatisfied with certain features of their daily life. These dissatisfactions arise in associations with other humans. Those dissatisfied often attempt to take action to modify the form of the associations that have led to dissatisfaction. In order to accomplish the task it often is necessary to develop new social systems or to modify the old one. The formation of crowds is but one of several lines of activity that may be taken to modify dissatisfying situations.

Crowd behavior is distinctive, but to emphasize the "abnormal" dimensions of crowd behavior appears to be fruitless. A more promising line of attack is one that conceptualizes the acting crowd as a social system that is distinctive in some ways from other social systems. It is a social system human beings adopt to take action with reference to other systems. As such, it is no more and no less pathological or bizarre than other systems they have developed.

NOTES

1. Neil J. Smelser, **Theory of Collective Behavior,** New York: Free Press, 1963.

2. Exceptions include Alan C. Kerckhoff, Kurt W. Back, and Norman Miller, "Sociometric Patterns in Hysterical Contagion," **Sociometry,** 28 (March, 1965), pp. 2-15; and Robert E. Forman, "Resignation as a Collective Behavior Response," **American Journal of Sociology,** 69 (November, 1963). pp. 385-390. An earlier exception is Seymour M. Lipset, **Agrarian Socialism,** Berkeley: University of California Press, 1950. His report of a rural protest movement contains little, if any, support for some of the more generally accepted propositions on the character of participants in protest collectivities. Perhaps this accounts for the lack of attention given it by those concerned with collective behavior.

3. Gustave LeBon, **The Crowd,** New York: Viking, 1960.

4. Ralph H. Turner, "Collective Behavior," in Robert E. L. Faris, editor, **Handbook of Modern Sociology,** Chicago: Rand McNally, 1964, p. 384, questions this view: "It is altogether possible that the search will ultimately undermine all of the traditional dynamic distinctions between collective behavior and organizational behavior and suggest that no special set of principles is required to deal with this subject matter." The framework offered by Turner is one of the few that does not imply that collective behavior is pathological behavior.

5. Robert K. Merton, "The Ambivalences of LeBon's **The Crowd,**" introduction to the Compass Books Edition of Gustave LeBon, **The Crowd,** New York: Viking, 1960, pp. v-xxxix.

6. LeBon, op. cit., p. 32, states, "Moreover, by the mere fact that he forms part of an organized crowd, a man descends several rungs in the ladder of civilization." And on p. 43, "It is not necessary that a crowd should be numerous for the faculty of seeing what is taking place before its eyes to be destroyed and for the real facts to be replaced by hallucinations unrelated to them.

7. Herbert Blumer, "Collective Behavior," in A. M. Lee, **New Outline of the Principles of Sociology,** New York: Barnes and Noble, 1946, p. 180. In a more recent statement Blumer has modified his position. Herbert Blumer, "Collective Behavior," in Joseph B. Gettler, editor, **Review of Sociology,** New York: Wiley, 1957, p. 131. "Latent with strong destructive and constructive potentialities the crowd is an important collectivity, particularly in societies undergoing transformation."

8. Smelser, op. cit., p. 72. Smelser's acceptance of LeBon's framework is indicated, p. 80, by the statement, "We hope to give more precise theoretical meaning to the insights of LeBon and others who have attempted to fathom the mysteries of these kinds of beliefs."

9. Roger W. Brown, "Mass Phenomena," in Gardner Lindzey, editor, **Handbook of Social Psychology,** II, Cambridge: Addison-Wesley, 1954, pp. 833-876.

10. Ralph H. Turner and Lewis M. Killian, **Collective Behavior,** Englewood Cliffs, N.J.: Prentice-Hall, 1957, esp. chap. 6.

11. Smelser, op. cit.; Rudolf Heberle, **Social Movements: An Introduction to Political Sociology,** New York: Appleton-Century-Crofts, 1951; and Stanley Lieberson and Arnold R. Silverman, "The Precipitants and Underlying Conditions of Race Riots," **American Sociological Review,** 30 (December, 1965), pp. 887-898.

12. The terms crowd and acting crowd will be used interchangeably; however, the acting crowd is only one type of crowd—the one most significant to the collective behavior process. Attention is directed specifically to the acting crowd but most of the propositions analyzed and offered are relevant to other forms of protesting collectivities.

13. Smelser, op. cit., pp. 152-153; G. E. Swanson, "A Preliminary Laboratory of the Acting Crowd," **American Sociological Review,** 18 (October, 1953), pp. 528-529; Kurt Lang and Gladys Engel Lang, **Collective Dynamics,** New York: Crowell, 1961, pp. 221-225; Ralph H. Turner and Lewis M. Killian **Collective Behavior,** Englewood Cliffs, N.J.: Prentice-Hall, 1957, p. 84. Most of the above note that suggestion is not a mechanism restricted to crowd situations but indicate it is of special importance in the crowd or other collective behavior situations. Turner and Killian, p. 84, state, "It [heightened suggestibility] amounts to a tendency to respond uncritically to suggestions that are consistent with the mood, imagery, and conception of appropriate action that have developed and assumed a normative character." Lang and Lang, p. 221, note, "The existence of a 'normal' suggestibility adds to the difficulty of explaining suggestibility in its contagious form." Smelser, p. 153, writes, "It should be stressed, however, that as an explanatory concept in collective behavior, suggestion should be limited to its appropriate place in the value-added process." Blumer, **New Outline,** p. 181, assigns suggestibility a more limited role than others. "It should be noted, however, that this suggestibility exists only along the line of the aroused impulses; suggestions made contrary to them are ignored."

14. Swanson, op. cit., p. 528.

15. While this theme is not always explicitly developed, the way material is presented usually emphasizes the "destructive" nature of the crowd. See Lang and Lang, op. cit., pp. 125-135; Smelser, op. cit., Chapter 8; Brown, op. cit., p. 846, clearly imputes destructive behavior to crowds by stating, "There may be lawless individuals whose brutal behavior in the mob is not completely discontinuous with their private lives." An exception is George Rudé, **The Crowd in History, 1730-1848,** New York: Wiley, 1964, p. 255, "Destruction of property, then, is a constant feature of the pre-industrial crowd; but not the destruction of human lives".

16. Rudé, op. cit., p. 59.

17. Ibid., p. 256.

18. This generalization appears to hold for mutinies

also. See T. H. McGuffie, **Stories of Famous Mutinies**, London: Arthur Barker, 1966.

19. Lang and Lang, op. cit., p. 128.

20. Ibid., p. 129.

21. Ibid., p. 129. For a more recent and detailed account of reciprocal violence see: Fred C. Shapiro and James W. Sullivan, **Race Riots New York 1964**, New York: Crowell, 1964, esp. pp. 50, 57, 60-61, 83, 130, and 141.

22. Chicago Commission on Race Relations, **The Negro in Chicago**, Chicago: U. of Chicago, 1922.

23. LeBon, op. cit., pp. 160-165.

25. Rudé, op. cit.

25. Brown op. cit., p. 846, "There are, of course, mobs lacking any clear leadership that are nevertheless homogeneously irrational," Lang and Lang, op. cit., p. 32, "There is an incontestable bit of truth in this contention that people in groups are often less rational than individuals on their own." Smelser, op. cit., Chapter 5. Smelser does not employ the concepts rational and irrational. However in this discussion of belief systems he employs the concept "hysterical beliefs" in much the same manner others have used irrationality.

26. Daniel Katz, "The Psychology of the Crowd." In J. P. Guilford, editor, **Fields of Psychology**, New York: D. Van Nostrand, 1940, p. 160; and Turner and Killian, op. cit., pp. 16-17, both indicate that the concept rationality is of little utility.

27. Katz, op. cit., p.180.

28. Alvin W. Gouldner, **Wildcat Strike**, Yellow Springs, Ohio: Antioch Press, 1954, pp. 18-26.

29. Everett D. Martin, **The Behavior of Crowds**, New York: Norton, 1920, p. 92. Elsewhere, p. 6, he states, "A crowd is a device for indulging ourselves in a kind of temporary insanity by all going crazy together." Lang and Lang, op. cit., p. 32, "This view that the 'crowd' brings pathological elements to the fore is more than an ideological assumption. It has driven home with some force the observation that large unities often act irrationally and under the impact of emotion." Smelser, op. cit., by his excessive use of phrases like hysterical beliefs, wish fulfillment beliefs, hallucinations, short-circuiting process and craze adopts a stance highly compatible with those who "explain"crowd behavior as a form of mental disturbance.

30. Edwin M. Lemert, "Paranoia and the Dynamics of Exclusion," **Sociometry**, 25 (March, 1962), p. 6.

31. Carl J. Couch, "Interaction and Protest," paper presented at 1967 National Meetings of American sociological Association (mimeograph); Lipset, op. cit., observed that the active participants of a movement tended to be those with some prior leadership status.

32. George Rudé, op. cit., p. 204.

33. Robert H. Somers, "The Mainsprings of the Rebellion: A Survey of Berkeley Students in November, 1964," in Seymour M. Lipset and Sheldon S. Wolin, editors, **The Berkeley Student Revolt**, New York: Doubleday, 1965, p. 544.

34. Alex Inkeles, "Industrial Man: The Relation of Status to Experience, Perception, and Value," **American Journal of Sociology**, 66 (July, 1960), pp. 1-31.

35. Clark Kerr and Abraham Siegel, "The Interindustry Propensity to Strike—an International Comparison," in Arthur Kornhauser et al., **Industrial Conflict**, New York: McGraw-Hill, 1954, p. 190.

36. Herbert Blumer, **New Outline**, p. 180. This proposition is implicitly accepted by those who advance a "convergence theory" interpretation of collective behavior. See Turner, op. cit., for a critique of this approach.

37. Gordon W. Allport and Leo Postman, **The Psychology of Rumor**, New York: Henry Holt, 1947, p. 191.

38. Arthur F. Raper, **The Tragedy of Lynching**, Chapel Hill: University of North Carolina Press, 1933, p. 226.

39. Rudé, op. cit.

40. Blumer, **New Outline**, p. 180, "Such an individual (typical member of a crowd) loses ordinary critical understanding and self-control as he enters into rapport with other crowd members and becomes infused by the collective excitement which dominates them." Lang and Lang, op. cit., p. 143, take an ambivalent position, "The extent to which individuals actually lose a clear awareness of what they are doing cannot be determined with any degree of finality."

41. Turner, op. cit., p. 386.

topic 21
collective behavior: riots, insurrections, and rebellions

Common sense tempts us to interpret the riot as something irrational and senseless, and moreover, as something that is characteristic of the "lower" classes. Such conventional views are not confined to popular folklore; the riots that devastated Watts in 1965 were depicted by the authors of a state-sponsored investigation as "a spasm—an insensate rage of destruction." Riots are also frequently construed as hopeless and useless.

Yet it may be argued that, for all of their bloodiness and tragedy, the urban riots in America's ghettos and barrios during the 1960s were neither formless and incoherent **nor** altogether senseless and futile.

Although often a violent, destructive, and deadly form of collective behavior, there is another and revealing side to them. In the first place, riots have not been confined to our times. They have a secure niche in the long history of American violence. As Brown points out, "Our cities have been in a state of more or less continuous turmoil since the colonial period." What is more, rioting has not been confined to the lower classes, and it has not always been useless. Recall the anti-British maritime riots in the colonies in the 1760s, for instance, and the later riotous dissent against such English colonial policies as the Stamp Act. Recall, too, our long history of labor riots (the Haymarket Riot in Chicago in 1886 and the Ludlow, Colorado, massacre in 1914, for example) or the recurrent and ill-fated desperation rebellions on the part of black slaves early in the nineteenth century.

Robert Blauner speaks for many discerning students of riots and rebellions when he asks us to search for the **meanings** behind riots in black ghettos. Thus the Watts riots, he argues, spoke for ghetto people trying desperately to say something, something like this: "We have abided indignity and frustration long enough. It is time we insist upon becoming citizens in our own right rather than natives dominated by colonial masters." The authors of the **Report of the National Advisory Commission on Civil Disorders** came to a similar conclusion: Their examination of twenty-four riots revealed a typical pattern of "deeply held grievances which were widely shared by many members of the Negro community," grievances that, in all the cities, "related to prejudice, discrimination, severely disadvantaged living conditions, and a general sense of frustration about their inability to change those conditions."

Each of the articles in this section addresses itself to violent forms of collective behavior. The authors—Ralph Conant, Martin Oppenheimer, and Hugh Graham and Ted Gurr—variously search for the logic of events or the "scenarios" that culminate in rebellions, insurrections, or riots. Yet all, however sympathetic to the frustrations and grievances that actuate such violent behavior, appear to agree in the end that, as Graham and Gurr conclude, revolutionary victory is unlikely in the modern postindustrial state—that, moreover, "the prolonged use of force or violence to advance the interests of any segmental group may impede and quite possibly preclude reform."

chapter 48
rioting, insurrection, and civil disobedience
ralph w. conant

Rioting is a spontaneous outburst of group violence characterized by excitement mixed with rage. The outburst is usually directed against alleged perpetrators of injustice or gross misusers of political power. The typical rioter has no premeditated purpose, plan, or direction, although systematic looting, arson, and attack on persons may occur once the riot is underway. Also, criminals and conspirators may expand their routine activities in the wake of the riot chaos. While it is quite clear that riots are unpremeditated outbursts, they are not as a rule senseless outbursts. The rage behind riots is a shared rage growing out of specific rage-inducing experiences. In the United States, the rage felt by Negroes (increasingly manifested in ghetto riots) is based on centuries of oppression, and in latter times on discriminatory practices that frustrate equal opportunity to social, economic, and political goals. While all riots stem from conflicts in society similar to those that inspire civil disobedience, they ordinarily do not develop directly from specific acts of civil disobedience. Yet repeated failures of civil disobedience to achieve sought-after goals can and often do result in frustrations that provide fertile ground for the violent outbursts we call riots.

The factors universally associated with the

From **American Scholar**, Summer 1968. Reprinted by permission of the author.

occurrence and course of any riot are the following: (1) preconditions, (2) riot phases, and (3) social control. The discussion here is drawn from a review of the literature of collective behavior as well as studies currently underway at the Lemberg Center for the Study of Violence at Brandeis University.

THE PRECONDITIONS OF RIOT: VALUE CONFLICTS

All riots stem from intense conflicts within the value systems that stabilize the social and political processes of a nation. The ghetto riot is a concrete case of a group attempt to restructure value conflicts and clarify social relationships in a short time by deviant means.

There are two classes of value conflicts, each of which gives rise to a different kind of struggle. The first calls for normative readjustment in which the dominant values of a society are being inequitably applied. In this case, the aggrieved groups protest, and if protest fails to attain readjustment, they riot.

The antidraft rioter at the time of the Civil War was protesting the plight of the common man who could not, like his wealthier compatriots, buy his way out of the draft. American egalitarian values were not being applied across the board. The readjustment came only after the intensity of the riots stimulated public concern to force a change.

The contemporary ghetto riots grow out of the failure of the civil rights movement to achieve normative readjustment for black people through nonviolent protest. This failure has produced lines of cleavage which, if intensified, will result in the second type of value conflict, namely, value readjustment.

In this case, the dominant values of the society are brought under severe pressure for change. The social movement that organizes the activities of an aggrieved sector of the population, having given up hope for benefiting from the going value system, sets up a new configuration of values. The movement becomes revolutionary. When Americans gave up hope of benefiting from the English institutions of the monarchy and the colonial system, they set up their own egalitarian value system and staged a revolution.

Now, Black Power and Black Nationalist leaders are beginning to move in the direction of value readjustment. They are talking about organizing their people on the basis of separatist and collectivist values and they are moving away from the melting pot individualistic values of our country, which are not working for them.

The Hostile Belief System

An aggrieved population erupts into violence on the basis of preexisting hostile belief. During the anti-Catholic riots in the early part of the nineteenth century, the rioters really believed that the Pope, in Rome, was trying to take over the country. The anti-Negro rioters in Chicago and East St. Louis (and even in Detroit in 1943) really believed that Negroes were trying to appropriate their jobs and rape their women and kill their men.

Today, many rioters in black ghettos really believe in the malevolence of white society, its duplicity, and its basic commitment to oppressing Negroes. An important component of the hostile belief system is that the expected behavior of the identified adversary is seen as extraordinary—that is, beyond the pale of accepted norms. In the black ghettos, people are convinced, for example, that the police will behave toward them with extraordinary verbal incivility and physical brutality, far beyond any incivility and brutality displayed toward whites in similar circumstances.

The hostile belief system is connected, on the one hand, with the value conflict, and, on the other, with the incident that precipitates a riot. It embodies the value conflict, giving it form, substance, and energy. It sets the stage for the precipi-

tating incident, which then becomes a concrete illustration of the beliefs. A police officer shooting and killing a young black suspected car thief (as in San Francisco in September, 1966), or beating and bloodying a black taxi driver (as in Newark in July, 1967), confirms and dramatizes the expectations incorporated into the hostile beliefs and triggers the uprising.

Hostile beliefs bear varying relations to "reality." Their systemization means that in some aspects they are incorrect exaggerations; in others, very close to the truth. In the 1830s, the Catholic Church wanted more power and influence locally, but it did not, consciously, want to take over the country. Today, large numbers of white people want to keep Negroes where they are by allowing them to advance only gradually. But they do not, at least consciously, want to oppress them.

Relative Deprivation

An important and almost universal causal factor in riots is a perception of real or imagined deprivation in relation to other groups in the society. As James R. Hundley has put it, the aggrieved see a gap between the conditions in which they find themselves and what could be achieved given a set of opportunities. Ghetto residents in the United States use middle-class suburban living as a comparative point, and they feel acutely deprived. The areas of relative deprivation for the black American are pervasively economic, political, and social.

Obstacles to Change

Another universal causal factor behind riots is the lack of effective channels for bringing about change. Stanley Lieberson and Arnold Silverman, in their study of riots in United States cities between 1910 and 1961, note a correlation between cities in which riots have occurred and cities that elect officials at large rather than from wards. In this situation, Negroes are not likely to have adequate representation, if any. The result is that they feel deprived of a local political voice and are in fact deprived of a potential channel through which to air grievances. An aggrieved population with no access to grievance channels is bound to resort to rioting if one or more of their grievances become dramatized in a precipitating incident.

Hope of Reward

While riot participants do not ordinarily think much in advance about the possible outcome of a riot, still those who participate harbor hopes, however vague, that extreme and violent behavior may bring about desired changes. Certainly the contagion effect had a significant role in the crescendo of ghetto riots in the United States during 1967. Part of the spirit was that things could not be made much worse by rioting, and riots might achieve unexpected concessions from influential whites. Any hard-pressed people are riot-prone and the more so if they see others like themselves making gains from rioting. What happens is spontaneous, but hope raises the combustion potential.

Communication

Ease of communication among potential rioters is less a precondition of riot than a necessary condition to the spread of riot, once started. Riots tend to occur in cities during warm weather when people are likely to be congregated in the streets and disengaged from normal daily activities.

THE PHASES OF A RIOT

A riot is a dynamic process which goes through different stages of development. If the preconditions described above exist, if a value conflict intensifies, hostile beliefs flourish, an incident that exemplifies the hostile beliefs occurs, communications are inadequate and rum inflames feelings of resentment to a fever pitch, the process will get started. How far it will go depends upon a further process of interaction between the local authorities and an aroused community.

There are four stages within the riot process. Not all local civil disturbances go through all four stages; in fact, the majority do not reach stage three. It is still not certain at what point in the process it is appropriate to use the word "riot" to describe the event. In fact more information is needed about the process and better reporting of the phase structure itself.

Phase 1. The Precipitating Incident

All riots begin with a precipitating event, which is usually a gesture, event, or act by the adversary that is seen by the aggrieved community as concrete evidence of the injustice or relative deprivation that is the substance of the hostility and rage felt by the aggrieved. The incident is inflammatory because it is typical of the adversary's behavior toward the aggrieved and responsible for the conditions suffered by the aggrieved. The incident is also taken as an excuse for striking back with "justified" violence in behavior akin to rage.

The event may be distorted by rumor and made to seem more inflammatory than it actually is. In communities where the level of grievances is high, a seemingly minor incident may set off a riot; conversely, when the grievance level is low, a more dramatic event may be required to touch off the trouble.

A significant aspect of the precipitating event, besides its inflammatory nature, is the fact that it draws together a large number of people. Hundley explains that some come out of curiosity; others because they have heard rumors about the precipitating event; still others because they happen to be in the vicinity. Some of the converging crowd are instigators or agitators who are attempting to get a riot started; others come to exploit the situation and use the crowd as a cover for deviant activities. Local officials, church and civic leaders, come because they see it as their duty to try to control the violent outburst.

Phase 2. Confrontation

Following the instigating incident, the local population swarms to the scene. A process of "keynoting" begins to take place. Potential riot promoters begin to articulate the rage accumulating in the crowd, and they vie with each other in suggesting violent courses of action. Others, frequently recognized ghetto leaders, suggest that the crowd disband to let tempers cool and to allow time for a more considered course of action. Law enforcement officers appear and try to disrupt the "keynoting" process by ordering and forcing the crowd to disperse. More often than not, their behavior, which will be discussed below, serves to elevate one or another hostile "keynoter" to a position of dominance, thus flipping the riot process into the next phase.

The outcome of phase 2 is clearly of crucial importance. The temper of the crowd may dissipate spontaneously, or escalate explosively. The response of civil authorities at this point is also crucial. If representatives of local authority appear, listen to complaints, and suggest some responsive method for dealing with them, the agitation tends to subside: A "let's wait and see" attitude takes over. If they fail to show up and are represented only by the police, the level of agitation tends to rise.

How the news media handle phase 2 has a critical effect on the course of the riot. During the "sensationalizing" era of a few years ago in the United States, almost any street confrontation was likely to be reported as a "riot." In the current policy of "restraint," a street confrontation may not be reported at all. Neither policy is appropriate. A policy of "adequate communication" is needed. The grievances stemming from the precipitating incident and agitating the crowd should be identified. The response of local authorities should be described. The adversary relations and their possible resolutions, violent or nonviolent, should be laid out insofar as possible.

Phase 3. Roman Holiday

If hostile "keynoting" reaches a sufficient crescendo in urban ghetto riots, a quantum jump in the riot process occurs and the threshold of phase 3 is crossed. Usually the crowd leaves the scene of the street confrontation and reassembles elsewhere. Older persons drop out for the time being and young people take over the action. They display an angry intoxication indistinguishable from glee. They hurl rocks and bricks and bottles at white-owned stores and at cars containing whites or police, wildly cheering every hit. They taunt law enforcement personnel, risk capture, and generally act out routine scenarios featuring the sortie, the ambush, and the escape—the classic triad of violent action that they have seen whites go through endlessly on TV. They set the stage for looting, but are usually too involved in "the chase" and are too excited for systematic plunder. That action comes later in phase 3, when first younger, then older, caught up on the Roman Holiday, and angered by tales of police brutality toward the kids, join in the spirit of righting ancient wrongs.

Phase 3 has a game structure. It is like a sport somehow gone astray but still subject to correction. Partly this openness derives from the "King-for-a-day" carnival climate. Partly it is based on the intense ambivalence of black people toward the white system and its symbolic representatives; its hated stores and their beloved contents, its despised police and their admired weaponry, its unregenerate bigots and its exemplary civil rights advocates, now increasingly under suspicion. Because of the ambivalence, action and motive are unstable. Middle-class or upwardly mobile Negroes become militants overnight. Youths on the rampage one day put on white hats and armbands to "cool the neighborhood" the next. It is because of the ambivalence felt by Negroes, not only toward whites but toward violence itself, that so few phase 3 disturbances pass over into phase 4.

Phase 4. Siege

If a city's value conflict continues to be expressed by admonishment from local authorities and violent suppression of the Roman Holiday behavior in the ghetto, the riot process will be kicked over into phase 4. The adversary relations between ghetto dwellers and local and City Hall whites reach such a degree of polarization that no direct communications of any kind can be established. Communications, such as they are, consist of symbolic, warlike acts. State and federal military assistance is summoned for even more violent repression. A curfew is declared. The ghetto is subjected to a state of siege. Citizens can no longer move freely into and out of their neighborhoods. Forces within the ghetto, now increasingly composed of adults, throw fire bombs at white-owned establishments and disrupt fire fighting. Snipers attack invading paramilitary forces. The siege runs its course, like a Greek tragedy, until both sides tire of this fruitless and devastating way of solving a conflict.

SOCIAL CONTROL

Studies of past and present riots show that the collective hostility of a community breaks out as a result of inattention to the value conflict (the long-range causes) and as a result of failures in social control (immediate causation). These failures are of two sorts: undercontrol and overcontrol. In the condition of undercontrol, law enforcement personnel are insufficiently active. Although the condition may be brought about in various ways, the effect is always the same. The dissident group, noting the weakness of the authorities, seizes the opportunity to express its hostility. The inactivity of the police functions as an invitation to act out long-suppressed feelings, free of the social consequences of illegal behavior.

In some communities, as in the 1968 Detroit riot, undercontrol during early phase 3 produces an efflorescence of looting and is then suddenly replaced with overcontrol. In other communities overcontrol is instituted early, during phase 2. Local and state police are rushed to the scene of the confrontation and begin to manhandle everyone in sight. Since the action is out of proportion to the event, it generates an intense reaction. If overcontrol is sufficiently repressive, as in the 1967 Milwaukee riot, where a 24-hour curfew was ordered early in phase 3 and the National Guard summoned, the disturbances are quieted. In Milwaukee, the ghetto was placed under a state of siege as the Roman Holiday was beginning to take hold in the community. No "catharsis" occurred and there was no improvement in ghetto-City Hall communications. The consequences of such premature repression cannot yet be discerned. Short of the use of overwhelming force, over-control usually leads to increased violence. The black people in the ghetto see the police as violent and strike back with increased intensity. Studies being conducted currently at the Lemberg Center show that in the majority of instances, police violence toward ghetto residents precedes and supersedes ghetto violence.

An adequate law enforcement response requires an effective police presence when illegal activities, such as looting, take place. Arrests can and should be made, without cruelty. It is not necessary that all offenders be caught and arrested to show that authorities intend to maintain order. Crowds can be broken up or contained through a variety of techniques not based on clubbing or shooting. The avoidance of both undercontrol and overcontrol is a matter of police training for riot control. This was the deliberate pattern of police response in several cities (notably Pittsburgh) to the riots following the assassination of Martin Luther King in April [1968].

Commenting on the interaction between a riot crowd and social control agencies, Hundley observes (1) that the presence of police tends to create an event, provide a focal point, and draw people together for easy rumor transmittal; (2) that the result of too few police is uncontrolled deviant behavior; (3) that a legitimate police activity (from the standpoint of riot participants) will not escalate the incident, but even if the original police activity is seen as legitimate, policemen observed being rude, unfair, or brutal at the scene may touch off a riot; (4) success of a police withdrawal during a riot depends upon officials contacting the legitimate leaders of the community and allowing them to exert social control; (5) when officials do not know the community leaders (or no effective ones are available), their withdrawal simply allows the instigators and exploiters to create or continue the riot; (6) the presence of police who do not exert control promotes the emergence of norms that encourage deviant activity.

Hundley adds these further observations on social control factors: (1) the sooner help comes from outside control agencies, the sooner the riot stops, although we think a riot can be stopped too soon, before catharsis or settlement of grievances

can occur. Hundley's next point, however, takes this matter into account: (2) the sooner the larger community seeks out real ghetto leaders and satisfies their grievances, the sooner the riot stops. (3) The sooner the audience ceases watching the riot activity, the sooner the riot disappears. (4) The greater degree of "normalcy" maintained in the community during the riot, the more likely it is that the riot will remain small or cease.

CIVIL INSURRECTION

When community grievances go unresolved for long periods of time and efforts at communication and/or negotiation seem unproductive or hopeless, despair in the aggrieved community may impel established, aspiring, or self-appointed leaders to organize acts of rebellion against civil authorities. Such acts constitute insurrection and differ from riots in that exceptions are riots that are instigated by insurrectionists.

Although insurrection is deliberate rebellion, the aim of the insurrectionist, unlike that of the revolutionary, is to put down persons in power, to force abandonment of obnoxious policies or adoption of desirable ones. The insurrectionist is not out to overthrow the system. (The organizers of the Boston Tea Party were insurrectionists, they were not yet revolutionaries.) Like the civil disobedient (or the rioter), the insurrectionist will settle for some specific adjustment in the system, such as a change in political leadership, increased representation in the system, repeal of an objectionable law, or abandonment of an inequitable policy. The revolutionary has lost hope for any effective participation in the existing system (as had the American revolutionaries by 1776) and presses for a total overthrow.

Civil insurrection is in a stage of civil protest that develops from the same set of conditions that inspire acts of civil disobedience or riot. Riots do not turn into insurrection, although insurrectionists are often encouraged by riots to employ organized violence as a means to attain sought-after goals. The participants in acts of civil disobedience and riots are obviously seen by insurrectionists as potential participants in organized acts of violent protest. Indeed, the disobedients and the rioters may themselves be converted to insurrection tactics, not by existing insurrectionists, but by disillusionment and frustration in the other courses of action.

Civil disobedience and insurrection, both of which are deliberate acts, characteristically involve relatively few of the aggrieved population, because it is hard to get ordinary people to participate in planned disobedience of the law (and run the risk of punishment) or premeditated acts of violence (and run the double risk of physical harm and punishment). Also the various social control mechanisms, aside from the law enforcement agencies, tend to keep most people from willful, premeditated violence and disobedience. Riots, on the other hand, may involve large numbers of people, many of whom are usually law abiding, not because a riot is any more acceptable than insurrection or civil disobedience, but because these are irresistible elements of contagious emotion rooted in commonly shared and commonly repressed feelings of frustration and rage. These feelings of frustration and rage are linked to and grow out of hostile beliefs about the adversary, and in the early stages of a riot are inflamed by some incident that seems to be an example of the adversary's typical behavior. The incident becomes an excuse for an angry, concerted outburst, which can spread very rapidly in the aggrieved community and rationalize otherwise unacceptable acts. Law-abiding citizens who participate in a riot are not so easy to organize for insurrection. Persons who can be recruited for organized acts of violent protest are more likely to be those who have already become involved in some form of criminal activity as an individual, private (perhaps unconscious) protest against a hostile society. It may also be easier to organize insurrection in a community with an established tradition of either rioting or insurgency.

THE JUSTIFICATION OF CIVIL PROTEST

There is substantial agreement among legal and political thinkers that nonviolent challenges to the policies and laws of civil authority are an indispensable mechanism of corrective change in a democratic society. Insofar as possible, procedures for challenge which may involve open and deliberate disobedience should be built into the laws and policies of the system, for such procedures give the system a quality of resilience and flexibility, the capacity to absorb constructive attack from within.

As George Lakay has pointed out, one great strength of democratic institutions is that they build a degree of conflict into the decision-making structure just so that conflicts can be resolved publicly and without violence. Adequately designed democratic institutions deliberately reflect shifting views and power relations or interest

groups and the normal workings of compromise and settlement, and equilibrium is usually maintained. Civil disobedience, and other forms of civil protest, are resorted to when political adversaries exhaust means of compromise in the political arena. Then the less powerful of the adversaries is forced to carry his challenge into a legal procedure or to the public in a show of protest.

Agreement on a policy of deliberate tolerance of peaceful challenge does not imply automatic agreement on what conditions justify challenges that involve disobedience. Moreover, agreement on a policy of tolerance toward nonviolent civil disobedience bears no necessary relationship at all to the question of the justification of civil protest involving violence, as riots and insurrection always do.

Nonviolent civil disobedience is justified under the following circumstances:

1. When an oppressed group is deprived of lawful channels for remedying its condition; conversely, a resort to civil disobedience is never politically legitimate where methods of due process in both the legal and political systems are available as remedies.
2. As a means of resisting or refusing to participate in an obvious and intolerable evil perpetrated by civil authorities (for example, a policy of genocide or enslavement).
3. When government takes or condones actions that are inconsistent with values on which the society and the political system are built, and thus violates the basic assumptions on which the regime's legitimacy rests.
4. When it is certain that the law or policy in question violates the constitution of the regime and, therefore, would be ruled unconstitutional by proper authority if challenged.
5. When a change in law or policy is demanded by social or economic need in the community and the normal procedures of law and politics are inadequate, obstructed, or held captive by antilegal forces.
6. When the actions of government have become so obnoxious to one's own personal ethics (value system) that one would feel hypocritical in submitting to a law that enforces these actions: for example, the Fugitive Slave Law.

It seems to me that a citizen is justified in originating or participating in an act of civil disobedience under any of these circumstances, and, as Herbert Kelman has argued, that an act of civil disobedience in such circumstances should be generally regarded as obligatory in terms of the highest principles of citizenship. This does not mean that acts of civil disobedience should be ignored by civil authorities; on the contrary, aside from the damage such a policy would do to effectiveness of the act of civil disobedience, it must be considered the obligation of the regime to punish a law breaker so long as the violated law is in force. As William Buckley has argued, it is the individual's right to refuse to go along with his community, but the community, not the individual, must specify the consequences. For the regime to act otherwise would be to concede the right of personal veto over every act of government. At the same time, a conscientious challenge to civil authority (with full expectation of punishment) aimed at repairing a serious flaw in the system of justice is a step every citizen should know how to decide to take.

Americans like to think of themselves as a peace-loving people, yet violence is and always has been an important and sometimes indispensable instrument of social, economic and political change in our national history. We do not need to be reminded of the role it has played in United States foreign policy and in domestic relations.

The fact is that Americans are both peace-loving and willing to resort to violence when other avenues of goal achievement seem closed or ineffective. In our national history violence was the ultimate instrument in our conquest of the lands on the North American continent that now comprise the nation. Violence freed the American colonists from British rule and later insured freedom of the seas (1812-1815). Violence abolished slavery, established the bargaining rights of labor, twice put

down threatening tyrannies in Europe and once in the Asian Pacific. In the present day, violence is the unintended instrument of black citizens to break through oppressive discrimination in housing, equipment, education, and political rights.

Americans have always taken the position that violence could be justified as an instrument of last resort in the achievement of critical national goals or in the face of external threat.

While it is true that we have always felt most comfortable about government-sponsored violence and especially violence in response to an external threat, we have often rationalized post factum the use of violence by aggrieved segments of the population when the cause was regarded as a just one in terms of our deeply held egalitarian values. The antidraft riots during the Civil War are one example; labor strife that finally led to legitimizing workers' bargaining rights is another. Two or three generations from now, the ghetto riots (and even the spasmodic insurrection that is bound to follow) will be seen as having contributed to the perfection of our system of egalitarian values. Thus, I conclude that violence in the cause of hewing to our most cherished goals of freedom, justice, and equal opportunity for all our citizens is and will remain as indispensable a corrective ingredient in our system as peaceful acts of civil disobedience. The sole qualification is that all other avenues of legitimate and peaceful change first be substantially closed, exhausted, or ineffective.

When an aggrieved segment of the population finds it necessary to resist, riot, or commit deliberate acts of insurrection, the government must respond firmly to enforce the law, to protect people and property from the consequences of violence, but it must, with equal energy and dedication, seek out the causes of the outbursts and move speedily to rectify any injustices that are found at the root of the trouble.

chapter 49
the urban guerrilla
martin oppenheimer

What are the real prospects for guerrilla warfare in the urban black ghetto? A 1967 Harlem handbill states, "There is but one way to end this suffering and that is by Black Revolution. Our Revolution is a unity of the Black Man wherever he may be. . . . When we unite we can end our suffering. Don't riot, join the revolution!" I. F. Stone, on August 19, 1968, commented: "We must be prepared to see first of all that we face a black revolt; secondly, that the black ghettos regard the white police as an occupying army; thirdly, that guerrilla war against this army has begun. . . . The effect of the ambushes which have begun to occur in various cities is to deepen police hatred . . . and therefore to stimulate those very excesses and brutalities which have made the police a hated enemy."[1]

On the other extreme, as it were, are warnings emanating from police and army circles. The **New Republic** (January 27, 1968) quotes a Colonel Robert B. Rigg, writing in the January 1968 **Army** magazine, as predicting "scenes of destruction approaching those of Stalingrad in World War II." Colonel Rigg's viewpoint seems to be that "in the next decade at least one major metropolitan area could be faced with guerrilla warfare requiring sizable United States army elements."

If we assume there will in fact be further disorders in our urban ghettos in the years to come, given the general failure of society to solve the problems of the poor and of the black community, and that some of these disorders may well take the form of paramilitary outbursts, what is the prognosis for such insurrectionary attempts?

I assume first of all that a black rebellion would be a genuinely popular uprising and might be able to take over militarily the black ghetto areas of some cities. But if this were to take place, it would be without any logistical base in the countryside or abroad, and the urban uprisings would be territorially and logistically isolated. A further assumption is that of the Black Power advocates themselves, namely, that we live in a basically racist society which would not hesitate to counter with a reactionary, completely military solution to black paramilitary activity. There is ample evidence to support the idea that even racially and culturally similar groups do not balk at such measures. If a serious insurrection were to take place, there is little doubt (at least in my mind) that this would unleash the barely latent hostilities of a large sector of white society, which would support repressive measures. In addition to being isolated in the cities, the black guerrila would confront a government more or less in a position to move in a unified fashion against him. In brief, the position the black guerrilla is in is as bad as some of the worst examples of revolt in history (for example, the Warsaw Ghetto) and is certainly in no way analogous to the more optimal situations (Caracas in 1958, or Petrograd in 1917).

The latter were offensive (revolutionary) in the sense that the existing government was to be replaced; a black rebellion would in all likelihood be, like the Warsaw Ghetto uprising, **defensive**, meaning that it would be a reaction to further encroachments on the ghetto population by the status quo—hence an insurrection of desperation. (An alternative strategy, that of the "interurban guerrilla," will be explored later.)

A brief examination of some cases that roughly approximate the situation of the defensive black guerrilla in the United States will show, I think, that unless the social structure becomes far weaker than we have reason to believe it will in the near future, a defensive black insurrection is doomed from a military point of view.

Some information was gathered covering six cases of urban uprisings, all but one in this century. Excluded from these cases were such short-lived risings as those in Berlin and Poznan in June 1953 and June 1956, respectively; also excluded were general rebellions of which the urban uprising was only one part—for example, the Hungarian rebellion of 1956 or the Irish Revolution of 1919—and urban uprisings such as Petrograd and Caracas, where the rebels were neither isolated nor confronted with a unified-power structure.

The following criteria were used in this selection, which, it should be emphasized, is illustrative

CASE AND DATES	CASUALTIES
The Paris Commune (March 28-May 28, 1871)	20,000 to 30,000 dead vs. 83 officers and 794 men of the Versaillese government
The Easter Rising (Dublin) (April 24-29, 1916)	No figures available
Shangai, China (February 21-April 13, 1927)	About 5,000 dead
Vienna, Austria (February 12-17, 1934)	1,500 to 2,000 dead vs. 102 Heimwehr
Warsaw Ghetto (April 19-May 15, 1943)	Several thousand killed, 56,000 deported, vs. about 20 Germans
Warsaw Uprising (July 31-October 2, 1944)	100,000 to 250,000 dead

rather than a sampling. First, each uprising was at minimum a guerrilla outbreak, backed by a significant sector of the local urban population—that is, each was a genuinely popular "rising." Second, in each case the rising developed into a rebellion which successfully took over an entire city or a large sector thereof. Third, the rebels in each case were isolated, either acting totally alone, or effectively separated from outside support. Fourth, in these illustrations the government continued to function effectively at least outside the city, and managed to move in a unified fashion against the rebels within a short time. These are, in fact, the conditions confronting Black Power strategists when they talk about paramilitary activity of an insurrectionary kind.

The Paris Commune, March 28-May 28, 1871

After the capitulation of Paris to the Prussians on January 8, 1871, the Prussian troops remained on the outskirts of the city, preferring to let the conservative Thiers government disarm the more popularly based National Guard which was mainly working class in composition. When the government attempted to do so on March 18, the National Guard resisted, and on the 28th the Commune was proclaimed. The official government withdrew to Versailles, and together with the Prussians beseiged the city. The Commune held fast for two months but was finally overwhelmed by the troops of Versailles, with the Prussians playing a relatively passive role. A brutal massacre followed; Frank Jellinek has pointed out that the whole Jacobin "terror" during the French Revolution executed 2,596 people in Paris; in the Commune between 20,000 and 30,000 men, women, and children fell. How many of these were victims of the massacre is unknown. Over 30,000 people were subsequently imprisoned. The Versaillese forces lost 83 officers and 794 men killed.[2]

The Easter Rising, Dublin, April 24-29, 1916

Intense repression of Irish nationalism from 1914 to 1916 had built up considerable resentment in the population, and by the fall of 1915 the Irish Volunteers, military arm of the Irish Republican Brotherhood, were drilling and marching openly in many parts of the country, including Dublin. An uprising was fixed for Easter Sunday 1916, but was countermanded at the last minute by the national organization, led by moderates. The Dublin organization, James Connolly's working-class-oriented Citizens' Army, determined to go ahead anyway, and the rebellion broke out on Monday, April 24, with the swift seizure of the Post Office and other key points, and the proclamation of the Republic. Some one thousand to fifteen hundred armed men and women participated. British troops were rushed to the city from throughout the country, and they gradually forced their way into insurgent areas, backed by artillery fire and raiding parties which took heavy casualties among civilian noncombatants. On Saturday, April 29, the surviving Citizens' Army soldiers surrendered. Connolly himself was severely wounded. Courts-martial quickly followed, and from May 3 to 12, fifteen of the ringleaders, including Connolly, were executed. In 1919 the armed struggle was renewed on a nationwide basis, resulting two years later in an ambiguous treaty with the British. This was followed by a civil war which lasted two more years. Precise casualty figures on the Easter rising are not available.

Shanghai, February 21-April 13, 1927

In response to Chiang Kai-shek's military advance from the north with a revolutionary army, the workers of Shanghai staged a general strike on February 19, 1927, to undermine the local warlord and aid Chiang. In response, execution squads were set up on the streets, and after this terror an insurrection began on February 21. Chiang, who was basically hostile to the working-class forces, waited on the outskirts of the city, and the insurrection was suppressed two days later. While Chiang continued to engage himself in mopping-up operations outside the city, the workers again struck on March 21. Again Chiang did not move. This strike also led to an insurrection which succeeded in taking over the city, and Chiang was welcomed as a liberator. But on April 12 Chiang, aided by foreign troops and gangsters, began a reign of terror against working-class, trade union, and communist organizations. After sporadic resistance, the revolutionists were wiped out by Chiang's forces within twenty-four hours. O. Edmund Clubb estimates that about five thousand radicals, unionists, and the like were massacred.[3]

Vienna, February 12-17, 1934

The Austrian Socialist party had been desperately trying to work out a common front against the Nazis with the Dollfuss regime, despite the latter's physical attacks on the socialists in various parts of the country. The Viennese socialists, representing the city's working class in the main, finally agreed to rise in arms if the Dollfuss government attempted further suppression of workers' organizations in the city. On February 12 the Heimwehr, Dollfuss' military arm, raided Viennese workers' clubs and arrested many leading socialist figures. Armed resistance began when Dollfuss invaded, interestingly, the worker-controlled public housing projects, and fired on the projects with howitzers and mortars. After three days of heavy fighting the survivors were forced to surrender or were overpowered, with some leaders fleeing the country. Nine leaders of the defensive "insurrection" were immediately hanged, and thousands were imprisoned in concentration camps. Some fifteen hundred to two thousand people had been killed, as against 102 soldiers of the Heimwehr.

The Warsaw Ghetto, April 19-May 15, 1943

In the fall of 1942, after only seventy thousand of an original population of 400,000 remained in the Jewish ghetto of Warsaw, the Jewish organizations decided to resist further deportations militarily. The ghetto was more or less in Jewish hands to begin with, and when Weapons-SS raiding parties entered to liquidate the population on the 19th, they were met with gunfire. Only some fifteen hundred Jews were organized into military units, with less equipment among them than in a company of infantry (about a hundred rifles, a few machine guns, a few hundred revolvers). SS and police units numbered two to three thousand. Several thousand Jews were killed in the fighting, some five to six thousand escaped into the surrounding countryside (many to be captured and killed later), and 56,000 were deported to extermination camps. When the Russians arrived in January, 1945, only two hundred Jews remained alive in the city.

An interesting historical note for those who believe that in some sense ghetto home rule (including self-policing) is desirable, is that the Warsaw Ghetto was, from 1940 to 1943, virtually a Jewish state. "Yiddish-speaking policemen were a direct consequence of the German decision to establish a ghetto, and in that respect they became as necessary as any other group . . . ."[4] This self-rule, wherever it existed among Jews, actually contributed to their destruction by creating a mechanism which the Nazis could and did use to do their work. A similar example occurs in the story of **The Bridge on the River Kwai**, when the discipline and morale infused by a British officer are used by the Japanese to help their military efforts in destroying other British units.

A ghetto is particularly vulnerable to hunger

and disease, especially when enforced by a besieg-
ing army (as in Warsaw or the Paris Commune). In
Paris the people ate rats and shoelaces; in Warsaw
hunger and typhus resulted in five thousand deaths
each month in the year prior to the ghetto uprising.
"By decreasing and choking off the food supply,
the Germans were able to turn the ghettos into
death traps. And that is what they did."[5] Raul Hilberg reports that in the winter of 1941-42 the
sewage pipes froze, toilets became useless, and human excrement was dumped into the streets with
the garbage. Cases of cannibalism were reported.
Between 500,000 and 600,000 Jews died in Polish
ghettos and labor camps before the extermination
camps went into operation.

The Warsaw Uprising, July 31-October 2, 1944

As Russian troops approached Warsaw, an
underground army, with agreement of the Soviets,
rose up to throw out the Germans and divert German troops from the Russian flanks. Preparations
were relatively open, as the Germans ignored violations of many regulations. There was a virtual vacuum of power in the city, and the underground was
able to take over large sectors of it very quickly.
The Russians, however, did not come to the aid of
the uprising for political reasons, and the German
occupying troops were soon able to make serious
inroads into the city. Despite several extremely
risky British and American air drops of supplies
(and ultimately even Russian ones, though they
neglected parachutes so that all supplies were destroyed as they hit the ground), the underground
was forced to surrender. The Germans had deported
some 200,000 hostages to nearby concentration
camps by this time; estimates of total Warsaw casualties for the two-month battle range from 100,000
to 250,000 killed.

Note that in most of these cases the rebels had
no illusions about winning outside aid. In three of
the cases (the Easter Rising, Shanghai, and the Warsaw Uprising) the rebels moved on the false assumption that aid would be forthcoming, and in two
others they moved only in desperation, with no
real hope of success. Even the Paris Commune
hoped that the remainder of the country would
organize communes to come to its aid. Furthermore, in five of the six cases, the actual outbreak
of the rebellion took place only as a defensive measure against severe encroachments by the dominant
power, and would probably not have occurred at
all without this repression. The Warsaw Uprising is
the only exception to this. And, in three of the

cases, the rebellion was against foreigners. Perhaps
it can be argued that the American white power
structure is basically foreign to the black population, but having a clearly foreign oppressor does
seem to make it easier to unite the population for
rebellion.

Given this sort of dismal evidence, why has so
much attention been given by the white press, and
by some spokesmen in Black Power circles, to
paramilitary potentials? There are three possible
interpretations for this fascination (apart from the
view that the police and the military display alarm
in order to justify their existence and their appro-
priations). First, paramilitary affairs in the black
ghetto may be largely a creation of the press which
has resulted in a self-fulfilling prophecy. For the
white community, which seems to require a rationale for abandoning the civil rights movement and
refusing significant aid to urban areas, the urban
riot has become highly functional. The attention
given by the white press to what has been until recently the peripheral phenomenon of paramilitary
Black Power is equally if not more functional. For
lower middle-class people in the suburbs who have
long repressed itchy trigger fingers, talk of urban
risings by the black population affords an outlet
for repressed hostilities which can only be exceeded
by an actual outbreak of warfare. For the black
community, the large-scale attention focused upon
a small minority of paramilitary types seems evidence that such activity may in fact be dangerous,
hence effective as a threat with which to coerce
white power structures. Such a view is useful for
paramilitary recruiters.

A second, related, interpretation has to do
with the "machismo" so important to downtrodden
males in any oppressed culture.

A third interpretation, which is by now a cli-
ché in social science as well as informed lay circles,
has to do with the desperation born of the apparent failure of both conventional politics and nonviolent direct action to secure significant changes
in the condition of the American Negro. As a result, many black leaders have been forced to the
conclusion that, for the time being at least, the
civil rights movement is dead and that Black Power—
the cultural, social, and economic autonomy (and,
given the ghettoized character of the black population, territorial autonomy) of blacks—is the only
viable strategy. Black Power is a vague concept because it is a new movement. It should not be surprising that some of its advocates demand violent
or military tactics. We must remember that it took

from about 1825 to the publication, in 1896, of Herzl's **The Jewish State** for Jews even to begin to clarify the issue of "Jewish Power," and that, almost from the beginnings of Zionism, many Zionist as well as non-Zionist ghetto groups had paramilitary auxiliaries.

A SCENARIO

Despite the pessimistic military prognosis for a black revolution, it "might be attempted in the face of overwhelming odds and without regard to the terrible consequences."[6] Let us see, by the use of a crude scenario, how a defensive black insurrection, born of desperation, might develop. Obviously, any knowledgeable person could add all sorts of complications and refinements to such a scenario by including various technological considerations. Nevertheless, I believe the basic issues can be clearly made to appear in such a semifictional presentation.

■

It was a hot Friday evening in August, 1969, in the north Philadelphia ghetto. In the third incident in as many weeks, police halted a car belonging to members of the "Black Liberation Front," and, when one of the blacks was slow to get out of the car, police opened fire. Two of the car's occupants were hit; a third returned the fire with an automatic carbine, and an officer was hit. An "assist officer" call went out and soon a several-block area was surrounded by "red cars." Meanwhile, the surviving BLF fighter disappeared. The appearance of the police cars drew catcalls from the young people of the area, and when police attempted to place two youngsters under arrest, a minor riot broke out. Other BLF members had by then been alerted, and within a half hour a small mob was moving on the precinct station.

Meanwhile, a half dozen "triads" of BLF irregulars opened fire on traffic patrolmen and police cars at as many locations in north and west Philadelphia, and other units of less than a dozen men each began to smash store windows along Columbia and Ridge Avenues, the principal ghetto merchant centers. An outraged mob of blacks, at a BLF street-corner rally at 52nd and Market Streets, occupied the train station there and took over the control point of the suburban trains. A trained BLF technician halted the Paoli (suburban) Local.

Almost simultaneously, "Radio Black Liberation" went on the air to declare martial law in north and west Philadelphia, and to announce the formation of a revolutionary government for the defense of the area against further atrocities by the white police "pigs." Control points were established, and whites attempting to enter the area by car or bus were fired on and turned back. "Radio Black Liberation" announced the capture of over one thousand white businessmen and professionals from the Paoli Local. The North Philadelphia Station of the Pennsylvania Railroad was captured after an exchange of gunfire with railway police, and train service to New York City was cut. Irregular BLF units intercepted underground telephone and electricity conduits, and all electricity in Philadelphia, plus a ten-county area in southeastern Pennsylvania and southern New Jersey, was cut off. City Hall, some fifteen blocks from the rebel-held area, was attacked by terrorist groups, and an explosion rocked the police station at 8th and Race, a similar distance from the north Philadelphia ghetto. The police communications system was knocked out, and there were heavy police casualties. North and west Philadelphia, with a total black population of about 400,000 (and less than 100,000 whites), was effectively under rebel control.

BLF activities had been under surveillance for some time. Months before, the Philadelphia Police Commissioner had developed contingency plans in case of a serious uprising, in careful collaboration with state and federal officials. Hints of black unrest had appeared in the local press, and the usual electronic devices, though unconstitutional, kept interested parties informed of most BLF activities. Gun sales in the suburbs and white areas adjacent to the ghetto rocketed; when the Paoli Local was stopped, a few white businessmen even took revolvers and carbines from their attaché cases and managed to scare the rebels off the train station platforms. Thus, while the train remained an isolated hostage in a hostile ghetto, it remained "free." The passengers went hungry that night and the succeeding day; a handful of black passengers was executed.

National Guard units, "trained up" to urban guerrilla warfare duty, and virtually all white, were moved in quickly to confront the rebel control points all along the borders between north and west Philadelphia and the rest of the city. Police cut off the city water supply to the ghetto area, and auxiliary electricity and telephone systems restored service to the remainder of the city and outlying counties. Special Forces units moved by boat to the bridges of the Schuylkill River and cut off communications between north and west Philadelphia. Helicopters began twenty-four-hour surveillance of the rebel areas—the rebels managed to shoot down several of them. By 4 A.M. Saturday morning the rebel area, cut in half, lay in total darkness, surrounded by a division of the Pennsylvania National Guard. "Radio Black Liberation" was effectively forced off the air as its generators carried it only to a fifty-block area. No food supplies of any kind were delivered to the ghetto area Saturday. The Paoli Local, isolated but free, was soon reinforced by pinpoint parachutists of the 110th Airborne, who shot their way out of the station to "liberate" a block area on each side. Helicopters using flamethrowers prepared the way; extensive fires soon raged in west Philadelphia—there was of course no fire service, and no water.

By noon Saturday, dissension in rebel ranks began to build as deputations of neighbors pleaded for surrender. There was no milk, no bread, no water; the sewage system was hopelessly backed up, and the almost negligible medical personnel left in the area warned of imminent epidemics. Looting of stores was complete, but the food supplies could not last long. Outbreaks in other Northern cities, which the BLF had hoped for, either failed to materialize or were similarly isolated. In any case, the rebels received no accurate information from the outside, and they could not even know of the protests entered on their behalf by several African nations. (The Soviet Union remained silent, having just suffered a reprimand from the United Nations General Assembly for its intervention in the internal affairs of Rumania.)

At 2 P.M. on Saturday, deputations of National Guard officers, including Negro officers, made appearances in both west and north Philadelphia. Upon being taken to rebel headquarters, they stated that unless the rebels surrendered unconditionally by 5 P.M., artillery units would proceed to demolish north Philadelphia block by block. The rebel command repeated the famous utterance made by the United States commander at Bastogne, in World War II, adding, "What the hell, it's cheaper than urban renewal."

Meanwhile, however, two other events in the city came to light in the press (which appeared that day as usual, with appeals for law and order which were dropped into the ghetto area). First, south Philadelphia, the location of Philadelphia's third black community, was placed under martial law—a pass system was instituted, and several hundred potential "troublemakers" were quickly arrested

and shipped to a neighboring county jail, which had been taken over by a National Guard battalion. Second, at the border of north Philadelphia and neighboring Kensington, National Guard units were alternated with units of the Kensington Citizens' Militia, which, unlike the National Guard, began a tactic of quick hit-and-run invasions of the rebel-controlled area. Several dozen blacks were killed in these raids, which demolished, by explosive, several tenements. Eleven militiamen fell casualty to the rebels. By 3 P.M. Saturday, eight blocks were evacuated and left in the hands of the Kensington Militia, while no blocks were gained anywhere against the National Guard and the Airborne troops.

Promptly at 5 P.M. a field artillery battalion of the 1st Army, headquartered at Fort Dix, entrenched itself in a schoolyard ten blocks below the ghetto area and proceeded to level the area bordered by Broad, Columbia, 15th, and Jefferson Streets, in the heart of north Philadelphia. A half hour later an Air Force jet dropped napalm on the Muslim Mosque on Lancaster Avenue in west Philadelphia, starting an uncontrollable fire.

Events after that time were indistinct. It would seem that a crowd of black women, some armed, overran the rebel post at Presbyterian Hospital in west Philadelphia and surrendered to the National Guard. Except for one public housing project, in which snipers continued activity until Sunday morning, west Philadelphia was occupied by midnight. North Philadelphia held out longer because of fear of the Kensington Militia, but word of this finally leaked out through the City's Human Relations Commission, and the Militia was withdrawn; a committee of Negro ministers surrendered the area to the Guard in a brief, prayerful ceremony at noon Sunday. The "Philadelphia Commune" was over, less than forty-eight hours after it began.

More than two thousand "rebels," most of them women and children, perished, as against some one hundred Guardsmen (mostly victims of sniper fire), some dozen Airborne, and two dozen civilians (in the battle of the Paoli Local), eleven Kensington Militiamen, and twenty police officers.

■

This sort of outcome has been the common fate of isolated urban uprisings. Coordinated uprisings in many cities would complicate matters, of course; so would supporting paramilitary actions (including, perhaps, seizures of public buildings and even police stations) by left-wing students. But so long as the general public (including about 800,000 members of the National Rifle Association) is prepared to support the government, even a larger-scale uprising can have hardly any other result.

There is a possible exception; if, in a preconsensus "liberal" stage the government acts inconclusively, the rebellion might last longer. But, again given the prognosis of general public hostility to the aims of the rebels, pressure on the government from the Right would probably be so extreme that a military solution might be forced. If the government continued to vacillate, a threatened right-wing coup (or, at minimum, right-wing vigilante action) would force the government to "clean up the mess" rather than be forced from office.

Let us suppose, however, that the Philadelphia Commune had been able to hold out for a few more days, and that the government had proposed a negotiated settlement. What might the rebels have demanded? It is difficult to say, particularly since the black community is itself divided on broad strategy. But one might suppose the following kinds of demands: (1) Self-government with the election of a black mayor and council in the black-held area. (2) Expropriation of all white-owned businesses, with ownership passing to the community (socialization). (3) Black autonomy over all institutions in the rebel area, including public schools, welfare institutions, and housing. (4) Political recognition as a separate city-state, or perhaps in cooperation with other such communes, as a nation, with diplomatic representation. (5) Free passage to and from work in white areas, with economic relationships roughly approximating those of the "common market," that is, a common monetary standard, trade agreements, no tariffs, and so on.

Such an arrangement is not dangerous to white society in any fundamental way, and in fact is one of the Establishment strategies. Demographically, black government is in the cards for many American cities anyway, so long as city-county consolidation (the abolition of artificial city boundaries) is resisted by the suburbs. With the exception of the landlord and small-merchant class (and a few larger distributors like those of dairy products, who would have to give way to black cooperatives), the advantages to the economy would probably outweigh the disadvantages. White society might still be able to hire black mercenaries to fight its colonial wars. And a wasteful welfare establishment could be dismantled in much the same way as with a guaranteed minimum income, except that the black community alone would have to generate that income, rather than the whole nation.

In the short run, most of the economic disadvantages of the plan would be to the black community. Many more would be unemployed before whites caught on to the advantages (and basically harmless nature) of the black-controlled internal neocolony. It would take some years before enough capital could be generated inside the black community to reach the "take-off" point of economic development, and black businesses (whether privately controlled or socially owned and controlled) would then have to confront the problem of competition with white businesses which would probably be discriminatory. This new discrimination could only be overcome by competing economically, which would in all probability mean cutting labor costs and installing labor-saving machinery. The black community would then have an unemployment rate roughly similar to its rate at present, but at a higher level of expectation. In terms of **general** economic conditions it would continue to be dependent on the white economy because of its need to trade with the outside world.

Trotsky once said you cannot have socialism in one country. Nor can you have it, isolated, in one ghetto or even in a set of ghettos. The economic future of the black American is, for better or worse, tied to a national and, in fact, an international economy. Separate economies are no longer viable even if they were not prevented by the dominant social order for racist reasons. (One can imagine how racists would use the fact that blacks were economically and politically no longer a part of the United States.)

Black Power circles have mentioned an alternative form of paramilitary activity in the urban context—the longer-range revolutionary underground, possibly including terrorism, sabotage, and even small, mobile guerrilla bands, all of this being carried on over a longer period of years. The objective of such a strategy would be similar to that of Debray in Latin America: to create such social havoc that the structure of society would be subverted. With such subversion, and the inability of the regime to cope with the problems created by it, other elements of society would also become disaffected, and the guerrilla movement would in this way gradually grow to a point where an attempt to overthrow the entire government might be made. This strategy would assume some allies among whites.

Such a prognosis makes more sense. "The new

concept is lightning campaigns conducted in highly
sensitive urban communities with the paralysis
reaching the small communities and spreading to
the farm areas. . . . It dislocates the organs of harmony and order and reduces central power to the
level of a helpless, sprawling, octopus. . . . The factory workers will be afraid to venture out on the
streets to report to their jobs. . . . Violence and
terror will spread like a firestorm. A clash will
occur inside the armed forces. . . . U.S. forces will
be spread too thin for effective action. . . . The
economy will fall into a state of chaos."[7]

The obstacles to this strategy, unlike that of
the insurrectionary outbreak as such, are not as
serious as the House Committee on Un-American
Activities might think—it is questionable that
"there is little doubt that such an uprising could be
effectively and quickly controlled." It is not true,
either, that "the ghetto could be isolated and the
guerrillas effectively bottled up," unless all ghettos
were turned into concentration camps—which
would create precisely the conditions for immediate, widespread insurrection that some militants
might like. Nor is it true that "a guerrilla war based
on racial lines would never be supported by any
sizable number of Negroes" especially if the Committee's suggestion that the ghetto should be isolated and "search and seizure operations . . . instituted" is followed.[8]

What HCUA has done is to support the idea
that an actual outbreak of insurrection at present
would be suicidal. But it has not effectively demolished the arguments for a gradual buildup, beginning with terrorism and sabotage on a small scale.
Indeed, it supports such a strategy by pointing
(accurately, I think) to the way our government
would react once such a campaign were begun:
"most civil liberties would have to be suspended . . .
the population of the ghetto would be classified
through an office for the 'control and organization
of the inhabitants.' . . ." We might even see the
institution of puppet governments, and puppet
police, and, of course, "The McCarran Act provides
for various detention centers." This, then, is the
sure road to the subversion of the country, and to
a revolution—or a counter-revolution. Who will
have been chiefly responsible, the rebels or the
police state created to control them?

THE INTERURBAN GUERRILLA

Let us look at a scenario of an interurban guerrilla campaign, devised as a strategy to subvert society and create a revolutionary situation.

■

By 1972 the Black Liberation Front had established small followings in virtually every black
ghetto from Boston to Washington, D.C., including
elements numerically strong enough to form small
guerrilla bands in most larger cities of that megalopolis. The strategy of the BLF followed traditional
resistance or revolutionary underground lines: small
triads consisting of one "leader," one "agit-prop"
(agitation and propaganda), and one "org-man"
(organizational work) were in touch with district
triads through only one man (to reduce the risk of
informers); each district was in contact with an
area triad, each area with a region, and so forth,
all the way up to the top. The capture of any member would involve, at most, the other members of
his triad, and by that time security procedures
would warn others to change location, names, and
identity papers. Each triad, in addition, had special
functions: supply, intelligence, assault, training, or
"underground railway" for smuggling people in
and out of Mexico, Canada, and other points farther away (Cuba, for example). Assault units often
were smuggled to Canada, trained in sabotage and
terror methods (in Quebec province), and then returned. Other training areas included isolated farms
in Pennsylvania, the Adirondacks, and the Catskills.

Only assault units were fully armed; other
units had some arms, but their operations did not
require extensive violence, thus minimizing legal
risks. The assault teams as well as other units were
required to manufacture most of their own sabotage equipment; supply units functioned only to
obtain special equipment such as radios, trucks,
machine guns, and larger stores of explosives. "Normal" arms were purchased in small quantities over
the counter or occasionally looted from sporting-
goods stores, or seized from "the man on the beat"
(who was gradually replaced throughout the country by mobile police units).

The main operating areas for the BLF guerrilla
bands were the larger cities, especially its police
and government operations, with some attention
to nearby army and naval bases; later, industrial
sites were targeted. The objective was to "get
whitey out" by dislocating his system. Two methods of operation were used chiefly: night attacks,
using a large ghetto as a base, then returning singly
to that base to merge with the population (including holding down a regular job). Police found it
difficult to track single fighters back into enemy
"jungle." The second method was to base small

bands in nearby cities, move them to a point of attack, and then out of that area to other nearby cities (usually smaller, less significant, and more neglected by enforcement officials). For example, in the attack on West Point of Christmas Day, 1972, ten triads converged from as many small cities, and dispersed to as many others. To this day, enforcement officials do not know who came from what city, or who went where—all that is known is that at least Poughkeepsie, Beacon, Newburgh, Nyack, Ossining, Peekskill, and White Plains were involved. Each had a black ghetto; each had proto-political "disturbances" in the late sixties, and none had its problems significantly dealt with, much less solved, by 1972.

Between 1970 and 1973, ambushes of law enforcement agents increased rapidly; by 1972 one-man police cars were no longer used in the megalopolis. Even state police traveled in pairs on highway and turnpike patrol duty. Nevertheless, an average of five police teams were attacked every week during the last six months of 1972.

By early 1973 the BLF felt itself strong enough to expand operations. In April of that year eight police stations, two National Guard armories, three city jails, and a minimum-security federal prison were raided. All weapons were taken, and all prisoners released from jails. Martial law had to be declared in four cities, and one division of army troops was recalled from Germany. The President was unable to promise the military dictator of Thailand further military aid—the President's inauguration, significantly, had had to be moved from Washington, as his nomination was moved from San Francisco the summer before, in response to general strikes by the black populations in those cities.

Sabotage of industrial production began that spring. Behind the scenes, industrial leaders demanded action to halt the rapidly mounting economic chaos, and military men called the President's attention to the fact that most military stockades were now overflowing with black soldiers and their white "peacenik" friends. The naval facility at Newport News was heavily damaged by sabotage, which coincided with riots in two state prisons (allegedly instigated by Muslims) and a Marine Corps brig. The assassination of the Governor of Virginia further served to undermine law and order. Several banks were "hit" for funds to carry out BLF actions.

The national response to this situation was mixed. On the left, liberals and radicals called for full implementation of the "political program" of the BLF, which demanded a pullout of white power from black ghettos, and the socialization of the ghettos. In addition, realizing the limits of the ghetto economy, white radicals demanded the nationalization of basic industries and their full assistance to the black economy without strings attached.

In the political center, such groups as Americans for Democratic Action and the Urban Coalition, as well as many trade unions, demanded a "war on two fronts," the establishment of law and order, and social measures to alleviate the ghetto's problems. These programs included a guaranteed income, local control over urban renewal, decentralization of education and welfare, with control to be handed over to local citizen groups, an extensive "Freedom Budget," and better-trained and better-paid police. The Wall Street Journal considered this a "realistic" program.

On the right, vigilante and "neighborhood defense" groups sprang up by the hundreds. The National Rifle Association and the American Legion merged to form the largest paramilitary organization in world history. On the ultra-right, the Minutemen flourished.

Crisis after crisis virtually immobilized organized religion and the multiversity. It was no longer possible to recruit theology students to serve local (especially surburban) churches and synagogues. The universities were riddled with unrest and demands for student and faculty power. Almost every professional organization in the country, from social workers and sociologists to physicists and political scientists, had "left" caucuses which demanded an end to "serving the establishment" and a reorientation of professions and the universities to "human needs," which they often saw as revolution. The universities became training centers for direct action and nonviolent resistance. There was a massive revival of protest art, writing, and theater.

As right-wing vigilante terror increased against blacks and the Left, countergroups of the "armed defense" type were organized. These groups, Left and Right, frequently clashed in bloody street battles. The police could no longer cope with the number of demonstrations and counterdemonstrations, so they relied more heavily on new technological innovations, like special gases. This resulted in escalation, as private and public armies began to experiment with countermeasures.

At the root of this chaotic picture was the simple fact that the BLF, various student New Left groups, and even groups on the right had real problems which the government was not able to solve.

The more militancy there was, the more real reforms were resisted by Congress; the more reforms were resisted, the more militant the protests became. Any semblance of "concensus" politics had disappeared by 1973. In the 1974 elections, no party would have a working majority in Congress.

Augmenting the "real" problems were those stemming from the protracted guerrilla warfare of the BLF. It became impossible to distinguish the causes of problems—the disruption of society by the BLF and by the countermilitancy of the Right, became indistinguishable from other causes, and from each other. There was an increasing clamor among middle-class Americans for a strong man to lead the country out of disaster. White radical groups vacillated between preparing for an underground existence, packing bags for Canada, engaging in electoral activity to counter the Right, and trying to build broad "united fronts" to stop fascism.

On July 4, 1973, the Black Liberation Front held a "Congress of Black Americans for Home Rule" in Harlem. The Minutemen scheduled a march on Washington. The Huks took Manila. Black troopers of the 98th Airborne mutinied and destroyed two airbases. The Chief Justice of the Supreme Court and the Ambassador to the United Nations both resigned and flew to Switzerland. After turning the defense of the capital over to General Westmoreland, the President moved quickly to appoint a bipartisan commission "to investigate and make recommendations . . . including the basic causes and factors."[9]

■

The outcome is open; such a development has never occurred in Western, urban, industrialized society. The prognosis, perhaps fantastic, is not impossible given what we find in many strata of the population: a resistance to giving up anything in order to solve problems. Problem-solving does require some surrender of vested interests. Failing that, structural strain will increase, with collective behavior appropriate to historical circumstances. At this point, the logical and historical next step for the urban black, after protopolitical activities such as rioting, would seem to be some kind of paramilitary action.

The options for the black urban guerrilla are these: (1) Insurrection now, with nearly certain repression and a catastrophic setback for any black protest movement. (2) A gradual build-up of subversion, with the possibility of total repression at virtually any point, resulting either in an insurrection of desperation or in an insurrection at what the rebels deem to be the culminating point of the subversion of the society. (3) The possible defeats of both of those insurrections—the first, because it is an insurrection of desperation and is not calculated to win, the second as the result of defeat in what is virtually a civil war. (4) Victory in the civil war, and the creation of (in all probability) some sort of interracial regime along authoritarian-leftist lines.

If the road to urban revolution is to be anything but an adventure, it will begin with terror and sabotage (assuming the exclusion of democratic processes as a feasible strategy). As soon as these methods become organized by secret societies, however, the terrorist groups are susceptible to infiltration and provocation—this is what can destroy the revolution at its inception, not search and seizure missions or concentration camps. But in a larger sense, guerrillas cannot be suppressed unless the problems that create them are dealt with effectively, for guerrillas will always be replaced by other guerrillas as long as the problems of oppression remain.

The ultimate answer to urban insurrection, or to the potential for it which lies in gradual subversion beginning with terror, is not the House Committee or the FBI or the "Civil Disobedience Squad." It is not Mace, foam, barbed wire, electronic eavesdropping, helicopters, or informers. It is solving problems.

NOTES

1. I. F. Stone's Weekly, August 19, 1968.
2. Frank Jellinek, The Paris Commune of 1871, London, Gollancz, 1937.
3. O. Edmund Clubb, Twentieth-Century China, New York, Columbia University Press, 1964.
4. Gerd Korman, "The Setting," New University Thought, vol. 6 (March-April 1968), Special Commemoration Issue for the 25th Anniversary of the Warsaw Ghetto Uprising, 7.
5. Raul Hilberg, The Destruction of the European Jews, Chicago, Quadrangle Books, 1961, pp. 168-174.
6. Lewis M. Killian, The Impossible Revolution: Black Power and the American Dream, New York, Random House, 1968.
7. Robert F. Williams, quoted in Committee on Un-American Activities, U.S. House of Representatives, Guerrilla Warfare Advocates in the U.S., Washington, U.S. Government Printing Office, 1968, p. 19.
8. Committee on Un-American Activities, pp. 57-58.
9. National Advisory Commission, Report, p. 534.

chapter 50
violence
in america
hugh davis graham
and ted robert gurr

Does violence succeed? The inheritors of the doctrines of Frantz Fanon and "Ché" Guevara assert that if those who use it are sufficiently dedicated, revolution can always be accomplished. Many vehement advocates of civil order and strategists of counterinsurgency hold essentially the same faith: that sufficient use of public violence will deter private violence. This fundamental agreement of Left and Right on the effectiveness of force for modifying others' behavior is striking. But to what extent is it supported by theory and by historical evidence?

The two most fundamental human responses to the use of force are to flee or to fight. This assertion rests on rather good psychological and ethological evidence about human and animal aggression. Force threatens and angers men, especially if they believe it to be illegitimate or unjust. Threatened, they will defend themselves if they can, flee if they cannot. Angered, they have an innate disposition to retaliate in kind. Thus men who fear assault attempt to arm themselves, and two-thirds or more of white Americans think that black looters and arsonists should be shot. Governments facing violent protest often regard compromise as evi-

dence of weakness and devote additional resources to counterforce. Yet if a government responds to the threat or use of violence with greater force, its effects in many circumstances are identical with the effects that dictated its actions: Its opponents will, if they can, resort to greater force.

There are only two inherent limitations on such an escalating spiral of force and counterforce: the exhaustion of one side's resources for force, or the attainment by one of the capacity for genocidal victory. There are societal and psychological limitations as well, but they require tacit bonds between opponents: One's acceptance of the ultimate authority of the other, arbitration of the conflict by neutral authority, recognition of mutual interest that makes bargaining possible, or the perception that acquiescence to a powerful opponent will have less harmful consequences than resisting to certain death. In the absence of such bases for cooperation, regimes and their opponents are likely to engage in violent conflict to the limit of their respective abilities.[1]

To the extent that this argument is accurate, it suggests one kind of circumstance in which violence succeeds: that in which one group so overpowers its opponents that they have no choice short of death but to desist. When they do resist to the death, the result is a Carthaginian peace. History records many instances of successful uses of overpowering force. Not surprisingly, the list of

From Violence in America—Historical and Comparative Perspectives. Report to the National Commission on the Causes and Prevention of Violence, June 1969. U.S. Government Printing Office, Washington, D.C.

successful governmental uses of force against opponents is much longer than the list of dissident successes against government, because most governments have much greater capacities for force, provided they keep the loyalty of their generals and
soldiers. Some dissident successes discussed in this
volume include the French, American, Nazi, and
Cuban Revolutions. Some governmental successes
include, in Britain, the suppression of the violent
phases of the Luddite and Chartist movements in
the nineteenth century; in Venezuela the Betan-
court regime's elimination of revolutionary terrorism; in the United States the North's victory in the
Civil War, and the quelling of riots and local rebellions, from the Whiskey Rebellion of 1794 to the
ghetto riots of the 1960s.

Governmental uses of force are likely to be
successful in quelling specific outbreaks of private
violence except in those rare circumstances when
the balance of force favors its opponents, or the
military defects. But the historical evidence also
suggests that governmental violence often succeeds
only in the short run. The government of Imperial
Russia quelled the revolution of 1905, but in doing
so intensified the hostilities of its opponents, who
mounted a successful revolution 12 years later,
after the government was weakened by a protracted and unsuccessful war. The North "won" the
Civil War, but in its very triumph created hostilities
that contributed to one of the greatest and most
successful waves of vigilante violence in our history.
The 17,000 Klansmen of the South today are neither peaceable nor content with the outcome of
the "War of Northern Aggression."[2] State or federal troops have been dispatched to quell violent
or near-violent labor conflict in more than 160 recorded instances in American history; they were
immediately successful in almost every case yet did
not significantly deter subsequent labor violence.

The long-range effectiveness of governmental
force in maintaining civil peace seems to depend
on three conditions . . .: public belief that governmental use of force is legitimate, consistent use of
that force, and remedial action for the grievances
that give rise to private violence. The decline of
violent working-class protest in nineteenth-century
England was predicated on an almost universal
popular acceptance of the legitimacy of the government, accompanied by the development of an
effective police system—whose popular acceptance
was enhanced by its minimal reliance on violence—
and by gradual resolution of working-class grievances. The Cuban case was quite the opposite: The

governmental response to private violence was ter-
roristic, inconsistent public violence that alienated
most Cubans from the Batista regime, with no significant attempts to reduce the grievances, mostly
political, that gave rise to rebellion.

We have assumed that private violence is "successful" in those extreme cases in which a government capitulates in the face of the superiority of
its opponents. This is not the only or necessarily
the best criterion of "success," though. A better
criterion is the extent to which the grievances that
give rise to collective protest and violence are resolved. Even revolutionary victories do not necessarily lead to complete success in these terms. The
American Revolution returned effective political
control to the hands of the colonists, but eventually led to an expansion of state and federal authority that diminished local autonomy to the point
that new rebellions broke out in many frontier
areas over essentially the same kinds of grievances
that had caused the revolution. The Bolshevik revolution ended Russia's participation in World War I,
which was perhaps the greatest immediate grievance
of the Russian people, and in the long run brought
great economic and social benefits; but the contingent costs of the subsequent civil war, famine, and
totalitarian political control were enormous. The
middle-class political discontents that fueled the
Cuban revolutionary movement, far from being
remedied, were intensified when the revolutionary
leaders used their power to effect a basic socio-
economic reconstruction of society that favored
themselves and the rural working classes.

If revolutionary victory is unlikely in the modern state, and uncertain of resolving the grievances
that give rise to revolutionary movements, are there
any circumstances in which less intensive private
violence is successful? We said above that the legitimacy of governmental force is one of the determinants of its effectiveness. The same principle applies to private violence: It can succeed when it is
widely regarded as legitimate. The vigilante movements of the American frontier had widespread
public support as a means for establishing order in
the absence of adequate law enforcement agencies,
and were generally successful. The Ku Klux Klan
of the Reconstruction era similarly had the sympathy of most white Southerners and was largely
effective in reestablishing and maintaining the prewar social and political status quo. The chronicles
of American labor violence, however, suggest that
violence was almost always ineffective for the
workers involved. In a very few instances there was

popular and state governmental support for the grievances of workers that had led to violent confrontations with employers, and in several of these cases state authority was used to impose solutions that favored the workers. But in the great majority of cases the public and officials did not accept the legitimacy of labor demands, and the more violent was conflict, the more disastrous were the consequences for the workers who took part. Union organizations involved in violent conflict seldom gained recognition, their supporters were harassed and often lost their jobs, and tens of thousands of workers and their families were forcibly deported from their homes and communities.

The same principle applies, with two qualifications, to peaceful public protest. If demonstrations are regarded as a legitimate way to express grievances, and if the grievances themselves are widely held to be justified, protest is likely to have positive effects. One of the qualifications is that if public opinion is neutral on an issue, protest demonstrations can have favorable effects. This appears to have been an initial consequence of the civil rights demonstrations of the early 1960s in the North. If public opinion is negative, however, demonstrations are likely to exacerbate popular hostility. During World War I, for example, pacifist demonstrators were repeatedly attacked, beaten, and in some cases lynched, with widespread public approval and sometimes official sanction. Contemporary civil rights demonstrations and activities in the South and in some northern cities have attracted similar responses.

The second qualification is that when violence occurs during protest activities, it is rather likely to alienate groups that are not fundamentally in sympathy with the protesters. We mentioned above the unfavorable consequences of labor violence for unions and their members, despite the fact that violence was more often initiated by employers than by workers. In the long run, federally enforced recognition and bargaining procedures were established, but this occurred only after labor violence had passed its climacteric, and moreover in circumstances in which no union leaders advocated violence. In England, comparably, basic political reforms were implemented not in direct response to Chartist protest, but long after its violent phase had passed.

The evidence supports one basic principle: Force and violence can be successful techniques of social control and persuasion when they have extensive popular support. If they do not, their advocacy and use are ultimately self-destructive, either as techniques of government or of opposition. The historical and contemporary evidence of the United States suggests that popular support tends to sanction violence in support of the status quo: the use of public violence to maintain public order, the use of private violence to maintain popular conceptions of social order when government cannot or will not. If these assertions are true—and not much evidence contradicts them—the prolonged use of force or violence to advance the interests of any segmental group may impede and quite possibly preclude reform. This conclusion should not be taken as an ethical judgment, despite its apparent correspondence with the "establishmentarian" viewpoint. It represents a fundamental trait of American and probably all mankind's character, one which is ignored by advocates of any political orientation at the risk of broken hopes, institutions, and lives.

To draw this conclusion is not to indict public force or all private violence as absolute social evils. In brief and obvious defense of public force, reforms cannot be made if order is wholly lacking, and reforms will not be made if those who have the means to make them feel their security constantly in jeopardy. And as for private violence, though it may bring out the worst in both its practitioners and its victims, it need not do so. Collective violence is after all a symptom of social malaise. It can be so regarded and the malaise treated as such, provided public-spirited men diagnose it correctly and have the will and means to work for a cure rather than to retaliate out of anger. Americans may be quick to self-righteous anger, but they also have retained some of the English genius for accommodation. Grudgingly and with much tumult, the dominant groups in American society have moved over enough to give the immigrant, the worker, the suffragette better—not the best—seats at the American feast of freedom and plenty. Many of them think the feast is bounteous enough for the dissatisfied students, the poor, the Indians, the blacks. Whether there is a place for the young militants who think the feast has gone rotten, no historical or comparative evidence we know of can answer, because absolute, revolutionary alienation from society has been very rare in the American past and no less rare in other pluralistic and abundant nations.

SOME ALTERNATIVES TO VIOLENCE

Political leaders faced with outbreaks or threats of collective violence can respond in the two general ways that we discussed above: They can strengthen systems of forceful social control, or they can exert public effort and encourage private efforts to alleviate conditions leading to discontent. Primary reliance on force has indeterminate outcomes at best. If popularly supported, public force will contain specific outbreaks of private violence, but is unlikely to prevent their recurrence. At worst, public force will so alienate a people that terrorist and revolutionary movements will arise to challenge and ultimately overthrow the regime. The teaching of comparative studies is that governments must be cautious in their reliance on force to maintain order, and consistent in the exercise of the modicum of force they choose to use. These are policies that require both appropriate leadership and well-trained, highly disciplined, and loyal military and police forces.

The effort to eliminate the conditions that lead to collective violence may tax the resources of a society, but it poses less serious problems than increased resort to force. American labor violence has been mitigated in the past 25 years partly by growing prosperity, but more consequentially because employers now have almost universally recognized unions and will negotiate wage issues and other grievances with them rather than retaliate against them. The movement toward recognition and negotiation was strongly reinforced when workers in most occupations were guaranteed the right to organize and bargain collectively in the National Labor Relations Act of 1935. Taft and Ross judge the act to have been effective not just because it established procedures but because of the concerted effort to enforce them by the National Labor Relations Board and the willingness of both employers and unions to recognize the Board's authority. Their willingness may be a testimony also to their own and public dismay at the destructiveness of earlier conflicts. It is worth emphasizing that in this situation the long-range consequences of conciliatory response was a decrease not increase in violent conflict. In fact, violence was chronic so long as union recognition was denied. The outcome suggests the inadequacy of arguments that concessions necessarily breed greater violence.

The history of English working-class protest supports these interpretations. In the nineteenth century, when England was transformed by an industrial revolution in which a highly competitive, laissez-faire market economy disrupted traditional employment patterns and led to sweatshop conditions for many urban workers, violent public protest then became chronic. Several conditions

averted what many Englishmen then feared as a threat of working-class revolt. One was economic growth itself, which led to a significant improvement in the standard of living of urban workers and to hopeful prospects shared by all classes. A second was the acceptance by upper-class political leaders of demands for political reform, and acceptance dictated by both principle and practicality that led to the enfranchisement and assimilation of the working classes into the English body politic. A third was a trend toward grudging toleration of, and ultimately the acceptance and encouragement of, working-class organization. Recognition of the right of workers to organize and bargain led to a flourishing not only of unions but of self-help organizations, cooperatives, and religious and educational groups, all of which together provided British workers with means to work toward the resolution of their discontents.

There were and are characteristics of English society that had no direct American parallels. Expectations of English workers were less high than those of ambitious immigrants to the United States. The English class structure, though more stratified and complex than the American, was generally accepted by all classes, seldom directly challenged. The laissez-faire sentiments of British employers were tempered by an acceptance of civic responsibilities that developed more quickly than it did in the United States, and as one consequence English labor violence never reached the intensity that it did in the United States. Working-class demands for political reform were predicated on the common assumption that governments could be changed and the power of the state used to ameliorate the economic grievances of workers. Though the parallels are not exact, the English experience seems to suggest some general lessons for the contemporary United States: Civil peace was established through a judicious, perhaps fortuitous, combination of governmental and political reform, and institutional development among the aggrieved classes of society.

Intensely discontented men are not will-less pawns in a game of social chess. They also have alternatives, of which violence is usually the last, the most desperate, and in most circumstances least likely of success. Peaceful protest, conducted publicly and through conventional political channels, is a traditional American option. As one of the world's most pluralistic societies, we have repeatedly albeit reluctantly accommodated ourselves to discontented groups using interest and pressure-group tactics within the political process as a means of leverage for change. But it also is an American characteristic to resist demonstrative demands, however legal and peaceful, if they seem to challenge our basic beliefs and personal positions. Public protest in the United States is a slow and unwieldy instrument of social change that sometimes inspires more obdurate resistance than favorable change.[3]

Another kind of group response to intense stresses and discontents is called "defensive adaptation" by Bernard Siegel. It is essentially an inward-turning, nonviolent response motivated by a desire to build and maintain a group's cultural integrity in the face of hostile pressures. The defensive group is characterized by centralization of authority; attempts to set the group apart by emphasizing symbols of group identity; and minimization of members' contacts with other groups. It is an especially common reaction among ethnic and religious groups whose members see their social environments as permanently hostile, depreciating, and powerful. Such adaptations are apparent, for example, among some Pueblo Indians, Black Muslims, and Amish, and many minority groups in other nations. This kind of defensive withdrawal may lead to violence when outside groups press too closely in on the defensive group, but it is typically a response that minimizes violent conflict. Although the defensive group provides its members some, essentially social and psychological, satisfactions, it seldom can provide them with substantial economic benefits or political means by which they can promote their causes vis-a-vis hostile external groups.

A third general kind of response is the development of discontented groups of positive, socially integrative means for the satisfaction of their members' unsatisfied expectations. This response has characterized most discontented groups throughout Western history. In England, social protest was institutionalized through the trade unions, cooperative societies, and other self-help activities. In continental Europe, the discontent of the urban workers and petit bourgeoisie led to the organization of fraternal societies, unions, and political parties, which provided some intrinsic satisfactions for their members and which could channel demands more or less effectively to employers and

into the political system. In the United States the chronic local uprisings of the late eighteenth, the nineteenth, and the early twentieth century—such as the Shay, Whiskey, Dorr, and Green Corn Rebellions—have been largely superseded by organized, conventional political manifestations of local and regional interests. Labor violence similarly declined in the United States and England once trade unions were organized and recognized.

The contemporary efforts of black Americans to develop effective community organizations, and their demands for greater control of community affairs, seem to be squarely in this tradition. So are demands of student protesters for greater participation in university affairs, attempts of white urban citizens to create new neighborhood organizations, and the impulse of middle-class Americans to move to the suburbs where they can exercise greater control over the local government.

The initial effects of the organization of functional and community groups for self-help may be increased conflict, especially if the economic and political establishments attempt to subvert their efforts. But if these new organizations receive public and private cooperation and sufficient resources to carry out their activities, the prospects for violence are likely to be reduced. The social costs of this kind of group response seem much less than those of public and private violence. The human benefits are likely to be far greater than those attained through private violence or defensive withdrawal. . . .

NOTES

1. This discussion is drawn from arguments and evidence in Ted Robert Gurr, **Why Men Rebel** (Princeton: Princeton University Press, 1969), chap. 8. The survey datum is from Hazel Erskine, "The Polls: Demonstrations and Race Riots," **Public Opinion Quarterly** (Winter 1967-1968), 655-677.

2. On Klan membership in 1967, see U.S. Congress, House Un-American Activities Committee, **The Present-Day Ku Klux Klan Movement** (Washington, D.C.: Government Printing Office, 1967), p. 62.

3. Kenneth E. Boulding makes the same point in a discussion of the possible consequences of antiwar protest, in "Reflections on Protest," **Bulletin of the Atomic Scientists**, 21 (October 1965), 18-20.

topic 22

revolutions of rising expectations: the third-world peoples and the road to modernity

The term **third world** is for many a stirring, perhaps an electrifying one, evoking an image of dark-skinned peoples in underdeveloped lands on the verge of the explosive growth that culminates in modernization. But this imagery is not precise enough for the student of society and social change if his analyses are to be fruitful and his understanding truly rewarding. The term **third world** is even vaguer than the label **industrial** as applied to the developed countries of the world. For all of their often striking unlikenesses in history, language, normative structure, religion, and fundamental ethos, such industrial giants as Japan, West Germany, the Soviet Union, France, the United States, and England are essentially more like one another in terms of economic, technological, bureaucratic, and educational structure than are the heterogeneous underdeveloped nations.

Whatever its shortcomings, however, the designation third world possesses one measure of empirical validity. For despite their diversity, virtually all of the third-world peoples share one central and unhappy circumstance in common: they are desperately poor. Worse still, this poverty, is getting worse, as the gap between rich nations and poor nations widens. The rich are literally getting richer and more powerful, and the poor poorer and more powerless with each passing year. An economist, Barbara Ward, sums it up:

> Our world today is dominated by a complex and tragic division.
> One part of mankind has undergone the revolutions of modern-
> ization and has emerged on the other side to a pattern of great
> and increasing wealth. But most of the rest of mankind has
> yet to achieve any of the revolutions: they are caught off bal-
> ance before the great movement of economic and social momen-
> tum can be launched. Their old traditional world is dying. This
> being so, the gap between the rich and the poor has become
> inevitably the most tragic and urgent problem of our day.

There are no easy solutions to the problem, primarily because a tradition-infused, change-resistant value system prevails in so many of the third-world's communal cultures: The psychology and the will-to-change required for the revolution of modernity is absent.

But there are other factors. Most of the third-world countries are running a losing race between "stork and plow"—between explosive population growth and the capacity to produce sufficient food to stave off mass starvation or, at best, massive malnutrition. Related to this is the dangerous dependence upon one- or two-crop economies.

Furthermore, there is in third-world countries the possibility—in many cases the distinct probability—of recurrent revolutions, juntas, and **coups d'etat** accompanied, frequently, by totalitarian regimes, ruthless suppression or elimination of opposition, and the tendency to seek warlike instead of peaceful solutions to rivalries with neighboring nations. And on top of that there is the temptation for the big powers to play a dangerous game of chess with this and that hapless Vietnam, India, Pakistan, Nicaragua, or Cambodia.

Of the three essays that comprise this section, the first, by Rainer Shickele, may strike many readers as naively hopeful. But if Shickele appears too optimistic in believing that progressive leaders will emerge in the third world, he is correct in pointing out that the greatest challenge to mankind during the next few centuries will be the showdown battle between technology and science on the one hand and humanist ideology on the other. For if science and technology have indeed given man the power to obilterate poverty, they have also given him the power to destroy himself by instant mass murder.

Like Schickele, Eric Hoffer points out the similarities and the differences between the industrial revolution in the West and the revolution of modernity in the third world—in this case Asia. Hoffer is particularly attentive to the psychological consequences of the sudden sense of freedom and autonomy that has been thrust on so many Asians. Robert Heilbronner's piece may be construed by some as unduly despairing. But in fact his synopsis of the almost insurmountable obstacles confronting the modernization process is starkly realistic.

chapter 51
agrarian revolution and economic progress
rainer schickele

We are witnessing a drama of breathtaking sweep throughout the newly developing world.

We are in the second act on which the curtain rose after World War II. The first act started in the wake of the French and American revolutions, around the year 1800. The center of the stage in the first act was Europe and North America. In the second act, it has shifted from the West to the East and South, to Asia, Africa, and Latin America.

The central protagonist is the worker, the peasant, the small craftsman, the clerk, the poor man working in the factory, field, workshop, and office. The plot of the drama deals with his frustrations and triumphs as he struggles along his way from subservience to human dignity and citizenship, from poverty to wealth, under the guiding spirit of humanist ideology, of democracy and the equality of man.

THE INDUSTRIAL REVOLUTION OF THE WEST

In the first act, during the Industrial Revolution up to World War II, technology brought about a tremendous increase in productivity. Application of science to the production processes increased the capacity of people to produce so much that,

From Rainer Schickele, Agrarian Revolution and Economic Progress (New York: Praeger, 1968). Reprinted by permission of Praeger Publishers, Inc.

for the first time in the history of mankind, it became possible to wipe out hunger and poverty. The humanist ideology taught people that the purpose of an economic system is the creation of wealth for the satisfaction of human wants, and that men are created equal. This means that men of all races and creeds have a basic human right to equality of opportunity and civic dignity, that the satisfaction of the human wants of the poor is as important as that of the rich, and that degrading poverty is incompatible with the principle of human rights in a modern democracy.

The economic system during the Industrial Revolution was based mainly upon private entrepreneurs. Although producers were always subject to various public policies and regulations, these were in the beginning formulated in the interest of industrial producers and of commerce with no regard for expanding also the opportunities for the millions of poor workers employed at starvation wages and working under most horrible sweatshop conditions. During the nineteenth century, many people became rich, but many, many more people remained extremely poor. As late as the middle of the twentieth century, the richest of the Western industrial countries still had far too many families living in poverty, in the midst of plenty.

This weakness of the private enterprise system in distributing its rising output to also meet the needs of the poor became apparent as early as the middle of the nineteenth century. Our drama's hero, the worker, farmer, or small craftsman, with the help of philosophers and economists, came forth with the proposal of an alternative economic system, that of state enterprise, whose purpose was to create wealth for the satisfaction of human wants according to physical and social need rather than ability to pay. It was, however, only as late as the 1920s, and only in one country, Russia, that a centralized state enterprise system was actually put into practice during the first act of our drama. It performed well in reducing abject poverty among the masses of the people, but was much less successful in the task of increasing productivity, particularly in agriculture.

The hero, when he saw more than half a century go by without any Western country adopting the state enterprise system, began struggling for a fundamental reform, for a reorientation of the private enterprise system which would strengthen its performance in satisfying the human wants of the poor, without weakening its performance in producing wealth. In their political ascendancy, people assigned to the state the responsibility for guiding the private enterprise economy with social and economic welfare policies so as to reduce poverty and give equal opportunities to the poor for education, health, and bargaining power in the market. These policies compensated, at least in part, for the lack of the market system's response to the needs of the poor, and still preserved the incentives and initiatives of private enterprise in production.

This "mixed economy" where private enterprise produces and trades within a framework of public policies and controls designed to promote the economic welfare of people as a whole, and particularly of the poor and disadvantaged, achieved a dramatic breakthrough in most of the Western industrialized countries during the 1920s and 1930s. In the Scandinavian countries, poverty has almost been wiped out, private enterprise is producing efficiently and profitably and living standards are among the highest in Europe. Also, in many of the other Western industrialized countries, the extent of poverty has been reduced more or less depending on the scope and efficiency of the public policies for equalizing opportunities and reducing poverty. There remains no economic or moral justification for poverty in an industrially developed affluent society where excess production capacity and surpluses are more troublesome than shortages. So our drama's hero continues his struggle in the West, but with a strong stance which promises to bring him soon within reach of his economic goal—the abolition of poverty.

This is the stage of affairs, the scenery and the stage of the plot at the end of the drama's Act I, the Industrial Revolution of the West.

THE AGRARIAN REVOLUTION OF THE NEWLY DEVELOPING WORLD

As the curtain rises on Act II around the year 1950, the Agrarian Revolution of the East and South has started. The scene is the vast region of Asia, Africa, and South America, a rural region where most people live on farms and in villages and derive their livelihood from agriculture. Here, 800 to 900 million people achieved political independence from colonial rule in recent years, and another 400 million people are bringing about fundamental changes in their old traditional governments. Of the 1.25 billion people in this newly developing part of the world, 90 percent live in countries with an average per capita income of less than $200 per year. This simply means that the vast majority of the people are very poor indeed.

The people want to consummate their newly won political independence and strive toward their new aspirations of human dignity, freedom as responsible citizens, and equality of opportunity. This means they must raise their production and do so for the main purpose of reducing poverty.

The hero finds himself in a state of deep and widespread poverty. His trials deal with finding ways of harnessing the wealth-creating drive of private enterprise within a framework of governmental policies that satisfy the human wants of the poor, in order to unleash the pent-up capacities and energies of the people which are now stunted, suppressed by lack of education, health, food, and other bare necessities of life.

The drama's hero is not a heroic character. He takes on the shape of many different persons in all walks of life. He appears as an Indian farmer, overlooking his fields parched by the drought of the failing monsoon, with his wife, children and grandparents. Where will the food come from to keep his family alive? He appears as an office clerk in Nigeria who was fired by the manager to make room for a cousin, and who cannot find another job because he comes from the wrong tribe. He appears as a woman in a textile factory in Malaysia, a fisherman in Haiti, a blacksmith in the northeast of Brazil—and whenever some little thing goes wrong he is down and out. There are so many little things over which he has no control and which can go wrong for him, because he has no influence over his environment, no influence with his employer, landlord, or creditor in the conduct of public and community affairs. But he knows that if he is given a chance, if he can get education, food, and other prime necessities of life, he can do well, and he has proven it again and again on the rare occasions when he did get a chance. He is determined to get this chance for the multitude of poor people everywhere.

There are leaders emerging who articulate the aspirations of the people, who educate them in political and economic matters, who organize them into cooperative groups and political parties, who are rapidly learning the art and science of modern politics and government. Some of these leaders come from poor families, from peasant farms and shantytowns; but many come from well-to-do families, from educated classes, from professional and civil service ranks and landed aristocracies. Gandhi, whose father and grandfather were chief ministers of several Indian states, shared the life of the poor voluntarily in the service to their cause. Nyerere was a teacher, Senghor a philosopher and poet, Cardenas a general, before they became great leaders of their people. They identified themselves with them, they came to political power with their support and held their confidence. This emergence of progressive leaders of the common people is proceeding everywhere, slowly in some places, faster in others. There is today no government, no group of rulers and wealthy merchants and landowners who do not sense the political ascendancy of the poor.

This pervasive spirit of the times is our drama's hero. This spirit is energized by the vision of man coming into his own, as an individual on equal terms with his brethren of all races, creeds, and nations, with equal opportunities to develop his talents, to apply his productive efforts, and to be treated with respect by other persons and by his government. This is the freedom aspect of this ideology; its counterpart, fully as indispensable, is the responsibility aspect— the vision of man as a member of the community, who accepts the obligation to serve the needs of society, who participates in public affairs as a responsible citizen with the community's interest at heart.

The practical meaning of this ideology, this spiritual credo of our time, is that the individual has the right to choose and act freely within the limits of compatibility with community welfare; and that the government, in its promotion and safeguarding of the community's welfare, exercises its power with the consent of the people at large, and within the limits of compatibility with individual freedom and dignity.

Who is the villian in our drama? The plantation owner with a whip? The feudal prince in his palace with wives in silk brocades and thousands of peasants in rags and abject servitude? The colonial administrator backed by mercenaries?

These characters are disappearing rapidly with the demise of colonial empires, the achievement of political independence, and the creation of representative democratic governments, although there are still areas where they are fighting covertly, but ruthlessly, for their power and social status.

The real antagonist is the old traditional spirit of privilege and power of the few over the many, of the elite over the "innately inferior," of the born aristocrat over the plebs, of the wealthy over the poor. This antagonist still has great strength which is rooted in past traditions of thousands of years. He also takes on the shape of many different persons in all walks of life. He appears as a peasant who has no respect for the dignity of his wife and mistreats her as a slave. How can his children grasp the belief in human dignity when they see their own mother mistreated? He appears as a government official who abuses the power of his office, who intimidates people and demands bribes. He appears as a landowner who keeps his tenants and laborers ignorant and poor and in debt to him, or as a foreman in a factory who bars his workers from advancement and keeps them in constant fear of dismissal.

This metaphoric prologue symbolizes the essence of the forces underlying modern economic development problems. For the first time in mankind's history, technology offers the possibility of producing enough for every man, woman, and child to live in decency, free from hunger and stultifying want. This constitutes the material base upon which a democratic society can be built embracing all the people rather than only a small elite.

GENERATORS OF PROGRESS

There are two powerful generators of economic development the humanist ideology, and science and technology.

The great moral force which ushered in the American and French revolutions of the late eighteenth century and shaped the concept of a modern democratic social system was rooted in the belief that men are created equal before God, or in worldly terms, that men are equal before the law and have equal rights for opportunities to develop their capacities, to reap the fruits of their productive efforts, and to participate in the shaping of their communities, in the molding of their institutions and governments. This idea is still an infant in world history's perspective, and is very new indeed to the traditional cultures of two thirds of the world population. But this humanist idea is on the march everywhere, is stirring in the minds and hearts of people throughout the world, and will continue to shape the history of mankind throughout the current and the coming centuries.

In the West, this humanist ideology transformed a feudal elite society into a democratic society of citizens in which universal suffrage, one-man, one-vote, became the revolutionary invention for making government responsible to the people. It transformed a highly restrictive and esoteric educational system for the privileged few into a universal, largely free, educational system for everyone. It abolished slavery and established a code of law and a system of courts before which every man was considered equal in his rights and responsibilities. It created the goal of people's economic welfare, of equitable sharing of the nation's wealth and opportunities, of abolition of hunger and poverty—a logical sequel to the abolition of slavery. These were tremendously powerful innovations which triggered a revolution of rising aspirations and unleashed pent-up energies of people for building a new society, new institutions and standards of behavior, new laws and forms of government. Even after 150 years of political potency in the Western industrial world, no one claims that this humanist ideology has found its full realization in modern Western society; it is still far from it. But since the middle of the current century, it has become the dominant world spirit and driving force. It is giving the direction, the orientation, for progress throughout the world, in the industrial West and newly developing agrarian countries alike.

Science and technology transformed the traditional production processes in industry, agriculture, and trade into instruments of amazing power for making the natural resources of the earth the servants of the material needs of man. In the industrial West, during the last hundred years, output per worker increased manyfold in every line of production. It created a large variety of new goods and services which were not even conceivable a hundred years ago. This application of a rapidly expanding science to practical production processes is now beginning to spread throughout the developing world, and is bringing about new attitudes of people toward their work, new forms of organization and group activities in production techniques, in market structures and government function. Science and technology have given man the power to abolish poverty, for the first time in history—but also to destroy himself by instantaneous mass murder. The greatest challenge to mankind in the coming centuries is to uphold the mastership of the humanist ideology, of the spiritual and moral values of modern society, over the application of technology, over the use of science in human affairs. This applies to the use of atomic energy as well as to the use of mechanization and automation.

These two great generators of progress, the humanist ideology and the scientific technology, are the West's constructive legacy to the newly developing regions of the world; they have to adopt them to their own peculiar conditions, but they need not invent them anew. Herein lies the hope for a victorious outcome of the race against time.

If progress lags too much, there is real danger of mankind losing control over technology. A serious disintegration of the spiritual power which the idea of the equality and dignity of man holds over our hearts and minds may readily lead to an atomic holocaust, or to a technocratic society of robots along the alpha-beta-gamma lines of Huxley's **Brave New World** or the nightmare of Orwell's **1984**.

The **material aspect** of the race against time is that between food and population, between production and poverty. Will we succeed in abolishing hunger and poverty fast enough to prevent a worldwide breakdown of interhuman and international relations, of national and world peace?

The **ideological aspect** is the question: Will people's faith in the humanist idea of the respect for our fellowman's and neighbor-nation's dignity and right of self-government withstand the frustrations and trials on the road to progress, or will this faith falter in us before a modicum of realization is reached?

These are the two basic disturbing aspects of the race against time which leaders must ponder honestly, at all levels, in all walks of life, in all countries throughout the world.

chapter 52
the awakening of asia
eric hoffer

The tendency is to ascribe the present revolutionary turmoil in Asia to Communist agitation, or see it as an upheaval against foreign domination or misrule by corrupt native governments. Though there is a large element of truth in these views they somehow fail to go to the heart of the matter. The nations of Asia have for uncounted centuries submitted to one conqueror after another and been misruled, looted, and bled by both foreign and native oppressors without letting out a peep. If then the masses are now rising in protest, it is not because domination and corruption have become unduly oppressive, but because the masses are not today what they were in the past. Something has happened to change their temper. We are told, it is true, that an awakening has taken place in Asia. But if this "awakening" is to be more than a metaphor, it must refer to specific changes in individual attitudes, inclinations, and aspirations. We ought to know what these changes are and how they were brought about.

The same is true of Communist agitation: its effectiveness in Asia is due less to the potency of its propaganda than to the temper of the people it tries to propagandize. When not backed by force, Communist propaganda can persuade people only of what they want to believe, and it can make

From **The Ordeal of Change** by Eric Hoffer. Reprinted by permission of Harper & Row, Publishers, Inc.

headway only when it gives people something they desperately desire. It seems obvious that we cannot begin to speculate on the state of affairs in Asia unless we have a fairly clear idea of the individual attitudes, inclinations, and, above all, desires prevailing there at present. What is it that the ill-fed, ill-clad, and ill-housed masses in China, India, Indonesia, etc., so desperately desire?

Economic theory can give only a dull and unconvincing answer. One thinks of the shouting and marching, and the sea of upturned faces one has seen in newsreels and photographs—grimacing, passionate faces, each framing a gaping mouth. One wonders what is going on behind these faces and what it is that the gaping mouths shout. Do they shout for bread, clothing, and houses? Do they clamor for the good things of life? Do they call for freedom and justice? No. The clamor that is rising all over the Orient is a clamor for pride. The masses in Asia will sacrifice every economic benefit they have, and their lives too, to satisfy their craving for pride. The sea of open mouths roars defiance and not economic grievances and demands. As we shall see, this clamorous craving for pride is a characteristic manifestation of the process of awakening, and it is by probing the nature of this process that we are most likely to reach the core of our problem.

To say that the impact of the West was a chief factor in the awakening of Asia is not to say that it was oppression and exploitation by the Western colonial powers that did it. For not only are oppression and exploitation an old story in Asia, but the colonial regimes of the British in India and of the Dutch in Indonesia were fairly beneficient—more so perhaps than any regime those countries ever had or are likely to have for some time. I am convinced that were the Western colonial powers a hundred times more beneficient, and had they been animated from the very beginning by the purest philanthropic motives, their impact on the Orient would still have had the fateful consequences we are witnessing at present. For Western influence, irrespective of its intentions, almost always brought about a fateful change wherever it penetrated, and it is this change that is at the root of the present revolutionary unrest.

The change I have in mind is of a specific nature—the weakening and cracking of the communal framework. Everywhere in Asia before the advent of Western influence the individual was integrated into a more or less compact group—a patriarchal family, a clan or a tribe, a cohesive rural or urban unit, a compact religious or political body. From birth to death the individual felt himself part of a continuous eternal whole. He never felt alone, never felt lost, and never saw himself as a speck of life floating in an eternity of nothingness. Western influence invariably tended to weaken or even destroy this corporate pattern. By trade, legislation, education, industrialization, and by example, it cracked and corroded the traditional way of life, and drained existing communal structures of their prestige and effectiveness. The Western colonial powers offered individual freedom. They tried to shake the Oriental out of his lethargy, rid him of his ossified traditionalism, and infect him with a craving for self-advancement. The result was not emancipation but isolation and exposure. An immature individual was torn from the warmth and security of a corporate existence and left orphaned and empty in a cold world. It was this shock of abandonment and exposure which brought about the awakening in Asia. The crumbling of a corporate body, with the abandonment of the individual to his own devices, is always a critical phase in social development. The newly emerging individual can attain some degree of stability and eventually become inured to the burdens and strains of an autonomous existence only when he is offered abundant opportunities for self-assertion or self-realization. He needs an environment in which achievement, acquisition, sheer action, or the de-

velopment of his capacities and talents seems within easy reach. It is only thus that he can acquire the self-confidence and self-esteem that make an individual existence bearable or even exhilarating.

Where self-confidence and self-esteem seem unattainable, the emerging individual becomes a highly explosive entity. He tries to derive a sense of confidence and of worth by embracing some absolute truth and by identifying himself with the spectacular doings of a leader or some collective body—be it a nation, a congregation, a party, or a mass movement. He and his like become a breeding ground of convulsions and upheavals that shake a society to its foundations. It needs a rare constellation of circumstances if the transition from a communal to an individual existence is to run its course without being diverted or reversed by catastrophic complications.

Europe at the turn of the fifteenth century witnessed a similar release of the individual from the corporate pattern of an all-embracing Church. At the beginning, the release was accidental. A weakened and discredited Church lost its hold on the minds and souls of the people of Europe. There, too, the emergence of the individual was less a deliberate emancipation than an abandonment. But how different were the attending circumstances then from what they are now in Asia! The emerging European individual at the end of the Middle Ages faced breathtaking vistas of new continents just discovered, new trade routes just opened, the prospect of fabulous empires yet to be stumbled upon and new knowledge unlocked by the introduction of paper and printing. The air was charged with great expectations and there was a feeling abroad that by the exercise of his capacities and talents and with the aid of good fortune the individual on his own was equal to any undertaking at home and across the sea.

Thus by a fortuitous combination of circumstances, the fateful change from a communal to an individual existence produced an outburst of vitality that has since been characteristic of the Occident and marks it off from any other civilization. Yet even so, the transition was not altogether smooth. The convulsions of the Reformation and Counter-Reformation stemmed from the fears and passionate intensities of people unequal to the burdens and strains of an individual existence.

No such exceptional combination of circumstances attended the crumbling of communal life in Asia. There the awakening of the individual occurred in a landscape strewn with the litter and rubble of centuries. Instead of being stirred and lured by breathtaking prospects and undreamt-of opportunities, he finds himself mired in a life that is stagnant, debilitated, and inordinately meager. It is a world where human life is the most plentiful and cheapest thing, and where millions of hungry hands grab at the meanest prize and meagerest morsel. It is, moreover, an illiterate world, where even rudimentary education confers distinction and lifts a man above the common run of toiling humanity. The articulate minority is thus prevented from acquiring a sense of usefulness and of worth by taking part in the world's work, and is condemned to the life of chattering, posturing pseudointellectuals.

The rabid extremist in present-day Asia is usually a man of some education who has a horror or manual labor and who develops a mortal hatred for a social order that denies him a position of command. Every student, every minor clerk and officeholder, every petty member of the professions feels himself one of the chosen. It is these wordy, futile people who set the tone in Asia. Living barren, useless lives, they are without self-confidence and self-respect, and their craving is for the illusion of weight and importance, and for the explosive substitutes of pride and faith.

It is chiefly to these pseudointellectuals that Communist Russia directs its appeal. It brings them the promise of membership in a ruling elite, the prospect of having a hand in the historical process, and, by its doctrinaire double-talk, provides them with a sense of weight and depth.

As to the illiterate masses, the appeal of Communist preaching does not lie in its "truths," but in the vague impression it conveys to them that they and Russia are partners in some tremendous, unprecedented undertaking—the building of a proud future that will surpass and put to naught all the "things that are."

■

The crucial fact about the awakening in Asia is that it did not come from an accession of strength. It was not brought about by a gradual or sudden increase of material, intellectual, or moral powers, but by the shock of abandonment and exposure. It was an awakening brought about by a poignant sense of weakness. And we must know something about the mentality and potentialities of the weak if we are to understand the present temper of the people in awakening Asia.

It has been often said that power corrupts. But it is perhaps equally important to realize that weakness, too, corrupts. Power corrupts the few, while weakness corrupts the many. Hatred, malice, rudeness, intolerance, and suspicion are the fruits of weakness. The resentment of the weak does not spring from any injustice done to them but from the sense of their inadequacy and impotence. We cannot win the weak by sharing our wealth with them. They feel our generosity as oppression. St. Vincent de Paul cautioned his disciples to deport themselves so that the poor "will forgive you the bread you give them." But this requires, in both giver and receiver, a vivid awareness of a God who is the father of all, and a living mastery of the religious idiom which we of this day do not, and perhaps cannot, have in full measure. Nor can we win the weak by sharing our hope, pride, or even hatred with them. We are too far ahead materially and too different in our historical experience to serve as an object of identification. Our healing gift to the weak is the capacity for self-help. We must learn how to impart to them the technical, social, and political skills which would enable them to get bread, human dignity, freedom, and strength by their own efforts.

My hunch is that in mastering the art or the technique of helping the weak to help themselves we shall solve some of the critical problems which confront us, not only in our foreign relations, but also in our domestic affairs.

chapter 53
counterrevolutionary
america
robert l. heilbroner

Is the United States fundamentally opposed to economic development? The question is outrageous. Did we not coin the phrase, "the revolution of rising expectations"? Have we not supported the cause of development more generously than any nation on earth, spent our intellectual energy on the problems of development, offered our expertise freely to the backward nations of the world? How can it possibly be suggested that the United States might be opposed to economic development?

The answer is that we are not at all opposed to what we conceive economic development to be. The process depicted by the "revolution of rising expectations" is a deeply attractive one. It conjures up the image of a peasant in some primitive land, leaning on his crude plow and looking to the horizon, where he sees dimly, but for the first time (and that is what is so revolutionary about it), the vision of a better life. From this electrifying vision comes the necessary catalysis to change an old and stagnant way of life. The pace of work quickens. Innovations, formerly feared and resisted, are now eagerly accepted. The obstacles are admittedly very great—whence the need for foreign assistance—but under the impetus of new hopes the economic

mechanism begins to turn faster, to gain traction against the environment. Slowly, but surely, the Great Ascent begins.

There is much that is admirable about this well-intentioned popular view of "the revolution of rising expectations." Unfortunately, there is more that is delusive about it. For the buoyant appeal of its rhetoric conceals or passes in silence over by far the larger part of the spectrum of realities of the development process. One of these is the certainty that the revolutionary aspect of development will not be limited to the realm of ideas, but will vent its fury on institutions, social classes, and innocent men and women. Another is the great likelihood that the ideas needed to guide the revolution will not only be affirmative and reasonable, but also destructive and fanatic. A third is the realization that revolutionary efforts cannot be made, and certainly cannot be sustained, by voluntary effort alone, but require an iron hand, in the spheres of both economic direction and political control. And the fourth and most difficult of these realities to face is the probability that the political force most likely to succeed in carrying through the gigantic historical transformation of development is some form of extreme national collectivism or Communism.

In a word, what our rhetoric fails to bring to our attention is the likelihood that development will require policies and programs repugnant to

From "Counterrevolutionary America," by Robert L. Heilbroner, in **Commentary**, 43:31-38, April 1967. Copyright © 1967 by Robert L. Heilbroner. Reprinted by permission of the American Jewish Committee, New York.

our "way of life," that it will bring to the fore governments hostile to our international objectives, and that its regnant ideology will bitterly oppose capitalism as a system of world economic power. If that is the case, we would have to think twice before denying that the United States was fundamentally opposed to economic development.

But is it the case? Must development lead in directions that go counter to the present American political philosophy? Let me try to indicate, albeit much too briefly and summarily, the reasons that lead me to answer that question as I do.

I begin with the cardinal point, often noted but still insufficiently appreciated, that the process called "economic development" is not primarily economic at all. We think of development as a campaign of production to be fought with budgets and monetary policies and measured with indices of output and income. But the development process is much wider and deeper than can be indicated by such statistics. To be sure, in the end what is hoped for is a tremendous rise in output. But this will not come to pass until a series of tasks, at once cruder and more delicate, simpler and infinitely more difficult, has been commenced and carried along a certain distance.

In most of the new nations of Africa, these tasks consist in establishing the very underpinnings of nationhood itself—in determining national borders, establishing national languages, arousing a basic national (as distinguished from tribal) self-consciousness. Before these steps have been taken, the African states will remain no more than names insecurely affixed to the map, not social entities capable of undertaking an enormous collective venture in economic change. In Asia, nationhood is generally much further advanced than in Africa, but here the main impediment to development is the miasma of apathy and fatalism, superstition and distrust that vitiates every attempt to improve hopelessly inefficient modes of work and patterns of resource use: While India starves, a quarter of the world's cow population devours Indian crops, exempt from either effective employment or slaughter because of sacred taboos. In still other areas, mainly Latin America, the principal handicap to development is not an absence of national identity or the presence of suffocating cultures (although the latter certainly plays its part), but the cramping and crippling inhibitions of obsolete social institutions and reactionary social classes. Where landholding rather than industrial activity is still the basis for social and economic power,

and where land is held essentially in fiefdoms rather than as productive real estate, it is not surprising that so much of society retains a medieval cast.

Thus, development is much more than a matter of encouraging economic growth within a given social structure. It is rather the **modernization** of that structure, a process of ideational, social, economic, and political change that requires the remaking of society in its most intimate as well as its most public attributes.[1] When we speak of the revolutionary nature of economic development, it is this kind of deeply penetrative change that we mean—change that reorganizes "normal" ways of thought, established patterns of family life, and structures of village authority as well as class and caste privilege.

What is so egregiously lacking in the great majority of the societies that are now attempting to make the Great Ascent is precisely this pervasive modernization. The trouble with India and Pakistan, with Brazil and Ecuador, with the Philippines and Ethiopia, is not merely that economic growth lags, or proceeds at some pitiable pace. This is only a symptom of deeper-lying ills. The trouble is that the social physiology of these nations remains so depressingly unchanged despite the flurry of economic planning on top. The all-encompassing ignorance and poverty of the rural regions, the unbridgeable gulf between the peasant and the urban elites, the resistive conservatism of the village elders, the unyielding traditionalism of family life—all these remain obdurately, maddeningly, disastrously unchanged. In the cities, a few modern buildings, sometimes brilliantly executed, give a deceptive patina of modernity, but once one journeys into the immense countryside, the terrible stasis overwhelms all.

To this vast landscape of apathy and ignorance one must now make an exception of the very greatest importance. It is the fact that a very few nations, all of them Communist, have succeeded in reaching into the lives and stirring the minds of precisely that body of the peasantry which constitutes the insuperable problem elsewhere. In our concentration on the politics, the betrayals, the successes and failures of the Russian, Chinese, and Cuban revolutions, we forget that their central motivation has been just such a war à l'outrance against the arch enemy of backwardness—not alone the backwardness of outmoded social superstructures but even more critically that of private inertia and traditionalism.

That the present is irreversibly and unqualifiedly freed from the dead hand of the past is, I think, beyond argument in the case of Russia. By this I do not only mean that Russia has made enormous economic strides. I refer rather to the gradual emancipation of its people from the "idiocy of rural life," their gradual entrance upon the stage of contemporary existence. This is not to hide in the smallest degree the continuing backwardness of the Russian countryside where now almost fifty—and formerly perhaps eighty—percent of the population lives. But even at its worst I do not think that life could now be described in the despairing terms that run through the Russian literature of our grandfathers' time. Here is Chekhov:

> During the summer and the winter there had been hours and days when it seemed as if these people [the peasants] lived worse than cattle, and it was terrible to be with them. They were coarse, dishonest, dirty, and drunken; they did not live at peace with one another but quarreled continually, because they feared, suspected, and despised one another. . . . Crushing labor that made the whole body ache at night, cruel winters, scanty crops, overcrowding, and no help, and nowhere to look for help.

It is less certain that the vise of the past has been loosened in China or Cuba. It may well be that Cuba has suffered a considerable economic decline, in part due to absurd planning, in part to our refusal to buy her main crop. The economic record of China is nearly as inscrutable as its political turmoil, and we may not know for many years whether the Chinese peasant is today better or worse off than before the revolution. Yet what strikes me as significant in both countries is something else. In Cuba it is the educational effort that, according to **The New York Times**, has constituted a major effort of the Castro regime. In China it is the unmistakable evidence—and here I lean not alone on the sympathetic accound of Edgar Snow but on the most horrified descriptions of the rampages of the Red Guards—that the younger generation is no longer fettered by the traditional view of things. The very fact that the Red Guards now revile their elders, an unthinkable defiance of age-old Chinese custom, is testimony of how deeply change has penetrated into the texture of Chinese life.

It is this herculean effort to reach and rally the great anonymous mass of the population that is **the great accomplishment of Communism**—even though

it is an accomplishment that is still only partially accomplished. For if the areas of the world afflicted with the self-perpetuating disease of backwardness are ever to rid themselves of its debilitating effects, I think it is likely to be not merely because antiquated social structures have been dismantled (although this is an essential precondition), but because some shock treatment like that of Communism has been administered to them.

By way of contrast to this all-out effort, however short it may have fallen of its goal, we must place the timidity of the effort to bring modernization to the peoples of the non-Communist world. Here again I do not merely speak of lagging rates of growth. I refer to the fact that illiteracy in the non-Communist countries of Asia and Central America is increasing (by some 200 million in the last decade) because it has been "impossible" to mount an educational effort that will keep pace with population growth. I refer to the absence of substantial land reform in Latin America, despite how many years of promises. I refer to the indifference or incompetence or corruption of governing elites: the incredible sheiks with their oildoms; the vague, well-meaning leaders of India unable to break the caste system, kill the cows, control the birthrate, reach the villages, house or employ the labor rotting on the streets; the cynical governments of South America, not one of which, according to Lleras Camargo, former president of Colombia, has ever prosecuted a single politican or industrialist for evasion of taxes. And not least, I refer to the fact that every movement that arises to correct these conditions is instantly identified as "Communist" and put down with every means at hand, while the United States clucks or nods approval.

To be sure, even in the most petrified societies, the modernization process is at work. If there were time, the solvent acids of the twentieth century would work their way on the ideas and institutions of the most inert or resistant countries. But what lacks in the twentieth century is time. The multitudes of the underdeveloped world have only in the past two decades been summoned to their reveille. The one thing that is certain about the revolution of rising expectations is that it is only in its inception, and that its pressures for justice and action will steadily mount as the voice of the twentieth century penetrates to villages and slums where it is still almost inaudible. It is not surprising that Princeton historian C. E. Black, surveying this labile world, estimates that we must anticipate "ten to fifteen revolutions a year for the foreseeable future in the less developed societies."

In itself, this prospect of mounting political restiveness enjoins the speediest possible time schedule for development. But this political urgency is many times compounded by that of the population problem. Like an immense river in flood, the number of human beings rises each year to wash away the levees of the preceding year's labors and to pose future requirements of monstrous proportions. To provide shelter for the three billion human beings who will arrive on earth in the next forty years will require as many dwellings as have been constructed since recorded history began. To feed them will take double the world's present output of food. To cope with the mass exodus from the overcrowded countryside will necessitate cities of grotesque size—Calcutta, now a cesspool of three to five millions, threatens us by the year 2000 with a prospective population of from thirty to sixty millions.

These horrific figures spell one importunate message: haste. That is the **mene mene, tekel upharsin** written on the walls of government planning offices around the world. Even if the miracle of the loop is realized—the new contraceptive device that promises the first real breakthrough in population control—we must set ourselves for at least another generation of rampant increase.

But how to achieve haste? How to convince the silent and disbelieving men, how to break through the distrustful glances of women in black shawls, how to overcome the overt hostility of landlords, the opposition of the Church, the petty bickerings of military cliques, the black-marketeering of commercial dealers? I suspect there is only one way. The conditions of backwardness must be attacked with the passion, the ruthlessness, and the messianic fury of a jehad, a Holy War. Only a campaign of an intensity and singlemindedness that must approach the ludicrous and the unbearable offers the chance to ride roughshod over the resistance of the rich and the poor alike and to open the way for the forcible implantation of those modern attitudes and techniques without which there will be no escape from the misery of underdevelopment.

I need hardly add that the cost of this modernization process has been and will be horrendous. If Communism is the great modernizer, it is certainly not a benign agent of change. Stalin may well have exceeded Hitler as a mass executioner. Free inquiry in China has been supplanted by dogma and catechism; even in Russia nothing like freedom of criticism or of personal expression is allowed. Furthermore, the economic cost of industrialization in both countries has been at least as severe as that imposed by primitive capitalism.

Yet one must count the gains as well as the losses. Hundreds of millions who would have been confined to the narrow cells of changeless lives have been liberated from prisons they did not even know existed. Class structures that elevated the flighty or irresponsible have been supplanted by others that have promoted the ambitious and the dedicated. Economic systems that gave rise to luxury and poverty have given way to systems that provide a rough distributional justice. Above all, the prospect of a new future has been opened. It is this that lifts the current ordeal in China above the level of pure horror. The number of human beings in that country who have perished over the past centuries from hunger or neglect, is beyond computation. The present revolution may add its dreadful increment to this number. But it also holds out the hope that China may finally have been galvanized into social, political, and economic attitudes that for the first time make its modernization a possibility.

Two questions must be answered when we dare to risk so favorable a verdict on Communism as a modernizing agency. The first is whether the result is worth the cost, whether the possible—by no means assured—escape from underdevelopment is worth the lives that will be squandered to achieve it.

I do not know how one measures the moral price of historical victories or how one can ever decide that a diffuse gain is worth a sharp and particular loss. I only know that the way in which we ordinarily keep the books of history is wrong. No one is now toting up the balance of the wretches who starve in India, or the peasants of Northeastern Brazil who live in the swamps on crabs, or the undernourished and permanently stunted children of Hong Kong or Honduras. Their sufferings go unrecorded, and are not present to counterbalance the scales when the furies of revolution strike down their victims. Barrington Moore has made a nice calculation that bears on this problem. Taking as the weight in one pan the 35,000 to 40,000 persons who lost their lives—mainly for no fault of theirs—as a result of the Terror during the French Revolution, he asks what would have been the death rate from preventable starvation and injustice under the **ancien régime** to balance the scales.

"Offhand," he writes, "it seems unlikely that this would be very much below the proportion of .0010 which [the] figure of 40,000 yields when set against an estimated population of 24 million."[2]

It is unjust to charge the ancien régime in Russia with ten million preventable deaths? I think it not unreasonable. To charge the authorities in pre-revolutionary China with equally vast and preventable degradations? Theodore White, writing in 1946, had this to say: ". . . some scholars think that China is perhaps the only country in the world where the people eat less, live more bitterly, and are clothed worse than they were five hundred years ago."[3]

I do not recommend such a calculus of corpses—indeed, I am aware of the license it gives to the unscrupulous—but I raise it to show the onesidedness of our protestations against the brutality and violence of revolutions. In this regard, it is chastening to recall the multitudes who have been killed or mutilated by the Church which is now the first to protest against the excesses of Communism.

But there is an even more terrible second question to be asked. It is clear beyond doubt, however awkward it may be for our moralizing propensities, that historians excuse horror that succeeds; and that we write our comfortable books of moral philosophy, seated atop a mound of victims—slaves, serfs, laboring men and women, heretics, dissenters—who were crushed in the course of preparing the way for our triumphal entry into existence. But at least we are here to vindicate the carnage. What if we were not? What if the revolutions grind flesh and blood and produce nothing, if the end of the convulsion is not exhilaration but exhaustion, not triumph but defeat?

Before this possibility—which has been realized more than once in history—one stands mute. Mute, but not paralyzed. For there is the necessity of calculating what is likely to happen in the absence of the revolution whose prospective excesses hold us back. Here one must weigh what has been done to remedy underdevelopment—and what has not been done—in the past twenty years; how much time there remains before the population flood enforces its own ultimate solution; what is the likelihood of bringing modernization without the frenzied assault that Communism seems most capable of mounting. As I make this mental calculation I arrive at an answer which is even more painful than that of revolution. I see the alternative as the continuation, without substantial relief—and indeed with a substantial chance of deterioration—of the misery and meanness of life as it is now lived in the sinkhole of the world's backward regions.

I have put the case for the necessity of revolution as strongly as possible, but I must now widen the options beyond the stark alternatives I have posed. To begin with, there are areas of the world where the immediate tasks are so far-reaching that little more can be expected for some decades than the primary missions of national identification and unification. Most of the new African states fall into this category. These states may suffer capitalist, Communist, Fascist, or other kinds of regimes during the remainder of this century, but whatever the nominal ideology in the saddle, the job at hand will be that of military and political nation-making.

There is another group of nations, less easy to identify, but much more important in the scale of events, where my analysis also does not apply. These are countries where the pressures of population growth seem sufficiently mild, or the existing political and social framework sufficiently adaptable, to allow for the hope of considerable progress without resort to violence. Greece, Turkey, Chile, Argentina, Mexico, may be representatives of nations in this precarious but enviable situation. Some of them, incidentally, have already had revolutions of modernizing intent—fortunately for them in a day when the United States was not so frightened or so powerful as to be able to repress them.

In other words, the great arena of desperation to which the revolutionizing impetus of Communism seems most applicable is primarily the crowded land masses and archipelagoes of Southeast Asia and the impoverished areas of Central and South America. But even here, there is the possibility that the task of modernization may be undertaken by non-Communist elites. There is always the example of indigenous, independent leaders who rise up out of nowhere to overturn the established framework and to galvanize the masses—a Gandhi, a Martí, a pre-1958 Castro. Or there is that fertile ground for the breeding of national leaders—the army, as witness Ataturk or Nasser, among many.[4]

Thus there is certainly no inherent necessity that the revolutions of modernization be led by Communists. But it is well to bear two thoughts in mind when we consider the likely course of non-Communist revolutionary sweeps. The first is the nature of the mobilizing appeal of any successful revolutionary elite. Is it the austere banner of saving and investment that waves over the heads of the shouting marchers in Jakarta and Bombay, Cairo and Havana? It most certainly is not. The banner of economic development is that of nationalism, with its promise of personal immortality and collective majesty. It seems beyond question that a feverish nationalism will charge the atmosphere of any nation, Communist or not, that tries to make the Great Ascent—and as a result we must expect the symptoms of nationalism along with the disease: exaggerated zenophobia, a thin-skinned national sensitivity, a search for enemies as well as a glorification of the state.

These symptoms, which we have already seen in every quarter of the globe, make it impossible to expect easy and amicable relations between the developing states and the colossi of the developed world. No conceivable response on the part of America or Europe or, for that matter, Russia, will be able to play up to the vanities or salve the irritations of the emerging nations, much less satisfy their demands for help. Thus, we must anticipate an anti-American, or anti-Western, possibly even anti-white animus from any nation in the throes of modernization, even if it is not parroting Communist dogma.

Then there is a second caution as to the prospects for non-Communist revolutions. This is the question of what ideas and policies will guide their revolutionary efforts. Revolutions, especially if their whole orientation is to the future, require philosophy equally as much as force. It is here, of course, that Communism finds its special strength. The vocabulary in which it speaks—a vocabulary of class domination, of domestic and international exploitation—is rich in meaning to the backward nations. The view of history it espouses provides the support of historical inevitability to the fallible efforts of struggling leaders. Not least, the very dogmatic certitude and ritualistic repetition that stick in the craw of the Western observer offer the psychological assurances on which an unquestioning faith can be maintained.

If a non-Communist elite is to persevere in tasks that will prove Sisyphean in difficulty, it will also have to offer a philosophical interpretation of its role as convincing and elevating, and a diagnosis of social and economic requirements as sharp and simplistic, as that of Communism. Further, its will to succeed at whatever cost must be as firm as that of the Marxists. It is not impossible that such a philosophy can be developed, more or less independent of formal Marxian conceptions. It is likely, however, to resemble the creed of Communism far more than that of the West. Political liberty, economic freedom, and constitutional law

may be the great achievements and the great issues of the most advanced nations, but to the least developed lands they are only dim abstractions, or worse, rationalizations behind which the great powers play their imperialist tricks or protect the privileges of their monied classes.

Thus, even if for many reason we should prefer the advent of non-Communist modernizing elites, we must realize that they too will present the United States with programs and policies antipathetic to much that America "believes in" and hostile to America as a world power. The leadership needed to mount a jehad against backwardness—and it is my main premise that only a Holy War will begin modernization in our time—will be forced to expound a philosophy that approves authoritarian and collectivist measures at home and that utilizes as the target for its national resentment abroad the towering villains of the world, of which the United States is now Number One.

All this confronts American policymakers and public opinion with a dilemma of a totally unforeseen kind. On the one hand we are eager to assist in the rescue of the great majority of mankind from conditions that we recognize as dreadful and ultimately dangerous. On the other hand, we seem to be committed, especially in the underdeveloped areas, to a policy of defeating Communism wherever it is within our military capacity to do so, and of repressing movements that might become Communist if they were allowed to follow their internal dynamics. Thus, we have on the one side the record of Point Four, the Peace Corps, and foreign aid generally; and on the other, Guatemala, Cuba, the Dominican Republic, and now Vietnam.

That these two policies might be in any way mutually incompatible, that economic development might contain revolutionary implications infinitely more far-reaching than those we have so blandly endorsed in the name of rising expectations, that Communism or a radical national collectivism might be the only vehicles for modernization in many key areas of the world—these are dilemmas we have never faced. Now I suggest that we do face them, and that we begin to examine in a serious way ideas that have hitherto been considered blasphemous, if not near-traitorous.

Suppose that most of Southeast Asia and much of Latin America were to go Communist, or to become controlled by revolutionary governments that espoused collectivist ideologies and vented extreme anti-American sentiments. Would this constitute a mortal threat to the United States?

I think it fair to claim that the purely **military** danger posed by such an eventuality would be slight. Given the present and prospective capabilities of the backward world, the addition of hundreds of millions of citizens to the potential armies of Communism would mean nothing when there was no way of deploying them against us. The prospect of an invasion by Communist hordes—the specter that frightened Europe after World War II with some (although retrospectively, not too much) realism—would be no more than a phantasm when applied to Asia or South America or Africa.

More important, the nuclear or conventional military power of Communism would not be materially increased by the armaments capacities of these areas for many years. By way of indication, the total consumption of energy of all kinds (in terms of coal equivalent) for Afghanistan, Bolivia, Brazil, Burma, Ceylon, Colombia, Costa Rica, Dominican Republic, Ecuador, El Salvador, Ethiopia, Guatemala, Haiti, Honduras, India, Indonesia, Iran, Iraq, Korea, Lebanon, Nicaragua, Pakistan, Paraguay, Peru, Philippines, U.A.R., Uruguay, and Venezuela is less than that annually consumed by West Germany alone. The total steel output of these countries is one-tenth of U.S. annual production. Thus, even the total communization of the backward world would not effectively alter the present balance of military strength in the world.

However small the military threat, it is undeniably true that a Communist or radical collectivist engulfment of these countries would cost us the loss of billions of dollars of capital invested there. Of our roughly $50 billions in overseas investment, some $10 billions are in mining, oil, utility, and manufacturing facilities in Latin America, some $4 billions in Asia including the Near East, and about $2 billions in Africa. To lose these assets would deal a heavy blow to a number of large corporations, particularly in oil, and would cost the nation as a whole the loss of some $3 or $4 billions a year in earnings from those areas.

A Marxist might conclude that the economic interests of a capitalist nation would find such a prospective loss insupportable, and that it would be "forced" to go to war. I do not think this is a warranted assumption, although it is undoubtedly a risk. Against a Gross National Product that is approaching ¾ of a trillion dollars and with total corporate assets over $1.3 trillions, the loss of even the whole $16 billions in the vulnerable areas should be manageable economically. Whether such a takeover could be resisted politically—that is,

whether the red flag of Communism could be successfully waved by the corporate interests—is another question. I do not myself believe that the corporate elite is particularly war-minded—not nearly so much so as the military or the congressional—or that corporate seizures would be a suitable issue for purposes of drumming up interventionist sentiment.

By these remarks I do not wish airily to dismiss the dangers of a Communist avalanche in the backward nations. There would be dangers, not least those of an American hysteria. Rather, I want only to assert that the threats of a military or economic kind would not be insuperable, as they might well be if Europe were to succumb to a hostile regime.

But is that not the very point? it will be asked. Would not a Communist success in a few backward nations lead to successes in others, and thus by degrees engulf the entire world, until the United States and perhaps Europe were fortresses beseiged on a hostile planet?

I think the answer to this fear is twofold. First, as many beside myself have argued, it is now clear that Communism, far from constituting a single unified movement with a common aim and dovetailing interests, is a movement in which similarities of economic and political structure and ideology are more than outweighed by divergencies of national interest and character. Two bloody wars have demonstrated that in the case of capitalism, structural similarities between nations do not prevent mortal combat. As with capitalism, so with Communism. Russian Communists have already been engaged in skirmishes with Polish and Hungarian Communists, have nearly come to blows with Yugoslavia, and now stand poised at the threshold of open fighting with China. Only in the mind of the **Daily News** (and perhaps still the State Department) does it seem possible, in the face of this spectacle, to refer to the unified machinations of "international Communism" or the "Sino-Soviet bloc."

The realities, I believe, point in a very different direction. A world in which Communist governments were engaged in the enormous task of trying to modernize the worst areas of Asia, Latin America, and Africa would be a world in which sharp differences of national interest were certain to arise within these continental areas. The outlook would be for frictions and conflicts to develop among Communist nations with equal frequency as they developed between those nations and their non-Communist neighbors. A long period of jockeying for power and command over resources, rather than anything like a unified sharing of power and resources, seems unavoidable in the developing continents. This would not preclude a continuous barrage of anti-American propaganda, but it would certainly impede a movement to exert a coordinated Communist influence over these areas.

Second, it seems essential to distinguish among the causes of dangerous national and international behavior those that can be traced to the tenets of Communism and those that must be located elsewhere. "Do not talk to me about Communism and capitalism," said a Hungarian economist with whom I had lunch this winter. "Talk to me about rich nations and poor ones."

I think it is wealth and poverty, and not Communism or capitalism, that establishes much of the tone and tension of international relations. For that reason I would expect Communism in the backward nations (or national collectivism, if that emerges in the place of Communism) to be strident, belligerent, and insecure. If these regimes fail—as they may—their rhetoric may become hysterical and their behavior uncontrolled, although of small consequence. But if they succeed, which I believe they can, many of these traits should recede. Russia, Yugoslavia, or Poland are simply not to be compared, either by way of internal pronouncement or external behavior, with China, or, on a smaller scale, Cuba. Modernization brings, among other things, a waning of the stereotypes, commandments, and flagellations so characteristic of (and so necessary to) a nation engaged in the effort to alter itself from top to bottom. The idiom of ceaseless revolution becomes less relevant—even faintly embarrassing—to a nation that begins to be pleased with itself. Then, too, it seems reasonable to suppose that the vituperative quality of Communist invective would show some signs of abating were the United States to modify its own dogmatic attitude and to forego its own wearisome clichés about the nature of Communism.

I doubt there are many who will find these arguments wholly reassuring. They are not. It would be folly to imagine that the next generation or two, when Communism or national collectivism in the underdeveloped areas passes through its jehad stage, will be a time of international safety. But as always in these matters, it is only by a comparison with the alternatives that one can choose the preferable course. The prospect that I have offered as a plausible scenario of the future must be placed against that which results from a pursuit of our present course. And here I see two dangers of even greater magnitude: (1) the prospect of many more Vietnams, as radical movements assert themselves in other areas of the world; and (2) a continuation of the present inability of the most impoverished areas to modernize, with the prospect of an eventual human catastrophe on an unimaginable scale.

Nevertheless, there is a threat in the specter of a Communist or near-Communist supremacy in the underdeveloped world. It is that the rise of Communism would signal the end of capitalism as the dominant world order, and would force the acknowledgment that America no longer constituted the model on which the future of world civilization would be mainly based. In this way, as I have written before, the existence of Communism frightens American capitalism as the rise of Protestantism frightened the Catholic Church, or the French Revolution the English aristocracy.

It is, I think, the fear of losing our place in the sun, of finding ourselves at bay, that motivates a great deal of the anti-Communism on which so much of American foreign policy seems to be founded. In this regard I note that the nations of Europe, most of them profoundly more conservative than America in their social and economic dispositions, have made their peace with Communism far more intelligently and easily than we, and I conclude that this is in no small part due to their admission that they are no longer the leaders of the world.

The great question in our own nation is whether we can accept a similar scaling down of our position in history. This would entail many profound changes in outlook and policy. It would mean the recognition that Communism, which may indeed represent a retrogressive movement in the West, where it should continue to be resisted with full energies, may nonetheless represent a progressive movement in the backward areas, where its advent may be the only chance these areas have of escaping misery. Collaterally, it means the recognition that "our side" has neither the political will, nor the ideological wish, nor the stomach for directing those changes that the backward world must make if it is ever to cease being backward. It would undoubtedly entail a more isolationist policy for the United States vis-à-vis the developing continents, and a greater willingness to permit revolutions there to work their way without our interference. It would mean in our daily political life the admission that the ideological battle of capitalism and Communism had passed its point of usefulness or relevance, and that religious diatribe must give way to the pragmatic dialogue of the age of science and technology.

I do not know how to estimate the chances of effecting such deepseated changes in the American outlook. It may be that the pull of vested interests, the inertia of bureaucracy, plus a certain lurking fundamentalism that regards Communism as an evil which admits of no discussion—the anti-Christ —will maintain America on its present course, with consequences that I find frightening to contemplate. But I believe that our attitudes are not hopelessly frozen. I detect, both above and below, signs that our present view of Communism is not longer wholly tenable and that it must be replaced with a new assessment if we are to remain maneuverable in action and cogent in discourse.

Two actions may help speed along this long overdue modernization of our own thought. The first is a continuation of the gradual thawing and convergence of American and Russian views and interests—a rapprochement that is proceeding slowly and hesitantly, but with a discernible momentum. Here the initiative must come from Russia as well as from ourselves.

The other action is for us alone to take. It is the public airing of the consequences of our blind anti-Communism for the underdeveloped world. It must be said aloud that our present policy prefers the absence of development to the chance for Communism—which is to say that we prefer hunger and want and the existing inadequate assaults against the causes of hunger and want to any regime that declares its hostility to capitalism. There are strong American currents of humanitarianism that can be directed as a counterforce to this profoundly antihumanitarian view. But for this counterforce to become mobilized it will be necessary to put fearlessly the outrageous question with which I began: Is the United States fundamentally opposed to economic development?

topic 23

black skins, brown skins, red skins: the hyphenated americans

To be dark skinned: Only those whose skin pigmentation is other than white can comprehend the full poignancy of the Black Panther's anguished lament.

> I did all the right things. I got a job and a car, and I was wear-
> ing a suit and getting good pay . . . [but] I might as well have
> had my hairguard on and my purple pants, because when I
> walked down the street I was just another nigger . . . see . . .
> just another nigger [Don Cox, Black Panther Field Marshall].

Whether they are brown or red or black, and no matter what their occupational and educational levels, those whose skin is not white are continually confronted in one way or another by the seemingly ineradicable wall of racism that effectively thwarts full partici- pation in a way of life taken for granted by all but a handful of the white-skinned majority. Prejudice, rejection, and hostility are a way of life for them. So is powerlessness.

In a very real sense they are domestic colonials—third-world peoples at home. They too have been seduced by a revolution of rising expectations—Supreme Court decisions that have "guaranteed" them legal and educational equality, labor-union assurances of equal opportunities, and the dazzling promises of political campaign speeches. The failure, relative or absolute, of their aspirations has fostered the gnawing suspicion that their dreams will never come true.

To be a dark-skinned American is to be a hyphenated American, a marginal man who is neither fully accepted nor absolutely rejected by the dominant society. But to be a hyphenated American today is a different thing from being yesterday's Irish- or Italo- or Polish-American. For one thing, the immigrant Americans were not, like the Afro- American and the Indian, a conqurered people. Although many immigrants were be- wildered and demoralized by their sordid working and living conditions, their children and their grandchildren have by and large been able to make the leap to the comforts of middle-class life. No so for the vast majority of our dark-skinned minorities. Even the few, blacks in particular, who have "made it" in economic or occupational terms have been repeatedly rebuffed in social and psychological terms by "whitey" or "Charlie," by "the man."

What, then, is the answer? How are we to shatter the vicious circle of unemployment or underemployment; of grinding poverty; of dilapidated, overcrowded, unheated homes in decaying barrios, reservations, and slums; of large, undernourished, and often fatherless families, of children who are quickly defined as school failures and then quit school, thus depriving themselves of the only effective avenue to occupational and economic mobility; and, above all, of institutionalized prejudice and racism that denies social, legal, and interpersonal equality?

Three of the five articles in this section relate to blacks, but much that is said in each may be generalized to America's second most populous minority, the Mexican-American, and to its oldest inhabitants, the Indians. Charles Hamilton's essay reminds us that the white radical as much as the white liberal and moderate has a great deal to learn about the plight and the psychology of the black—as well as about the most pragmatic scenario for progress. In their article, Frances Piven and Richard Cloward ask whether truly effective gains are in the offing for the black in the face of increasingly organized and potent resistance on the part of white special-interest blocs. Richard Hatcher, one of the nation's first Negro mayors, compares the various options open to Afro-Americans—violent confrontation, geographic separation, or coexistence—and opts for the latter.

The final two selections relating, respectively, to the American Indian and the Chicano, are of a piece with the first three in their assessment of the odds confronting the minority American in his efforts to escape his underdog plight. The authors of "Where the Real Poverty Is" document the fact that the Indian's situation is the most abject of all—and perhaps the most nearly hopeless. Carey McWilliams points out that the Anglo world with which the Mexican-American must grapple is just as hostile and resistant to change as the white man's world is to the native American and "the man's" is to the black.

chapter 54
the black revolution: a primer for white liberals
charles v. hamilton

Among the Americans who have been most confused, distressed, and even disgusted by recent manifestations of the Black Revolution are many of those whites who have traditionally been known as liberals, and who have long been committed to the betterment of race relations and the attainment of civil rights in such fields as employment, education, and housing.

By word and deed, Black Power advocates—and I am one—have brought tension, uncertainty, and pain to the ranks of liberals. A few liberals have become active, outspoken opponents of the Black Revolution. Many are washing their hands entirely of "the race issue." Still others, while maintaining their commitment to civil rights, are plainly perplexed by the new issues raised by black militants.

It is an uncomfortable state of affairs, and one that is often depicted as dangerous to society. Yet I believe that the processes now at work can lead to constructive results—provided we are willing to examine those processes, understand them, and adapt ourselves to the changes that may be necessary.

In attempting to assess, briefly, some aspects of the Black Revolution that have proven so troublesome to white liberals, I will try not to repeat

From **The Progressive**, January 1969. Reprinted by permission.

the points made by James Farmer in his article, "Are White Liberals Obsolete in the Black Struggle?" in **The Progressive** for January, 1968. I am in full agreement with those points. My comments will attempt to extend Mr. Farmer's discussion.

White liberals should recognize that their discomfort is well-founded: The Black Revolution challenges—and, indeed, rejects—many of the values they hold dear. To an extent that even most liberals fail to recognize, these values have been broadly accepted by much (though not all) of American society. They are the values of individual freedom and equality, founded on John Locke's doctrine that man is basically rational, capable of knowing his self-interest and capable of reaching an accommodation based on that self-interest.

In the realm of race relations, these principles are articulated in terms of color blindness. ("We don't hire on the basis of color; we hire on the basis of merit.") Racial integration is regarded as a highly desirable goal and one that is consciously sought.

Politics, in the liberal tradition, is seen as a protracted process. Men bargain, negotiate, and ultimately reach a compromise. Consensus is presumed, and political conflict is confined to certain predetermined rules of the game. Change is expected to be gradual, and the goal of objectivity is sought. Passion and subjectivity are eschewed. Considerable reliance is placed on discussion, debate—dialogue.

There is an assumption that social problems can be resolved, especially if all parties are sincere and work "within the system."

There is an assumption, too, that "law" must be obeyed, and that "law" (meaning, of course, particular legal statutes) is made by legitimate processes. The authority of law-making bodies is not to be questioned; their particular decrees and statutes, perhaps, but not their fundamental authority to issue such decrees and statutes.

If one wishes to change the particular outputs, one does so "legally"—that is, by resort to the courts and the ballot box, primarily, and by pressure-group lobbying in the legislature, although this last approach is suspect; it smacks of undue favors and "dirty politics." Liberal concern about "dirty politics" has led to a spate of reforms aimed at democratizing the political process: referendum, initiative, recall; party primaries; blue-ribbon reform candidates; antipatronage measures. (It has been pointed out too infrequently that many of these liberal reforms have operated against the interests of masses of black people.)

All this is part of the liberal approach to politics in America. And black Americans have for years subscribed to this egalitarian, libertarian orientation. Their goal has been to enter the mainstream of the American polity by pursuing the liberal principle of legitimacy. But after years of fashioning alliances with liberals along these lines, the black masses find themselves confronted with the fact that they have not only failed to improve their condition, but that they have steadily lost ground in relation to the progress of whites.

The various educational systems, in the more liberal North as well as in the South, have failed to come to terms with the cultural (as well as the educational) needs of black children. Northern liberals showed no concern about the deficiencies in textbooks until black parents and students began to call this to their attention. The liberals had assumed the superior efficacy of **their** approach to education, and were convinced it would behoove black children to take advantage of it—even if they had to be bused across town to do so. It never occurred to those white liberals, that their standardized tests might be culturally biased. And even if they were, were not the little black children "culturally disadvantaged," "slow learners," "high risks"?

The liberals never gave much thought to the ultimate effect on black people of years of urban renewal; many were on the faculties of universities using urban renewal to relieve their "land-locked" condition. Some liberal professors raised their voice against the destruction of black neighborhoods. But most of the social scientists, more interested in their methodology and their correlations than in the social product (some call it value-free social science), took no interest in black community participation in urban renewal decision-making.

Today, some of these faculties are trying to rush relevancy by adding courses dealing with black America to their curricula. They are groping to understand the demands of black student groups on the campuses, and many of the white liberal professors now find they are simply not relevant to a vast segment, an important segment, of this society—precisely because **their** (not just the students') education has been blindly incomplete.

Black people have been complacent about police brutality for years, and many white liberals did not get "up-tight" about this issue until they began protesting against the war in Vietnam and experiencing the brutality themselves. Antiwar demonstrators have often described police tactics as "unbelievable," but they have been quite believable to black people. I would suggest that if those same white liberals were to start protesting this country's policies and practices toward South Africa, they would rub up against the same firm billy clubs. It is most instructive, incidentally, that white liberal America is not overly concerned about the economic support of South Africa's apartheid system offered by interests in this country. But this may become the next liberal fad (when the Vietnam war is over).

The point I want to make is that the white liberals' approach to problems of race in this country have not been as viable as many would like to think. Their agenda simply has not been as enlightened as a first guess would indicate. And this has been the case largely because they have been operating under a principle of legitimacy not particularly applicable to the development of black people. The general approach has specific relevance for a relatively secure, relatively "anchored" group, and it is capable of manipulating the system to permit a few to make it—as a few blacks have.

White liberals have never come to terms with the phenomenon of **institutionalized** racism in this country. It was Stokely Carmichael who broached this subject in the present-day context, and he was **followed** by the President's Commission on Civil Disorders (Kerner Commission). It is small wonder that few black people could get excited about the commission's report. It merely articulated what many of us had been saying for years, and if many white liberals did not know it, then it is apparent they were operating on a different set of principles and premises.

I am suggesting that black people are pursuing a principle of legitimacy outside the traditional liberal framework—one that is concerned with **group** development, and that does not presume the existence of a consensus, especially on matters regarding race. This principle is very color conscious. ("We want black principals to head schools in the black communities.") Racial integration is not regarded as a matter of immediate, high priority, because it is recognized that before any group can enter the open society it must first close ranks. Prolonged debate, discussion—dialogue—are luxuries which frequently cannot be afforded.

This principle is most usually associated with a society on the make, with a people coming out from under colonial rule into political independence and economic development. In the present-day American context, it is manifested in demands for black community control of schools and law enforcement agencies; in such moves as black ownership of businesses in the black community.

Pursuing this principle, black people cannot assume the Lockeian notion of the rationality of man; in fact, in regard to race, they must assume that Western, Anglo-Saxon man might well be irreconcilably irrational. Politics as a protracted process becomes only a frustrating exercise, especially when one realizes the extent to which black people have been **systematically** excluded from decision-making.

The goal of the Black Revolution is development, and those institutions in society which put as much stock in procedures as in performance must be looked upon as obstacles to that goal.

Black people understand that the best way to pursue the fulfillment of their potentiality is to start from a firm base of self-awareness and identity. When liberals tell them to forget race and think of themselves only as Americans, they know that this is an invitation which only those in power can entertain—an invitation to cultural absorption. And such absorption will occur while other groups in the society protect and maintain their own cultural identity.

It is important to point out that in examining the contrast between liberal values and those of the Black Revolution, I am discussing two principles of **legitimacy**: One is not legitimate and the other illegitimate. Rather, one is more valid than

the other for a previously colonized people set on rapid social change and development. The concerns and motivations of such people often simply do not coincide with those of people proceeding under an egalitarian, libertarian principle. Herein, I suggest, lies the major tension between white liberals and advocates of Black Power. Black Power groups must be viewed as new, relevant intermediary groups for a people who no longer trust the established, traditional, frequently liberal-oriented associations.

Should one conclude that black people have more in common with white conservatives than with liberals? Conservatives oppose busing and are resistant to open housing; they see Black Power as a modern-day extension of Booker T. Washington— a misreading of both Mr. Washington and Black Power.

A close examination will reveal, however, that ultimately the advocates of Black Power still have more in common with liberals than with conservatives. The former recognize, for example, the importance of the federal government's role in the development of black communities—a role as crucial, in its way, as the input of external economic resources and technical assistance for the development of previously colonized countries. Conservatives, with their basically anticentrist and antigovernment views (i.e., antigovernment for all but themselves), offer no useful partnership to the Black Revolution. They see Black Power as decentralist, when, in fact, it is an effort to build a more meaningful central relationship.

There is nothing irreconcilable about black people pursuing their own principle of legitimacy and subsequently taking their place as full-fledged members of the American pluralist society. This process, in itself, would lead to a vast transformation of the system. I see this process as comparable to new nations of Africa and Asia gaining their political independence, then adopting a particular principle of development and ultimately assuming their places as developed members of the society of nations.

The more dynamic the process of social change and the more we are personally involved in it, the more difficult it is to see such change in its overall, long-term developmental stages—and the easier it is to "lose our cool." But such is the challenge to those who would understand system transformation in a modern, industrial, heterogeneous society and who would create—during that delicate period of transformation—necessary and vital forms of communication and cooperation.

chapter 55
what chance
for
black power?
frances fox piven
and richard a. cloward

If there is a lesson in America's pluralistic history, it is that the ability of an outcaste minority to advance in the face of majority prejudices partly depends upon its ability to develop countervailing power. It is extraordinary that so conventional an idea has evoked so bitter a controversy in the civil rights community. For, stripped of rhetoric, the idea of "black power" merely emphasizes the need to augment Negro influence by developing separatist institutions, ranging from economic enterprise to political organization.

Older civil rights organizations take umbrage at the separatist impulse because it appears to repudiate the principle of integration. Considering that ethnic labor unions, ethnic political machines, and other ethnic institutions have been essential to the rise of various minorities, it is puzzling to hear it said that Negroes must restrain themselves from following the same course. Indeed, those institutions in the black community which are "integrated"—whether political organizations, the rackets, or social welfare agencies—actually contribute to black impotence, for they are integrated only in the sense that they are dominated by whites and serve white interests.

Those who are dismayed by the separatist

From The New Republic, 158, March 30, 1968. Reprinted by permission of The New Republic, ©1968, Harrison-Blaine of New Jersey, Inc.

position also fear that it will alienate liberal and labor allies. Blacks are a minority, to be sure, and cannot go it alone. But neither will they ever be more than a nominal participant in coalitions unless they are better organized; rather, their leaders will serve mostly to legitimize programs from which others benefit. An organized group need not sit about debating the pros and cons of seeking allies; it will be sought out by others, and offered genuine concessions because it has strength to bring to any alliance. Those who now urge color-blind coalition are unable to show why the black poor would have more effective leverage in future alliances than they have had in the past.

Before damning black power for its principles or dooming it for its strategy, one should look at what the Negro has so far achieved without power, and what the future holds if his powerlessness persists.

The upheavals which are sometimes called "the Negro revolution"—the civil rights protests, the spreading violence in the cities, and the controversy over black power—are reflections of economic changes. When old patterns are rapidly undermined, dislocating masses of people, disorder often follows.

No group has been more acutely affected by technological change than the Negro, although the middle class and the poor have been affected quite differently. Educated Negroes are in demand in professional, scientific, and technical occupations because of the growing need for skilled manpower. Since the end of World War II, the proportion of Negro families earning between $5,000 and $7,000 (in 1965 dollars adjusted for price changes) almost trebled and now approximates the proportion of whites in that income class. The proportion earning between $7,000 and $10,000 did treble and is now about two-thirds of the proportion of whites in that income group.

It was this rising class that launched the civil rights movement, especially the young of a newly arriving Southern bourgeoisie. As is often the case, ascending economic fortunes had themselves generated expectations which outpaced the actual rate of advance. Thus Negro colleges, once training grounds for a segregated elite, suddenly disgorged cadres to lead boycotts, freedom rides, and sit-ins. Nor was this economic discrepancy the only source of discontent. A segregated society also deprived them of the symbols of prestige which normally accompany higher economic status. Spurred by these status discrepancies, the movement focused much of its energy on desegregating lunch counters and public accommodations.

Much of what was aspired to has been achieved —the legal symbolic representations that American institutions were made "for whites only" are crumbling. That these features of our social life are collapsing so quickly (as these things go) is a mark of the extent to which they had become outmoded as a result of economic changes.

■

For the mass of black poor, however, the technological revolution has had less happy consequences. Although the proportion of poor families has dropped considerably in the past two decades, more than half of the black families in America still have incomes of less than $5,000, and one in four subsists on less than $3,000. Furthermore, apparent increases in income are often offset by the forced migration to the cities, where it costs more to live. Most ominous, the technological advances which made old patterns of segregation obsolete are also making a substantial segment of the black poor obsolete. Southern Negro sharecroppers, driven off the land by machines, can now eat at a desegregated lunch counter, take a desegregated interstate bus North, and arrive in a city with a fair employment ordinance—but no jobs. The mechanization of the farms they left is

matched in the cities by the automation and decentralization of industry. Wherever black people are concentrated, North or South, true rates of unemployment (both those looking for work and those who have given up) range from 20 to 50 percent.

In the rural South, the more fortunate among the unemployed barely subsist on federal surplus commodities; the less fortunate starve. If they could get on the welfare rolls, people would have a bit of money, but they are kept off by a tangle of exclusionary laws, bureaucratic obstacles, and just plain illegal rejections. Feared at the polls and no longer needed in the fields, they are told to go North. As it happens, the women and children are more likely to get on the welfare rolls in the North, provided that their men "desert" them first. And so unemployed husbands and fathers stand about "in hiding" on every ghetto street corner. Meanwhile welfare administrators and politicans curry public favor by promoting job training for welfare mothers—but not for their men. At that, the women are trained for jobs that don't exist, or won't for long. The work they do get is in low-paid, dead-end jobs: in 1966, Negroes composed 42 percent of the private household work force and 25 percent of nonfarm laborers. Poor blacks, in brief, are being shut out of the economic system. They have progressed from slave labor to cheap labor to no labor at all.

The violence in the cities is the response of the black poor to their new social and economic condition, just as the civil rights protests were the response of the black middle class to their changing condition. It is not that poverty or unemployment produces mass discontent and violence, for if this were so no society could be stable. Rather, massive economic displacement may have a reverberative effect on other institutions, weakening their capacity to regulate sentiments and behavior, and culminating finally in violence.

The most obvious reverberation is the shift of populations from rural to urban areas. Blacks have become an urban people in just two or three decades, and this has set them loose from existing structures of social control. Although a repressive, feudalistic system persists in the South, a great many Negroes have been liberated from it just by no longer being there. Nor have they been absorbed by the main regulatory institutions of the city, especially the economic system. Ghetto institutions, such as churches and political machines, have also not incorporated them. Furthermore, the press of numbers is disrupting traditional accommodations upon which racial peace depends; the boundaries of previously sacrosanct white neighborhoods and schools are being breached, and white political power in city halls is threatened. When tensions rise as institutional controls weaken, the eruption of violence should not be surprising.

The splintering off of a segment of the civil rights movement—symbolized by the raised black fist and the cry of "black power"—is also a response to these upheavals. New conditions of life, by altering mass attitudes, undercut old patterns of leadership. Traditional Negro elites who have maintained their hegemony by serving as the agents of white power and resources are being challenged by new aspirants to leadership whose insistent nationalism reflects the current mood of discontent. And whatever else may be said of its rhetoric —the language of violence and the allusions to revolution—black power, by calling on people to be, feel, think, and act black, is fostering a new sense of community in the ghetto, especially among the young. This is a hopeful trend, for solidarity is one prerequisite to the political power without which the mass of black poor cannot advance economically.

■

There is no doubt that major governmental action will be taken to deal with disruptions in the cities. Corporation executives and mayors, union officials and presidential aspirants—men whose interests are in one way or another threatened by urban disorder—are agreed in demanding federal programs to stem rising municipal costs, "crime in the streets," and riots. But while this "urban coalition" wants to ease urban trouble, the groups it includes have interests quite at odds with those of the black poor. And experience shows that the poor have good reason to be apprehensive about programs formed in their name by the powerful.

To appreciate the grounds for apprehension, look at the differences between government programs for the organized and unorganized poor. In response to the crisis in the thirties, the federal government proclaimed its responsibility for the poor but promulgated legislation favoring those of the urban poor who, already partly organized in unions and political machines, were important to the newly formed Democratic coalition. Political leaders pressed through a series of social welfare measures designed to protect the urban worker—

unemployment compensation, old age and survivors' insurance, and housing subsidies for those with moderate incomes. More important, workers got concessions that nourished their organizations, especially the Wagner Act, which gave them the right to bargain collectively and thus made the growth and stabilization of unions possible—membership expanded from three million in 1930 to 14 million in 1945. In this way, the working classes were able to make gains in the economic system, and to guard governmental programs designed for them.

The poor who lacked political power were left behind. The worst poverty still exists among those who did not win collective bargaining rights by legislation, such as agricultural laborers. In the cities, the still unorganized black masses continue to be victimized by programs ostensibly intended for their benefit. Consider, for example, the public welfare programs enacted in 1935 which promised decent subsistence for everyone; three decades later, the average family of four on ADC (Aid to Dependent Children) gets only $1,800 a year. The Public Housing Act of 1937 proclaimed the goal of providing decent housing for the poor; today there are about 10 million substandard dwelling units in the country, for only 600,000 units of public housing have been constructed. Our national policy of full employment, enunciated by legislation in 1946, has proved to be meaningless rhetoric.

Worse yet, manifestly egalitarian measures have been turned against the poor. Federal agricultural subsidies, established to aid all farmers, actually helped to bankrupt small ones and enrich large ones. The Housing Act of 1949 asserted the right of every American to "a decent and standard dwelling unit," but initiated the Urban Renewal Program that destroyed 350,000 low-rental housing units in the course of reclaiming slum neighborhoods for commercial facilities and better-off residents. Several hundred thousand more low-rental homes were demolished during the same period by public works and federal highway construction—programs also put forward under the banner of improving the urban environment. Indeed, these programs, "for the community as a whole" have succeeded in destroying more low-rental units than government has constructed since the Public Housing Act was passed.

Finally, what concessions the unorganized poor did get actually inhibited their capacity for political action. This is especially true of public welfare and public housing programs in which benefits are made conditonal on complaint behavior by recipients. The poor, dealt with as supplicants by functionaries who can evict them or cut off their checks at will, are rendered more helpless in exchange for the benefits they receive.

New proclamations about action to help the poor are now being made, and new programs discussed. But what reason is there to suppose that these measures will not also be tokenistic, or turned to serve the interests of other groups, or designed to intimidate the recipients still more? For the simple truth is that governmental action has not worked for the unorganized poor and is not likely to work for them in the future unless they become a political force in initiating and shaping it.

■

But the prospects for black urban power, as we have just defined them, rest on the erroneous assumption that American politics are formed by voting numbers alone. The conventions of electoral politics are regularly subverted in many ways. Those already holding power will not yield the spoils of office quickly or easily to new majorities. Even when official representation is achieved, responsiveness by government requires a constituency capable of watching over and pressuring officials. To be sure, blacks will assume nominal power in the cities because of the sheer weight of their numbers; but compared to earlier groups, blacks have few organizational ropes to keep rein on their leaders. Black officials will find themselves confronted by a variety of well-organized white groups —such as unions of public employees—who have the power to obstruct the business of government. They will be pressed to defer to these white interests, and an unorganized black constituency will give them the slack to do it. Although it may be too soon to draw conclusions, the first statements and appointments of Cleveland's newly elected black mayor suggest just such conciliation of whites.

Moreover, local government has been greatly weakened since the heyday of the ethnic urban machine. Localities now collect a mere seven percent of tax revenues, while the federal government collects two-thirds. This fiscal weakness underlies the great vulnerability of local government to national centralized power, reflected both in the schemes for intervention by national corporations and in new encroachments by the federal government under the guise of metropolitan planning.

The national government is using its multitude of existing programs for localities to form a new system of metropolitan-wide bureaucracies. This new level of government will impose federal policies on localities in the course of channeling grants-in-aid to them.

The need for metro administration is commonly justified on the ground that the concentration of people in sprawling urban areas has produced a host of problems—transportation, water supply, pollution control—which transcend narrow municipal boundaries. The solution of these problems is said to require programs planned and implemented on a metropolitan basis. For some problems, perhaps so; however, many urban problems remain unsolved, not for lack of area-wide planning, but for lack of political will. That communities do not apply for federal funds to build public housing needs no explanation beyond local reluctance to house the poor and black. Nevertheless, metro bureaucracies are emerging, and they will supersede the cities just as blacks come to power.

Whose interests will the federal metro agencies reflect? It takes no special acumen to see the answer. Their policies will be formed in deference to the inner-city and suburban whites who are an overwhelming majority in the metro region. Thus programs for the inner city will be designed to protect and ease the ethnic working classes, the residual middle class, and corporate groups with heavy property investments in the core. And there will be suburban services and facilities to meet the needs of decentralizing industry and white residents, whose electoral power now exceeds that of inner-city populations. Judging from the past, programs for blacks will be designed to treat their presumed deficiencies—to engender "good work habits and incentives," strengthen family life, improve mental health.

If the black middle class has so far benefited from technological change, it will prosper even more from the corporate-metro solutions to the urban crisis. To smooth the path of intervention, the black middle class will be absorbed into white corporate and metropolitan agencies. It should not be surprising, therefore, that these new approaches are already being hailed by Negro elites. The rationale given is that they will further integration—metropolitanism is said to be the way to breach the wall between ghetto and suburb in housing and education, and corporate programs the way to promote economic integration. But as metropolitan administrations take control, they are not likely to promote the dispersal of blacks to white neighborhoods in the face of resistance by an area-wide majority; meanwhile, white corporate control will be extended to the ghetto. Thus these new systems will enable whites, even as the ideal of integration is invoked, to maintain political and economic hegemony over the black masses.

The black poor, then, have few prospects for political or economic advancement. Because of the current disruptions, they will get a few concessions to restore tranquility. But once the cities are tranquilized, what then? As we have said, the main chance for black power is in the cities, but the odds are lengthening. If there is a question to be debated, it is not whether the idea of black power is desirable; it is whether the power of this idea can prevail in the face of the continuing centralization of corporate and federal power over the city.

chapter 56
age of a new humanity
richard hatcher

THE MEANING OF BLACK POWER

Black Power: That is what I would like to talk to you about this evening. When Stokely Carmichael shouted "black power" in that Mississippi school yard, he performed a mystic function that some poet must always perform at the proper moment in history. He gave voice, he gave a name to a development in the life of black America which was happening anyway, and which needed naming so that we could talk about it and so that we could think about it. I say he named it rather than created it because the movement towards black power under other names has had a long and honorable past. If it has become the dominant tone of our emotions in the last two or three years, that is only because, like the proverbial snowball, the accretion of time and frustration has turned incipience into actuality, has made of a snowball an avalanche. I want, today, to look at these two words, "black" and "power" from the vantage point of a man who has had some connection with both words. It is beyond dispute that I am black—and I am too modest to say beautiful. It is also true that, for more than a year now, I have held a position with at least a modicum of power. It is a good time, then, at the end of the first year of my administration as Mayor

Reprinted by permission of **Freedomways** magazine, vol. 9, no. 2, 1969. Published at 799 Broadway, New York City.

of Gary to examine what "black power" has meant to me. My blackness has been the dominant fact of my life's experience, as it is the dominant fact of life of every black man in America, perhaps in the world. James Baldwin, with his usual brilliance and cogency, describes the condition in his famous essay "Stranger in the Village" in which he discusses his experience as a black man in a little Swiss village.

For this village, even were it incomparably more remote and incredibly more primitive, is in the West, the West on which I have been so strangely grafted. These people cannot be, from the point of view of power, strangers anywhere in the world. They have made the modern world, in effect, even if they do not know it. The most illiterate among them is related in a way that I am not, to Dante, to Shakespeare, to Michelangelo, da Vinci, Rembrandt and Racine. A cathedral at Chartres says something to them that it cannot say to me, as indeed, with the Empire State Building, should anyone here ever see it. Out of their hymns and dances come Beethoven and Bach. Go back a few centuries, and they are in their full glory; but I am in Africa watching the conquerors arrive.

And because of the white man's rape of Africa, because of the suffering of slavery, because of the

long and barbarous history of segregation and discrimination, black people are strangers in this, the
American Village. And because white people and
white Europeans have developed the ideology of
racism to justify the sociological and historical experiences I have mentioned, I am a stranger in this
village. But, from another point of view, because I
am a man and because I have been reared on the
words, though not the facts, of Christianity and
democracy, I am also an inhabitant, and, in a
strange sort of way, a citizen of the village. Much
of the history of black America is dominated precisely by this contradiction. We have been told one
thing—democracy, freedom—we hold these truths
to be self-evident, that all men are created equal;
we have lived quite another—slavery,the Ku Klux
Klan, white liberals so concerned with black people that they will tell them exactly what they
ought to want, schools that don't teach us, promises from the Supreme Court which turn to ashes in
strikes against Ocean Hill-Brownsville in New York.

And I say to you, that is why we have been
forced to fall back on our own resources, for you
cannot be a stranger always. To be continuously
strange is to pay a psychological price so great that
no people can endure it forever. When black America, then, turns to blackness, to what Africa has
for a long time called Negritude, we have no apologies to make. From the time that I was a little
child, before I ever heard of Othello, or, for that
matter, Shakespeare, I knew I was black. No wonder, then, that as a grown man, I must turn to the
words of Leopold Senghor, the black African poet
from Senegal, or to those of Langston Hughes or
Arna Bontemps, or LeRoi Jones or Gwendolyn
Brooks. From the time that I was a little child, before I ever heard of Beethoven or Bach, I knew I
was black. No wonder, then, that I turn to Jimi
Hendrix and Aretha Franklin, and that I recall with
anger the black American symphony conductor
Dean Dixon, who had to go abroad to practice his
art. From the time that I was a child, and before I
ever heard of Paul Bunyon or George Washington,
I knew that I was black. No wonder, then, that as a
grown man I turned to John Henry and Jomo Ken-
yatta and W. E. B. Du Bois, I will stop being a
stranger, because I will recall that, though a stranger in the village, I have lived here nonetheless; and
I have history here and elsewhere, as in Africa, and
that history will make me less the stranger. We
assert what we are and we may wear a dashiki and
look with favor on a "natural." Being ourselves will
make us less the stranger. We tried being like the
so-called natives and were not allowed to be like

them, so we must turn to our own resources. Baldwin goes on to say that the black man insists by
whatever means he finds at his disposal that the
white man cease to regard him as an exotic rarity
and recognize him as a human being.

And so, my experience with the word "black"
is that of all black people. Being black has made me
a stranger, being black has dominated my life. I
cannot, nor would I wish to reject my blackness,
and so I turn what the white world has attempted
to make into a handicap, precisely into its opposite. Black America is fortunate in that our culture
is more than rich enough so that we can find in
blackness an advantage, a source of pride, a way to
end our estrangement. But there is another side to
this. Even though I may find in Negritude and in
black culture a way not to be so strange any longer,
especially strange to myself, that is not enough. My
estrangement has also included my powerlessness.
I have not only been a stranger in the village but I
have also been a stranger without power. There are
times in history when strangers have had sufficient
power to keep themselves at least supplied with the
necessities for decent living. This has been true of
many who came to these shores as strangers; as,
after a generation or so, the Irish and the Italians
and so on. It has not been the case with black
Americans. Because our strangeness has provided
the others with the chief source for hewing of
wood and the drawing of water, because black people have had no power, because the ideology of
racism has permitted white Americans to think it
natural, we have been exploited and used, deprived
of the minimum wherewithal for a decent life.
Sometimes we have been deprived of our best
brains, all for the aggrandizement and enrichment
of others. And that is why pride in being black is
really not enough for our survival. That is why we
have had increasingly to turn attention to a means
of wresting from the majority, not only a new perception of our humanity, but also a new place in
the nation, so that we can enforce our demands for
the satisfaction of our needs.

This is nothing new. The African chief, Cin-
que, sought power when he led a mutiny on the
slave ship, Amistad, in 1839. And Nat Turner was
quite explicit when he said that the reason for his
revolt was to strike terror into the hearts of the
planters, and thus have the power to establish a
black community in the dismal swamp. L'Ouver-
ture knew about the need for power and so did, in
more recent history, such often unheeded thinkers
as W. E. B. Du Bois and Paul Robeson, or for that
matter, Marcus Garvey. There is nothing new in the

search for power by black Americans. What is new, perhaps, is that our search has been intensified because we have combined pride in being black with that search for power; and that we have found, in various stages of our experience, power shared with the majority does not seem to work. Power means, quite simply, a force strong enough so that you can get whatever it is you need. Let me recall that in the last two decades we have tried all sorts of ways of achieving power. The Brown Decision by the United States Supreme Court concerning equal education represented an effort to use the power of the courts to win needed improvement in the lives of black children. We won that skirmish, but we have discovered almost fifteen years laters that there was not enough strength in the **power** of the courts to guarantee any fundamental change in the education of black children. Legal power, which helped a little, did not help enough.

Dr. Martin Luther King tried another form of power. Beginning with the Montgomery bus boycott of 1955, Dr. King tried with all of his skill and all of his dedication—indeed he gave his life for it—to use the nonviolent power of black masses to achieve their needs. An eloquent man, he said it much better than I can hope to do. In writing for **Liberation** magazine in 1959, Dr. King said, "There is more power in socially organized masses on the march than there is in guns in the hands of a desperate few. All history teaches us that, like a turbulent ocean beating great cliffs into fragments of rock, the determined movement of people incessantly demanding their rights always disintegrates the old order. This is the social lever which will force open the door to freedom. The powerful weapons are the voices, the feet and the bodies of dedicated, united people, moving without rest towards a just goal."

This too, was an expression of black power though we did not then call it such; but this form of power in and of itself was also found inadequate to meet our needs. Nine years after he had written those words Dr. King had fallen to the assassin's bullet. Nine years after he had written those words, though segregation was a little less blatant in the south, though more black people had found their way to the voting booth in the south, the bulk of black America, living in the horror of the crowded, firetrap, haunted ghettos of the north, had not advanced. This society, it would appear, was not prepared to yield easily to the needs of black America, and so the search for a lever, for an effective means of achieving power, had to go on. something that was taught to us by Malcolm X

and LeRoi Jones and Rap Brown and Eldridge Cleaver. We learn that when the stranger allies himself with the so-called natives, to return to Baldwin's metaphor, "It is very hard for the stranger to play anything but a secondary role." In the many struggles black Americans carried on with white people, we found all too often that well-meaning whites nevertheless conceived of us as strangers, assigned to us the role of strangers in our own struggle; and thus, well-meaning white people knew what was good for us better than we did. They knew what our feelings about things ought to be better than we did; and I say that many of these men and women were well-meaning, because history records that they worked very hard and often sacrificed a great deal for our causes. And I cannot forget that it was white Goodman and white Schwerner who died along with black Chaney in the red dirt of Mississippi. But it takes nothing away from their heroism or dedication to say that they were always, willingly or not, the natives and we were always the strangers. To stop being strangers, we have to find the road to power ourselves. Whether or not one fully accepts other aspects of the thought of Frantz Fanon, it is clear that rising black consciousness requires that we be led by our own, determine our own destiny, recognize our own needs, and that white Americans have quite another task to perform, perhaps an impossible one; which is to work to cure the sickness of racism among their own people.

Efforts at achieving power in various forms combined with the rising tide of black self-confidence, then, brings us to the heart of the problem faced by Black America today, and to the heart of my own problems as a man who, as I said, has achieved some modicum of power. It is clear that pride in blackness and all that this implies, from a revival of black history and other Afro-American studies to a new appreciation of the beauty of our women, to being led on the road to a better life by black leaders, is an absolute necessity. This we are beginning to do. We have not yet, however, solved the riddle as to what lever can provide the power that we need to wrest a better way of life from the power structure within the total society.

WHAT ARE THE OPTIONS FOR BLACK AMERICANS?

We have a number of options, and I would like to discuss a few of these now, including the one about which I am most knowledgeable. One option is, of course, to leave, to return not only spiritually, but physically to the lands of our African heritage. No doubt, some will choose that solution, but it cannot be a solution for most of us. There are physical problems as to where such a massive migration would go and cultural ones stemming from our distance from African cultures. But there are also other aspects. We own a good part of these United States, not physically, but morally; and our sweat has gone to make the railroads run and to make cotton king; and our brains helped to build Washington, D.C., and make heart transplants possible; our talents have helped enrich the music, the stage, and the poetry of the nation; our blood has been shed in too many wars, including the fiasco in which we are now engaged. So, we have a great investment in this nation, one that we ought not be forced to give up; and our power ought to give us our rightful share in what we have wrought. Therefore, I, for one, choose not to leave.

There is another approach. We can demand a piece of the nation for ourselves. We can demand five or six states as the territory for a black nation, or we can carve out the old ghetto in each city as our own turf. This has possibilities. It has been explored by many thinkers, both black and white, including so thoughtful a man as W. H. Ferry, President of the Center for the Study of Democratic Institutions. Ferry writes in the **Saturday Review** of June 15, 1968, "But what black town wants most, white town cannot give it. Black town wants independence and the authority to run its own affairs. It wants to recover its manhood, self-love, and to develop its ability to conduct a self-reliant community." A successful plan for coexistence, that is, between black town and white town, to use Ferry's terms, will not bring utopia into being in black town. Autonomous, interdependent black town will be no better and no worse than other parts of the urban scene. Blacks can be expected to exploit blacks, even as whites exploit whites. It may be less demeaning to be robbed by a soul brother, but it leaves the belly just as empty.

Speaking of coexistence, I'm sure you've all heard of the situation where the lion and the lamb were put in a cage together to show that coexistence was possible. Each day, people would come by to see the lion and the lamb in the cage together as it was a very amazing thing. Finally, one of the employees there went up to the keeper of the cage and said, "You've just got to explain to me how this can be—how a lion and a lamb can coexist so peacefully together." The man in charge of the cage said, "Well, you see, it's very easy. Every morning we put in a new lamb."

I think that coexistence is possible. I do not reject this form of power either on moral grounds or on grounds of feasibility. I have not seen any evidence within this society that black America can get such community without first achieving the tremendous power necessary to force them into existence. The white power structure, which pinches the pennies from Model Cities plans and Head Start programs will not readily give up control of major sections of New York, Chicago, and Los Angeles. The slum lords who live in pretty suburbs on the profits they make from the hellholes in the ghettos will not turn their hovels over to other owners for the asking. Black towns are intriguing, but they evade the question, for we must, should we decide we want them, first find the power to get them.

Now there is also the **power of violence**, in direct opposition to the kind of power that Dr. King sought to use. I do not wish here to discuss this form of power. Rather, I want to ask about the efficiency of the use of street violence, about its ability to achieve results. Like it or not, violence cannot readily be dismissed as a source of power. It is true beyond dispute that the white section of the nation sat up and listened hard when it heard the fire engines racing to Hough, to Watts, to Harlem, and to Chicago's west side. I am afraid that, to date, this form of power has not paid off very much. White America talks better about what it **ought** to do, but such talk has been around for a long time. It is hardly new. In fact, all that street violence has produced so far is more white talk and burned-out ghettos. The Kerner Report is a very nice piece of rhetoric which has not fed one black mouth. I do not reject violence out of hand but I have yet to see how it becomes a useful level for power.

POLITICAL POWER FOR BLACK AMERICA

Let me turn, finally, to the kind of power that I know most about, and that is **political power** in cities of large black population. I think it is clear in the first place that my election as Mayor of Gary has done something for Gary's black community, insofar as its pride and sense of self are concerned. While we may still be strangers in our village, it surely makes us feel less strange that one of us has been chosen to head the village government. I recall when I was running for office that the questions that were always asked of me were, first of all, "Do you think that we're ready?" And, of course I, at that point, would always quote Tom Mboya, "Ready or not, here we come." The other question was, "Do you really think that you're qualified to be mayor of Gary?" I was very naive at the time and I would always talk about those things that I thought qualified me to be mayor of their community—my education, my training, my experience as a prosecutor, and on and on. But I soon learned that those were not the kinds of qualifications that they were interested in. So then, I got smart and when someone would ask me that question I'd say, "Well, I don't know whether I'm qualified or not but let's talk about some of the other mayors that Gary has had." And I would ask, "Did you know that the first mayor of Gary, a man named Tom Knotts, was elected in 1906, was arrested 14 times in his first two years in office for corruption?" And they would say, "No, I didn't know about that." Then I would say, "Gary had another mayor named Daryl Johnson who was elected mayor of that city and went to prison for four years and came back and was elected mayor of that city again. Did you know that?" They would say, "No, I didn't know about that, either." So then, I would tell them that more recently, we had another mayor who was caught doing something that he should not have been doing and he went to the federal penitentiary for three years and now he's back supporting my opponent. "Did you know about that?" They'd say, "No, I didn't know about that, either." I'd say, "Well, if you compare me to those fellows, I just very well could be the most qualified person ever to run for mayor."

But, because the black people in Gary got themselves together, some good has resulted. Some local efforts are being made to make certain that they will not be exploited quite so mercilessly, that they will get their share of whatever they have coming to the extent that anything is available; but right there is the rub. I may be the Mayor of Gary, but I cannot, by that token, guarantee that black people will share in the unbelievable profits of the United States Steel Corporation which dominates our city's economic life. I am the Mayor of Gary and I cannot stop a war in Vietnam which strains the national treasury to such an extent that only very limited programs are available to the city for the reconstruction of its black community. I am the Mayor of Gary, and I was elected as a Democrat, but I am not able to sway the white Democratic Party so that it will reverse the present trend of national priorities and make the need of the black communities first on the list. I am the Mayor of Gary, but I cannot change the fact that our schools are too poorly funded from state or nation,

or even local sources of revenue, to provide the catch-up educational process the city needs in order to bring our black youngsters up to educational standards. I want to confide a further problem to you. I am the Mayor of Gary and, thus, I am the mayor of all the people of the city, and I would like to do my best for all of them, black or white. But, you know, what I cannot do for black brothers, I cannot do for white people either, try as I might. The black community's needs are infinitely greater, but the white community in our city is not without problems. For the same reasons which prevent me from solving many of the black problems, I cannot solve many of the white ones either. Neither could my white predecessors. Though I have some local political power, it becomes clear to me that this is not enough and that the power structure of this society is not prepared to give up enough of its profits to solve the living problems of blacks or whites.

Although black kids in Gary are badly educated, white ones are not getting nearly what they should, either. Although black communities are devoid of parks and play spaces, white communities do not have adequate park facilities, either. Rumor has it that there are a few white people in Gary who wish to disaffiliate from the municipality, a predominantly white section of the city, because they "don't like what's going on in City Hall." It seems that while they were able to stomach the jailings of several earlier mayors and one form or another of municipal corruption, they just cannot abide whatever it is that a black mayor is doing; though not one has accused him of appropriating for himself one dishonest penny. I would warn these white citizens that disaffiliation will not solve one single problem for them except, perhaps, their hurt racial pride; for the fact of the matter is that the local political lever for power, black or white, can only do very limited things, that it cannot really solve the problems faced by the American city until the entire power structure is in some way forced to yield to the people what the people need and what the people deserve.

On the question of power, it becomes more and more apparent it cannot be left at the level of parochial power. Even if it were possible to establish the black towns that Ferry talks about, black people would not have control over the basic economic, foreign policy, or social welfare priority decisions which would determine the welfare of the black people as well as whites. Black towns might make us feel better, and that is terribly important, so I do not reject such ideas, but they will not make us live much better. What is true of black power is also true of other forms of group power. Our campuses, for example, have seen a demand for student power which has a great deal of legitimacy. Surely, students ought to play a much larger role in the life of a university which is their community for four or more years; but student power will not, by itself, change the national system of priorities in which education runs far behind spending for super weapons of destruction, in which drafting young men for wars is more important than letting them continue their studies beyond a bachelor degree so that they can apply their knowledge to the alleviation of human suffering. Student power, like black power, like youth power, like neighborhood power, like other forms of parochial power, can only achieve very limited gains. And so, where does this leave us? Am I rejecting the drive for black power? Am I hopelessly saying that nothing we may do can be of use? The answer is a clear and decisive No. The drive for black power is an essential, for it will help to end our strangeness in the village and I think that to be absolutely necessary.

And so, I support all forms of black power which will help black America to define itself, to recapture its heritage, to assert its ability, to realize its most immediate demands. I don't think it's immodest on my part to say that Gary's black children will be richer and stronger human beings for the knowledge that one of their own can govern the city, for the knowledge that their mothers and fathers were able to get themselves together enough to elect one of their own and, thus, assert their dignity. Nor is it immodest to say that Gary's black community is being given, for the first time in its history, some of the attention and concern which it so richly deserves, and that the lives of black men and women will be somewhat the better for it and the city will be somewhat the greater for it.

These are among the things which black power can do and ought to do and must do. But, beyond that, if I look to the alleviation of our poverty and the improvement of our standard of life, logic compels me to place hope in the eventual coming together of the demands for power by people of many sorts. I see hope in the rising tide of student militancy if that militancy is carried, in time, from the campuses into the communities across the nation.

I see hope in the demands of Spanish-speaking Americans for their share of the power. I see hope in the growing radicalism of the young who de-

mand youth power and no longer are content to accept a dehumanized status quo. I see our only hope for a decent society in the coming together some time in the future of all these demands for partial and parochial power into a total demand for people power.

In the essay which I have already quoted, Baldwin concludes with the following: "No road whatever will lead Americans back to the simplicity of this European village, for white men still have the luxury of looking on me as a stranger. I am not really a stranger any longer for any American alive. One of the things that distinguishes Americans from other people is that no other people has ever been so deeply involved in the lives of black men and vice versa. It is precisely this black-white experience which may prove of indispensable value to us in the world we face today. This world is white no longer and it will never be white again."

That is what we hope America will realize as we achieve more and more power which our blackness demands. As we try to save ourselves, if we achieve the full potential of what black power can do, then it will be up to the rest of America, white, Spanish-speaking, student, youth, and so on, to join us in the establishment of the power of the people in a world in which none are strangers. If they fail, or if we fail, we may have no way left to live in this country. If they can succeed and if we can succeed, if the People can wrest control from the hands of the economic overlords and the political self-servers, the rich and the powerful, then, and only then, do we have some hope that the good society can be ours.

One of the finest black poets, Margaret Walker, ends her poem "For My People" with a kind of incantation to the future. Let me cite it here in closing, for her vision, the vision of a black woman, wrote these words more than a quarter of a century ago and they still hold true.

Let a new earth rise, let another world be born,
Let a bloody peace be written in the sky,
Let a second generation full of courage issue forth,
Let a people loving freedom come to growth,
Let a beauty full of healing and a strength of final clenching
Be the pulsing in our spirits and our blood.
Let the martial songs be written,
Let the dirges disappear,
Let a race of men now arise and take control!

"A race of men" Margaret Walker says, and I say: Let us turn the promise of America into real progress; let us turn the dream into reality; for the sake of God, for the sake of man, for the sake of America, let's get ourselves together.

chapter 57
where the real poverty is:
plight of
american indians
u.s. news & world report

The American Indians—long out of sight and out of mind on their isolated reservations—are getting a fresh burst of attention in Washington.

Congress is being asked to vote more money for Indians' need. More help through the antipoverty program also is promised.

A committee of the Senate has jumped on the Bureau of Indian Affairs for its handling of education and other matters on reservations. Top officials of the Bureau met in Santa Fe, New Mexico, April 12-15 [1966] to begin an overhaul of the agency.

If Indians themselves take the promise of better days ahead with a large grain of salt, the reason is not far to seek. They have been promised better things ever since the white man began to move westward two centuries ago.

Today, abject poverty is a way of life for the average Indian. Yet the antipoverty dollars and workers that abound in big-city slums are just beginning to move to Indian reservations.

So-called **de facto** segregation existed in Indian schools long before civil rights advocates coined the phrase. It still is the rule, not the exception. Yet, there's no busing of large numbers of white children to integrate Indian classrooms.

Reprinted from **U.S. News & World Report,** April 25, 1966. Copyright (1966) U.S. News & World Report, Inc.

And medical care? On southwestern reservations, thousands of Indians are blind, or going blind, from trachoma, an eye disease. But government health services for Indians have been spread too thin to control the disease.

A LOOK AT ONE TRIBE

Typical of the plight of many tribes today is that of the Navajos. Their reservation is located in the northeastern corner of Arizona, with some land extending eastward into New Mexico and northward into Utah.

The Navajo reservation is a vast desolate land—15 million acres of desert, semiarid plains, and mountains. Here live more than one-fourth of all Indians on reservations today. Life for them contrasts sharply with that in the affluent society of the white man in such cities as Phoenix, Albuquerque, and Denver, each only a few hours' drive away.

Living within the vastness of Navajo land is a population somewhere between 106,000 and 120,000. An exact count is not possible because many families in remote areas have children without reporting them. A total of 380,000 Indians are on U.S. reservations.

When the Navajos roamed the Southwest at will, they were a proud and self-sufficient tribe. Their freedom ended with "The Long Walk" in 1865. That year, Col. Kit Carson and his troopers climaxed a ruthless, scorched-earth campaign against the Navajos by rounding up 9,000 of their men, women, and children. This band was marched 300 miles to Fort Sumner, in New Mexico. The Navajos spent three years in exile.

In 1868, the U.S. government signed a treaty with the Navajos and returned them to a reservation in their homeland. Over the years, the reservation has been expanded to its present 15 million acres.

DINEH AND THE ANGLOS

The Navajos still are a proud people. They call themselves **Dineh**, which means "the people." Americans are called "Anglos."

Navajos consider themselves superior to other Indians and other races. But tribal leaders at Window Rock, capital of the reservation, grapple with problems as monumental as those in many an underdeveloped country.

Poverty is widespread. While an income of below $3,000 a year may mean poverty in the "Great Society" of the white man, a Navajo family with that kind of money is well-to-do in the eyes of other Navajos.

Illiteracy is the rule rather than the exception. Under the 1868 treaty, the U.S. government is supposed to give Navajo children a free education. Even so, 7 out of 10 adults are unable to read or write the English language.

Unemployment on the reservation is so high as to make so-called pockets of poverty in other parts of the United States look prosperous. Raymond Nakai, tribal chairman, estimates that 19,000 are jobless out of a total work force of 30,000.

Housing is substandard by any measure. Most Navajo families live in hogans—small, circular huts of log and adobe without running water or electricity. Others live in frame houses that, if anything, are less adequate than the hogans.

Infant mortality is high. It averages out at 40.3 deaths per thousand births in the first year of life. That compares to a U.S. average of 25.3.

Yet, despite high infant mortality, Navajo leaders face a population explosion. Numbers are increasing at the rate of about 3 to 4 percent a year. The U.S. average is 1.5 percent.

The federal government has been spending more than 50 million dollars a year to improve the Navajos' lot. Most of this, 36.7 million this year, is spent by the Bureau of Indian Affairs, known simply as the BIA. The rest is spent by the U.S. Public Health Service.

KILL AND CURE

Says a BIA official: "People often ask: 'You've been running Indian affairs for 150 years. Why haven't you made more progress?' They forget that for the first 100 of these years we were busy killing off Indians, rounding them up, and pushing them as far out of the way as possible onto reservations in isolated areas. Only in the last generation have we made any real effort to bring the Indians into modern life."

BIA's major effort on the reservation is education. There are 48 boarding schools on the reservation. Nearly half the Navajo children must attend these because distances are too great to bus them to and from their homes. Other children go to BIA day schools and to mission schools. A few attend public schools with white children.

School attendance has improved markedly in recent years. In the 1951-52 school year, only 13,135 were in class out of a school-age population of 26,336. In the 1964-65 school year, the comparable figures were 40,256 out of 45,969. Still, that leaves nearly 6,000 children outside classrooms.

Large numbers of children arrive at school age speaking only Navajo. To help them overcome this handicap, the Bureau has preschool classes in which 6-year-olds get a year of training in the English language.

Despite all the money spent on schools, many Navajo leaders feel that the educational effort misses the mark.

A NAVAJO'S STORY

One of these is Peter McDonald, a Navajo who left the reservation to get a college education and a good job, but has returned to try to help his people.

The trouble with BIA schooling, as Mr. McDonald sees it, is that the Indian children are taught "to be like a white man, and think like a white man." The result, says Mr. McDonald: "They completely lose their self-identity as Navajos. They can't live within their own culture and they can't live in the affluent society of the white man. So you get mixed-up kids, and they give up. This is happening to many of our young people between the ages of 16 and 30."

Mr. McDonald knows from personal experience what it is like to be poor and mixed up. He dropped out of school in the sixth grade. First, he studied with his grandfather to be a medicine man —a profession still widely accepted by the Navajos.

Many an educated Navajo believes that a medicine man can cure illnesses that defy modern medicine.

At the age of 15, Mr. McDonald joined the Marine Corps. After his discharge, he completed the equivalent of four years of high school in one year. Then he got a degree in electrical engineering at the University of Oklahoma. He worked for seven years for Hughes Aircraft Company. During that time, he won a master's degree at the University of California at Los Angeles.

Three years ago, Mr. McDonald left a promising career in industry and came back to the reservation to work for betterment of his people. He now heads the Navajos' antipoverty program, which gets its funds from the Office of Economic Opportunity in Washington.

OPENING ROUNDS

The "war on poverty" is off to a small start on the Navajo reservation. Mr. McDonald thinks it offers the best opportunity Indians have had to lick their basic problems.

Operation Head Start, funded with $500,000, now is under way at 25 locations with 700 children enrolled. Mr. McDonald says it is a big improvement over the preschools of the BIA because children can begin learning English sooner. He has asked for 2.5 million dollars to expand Head Start to at least 3,000 children at 150 locations.

Mr. McDonald is determined to get a college on Navajo land because: "No matter how much we do in economic development, so long as we don't have a college on the reservation, this place will never blossom." He hopes to get $27,000 in antipoverty funds for a study that will lead to establishment of a junior college.

Most important, tribal leaders say, is a manpower development and training program. They have asked for 20 million dollars from the Office of Economic Opportunity to finance such a program.

Training programs of the past, in Mr. McDonald's view, "have only created a sense of frustration because, for all the talk, we're not getting people to the job or jobs to the people. Those who are trained often can't land a job because they don't have the apprenticeship, or the union qualifications."

What is needed, according to Navajo leaders, is a plan to take the unskilled Navajo all the way through testing, counseling, remedial education, on-the-job training, apprenticeship and finally into the job itself.

RICHEST OF THE POOR

For all their individual poverty, the Navajos are far better off than most other tribes. Their land is rich in minerals—coal, gas, oil, uranium, helium. Bonuses and royalties of more than $200 million have poured into the tribal treasury since 1950. Of this, about $85 million remains.

But mineral income has been declining and tribal spending has been increasing. This year the tribal budget is $26 million, against income of only a little more than $11 million.

"At the rate we're going, we'll be broke in about five years," says a member of the tribal council.

A big hope of Navajo leaders is that the tribe can attract enough industry to the reservation to provide jobs for at least some of the 19,000 now unemployed. A small beginning has been made.

At Shiprock, New Mexico, 300 young Navajo women now are in a work-training program in a plant of the Fairchild Semiconductor division of Fairchild Camera & Instrument Corporation.

Sixty women work at a B.V.D. Company plant in Winslow, Arizona, south of the reservation. If the Navajo women show that they are able machine operators, the B.V.D. Company may establish several plants on the reservation. According to BIA officials, the women have been turning out T-shirts at a rate 30 percent above expectations.

For the future, 30 to 40 firms have expressed interest in putting plants on the reservation. Of these, 11 have shown "strong interest" and negotiations now are in progress with six of them.

If all 11 companies should go through with plans discussed, between 5,000 and 11,000 jobs would be created.

MINING THE COAL

The tribe also is beginning to cash in on its coal reserves, estimated at 758 million tons and one of the largest remaining deposits in the United States. Until recently, this coal supply had been untapped because it was so low in quality that shipping it any distance was uneconomic.

But now, with long-distance transmission of electricity possible through new developments, steam generating plants are being built at mine sites.

Already in operation are three plants of the Arizona Public Service Company.

On April 12, negotiations were completed for two giant steam generation plants that will tap Navajo coal beds. A group of 21 private and public electric utilites known as WEST will build the plants—at Farmington, New Mexico, and at Mohave, Nevada. The latter plant is to get coal from the reservation through a coal-slurry pipeline.

"These two plants, along with those already in operation, will make the Four Corners as big as any power center in the United States," says Washington lawyer Norman M. Littell, general counsel and claims attorney for the Navajos. Four Corners is the area where the states of Arizona, New Mexico, Colorado, and Utah meet.

Thus, the outlook is not all bleak at Window Rock where Navajo leaders try to cope with the present and plan for the future.

Control of Navajo affairs rests in the tribal council, made up of 74 representatives elected from 97 chapters on the reservation. Because so many Navajos are illiterate, ballots present both names and pictures of the candidates.

Politicking is one lesson that the Navajos have leared well from the whites. Elections are to be held in November, and already the air at Window Rock is filled with charges and countercharges of corruption and inefficiency.

This preoccupation with politics hampers the Navajos, according to J. Bruce Wiley, a Denver management consultant who advises the tribe on its antipoverty program.

"The trouble is that anything one faction suggests is prima facie evidence to the opposing faction that it is no good," says Mr. Wiley. "Until real leadership emerges, we're going to have practically no progress at all."

THE COUNCIL IN SESSION

The tribal council meets four times a year at Window Rock in a round, hogan-shaped building with huge, polished wooden beams radiating outward from the center. The white plaster walls are adorned with frescos of Navajo life and history.

The men dress in their go-to-town uniform of cowboy boots, Levis, plaid shirts, short jackets, and Western hats.

Older women wear long skirts of flowered cotton or pleated satin with overblouses of velvet, topped off by colorful hand-woven shawls. Younger women wear blouses cut like cowboy shirts with flared skirts or tapered slacks.

Old ways on the reservation are undergoing gradual change. While a herd of sheep still is the major status symbol and evidence of wealth among the older Navajos, younger ones seem to prefer a new status symbol—the pickup truck, preferably blue or light green.

Some of the younger generation are getting away to college. There is a scholarship fund derived from interest on 10 million dollars on deposit in the U.S. Treasury. In the 1964-65 academic year, 536 Navajos entered college. Of these, 122 dropped out. In the current year, 596 are in college.

THE RELOCATION PROGRAM

As with other Indian tribes, there have been attempts to move Navajos off the reservation into the mainstream of U.S. life.

Under the "direct employment-assistance program" started in 1952, a total of 6,500 Navajo men and women have been relocated in such areas as San Francisco, Los Angeles, Denver, Dallas, Chicago, and Cleveland. The government pays transportation and initial living expenses and helps the Navajo find a home and a job.

A BIA official estimates that about one-third have returned to the reservation. Mr. McDonald, however, puts the figure closer to 50 percent and says: "One reason for this failure is that people from the reservation haven't learned to live with people outside. As a result, many have tagged relocation as not the right thing to do. Now others don't want to leave because they feel the program is unsuccessful."

But basically, says Mr. McDonald, most Navajos feel that "the reservation is their home and they want to make a go of this place."

BOOTSTRAP BUSINESSES

One of the most hopeful omens for the future has been the success of the Navajos in self-help projects, says Graham Holmes, BIA superintendent on the reservation.

One such project is the 10-million-dollar sawmill of the Navajo Forest Products Industries north of Window Rock. This enterprise is owned by the tribe and managed by a group of Navajos and outside experts. The sawmill, largest in New Mexico, employs 450 persons. More than 90 percent are Navajos. Annual payroll is 1.5 million dollars.

In 1965, the sawmill did a gross business of 3.5 million dollars and had a net profit of $450,000. Profits were plowed back into the business.

Other tribal enterprises include two restaurants, a gift shop, and a one-third interest in a Window Rock bank.

The tribe also gets a share of the profits from several motels in Arizona and New Mexico. And the tribe has $100,000 invested in a marina on Lake Powell, the reservoir behind Glen Canyon Dam, recently completed on the Colorado River.

A major enterprise is the Navajo Tribal Utility Authority, launched in 1960: It now has 212 employees, and 1,367 customers for gas, 4,029 for electricity, and 980 for water and sewerage.

This fledgling utility, admittedly, has made only a tiny beginning on this vast reservation. Tribal leaders, however, are optimistic about its future. They say that, as more jobs are created, living standards will rise, and there will be more utility customers. The result will be more jobs in the utility.

Clearly, this illustrates the basic problem for the Navajos: how to start an economic cycle that will feed on itself, generating more and more jobs and better and better living conditions.

BROKEN PROMISES

Another problem, says Navajo leaders, is that the white man still tries to push the Indian around on occasion. As an immediate example, they point to a big irrigation project promised for the reservation from the government's development of the San Juan River.

When the project was authorized by Congress, the tribe was promised enough water to irrigate 110,630 acres—enough to support more than 1,000 families. Now, say tribal leaders, the government wants to provide only enough water for around 75,000 acres, taking the rest of the water to augment supplies for areas in New Mexico, mainly Albuquerque.

Officials of the Interior Department, which is in charge of the work, say the project is being re-studied to determine the feasibility of irrigation of all the acreage first planned.

The project is now under construction with enough water due to arrive in 1971 to irrigate 10,000 acres. Target date for finishing the project is 1980.

Is there any solution in sight for the problems of American Indians?

One man who has spent a lifetime working with the Indians says that the most important step that could be taken to solve their problem would be to make the Bureau of Indian Affairs an independent agency because: "As long as the Bureau is in the Department of the Interior, its policies will change with every Administration and every whim of politicians in Washington."

With a more stable policy toward Indians, said this man, business and industry would be more likely to bring jobs to reservations.

"A TERRIFIC POTENTIAL"

The need for jobs on the reservations is one thing on which there is widespread agreement. Says Mr. Wiley, the management consultant working with the Navajos: "The actual potential for development is terrific. If I had guts enough to break loose from my status symbols, pull out and come here, not only could I become a millionaire, but I could start any one of a half dozen industries that could employ many hundreds of Navajos."

Thus, Mr. Wiley poses the big question: Will business and industry leaders take a chance in this desolate land where the latest status symbol is a pickup truck?

chapter 58
the mexican problem
carey mcwilliams

The third largest ethnic minority in the United States, Mexicans have long been a source of major concern, not to themselves but to those in whose midst they live. The majority's concern relates to the undeniable fact that—measured in terms of "acculturation" and "assimilation" as these concepts have been applied to European immigrants—Mexicans are among the least "Americanized" of the ethnic groups which make up the population of the United States today. If one uses income, employment, health and educational levels as a basis of comparison, Mexicans are clearly a disadvantaged group. And in this respect, Mexicans are remarkably homogeneous; that is, there is relatively little differentiation among them on socio-economic lines (although this situation is now changing). Based on a study of the 1950 census, Donald J. Bogue concludes that of all ethnic groups in the United States, Mexicans constitute "the only ethnic group for which a comparison of the characteristics of the first and second generation fails to show a substantial intergenerational rise in socio-economic status" or, to put it another way, Mexicans do not **seem** to be rising in status.

Majorities, of course, have a tendency to blame

Reprinted by permission of the publisher from Carey McWilliams, **The Mexicans in America** (New York: Teachers College Press, 1968; copyright 1968 by Teachers College, Columbia University), pp. 16-23.

minorities for whatever is wrong in the relationship between the majority and the particular minority. It is not surprising, therefore, that most of the social theorizing about Mexicans has, in one way or another, inclined to the view that the ethnic characteristics of Mexicans as Mexicans account for their disadvantaged status. One group of theorists, for example, stresses the importance of a deeply rooted conflict of values. The Mexican, according to these theorists, is not achievement-oriented, which is a way of saying that he is not properly motivated, which, again, is a way of saying that he is lazy. It is said that the culture from which he derives is more concerned with "being" than with "doing"; that it places more emphasis on the present than the future, etc. It is also said that the Mexican is "tradition directed" and that his resistance to the demands of the host culture—the culture that he finds in the Southwest—generates resentment, which in turn drains him of emotional energy. For example, a frequent complaint against the Mexican in the Southwest is that he is "apathetic." That a conflict of values does exist, and that this conflict has some bearing on the disadvantaged position of the Mexican, may be conceded. But simpler, more basic factors should receive primary stress. If you listened to Anglo-Americans in the Southwest you would be forced to conclude that "everything that is **Mexican** about the Mexican-American is problematic, a liability and a barrier."[1] The problem, to the extent that there is one, is not to be found, at least not exclusively, in a conflict of values, and it is certainly not to be found in the Mexican as a Mexican. Rather it is implicit in the experience of the Mexican in the Southwest; it is an aspect of the relationship between Anglo and Hispano—majority and minority —in that region.

To begin with, one must recognize—and continue to emphasize—that such concepts as "acculturation" and "assimilation" were derived from the study of European immigration and are not entirely applicable to the Mexican experience. They relate, that is, to a different "model." Studies of European immigration have assumed that the immigrant, being cut off from his roots, had no alternative but to "assimilate" the prevailing cultural pattern, that is, adopt it as his own. This in turn assumes that "Europe" and "America" are two quite separate cultural entities. But Mexicans do not have the same feeling for the Southwest that European immigrants have for areas in which they have settled.

Mexicans have been able to move "north from Mexico" while remaining at all times within a familiar physical and cultural environment. They have been able to travel from one end of the Southwest to the other, to live and work in these areas, while at all times continuing to speak Spanish. Furthermore, they can "commute," as many do, from one side of the border, where they live, to the other side, where they work. In the past, the absence of American citizenship has not been a barrier in many types of employment. In many instances, there has been no special incentive to acquire citizenship. The fact is that large parts of Mexico have been part of the labor market of the Southwest. The jobs have been on one side of the border, the workers on the other. Unlike European immigrants, Mexicans have often been uncertain about their permanent intentions; basically they feel at home, in varying degrees, on both sides of the border. "Unlike the immigrant from Europe," writes Dr. John M. Sharp of Texas Western College, "the Mexican-American is by no means willing to abandon his ancient cultural and linguistic heritage, in which he takes—however inarticulately —traditional pride, to accept the cultural pattern common to native speakers of English in our nation."[2]

Originally—and typically—most Mexican immigrants were employed in large numbers in particular industries; desert cement plants, mines, railroads, etc., which were isolated from large centers of population and which needed large amounts of relatively cheap and unskilled labor. In agriculture, Mexicans have worked, in large numbers, as part of migratory farm labor pools, which again implies a degree of group isolation. Constant mobility interrupts opportunities for "acculturation." So does geographic isolation from large centers of population. So does the fact that Mexicans have tended to work in "gangs," in a limited range of occupations, which has meant, in effect, working with other Spanish-speaking Mexicans under the supervision of a Spanish-speaking Mexican "boss" or "foreman." Much Mexican employment has been seasonal or casual in character, types of work in which there is a little opportunity to learn a special skill or to advance from a lower bracket of employment to a higher. "The history of the Southwest," writes Dr. Harland Padfield, "has been a seesaw battle on a technological chess board between vast labor pools of the Mexican hinterlands and the more technological and highly paid Anglo and Mexican-American northerner."[3] Until fairly recent times, Mexicans who migrated to the Southwest came from areas of limited educational opportunities in which it was not possible to learn or acquire a variety of occupational skills. And historically the Mexican immigrant came to areas in the Southwest which, not so many years ago, offered little in the way of educational opportunities. The first Mexican-American graduated from the grammar school in Nueces County, Texas, in 1904.

But nothing could be further from the truth than to characterize Mexicans as "lazy" or "apathetic." The contributions which Mexican labor has made to the economy of the Southwest are the best proof that Mexicans are anything but lazy. And the history of organized labor in the Southwest provides abundant documentation for the proposition that Mexican labor has been anything but "docile" or "apathetic." Mexican workers have conducted strikes of historic interest and major economic importance in the various industries in which they have been employed. In the conduct of these strikes they have shown remarkable courage and determination and militancy. Indeed it was the tendency of Mexicans to organize and thereby seek to improve their living and working conditions that resulted in the first efforts to remove them from relief rolls and "repatriate" them to Mexico.[4] And it should be emphasized that the American Federation of Labor was for years opposed to Mexican immigration and failed to organize Mexicans once they had settled here. Many unions, over a period of years, excluded Mexicans from membership. In fact, organized labor's strategy was to monopolize the better paying, skilled jobs for its members. Not only were these categories of work easier to organize than the unskilled, seasonal, and casual types of employment, but by shunting Mexicans into these jobs it was possible to create a kind of labor hierarchy in which the Mexicans were restricted to the least desirable, lowest paid, least skilled types of work. Organized labor certainly did very little, in the early period, to assist in the "acculturation" or "assimilation" of the Mexican.

THE HISPANO "LANGUAGE PROBLEM"

Those who inveigh against the Mexican's "backwardness" usually point to the "language problem" as the major cause. With most Mexicans, Spanish is the language of the home. Mexican immigrants have settled in Spanish-speaking communities, they have attended Spanish-language movies, Masses are usually conducted (or were in the past) in Spanish at the local parish church, and immigrant Mexicans have generally read Spanish-language newspapers. Geographical and occupational segregation have fostered cultural isolation. In the past there have been few incentives to abandon Spanish or, to put it another way, to learn English. Then, too, Mexicans have a thoroughly understandable pride in their Spanish background and in their cultural inheritance, and the Spanish language, of course, has been the carrier of this tradition. The Mexican Revolution (1910-1920) added to this feeling of pride in the Mexican-Spanish inheritance. It is not surprising, therefore, that most Mexicans identify with "la raza," which is their way of referring to the Spanish-speaking. Mexican families tend to be large, family ties are strong, and the Mexican family is of the large or extended variety, that is, more individuals are included in it or regarded as belonging to it than would be the case with Anglo-American families. In the Southwest, as Margaret Mead puts it, "to be Spanish-American is to belong to a **familia**." In California, in the early period, the most important type of family was the ranchero or ranch family; families were identified with a particular ranchero. In New Mexico, families were identified with particular villages. In many New Mexico villages, family ties remain remarkably strong; certain villages are virtually identical with certain families. Social and economic discrimination, as well as geographical isolation, have held the Spanish-speaking together, strengthened family ties, and preserved traditional ways of doing things. Most Mexicans are poor and, as one of them has said, "by sticking together we can sustain a lot of poverty."

This background must be kept in mind in discussing the "language problem." A report of the National Education Association, written in 1966, properly characterizes the so-called "language problem" as "the most acute educational problem" in the Southwest.[5] The nature of the problem can be summarized by paraphrasing the major conclusions of the report. In parts of the Southwest, as in Texas, instruction in the English language is mandatory, except, of course, in foreign language classes. In some schools the speaking of Spanish is forbidden both in the classrooms and on the playgrounds, and not infrequently students have been punished for lapsing into Spanish. In such an educational setting, the Spanish-speaking student is at a great disadvantage. On entering school, he may know some English but has used it infrequently. The language of the home, of his childhood, of his first years, of the neighborhood and community in which he resides, is Spanish. His environment, his experiences, his very personality, have been shaped by it. Not surprisingly, the Mexican student tends to fall behind in the first grade, and each passing year finds him further "retarded." This in turn creates a kind of "educational discrimination." It has, for example, resulted in classes for "slow learners," often made up largely of Mexican youngsters. De facto schools, based on residential segregation, contribute to the same end. As a result of the language handicap, the Spanish-speaking student has been placed at an educational disadvantage, which in turn has resulted in occupational and economic handicaps. The NEA's basic recommendations suggest the nature of the real problem: bilingual instruction in preschool programs and early grades; the teaching of English as a second language; emphasis on the reading, writing, and speaking of good Spanish, since Mexican-American children are often illiterate in it. What a close reading of the NEA report suggests is that the old Spanish borderlands are today, as they always have been, an area of cultural fusion or interpenetration. Spanish-Mexican cultural influences are now too deeply implanted ever to be entirely uprooted even if this were desirable, which it is not. As Dr. Manual H. Guerra puts it, Mexican-Americans have a bond with Mexico which transcends the older Anglo-American educational theories.

We do not want to give up the Spanish language, pray to God in English, substitute mashed potatoes for frijoles or "junk" our piñatas. Rather we want to bring all of these values to American society as our contribution to the diversity and wealth of our country. Rather than the melting pot, we believe in the heterogeneity of American society, including the give and take with other peoples and other cultures.

Today it is generally recognized that what used to be called "the language problem" is really an educational problem, and that the solution rests with the school system. For example, the U. S. Office of Education has set up a special program to help and advise school systems in the Southwest in their efforts to adjust policies and teaching techniques to improve the instruction of Spanish-speaking youngsters.

In considering the disadvantaged position of the Mexican in the Southwest, one must never forget that this position is an aspect of the Mexican's poverty. The poor are always disadvantaged and most Mexicans are poor. The homes of the poor have fewer cultural "advantages," such as books and paintings and recordings, etc., than do the homes of the well-to-do. With the Mexican-American there is a "poverty handicap" as well as a language handicap. Representative Henry Gonzalez, who is of Mexican-American background, puts it this way: Mexican-Americans "live in an enormous belt of poverty beginning in east Texas, sweeping down through south Texas and the Rio Grande Valley, and stretching west into New Mexico, Arizona, Colorado, and Southern California." This vast region has been called "a thousand miles of poverty," and so it is, for the Spanish-speaking. What Lyle Saunders wrote about the Spanish-speaking some years ago is still true:

Everywhere . . . there is poverty. Not all Spanish-speaking are poor, but in general more of them are poor than is true for any other group. . . . If one were to attempt to characterize the condition of the Spanish-speaking . . . he would be forced to say that, in general, and for nearly any index of socio-economic status that might be devised, the Spanish-speaking people are found to occupy a less desirable position than the Anglos or the population as a whole.

SOCIAL DISCRIMINATION AGAINST HISPANOS

Another factor, closely related to the Mexican's poverty, helps account for his disadvantaged status. In the Southwest, Mexicans have never been subjected to the same degree or kinds of social discrimination which have been practiced, for example, against Negroes in the Deep South. But anti-Mexican discrimination exists and, not so many years ago, was quite common. In a recent speech Representative Henry Gonzalez, who is himself of Spanish-speaking background—he represents a San Antonio, Texas, constituency—reminded his colleagues in the House that when he was seven years old he was turned away from a public swimming pool in Terrell Wells, Texas, because he was a Mexican-American; he also told them that he vividly remembers signs which appeared in many shops which read "No Mexicans Served."[6] The brilliant young Mexican-American writer, John Rechy, born in El Paso's southside, of Mexican immigrant parents, provides some illuminating insights on social discrimination against the Spanish-speaking.

Prejudice against the Mexican is sometimes subtly, sometimes blatantly, manifest; whatever its form, it permeates the Southwest air as smog permeates downtown Los Angeles. . . . As early as kindergarten, I heard Mexican-Americans like myself referred to as 'greasers. . . . A Mexican-American child growing up in this atmosphere of implied inferiority and 'differences'—knowing that if he gets through high school at all he will have to go out and work immediately—quickly becomes aware of his bleak future.[7]

For the most part, present-day discrimination against the Spanish-speaking tends to assume rather subtle forms. But not always, and not everywhere. For example, Dr. Theodore W. Parsons conducted a three-year study of an agricultural town in central California which he refers to as "Guadalupe" although that is not the name of the town. Discrimination in the schools was evident, but the community leaders and those who ran the schools seemed to be unaware of it. A Chamber of Commerce Committee saw to it that the annual artichoke festival "Queen" was always an Anglo-American; the Mexican candidate was always selected as her attendant. Two of three churches in the community did not accept Mexicans. At the Catholic Church, the Mexicans customarily attended a separate mass and the priest's sermon to them was different in content and tone from that given to the Anglo group. When both groups were in church at the same time, on special occasions, the Mexicans sat at the rear of the church or stood if seating was inadequate. At school graduation, the Mexicans marched in last and sat at the rear of the platform. "In general," Dr. Parsons found, "Anglo informants characterized the Mexican villagers as being immoral, violent, and given to fighting, dirty, unintelligent, improvident, irresponsible and lazy. . . . Mexican informants often described Anglos as being unsympathetic, aggressive, interested only in themselves, cold and demanding. . . . Not one of the several hundred people contacted during the field investigation had ever visited a home outside of his own ethnic group."[8] In social environments of the type described by Rechy in El Paso and Parsons in "Guadalupe"—and these are typical situations—it is not surprising that Spanish-speaking students should feel resentment or that this resentment should often find expression in a determination to speak Spanish both as a mark of protest against Anglo discrimination and as a means of demonstrating loyalty to "la raza," to one's own people.

To sum up, the disadvantaged status of the Mexican in the Southwest is primarily to be explained in terms of quite specific social, geographic, economic and historical considerations, rather than by attempts to attribute to Mexicans traits and characteristics which, to the extent that they exist, are consequences of the poverty and deprivation which have too long prevailed among the Spanish-speaking.

Those people today, writes Dr. Julian Samora of the University of Notre Dame, who claim that the Spanish-speaking are unindustrious, unambitious, and do not 'take to education' need but review the history of this population in the United States. . . . We find a people who came to this country in the (early) 1600's and 1700's; who established a folk society based on European traditions; who were isolated geographically and therefore culturally from the mainstream of western civilization; who lived a relatively 'slow' life based on agriculture and the seasons; who had no particular need for education as we know it today; who, when conquered, were not assisted by the conquerors to make an adjustment to the new society; and who, when faced with the com-

petition of the dominant society, could do little but withdraw into further isolation. When educational facilities were finally established, the Spanish-Americans could not be expected to flock to the institutions since essentially these were not an integral part of their culture. Even today, although facilities are generally adequate, the consequences of the long historical tradition are evident. This whole picture for the Southwest was compounded further by the influx of a large number of immigrants (generally speaking, peasant, rural, uneducated, of lower socio-economic status) from Mexico who also did not have the tradition of public education in their background. The latter immigration, however, faced not only the same general problem of the previous group, but on top of it was heaped the scourge of discrimination and segregation.[9]

NOTES

1. "An Evaluation and Critique of The Mexican American Studies Project," A Ford Foundation Grant Extended to the University of California at Los Angeles, p. 7. An undated pamphlet, prepared by Dr. Manuel H. Guerra and Dr. Y. Arturo Cabrera for the Education Council of the Mexican American Political Association, Los Angeles.

2. "The Invisible Minority: Report of the NEA-Tucson Survey on the Teaching of Spanish to the Spanish-Speaking." Published by Department of Rural Education, National Education Association, Washington, D.C., 1966, p. 5.

3. "Social Foundations of Rural Poverty in the Southwest," a paper presented by Dr. Harland Padfield, at hearings of the National Advisory Commission on Rural Poverty, Tucson, Arizona, January 26-27, 1967, p. 10.

4. North from Mexico: The Spanish-Speaking People of the United States by Carey McWilliams, J. B. Lippincott Company, 1948, p. 190, p. 193.

5. The Invisible Minority: Report of the NEA-Tucson Survey on the Teaching of Spanish to the Spanish-Speaking, published by Department of Rural Education, National Education Association, Washington, D.C., 1966, Foreword, p. v.

6. Congressional Record, June 12, 1967, p. H. 7010.

7. The Nation, October 10, 1959; see also his fine article "El Paso de Norte," Evergreen Review, Autumn, 1958.

8. From "Guadalupe," a 429-page doctoral dissertation by Dr. Theodore W. Parsons, 1966, on file at Stanford University (it will be published in shorter form by Holt, Rinehart and Winston as one of the "Case Studies in Cultural Anthropology" series edited by Dr. George D. Spindler).

9. Quoted in Congressional Record, January 17, 1967, p. S-357.

topic 24

contracultural dissent: rebellion against the future

"So foul a sky," Shakespeare's King John warns us, "clears not without a storm."
Is today's sky foul? Has our posturban, postindustrial society—its system of allocating power and status, its treatment of its minorities and its poor, its ways of dealing with its environment, its military posture, its schools, and its notions of the good life—fallen far short of its promise? Many Americans, in particular young Americans, think so. Is a storm in the offing? Will there be an out-and-out collision and showdown between those who defend the old way of life and those who champion the new? Will our metaphorical skies be cleared? Is the prospect of fundamental and enduring changes in our values, norms, goals, esthetics, and life styles a mere fantasy? Again there are many—let us label them contracultural youth—who believe that there are indeed changes in the wind. Listen to Jerry Rubin (1969):

> Young whites are dropping out of white society. We are getting
> our heads straight, creating new identities. We're dropping out
> of middle-class institutions, leaving their schools, running away
> from their homes, and forming our own communities. We are
> becoming the new niggers.

What are the elementary sources of contracultural dissent? Is this discontent a legitimate expression of a deepfelt grievance, or is it merely an ego trip? Is what has variously been labeled "the counterculture" and "Consciousness III" a passing fad? Is it something that has been exaggerated beyond all reason—a myth with its own fantasies and mystique? Is it self-defeating? Will it be co-opted by such arms of the establishment as Madison Avenue, the mass media, and the industrial bureaucracies?
It is to these and similar questions that the authors of the three articles that follow address themselves. Instead of focusing on such singular facets of youth dissent as the drug culture, the new morality, or the underground newspaper, the authors choose to analyze the more comprehensive manifestations and the underlying sources of contracultural dissent.
The first selection, by Donald McDonald, pinpoints both the more specific attributes

and the elementary sources of youth dissent and concludes that the cultural revolution of the young will succeed—that their revolution will, without resorting to violent confrontation politics, "work profound and permanent change." Erazim Kohák advises that our affluent society makes a youth revolution "not only possible but virtually necessary," for a postindustrial social system such as ours has no truly significant role for its young; yet for society's sake as much as theirs, it is imperative that they play substantial and responsible roles. The final piece, by Peter Berger and Brigitte Berger, takes a variant tack. Although they are not unsympathetic to the youth rebellion, they conclude that it may, in effect, become self-defeating. The reader will have to decide for himself whether their somewhat startling prognosis will in fact be substantiated by events during the next several decades.

Few summary statements of the elemental thrust of contracultural dissent are more succinct than that voiced by the anonymous authors of the "Port Huron Statement" of 1962:

Men have unrealized potential for self-cultivation, self-direction, self-understanding, and creativity. It is this potential that we regard as crucial and to which we appeal, not to the human potentiality for violence, unreason, and submission to authority. . . . We seek the establishment of a democracy of individual participation, governed by two central aims: that the individual share in those social decisions determining the quality and direction of his life; that society be organized to encourage independence in men and provide the media for their common participation.

chapter 59
youth
donald mcdonald

Are our rebellious youth "fixated at the temper tantrum stage"—or are they "the first generation born in a new country"?

■

For every assertion made about American youth, there exists, it seems, an exact denial. Bruno Bettelheim talks about rebellious youth being "fixated at the temper tantrum stage," but Margaret Mead takes hope in "the young people who are rebelling all around the world, rebelling against whatever forms the governmental and educational systems take"; these youth "are like the first generation born in a new country" while their elders are "immigrants from an earlier world living in an age essentially different from anything we knew before." A **Fortune** poll finds that youth are significantly changing their values, but a Gallup poll declares that youth are really not very radical. Two University of Southern California researchers discover that talk of a generation gap is exaggerated, but Miss Mead says there is a "deep, new, unprecedented, worldwide generation gap." Premarital sexual activity is said to be rampant among youth,

but it is also said that, while today's youth talks more about sex, they are no more sexually active than were the youth of previous generations. Youth are alleged to be at once sick and sane; alienated and involved; political and apolitical; arrogant and humble; naive and sophisticated; immoral and religious; obscene and pure; selfish and generous; violent and gentle; cynical and idealistic.

These contradictions do indeed exist in each person, and various youth groups do reflect various —sometimes opposed—values, attitudes, convictions. These contradictions also reflect different values in those judging youth. What strikes one observer as "youthful arrogance" seems to another "refreshing candor." Where one critic discovers a "pathological condition" in young people, another rejoices in the "sanity" of youth's rejection of a "sick society." The "anarchism" that sends shivers down the spines of some adults is welcomed by others as a sign of "healthy antiauthoritarianism." What looks like "cultural nihilism" from one quarter, looks like the emergence of an authentic "counterculture" from another.

In this situation one cannot make even modest assertions about youth without fear of contradiction. All generalizations are vulnerable. Nevertheless, something as convulsive, as fascinating, and as inescapably important as the actions of American youth imposes on one an effort to understand, to discern pattern and direction. This report is an ef-

Reprinted, with permission, from the August 1970 issue of **The Center Magazine**, a publication of the Center for the Study of Democratic Institutions in Santa Barbara, California.

fort to comprehend what is happening on the youth scene, why it is happening, and its meaning. By "youth" I mean those between the ages of fifteen and twenty-five. There are obvious differences —in values, attitudes, experience—between fifteen- and twenty-five-year-olds, but the differences due to age may be far less significant than the similarities all across this age span.

I intend to use numbers sparingly, if at all, in this report. Not that numbers are not available or that numbers are not important. They are available and they can be useful, especially to historians. But numbers are misleading when used as an index of ideas and ideological change; cultural transformations; ferment in values, attitudes, opinions; the character and direction of movements. And, as a basis for prophesy, the numbers game is an exercise in self-delusion. Clark Kerr, the former president of the University of California, wrote in June, 1967— three and a half years after the first student confrontation on the Berkeley campus—that "the great wave of student confrontations now seems to be passing. . . . New leaders are arising [not from the revolutionaries or the bohemians, but] from . . . the New Collegiate group [which] has as one of its characteristics devotion to the campus and willingness to work with and through the campus power structure. . . . They are setting the tone of this generation." He referred to the "overtold story . . . about the 'filthy nine' (only four of them students) who constituted the totality of the much-publicized Filthy Speech Movement on the Berkeley campus." Mr. Kerr's profound misperception of the meaning of what has been happening on the Berkeley campus since 1963 is not because he did not have in 1967 the advantage of our hindsight in 1970. It is because he thought there was a direct correlation between number and meaning.

Jerry Rubin's book Do It! sold ninety-six thousand copies before publication date and there are one hundred and eighty thousand copies now in print. A half million young people attended the Woodstock festival. Almost another half million were at the November l5, 1969, Peace Mobilization in Washington. Undoubtedly these are impressive statistics, but they are useful only because they suggest that something important may be happening among American youth. The Nixon administration furnished us with a classic illustration of how not to read numbers. The federal government sent up a military helicopter to take pictures of the Peace Mobilization rally, then put a team of photo interpreters to work counting the dots on a greatly enlarged print of the scene in order to prove that not five hundred thousand but only four hundred and fifty-three thousand, or whatever, came to Washington to protest President Nixon's Vietnam policy.

One professor of psychology plays a different game. He begins by dividing all American youth into college and noncollege youth. He then divides college youth into those attending elite colleges and those attending nonelite colleges. He next divides those attending the elite colleges into political and nonpolitical students. The political students he divides into moderate liberals and radical activists. Finally, he divides the radical activists into nonviolent and violent students. His conclusion is that this very small minority of college students— the violent, radical, political activists attending elite schools—are not representative of what he calls the "youthful revolution." Such reductionism, and the conclusion drawn from it, ignores several far more valid and significant facts: (1) the historically crucial role that small minorities have always played in revolutionary times; (2) the majority of students, while they do not support or encourage violence, do not oppose it either, not even when it occurs on their own campuses; and (3) the sympathy and even temporary alliance of the majority is spontaneously given when police are called in by school administrators.

Erik Erikson has noted that if a small group of militantly agitated youths "sets out to agitate on a large scale, it often succeeds way beyond its numerical strength or political foresight because it draws out and inflames the latent aggravations of that majority of young people who would otherwise choose only banal and transient ways of voicing dissent or displaying conflict." Erikson has also noted that where youthful challenge "is met with the deployment of a hired force that does not hesitate to vent all the frustrated anger shunned by the privileged, the ethical weakness in delegating violence immediately arouses the solidarity of those larger numbers of students who would not otherwise be attracted by amoral stratagems."

■

Not all youth are involved in all aspects of the youth scene and not all who are involved in particular aspects of it are involved with the same degree of intensity and on the same level of sophistication and commitment. But few youth are not involved in at least one of the following phenomena:

1. Assertion of autonomy in matters of appearance, taste, morals, and values, combined with the ability to make one's convictions stick. Although a number of studies seem to indicate that many young people reflect the views of their parents, at least in matters of politics and ideology, the really salient fact is that in cultural, moral, and ethical matters, young people have sharply diverged from the adult generation; in their politics and ideology they are moving steadily in the direction of deeper radicalization. Increasingly the arguments one hears from young people are no longer concerned with the degree of radicalization deemed necessary but whether politics itself, no matter how radical, is a serious option and to what extent violence can be justified on tactical, strategic, and ethical grounds. The point here is that not only the specific content of young people's life style but also the autonomy with which it is being developed represent something indomitable emerging from American youth.

2. The demand for relevance in education as illustrated by a gathering revolt against the lecture and the authority-in-the-classroom figure; a demand for seminars; the rise of free high schools and free universities; insistence on systemic flexibility in the forms of education in which life in the community, work, travel, are all thought to be educational experiences at least as authentic as the conventional classroom, laboratory, and library models. Herbert Kohl's little book, **The Open Classroom**, is a practical expression of interim arrangements that high school teachers and students can adopt pending the open school and eventually the open school system. Last winter, **The New York Times** reported that a group of about thirty of the most brilliant students had withdrawn from half a dozen Milwaukee high schools to form their own school in association with a professor from the University of Wisconsin. Whether or not they had read anthropologist George Pettitt's book, **Prisoners of Culture**, they were echoing his conviction that "no existing school system meets the educational needs of contemporary man." The Milwaukee experience is not isolated; it is becoming typical and has the unmistakable air of a harbinger. HIGH SCHOOL UNREST RISES, ALARMING U.S. EDUCATORS was a headline in **The New York Times,** and not all the unrest is racial in nature. In fact, only one-third of a sample survey of three hundred and sixty-one high school disturbances could be traced to racial troubles; the rest were concerned with political issues, dress regulations, discipline, and educational reforms.

3. Uncompromising resistance to the militarization of life and to war as an instrument of foreign policy. Indeed, "resistance" is not an adequate word to describe the attitude of youth toward war. They find it obscene, absurd, ethically outrageous.

4. Identification with the poor. In its early stages, this identification is verified by young people giving up their vacations to work with blacks, with sharecroppers, with grape-pickers. Later, the identification is expressed in demands for radical restructuring of society because of the growing conviction of young people that poverty is not an accidental and passing phenomenon but is endemic to our society.

5. A personalist-communalist orientation. Full development as a person is perceived as possible only within a community. The communities vary from an off-campus house rented by a dozen students, to a tribal commune in the hills of California, to a family of tribes in New Mexico. What is held in common not only by those living in communities but by others as well is an almost monastic attitude toward economic reward, and a rejection of the competitive imperative of American society in which getting ahead can only be accomplished at the expense of someone else's falling behind.

6. Alienation. Though "alienation" is a term that covers a spectrum from pathological disorientation to moods of disaffection, its conventional meaning rather accurately describes the experience of young people: an estrangement from the values of one's society and a sense of the meaninglessness of life and one's role in it. Seymour Halleck, the director of student psychiatry at the University of Wisconsin, has said that while probably less than four percent of college students suffer alienation in a form severe enough to cause them to seek psychiatric help, about half the students seeking help are alienated. "An increasing number of college students who consult psychiatrists," Dr. Halleck wrote several years ago, "complain of vague feelings of apathy, boredom, meaninglessness, and chronic unhappiness. Such complaints are best understood in terms of the concept of alienation." But many students who will never visit a psychiatrist recognize these feelings, because they too have experienced them in varying degrees of intensity. Such students are perhaps best described as "alienable" rather than "alienated."

7. An ambivalent attitude toward tradition

and history. A common complaint directed against young people is that they are ignorant of the lessons that history can teach them and contemptuous not only of history but of humane traditions. What youth seem to resent most is the attempt by their elders to invoke the past and tradition as an automatic touchstone for all of contemporary thought and as a restraint on radical activism directed at present social injustices because, in the elders' view, youth's newly discovered injustices are the same old injustices that have plagued mankind from time immemorial. They also question the humaneness of at least the most recent chapters of the human tradition: "In the last fifty years," Ronald D. Laing writes in **The Politics of Experience,** "we human beings have slaughtered by our own hands coming on for one hundred million of our species."

∎

No one- or two-factor analysis can serve to explain something as complex as the contemporary American youth scene. There appears to be a convergence of a number of trends, ideas, movements, and convictions whose time has come. The convergence is occurring against a background and in a context of certain historical realities that evoke, reinforce, and, as it were, objectify the gathering convictions. This confluence finds its most dramatic expression in the youth; indeed, the confluence **is** the experience of youth.

The following are some of the important elements, the convergent realities, that together begin to explain why the "youth scene" is happening.

The Age of Affluence

Granted all the slipperiness and ambiguousness of the term, there is relative affluence for many youth and the removal of the specter of destitution for most. Youth who have not experienced want cannot understand their parents' anxiety to achieve economic security. It is easy to be critical of parents. Even when the criticism is not expressed, its presence introduces distance between young people and their parents. In such an age, the pressure to secure a job immediately after high school or college does not exist for many. They view work as a factor in human development rather than as a means of sheer survival. They are also able to extend the moratorium during which they can assess their position, experiment with behavior patterns, and begin to take those steps that lead

from adolescence to adulthood. But this also means a prolongation of dependence on parents for food, clothing, shelter, medical care, and, along with continuing dependence, a continuing, sometimes cumulative, resentment of parents and a generalized resentment of the whole adult generation. "Mere dependence on an older generation," Erikson writes, "comes to symbolize a despised colonial heritage. . . . And has youth not learned from psychoanalysis to look at man's prolonged childhood dependence as an evolutionary fact artificially protracted by adults in order to subvert the radiance of children and the vigor of youth and to confirm the molds of adult self-images?"

The Atomic Age

Youth born in the year of Hiroshima and Nagasaki are now twenty-five years old. An entire generation has grown up in the shadow of the mushroom cloud, with the constant reminder that we can reduce the planet to a radioactive cinder.

The Cold War

To youth, the twenty-five-year Cold War against communism that has cost American taxpayers one trillion dollars in arms and whose chief article of faith is that it is better to be dead than Red, seems incomprehensible. To them it represents the older generation's irrational response to largely self-induced fears.

The Hot Wars

Korea, the Dominican Republic, Cuba, Guatemala, Vietnam, Cambodia. Both the vanguard and the bulk of the antiwar movement have been made up of youth. Though the movement has taken many forms—from Eugene McCarthy's Children's Crusade in 1967 and 1968, to the Peace Moratorium and Peace Mobilization, to the politics of rage and the politics of outrage—the moral sensibilities of the young have been deeply shocked by the conduct of the United States government in the world community. One of the effects on youth has been, ironically, their adoption of the code and manner of the state.

Even when he seeks to resist the violence and irrationality of the state," Norman Cousins writes, "he tends to speak the language of the state and to adopt its own temper. The problem of youth today is the problem of the total society—how best to return to the rule and style of reason. The taming of men cannot be separated from the taming of nations. . . . The government of the United States was conceived by men who believed it possible for a nation to become a moral instrument. They rejected the notion of a double standard under which the state can itself be immoral, mendacious, brutal, or irrational while demanding that its citizens adhere to a code of responsibility and reason.

The Inversion of National Priorities

Young people are informed that a single Apollo mission to the moon costs $375 million. They have been told by the General Accounting Office that the Defense Department is now proceeding on one hundred and thirty new strategic and tactical weapons systems costing $140 billion. They know that arms and space programs account for seventy percent of available federal expenditures each year. And they know that mental hospitals are overcrowded, that not even minimal custodial care is being given to the mentally ill; that many elderly people live in squalor; that the urban ghettos are hells; and that the air and water resources of the nation continue to be wasted and polluted. A year ago, Republican Congressman W. E. Brock, of Tennessee, released the report that he and twenty-two of his Republican colleagues in the House of Representatives had made following their tour of fifty American universities, where they talked with more than a thousand students. The purpose of the visits was to ascertain student views with the hope that they might understand the causes of campus unrest. Mr. Brock and his fellow congressmen returned to Washington profoundly impressed by the seriousness, insight, and responsibility of the vast majority of students. They also warned that while most students "are not poised on the edge of revolution," many "can be radicalized when violence or confrontation on campus occurs. Also disillusionment in our system by students can grow, even without violence, if we place one label on all students and fail to understand that they raise many areas of legitimate concern." Among the areas of "legitimate concern" Congressman Brock found among the students were misplaced priorities; racism; the military-industrial complex; American imperialism; police-state tactics and atmosphere; economic oppression; poverty; Vietnam; the military draft; materialism; overreaction by adults; hypocrisy of adults; failure of mass media to report accurately or sensitively; faculty

who put grant-getting and research ahead of teaching; the irrelevance of course material in the classroom.

The Technological Revolution

Among other things, the technological revolution deprives increasing numbers of young people of the opportunity to get into humanly satisfying work, and imposes the iron logic of the technological imperative on a society in which human needs, since they cannot be qualified and computerized, are neglected. Bruno Bettelheim, who on other occasions has angered many young people by what they think is his insensitivity to their justified grievances, has said that society has made youth "obsolete," thus imposing great frustrations on the young. The adolescent yearns for an adulthood that is being postponed, on the one hand, by a technologized society that has no use for his services and, on the other, by an educational system that "has brought incredibly large numbers to the academic life who do not find their self-realization through study or intellectual adventure." Paul Goodman asks:

> How can young people think of a future community when they themselves have no present world, no profession or other job in it, and no trust in other human beings? Contemporary conditions of life have certainly deprived people—and especially young people—of a meaningful world in which they can act and find themselves. . . . Old people are shunted out of sight at an increasingly earlier age; young people are kept on ice till an increasingly later age.

Television

Television's daily and documentary journalism, imperfect as it is, furnishes a bond among youth in the form of instant and continuous awareness and consciousness of themselves as sharing the same passions, values, friends, and enemies. For the first time youth are one and are conscious of their unity. Television is also the essential carrier for activists. No movement can hope to succeed if it is denied access to the television cameras of a nation, a fact Mayor Daley of Chicago and his police understood when they harassed television reporters of the street violence at the 1968 Democratic Convention; a fact Jerry Rubin patiently reminds his followers of again and again and personally demonstrates with antics designed to attract the attention of television newsmen; a fact the Peace Mobilization organizers in Washington recognized when the three national television networks provided only brief spot coverage of the massive November 15th rally [in 1969], thus depriving the peace movement of the psychological lift that the magnitude and spirit of the Washington rally would have given it around the nation. Finally, a generation that has grown up in front of the television screen has had what might be called a Gestalt-like experience in which emotional involvement plays an important role, the sense of reality is holistic rather than fragmented, and what one sees for oneself is far more credible than what one hears from one's political leaders. Such an experience is exactly suited to the tasks confronting a young political-social activist. Such an experience also makes repugnant to the student the schools' organization of education as a series of exposures to narrow bands of specialized knowledge, or "intellectual disciplines."

Existentialism

Whether or not young people can trace their existentialism to Jaspers and Heidegger, to Sartre or Marcel, does not seem to be very important. What is important is that youth are heavily existentialist in valuing immediate experience and the concrete over reflection and the abstract, in putting their primary trust in the former rather than the latter as guides to ethical behavior, and in their conviction that there has been, in Maslow's words, a "total collapse of all sources of values outside the individual," that there is "no place else to turn but inward, to the self, as the locus of values." While there was much that was modish in existentialism, particularly in postwar French existentialism, the questions taken up by existentialists concern the purpose of life, and death, anxiety, meaninglessness, the fate of man in mass society, all questions that academic philosophers have been ignoring in their pursuit of analytic philosophy, linguistics and semantics, logical empiricism, and structuralism. Again, young people are repelled not by philosophy or the intellectual life as such but by the kind of arid and abstract intellectualizing that has characterized whole departments of philosophy in the universities. Whatever life is, they reason, it is not that. Warren Bennis, the former executive vice president of the State University of New York at Buffalo, predicts that in future education "truth will be defined more in existential and less in rationalist terms; more by experience and less by data."

The Rigidity of Basic Social Institutions

It is undoubtedly the nature of institutions to be slow to change. What young people object to more than the slowness of change in the schools, churches, political parties, is the fact that youth are denied a part in the decision-making process of those institutions. This they interpret as an essential in the adult strategy of prolonging adolescence. The further practical effect is to postpone indefinitely the changes youth see as necessary. Against their own awareness of their needs for self-expression, self-development, and independence, and against their sensitivity to the social injustices they see all around them, young people confront a rigidity of institutional life that strikes many of them as at best ignorance and at worst cold contempt. Their response is to seek alternatives: free schools in place of the closed system; meditation, sometimes indistinguishable from self-hypnosis, in place of religion; confrontation in place of party politics. The performance of the Democratic Party at the 1968 National Convention was institutional rigidity in its classic form. After a series of primary elections in which youth played a major part and in which the Democratic voters overwhelmingly registered their disapproval of Lyndon Johnson's Vietnam policy, the Democratic Party nominated for President the chief apologist of that policy.

Art and Craft Technology

With the advent of inexpensive tape recorders and other electronic gear, printing techniques, highly portable musical instruments, youth have the technical equipment to translate almost instantly into art forms (song, light-and-sound shows, underground press) the creative energies and imaginative inspirations that are the special gift of the young. In turn, this adds to the growth of a consciously independent life- and art-style.

Literature

In the last twenty-five years, there has emerged an impressively large body of literature which, through its analysis of institutional and social life, its criticism of society, and its perception of the special social-psychological ambience of the young, verifies for youth the validity of their judgments drawn from personal experience. This consciousness that their experience is widely shared with others and, indeed, that its meaning is even more profound than they had suspected strengthens their conviction. They believe their insight is deepened by writers like Paul Goodman, Edgar Z. Friedenberg, Ronald Laing, Erik Erikson, John Holt, Erich Fromm, Kenneth Keniston, Abraham Maslow, Gabriel Marcel, Lewis Mumford, Peter Marin, Herbert Kohl, Theodore Roszak, William Barrett, Christopher Lasch, William Appleman Williams, Robert Paul Wolff, Carl Oglesby, Herbert Marcuse, Norman Mailer, I. F. Stone, Irving Howe, Robert Heilbroner, Christopher Jencks, Michael Walzer, Tom Hayden, Jerry Rubin, John Kenneth Galbraith. Though there are great differences—in thought, tone, style, position—between a Jerry Rubin and a John Kenneth Galbraith, between an Erik Erikson and a Herbert Marcuse, what together these writers represent is a powerful criticism of contemporary society, of the distribution of power within the society, of the increasing dehumanization and depersonalization of life, and of the older generation's arrangement for youth of the terms of admission into adult society. Even the titles of some of their books reflect their temper: **One-Dimensional Man; Man Against Mass Society; Irrational Man; The Divided Self; Problematic Man; Man Alone; The Making of a Counter-Culture.** Some of this literature speaks for youth. All of it speaks to them.

■

Historians deal with meaning; prophets and meteorologists with prediction. It is too early for history, too soon for predictions. But contemporary American youth and society itself are having convulsions. One must try to wrest from the times some present meaning. Prudence is still a virtue, and political and social prudence still a necessity. Perhaps some of the meaning can come through when young people speak for themselves, with occasional interspersions from older people.

Billy Digger, in a Haight-Ashbury paper, circa 1967, writes of a school teacher talking to a classroom "cramped with sitting, suffocating children." She says:

Don't talk, children. Sit there and listen to me for the next six hours, for the next five days, the next forty weeks. If you successfully pass through the first eight years of imprisonment, you can do four more years in high school. Then, if you are intelligent, fortunate, and have enough money you can do four more years in a university. Then you can graduate

and proudly be imprisoned in offices, factories, and institutions throughout the world until, at long last, you are sixty-five. Then you are free to take off more than two in a row.

Herbert Kohl, in **The Open Classroom:**

For most American children there is essentially one public-school system in the United States and it is authoritarian and oppressive. Power is a problem for all of us. The development of open, democratic modes of existence is essentially the problem of abandoning the authoritarian use of power and of providing workable alternatives. That is a problem that must be faced by all individuals and institutions that presume to teach.

Edgar Z. Friedenberg, in **Coming of Age in America:**

Compulsory school attendance is provided by a law which recognizes no obligation of the school that the student can enforce. He cannot petition to withdraw if the school is inferior, does not maintain standards, or treats him brutally. . . . What is learned in high school . . . depends far less on what is taught than on what one actually experiences in the place.

A Harvard sophomore:

If I had been brought up in Nazi Germany—supposing I wasn't Jewish—I think I would have had an absolute set of values, that is to say, Nazism, to believe in. In modern American society, particularly in the upper-middle class, a very liberal group, where I'm given no religious background, where my parents always said to me, 'If you want to go to Sunday School, you can,' or, 'If you want to take music lessons, you can,' but 'It's up to you,' where they never did force any arbitrary system of values on me—what I find is that with so much freedom, I'm left with no value system, and in certain ways I wish I had had a value system forced on me, so that I could have something to believe in.

Professor George Wald, Nobel Laureate of Harvard:

I don't think affluence has much to do with it. Permissiveness perhaps. But it's a negative kind of permissiveness. It's a permissiveness that comes from parents having nothing, no creed, no philosophy to believe in, absolutely no idea of where they are. We have desperately to find our way back to human values. I would even say to religion. There's nothing supernatural in my mind. Nature is my religion, and it's enough for me. . . . What I mean is: we need some widely shared view of the place of man in the universe.

Tom Hayden, a founder of Students for a Democratic Society, and one of the Chicago Seven in the 1969-70 conspiracy trial:

> I was encouraged by the election of John Kennedy in 1960 and especially by the erection of the Peace Corps. Then the Peace Corps became wedded to American foreign policy. We went to Mississippi to fight for civil rights with confidence that the country was behind us. We discovered that the law serves power. These feelings were deepened by the outbreaks in Northern cities and by the failure of the government to satisfy grievances in the ghetto. Most important was the war in Vietnam. At first, we believed in dialogue, but the officials wouldn't conduct reasonable dialogue. Regardless of police violence or repression, the student movement will not go away but will accelerate, using any tactics that seem suitable to stop the Vietnam aggression and begin the process of social change at home.

James S. Kunen in 1968, in the **Atlantic Monthly:**

> What's happening at Columbia University is not a revolution but a counterattack. We are fighting to recapture a school from business and war and rededicate it to learning and life. Right now nobody controls Columbia, but if we get it, we will never give it back. And there are five million college students in the country watching us. And a lot of them have just about had it with the Biggees

Maureen Hanlon, twenty-one-year-old University of California senior and sorority girl, after the National Guard's killing of four Kent State University students in an antiwar campus demonstration:

> I never wanted to consider violence before, but it just might work. Nothing else has.

Ethel C. Romm, reporting (in **Editor & Publisher**) on the Woodstock rock festival in 1969:

> Monumental drug usage was the festival's hallmark. At least ninety percent of the crowd was smoking marijuana. . . . It seems evident that perhaps fifty percent were using LSD, methedrine, hashish, mescaline. . . . Once fearful of "those hippies," shopkeepers found they always said "please," seldom helped themselves to items like the typical summer tourist. One state trooper after another said: "I never heard so many 'excuse me's' in my ten years in uniform." "This traffic jam is eight miles long and no one has leaned on a horn. Can you believe that?" "Not a knifing or a stabbing. . . ." They made many, many friends in our area, including the sheriff who, according to our paper this morning, has invited them back next year.

These are selected quotations. But they are typical. They could be multiplied a hundredfold. What they confirm is the belief that a cultural revolution is taking place in America; that it is almost exclusively a youthful cultural revolution; that the young are quite unconcerned with conventional party politics; and that a steady radicalization of the young has been taking place, beginning roughly at the time of the assassination of John F. Kennedy and increasing in volume and tempo with their realization that social, political, and economic conditions are not susceptible to any structural or systemic change through dialogue, electoral politics, or the pressure of public opinion. (It is difficult to think of any radical militants who were, so to speak, "born that way." Certainly Tom Hayden, Jerry Rubin, Carl Oglesby were not. Their experience has become the experience of countless young people: It is the familiar radicalization process that begins with idealistic faith and hope in the American system, proceeds through disillusion and frustration, and ends in cynicism, in confrontation, in violence perhaps, and, beyond that, in anarchism and nihilism.)

Bruno Bettelheim is convinced that the more extreme of young militants are raging against a chaos that is within themselves, not the world. "While consciously they demand freedom and participation, unconsciously their commitment to Mao and leaders like him suggests their desperate need for controls from the outside, since without them they cannot bring order to their own inner chaos."

To the criticism that Dr. Bettelheim is insensitive to social injustices and the imperviousness of social institutions, Bettelheim replies: "One should go along with the Establishment if it is halfway reasonable; any Establishment is only halfway reasonable." And he returns to his conviction that "the militant is more motivated by his inner anger than by the wrongs of society."

"It is very easy to say, 'I want a just society,'" according to Dr. Bettelheim, "but that is not idealism. Adolescents make tremendously high moral demands on others. . . . Idealism is when you put your ideas into practice, at some expense and hardship to yourself."

It is when he assumes that the youthful dissenters have not undergone "expense and hardship" on behalf of their idealism and when he discusses dissent almost wholly in terms of clinical pathology that one begins to grow cautious about Dr. Bettelheim's diagnosis.

A more profound clarification of "the emotional roots of youthful dissent" has been provided by another psychoanalyst, Erik Erikson, in his "Reflections on the Dissent of Contemporary Youth" (Daedalus, Winter, 1970). Although Erikson is principally concerned with trying to understand youthful dissent in the light of his theory of human development and is not an uncritical apologist for youth, he grants them the grounds for the repugnance they feel for society:

Adaptive social processes must protect and support ego development in childhood and give strength and direction to adolescent identity. But while the complementarity of individual and societal processes has been acknowledged and studied, questions in regard to the potential arbitrariness of all systems of power have remained. This questioning has, in fact, been vastly intensified in recent years with the increasing awareness of the use (or misuse) to which large-scale organization puts individual inventiveness and valor. The most affluent and progressive systems seem to thrive at the expense of individual values: their costliness may become apparent in the restriction of spontaneity in the midst of a system extolling individual freedom; in the standardization of information in the midst of a universal communications industry; and, worse, in new and numbing denials in the midst of universal enlightenment.

He continues:

Modern youth has grown up with the fact that an affluent civilization can learn to become relatively peaceful and neighborly in large areas of its existence and yet delegate the greatest destructive power that ever existed to nuclear monsters scientifically created and loyally serviced by well-adjusted experts and technicians. Not that most young people any more than most adults can keep this paradox in the center of attention for any length of time; but was it not psychoanalysis which taught that man is responsible for what he represses or attempts to remain unaware of?

The legitimacy of violence becomes the greatest single issue in the ideological struggle of youth today. It can come to sharpest awareness in those young men who must be prepared to see themselves or their friends inducted into a "service" that legitimizes what appears to be the senseless continuation of colonial wars. Most of them decide to fulfill traditional expectations of duty and heroism. Some object conscientiously. . . . A few turn furiously against the system; but if they seem totally committed to a negative utopia in which the existing world must come to an end before anything can live, one should remember that they have grown up in a setting in which adult happiness-as-usual did not exclude the minute-by-minute potential of a nuclear holocaust—and an end of mankind as we know it.

Dr. Erikson remarks toward the end of the article that when young people "hide their true identity behind dark glasses and ubiquitous hair and at the same time flaunt a negative identity often way beyond their emotional means," this may be a "negation of the three developmental necessities marking the termination of adolescence: an identity tied to some competence; a sexuality bound to a style of intimacy; and the anticipation of becoming, before long, responsible for the next generation."

He offers one piece of "therapeutic" advice at the end of his diagnosis. It is based on a belief that the future

will force on young adults not only new styles of parenthood, but also the responsibility of being, indeed, their younger brothers' and sisters' keepers. After all the remarkable service which some of our young people have rendered to the underprivileged and underdeveloped on the periphery of their lives, they may have to learn that to be a young person under conditions of rapid change means to assume responsibility for younger persons nearby, and this in ways impossible to perform by older people and least of all by parents. This is prophetically anticipated in the transient brotherhoods and sisterhoods of today—even if such caring for one another is at times only a sporadic and romantic phenomenon. . . .

If the older young people could find the courage in themselves—and encouragement and guidance from their elders—to institutionalize their responsibility for the younger young, we might see quite different images of both youth and young adulthood emerge than those we now know. New models of fraternal behavior may come to replace those images of comradeship and courage that have been tied in the past to military service and probably have contributed to the glorification of a kind of warfare doomed to become obsolete in our time; and they may come to continue the extraordinary work, both inspired and concrete, done in the last few decades by pioneering youth groups on a variety of frontiers. This, in turn, would make it possible for adults to contribute true knowledge and genuine experience without assuming an authoritative stance beyond their actual competence and genuine inner authority.

Dr. Erikson's "therapy" is corroborated from many sources. In Dr. Halleck's study of student alienation, he came to the conclusion that there would be far less of it if young people had more genuine contacts with adults. "A student can spend months on a large campus without having a conversation with a person over thirty," Dr. Halleck said.

Urie Bronfenbrenner, a professor of psychology and child development at Cornell University, has just completed a comparative study of American and Soviet approaches to child-rearing (**Two Worlds of Childhood/U.S. and U.S.S.R.**). "You become human," Dr. Bronfenbrenner said in an interview with **The New York Times'** Israel Shenker, "by contact with others older than yourself, who enable you by interaction with them to acquire a personality. Without older children or adults, you wind up—by default—in an age-segregated peer group centering on momentary gratification and

anti-social behavior. The result is a generation which has not learned what compassion is, and compassion is essential for survival." He found in Russia that one generation has great concern for the next. By contrast:

The pattern of life in Western society does not permit people to become interested in children. While we [Americans] talk a great deal about being a child-oriented society, we're markedly and dangerously neglectful of children. The amount of time spent at work and going to work, and the social obligations imposed by many occupations and professions effectively exclude time for one's children. Architects plan houses so that parents cannot see their children at play. . . . American children are disappearing from view and therefore from the social conscience. Permissiveness is lack of concern, and one way to get freedom is not to care. The one thing a Russian child can never feel is that he isn't loved. Parents and children are thrown together by the housing shortage; it's impossible to send the children off to another part of the house. There isn't another part.

One of the premises of Dr. Erikson's "therapeutic suggestion"—that, with respect to the young, adults cannot assume an authoritative stance beyond their competence and genuine inner authority—is reinforced by Rudolf Dreikurs, a professor of psychiatry at the Chicago Medical School. Dr. Dreikurs states flatly that the autocratic society is dead and that university presidents, high school principals, teachers, and parents still have to learn this. "We can no longer run schools for our children," he says. "We have to get their participation in decision-making." He predicts that many universities will close and there will be more rebellion and conflict in schools and families until responsibility is shared by all. "The autocratic demand for submission no longer holds. No harmony is possible without equality and mutual respect."

The question that puzzles adults is why college and university students apparently feel so little affection or loyalty for their schools that they can look on with equanimity when their more militant fellow students set fire to campus buildings. Part of the explanation may lie in the reluctance of administrators and teachers to share decision-making; part of it in the fact noted by Dr. Halleck—that students can spend months on a campus with no personal contact with anyone over thirty; part in the fact that students see university and society as mirror images and collaborators. Paul Goodman, in a letter a year ago to The New York Times Magazine, offers another explanation:

> The majority of so-called students in American colleges do not want to be there and ought not to be. An academic environment is not the appropriate means of education for most young people, including most of the bright. The present expanded university is coercive in its very nature; the young have to go there for various well-known reasons—none of which is necessary for their well-being or for the well-being of society. Then when militants defy the coercive institution and shout "Shut it down!" the majority are coolly complacent because they don't care for the place either. . . . Every one of these campus disorders is essentially a prison riot. If the colleges were truly voluntary associations, the disorders would never occur or would be immediately quelled by the actions of the members who would protect what they love.

■

A persistent question—on the minds of adults, if not young people—is whether there will be a violent political revolution in the classic sense of a seizure of the political and governing power in the society, and a rearrangement of the distribution of that power. When the question is asked that way, the answer must almost inevitably be no. Even if the young people were not disorganized, even if they were not splintered into liberals and radicals, crazies and destructivists, their seizure capabilities are almost nil. But their capacity for disruption through confrontation and through hit-and-run terrorism (actual and threatened) has already been demonstrated. However, disruption does not necessarily lead to seizure of political power, nor does it hold much promise of radicalizing and enlisting the sympathies of the massive middle class in the American society. Far from it. American industrial workers and their sons have shown that, if provoked, they will protect their jobs by any means from the threats posed by antiwar demonstrators; and they are joined by craft construction workers who are determined to keep blacks out of their unions.

If violent confrontation politics persist and intensify and if society becomes ungovernable and human life is in constant jeopardy, what seems most likely is a militarily imposed "order," a more or less continuing garrison existence under martial law. According to Irving Howe, violent confrontation politics will only awaken sleeping dogs it would be well to let lie.

The political revolution question can be asked in a more realistic, but perhaps unanswerable, way: Is the youthful cultural revolution so deep, pervasive, and irresistible that it will, in time, work similarly deep, pervasive, and irresistible changes in the political and economic life of the American society? Even posing the question that way is not entirely satisfactory, since it implies that the cultural revolution can be thought of as purely cultural, with no political character and no ideological content. Young people do not come in such neat, exclusive categories. But the cultural character of their revolution, the ethical, moral, psychological, and aesthetic qualities that are summed up in the word "life-style," may in the end—if the society can hold itself together long enough—work profound and permanent change. Much will depend on the extent to which the activists will carry their political militancy and the way in which the adult community will respond to both the political militancy and the cultural innovations.

Admittedly there is little justification for thinking that the young people will exercise restraint or that their elders will exhibit understanding. There may be symbolic speech in the politics of confrontation and the counterpolitics of repression. And such symbolism may be a necessary prelude to dialogue, but it is not dialogue. As this is written, the American college students, almost as one, are enraged by the Ohio National Guard's killing of four Kent State University students who had gathered on their own campus to protest President Nixon's spreading of the war into Cambodia. The killing followed by a few days Mr. Nixon's characterization of campus antiwar protesters as "bums."

Other adult responses to the young, though less lethal and dramatic, are no less adamant. The severity of marijuana laws, the writing of new constitutionally dubious conspiracy laws, the refusal of senior faculty members to let university students have a genuine voice in the way their educational program is conducted, the manner in which Chicago police were absolved for the brutality they visited on the young and the innocent bystanders on the streets during the 1968 Democratic Convention—all these adult reactions must seem to the young to constitute an insurmountable barrier between themselves and their elders.

One thinks of Oswald Spengler's description of younger and older cultures in **The Decline of the West**:

> By the term "historical pseudomorphosis" I propose to designate those cases in which an older alien culture lies so massively over the land that a young culture cannot get its breath and fails not only to achieve pure and specific expression-forms, but even to develop fully its own self-consciousness. All that wells up from the depths of the young soul is cast in the old molds, young feelings stiffen in senile practices, and instead of expanding its own creative power, it can only hate the distant power with a hate that grows to be monstrous.

But the young today are in fact achieving their own "pure and specific expression-forms," they are developing fully their "own self-consciousness." The autocratic society, as Dr. Dreikurs said, is dead (though a lot more heads will undoubtedly be bloodied before its death is universally recognized).

Also, the young have already forced many reluctant college and university administrations and faculties to make reforms that these educators now acknowledge were long overdue. One is therefore entitled to entertain the hope that in the cultural revolution both the young and the old will find it possible to accommodate each other, and in the accommodation perhaps learn to trust each other and, in that trust, to make the nation's political behavior square with the youth-heightened moral vision, and its economic arrangements coincide with the official rhetoric about equality of opportunity.

Almost a hundred and fifty years ago, Alexis de Tocqueville wrote, in **Democracy in America,** something that is especially appropriate today as we seek not only for meaning but also for some hope from the contemporary scene:

"It is evident to all alike," de Tocqueville wrote, "that a great democratic revolution is going on among us, but all do not look at it in the same light. To some it appears to be novel but accidental, and, as such, they hope it may still be checked; to others it seems irresistible, because it is the most uniform, the most ancient, and the most permanent tendency that is to be found in history."

chapter 60
being young in a postindustrial society:
erazim v. kohák

Whatever is happening on campus, it is not a revolution in any recognizable sense. A revolution must have an independent socioeconomic base, and the "youth revolution" conspicuously lacks that. Its proponents do not constitute a class, definable in terms of a specific mode of production and capable of offering an alternative mode of meeting men's physical and social needs. Nor do the young have a set of structural proposals that they could put into effect if they were to seize power—or, for that matter, an organization capable of seizing it. The campus upheavals have created a violent, destructive fringe, but the campus mood as a whole is not that. It is a mood of concern and acute alienation, and the upheaval in which it results, while capable of affecting national policy and causing temporary disruption of academic processes, can be represented as a "revolution" only rhetorically, either to justify or provoke repressive measures. For purposes of social analysis it might be more accurate to describe it as a sort of **mutiny**—a bewildered, explosive refusal to continue functioning within a system that has become increasingly alien and alienating.

For this reason, social conditions that shaped the campus upheavals might well prove more significant than the immediate causes sparking this or that explosion. Those causes are real, urgent—and

From Dissent, February 1971. Reprinted by permission.

familiar enough. American foreign and domestic policies are passing through a fundamental crisis. It is not simply a matter of specific setbacks like the Bay of Pigs fiasco or the bloody stalemate in Vietnam, or the discovery of poverty and discrimination at home. Rather, basic conceptions which have guided American public policy since the thirties have proved inadequate in the complex world of the sixties. As at the time of the analogous failure of isolationism and **laissez faire** in the early thirties, America is retaining its basic commitment, foreign and domestic, and the young serve as the leading edge of frustration.

But while there are clear parallels between the failure of isolationism and **laissez faire** in the thirties and the present failure of anti-Communism and Keynesianism, there are basic differences as well, and these need to be explained in terms of changing conditions rather than recurrent causes. Perhaps the most significant difference is that while in the thirties the revolting young were very much part of a wide upsurge in the whole society, today they are strangely isolated in a world of their own. In the thirties, the "people" of campus rhetoric had a definite empirical counterpart—union workers, dust-bowl farmers, depressed urban middle class. Today, "the people" is largely a mystified concept. The empirical people are to a large extent middle America—as a revolutionary mass they exist primarily in campus imagination.

The impact of campus mutiny on national policy has been significant, but largely indirect. With a few exceptions like the "frontlash" project, the overt content of the youth revolt has tended to create an isolated subculture of youthful imagination rather than significant alternatives for the public world. Not the fact but the form of the youth revolt raises a question about conditions rather than causes—the place of the young in a postindustrial society.

■

What precisely is the youth "revolution"? A great part of the confusion may be due to the fact that it isn't anything precisely. It is an amorphous, discontinuous series of outbursts, which attach themselves to anything from fads in dress and music to radical activism. Their common denominator is distress rather than demand, loneliness rather than confidence.

The positive traits of campus upheaval are common to youth movements of all ages. Any youth movement must stress the special problems and assets of the young—their lack of a firm place in society, their spontaneity, enthusiasm, and idealism. It must degrade those qualities the young do not ordinarily possess, such as skill, persistence, competence; and avoid problems the young normally do not face, such as assuring daily sustenance, public safety, or long-range planning. Youth movements invariably tinge their idealism with a sense of bitter disillusion: brought up on the ideals of their society, the young tend to be shocked by its realities, whether capitalist, Communist, or socialist. The young share a common sense of being in the society but not of it, thereby reflecting quite accurately their relation to the economy. And for entirely understandable reasons, the young have often shared a sense of mission to redeem their society with their spontaneity and dedication, coupled with a conviction that this cannot be done by humdrum means. Work is vain, dedication and drama alone avail.

In addition to the common traits of adolescence, present-day youth movements share a common perspective of posttechnological affluence. This is a bit more surprising. Even in America, the affluent society is at best 20 years old and remains a class phenomenon. The "affluent young" on state college campuses are, objectively, anything but affluent.

Yet affluence is a state of mind as much as a level of consumption. It reflects relative freedom from ordinary economic cares and preoccupations: in terms of the most elementary immediate experience, it is the mentality of the man who can ask himself, what shall I do today?—and does not receive an immediate, unequivocal answer in terms of daily need. In this sense, affluence can reflect, as in America and Western Europe, the condition of a society whose total productive capacity exceeds its total needs. But it can also reflect the added productive capacity represented by a team of horses in a village where the family cow pulls the plow by day and gives milk at night. In the "socialist" countries of Eastern Europe, comprehensive medical and social care, embracing everything from job security to free vacation tours, creates symptoms of affluence in spite of rather low standards of consumption. Finally, the isolation of the academic community from daily demands, required for academic work, may help to create a very distinctly affluent perspective.

The place of the young in a society that accepts the affluent model as normative is significantly different from that in a society of scarcity. An affluent society provides for its young a far greater degree of autonomy from many pressing daily occupations, not only objectively but also because it expects far less from the young in terms of cooperation in securing food, shelter, and even an atmosphere of cooperation within the family unit. Unlike his counterpart in the 1820s, a romantic rebel today can "drop out" almost completely for extended periods of time while still enjoying much of the affluence, security, and mobility of an advanced society.

To be sure, there have always been young men who enjoyed this privilege, but in the past they have been relatively few. Being a revolutionary, if we are to trust Cohn-Bendit, is a great way to live; but it requires the time and leisure of a student, and in the past students have constituted a miniscule proportion of the young. Today, some 50 percent of young Americans go on to some form of higher training, only entering the labor force between 18 and 26. For some years after ceasing to be children they are effectively excluded from assuming adult social roles. The youth "revolution" today can be a mass phenomenon because there is a mass of the young that has the objective prerequisites for engaging in it.

The affluent society makes a youth "revolution" not only possible but virtually necessary. The reason is not simply the inevitable discrepancy between expectations of affluence and objective reality. Even when affluence is quite objective —or perhaps especially when that is the case—the place of the young in society becomes precarious. Given the high degree of skill demanded by modern production, the young have little opportunity for significant participation in the work of the society. They may be enthusiastic—but in economic terms they constitute seasonal unskilled labor. At the same time technological sophistication eliminates many of the marginal tasks that had traditionally provided a bridge between play and work, and where it does not, it makes them appear onerous and insignificant. At a time in life when a young person most acutely experiences the need for a socially significant role to establish his personal identity, a society patterned on the affluent model consigns him to the role of an object of indulgence. It is not surprising that the young seek to establish their distinct identity either by dropping out or by adopting the mock-heroic role of the rebel.

There would be something radically wrong if, for some ten years after ceasing to be children, the young continued to accept without protest the role of pampered children. But there is also something radically wrong with a social model which offers them this role.

∎

These observations leave the question of fact unanswered but they do suggest an answer to the question of method. First of all, they establish the lesson of Karl Marx: There is a definite connection between technology and ideology, between the modes and means of production and the modes and means of social existence.

Economic dependence, however, is a necessary but not a sufficient explanatory principle. Analogous economic development is compatible with more than one form of social organization and behavior. A catalytic principle is needed to explain why particular forms emerge at a particular time and place. In part, to be sure, the reasons are historical—the economic prerequisites for a campus revolt existed in the fifties, but America's confidence in the ability of its leadership to cope with the problems of the time did much to prevent an explosion. Only with the loss of confidence— brought about by the failure of basic policies and signalized by the death of a President—did the inherent tensions actually erupt. But an ad hoc explanation deals with causes rather than condi-

tions—for understanding conditions, a generic catalytic principle is needed.

Campus revolutionaries tend to find such a catalyst in the Sombartian principle of power struggle which Lenin singled out as the key to his interpretation of Marxism. Its appeal is understandable enough: Struggle, especially the rather indefinite "revolutionary" struggle, is a form of activity that places a premium on the assets of youth. As an analytic tool, however, the Leninist emphasis, more familiar in the West as the "cold-war perspective," is viciously counterproductive. Seeing everything, in R. Roland's words, "from the viewpoint of an army commander" obscures both the complexity of social problems and possibilities of solution. The social strategy of such "Leninism" is to transform problems to be solved into struggles to be won and enemies to be destroyed. Effective in mobilizing energies for battle, it is unable to use them except to do battle: Leninist regimes, having won power, are notoriously incapable of building free, just societies—instead, they are borne into the fratricidal process Stalin described as "intensification of class struggle **following** the Revolution."

For purposes of social analysis and construction, a different historical conception is more helpful. Engels suggests it in his letter to Bloch in 1894 when he writes that his and Marx's preoccupation with economics and revolution was an understandable but unfortunate oversimplification. The structure of society is not a passive reflection of productive relations, but rather a product of the dialectical interaction of economic and ideological factors. Technology alone does not guarantee smooth social functioning or cause social crises. Neither does ideology alone. The crucial factor is their interrelation: A society can function smoothly if its productive processes can meets its physical needs—and if its images of man and society are capable of rationalizing those processes. Ideological appropriation of physical reality is the catalyst—struggle is incidental to it. Social crises reflect a discrepancy between technology and ideology, while social progress is a process of mutual adjustment rather than of forcible imposition of one factor on the other.

This reading of Marxism provides us with the methodological tool for understanding phenomena like the youth "revolution." The Leninist linear reading cannot explain it: Neither internal nor international issues fit the pattern of worldwide struggle ranking the "good guys" against "bad guys." There are problems to be solved rather than unequivocal "struggles" between good and evil. In particular, the mutiny of the young is not an extension of a struggle between Soviet and/or Chinese "socialist" power and American "capitalist" power. Rather, it reflects a dialectic of ideology and technology. The place and image of being young in postindustrial society is far more relevant for understanding the youth "revolution" than the opposition of "revolution" and "reaction."

We need to suspend the fierce imagery of campus rhetoriticians and their construction-site opponents. We need rather to ask about the relation of ideology and technology in concrete human experience. First, what is the impact of technological change on the experience of being young? Second, what are the ideological tools in terms of which the young seek to appropriate that change? And, finally, how would our image of man and society have to change to be capable of rationalizing new productive relations, and how would those relations have to be ordered to safeguard the values represented by that image?

To describe the impact of the scientific-technological revolution as "alienation" is accurate but not very helpful. Certainly the young—and for the matter humans **qua** human—find the postindustrial society alien: bewildering, incomprehensible, threatening. Men appropriate their world through the double process of conceptualization and manipulation. The world becomes familiar as men handle it, work in it and with it, and as they incorporate it in an overall world view. These processes have in fact broken down—but the question is precisely where and how.

The technological-scientific revolution has changed the role of the young by creating a need for extended training periods while at the same time obscuring the relation between training and practice, effort and effect. This is a generic feature of technological complexity. Putting it quite crudely, a subsistence farmer literally eats what he grows: His toil and aching muscles have an immediate personal significance in the feel of a full stomach. His production is not pointless activity, his product not soulless commodity.

The factory worker's experience is different. There is little visible link between the effort he exerts and its effect on his immediate social world. His is alienated labor: effort dissociated from effect. A basic problem for any society beyond subsistence level is one of providing compensatory mechanisms for technological alienation. The industrial age dealt with it in part through the

wage system. If the wage functioned objectively, as an instrument for control of labor and distribution, its subjective significance was no less important: The wage packet functioned as a link between effort and effect, translating labor into needed goods. Theoretically, an adequate wage could compensate for technological alienation. The concern of the unions with wages—or of the individual worker with what Karl Marx, living on an unearned income, perceived as "soulless commodity," was not an expression of the greed and materialism of the unenlightened proletariat. It was an expression of concern. The cash nexus may have been a symbol of alienation, but it was also one of its compensating factors.

In the postindustrial age the dissociation of effort and effect increases sharply while the compensating mechanisms become obscured and obsolete. As goods become widely available and payment effectively invisible in a tangle of delayed payment and paper accounting, the significance of effort diminishes. Effort appears pointless, goods become soulless commodity. The split between effort and effect, the two poles of personal identity, becomes endemic.

In the age of scarcity, liberals assumed that once the goods of daily life become available with minimum effort, human life would be freed from drudgery, and human energy would flow into "creative" tasks. They did not anticipate the secondary effect: that human life will be deprived of the token tasks through which man builds a sense of self-confident identity, relates effort and effect, and gains the habits of work demanded by creative effort: in short, that man, no longer forced to manipulate his world, will lose the ability to conceptualize it.

In the postindustrial age, a quasi-magical relation of push-button and instant product replaces effort as the basic, experienced link between man and his world. It not only expresses but also reinforces human alienation in a machine world.

The academic intelligentsia—especially the students—experience the effect of technological alienation most acutely. Young intellectuals are the segment of the population most completely deprived of—or liberated from—the need and opportunity of handling the world, of linking matter and meaning through effort. Academic effort is real enough and its effects far reaching, but its connection with need is seldom acted out.

Alienation is finally the result of a sense of the ineffectiveness of effort and anonymity of effect:

the gnawing suspicion that what a man does has no relation to what he hopes for or enjoys, and, conversely, that the things he enjoys and hopes for are a fortuitous product of anonymous forces. Students are not alone in experiencing it: It is the problem of the least as well as the most privileged. It has always been the problem of the children of the aristocracy; today it is a problem for national and racial minorities whose traditional forms of effort are not sufficiently sophisticated to produce an effect in a postindustrial society. It is also the problem of women, displaced by technology from traditional roles but barred by old habits of thought and work from assuming new ones. It is the problem of humans in a society in which significant roles appear to be reserved for machines.

■

Though creating an explosive situation, alienation itself does not bring about the explosion. In the America of Eisenhower and Kennedy it was effectively compensated by the faith that though the forces may be anonymous they are effective and benign. The explosion came when the basic concepts of the Eisenhower era, anti-Communism and Keynesianism, the struggle against totlitarianism abroad and scarcity at home proved inapplicable to new problems. For in the sixties the problem was no longer simply one of "stopping Communism" but rather of creating a viable democratic alternative, no longer one of raising the GNP but rather of distributing affluence.

The quixotic nature of the campus mutiny, however, may well be due to the fact that the ideological alternatives available to the campus are still geared to the realities of the age of scarcity in which total need vastly exceeded total productive capacity. Within such a matrix, any effort is in principle significant as contributing to total capacity—the secret of Adam Smith's invisible hand. Within such a matrix, society is inevitably polarized between drones and drudges—those whose needs are met and those whose needs, because of inadequate total capacity, must remain unmet.

Campus ideologies today reflect this matrix far more than the realities of a postindustrial society. One alternative articulates the situation of the drudges for whom work is drudgery but inevitable. Its strategy is to make virtue out of necessity by stressing the inherent nobility of work and desirability of the compensations it offers. Freedom

from drudgery, impossible in any case, is presented as decadent, and experienced as unnecessary: The drones make the decisions and bear the responsibility.

The second alternative articulates the experience of the drones, making a virtue out of privilege. In the experience of the drone, work is unnecessary, for his physical and social needs are met by drudges. From this perspective the proper pursuit of man is not work but pure, spontaneous self-expression. Any concern with needs is degrading, and as the ideal of the drudges is a society in which all men labor and none is exempt, the ideal of the drones is a society in which all are aristocrats and no man labors.

The first alternative is represented by puritan and proletarian ideologies, by Ayn Rand's objectivism of but a few years ago and the present cult of Third World revolutionism. Both are profoundly conservative: Both see affluence as the villain and the solution as a reversion to a simpler age. In the objectivist utopia, complexity of technological relations is resolved through strict accounting. Nothing is allowed to appear "free"; everything must be paid for individually. Effort is never anonymous or social; it is always individual, tied to individual needs. In the Third World version, effort becomes radically social and heroic, either by substituting guerrilla warfare for productive activity or by making productive activity heroic. Thus the harvest becomes the "battle for the grain," manufacture becomes a "struggle to fulfill the plan." There is much talk of duty, little of freedom.

The appeal of the proletarian/puritan approach lies largely in its recognition of the need to make effort significant—and of the uses of adversity in achieving this. But for good or bad, neither its puritan nor proletarian version is viable in an affluent society. The heroic model failed disastrously even in much less developed Eastern Europe. It invokes a "struggle" that is theoretic and abstract, though the work it demands is all too immediate and concrete. "Moral incentives," paradoxically dear to materialist theoreticians, proved at best partly effective, and only in situations in which the theoretical struggle had a practical counterpart. On campus, this heroic approach has produced mock-heroics. The puritan version did not even have an opportunity to fail. Technological complexity makes Ayn Rand's simplification impossible in principle.

In a sense, the utopian/aristocratic approach is much more congenial to the experience of the young in postindustrial society. On campus, obligations appear and often are conventional, and the effort required to meet them appears arbitrary. A strategy that seeks not to make effort significant but to eliminate it is much more appealing, especially if linked to a vision of spontaneous activity as the genuinely human pursuit.

In a very crude version, this is the alternative offered by Madison Avenue. Its logic is simple: Since in an affluent society production is justified by replacement of effort rather than meeting of needs, Madison Avenue holds out the vision of effortlessness as the way to fulfillment. Have, not do.

This approach has had a remarkable impact on America. Not only do a great many of the young consider having to exert effort the chief source of their alienation, but a great many adults, including educators, see the solution to youth protest in making things easier, in doing for the young more and more of what they can do for themselves. Perhaps the most striking testimony to the effectiveness of Madison Avenue is that parents who have "liberated" their children from virtually every opportunity to assume responsibility and whose children are "still" restless, frequently share the conviction that their children need even more freedom from responsibility, more done for them.

In this crude version, this self-destructive aristocratic utopia is persuasive because it reflects rather than challenges the position of man as consumer in an industrially mature society. It is self-destructive because the consumer is also the producer, and the habits of effortlessness and dependence may be virtues in the consumer but are vices in the producer. A modern utopia need not be a utopia for drudges, but it does have to be a utopia of producers rather than of conspicuous consumers.

The problem of man as producer, absent in the Madison Avenue utopia, is very much present in the rather more sophisticated version presented by neo-Marxists like Herbert Marcuse. As interpreted on campus, Marcuse shares the Madison Avenue conviction that the effortless utopia is possible and desirable, and that our failure is the failure to realize it. Thus the mutiny of the young against purposive effort is legitimate, not only because effort has been misdirected but because it is gratuitous.

Marcuse in effect radicalizes Marx in a rather interesting way. In the famous passage in **Kapital** Marx distinguishes the realm of necessity and the

real of freedom, and his reference to a short workday suggests that what he had in mind was economically necessary activity and free-time activity respectively. In Marx, the realm of freedom makes the realm of necessity meaningful: Man works in order to enjoy freedom from need. In turn, the realm of necessity makes the realm of freedom possible: The achievements of work win man leisure. According to Marcuse, the realm of necessity has become superfluous: Technology is at least in principle capable of replacing all necessary activity. Human life is in principle capable of becoming entirely a realm of spontaneous, unnecessary activity. Only old habits, psychological and institutional, stand in the way.

Marcuse's estimate of the possibilities of technology may or may not be accurate. The odds are against it: The construction, servicing, and control of an economic system so sophisticated that it could meet all productive and distributive needs is likely to demand more rather than less skill, discipline, and dependability on the part of labor. Reliance on spontaneity is notoriously more compatible with beachcombing than with sophisticated technology.

But even were it technologically feasible, Marcuse's vision would remain problematic. Marcuse is right in seeing work performed under alien, arbitrary constraint as senseless drudgery. But it is not at all clear that its aristocratic opposite, the spontaneous activity "liberated" from all external motives, is the alternative. Traditionally, those sectors of the population which have most closely approximated such "liberation"—the children of the aristocracy, the children of the superrich, and now the children of the affluent—have constituted the most frustrated, decadent, and alienated sector of society. Effort becomes meaningful not by becoming unnecessary, but by becoming purposeful and effective. The dichotomy of drudgery and leisure leaves out the uniquely human alternative, necessary work, freely undertaken for good and sufficient reason.

This is the democratic alternative. Even if Marx's scheme of necessity and freedom were economically invalid—which is far from evident—it would still retain its social and psychological validity. Freedom is not empty when it is won through ability to meet necessity through effort—when it is based on democratic work. As long as it is based on dependence on others, whether slaves or robots, it is alienation. Necessity can become meaningful rather than oppressive when man appropriates it as a means of freedom: When it is simply met by the efforts of others, it remains degrading. Marx's hopes for the redeeming role of the proletariat were based on the fact that the proletariat wins its freedom by meeting its own needs through its own labor, not by dependence on others, and so need not itself become an exploiting class.

Marcuse himself may well be trying to say something very similar—that work becomes meaningful when it serves a purpose rather than an external demand. His emphasis on an aesthetic perspective of man and world, his insistence on speaking of **surplus** repression, all hint in this direction. But that has not been his impact on campus. There the lesson of Marcuse has become virtually indistinguishable from the lesson of Madison Avenue: Effort is degrading and objectively unnecessary, demanded only by old-fashioned administrators and equally old-fashioned superegos. Hence the response is the "Great Refusal"—chemical or political—to destroy the system which makes demands without, presumably, disrupting the flow of benefits from a self-operating technology, and the "new sensibility" which will replace inner need for effort with instant self-realization. From this perspective, work is polarized between the abstractions of drudgery and play, and the young—some of them—see play as their birthright.

Marcuse's recent loss of popularity on campus may well be due to his misgivings about this bowdlerized version of his ideas. But the misgivings come too late: Utopian ideology has inseparably associated all effort with the problems it seeks to resolve. Any effort to resolve them perpetuates them because it perpetuates the age of effort rather than ushering in the age of spontaneity. The only truly "radical" approach is to reject the problems and solutions alike, to withdraw from the world of effort into the world of sensibility.

This version of the utopian ideology fits rather neatly with the campus version of the ideology of heroic effort. Revolution is the praxis of utopia: Since problems have to be surpassed rather than solved, "revolutionary" symbolic acts are appropriate. Closing down the University might not improve the quality of education just as "offing the pigs" might not contribute to a more humane and equitable assurance of public safety, but it will render social problems insoluble—and so force the society to transcend them.

The success of the new revolutionary-utopian synthesis on campus is due not to any ability to solve the problems of the young but rather to its ability to rationalize them. But while the revolutionary utopianism does accurately reflect the experience of the young, it does nothing to change it. Read in revolutionary-utopian terms, social issues and personal problems may become at once comprehensible and insoluble. The shift in campus strategy makes the point clearly. Social issues have become accessible to campus concern through a translation from the terms of the external world into the terms of emotions, attitudes, and feelings. The issues are real, but the campus "radicalizes" them—makes them subjective, highly general, and charged with the emotions of personal problems. Thus the very real problem of minorities in an increasingly homogeneous society has become the problem of "racism" rather than civil rights, the solution an equivalent of dropping out and turning on—black separatism and black consciousness. Similarly, the complex issues of the place of women in society became the question of "sexism," and even urgent questions of public safety at home and abroad have turned into emotional issues of being "for peace," for "love," "against oppression," or hating "racist, sexist, imperialist pig America." The translation is not always this extreme, and there are still a great many students struggling to retain their hold on reality, but the direction of the revolutionary-utopian ideology is unmistakable and powerful because it makes problems appear amenable to the strategy available to the young—dropping out and turning on.

Yet the demand for "immediate abolition of racism, sexism, imperialism, and pollution" will necessarily be frustrated. It can lead only to greater and greater frustration, sharper and sharper confrontation—and ultimately to repression, whether by reaction or revolution, since even "the revolution" could not meet its own demands. (This is but one sense in which revolution and counterrevolution become equivalents.) The revolutionary-utopian ideology has given the young a superficial sense of instant significance, but the cost is damnably high. The basic problem of rationalizing postindustrial production has disappeared behind a revolutionary-utopian smoke screen. An ideology simply reflecting the conditions of production is not enough. Nor is an ideology that simply reaffirms a perennial ideal. What is needed is an ideology that could play the role of a catalyst between ideals and the realities of the postindustrial age.

■

Prerequisites for a catalytic ideology do exist today. In spite of the appeal of the revolutionary-utopian strategy, the great escape was not and is not what the great majority of students seek to achieve. The problem, after all, is not that the young refuse to accept the role of pampered, useless children: That was always the positive moment in their mutiny. **The problem is that the society has no real role for its young.** The policy emerging from recent confrontations—roughly, to push off the young into even more luxurious academic sandlots while stationing armed guards around them—is counterproductive. The young have a right to a significant role in society, not only for their own sake but for the sake of society as well. A catalytic ideology would have to be capable of providing social roles both objectively significant and experienced as such.

The objective problem can be solved because it is not simply a matter of technology but of its ideological appropriation as well. Effort loses objective significance not simply because postindustrial society can produce more than it needs, but because it is unable to use its productive capacity to improve the quality of life. A capitalist economy is inevitably bound to reinvest for profit, creating an inflation of unneeded goods, but it lacks the mechanisms to channel its surplus capacity to meet the need for a distribution of affluence —public health, education, housing. When Adam Smith's invisible hand ceases to function with the overcoming of social scarcity, a capitalist society has no way of replacing it. The result is the paradoxical situation of effort invested so that one part of the society would not have to roll up car windows by hand while another part remains deprived of essential services.

Nothing in the nature of postindustrial production demands such a society. Continued reinvestment in surplus production is economically as well as socially undesirable. It has an inflationary effect on the economy as well as on skill levels demanded of the labor force. It creates social and environmental problems not only morally bad but also economically damaging. Modern production requires a social structure capable of coordinating national productive effort, channeling investment into areas of need, and preventing major dislocation of the economy by irresponsible decisions. A postindustrial society requires a socialist social structure to make effort objectively meaningful.

The inherent danger of socialism, however, is that in establishing a social machinery for eco-

nomic direction it creates a concentration of power —the coercive power of the state and the power of focused economy—far beyond anything capitalism dreamed of and makes men far more dependent than free. Campus rebels, while aware of the limitations of capitalist economy, have been blissfully ignorant of this tendency of socialism. A catalytic ideology would need to take it into account, and counter it with a consistent, radical demand for democracy. The first priority of socialism must be to safeguard rights of free critique, free press, vigorous dissent, individual responsibility and initiative. It has to be democratic both in outline and detail, striving to achieve maximum participation—giving each man an opportunity to function as a member of a community rather than as its beneficiary of victim.

Student slogans about participation grope in this direction. It might be more efficient to have a state agency build low-cost housing than to organize a tenants' cooperative through which to channel funds, but the rebelling young are beginning to recognize that the efficiency is self-defeating. The same is true of community clinics and college dormitories. While social action is necessary to make individual action effective, it is not sufficient —it is the individual action, what Marx called "socially useful labor," which gives men confidence in their identity and a sense of social participation, and can transform campus mutineers into a positive social force.

Postindustrial productive relations create conditions for democracy as a life-style and not only a political system. To a great extent, the complexity of postindustrial production eliminates economic justification for both the class of drudges and the class of idlers. Income differences tend to be quantitative, differences of earned income. Within a socialist structure, a technologically advanced society can be a classless society of wage earners rather than a society polarized between owners and the owned.

But the anarchist/authoritarian temper of the campus mutiny suggests that posttechnological production does not create the psychological conditions for democracy. Rather, it tends to create habits of dependence, irresponsibility, and anonymity, directly contrary to habits required for a democratic life-style. Here a conscious attack is needed. Neither indulgence nor repression is relevant. What is needed is the democratic opportunity **to do**, to accept responsibility and participate in the work of the society, from shared family responsibilities to opportunities for dealing with political and social problems.

In terms of the campus, this justifies the entire range of student participation in academic administration and services, as well as off-campus involvement. But the basic need is to make the students' professional work significant. A student's personal identity is first of all that of a student—and if this is experienced as trivial or insignificant, no amount of marginal activity can replace the self-esteem lost through deprecation of the primary role. Making study significant does not mean making it "relevant" in a fashionable sense of the word by restricting it to the narrow horizons of students' immediate experience. Such strategy may keep students amused, but it gives them little sense of the importance of their work—or of themselves as engaged in it. Rather, making study significant means taking students seriously, showing them the same respect scholars show their colleagues. The scholarship presented in courses deserves to be thorough, and the standards demanded high. Expecting a faculty to teach and paying it for teaching, and expecting students to study and rewarding them for it, are prime requisites. Utilizing the skills of graduates in social service rather than surplus production is their counterpart.

None of this, to be sure, speaks directly to the problems raised by student rebels. Those problems are cosmic ones, stated in intensely personal terms. Any concrete social action will necessarily disappoint them. A person stripped of all the accouterments of personal identity—of skills, interests, obligations—may well be permanently alienated simply because he has lost the ability to function in any social context.

There are signs that Americans are becoming aware of the continuity between responsibility and self-respect. Even on campus, there is increasing evidence of a sorting out process which separates the desperate from the concerned. It is by no means an automatic development, but it is a possible and a promising one. Given a consistent commitment on the part of all who deal with the young to provide opportunities for participation and assumption of responsibility and an equally consistent resistance to the clamor of the frightened for fewer demands and greater "freedom," it is a development that can effectively compensate for the technological displacement of the young.

Nothing in the nature of postindustrial production guarantees this: quite the contrary, it is entirely possible for most parents and the society as a whole to deprive the young of all participation. But there is everything to make a meaningful participation possible. The mutiny of the young need not end in irrelevance and repression. The displacement of the young that produces it is not simply the result of a technology that makes effort unnecessary, but also of an obsolete ideology that regards it as heroic—and onerous. Socialist recognition of social rights and democratic recognition of individual responsibility make another conception possible: democratic work as the self-expression of a free man in a just society. The growing disillusion of the majority of students with the heroics of their over-thirty ideological mentors, their growing involvement in social, political, and academic processes and their evident concern with the realities rather than the psychodrama of social change hold out hope for a democratic alternative to violence and repression. They deserve our support. If they can win the freedom to accept responsibility and show a willingness to accept being young not as a privilege or an onus, but as a valid, responsible way of participating in social existence, the youth revolution will become unnecessary. It will also succeed.

chapter 61
the blueing
of america
peter l. berger
and brigitte berger

A sizable segment of the American intelligent-sia has been on a kick of revolution talk for the last few years. Only very recently this talk was carried on in a predominantly Left mood, generating fantasies of political revolution colored red or black. The mood appears to have shifted somewhat. Now the talk has shifted to cultural revolution. Gentle grass is pushing up through the cement. It is "the kids," hair and all, who will be our salvation. But what the two types of revolution talk have in common is a sovereign disregard for the realities of technological society in general, and for the realities of class and power in America.

Only the most religious readers of leftist publications could ever believe that a political revolution from the Left had the slightest prospects in America. The so-called black revolution is at a dividing fork, of which we shall speak in a moment. But as to the putatively green revolution, we think that the following will be its most probable result: It will accelerate social mobility in America, giving new opportunities for upward movement of lower-middle-class and working-class people, and in the process will change the ethnic and religious composition of the higher classes. Put differently: Far from "greening" America, the alleged cultural revo-

From The New Republic, April 3, 1971. Reprinted by permission of The New Republic, © 1971, Harrison-Blaine of New Jersey, Inc.

lution will serve to strengthen the vitality of the technological society against which it is directed, and will further the interests of precisely those social strata that are least touched by its currently celebrated transformations of consciousness.

The cultural revolution is not taking place in a social vacuum, but has a specific location in a society that is organized in terms of classes. The cadres of the revolution, not exclusively but predominantly, are the college-educated children of the upper-middle class. Ethnically, they tend to be WASPs and Jews. Religiously, the former tend to belong to the main-line Protestant denominations, rather than to the more fundamentalist or sectarian groups. The natural focus of the revolution is the campus (more precisely, the type of campus attended by this population), and such satellite communities as have been springing up on its fringes. In other words, the revolution is taking place, or minimally has its center, in a subculture of upper-middle-class youth.

The revolution has not created this subculture. Youth, as we know it today, is a product of technological and economic forces intimately tied to the dynamics of modern industrialism, as is the educational system within which the bulk of contemporary youth is concentrated for ever-longer periods of life. What is true in the current interpretations is that some quite dramatic transformations of consciousness have been taking place in this sociocultural ambience. These changes are too recent, and too much affected by distortive mass-media coverage, to allow for definitive description. It is difficult to say which manifestations are only transitory and which are intrinsic features likely to persist over time. Drugs are a case in point. So is the remarkable upsurge of interest in religion and the occult. However, one statement can be made with fair assurance: The cultural revolution has defined itself in diametric opposition to some of the basic values of bourgeois society, those values that since Max Weber have commonly been referred to as the "Protestant ethic"—discipline, achievement, and faith in the onward-and-upward thrust of technological society. These same values are now perceived as "repression" and "hypocrisy," and the very promises of technological society are rejected as illusionary or downright immoral. A hedonistic ethic is proclaimed in opposition to the "Protestant" one, designed to "liberate" the individual from the bourgeois inhibitions in all areas of life, from sexuality through aesthetic experience to the manner in which careers are planned. Achievement is perceived as futility and "alienation," its ethos as "uptight" and, in the final analysis, inimical to life. Implied in all this is a radical aversion to capitalism and the class society that it has engendered, thus rendering the subculture open to leftist ideology of one kind or another.

Its radicalism, though, is much more far-reaching than that of ordinary, politically defined leftism. It is not simply in opposition to the particular form of technological society embodied in bourgeois capitalism but to the very idea of technological society. The rhetoric is Rousseauean rather than Jacobin; the imagery of salvation is intensely bucolic; the troops of the revolution are not the toiling masses of the Marxist prophecy but naked children of nature dancing to the tune of primitive drums.

■

When people produce a utopia of childhood it is a good idea to ask what their own childhood has been like. In this instance, the answer is not difficult. As Philippe Ariès has brilliantly shown, one of the major cultural accomplishments of the bourgeoisie has been the dramatic transformation of the structure of childhood, in theory as well as in practice. Coupled with the steep decline in child mortality and morbidity that has been brought about by modern medicine and nutrition, this transforma-

tion is one of the fundamental facts of modern society. A new childhood has come into being, probably happier than any previous one in human society. Its impact, however, must be seen in conjunction with another fundamental fact of modern society—namely, the increasing bureaucratization of all areas of social life. We would see the turmoil of youth today as being rooted in the clash between these two facts—paraphrasing Max Weber, in the clash between the new "spirit of childhood" and the "spirit of bureaucracy." However one may wish to judge the merits of either fact, both are probably here to stay. Logically enough, the clash almost invariably erupts when the graduates of the new childhood first encounter bureaucracy in their own life—to wit, in the educational system.

The matrix of the green revolution has been a class-specific youth culture. By definition, this constitutes a biographical way station. Long-haired or not, **everyone**, alas, gets older. This indubitable biological fact has been used by exasperated over-thirty observers to support their hope that the new youth culture may be but a noisier version of the old American pattern of sowing wild oats. Very probably this is true for many young rebels, especially those who indulge in the external paraphernalia and gestures of the youth culture without fully entering into its new consciousness. But there is evidence that for an as yet unknown number, the way station is becoming a place of permanent settlement. For an apparently growing number there is a movement **from youth culture to counterculture**. These are the ones who drop out permanently. For yet others, passage through the youth culture leaves, at any rate, certain permanent effects, not only in their private lives but in their occupational careers. As with the Puritanism that gave birth to the bourgeois culture of America, this movement too has its fully accredited saints and those who only venture upon a **halfway covenant**. The former, in grim righteousness, become sandal makers in Isla Vista. The latter at least repudiate the more obviously devilish careers within "the system"—namely, those in scientific technology, business, and government that lead to positions of status and privilege in the society. They do not drop out, but at least they shift their majors—in the main, to the humanities and the social sciences, as we have recently seen in academic statistics.

The overall effects of all this will, obviously, depend on the magnitude of these changes. To gauge the effects, however, one will have to relate them to the class and occupational structures of the society. For those who become permanent residents of the counterculture, and most probably for their children, the effect is one of downward social mobility. This need not be the case for the halfway greeners (at least as long as the society is ready to subsidize, in one way or another, poets, T-group leaders and humanistic sociologists). But they too will have been deflected from those occupational careers (in business, government, technology, and science) that continue to lead to the higher positions in a modern society.

What we must keep in mind is that whatever cultural changes may be going on in this or that group, the personnel requirements of a technological society not only continue but actually expand. The notion that as a result of automation fewer and fewer people will be required to keep the technological society going, thus allowing the others to do their own thing and nevertheless enjoy the blessings of electricity, is in contradiction to all the known facts. Automation has resulted in changes in the occupational structure, displacing various categories of lower-skilled labor, but it has in no way reduced the number of people required to keep the society going. On the contrary, it has increased the requirements for scientific, technological, and (last but not least) bureaucratic personnel. (The recent decline in science and engineering jobs is due to recession, and does not affect the long-term needs of the society.) The positions disdained by the aforementioned upper-middle-class individuals will therefore have to be filled by someone else. The upshot is simple: **There will be new "room at the top."**

Who is most likely to benefit from this sociological windfall? It will be the newly college-educated children of the lower-middle and working classes. To say this, we need not assume that they remain untouched by their contact with the youth culture during their school years. Their sexual mores, their aesthetic tastes, even their political opinions might become permanently altered as compared with those of their parents. We do assume, though, that they will, now as before, reject the antiachievement ethos of the cultural revolution. They may take positions in intercourse that are frowned upon by Thomas Aquinas, they may continue to listen to hard rock on their hi-fi's, and they may have fewer racial prejudices. But all these cultural acquisitions are, as it were, functionally irrelevant to making it in the technocracy. Very few of them will become sandal makers or farmers on communes in Vermont. We suspect that not too

many more will become humanistic sociologists.

Precisely those classes that remain most untouched by what is considered to be the revolutionary tide in contemporary America face **new prospects of upward social mobility.** Thus, the "revolution" (hardly the word) is not at all where it seems to be, which should not surprise anyone. The very word **avant-garde** suggests that one ought to look behind it for what is to follow—and there is no point asking the **avant-gardistes**, whose eyes are steadfastly looking forward. Not even the Jacobins paid attention to the grubby tradesmen waiting to climb up over their shoulders. A technological society, given a climate of reasonable tolerance (mainly a function of affluence), can afford a sizable number of sandal makers. Its "knowledge industry" (to use Fritz Machlup's term) has a large "software" division, which can employ considerable quantities of English majors. And, of course, the educational system provides a major source of employment for nontechnocratic personnel. To this may be added the expanding fields of entertainment and therapy, in all their forms. All the same, quite different people are needed to occupy the society's command posts and to keep its engines running. These people will have to retain the essentials of the old Protestant ethic—discipline, achievement orientation, and also a measure of freedom from gnawing self-doubt. If such people are no longer available in one population reservoir, another reservoir will have to be tapped.

■

There is no reason to think that "the system" will be unable to make the necessary accommodations. If Yale should become hopelessly greened, Wall Street will get used to recruits from Fordham or Wichita State. Italians will have no trouble running the RAND Corporation, Baptists the space program. Political personnel will change in the wake of social mobility. It is quite possible that the White House may soon have its first Polish occupant (or, for that matter, its first Greek). Far from weakening the class system, these changes will greatly strengthen it, moving new talent upward and preventing rigidity at the top (though, probably, having little effect at the **very** top). Nor will either the mechanics or the rewards of social mobility change in any significant degree. A name on the door will still rate a Bigelow on the floor; only there will be fewer WASP and fewer Jewish names. Whatever other troubles "the system" may face, from pollution to Russian ICBMs, it will not have to worry about its being brought to a standstill by the cultural revolution.

It is, of course, possible to conceive of such economic or political shocks to "the system" that technological society, as we have known it in America, might collapse, or at least seriously deteriorate. Ecological catastrophe on a broad scale, massive malfunction of the capitalist economy, or an escalation of terrorism and counterterror would be cases in point. Despite the currently fashionable prophecies of doom for American society, we regard these eventualities as very unlikely. If any of them should take place after all, it goes without saying that the class system would stop operating in its present form. But whatever else would then be happening in America, it would **not** be the green revolution. In the even remoter eventuality of a socialist society in this country, we would know where to look for our greeners—in "rehabilitation camps," along the lines of Castro's Isle of Pines.

We have been assuming that the children of the lower-middle and working classes remain relatively unbitten by the "greening" bug—at least sufficiently unbitten so as not to interfere with their aspirations of mobility. If they too should drop out, there would be literally no one left to mind the technological store. But it is not very easy to envisage this. America falling back to the status of an underdeveloped society? Grass growing over the computers? A totalitarian society, in which the few remaining "uptight" people run the technocracy, while the rest just groove? Or could it be Mongolian ponies grazing on the White House lawn? Even if the great bulk of Americans were to become "beautiful people," however, the rest of the world is most unlikely to follow suit. So far in history, the uglies have regularly won out over the "beautiful people." They probably would again this time.

The evidence does not point in this direction. The data we have on the dynamics of class in a number of European countries would suggest that the American case may not be all that unique. Both England and western Germany have been undergoing changes in their class structures very similar to those projected by us, with new reservoirs of lower-middle-class and working-class populations supplying the personnel requirements of a technological society no longer served adequately by the old elites.

What we have described as a plausible scenario is not terribly dramatic, at least compared with the revolutionary visions that intellectuals so often thrive on. Nor are we dealing with a process unique in history. Vilfredo Pareto called this type of process the "circulation of elites." Pareto emphasized (rightly, we think) that such circulation is essential if a society is going to survive. In a Paretian perspective, much of the green revolution would have to be seen in terms of decadence (which, let us remark in passing, is not necessarily a value judgment —some very impressive flowerings of human creativity have been decadent in the same sociological sense).

But even Marx may, in a paradoxical manner, be proven right in the end. It may be the blue-collar masses that are, at last, coming into their own. "Power to the people!"—nothing less than that. The "class struggle" may be approaching a new phase, with the children of the working class victorious. These days we can see their banner all over the place. It is the American flag. In that perspective, the peace emblem is the old bourgeoisie, declining in the face of a more robust adversary. Robustness here refers, above all, to consciousness —not only to a continuing achievement ethos, but to a self-confidence not unduly worried by unending self-examination and by a basically intact faith in the possibilities of engineering reality. Again, it would not be the first time in history that a declining class leaned toward pacifism, as to the "beautiful things" of aesthetic experience. Seen by that class, of course, the blue-collar masses moving in suffer from considerable aesthetic deficiencies.

"Revolutionary" America? Perhaps, in a way. We may be on the eve of its blueing.

topic 25

the cultural revolution:
the new music,
the underground press,
and pop culture

There is an insurrection afoot—a cultural rebellion. Confined in the beginning to such contracultural epicenters as San Francisco's Haight-Ashbury, the East Village in New York, and Venice West in Los Angeles, its impulses—on the wings of Bob Dylan, Janis Joplin, Jimi Hendrix, the Airplane, and **The Great Speckled Bird**—have radiated all over the country. The cultural convulsion is revolutionizing the tastes and life styles of millions of young Americans and their counterparts in industrial societies elsewhere.

What a far cry from the climate of two decades ago! In the 1950s intellectuals and sociologists (some without portfolio) were fond of assailing what was invidiously labeled **mass culture**. A host of social analysts attacked such hyperconformist species as the suburbanite, the other-directed organization man, the generation of white-collar bureaucrats, and the apathetic college generation of the "silent fifties." Actuating their apprehensiveness was the fear summarized by Dwight Mcdonald: "The tendency of modern industrial society . . . is to transform the individual into the mass man."

It is perhaps too soon to prophesy whether the future holds an Orwellian sort of mass man addicted to soap-opera fare in music, drama, literature, and the cinema, or whether a vigorous, new, and creative cultural renascence is in the offing. But surely the most revealing clues are readily at hand in the form of the underground press, pop culture, and particularly the new music. Of all the media of expression that personify the very essence of youth dissent, none—hair, clothes, and argot among them—is more revealing than the new music.

Contracultural dissent did not develop overnight. It has its roots in such early-day pockets of bohemianism as the Left Bank in Paris, New York's Greenwich Village, and the later Beat and Hippie movements. Similarly, the new music traces a long ancestry, back to Negro blues, country and western, and bluegrass music; later came such pioneers as Elvis Presley, Chuck Berry, and Buddy Holly, followed more recently by Paul Butterfield, Bob Dylan, the Rolling Stones, and—perhaps most crucially of all—the Beatles. The major transformation from the old style to the new took place in the middle 1960s when, on the heels of a revival of folk singing, performers like Dylan began to compose and sing their own songs.

Consciously modeling himself on Woody Guthrie, the wandering minstrel of the

1930s, Dylan and his music expressed a variety of themes ranging from civil rights, the war in Vietnam, and the phantasmagoric world of youth, to a private world of drugs, love relationships, and personal freedom—paralleling the changing imagery and themes of contracultural dissent in general.

Central among these themes were antiwar protest, youth as victim, the plastic world created by technology, Madison Avenue, and Hollywood, and tripping out of a repressive society—"How happy life would be," the Amboy Dukes declared, "if all mankind would take the time to journey to the center of the mind." Ralph Gleason sums it all up: "The most immediate apparent change instituted by the new music is a new way of looking at things. We see it evidenced all around us. The old ways are going and a new set of assumptions is beginning to be worked out."

The authors of the three articles in this section focus, in turn, on the origins of the new music (Serge Denisoff and Mark Levine), the revolution in the underground media (Peggy Scott), and, on "Boobus Americanus," H. L. Mencken's term for the middle-American lowbrow who is at fundamental odds with virtually all that contracultural esthetics stands for. In the end, the reader must decide for himself which culture (if either) will prevail—the contraculture or the culture of the "great boob."

chapter 62
generations and counter-culture: a study in the ideology of music[*]
r. serge denisoff and mark h. levine

Karl Mannheim's sociology of knowledge rests upon the notion of "relationism," where truth is predicated upon situationally prescribed values of individuals or units in any social context (Mannheim, 1936:79). Generations in this schema are viewed as: "nothing more than a particular kind of identity or location, embracing related 'age groups' embedded in a historical-social process" (Mannheim, 1951:292). With this unique relationship to a historical time and place, generations are conceptualized as processing a distinct awareness akin to Marx's view of class consciousness. Each generation, Mannheim (1951:293) argues, has a different or "fresh contact" with custom, tradition, and political thought. Furthermore, in periods of rapid social change, generations are likely to develop highly distinctive outlooks and aims which conflict with those of older generations, thus leading to political youth movements as groups consciously emphasizing "their character as generational units" (Mannheim, 1951:309). T. B. Bottomore (1968:

101) has applied this conceptualization to the New Left in North America, writing:

> "Make love, not war" is hardly an exhortation directed to the elderly. The fact that radical movements are animated and led for the most part by university students is itself enough to establish that they are primarily manifestations of generational culture.

This view is predicated upon several assumptions, particularly the "end of ideology" thesis submitted by Bell (1963), Lipset (1963), and recently Boorstein (1969). Bell and Lipset, in their controversial treatise, advanced the argument that ideological movements of the Left were irrelevant after the 1950s due to the exigencies of international political polarization and the rise of the welfare state in the West. Moreover, Marx's Law of Immiseration, it was contended, had no persuasive power in the affluent societies of the West. While a number of critics came forth to challenge this thesis only staunch Marxist ideologues presented reaffirmations of their maligned position (see Waxman, 1968; Aptheker, 1960). Instead, most critiques were aimed at the "pluralistic and economic" assumptions offered by Bell and Lipset, generally ignoring radical alternatives. C. Wright Mills (1963:259), in his "Letters to the New Left," was one of the few to urge that intellectuals and stu-

This excerpt from "Generations and Counter-Culture: A Study in the Ideology of Music" by R. Serge Denisoff and Mark H. Levine is reprinted from Youth and Society, vol. 2, no. 1, September 1970, pp. 41-50, by permission of the publisher, Sage Publications, Inc.

*The authors wish to thank Stan Kanehara and Shelley Levine for their assistance in the preparation of this paper, presented at the annual meetings of the Pacific Sociological Assn., Anaheim, California, April 6, 1970.

dents should formulate "new theories of structural changes of and by human societies in our **epoch**." Despite Mills' desire for radical alternatives, he (1963:259) dismissed Marxism-Leninism, stating: "Forget Victorian Marxism except whenever you need it; and Lenin again (be careful)—Rosa Luxemburg, too." Since this famous open letter to the British New Left, nearly all the studies dealing with this political phenomenon have characterized it as nonideological. In fact, the New Left has come to idealize Camus' (1956:13-22) description of the rebel who affirms human solidarity and value without resorting to the Hegelian Absolute Truths. While contemporary North American Leftists were differentiated from their Stalinist, Trotskyist, and Socialist forerunners, they were nearly always characterized as carrying on the liberal, humanistic tradition of Roosevelt's New Dealism cherished by their parents, that is, the values of Jeffersonian and countervailing power as described by Galbraith, for example, "participatory democracy."[1]

Keniston (1967:120) indicates that political activists are "living out their parents' values in practice, and one study suggests that activists may be somewhere **closer** to their parents' values than nonactivists." The study (Flacks, 1967:68), cited by Keniston, of members of the Students for a Democratic Society (SDS) at the University of Chicago, noted:

> Most students who are involved in the movement . . . are involved in neither "conversion" from nor "rebellion" against the political perspectives of their fathers. A more supportable view suggests that the great majority of these students are attempting to fulfill and renew the political traditions of their families.

Early studies such as these by Keniston and Flacks appeared to imply that Mannheim's conceptualization of "generational units" was not totally applicable to the New Left. Accordingly, the generational conflict originally was most apparent between the Old Left and their New Left children. More recently, other investigations of the political attitudes of New Left adherents have come to question the "political socialization" hypothesis. Jansen et al. (1968), report that continuity of ideology and political activism is strongly influenced by the prestige of a university. Riley Dunlap (1969:21-22) found little support at the University of Oregon "for the socialization hypothesis, as the SDS activists do not appear to have very liberal parents."

In effect, these latter studies appear to indicate that while students in America's academically elite universities, such as the Ivy League schools, may be closely tied to the liberal cosmopolitan orientations of their parents, others in the same generational unit are not. As student discontent and antiwar sentiment are dispersed throughout the generational unit, the continuity hypothesis appears to be less valid.[2] Due to the sheer amorphousness of the present antiestablishment sentiment, extrapolation from university political groups and other organizations is limited in value. As Roszak (1969:xi) correctly observes, there is more to the generational unit than a "card carrying movement, with a headquarters, an executive board, and a file of official manifestoes." It appears that with the increasing polarization and internal fragmentation of sociopolitical publics, even what was nebulously termed the New Left is no longer a viable unit of analysis (see Rush and Denisoff, 1970). Externally, the New Left has been isolated from a number of legitimate political channels and institutions such as traditional liberal, peace, and civil rights lobbies. Only the foci of opposition to the Vietnam War has kept some segments of the New Left in touch with older protest groups. Internally, the New Left has been shattered by the emergence of the New Old Left and the so-called "counter-culture."

The New Old Left can be defined and characterized as being ideologically committed to either Mills' Labor Metaphysic, the idealization of the proletariat, or the neo-Leninism of International Third World organizations, such as the glorification of students and minority group members as vessels of social change. This newly emerging dogmatism has led to the inevitable internecine splintering so characteristic of sectarian movements (see Alexander, 1953:282-310). The New Left's shift to increased ideological agitation has pushed it away from its natural generational constituency. This trend was clearly evidenced at the November 15, 1969, New Mobilization Against the War (New Mobe) rallies in two central urban areas. The New Mobe marches were designed to give witness to public opposition to American participation in the Vietnamese Civil War. Demonstrators assembled in Washington, D.C., and San Francisco to express their opposition to the war in a manner similar to the Aldermaston East Peace March. Crowds exceeding 200,000 persons were reported in both cities. In San Francisco the tone of the rally can best be described as antidoctrinal and nonviolent. Speakers who invoked ideological solutions and tactics involving the use of force were soundly hissed and booed (Lembke and Hager, 1969:B) as evidenced by David Hillard, the Black Panther Party spokesman who, professing allegiance to the tenets of Marxism-Leninism, was hooted loudly when he remarked, "If you want peace, you've got to fight, fight, fight." Hillard received a like response following the statement, "You won't get peace by playing guitars or holding demonstrations like this." Other representatives of ideological organizations did not fare better. The greatest public accolades were reserved for apolitical speakers, particularly musicians.

Paul Schrade, a union official, labeled the Golden Gate Park rally, appropriately the site of the first be-in, "Woodstock West." This reference, of course, is to a rock festival held August 15, 1969, in upstate New York, attended by 300,000 to 500,000 youths. Here the participants lived on an open hillside, listening to their rock idols for three days and nights, with no buildings or conveniences. **Life** magazine reported:

> For three days nearly half a million people lived elbow to elbow in the most exposed, crowded, rain drenched, uncomfortable kind of community, and there wasn't so much as a fist fight. The whole world was watching, and never before had a hippie [sic] gathering been so large or so successful; so impressive.
>
> "There are a hell of a lot of us here. If we are going to make it, you had better remember that the guy next to you is your brother." Everybody remembered. Woodstock made it.

Given its success, Woodstock has been recurrently presented as evidence of the practicability of a new culture and social order. Noteworthy is the fact that Woodstock was apolitical; attempts by political activists to radicalize the milling throng went unheeded. The **Rolling Stone** (1969:24) recorded the following incident involving The Who, a leading rock band, and Yippie leader Abbie Hoffman:

> Hoffman leaped onto the stage, grabbed a microphone and announced that the festival was meaningless as long as White Panther Party leader and MC-5 manager John Sinclair was rotting in prison. Peter Townshend . . . [of The Who] . . . then clubbed Hoffman off the stage with his guitar. **That's the relationship of rock to politics** [italics added].

Woodstock generally has been described as a "victory for music and peace." A similar observation could be made of the moratorium rally in San Francisco. While the New Old Left drifts into the political esoterica of Marxsmanship, a large entity is becoming more potent: the counter-culture.

The counter-culture is an amorphous representation of the generational unit which cuts across educational and ideological boundaries. It constitutes a social entity which emerges en masse at given social events, such as demonstrations, rock festivals, love-ins, marches, and the like, and then melts away until the next such happening. As Roszak (1969:48-49) observes, the counter-culture is:

> Something in the nature of a medieval crusade: a variegated procession constantly in flux, acquiring and losing members all along the route of march. Often enough it finds its own identity in a nebulous symbol or song that seems to proclaim little more than "we are special . . . we are different . . . we are outward-bound from the old corruptions of the world." **Some join the troop** only for a brief while, long enough to enter an obvious and immediate struggle: a campus rebellion, an act of war-resistance, a demonstration against injustice [italics added].

The counter-culture is viewed as "experiential" rather than ideological, or as Roszak (1969:xi) describes it, "ectoplasmic Zeitgeist" in competition with "values and assumptions that have been in the mainstream of our society . . . since the scientific revolution." Thus, as Roszak sees it, the counter-culture is a product of the demands of technology and the new industrial state, as described by Ellul (1964) and Galbraith (1967), rather than the ideologically prescribed causes of alienation and immiseration.

The hub of the counter-culture, given its experiential nature, is the musical genre of rock, from whence come the heroes or high priests of counter-culture, the rock musicians. At the moratorium the greatest audience response was to rock music, one report (Lembke and Hager, 1969) correctly noting that the "most ecstatic response of the day [was] to several numbers by the San Francisco cast of the rock musical "Hair." The next largest outpouring was for the rock band of Crosby, Stills, Nash, and Young. After a prolonged standing ovation from an estimated 200,000 persons, Steve Stills walked up to the microphone, raised his arms with the now traditional V sign, and shouted: "Politics is bullshit! Richard Nixon is bullshit! Spiro Agnew is bullshit! Our music isn't bullshit" (Denisoff, n.d.). It was a sentiment nearly all of the crowd appeared to share. It is precisely this antipolitical attitude which characterizes the counter-culture. Given the nature of the counter-culture, even the broadest of political movements is not necessarily representative of the **entelechy** of the current generational unit. For example, even the most liberal estimates of antiwar demonstrations in America have not matched the turnout for the Woodstock Festival nor the Rolling Stones' free concert at Livermore, California. Similarly, the continuity hypothesis of Flacks, Keniston, and others, while true of their samples, does not begin to picture the generational unit described by Mannheim and, later, Bottomore. Instead, we must concur with Roszak, Leary, Carey, and others that "one is apt to find out more about their [young people's] ways by paying attention to pop music, which now knits together the whole thirteen to thirty age group" (Roszak, 1969: 291).

The thrust for this assertion is that while politics as an organizational phenomenon reflects less than a tenth of the present generational unit, rock music affects over eighty percent of this group. As such, we are proposing that Mannheim's notion of generational units in conflict can best be examined in terms of life styles and cultural leanings rather than conventional political ideologies.

Moreover, we would suggest that if indeed politics between generations are as similar as the above data suggest, then the so-called generation gap must lie elsewhere, perhaps in Roszak's counter-culture.

GENERATIONAL CONFLICT AND ROCK AND ROLL, 1950-1970

Rock and roll emerged during the 1950s as an aberrant, in the Mertonian sense, deviation, in that it connoted juvenile misconduct, not in the lyrics, but in the presentation of the material, such as the dress styles and stage presence of performers. The key word, here, was "roll," suggesting sexual intercourse. Lyrically, however, as will be explicated below, the notions of adolescent passage into adulthood and postponed gratification were stressed. The adult generation at this time objected to rock and roll as senseless and incoherent, and expressed "consternation as to how this genre could provoke such extraordinary interest" (see Green, 1965:204-228). As such, rock and roll was perceived by the

adult generation of the 1950s as deviating from the outward symbols of respectability and the basic normative order. Rock and roll, as opposed to the rock music of the next decade, did not question basic values or institutions. The fact that youngsters liked junk music was seen as a fad which they would pass out of upon entering adulthood (see Gillet, 1966:11-14; Gershman, 1969:1, 37; Keil, 1966:44-45).

In the 1960s rock music was nonconformist, in that it was viewed as urging social change. The stress of the music of the 1960s was upon lyrical content, setting the stage for "rock music's connection with politics and social issues" (Hilburn, 1970:21). Rock music was viewed, not as advocating a temporary role suspension, but rather as questioning basic values and institutions. For example, the sentiment of turn on, tune in, and drop out, found in some rock numbers, stresses total disaffiliation. Drugs, discussed in some songs, are also viewed as a barrier for later participation in the system.

More importantly, rock music has in time gained an intellectual respectability lacking in the 1950s. It was only in the late 1960s that scholarly interest was directed to this musical phenomenon. In the 1950s, serious musicians and adults in general denounced rock and roll as **déclassé** in an artistic and moral sense, whereas in the 1960s rock music has been seen as innovative and **classé**, but as politically and intellectually deviant.

Origins of Contemporary Rock

Contemporary rock music is the product of several **déclassé** subcultures and musical genres vis-à-vis middle America and popular music (see von Meier, n.d.; Gillett, 1966:11-14; Belz, 1969). Rock and roll was a direct spin-off from race music originally directed to urban Black ghettos. Another important strain of rock music is derived from "hillbilly," or the country and western genre, occasionally referred to as "shit-kickers" music, connoting the "barnyard quality" of the product. This genre, until recently, was primarily addressed to a rural, white audience in the southern and western parts of the United States.

The dominant or **kitsch** society's exposure to rock and roll was originally through so-called "cover" versions of Black material. Here popular as well as country singers would take race material and make it usable for their audience (see Friedenburg, 1963; Hentoff, 1956:12). This practice, it was argued, was necessary because of the emphasis on roll, or sex, in these original versions. For example, the Midnighters' "Work With Me Annie" was transformed to "Dance With Me Henry." "Shake, Rattle and Roll," was changed by Pat Boone and others to exclude obscene passages. Covering was not always moralistic, but overtly economic. For example, the Chords, a Negro group, recorded "Sh Boom" for the ghetto market. The Crew Cuts recorded the same inoffensive lyrics, added strings, and other kitsch trappings, and produced a million seller in the white or pop market.

In the country and western sphere a similar process took place with Bill Haley and, later, Elvis Presley taking Negro blues tunes and merging them into a semi-country or "rock-a-billy" style. Haley (Schonbert, 1956:10) explained this practice to one interviewer as follows: "Bad lyrics can have an effect on teenagers. I have always been careful to not use suggestive lyrics."

Despite the innocent lyrics, rock and roll was associated in the mass culture with various déclassé undertones. One of the original best-selling records in this genre was Bill Haley's "Rock Around the Clock," the theme song from the movie **Blackboard Jungle**. Equally, Presley's physical appearance greatly paralleled and furthered the American stereotype of a delinquent youth. David Riesman (1964:88) characterized "Elvis the Pelvis" as follows:

> Presley created a definitely "antiparent" outlook. His music—and he, himself—appeared somewhat insolent, slightly hoodlum.
>   Presley was a much more gifted musician than adults gave him credit for, but he antagonized the older generation. And that gave the younger generation something to hang on to which their usually permissive parents openly disliked.

Presley, as an examination of his early hits show, was not in any way a social or political dissenter. Only his outward appearance and his stage posture, or lack of it, offended adult sensibilities (see Denisoff and Levine, 1969). Yet the lyrics of Presley's songs continued the romantic love syndrome of less controversial crooners, as with "I Want You, I Need You, I Love You" and "Heartbreak Hotel," a classic statement of the rejected suitor. As Donald Horton's (1962:569-578) work suggests, nearly all popular songs during the mid fifties were addressed to ancient courtship motifs.

Early Rock Themes

Early rock music rarely went beyond "boy-meets-girl, loses-girl" themes. Occasionally some song dealing with adolescence or the music itself would become popular, but generally the music was totally in keeping with social norms. Chuck Berry was one of the few stars who recorded songs such as "Brown-Eyed Handsome Man," "Almost Grown," "Monkey Business," "Rock and Roll Music," and "Roll Over Beethoven" which questioned the status quo. The latter two pieces were direct attacks upon the more traditional musical tastes of an older generation as well as a reaffirmation of rock and roll:

> Don't care to hear 'em play a tango
> I'm in no mood to hear a mambo;
> It's 'way too early for a congo,
> So keep a rockin' that piano
> So I can hear some of that rock 'n' roll music
> ["Roll Over Beethoven," Arc Music].

The song continues to urge the listener to feel or experience the music and to "reel and rock" to its rhythmic beat. Some of his other recordings such as "Almost Grown" and "Monkey Business" stated the problems of adolescence, but concluded "Don't bother me, Leave me alone . . . I'm almost grown." Eddie Cochran's "Summertime Blues" is universally considered the first protest song in the rock genre. The piece is typical rock-a-billy or Presley style, emphasizing the hardships of part-time jobs, getting the car, and adolescence in general. The only political reference, however, was to the lack of enfranchisement:

> I'm gonna take my problem to the United Nations,
> I called my Congressman, but he said quote:
> "I'd like to help you son, But you're too young to vote"
> ["Summertime Blues," American Music Inc.].

Given the rather confused institutional references—congressman have little to do with the United Nations—and the song's ending, "there ain't no cure for the summertime blues," the protest value of this piece was symbolic at best.[3] This feature was characteristic of all of the quasi-protest songs of the early rock and roll period; indeed, most of the songs ended in resignation to cultural diffusion and parental domination. In fact, several

knowledgeable observers, such as Barzun and Riesman, have gone so far as to suggest that rock music
was little more than "background noise" selectively
turned on and off (see Robinson and Hirsch, 1969:
42-45; Denisoff and Levine, 1969).

One indication of the symbolic nature of the
music was the summary blacklisting of rock and
roll musicians for alleged "misconduct." Jerry Lee
Lewis' marriage to his teenage cousin resulted in
his removal from the playlists of the top forty stations. Yet, rock was generally viewed by adults as
beyond serious consideration and structurally
deviant. For many, the payola or bribery scandals
of the early 1960s only reaffirmed this belief. Sub-
stantiatively, it was not until the so-called folk
music revival (1958-1965) that lyrics began to
address political issues and social dissent.

INFLUENCE OF FOLK
GENRE ON PROTEST THEMES

Folk music, historically, has been utilized as a
vehicle for social protest (see Dunson, 1965; Rodnitzky, 1969:35-45; Denisoff, 1968b:228-247;
1969:183-197). In America it has been exploited
especially, but not exclusively, by the working
class or left-wing movements, particularly the Industrial Workers of the World and the Communist
Party. It was this latter movement which sowed
the seeds of the revival, although it never succeeded
in popularizing the folk genre itself. Folkniks, during the revival of the early 1960s, discovered the
songs of Woody Guthrie, Molly Jackson, The Almanac Singers, and, of course, Pete Seeger. In time,
they wrote songs about the social strains of their
period, rather than recalling the labor struggles of
the 1930s and the Spanish Civil War. The key
figure in this transition was Bob Dylan, who wrote
countless pieces decrying racial, political, and other
social dysfunctions.

Concomitant to the popularization of "protest
singers," particularly on college campuses, was the
rise of the Beatles, who revitalized the popular
music field. The Beatles, with their Skiffle tradition, covered early American blues recordings as
well as writing their own material. Originally, their
material was in the romantic love vein of "I Want
to Hold Your Hand" and "She Loves Me." Several
ex-folkniks, particularly the Byrds, a rock group,
melted the Dylan lyric into a Beatle-like arrangement, thus coming up with "folk-rock" (Belz,
1969:177; Dunson, 1966:12-17). In 1965, Dylan
followed suit, giving up politics and adopting an
electric rock band, a move which severed him from

his folk music mentors and the Old and New Left.
In his song "My Back Pages," Dylan dissents from
those who see song as "a cry for justice" and left-
wing ideology:

> Good and bad I define these terms
> Quite clear no doubt, somehow
> Ah, But I was so much older then
> I'm younger than that now
>   ["My Back Pages," Widmark and Sons].

Dylan's new popularity among top-forty audiences,
as well as that of the Byrds, produced a number of
imitators who tried to combine rock music with
protest songs. Among them, the best-known example is ex-Christy Minstrel Barry McGuire, who recorded "Eve of Destruction." This was a denunciation of the hypocrisy of the older generation and
a statement that if conditions did not improve,
nuclear annihilation was around the corner (see
Denisoff and Levine, 1969; Noebel, 1966:228-
231). Despite the sales of this controversial song,
few other blatantly political songs have been commercially successful. Indeed, overt political propaganda songs today are more in the realm of novelty
items, both right and left, than effective songs of
persuasion.[4] In recent years only John Lennon and
Yoko Ono's "Give Peace a Chance" has gone from
the political arena into the top forty. As we have
seen, rock music during its formative years incorporated a number of deviant elements from American society into a vehicle of the mass culture. Yet
unlike the classic notions of "massification" presented by Gessat and McDonald, the popularization
of rock music was in a particular generational unit
rather than the entire population, which in many
instances did not exhibit atomization.

Hippie Influence on Rock

Strikingly, in the later part of the sixties rock
music was strongly influenced by events in the
emerging hippie movement, the model of the counter-culture, with its stress on mind-expanding
drugs. Timothy Leary, the self-appointed prophet
and youth leader, portrayed (1968:355) the underground movement as preaching a message of "turn
on, tune in, drop out." In the drug culture, politics were generally deemed insignificant. What were
important were the weekend "happenings" at the
Fillmore Auditorium and the Avalon Ballroom. At
these events one was exposed to a total experience
in mixed media. Wolfe (1968:42) presents one
description of a night at the Avalon:

Evening at the Avalon provides plenty of the ear-splitting sound characteristic of the hippie band. Continuously changing light projections of liquid colors and protoplastic forms bathe the dancers. Their luminescent, striped and dotted clothes glow eerily amid the flashing lights. Symbols, concentric circles, and pictures of Indians and oriental priests are beamed onto the walls.

Suddenly, the fast, screaming music dies down to a soft love song and then gives way to a mournful Indian dirge. The light show changes. On one wall there is a picture of Buddha and on another a picture of Christ on the cross. Several hundred of the youngsters on the dance floor join hands. They sway back and forth in a trancelike state.

Rock music for the hippie cult was a religious experience in the tradition of William James and Aldous Huxley, and as described by William Sargant. One critic (Robinson, n.d.) notes:

Rock concerts are religious experiences and today's rock musicians and audience view the church in the regalness of their robes and mystical trappings.

More significantly, the music became a symbol for social alternatives, that is, a counter-culture. The music for both generational units became an expression or **zeitgeist** of the rejection of deferred gratification and of limiting traditional rites of passage. The music's trancelike quality was viewed as deterring students from scholastic achievement. Songs such as "White Rabbit" were described as urging listeners to drop out and into the drug culture. Most studies of rock music, to date, have converged upon the musical message of individual freedom, doing one's own thing, or the hang loose ethic. As Carey (1969:162) notes:

The overall preoccupation in the lyrics is with choice. Choice is mainly exercised in terms of freeing one's self from external constraints, whatever their source.

The lyrics imply two major choices, urging the listener to maximize his freedom in interpersonal relationships, and to drop out of conventional society. Dropping out is viewed as a positive thing. . . . Withdrawal is a response to the coerciveness of institutions and a decision not to collaborate with them.

The freedom of choice in rock numbers is both anti-intellectual and anti-ideological Rodnitzky (1969) relates:

Folk-rock . . . is becoming increasingly anti-intellectual. The new stress on the sensory effect of the music rather than the verbal message is one aspect of the increasing belief that truth must be felt rather than rationally grasped.

At a press conference the Jefferson Airplane stated (Glass, 1969:1), "Don't ask us about politics, we don't know anything about it. And what we did know, we just forgot." A once-political musical commentator described contemporary music as "a sensual experience . . . everything but an intellectual, theatrical presentation" (see Cohen, 1968-1969:11). Only a handful of rock musicians, it would appear, have strong political commitments or views which are translated into their songs. Country Joe and the Fish, the Fugs, and the now defunct Mothers of Invention were the overtly political in the rock genre.

Subversive Themes in Rock?

Despite the lack of political sentiment expressed in most rock songs, spokesmen of the older generation see the music as politically and socially subversive. The stress upon freedom and choice, cited by most observers as major tenets of the American Creed, has been described as statements of hedonism and license. In the 1950s, rock and roll was seen as an "expression of **hostile** rebellious youth" (see Belz, 1969:44). In recent years, rock music has come to be viewed as politically dissident and morally subversive. This is in keeping with Mannheim's suggestion that rapidity of social change leads to differential perception and ideological interpretation. As we have seen, musical styles in the last two decades changed with a rapidity not previously experienced. It appears that as musical changes occur, greater concern is expressed by those wedded to genres of the past.[5]

During the folk revival, this "youth rebellion" came to be seen as subversive by conservative groups such as the John Birch Society and, particularly, David Noebel of the Christian Crusade (Denisoff, 1969a; 1969b.63-64). More recently, adults have objected to rock music as an advocate of drugs and antiestablishment attitudes. The older generation's view of music has several fundamental historical roots. The first root of the older generation's view of popular music is the austere religious notion that nonreligious art is sinful (Denisoff, forthcoming). Early American clergy, as well as American fundamentalists today, saw secular music as the tool of the Devil. As such, the enjoyment of secular music, especially by the young, was viewed as Devil's work.

This demonic tenet of frontier Christianity leads to a second underlying cause for the "music is deviant" view: conspiracy. The Devil was perceived as engaging in a conspiratorial war for men's souls. He, of course, relied upon the tools of trickery and other machinations to achieve his goals. This is particularly true in the case of the youth, who, what with the image of the Pied Piper of Hamlin, has been seen as susceptible to corruption due to his unawareness of evil. Most recent discussions (Noebel, 1965:15) of rock music, by its opponents, have exhibited these two trends:

> Throw your Beatle and rock and roll records in the city dump. We have been unashamed of being labeled a Christian nation. . . . Let's make sure four mop-headed anti-Christ beatniks don't destroy our children's emotional and mental stability and ultimately destroy our nation as Plato warned in his **Republic**

A president (see Robinson and Hirsch, 1969:1) of a large independent chain of radio stations stated:

> We've had all we can stand of the record industry's glorifying marijuana, LSD, and sexual activity. The newest Beatles record has a line of 40,000 purple hearts in one arm. Is that what you want your children to listen to?

Art Linkletter (see Fong-Torres, 1969:20), appearing before a congressional committee, argued that rock and roll was little more than an inducement to take drugs:

> In the Top 40 half the songs are secret messages to the teen world to drop out, turn on, and groove with chemicals and light shows at discotheques. Most of the jackets of record albums are merely signboards of psychedelia.

One fundamental interpretation of these divergent views of rock music is provided in Mannheim's notion of relationism and generational units. That is, generational units perceive the ideology of the music in totally different ways: The following ex-

cerpt from an interview (Denisoff, 1968a) with the First Edition, a pop rock group, is illustrative of Mannheim's relationism:

> They [adolescents] . . . realize the average person outside of their age category does not put that depth into it and it's a way of saying, 'I know more than you do' because I read something into that . . . you don't even see.
>
> Records say things very plainly and in very plain words, but adults don't understand them either.

Belz and others appear sympathetic to this position, suggesting that adults have generally seen rock 'n' roll as lyrically senseless and incoherent, and could not understand how their children could enjoy this type of music. As such, rock music is believed to be a significant area of generational contention.

Rock and roll, as well as rock music, appealed to young people; neither appealed particularly to the adult generation, although rock music, given its more ideational or intellectual quality, does appeal to a wider age range than its forerunner. The generational conflict over music in the 1950s, we have argued, revolved around the representative and symbolic aspects of the music as well as its shady origins. The generational conflict of the present era no longer touches upon issues of symbolism or musical structure or the appearance of performers, but rather the debate focuses more on the lyrical content of the material.

In sum, we are suggesting that political indices of generational conflict, the socialization hypothesis presented by Flacks and others, have not been conclusive in regard to Mannheim's thesis of generational units and social protest. Instead, we have suggested that the counter-culture may be a more fruitful area of investigation vis-à-vis generational units. Moreover, it was indicated that rock music was an important factor in the life style of the counter-culture and, indeed, the entire generational unit.

Generational Units:
Music and Political Attitudes

The preceding discussion suggests a number of hypotheses, of which two are paramount: (1) Differentiations between generational units will be greater than in intragenerational units; (2) differentiations, if the counter-culture thesis is correct, will be greater between generational units in the sphere of rock music than in political attitudes. The first hypothesis is addressed to establishing or falsifying Mannheim's notion of generational units as being similar, rather than diversified, internally, and externally in opposition to the older or previous generational unit. The second hypothesis involves testing for greatest area of generational conflict, if any, in the areas of politics and music. If generational conflict is greater between two generational units, and music is the main area of dissension, we may then suggest that Mannheim's approach to generations may be the most useful, and that the counter-culture thesis may be more descriptive of the current generation than the political socialization studies.

In 1968 a random sample of 444 secondary school students and dropouts was drawn from a city in the metropolitan area of Vancouver, British Columbia (see Rush, Collinge, and Wyllie, 1969). The ages of individuals in this group ranged from thirteen to nineteen. According to some observers this age range is central to generational conflict and support for the counter-culture.

To facilitate a comparison of generations, 121 parents of those students and dropouts already selected were questioned. Along with the parents, 36 teachers and administrators from the schools covered in the sample were queried, bringing the total adult sample to 157.

As Tables 1 through 4 indicate, intragenerational conflict does not appear significant in either political or musical areas. Students do not tend to favor any particular political party more than their dropout counterparts. In musical tastes the differences between students and dropouts also were not significant with a majority favoring rock music. In sampling the parents and teachers of the aforementioned students and dropouts no significant difference was found in their political preferences as a generational unit. The adults tended to prefer the Liberal Party of Canada, as had their children and charges.

The findings presented in Tables 1, 2, 3, and 4 support Mannheim's hypothesis on the entelechy of a generational unit. Parents and teachers by and large did not like rock music, while their offspring overwhelmingly supported this musical genre. Respondents were also questioned with the aim of testing our second hypothesis dealing with counter-culture, namely that differences between generations will be substantially greater in the area of music than in politics. As the data in Tables 5 and 6 show, generational differences are exceedingly

prevalent in terms of the musical tastes of those sampled, while such is not the case with reference to political preferences, thereby supporting Roszak's counter-culture hypothesis. Among the adults, 96 percent of those sampled selected Broadway show, movie themes, classical, or religious music as their first or second choice in answer to an open-ended question "Which types of music do you like best?" while among the younger generational unit, these four types of music were selected in only one instance out of every eight.

In the younger generational unit, 87.9 percent choose rock and roll music as their first or second favorite choice of musical genres. In the adult sample, only 4 percent expressed such a choice. As

TABLE 1.
Student-Dropouts Intragenerational Unit Political Preferences

	COMMUNIST	SOCIALIST	LIBERAL	CONSERVATIVE	TOTAL
Students	10 (3.3)	50 (16.4)	216 (70.5)	30 (9.8)	306
Dropouts	0	7 (17.9)	29 (74.7)	3 (7.4)	39
Total	10	57	245	33	345

$x^2 = 1.63$ not significant.

TABLE 2.
Student-Dropouts Intragenerational Unit Musical Preferences

	ROCK MUSIC	SHOW AND CLASSIC	TOTAL
Students	280 (87.2)	41 (12.8)	321 (100.0)
Dropouts	34 (94.4)	2 (5.6)	36
Total	314	43	357

$x^2 = 1.24$ not significant.

TABLE 3.
Parent-Teacher Intragenerational Unit Political Preferences

	SOCIALIST[a]	LIBERAL	CONSERVATIVE	TOTAL
Student's parents	22 (25.0)	55 (62.5)	11 (12.5)	88
Dropout's parents	3 (12.0)	19 (76.0)	3 (12.0)	25
Teachers	6 (21.4)	22 (78.6)	0	28
Total	31	96	14	141

$x^2 = 6.32$ not significant.

[a]None of the respondents support the Communist Party. In the sphere of musical tastes the parent-teacher sample nearly always favored the musical offerings of the Broadway stage and the classics.

TABLE 4.
Parent-Teacher Intragenerational Unit Musical Preferences

	ROCK MUSIC	SHOW AND CLASSIC	TOTAL
Student's parents	4 (4.2)	91 (95.8)	95
Dropout's parents	1 (5.5)	18 (94.5)	19
Teachers	1 (2.8)	36 (97.2)	37
Total	6	145	151

x^2 = .5 not significant.

TABLE 5.
Generational Unit Differences in Musical Preferences

	ROCK MUSIC	SHOW AND CLASSIC	TOTAL
Students and dropouts	314 (87.9)	43 (12.1)	357
Adults	6 (4.0)	145 (96.0)	151
Total	320	188	508

x^2 = 319 significant at any level.

TABLE 6.
Generational Unit Differences in Political Preferences

	COM-MU-NIST	SO-CIAL-IST	LIB-ERAL	CON-SER-VA-TIVE	TOTAL
Students and dropouts	10 (2.9)	57 (16.5)	245 (71.0)	33 (9.6)	345
Parents and teachers	0 (0.0)	31 (22.0)	96 (68.1)	14 (9.9)	141
Total	10	88	341	47	486

x^2 = 4.83 not significant.

Table 5 illustrates, there is a significant difference (x^2 is 319) at any level between the older generational unit and the younger in musical preferences. The differences between parents-teachers, and students-dropouts in the political preferences is not statistically significant, x^2 = 4.83 at 3 degrees of freedom. This lack of significance is shown in Table 6.

These findings from a nonelitist sample of secondary school students and dropouts indicate that political preferences between generational units are pretty much the same. On the other hand, significant differences in so-called cultural areas are observable.

From the above findings, it would appear that Rozsak's counter-culture thesis has some empirical support; however, the authors urge caution in extrapolating from this sample. High school students are by and large more experientially oriented than their more intellectual collegiate counterparts. This factor, without doubt, skews the data toward Rozsak's antitechnology stance.

In addressing the political socialization issue, our data lend support to the Keniston and Flacks hypothesis of ideological continuity. Nevertheless, the age of the sample may be more favorable to this hypothesis as opposed to the findings of Dunlap and others. Also, the sample was of a predominantly middle- and upper-middle-class area.

The significant finding here, however tentative, is that generational conflict in the Mannheimian sense, may involve more than just the political sphere generally treated by those observing youth movements. As such, much benefit may be derived from looking at the cultural trends in youth culture such as music, films, and other experiential aspects of what may be a growing counter-culture.

NOTES

1. Interestingly, these same WASP students have turned their backs on the so-called Horatio Algier ideal or the American Dream.

2. While the campus remains the main staging ground for political protest, it is not directed by any one group or coalition of organizations. Campus antiwar protest is large in sentiment; however, this stance frequently has little to do with SDS and other political organizations.

3. A handful of other songs, more in the R&B tradition, raised the same issues of parental dominance. However, unlike "Summertime Blues," the Silhouettes record "Get a Job" was a song decrying the lack of work for young Black men.

4. A number of so-called protest songs have sporadically made their way to the top forty, particularly the Animals' "We Gotta Get Out of This Place" and "Sky Pilot"; Jody Miller's "Home of the Brave"; Sonny Bono's "Laugh at Me"; "Mr. Businessman" by Ray Stevens; "Two Plus Two" by Bob Seger; "Skip a Rope" by Hensen Cargill; "Universal Soldier" by Glen Campbell; and the Buffalo Springfield's "For What It's Worth." Only the latter piece was predominantly in the rock genre. Barry Sadler's pro-Administration "Ballad of the Green Berets" was put to an old Spanish Civil War march. Ironically, most proestablishment songs have been recorded either in country and western genre or in the middle media style of Frankie Laine and Pat Boone, neither having much to do with the top forty.

5. There is nothing particularly new in this proposition, as Plato once suggested, "The introduction of novel fashions in music is a thing to bear of as endangering the whole fabric of society." (See Plato, 1945:115.)

REFERENCES

ALEXANDER, R. J. (1953) "Splinter groups in American radical politics." *Social Research* 20 (October):282-310

APTHEKER, H. (1960) *The World of C. Wright Mills.* New York: Marzani & Munsell.

BELL, D. (1963) *End of Ideology: the Exhaustion of Political Ideas in the Fifties.* New York: Collier.

BELZ, C. (1969) *The Story of Rock.* New York: Oxford Univ. Press.

BOORSTEIN, D. (1969) *The Decline of Radicalism.* New York: Random House.

BOTTOMORE, T. B. (1968) *Critics of Society: Radical Thought in North America.* New York: Pantheon Books.

CAMUS, A. (1956) *The Rebel: An Essay on Man in Revolt.* New York: Alfred Knopf.

CAREY, J. T. (1969) "The ideology of autonomy in popular lyrics: a content analysis." *Psychiatry* (Fall): 150-163.

COHEN, J. (1969) "Interview with Roger McGuinn of the Byrds." *Sing Out* 18 (December/January): 11.

DENISOFF, R. S. (forthcoming) "The religious roots of the song of persuasion." *Western Folklore.*

 (1969a) "The ideology of the extreme right and folk music." California State College, Los Angeles. (mimeo)

 (1969b) "The proletarian renascence: the folkness of the ideological folk."*J. of Amer. Folklore* 82 (January/March): 63-64.

 (1969c) "Urban folk 'movement' research: value free?" *Western Folklore* 28 (July): 228-231.

 (1968a) *Interview at Vancouver,* July 27.

 (1968b) "Protest movements: class consciousness and the propaganda song." *Sociological Q.* 9 (Spring) :228-247.

DENISOFF, R. S. and LEVINE, M. H. (1969a) "The one-dimensional music: a research note." California State College, Los Angeles. Unpublished.

—— (1969b) "The popular protest song: the case of the 'Eve of Destruction.' " California State College, Los Angeles. (mimeo)

DUNLAP, R. (1969) "Family backgrounds of radical and conservative political activists at a non-elite university." Eugene: Univ. of Oregon. (mimeo)

DUNSON, J. (1966) "Folk rock: thunder without rain." *Sing Out* 15 (January):12-17.

—— (1965) *Freedom in the Air.* New York: International Publishers.

ELLUL, J. (1964) *The Technological Society.* Translated by J. W. Wilkinson. New York: Alfred Knopf.

FLACKS, R. (1967) "The liberated generation: an exploration of the roots of student protest." *J. of Social Issues* 23 (July).

FONG-TORRES, B. (1969) "Feds' dope circus: 'how much LSD do you take to be addicted?' " *Rolling Stone* (November 29):20.

FRIEDENBERG, E. (1963) *Coming of Age in America.* New York: Vintage.

GALBRAITH, J. K. (1967) *The New Industrial State.* Boston: Houghton-Mifflin.

GERSHMAN, M. (1969) "The blues once black, now a shade whiter." *Los Angeles Times Calendar* (January 19):1, 37.

GILLETT, C. (1966) "Just let me hear some of that rock and roll music." *Urban Rev.* 1 (December):11-14.

GLASS, W. (1969) "The history of rock and protest." California State College, Los Angeles. Unpublished.

GOLDBERG, H. (1968) "Contemporary culture innovations of youth: popular music." Presented at the annual meetings of the Amer. Psychological Assn., August 31.

GREEN, A. (1965) "Hillbilly music: source and symbol." *J. of Amer. Folklore* 78 (July/September):204-228.

HENTOFF, N. (1965) "Musicians argue values of rock and roll." *Downbeat* 23 (May 30):12.

HILBURN, R. (1970) "Rock enters 70's as the music champ." *Los Angeles Times Calendar* (January 4):21.

HORTON, D. (1962) "The dialogue of courtship in popular songs." *Amer. J. of Sociology* 62 (May):569-578.

JANSEN, D. et al. (1968) "Characteristics associated with campus social political action leadership." *J. of Counselling Psychology* 15 (November):552-562.

KAHN, R. (1969) "Rank and file student activism: a contextual test of three hypotheses." Presented at the meetings of the Amer. Sociological Assn., San Francisco.

KEIL, C. (1966) *Urban Blues.* Chicago: Univ. of Chicago Press, pp. 44-45.

KENISTON, K. (1967) "The sources of student dissent." *J. of Social Issues* 23 (July):120.

KENNEDY, P. (1969) "Woodstock '69." *Jazz and Pop* 8 (November):20-23.

LEARY, T. (1968) *Politics of Ectasy.* New York: Putnam.

LEMBKE, D. and HAGER, P. (1969) "Thousands parade quietly in San Francisco to show war frustration." *Los Angeles Times* (November 16):B.

LIFE (1969) "The great Woodstock rock trip." (special edition).

LIPSET, S. M. (1963) *Political Man.* Garden City: Anchor.

McCLENDON, G. (1969) Quoted in J. P. Robinson and P. Hirsch, "Teenage response to rock and roll protest songs." Presented at the meetings of the Amer. Sociological Assn., San Francisco, September.

MANNHEIM, K. (1951) "The sociological problem of generations," in P. Kecskemeti (ed.) *Essays on the Sociology of Knowledge.* London: Routledge and Kegan Paul.

——. (1936) *Ideology and Utopia: An Introduction to the Sociology of Knowledge.* New York: Harcourt, Brace, & World.

MARCUS, G. (1969) "The Woodstock festival." *Rolling Stone* (September 20):24.

MILLS, C. W. (1963) "The New Left," in I. Horowitz (ed.) *Power, Politics, and People: The Collected Essays of C. Wright Mills.* New York: Ballantine.

NOEBEL, D. A. (1966) *Rhythm, Riots, and Revolution.* Tulsa: Christian Crusade Publications.

——. (1965) *Communism, Hypnotism, and the Beatles* Tulsa: Christian Crusade Publications.

PLATO. (1945) *The Republic.* Trans. by F. M. Cornford. New York: Oxford Univ. Press.

RIESMAN, D. (1964) "What the Beatles prove about teenagers." *US News and World Report* (February 24):88.

ROBINSON, J. P. and HIRSCH, P. (1969) "It's the sound." *Psychology Today* 3 (October):42-45.

ROBINSON, R. (n.d.) *First Winter.* Buddah Records BSD: Liner Notes.

RODNITZKY, J. L. (1969a) "The evolution of the American protest song." *J. of Popular Culture* 3 (Summer): 35-45.

———. (1969b) "The new revivalism: American protest songs, 1945-68." Presented at the annual meeting of the Amer. Studies Assn., Toledo, Ohio, October 31.

ROSZAK, T. (1969) *The Making of Counter Culture: Reflections on the Technocratic Society and Its Youthful Opposition.* Garden City: Anchor Books.

RUSH, G., COLLINGE, F. B., and WYLLIE, R. W. (1969) *North Vancouver Adolescent Study.* Burnaby: Simon Fraser Univ.

RUSH, G. and DENISOFF, R. S. (1970) "A World to Win." *The Sociology of Ideological Movements.* New York: Appleton-Century-Crofts.

SCHONBERT, E. (1956) "You can't fool public, says Haley." *Downbeat* 23 (May 30):10.

SIMMONS, J. I. and WINOGRAD, B. (1966) *It's Happening.* Santa Barbara: Marclaird Publications.

VON MEIER, K. (n.d.) "The background and beginnings of rock and roll." Univ. of California. Unpublished.

WAXMAN, C. (1968) *The End of Ideology Debate.* New York: Funk & Wagnalls.

WOLFE, B. H. (1968) *The Hippies.* New York: Signet.

chapter 63
the underground press
peggy scott

The sixties have been showing themselves as times of revolution and change in almost every aspect of life. Beneath all of the uproar and activity there has been the voice of a new kind of reporter. At first this voice was barely audible but lately it has nearly become a shout. Underground newspapers are now a part of the American scene.

Two years ago there were not more than five known underground newspapers in the United States and Canada. Since then about 150 to 200 have sprung up. Of course no one is sure how many papers there are because their survival has depended somewhat upon their secretiveness. But lately this element of repression has changed. The underground press can no longer be said to be truly underground. Instead it is fast becoming a significant force in society. In March 1968, Newsweek and the Wall Street Journal reported that the underground press was growing in circulation and financial success. To support this statement they cite the fact that two new press syndicates have appeared which are the underground equivalents of the Associated Press and the United Press International. They are: (1) United Press Syndicate (UPS) which allows sixty papers to run its stories with credit lines attached, and (2) Liberation News Service (LNS) which sells news articles, reviews,

From **College Press Review**, Winter/Spring, 1969. Reprinted by permission.

and essays for $180 to subscribers. The main office of LNS, located in Washington, D.C., recently switched to teletype machines. The **Wall Street Journal** reported that there are 50 or more underground papers. **Newsweek** reported a more extensive 150 in circulation. Marshall Bloom of LNS told the **New York Times** that more than 200 had begun publication in the last two years. In addition he told **The Nation** that LNS handles 280 papers with 125 of these underground, 80 of them peace papers, and the rest college publications. Reader estimates have been placed at 33,000 by the **Wall Street Journal** and at 4.6 million by Bloom. Some of the papers are published only now and then and readership is in the hundreds. Others are weeklies with wide circulation. This group is dominated by the Big Three: **EVO**, 45,000 readers, **Berkley Barb**, 60,000, and the Los Angeles **Freep**, 85,000. In addition most of these papers have paid employees. In response to this report, Peter Werbe, coeditor of Detroit's underground paper, **The Fifth Estate**, said that this success would not spoil the underground press and that this was the first step in a guerrilla movement. Marvin Gibson, another underground editor replied:

It's going to get bigger all the time. There are going to be more and more papers that will give people coverage they're not getting—and will never get—from the daily papers.

The underground press is primarily a product of the younger generation; writers and readers alike are usually under thirty years old. Society has seen its younger counterpart reject outside control of music and politics. Now the young have taken another step and opened their own field of communication. One reason this action was taken was because they felt they had no voice in the Establishment press, as the regular news media are known. The **Paperbag**, an underground magazine of Los Angeles, views the situation in an editorial:

> All estimable magazines, they have their own particular slant and unfortunately they don't include much about the winds of change that are sweeping our country, and particularly the young people in it.

Some of the underground papers even see themselves as competitors with the Establishment press. This group includes the more radical papers such as the **East Village Other** of New York whose editor told a correspondent for the **San Francisco Chronicle**:

> America now finds itself split into two camps, two life cycles. A cultural evolution is taking place that will sweep the grey-haired masters into the garbage heap. Wisdom and time are on the side of youth.

Generally the papers take themselves seriously. They feel they are going to have a lasting effect on society. According to Wayne Hansen of Boston's **Avatar** the underground media are more than a mere fad:

> The twenties had Hemingway and Fitzgerald; the Beat Generation had Kerouac and Allen Ginsberg. But did you ever wonder where are the books of this generation? Today's writing is more immediate; you can't wait around for a publisher.

Another underground newspaperman, Allan Katzman, cofounder of **EVO**, states a similar opinion:

> Twenty years from now people will be able to look back and understand this period, get a good feel for what it must have been like, by reading **EVO**.

Just what is it that the young wish to say that is so important to them? There are many areas of general interest dealt with in the underground papers. The emphasis given to each of these areas depends upon the group editing the paper. But whether attention is given to sex, drugs, or politics, the aim is toward cultural changes in values and beliefs. The editors of the underground press claim that they are revealing the trends of the future, and that the future will be better because of their writing.

In its most radical form, the underground press is a close approximation of the beliefs of a group known as Students for a Democratic Society (SDS). This group has been so influential in the younger generation's "revolution" that it should be analyzed as to its proportionate effect upon the underground media. The objectives of the SDS are as follows: (1) to make Americans realize how "bad" our government is and to encourage resistance to it, (2) to make people distrust all institutions, (3) to end the Vietnam War, or even further, to end all war by overthrowing the governmental system that makes war necessary, and (4) to establish a highly decentralized government in which there are no monopolies or big institutions, and more localization of government.

A Boston girl has summed up the role of the underground press in accomplishing these objectives:

> Demonstrations give us no power, they simply alienate us from other people. We are more alone than ever. We ought to educate the people first so they understand what we are demonstrating against and why.

Views similar to those of the SDS are apparent in the underground media. This is not to say that this group is influencing all of the papers, but merely that the aforestated objectives are a general summation of the slant of the underground papers.

Several of the media have stated as one of their main purposes to expose the truth about what is happening in the world. Such an aim would tend to accomplish goals number one and two in the list of SDS objectives. **Naturally** if stories are reported in the underground paper that are ignored in the establishment press, a person becomes distrustful of the regular paper and of the whole governmental system under which it operates. In the pages of the **National Underground Review** of Village Station, New York, is an editorial statement concerning this situation:

The first thing you do is get mad. Mad at the evening news for distorting the real story. "I saw the tear gas. They can't say it wasn't used." But they do say it. And you get mad.

The editor of **EVO**, 26-year-old law student Peter Leggieri, has stated:

There is no such thing as free press in this country. There is **permitted** press—but what is permitted depends on the locality.

Another stated objective of the papers is simply to protest. This protest may be in any area of society and could work to achieve any of the stated SDS objectives. Thomas Pepper in **The Nation** has said of the underground press:

All these papers do is offer protest—it not only requires it, but depends on it.

The Worcester Punch of Worcester, Mass., has defined the reason for its beginning as "Protest to (against): political and social pro-peace—anticolonialism." Much of its protest is against the Vietnamese war. An editorial comment in one of these issues expresses dissatisfaction with the war policy of the United States.

The editors of **Punch** believe that the only feasible and moral alternative is for the U.S. to withdraw its forces from Vietnam and let the Vietnamese settle their own affairs. The U.S. is aggressing in a foreign country and should simply get out.

Another medium which offers a form of protest to the war is the **Win Peace and Freedom through Nonviolent Action** of New York City. The editors intend their magazine to be the voice of the peace movement, and it is totally devoted to this task. This magazine is published monthly by a group known as the War Resisters League. In addition to these war protesters there is the **Mother of Voices** of Amherst, Massachusetts, which proposes an end to the Vietnamese conflict as an immediate goal of the paper.

Protest can also be seen in the area of education. The underground press has been playing a role in attacks against the administrations of schools, the lack of constitutional rights, and the quality of education. One paper which is seeking to bring about revolutionary changes in university policy towards students is the **Free Press—Underground** of Columbia, Missouri. In an article by Steve Fuchs the administration is viewed as a restrictive power which is trying to control the students' lives. He charges:

Students are treated as objects to be manipulated and are not allowed to participate in the decision-making process of their University.

In the **Worcester Punch** is a report of the planning of a free university, an informal structure which could examine social problems not covered by textbooks. The article describes the type of institution conceived and closes with a promise of further coverage of the development of the project.

A few of the underground papers are primarily concerned with their effect on the regular news media of their area, whether it be on the campus or in the community at large. An example of this type of paper is **The Voice** of New York City, an extremely successful weekly. **The Voice** was begun to outdo the regular local press, particularly the **New York Times.** In contrast it is further left politically and more artistic than the **Times,** and it substitutes reviews of books, movies, the theatre, music, and the press for ordinary news reporting. New Yorkers, characteristically dissatisfied with American public life, have made a good audience for the paper. Another paper aimed at the establishment media is **The Worm** of Halifax. In answer to a question of why it was begun, David Smith, the editor, replied that there had been dissatisfaction with the **Dalhousie Gazette,** the university publication. He felt that "competition would breed improvement," and was successful in his attempt. According to Smith, the **Gazette** had been too involved in off campus news reporting before his paper was published. But after only five issues of **Worm, Gazette** student news content increased 27.8 percent.

Many of the underground papers are distinguishable from the establishment press by their literary and artistic content. This difference is due to the emphasis on creativity by some of the publications. One unique example of this type of paper is the **San Francisco Oracle** which is loaded with spiritualism and psychedelic artwork. Its stated aim is to encourage creative thought and expression. Another San Francisco underground paper, **Vanguard,** was initiated for the same purpose. The editor-publisher, Keith St. Clare, expresses his reason for starting the paper:

Lack of creative outlet available to San Francisco's tenderloin citizens, need for a literate, constructive homophile publication. . . .

Some of the young editors are sincerely devoted to this literary endeavor. But few are so dedicated as the coeditor of **The Warren-Forest Sun** of Detroit, John Sinclair, who says:

I'd like to have enough money from some source to publish **The Sun** regularly and in full color. We are dormant now with the paper but will return to publication as soon as we can find a backer who will pay the printing bill and distribute the paper. He can have all the money that comes in from it—all we want is a medium for our writing and artwork.

Often the papers will herald a certain protest and change movement such as the drive to repeal the Marijuana Tax Act of 1937. In an article entitled "Killer Weed," the **Paperbag** of Los Angeles slanders the law as stupid and biased and proposes that the first step in repealing it be the education of the public on marijuana's unharmful effects.

Perhaps the best summation of the aims of the underground paper at this point is that of a high school editor of the underground media. According to him there are two basic functions of the papers: (1) to permit and encourage nonconformity by being a sounding board for the complaints of any individual, and (2) to protest injustice.

But this summary would only include the milder expressions of the underground. A much more serious form exists which is aimed at the structure of American society. Papers which write at this level have an all-encompassing goal in mind— a cultural revolution. Many young radicals are disillusioned with the United States in every aspect of its way of life. They abhor materialism, distrust politics, disagree with the established moral standards, and reject the Establishment church. As a voice of these dismayed young people, the underground press is demanding an overthrow of the status quo and a new system according to new standards. In September, 1967, the **Open City** ran an editorial on this subject which stated:

We feel that it is time that each of the groups now in revolt against an increasingly monolithic social system learns that it has much more in common with the other groups than it previously knew. Perhaps this way the sep-

parate isolated rebellions which the Establishment finds comparatively easy to put down could be joined into one truly effective social and political uprising.

The **Illustrated Paper** defines its goal as

an anarchist revolution in our lives filled with good sex, good work. Artistic and intellectual activity and food, clothing, and shelter. . . .

And the **Worcester Punch** is more specific in its aims:

peace, civil rights, social reform, a third party to replace the status quo two parties. . . .

But these two papers are only representations of all the underground media. The very existence of these papers is based upon dissatisfaction with "the way things are" in our country. Perhaps the best summary of the general attitude of the young revolutionaries appeared in **Paperbag**:

We think all wars are a waste, that perhaps the churches need an overhaul, and that America needs new directions. We're convinced there's something more to life than the latest model car, the size of color T.V. sets, or the "good life" in the suburbs. And if there isn't, there sure as hell ought to be.

But though there is universal agreement that there should be a change, there is diversified opinion as to the type or degree of change in order. For instance, the **Paperbag** offers a subtle suggestion that the American economic system be replaced by a system that does not exploit the poor. The **Mother of Voices** carries this idea a step further by proposing a new type of community system in which people of similar outlooks help each other "make it in the world." In addition the paper presents a challenge for hippies to stop "living off" the so-called straight people and to begin producing their own food, clothing, shelter, and jobs. According to the paper, the type of society proposed is not a Utopia or an organization of communal farms. Instead it is a practical community in which people of similar interests live and work together. An even more radical approach is taken by the magazine **The Modern Utopian**. In the opinion of the editors almost every aspect of American life is in need of change. The ultimate goal would be a new society in which such things as group dating, permissible abortion, legalized drinking for all ages, and alcoholic beverages served at church parties are a part of everyday life. The magazine even carries the idea of group marriages. This idea is based on the theory that one can be a much happier person by sharing an emotional and sexual relationship with one person so why shouldn't this be increased by sharing it with more than one? The **Modern Utopian**, publishes reports of changes in American government such as the move to abolish capital punishment, developments in church-state separation, and court cases protesting laws of questionable social justice such as the jailing of chronic alcoholics. At times the magazine carries its proposals to extremes as in the suggestion that public toilets be "sexually integrated." The **Midpeninsula Observer** carries a unique article on a new type of drama, the guerrilla theatre. This would take the expressions of the underground directly to many people who might not be influenced or reached in any other way. The stage would be much like the medicine wagon or street corner theatres of the Old West, with touring companies as performers. The **Observer** advises that the plays be carefully designed to "reflect the sickness of our society." To do this the particular geographic, social, and political situation of the area in which a play is to be acted must be closely examined beforehand. In the opinion of the author, the underground could really benefit by utilizing this new type of medium. Whether or not it would benefit the radicals, it would undoubtedly be a significant new addition to American drama, especially if it could establish itself. Another paper which offers a bold proposal for a change is the **Washington Free Press** which advocates what it calls a Neo-American Church in which LSD and other drugs are used as sacraments.

Almost all of the papers are against the violence which characterizes American society, and would rather see a new situation in which peace is present. They take it very seriously and have proposed theories as to why it is flourishing in the United States. **The Paper** of East Lansing, Michigan, believes violence is due to (1) frontier tradition, (2) the fast-evolving sex revolution, (3) frustrations of a brain-washed society, and (4) our scapegoat type society which blames a certain group of people such as Negros for society's problems. Another magazine is much more "down to earth" in its opinion of why riots occur:

They riot because they're pissed off and

they're just looking for an excuse . . . because they hate cops and because cops are a symbol for all the unnamable frustration that comes from living in a tight ugly ghetto.

But even though the papers are concerned over violence in society, they are opposed to police. Many of them carry news reports of police brutality. In the **National Underground Review** there is an account of student resistance to police at Columbia University complete with a photograph of a young man with his head bleeding. The article states:

We are in this room with them [the police], singing, locked arms, and they stand behind us and over us with their little blackjacks which open you up. It's obviously some deep sexual or fantasy thing with them or they would stop beating on you out of sheer boredom.

Another story of police cruelty appeared in the **Midpeninsula Observer** which condemned the police for clubbing and squirting mace in the faces of demonstrators after they had been arrested. The **Mother of Voices** carried a short excerpt of the Surgeon General's report that mace is much more dangerous than the police are admitting.

Some of the papers go to greater lengths to criticize the police. These run editorials of up to two pages on the ridiculousness of policemen. An example of this type of criticism appeared in **The Paper**. There was a humorous editorial in one issue which emphasized the tendency of policemen to get carried away with their authority In the article are examples of incidents such as a policeman pronouncing a man dead and then screaming obscenities at a man who is certain the victim is only in shock. **The Paper** asks:

If man will let others die rather than appear wrong or "lose face"—you can imagine what they will do if someone (not themselves) is involved!

The article also protests against a society which is based upon fear, the fear of policemen. The author is enraged by the fact that America is supposed to be the most "civilized" nation because it has the most policemen.

One paper carries the hint of a bit of sympathy

for the police. The **Paperbag** expresses its attitude in this way:

> We think the police have a tough job but some cities are becoming police states with some of their policemen more incensed about long hair and beads than they are about thefts and muggings.

But the **Paperbag** also reminds its readers that all too often the police departments of our nation are guilty of much more than mere neglect. It charges that policemen have stolen property and taken lives. Several examples are cited.

Just as the subject matter of the papers is controversial, the journalistic methods of underground editors are bold. Humor is a device used in most of the papers in some form. In some it takes the form of a funny story, in others it may appear in cartoons or comic strips. But in every case it is aimed at the Establishment. The **National Underground Review** carries an account of a hippie marriage arrangement that most anyone would have to smile about. In the story the female partner in a free love relationship decides she wants to get married, much to the dismay of her mate. To compromise the conflict, he devises a system to satisfy both sides. He agrees to sign any papers for her if she will do the same for him. So after he signs the marriage license, she signs the following statement:

> We, the undersigned, hereby declare that the form of marriage which we went through . . . was not intended by us to have, and as far as we are concerned does not have any legal, social, or moral validity whatsoever.

He concludes by saying they are both very happy with this arrangement.

Humor also appears in cartoons and comic strips. The **Paperbag** is the primary example of the use of this method. One of its cartoons pictures two plump middle-aged couples seated in a living room; one of the wives is saying:

> We took LSD and Willard threw up.

Satire is another literary device used in the papers. Like the humor, it is directed at the establishment but it is much more bitter. A striking example of the use of satire appears on the front of the **Spokane Natural** Christmas issue. There is a picture of a skeleton mother and child with the caption:

Only 16 more bombing days till Christmas.

The **Washington Free Press** uses "cover satire" also. On the front of the May 8, 1968, paper is a poster which says "Zip Your Lip, America; Loose Talk is Dangerous." Under the poster is a quotation from a U.S. Court of Appeals judge disclaiming public speech by government employees, a headline from **The Evening Star** of Washington D.C. saying "U.S. Workers' Free Speech Curbed," and an excerpt of the First Amendment to the Constitution with a satirical addition at the end.

The most frequent and inflaming method of the underground press is the use of obscene language. A few of the papers reject vulgarity, among them the Los Angeles **Underground** and the **Anvil** of North Carolina, but these are in the minority. Most of them condone the use of dirty language. Allan Katzman of **EVO** expresses the general attitude in this statement:

> We're not based on perfection; we're based on our own reliable responses to what's going on. If at times we're extremely obscene, it's because we're feeling obscene. We're not afraid of expressing our feelings . . . it's journalism through your fingertips.

There have been many arrests made all over the country on obscenity charges against underground editors. One case occurred in Boston when **Avatar's** street hawkers were arrested in Harvard Square because of the language used in the paper. After the paper printed one of the verbs in letters four inches high and 58 arrests had been made, a local court ruled that the language used was not obscene at all. An agreement was finally reached whereby the paper could not be sold to those under 18. In recent months, Milwaukee and West Palm Beach papers have had cases of arrest.

Psychedelic artwork is present in most all of the underground papers. It is splashed across the covers of the **Spokane Natural**, the **San Francisco Oracle**, and the **Mother of Voices**. The colors and confusion would probably make little sense to the average American because it reminds one of what he has heard of a drug experience. Much of the artwork of the papers is probably shocking to "grownups" because it is the expression of sensual pleasures; sex in particular. This shock is intended and, once again, is a type of rebellion against the Establishment.

Another artistic method of underground media is the use of poetry. Sometimes it is simply a hu-

morous jab at high society as in the following excerpt titled "The Transplanted Heart."

> I carried in a china dish
> a special treat
> for the dinner guests
> who stabbed it with toothpicks—
> it wiggled like aspic
> "Tastes great! How'd you make it?"
> "I had an operation.
> I served a souvenir. . . ."

At other times the poetry is quite serious as when
it is written against war. **The Paper** of East Lansing,
Michigan, carries a short poem of this type:

> Our Leaders
> They burn bridges
> behind them
> these articulate shells
> of men
> not seeing the blackened
> structures remaining
> nor the pitiful bones
> of victims protruding
> from under
> scorched timber. . . .

From this selection one can feel the involvement
of the young author in one of America's most
serious problems. The simplicity of this poem
is reflective of the style of many underground
poems.

One of the most outrageous devices of the
underground press is their use of photographs that
the regular news media would reject. Most of these
are pictures of the horrid effects of war such as
napalm-scorched babies, beheaded Viet Cong soldiers, or piles of dead bodies. The **Mother of Voices**
uses this method in its effort to end the war. Other
types of shock photography are in the areas of sex,
which the **Berkeley Barb** illustrates, and racial violence, which **The Plain Truth** of Champaign, Illinois, uses.

The underground press is directed toward the
overthrow of the status quo. Not only does it write
stories and poems and print pictures to direct the
change but it uses a very practical method—classified ads. Some of the papers are quite bold in this
matter, for many of the requests are illegal. The
Washington Free Press carries a multitude of requests for lesbian partners in its classified section.
The **Berkeley Barb** even prints purported drug
advertisements:

HAVE YOU TRIED LSD in our convenient
take-home 6 packs? Ask for it by name at
Larry Blake's Rathskeller.

Because of the radical characteristics of the
underground media, one might be inclined to think
that only liberal, extremist hippies would comprise
its audience. But according to their editors, the
readers are much more diversified. A few of the
papers, when asked to describe their audiences, replied with hippie-like descriptions. These were the
Seed of Chicago and the **Illustrated Paper** of Mendocino, California. The **Spokane Natural** said that
hippies make up a large part of their audience but
that the paper was directed toward all types of
liberals and radicals. An even greater number of the
papers defined their audiences as high school and
college students and professionals, mature ones at
that! Some of these papers are **The Midpeninsula
Observer**, the **Mother of Voices**, the **North Carolina
Anvil**, and the **Worcester Punch**. Perhaps the most
surprising fact of all is that some of the editors
write for the "square, middle-class, Establishment,"
as does the **Underground Digest**. This is of course
to gain more sympathy among adults for the underground movement. But the success of such an
attempt is highly questionable.

Presumably, the underground press has had
significant effects on society. The regular college
newspapers have been becoming more militant in
responding to the underground papers. The administrations of their colleges and universities have
been in an uproar over: (1) extremely critical articles about state politics and politicians, (2) articles
in "bad taste," and (3) pornographic writing. Another effect has been that the underground press
has made society realize that the ordinary press
does not communicate with subcultures. The regular press speaks only to the majority—middle-class
Americans. In addition, the underground press has
demonstrated the deficiency of the American press,
even though it has not improved journalism.

One might question the opinion that the underground press has not improved journalism.
Those who say it has not attribute the reason to (1)
the lack of semblance of order or leadership, (2) no
definite directions for the future; haphazardness,
and (3) no sound economic support. Others criticize the underground press because of its dependence on protest. They believe the whole medium
would die if it could not speak against something
of significance. One paper carries a letter to the
editors by David Abernathy which criticizes this
paper (the **Midpeninsula Observer**) for using the

"worst features of 'the system' to undermine " 'the System.' " He accuses the paper of quoting politicians out of context to support its case against them and for redoing photographs so professionally that they are "masterpieces worthy of a top Madison Avenue huckster."

A few of the papers feel that they are beginning to be accepted by the general public. These would naturally be the less radical ones such as **Crawdaddy** of New York City and the **Spokane Natural**, the latter of which boasts of more local paid advertisements.

But whether they are being accepted or not, the underground newspapers are becoming a significant news medium in America. One might suppose that this new medium is having a strong influence upon its young readers just as the establishment press is supposed to have on older people. Perhaps in a few years the changes demanded by the young editors will come. If they do, one may be sure the papers will take much of the credit.

BIBLIOGRAPHY

ABERNATHY, David B. "Letters to Editors," *Midpeninsula Observer*, Vol. I (February, 1968), 2.

BRILLIANT, Ashleigh E. "The One Dollar Haight Divorce," *National Underground Review*, Vol. I (June, 1968), 12.

——— "Doing Our Thing," *Paperbag*, Vol. I (February, 1968), 6.

DREYER, Thorne. "Lower East Side United Against Pigs," *Washington Free Press*, Vol. II (August, 1968), 3.

———. "Fairmont Demonstrators Are Brutally Attacked," *Midpeninsula Observer*, Vol. II (August, 1968), 3.

FELDMAN, Samuel N. "Underground Newspapers: Their Aimes, Prospects, Procedures," *The School Press Review*, Vol. XLIII (March, 1968), 1.

———. "Free University Planned Here," *The Worcester Punch*, Vol. II (March, 1968), 2.

FREEL, Fred. "Killer-Weed," *Paperbag*, Vol. I (February, 1968), 32.

FUCHS, Steve. "What's To Be Done?" *Free Press Underground,* Vol. III (October, 1967), 2.

KITZES, Esther. "Before the Revolution Come the Words," *College Press Review*, Vol. VIII (Spring, 1968), 4.

KRONENBERGER, John. "What's Black and White and Pink and Green and Dirty and Read All Over," *Look*, Vol. XXXII (October, 1968), 20.

KUPFERBERG, Tuli. "How to Think about the Police," *The Paper*, Vol. III (January, 1968), 8.

LAMPA, William. "Our Leaders," *The Paper*, Vol. III (January, 1968), 7.

———. "Letters to the Editors," *The Worcester Punch*, Vol. II (March, 1968), 2.

——— "L.N.S.," *Mother of Voice*, Vol. I (June, 1968),

LOWENTHAL, Wolfe. "Cry if You're Getting Your Head Broken," *National Underground Review*, Vol. I (June, 1968), 7.

———. "Messages," *Berkeley Barb*, Vol. VI (May, 1968), 14.

MILLS, Margaret. "Guerrilla Theatre: great potential." *Midpeninsula Observer*, Vol. I (January, 1968), 4.

———. "News," *National Underground Review*, Vol. I (June, 1968), 15.

———. "News Digest of Social Change," *The Modern Utopian*, Vol. I (July-August, 1968), 7.

NOVICK, Peter. "Underground God," *Washington Free Press*, Vol. II (March, 1968), 10.

PEPPER, Thomas. "Underground Press: Growing Rich on the Hippie," *The Nation*, Vol. CCVI (April, 1968), 570.

PLATO, Jimmy. "Death Valley," *Mother of Voices*, Vol. I (June, 1968), 2.

PORCHE, Verandah. "The Transplanted Heart," *Mother of Voices*, Vol. I (March, 1968), 17.

RADER, Dotson. "Princeton Weekend with the S.D.S." *The New Republic*, Vol. CLVII (December, 1967), 15-16.

SHEA, Frank. "The Establishment: Hypocrisy on Half Shell," *Paperbag*, Vol. I (August, 1968), 28.

SURVEY of the Underground Press, conducted by Glen Kleine.

chapter 64
the great roob revolution
roger price

The word "rube" (from Reuben) was originally used by carnival people to identify the farmers, yokels, and assorted rural types who attended their itinerant bacchanal and who, thrust into the exotic atmosphere of the carnival, behaved badly. "Hey, rube!" was the classic cry for help used by the carnies when the locals began acting up.

In his own environment this old-time, or classic, rube possessed many virtues: courage, loyalty, honesty, and the basic virtue from which all others must stem—pride. The source of his pride was his ability to function. He could do things. He was dependable and self-confident. He was the yeoman longbowman at Crécy whose arrow storm destroyed the mounted chivalry of France. The classic rube withstood the unwithstandable winter at Valley Forge. He planted the fields and built the bridges and railroads of America. He was Harry Truman. He was okay.

But once the rube left the Midwest or Appalachia or Georgia or Vermont or wherever and went to the City, he became a misplaced person and he began to act badly again. He found himself in an anonymous urban society which neither challenged nor threatened him and which made no

demands on him except as a Consumer. He became a Roob, with a capital r.

A tragedy of the Roob's ascendancy is that it means the elimination of the classic rube.

The American Roob today is a different proposition. He is no longer mainly Celtic-Anglo-Saxon-Protestant. There are Italian Roobs, Jewish Roobs, Greek Roobs, Afro-Roobs, College Professor Roobs, Art Expert Roobs, and probably Junkie Roobs.

The Roob, whose ancestors have existed for millennia, is the eternal plebeian. His literary antecedents are Swift's Yahoo and Mencken's Boob. He is Ortega y Gasset's Mass Man. He is all the corporals in all the world's armies and he is always a product of the City. In Athens his progenitors murdered Socrates and condemned Aristotle; in Rome they demanded circuses and collaborated with Alaric; in Madrid they applauded the Inquisition and later Franco; in Paris they whooped it up around the guillotine; in London they beheaded Charles I; and in Berlin they almost Made It with Adolf Hitler. Time and again the latent Roob has appeared briefly in the foreground of history, never achieving power except as a mob and always being quickly repressed and condemned again to impotence.

But today in America the Roob, the mass man, has come into his own as a dynamic social force. For the first time his numbers are overwhelming, and he is consolidated. And for the first time he is affluent: As a result he has an appalling new weapon which he uses to impose his ideas and attitudes upon the total population. This weapon is his Purchasing Power. And pandering to it has become our largest national industry.

By exercising this power, the Roob is relentlessly pulling us all down to his level. He is eliminating all that is non-Roob in our culture. Gresham was right about more things than money when he said the Bad (completely) drives out the Good. More and more, the commonplace, the ordinary, and the vulgar are becoming national goals.

This is not the result of a master plan conceived by some misanthropic genius, but of economic evolution. As industrialization shortened the workweek, as fewer people were needed to produce food, leisure time increased radically, and the manufacture and sale of an increasing number of nonessential, frivolous items became necessary to keep the economy expanding. And so we began to turn more and more to Consumerism as an end in itself.

The Roob discovered in himself a great talent for consuming, a talent which would justify the sublimation of his personality into one overriding need—the need for Self-Gratification.

Accepting the concept of Self-Gratification and Fun as noble and moral imperatives, and ill-equipped to make decisions based on value, the Roob began automatically to react like a child or a savage to what the world eagerly offered him. If something sparkled or jangled, he said, "I like it." If not, he said, with considerably more vigor, "I don't like it!" He began, as children do, to define himself negatively ("Johnny won't eat mashed potatoes"; "Susan doesn't like meat"), and embraced an intellectual primitivism which requires no more intelligence than that possessed by a dog (a dog can easily say "I like it," "I don't like it").

In this two-orientational thought process, the phrase "I don't like it" has, as might be expected, become the more important. We are living in an age of "I don't like it."

In the planning of advertising or entertainment (and the two are becoming inseparable), no other factor is so important as "I don't like it." Great effort is made, not to introduce elements which might please, but to eliminate those which might "offend." If the producers of a TV show which presumes to have twenty million viewers receive ten letters complaining about something, pandemonium sets in. Meetings of top executives are held. Changes are ordered.

This literally does happen (yes, only ten letters can do it), but it is not as silly as it might seem because the Roob is already so standardized that if ten letters appear, usually written in pencil on ruled paper, it can be assumed that millions more have identical feelings: They didn't like it.

Although the hucksters who control the aptly named mass media think they are manipulating what they refer to as "the slobs," and although they spend millions on the latest scientific, Pavlovian methods, **they** are the ones who are being conditioned. When the Roob rings the bell, the media people are the ones who salivate. And so does American industry. All are caught in the trap of their own venality.

Manufacturers no longer aspire to make a "good" shoe or a "good" car. They try to make one for which there is an overwhelming demand. They have no interest in making or marketing a product for a small, specialized audience. All lust, with reason, for the mass sale; for with mass acceptance comes instant money and occasionally temporary celebrity. When that mass approval is withheld, the trip to the unemployment office, the couch or the A. A. meeting is inevitable.

If everybody doesn't want it, nobody gets it.
                              — Price's First Law

When I get scared and worried, I tell myself, "Janis, just have a good time." So I juice up real good and that's just what I have. . . . It's a damn sight better than being bored. — Janis Joplin [quoted in **The New York Times**, February 23, 1969].

BASIC DICTION

Basic Roobs seldom pronounce t or d or a final **g**. Actually they have trouble with most consonants and are inclined to swallow their vowels, which lends a certain depressing originality to their speech. In Southern California even newscasters say "wunnerful" and "anna-bioddicks" and "ineress-ting." The word "interesting," pronounced in this manner, with the accent on the third syllable, is the infallible mark of the Roob. Non-Roobs say "interesting." Other examples are:

fack: that which is self-evident: "Thassa fack"
fure: less, as in "I got fure cavidys since I use Cress"
present: chief executive: "Heeza present of our bank"
innaleckshul: show-offy, nondemocratic

thur: third person plural: "Thur goin' to the bob-bycue"

Pronesant: Methodist, Presbyterian, non-Catholic

hooya: as in "Hooya kiddin'?"

lug jury: use of high-class stuff

pleece: officers of the law (a favorite of Hubert Humphrey)

oney: alone, as in "It's oney me"

on juice: a citric drink

Amurkin: U.S. citizen

wotcher: as in "Wotcher doin' t'marr?"

whenjer: as in "Whenjer bus go?"

li-berry: place where books are stored

goff: a game

finey: as in "I finey got my draff notice"

jeet-jet?: "Have you had any food recently?"

nuculer: a big, big bomb as described by our Secretary of Defense, Mr. Laird

In cities on the Eastern seaboard many Basics ignore r's, substitute **d** for **th** and overemphasize internal **g**'s and **t**'s: "Ya brudda, da bah-tenda, he still goin' widda singga from Long Guyland, Hanh?"

In the South and Southwest the Roob tends to whine, producing a nasal sound commonly referred to, euphemistically, as a drawl. He accomplishes this by pronouncing all vowels except **e** as diphthongs: "aa-ee," "e," "hii-ee," "oh-uuu," "ee-yew."

BASIC VOCABULARY

Excluding proper names and the quasi-technical terms used in his job, the Basic's speaking vocabulary consists of no more than five hundred words. He will recognize, but never use, perhaps two thousand more. "Profound" is such a word. Also: "idolize," "remarkable," "massive," "tangible," and "subdue." None of these are adverbs. The Basic Roob never uses adverbs, and because of this he has introduced a linguistic atavism into our speech. When he wishes to qualify a verb, he says, "He was walkin' . . . slow like," using the original Middle English form, which in Elizabethan times became "slowlyke" and eventually "slowly." This retrogressive Roobism is probably the source of the excessively used "like" in the teenage and hip patois.

Although he is unswervingly hostile to real erudition or any sort of scholarship that does not pander to his myopic view of himself, the Roob occasionally wants to be considered "high-class" and feels the need to use "big words." He has the savage's belief that words have a reality of their own and feels that verbal complexities are a form

of ritual magic which, when uttered, are a legitimate substitute for knowledge. Unfortunately he doesn't know any big words except "Cinema-Scope," so he uses compound words such as "Insurancewise," "accident-prone," and "fun thing." A recent extension of this compulsion is the tendency to add extra syllables to existing words. In addition to making "interesting" a four-syllable word, the Roob now adds an extra syllable to "controversial," pronouncing it "con-tro-ver-see-al."

The Basic will often, especially when greeting his peers, use certain earthy expletives ("Gahdammit, Chief, you onna ball there, Boy?"), but there is no real Basic slang as such. He is, however, addicted to a number of condensed clichés which he uses in the belief that they add precision to his murky pronouncements:

fer free	be my guess
plus witch	gourmay dish
a person like yourself	cook-out
onna ball	irregardless
I buy that	no sweat
same difference	I could care less

BASIC CONVERSATION

Where the classic rube was traditionally taciturn or laconic, the Basic Roob is a talker. A Basic conversation consists of two or more of them taking turns reciting what has happened to them recently. In order of importance the subjects of these recitals are:

1. TV
2. How much they had to drink last Saturday night or last week or the time they were in Chicago
3. "Innaressting facks" about automobiles, prices of, routes, mileage
4. "Innaressting facks" about jobs
5. Sports (male only)
5a. Kids, home furnishings, hair sprays, other people's kids, home furnishings (female only)
6. Food, where eaten, size of portions, prices of
7. Opinions (usually "don't-like") about politics, celebs, and prices

INFORMATION

In spite of the Basic's compulsion to make instant and categoric judgments about everything, he has few points of reference upon which to base his opinions. Although the odds are five to one that he is a high school graduate, his lack of general information is bloodcurdling.

He recognizes a few names, but often has no specific idea of who they really are; he knows Hemingway was a writer, but does not know his first name or anything he ever wrote. Excluding a selected handful of television and film personalities, no more than four presidents and/or presidential aspirants, and a clutch of active sports figures, he knows with any degree of assurance only:

George Washington	Abe Lincoln
Tarzan	Freud
Napoleon	The Jolly Green Giant
Jesus Christ	Rembrandt
Snoopy	Winston Churchill
Picasso	David (& Goliath)
Shakespeare	A. Hitler
Hemingway	Billy Graham
Julius Caesar	Mickey Mouse

He will recall having heard of, but be totally unable to identify:

Charlemagne	Macbeth
J. Paul Getty	Robert McNamara
Hannibal	Benedict Arnold
Moby Dick	Ralph Bunche

He will never have heard of:

Polonius	Henri Matisse
Winnie-the-Pooh	David Ben-Gurion
Norman Podhoretz	Norman Cousins

BASIC HUMOR

The Basic is actually a good-natured person and has a sense of humor. Unfortunately his lack of information or data about the non-Roob aspects of the world drastically limits his ability to appreciate it. He automatically resents any jokes which he doesn't **understand**; however, he will laugh easily at those he does, including those which make fun of himself (but not of his culture).

He enjoys repeating dirty stories when he can remember them, and he will tell lengthy tales of the odd and often dreadful situations he has gotten into by overdrinking, but his real humor is expressed by teasing: "Hey, kid, you don't really want this ice cream cone, do ya?" "Hey, Mary Lou, watcher say we ditch ol' Harry, and me and you go to a mo-tel?"

When it comes to repartee (if that is the correct word), the Basic Roob has one all-purpose phrase which may be delivered in a variety of ways (flatly, sarcastically, quizzically) to suit any occasion. The phrase is "Are you kiddin'?"

BASIC STATUS SYMBOLS

Cameras (Roobs wear camera straps as if they were Legion of Honor ribbons). Formica. Combination stereo and color TV sets. Goldfish tanks with plastic plants and orange plastic castles. Wrist watches (male). Cultured pearls (female). Salt-and-pepper shakers shaped like female breasts. Nutcrackers shaped like female thighs. Lawn flamingoes. A real oil painting done by a female relative. Ash trays from Hawaii, Mexico, or the Caribbean.

BASIC DRINKS

Cola drinks and coffee. Bottled or canned beer. Seven and Seven (Seagram's 7 Crown and 7-Up), rye and ginger, vodka and orange juice.

BASIC CUISINE

For any special occasion, steak and only steak. Otherwise, french fried anything with ketchup. Barbecued anything. Instant anything. Pizzas, spaghetti, and constantly, at any place and any time, hamburgers! (The hot dog, it seems to me, is universally American and I have arbitrarily left it out.) Basics and their families eat a lot of cold cereals with milk, but seldom drink milk or eat cheese (except on a burger) after they're ten years old. In Chinese restaurants they eat egg roll, chow mein, and chop suey. They never order anything in a restaurant they haven't had before.

BASIC HOBBIES

In addition to talking and drinking, the Basic Roob is addicted to a number of other leisure-time activities. One of the more specialized of these hobbies is:

1. Gawking

Whenever there is a disaster, Roobs rush from their homes to their cars and within a matter of minutes they have clogged the highways, making it difficult if not impossible for legitimate personnel, ambulances, and fire trucks to get there.

Once at the Scene, they line up by the thousands and stare for hours at the building where the old lady was decapitated, at the spot in the ocean where the airplane crashed and sank with 125 on board, at the seven-car auto wreck.

They consider it a major triumph if they arrive in time to see actual bodies or blood. Strangely enough, many of them become queasy at the sight of blood, but this doesn't in the slightest deter them in their rush to view it.

If not restrained by police, they will grab buttons, fragments of the plane, even a victim's shoes, as "souvenirs." They snap each other's photos in front of the spot where the tragedy occurred. They buy hot dogs from the vendors who invariably show up (even at 3 A.M.). They drink whiskey from half-pint bottles. It's carnival time.

2. Bowling

Bowling is to Roobs what fox hunting was to the British aristocracy. It affords them a chance to drink and smoke while they exercise, and they can bring along their women.

3. General

Older Basics have an admirable tendency, inherited from their classic-rube parents, to build stuff. They have power tools; they build walls and patios in their backyards; they will rewire their houses and put together good hi-fi units; they rebuild automobiles, sometimes spending fantastic effort on ingenious and incredibly powerful monstrosities for display at drag strips; they operate and will often build their own boats.

Unfortunately many of their children, those who have been born in the City, are losing this instinct to do-it-themselves. They may buy or rent boats and they still have a strong interest in automobiles, but they seldom redesign them to any extent. They show their interest mostly by watering them with a hose on Saturday afternoons.

4. Seduction

When a Basic attempts to hustle a lady Basic, he first tries to get her drunk. Then he begins grabbing her and says "Aw, come on, what's the matter with you?" He considers this a very persuasive question and keeps grabbing and repeating it until he either succeeds or is rebuffed. (It works more often than not.)

5. The Vacation and the Weekend Trip

The Vacation is included under hobbies, but it is, for the Basic Roob, much more. It is a ritual. It is the one time that he is on his own, away from the job, away from the Box, but never, of course, away from himself.

Summer is the season for the great Roobmove. When June comes bustin' out all over, you can spot carfuls of them on every major artery, their faces set in a terrible look of purpose. Their purpose is, first, to Get There; second, to measure the gas mileage it took them to Get There.

What is the reason for this great migration? When did it all begin?

First, you must understand the awesome importance to Roobs of the Vacation or the Weekend Trip. An exhausting and dangerous drive on a crowded thruway to an equally crowded and overpriced resort is their claim to membership in the Leisure Class. They go in search of the Pepsi People, the Ale Men, the Swingers; and they live in deadly fear that they may take the wrong road, read the wrong travel ads and not see the turnoff to Marlboro country. They are afraid they will **miss something.**

The Roob believes with all his heart that somewhere along Route 12A all the Fun People are having a Fun Time under the benevolent eye of a recreation counselor. No right-minded Fun Person would ever isolate himself or seek his own diversions, for a Roob's identity is based on attendance at mass functions that require standing in line, such as a company barbecue or the opening of a snake farm.

He transports himself in candy-colored cars, with boxes of Kleenex in the rear window, plastic Jesi or monkeys suction-cupped to the dash and Esso maps unfolded in the front seat.

If you see a Roob on a winding road, you can be sure he is lost and forlornly seeking the safety of the turnpike.

His meccas are any state with "vacationland" printed on its license plates (or on the paper place mats in roadside restaurants). Or any Historical Landmark. Or any Authentic Reconstruction with attendants wearing period costumes. Or any World's Fair. Or any place he didn't see last year—because he knows the Fun People aren't **there.**

Triptime is a time for Fun Food: anything that comes in a wrapper, on a paper plate, with a flag on it, or is over eight inches high with a maraschino cherry on top. And (as always) hot dogs, hamburgers, and pizzas. A Roob child can smell a pizza at a distance of fifteen hundred yards with the wind against him. Roobs never eat the specialty of the region unless it has been breaded and deep-fried so that it tastes exactly like a french fry.

Their vacation pastimes include (1) littering, (2) eating, sleeping, or sitting in a Howard Johnson's, (3) squeezing into the most crowded part of a beach and greasing one another, (4) walking slowly and suspiciously down the main street of a resort town and comparing the menu prices posted in different windows, (5) spotting license plates from their home state and accosting the drivers, (6) sitting in their own cars overlooking any place called "scenic" and reading a newspaper, (7) buying postcards, and (8) buying fake Dresden figurines in a cut-rate Armenian store to remind them of the rugged coast of Maine.

Vacationing Roobs all look as if someone blew a bugle at 4 A.M. and they all got up and dressed in the dark. The females no longer wear men's shirts, Capri pants and rollers in their hair, but are now seen in "casual wear" as recommended by **Woman's Day**, the supermarket **Vogue**.

They wear mini-shifts, Bermudas, bell-bottomed slack suits made from flamboyant prints reminiscent of the rain forests. Halters. Large hats with Dacron ponytails attached and stacked-heel sandals. They like plastic articles in which forms of marine life can be embedded or any straw article with shells on it or Fun Jewelry shaped like flora or fauna. They carry satchelly handbags decorated with plastic flowers, alligators, or carrots and wear sunglasses encrusted with busted glass.

For noncasual occasions they have at least one pastel-colored outfit which is "matched": pink or powder-blue sweater, skirt, stubby shoes, and jacket with fur trim.

The males, in addition to their cameras, wear those sports shirts in inexplicable colors which,

even when new, look as if they've been washed twelve times and which cost $4.95. The amount a Basic pays for his shirts is in some way permanently impressed on his mind. He will spend $20 in a bar, buy a $3,800 car, a $600 color TV, but will never spend more than $6 on a shirt (unless he plays golf or is on a bowling team).

They wear the shirts tieless and coatless or with the collar folded over the lapels of their sports jackets. They wear caps with green plastic windows cut in the long visors. Turtlenecks and thin knit pullovers with strange symbols sewn on the pocket rim which vaguely suggest some Medieval Sport. They assert individuality with funny shoes and pencils and pens in their breast pockets. For more formal wear the male has a whole set of suits and accessories which are just like his cold-weather clothes except they are ventilated. The shirt is a mass of perforations called Wunda-weave. The shoes are toeless cordovans. The hat has several portholes in it. In short, the summer Roob is one big advertisement for Evaporation.

With each succeeding season the Roobs hurl themselves still more fiercely into the game of Musical Towns, bent on seeing every square inch of Everything. Constant mobility has become a way of life; instant somewhere-else a fact. Will it all end only when there are Dairy Queen stands and pizza parlors in Tibet and the equatorial pygmies are playing Pokerino and miniature golf? Probably. And now, of course, there's always the moon . . .

topic 26

images of the future

The Age of Aquarius . . . Walden II . . . 1984 . . . Brave New World. . . . Whatever label we would affix to it, the world of tomorrow is essentially a matter of guesswork. Granted, much of our conjecture about the future stems from painstaking and well-informed analyses of present trends. All the same, the sheer speed and magnitude of technological growth and the accelerating knowledge explosion is coupled with another factor that is problematical indeed: the omnipresent reality of cultural lag, which promises a gap between technoscientific breakthroughs and our capacity to master and profit from such advances. Thermonuclear holocausts, biological warfare, irreversible pollution, unlivable cities, and mass starvation are possibilities real enough to sober all but the most sanguine of optimists.

In attempting to analyze and predict the future, let us concentrate on two of its central qualities: the promise of technology on the one hand, and the threat of technological dehumanization on the other.

We may agree for instance with Daniel Bell that the computer will allow us to construct helpful models of the future, and yet, at the same time, recognize that such refined analytical techniques as game and decision theory, linear programming, simulation, systems analysis, and so on, appear to go hand in hand with a potential for debasing the idiosyncratic and autonomous qualities of man.

Few have spelled out the ominous aspects of this view more forcefully than Stuart Chase:

For the next generation we shall probably have to face a frightening multiplication of technologies. We must try to hold them within bounds of human toleration . . . . . The crucial factor is **time**. Has the human race time enough?

The dehumanizing, debasing potential of postmodernity does not end with the menace of technological alienation. There are the even more terrifying possibilities of accelerating technological unemployment and underemployment (with all that these entail in poverty and psychic misery) and of unbridled population explosions that will make life wretched in the more industrialized societies and wipe life out in the less developed countries. There is the distinct risk that we will at one and the same time despoil our remaining natural resources and deface our natural landscape. There is the likelihood of ever more deadly and inhumane wars, coupled with the increasing risk of thermonuclear extinction. Last, there is the chance that ever-increasing increments of power—economic, political, or military (or all three in combination)— may fall into the hands of ever-fewer people while the mass of mankind is simultaneously disenfranchised.

This, however, is only one side of the coin. The authors of our final three selections audit the other and more reassuring side. Yet if each of them —Erich Fromm, Kenneth Boulding, and the anonymous editors of **Liberation**—holds out the possibility of reform and ultimate salvation, each takes pains to warn us that the "megamachine" (to borrow Lewis Mumford's felicitous label) poses appallingly sinister, perhaps insurmountable, hurdles. All three would agree that the world is changing more profoundly than many of us recognize. And they would agree, too, that a deeply pessimistic, blanket rejection of technology is as simplistic and dangerous as the optimism that has prevailed in the past. "There is a very real danger," Murray Bookobin warns us, "that we will lose our perspective toward technology, that we will neglect its liberatory tendencies and, worse, submit fatalistically to its uses for destructive ends." It is still for us to choose.

chapter 65
toward a humanized technology
erich fromm

A specter is stalking in our midst whom only a few see with clarity. It is not the old ghost of communism or fascism. It is a new specter: a completely mechanized society, devoted to maximal material output and consumption, directed by computers; and in this social process, man himself is being transformed into a part of the total machine, well fed and entertained, yet passive, unalive, and with little feeling. With the victory of the new society, individualism and privacy will have disappeared; feelings toward others will be engineered by psychological conditioning and other devices, or drugs which also serve a new kind of introspective experience. As Zbigniew Brzezinski put it, "In the technetronic society the trend would seem to be towards the aggregation of the individual support of millions of uncoordinated citizens easily within the reach of magnetic and attractive personalities effectively exploiting the latest communication techniques to manipulate emotions and control reason."[1] This new form of society has been predicted in the form of fiction in Orwell's **1984** and Aldous Huxley's **Brave New World**.

Perhaps its most ominous aspect at present is that we seem to lose control over our own system.

We execute the decisions which our computer calculations make for us. We as human beings have no aims except producing and consuming more and more. We will nothing, nor do we not-will anything. We are threatened with extinction by nuclear weapons and with inner deadness by the passiveness which our exclusion from responsible decision making engenders.

How did it happen? How did man, at the very height of his victory over nature, become the prisoner of his own creation and in serious danger of destroying himself?

In the search of scientific truth, man came across knowledge that he could use for the domination of nature. He had tremendous success. But in the one-sided emphasis on technique and material consumption, man lost touch with himself, with life. Having lost religious faith and the humanistic values bound up with it, he concentrated on technical and material values and lost the capacity for deep emotional experiences, for the joy and sadness that accompany them. The machine he built became so powerful that it developed its own program, which now determines man's own thinking.

At the moment, one of the gravest symptoms of our system is the fact that our economy rests upon arms production (plus maintenance of the whole defense establishment) and on the principle of maximal consumption. We have a well-functioning economic system under the condition that we are producing goods which threaten us with physical destruction, that we transform the individual into a total passive consumer and thus deaden him, and that we have created a bureaucracy which makes the individual feel impotent.

Are we confronted with a tragic, insolvable dilemma? **Must we produce sick people in order to have a healthy economy, or can we use our material resources, our inventions, our computers to serve the ends of man? Must individuals be passive and dependent in order to have strong and well-functioning organizations?**

■

There is a growing polarization occurring in the United States and in the whole world: There are those who are attracted to force, "law and order," bureaucratic methods, and eventually to non-life, and those with a deep longing for life, for new attitudes rather than for ready-made schemes and blueprints. This new front is a movement which combines the wish for profound changes in our economic and social practice with changes in our psychic and spiritual approach to life. In its most general form, its aim is the activation of the individual, the restoration of man's control over the social system, the humanization of technology. It is a movement in the name of life, and it has such a broad and common base because the threat to life is today a threat not to one class, to one nation, but a threat to all.

■

Man, lacking the instinctual equipment of the animal, is not as well equipped for flight or for attack as animals are. He does not "know" infallibly, as the salmon knows where to return to the river in order to spawn its young and as many birds know where to go south in the winter and where to return in the summer. His decisions are **not made for him** by instinct. **He** has to make **them.** He is faced with alternatives and there is a risk of failure in every decision he makes. The price that man pays for consciousness is insecurity. He can stand his insecurity by being aware and accepting the human condition, and by the hope that he will not fail even though he has no guarantee for success. He has no certainty; the only certain prediction he can make is: "I shall die."

Man is born as a freak of nature, being within nature and yet transcending it. He has to find principles of action and decision making which replace the principles of instinct. He has to have a frame of orientation which permits him to organize a consistent picture of the world as a condition for consistent actions. He has to fight not only against the dangers of dying, starving, and being hurt, but also against another danger which is specifically human: that of becoming insane. In other words, he has to protect himself not only against the danger of losing his life but also against the danger of losing his mind. The human being, born under the conditions described here, would indeed go mad if he did not find a frame of reference which permitted him to feel at home in the world in some form and to escape the experience of utter helplessness, disorientation, and uprootedness. There are many ways in which man can find a solution to the task of staying alive and of remaining sane. Some are better than others and some are worse. By "better" is meant a way conducive to greater strength, clarity, joy, independence; and by "worse" the very opposite. But more important than finding the **better** solution is finding some solution which is viable.

■

In spite of the fact that there is a tragic disproportion between intellect and emotion at the present moment in industrial society, there is no denying the fact that the history of man is a history of growing awareness. This awareness refers to the facts of nature outside of himself as well as to his own nature. While man still wears blinders, in many respects his critical reason has discovered a great deal about the nature of the universe and the nature of man. He is still very much at the beginning of this process of discovery, and the crucial question is whether the destructive power which his present knowledge has given him will permit him to go on extending this knowledge to an extent which is unimaginable today, or whether he will destroy himself before he can build an ever-fuller picture of reality on the present foundations.

If this development is to take place, one condition is necessary: that the social contradictions and irrationalities which throughout most of man's history have forced upon him a "false consciousness"—in order to justify domination and submission respectively—disappear or at least are reduced to such a degree that the apology for the existent social order does not paralyze man's capacity for critical thought. Of course, this is not a matter of what is first and what is second. Awareness of existing reality and of alternatives for its improvement helps to change reality, and every improvement in reality helps the clarification of thought. Today, when scientific reasoning has reached a peak, the transformation of society, burdened by the inertia of previous circumstances, into a sane society could permit the average man to use his reason with the same objectivity to which we are accustomed from the scientists. This is a matter not primarily of superior intelligence but of the disappearance of irrationality from social life—an irrationality which necessarily leads to confusion of the mind.

STEPS TO THE HUMANIZATION OF TECHNOLOGICAL SOCIETY

If we are now to consider the possibility of humanizing the industrial society as it has developed in the second Industrial Revolution, we must begin by considering those institutions and methods which for economic as well as psychological reasons cannot be done away with without the total disruption of our society. These elements are: (1) The large-scale centralized enterprise as it has developed in the last decades in government, business, universities, hospitals, etc. This process of centralization is still continuing, and soon almost all major purposeful activities will be carried on by large systems. (2) Large-scale planning within each system, which results from the centralization. (3) Cybernation, that is cybernetics and automation, as the major theoretical and practical principle of control, with the computer as the most important element in automation.

But not only these three elements are here to stay. There is another element which appears in all social systems: the system Man. As I pointed out earlier, this does not mean that human nature is not malleable; it means that it allows only a limited number of potential structures, and confronts us with certain ascertainable alternatives. The most important alternative as far as the technological society is concerned is the following: If man is passive, bored, unfeeling, and one-sidedly cerebral, he develops pathological symptoms like anxiety, depression, depersonalization, indifference to life, and violence. Indeed, as Robert H. Davis wrote In a penetrating paper, "the long-range implications of a cybernated world for mental health are disturbing."[2] It is important to stress this point, since most planners deal with the human factor as one

which could adapt itself to any condition without causing any disturbances.

The possibilities which confront us are few and ascertainable. One possibility is that we continue in the direction we have taken. This would lead to such disturbances of the total system that either thermonuclear war or severe human pathology would be the outcome. The second possibility is the attempt to change that direction by force or violent revolution. This would lead to the breakdown of the whole system and violence and brutal dictatorship as a result. The third possibility is the humanization of the system, in such a way that it serves the purpose of man's well-being and growth, or in other words, his life process. In this case, the central elements of the second Industrial Revolution will be kept intact. The question is, Can this be done and what steps need to be taken to achieve it?

■

Given these general aims, what is the procedure of humanistic planning? **Computers should become a functional part in a life-oriental social system and not a cancer which begins to play havoc and eventually kills the system.** Machines or computers must become means for ends which are determined by man's reason and will. The values which determine the selection of facts and which influence the programming of the computer must be gained on the basis of the knowledge of human nature, its various possible manifestations, its optimal forms of development, and the real needs conducive to this development. That is to say, man, not technique, must become the ultimate source of values; optimal human development and not maximal production the criterion for all planning.[3]

WHAT IS THE NATURE OF "HUMANISTIC MANAGEMENT" AND ITS METHODS?

The basic principle of the humanistic management method is that, in spite of the bigness of the enterprises, centralized planning, and cybernation, the individual participant asserts himself toward the managers, circumstances, and machines, and ceases to be a powerless particle which has no active part in the process. Only by such affirmation of his will can the energies of the individual be liberated and his mental balance be restored.

The same principle of humanistic management can also be expressed in this way: While in alienated bureaucracy all power flows from above downward, in humanistic management there is a two-way street, the "subjects"[4] of the decision made above respond according to their own will and concerns; their response not only reaches the top decision makers but forces them to respond in turn. The "subjects" of decision making have a right to challenge the decision makers. Such a challenge would first of all require a rule that if a sufficient number of "subjects" demanded that the corresponding bureaucracy (on whatever level) answer questions, explain its procedures, the decision makers would respond to the demand.

∎

If the bureaucratic mode were changed from an alienated to a humanistic one, it would necessarily lead to a change in the type of manager who is successful. The defensive type of personality who clings to his bureaucratic image and who is afraid of being vulnerable and of confronting persons directly and openly would be at a disadvantage. On the other hand, the imaginative, non-frightened, responsive person would be successful if the method of management were changed. These considerations show how erroneous it is to speak of certain methods of management which cannot be changed because the managers "would not be willing or capable of changing them." What is left out here is the fact that new methods would constitute a selective principle for managers. This does not mean that most present managers would be replaced by the new type of manager. No doubt there are many who under the present system cannot utilize their responsive capacities and who will be able to do so once the system gives them a chance.

Among the objections to the idea of active participation of the individual in the enterprises in which he works, perhaps the most popular one is the statement that, in view of increasing cybernation, the working time of the individual will be so short and the time devoted to leisure so long that the activation of the individual will no longer need to take place in his work situation, but will be sufficiently accomplished during his leisure time. This idea, I believe, is based on an erroneous concept of human existence and of work. Man, even under the most favorable technological conditions, has to take the responsibility of producing food, clothing, housing, and all other material necessities. This means he has to work. Even if most physical labor is taken over by the machines, man has still to take

part in the process of the exchange between himself and nature; only if man were a disembodied being or an angel with no physical needs, would work completely disappear. Man, being in need of assimilating nature, of organizing and directing the process of material production, of distribution, of social organization, of responses to natural catastrophes, can never sit back and let things take care of themselves. Work in a technological society may not be a "curse" any more, but that paradisiacal state in which man does not have to take care of his material needs is a technological fantasy. Or will the solution be, as Brzezinski[5] predicts, that only the elite will have the privilege of working while the majority is busy with consumption? Indeed, that could be a solution to the problem, but it would reduce the majority to the status of slaves, in the paradoxical sense that they would become irresponsible and useless parasites, while the free man alone would have the right to live a full life, which includes work. **If man is passive in the process of production and organization, he will also be passive during his leisure time.** If he abdicates responsibility and participation in the process of sustaining life, he will acquire the passive role in all other spheres of life and be dependent on those who take care of him. We already see this happening today. Man has more leisure time than before, but most people show this passiveness in the leisure which is forced upon them by the method of alienated bureaucratism. Leisure time is mostly of the spectator or consumption type; rarely is it an expression of activeness.

∎

Our society, like many of the past, has accepted the principle "he who does not work should not eat." (Russian Communism has elevated this old principle into a "socialist" precept, phrasing it slightly differently.) The problem is not whether a man fulfills his social responsibility by contributing to the common good. In fact, in those cultures which have explicitly or implicitly accepted this norm, the rich, who did not have to work, were exempted from this principle, and the definition of a gentleman was a man who did not have to work in order to live in style. The problem is that any human being has an inalienable right to live regardless of whether or not he performs a social duty. Work and all other social obligations should be made sufficiently attractive to urge man to desire to accept his share of social responsibility, but he should not be forced to do so by the threat of starvation. If the latter principle is applied, society has no need to make work attractive and to fit its system to human needs. It is true that in many societies of the past the disproportion between the size of the population and the available techniques of production did not permit the freedom to dispense with the principle of what is, in fact, forced labor.

In the affluent industrial society there is no such problem, and yet even the members of the middle and upper classes are forced to follow norms laid down by the industrial system for fear of losing their jobs. Our industrial system does not give them as much leeway as it could. If they lose a job because they lack "the right spirit"—which means they are too independent, voice unpopular opinions, marry the "wrong" woman—they will have great difficulties in finding another job of equal rank, and getting a job of inferior rank implies that they and their families feel their personality has been degraded; they lose the new "friends" they had gained in the process of rising; they fear the scorn of their wives and the loss of respect from their children.

The point I want to make is to uphold the principle that a person has an inalienable right to live—a right to which no conditions are attached and which implies the right to receive the basic commodities necessary for life, the right to education and to medical care; he has a right to be treated at least as well as the owner of a dog, or a cat treats his pet, which does not have to "prove" anything in order to be fed. Provided this principle were accepted, if a man, woman, or adolescent could be sure that whatever he did his material existence would not be in jeopardy, the realm of human freedom would be immensely enhanced. Acceptance of this principle would also enable a person to change his occupation or profession by using one or more years in preparing himself for a new and, to him, more adequate activity. It happens that most people make a decision about their career at an age when they do not have the experience and judgment to know what activity is the most congenial to them. Perhaps in their midthirties they wake up to the fact that it is too late to start that activity which they now know would have been the right choice. In addition, no woman would be forced to remain unhappily married because she did not have what it takes even to prepare herself for a job at which she could make a living. No employee would be forced to accept conditions which to him are degrading or distasteful if he knew he would not starve during the time he looks for a job more to his liking. This problem is by no means solved by unemployment or welfare dole. As many have recognized, the bureaucratic methods employed here are humiliating to such a degree that many people are afraid of being forced into the dole-receiving sector of the population, and this fear is sufficient to deprive them of the freedom not to accept certain working conditions.

NOTES

1. "The Technetronic Society," Encounter, vol. 30, no. 1 (January, 1968), p. 19.

2. "The Advance of Cybernation: 1965-1985," in The Guaranteed Income, ed. by Robert Theobald (New York: Doubleday Anchor Books, 1967).

3. Hasan Ozbekhan has formulated the problem very succinctly: "What we have failed to do in all this is to ascribe operational meaning to the so-called desirables that motivate us, to question their intrinsic worth, to assess the long-range consequences of our aspirations and actions, to wonder whether the outcome we seem to be expecting does in fact correspond to that quality of life we say we are striving for—and whether our current actions will lead us there. In other words, in this writer's conception of planning we are in the deeper sense failing to plan." (Cf. the article by Hasan Ozbekhan, "The Triumph of Technology: 'Can' Implies 'Ought,'" System Development Corporation. I also gratefully acknowledge the suggestions I received by subsequent personal communication from Mr. Ozbekhan; furthermore, from Martin K. Starr and Raymond G. Brown.)

4. In the following, I shall call those subject to control by bureaucracy "subjects."

5. Zbigniew Brzezinski, "The Technetronic Society," Encounter, vol. 30, no. 1, (January, 1968).

chapter 66
after civilization, what?
kenneth e. boulding

We are living in what I call the second great change in the state of man. The first is the change from precivilized to civilized societies. The first five hundred thousand years or so of man's existence on earth were relatively uneventful. Compared with his present condition, he puttered along in an astonishingly stationary state. There may have been changes in language and culture which are not reflected in the artifacts, but if there were, these changes are lost to us. The evidence of the artifacts, however, is conclusive. Whatever changes there were, they were almost unbelievably slow. About ten thousand years ago, we begin to perceive an acceleration in the rate of change. This becomes very noticeable five thousand years ago with the development of the first civilization. The details of this first great change are probably beyond our recovery. However, we do know that it depended on two phenomena: the development of agriculture and the development of exploitation. Agriculture, that is, the domestication of crops and livestock and the planting of crops in fields, gave man a secure surplus of food from the food producer. In a hunting and fishing economy it seems to take the food producer all his time to produce enough

food for himself and his family. The moment we have agriculture, with its superior productivity of this form of employment of human resources, the food producer can produce more food than he and his family can eat. In some societies in these happy conditions, the food producer has simply relaxed and indulged himself with leisure. As soon, however, as we get politics, that is, exploitation, we begin to get cities and civilization. Civilization, it is clear from the origin of the word, is what happens in cities, and the city is dependent (in its early stages, at any rate) on the existence of a food surplus from the food producer and some organization which can take it away from him. With this food surplus, the political organization feeds kings, priests, armies, architects, and builders, and the city comes into being. Political science in its earliest form is the knowledge of how to take the food surplus away from the food producer without giving him very much in return.

Now I argue that we are in the middle of the second great change in the state of man, which is as drastic and as dramatic, and certainly as large as, if not larger than, the change from precivilized to civilized society. This I call the change from civilization to postcivilization. It is a strange irony that just at the moment when civilization has almost completed the conquest of precivilized societies, postcivilization has been treading heavily upon its heels. The student of civilization may soon find himself in the unfortunate position of the anthropologist who studies precivilized societies. Both are like the student of ice on a hot day—the subject matter melts away almost before he can study it.

These great changes can be thought of as a change of gear in the evolutionary process, resulting in progressive acceleration of the rate of evolutionary change. Even before the appearance of man on the earth, we can detect earlier evolutionary gear-shiftings. The formation of life obviously represented one such transition, the movement from the water to the land another, the development of the vertebrates another, and so on. Man himself represents a very large acceleration of the evolutionary process. Whether he evolved from preexisting forms, or landed from a space ship and was not able to get back to where he came from, is immaterial. Once he had arrived on earth, the process of evolution could go on within the confines of the human nervous system at a greatly accelerated rate. The human mind is an enormous mutation-selection process. Instead of mutation-selection process being confined, as it were, to the flesh, it can take place within the image, and hence, very rapid changes are possible. Man seems to have been pretty slow to exploit this potentiality, but one suspects that even with primitive man, the rate of change in the biosphere was much larger than it had been before, because of the appearance of what Teilhard de Chardin calls the noosphere, or sphere of knowledge.

Civilization represents a further acceleration of the rate of change, mainly because one of the main products of civilization is history. With the food surplus from agriculture it became possible to feed specialized scribes. With the development of writing, man did not have to depend on the uncertain memories of the aged for his records, and a great process of accumulation of social knowledge began. The past could now communicate, at least in one direction, with the present, and this enormously increased the range and possibility of enlargement of the contents of the human mind.

Out of civilization, however, comes science, which is a superior way of organizing the evolution of knowledge. We trace the first beginnings of science, of course, almost as far back as the beginning of civilization itself. Beginning about 1650, however, we begin to see the organization of science into a community of knowledge, and this leads again to an enormous acceleration of the rate of change. The world of 1650 is more remote to us than the world of ancient Egypt or Samaria would have been to the man of 1650. Already in the United States and Western Europe, in a smaller degree in Russia and in some other parts of the world, we see the beginnings of postcivilized society—a state of man as different from civilization as civilization is from savagery. What we really mean, therefore, by the anemic term "economic development" is the second great transition in the state of man. It is the movement from civilized to postcivilized society. It is nothing short of a major revolution in the human condition, and it does not represent a mere continuance and development of the old patterns of civilization.

As a dramatic illustration of the magnitude of the change, we can contemplate Indonesia. This is a country which has about the same extent, population, and per capita income as the Roman Empire at its height. For all I know it is producing a literature and an art at least comparable to that of the Augustan age. It is, therefore, a very good example of a country of high civilization. Because of this fact, it is one of the poorest countries in the world. It is desperately anxious to break out of its present condition. Jakarta is a city about the size of ancient Rome, though perhaps a little less splendid. All this points up the fact that the Roman Empire was a desperately poor and underdeveloped society. The Roman cities seem to have been always about three weeks away from starvation, and even at its height it is doubtful whether the Roman Empire ever had less than seventy-five to eighty percent of its population in agriculture.

Civilization, that is, is a state of society in which techniques are so poor that it takes about eighty percent of the population to feed the hundred percent. But we do have about twenty percent of the people who can be spared from food-producing to build Parthenons and cathedrals, to write literature and poetry, and fight wars. By contrast, in the United States today we are rapidly getting to the point where we can produce all our food with only ten percent of the population and still have large agricultural surpluses. But for the blessings of agricultural policy, we might soon be able to produce all our food with five percent of the population. It may even be that agriculture is on its way out altogether and that within another generation or so we will produce our food in a totally different way. Perhaps both fields and cows are merely relics of civilization, the vestiges of a vanishing age. This means, however, that even in our society, which is at a very early stage of postcivilization, we can now spare about ninety percent of the people to produce bathtubs, automobiles, H-bombs and all the other conveniences of life. Western Europe and Japan are coming along behind the United States very fast. The Russians, likewise, are advancing toward postcivilization, although by a very different road. At the moment their ideology is a handicap to them in some places—especially in agriculture, which still occupies forty-five percent of the people. And, if the Russians ever discover that super-peasants are a good deal more efficient than collective farms, they may cut away some of the ideology that hangs around their neck and move even more rapidly toward postcivilized society.

I'm not at all sure what postcivilization will look like but it will certainly be a worldwide society. Until very recently, each civilized society was a little island in a sea of barbarism which constantly threatened to overwhelm it. Civilization is haunted by the spectre of decline and fall, though it is noteworthy that in spite of the rise and fall of particular civilizations, civilization itself expanded steadily in geographical coverage, from its very beginnings. We must face the fact, however, that postcivilized society will be worldwide, if only because of its ease of communication and transportation. I flew last year from Idlewild to Brussels, and on glimpsing the new Brussels Airport out of the corner of my eye, I thought for a moment that we had come back and landed at Idlewild again.

The characteristic institutions of civilization are, as we have seen, first agriculture, then the city, then war, in the sense of clash of organized armed forces, and finally, inequality, the sharp contrast between the rich and the poor, between the city and the country, between the urbane and the rustic. The state is based very fundamentally on violence and exploitation, and the culture tends to be spiritually monolithic.

In postcivilization all these institutions suffer radical change. Agriculture, as we have seen, diminishes until it is a small proportion of the society; the city, likewise, in the classical sense, disintegrates. Los Angeles is perhaps the first example of the postcivilization, posturban agglomeration—under no stretch of the imagination could it be called a city. War, likewise, is an institution in process of disintegration. National defense as a social system has quite fundamentally broken down on a world scale. The ICBM and the nuclear warhead have made the nation-state as militarily obsolete as the city-state, for in no country now can the armed

forces preserve an area of internal peace by pushing violence to the outskirts. Poverty and inequality, likewise, are tending to disappear, at least on their traditional scale. In civilized societies the king or the emperor could live in a Versailles and the peasant in a hovel. In postcivilized society, it is almost impossible for the rich to consume on a scale which is more, let us say, than ten times that of the poor. There is no sense in having more than ten automobiles!

Another profound change in the passage from civilization to postcivilization is the change in the expectation of life. In civilized society, birth and death rates tend to be about forty per thousand and the expectation of life at birth is twenty-five years. In postcivilized society, the expectation of life at birth rises at least to seventy and perhaps beyond. It may be that we are on the edge of a biological revolution, just as dramatic and far-reaching as the discovery of atomic energy and that we may crack the problem of aging and prolong human life much beyond its present span. Whether or not, however, we go forward to Methuselah, the mere increase of the average age of death to seventy is a startling and far-reaching change. It means, for instance, that in an equilibrium population, the birth and death rates cannot be more than about fourteen per thousand. This unquestionably implies some form of conscious control of births. It means also that a much larger proportion of the population will be in later years.

It is perfectly possible to paint an antiutopia in which a postcivilized society appears as universally vulgar or dull. On the whole, however, I welcome postcivilization and I have really very little affection for civilization. In most precivilized societies the fact that the life of man is for the most part nasty, brutish, and short, does not prevent the poets and philosophers from sentimentalizing the noble savage. Similarly, we may expect the same kind of sentimentalizing of the noble Romans and civilized survivals like Winston Churchill. On the whole, though, I will not shed any tears over the grave of civilization any more than I will over precivilized society. The credit balance of postcivilization is large. It at least gives us a chance of a modest utopia, in which slavery, poverty, exploitation, gross inequality, war, and disease—these prime costs of civilization—will fall to the vanishing point.

What we have at the moment is a chance to make a transition to this modest utopia—a chance which is probably unique in the history of this planet. If we fail, the chance will probably not be repeated in this part of the universe. Whatever experiments may be going on elsewhere, the present moment indeed is unique in the whole four billion years of the history of the planet. In my more pessimistic moments, I think the chance is a slim one, and it may be that man will be written off as an unsuccessful experiment. We must look at the traps which lie along the path of the transition, which might prevent us from making it altogether.

The most urgent trap is, of course, the trap of war. War, as I have suggested, is an institution peculiarly characteristic of civilization. Precivilized societies have sporadic feuding and raiding, but they do not generally have permanent organized armed forces, and they do not generally develop conquest and empire; or if they do, they soon pass into a civilized form. An armed force is essentially a mobile city designed to throw things at another mobile or stationary city with presumably evil intent. As far as I know, not more than two or three civilizations have existed without war. The Mayans and the people of Mohenjodaro seem to have lived for fairly long periods without war, but this was an accident of their monopolistic situation and they unquestionably occupied themselves with other kinds of foolishness. If precivilized society, however, cannot afford war, postcivilized society can afford far too much of it, and hence will be forced to get rid of the institution because it is simply inappropriate to the technological age. The breakdown in the world social system of national defense really dates from about 1949, when the United States lost its monopoly of nuclear weapons. A system of national defense is only feasible if each nation is stronger at home than its enemies, so that it can preserve a relatively large area of peace within its critical boundaries. Such a system is only possible, however, if the range of the deadly missile is short and if the armed forces of each nation lose power rapidly as they move away from home. The technological developments of the twentieth century have destroyed these foundations of national defense, and have replaced it with another social system altogether, which is "deterrence."

"Deterrence" is a social system with properties very different from that of national defense, which it replaced. Under national defense, for instance, it is possible to use the armed forces; under "deterrence" is it not—that is, if the deterring forces are ever used, the system will have broken down. We live in a society with a positive possibility of irretrievable disaster—a probability which grows every

year. Herman Kahn recently said: "All we are doing is buying time, and we are doing nothing with the time that we buy." The armed forces of the world are caught in a technological process which not only destroys their own function, but threatens all of us. Even if a few of us do crawl out of the fallout shelters, it is by no means clear that we can put the world back together again. Even if the human race could survive one nuclear war, it is very doubtful that it could survive a second; and as the purpose of the first nuclear war would be to set up a political system which would produce the second, unless there is a radical change in attitude towards national defense, the prospects of the human race seem to be dim. Fortunately, "there is still time, brother," and evolution can still go on in the minds of men. The critical question is whether it can go on rapidly enough. The abolition of national defense, which is what we must face, is going to be a painful process, as we have come to rely on it to preserve many of the values which we hold dear. If the task can be perceived, however, by a sufficient number of people, there is a chance that we may avoid this trap before it is too late.

Even if we avoid the war trap, we may still fall into the population trap. Population control is an unsolved problem even for the developed areas of the world, which have moved the furthest towards postcivilization. An equilibrium of population in a stable postcivilized society may represent a fairly radical interference with ancient human institutions and freedoms. In a stable postcivilized society, as I have suggested, the birth and death rates must be of the order of fourteen per thousand, and the average number of children per family cannot much exceed two. There are many social institutions which might accomplish this end. So far, however, the only really sure-fire method of controlling population is starvation and misery.

In many parts of the world—indeed, for most of the human race for the moment—the impact of certain postcivilized techniques of civilized society has produced a crisis of growth, which may easily be fatal. In the tropics especially, with DDT and a few simple public-health measures, it is easy to reduce the death rate to nine or ten per thousand while the birth rate stays at forty per thousand. This means an annual increase of population of three percent **per annum**, almost all of it concentrated in the lower age groups. We see dramatic examples of this phenomenon in places like the West Indies, Ceylon, and Formosa; but thanks to the activity of the World Health Organization, it is taking place rapidly all over the tropical world. Perhaps the most important key to the transition to postcivilization is heavy investment in human resources—that is, in education. The conquest of disease and infant mortality, however, before the corresponding adjustment to the birth rate, produces enormous numbers of children in societies which do not have the resources to educate them—especially as those in the middle age groups, who after all must do all of the work of a society, come from the much smaller population of the pre-DDT era.

Even in the developed countries, population control presents a very serious problem. The United States, for instance, at the moment [1962] is increasing in population even more rapidly than India. The time when we thought that the mere increase in income would automatically solve the population problem has gone by. In the United States, and certain other societies in the early stages of postcivilization, the child has become an object of conspicuous domestic consumption. The consumption patterns of the American spending unit seem to follow a certain "gestalt" in which household capital accumulates in a certain order, such as the first car, the first child, the washer and dryer, the second child, the deep freeze, the third child, the second car, the fourth child, and so on. The richer we get, the more children we can afford to have and the more children we do have. We now seem to be able to afford an average of something like four children per family, and as, in a post-civilized society, these four children all survive, the population doubles every generation. A hundred years of this and even the United States is going to find itself uncomfortably crowded. It can be argued, indeed, that from the point of view of the amenities of life we are already well beyond the optimum population.

The third trap on the road to postcivilization is the technological trap. Our present technology is fundamentally suicidal. It is based on the extraction of concentrated deposits of fossil fuels and ores, which in the nature of things are exhaustible. Even at present rates of consumption, they will be exhausted in a time span which is not very long measured against human history and which is infinitesimally small on the geological time scale. If the rest of the world advances to American standards of consumption, these resources will disappear almost overnight. On this view economic development is the process of bringing closer the evil day when everything will be gone—all the oil, the coal, the ores—and we will have to go back to primitive agriculture and scratching in the woods.

There are indications, however, that suicidal technology is not absolutely necessary and that a permanent high-level technology is possible. Beginning in the early part of the twentieth century, it is possible to detect an antientropic movement in technology. This begins perhaps with the Haber process for the fixation of nitrogen from the air. A development of similar significance is the Dow process for the extraction of magnesium from the sea. Both these processes take the diffuse and concentrate it, instead of taking the concentrated and diffusing it, as do most processes of mining and economic production. These antientropic processes foreshadow a technology in which we shall draw all the materials we need from the virtually inexhaustible reservoirs of the sea and the air and draw our energy from controlled fusion—either artificially produced on the earth or from the sun.

This is why I so much resent spending half the world's income on armaments—because the more we do this, the less chance we have of making the transition to a stable, high-level society. The human race is in a precarious position on its planet and it should act accordingly. It has a chance, never to be repeated, of making its great transition, and if it fails, at least one good experiment in intelligence will have gone to waste. I suppose there are similar experiments of this nature going on in other parts of the universe; but I must confess to a hopelessly anthropocentric prejudice in favor of planet earth. It's a nice planet, and I'm in favor of it and I have no desire to see its principal inhabitant blow it up or starve it out.

When we look at the nature of possible remedies for our immediate problems, it seems clear that we all are engulfed in a profound and appallingly dangerous misallocation of our intellectual resources. The misallocation lies in the fact that although all our major problems are in social systems, we persist in regarding them as if they were essentially problems in physical or biological systems. We persist in regarding agricultural problems, for instance, as one of crops, whereas it is clearly fundamentally a problem of farmers. We persist in regarding the flood-control problem as a problem of the river and we even turn it over to army engineers, who treat the river as an enemy. A flood, however, is no problem at all to a river. It is a perfectly normal part of its way of life. The flood, essentially, is a problem of people and of social institutions, of architecture and zoning. Professor Gilbert White, of the University of Chicago, suggests that after spending over four billion dollars on flood control in this country, we are more in danger of major disasters than we were before. What we really mean by flood control is the substitution of a major disaster every fifty or one hundred years for minor inconveniences every five or ten.

In national defense we have fallen into exactly the same trap. We regard this as a problem in physical systems and in hardware, whereas it is essentially a problem in social systems. Here again, we are building into our societies the eventual certainty of total disaster. In face of the fact that war and peace is the major problem of our age, we are putting practically nothing into peace research; even when we do put money into arms control and disarmament research we spend sixty million dollars for Project Vela, which deals wholly with physical systems, and one hundred and fifty thousand on Project Vulcan, which deals with social systems and with unanswerable questions at that. When we look at biological and medical research, and still more, research into population, the disparity is just as striking. We persist in regarding disease as a biological problem, whereas it is fundamentally a biosocial system. Yet the number of sociologists in our medical schools can be counted almost on the fingers of one hand.

Nevertheless, in spite of the dangers, it is a wonderful age to live in, and I would not wish to be born in any other time. The wonderful and precious thing about the present moment is that there is still time—the Bomb hasn't gone off, the population explosion may be caught, the technological problem can, perhaps, be solved. If the human race is to survive, however, it will have to change more in its ways of thinking in the next twenty-five years than it has done in the last

twenty-five thousand. There is hope, however, in the fact that we are very far from having exhausted the capacity of this extraordinary organism that we call man. I once calculated the capacity of the human nervous system in terms of the number of different states it might assume, which is a very rough measure. This comes to two to the ten billionth power, assuming that each of our ten billion neurons is capable of only two states. This is a very large number. It would take you ninety years to write it down at the rate of one digit a second. If you want a standard of comparison, the total number of neutrinos, which are the smallest known particles, which could be packed into the known astronomical universe (this is the largest physical number I could think of) could easily be written down in three minutes. I find it hard to believe, therefore, that the capacity of the human organism has been exhausted.

What we have to do now, however, is to develop a new form of learning. We have to learn from rapidly changing systems. Ordinarily we learn from stable systems. It is because the world repeats itself that we catch on to the law of repetition. Learning from changing systems is perhaps another step in the acceleration of evolution that we have to take. I have been haunted by a remark which Norman Meier, the psychologist, made in a seminar a few months ago, when he said that a cat who jumps on a hot stove never jumps on a cold one. This seems precisely to describe the state we may be in today. We have jumped on a lot of hot stoves and now perhaps the cold stove is the only place on which to jump. In the rapidly changing system it is desperately easy to learn things which are no longer true. Perhaps the greatest task of applied social science at the moment is to study the conditions under which we learn from rapidly changing systems. If we can answer this question, there may still be hope for the human race.

chapter 67
tract for
the times
editors of liberation

The decline of independent radicalism and the gradual falling into silence of prophetic and rebellious voices is an ominous feature of the mid-twentieth century. Anxiety and apprehension have invaded the air we breathe. Advances in science and technology, which should have been our greatest triumphs, leave us stunned and uncertain as to whether human life and history have meaning.

Power is everywhere openly or secretly idolized. The threat of atomic or biological war, perhaps even the extinction of mankind, hangs over the earth. Hopes and ideals have become propaganda devices. But those who should furnish vision and direction are silent or echoing old ideas in which they scarcely believe themselves.

This failure of a new radicalism to emerge is an indication, it seems to us, that the stock of fundamental ideas on which the radical thinking of recent times has been predicated is badly in need of thorough reappraisal. Much of its inspiration appears to be used up. Old labels—principally in the Marxist and liberal traditions—simply do not apply any more, and the phrases which fifty years ago were guideposts to significant action have largely become empty patter and jargon.

The changes of recent years—represented by atomic power and by the beginnings of the Second

From **Liberation**, March 1963. Reprinted by permission.

Industrial Revolution and also by the rise of totalitarianism—have filled many thoughtful persons with the strong suspicion that the problems of today must be attacked on a much deeper level than traditional Marxists, Communists, and various kinds of Socialists and Anarchists have realized. Proposals and calls to action couched in the old terms fail any longer to inspire much hope or genuine humane enthusiasm, because large numbers of people are aware, or dimly sense, that they do not touch the roots of the trouble.

There is no point, for example, in reshuffling power, because the same old abuses still persist under new masters. The vast energy devoted to reconstructing government is wasted if in a short time the new structure becomes as impervious to fundamental human decency and ethics as the old one. There is no doubt that there are forms of property relationships which are oppressive and destructive of true community, but if these are altered and the average individual finds his life as dull and empty as ever and the enslavement of his hours just as great, little or nothing has been achieved.

It is increasingly evident that nineteenth century modes of thought are largely incapable of dealing with such questions. The changes which are going on in the modern world—which call into doubt many assumptions which almost all nineteenth century revolutionists and reformers took for granted—require also changes in our deepest modes of thought. We require a post-Soviet, post-H-bomb expression of the needs of today and a fresh vision of the world of peace, freedom, and brotherhood in which they can be met.

OUR ROOT TRADITIONS

In reexamining our thought—and especially the two great dominant traditions of liberalism and Marxism—we return in part again to root traditions from which we derive our values and standards. There are four of these:

1. There is an ancient Judeo-Christian prophetic tradition which gave men a vision of human dignity and a reign of righteousness, equality, and brotherhood on earth. It taught them that building such an order of life was their task, and that a society of justice and fraternity could be built by justice and love and not by any other means.

2. There is an American tradition—far from having been realized, often distorted, and all but lost—of a "nation conceived in liberty, and dedicated to the proposition that all men are created equal." It is a tradition which also emphasizes the dignity of man and asserts that government rests upon consent, and institutions are made for man, not man for institutions. Such names as Jefferson, Paine, Thoreau, Emerson, Debs, Randolph Bourne, the Quaker experiment in Pennsylvania, the Utopian community experiments, the Abolition movement, the Underground Railway, are associated with this tradition.

3. There is the heritage of the libertarian, democratic, antiwar, socialist, anarchist, and labor movements in Europe and the United States in the latter half of the nineteenth century and the early years of the twentieth. Multitudes of common people, the impoverished and distressed, believed that through these movements, with the help of modern science and technology, a "classless and warless world" had become possible and would in a comparatively short time be achieved.

4. There is a tradition of pacifism or nonviolence which has been exemplified throughout the centuries and in many parts of the world in great teachers and saints—or in such a figure as the Emperor Asoka—who have rejected war as accursed and unworthy of men and have insisted that injustice and violence cannot be overcome by injustice and violence but only by righteousness and peace. In particular, Gandhi stands in this tradition, not as an example to be slavishly imitated, but as a pioneer who in a series of great political and social experiments joined nonviolence and revolutionary collective action.

CRITIQUE OF LIBERALISM

In the light of these root traditions we can see that the greatness of liberalism has been its emphasis on humaneness and tolerance, its support of the liberties of the individual and its insistence on the free and inquiring mind and rejection of fanaticism and dogmatism. Its weakness has been its failure to come to grips with war, poverty, boredom, authoritarianism, and other great evils of the modern world. These problems it has tended optimistically to leave to "education" and "good will," both of which have so far proved incapable of dealing with them successfully. Liberalism has tried to diagnose our troubles without going to fundamentals—the inequalities and injustices upon which our present social order is based and which no "good will" can wish away.

This failure to raise the embarrassing questions has made liberalism often shallow, hypocritical, and dilettantish, all too often lacking in fundamental earnestness. Essentially the liberal accepts the existing order and wants to exploit it and share in it as much as the next man. At the same time he is troubled and wants the good conscience of repudiating its wrongs. Liberalism thus becomes a fashionable pose—for millionaires and generals as well as for intellectuals and editorial writers. It becomes a public ritual lacking roots in private life and behavior, and makes the liberal an easy prey of opportunism and expedience.

As against this liberal attitude a new quality of seriousness and personal honesty is necessary. In this respect what is wanted is not political liberalism but political fundamentalism. We are more interested in concrete situations than in rhetorical blueprints, in individual lives than in "global historical forces" which remain merely abstract. What matters to us is what happens to the individual human being—here and now. We will be just as flexible as the liberal, but we will strive to be more searching, and we will insist on spelling things out in terms of daily consequences, hour to hour, for everyone.

CRITIQUE OF MARXISM

Marxism, like liberalism, has much to teach, both positively and negatively. Its fundamental demand for economic justice and its attack on the problem of poverty are permanently valuable. It touches the source of much that is wrong with the world in exposing the property nerve. But many of its attitudes are those of the outmoded bourgeois epoch which it tried to repudiate. Marx was to a much greater degree than he himself realized a spokesman for nineteenth century thought patterns, now hopelessly out of date. His historical determinism, built up by analogy from now outmoded science, is an example. So also is the tendency to sacrifice the present for the future, so that human beings of today are regarded as pawns for bringing about something better in a tomorrow that never comes.

The most serious weaknesses of Marxism, however, are its omissions and its reactionary "realism" in respect to the instruments of revolution. Marx, for all his brilliant analysis of economic power, failed to analyze with equal profundity the questions of military and political power. Hence he underestimated the seriousness of the growth of the State and its emergence as an instrument of war and oppression. In trying to liberate mankind from economic slavery, he failed to see the looming horror of political slavery.

Closely related to this failure is Marx's inability to realize that social betterment cannot be brought about by the same old methods of force and chicanery characterizing the regimes which had to be overthrown precisely because they embodied such evils. It is an illuminating insight of pragmatism that means and ends condition each other reciprocally and that the ends must be built into the means. It is not sound, therefore, to expect to achieve peace through war, justice through violence, freedom through dictatorship, or civil liberties through slave labor camps. Such instruments create the social attitudes and habit patterns which they are ostensibly designed to remove. Dictatorship in any form, as well as spy systems, concentration camps, military conscription, restrictions on travel and censorship of books, papers, and political parties must all be decisively rejected. What this means is that a truly radical movement today—if it does not want to fall into the trap which the Russian Communist movement has fallen into—must take these ethical problems much more seriously than many nineteenth century thinkers did, and must commit itself to an essentially democratic and nonviolent strategy.

THE POLITICS OF THE FUTURE

One of the symptoms of our time is that many people are fed up with "politics"—by which they mean the whole machinery associated with political life. To become significant, politics must discover its ethical foundations and dynamic.

The politics of the future requires a creative synthesis of the individual ethical insights of the great religious leaders and the collective social concern of the great revolutionists.

It follows that we do not conceive the problem of revolution or the building of a better society as one of accumulating power, whether by legislative or other methods, to "capture the State," and then, presumably, to transform society and human beings as well. The national, sovereign, militarized and bureaucratic State and a bureaucratic collectivist economy are themselves evils to be avoided or abolished. Seizure of the war-making and repressive machinery of the State cannot be a step toward transforming society into a free and humanly satisfying pattern. It is the transformation of society by human decision and action that we seek. This is a more complex and human process in which power as ordinarily conceived plays a minor part. Political action in this context is, therefore, broadly conceived. It includes such developments as the Land Gift Movement in India and community and cooperative experiments in many lands. New political alignments in the narrower sense of the term may emerge from basic ethical and social changes, but preoccupation with or dependence upon the machinery of politics, or the violent seizure of power, are evils always to be avoided, and never more so than in the present crisis.

Similarly, we reject the faith in technology, industrialization, and centralization per se, characteristic of both the contemporary capitalist and Communist regimes. Our emphasis is rather on possibilities for decentralization, on direct participation of all workers or citizens in determining the conditions of life and work, and on the use of technology for human ends, rather than the subjection of man to the demands of technology.

From the synthesis of the ethical and the political emerges a new attitude toward utopianism in social and cultural thinking. Under the impact of Marxism, utopianism became virtually a term of abuse. But this attitude itself was narrow and misjudged the scientific method, not seeing that the essence of science is its openness to new and creative insights and its willingness to test them experimentally. The utopian attitude is one that is permanently needed in human affairs. It represents the growing edge of society and the creative imagination of a culture.

As we recognize more and more the imaginative and speculative element in mathematics and science and as the mechanical determinism of the last century passes away, the outmoded "scientific" aspect of nineteenth century Marxism will begin to disappear, and Marx will then appear in his true light as one of the great visionaries and utopian thinkers of that century. With new conditions, modifications of his utopian thinking are necessary and new utopias will appear, to furnish direction and incentives for action.

The world **can** move toward the abolition of war and toward a society built on responsible freedom, mutuality, and peace. Collective effort and struggle to achieve such a society should not be abandoned because the movements of an earlier day have been frustrated or wrecked.

The very presuppositions on which human relationships are based must be revolutionized. This makes it peculiarly difficult to live responsibly as individuals today and to carry on collective efforts for basic changes. In addition, the creation of a movement of dissent and social change in the United States is impeded by a sustained, war-based prosperity, with millions of unionists making a living at war jobs. This makes the task virtually as difficult in the United States as in Russia or other Communist-bloc countries.

The problem of war is one of special gravity for us, as for all our fellow men. It may be argued that for personal ethics there is no distinction between a war in which a few persons are killed at a time and one in which multitudes are wiped out. But from a sociological view, the H-bomb and what it symbolizes—possible extinction of the race itself —present mankind with a new situation. War is no longer an instrument of policy or a means to any rational end. For this reason, if for no other, a central part of any radical movement today is withdrawal of support from the military preparation and activities of **both** the dominant power blocs. Whatever differences may exist between Communist and "free world" regimes, in this decisive respect they are **equal** threats, two sides of the **same** threat to the survival of civilization. The H-bomb is not an instrument of peace in the hands of one and of war in the hands of the other. Nor is it a mere accidental excrescence in either of them but, rather, a logical outgrowth of their basic economic and social orders.

War and war preparation in the hands of any other power or group of powers is not a source of deliverance either. A Third Force based on military power would be reactionary and evil just as the present power blocs are. Any "Third Camp" or "Third Way" grouping of peoples must, therefore, be founded on an essentially nonmilitary, nonviolent base.

There are in Western Europe, Asia, Africa, and Latin America, peoples who live "in between" the two atomically armed power blocs. Of necessity, their prime objective is to keep from being drawn into either bloc and engulfed in the wars for which these Leviathans are arming. Nor can these peoples "in between" escape the peril by seeking to constitute a third atomically armed power bloc. Even if they were permitted by the dominant powers to achieve such military and economic independence as to constitute a decisive "balance," this would only serve to plunge the world into permanent war among **three** totalitarian tyrannies, on George Orwell's model in **1984**.

There are in noncommitted areas groups seeking to deal with the problems of economics and politics in a broader way and at a deeper ethical level. They seek to build not another Military Force but a Third Camp or Third Way. They are striving not only to avoid war but to build a socioeconomic order and culture different from both Communism and capitalism. Such groups as the Asian Socialist parties, the Gandhian Constructive Workers, and the Bhoodan movement of Vinoba Bhave in India illustrate this trend, as do the nonviolent responses to Colonialism in Africa. The June, 1953, workers' revolts in East Germany were part of a spontaneous movement in this direction.

Finally this does not in any degree imply preoccupation with affairs abroad to the neglect of developments in the United States. Nor does it mean concern with large-scale societal or governmental revolution to the neglect of the "one-man revolution" and of experiments in creative living by individuals, families, and small groups. Such activities are especially important and germinal. What happens in any significant sense in society as a whole is directly related, and to a great degree grows out of, what has already happened in the lives of individuals and small groups.

selected bibliography by topic

TOPIC 1. THE SOCIOLOGICAL ENTERPRISE: ITS SCOPE AND COMPASS

Some suggested book resources

BECKER, Howard et al. *For a Science of Social Man.* New York: Macmillan, 1954.

BERGER, Peter. "Sociology as an Individual Pastime." In *Invitation to Sociology: A Humanist Perspective.* Garden City, N.Y.: Doubleday, 1963.

BIERSTEDT, Robert. "Sociology and General Education." In *Sociology and Contemporary Education,* ed. Charles Page. New York: Random House, 1964.

BOTTOMORE, T. B. *Sociology: A Guide to Problems and Literature.* New York: Grove, 1972.

BRANSON, Leon. *The Political Context of Sociology.* Princeton, N.J.: Princeton University Press, 1961.

CAMERON, William Bruce. *Informal Sociology.* New York: Random House, 1963.

CHINOY, Ely. *Sociological Perspective.* New York: Random House, 1968.

DOBRINER, William. "The Sociological Perspective." In *Social Structures and Systems: A Sociological Overview.* Pacific Palisades, Calif.: Goodyear, 1969.

FYVEL, T.R., ed. *The Frontiers of Sociology.* London, England: Cohen and West, 1964.

HINKLE, Roscoe C. *The Development of Modern Sociology.* New York: Random House, 1954.

INKELES, Alex. "What is Sociology?" In *What is Sociology? An Introduction to the Discipline and Profession.* Englewood Cliffs, N.J.: Prentice—Hall, 1964.

KAPP, K. William. *Toward a Science of Man in Society.* The Hague: Martines Nijhof, 1961.

PARK, Peter. *Sociology Tomorrow.* New York: Pegasus, 1969.

RUNCIMAN, W. G. *Sociology in Its Place.* Cambridge: Cambridge University Press, 1970.

SEGERSTEDT, Torgony T. *The Nature of Social Reality.* Totowa: Bedminister press, 1966.

SINCLAIR, I. J., et al. *Sociology.* Englewood Cliffs, N.J.: Prentice-Hall, 1969.

TOPIC 2. THE SOCIOLOGICAL ENTERPRISE: MODES OF ANALYSIS

Some suggested periodical resources

BECKER, Howard S., and GEER, Blanche. "Participant Observation and Interviewing: A Comparison." *Human Organization* 16 (Fall 1957).

CAMERON, William Bruce. "The Elements of Statistical Confusion, or: What Does the Mean Mean?" *Bulletin* of the American Association of University Professors 43 (1957).

GOULDNER, Alvin W. "The Sociologist as Partisan." *American Sociologist* 3 (1968).

LAZARSFELD, Paul. "Attitude Surveys: What They Tell Us." In *"The American Soldier*—An Expository Review." *Public Opinion Quarterly* 13 (1949).

VOSS, Marvin L. "Pitfalls in Social Research: A Case Study." *American Sociologist* 1 (May 1966).

Some suggested book resources

DENZIN, Norman K., ed. *Sociological Methods.* Chicago: Aldine, 1970.

GREENWOOD, Ernest. *Experimental Sociology.* New York: King's Crown Press, 1947.

HAMMONE, Phillip E., ed. *Sociologists at Work: The Craft of Social Research.* Garden City, N.Y.: Doubleday, 1964.

LUNDBERG, George. *Social Research,* New York: Greenwood Press, 1968.

MADGE, John. *The Tools of Social Science.* Garden City, N.Y.: Doubleday, 1953.

MOSER, C. A., and KALTON, G. *Survey Methods in Social Investigation.* New York: Free Press, 1972.

SMELSER, Neil J., et al. "The Questions Sociologists Ask." In *Sociology.* Englewood Cliffs, N.J.: Prentice-Hall, 1969.

THOMLINSON, Ralph. *Sociological Concepts and Research.* New York: Random House, 1965.

WISEMAN, Jacqueline, and ARON, Marcia S. *Field Projects for Sociology Students.* Cambridge, Mass.: Schenkman, 1970.

ZETTERBERG, Hans L. *On Theory and Verification in Sociology.* Totowa: Bedminister Press, 1965.

TOPIC 3. THE SOCIOLOGICAL ENTERPRISE: ISSUES AND CONTROVERSIES

Some suggested periodical resources

DENZIN, Norman K. "Who Leads: Sociology or Society?" *American Sociologist* 5 (May 1970).

DOUD, Douglas F. "On Veblen, Mills, and the Decline of Criticism." *Dissent* 11 (Winter 1964).

GOVE, Walter R. "Should the Sociology Profession Take Moral Stands on Political Issues?" *The American Sociologist* 5 (August 1970).

GRAY, David J. "Value-free Sociology: a Doctrine of Hypocrisy and Irresponsibility." *The Sociological Quarterly* 9 (Spring 1968).

KOHL, Herbert. "Great Expectations." *New York Review of Books* (September 12, 1968).

Some suggested book resources

BECKER, Howard S. *Sociological Work.* Chicago: Aldine, 1970.

BOALT, Gunnar. *The Sociology of Research.* Carbondale: Southern Illinois University Press, 1969.

BRUYN, Severyn T. *The Human Perspective in Sociology.* Englewood Cliffs, N.J.: Prentice-Hall, 1966.

DOUGLAS, Jack D., ed. *The Relevance of Sociology.* New York: Appleton, 1970.

HOROWITZ, David, ed. *Radical Sociology.* San Francisco: Canfield Press, 1971.

MILLS, C. Wright. *Sociology and Pragmatism.* New York: Paine-Whitman, 1964.

MOTWANI, Kawai. *A Critique of Empiricism.* In *Sociology.* Bombay: Allied Publishers, 1967.

ROSS, Ralph. "The Nature of Science." In *Symbols and Civilization.* New York: Harcourt Brace Jovanovich, Harbinger edition, 1962.

STEIN, Maurice, and VIDICH, Arthur. *Sociology on Trial.* Englewood Cliffs, N.J.: Prentice-Hall, 1963.

TOPIC 4. THE CULTURAL DIMENSIONS OF EVERYDAY LIFE: THE CULTURAL IMPERATIVE

Some suggested periodical resources

BENNETT, John W. "Communal Brethren of the Great Plains." *Transaction* (December 1966).

BRIGGS, Jean L. "Kapluna Daughter: Living with Eskimos." *Transaction* (January 1970).

DRYFOSS, Robert J., Jr. "Two Tactics for Ethnic Survival—Eskimo and Indian." *Transaction* (January 1970).

HALL, Edward T. "The Silent Language." *Americas* 14 (February 1962).

HORTON, John. "Time and Cool People." *Transaction* (March/April 1967).

LYMAN, Stanford M. and SCOTT, Marvin B. "Territoriality: A Neglected Sociological Dimension." *Social Problems* 15 (1967).

MINER, Horace. "Body Ritual Among the Nacirema." *American Anthropologist* 58 (1956).

VOGT, Jon Z., and O'DEA, Thomas F. "A Comparative Study of the Role of Values in Two Southwestern Communities." *American Sociological Review* (1953).

Some suggested book resources

ARENSBERG, Conrad. *The Irish Countryman.* Garden City, N.Y.: Doubleday, 1968.

BARNETT, H. G. *Innovation: The Basis of Cultural Change.* New York: McGraw-Hill, 1967.

GAZAWAY, Rena. *The Longest Mile.* Garden City, N.Y.: Doubleday, 1969.

HALL, Edward T. *The Hidden Dimension.* Garden City, N.Y.: Doubleday, 1966.

HOEBEL, E. Adamson. "The Nature of Culture." In Harry L. Shapiro, ed., *Man, Culture, and Society.* New York: Oxford University Press, 1956.

HOGGART, Richard. "There's No Place Like Home—Working-Class Culture in London." In *The Uses of Literacy.* Boston: Beacon, 1961.

HOIJER, Harry. "Language and Writing." In Harry L. Shapiro, ed., *Man, Culture, and Society.* New York: Oxford University Press, 1956.

HOWELLS, William. *The Heathens.* Garden City, N.Y.: Doubleday, 1962.

KLUCKHOHN, Clyde. "The Concept of Culture." In *Mirror for Man.* New York: McGraw-Hill, 1949.

MIDDLETON, John, ed. *Magic, Witchcraft and Curing.* Garden City, N.Y.: Doubleday, 1967.

MURDOCK, George Peter. "How Culture Changes." In Harry L. Shapiro, ed., *Man, Culture, and Society.* New York: Oxford University Press, 1956.

OLIVER, Douglas. *Invitation to Anthropology.* Garden City, N.Y.: Doubleday, 1964.

WHITE, Leslie A. "Symbol, the Basis of Language and Culture." In *The Science of Culture.* New York: Farrar, Straus & Giroux, 1949.

TOPIC 5. THE CULTURAL DIMENSIONS OF EVERYDAY LIFE: SUBCULTURES AND CONTRACULTURES

Some suggested periodical resources

BRYAN, James H. "Apprenticeships in Prostitution." *Social Problems* 12 (Winter 1965).

DAVIDSON, Sara. "Open Land, Getting Back to the Communal Garden." *Harper's* (June 1970).

DIXON, Marlene. "The Restless Eagles: Women's Liberation." *Motive Magazine* (March-April 1969).

FINESTONE, Harold. "Cats, Kicks and Color." *Social Problems* 5 (1957).

HOWARD, John Robert. "The Flowering of the Hippie Movement." *The Annals* 382 (March 1969).

JACKMAN, Norman R., O'TOOLE, Richard, and GEIS, Gilbert. "The Self-Image of the Prostitute." *The Sociological Quarterly* 4 (Spring 1963).

KANTER, Rosabeth Moss. "Communes." *Psychology Today* 4 (July 1970).

LEVINE, Jack, and SPARES, James L. "An Analysis of the Underground Press." *Youth and Society* 2 (September 1970).

LEZNOFF, Maurice, and WESTLEY, M. A. "Overt and Covert Homosexuals." In "The Homosexual Community." *Social Problems* 3 (April 1956).

OTTO, Herbert A. "Communes: The Alternative Life-Style." *Saturday Review* (April 1971).

WEINBERG, S. Kirson, and AREND, Henry. "The Occupational Culture of the Boxer." *American Journal of Sociology* 57 (1952).

Some suggested book resources

ARNOLD, David O., ed. *The Sociology of Subcultures.* Berkeley: Glendessary Press, 1970.

BROWN, Claude. "The Subculture of Violence." In *Manchild in the Promised Land*. New York: Macmillan, 1965.

GOODMAN, Mitchell. *The Movement Toward a New America.* New York: Pilgrim Press, 1970, pp. 68-122, 433-747.

MINAR, David W., and GREER, Scott. *The Concept of Community.* Chicago: Aldine, 1970.

POLSKY, Ned. *Hustlers, Beats and Others.* Garden City, N.Y.: Doubleday, 1967.

SCOTT, Robert A., and DOUGLAS, Jack D., eds. *Theoretical Perspectives on Deviance.* New York: Basic Books, 1972.

SIMMONS, J. L. *Deviants.* Berkeley: Glendessary Press, 1969.

TOPIC 6. THE ACQUISITION OF PERSONALITY: INTERPERSONAL INTERACTION, SOCIAL ROLES, AND THE SOCIAL SELF

Some suggested periodical resources

BERGER, Bennett M. "The New Stage of American Man —Almost Endless Adolescence." *The New York Times Magazine* (November 2, 1969).

BRUNSWICK, Ann F. "What Generation Gap?" *American Journal of Sociology* 17 (Winter 1970).

HANNERZ, Ulf. "Roots of Black Manhood." *Transaction* 6 (October 1969).

HAWLEY, Andy. "A Man's View." *Motive Magazine* (March-April 1969).

KLAPP, Orrin B. "Social Types: Process and Structure" *American Sociological Review* 23 (1958).

RIESMAN, David. "Permissiveness and Sex Roles." *Journal of Marriage and the Family* 21 (August 1959).

WINICK, Charles. "Teen-agers, Satire and Mad." *Merrill-Palmer Quarterly of Behavior and Development* 8 (1952).

Some suggested book resources

ALLPORT, Gordon W. "Becoming Human." In *Becoming*. New Haven: Yale University Press, 1955.

BERGER, Peter. "Society in Man." In *Invitation to Sociology: A Humanist Perspective.* Garden City, N.Y.: Doubleday, 1963.

BLUMER, Herbert. "Symbolic Interaction." In Arnold Rose, ed., *Human Behavior and Social Processes.* Boston: Houghton Mifflin, 1962, pp. 179-184.

EISENSTADT, S. N. *From Generation to Generation.* New York: Free Press, 1964.

GOFFMAN, Erving. *The Presentation of Self in Everyday Life.* Garden City, N.Y.: Doubleday, 1959.

GOFFMAN, Erving. "Role Distance." In *Encounter*. Indianapolis: Bobbs-Merrill Co., 1961.

GOFFMAN, Erving. *Interaction Ritual.* Garden City, N.Y.: Doubleday, 1967.

HUNT, Robert, ed. *Personalities and Cultures.* Garden City, N.Y.: Doubleday, 1967.

JONAS, David, and KLEIN, Doris. *Man-Child: A Study of the Infantilization of Man.* New York: McGraw-Hill, 1971.

KLAPP, Orrin B. "Mockery of the Hero." In *Heroes, Villains, and Fools*. Englewood Cliffs, N.J.: Spectrum Books, 1962, chap. 7.

ROGERS, Carl. *On Becoming a Person.* Cambridge: The Riverside Press, 1961.

TALBOT, Toby, ed. *The World of the Child.* Garden City, N.Y.: Doubleday, 1967.

YOUNG, Leontine. *Life Among the Giants.* New York: McGraw-Hill, 1970.

TOPIC 7. THE ENDURING SELF AND THE CHANGING SELF: THE TOTAL INSTITUTION AND RESOCIALIZATION

Some suggested periodical resources

GARAHEDIAN, Peter G. "Socialization in the Prison Community." *Social Problems* 2 (Fall 1963).

GARFINKEL, Harold. "Conditions of Successful Degradation Ceremonies." *American Journal of Sociology* 61 (1956).

GERGEN, Kenneth J. "Multiple Identity." *Psychology Today* 5 (May 1972).

LIFTON, Robert J. "Thought Reform of Western Civilians in Chinese Communist Prisons." *Psychiatry* 19 (1956).

MOSKOS, Charles C., Jr. "Why Men Fight." *Transaction* 7 (November 1969).

Some suggested book resources

ARENDT, Hannah. *The Origins of Totalitarianism.* New York: Harcourt Brace Jovanovich, 1958.

AUBERT, Wilheim. *The Hidden Society.* Totowa: Bedminister Press, 1965.

BENNIS, W. G., et al., eds. *Interpersonal Dynamics.* Homewood: Dorsey, 1964.

BETTELHEIM, Bruno. *Symbolic Wounds.* London: Thames and Hudson, 1955.

GOFFMAN, Erving. *Asylums.* Garden City, N.Y.: Doubleday, 1961.

KAHLER, Erich. "Totalization and Terror." In *The Tower and the Abyss*. New York: Viking, Compass edition, 1967.

KOGON, Eugene. "Daily Routine in Buchenwald." In *The Theory and Practice of Hell*. New York: Farrar, Straus & Giroux, 1950.

KRIM, Seymour. "The Insanity Bit." In Seymour Krim, ed., *The Beats*. New York: Fawcett, 1960.

LIFTON, Robert J. "Methods of Forceful Indoctrination: Psychiatric Aspects of Chinese Communist Thought Reform." In M. R. Stein, A. J. Vidich, and David Manning White, eds., *Identity and Anxiety in Mass Society.* New York: Group for Advancement of Psychiatry, 1960, pp. 410-492.

LUCHTERHAND, Elmer. "Prison Behavior and Social System in the Nazi Concentration Camps." In Bernard Rosenberg, Israel Gener, and F. William Houton, eds., *Mass Society in Crisis.* New York: Macmillan, 1971, pp. 59-84.

SCHEIN, E. H. "Brainwashing." in W. G. Bennis, et al., eds., *Interpersonal Dynamics.* Homewood: Dorsey Press, 1964.

TOPIC 8. SOCIAL SYSTEMS: THE HUMAN GROUP

Some suggested book resources

BALES, Robert F. "Small Group Theory and Research." In R. K. Merton et al., eds., *Sociology Today.* New York: Basic Books, 1955.

CARTWRIGHT, Darwin, and ZANDER, Alvin, eds., *Group Dynamics.* New York: Harper & Row, 1960.

HARE, A. Paul. *Handbook of Small Group Research.* New York: Free Press, 1962.

HARE, A. Paul, BORGATTA, Edgar F., and BALES, Robert F., eds. *Small Groups.* New York: Knopf, 1955.

HOMANS, George C. *The Human Group.* New York: Harcourt Brace Jovanovich, 1950.

KLEIN, Josephine. *The Study of Groups.* London: Routledge & Kegan Paul, 1956.

LIEBOW, Elliot. "Friends and Networks." In *Tally's Corner.* Boston: Little, Brown, 1967, pp. 161-170.

MILLS, C. Wright. "The Great Salesroom." In *White Collar.* New York: Oxford University Press, 1961.

SHEPHERD, Clovis R. *Small Groups.* San Francisco: Chandler, 1969.

SHERIF, Muzafer. *Group Conflict and Co-operation.* London: Routledge & Kegan Paul, 1966.

SIMMEL, Georg. *The Web of Group Affiliations.* New York: Free Press, 1964.

THIBAUT, John W., and KELLEY, Harold H. *The Social Psychology of Groups.* New York: Wiley, 1959.

VAN DER HAAG, Ernest. "The Basic Tension of Group Membership." In *Passion and Social Constraint.* New York: Dell, Delta paperback edition, 1963, pp. 109-115.

WHYTE, William H., Jr. "The Organization Man." In *The Organization Man.* New York: Simon and Schuster, 1956, pp. 3-15.

TOPIC 9. THE HUMAN COMMUNITY: VIEWS FROM BELOW AND OUTSIDE

Some suggested periodical resources

DAVIS, Fred. "Why All of Us May Be Hippies Someday." *Transaction* (December 1967).

DUMONT, Matthew P. "Tavern Culture: The Sustenance of Homeless Men." *American Journal of Orthopsychiatry* 37 (October 1967).

The Modern Utopian. San Francisco: Alternatives Foundation, 1971, 1972.

Some suggested book resources

BINZEN, Peter. *Whitetown, U.S.A.* New York: Random House, 1970.

CAPLOVITZ, David. "East Harlem: The Merchant and the Low Income Consumer." In *The Poor Pay More.* New York: The Free Press, 1968.

CLARK, Kenneth B. "The Psychology of the Ghetto." In *Dark Ghetto.* New York: Harper & Row, 1965.

HEDGEPETH, William, and STOCK, Dennis. *The Alternative: Communal Life in New America.* New York: Macmillan, 1972.

Report of the National Advisory Commission on Civil Disorders, "The Future of the Cities." Washington, D.C.: U.S. Government Printing Office, 1968.

RICHTER, Peyton E., ed. *Utopias, Social Ideals and Communal Experiments.* Boston: Holbook Press, 1971.

SPECK, Ross V., et. al. *The New Families: Youth, Politics and the Politics of Drugs.* New York: Free Press, 1972.

SPIRO, Melford E. *Kibbutz.* New York: Shocken, 1970.

STEIN, Maurice R. *The Eclipse of Community.* Princeton, N.J.: Princeton University Press, 1960, chaps. 5-7.

SUTTLES, Gerald D. "The Social Order of the Slum." In *The Social Order of the Slum.* Chicago: University of Chicago Press, 1968.

ZABLOCKI, Benjamin. *The Joyful Community.* Baltimore: Penguin Books, 1971.

TOPIC 10. THE HUMAN COMMUNITY: SUBURB AND VILLAGE IN THE POSTURBAN WORLD

Some suggested periodical resources

BERGER, Bennett M. "The Myth of Suburbia." *Journal of Social Issues* 17 (1961).

DOBRINER, William M. "The Natural History of A Reluctant Suburb." *Yale Review* 49 (1960).

FRENCH, Robert Mills, and HADDEN, Jeffrey K. "Mobile Homes: Instant Suburbia or Transportable Slums?" *Social Problems* 16 (1968).

GANS, Herbert J. "An Anatomy of Suburbia." *New Society* 6 (September 28, 1967).

Time (March 1971). "Surburbia: The New American Plurality."

Some suggested book resources

CLARK, S. D. "The Suburban Community." In *Urbanism and the Changing Canadian Society.* Toronto: University of Toronto Press, 1961, pp. 20-30.

CLARK, S. D. "The Process of Suburban Development." In John Kramer, ed., *North American Suburbs.* Berkeley: Glendessary Press, 1972, pp. 19-30.

GANS, Herbert J. "Urbanism and Suburbanism as Ways of Life." In Arnold Rose, ed., *Human Behavior and Social Processes.* Boston: Houghton Mifflin, 1962, pp. 625-648

RINGER, Benjamin B. "Jewish-Gentile Relations in Lakeville." In *The Edge of Friendliness.* New York: Basic Books, 1967.

SEELEY, John R., SIM, R. Alexander, and LOOSLEY, Elizabeth W. *Crestwood Heights.* New York: Basic Books, 1956.

SPECTORSKY, A. C. "The Exurbanites." In *The Exurbanites.* Philadelphia: Lippincott, 1955, chaps. 1, 9.

STEIN, Maurice. "Suburbia—A Walk on the Mild Side." In *Voices of Dissent*. New York: Grove, Evergreen paperback ed., 1958, pp. 187-195.

WHYTE, William H. "The Case for Crowding." In *The Last Landscape*. Garden City, N.Y.: Doubleday, 1968.

WHYTE, William H. "The New Suburbia" and "The Consumer in Suburbia." In Lincoln H. Clark, ed., *Consumer Behavior*. New York: New York University Press, 1954, pp. 1-14.

WOOD, Robert C. "The Image of Suburbia." In *Suburbia, Its People and Their Politics*. Boston: Houghton Mifflin, 1958.

TOPIC 11. STRUCTURED SOCIAL INEQUALITY: THE UNDERCLASS IN AMERICA

Some suggested book resources

BLAUSTEIN, Arthur, and WOOCK, Roger. *Man Against Poverty*. New York: Random House, 1968.

CAPLOVITZ, David. "The Merchants and the Low Income Consumer." In *The Poor Pay More*. New York: Free Press, paperback edition, 1967, pp. 12-25.

ELMAN, Richard. *Poorhouse State*. New York: Dell, 1968.

GALBRAITH, John Kenneth. "The Disgrace of Poverty midst Affluence." In *The Affluent Society*. Boston: Houghton Mifflin Co., 1958, pp. 323-333.

GANS, Herbert J. "Male-Female Relationships in the Urban Village." In *The Urban Villagers, Group and Class in the Life of Italian-Americans*. New York: Free Press, 1962, pp. 47-53.

GLASER, Nathan. "A Sociologist's View of Poverty." In Margaret S. Gordon, ed., *Poverty in America*. San Francisco: Chandler, 1965, pp. 12-26.

GLAZER, Nona, and CREEDON, Carol F. *Children and Poverty*. Skokie, Ill.: Rand McNally, 1968.

GRIER, William H., and COBBS, Price M. "Acquiring Manhood." In *Black Rage*. New York: Basic Books, 1969, pp. 56-62.

HARRINGTON, Michael. "The Visible Land." In *The Other America*. New York: Macmillan, 1962.

KAMAROVSKY, Mirra. *Blue-Collar Marriage*. New York: Random House, 1962, pp. 25-30.

LIEBOW, Elliot. "Husbands and Wives." In *Tally's Corner*. Boston: Little, Brown, 1967, pp. 103-119.

LUMER, Hyman. "Why People are Poor." In *Poverty: Its Roots and Its Future*. New York: International Publishers, 1965, pp. 13-32.

MILLER, Herman P. *Poverty American Style*. Belmont: Wadsworth Publishing Co., 1966.

MILLER, Herman P. *Rich Man, Poor Man*. New York: T. Y. Crowell, 1971.

MOORE, Truman. "Shacktown, USA; Migrant Farm Labor." In *The Slaves We Rent*. New York: Random House and Paul R. Reynolds Inc., 1965.

PILISUK, Marc, and PILISUK, Phyllis. *Poor Americans: How the Poor White Live*. Chicago: Aldine, 1971.

SELIGMAN, Benjamin. *Permanent Poverty: An American Syndrome*. Chicago: Quadrangle, 1968.

SHOSTAK, Arthur B. *Blue Collar Life*. New York: Random House, 1969.

VALENTINE, Charles A. *Culture and Poverty*. Chicago: University of Chicago Press, 1968.

WILL, Robert E., and VATTER, Harold G. *Poverty in Affluence*. New York: Harcourt Brace Jovanovich, 1970.

TOPIC 12. THE ECONOMIC SECTOR: THE REALM OF POWER

Suggested periodical resources

HEILBRONER, Robert. "How the Pentagon Rules Us." *New York Review of Books* 15 (1970).

McDONALD, Donald. "Milatrism in America." *The Center Magazine* 3 (January 1970).

McGOVERN, George S., et al. "The People versus the Pentagon." *The Progressive* (June 1969).

MINNIS, Jack. "The Care and Feeding of Power Structures." *New University Thought* 5 (Summer 1964).

NEAL, Fred Warner. "Government by Myth." *The Center Magazine* 2 (November 1969).

The Progressive. "The Power of the Pentagon." 33 (June 1969).

RECHY, John. "The Army Fights an Idea." *The Nation* (January 12, 1970).

SHERRILL, Robert. "The War Machine." *Playboy* (May 1970).

SHOUP, General David M. "The New American Militarism." *The Atlantic* (April 1969).

STERN, Sol. "The Defense Intellectuals." *Ramparts* 5 (February 1967).

STONE, I. F. "McNamara and the Militarists." *New York Review of Books* (November 7, 1968).

STONE, Jeremy J. "How the Arms Race Works." *The Progressive* (June 1969).

Some suggested book resources

APTHEKER, Herbert. "Power in America." In *The World of C. Wright Mills*. New York: Marzani and Munsell, 1960.

BERLE, Adolf A. *Power*. New York: Harcourt Brace Jovanovich, 1969.

CHOMSKY, Noam. *American Power and the New Mandarins*. New York: Pantheon, 1969.

DOMHOFF, G. William. "The Control of the Corporate Economy." In *Who Rules America?* Englewood Cliffs, N.J.: Prentice-Hall, Spectrum Books, 1967, pp. 38-47.

DOMHOFF, G. William, and BALLARD, Hoyt B., eds. *C. Wright Mills and The Power Elite*. Boston: Beacon, 1969.

DONOVAN, James A. *Militarism, U.S.A.* New York: Scribner, 1970.

HACKER, Andrew. *The Corporation Take Over*. New York: Doubleday.

KOLKO, Gabriel. *Wealth and Power in America; An Analysis of Social Class and Income Distribution*. New York: Praeger.

KORNHAUSER, William. "Power Elite" or "Veto Groups." In Seymour M. Lipset and Leo Lowenthal, eds., *Culture and Social Character*. New York: Free Press, 1961.

MAILER, Norman. *The Armies of the Night*. New York: Norton, 1968.

MANSFIELD, Edwin, ed. *Monopoly Power and Economic Performance.* New York: Norton, 1968.

MELMAN, Seymour. *Our Depleted Society.* New York: Dell, 1966.

MELMAN, Seymour. *Pentagon Capitalism.* New York: McGraw-Hill, 1970.

MILLS, C. Wright. *The Power Elite.* New York: Oxford University Press, 1959.

PRESTHUS, Robert. *Men at the Top.* New York: Oxford University Press, 1964.

REICH, Michael, and FINKLEHOR, David. "The Military Industrial Complex: No Way Out." In Tom Christoffel, et al., eds., *Up Against the American Myth.* New York: Holt, Rinehart & Winston, 1970.

ROSE, Arnold. "The Power Structure." In *The Power Structure: Political Process in American Society.* New York: Oxford University Press, 1967.

STAPP, Andy. *Up Against the Brass.* New York: Simon & Schuster, 1970.

STIGLER, George J. "The Case Against Big Business." In Edwin Mansfield, ed., *Monopoly, Power and Economic Performance.* New York: Norton, pp. 3-12.

SWEEZY, Paul M. "Is There an American Ruling Class?" In *The Present as History: Essays and Reviews on Capitalism and Socialism.* New York: Monthly Review Press, 1962, pp. 127-138.

TOPIC 13. THE ECONOMIC SECTOR: THE BUREAUCRATIC ETHOS

Some suggested periodical resources

BENNIS, Warren G. "Beyond Bureaucracy." *Transaction* (July/August 1965).

SELIGMAN, Ben B. "Man, Work, and the Automated Feast." *Commentary* (July 1962).

Some suggested book resources

ARGYRIS, Chris. *Personality and Organization.* New York: Harper & Row, 1957.

BENDIX, Reinhard. "Individual Initiative and the Problem of Bureaucracy." In *Higher Civil Servants in American Society.* Boulder: University of Colorado Press, 1949.

BENNIS, Warren G. *Changing Organization.* New York: Holt, Rinehart & Winston, 1966.

BENNIS, Warren G. *American Bureaucracy.* New York: Transaction Books, 1970.

BENSMAN, Joseph, and ROSENBERG, Bernard. "The Meaning of Work in Bureaucratic Society." In Maurice R. Stein, Arthur Vidich, and David M. White, eds., *Identity and Anxiety.* New York: Free Press and Macmillan, 1960.

BLAU, Peter M. *Bureaucracy in Modern Society.* New York: Random House, 1956.

BLAU, Peter M. *The Dynamics of Bureaucracy.* Chicago: University of Chicago Press, 1967.

COHEN, Harry. *Demonics of Bureaucracy.* Iowa City: University of Iowa Press, 1965.

ELLUL, Jacques. "Techniques." In *The Technological Society.* New York: Random House, Vintage edition, 1967, pp. 3-6.

FINER, S. H. "Bureaucracy in the Army." In "The Political Strengths of the Military" in *The Man on Horseback.* London: Pall Mall Press Lted., 1962.

GOULDNER, Alvin. "Red Tape as a Social Problem." In Robert K. Merton et al., eds., *Reader in Bureaucracy.* New York: Free Press, 1952, pp. 410-418.

MARCUSE, Herbert. "Liberation from the Affluent Society." In D. Cooper, ed., *To Free a Generation.* New York: Collier, 1968, pp. 180-192.

MERTON, Robert E. "Bureaucratic Structure and Personality." In *Social Theory and Social Structure.* New York: Free Press and Macmillan, 1968.

MICHAEL, Donald M. "Some Speculations on the Social Impact of Technology." In D. Morse and A. Warner, eds., *Technical Innovations in Society.* New York: Columbia University Press, 1966.

PARKINSON, G. Northcote. "Parkinson's Law." In *Parkinson's Law: Other Studies in Administration.* Boston: Houghton Mifflin, 1951, pp. 2-13, 59-69.

PRESTHUS, Robert. *Organizational Society.* New York: Random House, Vintage edition.

PRESTHUS, Robert. "The Upward Mobiles in the Organizational Society." In *The Organizational Society.* New York: Random House, Vintage edition, pp. 164-182, 188-199.

ROGERS, David. "A Model of Bureaucratic Pathology." In *110 Livingston Street.* New York: Random House, 1968, pp. 267-277.

SHILS, Edward B. "Automation: Technology or Concept." In *Automation and Industrial Manpower.* New York: Holt, Rinehart & Winston, 1963, pp. 1-14.

TOPIC 14. THE ECONOMIC SECTOR: THE AGE OF CYBERNATION AND TECHNETRONIC MAN

Some suggested periodical resources

BAZALON, David T. "The 'New Class.'" *Commentary* 42 (August 1966).

BELL, Daniel. "Notes On the Post-Industrial Society." *The Public Interest* 6 (Winter 1967) and 7 (Spring 1967).

BRZEZINSKI, Zbigniew. "America in the Technetronic Age." *Encounter* 30 (January 1968).

CALDER, Nigel. "Tomorrow's Politics: The Control and Use of Technology." *The Nation* 200 (1965).

CARLETON, William G. "The Century of Technocracy." *Antioch Review* 25 (1965-1966).

FERRY, W. H. "The Technophiliacs." *The Center Magazine* 1 (July 1968).

GOULDNER, Helen P. "Children of the Laboratory." *Transaction* 4 (April 1967).

GRAUBARD, Allen. "One-Dimensional Pessimism: A Critique of Herbert Marcuse." *Dissent* 15 (1968).

GREEN, Harold P. "The New Technological Era." *Bulletin of the Atomic Scientists* 23 (November 1967).

HANDLIN, Oscar. "Science and Technology in Popular Culture." *Daedalus* 94 (1965).

HAVEMANN, Ernest. "Computers: Their Scope Today." *Playboy* 14 (October 1967).

LEKACHMAN, Robert. "The Automation Report." *Commentary* 41 (May 1966).

McCLINTOCK, Robert. "Machines and Vitalists: Reflections on the Ideology of Cybernetics." *American Scholar* 35 (1966).

MESTHENE, E. G. "How Technology Will Shape the Future." *Science* 161 (1968).

NISBET, Robert A. "The Year 2000 and All That." *Commentary* 45 (June 1968).

SOLOW, Robert M., and HEILBRONER, Robert L. "The Great Automation Question." *The Public Interest* 1 (Fall 1965).

WESTIN, Alan F. "The Snooping Machine." *Playboy* 15 (1968).

Some suggested book resources

BRZEZINSKI, Zbigniew. *Between Two Ages, America's Role in the Technetronic Era.* New York: Viking 1970.

BURKE, John G. *New Technology and Human Values.* Belmont: Wadsworth, 1966.

DECHERT, Charles R., ed. *The Social Impact of Cybernetics.* New York: Simon & Schuster, 1967.

ELLUL, Jacques. *The Technological Society.* New York: Random House, 1967.

FERKISS, Victor C. *Technological Man, The Myth and the Reality.* New York: Mentor, 1970.

FRANCOIS, Willam. *Automation: Industrialization Comes of Age.* New York: Crowell Collier Macmillan, 1964.

MARCUSE, Herbert. *One-Dimensional Man.* Boston: Beacon, 1964.

MESTHENE, Emmanual G. *Technological Change, Its Impact on Man and Society.* New York: Mentor, 1970.

MICHAEL, Donald M. "Some Speculations on the Social Impact of Technology." In D. Morse and A. Warner, eds., *Technological Innovations in Society.* New York: Columbia University Press, 1966.

PERRUCCI, Robert, and PILISUK, Mark. "The Meaning of the Cybernetic State." In Perrucci and Pilisuk, eds., *The Triple Revolution Emerging.* Boston: Little, Brown, 1971, pp. 157-173.

THEOBALD, Robert. *The Challenge of Abundance.* New York: Mentor, 1962.

ZIJDERVELD, Anton C. *The Abstract Society.* Garden City, N.Y.: Doubleday, 1971.

TOPIC 15. INSTITUTIONAL CHANGE: THE FAMILY IN TRANSFORMATION

Some suggested periodical resources

GOLDBERG, Marilyn Power. "The Economic Exploitation of Women." *The Review of Radical Political Economics* 11 (Spring 1970).

GORDON, Linda. "Families and the Oppression of Women." *The New England Free Press* (1971).

MACK, Delores. "Where the Black Matriarchy Theorists Went Wrong." *Psychology Today* (January 1971).

MILLER, S. M. "On Men: The Making of a Confused Middle-Class Husband." *Social Policy* 2 (July, August 1971).

MITCHELL, Juliet. "The Situation of Women." *New Left Review* 40 (November/December 1966).

Time (December 1970). "The American Family: Future Uncertain."

Some suggested book resources

FARBER, Seymour, and WILSON, Roger. *Potential of Women.* New York: McGraw-Hill, 1963.

GLASSER, Paul H., and GLASSER, Lois N. *Families in Crisis.* New York: Harper & Row, 1969.

GOODE, William J. *World Revolution and Family Patterns.* New York: Free Press, 1963.

GORDON, Albert I. *Intermarriage: Interfaith, Interracial, Interethnic.* Boston: Beacon, 1964.

KOMAROVSKY, Mirra. *Blue-Collar Marriage.* New York: Random House, 1964.

MILLET, Kate. *Sexual Politics.* Garden City, N.Y.: Doubleday, 1970.

MOORE, Barrington, Jr. "Thoughts on the Future of the Family." In *Political Power and Social Theory.* Cambridge: Harvard University Press, 1958, pp. 60-78.

Editors of *Ramparts. Conversations With the New Reality.* San Francisco: Canfield, 1971.

ROSZAK, Betty, and ROSZAK, Theodore. *Masculine/Feminine.* New York: Harper & Row, 1969.

SCHUR, Edwin. *Family and the Sexual Revolution.* Bloomington: Indiana University Press, 1964.

SKOLNICK, Arlene S., and SKOLNICK, Jerome H., eds. *Family in Transition.* Boston: Little, Brown, 1971.

SPIRO, Melford E. *Children of the Kibbutz.* New York: Schocken, 1965.

SULLEROT, Evelyne. *Woman, Society and Change.* New York: McGraw-Hill, 1971.

TOPIC 16. THE RELIGIOUS FACTOR: ZEN AND SECTS, BLACK MUSLIMS AND JESUS FREAKS

Some suggested periodical resources

ADAMS, Robert Lynn, and FOX, Robert John. "Mainlining Jesus: The New Trip." *Society* (February 1972).

BROWN, Norman O. "Apocalypse, The Place of Mystery in the Life of the Mind." *Harper's* (May 1961).

CATTON, William R., Jr. "What Kind of People Does a Religious Cult Attract?" *American Sociological Review* 22 (1957).

GLOCK, Charles Y., and STARK, Rodney. "Will Ethics be the Death of Christianity?" *Transaction* 7 (June 1968).

HAND, Thomas G. "The Challenge of Zen." *America* (February 8, 1969).

HARRIS, T. George. "A Conversation with Harvey Cox." *Psychology Today* 3 (April 1970).

HASTINGS, Philip V., and HOGE, Dean R. "Religious Change Among College Students Over Two Decades." *Social Forces* 49 (September 1970).

Hollywood Free Paper 3 (1971). "Jesus Loves You."

JOHNSON, Benton. "Theology and the Position of Pastors on Public Issues." *American Sociological Review* 32 (June 1967).

WHITE, Lynn, Jr. "The Historical Roots of our Ecologic Crisis." *Science* 155 (1967).

Some suggested book resources

BOYD, Malcolm. *The Underground Church.* Baltimore: Penguin, 1969.

COPPER, John Charles. *Religion in the Age of Aquarius.* Philadelphia: Westminster, 1971.

HADDEN, Jeffrey K. *The Gathering Storm in the Churches.* Garden City, N.Y.: Doubleday, 1969.

HADDEN, Jeffrey K. *Religion in Radical Transition.* Chicago: Aldine, 1971.

LENSKI, Gerhard. *The Religious Factor.* Garden City, N.Y.: Doubleday, 1968.

ROSS, Nancy Wilson. *Three Ways of Asian Wisdom, Hinduism, Buddhism, and Zen and their Significance for the West.* New York: Simon & Schuster, Clarion edition, 1969.

SNYDER, Gary. "Passage to More Than India." In *Earth House Hold.* New York: New Directions, 1968, pp. 106-116.

STREKER, Lowell D. *The Jesus Trip, Advent of the Jesus Freaks.* Nashville, Tenn.: Abingdon, 1971.

SUZUKI, D. T. *An Introduction to Zen Buddhism.* New York: Grove, 1964.

WHITE, John, ed. *The Highest State of Consciousness.* Garden City, N.Y.: Doubleday, 1972.

WILSON, Byron. *Religion in Secular Society: A Sociological Comment.* London: Watts, 1966.

WILSON, Byron. *Religious Sects.* New York: McGraw-Hill, 1972.

ZABLOCKI, Benjamin. *The Joyful Community.* Baltimore, Penguin, 1971.

KENNISTON, Kenneth. "Young Radicals: The Confrontation with Inequity." In *Young Radicals, Notes on Committed Youth.* New York: Harcourt Brace Jovanovich, Harvest edition, 1968, pp. 125-140.

NEWFIELD, Jack. "The Movement." In *A Prophetic Minority.* New York: The New American Library, Signet paperback edition, 1967, pp. 19-24.

OGLESBY, Carl. *New Left Reader.* New York: Grove, 1969.

OVERSTREET, Harry, and OVERSTREET, Bonaro. *Strange Tactics of Extremism.* New York: Norton, 1964.

PETTIGREW, Thomas F., and RILEY, Robert T. "The Social Psychology of the Wallace Movements." In *Racially Separate or Together?* New York: McGraw-Hill, 1971, pp. 231-256.

SCHWARTZ, Barry, and DISOH, Robert. *White Racism.* New York: Dell, 1970.

STILLMAN, Edmund, and PFAFF, William. *Politics of Hysteria.* New York: Harper & Row, 1964.

TOPIC 17. THE INSTITUTIONAL MATRIX: THE POLITICAL REALM

Some suggested periodical resources

Journal of Social Issues 27 (1971). "The New Left and the Old."

McDERMOTT, John. "Thoughts on the Movement." *Viet Report* (September/October 1967).

OGLESBY, Carl. "Let Us Shape the Future." *Liberation* (January 1966).

Some suggested book resources

BELL, Daniel. *The Radical Right.* Garden City, N.Y.: Doubleday, 1963.

BOOKCHIN, Murray. *Post-Scarcity Anarchism.* Berkeley: Ramparts Press, 1971.

BOTTOMORE, T. B. *Critics of Society: Radical Thought in North America.* New York: Random House, 1969.

DAHL, Robert A. *After the Revolution?* New Haven: Yale University Press, 1970.

EPSTEIN, Benjamin, and FORSTER, Arnold. *The Radical Right.* New York: Random House, 1967.

FANON, Frantz. *Black Skin, White Masks.* New York: Grove, 1967.

FLACKS, Richard. "Revolt of the Young Intelligentsia: Revolutionary Class Consciousness in Post-Scarcity America." In Roderica Aya and Norman Miller, eds., *The New American Revolution.* New York: Free Press, 1971, pp. 223-259.

FRIEDENBERG, Edgar Z. *The Anti-American Generation.* Chicago: Aldine, 1971.

HARRINGTON, MICHAEL. "The Mystical Militants." In *Thoughts of Young Radicals.* New York: Pitman, 1966, pp. 66-73.

HARRINGTON, Michael. *Toward a Democratic Left.* New York: Macmillan, 1970.

HUTCHINS, Francis G. "A View from Harvard: Radicals vs. Liberals." In Irving L. Horowitz, ed., *The Troubled Conscience.* Los Angeles, Calif.: James E. Freel, 1971, pp. 98-100.

TOPIC 18. THE EDUCATIONAL ESTABLISHMENT: THE PRECOLLEGE SCENARIO

Some suggested periodical resources

COHEN, David K. "Public Schools: The Next Decade." *Dissent* (April 1971).

COLEMAN, James S. "The Children Have Outgrown The Schools." *Psychology Today* 5 (February 1972).

DIVOKY, Diane. "New York's Mini-Schools, Small Miracles, Big Troubles." *Saturday Review* (December 18, 1971.

HOWE, Florence, and LAUTER Paul. "How the School System is Rigged for Failure." *New York Review of Books.* (June 8, 1970).

ILLICH, Ivan. "After Deschooling, What?" *Social Policy* (September/October 1971).

ILLICH, Ivan. "Schooling: The Ritual of Progress." *New York Review of Books* (December 3, 1970).

ILLICH, Ivan. "The Alternative to Schooling." *Saturday Review* (June 1971).

Saturday Review (April 29, 1972), 32-58. *Education* Section.

This Magazine is About Schools. Quarterly journal (1971, 1972, 1973).

Some suggested book resources

FANTINI, Mario. *Community Control and the Urban Schools.* New York: Praeger, 1970.

GROSS, Ronald and Beatrice, eds. *Radical School Reform.* New York: Simon & Schuster, 1969.

HERNDON, James. *How to Survive in Your Native Land.* New York: Bantam, 1972.

HERNDON, James. *The Way It Spozed to Be.* New York: Simon & Schuster, 1968.

HOLT, John. *The Under-Achieving School.* New York: Dell, Delta Books, 1970.

HOLT, John. *What Do I Do Monday?* New York: Dutton, 1970.

JENCKS, Christopher. "The Future of American Education." In Irving Howe, ed., *The Radical Papers.* New York: Doubleday, 1966; and New York: Dissent Publishing Association, 1966, pp. 273-295.

JOSEPH, Stephen M. *The Me Nobody Knows*. Cleveland: World Publishing, 1969.

KOERNER, James D. *Who Controls American Education?* Boston: Beacon, 1968.

KOZOL, Jonathan. *Death at an Early Age*. Boston: Houghton Mifflin, 1967

LEONARD, George B. *Education and Ecstasy*. New York: Dell, Delta edition, 1968.

MOUSTAKAS, Clark. *The Authentic Teacher*. New York: Howard Doyle, 1966.

NEILL, A. A. *Freedom, Not License*. New York: Hart, 1966.

NEILL, A. S. *Summerhill*. New York: Hart, 1960.

POSTMAN, Neil, and WEINGARTNER, Charles. *Teaching as a Subversive Activity*. New York: Dell, 1971.

REIMER, Everett. *School is Dead*. Garden City, N.Y.: Doubleday, 1971.

ROTHMAN, Esther. *The Angel Inside Went Sour*. New York: Bantam, 1972.

SCHREIBER, Daniel. *Profile of the School Dropout*. New York: Random House, 1968.

SIZER, Theodore R. "The Schools in the City." In James G. Wilson, ed., *The Metropolitan Enigma*. Cambridge: Harvard University Press, 1968.

TOPIC 19. THE EDUCATIONAL ESTABLISHMENT: THE REALM OF HIGHER EDUCATION

Some suggested periodical resources

BECKER, Howard S. "What Do They Really Learn in College?" *Transaction* 1 (May 1964).

CARTER, Larry. "University of California at Santa Cruz: New Deal for Undergraduates." *Science* 71 (January 15, 1971).

ILLICH, Ivan. "Schooling: The Ritual of Progress." *New York Review of Books* (December 3, 1970).

ILLICH, Ivan. "Education Without School: How It Can Be Done." *New York Review of Books* (January 7, 1971).

JEROME, Judson. "The Living-Learning Community." *Change* (September 1971).

NOVAK, Michael. "Experiment at Old Westbury." *Commonweal* 89 (January 31, 1969).

PERRY, J. B., et al. "Patterns of Student Participation in a Free University." *Youth and Society* 3 (December 1971).

WICKER, Tom. "America and Its Colleges: End of An Affair." *Change* (September 1971).

Some suggested book resources

CONNERY, Robert H. *The Corporation and the Campus*. New York: Praeger, 1970.

FRANCOIS, William. *Automation*. New York: Macmillan, 1964.

FRANKEL, Charles. *Education and the Barricades*. New York: Norton, 1969.

HALSEY, A. H. *Education, Economy and Society*. New York: Free Press, 1961.

JENCKS, Christopher, and RIESMAN, David. *The Academic Revolution*. Garden City, N.Y.: Doubleday, 1969.

MARCSON, Simon. *Automation, Alienation, and Anomie*. New York: Harper & Row, 1970.

MAYHEW, Lewis B. "The Future Undergraduate Curriculum." In Alvin C. Eurich, ed., *Campus 1980*. New York: Dell, 1968.

MICHAEL, Donald N. *Future Society*. Chicago: Aldine, 1970.

RIDGEWAY, James. *The Closed Corporation, American Universities in Crisis*. New York: Ballantine, 1969.

RIESMAN, David, and JENCKS, Christopher. "The College as an Initiation Rite." In Nevitt Sanford, ed., *The American College*. New York: Willey, 1962.

STEMBER, Charles H. "Education and Attitude Change." In *Education and Attitude Change*. New York: American Jewish Committee, 1961.

STROUP, H. *Bureaucracy in Higher Education*. New York: Free Press, 1965.

TERBORTH, George. *Automation Hysteria*. New York: Norton, 1966.

TUSSMAN, Joseph. *Experiment at Berkeley*. New York: Oxford University Press, 1969.

TOPIC 20. COLLECTIVE BEHAVIOR: FADS AND FASHIONS IN LIFE STYLES

Some suggested book resources

BLUMER, Herbert. "Outline of Collective Behavior." In Robert R. Evans, ed., *Readings in Collective Behavior*. Skokie, Ill.: Rand McNally, 1969.

BUCKNER, H. Taylor. "A Theory of Rumor Transmission." In Robert R. Evans, ed., *Readings in Collective Behavior*. Skokie, Ill.: Rand McNally, 1969.

GARDNER, Martin. *Fads and Fallacies in the Name of Science*. New York: Dover, 1957.

SHELLOW, Robert, and ROEMER, Derek V. "The Riot That Didn't Happen." In Robert R. Evans, ed., *Readings in Collective Behavior*. Skokie, Ill.: Rand McNally, 1969.

SHIBUTANI, T. "Humor as a Collective Transaction." In *Improvised News, A Sociological Study of Humor*. Indianapolis: Bobbs-Merril, 1966.

SHIBUTANI, T., ed. *Human Nature and Collective Behavior*. Englewood Cliffs, N.J.: Prentice-Hall, 1970.

SMELSER, Neill J. *Theory of Collective Behavior*. New York: Free Press, 1962.

TURNER, Ralph R. "New Theoretical Frameworks." In Robert R. Evans, ed., *Readings in Collective Behavior*. Skokie, Ill.: Rand McNally, 1969.

TURNER, Ralph, and KILLIAN, L. M. *Collective Behavior*. Englewood Cliffs, N.J.: Prentice-Hall, 1957.

WATTS, William A., and WHITTAKER, David. "Free Speech Advocates at Berkeley." In Robert R. Evans, ed., *Readings in Collective Behavior*. Skokie, Ill.: Rand McNally, 1969.

WOLFE, Tom. *Kandy Kolored Tangerine-Flake Streamline Baby*. New York: Farrar, Straus & Giroux, 1965.

WOLFE, Tom. *Electric Kool-Aid Acid Test*. New York: Farrar, Straus & Giroux, 1968.

WOLFE, Tom. *Pump House Gang*. New York: Farrar, Straus & Giroux, 1968.

TOPIC 21. COLLECTIVE BEHAVIOR: RIOTS, INSURRECTIONS, AND REBELLIONS

Some suggested book resources:

ARENDT, Hannah. *On Violence*. New York: Harcourt Brace Jovanovich, 1969.

BANFIELD, Richard C. "Rioting Mainly for Fun and Profit." In James Q. Wilson, ed., *The Metropolitan Enigma.* Cambridge: Harvard University Press, 1968.

BRINTON, Crane. *Anatomy of Revolution.* New York: Random House, 1957.

CONNERY, Robert H. *Urban Riots.* New York: Random House, 1969.

ECKSTEIN, Harry, ed. *Internal War.* New York: Free Press, 1964.

FANON, Frantz. *Toward the African Revolution.* New York: Grove, 1968

GUEVARA, Ernesto [Ché]. *Guerrila Warfare.* New York: Monthly Review, 1961.

GUEVARA, Ernesto [Ché]. *Complete Bolivian Diaries of Che Guevara and Other Captured Documents.* New York: Stein and Day, 1969.

HOFFER, Eric. *The True Believer.* New York: Harper & Row, 1951.

HOFFMAN, Abbie. *Revolution For the Hell of It.* New York: Dial, 1968.

LEIDEN, Carl, and SCHMITT, Karl. *Politics of Violence.* Englewood Cliffs, N.J.: Prentice-Hall, 1968.

OPPENHEIMER, Martin. *Urban Guerilla.* Chicago: Quadrangle, 1969.

ROSE, Tom, ed. *Violence in America: A Historical and Contemporary Reader.* New York: Random House, 1970.

SHAULL, Richard. "The Search for a New Style of Life." In Carl Oglesby and Richard Shaull, *Containment and Change.* New York: Macmillan, 1967, pp. 184-198.

SKOLNICK, Jerome H. "The Politics of Confrontation." In *The Politics of Protest.* New York: Ballantine, 1969.

TOBER, Rober. *War of the Flea: A Story of Guerrilla Warfare.* New York: Citadel, 1970.

TOPIC 22. REVOLUTIONS OF RISING EXPECTATIONS: THE THIRD-WORLD PEOPLES AND THE ROAD TO MODERNITY

Some suggested book resources

FANON, Frantz. *Dying Colonialism.* New York: Grove, 1967.

FANON, Frantz. "Concerning Violence." In *The Wretched of the Earth.* New York: Grove, Evergreen edition, 1968, pp. 29-38.

HEILBRONER, Robert L. *The Great Ascent.* New York: Harper & Row, 1963.

KENNER, Martin, and PETROS, James. *Fidel Castro Speaks.* New York: Grove, 1970.

LIFTON, Robert J., ed. *America and the Asian Revolutions.* Chicago: Aldine, 1970.

McGRATH, Edward. *Is American Democracy Exportable?* New York: Free Press, 1968.

MILLER, Norman, and AYA, Roderick, ed. *National Liberation: Revolution in the Third World.* New York: Free Press, 1971.

MILLIKAN, Max F., and BLACKMER, Donald L. *Emerging Nations: Their Growth and American Policy.* Boston: Little, Brown, 1970.

NIEBUHR, Reinhold, and SIGMUND, Paul E. *The Democratic Experience.* New York: Praeger, 1969.

SILVERT, Kalman H. *Conflict Society: Reaction and Revolution in Latin America.* New York: Harper & Row, 1968.

STAVENHAGEN, Rodolfo. *Agrarian Problems and Peasant Movements in Latin America.* Garden City, N.Y.: Doubleday, 1970.

TABB, William K. "The Black Ghetto as Colony." In *The Political Economy of the Black Ghetto.* New York: Norton, 1970, pp. 21-34.

TURNBULL, Colin. *The Lonely African.* New York: Simon & Schuster, 1962.

WALLERSTEIN, Immanuel. *Africa: The Politics of Unity.* New York: Random House, 1969.

WARD, Barbara. *The Rich Nations and the Poor Nations.* New York: Norton, 1962.

TOPIC 23. BLACK SKINS, BROWN SKINS, RED SKINS: THE HYPHENATED AMERICANS

Some suggested periodical resources

HARDING, Vincent. "The Afro-American Past and the American Present." *Motive* (April 1968).

JOSEPHY, Alvin M., Jr. "Indians in History." *The Atlantic* (June 1970).

LEMAN, Beverly. "Social Control of the American Ghetto." *Viet-Report* 3 (Summer 1968).

STEEL, Ronald. "Letter from Oakland: The Panthers." *New York Review of Books* 13 (September 11, 1969).

WILKINSON, Doris. "Coming of Age in a Racist Society: The Whitening of America." *Youth and Society* 3 (September 1971).

Some suggested book resources

BOGGS, James and Grace. *Racism and the Class Struggle.* New York: Monthly Review Press, 1970.

BORGESE, Elizabeth M. "The Other Hill." In Irving L. Horowitz, ed., *The Troubled Conscience.* Los Angeles: James E. Freel, 1971, pp. 276-301.

BUCKMASTER, Henrietta. *Let My People Go.* Boston: Beacon, 1941.

CARMICHAEL, Stokely, and HAMILTON, Charles V. *Black Power: The Politics of Liberation in America.* New York: Random House, 1968.

CLEAVER, Eldridge. *Soul on Ice.* New York: McGraw-Hill, 1968.

CRUSE, Harold. *Rebellion or Revolution.* New York: Apollo, 1968.

GALARZA, Ernesto. *Merchants of Labor.* Skokie, Ill.: Rand McNally, 1966.

GOODMAN, Mitchell, ed. *The Movement Toward a New America.* New York: United Church Press, 1970, pp. 124-258.

GREGORY, Dick. *Nigger.* New York: McGraw-Hill, 1970.

GRIER, William H., and COBBS, Price M. *Black Rage.* New York: Basic Books, 1968.

HENTOFF, Nat. *Our Children are Dying.* New York: School Book Services, 1966.

LESTER, Julius. *Look Out Whitey—Black Powers' Gon' Get Your Mama.* New York: Grove, 1969.

LEVINE, Stuart, and LURIE, Nancy O. *The American Indian Today.* Baltimore: Penguin, 1970.

LIEBOW, Elliot. *Tally's Corner: A Study of Negro Streetcorner Men.* Boston: Little, Brown, 1967.

LINCOLN, C. Eric. *The Black Muslims in America.* Boston: Beacon, 1961.

McWILLIAMS, Carey. *North From Mexico.* New York: Greenwood, 1949.

McWILLIAMS, Carey. *Brothers Under the Skin.* Boston: Little, Brown, 1951.

McWILLIAMS, Carey. *The Mexicans in America.* New York: Teachers College, 1968.

MALCOLM X, *Autobiography of Malcolm X.* New York: Grove, 1965.

MOQUIN, Wayne, and VAN DOREN, Charles. *A Documentary History of the Mexican Americans.* New York: Bantam, 1972.

REICH, Michael. "The Economics of Racism." In Richard C. Edwards, Michael Reich, and Thomas E. Weisskopf, eds., *The Capitalist System.* Englewood Cliffs, N.J.: Prentice-Hall, 1972, pp. 313-326.

SPEAR, Allan H. *Black Chicago: The Making of a Negro Ghetto.* Chicago: University of Chicago Press, 1969.

TOPIC 24. CONTRACULTURAL DISSENT: REBELLION AGAINST THE FUTURE

Some suggested periodical resources

BRONOWSKI, J. "Protest—Past and Present." *The American Scholar* 38 (Autumn 1969).

BROWN, Michael E. "The Condemnation and Persecution of the Hippies." *Transaction* 6 (September 1969).

CAPOUYA, Emil. "The Myth of Ecstatic Commentary." *Nation* (1971).

FLACKS, Richard. "Social and Cultural Meanings of Student Revolt: Some Informal Comparative Observations." *Social Problems* 17 (Winter 1970).

FRIEDENBERG, Edgar Z. "Current Patterns of Generational Conflict." *Journal of Social Issues* 25 (April 1969).

HANNERZ, Ulf. "Roots of Black Manhood." *Transaction* 6 (October 1969).

KOPKIND, Andrew. *"The Greening of America:* Beyond the Valley of the Heads." *Ramparts* (1971).

LIPSET, S. M. "Students and Politics in Comparative Perspective." *Daedalus* 91 (1968).

LIPSET, S. M., and RABB, Earl. "The Non-Generation Gap." *Commentary* (August 1970).

LOFLAND, John. "The New Segregation: A Perspective on Age Categories in America." *Journal of Higher Education* 39 (March 1968).

LUBELL, Samuel. "That 'Generation Gap,' " *The Public Interest* 52 (Fall 1968).

MOLLER, Herbert. "Youth as a Force in the Modern World." *Comparative Studies in History* 10 (April 1968).

NOVAK, Michael. "The Greening of Consciousness III." *Commonweal Magazine* (1970).

PITTS, Jesse. "The Counter Culture: Tranquilizer or Revolutionary Ideology?" *Dissent* (June 1970).

SLATER, Philip E. "Cultures in Collision." *Psychology Today* 4 (July 1970).

WATTS, William A., and WHITTAKER, David. "Profile of a Non-Conformist Youth Culture." *Sociology of Education* 41 (Spring 1968).

Some suggested book resources

ALDRIDGE, John W. *In the Country of the Young.* New York: Harper & Row, 1970.

FLACKS, Richard. "Who Protests: The Social Bases of the Student Movement." In J. Foster and D. Long, eds., *Protest! Student Activism in America.* New York: Morrow, 1970, pp. 134-157.

FOX, Jack V. *Youth Quake.* New York: Cowles, 1967.

GOODMAN, Mitchell. *The Movement Toward a New America.* Philadelphia: Pilgrim Press, 1970.

HEIRICH, Max. *Conflict on the Campus.* New York: Columbia University Press, 1971.

KELLY, Kevin D. *Youth, Humanism and Technology.* New York: Basic Books, 1972.

KENISTON, Kenneth. *The Young Radicals.* New York: Harcourt Brace Jovanovich, 1968.

MANNING, Peter K., and TRUZZI, Marcello, eds. *Youth and Sociology.* Englewood Cliffs, N.J.: Prentice-Hall, 1972.

NEWFIELD, Jack. *A Prophetic Minority.* New York: New American Library, Signet edition, 1967.

REICH, Charles. *The Greening of America.* New York: Random House, 1970.

ROSZAK, Theodore. *The Making of a Counter Culture.* Garden City, N.Y.: Doubleday, 1969.

TOFFLER, Alvin. *Future Shock.* New York: Random House, Bantom edition, 1971, chaps. 13, 14.

TOPIC 25. THE CULTURAL REVOLUTION: THE NEW MUSIC, THE UNDERGROUND PRESS, AND POP CULTURE

Some suggested periodical resources

CANADY, John. "Pop Art Sells On and On—Why?" *New York Times Magazine.* (May 31, 1964).

GEHMAN, Ralph. "It's Just Plain Mad." *Coronet* 68 (1960).

GLEASON, Ralph. "Bob Dylan and the Children's Crusade." *Ramparts* (1966).

GOODMAN, Paul. "Sub-Language as Social Badge." *Dissent* (December 1971).

GOODWIN, Donald A. "The De-fused Revolution: the Underground Press Sells Out." *notes from below* 2 (May 1972).

HESS, Thomas. "Pop and Public." *Art News* (November 1963).

HOLDEN, Joan. "The Woodstock Movie: A $4 Revolution." *Ramparts* (1970).

HOROWITZ, Irving Louis. "Rock and Rebellion." *Commonweal* (February 1971).

IRWIN, David. "Pop Art and Surrealism." *Studio International* (May 1966).

LEIMBACKER, Ed. "The Crash of the Jefferson Airplane." *Ramparts* (1969).

LEVINSON, Sandra. "Sexploitation in the Underground Press." *Ramparts* (1969).

LYDON, Michael. "Chuck Berry and the Days of Rock and Roll." *Ramparts* (1969).

MANAGO, B. R. "Mad: Out of the Comic Rack and into Satire." *Add One* 1 (1962).

MIDDLEBROOK, Jonathan. "Television: The Medium of Contempt." *Ramparts* (1968).

MOREHART, Malcolm B. "Pop goes the Easel." *East Villager* (April 1972).

ROSENBERG, Harold. "The Game of Illusion." *The New Yorker* (November 24, 1962).

ROSENBLUM, Robert. "Pop Art and Non-Pop Art." *Art and Literature* (Summer 1965).

SANDLER, Irving. "The New Cool-Art." *Art in America* (1965).

SCOTT, Ashmead. "Horror Comics Come Alive." *East Villager* (November 1971).

TAYLOR, A. J. W. "Beatlemania—A Study in Adolescent Enthusiasm." *British Journal of Social and Clinical Psychology* 5 (1966).

TILLIM, Sidney. "Further Observations on the Pop Phenomenon." *Artforum* 4 (1966).

Some suggested book resources

FEIFFER, Jules. *The Great Comic Book Heroes.* New York: Dial, 1965.

GOODMAN, Mitchell. *The Movement Toward a New America.* Philadelphia: Pilgrim Press, 1970, pp. 372-432.

LIPPARD, Lucy R. *Pop Art.* New York: Praeger, 1966.

LOWENTHAL, Leo. *Literature, Popular Culture and Society.* San Diego: Pacific Books, 1968.

McLUHAN, H. Marshall. *Understanding Media.* New York: McGraw-Hill, 1968.

MELLY, George. *Revolt Into Style: The Pop Arts.* Garden City, N.Y.: Doubleday, 1970.

SKORNA, Harry J. *Television and Society: An Inquest and Agenda for Improvement* New York: McGraw-Hill, 1965.

WARSHOW, Robert. "Movie Chronicle: The Westerner." In *The Immediate Experience.* Garden City, N.Y.: Doubleday, 1962.

WINICK, Charles. "Arts and the Man: Movers and Shakers." In *The New People: Desexualization in American Life.* New York: Pegasus, 1969, pp. 15-31.

TOPIC 26. IMAGES OF THE FUTURE

Some suggested periodical resources

BATES, Frederick L. "Social Trends in a Leisure Society." *The Futurist* (February 1971).

FRANCIS, Roy G. "Problems of Tomorrow Kapow! An Argument and a Forecast." *Social Problems* 12 (1965).

MARCUSE, Herbert. "The Movement in a New Era of Repression: An Assessment." *Berekley Journal of Sociology* (1971).

The Modern Utopian 1 (1972). "Technology and Utopia."

The Modern Utopian 1 (1972). "Land of the Free."

NAGAI, Yonosuke. "The United States is Disintegrating." *Psychology Today* 5 (May 1972).

TURING, Alan M. "Psycho-Culture, Self-Directed Man." *The Modern Utopian* 1 (1972).

Some suggested book resources

BARBER, Benjamin R. *Superman and Common Men.* New York: Praeger, 1971.

BELL, Daniel, ed. *Toward the Year 2000.* Boston: Houghton Mifflin, 1968.

BRZEZINSKI, Zbigniew. *Between Two Ages.* New York: Viking, 1971.

COOPER, David, ed. *To Free a Generation: The Dialectics of Liberation.* New York: Macmillan, 1972.

DRUCKER, R. F. *The Age of Discontinuity.* New York: Harper & Row, 1969.

DUBOS, René. "The New Pessimism." In *So Human an Animal.* New York: Scribner 1968, pp. 9-18.

DUCHENE, Francois, ed. *The Endless Crisis.* New York: Simon & Schuster, 1970.

Foreign Policy Association, eds. *Toward the Year Two Thousand Eighteen.* New York: Cowles, 1968.

GOODMAN, Paul. "Like a Conquered Province." In *Like a Conquered Province.* New York: Random House, 1967.

HANNA, Thomas. *Bodies in Revolt.* New York: Dell, Delta edition, 1972.

KAHN, Herman, and WIENER, Anthony J. "Science and Technology: A Framework for Speculation." In *The Year 2000.* New York: Macmillan, 1967, pp. 50-57.

KOSTALANETZ, R. "Radical Thought for Our Times." In *Beyond Left and Right.* New York: Morrow, 1968.

LUKACS, John A. *The Passing of the Modern Age.* New York: Harper & Row, 1969.

MICHAEL, Donald N. *The Unprepared Society: Planning for a Precarious Future.* New York: Basic Books, 1968.

REMMLING, Gunter W. "Dimensions of the Modern Mentality." In *Road to Suspicion.* New York: Appleton, 1967, pp. 3-10.

SYKES, Gerald. *The Cool Millenium.* Englewood Cliffs, N.J.: Prentice-Hall, 1967.

THEOBALD, Robert. "Glimpses of an Alternative Future." In *An Alternative Future for America II.* Chicago: The Swallow Press, 1970, pp. 43-54.

WINTER, Gibson. *Being Free: Reflections on America's Cultural Revolution.* New York: Macmillan, 1972.

WYLIE, Philip. *The Magic Animal.* Garden City, N.Y. Doubleday, 1968.

index